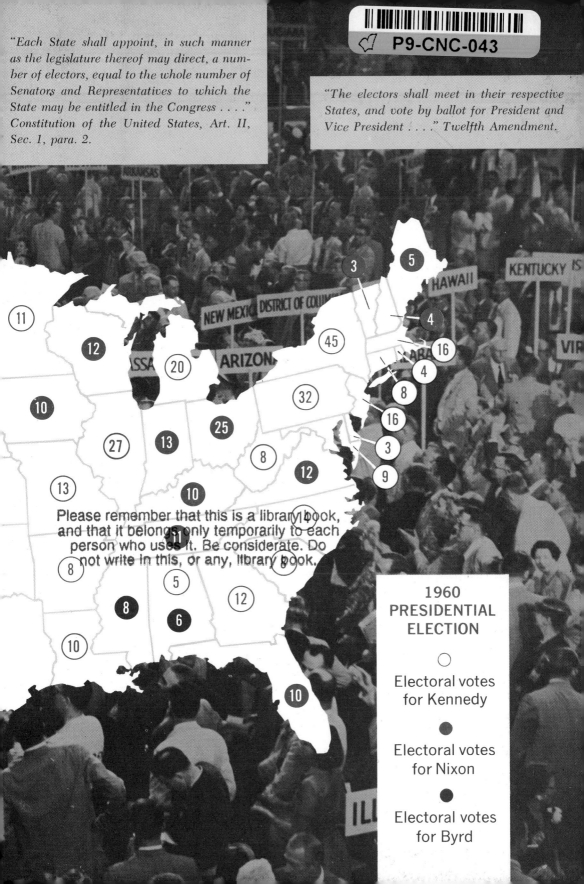

"Each State shall appoint, in such manner as the legislature thereof may direct, a number of electors, equal to the whole number of Senators and Representatives to which the State may be entitled in the Congress . . . ." Constitution of the United States, Art. II, Sec. 1, para. 2.

"The electors shall meet in their respective States, and vote by ballot for President and Vice President . . . ." Twelfth Amendment.

P9-CNC-043

Please remember that this is a library book, and that it belongs only temporarily to each person who uses it. Be considerate. Do not write in this, or any, library book.

1960 PRESIDENTIAL ELECTION

○ Electoral votes for Kennedy

● Electoral votes for Nixon

● Electoral votes for Byrd

The American System of Government

McGraw-Hill Series in Political Science

Joseph P. Harris, Consulting Editor

McGRAW-HILL *Book Company, Inc.*

New York Toronto London

THE

AMERICAN

SYSTEM

OF GOVERNMENT

JOHN H. FERGUSON
Professor of Political Science and
Director, Institute of Public Administration
The Pennsylvania State University

DEAN E. McHENRY
Professor of Political Science
University of California, Los Angeles and
Chancellor, University of California, Santa Cruz

Seventh Edition   1963

*This book is set in Electra, the
second of many type faces designed
by William A. Dwiggins for
Linotype. The display heads are
Spartan Heavy and Futura Bold.
The illustrations were designed by Edward Malsberg
and executed by Edward Malsberg and Felix Cooper.*

Preface

More than a decade and a half have passed since the first edition of this book appeared. The years since 1947 have been disillusioning in several ways. The wartime partnership of Russia and the United States has hardened into the deadlock of cold war. The United Nations has not brought the peace and security envisioned by the founders at San Francisco. The peoples of the world live in the shadow of the missile and the hydrogen bomb. Many stubborn domestic problems defy easy solution. Our state and local governments modernize with painful slowness.

Nevertheless, there is some basis for optimism. The nation has enjoyed a long period of economic prosperity. Our national, state, and local governments have demonstrated increasingly their ability to administer expanding services honestly and efficiently. We are learning, albeit slowly, how to help less developed countries along the road of social and economic progress. Despite the threatening international picture, the powers have been able to avoid big wars. The threat to personal freedom typified by "McCarthyism" passed without doing irreparable harm. Americans voted in unprecedented numbers during the presidential contest of 1960 and again in the congressional and state elections of 1962. Our state and local governments are showing signs of modernizing.

In this seventh edition, *The American System of Government* has been revised thoroughly to bring it up to date. New materials cover such timely topics as civil rights, reapportionment, Medicare, Peace Corps, Common Market, disarmament, United Nations operations in the Congo, food and drug regulation, Federal aid to education, and new farm legislation. New developments at state and local levels are also noted. Special attention is given to the rapid growth of state departments of administration, the federated-district plan of government for metropolitan areas, and the spreading interest shown in unified state court systems.

As in earlier editions, this text is organized along conventional lines in that it deals with national, state, and local governments in separate sections. The first part deals with historical backgrounds, general principles, and other essentials. The second part includes a discussion of Congress, the presidency, the courts, administrative organization, and the civil service. The third group of chapters is concerned with Federal powers and functions. The final section contains a concise treatment of state and local governments. This section has been kept brief so that instructors may supplement it with materials bearing upon the state in which they may be located. As an aid to this end, the final chapter contains a revised list of references dealing with particular states.

For those who desire a general introduction to the government of the United States and full coverage of national institutions and functions without state and local, the first three parts are available in a separate volume entitled *The American Federal Government*, the seventh edition of which is published simultaneously with this book.

To meet the demand for a briefer treatment of the whole compass of the government of the United States, the authors have prepared *Elements of American Government*, which is similar in scope but considerably more compact and simpler than *The American System of Government*.

Ten filmstrips designed to accompany these texts are available from the Text-Film Department, McGraw-Hill Book Company.

Students who wish additional guidance and self-help material may obtain through their bookstores the *Study Guide in American Government* by W. V. Holloway and Emile B. Ader, of the University of Tulsa. Newly revised to accompany the present editions of the texts, the student guide can serve as a valuable supplement.

Colleagues and librarians of The Pennsylvania State University and the University of California have aided us in countless ways. We are deeply grateful for the many comments received from instructors and students who have used our texts.

John H. Ferguson
Dean E. McHenry

Contents

FEDERAL POWERS AND FUNCTIONS

STATE AND LOCAL GOVERNMENTS

APPENDIXES

CREDITS FOR CHAPTER-OPENING PHOTOGRAPHS

Chapter One: Statue of Liberty; courtesy of the Port of New York Authority.

Chapter Two: Virginia tobacco wharf, from an eighteenth-century map; courtesy of the Bettman Archive.

Chapter Three: Independence Hall; courtesy of the Pennsylvania Historical and Museum Commission.

Chapter Four: The Constitution of the United States; Brown Bros.

Chapter Five: William F. Quinn being sworn in as first governor of the state of Hawaii.

Chapter Six: Trucks on highway; Portland Cement Association.

Chapter Seven: The Liberty Bell, in Independence Hall; courtesy of the National Park Service.

Chapter Eight: Courtroom scene; *The Verdict Is Yours.*

Chapter Nine: Immigrants' first view of New York; Wide World Photos.

Chapter Ten: Voters at political rally; Wide World Photos.

Chapter Eleven: A former president cheered at political convention; Wide World Photos.

Chapter Twelve: Oldest voter casting vote; Wide World Photos.

Chapter Thirteen: The Capitol; photo by Abbie Rowe, courtesy of the National Park Service.

Chapter Fourteen: Congressional clerk assigning bill a number; St. Louis *Post-Dispatch*, from Black Star.

Chapter Fifteen: White House and Washington Monument; courtesy of the White House Office.

Chapter Sixteen: President delivering State of the Union message to Congress; Harris and Ewing.

Chapter Seventeen: Interior of United States Supreme Court; *U.S. News and World Report.*

Chapter Eighteen: Office in the Pentagon; official U.S. Department of Defense photo.

Chapter Nineteen: New York City mailmen about to leave on their rounds; Wide World Photos.

Chapter Twenty: Coins; Ewing Galloway.

Chapter Twenty-one: Federal Reserve Building; Wide World Photos.

Chapter Twenty-two: U.S. State Department courier boarding a plane; Wide World Photos.

Chapter Twenty-three: United Nations headquarters; courtesy of the United Nations.

Chapter Twenty-four: Marching soldiers; Wide World Photos.

Chapter Twenty-five: Unloading sugar from Hawaii at Brooklyn docks; Wide World Photos.

Chapter Twenty-six: Ross Dam and powerhouse; Seattle City Light.

Chapter Twenty-seven: Change of shift at a steel plant; Black Star.

Chapter Twenty-eight: Growing wheat; J. L. Charlton, from Black Star.

Chapter Twenty-nine: Nebraska State Capitol; courtesy of the Division of Nebraska Resources.

Chapter Thirty: Connecticut state legislature, with electric roll call; *Hartford Times* photo by Einar G. Chindmark.

Chapter Thirty-one: Governor's car; courtesy of the New York State Department of Commerce.

Chapter Thirty-two: Empty courtroom; courtesy of the County of Westchester, New York.

Chapter Thirty-three: Firemen fighting blaze; Wide World Photos.

Chapter Thirty-four: Cuyahoga County Courthouse; Ewing Galloway.

Chapter Thirty-five: Filling station protesting state tax increase; Wide World Photos.

Chapter Thirty-six: State trooper; courtesy of Washington State Patrol.

Chapter Thirty-seven: City sanitation worker; Wide World Photos.

Chapter Thirty-eight: Back alley; courtesy of the New York City Housing Authority.

The American System of Government

McGraw-Hill Series in Political Science
Joseph P. Harris, *Consulting Editor*

Part One

Essentials of American Government

Chapter One

Political Institutions and Ideas

Politics is intimate, not a pageant in a remote marble capitol; it has to do with the lives and safety of your family and yourself; with whether you can afford to marry; or if you're married, whether you can afford to have children. Politics is the instrument which determines not only whether the cows which furnish your milk are free from tuberculosis, and if there shall be benches in the park, but whether your son will have to die on a battlefield, or whether you yourself will vaporize in a blast of improved nuclear fission.

The man who never takes sides, who never votes, never signs a petition, never speaks his mind, is a civic drone. Panics, depressions and wars come to him like weather. He suddenly peers out of his window and says, "Look, it's warring."

NORMAN CORWIN[1]

Arnold J. Toynbee, the eminent British historian, records twenty-one major civilizations in the history of mankind. To these must be added a larger, but unknown, number of primitive societies. Political institutions with authority to make and enforce laws—in other words, governments—have been common to both civilized and primitive societies. Although forms and procedures have differed, evidence accumulated by social scientists indicates that some form of government is essential to successful group life.

Governments, like other social institutions, vary greatly; indeed it is not possible to find identical forms and procedures in the governments of any two societies. Differences are explained by such factors as

[1] "One World or None?" *New Zealand Listener* (October 25, 1946), p. 10.

geography, climate, history, customs, resources, and degree of enlightenment.
Shaped by forces like these, distinctive governments have evolved in each country, and
constitutional forms that are successful in
one place might fail quite miserably in
another.

Not only do political institutions vary
but they are constantly in the process of
adaptation and change. In Great Britain,
for example, power has passed from King
to Parliament, the House of Commons has
taken predominance from the House of
Lords, and tight control of empire has been
replaced by a commonwealth relationship
based on shared responsibility and mutual
consent.

Similar transformation has taken place
in the United States. The nation now commands the devotion formerly reserved for
particular states. The negative individualism
of old is being replaced by a new attachment to positive government. The electorate
has expanded until it represents almost universal adult suffrage. Pressure groups have
become nationally organized, vocal, and
very powerful. Political parties have become
indispensable adjuncts of government. The
electoral college is withering away. The
Presidency has attained a commanding position. And, for good or ill, more changes are
in sight.

POLITICAL DIVISIONS OF THE WORLD

The modern national state is a product of
gradual evolution. The basic social unit of
primitive man was the family or kinship
group. Families, clans, and tribes were
united by commerce, conquest, and alliances, and the early kingdoms made their
appearance. Then the city-state emerged as
the major political unit of the Mediterranean world. After a period dominated by the
Roman Empire, Europe entered the feudal

era, in which political authority was frag-
mented. Feudalism ended gradually with
the merging of principalities and city-states
into larger and larger kingdoms, until the
modern national-state system became dis-
cernible during the latter part of the seventeenth century. Although the national state
is today the dominant political unit, some
attention must be given to lesser units, such
as dominions, protectorates, trust territories,
and colonies.

National States. About a hundred national states exist at present. From a legal
point of view, they may be defined as permanent associations of people politically
organized upon a definite territory and ha-
bitually obeying the same autonomous government. For a state to exist, then, the following elements must be present: (1) population, (2) territory, (3) political organization or government, (4) sovereignty, and
(5) unity sufficient to bind the community
together for sustained collective action.

The state may have a large or small *population*. India has over 438,000,000, whereas
Iceland has only about 176,000. Yet both
are national states with membership in the
United Nations and diplomatic representation abroad.

Likewise, a state may have much or little
territory. Luxembourg, with 999 square
miles, is a member of the family of nations
along with the Union of Soviet Socialist
Republics, which has nearly 8,600,000
square miles of territory.

A state's *political organization* may take
any form, but it must be powerful and
stable enough to command obedience and
to fulfill the international obligations of
statehood.

Sovereignty is the most controversial element. The term means "supreme temporal
power." All authorities agree that it must
exist if a state is to be recognized. Where
sovereignty rests and by whom it is exer-

MAJOR POLITICAL UNITS OF THE WORLD

Status as of November 15, 1962

UN—member United Nations
US—recognized by United States

CN—member Commonwealth of Nations
FC—member French Community
AS—member Organization of American States

NATIONAL STATES (in order of population)

CHINA (Communist)				CHINA (Nationalist)	UN	US		IVORY COAST	UN	US	FC
INDIA	UN	US	CN	AUSTRALIA	UN	US	CN	DOMINICAN REPUBLIC	UN	US	AS
SOVIET UNION	UN	US		ALGERIA	UN	US	FC	LAOS	UN	US	
UNITED STATES	UN		AS	SUDAN	UN	US		GUINEA	UN	US	
PAKISTAN	UN	US	CN	HUNGARY	UN	US		IRELAND	UN	US	
JAPAN	UN	US		CEYLON	UN	US	CN	URUGUAY	UN	US	AS
INDONESIA	UN	US		TANGANYIKA	UN	US	CN	REPUBLIC OF RWANDA	UN	US	
BRAZIL	UN	US	AS	NEPAL	UN	US		EL SALVADOR	UN	US	AS
GERMANY (West)		US		PORTUGAL	UN	US		NIGER	UN	US	FC
UNITED KINGDOM	UN	US	CN	BELGIUM	UN	US		CHAD	UN	US	FC
ITALY	UN	US		GREECE	UN	US		LIBERIA	UN	US	
FRANCE	UN	US	FC	KOREA (North)				SOMALIA	UN	US	
MEXICO	UN	US	AS	BULGARIA	UN	US		SIERRA LEONE	UN	US	CN
NIGERIA	UN	US	CN	CHILE	UN	US	AS	NEW ZEALAND	UN	US	CN
SPAIN	UN	US		SWEDEN	UN	US		SENEGAL	UN	US	FC
POLAND	UN	US		AUSTRIA	UN	US		KINGDOM OF BURUNDI	UN	US	
TURKEY	UN	US		IRAQ	UN	US		ISRAEL	UN	US	
PHILIPPINES	UN	US		MALAYA	UN	US	CN	HONDURAS	UN	US	AS
UNITED ARAB REPUBLIC	UN	US		CUBA	UN		AS	PARAGUAY	UN	US	AS
THAILAND	UN	US		VENEZUELA	UN	US	AS	DAHOMEY	UN	US	FC
KOREA (South)		US		GHANA	UN	US	CN	JORDAN	UN	US	
ETHIOPIA	UN	US		UGANDA	UN	US	CN	LEBANON	UN	US	
ARGENTINA	UN	US	AS	SAUDI ARABIA	UN	US		ALBANIA	UN		
BURMA	UN	US		SWITZERLAND		US		NICARAGUA	UN	US	AS
IRAN	UN	US		MALAGASY REPUBLIC	UN	US	FC	TOGO	UN	US	FC
YUGOSLAVIA	UN	US		YEMEN	UN	US		LIBYA	UN	US	
RUMANIA	UN	US		CAMBODIA	UN	US		CENTRAL AFRICAN			
CANADA	UN	US	CN	DENMARK	UN	US		REPUBLIC	UN	US	FC
GERMANY (East)				SYRIA	UN	US		COSTA RICA	UN	US	AS
VIETNAM (North)				FINLAND	UN	US		PANAMA	UN	US	AS
REPUBLIC OF SOUTH AFRICA	UN	US		ECUADOR	UN	US	AS	CONGO (ex-French)	UN	US	FC
VIETNAM (South)		US		TUNISIA	UN	US		MAURITANIA	UN	US	FC
COLOMBIA	UN	US	AS	GUATEMALA	UN	US	AS	CYPRUS	UN	US	
CONGO (ex-Belgian)	UN	US		MALI (SOUDAN)	UN	US		GABON	UN	US	FC
CZECHOSLOVAKIA	UN	US		NORWAY	UN	US		KUWAIT		US	
AFGHANISTAN	UN	US		HAITI	UN	US	AS	LUXEMBOURG	UN	US	
MOROCCO	UN	US		UPPER VOLTA	UN	US	FC	ICELAND	UN	US	
NETHERLANDS	UN	US		BOLIVIA	UN	US	AS				
PERU	UN	US	AS	CAMEROUN	UN	US	FC				

UNITED NATIONS TRUST TERRITORIES (by Trustee)

UNITED STATES	UNITED KINGDOM	AUSTRALIA	AUSTRALIA, NEW ZEALAND, AND UNITED KINGDOM
Carolines	Cameroons	New Guinea	
Marianas			
Marshall Islands			Nauru

MAJOR COLONIES* AND PROTECTORATES (by Controlling Power†)

UNITED STATES	AUSTRALIA	FRANCE	UNITED KINGDOM		PORTUGAL	NETHERLANDS
Puerto Rico‡	Papua	Reunion	Aden	Malta	Angola	Surinam & Antilles
			Basutoland	North Borneo	Mozambique	
			Bechuanaland	Rhodesias & Nyasaland‡	Portuguese Guinea	
			Fiji	Sarawak	Timor	
			Gambia	Singapore‡		
			Hong Kong	Trinidad & Tobago‡		
			Jamaica‡	West Indies		
			Kenya	Zanzibar		
			Mauritius			

*Above 300,000 in populaton.
†Excludes powers with contiguous territories under their control, such as Sinkiang and Tibet by China, and some of the European and Asian "republics" by the U.S.S.R., which resemble colonies in many respects.
‡Substantially self-governing.

cised are vital questions. It may rest in an emperor or monarch, as in the days of Caesar or Henry VIII. Or it may repose in a church, feudal lords, the people (as in the United States), a parliament, a class (as in the Soviet Union), or in the state itself conceived as an ideal person (as in fascist Italy under Mussolini). Theoretical location of sovereignty often differs from its actual situs, but all agree that a supreme authority must exist somewhere.

Unity is the most basic of all the elements. Its absence explains many historical phenomena. Lack of a full measure of unity was one of the difficulties encountered in molding the original thirteen colonies into an effective nation. Lack of unity also helps explain why the peoples of India, China, and parts of Africa have been slow to develop over-all political institutions. It accounts, in part, for the recent split between India and Pakistan, for many of the difficulties encountered by advocates of a United States of Europe, world federation, or some other form of world government. Before such heroic goals can be attained, there must exist a consciousness of unity that will ensure the cooperation required to fulfill the purposes of community life.

States decide among themselves whether a political unit possesses the attributes of statehood. Unanimity is unnecessary, but "recognition" by the more powerful nations usually is indispensable. Recognition is followed normally by exchange of diplomats, negotiation of treaties, and, perhaps, admission to the United Nations. Following recognition, the newcomer is considered an international personality with all the rights, privileges, and immunities of international law.

Dominions. A dominion is a territory having autonomy in the conduct of its internal and external affairs, but maintaining a degree of affiliation with a mother country.

The idea of dominion status grew out of British experience in granting larger and larger powers of self-government to Canada and other former colonies.

Now the United Kingdom, Canada, Australia, New Zealand, India, Pakistan, Ceylon, Malaya, Ghana, Nigeria, Cyprus, Tanganyika, Sierra Leone, Uganda, Jamaica, and Trinidad-Tobago are national states that have chosen, for a variety of reasons, to remain associated with the United Kingdom and one another through the Commonwealth of Nations. In 1952 the United States arranged commonwealth status with Puerto Rico, a former colony. Meanwhile, with old-fashioned colonialism under fire in many parts of the world, more dominion-type arrangements may be in the offing.

Protectorates. A protectorate is controlled by another power, usually through military, economic, and financial ties, but has not been formally annexed by the controlling power. Tonga, in the Pacific, and Uganda, in Africa, are British protectorates. Although the United States acknowledges no formal protectorates, her influence over Haiti, Dominican Republic, Panama, and Cuba at times resembles that relationship.

Trust Territories. The mandate system was devised after the First World War to administer territories taken by the victorious Allies from the defeated Central Powers. Under this arrangement, responsibility for control of such areas was given to the League of Nations, which then made some "advanced" state guardian of each area on behalf of the League.

The United Nations Charter created the Trusteeship Council to supervise a new plan resembling the mandate system. The Charter placed no specific territories under trust, but left that to subsequent negotiations between the UN and the powers which control dependent areas. Australia, Belgium, France, New Zealand, and the United

Kingdom received UN approval of trust agreements they submitted for territories formerly held by them under League mandate. The Union of South Africa refused to submit a trust plan for Southwest Africa, which it hoped to annex.

The United States was given trusteeship over the former Japanese mandates of the North Pacific—the Caroline, Mariana, and Marshall Islands. Italy was assigned a temporary trust over the former Italian Somaliland.

The administering powers have now granted self-government and independence to most of their former trust territories. The trusteeship chapters of the Charter have enduring importance, however, for they state principles which are appropriate to govern all colonial administration, whether within the trust system or not.

Colonies. In colonies sovereignty is exercised by a parent national state. Most colonies are geographically separated from their sovereign. European powers hold the greatest number of colonial possessions. Actually, most colonies have been granted some degree of self-government, ranging from nearly complete internal autonomy to meager participation in local affairs. The United States has refrained from using the term "colony," and persists in calling its dependent areas "territories." Nevertheless, the status of the Virgin Islands and of Samoa is not unlike that of a British colony like the Bahamas or a French colony like New Caledonia.

Nationalism. To understand the attitude of peoples toward their political units and their behavior and aspirations, it is necessary to understand what Frederick L. Schuman calls "the cult of the nation-state." The spirit of nationalism drives a national state to glorify its own race, culture, institutions, ideals, and purposes. In its harmless form nationalism leads to commemoration of heroes and history in storybook, song,

and dance. In its dangerous form it leads to jingoism, economic autarchy, violation of the rights of neighbors, and war. Persistence of extreme nationalist spirit constitutes a formidable barrier to international cooperation.

Nationalism operates also as a separatist influence within national states. In the 1930s, Sudeten German propaganda was a grave threat to Czechoslovakian unity. Between the two world wars, Yugoslavia was weakened by Croat nationalist aspirations for autonomy or a separate national state. The boundaries of a national state can rarely be drawn so perfectly that they include only persons of a common linguistic, cultural, ethnic, and religious background. The presence of any minority may lead to separatist agitation.

The nationalist spirit also stirs colonial peoples to revolt against their imperial masters. It drove Egyptian students to demonstrate against British "protection." It induced Indonesians to fight to the death against Netherlands forces. It whetted the will of the Annamese to expel their French overlords from Indochina. It led the Irish to demand and receive independence, despite the economic and other advantages of the British connection. It led Hungarians to revolt against Soviet domination. A rising nationalist spirit has played a large part in the achievement, during the postwar period, of national statehood by India, Pakistan, Burma, and a host of African states.

One of the great tasks of the present age is to reconcile nationalist aspirations with the preeminent fact that this is an interdependent world. Nationalism can be tolerated, even encouraged, up to the point where its exercise invades the rights and security of other peoples. For China or India a new nationalism may serve to unite diverse elements and thereby promote social and economic progress. For the major nations a new patriotism is needed—one devoted to internationalism and a conviction that all peoples of the earth can live together in peace and security.

World Organization. Although the nation-state has dominated the world scene for nearly three hundred years, there has been a parallel development of international consciousness and institutions. The International Telecommunications Union, the Universal Postal Union, the Pan American Union, the League of Nations, and the United Nations are tangible evidences of this trend.

Of the dozens of private and public international organizations today, the United Nations is paramount. The UN is not the government of a new world state but merely an association of national states formed for consultation and cooperative action. Membership is not compulsory, and the UN must work through governments of national states. In joining, however, member states limit their freedom of action and pledge their support to UN principles and decisions.

FORMS OF GOVERNMENT

An observer of today's governments is impressed with both their variety and similarity. He might classify them as unitary or federal, parliamentary or presidential, authoritarian or democratic. Or he might group them according to whether their constitutions are rigid or flexible.

Unitary or Federal. A government is *unitary* when the powers of government are concentrated in a single central government, with legal omnipotence over all territory within its boundaries. Local governments usually exist, but they are creatures of the central government and act as its administrative agents. Most national states have governments of this type. Examples

are Cuba, Belgium, France, Great Britain, Italy, and Japan. This form is also found within most of our fifty states and American territories like Puerto Rico.

A government is *federal* if political authority is divided between self-governing parts and the central whole, each operating within its sphere of action as defined in the constitution. The geographic subdivisions and their governments are not mere creatures of the central government, but share power and responsibility with it. Although the idea of federalism is old, the adoption of the federal system by the United States encouraged its use by other nations. Canada, Australia, Mexico, Brazil, and Switzerland are among the countries that use this form.

A weak federation is often called a "confederation." Under such an association, or league of sovereign states, the central government has limited powers, while the member states retain great autonomy and authority. Examples are the American states under the Articles of Confederation and the Confederate States of America during the Civil War. Some look upon the League of Nations and the United Nations as weak confederations.

Parliamentary or Presidential. In the *parliamentary* form, executive powers are exercised by a prime minister and his cabinet, who are usually members of parliament and continue to hold ministerial office as long as their policies are supported by a majority of parliament. This form is characterized by a weak titular executive like the British King or the president of Italy. In recent years the parliamentary form has often been designated the "cabinet" form. The latter term properly emphasizes the fact that, although parliament is the ultimate master, in Great Britain party discipline has become so rigid that a cabinet rarely can be overthrown by vote of lack of confidence. The parliamentary form is also used in most of the countries of Europe and the British Commonwealth.

In the *presidential* form the principal branches of government—executive, legislative, and judicial—are separated. The separation is almost invariably prescribed in a written constitution. The chief executive generally is elected, and he continues in office to the expiration of his term, regardless of the support given him by the legislative branch. The legislature, executive, and judiciary are coordinate branches, and each has its own constitutional authority. Although much criticized in recent years for its proclivity for stalemate, the presidential form has been continued in most of the countries that have adopted it. This form of government is found in the United States, its fifty states, most of the Latin-American republics, and a few other countries.

The *plural* executive, although less widely used, is attracting renewed interest. Known also as the "executive council" or "collegial" executive, it has long been used in Switzerland and was recently adopted in Uruguay. Selected by either parliament or popular election, councilors divide executive power among themselves, often on a bi- or multiparty basis. The commission plan of municipal and county government in the American states is somewhat similar.

Authoritarian or Democratic. An *authoritarian* or *dictatorial* form is one in which political authority is exercised by a single individual or a small group. This form is probably the oldest one known to man. Whether the social unit was the family, clan, tribe, city-state, or empire, power tended to gravitate to one or a few individuals who ruled with varying degrees of moderation. Even in "democratic" Athens, power was exercised by citizens who made up only a comparatively small proportion of the population. Absolute monarchs, so common during the Middle Ages, still exist in some semifeudal states.

The newest form of autocracy is the totalitarian national state. This concentrates power in one or a few who organize the state for total and undeviating devotion to the public will as expressed through its leaders. Mass support is mobilized through propaganda, a single highly disciplined political party, the secret police, ruthless suppression of dissent, and a high level of state activity to promote economic and social welfare or enhance national power and prestige. Examples are Italy under Mussolini, Germany under Hitler, prewar Japan, Spain under Franco, and the Soviet Union.

The *democratic* form is the one best known to Americans. Where it prevails, government is based on the consent of the governed, as expressed through constitutions, elections, and public opinion. Precautions are taken to keep power responsible, or limited; dissent is tolerated and even encouraged; and individual rights are given special safeguards.

A distinction is made between *direct*, or *pure*, democracy and representative democracy. In the former, citizens assemble periodically and perform the functions usually assigned to legislatures. Examples are found in ancient Greece and Rome, in the *Landesgemeinde* of some Swiss cantons, and in New England town meetings. Direct democracy is practicable only in small units where population is sparse and homogeneous and the issues are fairly simple. It is seldom used by modern national, state, and municipal governments, except in the form of the initiative, referendum, and other plebiscites.

In a *representative* democracy, the voters wield influence through officials selected to express and enforce their will. This system originated in the medieval states of Western Europe, was perfected in Great Britain, and is now widely practiced throughout the world.

The term "democratic" has other meanings. Some associate democracy with capitalism and argue that democratic forms of government cannot exist if government interferes much with private enterprise or goes into business itself. Others insist that there is more democracy, rather than less, where government expands services to equalize opportunities, surrounds profit-seeking business with greater controls, or undertakes to own and operate basic industries. Confusion is compounded when communists speak of their countries as "peoples' democratic republics," meaning by this that the proletariat has liquidated the exploiting classes and now operates the state by authoritarian measures. Precise definition is obviously impossible when the term "democracy" is used to describe social and economic systems as well as political ones. But if definition is confined to political systems, the essentials of democratic government are as stated.

In the twentieth century, the rise of *communism* and *fascism* as prevailing ideologies in several countries poses difficult problems of classification. Strictly speaking, they are not forms of government, but combinations of various social, economic, and political doctrines. Both vary widely in theory and practice. Both are authoritarian.

Modern communism, as practiced in the Soviet Union, is based on the writings of Marx, Lenin, and Stalin. Claiming that history teaches the inevitability of a class conflict whereby the propertied classes dominate and exploit the masses, communist leaders set out to establish a socialist system. Ruthless measures and dictatorship, communists argue, were essential to achieve this result and ensure its success. Someday, however, the state will wither away, leaving a democratic and classless society. Many communists give the impression that force and violence are essential to attain their goals; others deny that these methods are required, especially where change is possible through democratic processes.

To people outside the Soviet Union it became uncertain whether communism would be allowed to compete for acceptance with other ideologies or whether it was an instrument for extending Soviet power and influence.

Fascism grew to great power in Italy and Germany between the two world wars and has been a force in other sectors. This was a revolt of the conservative and nationalist elements against parliamentarians, radicals of the left, and internationalists. Liberal democracy gave way to dictatorship and ruthless suppression of dissidents. The nation became the supreme object of devotion and effort. Although private ownership of property and industry, trade unions, and the church and other private associations were permitted, they were subordinated to the paramount interest of the state.

As with communism, outsiders were given the impression that fascism at home meant national aggrandizement abroad. Ensuing tension erupted in war, the aftermath of which plagues the world.

Constitutions: Rigid or Flexible. Modern constitutionalism, which requires governments to conduct their affairs according to fundamental laws and practices, dates from the American and French Revolutions. Formerly, constitutions often were classed as either *written* or *unwritten*, but experience demonstrates that few, if any, are wholly one or the other.

The British constitution, classic example of the unwritten kind, consists of certain major statutes, court decisions, great settlements, and administrative ordinances, as well as customs. It is unwritten only in the sense that there is no single document which can be called the British constitution. The American Constitution, leading example of the written type, includes customs and usages and interpretations that are not part of the formal document.

The distinction between *rigid* and *flexible* constitutions is more meaningful and useful: it places emphasis on the amending process. Judgment could be made on the text of the amending clause, but the thorough student of government will wish to know how the clause operates in practice. Australia and Switzerland have similar procedures for formal amendment (proposal by parliament, ratification by popular vote), yet Australia adopts fewer than one per decade and Switzerland adopts dozens. The degree of rigidity or flexibility is also determined by the availability and use of other means of constitutional change, such as custom and usage, statutory elaboration, and judicial interpretation.

Constitutions may be classified as those that are *supreme* over the legislature and those that are *subordinate* to it. The supreme constitution is amended only by an extraordinary procedure that involves more than the legislature alone; the subordinate type may be altered by the legislature alone. Nearly all of the American states, requiring popular ratification of constitutional amendments, have supreme constitutions. The Union of South Africa, which vests the power to change in Parliament alone, has a subordinate constitution.

FUNCTIONS OF GOVERNMENT

Although the role of government is highly controversial, there is general agreement over certain essential, or minimum, functions. All argee that only government should

be permitted to enact laws and back them with sufficient force to compel acceptance and obedience. It is also generally agreed that governments should provide courts for the settlement of private controversies, protect life and property, defend the community from attack, conduct foreign relations, provide a medium of exchange and a postal system, and restrain individual, group, and commercial excesses.

If government would confine itself to these activities, its role would be largely that of lawgiver, judge, policeman, and soldier. But few modern governments stop at this point. Instead, they have become gigantic regulatory and service institutions. This transition has been accompanied by diverse ideologies and vehement controversy.

Antistatism. *Anarchism* is a school of thought that seeks the complete elimination of the state and its replacement by free and spontaneous cooperation among individuals and groups. Anarchists regard the state as an instrument of domination and exploitation by the propertied classes. Most of them expect that the new society will come into being by revolutionary action, but no new government or coercive system will replace the old.

Anarchism has never become the gospel of the masses, but its proponents often touch a responsive chord in people concerned over the expanding authority of modern governments. Communists who expect the state to wither away and leave a democratic classless society operating through voluntary cooperation may also properly be called anarchists.

Syndicalism holds somewhat similar views concerning the role of the state. Using the general strike as a method of seizing power, the syndicalist would establish in place of the state a series of industries managed by the workers. These industries would be federated on a functional basis; most syndicalists would permit this federation to exercise some coercive powers, particularly in the transitional period.

Individualism. The laissez-faire individualist regards the state as a necessary evil. He would have it perform only the minimum or essential functions, leaving promotion and regulation of the economic order to private enterprise and natural economic forces. That government is best, says a modern individualist, which governs least. To him government constantly threatens individual freedom and private initiative. Economic *laissez faire*, once the creed of radicals, has become the doctrine of conservatism, or even of reaction.

To be consistent, advocates of *laissez faire* must accept the withdrawal of nearly all forms of government support and paternalism. He who wants natural economic laws to govern production, distribution, and exchange must give up the protective tariff, governmental subsidy, marketing aids, and other services to business and agriculture. He must be prepared for the inequality that will result from unregulated operation of a "survival of the fittest" plan.

Individualism has a tremendous appeal to many Americans. It played a great part in the development of the country, in the early settlement of the East coast, in pushing back the frontiers to the West. It has been allied in many ways to opposition to state interference in individual opinions and conduct. Like many slogans, "free enterprise" is both appealing and vague, and its full implications are rarely examined.

Progressivism. A middle way between individualist and collectivist views on governmental functions is advocated by a diverse group known by such designations as "progressives," "liberals," "new dealers," and proponents of the "welfare state." In one sense they seek to revive the utilitarian ideals of the greatest good to the greatest number. Supporters of this social-welfare

point of view, although critical of the abuses of private enterprise and the profit motive, do not advocate socialism. Rather, they seek to reform and strengthen the existing economic system by expanding governmental functions if necessary.

In addition to the minimum functions, they would have government regulate, stimulate, coordinate, plan, and supervise the national economy. Some utilities would come under public ownership, and government would accept responsibility for providing full employment, social security, and housing. The progressives also favor expanded public-health, education, and nutrition programs. To promote social justice, they often encourage nonbusiness groups, especially labor, farmers, and consumers. All these objectives have won wide acceptance in the United States.

Collectivism. Socialist thought varies widely, but a basic tenet is belief in public ownership of the principal means of production, exchange, and distribution. Some socialists derive their doctrine from the writings of Marx and Engels, but there are many sources. Socialists condemn the capitalist system for concentrating wealth in the hands of a few and producing recurring wars and depressions. Upon winning power through the ballot box, most socialists anticipate a gradual transformation of the economic system from capitalism to socialism. Revolutionary socialists expect to win power only by violence, and hence predict a rapid transition to the new society.

Although socialist philosophy has made great headway in many countries, it has never become a major political movement in the United States. The Labor parties of Great Britain, Australia, and New Zealand profess a mild socialist doctrine and have been able to put into force much of their programs. Social Democratic and Socialist parties of European countries have played a major part in Continental politics for decades. The lack of headway in the United States may be explained by the relatively high standard of living and the frequency with which the old parties borrow planks from Socialist platforms to solve persistent problems.

Under the democratic-state socialist scheme, as envisaged by socialists in British and Western European countries, the government would nationalize credit and banking, transportation and communication, and the principal production industries. Central planning of the economic life of the country would tolerate such private enterprise as conformed to the plan.

Russian Communists to date have behaved much like state socialists, except that their methods have been more revolutionary and less private ownership is tolerated. Instead of withering away, the state has reached a new high in functions performed and obedience exacted.

Fascism as practiced in Italy and Germany was clearly in the collectivist rather than the individualist tradition. While permitting private property and associations, the state demanded total control, loyalty, and obedience—hence the term "totalitarian." Generally the fascist dictators found it unnecessary to socialize industry for their control was effective without going to that extreme.

THE ROLE OF POLITICAL SCIENCE

Something as old as government quite naturally has been given much thought and study. The large body of theory and knowledge which has been accumulated and verified justifies the term "political science." The political scientist is primarily concerned with the nature of authority, the institutions by which authority is expressed, the methods by which social control is achieved, and the aims and results of social control. Aware that authority is expressed in diverse ways, the political scientist is chiefly concerned with government and law.

Divisions of Political Science. Toward the end of the last century, colleges and universities in the United States began to offer political science as a separate discipline. Today the subject encompasses political theory, public law, comparative government, governments of particular nations, public administration, international relations, political parties, elections, and public opinion. Closely related are the disciplines of philosophy, history, anthropology, sociology, and economics. As a practical matter, the political scientist serves his profession as a scholar, teacher, author, public official, administrator, lawyer, consultant, or researcher. Opportunities are numerous for the well qualified.

Expanding Frontiers. Public authority surrounds the modern American in ways undreamed of by his forefathers. It may take the form of a new restraint, a tax, a service, or as a conscriptor of person and property. Whatever its form, authority as expressed through government makes itself felt upon Americans today from cradle to grave. To an American removed from pioneer days by only one or a very few generations, this growing authority over his life is greeted with mixed, and often hostile, emotions. But chafe as he will, the role of government expands.

This was once a nation devoted to laissez-faire principles; now Americans look increasingly to government for guidance and assistance in solving their economic problems. Public authority accepts responsibility today for stimulating, planning, regulating, and coordinating the economy of the nation. Read a recent political-party platform and note the promises made to business, labor, farmers, homeowners, consumers, and the rest. Note also the pledges made to provide full employment, control prices, plan for careful use of natural resources, and sustain

"I wish political science was as advanced as medical science, Doc . . . you got more words that nobody knows the meaning of . . ."

(Used by permission of George Lichty and the Chicago Sun-Times Syndicate.)

general prosperity. The day is gone when government will stand idly by and let the economy run its "natural" course from "boom to bust."

Similar trends are at work in the social realm. Next to military preparations, public-aided education is the largest consumer of the tax dollar, and more money is demanded. Social security, assistance to the needy, health programs, veterans' assistance, public housing, special programs for the mentally and physically handicapped, safe and efficient utility services—all this and much more is expected of today's governments.

As American society grows more complex, the mere task of safeguarding life and property demands more and more public authority. Highway police were not needed to patrol dirt roads; only a rudimentary police was needed when cities and villages were small; the Federal Bureau of Investi-

gation (FBI) is of recent vintage; modern fire-fighting units have taken the place of volunteer bucket brigades; and thousands of large and diversified prisons and correctional institutions supplement the ancient town lockup.

In the fields of foreign affairs and national defense authority manifests itself most conspicuously to twentieth-century Americans. The safety once enjoyed by isolation from Europe and Asia is a thing of the past. With its demise have come three major wars since 1898 and continuous fear of bigger and more devastating conflicts. Huge military establishments, unprecedented public expenditures, high taxes, and conscription have become commonplace. Unless feelings of national insecurity can be diminished, public authority is certain to grow and demand greater sacrifices.

Role of the Citizen. The citizen, as well as the political scientist, is concerned over the extension of authority. If government is autocratic, the citizen is limited in what he can do, but under a democracy he has a decisive role to play. The citizen must look to himself to make sure he is informed. This should be easier today than formerly because of the availability of radio, television, the press, and other mass media. But for most people it is harder to keep informed because of the increasing number and complexity of issues.

The citizen must also learn to make wise choices. If he remains content to ratify by his votes the candidates proposed by political machines and vested interests, he must not expect honest government; if he votes for a demagogue, he will jeopardize his own rights as well as those of others; or if he votes blindly on referendum and initiative proposals, he must not be surprised if his government fails to meet some of his most urgent needs.

A citizen must also learn how and when

to protest or give support. Well-organized protests at the right time can reform governments, change policies, and prevent abuse of power. But it is often easier to shout "Throw the rascals out" than it is to work for a cause. Pure water supply, better schools, a competent civil service, effective business regulation, adequate mental hospitals, and other benefits require active and continuous support.

The citizen needs to become a politican in the best sense of that term. Political parties starve for want of qualified and enthusiastic workers; pressure groups beg for aid and assistance; candidates and officials covet public interest and support; letters, telegrams, and interviews are needed and welcomed; qualified speechmakers are scarce; and more and better candidates are desperately needed. All this takes time, money, and interest, but democratic government flourishes or languishes in proportion to the number and quality of its lay politicians.

Political science lays a special claim on college and university students. The public will look to them for leadership and guidance. With government playing an increasingly vital part, the leaders of tomorrow must be able to understand, interpret, and direct forces that may improve or plague the lot of man. Effective citizenship is much more than a civic duty; it is also an opportunity for service richly rewarding in human satisfactions.

FOR FURTHER READING

Brecht, Arnold: *Political Theory: The Foundations of Twentieth Century Political Thought* (Princeton, N.J.: Princeton University Press, 1959).

Brewster, R. Wallace: *Government in Modern Society* (Boston: Houghton Mifflin, 1958).

Bryce, James: *Modern Democracies* (New York: Macmillan, 2 vols., 1921).

Cantril, Hadley: *Human Nature and Political Systems* (New Brunswick, N.J.: Rutgers University Press, 1961).

Carter, Gwendolen M., and John H. Herz: *Government and Politics in the Twentieth Century* (New York: Praeger, 1961).

Cohen, Carl: *Communism, Fascism, and Democracy: The Theoretical Foundations* (New York: Random House, 1962).

Dahl, Robert A.: *A Preface to Democratic Theory* (Chicago: University of Chicago Press, 1956).

Ebenstein, William: *Today's Isms* (Englewood Cliffs, N.J.: Prentice-Hall, 2d ed., 1958).

Friedman, W.: *Law in a Changing Society* (Berkeley and Los Angeles: University of California Press, 1959).

Hall, H. Duncan: *Mandates, Dependencies and Trusteeships* (New York: Carnegie Endowment, 1948).

Hallowell, John H.: *Main Currents in Modern Political Thought* (New York: Holt, 1950).

Hayes, Carlton J. H.: *The Historical Evolution of Modern Nationalism* (New York: Macmillan, 1948).

————: *Nationalism: A Religion* (New York: Macmillan, 1960).

Hitchner, Dell G., and William H. Harbold: *Modern Government: A Survey of Political Science* (New York: Dodd, Mead, 1962).

Hyneman, Charles S.: *The Study of Politics: The Present State of American Political Science* (Urbana, Ill.: University of Illinois Press, 1959).

Lipson, Leslie: *The Great Issues of Politics* (Englewood Cliffs, N.J.: Prentice-Hall, 1954).

MacIver, Robert M.: *The Web of Government* (New York: Macmillan, 1947).

Mayo, Henry D.: *An Introduction to Democratic Theory* (New York: Oxford, 1960).

Peaslee, Amos J.: *Constitutions of Nations* (The Hague, Netherlands: Nijhoff, 2d ed., 3 vols., 1956).

Pennock, J. Roland: *Liberal Democracy: Its Merits and Prospects* (New York: Rinehart, 1950).

Rodee, Carlton, T. J. Anderson, and C. Q. Christol: *Introduction to Political Science* (New York: McGraw-Hill, 1957).

Rossiter, Clinton: *Conservatism in America* (New York: Knopf, 1955).

Tocqueville, Alexis de: *Democracy in America* (New York: Knopf, 2 vols., 1945).

Van Dyke, Vernon: *Political Science: A Philosophical Analysis* (Palo Alto, Calif.: Stanford University Press, 1960).

Wheare, Kenneth C.: *Federal Government* (New York: Oxford, 3d ed., 1953).

————: *Modern Constitutions* (New York: Oxford, 1951).

REVIEW QUESTIONS

1. How does the national state differ from political units of other types in the modern world?

2. Distinguish between the terms "state" and "government."

3. What did Aristotle have in mind when he said that man is by nature a political animal?

4. What evidence is there that nationalism is a powerful force today? What evidence is there that nationalism is on the decline?

5. What factors are present in today's world that are forcing new political alignments and shaping new political institutions?

6. Compare the authority and function of the executive, legislative, and judicial branches under the presidential and parliamentary forms of government.

7. Distinguish between the federal and unitary forms of government, and give examples of each.

8. Of the various forms of government, why has democracy been practiced in comparatively few places and for relatively short periods of time?

9. Distinguish between individualism, collectivism, and progressivism.

10. How can the drift from individualism to varying degrees of collectivism in the United States and elsewhere be explained?

11. How does political science differ from history, philosophy, anthropology, economics, and sociology?

12. The late Elihu Root said, "The principal ground for reproach against any American citizen should be that he is not a politician." What did he have in mind? Do you agree or disagree?

13. Do you agree with James Bryce's statement that "No government demands so much from the citizens as Democracy and none gives back so much"?

14. What evidence is there to support Norman Corwin's statement, "Politics is intimate, not a pageant in a remote marble capitol"?

Chapter Two

Colonization,

Independence,

and Confederation

*In exploring the highways and byways of American
politics, I have been drawn to the conclusion that there
is more real conservation of ancient English institutions
in the rich geological strata of American politics—
at the state and county level, perhaps, even more
than at the federal level—than there is in England
itself. Americans come to Britain to see the roots of
their political system in the past and find much to inspire
them in the symbols and relics and ritual and
medieval mummery of one sort or another. But to see
many historic British institutions working more
robustly than they have worked in Britain for years and
to rediscover the type of political conflict which
characterized so much of British history, Englishmen
should go to the new world.*

KEITH KYLE[1]

American institutions, like those of other nations, have their origin deeply embedded in the past. Political institutions developed in four important periods: the colonial, the revolutionary, the confederation, and the constitutional. A brief historical review of government during the first three periods is essential to understand the constitutional

[1] "America: Curator of British Political Relics," *American Heritage*, vol. 9 (December, 1957), p. 12.

period, the subject of succeeding chapters. Such a review should increase respect for the past and understanding of the present. It also should foster the wise evaluation so badly needed in modern times.

COLONIZATION

Basis of Great Britain's Title to America.
Christopher Columbus discovered the West Indies in 1492, but John Cabot, an Ital-

ian in the service of England, was first to explore what is now the eastern coastline of the United States. Although unwilling to assist Columbus, King Henry VII of England quickly realized the importance of his discovery and in 1496 commissioned Cabot to "seek out, discover and find whatsoever isles, countries, regions or provinces of the heathen and infidels whatsoever they be, and in what part of the world soever they be, which before this time have been unknown to all Christians" and "to set up our banners and ensigns in every village, town, castle, isle, or mainland of them newly found." Cabot by 1498 had discovered Newfoundland and sailed southward along the eastern coast of America to what is now the Maryland-Virginia border. England's title in the New World was thus based upon the law of discovery and conquest.

Spanish explorers established similar title to what is now Florida, the Southwest, and western parts of America; French explorers planted their flag in the regions of Nova Scotia, the St. Lawrence River, the Great Lakes, and the Mississippi Valley to the Gulf of Mexico; while Dutchmen claimed the valleys of the Hudson and Delaware Rivers.

Rights of the Indians. Contrary to popular beliefs about their nomadic nature, Indians were found to occupy well-defined areas wherever the early explorers ventured. Tribes belonging to the Iroquois family, for example, inhabited the Great Lake and St. Lawrence region; those related to the Sioux family occupied the north central area; and those of the Muskhogean were settled in the southeast.

European nations claimed the right of *dominion* over lands held by Indian tribes in consequence of discovery but acknowledged that the Indians had the right of *occupancy*. This meant that European states asserted the right to colonize and manage

external affairs, while the Indians retained ownership of their lands with complete authority over internal tribal matters. This led the colonists to treat with the Indian tribes as "nations" and call their chiefs, or sachems, "kings." Although the whites brutally treated and exploited the Indians, they paid for most of the land and arranged transfers by solemn treaties.

Making North America British. The discovery of America stimulated many attempts at colonization. The first permanent settlement was at Jamestown, Virginia, in 1607. The Pilgrim Fathers established the second settlement at Plymouth, Massachusetts, in 1620. A series of settlements along the Atlantic seaboard made Georgia the thirteenth colony, in 1732.

Dutch, Swedes, French, and Spaniards all played their parts in colonizing America, but the British soon acquired a controlling influence. By conquering Holland's colonies (New Netherlands) in 1664, England acquired dominion over all the Atlantic seaboard from the Gulf of St. Lawrence to Florida. At the end of the French and Indian War, in 1763, England had eliminated Spanish control over Florida and French control over all of France's possessions in North America east of the Mississippi River. Thus, on the eve of the American Revolution, England controlled the present United States east of the Mississippi River.

Three Types of Colonies. Legal authorization was necessary to establish colonies in America. This was granted by the King in charters issued to trading companies, individuals, or groups of colonists. The charters authorized three types of colonial governments: royal (often called crown), proprietary, and charter (sometimes called corporate). The colonial governments are listed and described in the table on the Status of Colonial Governments on page 19.

Royal Colonies. Royal colonies, the most

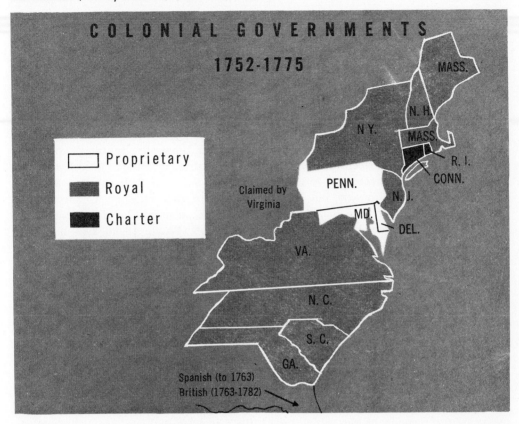

COLONIAL GOVERNMENTS

1752-1775

Proprietary

Royal

Charter

Claimed by Virginia

PENN.

MASS.

N.H.

N.Y.

MASS.

R.I.

CONN.

N.J.

MD.

DEL.

VA.

N.C.

S.C.

GA.

Spanish (to 1763)
British (1763-1782)

numerous, included New Hampshire, New York, New Jersey, Virginia, North Carolina, South Carolina, Georgia, and Massachusetts (after 1691). Charters granted to persons establishing these colonies were subsequently canceled[1] or withdrawn, establishing the King's control through commissions and instructions issued to governors.

The commissions were very much alike. They appointed a governor as the King's representative, or deputy, to carry out instructions. They provided for a council of men appointed by the Crown or governor to serve as an upper house of the legislature and assist the governor. Subject to the Crown's approval, the governor might suspend members of council from office, and,

in case of vacancies, appoint others. The commissions also authorized a general assembly of representatives to be chosen by the voters and a system of courts whose judges were appointed by the governor with the advice of council. Laws enacted by the legislature required the approval of the Crown, and appeals could be taken from the highest colonial court to the King in Council. The royal colonies were organized in this manner from shortly after their establishment until 1775.

Proprietary Colonies. At the time of the Revolution, Maryland, Delaware, and Pennsylvania were proprietary colonies. Lord Baltimore and William Penn, proprietors of these three colonies, and their heirs enjoyed absolute proprietorship of the territory. Charters authorized the proprietors to ap-

[1] Massachusetts, however, restored her charter as an instrument of government in 1775.

point governors and other officers, establish legislatures, create courts and appoint judges, set up local governments, and exercise the prerogatives that in royal colonies belonged to the Crown.

In Delaware and Maryland, the legislatures were bicameral: each upper house, called a council, had members appointed by the proprietor; each lower house had representatives elected by freemen. Pennsylvania's legislature was unicameral; the council had no legislative powers but served merely as an advisory body to the governor. Laws (except in Maryland) were subject to veto by the Crown. Appeals could be taken from the highest colonial court to the King in Council.

Charter Colonies. In the colonies of Rhode Island and Connecticut charters were granted to the colonists as a group after they had settled. The British government had no authority to interfere with their administration. These colonies were organized altogether upon popular and democratic principles: governors were elected annually by the freemen of the colony, and while they were supposed to be acceptable to the Crown, approval was seldom sought. The freemen chose members of both branches of the legislature. Acts of the legislature were neither subject to the governor's veto nor sent to England for approval. Judges and all other officers were appointed by the legislature, although appeals could be taken from the highest colonial courts to the King in Council.

Colonists cherished these charters, which allowed almost complete autonomy and spared them many of the excesses of royal governors suffered by neighbors. A story familiar to New Englanders illustrates the extent to which charters were treasured. In 1685, King James issued an order for the repeal of Connecticut's charter. The colony offered its submission, and in 1687 Sir Edmund Andros went to Hartford and, in the name of the Crown, declared the government dissolved. The charter was not surrendered, however, but secreted in an oak tree which is now displayed to sight-seers. Immediately after the revolution of 1688, the people resumed the exercise of all its powers. Succeeding British monarchs silently permitted this without struggle or resistance. Unlike most of the colonies that adopted new constitutions after the Declaration of Independence, Connecticut retained her charter as a fundamental law until 1818; Rhode Island kept hers until Dorr's Rebellion, in 1842. Had all the colonies been allowed so much autonomy and independence, some believe the Revolution would not have occurred.

New England Towns. In the New England colonies the principal unit of local government was the town (elsewhere called township). Counties existed but played a minor role, handling chiefly such matters as the administration of justice and the militia. Town government predominated because the first colonists came, not as individuals, but as church congregations or groups seeking religious freedom. Once here, the rugged soil, rigorous climate, and the presence of hostile Indians and wild animals encouraged small-scale farming, manufacturing, trading, fishing, and residence in compact communities. Towns were wholly rural, wholly urban, or sometimes partly rural and urban. They were incorporated with boundaries and powers defined by the colonial legislature.

Governmentally, the towns were pure, or direct, democracies. Town meetings, which were advertised meetings of voters, convened once a year or oftener. (In the early days, nonattendance was punishable by fine.) These gatherings enacted laws and chose officials to manage local business. Between town meetings, an elected board of

STATUS OF COLONIAL GOVERNMENTS IN 1775

GOVERNMENT	NAME AND FOUNDER	DATE FOUNDED
CHARTER (self-governing)		
• CHARTER granted directly to colonists.	Rhode Island, Roger Williams	1636
• GOVERNORS chosen by freemen for 1-year term.	Connecticut, Emigrants from Massachusetts	1636
• LEGISLATURE bicameral: both houses elected by freemen for 1-year terms.		
• JUDGES appointed by governor in council.		
• CROWN could not veto laws, but cases could be appealed from highest colonial court to King in Council.		
PROPRIETARY		
• PROPRIETOR owned colony but acknowledged sovereignty of King of England.	Maryland, Lord Baltimore	1634
	Delaware, Swedes	1638
• GOVERNOR appointed by proprietor.	Pennsylvania, William Penn	1681
• LEGISLATURE bicameral (except in Pennsylvania). Upper house appointed by proprietor. Lower house elected by freemen. Laws (except those of Maryland) were subject to approval and veto by Crown.		
• JUDGES appointed by governor and council. Appeals could be taken to King in Council.		
ROYAL		
• CROWN controlled directly by commissions and instructions to colonial government.	Virginia, London Company	1607
	Massachusetts, Puritans of the Massachusetts Bay Colony	1628
• GOVERNOR appointed by Crown and acted as King's deputy.	New Hampshire, John Mason	1629
	North Carolina ⎰ Eight South Carolina ⎱ nobles	1663
• LEGISLATURE bicameral (except in Georgia). Upper house appointed by King, lower house elected by freemen. Upper house acted as governor's council. All laws subject to approval and veto by Crown.	New York, Duke of York	1664
	New Jersey, Berkeley and Carteret	1664
• JUDGES appointed by governor. Appeals could be taken to King in Council.	Georgia, James Oglethorpe	1732

selectmen, with a town clerk and constable, managed affairs. Other officers were treasurer; assessor; surveyor of highways; the tithingman, a kind of Sunday constable who saw that people came to church and with foxtail wand kept them awake during sermons; the fence viewer, who supervised erection of boundary fences between adjoining properties; the hog reeve, who saw that rings were kept in noses of swine running at large; the field driver, who impounded stray cattle; the pound keeper, who caught and attended stray dogs; overseers of the poor; town criers; and many others. Besides providing local self-government, the town was a convenient electoral unit, with district representatives to the colonial legislature chosen at its open meetings.

The system was not without defects. Town powers were ill defined, and the right to take part in government was strictly limited to property owners. Too often, petty issues claimed excessive attention at meetings, and voters were selfishly parochial in their actions. The moderator might dominate proceedings arbitrarily, or defer to the more wealthy and influential landowners.

Nevertheless, these gatherings of voters —for social as well as political purposes— became deeply rooted in the affections of the people. "Town meeting" represents an ideal of direct democratic discussion and decision everywhere, and the old machinery is jealously maintained today in the more rural parts of New England. In more thickly settled sections, where the population is heterogeneous, modifications have occurred.

Southern Counties. In the southern colonies, town government never took root. The county was the primary unit of local government and administration. These colonies were settled more by individual entrepreneurs than by dissenting congregations; wild animals were scarce; and there were comparatively few hostile Indians. The land and climate were suitable for large-scale agriculture, particularly tobacco, cotton, indigo, and rice. Instead of homogeneous, compact communities, the plantation system necessitated a unit of local government larger than in the north.

At first plantation owners attended to local matters. Later, parishes served as both ecclesiastical and civil districts. These were governed by a vestry, consisting usually of several "select men" chosen by the parishioners, the minister, and churchwardens. A strong system of local government failed to develop, and before long the parish was overshadowed by the county.

Southern counties had no popular assembly, and so they were less democratic than northern towns. The principal officers were lieutenant, sheriff, justices of the peace, and coroners. County officers were appointed by the governor upon the recommendations of the justices of the peace. These justices, ordinarily a self-perpetuating body of aristocratic planters, dominated county governments. Thus controlled, the county became the unit of representation in the colonial assembly and of military, judicial, highway, and fiscal administration.

Local Government in the Middle Colonies. In the middle colonies, both towns and counties performed important functions. New York and New Jersey towns, resembling those of New England, played the larger role; in Pennsylvania and Delaware, the county predominated. The latter colonies originated the practice of electing county officers, particularly governing boards, similar to those now found in counties.

Cities during the Colonial Period. Within themselves the colonies were unitary. Large cities did not exist. As late as the Revolution, only about 3 per cent of the population lived in twenty-four boroughs (or cities), then in existence. These were established by charters issued by colonial governors and included New York (the oldest), Albany, Philadelphia, Annapolis, Norfolk, and smaller places mainly in Pennsylvania and New Jersey. In New England urban areas, such as Boston, the town-meeting system was adapted to municipal needs.

The principal governing authority in most boroughs was the common council composed of a mayor and recorder, both appointed by the governor, a small number of aldermen, and a larger number of councilmen elected by the voters. The common council controlled matters of administration, while the mayor and aldermen had additional judicial functions.

Three of the boroughs—Philadelphia, Annapolis, and Norfolk—were governed as "close corporations." Their aldermen and councilmen held positions for life, while the mayor and recorder were chosen by the common council from among the aldermen. Vacancies among the aldermen were filled by the common council, and among the councilmen by the mayor, recorder, and aldermen. These governing bodies were thus self-perpetuating and lacked the democratic features of other colonial-borough and present-day municipal governments.

The Good and Bad of Colonial Status. Certain advantages flowed from colonial status. Since most white inhabitants were British subjects, there was a common tradition, culture, language, and citizenship. Every colonist had a right to inhabit or inherit land in any other colony. The common law, with its invaluable guaranties of personal liberty, was the birthright and inheritance of all. Since appeals from local courts were taken to the King in Council, the law in the colonies was uniform in fundamental principles. England provided

protection from attacks by foreigners and pirates, handled foreign relations, helped defend against the Indians, counseled on questions of internal policy, and assisted with the administration of local laws. England retained control over commerce among the colonies and with foreign nations. Although this was often irritating, it did prevent intercolonial trade barriers. England also provided a uniform currency and an intercolonial postal service.

The most serious disadvantages of colonial status were: the colonies followed the fate of England in war or peace[1]; they were subject to the arbitrary whims and caprice of British kings and their agents; and Parliament might enact legislation detrimental to the best interests of the colonists without their knowledge or participation.

INDEPENDENCE

Disputes with Great Britain. The founding of Jamestown was separated from the Declaration of Independence by 169 years. During this time, incessant disputes arose between the colonists and representatives of the British government, particularly the royal governors, who often were of weak character. Many disputes were local, involving taxing proprietary lands, extending the franchise, importing convicts, raising troops, issuing paper money, organizing banks on insecure foundations, and establishing courts of law.

More serious quarrels arose when England enacted legislation monopolizing trade with the colonies, restricting the production and exportation of certain commodities (such as wool, wool products, and iron manufactures) to provide protection to manufacturers in England, and taxing colonists for the gen-

[1] For example, the war with France and her allies which lasted for over 50 years (1690–1748).

eral support of colonial administration. Colonial legislatures disobeyed obnoxious laws and orders, withheld appropriations for salaries of officials and soldiers until their demands were met, or addressed petitions to the home government. After the ascension of King George III, in 1760, Great Britain decided to deal firmly with her high-spirited and recalcitrant subjects in America. This fanned resentment to revolutionary fervor. Conciliation having failed by 1776, the colonists had a grim choice: submission or rebellion.

Committees of Correspondence. On the eve of their revolt, the colonists found, in England, a determined regime and, on this side of the Atlantic, all governmental machinery in the hands of loyal appointees of the King, except in Rhode Island and Connecticut. How, then, could fellow colonists express their opposition and form a "united front?" They found their answer in a system of committees of correspondence. Samuel Adams organized the first such committee in Boston in 1772. These groups hatched what was called by a bitter critic the "foulest, subtlest, and most venomous serpent ever issued from the egg of sedition."

Within one year almost every town in Massachusetts had similar committees and, encouraged by such events as the Boston Tea Party, they quickly spread to other colonies. By the end of 1773 a complete network of committees was organized to perform many of the same functions as modern political parties. They exchanged ideas and information and took over the management of town, county, and colonial affairs. Later, they elected the Continental Congress and provided an agency to enforce its decisions.

Thus, although the regularly constituted British-controlled governmental machinery remained, an extralegal system grew beside it, sapping its authority. A Tory later said that the work of the committees was "the source of the rebellion," and one present-day writer[1] has said:

The committees of correspondence that made the American Revolution possible were the town committees dominated by local "Sam Adamses" who were in close touch with Boston and other centers of radicalism. . . . Without their aid it is doubtful if the first Continental Congress would have been held in 1774 and the revolutionary movement in the colonies brought to its fruition in the Declaration of Independence. They made possible the domination of a great part of British America by cliques of radical patriots who looked to Sam Adams for leadership against the mother country. . . . After 1774, the colonies fairly bristled with hot-tempered Lib erty Boys, who, instead of calling themselves Sons of Liberty [as those who had previously resisted the Stamp Act called themselves], were now known as the committees of correspondence. But under whatever name these patriots worked, their purpose remained the same: to defend colonial liberty with arms rather than submit to British "tyranny."

The First Continental Congress. British attempts to punish the people of Massachusetts, who were more rebellious than others, united the colonies. On June 17, 1774, Massachusetts issued a call proposing that each colony appoint delegates to a conference to consider relations with England. In response, delegates from every colony except Georgia met in Philadelphia on September 5, 1774. The assemblage, which included the ablest men in the colonies, called itself the First Continental Congress. The delegates could not have been chosen by the regularly established colonial governments, which were still under the domination of Great Britain. Rather, they were

[1] John E. Miller, *Sam Adams, Pioneer of Propaganda* (Boston: Little, Brown, 1936), pp. 271–272. Quoted by permission of Little, Brown & Company and *Atlantic Monthly*.

appointed or elected by local committees, state conventions called by the local committees, or by state legislatures in which the revolutionary elements dominated. The delegates styled themselves "the delegates appointed by the good people of these colonies."

The Congress adopted an impressive Declaration of Rights, called for repeal of obnoxious legislation passed since 1763, agreed to stop the importation and consumption of British goods, and established a continental association to enforce the boycott. The association was a system of committees elected in towns, cities, and counties, supervised by colonial committees of correspondence, to detect and black-list parties caught violating the boycott. Before adjourning on October 26, Congress agreed to convene again in May, 1775, unless grievances had been redressed.

The Second Continental Congress. Great Britain replied to these developments with more repressive measures. Massachusetts prepared for war, and before another Congress met, blood had been shed at Concord and Lexington. The Second Continental Congress, which convened in Carpenters' Hall in Philadelphia on May 10, 1775, was a unicameral body comprised of practically the same men who had met earlier. Georgia, which had not sent delegates to the earlier Congress, did so during the summer. As before, delegates were chosen by popular conventions of the people of the various states or by the popular branches of the state legislatures. After the Declaration of Independence and the establishment of new state governments, the delegates were appointed by the legislatures of the states. Though "unique among the legislatures of history in that it had no authority to pass laws, no powers for enforcing the measures it did take, no means of raising money except printing, begging or borrowing,"[1] the Continental Congress served as the official organ of government for the united colonies until March, 1781, when the Articles of Confederation became effective. It was America's first national government.

The Declaration of Independence. When the Congress met in May, 1775, few desired or advocated independence. Washington, who had been appointed Commander in Chief of the colonial forces in July, 1775, said a year later: "When I took command of the army, I abhorred the idea of independence; now, I am convinced, nothing else will save us." Others had reached the same conclusion. Accordingly, Congress, on June 11, 1776, approved the appointment of a committee of five, with Thomas Jefferson as chairman, to draft a declaration of independence. A resolution to declare independence, introduced by Richard Henry Lee of Virginia, was approved by unanimous vote of Congress on July 2. The entire Declaration, approved two days later, became the "birth certificate of the American nation."[2]

Creation by Declaration of a Nation with de Facto Status. Two important questions of constitutional law were raised by the Declaration. The document declared "That these United Colonies are . . . absolved from all allegiance to the British Crown, and that all political connection between them and the state of Great Britain, is and ought to be totally dissolved. . . ." Did this destroy British sovereignty, as it announced, or did the colonies remain merely in a state of rebellion until the end

[1] Lynn Montross, *The Reluctant Rebels: The Story of the Continental Congress*, 1774–1789 (New York: Harper, 1950), p. 8.

[2] The full text of the Declaration of Independence is Appendix I.

of the war? The American view has been that the Declaration made them independent and sovereign both internally and externally; hence all steps taken by Congress after that date had the sanction of law. This view was pointedly stated by Justice Story:

The Declaration of Independence has . . . always been treated as an act of paramount and sovereign authority, complete and perfect *per se*, and *ipso facto* working an entire dissolution of all political connection with, and allegiance to, Great Britain. And this, not merely as a practical fact, but in a legal and constitutional view of the matter by the courts of justice.[1]

From the standpoint of international law, however, since foreign governments, with the exception of France and the Netherlands, refused to recognize or receive their ministers, the United Colonies remained in a *de facto* status until 1783. After this their status became *de jure*. This meant that, although Great Britain's sovereignty was doubtful, the United States was, nevertheless, not entitled to all the rights and privileges of nationhood until the rebellion terminated in its favor.

One Nation Created—Not Thirteen. Was one nation, or were thirteen nations, brought into existence by the Declaration? If one, then only the central government had authority to levy war; send and receive ambassadors, ministers, and consuls; and make treaties. If thirteen, then all were competent to do these things. The words of the Declaration are so ambiguous that they permit two interpretations. States' rights advocates called attention to these words: ". . . these United Colonies are, and of right ought to be *free and independent states* . . . and that as *free and independent states* . . . *they* have full power to levy war, conclude peace, and contract alliances, es-

tablish commerce, and do all other acts and things which independent states may of right do."[2] Nationalists stressed the statement that the Declaration was made "in the name and by authority of the good people of these colonies" by "the representatives of the United States of America, in general Congress assembled." To quote Justice Story, a stanch nationalist, again:

It [the Declaration of Independence] was not an act done by the State governments then organized, nor by persons chosen by them. It was emphatically the act of the whole *people* of the united colonies, by the instrumentality of their representatives, chosen for that among other purposes. . . . It was an act of original, inherent sovereignty by the people themselves, resulting from their right to change the form of government, and to institute a new one, whenever necessary for their safety and happiness. . . . It was, therefore, the achievement of the whole for the benefit of the whole.[3]

Provincialism was strong; the newly created states were as jealous of each other as of Great Britain; the Congress was weak and at the mercy of the states; and many of the states behaved as if they were sovereign. Nevertheless, in American law the theory has prevailed that a nation was created by the Declaration and the states remained sovereign only in the sense that in matters of a local nature they were self-governing. Of this the Supreme Court said in a twentieth-century decision [*United States v. Curtiss-Wright Export Corp.*, 299 U.S. 304 (1936)]:

As a result of the separation from Great Britain by the colonies, acting as a unit, the powers of external sovereignty passed from the Crown not to the colonies severally, but to the colonies in their collective and corporate capacity as the United States of America. Even before the Declaration, the colonies were a unit in foreign affairs, acting

[1] Joseph Story, *Commentaries on the Constitution of the United States* (Boston: Little, Brown, 2 vols., 1873), vol. 1, pp. 149–150.

[2] Italics are the authors'.

[3] *Ibid.*, p. 149.

through a common agency—namely, the Continental Congress, composed of delegates from the thirteen colonies. That agency exercised the powers of war and peace, raised an army, created a navy, and finally adopted the Declaration of Independence. Rulers come and go; governments end and forms of government change; but sovereignty survives. A political society cannot endure without a supreme will somewhere. Sovereignty is never held in suspense. When, therefore, the external sovereignty of Great Britain in respect of the colonies ceased, it immediately passed to the Union.

Converting Colonies into States. As events moved toward a showdown in 1775, crises developed in the internal affairs of the colonies, calling for much reorganization. The flight of most of the royal governors and other officials left many royal colonies without any official governments. In other instances, as in Massachusetts, resistance to British authorities made new arrangements necessary. Congress recommended that the states adopt "such governments as shall, in the opinion of the representatives of the people, best conduce to the happiness and safety of their constituents." Since no machinery existed with which to make the transition, Congress recommended that new governments be established by "assemblies or conventions," and most of the states followed this counsel. Charters of Rhode Island and Connecticut, however, needed only minor revisions, and Massachusetts slipped back to its 1691 charter, using it until 1780. For the first time in history a large group of communities had begun the formation of their own governments under written constitutions. As they did so, they began to refer to themselves as "states" rather than "colonies."

Provisions of the New State Constitutions. The new state documents, for the most part, carried forward the main outlines of colonial arrangements. Seven of them contained bills of rights; all restricted the suffrage. All established three branches of government; each was supposedly independent of the others, but in practice the popularly elected lower house became supreme. Reflecting the colonies' dislike of governors, the new constitutions deprived executives of many powers of the colonial period. Executives were elected by the people in four states, by the legislature in the others, and customarily for terms of one year. Only in Massachusetts was the governor given the veto, and that could be overridden by two-thirds of the legislature. In Pennsylvania and Georgia the legislature was unicameral, but the other states followed the colonial two-house system. The lower house, variously called house of burgesses, house of commons, or house of representatives, was almost exactly like that of colonial times; members, elected by the voters, served for one-year terms. Lower houses retained the treasured prerogative of originating tax measures. The upper house, called the legislative council in New Jersey and Delaware and the senate or council elsewhere, was, as a rule, elected by the voters or the lower house for terms varying from one to five years. The senate was smaller than the house for terms varying from one to five terms, and with more exacting qualifications. The senate became typed as representing propertied interests, and the house, the people of the state.

Judiciaries, too, reflected the revolutionary ideas of the people. The selection of judges was changed from appointment by colonial governors to election by state legislatures or appointment by popularly controlled executives. Georgia went so far as to provide for popular election—the method followed by most states today. Appointment was commonly for short terms, and judges were usually subject to removal by the legislatures. Court systems and procedures remained about as they had been. First, there were local peace magistrates and local inferior courts for the trial of petty civil cases and offenses. Above these stood a central court (analogous to our county or district courts of common pleas, quarter session, oyer and terminer, etc.) with civil and criminal jurisdiction over more serious cases. At the top stood a supreme court of review.

CONFEDERATION

Adoption of the Articles. Both the First and Second Continental Congresses met and functioned without constitutions. Created to meet an emergency, they were considered temporary agencies. When war appeared imminent and independence desirable, the central government had to be placed on a firm and permanent basis. On June 12, 1776, the day after a committee was appointed to prepare a declaration of independence, Congress appointed another committee consisting of one member from each colony "to prepare and digest the form of a confederation to be entered into between these colonies."

The committee reported a month later, and the plan was debated off and on until approved by Congress on November 17, 1777. All but Delaware and Maryland ratified in 1778. Holding out for assurances over the proper distribution and control of the territories west of the Allegheny Mountains, Delaware ratified in 1779, while Maryland delayed until March 1, 1781, on which date the Articles went into effect. They were the first constitution of the United States of America.[1]

Nature of the Confederation. It has been observed that, from a legal point of view, the Declaration of Independence created one nation, rather than thirteen, and it was suggested that in practice Congress was almost completely at the mercy of the states. The

[1] The text of the Articles is Appendix II.

Articles removed all pretense about the nature of the new government and demonstrated that the radicals were still in the saddle.

The Articles were adopted by "delegates of the states," and Article III stated that the "states . . . severally enter into a firm league of friendship with each other." This was not a union of the people of the colonies considered as a whole, but a league of states. They bound themselves together "for their common defense, the security of their liberties, and their mutual and general welfare," but each retained "sovereignty, freedom and independence, and every power, jurisdiction and right, which is [was] not expressly delegated to the United States, in Congress assembled." The Articles were thus another reflection of the radicals' abhorrence of strong government.

Government Established. The governmental machinery authorized by the Articles was meager indeed. Congress was the sole organ of government. There was no executive branch, but Congress was authorized to appoint such committees and "civil officers" as executive business required, and they were to perform their duties under its direction. There was no separate judicial branch. Federal courts were authorized only "for the trial of piracies and felonies committed on the high seas," for "reviewing and determining finally appeals in all cases of captures," and for the settlement of disputes between the states.

The Congress was unicameral and comprised not less than two nor more than seven delegates from each state appointed annually by the legislatures. No person could be a delegate for more than three years in any term of six years. Delegates were paid by the states, if at all; they voted by states, with each state having one vote; and they could be recalled and replaced at any time. Sessions were seldom attended by

STRUCTURE OF GOVERNMENT UNDER ARTICLES OF CONFEDERATION
1781-1789

INDIVIDUAL CITIZENS
(whom Congress could reach only through their respective states)

THIRTEEN SOVEREIGN STATES

CONGRESS

Unicameral. Each state had one vote with two to seven delegates.

Powers limited. Could conduct war and foreign affairs, request money and men from the states, conduct postal service, regulate Indian affairs. Other powers with consent of nine states, viz., borrow and coin money, make treaties, fix size of army and navy, pass a budget. Lacked power to regulate commerce, or to levy taxes.

LEGISLATIVE BRANCH

Officers appointed by Congress to do some of its executive work, i.e., foreign secretary, secretary of war, etc.

Committee of States to conduct affairs between sessions of Congress.

Articles of Confederation and Perpetual Union

Fundamental written law upon which the structure of government was based

In the relatively simple government established under the Articles of Confederation, the central government was weak and dependent upon the states. [Adapted from Shephard L. Whitman, *Visual Outline of American Government*, Student Outline Series (New York: Longmans, 1933). Used by permission of David McKay Company, Inc.]

one-third of the delegates the rules permitted, and as few as one-eighth of the entire body could negate resolutions.

Powers of Congress. The central government was given many of the powers wielded by the British government during the colonial period. No implied powers were granted; rather, Congress had only powers "expressly delegated." Some of them were to declare war and conclude peace; conduct foreign relations, including sending ambassadors and making treaties; requisition revenue from the states in proportion to the value of their land; requisition soldiers in proportion to the number of white inhabitants in each state; borrow money, emit bills of credit, and coin money; build and equip a navy; settle disputes between the states; establish a postal system; regulate weights and measures; create courts for limited purposes; and appoint committees and officers. The most important of these powers, including the addition of amendments, could be exercised only with the concurrence of all the states, while the others required the approval of at least nine state delegations.

Obligations of States. On their part, the states pledged themselves to observe their obligations and the orders of Congress; extend full rights to one another's citizens; give full faith and credit to the records, acts, and judicial proceedings of every other state; deliver up fugitives from justice to each other; submit their disputes to Congress for settlement; and allow open intercourse and commerce between the states. Retaining all powers not granted to Congress, the states were left with primary responsibility for protecting life and property and promoting the general welfare.

Weaknesses of the Confederation. Adoption of the Articles evoked great jubilation, but the weaknesses of the Confederation were soon shown. The fundamental defect was the dependence of Congress upon the good will of the states. With a public debt of over 40 million dollars and current obligations to meet, Congress, powerless to lay and collect taxes, could only requisition and urge the states to forward their quotas. Impoverished by war, harassed by social distress, and jealous of their prerogatives, the states either could not or would not pay their assessments. Of a total of $15,670,000 requisitioned between 1781 and 1786, only $2,419,000 were supplied. Georgia and North Carolina paid not a cent.

Congress was equally incapable of regulating interstate commerce, with the result that the states surrounded themselves with trade barriers, hampering the free flow of commerce. Without power to regulate foreign commerce, Congress could not compete with European rivals who discriminated against American trade. Possessing authority to coin money, Congress was prevented from doing so; hence a uniform system of currency did not exist and the states were flooded with paper money and currency of dubious value. Property holders and the commercial classes felt insecure because states could impair the obligation of contracts without external restraint.

The states developed increasing disregard for the central government. Knowing that they were usurping powers of Congress, some states regulated relations with the Indians. Others sent agents abroad for the negotiation of agreements and treaties. Most states organized their own navies and armies, and some conducted war outside their jurisdiction without the consent of Congress. With lagging interest in union, and without sustained organizational support from the radicals who gave it birth, the Congress became increasingly helpless. Only by the determined and strenuous efforts of a few men was it held together at all. Some members left in disgust.

Two amendments, to authorize Congress to levy tariff duties on imports, missed ratification by only one state—Rhode Island on the first occasion, New York on the second. All other attempts to improve the Articles having failed, some of the states were on the verge of civil war by the end of 1786. In Shays' Rebellion (1786) a multitude of angry debtors attempted to stop the collection of debts and taxes by preventing judges from holding court in several parts of Massachusetts. At one time it looked as if the state government might be overwhelmed. Although suppressed, the incident frightened the leaders and conservative elements into improving the framework of government and strengthening central government.

Achievements of the Confederation. Congress met annually in Philadelphia or other cities. It created standing administrative committees to handle foreign, financial, military, and naval affairs, which proved to be the forerunners of our present departments of State, Treasury, and Defense. The Congress preserved the idea of union until our present Constitution was adopted; it concluded the war and negotiated peace with England; it established diplomatic and consular relations with foreign powers, sending abroad, as representatives of the new republic, such distinguished statesmen as Silas Deane, Benjamin Franklin, Thomas Jefferson, and John Adams; and it assisted with the formation and adoption of the present Constitution. Its most brilliant achievement was the enactment of the Northwest Ordinance in 1787, by which the territory between the Alleghenies and the Mississippi, ceded to the United States by the states after the adoption of the Articles, was to be organized and governed. The colonial governments, so set up provided models followed later in organizing territories and states west of the Mississippi, Alaska, Hawaii, the Philippines, Puerto Rico, and the Virgin Islands.

These achievements indicate that in spite of its weaknesses the Confederation had much to its credit. Some scholars who have recently studied the period contend that the picture given to us by conservatives and Federalists has overdrawn the difficulties of the time and the shortcomings of the Confederation Congress. Professor Merrill Jensen,[1] for example, contends that, far from being a period of disillusionment and disintegration, the period that followed the

Revolution was one of "exuberant optimism" over newly found independence and the boundless opportunities that lay ahead. Instead of the general depression and distress pictured by the Federalists, Professor Jensen insists the period was one of social reform, economic progress, and cultural advancement. Trade barriers between the states, he says, "were the exception rather than the rule" and fewer than exist today.[2] National credit was "sound"; national debt was "fantastically low" when compared with that of most countries today; money received by the Confederation government was carefully spent; and many of the states were more successful in managing the creditor-debtor problem than has been generally believed.

Be this as it may, even the champions of confederation conceded the necessity for reform. The question was not whether the central government should have greater powers, but whether it should remain dependent on the states. The controversy was intense, as it is today over what powers should be given the United Nations. In the end the nationalists triumphed over the radicals who had precipitated the Revolution, dominated the state governments, and established and defended the Articles of Confederation. The movement for constitutional revision took tangible form in 1785 when two states took the initiative.

The Conference at Alexandria. Ignoring Congress, Maryland and Virginia, after incessant disputes over tariffs and navigation on the Potomac and adjoining waters, agreed to confer about those problems. Both appointed commissioners who met first at Alexandria, Virginia, then at Washington's home at Mount Vernon, in March, 1785. The commissioners formed a plan which contemplated uniform import duties and regulation of commerce and currency

[1] *The New Nation: A History of the United States during the Confederation, 1781–1789* (New York: Knopf, 1950).

[2] *Ibid.*, p. 340.

in the two states. Realizing that other states might be interested in these problems, they recommended that they be invited to meet at some future time.

The Annapolis Convention. Upon receipt of its commissioners' report, the Virginia legislature proposed that commissioners from all the states meet at Annapolis for the purpose of considering the trade and commerce of the United States as a whole. Representatives of only five states appeared at the opening of the convention in September, 1786, but others had been appointed. When, after three weeks, the

others did not appear, the delegates passed a resolution proposing that in 1787 another convention be called to meet in Philadelphia to consider the state of the union. Congress was slow to approve this plan, but six states appointed delegates to the proposed Philadelphia Convention. Finally, on February 21, 1787, Congress recommended that the convention be held, in terms that ignored the Annapolis movement but set the same place and date. All states, save Rhode Island, appointed delegates to attend the convention which formulated the present Constitution.

FOR FURTHER READING

Adams, Randolph G.: *Political Ideas of the American Revolution* (New York: Facsimile Library, 1939).

Alden, John Richard: *The American Revolution, 1775–1783* (New York: Harper, 1954).

Allen, H. C.: *Great Britain and the United States: A History of Anglo-American Relations (1783–1952)* (New York: St. Martin's, 1955).

Andrews, Charles M.: *The Colonial Background of the American Revolution* (New Haven, Conn.: Yale University Press, 1924).

Beard, Charles A., and Mary R. Beard: *The Rise of American Civilization* (New York: Macmillan, rev. and enl. ed., 4 vols., 1927–1942).

Becker, Carl: *The Declaration of Independence* (New York: Harcourt, Brace, 1922).

Benson, Lee: *Turner and Beard: Historical Writing Reconsidered* (New York: Free Press, 1960).

Bridenbaugh, Carl: *Cities in Revolt: Urban Life in America, 1743–1776* (New York: Knopf, 1955).

Brown, Robert E.: *Middle-class Democracy and the Revolution in Massachusetts* (Ithaca, N.Y.: Cornell University Press, 1955).

Burnett, Edmund C.: *The Continental Congress* (New York: Macmillan, 1941).

Channing, Edward: *Town and County Government in the English Colonies of North America* (Baltimore: Johns Hopkins Press, 1884).

Dumbault, Edward: *The Declaration of Independence and What It Means Today* (Norman, Okla.: University of Oklahoma Press, 1950).

Ferguson, E. James: *The Power of the Purse* (Chapel Hill, N.C.: University of North Carolina Press, 1961).

Gipson, Lawrence Henry: *The Coming of the Revolution, 1763–1775* (New York: Harper, 1954).

Griffith, Ernest S.: *History of American City Government: The Colonial Period* (New York: Oxford, 1938).

Hagan, William T.: *American Indians* (Chicago: University of Chicago Press, 1961).

Miller, John C.: *Triumph of Freedom, 1775–1783* (Boston: Little, Brown, 1948).

Montross, Lynn: *The Reluctant Rebels, The Story of the Continental Congress, 1774–1789* (New York: Harper, 1950).

Nevins, Allan: *The American States during and after the Revolution* (New York: Macmillan, 1924).

Osgood, Herbert L.: *The American Colonies in the 17th Century* (New York: Columbia University Press, 4 vols., 1924–1925).

Richeson, Charles R.: *British Politics and the Revolution* (Norman, Okla.: University of Oklahoma Press, 1954).

Robson, E.: *American Revolution in Its Political and Military Aspects, 1763–1783* (New York: Oxford, 1955).

Rossiter, Clinton: *Seedtime of the Republic* (New York: Harcourt, Brace, 1952).

Saunders, Jennings B.: *Evolution of the Executive Departments of the Continental Congress,*

1774–1789 (Chapel Hill, N.C.: University of North Carolina Press, 1935).

Thorpe, Francis N.: *The Federal and State Constitutions, Colonial Charters, and Other Organic Laws of the States, Territories, and Colonies* . . . , H. Doc. 357, 59th Cong., 2d Sess. (7 vols., 1909).

REVIEW QUESTIONS

1. What was the basis of Great Britain's title to American possessions in the New World? Can national states acquire titles today in the same manner?

2. What rights were accorded to American Indians by colonizing powers during the early period of American history? What practical difference does it make today how American Indians were treated in earlier times?

3. Distinguish between the three types of colonies established by Great Britain in the New World. Why were three types established rather than one?

4. What were some of the important similarities and differences in colonial governments? In state governments established during the revolutionary period?

5. What were the principal disputes with Great Britain that led to the Revolutionary War?

6. Trace the procedure by which the American Revolution was organized and consummated. How do you explain the fact that Great Britain found it impossible to restrain and subdue rebellion within her empire?

7. Compare the central government of the revolutionary period with that established by the Articles of Confederation.

8. Did the Declaration of Independence create one nation or thirteen of them? What practical difference did it make whether one or thirteen nations were created?

9. What were the weaknesses and achievements under the Articles of Confederation?

10. Do you agree with Merrill Jensen's contention that the Articles of Confederation were more desirable and effective than has been generally believed?

11. Identify some of the significant features of American government which were inherited from Great Britain.

12. Trace the steps by which the Constitutional Convention of 1787 was called.

Chapter Three

Framing and Adopting the Constitution

*I agree to this constitution with all its faults, if they
are such; because I think a general Government
necessary for us, and there is no form of Government
but what may be a blessing to the people if well
administered, and believe farther that this is likely to
be well administered for a course of years, and can
only end in Despotism, as other forms have done before
it, when the people shall have become so corrupted
as to need despotic Government, being incapable
of any other. I doubt too whether any other Convention we
can obtain, may be able to make a better Constitution.
For when you assemble a number of men to have the
advantage of their joint wisdom, you inevitably
assemble with those men, all their prejudices, their
passions, their errors of opinion, their local interests, and
their selfish views. From such an assembly can a
perfect production be expected? . . . Thus I consent,
Sir, to this Constitution because I expect no better,
and because I am not sure, that it is not the best.*

BENJAMIN FRANKLIN[1]

The Annapolis Convention was followed
by a fast-moving series of events. Slightly
more than a year later, the Constitution had
been drafted, signed, and referred to the
states for ratification.

With recommendations of the Annapolis
Convention in hand, and with knowledge
that several states had already appointed
delegates, Congress adopted a resolution on
February 21, 1787, calling upon the states
to send delegates to Philadelphia to meet
on the second Monday in May

. . . for the sole and express purpose of re-
vising the Articles of Confederation and reporting to Congress and the several legislatures such alterations and provisions therein
as shall when agreed to in Congress and
confirmed by the states render the federal

[1] Statement read at the Constitutional Convention by James Wilson on Monday, September 17,
1787. Charles C. Tansill (ed.), *Documents Illus-*
trative of the Formation of the Union of the
American States, H. Doc. 398, 69th Cong., 1st
Sess. (1927), pp. 739–740.

constitution adequate to the exigencies of Government & the preservation of the Union.

THE CONSTITUTIONAL CONVENTION

Delegates were promptly appointed in eleven of the states by legislatures or governors. New Hampshire was favorably disposed, but owing to local conditions failed to act before the convention was well under way. Rhode Island, controlled by radicals who feared further centralization of power, refused to send delegates. Credentials authorized the delegates to proceed to Philadelphia to join with others in "devising, deliberating on, and discussing," to quote from credentials given the Pennsylvania delegation, "all such alterations and further Provisions, as may be necessary to render the federal Constitution fully adequate to the exigencies of the Union. . . ."[1]

Personnel of the Convention. Seventy-four delegates were appointed; fifty-five put in an appearance at some time or other; an average of thirty were present at the sessions; and, at the close, thirty-nine signed the completed document. Thomas Jefferson and John Adams were in Europe on diplomatic missions or they surely would have been appointed. Patrick Henry "smelt a rat"[2] and declined appointment. Richard Henry Lee, then attending the sessions of Congress in New York, said that, because

he was a member of Congress, he ought not to participate in the convention. John Jay declined; Samuel Adams and John Hancock were not appointed because of their well-known hostility to strengthening the central government; while Thomas Paine had gone to Europe.

Otherwise, nearly all the important leaders of the country were designated to attend. The most distinguished figure was George Washington, still "first in the hearts of his countrymen." Others of prominence were James Madison, Edmund Randolph, and George Mason, of Virginia; Benjamin Franklin, Robert Morris, James Wilson, and Gouverneur Morris, of Pennsylvania; John Rutledge and Charles Pinckney, of South Carolina; Oliver Ellsworth, William Samuel Johnson, and Roger Sherman, of Connecticut; Rufus King, of Massachusetts; Alexander Hamilton, of New York; William Paterson, of New Jersey; and John Dickinson, of Delaware.

Qualifications of the Delegates. The delegates were, on the whole, young. Franklin, the oldest, was eighty-one; Dayton (New Jersey), the youngest, was twenty-six; fourteen were fifty or over; twenty-one were less than forty. The average age was forty-two. Most of the delegates came from the educated and professional classes. Twenty-five were college men, and thirty-three had studied law. Most outstanding of all was their wide experience in public affairs. To illustrate: seven had been state governors, forty-six had served in colonial or state legislatures, and forty-two had been delegates to the Continental Congress.

According to the late Charles A. Beard, most of the delegates came from the coastal region and belonged to the professional and propertied classes. The hinterland and poorer classes were underrepresented. The movement for a new constitution was a "conservative counter revolution" aimed at halting the

[1] Copies of credentials furnished several delegations may be found in Charles C. Tansill (ed.), *Documents Illustrative of the Formation of the Union of the American States,* H. Doc. 398, 69th Cong., 1st Sess. (1927), pp. 55–84.

[2] The "rat" apparently was a suspicion that the nationalists intended doing more than revise the Articles. More particularly, his opposition to the movement for revision was based upon a fear that Northern statesmen would carry out a project begun by John Jay whereby navigation rights on the Mississippi would be sacrificed to Spain to the detriment of the South. Moses C. Tyler, *Patrick Henry* (New York: Houghton Mifflin, 1915), pp. 298–312.

tide of radicalism then rising from demands of persons without property or right to vote. The Constitution was an economic document drawn by a consolidated economic group with property interests at stake.

Recent scholars challenge Beard's economic interpretation.[1] After studying colonial Massachusetts, Prof. Robert E. Brown insists that Beard overstressed class conflict. In his opinion, the Revolution was not accompanied by social upheaval in which the poor were arrayed against the well-to-do.

Prof. Forrest McDonald challenges Beard on the basis of an impressive appraisal of the economic interests of fifty-five delegates who attended the Constitutional Convention. According to him, a fourth had voted in their state legislatures for paper money and/or debtor-relief laws. Another fourth had economic interests that were adversely affected by the Constitution they helped write. Farm properties, and not—as Beard claimed— mercantile, manufacturing, and public securities, were the most common and important holdings of the delegates. At the Convention, they did not act as a consolidated economic group; each delegate was a "unique human being" responding to his own philosophy as well as to material interests. More decisive than economic interests, McDonald states, were the interests and outlooks of the states and localities represented.

More studies are needed before the merits of the arguments can be finally assessed. Whatever the outcome, experience has demonstrated that the Constitution was a cautious and conservative document. However, it provided for a more popular style of government than existed at that time in any other important country.

Estimates of the Delegates. Much praise has been heaped upon those who wrote the Constitution. Jefferson, writing from Paris, characterized them as "an assembly of demi-gods." A French chargé, writing to his government, said, ". . . if all the delegates named for this Philadelphia Convention are present, one will never have seen, even in Europe, an assembly more respectable for talents, knowledge, disinterestedness and patriotism than those who will compose it."[2] Charles A. Beard has written:

It was a truly remarkable assembly of men that gathered in Philadelphia on May 14, 1787, to undertake the work of reconstructing the American system of government. It is not merely patriotic pride that compels one to assert that never in the history of assemblies has there been a convention of men richer in political experience and in practical knowledge, or endowed with a profounder insight into the springs of human action and the intimate essence of government. It is indeed an astounding fact that at one time so many men skilled in statecraft could be found on the very frontiers of civilization among a population numbering about four million whites. It is no less a cause for admiration that their instrument of government should have survived the trials and crises of a century that saw the wreck of more than a score of paper constitutions.[3]

Perhaps Professor Farrand, a distinguished historian of the Constitution, is near the truth when he concludes:

[1] For Beard's views, see *An Economic Interpretation of the Constitution of the United States* (New York: Macmillan, 1939 ed.). For recent critical views, see Robert E. Brown, *Charles A. Beard and the Constitution: A Critical Analysis of "An Economic Interpretation of the Constitution"* (Princeton, N.J.: Princeton University Press, 1956), and Forrest McDonald, *We the People, The Economic Origins of the Constitution* (Chicago: University of Chicago Press, 1958).

[2] Quoted in Homer C. Hockett, *The Constitutional History of the United States, 1776–1826* (New York: Macmillan, 2 vols., 1939), vol. 1, p. 206.

[3] *The Supreme Court and the Constitution* (New York: Macmillan, 1912), pp. 86–87. Quoted by permission of The Macmillan Company, publishers.

Great men there were, it is true, but the convention as a whole was composed of men such as would be appointed to a similar gathering at the present time: professional men, business men and gentlemen of leisure; patriotic statesmen and clever, scheming politicians; some trained by experience and study for the task before them, and others utterly unfit. It was essentially a representative body, taking possibly a somewhat higher tone from the social conditions of the time, the seriousness of the crisis, and the character of the leaders.[1]

Organization of the Convention. On the appointed second Monday—May 14, 1787 —delegates from several states gathered in Independence Hall at Philadelphia. Here Congress had sat and the Declaration of Independence had been adopted. Because representatives from a majority of states failed to appear, the delegates adjourned daily until May 25, when a quorum was present.

The Convention organized immediately. Its first act was to choose a president. Franklin was a logical choice because of his age, reputation, and presidency of the state in whose capital the Convention was held. He withdrew, however, whereupon the Pennsylvania delegation placed Washington's name in nomination. He was promptly and unanimously elected. Major William Jackson, a former assistant secretary of war who had actively sought the position, was chosen secretary. Other minor officers were appointed, and rules were formulated. Rules provided that each state delegation have one vote, that a majority of the states should constitute a quorum, and that the proceedings be kept secret. Precautions were taken against "leaks." Sentries stood at doors to prevent eavesdropping, and according to the Beards, "they even had a

discreet colleague accompany the aged Franklin to his convivial dinners with a view to checking that amiable gentleman whenever, in unguarded moments, he threatened to divulge secrets of state."[2] In spite of precautions, the pledge to secrecy appears to have been broken.

Records of the Convention. Jackson's minutes consist of the formal journal of the Convention, the journal of the Committee of the Whole House, and records of votes cast.[3] The minutes contain a bare record of events and reveal little about the debates. They were kept in an untidy manner, and historians have found them frequently in error. Before the Convention adjourned, the secretary was directed to leave his papers with Washington, who was instructed to keep them until further directed by Congress. Washington deposited them with the Department of State in 1796, where they remained untouched until 1818, when Congress ordered them printed.[4]

Fortunately for posterity, notes were kept by several of the delegates. Madison's proved the most complete and reliable. They were purchased by Congress after Madison's death in 1836 and published in 1840 under the title of *The Papers of James Madison.*[5] Immediately they became the

---

[1] Max Farrand, *The Framing of the Constitution of the United States* (New Haven, Conn.: Yale University Press, 1940), pp. 40–41.

[2] Charles A. Beard and Mary R. Beard, *The Rise of American Civilization* (New York: Macmillan, 4 vols., 1927–1942), vol. 1, 312. Quoted by permission of The Macmillan Company, publishers.

[3] The originals of most of these may be found at present in the National Archives, Washington, D.C.

[4] They may be consulted in many libraries under the title of *Journal, Acts and Proceedings of the Convention, . . . which formed the Constitution of the United States* (Boston: T. B. Wait, 1819).

[5] The most pertinent documents, including Madison's notes, may be found in *Documents Illustrative of the Formation of the Union of the American States,* previously cited.

PLANS BEFORE THE CONSTITUTIONAL CONVENTION*

RANDOLPH, VIRGINIA	PATERSON, NEW JERSEY	PINCKNEY, SOUTH CAROLINA
LEGISLATIVE		
Bicameral. One house popularly elected; second chosen by first from nominees of state legislatures	Unicameral. Delegates to be chosen by state legislatures	Bicameral. House of Delegates elected by people on basis of population (Negroes counting three-fifths); Senate elected by House of Delegates from four districts
Voting based on money contributions or free population or both	Each state one vote	Each delegate and senator to have one vote
Powers of Congress broad	Powers of Congress enlarged; states to collect taxes but Congress to act if states default	Powers of Congress broad
EXECUTIVE		
Single executive chosen by Congress for one term only	Plural executive chosen by Congress for one term only	President elected by Congress annually
Authority to execute laws and exercise executive rights vested in Confederation Congress	Authority to execute laws, appoint, direct military operations	
JUDICIAL		
Supreme and inferior courts; judges appointed by Congress for life; Council of Revision to exercise a suspensive veto over acts of the national and state legislatures	Supreme court only; judges appointed by plural executive for life	A Federal court; admiralty courts might be established by Congress in each state; judges appointed for life
FEDERAL-STATE RELATIONS		
Federal government to admit new states and guarantee republican form of government; Federal government to negative state laws incompatible with the Union; also to use force against any state failing to fulfill its duty	Acts of Congress and treaties "supreme law of the respective states"; conflicting state laws forbidden; Federal executive to use force against noncooperative states	Federal governments to admit new states; states prohibited from keeping troops of war, entering into compacts, etc.; state laws to be approved by Federal legislature before becoming effective

* For texts of these plans, see Max Farrand (ed.), "The Records of the Federal Convention of 1787" (New Haven, Conn.: Yale University Press, 3 vols., 1911), vol. 3, pp. 593-631.

HAMILTON, NEW YORK

Bicameral
Assembly elected by people on basis of population; terms, 3 years; Senate elected for life terms by electors chosen by people

Congress to have power to pass all laws deemed necessary to common defense and general welfare of Union; Senate alone to declare war, approve treaties and appointments

President elected for life term by electors chosen by people within each state

Powers included veto, execution of laws, war, treaties, appointments, pardons

Supreme court appointed by President with consent of Senate for life terms; legislature given power to institute courts in each state

State laws contrary to Constitution are void; governors of states appointed by Federal government and have veto over state legislation; a special court provided to hear controversies arising between United States and particular states over territories

most authoritative source of information about the Convention. One should note that official records of the Convention were unavailable to those who construed the Constitution for thirty years, and Madison's illuminating papers were unavailable for more than half a century.

The Virginia Plan. On May 29 the Convention resolved itself into a committee of the whole to hear and consider various plans and proposals. The first and most important question was whether merely to revise the Articles or to construct a truly national government. The committee promptly decided in favor of a national government. Thereupon Governor Edmund Randolph of Virginia presented a plan prepared under the leadership of Madison. The Virginia Plan represented the large-state group and those favoring a strong central government and contemplated a complete overhauling of the Articles. Details of this and other plans presented are compared in the table of Plans before the Constitutional Convention.

The Virginia Plan was discussed for two weeks. Critics contended that it contemplated too great a departure from the Articles and placed the small states in a position of inequality. Had the plan been adopted as proposed, Virginia, for example, would have had fifteen or sixteen representatives in Congress, while Georgia, Delaware, and Rhode Island would each have had only two or three. This plan would have given the large states control over all three branches of government.

The New Jersey and Other Plans. Objections led to counterproposals. Chief of these were the New Jersey, Pinckney, and Hamilton Plans. The New Jersey Plan, presented on June 15 by William Paterson, received most consideration. It contemplated a less radical departure from the Articles than the Virginia Plan and won the support of confederationists and small-state delegations. After four days of debate, the committee of the whole voted 7 to 3 to reject it in favor of something more akin to the proposals made by Governor Randolph of Virginia.

The Critical Period. After endorsing the Virginia Plan, the Convention reconstituted itself to consider the report of the committee of the whole. The next five weeks were crucial. On several occasions the Convention appeared ready to go on the rocks. Martin of Maryland reported, on June 28, that it was on the verge of dissolution, "scarce held together by the strength of a hair," and Franklin proposed that the Convention henceforth open its sessions with prayers. Hamilton and others thought that to start at that late date would bring on "some disagreeable animadversions" and lead the public to believe that the Convention was split with dissension. Another delegate observed that the true cause was that the Convention had no funds with which to hire a preacher. Whatever the reason, the suggestion was not followed, but the delegates found ways of compromising their differences.

The Connecticut Compromise. The Constitution has been referred to as a "bundle of compromises." The crucial question was: How erect a government strong enough to meet the exigencies of the hour which would not "swallow up" the states nor place the small ones at the mercy of the larger?

The nationalists argued that, since state sovereignty had been the fundamental weakness of the Articles, a new government to be strong must derive its authority directly from the people. They pleaded for representation proportionate in both houses to population or tax contribution or both. Small-state delegates, on the other hand, made it clear that they would never enter

a union which impaired their identity and equality. Said Dickinson of Delaware, "We would sooner submit to a foreign power, than to submit to be deprived of an equality of suffrage, in both branches of the legislature, and thereby thrown under the dominion of the larger states."[1] The solution of this impasse was an absolute prerequisite to further progress.

Day after day the issue was debated until finally, as hope ebbed, Dr. Johnson, of Connecticut, renewed a suggestion previously made which led to a solution. Said he:

The controversy must be endless whilst Gentlemen differ in the grounds of their arguments; Those on one side considering the States as districts of people composing one political Society; those on the other considering them as so many political societies. . . . On the whole . . . in some respects the States are to be considered in their political capacity, and in others as districts of individual citizens, the two ideas embraced on different sides, instead of being opposed to each other, ought to be combined; that in *one* branch the *people,* ought to be represented; in the *other,* the *States.*[2]

Days later a committee of eleven, one from each state represented, was appointed to effect a compromise along the lines suggested by Dr. Johnson. They reported, and after ten days more of bitter debate the Convention agreed to representation in proportion to population in the House of Representatives and equal representation of the states in the Senate, with the proviso that all revenue bills must originate in the House. However, the small-state delegations insisted on some guaranty that, once the new government was established, their equality in the Senate would not be

[1] Farrand, *The Records of the Federal Convention of 1787,* vol. 1, p. 242.

[2] *Ibid.,* vol. 1, pp. 461–462. This was Madison's rendition of Dr. Johnson's remarks.

changed. Accordingly, a provision was inserted in the amendment article (Article V) stating that no amendment might ever be made to the Constitution to deprive any state of equal representation in the Senate without its consent. This is the only unamendable provision of the Constitution.

The Three-fifths Compromise. No less fundamental than the dispute between large and small states was one involving the economic interests of the sections. Underlying debate was a deep-seated conflict between the planting interests of the South, founded on slave labor, and the commercial and industrial interests of the North.

The six slave states, for obvious reasons, wanted the slaves counted for representation but not for determining their share of direct taxes. Northern delegates contended it was unfair to include slaves for representation inasmuch as they were not in law and fact equal with freemen. Moreover, to count them equally would make it possible for Southern states to increase their representation by importing more slaves. Naturally, Northern delegates wanted slaves counted when allocating quotas for direct taxes. In the end, Southern delegates agreed that three-fifths of all slaves would be counted in apportioning representatives provided they would be counted similarly when apportioning direct taxes.[1]

[1] The Fourteenth Amendment, adopted after the Civil War (1868), modified this provision by requiring that all persons, Negro as well as white, should be counted when determining the number of representatives to which each state is entitled. Although the Fourteenth Amendment said nothing about changing the basis for apportioning direct taxes, the three-fifth ratio became meaningless with the abolition of slavery.

There is reason to suspect that this compromise proved more advantageous to the North than to the South, inasmuch as Southern states had their representation diminished by the provision for a period extending from 1789 to 1860, whereas

Commerce and Slave-trade Compromise. Sectionalism showed itself on another important question. Delegates from New England and the middle states, where manufacturing, trade, and shipping interests dominated, were determined that the central government have adequate powers to regulate interstate and foreign commerce. The planters of the South, however, feared that a government with these powers would prohibit the importation of slaves and make commercial agreements with foreign states which would adversely affect their interests.

Ultimately, Congress won plenary power "to regulate commerce with foreign nations and among the several states," and the President was empowered to negotiate treaties. The South was placated by two provisions: (1) The slave trade was not to be prohibited for 20 years; (2) treaties must receive the approval of two-thirds of the Senate. Insertion of the provision forbidding export taxes helped allay the fears of Southern delegates.

Concluding Sessions. By July 26, the substance of the future Constitution was formulated into twenty-six resolutions and referred to a five-man Committee of Detail. The Convention then recessed until August 6, when it reassembled to receive the committee's report. For the next five weeks the Convention labored five or six hours daily, discussing article by article, section by section.

Finally, on September 8, a Committee on Style was appointed to "revise the style of and arrange the articles which had been agreed to by the house." The committee arranged the document in its present form (excepting the amendments) and on September 13 reported it in the handwriting of its chairman, Gouverneur Morris.

direct taxes were levied only four times prior to the Civil War and on each occasion remained in effect for only a short time.

The Constitution was formally adopted on the fifteenth and, two days later, was signed by thirty-nine of the delegates present—all but Gerry, Mason, and Randolph[1]—whereupon the Convention adjourned.

Sources of the Constitution. For a long time there was a tendency in the United States to regard the Constitution as a new invention in political science. This impression was conveyed by the famous remark of the great English statesman William Gladstone when he observed that "as the British Constitution is the most subtle organism which has proceeded from the womb and the long gestation of progressive history, so the American Constitution is the most wonderful work ever struck off at a given time by the brain and purpose of man." Instead of being "struck off at a given time," it had roots that were deep in the past.

In fact, there was little in the Constitution that was new. The men who wrote the document understood the governments of antiquity, the English constitution, and the governments of western Europe. They were also familiar with the political writings of the period, the most outstanding of which were Blackstone's *Commentaries on the Laws of England*, John Locke's *Two Treatises on Government*, Montesquieu's *Spirit of Laws*, and Rousseau's *Social Contract*. The best read among them also knew the seventeenth-century works—Thomas Hobbes's *Leviathan* and James Harrington's *The Commonwealth of Oceana*—that influenced both colonial institutions and the ideas of later writers. They were saturated with the revolutionary literature that some of their contemporaries, including some of those

[1] These men were in agreement with most of the Constitution but believed provision should have been made for a second convention to discuss criticisms and suggestions made during the process of ratification.

at the Convention, helped write and disseminate.

Of more immediate importance, however, were the records and experiences of the Continental Congress, the Articles of Confederation, the state constitutions adopted after 1775, and the colonial charters and governments. Virtually every provision of the Constitution is identical with, or similar to, words and phrases to be found in colonial and revolutionary documents. A comparison of phrases from the Articles of Confederation, the Constitution of Massachusetts, and the Constitution is shown in the table entitled Derivation of Constitutional Phrases.

The Constitution was not, therefore, "solely the product" of the "creative wisdom" of the founding fathers. It is more accurate to say the Constitution was a digest of the most approved principles and provisions of the charters of government with which the authors of the Constitution were acquainted.

THE CAMPAIGN FOR RATIFICATION

Weaknesses of Articles Overcome. Since the purpose of the Convention was to revise and improve the Articles and the Constitution begins by referring to a "more perfect union," one might inquire: How were the weaknesses of the Articles overcome? This question is answered in parallel columns on page 44.

Ratification Procedure. The Convention had been called to consider and suggest amendments to the Articles. Had the Articles been followed, Congress would have had to approve all the changes contained in the new Constitution and refer them to the legislature of each state before they could go into effect. Rather than follow this procedure, the Convention recommended one that was without legal sanction. It placed in the body of the Con-

DERIVATION OF CONSTITUTIONAL PHRASES

PHRASES FROM THE CONSTITUTION

"We, the people of the United States . . . do ordain and establish this Constitution for the United States of America."

* * * * * * * * * * * * * * * * *

"Judgment . . . shall not extend further than to removal from office and disqualification to hold and enjoy any office of honor, trust or profit under the United States; but the party convicted shall, nevertheless, be liable and subject to indictment, trial, judgment and punishment according to law."

* * * * * * * * * * * * * * * * *

"All bills for raising revenue shall originate in the House of Representatives; but the Senate may propose or concur with amendments as on other bills."

* * * * * * * * * * * * * * * * *

Congress shall have power to "fix the standard of weights and measures."

* * * * * * * * * * * * * * * * *

Congress shall have power "to make rules for the government and regulation of the land and naval forces."

* * * * * * * * * * * * * * * * *

"No title of nobility shall be granted by the United States; and no person holding any office of profit or trust under them shall, without the consent of the Congress, accept of any present, emolument, office, or title, of any kind whatever, from any king, prince, or foreign state."

COMPARABLE PHRASES

"We . . . the people of Massachusetts . . . do . . . ordain and establish the following . . . as the Constitution of the Commonwealth of Massachusetts."
(MASSACHUSETTS CONSTITUTION)

* * * * * * * * * * * * * * * * *

"Judgment shall not extend further than to removal from office and disqualification to hold or enjoy any place of honor, trust, or profit under this Commonwealth; but the party so convicted shall be, nevertheless, liable to indictment, trial, judgment and punishment, according to the laws of the land."
(MASSACHUSETTS CONSTITUTION)

* * * * * * * * * * * * * * * * *

"All money bills shall originate in the House of Representatives; but the Senate may propose or concur with amendments as on other bills."
(MASSACHUSETTS CONSTITUTION)

* * * * * * * * * * * * * * * * *

Congress shall have the power of "fixing the standard of weights and measures throughout the United States."
(ARTICLES OF CONFEDERATION)

* * * * * * * * * * * * * * * * *

Congress shall have the power of "making rules for the government and regulation of the said land and naval forces. . . ."
(ARTICLES OF CONFEDERATION)

* * * * * * * * * * * * * * * * *

"Nor shall any person holding any office of profit or trust under the United States, or any of them, accept of any present, emolument, office or title of any kind whatsoever from any king, prince, or foreign state; nor shall the United States in Congress assembled, or any of them, grant any title of nobility."
(ARTICLES OF CONFEDERATION)

stitution itself (Article VII) a provision declaring that ratification by conventions of the people of nine states would establish the Constitution.

The document was then sent to the Confederation Congress with the advice that the Congress approve it and refer it to the state legislatures which, in turn, should pass it along to conventions of the people in the separate states. It was also suggested that, when nine conventions had approved, Congress should put the new government into operation and go out of existence. Of this action on the part of the Convention Professor Burgess wrote:

What they [the Convention] actually did, stripped of all fiction and verbiage, was to assume constituent powers, ordain a Constitution of government and of liberty, and demand the *plébiscite* thereon, over the heads of all existing legally organized powers. Had Julius or Napoleon committed these acts, they would have been pronounced *coups d'état*. Looked at from the side of the people exercising the *plébiscite*, we term the movement revolution.[1]

Several considerations prompted this presumptuousness on the part of the Convention. The nationalists had triumphed at the Convention and they wanted to eliminate as many obstacles to acceptance as possible. Their greatest fear was that one or two state delegations in the discredited Congress would stymie action there or that one or two state legislatures would obstruct ratification. This was a real danger because Rhode Island had not been represented at all at the Convention, most of the New York delegation had left the Convention as a protest against its proceedings, and a number of delegates had spoken in opposition to the Constitution and the proposed method of ratification. The only chance of

[1] John W. Burgess, *Political Science and Comparative Constitutional Law* (Boston: Ginn, 2 vols., 1902), vol. 1, p. 105.

success was that Congress would obediently refer the new Constitution to the states and that nine of them would provide for conventions. Besides improving the possibility of adoption, reference to conventions elected by the voters especially for the purpose of considering the Constitution would give greater validity to the words "We, the people . . . do ordain and establish this Constitution." It would also emphasize the outstanding difference between the Constitution and the Articles, viz., that this was a union of the people and not of the states. The leaders believed that the gravity of the emergency justified circumventing the Articles.

Federalists and Antifederalists. The contest over adoption of the Constitution split leaders and populace into two factions: Federalists, who favored ratification, and Antifederalists, who opposed it. The contest was intense and bitter. The campaign for ratification was led largely by those who had attended the convention. Federalist sympathies were strongest in comparatively weak states—Delaware, New Jersey, Connecticut, Georgia, and Maryland. Sentiment was sharply divided in Pennsylvania, Massachusetts, South Carolina, and New Hampshire. Federalists were weakest in Virginia, New York, North Carolina, and Rhode Island.

Conspicuous among leaders of the Antifederalists were some of the "Old Patriots" of the Revolution, including Patrick Henry, Richard Henry Lee, Samuel Adams, George Mason, and Elbridge Gerry. The late Charles A. Beard argued that the Federalists had social status, wealth, and professional abilities on their side and represented mainly the Atlantic seaboard; while the Antifederalists were chiefly back-country pioneers and small farmers who distrusted the "upper" classes and had, themselves, only meager material resources. Generally speaking, as Beard expresses it, the opposition "could do nothing but gnash their teeth."[1] They were weakened by property-holding and tax-paying qualifications for voting and the difficulty of getting country voters out for elections in late fall and winter. His critics claim this places too much emphasis on class consciousness and conflict. Whatever the reasons, the Antifederalists lost despite the widespread lack of enthusiasm for the new constitution.

Criticisms of the Proposed Constitution. The Federalists stressed the weaknesses of the Articles and labored to convince the people that the choice was the proposed Constitution or anarchy, chaos, and possibly civil war. Complaints were heard concerning almost every provision of the proposed document. The pious complained that the Constitution nowhere recognized the existence of God. Many who otherwise favored a stronger government strenuously objected to the fact that they must accept or reject the document with no opportunity to amend it prior to final action. Others were opposed because the Convention had exceeded its instructions and recommended adoption contrary to the method required by the Articles. Many contended that the President would become a monarch because he would serve for an indefinite number of terms.

Patriots like Patrick Henry and Richard Henry Lee, noting that the document contained no bill of rights, dwelt upon dangers to liberty. The courts, it was feared, would usurp the powers and functions of state judiciaries. Paper-money advocates believed that the central government would upset the gains they had made through their state governments. Southerners were alarmed lest commercial interests of the North dominate the Congress and use the treaty, tax, and commerce powers to the detriment of their sectional interests. Northerners made a

[1] Beard, *The Supreme Court and the Constitution*, p. 102.

moral issue of concessions to the slave trade; while residents of larger states argued that too much had been conceded to the small states. The most persistent theme was that the states would be destroyed and the central government would become a tyrannical overlord. To offset these objections, the Federalists yielded to the extent of promising the addition of a bill of rights as soon as the new government was organized. Without this concession the Constitution might never have been adopted.

Ratification Completed. Upon the adjournment of the Convention on September 15, the document was sent to Congress, then meeting in New York City. There it was received without enthusiasm. After all, it was expecting a great deal to ask Congress "to light its own funeral pyre," as Bancroft has said. Nevertheless, Congress obediently (on September 28, 1787) adopted a resolution transmitting the document to the state legislatures to be submitted by them to state conventions. One state after another enacted legislation authorizing the election of delegates to attend the conventions.

Voters in most of the states chose delegates during the fall and winter of 1787–1788. The number of delegates attending the state conventions varied from about 30 in Delaware to about 355 in Massachusetts. Delaware, one of the small states that had been appeased by the Connecticut Compromise, was the first to ratify. The order of ratification and division of votes was as follows: (1) Delaware, December 7, 1787, unanimous; (2) Pennsylvannia, December 12, 1787, 46–23; (3) New Jersey, December 19, 1787, unanimous; (4) Georgia, January 2, 1788, unanimous; (5) Connecticut, January 9, 1788, 128–40; (6) Massachusetts, February 6, 1788, 187–168; (7) Maryland, April 28, 1788, 63–11; (8) South

THE ARTICLES AND THE CONSTITUTION

WEAKNESSES OF THE ARTICLES	HOW OVERCOME BY CONSTITUTION
1. States were sovereign.	**1.** People of the whole nation were made sovereign. A federal union from which secession was impossible was created, and the Federal Constitution and laws were made the supreme law of the land.
2. No independent executive.	**2.** Article II provides for President chosen indirectly by the voters. President is given "the executive power"; he is made Commander in Chief of the Army and Navy, and he may take all steps necessary to see that laws are faithfully executed.
3. No Federal courts. Federal laws enforced by state courts.	**3.** Separate system of Federal courts provided by Article III with authority to enforce Federal laws and annul state laws inconsistent with Federal Constitution or laws.
4. No power to collect taxes.	**4.** Article I, Section 8, empowers Congress to "lay and collect taxes, duties, imposts and excises."
5. No power over interstate and foreign commerce.	**5.** Article I, Section 8, gives Congress power to regulate commerce with foreign nations, among the several states, and with Indian tribes.
6. Congress an assembly of delegates who were chosen by state legislatures, were expected to vote as instructed, and could be recalled.	**6.** Congress composed of representatives who have definite tenure and can act in any manner they choose. House of Representatives chosen by direct vote of people, Senate by state legislatures (now direct popular vote).
7. Articles could be amended only by consent of all the states.	**7.** Constitution can be amended with approval of three-fourths of states.
8. Congress had only specifically delegated powers.	**8.** Congress given implied, as well as delegated, powers.
9. Central government could not act directly upon people.	**9.** Central government exercises its powers directly upon the people and concurrently with state governments.

44

Carolina, May 23, 1788, 149–73; (9) New Hampshire, June 21, 1788, 57–46; (10) Virginia, June 25, 1788, 89–79; (11) New York, July 26, 1788, 30–27; (12) North Carolina, November 21, 1789, 184–77; and (13) Rhode Island, May 29, 1790, 34–32.

Campaigns in Virginia and New York. Nine states, sufficient to make the Constitution effective, ratified by the middle of June, 1788, but two of the largest states, Virginia and New York, were not among them. Because their adherence was necessary if the new union were to be successful, all eyes were upon their constitutional conventions.

Virginia. The debate in the Virginia convention was one of the most celebrated in our history. Patrick Henry led the opposition. He was supported in the convention by such celebrities as George Mason, William Grayson, and James Monroe; while outside, Richard Henry Lee worked sedulously against adoption. It was no easy task to engage such a brilliant orator as Patrick Henry in forensic combat, but Madison did so and once more distinguished himself.

Madison was ably supported by John Marshall, then a young man of thirty-two, and Edmund Randolph. Although the latter was one of the three who had refused to sign the Constitution, he had since been won over to the Federalist cause. Washington was not a delegate; but his influence was great. The Federalists prevailed by a majority of ten votes, but not without promising the addition of a bill of rights.

New York. In New York the campaign was intense and bitter and the outcome doubtful. When the Constitution was published, the opposition was overwhelming. The prospect of defeat led Alexander Hamilton to induce Madison and John Jay to join him in publishing a series of anonymous essays defending the new instrument.

Gouverneur Morris was asked to join, but he declined. Historians agree that Hamilton wrote the great majority of the essays.

During the winter of 1787–1788—before the convention met in Albany—seventy-seven essays entitled *The Federalist* and signed first "a Citizen of New York," then "Publius," appeared in the New York press. These, plus eight others (making a total of eighty-five), were later published in book form under the same title. The essays won much support for the Constitution in New York and are considered the ablest exposition of the principles underlying the Constitution and one of the world's greatest treatises on government. After five weeks of acrimonious debate, the New York convention ratified the Constitution by the narrow margin of three votes, upon condition that a bill of rights be added at the earliest possible moment.

Popular Participation in Adoption of the Constitution. The Constitution begins by saying "We, the people . . . do ordain and establish this Constitution . . . ," and much has been said about popular sovereignty. This undoubtedly obtained in a juristic or legal sense, but nevertheless it is an exaggeration of what actually occurred.

Actually, comparatively few people participated directly in the adoption of the Constitution. The suggestion to call a constitutional convention was not submitted to popular vote. Delegates to the Philadelphia Convention were not elected by the voters but, rather, were appointed by the legislatures and governors. Finally, the Constitution was not submitted to the voters for popular approval. The only point at which the voters were allowed to participate directly was in choosing delegates to attend the state conventions which ratified the Constitution.

Only a few people—estimated at 160,-000—participated in the choice of dele-

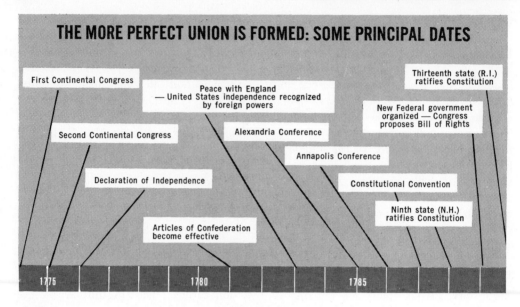

THE MORE PERFECT UNION IS FORMED: SOME PRINCIPAL DATES

First Continental Congress

Peace with England
— United States independence recognized
by foreign powers

Thirteenth state (R.I.)
ratifies Constitution

New Federal government
organized — Congress
proposes Bill of Rights

Second Continental Congress

Alexandria Conference

Annapolis Conference

Declaration of Independence

Constitutional Convention

Ninth state (N.H.)
ratifies Constitution

Articles of Confederation
become effective

1776   1780   1785

gates. Of these probably not more than 100,000 favored adoption. Indeed, some historians believe that the Constitution would have failed of adoption had it been submitted to popular referendum.

THE "MORE PERFECT" UNION

The National Government Organized. The addition of Virginia and New York brought eleven states under the "new roof," whereupon the old Congress took steps to establish the new government. The informal organization of the old Congress was maintained until May 2, 1789, but for lack of a quorum it transacted no official business after October, 1788. On September 13, 1788, Congress chose New York as the capital city and designated the first Wednesday in January for the states to choose presidential electors, the first Wednesday in February for electors to meet in their respective states and vote for President, and the first Wednesday in March for the inauguration of the new government.

Electors were chosen and met accordingly; twenty-two senators and fifty-nine representatives were duly elected, and the first Congress assembled on March 4, 1789, in Federal Hall on Wall Street. Lacking a quorum, Congress transacted no business until April 6. Then the electoral votes were counted by the Senate presiding officer before a joint session of Congress. George Washington was found to have been elected President by unanimous vote and John Adams Vice President by a substantial majority. After a historic trip from his home at Mount Vernon to the new capital, Washington was inaugurated on April 30.

The new Congress created and defined the powers, duties, and jurisdiction of the administrative and judicial branches of government, while the new President concerned himself with the selection of persons to fill the numerous offices. The promised bill of rights was proposed on September 25, 1789. North Carolina ratified the Constitution in November. Rhode Island ratified in May after Congress had threatened to deprive her of trading with the Union and after secesson had been widely discussed in several counties where Federalist sentiment was strong.

FOR FURTHER READING

Beard, Charles A.: *An Economic Interpretation of the Constitution of the United States* (New York: Macmillan, 1913).

————: *The Supreme Court and the Constitution* (New York: Macmillan, 1912).

Brant, Irving: *James Madison, the Nationalist, 1780–1787* (Indianapolis: Bobbs-Merrill, 1948).

Brown, Robert E.: *Charles Beard and the Constitution: A Critical Analysis of 'An Economic Interpretation of the Constitution'* (Princeton, N.J.: Princeton University Press, 1956).

————: *Middle-class Democracy and the Revolution in Massachusetts, 1691–1780* (Ithaca, N.Y.: Cornell University Press, 1955).

Butzner, Jane: *Constitutional Chaff: Rejected Suggestions of the Constitutional Convention of 1787* (New York: Columbia University Press, 1941).

Dietze, Gottfried: *The Federalist, A Classic on Federalism and Free Government* (Baltimore: Johns Hopkins Press, 1960).

Elliott, Jonathan (ed.): *Debates in the Several State Conventions on the Adoption of the Federal Constitution* (Washington, D.C.: printed by the editor, 2d ed., 5 vols., 1836–1845).

Farrand, Max: *The Framing of the Constitution of the United States* (New Haven, Conn.: Yale University Press, 1940 printing).

———— (ed.): *The Records of the Federal Convention of 1787* (New Haven, Conn.: Yale University Press, 3 vols., 1911).

Hamilton, Alexander, et al. (ed. by Paul L. Ford): *The Federalist* (New York: Holt, 1898).

Kohn, Hans: *American Nationalism: An Interpretative Essay* (New York: Macmillan, 1957).

Long, Breckenridge: *Genesis of the Constitution of the United States of America* (New York: Macmillan, 1926).

Main, Jackson Turner: *The Antifederalists: Critics of the Constitution, 1781–88* (Chapel Hill, N. C.: University of North Carolina Press, 1962).

McDonald, Forrest: *We the People, The Economic Origins of the Constitution* (Chicago: University of Chicago Press, 1958).

Miller, John C.: *The Federalist Era, 1789–1801* (New York: Harper, 1960).

Morgan, Edmund S.: *The Birth of the Republic, 1763–89* (Chicago: University of Chicago Press, 1956).

Prescott, Arthur T. (comp.): *Drafting the Federal Constitution* (Baton Rouge, La.: Louisiana State University Press, 1941).

Rodick, Burleigh Cushing: *American Constitutional Custom: A Forgotten Factor in the Founding* (New York: Philosophical Library, 1953).

Rutland, Robert Allen: *The Birth of the Bill of Rights* (Chapel Hill, N.C.: University of North Carolina Press, 1955).

Schuyler, Robert L.: *The Constitution of the United States: An Historical Survey of Its Formation* (New York: Macmillan, 1923).

Stevens, Charles E.: *Sources of the Constitution of the United States* (New York: Macmillan, 1894).

Tansill, Charles C. (ed.): *Documents Illustrative of the Formation of the Union of the American States,* H. Doc. 398, 69th Cong., 1st Sess. (1927).

Umbreit, Kenneth B.: *Founding Fathers: Men Who Shaped Our Tradition* (New York: Harper, 1941).

Van Doren, Carl: *The Great Rehearsal: The Story of the Making and Ratifying of the Constitution of the United States* (New York: Viking, 1948).

REVIEW QUESTIONS

1. Trace the steps by which the Constitution was drafted and ratified.

2. Characterize the delegates who attended the Constitutional Convention. What influence did these characteristics have upon Convention proceedings and the Constitution?

3. What features of the Virginia Plan were

adopted by the Constitutional Convention? The New Jersey Plan? Other plans?

4. What conflicts of interest manifested themselves at the Constitutional Convention? How were these reconciled? Who got the better of the compromises?

5. Upon what important sources of theory and experience did those who wrote the Constitution draw?

6. In what ways was the Constitution "more perfect" than the Articles of Confederation?

7. What were the basic differences of opinion and interest between those who favored the Constitution and those who opposed it?

8. Comment upon the role played by each of the following in framing and adopting the Constitution: *The Federalist Papers*, George Washington, James Madison, Gouverneur Morris, Benjamin Franklin, Samuel Adams, Patrick Henry, Thomas Jefferson, Alexander Hamilton.

9. How do you explain the fact that only a comparatively small number of people participated in framing and adopting the Constitution?

10. Trace the steps by which the new national government was put into operation.

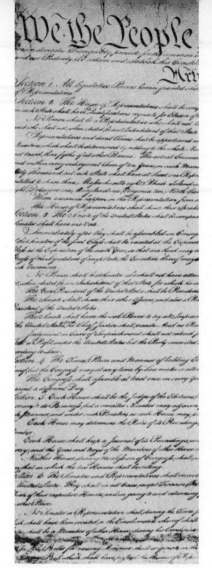

Chapter Four

Constitutional Principles and Methods of Change

Some men look at constitutions with sanctimonious
reverence and deem them like the ark of the covenant,
too sacred to be touched. . . . But the laws and
institutions must go hand in hand with the progress
of the human mind. . . . We might as well require
a man to wear still the coat which fitted him when a boy
as civilized society to remain ever under the regimen
of their barbarous ancestors. . . . Each generation . . .
has a right to choose for itself the form of government
it believes most promotive of its own happiness.

THOMAS JEFFERSON[1]

In contrast to the Declaration of Independence, the Constitution is not a revolutionary document. The simple aim of its authors was to establish a strong, central government.

What they came up with is extremely brief, especially as compared to the detail in state constitutions. The major provisions reflect the preoccupation of the framers with certain fundamentals which they regarded as crucial.

The principles upon which they agreed are described in this chapter. Also reviewed are the methods by which the Constitution has been adapted to changing conditions.

[1] Quoted in Saul K. Padover, *Thomas Jefferson on Democracy* (New York: The New American Library of World Literature, Inc., 2d printing, 1949), p. 67.

PRINCIPLES

Popular Sovereignty. Sovereignty, the authority and power to command and coerce all others, resides somewhere in every fully developed national state. During the colonial period, the King and Parliament of England were sovereign. The Revolution suspended Great Britain's sovereignty, the colonists claiming they were supreme. Under the Articles of Confederation, each of the thirteen states enjoyed ultimate authority. But adoption of the Constitution transferred sovereignty to the people of the country. The preamble declares that "We, the People of the United States . . . do ordain and establish this Constitution for the United States of America," and the presumption of popular sovereignty runs throughout the document. Accordingly, when a sufficient number of qualified voters act in unison, there is no legal limit to their power. They reign in the American political world, said de Tocqueville, "as the Deity does in the Universe."

Sovereign: People of the Whole Nation? This principle is clear, but applying it has led to several controversies. One of the first and most troublesome arose between nationalists and advocates of state rights. The latter, with John C. Calhoun as their ablest spokesman, admitted that the people were sovereign; but they contended that the people within each state had ultimate legal authority—even to withdraw from the Union if they wished.

The nationalists contended that sovereignty resided with the people as a whole, regardless of state lines. It followed that people within a particular state must, ultimately, bow to the authority of all the people. Their arguments prevailed, but only as an outcome of the terrible bloodshed and strife of the Civil War.

Sovereign: Only Some of the People? Another controversy questions the nature of the franchise. The people are sovereign. But which people? How many of them? The courts have held that the word "people," as used in the preamble, is synonymous with "citizens"; hence, aliens and nationals do not share sovereignty. But how many citizens exercise the rights of sovereignty? In practice, only those who vote or, at most, all those who are eligible to vote.

Suppose that only a few are eligible to vote, as was the case during the formative years of the nation. Is the minority that holds political power obliged to extend the suffrage? The answer is that, at any given time, sovereignty resides in the body of qualified voters who are competent to participate in amending the Constitution; voting is a privilege extended at the discretion of those who presently exercise power; the unenfranchised have no legal right to vote. Thus, youths under voting age, Negroes before the Civil War, women before they were enfranchised, and millions of others who fail to qualify are not among the "people" in whom sovereignty resides.

Popular Sovereignty and the Right to Revolt. A third controversy, still heard, revolves around the question of whether the people have a legal right to revolt. Logically, if the voters are sovereign, it would seem that they can do anything they please, whether by peaceful or other means. Being reasonable and peace-loving people, they will normally use existing political machinery to express their will. But suppose only a few possess the franchise and will not enact legislation to enfranchise the masses. Or suppose that the administration in power acts dictatorially, suppressing liberties and otherwise ignoring the Constitution. What then? Have the people, or groups of them, the right to revolt?

Opinion divides on this thorny question. During the early years of the Republic the right of revolution was stanchly defended, doubtless to justify the revolt from England but also because it accorded with the democratic theory then pervading the political atmosphere. Typical of the expressions were the words of the Declaration of Independence which run:

We hold these truths to be self-evident. . . . That whenever any Form of Government becomes destructive of these ends, it is the Right of the People to alter or to abolish it, and to institute new Government, laying its foundation on such principles and organizing its powers in such form, as to them shall seem most likely to effect their Safety and Happiness.

The thought was more colorfully stated by Thomas Jefferson in a letter prompted by Shays' Rebellion, in Massachusetts:[1]

. . . God forbid that we should ever be 20 years without such a rebellion. The people cannot be all, & always, well informed. The part which is wrong will be discontented in proportion to the importance of the facts they misconceive. If they remain quiet under such misconceptions it is a lethargy, the forerunner of death to the public liberty. We have had 13. states independent 11. years. There has been one rebellion. That comes to one rebellion in a century & a half for each state. What country before ever existed a century & a half without a rebellion? & what country can preserve its liberties if their rulers are not warned from time to time that their people preserve the spirit of resistance? Let them take arms. The remedy is to set them right as to facts, pardon & pacify them. What signify a few lives lost in a century or two? The tree of liberty must be refreshed from time to time with the blood of patriots & tyrants. It is its natural manure. . . .

[1] Letter to James Madison quoted in Dumas Malone, *Jefferson and the Rights of Man* (Boston: Little, Brown, 1951), pp. 165–166.

FUNDAMENTAL PRINCIPLES OF THE CONSTITUTION

E PLURIBUS UNUM

CONSTITUTION OF THE UNITED STATES

POPULAR SOVEREIGNTY

REPRESENTATIVE SYSTEM

SEPARATION OF POWERS

CIVILIAN SUPREMACY

LIMITED GOVERNMENT

FEDERAL SYSTEM

JUDICIAL REVIEW

As memory of the Revolution dimmed, however, less emphasis was placed on the right of revolution and more on the right of existing governments to maintain law and order. In a 1950 decision upholding the conviction of eleven Communists for conspiracy to teach and advocate the overthrow of government by force (*Dennis v. United States,* 341 U.S. 501), a majority of the Supreme Court said:

That it is within the *power* of the Congress to protect the Government of the United States from armed rebellion is a proposition which requires little discussion. Whatever theoretical merit there may be to the argument that there is a "right" to rebellion against dictatorial governments is without force where the existing structure of the government provides for peaceful and orderly change. We reject any principle of governmental helplessness in the face of preparation for revolution, which principle, carried to its logical conclusion, must lead to anarchy. No one could conceive that it is not within the power of government to prohibit acts intended to overthrow the Government by force and violence.

Despite this opinion, the early American view has strong defenders. Said Justice Hugo Black in a recent dissent [*In Re Anastaplo*, 366 U.S. 82 (1961)]:

Since the beginning of history there have been governments that have engaged in practices against the people so bad, so cruel, so unjust and so destructive of the individual dignity of men and women that the "right of revolution" was all the people had left to free themselves. As simple illustrations, one government almost 2,000 years ago burned Christians upon fiery crosses and another government, during this very century, burned Jews in crematories. I venture the suggestion that there are countless multitudes in this country, and all over the world, who would join Anastaplo's belief in the right of people to resist by force tyrannical governments like those.

Although denying that Americans have the legal right to revolt, a majority of the Supreme Court has distinguished between theoretical belief and revolutionary action and limited punishment to the latter [*Yates v. United States*, 354 U.S. 298 (1957)].

A Federal System. As noted in Chapter I, a state may be organized on a unitary basis, as a confederation, or as a federal union. The circumstances in 1787 precluded a unitary system; the only choice lay between continuing and strengthening the confederation or building a federal union.

The American federal union, though severely strained by the Civil War, has stood the test of over a century and a half. It is today the oldest federal union in existence. So successful has it been that many other countries have followed the American model. Some people now visualize a world organized on a federal basis.

National Supremacy. In a federal system, jurisdictional conflicts are bound to arise between the central and regional governments. Experience with them demonstrates that federal law must be paramount. Otherwise, the people of the nation will be at the mercy of the inhabitants of individual states. Realizing this, the founding fathers never doubted the necessity of subordinating state to Federal laws if and when the two conflicted. Accordingly, they stipulated that the Federal Constitution, acts of Congress, and treaties were the "supreme law of the land." A conflict between Federal and state law is usually decided by Federal courts.

A Representative System. The Constitution established a representative democracy. Town meetings are still held in a few New England communities. The referendum, initiative, and recall are used in a number of states. But, on the whole, representatives chosen directly or indirectly by the voters run American government. This is especially true of the Federal government; voters may not initiate laws of the nation as they may of a number of states and cities. Laws cannot be enacted by referendum, though Congress can stipulate that referendums be used to help determine when certain legislative provisions will become effective. Voters are not permitted to recall Federal officers.

Indeed, on only three occasions does the electorate participate directly in Federal affairs, viz., when voting for representatives, United States senators, and electors to choose the President and Vice President. Once chosen, matters of national government are in their hands.

Civilian Supremacy over the Military. Those who founded the American republic believed that large military establishments and tyranny went hand in hand. This view, advanced in the writings of the leading political theorists of the period, like Locke, Rousseau, Montesquieu, Coke, and Blackstone, was confirmed by the behavior of British troops in the colonies. It is not surprising, therefore, to find listed in the charges made against King George III by the Declaration of Independence: "He has kept among us, in times of peace, Standing Armies, without the Consent of our legislature. He has affected to render the Military independent of and superior to the Civil Power."

The Constitutional Convention of 1787 gave broad military powers to the President and Congress, but it also provided safeguards. Only Congress could declare war; all revenue bills must originate in the more popular house of Congress; no money could be spent except as appropriated by Congress; no money could be appropriated for an army for longer than two years; suspension of the writ of habeas corpus was limited; and the states were left with authority to officer and train militias. During the debates over its ratification, advocates of the Constitution agreed to amendments which would go further and provide guaranties against quartering troops in any house without the consent of the owner and to assure people of the right to keep and bear arms. These guaranties were incorporated in the Second and Third Amendments.

Thoroughly entrenched by Constitution and long experience, the principle of civilian supremacy has not been challenged directly. But involvements in wars and international politics since 1898 have increased American military commitments; the defense establishment has grown enormously; military personnel, active and retired, has integrated itself with all phases of economic, social, and political life; the military bureaucracy, with the aid of veterans' and other patriotic societies and supporting interests, has become a powerful pressure group; conscription has become an accepted accompaniment of war and widely advocated as a desirable peacetime institu-tion; and state militias have come increasingly under Federal dominance.

In consequence, many voices are raised lest the principle of civilian supremacy be lost. The principle still has vigor, however, as indicated by President Truman's dramatic dismissal in 1951 of five-star General MacArthur from his command in Japan and Korea. Vigor also is indicated by the zeal of congressional committees in investigating and reviewing military affairs.

Limited Government. Government is a necessity, but it implies coercion and restraint. How secure enough governmental authority without creating an agency abusive of liberty? The problem is as old as human society. Those who adopted the Constitution thought they had an answer to the paradox: (1) They assumed the people were sovereign. (2) The organization and powers of their governments were set forth in written documents in language as plain as they could command. (3) After carefully stating what powers they wished the Federal government to exercise, they left all residual powers to the states or to the people. (4) The three branches of government were separated and made to operate with elaborate checks and balances. (5) Both Federal and state governments were specifically forbidden to perform certain acts. (6) The military was subordinated to civilian control. (7) Individual and personal rights were protected against invasion by either Federal or state governments. (8) Powers could be exercised only by elected officers or those duly appointed by officials chosen by the voters. (9) They provided that constitutional amendments could not be added unless desired by an overwhelming majority of the voters.

American governments, the states in particular, have frequently ignored injustices perpetrated by groups of citizens against races and minorities, and have occasionally themselves been guilty of violating human liberties. On the whole, however, the record is good.

Emphasis upon keeping government limited has declined in favor of sentiment for bigger, stronger governments. The industrial revolution, wars, depressions, and threats of communism and fascism have led many to fear their consequences more than they fear strong government. To these people government has become the champion and protector of values and welfare. While professing respect for personal rights, many of the new schools are impatient with traditional restraints that impede prompt and vigorous governmental action.

Can American governments continue to meet recurring crises, provide the expected manifold services, but avoid becoming dictatorial? British and American experience suggests that they can, although emergencies do weaken the bulwarks of personal liberty and democratic control.

Separation of Powers. The three powers (or branches) of government may be united or separated. Where the parliamentary form exists, parliament is the central agency; the real executive, the prime minister and his cabinet, is selected by parliament from its own membership; and courts may not declare acts of the legislature unconstitutional. In dictatorships, powers are either united in the executive branch or, although technically separated, become completely subordinate to it. Where powers are separated, each branch has its own powers and prerogatives to restrain the other branches, thus creating a check-and-balance system. The latter has been considered by many to be a safeguard against tyranny.

Origin of Doctrine. Colonial statesmen had read the Englishman John Locke and the Frenchman Montesquieu on the separation of powers. Their experience with autocratic British kings and colonial governors

made them receptive to the theory. Consequently, this feature was incorporated into every state constitution adopted during the Revolution. A classic expression of the doctrine is found in the constitution of Massachusetts:

In the government of this commonwealth, the legislative department shall never exercise the executive and judicial powers, or either of them: the executive shall never exercise the legislative and judicial powers, or either of them: the judicial shall never exercise the legislative and executive powers, or either of them: to the end that it may be a government of laws, and not of men.

With widespread distrust of political power generally, and of a national government in particular, it was inevitable that powers should be separated in the new Constitution.

Constitutional Basis. Unlike the constitution of Massachusetts, quoted above, the Federal Constitution does not state categorically that the powers are and must remain separated. That they are separated is because of language used in creating the three branches: Article I starts off, "*All* legislative powers herein granted shall be vested in a Congress." Article II begins with the statement that "*The* executive power shall be vested in a President." And Article III states that "*The* judicial power . . . shall be vested in one Supreme Court, and in such inferior courts as Congress may from time to time ordain and establish."[1] This inclusive and exclusive language, coupled with the fact that the powers are set forth in three different articles, provides the constitutional basis for their separation.

Checks and Balances. Separation of powers is implemented by elaborate checks and balances. To mention only a few: Congress

---

[1] Italics are the authors'.

is checked by the requirement that laws must receive the approval of both houses, by the President's veto, and by the power of judicial review. The President is checked by the fact that he cannot enact laws, that no money may be spent except in accordance with appropriations made by law, that Congress can override his veto, that he can be impeached, that treaties must be approved and appointments confirmed by the Senate, and by judicial review. The judicial branch is checked by the power retained by the people to amend the Constitution, by the power of the President with the advice and consent of the Senate to appoint judges, by the fact that judges can be impeached, and by the provision that permits Congress to determine the size of courts and limit their appellate jurisdiction.

Criticisms of Separation of Powers. The doctrine of separation of powers has many apologists; it also has its critics. Some think that one, or more than one, of the branches acquires too much influence. They complain that the President, by use of television, radio, motion pictures, press conferences, patronage, and a widespread bureaucracy, often dominates Congress. Critics also allege that the President, by administrative decrees and control over judicial appointments, often gains the upper hand over the judicial branch. Legislative interference with administration is criticized too. The courts have been accused of usurping authority which properly belongs to Congress and the President.

There is some truth to these contentions, but it would be impossible to devise a workable system without a considerable number of interrelationships between the three branches. Moreover, existing checks and balances tend to restrain, with the result that over a period of time each branch manages to "hold its own" in relation to the others.

Another group of critics decries separation as frustrating leadership and producing stalemates. They note that under the American system the President may be of one political party and Congress of another, with little being accomplished. They also point out that the courts may construe the Constitution so narrowly as to frustrate both the President and Congress. They see advantages in the British system, with all branches united and accountable to Parliament led by the Prime Minister and his cabinet.

Unifying Devices. These criticisms have much validity. But there are factors that tend to unify the three branches. Most important is the political party. Another is the President's power to initate legislation, send messages to Congress, defend measures before committees, appeal and maneuver for public support, labor with individual congressmen, and threaten to withhold patronage. If both the President and Congress persist, the courts can be brought to a more accommodating point of view, or constitutional amendments can be sought.

In spite of these unifying devices, comparison with the British form leads to the conclusion that effective leadership is less likely to exist in the United States, except possibly during emergencies. In the past, however, Americans have not been conspicuously desirous of executive leadership. Various proposals have been made to ensure greater presidential leadership, but early enactment of any seems unlikely. If the emphasis upon a positive governmental program persists, however, the situation may change and modify the traditional patterns of checks and balances.

Judicial Review. The Constitution does not say what should happen if it is violated by the President, Congress, or the courts. The President may veto acts of Congress he considers in conflict with the Constitution. Likewise, Congress can retaliate in many ways against a President who violates the Constitution. Both the President and Congress have ways to reprimand Federal courts for conduct and decisions they consider contrary to the Constitution.

These checks operate continuously, and usually without great publicity or discussion. But early in American history the courts undertook to declare acts of Congress unconstitutional, and this has occasioned violent controversy. Acceptance of the principle of judicial review has made the Supreme Court the most powerful judicial agency in the world. Other countries have emulated American practice, but in none have the courts played such an important role as in the United States.

Judicial Review Intended. Because the Constitution does not specifically grant the power of judicial review and courts' decisions have often irritated Congress, the President, and large sectors of the public, the courts' right to exercise the prerogative has been challenged. The controversy motivated intensive historical research on the origin of the practice and the intent of those who wrote the Constitution.

Evidence reveals that judicial review as we know it emerged with the adoption of written constitutions by the American states after their break with England in 1776; the majority at the Constitutional Convention favored judicial review. Why, then, was no specific provision made for it? The framers of the Constitution believed the power to be clearly implied from language used.

Constitutional Basis for Judicial Review. One of the pertinent provisions is found in Article VI, which reads, in part, "This *Constitution,* and the *Laws* of the United States *which shall be made in pursuance thereof;* and all Treaties made, or which shall be made, under the authority of the United

States, shall be the supreme law of the land. . . ."[1] Another relevant provision is Article III, Section 2, which says, "The judicial power shall extend to all cases, in law and equity, arising under this Constitution, the laws of the United States, and treaties made, or which shall be made, under their authority. . . ."

The Supreme Court faced the issue for the first time in *Marbury v. Madison.* Congress had provided in the Judiciary Act of 1789 that requests for writs of mandamus (judicial orders commanding government officials to perform duties required by law) might originate in the Supreme Court. On the night of March 3, 1801, Marbury had been appointed justice of peace for the District of Columbia by President Adams, whose term expired before the commission was delivered. The incoming President, Jefferson, and his Secretary of State, Madison, refused to deliver the commission to Marbury, who immediately petitioned the Supreme Court for the writ of mandamus permitted by the Judiciary Act of 1789. Chief Justice Marshall wrote the opinion for the Court. After saying that he thought Marbury was entitled to the commission, Marshall declared the Supreme Court was without authority to grant a writ compelling its delivery. The Judiciary Act of 1789 had enlarged the original jurisdiction of the Supreme Court as prescribed by the Constitution, and therefore it was null and void.

Chief Justice Marshall's justification is based upon the following assumptions: (1) The Constitution is a written document that clearly defines and limits the powers of government; (2) the Constitution is a fundamental law and superior to ordinary legislative enactments; (3) an act of the legislature contrary to the fundamental law is void and therefore cannot bind the

[1] Italics are the authors'.

SUPREME COURT CASES
DECLARING UNITED STATES LAWS UNCONSTITUTIONAL

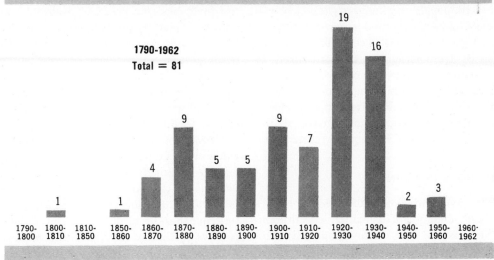

1790-1962
Total = 81

Although judicial review of legislation is an important feature of American government, the number of Federal statutes voided by the court is not, in most decades, large.

courts; (4) the judicial power, together with oaths to uphold the Constitution that judges take, requires that the courts so declare when they believe acts of Congress violate the Constitution. Although Marshall's reasoning has been criticized and his facts termed inaccurate, the principle of judicial review was firmly embedded in the American system of government.

Experience with Judicial Review. In eighty or more cases the Supreme Court has declared Federal statutes unconstitutional in whole or in part. After the Marbury decision, fifty-four years elapsed before another statute was invalidated by the famous Dred Scott case [*Scott v. Sandford*, 19 How. 393 (U.S. 1857)]. In that instance, a divided court declared the Missouri Compromise of 1820 unconstitutional and by doing so intensified the situation that later erupted into the Civil War. The timetable of court reversals is shown in the chart given above. Only two reversals led to

amendments: the Dred Scott decision led to the Thirteenth and Fourteenth Amendments; the decision in *Pollock v. Farmers' Loan & Trust Co.* [158 U.S. 601 (1895)] was overcome by the Sixteenth Amendment. A number of cases dealt with large questions of public policy, such as legal tender, child labor, minimum wages for women, Federal taxation of state agencies, and the regulation of large-scale businesses.

Many complain that, with judicial review, the Supreme Court has expanded its authority and become a nonelective superlegislature. Some insist that the Court has shown undue partiality for property rights and excessive dependence upon legal formulas which seriously retard social progress. As evidence, critics offer the number of cases wherein the courts have declared welfare legislation unconstitutional but later, in response to popular insistence, reversed their decisions.

There is validity to such criticisms, but

few in the United States advocate complete abandonment of judicial review. Various reforms have been suggested, but none has evoked popular enthusiasm. Experience in the United States and elsewhere suggests that the courts may check political departments temporarily but they are likely to accommodate eventually if pressures are intense and persistent. Important change in the practice of judicial review will depend upon the degree of judicial restraint and the intensity and duration of future crises.

METHODS OF CHANGE

The American Constitution is the world's classic example of a written constitution. Nevertheless, only cursory examination discloses many unwritten features. Many of the most conspicuous features of the American system of government have no apparent constitutional foundation but have been added over the years by interpretation, custom, and usage.

Amendment. The most obvious manner by which the Constitution may be changed is by adding amendments as provided for in Article V:

> The Congress, whenever two thirds of both Houses shall deem it necessary, shall propose amendments to this Constitution, or, on the application of the legislatures of two thirds of the several States, shall call a convention for proposing amendments, which, in either case, shall be valid to all intents and purposes, as part of this Constitution, when ratified by the legislatures of three fourths of the several States, or by conventions in three fourths thereof, as the one or the other mode of ratification may be proposed by the Congress; provided that no amendment which may be made prior to the year one thousand eight hundred and eight shall in any manner affect the first and fourth clauses in the ninth section of the first article; and that no State, without its consent, shall be deprived of its equal suffrage in the Senate.

Two observations of a general character may be made: (1) The proposal and ratification of amendments are solely legislative functions—the President need not sign proposed amendments before they are sent to the states, nor do the state governors need to sign instruments of ratification. (2) Except for the provision that a state's equality of representation cannot be diminished without its consent, any provision can be legally altered by amendment.[1]

Proposal of Amendments. Article V provides two methods by which amendments may be proposed: by a two-thirds vote of both houses of Congress; by a convention called after receiving petitions from legislatures in two-thirds of the states. Out of thousands of resolutions introduced in Congress, only twenty-nine have mustered the two-thirds vote of both houses (two-thirds of the members present, assuming the presence of a quorum—not necessarily two-thirds of the total membership.)[2] None has been proposed by the alternate method of constitutional convention.

If Congress is unwilling to submit amendments to the states, the state legislatures may force action by petitioning Congress to call a constitutional convention. Petitions have been addressed to Congress on many occasions. Some of these have been general in character, asking only that a convention be called. Others have urged calling a convention to consider specific matters such as outlawing polygamy, direct election of the President and Vice President, control of

[1] Observe, however, that prior to 1808, amendments could not be made to the first and fourth clauses in the ninth section of Article I, clauses which permitted the slave trade for a period of twenty years after the adoption of the Constitution and stipulated that direct taxes must be apportioned among the states on the basis of population. These exceptions are no longer of importance.

[2] For those proposed but unratified, see last page of Appendix III.

AMENDMENT PROCEDURE

METHOD OF PROPOSAL*	METHODS OF RATIFICATION†
By two-thirds vote of both houses of Congress (method used to propose all 29 amendments)	Legislatures in three-fourths (38) of the states (method used to ratify first 20, 22d, and 23rd amendments); or
By constitutional convention called by Congress when petitioned to do so by two-thirds (34) of the states (method unused to date)	Conventions in three-fourths (38) of the states (method used to ratify 1 amendment—the 21st).

* Either method may be used.
† States may select either method unless Congress specifies which should be followed.

trusts, and direct election of senators. Petitions have never been received concerning any one subject from as many as two-thirds of the states, but enough were submitted urging the direct election of senators to play an important, if not decisive, role in forcing the submission of the Seventeenth Amendment. If two-thirds of the states were to petition, Congress would be obliged to call a convention.

Ratification. Two methods of ratification are provided, viz., by legislatures in three-fourths of the states or by conventions in a similar number of the states. Congress may indicate the method of ratification to be followed, as in proposing that the twenty-first be considered in conventions. Failure to express preference leaves the states free to choose either one. States must use either legislatures or conventions—nothing else may be substituted—and the decision to ratify is irrevocable [*Hawke v. Smith*, 253 U.S. 221, 231 (1920)]. Rejection, however, does not preclude reconsideration of the proposal by the same legislature or convention or subsequent ones.

The usual procedure is for the governor of the state, upon receipt of a joint resolution of Congress, to refer the matter to the state legislature. If the resolution calls for conventions, the state legislature usually enacts the necessary authorization, stating where and when the convention will be held, the number of delegates, etc. If conventions are not specified, the legislature may consider the amendment at any time. Ratification is legally consummated the moment the requisite three-fourths of the states ratify.

Thus far, all but one of the twenty-three amendments have been approved by state legislatures. This method is simpler and less expensive, inasmuch as legislatures are or will be in session anyway. The convention method might be somewhat faster because the convention is called for a single purpose; legislatures have many matters to deal with and may be precariously divided along party lines. The convention method more likely reflects public opinion because delegates are chosen after a pro and con campaign on a particular issue.

The principal motive of Congress in requiring that the Twenty-first Amendment be ratified by conventions seems to have been the desire for speedy action when public opinion, as expressed in the election of a Democratic President and Congress in 1932, was sympathetic to repeal of prohibition.

Time Required for Ratification. Ratification of an amendment may take place a few months or many years after its proposal. Congress placed a time limit of seven years in the Eighteenth, Twentieth, Twenty-first, Twenty-second, and Twenty-third Amendments. This encouraged the belief that amendments "died of old age" unless a time limit was stated, and the Supreme Court upheld this view [*Dillon v. Gloss,* 256 U.S. 368 (1921)]. But in 1939 the Court ruled differently [*Coleman v. Miller,* 307 U.S. 433]. Holding that the child-labor amendment was still "alive" after fifteen years, the Supreme Court said that the question of a time limit is political. Being such, Congress, and not the courts, must decide what is a reasonable period. Congress may limit the period for ratification to any number of years; otherwise, proposed amendments are before the states indefinitely.

Apparently a state could ratify any of the six amendments that remain unratified by the requisite number of states. On one occasion Ohio ratified an amendment proposed eighty years earlier. Connecticut, Georgia, and Massachusetts, somewhat embarrassed upon finding that they had never done so, ratified the first ten amendments as recently as 1939. The time required for ratification has been rather short, varying from three years and eleven months for the Twenty-second Amendment to seven months for the Twelfth. The Twenty-third was ratified in nearly record-breaking time: slightly over nine months.

The First Twelve Amendments. The first ten amendments, the famous Bill of Rights, were proposed by the first Congress to fulfill the pledge made by the Federalists to ensure adoption of the Constitution. They restrict the national government, not the states [*Barron v. Baltimore,* 7 Pet. 243 (U.S. 1833)].

The eleventh was added after the states had been incensed by the Supreme Court's decision holding that Article III of the Constitution permitted states to be sued in Federal courts [*Chisholm v. Georgia,* 2 Dall. 419 (U.S. 1793)]. The amendment was intended to guarantee that a "sovereign" state would never again be summoned before the Federal judiciary as had Georgia in the case cited.

The Twelfth Amendment grew out of the election of 1800, in which Jefferson and Burr defeated Adams and Pinckney. The electoral college discovered that, by voting for the President and Vice President on the same ballot, as Article II required, Jefferson and Burr had the same number of votes. Everyone understood Jefferson to have been the candidate for President and Burr the candidate for Vice President. But the tie threw the election to the House of Representatives. To ensure that this would never happen again, the Twelfth Amendment was proposed and promptly ratified.

The Civil War Amendments. The next three amendments grew out of the Civil War. The thirteenth prohibited slavery; the fourteenth defined citizenship, forbade states to deprive persons of life, liberty, and property without due process of law, forbade states to deny anyone equal protection of the law, and provided a method of punishing states which deny adult male citizens the right to vote. This punishment —reduction of representatives in Congress proportionate to the number of citizens denied the right to vote—has never been enforced because of its political implications. The late Senator Borah sponsored an amendment to repeal this unenforced section of the Fourteenth Amendment. The effort failed, but there is still some sentiment for the proposal.

The Fifteenth Amendment specifically forbade the Federal government and the states from denying the right to vote because of race, color, or previous condition of servitude. Unlike the unenforced section of the Fourteenth Amendment, which requires Congress to impose a political penalty upon states, the Fifteenth Amendment is enforced by the courts.

These three amendments were added by questionable methods. The thirteenth was approved with the help of West Virginia, whose secession from Virginia was of dubious legality, and with the aid of carpetbag legislatures in several Southern states. The fourteenth and fifteenth were ratified by making their approval a prerequisite for readmission of Southern states to full rights in the Union.

Sixteenth to Nineteenth Amendments. Forty-three years elapsed before additional amendments were added. Many people had become convinced that the Constitution might never again be changed by the amendment procedure. The next amendment overcame a decision of the Supreme Court which held that income taxes were direct taxes and must be apportioned among the states on the basis of population [*Pollock v. Farmers' Loan & Trust Co.*, 158 U.S. 601 (1895)]. Since this precluded graduated income taxes based upon the capacity of people to pay, the Sixteenth Amendment was added.

The graduated income tax has become the Federal government's chief source of revenue. In recent years its rates have so risen that a movement has been started to repeal the amendment. Those favoring repeal would add a substitute establishing a ceiling of 25 per cent on income, inheritance, and gift taxes levied by Congress.

Since 1939, about half of the states have acted favorably upon a resolution calling upon Congress to call a constitutional convention to consider the substitute measure. Several states have since rescinded their approval, leaving about fifteen on record as favoring the substitute.

The Seventeenth Amendment, added in 1913, transferred election of United States senators from state legislatures to the voters. The eighteenth was proposed after the United States entered the First World War and ratified two months after the armistice. It added Federal power to that of the states to eliminate the evils of the liquor traffic. The nineteenth resulted from years of agitation on the part of feminist leaders and organizations clamoring for legal recognition of women's right to vote. Although many states had granted women the privilege of voting, an amendment was necessary to ensure suffrage throughout the nation.

Recent Amendments. The Twentieth Amendment added three procedural changes. Formerly, Congress convened regularly on the first Monday in December and remained in session as long as it pleased. This was the "long session." But when it convened the following December, Congress could remain in session only until March 4, at which time the terms of all the representatives and one-third of the senators expired. This was the "short session."

Meanwhile, in the November preceding the short session, all of the seats of the House of Representatives and one-third of the Senate seats had been put to election. Although some of the incumbents had been defeated for reelection, they nevertheless convened with the rest in December and continued to serve throughout the short session, i.e., until the following March 4. Continuing to serve for four months after defeat caused them to be dubbed "lame ducks." While the lame ducks served throughout the short session, new members chosen in the preceding November remained out of office. Since their terms began on March 4, they could be called into special session at any time after that date, but if the President did not call a special session, they regularly convened in the following December—thirteen months after election.

The Twentieth Amendment ended all terms on January 3 and provided that Congress convene regularly on the same date. This means that both sessions of a Congress can be "long" and that only two months elapse between election and the commencement of duties. The second provision of the amendment moved the President's inauguration from March 4 to January 20. A third empowered Congress to provide for choosing a President and Vice President should something happen to prevent those elected in November of an election year from being inaugurated on the following January 20. This was intended to overcome embarrassment such as occurred in the famous Hayes-Tilden contest of 1876, in which the outcome was uncertain until a few hours of the date of inauguration.

The Twenty-first Amendment ended prohibition, which had imposed gigantic responsibilities upon the national, state, and local governments. Controversy had raged for more than two decades over the desirability of attempting to interfere with personal liberty by forbidding the manufacture, transportation, and sale of intoxicating beverages. The depression following the stock-market crash of 1929 brought an economic and social revolution which placed the critics of prohibition in positions of power. The result was the Twenty-first Amendment, which repealed the eighteenth and gave the states long-coveted authority to control interstate shipments of intoxicating liquors.

The Twenty-second Amendment came as a political reaction to the breach made by Franklin D. Roosevelt in the two-term tradition. Proposed in March, 1947, by the required two-thirds of both houses of Congress, the amendment was ratified by the thirty-sixth state in February, 1951.

This change made it impossible for any successor to President Harry S. Truman to be elected more than twice. In the event a Vice President succeeds to the office of President during the first two years of a term, he may be elected to fill the Presidency only once. If he succeeds during the last two years of a term, he may be elected twice. Thus someone might hold the office of President for a maximum of ten years.

It is too early to calculate the full effect of this amendment. Opposition was neither strong nor vocal, but thoughtful students point out that the amendment is almost certain to reduce the President's ability to lead Congress and his party, especially during the last half of his second term. Some believe that this fear became a reality in President Dwight D. Eisenhower's second term.

The Twenty-third Amendment had only one objective: to permit residents of the District of Columbia to vote in presidential elections.

Amendments Few and Hard to Obtain. One is impressed by the infrequency with which amendments have been added. Omitting the first ten, which were adopted within a short time after the Constitution became effective, an amendment has been adopted about every thirteen years. But this is too favorable a picture. The thirteenth, fourteenth, and fifteenth were ratified under questionable circumstances. If these are omitted, the record is one amendment added approximately every 17 years.

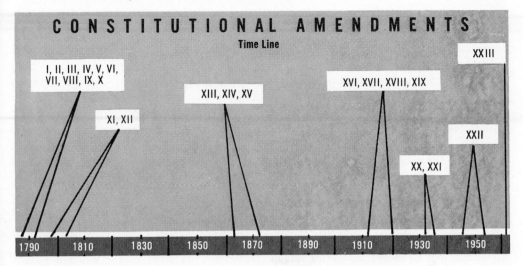

CONSTITUTIONAL AMENDMENTS
Time Line

I, II, III, IV, V, VI, VII, VIII, IX, X

XI, XII

XIII, XIV, XV

XVI, XVII, XVIII, XIX

XX, XXI

XXII

XXIII

| 1790 | 1810 | 1830 | 1850 | 1870 | 1890 | 1910 | 1930 | 1950 |

The most striking feature shown here is that Federal constitutional amendments come in groups, often with long intervals between.

Although amendments can be speedily proposed and ratified, as illustrated by the twelfth, opinion must be overwhelmingly in favor of a proposal before this can happen. Proponents must marshal a two-thirds vote in both houses, or a total of 292 votes in the lower house and 67 votes in the Senate, if the total membership is present. Opponents, on the other hand, may block a proposal with one-third of the membership in only *one* of the houses (146 votes in the House or 34 in the Senate).

The situation is worse when it comes to ratification. Proponents must obtain affirmative action in both houses of state legislatures in thirty-eight states (except in the state of Nebraska, where the legislature is unicameral), or a total of seventy-six separate legislative bodies, while opponents need to induce only *one* house in thirteen different states to block ratification. Thus a small minority, estimated by some to be as low as 5 per cent of the population, can permanently defeat an amendment desired by a considerable majority of the people. This is particularly true with an amendment likely to affect adversely the special interests of some geographic section of the country.

The magnitude of the effort involved has undoubtedly deterred more frequent use of the amending procedure. Where merely a different interpretation of a general phrase is desired, those interested in altering the Constitution are likely to put pressure on the courts rather than resort to the amendment procedure. This was the case during the controversy over slavery, legal tender, child labor, the New Deal, and race segregation.

Proposals to Change Amendment Procedure. Many advocate simplification of the amending procedure. The most frequent suggestions are that the proposal of amendments require only a majority vote in both houses of Congress and ratification require the approval of two-thirds (rather than three-fourths) of the states, a simple majority of states, or a majority of the people voting by referendum in a majority of the states. Thus far it has been impossible to evoke enthusiasm for any of the suggestions. A determined minority, anticipating certain amendments that would be sure to follow, would probably resist simplifying the amendment procedure as strenuously as it would oppose specific amendments.

Other Suggested Amendments. Congressmen propose numerous amendments and state legislatures often petition for a national convention to consider suggested amendments. Proposals such as these are referred to the judiciary committees of the two houses but seldom are given serious consideration. In 1924 Congress proposed an amendment, since ratified by twenty-eight states, that would permit Federal regulation of child labor. In 1962 Congress proposed an amendment to abolish tax-paying qualifications for persons who vote for Federal officers.

Other proposed amendments which have some support include: granting home rule, or statehood, for the District of Columbia; reducing the voting age to eighteen; abolishing the electoral college; limiting presidential use of executive agreements and the scope of treaties; outlawing lynching; restricting the use of literacy tests in qualifying voters; lengthening the terms of congressmen to four years; repealing the Twenty-second Amendment; limiting Federal income, estate, and gift taxes to 25 per cent; fixing the number of Supreme Court justices; and limiting congressional authority over the appellate jurisdiction of the Federal courts.

Judicial Interpretation. As already intimated, a constitution also grows and changes by judicial interpretation. This is particularly true of the American Federal Constitution, written in concise, general words and phrases which admit varying interpretations. Almost every clause of the Constitution has been before the courts,

---

¹ Texts of the two proposals mentioned, which are before the states for ratification, are given at the end of Appendix III.

and it is chiefly from court decisions that an understanding of the document must be derived. Former Chief Justice Hughes epitomized the situation when he said, "We are under the Constitution, but the Constitution is what the judges say it is."

A few illustrations clarify his meaning. The preamble, the courts have held, does not convey a grant of power; it is merely a declaration of purpose. A tax on incomes is a direct tax rather than an indirect one. Congress can create corporations, such as banks, to carry out its delegated powers. The Constitution does not follow the flag into newly acquired territories. The first ten amendments apply to the national government only. The courts may declare acts of Congress unconstitutional. A Federal petit jury must consist of twelve persons.

Ordinarily, in deciding cases, the courts follow the rule of stare decisis; i.e., they decide as they did in previous cases unless there is some compelling reason for them not to do so. This practice permits the formation of a body of "judge-made law." But judges may depart from precedents, and these changes of opinion have the same effect, at least temporarily, as formal amendments.

American history is strewn with conspicuous instances of court reversals. In 1932 Justice Brandeis listed forty important instances wherein the Supreme Court had reversed itself or drastically modified its decisions [*Burnet* v. *Coronado Oil and Gas Co.*, 285 U.S. 393 (1932)]. Since his listing, more reversals have occurred than during any previous period of equal length.

Since 1936 the Supreme Court has reversed or greatly modified its interpretations of at least four of the most controversial provisions of the Constitution—the tax power, the commerce power, and the Fifth and the Fourteenth Amendments.

Indeed, constitutional lawyers of three

decades ago would scarcely recognize the Constitution today. Then, Congress could not regulate manufacturing, mining, the generation of electric power, and agricultural production because they had no direct effect upon interstate commerce; now, they are admitted to have sufficient effect upon interstate commerce to permit Federal control. Then, Congress could not tax state instrumentalities and their employees, nor could states tax Federal employees; now, most of these intergovernmental immunities are gone. Then, states deprived liberty without due process of law by fixing minimum wages for women; today, they do not. Then, a primary was not an election; now it is. If one were forced to decide which has had the greater influence in shaping American institutions, the amendment article or judicial interpretation, a strong case could be made for the latter.

Legislative Elaboration. The Constitution is also what Congress says it is. Simple, general phrases may be elaborated by statutes to give them unexpected meaning. Where this occurs, the effect is often as significant as if amendments were formally enacted. The principal basis for congressional elaboration has been the implied power that authorizes the enactment of all laws that are "necessary and proper" to carry delegated powers into effect.

Illustrations of the use of this power are legion. Executive departments are anticipated by three casual references in the Constitution, but no direct authority to create them is given. Believing them necessary and proper for effective administration, Congress has not hesitated to legislate them into existence. Nowhere does the Constitution prescribe the precise manner for selecting inferior officers of the government. Article II, Section 2, states that their appointment may be vested in the President alone, in the courts of law, or in the heads of departments. Nevertheless, Congress many years ago enacted a civil service law which provided, among other things, for the creation of a Civil Service Commission and the recruitment of thousands of employees from ratings made in competitive examinations. The Constitution anticipates that the circumstance might arise when both the President and Vice President might be removed from office and authorizes Congress then to provide for the choice of a Chief Executive. The provision was elaborated by the Presidential Succession Act of 1886 and, more recently, the Act of July 18, 1947. The latter provides that first the Speaker, then the President pro tempore of the Senate, then department heads should become President in the order of the departments' establishment.

By broadly interpreting its powers, Congress has established and implemented a huge defense establishment; created dozens of administrative boards and bureaus; annexed a far-flung empire; entered into education, banking, insurance, construction, transportation, and generating electric power; and found authority to regulate the economic and social life of a highly industrialized and complicated nation.

Executive Interpretation. The courts and Congress have no monopoly on the right to construe the Constitution. Over the years Presidents have insisted that the document meant what they said it did, and their views have frequently prevailed. Jefferson, while admitting that his power to do so was doubtful, acquired Louisiana without prior authorization by Congress. Lincoln insisted that the Southern states had never been out of the Union. Johnson, Wilson, and Franklin D. Roosevelt contended that Congress could not restrict the removal of executive employees. Cleveland asserted the right to use Federal troops within a state to enforce Federal law or protect Federal property.

Theodore Roosevelt maintained that he could agree to supervise collection of Santo Domingo customs by executive agreement, rather than by treaty as many in Congress preferred. Wilson asserted the right to arm merchantmen in spite of congressional opposition. Coolidge defended his refusal to send troops into a state to maintain order merely because a state legislature or governor asked him to do so.

Various presidents have insisted that they were justified in sending armed forces anywhere in the world to protect American lives and property without obtaining legislative approval. Franklin D. Roosevelt successfully contended that the Constitution was broad enough to justify a far-reaching program of recovery and reform. Illustrations could be multiplied, but these suggest that the Chief Executive has played a significant role in modifying and expanding the Constitution.

Custom and Usage. Many of the unwritten provisions of the Constitution have been added by custom and usage. Political parties are not mentioned in the Constitution but long ago became indispensable institutions. The electoral college, though looked upon as a brilliant invention by the framers of the Constitution, ceased functioning as originally intended as early as 1796. The President's Cabinet is almost entirely the product of custom. Legislative committees are not authorized in the Constitution, but custom and usage have made them as permanent as if they were, and custom decrees that members of the House of Representatives should be residents of the districts from which they are chosen.

The Constitution a Living Document. Originally only a skeletal framework of government, the Constitution became a "living" document. Though written and infrequently amended, it has kept pace with the American people, allowing much freedom while providing the machinery to maintain order, resolve domestic problems with a minimum of violence, and realize national aspirations.

Occasionally a voice is raised calling for a complete revision of the famous document. Frequently, dissatisfied minorities clamor for drastic alterations. The latter may get their wish if revolutionary conditions prevail for a prolonged period of time. If such conditions can be avoided, total revision seems improbable. As in the past, the Constitution is more likely to be adapted to changing needs and conditions by interpretation, custom, and usage.

FOR FURTHER READING

Ames, Herman V.: "The Proposed Amendments to the Constitution . . . during the First Century of Its History" in Annual Report of the American Historical Association for the Year 1896 (Washington, D.C.: vol. 2, 1897).

Beard, Charles A.: The Supreme Court and the Constitution (New York: Macmillan, 1912).

Brown, Everett S.: Ratification of the Twenty-first Amendment to the Constitution of the United States: State Convention Records and Laws (Ann Arbor, Mich.: University of Michigan Press, 1938).

Carr, Robert K.: The Supreme Court and Judicial Review (New York: Rinehart, 1942).

Corwin, Edward S.: Court over Constitution: A Study of Judicial Review as an Instrument of Popular Government (Princeton, N.J.: Princeton University Press, 1938).

Crosskey, W. W.: Politics and the Constitution in the History of the United States (Chicago: University of Chicago Press, 2 vols., 1953).

Graham, George A.: America's Capacity to Govern (Tuscaloosa, Ala.: University of Alabama Press, 1960).

Haines, Charles G.: The American Doctrine of Judicial Supremacy (Berkeley and Los Angeles, Calif.: University of California Press, 2d ed., 1932).

————: The Role of the Supreme Court in American Government and Politics, 1789–1835 (Berkeley and Los Angeles, Calif.: University of California Press, 1944).

―――― and Foster H. Sherwood: *The Role of the Supreme Court in American Government and Politics, 1835–1864* (Berkeley and Los Angeles, Calif.: University of California Press, 1957).

Hazlitt, Henry: *A New Constitution Now* (New York: McGraw-Hill, 1942).

Hehmeyer, Alexander: *Time for a Change: A Proposal for a Second Constitutional Convention* (New York: Rinehart, 1943).

Heller, Francis H.: *The Sixth Amendment to the Constitution of the United States: A Study in Constitutional Development* (Lawrence, Kans.: University of Kansas Press, 1951).

Horwill, Herbert W.: *Usages of the American Constitution* (New York: Oxford, 1925).

James, Joseph B.: *The Framing of the Fourteenth Amendment* (Urbana, Ill.: University of Illinois Press, 1956).

McBain, Howard L.: *The Living Constitution: A Consideration of the Realities and Legends of Our Fundamental Law* (New York: Macmillan, 1934).

McWhinney, Edward: *Judicial Review in the English Speaking World* (Toronto: University of Toronto Press, 1956).

Merriam, Charles E.: *The Written Constitution and the Unwritten Attitude* (New York: Richard R. Smith, 1931).

Munro, William B.: *The Makers of the Unwritten Constitution* (New York: Macmillan, 1930).

Musmanno, Michael A.: *Proposed Amendments to the Constitution . . .* , H. Doc. 551, 70th Cong., 2d Sess. (1929).

Myers, Denys P.: *The Process of Constitutional Amendment*, S. Doc. 314, 76th Cong., 3d Sess. (1941).

Orfield, Lester B.: *Amending the Federal Constitution* (Chicago: Callaghan, 1942).

Padover, Saul K.: *The Genius of America: Men and Ideas That Shaped the American Mind* (New York: McGraw-Hill, 1962).

Patterson, Bennett B.: *The Forgotten Ninth Amendment: A Call for Legislative and Judicial Recognition of Rights under Social Conditions Today* (Indianapolis: Bobbs-Merrill, 1955).

Read, Conyers (ed.): *The Constitution Reconsidered* (New York: Columbia University Press, 1938).

Schwartz, Bernard: *The Supreme Court: Constitutional Revolution in Retrospect* (New York: Ronald, 1957).

Swisher, Carl B.: *The Growth of Constitutional Power in the United States* (Chicago: University of Chicago Press, 1946).

―――――: *American Constitutional Development* (Boston: Houghton Mifflin, 1943).

Tansill, Charles C. (ed.): *Proposed Amendments to the Constitution Introduced in Congress, December 4, 1899–July 2, 1926*, S. Doc. 93, 69th Cong., 1st Sess. (1926).

Ten Broek, Jacobus: *The Antislavery Origins of the Fourteenth Amendment* (Berkeley and Los Angeles, Calif.: University of California Press, 1951).

Warren, Charles: *Congress, the Constitution, and the Supreme Court* (Boston: Little, Brown, 1925).

REVIEW QUESTIONS

1. What is the constitutional basis for each of the principles discussed in this chapter?

2. Of what practical significance is the principle of popular sovereignty today?

3. What circumstances led the founding fathers to prefer a Federal system to one that was unitary?

4. How does the representative system of government differ from a pure, or direct, democracy? What are the advantages and disadvantages of each?

5. Do you think our system of government has enough safeguards to ensure that the military can be kept permanently subordinated to civilian authority?

6. Defend and criticize the Supreme Court's decision in *Marbury v. Madison*.

7. How do you explain the comparatively large increase in the number of laws declared unconstitutional during the period 1920–1940? How do you explain the decrease since 1940?

8. Defend and criticize the doctrine of separation of powers.

9. On the whole, has judicial review been beneficial or harmful to the welfare of the American people?

10. Explain the procedure by which each of the amendments to the Constitution was added. Should any of the amendments which were proposed by Congress but which remain unratified by the required number of states be added to the Constitution?

11. Give examples of changes made in the American system of government by methods other than amendment.

12. Of the constitutional amendments now under consideration in and out of Congress, which should be added to the Constitution?

Chapter Five

The Federal Union and Its Parts

Now over the years, due in part to our decentralized system, we have come to recognize that most problems can be approached in many reasonable ways. Our constitutional checks and balances, our State and Territorial governments, our multiplicity of county and municipal governing bodies, our emphasis upon individual initiative and community responsibility, encourage unlimited experimentation in the solving of America's problems. Through this diversified approach, the effect of errors is restrained, calamitous mistakes are avoided, the general good is more surely determined, and the self-governing genius of our people is perpetually renewed.

DWIGHT D. EISENHOWER[1]

A *federal state* divides authority between self-governing parts and the central whole; each part operates in its sphere as defined in fundamental law. Among federal states of the modern world are the United States of America, Switzerland, Canada, and the

[1] Address to conference of state governors in Williamsburg, Virginia, June 24, 1957. U.S. President, Joint Federal-State Action Committee, *Progress Report No. 1* (December, 1957), p. 17.

Commonwealth of Australia. A *unitary state* concentrates power in a single central government having legal omnipotence over all territory within the state. In practice, such governments usually delegate some functions to local units. Examples of unitary states in recent times include France, Great Britain, and most of the smaller nations.

Under the federal arrangement, matters considered of primary importance to the

country as a whole are assigned to the national government. Usually these include foreign relations, defense, foreign commerce, and a monetary system. Functions deemed principally of local interest are given to provincial (in United States, state) governments. Local affairs include such matters as regulation of local commerce, public education, and roads and highways. All federal systems find it difficult to distribute powers between central and local governments on a permanently satisfactory basis. Changing conditions often make obsolete the distribution of powers; hence, constitutional crises recur in countries using the federal plan.

FEDERALISM IN THEORY AND PRACTICE

History of Federalism. Federalism has been practiced since ancient times. Greek city-states united into leagues for common worship and to resist common enemies. In medieval times three notable confederations were established. The Lombard League was formed by northern Italian cities to resist the Hohenstaufens. In northern Germany the Hanseatic League achieved considerable commercial and political strength. The Netherlands Confederation bound the northern lowland provinces through the years of Spanish oppression.

The forerunner of modern federations was the old Swiss Confederation, which the authors of *The Federalist* mentioned frequently. The launching of the United States dramatically drew the attention of the modern world to the possibilities of federalism. Historical precedent contributed little guidance to build the first truly federal constitution and solve the difficult problems of distributing powers between national and state governments. It is remarkable, therefore, that the founding fathers framed a fundamental law that, with few amendments, has adapted to a century and three-quarters of revolutionary change.

What does the map of the world reveal about nations with a federal form of government? Nearly all countries of very large area have adopted the federal principle. Among the far-flung nations using federalism in one form or another are United States, Canada, Australia, Mexico, Brazil, Argentina, the Soviet Union, India, and Pakistan. Historical or ethnic factors have made unitary government impossible in virtually all the modern nations that have federal systems. The American states sought effective unity on common problems but individuality in local affairs. Switzerland is a quadrilingual country, with strong traditions of cantonal self-government. The First Reich (1871–1918) and Second Reich (1918–1933) eras in Germany found federation an appropriate device in transition from individual principalities to the centralized, totalitarian state. Canada and Australia were made up of former colonies of Great Britain; in each the geographic extent and historical separation ruled out the unitary form. In Canada the French problem made federation even more necessary. The polyglot population, scattered lands, and large area of Russia dictated federal form, if not spirit.

In two of the four Latin-American federations, Mexico and Venezuela, the adoption of federalism reflected a desire to imitate the liberal institutions of the United States. Strong reasons existed for the use of the federal plan in Argentina and Brazil, but in recent years, repeated national intervention in state affairs has rendered their federalism less meaningful. Following the Second World War, the federal principle was useful in launching new governments for India, Pakistan, Burma, Yugoslavia, Western Germany, and Indonesia, although the last mentioned subsequently became a unitary state.

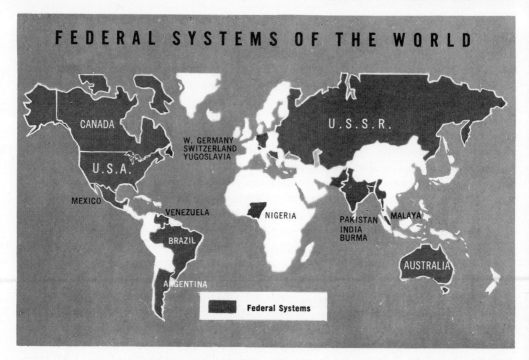

FEDERAL SYSTEMS OF THE WORLD

CANADA

W. GERMANY
SWITZERLAND
YUGOSLAVIA

U.S.S.R.

U.S.A.

MEXICO

VENEZUELA   NIGERIA   PAKISTAN   MALAYA
                                INDIA
BRAZIL   BURMA

ARGENTINA   AUSTRALIA

Federal Systems

The sixteen nations named are deemed by the authors to be federal in form, although not invariably in spirit. Two nations that are sometimes listed as federations
—the Netherlands and the Republic of South Africa—we classify as unitary.

Advantages to the United States. The American states were unprepared in 1787 to surrender their powers to a unitary central government. Federalism is retained because of certain merits. First, it secures the benefits of local self-government and civic training. Often the best judges of a public function are those close to it. Services may be adapted to suit community needs. City hall, county courthouse, or state capitol elicit more responsibility and participation than a far-off national capitol.

Second, it allows flexibility for experimentation and adaptation to areas with dissimilar interests and populations. If North Dakota wishes to try writing state hail insurance, it may gain experience useful to other states and the national government. State experiments in social insurance or other fields may provide data to build a sound policy for the Federal government. An agrarian state encounters problems vastly different from those of an industrial state. A French-speaking Catholic province of Canada differs from an English-speaking Protestant one in approaching many social problems; a federal system allows each to manage local affairs to suit itself.

Third, it provides stability, and it safeguards individual rights. Differing election dates and varied issues mean a less drastic turnover of officeholders than under the unitary system. An all-powerful central government might sweep away rights of individuals and minorities, but division of authority between state and national units provides a dual protection.

Fourth, it is an effective compromise between fractionalization into many small nations and the centralization that destroys local autonomy. To break up the American republic of today into fifty small nations is unthinkable, and most Americans would reject centralization of all authority in Washington. The effectiveness of the compromise hinges upon either having static conditions (a natural impossibility) or possessing a fundamental law sufficiently elastic to allow the changes persistently demanded by the public but without yielding to momentary gusts of passion. The American federal system has proved adaptable to the needs of a growing people and a dynamic society.

Shortcomings of American Federalism. To heap unstinted praise upon federalism and close our eyes to its several shortcomings would be useless. Distribution of powers between two levels of government on a permanently satisfactory basis is impossible. Technological developments, economic conditions, wars, and social changes alter the problems of government; they may call for a reallocation of responsibilities for particular public services. If the constitution in which powers are assigned is precise and inflexible, there may be great dissatisfaction over the resulting social lag.

Critical periods arose in American history when problems clearly national in scope were held not subject to Federal legislation. Three Federal attempts to curb the evils of child labor were declared unconstitutional before the wages-and-hours law of 1938 was found valid. In the United States the national and state powers were defined in very general terms. Federal authority has expanded mainly through the Supreme Court's liberalized interpretations of national powers.

Second, diffusion of authority leads to delay and deadlock in critical times. In war and economic depression, parts divide against themselves and lack the unity needed to solve the great issues at hand. The sense of corporate unity that has enveloped the nation during its major wars and the broad nature of the war powers have caused less embarrassment than some domestic crises, such as the depression of the early 1930s.

Third, confusion arises from the lack of uniformity in laws, and extra expense is incurred in maintaining two levels of government. Some progress has been made toward securing uniform state legislation in certain fields, but the diversity of state law is enormous. An insurance company operating nationwide, for example, incurs great expense in meeting the requirements of our fifty state laws. Often it is said that two levels of government are more expensive than one. Certain costs are duplicated, but whether the unitary form would be cheaper is speculative.

Although still one of the world's leading exponents of federalism, the United States has profoundly changed its own system, chiefly by expanding central authority at the expense of local autonomy.

Federalism Reconsidered. More than seventeen decades after the American federal system opened for business, Congress created a body to study its operation. The Commission on Intergovernmental Relations was established in 1953 to examine the roles of the Federal government and the states. It consisted of twenty-five members; fifteen were appointed by the President, five by the President of the Senate, and five by the Speaker of the House. After some difficulty in finding adequate leadership, the Commission settled down to work under the chairmanship of Meyer Kestnbaum. It established study and advisory committees in each of the functional and fiscal areas principally involved in Federal-state relations. Fifteen separate studies were published, in addition to the annual report.[1]

The report of the Commission reads at some points like a "states' rights" tract, but most of its recommendations are moderate and indicate a willingness to build upon the experience of the past. There is a careful review of the beginnings of the federal system, the role of the states, jurisdictional problems relating to Federal and state functions, and fiscal relationships such as the grant-in-aid. The latter part of the report describes functions and makes specific recommendations for major changes, including increased state participation in soil and agricultural conservation, larger Federal grants for highways (and reduced supervision), and a revised formula for old-age assistance payments to the states.

Among the controversial items, the Commission reported adversely on the proposed Federal aid to elementary and secondary education. It stressed the difficulty posed by the fact that 12 per cent of the nation's children attend nonpublic schools. It found objection to dealing directly with school districts and also to transmitting Federal grants through state governments.

To focus continuous attention on the problems of intergovernmental relations, the Commission suggested that a special assistant in the Executive Office of the President be given coordinating responsibilities. An "advisory board," appointed by the President, would meet from time to time and provide counsel in the interlevel area. Several recommendations pointed to the need for careful review and coordination, especially of fiscal aspects of Federal-state relations. In the natural-resources field, the Commission supported a per-manent "board of coordination and review" to advise the national government on policy and state cooperation.

The *Report* is an important milestone in the evolution of American federalism. In emphasizing the need for virile state governments it hoped to help correct a quarter of a century of tendencies toward ever greater centralization. But the commissioners did not agree in all matters. Some, particularly the former governors, would like the Supreme Court decisions permitting the fuller exercise of Federal powers reversed.[2] Others, led by the "liberal" senators, believe that the Federal government must continue to extend its role in serving the general welfare of the whole people.[3]

The Commission was scarcely designed to make daring imaginative proposals. Compared with its Canadian counterpart, the Royal Commission on Dominion-Provincial Relations, the United States Commission appears to have been too large and bound down with representatives of particular interests—congressional, state, partisan, and other. The divergent groups did not achieve a desirable meeting of minds and agreement on ways and means of modernizing the federal system. Nevertheless the studies made under the Commission, plus surveys made in selected states, are a foundation upon which sound policies and programs in Federal-state relations can be based.[4]

In 1957 President Eisenhower invited

---

[1] U.S. Commission on Intergovernmental Relations, *Report* . . . (1955). The full list of publications appears on p. 295 of the report.

[2] *Ibid.*, pp. 59–60, footnotes 1 and 2. Six former governors were members of the Commission.

[3] *Ibid.*, pp. 277–279, for dissent of Senator Morse. On many of his separate statements and dissents on specific topics, he was joined by Senator Humphrey.

[4] The best brief description of the Commission's work is William Anderson, "The Commission on Intergovernmental Relations and the United States Federal System," *Journal of Politics*, vol. 18 (May, 1956), pp. 211–231.

WEIGHING FEDERALISM

LOCAL CONTROL	FEDERAL CONTROL

ADVANTAGES

LOCAL CONTROL

1. Promotes local unity, sense of neighborhood responsibility, spirit of self-reliance, and capacity for group action.

2. Secures close adaptation of public services to local needs.

3. Promotes and safeguards freedom, democracy, and responsible government.

4. Promotes socially beneficial intercommunity competition.

5. Permits safe experimentation with new forms and methods of government, thus fostering a gradual improvement in government throughout the country.

6. Promotes political stability.

7. Promotes national unity and national security.

8. Relieves the national government of congestion of business.

FEDERAL CONTROL

1. Unifies the nation.

2. Provides for the common or national needs of the population and for a coordinated development of the nation's resources.

3. Safeguards the nation's independence.

4. Safeguards the liberties of the people in a democratic country and provides for an equality of social, economic, and educational opportunities in the various sections of the country.

5. Responds quickly to changed national situations and takes care of national emergencies.

6. Is more efficient and economical in many respects than are local governments.

7. Gives common direction to local governments, impels them to maintain minimum standards of public service, and helps them to operate more efficiently.

DISADVANTAGES

LOCAL CONTROL

1. Results in an inefficient and an uneconomic management of local affairs.

2. Fosters local autocratic rule by petty officials and powerful minority groups.

3. Breeds narrow parochialism and produces national and regional disunity and disorganization.

4. Results in extreme inequality in the standards of public service and protection of civil rights throughout the country or the region.

5. Produces inertia and extreme rigidity in the organization and operation of the government.

6. Lessens national security.

FEDERAL CONTROL

1. Promotes a rule of an irresponsible national bureaucracy and destroys democracy.

2. Results in a neglect of local needs.

3. Destroys local civic interest, initiative, and responsibility, individual freedom and self-reliance.

4. Results in the instability of governmental policies, and of the government itself.

5. Results in inefficiency and waste.

6. Produces a congestion of business, industry, arts, and culture in the capital and the economic and cultural decay of the rest of the country.

7. Weakens national unity and national security.

Condensed from Paul Studenski and Paul R. Mort, "Centralized vs. Decentralized Government in Relation to Democracy" (New York: Teachers College, Columbia University, 1941).

the governors to join with him in forming a task force to work on functional and financial problems of intergovernmental relations. In 1959 it was given statutory status as the Advisory Commission on Intergovernmental Relations. It consists of twenty-six members drawn from national, state, and local governments. They consider problems affecting the various levels of government, with special emphasis on grant problems and the fiscal aspects of Federal-state-local relations.

DISTRIBUTION OF POWERS

Specific National Powers. The national government possesses only those powers specifically delegated to it, or reasonably to be inferred from the Constitution. The Tenth Amendment declares: "The powers not delegated to the United States by the Constitution, nor prohibited by it to the States, are reserved to the States respectively, or to the people."

The major Federal powers are enumerated as powers of Congress in Article I, Section 8. They are shown in the table of Examples of the Distribution of Powers in the American Federal System. Other Federal powers are provided for elsewhere in the Constitution.

The national government today appears to possess powers not exercised in the years following 1789. This does not disprove the fact that the United States has a central government of enumerated powers only. Some of the Federal powers, especially tax and commerce, have grown tremendously in scope; the Constitution has shown great capacity for adaptation to changed conditions. Nevertheless, every activity of the national government must be justified under one or more of the specifically delegated powers. Congress lacks a general welfare

power, under which to do anything required by the public interest. Each act of Congress must be hung upon a constitutional "hook" —commerce, tax, monetary, or other. If no constitutional delegation can be found, or if one is improperly used, the legislation may be attacked as unconstitutional. The fact that Congress possesses only powers specifically delegated to it, or reasonably inferred, is one of the outstanding features of American government.

Implied Powers. After the list of powers of Congress given in Article I, Section 8, the Constitution grants Congress authority to "make all Laws which shall be necessary and proper for carrying into execution the foregoing powers, and all other powers vested by this Constitution in the government of the United States, or in any department or officer thereof." This "elastic" or "necessary and proper" clause has evoked much controversy over the breadth of national authority.

The "strict constructionalist" versus "broad constructionalist" conflict over this point has raged at several periods. What unspecified powers might reasonably be implied from those specifically delegated? Hamilton and his followers claimed that Congress possessed much authority in addition to the powers explicitly stated. Jefferson and his supporters insisted that Federal powers should be interpreted by the letter of the Constitution; no authority could be exercised unless specifically delegated.

Under John Marshall, Chief Justice from 1801 to 1835, the Supreme Court supported broad interpretation. The most celebrated case was *McCulloch v. Maryland.* [4 Wheat. 316 (U.S. 1819)]. Maryland had levied a tax upon notes issued by the Baltimore branch of the second United States Bank. The cashier refused to pay the tax. Two principal questions were posed. First, may the United States charter such a bank? The Court answered that it might do so under the congressional power to coin money and to regulate the value thereof. Marshall argued:

We admit, as all must admit, that the powers of the government are limited, and that its limits are not to be transcended. But we think the sound construction of the Constitution must allow to the national legislature that discretion, with respect to the means by which the powers it confers are to be carried into execution, which will enable that body to perform the high duties assigned to it, in the manner most beneficial to the people. Let the end be legitimate, let it be within the scope of the Constitution, and all means which are appropriate, which are plainly adapted to that end, which are not prohibited, but consistent with the the letter and spirit of the Constitution, are constitutional. . . .

Another question involved the power of the state to tax the issue of the bank. The Court denied to the state any authority to tax a Federal instrumentality on the ground that the "power to tax involves the power to destroy."

The ultimate decision on the validity of invoking implied power in a given instance is rendered by the United States Supreme Court. In its decisions regarding the scope of national power the Court has been far from consistent. The Court in some areas and at certain periods has permitted great latitude. In other fields and at other times the Court has held Congress to the letter of the fundamental law.

Lines of legal precedent on both sides of many issues before the Court have developed over a century and a half. Therefore, a judge predisposed for or against expansion of Federal power easily finds important cases to support his decision. Wanting to interpret national power narrowly, he cites as authority cases from the Taney or Taft eras in the Court. He justified the broad construction of Federal authority by citing from Marshall and Stone epochs.

Powers of the State. The state governments possess an indefinite grant of the remaining powers neither given to the Federal government nor prohibited to the states. The Tenth Amendment indicates the sweeping nature of this authority. But Article I, Section 10, forbids the states to make treaties, emit bills of credit, make other than gold and silver legal tender, pass a bill of attainder, pass an ex post facto law, impair the obligation of contracts, grant titles of nobility, tax imports or exports, lay tonnage taxes, keep troops or warships in peace time, or make compacts without congressional approval.

Being residual in nature, state powers are broader than those of the Federal government. States are assumed to have all authority not prohibited in Federal or state constitutions. The principal state power, the police power, gives the state sanction to provide for the health, morals, safety, and welfare of its people.

All governmental power cannot be classified exclusively into Federal or state categories. Some powers are shared by the two levels of government; these are usually called "concurrent powers." For example, both state and Federal governments set standards of weights and measures, tax and borrow, and enact bankruptcy laws.

The Supreme Law of the Land. The supremacy of the Federal Constitution, and of national law within its sphere, is assured by Article VI, clause 2, which provides:

This Constitution, and the laws of the United States which shall be made in pursuance thereof; and all treaties made, or

EXAMPLES OF THE DISTRIBUTION OF POWERS IN THE AMERICAN FEDERAL SYSTEM

POWERS DELEGATED

	FEDERAL	STATE
To make and enforce laws	X	X
To conduct elections		X
To tax	X	X
To spend money to provide for general welfare	X	X
To borrow money	X	X
To regulate interstate and foreign commerce	X	
To coin money	X	
To fix standards of weights and measures	X	
To establish post offices and post roads	X	
To grant patents and copyrights	X	
To establish and maintain courts	X	X
To define and punish piracies and felonies on the high seas	X	
To declare war, grant letters of marque and reprisal	X	
To raise and support an army	X	
To maintain a navy	X	
To provide for militia	X	
To conduct foreign relations	X	
To govern territories	X	
To ratify amendments		X
To charter banks and other corporations	X	X
To take property for public purposes	X	X
To regulate intrastate commerce		X
To establish local governments		X
To protect health, safety, and morals		X
To change state constitutions and governments		X

POWERS PROHIBITED

	FEDERAL	STATE
May not impose direct taxes disproportionate to population and states	X	
May not impose nonuniform indirect taxes	X	
May not tax exports	X	X
May not give preference to one state over another in matters of commerce	X	
May not grant titles of nobility	X	X
May not enter into treaties		X
May not coin money, keep troops or ships of war in time of peace		X
May not pass laws impairing obligation of contract		X
May not tax imports		X
May not change state boundaries without consent of states involved	X	
May not abridge guaranties contained in Bill of Rights	X	
May not permit slavery	X	X
May not deny persons equal protection of the laws		X
May not prevent persons from voting because of race, color, or sex		X
May not violate Federal Constitution or obstruct Federal laws		X

which shall be made, under the authority of the United States, shall be the supreme law of the land; and the judges in every State shall be bound thereby, anything in the constitution or laws of any State to the contrary notwithstanding.

This clause expresses the spirit of the Union. The Federal Constitution is paramount over all other forms of law, state or national. Federal law, if validly enacted under the Constitution, ranks above state law. State laws that conflict with valid Federal laws or treaties may be adjudged unconstitutional on such grounds. An officer of the Federal government or a private citizen can institute such a suit in Federal court. If the court finds the state law in conflict, the law is unenforceable. Failure of a state to respect the decision justifies the use of military force by the Federal government. The first occasion upon which a state law was declared unconstitutional by the United States Supreme Court was that of *Fletcher v. Peck* [6 Cranch 87 (U.S. 1810)], wherein an act of Georgia was at issue. Since then, several hundred state laws have failed the test of constitutionality. Fortunately, the Federal government has seldom had to resort to force.

A new phase of national supremacy may be opened in the Tennessee apportionment case, *Baker v. Carr* [369 U.S. 186 (1962)]. The decision brought state legislative redistricting within the purview of the Federal courts under the equal protection clause of the Fourteenth Amendment. One commentator said that in this case "the Court probably handed down its most important decision since *Marbury v. Madison*."[1]

[1] Ruth C. Silva, "Apportionment in New York, Part One: The Legal Aspects of Reapportionment and Redistricting: Baker v. Carr," *Fordham Law Review*, vol. 30 (April, 1962), p. 581.

The Tennessee constitution requires the reapportionment of legislative representation every ten years, taking into account the number of voters in the several counties. Petitioners alleged that a 1901 statute and subsequent failure to reapportion, despite growth and relocation of population, constituted denial of equal protection. Their complaint was dismissed in a lower Federal court.

In overruling the lower court, the Supreme Court held (1) that the Federal courts have jurisdiction over cases involving state legislative districting, (2) that the appellants had a justiciable cause of action on which they were entitled to seek relief, and (3) that petitioners were competent to bring suit. The Tennessee law was not declared unconstitutional; the lower court was directed to try the case.

The majority opinion distinguished between this case and others ruled nonjusticiable as posing "political questions" under the republican form of government clause. The Court said: " . . . it is the relationship between the judiciary and the coordinate branches of the Federal Government, and not the Federal judiciary's relationship to the States, which gives rise to the 'political question'. "

Strong dissenting opinions were filed by two justices. They protested against judicial intervention "in the essentially political conflict of forces. . . ." There can be no doubt that *Baker v. Carr* will change the Federal-state balance, but the extent cannot be determined before settlement of the many suits filed in the various states.

UNITS OF AMERICAN GOVERNMENT

Number and Diversity of Units. The American federal system proves most confusing in its multiplicity of units of government and the diversity of their names, powers, and duties. The two major levels are Federal and state. Legally the state possesses all the power exercised by both state and local governments; in practice, however, it delegates both powers and functions to many political subdivisions.

The full list of these local units astonishes the average citizen. How can he find the precise government unit charged with the service about which the seeks information? Actually the total of governmental units declined 34 per cent between 1942 and 1957, and nearly 11 per cent between 1957 and 1962, according to the Bureau of the Census.

The States. The states vary greatly in area, population, and wealth. Their equality in the Union is like the dictum that all men are created equal: politically it is so in one sense, but each individual is endowed differently in physique, in abilities, and in his share of the world's goods. In area the states vary from Rhode Island, with 1,214 square miles, to Alaska, with 586,400; in population (1960 census) they range from Alaska, with 266,167, to New York, with 16,782,304. In wealth some far outstrip others in resources, access to markets, and industrial facilities. Pressure for Federal aid often is most intense from the poorer states, and Federal grants correct some of the inequalities between states.

Local Governments. All states except Alaska, Connecticut, and Rhode Island have counties or parishes. The importance of the county varies considerably. In the South, West, and Middle Atlantic areas, counties are major units of local government; in New England, with a minimum of functions, they exist largely for administrative convenience. The New England town embraces rural and urban territories and has broad governmental functions. The Middle Western township is a distant cousin, primarily rural, and with less-important powers and duties. School and other special districts usually have the power

to tax, and they constitute an important category of governmental units.

ADMISSION OF STATES TO THE UNION

The thirteen states existing at the time of the Constitutional Convention were offered charter membership in the Union. After eleven states ratified the Constitution, the new government was declared in operation; North Carolina and Rhode Island finally ratified in 1789 and 1790. The union of thirteen states lasted only one year. New states joined each decade until 1912, when the last contiguous continental territories, Arizona and New Mexico, were admitted. Alaska's admission in 1958 and Hawaii's in 1959 have reopened the statehood door.

Admission Procedure. Procedure for the admission of new states is well established; Article IV, Section 3, gives Congress sole power. The major restriction is that territory of existing states may not be taken without consent.

The admission process normally has involved five steps: (1) A territorial government is organized. (2) The territory applies to Congress for admission to the Union. (3) Congress enacts an "enabling act" outlining procedure for framing the constitution. (4) The territory frames a constitution. (5) Congress passes a resolution of admission.

Several territories, including Tennessee, Michigan, Oregon, and California, have achieved statehood through a process that eliminated one or more of the steps. The "Tennessee Plan," followed by Alaska, involves drafting a state constitution without congressional authorization and electing unofficial United States senators and representatives who proceed to the national Capitol and lobby for admission to the Union.

Conditions for Admission? Congress has withheld admission from would-be states until certain conditions are met. However,

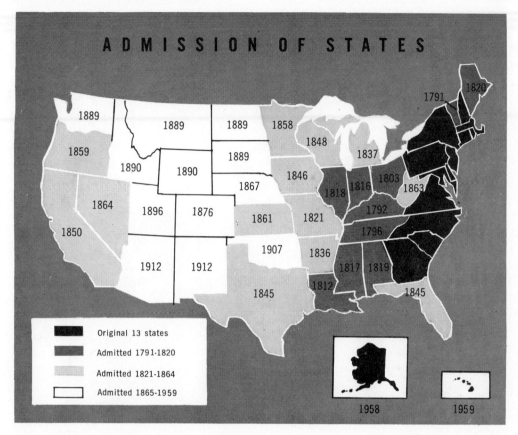

ADMISSION OF STATES

1791 1820
1889 1889 1889 1858
1859 1848 1837
1890 1889
1864 1890 1890 1846 1818 1816 1803 1863
1867 1792
1896 1876 1861 1821 1796
1850 1907 1836
1912 1912 1817 1819
1845 1812 1845

Original 13 states
Admitted 1791-1820
Admitted 1821-1864
Admitted 1865-1959

1958   1959

no conditions pertaining to internal matters can be enforced after the admission of the state. Once admitted, the state is equal to all other states, and may not be bound by prior commitments.[1] On the other hand, conditions imposed with regard to disposition of Federal lands ceded to states and other matters under Federal jurisdiction are enforceable.

Imposing conditions on new states began with the admission of Ohio. Acts of admission usually described the status of each new one as "on an equal footing with the original states," but Congress repeatedly placed detailed conditions. Utah, on admission in 1896, was required to forbid polygamy and

[1] The leading case in this field is *Coyle v. Smith*, 221 U.S. 559 (1911).

to assure nonsectarian public schools. Oklahoma, as a condition of admission in 1907, promised to leave its capital in Guthrie for a period of years. But four years later the state removed the capital to Oklahoma City. When appealed to the United States Supreme Court, this restriction on Oklahoma was declared invalid on the ground that all states are politically equal and have full control over their internal affairs. The enabling act to admit Arizona was vetoed by President Taft in 1911 because he objected to a provision for recall of the judiciary. An amended act was passed to eliminate the disputed clause, but after admission in 1912, Arizona promptly restored provisions for recalling its judges, which are still in effect.

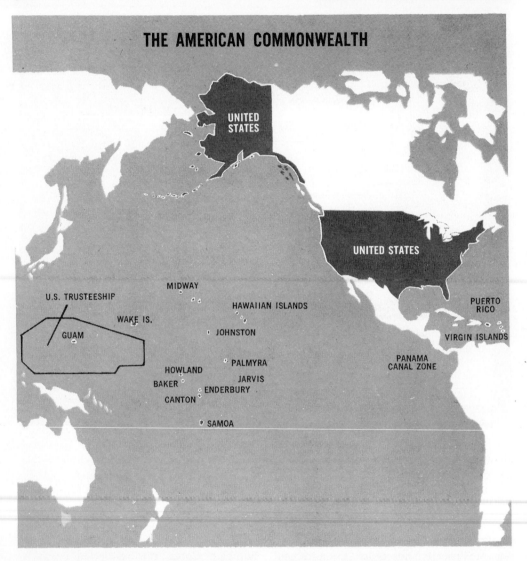

THE AMERICAN COMMONWEALTH

UNITED
STATES

UNITED STATES

MIDWAY

U.S. TRUSTEESHIP

HAWAIIAN ISLANDS

PUERTO
RICO

WAKE IS.

GUAM

JOHNSTON

VIRGIN ISLANDS

PALMYRA

HOWLAND

PANAMA
CANAL ZONE

BAKER   JARVIS
          ENDERBURY

CANTON

SAMOA

Campaigns for Statehood. Nearly a half century after the last contiguous territories of continental United States became states, serious consideration was given to the admission of Hawaii and Alaska. Their important roles and loyalty during the Second World War added much weight to their claims. In Puerto Rico sentiment appears divided sharply between independence and statehood; an ambiguous "Commonwealth" status exists at present.

Agitation for statehood had been incessant for a generation in Hawaii and Alaska. Plebiscites amply demonstrated eagerness for statehood; both drafted constitutions. For statehood, it was argued: historically, territories have been admitted after a period of tutelage; their citizens, as American citizens, were entitled to equal rights and participation in government; continued territorial status was contrary to the democratic ideal over which Americans have been so effusive; Congress discriminated against them, particularly when appropriating funds for public works; they were controlled by a Congress in which they had no vote, by a President whom they could not help elect, and by a Constitution they were not allowed to help amend; they paid the same Federal taxes as did citizens on the mainland; their sons were drafted; and they were qualified by character, education, and experience to assume the full obligations arising from statehood.

The chief objections were that the process of Americanization had not gone far enough, especially in Hawaii, where there are many of oriental ancestry, and it was unfair to give the territories equality of voting power in the Senate with existing large states. In times past, the Armed Forces had objected because they thought statehood would subject their handling of bases and installations to more civilian controls.

Recent Presidents, Republican and Democratic party platforms, and the Conference of State Governors urged statehood for both territories. Increasingly favorable sentiment was expressed in Congress. A statehood bill passed the House in 1950 but was blocked in the Senate. Action was stymied by several factors, such as fear on the part of Southern senators that statehood would increase the voting strength of those favoring Federal civil-rights legislation and alarm among some economic interests in the territories that they would not fare so well if regulated by state governments.

The State of Alaska. Separated from the state of Washington by a 400-mile corridor belonging to Canada, Alaska was the first noncontiguous territory. Its vast sprawling domain encompasses 586,400 square miles —an area more than twice as large as Texas, thirteen times as large as Pennsylvannia, and three and one-half times as large as California.

Shortly after its purchase from Russia in 1867, Alaska became an incorporated territory, but it remained unorganized until 1884. Both fundamental and formal rights were protected by the Constitution. All general laws of Congress applied unless they specifically stated otherwise. Residents had no vote in presidential elections. They were represented in Congress by a delegate, elected every two years, who had a seat in the House of Representatives but no vote.

When Alaska was acquired, the treaty provided that inhabitants who wished to retain their Russian allegiance should depart within three years. All others, except "uncivilized" native tribes, were collectively naturalized, and their children born subsequently became citizens by birth. Members of the "uncivilized" tribes were considered wards of the Federal government until 1924, when they were collectively naturalized.

Congress passed the act of admission in July, 1958, and Alaska accepted its new status by overwhelming popular vote the following month. The forty-ninth state entered the Union with one of the most modern constitutions ever drafted. It retains the bicameral legislature, makes the gover-

---

TERRITORY OF ALASKA

SAMPLE BALLOT

FOR

RATIFICATION OF THE CONSTITUTION AND OF CONVENTION ORDINANCES

Mark "X" in the square opposite the word "yes" if you favor the proposition.
Mark "X" in the square opposite the word "no" if you oppose the proposition.

Proposition No. 1— RATIFICATION OF CONSTITUTION:

| Shall the Constitution for the State of Alaska prepared and agreed upon by the Alaska Constitutional Convention be adopted? | YES ☐ |
| | NO ☐ |

Proposition No. 2— ALASKA-TENNESSEE PLAN:

| Shall Ordinance Number Two (Alaska-Tennessee Plan) of the Alaska Constitutional Convention, calling for the immediate election of two United States Senators and one United States Representative, be adopted? | YES ☐ |
| | NO ☐ |

Alaska used this ballot in 1956 to ratify its constitution and move for statehood without waiting for an enabling act of Congress.

norship elective, and gives a full grant of power to the state government to control its resources and regulate its affairs.

The Fiftieth State, Hawaii. Twenty-four hundred miles southwest from San Francisco lie the islands that constitute the new State of Hawaii. In March, 1959, Congress adopted an act of admission making the former territory the fiftieth state. The formalities of proclamation and the beginning of state government required months. The capital, Honolulu, is located on Oahu; there are seven other principal islands. The total area, including the small outlying islands, is about twice the combined size of Delaware and Rhode Island.

Before annexation in 1898, Hawaii was an independent republic with a long tradition of monarchial rule. It became an incorporated territory by the Organic Act of 1900. Though citizens, its people had no vote in presidential elections, and their only representative in Congress was a delegate, chosen by the voters every two years, who had a nonvoting seat in the House of Representatives. General laws of Congress applied unless exception was expressly made. Both fundamental and formal rights were guaranteed in the territory.

The state constitution, drafted by a convention in 1950, went into effect when statehood was proclaimed in 1959. It is a modern charter of good form and modest length, but with fewer innovations than the constitution of Alaska. Institutions of the territorial era were carried over and transformed. The legislature is bicameral, with houses elective in the usual way. The only elective executive officers are the governor and the lieutenant governor. The number of executive departments is limited to twenty. Judges of the state court system are appointed by the governor.

Because of the unique racial composition of Hawaii, its political tendencies were watched with interest. The first congressional delegation sent to Washington consisted of one senator of Chinese, one senator of European, and one representative of Japanese ancestry. One senator was a Republican; the other senator and the House member were Democrats. In the presidential election of 1960 the Republican and Democratic tickets were nearly tied. Its 1960 population of 632,772 entitles Hawaii to two House seats and four electoral votes during the sixties.

AMERICAN TERRITORIES

Since the Second World War, the world has given much attention to dependent areas, territories inhabited by people unable to stand wholly on their own. The Charter of the United Nations sets the goal of independence or self-government for dependent peoples everywhere. However, colonial revolt continues on most continents.

Americans are inclined to stand aloof or even to criticize colonialism in sweeping terms. Yet the colonial problems of the United States are many. Alaska and Hawaii had to struggle long for statehood. Gunshots in Washington, D.C., in the 1950s are striking evidence that not all Puerto Ricans are content with "commonwealth status." Other territories call to the national capital for aid, protection, and home rule.

Power to Acquire and Govern. Authority to acquire territory from foreign nations is implied largely from the war and treaty powers. The acquisition of unclaimed territory by discovery is inherent in the sovereignty of the United States. Authority to acquire within existing limits of the United States is implied from both the spending power and the provisions, noted below, conferring power to govern territories. The Constitution assumes that territory acquired within the states will be either ceded by the states or purchased from them or from private parties.

The power to govern territory comes from two provisions. Article I, Section 8, says Congress shall have power

. . . to exercise exclusive legislation in all cases whatsoever, over such district (not exceeding ten miles square) as may, by cession of particular States, and the acceptance of Congress, become the seat of the government of the United States, and to exercise like authority over all places purchased by the consent of the legislature of the State in which the same shall be, for the erection of forts, magazines, arsenals, dock-yards, and other needful buildings . . .

The second provision is in Article IV, Section 3: "Congress shall have power to dispose of and make all needful rules and regulations respecting the territory . . . belonging to the United States."

Thus Congress has exclusive jurisdiction over the overseas territories plus the District of Columbia, ceded by Maryland. Within the states, though, it is continually necessary to determine whether state or Federal law applies to each government-owned army camp, veterans' home, shipyard, arsenal, post office, or other area. Under the terms of Article I, Section 8, cited above, Federal jurisdiction is exclusive only over places purchased with the consent of the legislature of the state in which they are situated. If purchased without state approval, as is often the case, both Federal and state law would be applicable.

Status of Territories. If Congress expressly declares that a territory is incorporated into the United States, or by a series of acts implies this intention, the courts decree the territory *incorporated*. At the present time only the District of Columbia is an incorporated territory. Other American territories are *unincorporated*.

Supervision of Territories. Congress has complete dominion over territorial affairs. It may legislate not only concerning external affairs of the territory but also on other subjects considered within the scope of state legislation. In practice, however, local problems are usually turned over to a territorial government, with Congress retaining the right to abrogate any acts of the territorial legislature.

Administrative responsibility is now centered mainly in the Office of Territories, Department of the Interior. In years past the Army and Navy operated many territories, but the prevailing policy favors civilian rather than military control except in vital defense areas.

Nearly all Federal departments and agencies carry on operations within the various territories. For the most part, each goes its own way without clearing through either a central agency in Washington or the territorial governor's office.

The first Hoover Commission surveyed and criticized management of territorial affairs and recommended that Congress undertake a comprehensive study of the problem. One suggestion was to transfer all territorial and occupational duties from the Armed Forces to a special secretary reporting directly to the Secretary of Defense. A more favored alternative was to create a special Administration of Overseas Affairs with jurisdiction over all territorial and occupational activities abroad except State Department diplomatic and consular services. The assignment to Interior of supervisory responsibility over most of the populated American territories is a step in the direction indicated, but it falls short of the goal sketched by the Hoover Commission.

District of Columbia. In the District of Columbia there is no locally elected executive or legislature. Administration is the responsibility of a three-man Board of Commissioners appointed by the President with Senate approval. The judiciary (described in Chapter 17) consists of Federal and territorial courts. Congress now does all the lawmaking, although it has power to grant greater home rule and the Hoover Commission and many impartial bodies have recommended that it do so. Those in favor believe that it is ludicrous for the legislature of one of the most powerful nations of the world to decide comparatively petty issues for the District. Some of the opposition, on the other hand, fears that greater home rule might result in a flare-up of latent racial problems.

Statehood has long been advocated as the appropriate goal for incorporated territories. Congress can admit others by statute, but a constitutional amendment would be required for the District of Columbia because of the clause which says that Congress shall "exercise exclusive legislation in all cases

PRINCIPAL AMERICAN TERRITORIES

Territory	Date acquired	Status before acquisition	How acquired	Citizenship of natives	Legislature (elected by people)	Executive (appointed by President)
INCORPORATED:						
• DISTRICT OF COLUMBIA	1790	Part of Maryland	Donated	U.S. citizens	U.S. Congress	3 commissioners, 3-year terms
UNINCORPORATED						
• GUAM	1898	Spanish colony	War and treaty	U.S. citizens by collective naturalization, 1950	Unicameral	Governor, 4-year term
• PANAMA CANAL ZONE	1904	Territory of Panama	Perpetual lease and annual payment	Not U.S. citizens	None	Governor, 4-year term
• PUERTO RICO	1898	Spanish colony	War and treaty	U.S. citizens by collective naturalization	Senate and House	Governor, elected by voters, 4-year term
• SAMOAN ISLANDS	1904	Independent	Treaty with native chiefs	Not U.S. citizens	None	Governor, 4-year term
• VIRGIN ISLANDS	1917	Danish colony	Purchase by treaty	U.S. citizens by collective naturalization, 1927	Unicameral	Governor, indefinite term
• Trust territory of the PACIFIC ISLANDS	1947	Japanese mandates	Conquest and UN trust	Not U.S. citizens	None	High Commissioner, indefinite term

whatsoever" over the area. Meanwhile its citizens have no elective local council and no member of Congress. Under the Twenty-third Amendment, ratified in 1961, the District is now permitted to participate in presidential elections.

Commonwealth of Puerto Rico. Among the American territories the island of Puerto Rico is a somewhat special case, having more autonomy than the others. Known since July, 1952, as the Commonwealth of Puerto Rico, this territory has undergone a social betterment and economic expansion program popularly known as "Operation Bootstrap." Its new constitution provides for popular election of a governor and a bicameral legislature. The judiciary consists of a Federal district court and territorial courts.

A new bill of rights adds some significant features: wire tapping is expressly forbidden, the death penalty shall not exist, the military shall always be subordinate to civil authority, and the employment of children under fourteen is forbidden in occupations prejudicial to health. Certain "human rights," such as the right to have a free public education, to obtain work, to have a standard of living adequate for oneself and one's family, and to have social security, were included in the draft constitution approved by the voters, but the American Congress forced deletion of most of them.

Adoption of commonwealth status has moderated sentiment on the island for statehood and independence, but unless some of the nearly desperate economic and social problems are solved, demands for greater reforms will continue.

Puerto Rico is represented in Congress by a resident commissioner, who is elected and has a four-year term. He has a voice but no vote in the House of Representatives.

Other Territories. The lesser territories have a wide variety of political forms and problems. The Virgin Islands have a single governor appointed by the President and a legislative body elected by the people of the three islands.

The Panama Canal Zone is a territory leased in perpetuity from the Republic of Panama. Executive power rests in a governor, who is also president of the Panama Canal Company. There is no local legislature. A court of the district-court level serves the Zone.

Guam and Samoa are now under civilian rule after considerable periods of Navy government. Guam has its own courts and a unicameral legislature of modest powers.

Other Pacific islands fall into three categories. Naval reservations are maintained on Midway, Wake, Kingman Reef, and Johnston. The Office of Territories of the Department of Interior administers Jarvis, Baker, Howland, Canton, and Enderbury—the last two jointly with Great Britain. The Trust Territory of the Pacific, consisting of the Marshall, Caroline, and Mariana Islands, is administered by a high commissioner acting under a United Nations trusteeship agreement. The nature of this trusteeship system is examined in Chapter 23.

Democratic Trends. American acquisition and control of territories and their peoples has often been seriously criticized at home and abroad. To many it appears contradictory for a democracy to hold and control subject people. Although American policy has been paternalistic and usually humane, it has been slow to encourage self-government and self-determination. Recent years have witnessed some shift in policy. Independence for the Philippines was a dramatic step.

New encouragement has come from Alaskan and Hawaiian statehood. The District of Columbia has moved closer to self-rule. Puerto Ricans were permitted to choose their governor and later became a commonwealth with a constitution granting greater autonomy. In the Pacific islands, naval governors have been displaced by civilian ones. Supervisory authority has been shifted from military departments to the Interior. Citizenship has been granted to most people in the territories.

Territories have been encouraged to examine their needs and express their desires. Studies seeking ways of more clearly delimiting Federal and local authority have been made. The United Nations has given non-self-governing people everywhere a medium through which world opinion can be brought to bear upon their status and problems. The acid test for the United States, however, is how promptly its most advanced territory—the District of Columbia—will now be awarded the rights of full self-government.

RESTRICTIONS ON THE STATES

Some prohibitions of state action were necessary to protect the Federal government against state encroachments and ensure its supremacy in national matters. Others were deemed necessary to assure individual rights against attack by the states. Powers denied to the states include those listed in Article I, Section 10. The Fourteenth Amendment contains the most sweeping prohibitions; the Fifteenth Amendment also restrains states from withholding suffrage rights because of race, color, or previous condition of servitude; and the Nineteenth Amendment prevents denying the right to vote because of sex.

Treaties and Compacts. Two provisions in Article I, Section 10, forbid states to enter into special arrangements with foreign nations and ensure Federal control over interstate agreements. No state may enter into a treaty, alliance, or confedera-

tion. This is an unconditional prohibition, making Federal control exclusive in foreign relations. This clause was used frequently during and after the Civil War to sustain the Northern contention that states have no right to secede from the Union. It prevents New York from making a treaty with Canada with respect to the St. Lawrence waterway. It forbids Texas to join a league of nations or a Pan-American union.

Congress may permit an agreement or compact with another state or foreign power. Informal "gentlemen's agreements" between state governors and foreign governments are rare, but not unknown. On the other hand, many interstate compacts have been negotiated and approved by Congress. A very lively interest in this device has developed during the last two decades. It will be evaluated in the next chapter.

Denial of Monetary Powers. No money may be coined by states; nothing but gold and silver coin may be made legal tender for paying debts; and no bills of credit may be emitted. The courts have held that money means gold, silver, and copper coin and also that coinage involves molding a metallic substance of intrinsic value.[1] During the Revolution and Confederation, the variety of moneys and the disparity of values were so great that the need for a uniform medium of exchange, with value controlled by the national government, became urgent. States have not been inclined to interfere in this field; the issuance of sales-tax tokens started some arguments, but it is now generally agreed that these do not constitute coin.

Since the Constitution forbids states to make other than gold and silver coin legal tender in payment of debts, state experimentation in monetary reform is curbed.

[1] *Griswold v. Hepburn*, 63 Ky. 20 (1865). For a fuller discussion of Federal fiscal power, see Chap. 21.

Notes issued by state banks continue to circulate, but no state can force their acceptance. Congress alone retains the authority to establish other forms of legal tender. Thus a "United States note" may be inscribed "This note is legal tender at its face value for all debts, public and private" without any mention of gold or silver. If monetary reformers sought to issue "prosperity certificates," no state could compel their acceptance.

Issuing scrip is probably also forbidden by the constitutional provision that no state shall emit bills of credit. A bill of credit is a paper medium issued by a state and intended to circulate as money. State-bank notes continued to circulate until taxed out of existence by the Federal government in the 1860s. The dated stamp scrip or warrants proposed under the "Retirement Life Payments" scheme which the California electorate defeated in 1938, 1939, and 1942 might have been deemed bills of credit by the courts. The Canadian province of Alberta, under its "social credit" administration, in 1936 paid road workers with "prosperity certificates"; these might have been called a violation of the bills of credit prohibition if an American state had issued them. This provision in the Constitution shows appreciation for the economic principle, known as Gresham's law, that the cheaper of two mediums of exchange tends to displace the dearer when the two circulate side by side.

Limitation of State War Powers. Three points among the list of restrictions spell out the states' authority in war. They forbid states to issue letters of marque and reprisal; Article I, Section 8, of the Constitution authorizes Congress to grant such documents. A letter of marque and reprisal empowers the holder to privateer and prey upon the commerce of another nation. Because privateering may involve a country in war, the power wisely was reserved for the level of government controlling foreign relations.

States also are denied the right to keep troops or ships of war without consent of Congress. This does not prevent the maintenance of a state militia deemed necessary to quell insurrection too strong for civil authorities. Since the First World War, the state militias have been organized as units of the National Guard, under joint Federal-state auspices. The restriction aimed to prevent the development of state armies and navies and ensure Federal supremacy in defense. During the Second World War, Congress authorized states to form militia and guard units outside the National Guard organization.

The final restraint, forbidding a state to engage in war unless actually invaded, is of little practical importance today. It may have deterred state officers from provocative incidents in times past. Clearly, the states should not compromise the position of the Federal government by rash actions on their international boundaries.

Limitations on State Tax Power. The Constitution forbade Congress to discriminate between states and ports in matters of regulation and taxation. It was fitting, therefore, that unfair uses of state tax powers should be prohibited. States were denied the right to tax imports or exports. Goods might be taxed by a state before shipment to another state or after arrival from another state. But what constitutes arrival? The courts developed an "original-package" doctrine under which a commodity leaves the channel of trade only when the original box, bale, or carton in which it was shipped is opened. Only then is it taxable by the state. Reasonable state inspection fees may be collected on exported or imported goods, but interstate commerce may not be burdened by state taxation.

State tonnage duties on ships are prohibited except by congressional consent. This tax, on the basis of tonnage capacity of a vessel, is charged for entering or leaving a port. It should be distinguished from a wharfage charge or fee, which may be collected from a ship for services.

The implied restriction, derived from the very nature of the Federal system, that states cannot tax Federal instrumentalities and the Federal government cannot tax states is of very great importance. It was stated in *McCulloch v. Maryland* (1819) in terms of the "power to tax involves the power to destroy." The list of exemptions from state taxation expanded greatly, including not only Federal property, but also Federal salaries, gasoline used by Federal agencies, and income from Federal bonds. Finally, in 1939, the Supreme Court began to narrow the field of reciprocal immunity.

The Fourteenth Amendment, Section 4, forbids states to assume or pay any debt or obligation incurred in aid of insurrection or rebellion against the United States. Such debts are declared illegal and void.

Protection of Personal and Property Rights. As noted in Chapter 7, states must not violate personal and property rights, nor pass ex post facto laws, bills of attainder, or laws impairing the obligation of contract. They may not deny due process of law, deprive persons of equal protection under the law, or abridge the privileges and immunities of citizens. When states violate liberties, a Federal question arises and justifies resort to Federal courts. While this provides only a legal remedy, experience has demonstrated the wisdom of subjecting member units of the Federal union to constitutional limitations enforceable by the central government.

Suffrage Restrictions. In its original form the Constitution empowered the states to determine who might vote in Federal and state elections. The electorate for Federal officers was declared to be the same in each state as that for the more numerous branch of the state legislature. The Fifteenth and Nineteenth Amendments altered this; Section 2 of the Fourteenth Amendment contained a penalty which might be invoked against states disfranchising a proportion of the male population.

The Fifteenth Amendment declares simply: "The right of citizens of the United States to vote shall not be denied or abridged by the United States or by any State on account of race, color, or previous condition of servitude." Congress has authority to enforce this provision by appropriate legislation. The meaning is clear, and the amendment has been used to stop attempts to restrain Negro participation in elections. Indirect ways have been developed, however, to bar colored people on grounds of illiteracy, nonpayment of poll taxes, and similar devices.

The Nineteenth Amendment banning discrimination on account of sex effectively ended all state denial of woman suffrage. As the amendment refers only to the right to vote, several states continue to bar women from jury duty.

The penalty in the Fourteenth Amendment, of reducing a state's representation in the House of Representatives in the proportion as adult (twenty-one years of age) male citizens are denied the right to vote, has never been invoked by Congress.

FEDERAL OBLIGATIONS TO THE STATES

Federal guaranties to the states are not numerous but are of considerable importance. The Federal government is bound to (1) respect the territorial integrity of existing states in admitting new states, (2) guarantee a republican form of government to the states, (3) protect states against domestic violence and foreign invasions, (4) leave intact the constitutional grant of two senators for each state, and (5) forbid suit against states by individuals in the Federal courts.

Territorial Integrity of the States. Under the terms of Article IV, Section 3, clause 1:

New States may be admitted by the Congress into this Union; but no new State shall be formed or erected within the jurisdiction of any other State; nor any State be formed by the junction of two or more States, or parts of States, without the consent of the legislatures of the States concerned as well as of the Congress.

Congress has great powers over admission, but it cannot enforce conditions upon purely state matters. The territorial integrity of states was much discussed in the Constitutional Convention. The language agreed upon has been interpreted to mean that the territory of no state may be taken without its consent.

Actually several states, formed from parts of others, have been admitted. Kentucky, formerly a part of Virginia, secured that state's approval, and Congress admitted it as a separate state in 1792. Tennessee was formed in 1796, after North Carolina ceded its area to the United States. Vermont was admitted to the Union in 1791, in spite of New York's claims. Massachusetts agreed to Maine's separation in advance of that state's admission in 1820. West Virginia's separation from Virginia was authorized by a "rump," or irregular, legislature of Virginia during the Civil War.

Although continental territory of the United States (except that in the District of Columbia) is fully organized into states, occasionally proposals are made for creating a new state out of a portion of existing states. During 1941–1942 an amusing plan was advanced for the formation of a forty-ninth state called "Jefferson" out of the counties of southern Oregon and northern California. Schemes to create city-states of Chicago or New York have been suggested. Before Congress could admit any such new state, the existing states concerned would have to approve.

A Republican Form of Government. "The United States shall guarantee to every State in this Union a republican form of government. . . ." This statement appears in Article IV, Section 4. Several students have attempted to explain what the founding fathers meant by the provision. They say it means representative government, the form used in 1789, or democratic government with broad suffrage rights. No one is likely to secure a precise answer. The courts regard the question as political and decline to rule whether a given state government meets the requirements imposed by the Constitution. The matter is left for the Congress and the President to determine.

The President may indicate his choice between two rival regimes by using troops to protect or restore order, as in Dorr's Rebellion, in Rhode Island [*Luther v. Borden*, 7 How. 1 (U.S. 1849)]. Congress may announce its acceptance or rejection of a particular state regime by seating or refusing to seat its senators and representatives, as it often did in the reconstruction era. During Huey Long's predominance over Louisiana, Congress was urged to refuse seats to Louisiana legislators on the ground that they came from a state without a republican form of government. No action was taken.

Arguing that "republican form" meant representative government, a corporation in Oregon sought to prove in the courts that the initiative and referendum deprived the state of its lawful authority. The Supreme Court indicated the political character of the question and declared that Congress could so determine through acceptance or rejection of senators and representatives. [*Pacific States Tel. & Tel. Co. v. Congress*, 223 U.S. 118 (1912)].

Defense against Invasion and Violence.
The latter part of Article IV, Section 4, requires that the United States ". . . shall protect each of them against invasion; and, on application of the legislature, or of the executive (when the legislature cannot be convened) against domestic violence." This restatement of the Federal obligation to protect against foreign enemies is the logical companion to the prohibition of state armies and navies deriving from the Federal war power.

When does domestic violence reach a point that requires Federal intervention? The President decides this. Normally he sends Federal troops only after a request from the governor or legislature of the state concerned or when Federal law or Federal property is violated. President Cleveland broke the Pullman strike of 1894 with troops sent into Chicago over the protest of Governor J. P. Altgeld of Illinois. Cleveland used the grounds of protecting the mails and freeing interstate commerce of obstructions. President Eisenhower, in 1957, both "federalized" the Arkansas National Guard and called in Army units to enforce a Federal court order on desegregation in Little Rock, Arkansas, schools. He did this only after Governor Orval Faubus used the National Guard to prevent Negro students from entering a high school that had previously served white pupils only.

Equal Representation in the Senate. No state may be denied equal representation in the United States Senate without its own consent, which is never likely to be given. The Constitution says this portion of the fundamental law cannot be amended; it is an "entrenched clause."

State Immunity from Suit. The original Constitution left the way open for the national judiciary to assume jurisdiction over suits between a state and citizens of another state. The decision of the Supreme Court in *Chisholm v. Georgia* [2 Dall. 419 (U.S. 1793)], upholding a citizen's suit against the state, stirred up a storm of disapproval. Finally, in 1798, the Eleventh Amendment, outlawing such suits, was ratified. This amendment prohibits a state from being sued in Federal courts by an individual without consent given by law. Lacking such consent, the individual may seek remedy through legislative action on a "claim" bill.

STATE OBLIGATIONS TO THE UNION

Elections of Federal Officials. There is no separate Federal election machinery provided for in the Constitution, so states are obliged to conduct elections for Federal officials. Presidential electors are chosen in each state in whatever manner the state legislature directs. All states now use the direct-election method. Members of the House of Representatives are elected by the people, in most cases from single-member districts. Senators, under the Seventeenth Amendment, are elected at large in each state. For all three offices the suffrage requirements for voters are identical to those for the more numerous branch of the state legislature. Each state decides the method of nominating, if any, to be employed. Congress has set a common election date for Federal officers.

Participation in Amending Process.
States are obliged to participate in the Federal constitutional amending process. One method of proposing amendments (Federal constitutional convention) and both schemes of ratification (state legislatures and state conventions) require such participation.

FOR FURTHER READING

Federalism

Anderson, William: *The Nation and the States, Rivals or Partners?* (Minneapolis: University of Minnesota Press, 1955).

Benson, George C. S., et al.: *Essays in Federalism* (Claremont, Calif.: Institute for Studies in Federalism, Claremont Men's College, 1961).

Bowie, Robert R., and C. J. Friedrich (eds.): *Studies in Federalism* (Boston: Little, Brown, 1954).

Bryce, James: *The American Commonwealth* (New York: Macmillan, rev. ed., 2 vols., 1889).

Livingston, William S.: *Federalism and Constitutional Change* (New York: Oxford, 1956).

Macmahon, Arthur W. (ed.): *Federalism Mature and Emergent* (New York: Doubleday, 1955).

Pound, Roscoe, and others: *Federalism as a Democratic Process* (New Brunswick, N.J.: Rutgers University Press, 1942).

Studenski, Paul, and Paul R. Mort: *Centralized vs. Decentralized Government in Relation to Democracy* (New York: Teachers College, Columbia University, 1941).

Tocqueville, Alexis de: *Democracy in America* (New York: Knopf, 2 vols., 1945).

U.S. Commission on Intergovernmental Relations: *Report . . .* (1955). In addition, fifteen separate studies were issued.

Wheare, Kenneth C.: *Federal Government* (New York: Oxford, 3d ed., 1953).

Territories

Coulter, John Wesley: *The Pacific Dependencies of the United States* (New York: Macmillan, 1957).

Hancock, Ralph: *Puerto Rico, a Success Story* (Princeton, N.J.: Van Nostrand, 1960).

Hawaii Statehood Commission: *The State of Hawaii* (Honolulu: the Commission, 1956).

Hilscher, Robert H.: *Alaska Now* (Boston: Little, Brown, 1948).

Lind, Andrew W.: *Hawaii's People* (Honolulu: University of Hawaii Press, 1955).

Oliver, Douglas L.: *The Pacific Islands* (Cambridge, Mass.: Harvard University Press, 1951).

Padelford, Norman J.: *The Panama Canal in Peace and War* (New York: Macmillan, 1942).

Pomeroy, Earl S.: *Pacific Outpost: American Strategy in Guam and Micronesia* (Stanford, Calif.: Stanford University Press, 1956).

Pratt, Julius W.: *America's Colonial Experiment* (New York: Prentice-Hall, 1950).

Smith, Robert Aura: *Philippine Freedom, 1946–1958* (New York: Columbia University Press, 1958).

Snead, Mabelle C.: *Territorial Possessions of the United States* (New York: Vantage, 1954).

Trumbull, Robert: *Paradise in Trust: A Report on Americans in Micronesia, 1946–58* (New York: Sloane, 1959).

U.S. Commission on Organization of the Executive Branch of Government (first Hoover Commission): *Overseas Administration, Federal-State Relations, Federal Research* (1949).

REVIEW QUESTIONS

1. What reasons can you give in support of James Bryce's thesis that federalism is the "only possible form" for the United States? Why would a centralized system be "inexpedient" or "unworkable"?

2. The late Carl Becker described our Federal system as "the most complicated, stable, toughly resistant and impregnable political structure ever devised by any people." Discuss.

3. Define federalism. Where and why is it used?

4. What powers has the national government?

What powers have the states? What is the "necessary and proper" clause?

5. What comprises the "supreme law of the land" in the United States?

6. Critics often advocate reduction in the number of governmental units in the United States. How could the number of states be reduced? In your state, how can the number of counties, municipalities, districts, and other units be cut down? What change has taken place in the last decade?

7. If Puerto Rico should be admitted as a

state, what conditions validly can be imposed upon it?

8. What Federal constitutional restrictions limit the freedom of action of the several states?

9. List the Federal obligations to the states and explain what they mean today.

10. What obligations to the Federal government have the states?

11. What was the Commission on Intergovernmental Relations, and what did it accomplish?

12. Describe the process of admitting a new state. What is the Tennessee Plan?

13. Explain the authority of the national government to acquire and govern territories.

14. What are the principal distinctions between incorporated and unincorporated territories?

Chapter Six

Interstate and
Federal-State Relations

To many, the expanding powers of the National
Government seemed destined to reduce the States to mere
administrative provinces. This prospect was sharpened
by Supreme Court decisions which appeared to have
the effect of removing almost all significant limitations
on the expansion of National activities. It was often
aggravated by the conviction that many of the newer
activities constituted invasions of individual freedom
and ought not to be undertaken by any level of government.
Thus the fear of usurpation of State rights was frequently
combined with the fear of undue paternalism.

On the other hand, many who had welcomed the
expansion of National authority began to wonder if
our system of federalism had become an obstacle to
effective government. Their fear was that our form of
government would prove too slow-moving and cumbersome
to deal with the intricate social and economic problems
of an increasingly independent society and to cope with
authoritarian regimes of the Fascist, Nazi, and Communist
varieties. Our government system must be remodeled,
many thought, if it is to be adjusted properly to
20th-century conditions.

The Commission views both positions as extremes.

U.S. COMMISSION ON INTERGOVERNMENTAL RELATIONS[1]

The proof of a political system is in its operation. How has our federalism worked? Have the states really honored their obligations to one another? Have they developed a capacity for cooperative endeavor among themselves? Most crucial of all, how has the Federal-state relationship worked in practice? Will the obvious shift toward more centralized government stop short of weakening the states so that they are no longer vital self-governing parts of a true federal union?

INTERSTATE RELATIONS

Constitutional Interstate Obligations. The Constitution imposes upon each state certain obligations to all other states. The principal interstate duties are enumerated in

[1] *Report . . .* (1955), p. 2.

93

Article IV, which is devoted to states' relations. Outlined in general form only, it has remained for the courts to expound the meaning of the particular obligation in specific terms.

Full Faith and Credit. The first among these interstate obligations is in Article IV, Section 1, reading:

Full faith and credit shall be given in each State to the public acts, records, and judicial proceedings of every other State. And the Congress may by general laws prescribe the manner in which such acts, records, and proceedings shall be proved, and the effect thereof.

In 1804 Congress extended this to cover acts, records, and proceedings. Federal courts, also, are bound to give state-court decisions full faith and credit.

"Full faith and credit" means that every state must accept another state's statutes, charters, deeds, vital records, judicial decisions, and court records. For example, an ordinary civil judgment of Iowa courts ordering Smith to pay Brown $1,000 will be enforced by Kansas courts without an examination of the case on its merits, but merely after a determination of the authenticity of the original judgment. A Massachusetts marriage license is proof of wedded status in Pennsylvania. A Texas birth certificate may be used in Oregon to establish date of birth. A will properly drawn in Idaho is binding in the courts of Wyoming.

There are two notable exceptions to full faith and credit. First, the clause does not cover state proceedings under *criminal law*. A person convicted of a crime in Alabama is not punished for it in Kentucky. Such cases are handled through extradition, under which the state to which a fugitive from justice has fled delivers him up to the state where the crime was committed.

Second, *divorce decrees* granted by courts of a state in which neither party has a bona fide residence sometimes are not accepted by the courts of other states. Mr. and Mrs. A, who have lived together in New York, separate. Mr. A proceeds to Nevada where, after a few weeks, he is granted a divorce, without summons to Mrs. A. Returning to New York, Mr. A remarries. The second Mrs. A bears two children. Ten years later Mr. A dies. The first Mrs. A demands and is granted the whole of Mr. A's estate on the ground that their marriage was never legally dissolved under the laws of New York. The late Mr. A is adjudged a bigamist, his children and their mother are left penniless, and the children have the stigma of illegitimacy. Divorces granted in the state in which a couple have been domiciled are valid; even those issued by a state in which one of the parties has actual residence generally are accepted, if proper procedure is followed.[1]

Privileges and Immunities. The provision that the citizens of each state are guaranteed the privileges and immunities of citizens of the several states protects against interstate discrimination. This clause assures the citizen of one state the right to be protected, to travel, to reside, to secure habeas corpus, to sue in courts, to make contracts, to marry, to hold property, to enjoy tax equality, and to engage in trade or business in any other state.

Such guaranties help to make this one instead of many nations. The courts have invalidated several attempts by states to give their own citizens rights denied to citizens of other states. During the 1930s, proposals were made in states of the Pacific

[1] The status of out-of-home-state divorces has been much controverted in recent years. Two leading cases are *Williams v. North Carolina* [325 U.S. 226 (1945)] and *Vanderbilt v. Vanderbilt* [354 U.S. 416 (1956)]. The states with the shortest residence requirement before filing suit for divorce are Idaho, six weeks; Nevada, six weeks; Wyoming, sixty days; Arkansas, three months; and Utah, three months.

Southwest to curb the influx of migrants from drought and dust-bowl areas. States may require residence for a given period to achieve the right of suffrage, or to secure eligibility to poor relief. No state, however, can directly forbid indigent migrants to enter. Local authorities used vagrancy ordinances, and private individuals and groups conspired to frighten the migrants away. California forbade by law the transportation of indigent persons into its area, but the statute was declared unconstitutional.[1]

Are the rights of resident citizens and of citizens of other states precisely equal? There are three major exceptions and a number of minor ones to the application of the privileges-and-immunities clause. First, corporations are not considered citizens under this clause, so out-of-state concerns may be burdened with discriminatory legislation. But states are subject to restraint in this field under the due-process clause of the Fourteenth Amendment.

Second, the right to engage in certain professions or businesses may be restricted by state law to citizens who have resided in the state for a given time. Admission to the bar or to the practice of medicine in one state does not thereby secure the right to practice in all states.[2]

Third, the privileges of sharing in the property or proprietary functions of a state may be denied to a nonresident, or offered on a very different basis. A state university may require payment of a tuition fee by a nonresident, although none is collected from residents. For example, a state university may charge $250 per semester tuition for out-of-state students and none for its own residents. States customarily charge

[1] *Edwards v. California*, 314 U.S. 160 (1941). The majority opinion rejected the law on grounds of obstruction of interstate commerce.

[2] For details see Council of State Governments, *Occupational Licensing Legislation in the States* (Chicago: the Council, 1952).

nonresidents much higher fees for fish and game licenses than they do residents; one state charged local sportsmen $2 for a season permit covering all fish and game, and an out-of-state person $50 for the same privilege.

Extradition of Fugitives. The process of extradition is explained clearly in the second clause of Article IV, Section 2:

A person charged in any State with treason, felony, or other crime, who shall flee from justice, and be found in another State, shall, on demand of the executive authority of the state from which he fled, be delivered up, to be removed to the State having jurisdiction of the crime.

This is similar to international extradition except that between nations it is carried out under treaty. Any violation of state law, whether felony or misdemeanor, may be the basis for a request for rendition. Any person charged with a crime who leaves the state in which the alleged crime was committed may be extradited, whether he deliberately fled or not. Federal law extends extradition to territories.

Ordinarily the process works smoothly. Congress has directed that the governor of a state or territory "shall" detain the fugitive for whom extradition is asked. The governor of the state from which the accused person fled is notified when he is located. The formal request for rendition then follows. Usually the governor delivers up the fugitive without question, but occasionally he examines the facts and refuses. This refusal may occur when an executive distrusts the system of justice in the state making the request, as was the situation in *I Am a Fugitive from a Chain Gang*. It may be due to humanitarian considerations, such as a long record of reformed living. No court or officer can force a governor to render up a person if the governor refuses the request of extradition.

Interstate Cooperation. *Compacts.* The Constitution provides for interstate relations largely in negative, prohibitory terms. Even the provision for interstate compacts in Article I, Section 10, is in the form of a prohibition: "No State shall, without the consent of Congress . . . enter into any agreement or compact with another state. . . ." Normally a compact is negotiated between representatives of state executives, ratified by the states concerned, and submitted to Congress for consent, which is given by law.

Increasingly Congress has consented in advance to a compact or an idea for a com-

pact; sometimes no compact or state ratification has followed. By 1960 around one hundred compacts had been authorized by Congress; about sixty became effective through state ratification. Most interstate compacts deal with relatively minor matters-especially with boundary lines, rivers, harbors, waterways, bridges, and the like. During the last thirty-five years several compacts have dealt with important economic and governmental problems.

Although best known among interstate compacts, the New York Port Authority is scarcely typical. Negotiated between New York and New Jersey in 1920, it was ap-

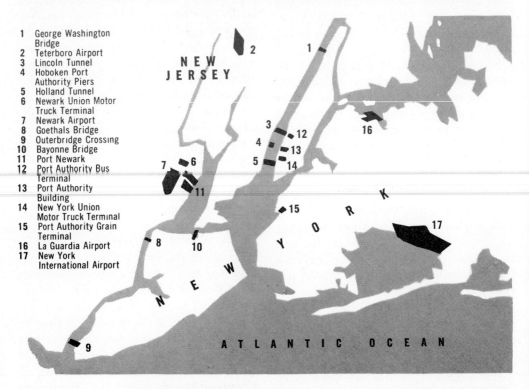

PORT OF NEW YORK AUTHORITY: PRINCIPAL PHYSICAL FACILITIES

1 George Washington Bridge
2 Teterboro Airport
3 Lincoln Tunnel
4 Hoboken Port Authority Piers
5 Holland Tunnel
6 Newark Union Motor Truck Terminal
7 Newark Airport
8 Goethals Bridge
9 Outerbridge Crossing
10 Bayonne Bridge
11 Port Newark
12 Port Authority Bus Terminal
13 Port Authority Building
14 New York Union Motor Truck Terminal
15 Port Authority Grain Terminal
16 La Guardia Airport
17 New York International Airport

This vast interstate enterprise plays a crucial role in the communications of the New York metropolitan area.

proved by Congress in 1921. The original plan was to provide an agency for the coordinated development of the metropolitan port facilities of America's leading harbor. Initially the authority was unable to get railroads, shipping lines, and others to cooperate in its comprehensive plan. But it scored a conspicuous success in building and maintaining bridge and tunnel facilities across the Hudson River. It also operates airports, rail and truck freight terminals, and the world's largest bus terminal. The authority is directed by twelve commissioners, six from each state. The commissioners are unsalaried; they place responsibility for the operation of the vast enterprise on well-paid career officials.

The authority does not have great powers of its own. Each major construction project requires the statutory approval of New York and New Jersey; the governors of the two states have veto power over acts of the authority. Its immunity from Federal review is now being tested in the courts. The executive director of the authority was cited for contempt of the House of Representatives after he refused, on direct order of the two governors, to produce records relating to internal management.

The Interstate Oil Compact is an outstanding attempt to stabilize a chaotic industry by interstate action. Negotiated by representatives of nine states in early 1935, the compact was ratified by Texas, Oklahoma, Kansas, New Mexico, Illinois, and Colorado. Congress consented later in 1935 and renewed it biennially to 1943 and every four years since. More states joined, making thirty active and three associate members by 1962. The purpose of compact is prevention of oil and gas waste. The text of the compact does not mention control of production, the establishment and enforcement of quotas being left to the member states. The oil compact has suffered in ef-

fectiveness because of California's unwillingness to ratify. For an industry as competitive as petroleum it may be regarded as a modest success.

The Crime Compact of 1934, given blanket approval by Congress the same year, is the most widely accepted. By 1951, all the then forty-eight states had ratified this agreement for interstate supervision of parolees and probationers. The reform of released convicts inevitably is complicated by the notoriety an ex-criminal achieves in his home community. Previously it has been difficult or impossible to provide proper parole facilities in other states. Now an ex-convict may have a chance to start anew under favorable circumstances and proper supervision in a state of his choice.

A new field for the compact is education. Forced by judicial decisions to offer equal professional training for Negroes, several states formed the Southern Regional Educational Compact in 1948. By 1962, sixteen states had joined. The arrangement is simple. States with high-quality institutions for training in medicine, dentistry, law, veterinary medicine, and other professional fields agree to accept students (colored or white) from states lacking facilities. The bill is paid by the state of the student's residence. This contract-for-service system makes available to each state, for thousands of dollars, services that would cost millions to duplicate. The Western Regional Education Compact, approved in 1953, has thirteen members and provides medical, dental, and veterinary medical training programs. The initial success of these ventures suggests a wide range of new uses for the compact idea.

Evaluation of the Compact Method. This device for attacking regional problems is likely to succeed mainly in restricted areas and in noncontroversial fields. The compact is inflexible and difficult to amend.

Commissions created by compacts enjoy little discretionary authority and rarely have power of enforcement. One state involved in the subject covered by the compact may stifle the whole project by refusing to ratify. Like a confederation requiring unanimous consent before acting, the compact scheme may be foredoomed to failure because a small minority may veto the majority will. Even when the necessary states ratify, Congress may withhold consent, as it has from the New England flood-control compacts. If enforcement action is required, it may not be uniform in the participating states.

Granting these objections, the compact is useful in solving problems falling between Federal and single-state jurisdiction and competence. It is no cure-all, no panacea for all ills. It may serve as a method through which states with common problems may work together on a modest cooperative basis. The Supreme Court in 1951 ruled that a state's obligations under a compact cannot be terminated by action of state courts [*West Virginia ex rel. Dyer v. Sims*, 341 U.S. 22 (1951)].

Many interstate agreements are made effective without congressional action. Executive arrangements, more informal than compacts, often suffice to ensure parallel action between two or more states. Usually these are mere agreements to follow the principles of reciprocity, to give assurances that each will treat the other with fairness and equality.

Uniform State Laws. Uniform state action is another road to interstate cooperation. Founded in 1892, the National Conference of Commissioners on Uniform State Laws is the leading organization promoting action in this field. The conference has representatives from each state, appointed by the governor; it is financed by state appropriations, by the American Bar Association and other bodies. Conference subcommittees have devised, and the general body has ratified, more than a hundred acts. Several other national groups have had wide acceptance among the states.

Three laws—Negotiable Instruments, Warehouse Receipts, and Stock Transfer—have been adopted by all states and most territories, but the typical act on the conference list has been adopted by only one-half of the states. Uniform laws simplify the task of doing business across state lines. Unfortunately, state legislatures often amend the proposed acts. A drastically amended uniform law has little advantage over one of homespun origin. Moreover, despite a clause declaring for uniform interpretation, courts of various states give diverse interpretations to uniform laws. Professor Grant has suggested that state adoption of Federal laws may ensure truer uniformity. Where this happens, statutes are uniform and a common system of interpretation may prevail.[1]

The Council of State Governments. Since a large number of interstate problems need solution, it is surprising that the first general, continuing, interstate organization was not established until 1925. The parent organization was called the American Legislators' Association; in 1935, it fostered the establishment of the Council of State Governments, with broad functions.[2]

The council provides the secretariat for the Governors' Conference, the American Legislators' Association, the Conference of Chief Justices, the National Association of Attorneys General, the National Association of Secretaries of State, and other bodies. It cooperates with the National Conference of Commissioners on Uniform State Laws

[1] J. A. C. Grant, "The Search for Uniformity of Law," *American Political Science Review*, vol. 32 (December, 1938), pp. 1082–1098.

[2] For history and functions of the council, see the current issue of *The Book of the States*, published biennially in Chicago.

and many other bodies of public officials. It publishes a monthly magazine, *State Government,* the only journal exclusively in this field.

The council is governed by a board of managers; each state contributing to its support appoints one member; associated groups also are represented. Every two years it holds a general assembly, to which each participating state sends one senator, one representative, and one administrator. State and national problems of the broadest character are considered. All states take part in the work, the participation of each being directed by its state commission on interstate cooperation, established by state law and composed of members of the legislature and representatives of the executive branch.

These commissions on interstate cooperation alert the states to the work of the council and interstate problems generally; they provide a mechanism through which the states may be represented at national and regional conferences on particular interstate problems. State trade barriers have been an important target. After national and regional conferences on trade walls, state representatives helped to repeal some existing barriers and defeat proposed new ones. Interstate action has dealt with relief, crimes, fisheries, water pollution, conservation of natural resources, and other problems. The Council of State Governments in its first two decades secured participation of all of the states, focused national attention on the gravity of interstate problems, and provided machinery for solving many problems.

Interstate Discrimination. *State Trade Barriers.* One of the primary motives in forming the Union was elimination of state tariff barriers. It was recognized that walls around states would endanger prosperity and unity. The founding fathers drew with great care the sections of the Constitution prohibiting state duties on imports and exports and assuring the Federal government of paramount power over interstate and foreign commerce. But the states over the years have managed to build up a large number of trade walls. The condition became particularly alarming during the 1930s, when discriminatory and counterdiscriminatory legislation reached state statute books with regularity.

What is a state trade barrier? It may be a statute, regulation, or practice that operates unfairly or to the disadvantage of persons, products, or services coming from sister states and to the advantage of local residents. Under the guise of protecting the health, morals, safety, and welfare of the people of a state, a law will require inspection and quarantine of plant and animal life. This requirement sounds legitimate, but it may be so enforced as to deny access to the state's market to out-of-state nurserymen or stock raisers. For example, New York state, seeking to curb Bang's disease, imposed a very rigid inspection on cattle shipped into the state, even though it did little to clean up infected herds at home. If New York inspectors reject Louisiana cattle, then Louisiana may retaliate with a quarantine embargo. This could lead to a complete ban on movement of plant and animal life between New York and Louisiana.

State laws governing motor vehicles, especially trucks, establish such diverse standards that out-of-state truckers cannot meet the requirements without excessive cost. State taxes and fees in other fields often stymie out-of-state competition. This practice is common in the alcoholic-beverage field, over which the Twenty-first Amendment gives states special powers. Differentials to favor local manufacturers or products are established through high license fees for importing or selling in the state.

The TRAILER to fit all State Laws

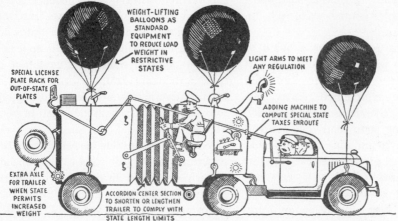

The interstate trucking industry is adversely affected by many state trade barriers. (Fruehauf Trailer Company.)

Discrimination against out-of-state wine is carried on by high excise taxes for imported and low taxes for native-produced beverages. Most states have general laws which give resident producers and vendors an advantage when selling to the state and its agencies.

Removing trade barriers requires action by the states themselves, but the Federal government can assist. Much progress has been made in this direction. After a careful analysis of the legal situation, the late Robert H. Jackson, when Solicitor General, suggested congressional action:[1]

We must not forget that while the commerce clause of itself will not keep open the channels of interstate trade, the Congress has a wide choice of means to use the grant of power effectively to achieve that end.

He pointed out that the more obvious discriminations by states might be curbed through litigation in the Federal courts, but Congress must provide a statutory basis for a more general and positive attack. The dangerous trend toward "Balkanization" by erecting trade barriers, which gained much support during the Depression, has been successfully halted and even reversed, but much state legislation of a restrictive character still exists.

Tax Competition. Connected with the general trade-barrier problem are the tax discriminations used by some states against other states and out-of-state producers, plus the tax factors which aid residents and producers. States often exempt businesses from taxes in order to induce them to move to or remain in the state. Florida once made a bid for rich and aged persons by providing in her constitution that no inheritance tax could be enacted.[2] Taxes that retaliate against other states by levies on insurance premiums, liquor, and other things are common. Conflicts often arise between states over the share of a large estate taxable by each. The state in which the deceased person has been domiciled generally has the

[1] Robert H. Jackson, "The Supreme Court and Interstate Barriers," *Annals of the American Academy*, vol. 207 (January, 1940), pp. 70–79, at p. 78.

[2] Eventually Florida was induced to abandon this form of tax competition by a Federal law setting up a credit for state taxation. See discussion of the tax-offset device, pp. 109–110.

best claim, but other states in which portions of the estate are located may claim the right to tax them.

State sales taxes are sidestepped by people making large purchases out of state. To plug this loophole, several states have levied "use" taxes, requiring payment of the equivalent of the sales tax before an article may be used. If a citizen of California buys an automobile in Michigan, California requires that he pay either the California sales tax or use tax before it can be licensed in the state. Exceptionally heavy taxes may be charged against out-of-state corporations. Dairying states have taxed oleomargarine to discourage consumption of vegetable fats and to promote the sale of butterfat. States have engaged in open warfare through alcoholic-beverage taxes which have favored home-produced liquors and applied heavy and retaliatory taxes on liquors from out of state.

FEDERAL-STATE RELATIONS

"Centralization" refers to the relationship between different levels of government. The process of centralization involves assumption by the higher level of government of both activities and authority from the lower level.

Federal centralization is the tendency for the national government to influence or control functions and fields formerly considered under state jurisdiction. "State centralization" describes the process of state assumption of authority over former local activities.

The relations between nation and state could not remain static over 170 years. Changing social and economic conditions require reallocation of responsibilities; virtually all these changes have strengthened the national government at the expense of the states. The states also have new and expanded functions, sometimes taken over from local units. The general tendency, however, has been in the direction of greater Federal centralization.

This section will examine devices and avenues through which Federal authority over the states or former state functions have developed, and appraise some of the expedients to which the states have resorted to correct their own inadequacies.

Federal Grants-in-Aid. A study by a committee of the Council of State Governments defined Federal grants-in-aid as:

. . . payments made by the national government to state and local governments, subject to certain conditions, for the support of activities administered by the states and their political subdivisions.[1]

The term includes both regular grants, which are "permanent" or recurring, and emergency grants, which are temporary and extraordinary. The term "grants-in-aid" does *not* include the following payments: (1) shared revenues, collected by the Federal government and paid in whole or in part to state or local governments; (2) payments in lieu of taxes, through which the nation reimburses the states and localities for services for which they cannot tax Federal property; (3) payments for contractual services performed by the United States government; (4) payments of cash loans; (5) payments to individuals within states, as in the National Guard.

Nature of Subsidy System. The earliest grants to states were in land or money, without the imposition of conditions on their use. Present-day grants are almost wholly *conditional.* They are made for specified purposes and are subject to conditions stipulated by Congress or the administering agency.

Other federal nations, such as Australia

[1] Council of State Governments, *Federal Grants-in-Aid* (Chicago: the Council, 1949), p. 29.

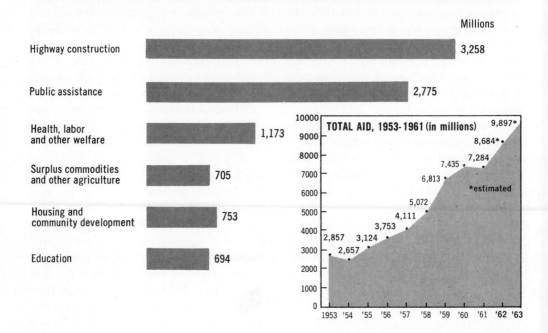

FEDERAL AID TO STATE AND LOCAL GOVERNMENTS
Budget expenditures in 1963, estimated

Millions

Highway construction	3,258
Public assistance	2,775
Health, labor and other welfare	1,173
Surplus commodities and other agriculture	705
Housing and community development	753
Education	694

TOTAL AID, 1953-1961 (in millions)

9,897*
8,684*
7,284
7,435
6,813
*estimated
5,072
4,111
3,753
3,124
2,857
2,657

1953 '54 '55 '56 '57 '58 '59 '60 '61 '62 '63

There are now approximately twenty-five aided functions; several proposals for new Federal grants are pending. [Bureau of the Budget.]

and Canada, make extensive use of "unconditional" grants to states or provinces; this type of grant is for general purposes with no detailed specifications. The Commission on Intergovernmental Relations, in 1955, rejected the idea of subventions for general state purposes, fearing that the net effect would be increased centralization.

The constitutional justification for Federal grants is found both in the power of Congress to dispose of territory and other property and in its power to tax and spend. (For fuller consideration of powers aspect, see p. 82.) In 1923 the Supreme Court had for the first time cases involving a modern conditional grant, the maternal and child health program. The act was chal-

lenged as invading state power and burdening disproportionately the taxpayers of the several states. The court did not provide direct answers to the issues, but it did refuse to declare the aid program void and made impossible the challenge by state or taxpayer of the validity of such an expenditure [*Massachusetts v. Mellon*, 262 U.S. 447 (1923)]. Subsequent cases have resulted in similar verdicts. Power to tax and spend for Federal grants appears to be fully assured.

Today there are some twenty-five aided functions, and several proposals for new Federal grants are pending. Arguments for and against grants-in-aid will be considered in a subsequent section, but a general explanation of why the Federal government has this device is in place here. Perhaps the greatest impetus comes from a desire to finance more and improved services by taxing on the broad base of the whole nation and spending in the areas of greatest need. The grant-in-aid offers a middle ground between direct Federal assumption of certain state and local functions and their continuation under exclusive state and local financing, with haphazard coverage and diverse standards. This achieves national minimum standards, yet retains most of the benefits of administration close to the people.

Services Aided by Federal Grants. In recent years the largest regular Federal grants-in-aid (excluding shared revenues, emergency grants, and payments to individuals within states) have been for old-age assistance, highways, aid to dependent children, unemployment-insurance and employment service, hospital construction, school-lunch program, and surplus agricultural.[1]

Lesser grants were made for agricultural experiment stations, agricultural extension work, cooperative projects in marketing, forestry cooperation, airport program, wildlife conservation, agricultural colleges, venereal-disease control, tuberculosis control, general health assistance, mental-health activities, heart-disease control, cancer control, maternal and child health, aid to crippled children, child welfare, aid to the blind, vocational rehabilitation, housing, veterans' training, and some minor functions.

Grants-in-aid have increased tremendously. In 1911–1912 their total scarcely exceeded 5 million dollars for regular, permanent functions; during the 1950s they were about 2½ billion dollars annually. All

[1] For latest figures, see U.S. Secretary of the Treasury, *Annual Report on the State of Finances . . .* (annual).

forms of Federal grants, including grants-in-aid, shared revenues, emergency grants, and payments to individuals within states, approached 4 billion dollars per year.

Conditions Attached to Federal Grants. The basis of allocation, the state contribution, and the extent of Federal control depend upon the nature of the service aided and the temper of Congress when the grant is authorized. The basis of allocation may be equal among the states, according to need, number aided, rural population, total population, or some other formula or combination. Generally Congress requires that a state match the Federal contribution with a state contribution. The state appropriation often is required on a dollar-for-dollar basis. Sometimes it must be more or less, and occasionally no matching is required.

Federal administrative controls vary greatly. Sweeping supervisory powers are exercised by Federal road officials over the construction of federally aided state highways. Control by Federal authorities over educational services and agricultural experiment stations is almost nil.

It would be poor policy for the Federal government to hand out money without some method of checking the stewardship of the states in spending it. On the other hand, petty and detailed checking is likely to produce resentment. Constant Federal pressure has done much to keep the spoils system out of state unemployment-insurance administration, and from state welfare agencies. Under the second Hatch Act, Congress attempted to keep state and local employees in federally aided functions out of politics. However, the law is so sweeping in its coverage that many believe it invades civil rights.

Equalization through Variable Grants. Grants deviating from apportionment of equal amounts for each state and a standard

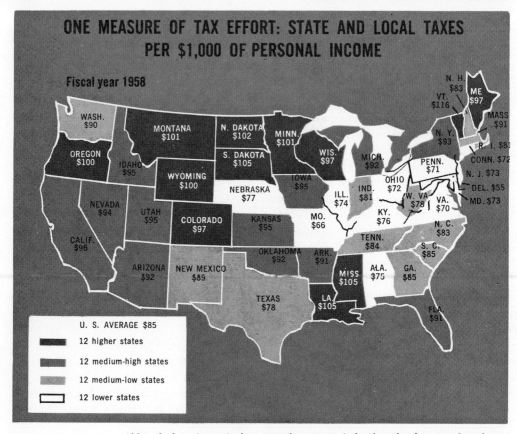

ONE MEASURE OF TAX EFFORT: STATE AND LOCAL TAXES PER $1,000 OF PERSONAL INCOME

Fiscal year 1958

N. H. $83
VT. $116
ME $97
MASS $91
R. I. $81
CONN. $72
N. J. $73
DEL. $55
MD. $73
N. Y $93

WASH. $90
MONTANA $101
N. DAKOTA $102
MINN. $101
WIS. $97
MICH. $92
PENN. $71
OREGON $100
IDAHO $95
S. DAKOTA $105
OHIO $72
WYOMING $100
IOWA $95
IND. $81
W. VA $78
VA. $70
NEBRASKA $77
ILL. $74
NEVADA $94
UTAH $95
COLORADO $97
KANSAS $95
MO. $66
KY. $76
N. C. $83
CALIF. $96
TENN. $84
S. C. $85
OKLAHOMA $92
ARK. $91
ARIZONA $92
NEW MEXICO $89
MISS $105
ALA. $75
GA. $85
TEXAS $78
LA. $105
FLA $91

U. S. AVERAGE $85
12 higher states
12 medium-high states
12 medium-low states
12 lower states

Although there is no single accepted means to judge how hard a state is trying to finance its own services, one good criterion is the ratio of state and local taxes to the aggregate income payments received by residents of the state in a given year. The states shaded black are making the greatest effort; those shown in white are making the least. [Data from U.S. Bureau of the Census.]

matching formula might be considered variable. Such adjustments take into account need, both for financial aid and for the services provided. Many programs are deficient so far as equalizing tendencies in existing apportionment and matching rules are concerned. For example, hospital-construction grants require $2 from the state for each $1 from the Federal government, although apportionment favors states with low per capita income. The "open end" method allocates public-assistance grants, with no limit on the amount of Federal

aid to each state, and commits the Federal government to pay a fixed proportion of the total state expenditures for this purpose. This led to far larger grants to the wealthier states. To correct this in part, the Federal government pays 80 per cent of the lowest monthly payments, and one-half of the payments above this amount, up to a fixed maximum, after which the state pays all above the maximum.

How do per capita grants compare with per capita income? Some of the richest states, such as Nevada, Montana, Wyoming,

North Dakota, Colorado, California, and Washington, are among the largest recipients of Federal subsidies in proportion to population. The states with lowest per capita income, such as Virginia, North Carolina, Kentucky, and Mississippi, are near the bottom in Federal aid received.[1]

Even when allowance is made for the highway and airport programs favoring the sparsely populated areas of the West, Federal aid at present does not aid the neediest states as much at its proponents desire. This condition arises in part from inability of states with the least resources to raise matching funds. In their efforts to secure such funds, there is grave danger that states may neglect unaided functions.

These considerations have focused attention on constructing variable-grant formulas in education, health, and assistance fields. These formulas are so complex that no attempt will be made to decribe them here. The report of the Council of State Governments highlights the problem of measuring the states' fiscal capacity and tax effort expended to raise their own funds.

Perhaps the simplest and most acceptable way to judge fiscal capacity is to use per capita income, with some adjustment for goods produced for home use and tax payments. Tax effort is harder to estimate, for there is considerable variation in state tax structures and rates. The Commission on Intergovernmental Relations rejected a general formula but recognized the need for equalizing programs which would not otherwise reach low-income states.

May states withdraw their support for functions which receive Federal aid, thus shifting the cost to the Federal government? This can be avoided by requiring maintenance of support at the same level reached in earlier years. Or, as contained

[1] Council of State Governments, *op. cit.*, p. 85.

in the aid-to-general-education bill passed by the Senate in the Eightieth Congress, a definite percentage of aggregate income is specified for the function. Will such controls tempt states to starve unaided functions and spend extravagantly on aided ones? This might be curbed by establishing a ratio between state collections and state fiscal capacity and requiring a state to tax up to a minimum standard to be eligible for Federal aid. Such a requirement is highly unlikely.

There are many other questions regarding equalization among states. Should Congress establish a maximum Federal contribution for an aided function? Should the grant-in-aid formula be in the law or left to the discretion of the administrator? Answers are needed before the present haphazard grant-in-aid programs achieve the goal of equalization.[2]

Appraisal of Federal Grants. Conditional grants-in-aid have both coercive and cooperative aspects. The bait of money is so attractive that rarely does a state resist the impulse to accept. Actually, the central government is only offering to provide something the state might not be able to afford. The clear alternative to Federal grants, if services are to be standardized at a high level, is direct Federal assumption of the many functions. The grant system postpones or renders unnecessary that more drastic step toward centralization. It implies a virtue in local administration, but insists upon uniform minimum standards. Paradoxically, Federal grants to states are both a step toward centralization and a substitute for centralization.

Many unsolved problems concerning

[2] For further reading, see especially Byron L. Johnson, *The Principle of Equalization Applied to the Allocation of Grants-in-Aid*, Bureau of Research and Statistics Memorandum No. 66 (Social Security Administration, 1947).

FEDERAL GRANTS-IN-AID
A Balance Sheet

ASSETS	LIABILITIES
Is useful device to join levels of government in common enterprise.	Permits Federal government to enter fields denied to it by Constitution.
Provides way to finance key services beyond capacity of states and local governments.	Is spent for local, not national, purposes, thus leading to sectional jealousies and jockeying for benefits.
Helps redistribute income and promotes progressive taxation.	Places unfair tax burden on some states to support services in others.
Improves state and local standards of administration.	Leads to extravagant spending by both Federal government and by states.
Provides substitute for direct national assumption of functions.	Distorts state budgets and tends to destroy budgetary control.
Induces state and local governments to enter neglected fields.	Violates doctrine that government which spends moneys should collect.
Involves two levels of government in checking upon extravagance.	Brings Federal control of local activities and builds bureaucracy.
Ensures a national minimum of services and performance level.	Will lead to Federal monopoly of tax power, destroy local independence.

SOURCE: Condensed from Council of State Governments, "Federal Grants-in-Aid" (Chicago: The Council, 1949), pp. 41-42.

grants-in-aid remain. Professor Harris has called attention to deficiencies in the system of distributing grants.[1] State and local budgets have been distorted; unaided services have suffered, particularly in the poorer states; vocational education is expanded abnormally, while in the poorer states general elementary education languishes; old-age assistance booms, while general relief in many states has been curtailed.

The different methods of allocating

[1] Joseph P. Harris, "The Future of Grants-in-Aid," *Annals of the American Academy*, vol. 207 (January, 1940), pp. 14–26.

Federal aid to the states are in most instances reasonably satisfactory and well designed to accomplish the purposes of Congress in making the grant. Federal aid for old-age assistance, however, has been severely criticized. Its provision for matching, without limitation as to the amount which may be allocated to individual states, has resulted in greater aid to the wealthier states. Distribution is in proportion to wealth, not need. Many proposals have been made to revise the formula to take into account the financial needs of the several states, thus enabling the poorer states to raise their standards.

Although only a small beginning has been made, the next great step in the Federal grant program probably will be toward aid for general education. As early as 1938 an Advisory Committee on Education, appointed by President Roosevelt, recommended Federal aid to equalize educational opportunity in the several states. The 1955 White House Conference on Education strongly endorsed Federal aid, and President Eisenhower recommended it.

Congress finally broke the log jam when it passed the National Defense Education Act of 1958. Spurred by Russia's demonstrated success in science, Congress authorized grants-in-aid for: (1) strengthening instruction in science, mathematics, and modern foreign languages; (2) improving guidance, counseling, and testing programs in public secondary schools; (3) research and experimentation in educational television; (4) area vocational-educational programs; and (5) improving state educational-statistical services. This legislation also broke new ground by authorizing loans and grants to colleges and universities and to worthy students.

Shortly after taking office, President Kennedy proposed to Congress the enactment of legislation to aid construction of public schools and increase teachers' salaries. Again in 1962 the President urged Federal aid to education, but in both sessions any grants to states for general educational purposes were defeated. Opposition to the appropriations came chiefly from two sources: (1) those, primarily from the South, who refused to accept the desegregation features of the bills, and (2) the advocates of parochial schools who opposed the funds' going exclusively to public schools. Aid to higher education proved less controversial; House and Senate passed different versions but they were unreconciled at the end of the Congress.

The major argument against Federal grants to the states is that they benefit the poorer states at the expense of the wealthier ones. The following attack, voiced in 1932 by James M. Beck, former Solicitor General and ex-congressman, echoes today:

> . . . the great incentive and principal cause of these subsidies is the persistent desire of the smaller agricultural states of the South and West, with their wholly disproportionate representation in the Senate, to milk for the benefit of these sections the larger and wealthier industrial states.[1]

Despite such attacks the grant system has grown and flourished. It has raised standards of essential services and provided an effective substitute for drastic centralization.

Other Forms of Federal Aid. There are several other forms of Federal aid to states. Some of these are shared revenues, in lieu payments, contractual arrangements, loans, and payments to individuals within states.

Most of the existing shared-revenue arrangements were made because the Federal government acknowledged an obligation to contribute to a state or local government. Federal revenues from national forests, mineral leases on the public domain, hunters of migratory birds, leases on flood-control lands, leases of federally owned power sites—all these are shared with state or local governments. Since most Federal agencies do not pay state or local taxes, it is only fair that some contribution be made.

In some counties of Western states more than 90 per cent of the land area is owned by Federal agencies; in 1957, the percentage of federally owned land areas was as follows: Nevada, 88; Utah, 69; Arizona, 45; Idaho, 65; Oregon, 51; Wyoming, 48; and California, 46. The laws permitting in lieu payments and shared revenues are so diverse that many cases of rank injustice

[1] James M. Beck, *Our Wonderland of Bureaucracy* (New York: Macmillan, 1932), p. 225. Used by permission of The Macmillan Company, publishers.

"Shoo!"

Herblock makes the case for Federal aid to education.
[From *Herblock's Here and Now* (Simon & Schuster).]

can easily be found. For example, the Armed Forces make no in lieu payments, cities, counties, and states in which large military reservations are located may be called upon to expand services at the very time when Federal land purchases reduce their tax bases.

Offshore Resources. In 1947, the Supreme Court's verdict in *United States v. California* (332 U.S. 19) gave the Federal government control over lands lying under the marginal sea. Representatives of the states were alarmed lest Congress assert Federal control not only over the coastal belt but over all submerged lands, previously submerged lands, and inland waterways. Such an interpretation would affect every state.

It might cast doubt on the ownership of much land and many improvements.

California, Texas, and Louisiana led in getting Congress to quitclaim the disputed lands to the states. Fabulous petroleum resources of the marginal sea were at stake. The House passed such a bill in 1948, but the Senate did not act. In 1952, after defeating a proposal to use revenues derived from Federal control for aid to schools ("oil for the lamps of learning"), Congress enacted legislation giving the states control. President Truman vetoed the bill, branding it an "outright gift" of immensely valuable resources to a few coastal states. The Eighty-third Congress enacted, and President Eisenhower signed, legislation returning the tidelands to the states.[1]

Contracts. Strictly speaking, a contractual arrangement under which a Federal agency pays a state agency for certain services is not Federal aid. Examples are numerous. In 1946 Congress provided for remunerating states for apprenticeship training furnished by state and local agencies. The GI Bill of Rights authorized veterans' unemployment allowances, administered under contract with state employment departments, and provided for educational benefits for veterans, which, if obtained in state colleges and universities, involved Federal payments to states.

The National Guard is in a class by itself. Once grouped with federally aided state services, it now is so fully under Federal control that at most it could be called a cooperative activity. Federal funds are paid out directly to individuals. States have certain powers over their National Guard units and certain obligations to provide facilities.

[1] For additional discussion of this problem, see Chap. 28. Good sources are E. R. Bartley, *The Tidelands Oil Controversy* (Austin, Tex.: University of Texas Press, 1953), and Robert J. Harris, "States' Rights and Vested Interests," *Journal of Politics*, vol. 15 (November, 1953), pp. 457–471.

Federal Credits for State Taxation. The Federal government encourages states along desired lines by another use of the tax power known as "tax offset," or Federal credits for state taxation. This involves levying a Federal tax but provides that the United States will collect only a portion of the original rate if the state levies a similar tax for an approved purpose.

The device was employed first in the Federal estate tax of 1924 which gave credit up to 80 per cent to taxpayers who paid a state inheritance tax. Its operation is best shown by example: Suppose Mr. A. M. Welloff died in Illinois, leaving to his daughter, Miss Welloff, a large estate on which the Federal death duty was calculated at $10,000. If Illinois collected as much as $8,000 in state inheritance taxes, then the United States waived that amount and collected only $2,000 on the estate. Prior to the Federal law, several states did not tax inheritances; Florida even advertised for the rich to retire there and escape this burden. Had Welloff died in Florida after 1924 and before Florida finally adopted an inheritance-tax law, the tax paid on his estate would have been $10,000, but all would have gone to the Federal government. Naturally, states hastened to enact laws to take advantage of this offset; now Nevada is the only taxless paradise where the rich can die without concern for death duties.

The Unemployment-insurance Offset. A decade passed before the tax offset was used again. During the prolonged discussions preceding enactment of the Social Security Act, the idea of using the sanction of tax offset to ensure state cooperation was proposed. The plan was adopted for unemployment insurance, the administration being left to the states but subject to extensive Federal controls through a grant-in-aid for administrative purposes.

The Social Security Act of 1935 levied

McClanahan, in the Dallas News

Look Behind the Back!

McClanahan warns that Federal aid may be accompanied by Federal control. (Courtesy of the Dallas News.)

a Federal tax on the payrolls of employers of eight or more persons. This tax, which began at 1 per cent and ultimately increased to 3 per cent, is collected in full from employers doing business in states that have no "approved" system of unemployment compensation; in states with an insurance scheme approved by the Social Security Administration, the Federal government waives 90 per cent of its tax and collects only 10 per cent.

For example, the Nuform Bustle Company of Des Moines would have to pay 3 per cent on its payroll to the United States Treasury if Iowa had no approved unemployment-insurance scheme, and employees would receive no benefits if they became unemployed. Since Iowa adopted a proper unemployment-compensation plan, however, the company pays only 3/10 of 1 per cent to the Federal government, plus whatever state tax may be levied, and has the satisfaction of seeing its employees protected in layoff seasons. All states promptly enacted unemployment-compensation laws to take advantage of this arrangement.

Evaluation of the Tax Offset. After the Supreme Court approved this exercise of the tax power,[1] renewed attention was directed toward the potentialities of the device. In the two instances where used, the tax offset proved so powerful that it virtually forced uniform state action. There were compelling reasons for adopting this coercive device in both cases. States with inheritance taxes were seriously threatened by Florida's open bid for wealthy persons to establish residence. Interstate competition for business and industry was so keen that only one state, Wisconsin, enacted the necessary tax and got unemployment insurance under way prior to 1935. The Federal law served as an umbrella, permitting each of the states to enact unemployment-compensation laws without fear of driving industries to other states.

Congress is likely to use sparingly a weapon so powerful as the tax-credit device. Important as they are, Federal grants-in-aid and other methods of inducing states to take desired action are less compelling because applying Federal credits for state taxation has the sanction of forfeiture of tax revenues by a state unwilling to cooperate.

Federal Cooperation and Expansion. *Restricting Lanes of Interstate Commerce.* By exercising its power over commerce,

Congress may help states to control some problems over which they otherwise could not make their control effective. The United States either refuses to allow passage, in or out of a state, of a certain commodity that the state seeks to prohibit or makes the commodity subject to the laws of the state immediately upon arrival.

Liquor provided the earliest experience with this form of cooperation. After the court ruled in 1890 that a state prohibition law could not apply to liquor in interstate commerce [*Leisy & Co. v. Hardin,* 135 U.S. 100 (1890)], Congress enacted the Wilson Act. This subjected liquor shipments into states to state regulation from the time of arrival. The act was upheld in the courts [*In re Rahrer,* 140 U.S. 545 (1891)]. The method of "divestment" used in the Wilson Act was later used to subject to state regulation game birds and animals (1900), oleomargarine (1902), misbranded gold and silver (1906), plant life under quarantine (1926), convict-made goods (1929), and prize-fight films (1940).[2]

A stronger type of divestment occurs when the Federal government prohibits the movement of goods *into* a state in violation of state law. The Webb-Kenyon Act of 1913 forbade transportation of liquor into states forbidding its use. Dormant during nationwide prohibition, the same principle was written into the Twenty-first Amendment, Section 2, thus:

> The transportation or importation into any State, Territory, or possession of the United States for delivery or use therein of intoxicating liquors, in violation of the laws thereof, is hereby prohibited.

The Webb-Kenyon method was also used in the Ashurst-Sumners Act of 1935, which

---

[1] *Steward Mach. Co. v. Davis,* 301 U.S. 548 (1937). The Court held the tax was an excise tax, the classification of employers was reasonable, and the state did not surrender any powers essential to sovereignty.

[2] Joseph E. Kallenbach, *Federal Cooperation with the States under the Commerce Clause* (Ann Arbor, Mich.: University of Michigan Press, 1942), pp. 112–199.

banned the transportation of prison-made goods in violation of state law. After the Supreme Court held this law valid [*Kentucky Whip & Collar Co. v. Illinois Cent.*, 299 U.S. 334 (1937)], hope was then aroused that Congress might be able to ban the products of child labor from states prohibiting their sale. Instead, Congress chose to regulate child labor directly and uniformly through the Fair Labor Standards Act of 1938. In 1940 a second Ashurst-Sumners Act placed an absolute prohibition on all shipment of prison-made goods in interstate commerce.

A third type of Federal restriction bans the movement of goods and persons *from* a state in violation of that state's law. This variety of control has been extended to automobile theft (1919), other stolen property (1934), kidnaped persons (1932), and fugitive felons (1934).[1]

After the oil-control features of the National Industrial Recovery Act of 1933 were declared unconstitutional,[2] Congress forbade shipments of petroleum in interstate commerce in excess of quotas set by state law.[3] This legislation assists oil-producing states in enforcing their laws relating to the production of petroleum and helps achieve the conservation goals anticipated in the Interstate Oil Compact.

Since 1949, the Federal government has helped state authorities locate evaders of state cigarette taxes by requiring sellers in interstate commerce to file monthly reports on sales to nondistributors.

The cooperative nature of this device has been demonstrated in the various examples of its use. In most cases it makes possible more effective state control, instead of displacing state with Federal authority.

Cooperative and Reciprocal Arrangements. State and Federal governments have made other voluntary cooperative arrangements. Cooperation may be consultation between Federal and state officials to exchange information and plan common or interrelated functions. State departments of agriculture usually act in close harmony with the United States Department of Agriculture. The Federal Department of Labor holds an annual conference to which state labor officials are invited and where they are encouraged to interchange ideas.

Relying upon its power to spend money, Congress has established many research and informational services which may induce states to undertake programs of action or raise standards of performance for existing activities. Jane Perry Clark has called this "informational inducement."[4]

Another little-noticed field of cooperation is reciprocal use of officials by Federal and state governments. Many state constitutions forbid state officers (to be distinguished from employees) from holding Federal posts, but a considerable development has occurred despite this limitation. Federal use of state employees and agencies is the more extensive. During the First and Second World Wars conscription was federally supervised but locally administered by state appointees. State prohibition-enforcement agents, during the era of the Eighteenth Amendment, often were made part-time Federal officers. Direct state use of Federal officials is less preferred, but Federal forest rangers may enforce state fish and game laws, and FBI agents frequently apprehend violators of state criminal laws. The county agent or farm advisor performs functions

---

[1] *Ibid.*, pp. 315–331.

[2] *Panama Refining Co. v. Ryan*, 293 U.S. 388 (1935). The grounds were excessive delegation of legislative authority to the President.

[3] The Connally Act of 1935, 49 Stat. 30, was renewed in 1937 and 1939, and made permanent in 1942, 56 Stat. 381.

[4] Jane Perry Clark, *The Rise of a New Federalism* (New York: Columbia University Press, 1938).

for three levels of government—national, state, and county.

Federal-Local Relations. Before 1933, contracts between the Federal government, cities, and counties were largely informal. Federal marshals and district attorneys worked with sheriffs, police chiefs, and prosecutors; the Office of Education issued publications and otherwise served local school districts; cities and counties helped enforce federally fixed standards of weights and measures; but the relationship was seldom direct and formal.

The picture has now changed. Recent legislation permits the use of Federal aid in building highways within cities. The United States Housing Authority makes grants to municipal and county housing authorities for the construction of locally owned and managed projects. Indeed, Federal-local contacts have become so numerous that some fear Federal domination.

Direct Federal Expansion of Activities. More than all others combined, broadened interpretation of Federal powers has been the avenue of Federal encroachment on former state functions. An astounding expansion of Federal activities has taken place during the last thirty years. The accomplishment and justification of this expansion may best be studied in connection with the Federal powers concerned. The commerce power now extends Federal control to every sort of transportation and communication, to manufacturing, mining, and other businesses that affect interstate commerce. Next in importance comes the tax power and its implied companion, the spending power. The tax power justifies the grant-in-aid, the tax offset, expenditures for research and informational services; it is also used for regulatory purposes.

Through its monetary power, the Federal government has extended its activities into such diverse fields as incorporating credit unions, insuring bank deposits, chartering and regulating savings and loan associations, and participating in international stabilization funds. Congress has used the war power to justify in part the great regional-planning scheme of the Tennessee Valley Authority and to authorize broad wartime controls covering production, transportation, distribution, conscription, and nearly every aspect of economic and social life in the country. Even the treaty power has been used to expand Federal authority.

Proposed Reform of the Federal System. *State Lines and Administrative Areas.* State boundaries today are products of historical factors, early transportation limits, and other forces, many of which are no longer valid. Criminals and diseases, both plagues of man, do not respect state lines. They may be handled effectively through either cooperative effort of two or more states or Federal action. Some students of Federal problems suggest that the answer to many interstate difficulties is to redraw state lines, creating a smaller number of regional states coinciding with economic and physiographic realities. One form of regional action is secured through interstate compact or informal agreement of neighboring states on a common program for meeting a problem. The Colorado River Compact and some of the recent river-pollution compacts are examples.

The Federal government sets up various administrative areas to aid in the execution of national law; most of these groupings respect state lines but combine several states for administrative convenience. An independent Federal agency like the Tennessee Valley Authority has broad planning powers over an area including portions of several states, and it may be a forerunner of other regional projects under Federal auspices. This practice is open to the objection, as in all Federal plans, that the people of the area have no direct voice in the management of the scheme. If the Missouri Valley Authority were authorized, for example, the state officials in the areas fear that the states might lose power to decide many questions important to their future. Standardizing all Federal administrative areas might be advantageous, but getting small states to consolidate with others appears virtually impossible, given the constitutional inviolability of the territory of a state.

Alterations in the Federal System. Various proposals have been made for recasting the balance between nation and states. Some have urged that the Federal government be given full general police power— to provide for the health, morals, safety, and welfare of the people. This scheme would require a constitutional amendment, exceedingly difficult to secure. Assigning such a sweeping power to the Federal government would transform our system into a unitary one for all practical purposes.

A second school of thought, which prevailed throughout the New Deal era, argues that the language of the Constitution confers sufficient authority upon the Federal government to deal with national problems. It maintains that the courts erred between 1933 and 1936 in narrowly construing Federal powers, but that this mistake has since been corrected through broad construction. Therefore, the constitutional crisis is over, for time and the new court personnel have combined to produce liberalized decisions. This policy comprehends no sudden changes in existing forms. It calls for the remodeling of practices and rejuvenation within the old framework.

Finally, there are the vigilant states' righters and decentralists who see local self-government giving way to growing state and Federal centralization. The more rabid expend their energies shouting invectives at the Federal octopus. The more thoughtful stress the desirability of improving state administration and legislation and using interstate organizations and arrangements to a greater degree.

How Much Centralization? Those favoring greater centralization raise many valid objections to the federal system as we have it. It does produce indefensible inequality in an essential public service like education. It provides an outlet for narrow sectional feelings, as evidenced by state trade barriers. It makes difficult the prompt solution of national problems on a national basis. The late Harold J. Laski once condemned our "obsolescent federalism" in these terms:

> But a contracting capitalism cannot afford the luxury of federalism. It is insufficiently positive in character; it does not provide for sufficient rapidity of action; it inhibits the emergence of necessary standards of uniformity; it relies upon compacts and compromises which take insufficient account of the urgent category of time; it leaves the backward areas a restraint, at once parasitic and poisonous, on those which seek to move forward; not least, its psychological results, especially in an age of crisis, are depressing to a democracy that needs the drama of positive achievement to retain its faith.[1]

The dangers from excessive centralization may be worse. In a country huge in area and population, a distant national bureaucracy is not likely to understand local needs. Civic interest and participation in government may be reduced in proportion to the size of the political unit and the distance from the seat of power. Alexis de Tocqueville, an early foreign observer of this new republic, wrote more than a hundred years ago one of the strongest arguments for decentralization:

[1] Harold J. Laski, "The Obsolescence of Federalism," *New Republic*, vol. 98 (May 3, 1939), pp. 367–369.

The case of the Unsuccessful Iceman

An iceman who took the long way around delivering a cake of ice on a hot day would find that he didn't have much ice left to be delivered. It's the same with the tax dollars we send to Washington earmarked for "local improvements". A lot of the money melts away in Washington before it ever gets back home. It pays the cost of administering the huge local aid program, for bureaucrats' offices, typewriters, salaries and the inevitable red tape.

Doesn't it make more sense to let Washington handle national affairs such as defense and postal service, and let local communities handle their own local improvements? That way communities will gain the most from their local improvement tax dollars. And we could get rid of some costly, tax-consuming federal agencies. If that makes good sense to you, why not write your Congressman about it?

The Timken Roller Bearing Company
Canton 6, Ohio

Although the case against the increasing Federal role in state and local programs is effectively presented, as in the advertisement above, Federal aid continues to expand. (Timken Roller Bearing Company.)

But I am of the opinion that a central administration is fit only to enervate the nations in which it exists, by incessantly diminishing their local spirit. Although such an administration can bring together, on a given point, all the disposable resources of a people, it injures the renewal of those resources. It may insure a victory in the hour of strife, but it gradually relaxes the sinews of strength. It may help admirably the transient greatness of a man, but not the durable prosperity of a nation.[1]

[1] Alexis de Tocqueville, *Democracy in America* (New York: Knopf, 2 vols., 1945), vol. 1, p. 87.

The answer for America probably lies in the middle ground. Federal centralization will continue to reduce the relative importance of the states as national control over insurance, public utilities, agriculture, social services, and general business increases. Grants-in-aid may expand to general education and other fields, reemphasizing that, although Federal financing and control over policy are mounting, the state and its local subdivisions still play an important role in administering functions close to the people served.

FOR FURTHER READING

See also works listed after preceding chapter.

Ball, Vaughn C., and others: "The Uniform Laws Movement: Symposium," *Ohio State Law Journal*, vol. 9 (Autumn, 1948), pp. 551–688.

Benson, George C. S.: *The New Centralization* (New York: Rinehart, 1941).

Bird, Frederick L.: *A Study of the Port of New York Authority: Its Purpose—Its Accomplishments—Its Plans for the Future* (New York: Dun & Bradstreet, 1949).

Clark, Jane Perry: *The Rise of a New Federalism* (New York: Columbia University Press, 1938).

Connery, Robert H., and Richard H. Leach: *The Federal Government and Metropolitan Areas* (Cambridge, Mass.: Harvard University Press, 1960).

Council of State Governments: *Federal Grants-in-Aid, Report of the Committee on. . . .* (Chicago: the Council, 1949).

———: *Interstate Compacts, 1783–1956* (Chicago: the Council, 1956).

———: *The Book of the States* (Chicago: the Council, biennial).

———: *State Government* (Chicago: the Council, monthly).

Eisner, Mark, and others: *Tax Barriers to Trade* (Philadelphia: Tax Institute, 1941).

Graves, W. Brooke: *Uniform State Action* (Chapel Hill, N.C.: The University of North Carolina Press, 1934).

Kallenbach, Joseph E.: *Federal Cooperation with the States under the Commerce Clause* (Ann Arbor, Mich.: University of Michigan Press, 1942).

Key, V. O.: *The Administration of Federal Grants to States* (Chicago: Public Administration Service, 1937).

Leach, Richard H., and Redding S. Sugg: *The Administration of Interstate Compacts* (Baton Rouge, La.: Louisiana State University Press, 1959).

Notz, Rebecca L.: *Federal Grants-in-Aid to States* (Chicago: Council of State Governments, 1956).

Roberts, Elliott: *One River—Seven States: TVA-State Relations in the Development of the Tennessee River* (Knoxville, Tenn.: University of Tennessee, Bureau of Public Administration, 1955).

Roettinger, Ruth L.: *The Supreme Court and State Police Power: A Study in Federalism* (Washington, D.C.: Public Affairs Press, 1957).

Schmidhauser, John R.: *The Supreme Court as Final Arbiter in Federal-State Relations* (Chapel Hill, N.C.: University of North Carolina Press, 1958).

Thursby, Vincent V.: *Interstate Cooperation: A Study of the Interstate Compact* (Washington, D.C.: Public Affairs Press, 1953).

U.S. House of Representatives, Committee on Government Operations: *Intergovernmental Relations in the U.S.: A Selected Bibliography*, 84th Cong., 2d Sess. (1956).

White, Leonard D.: *The States and the Nation* (Baton Rouge, La.: Louisiana State University Press, 1953).

Zimmerman, Frederick L., and Wendell Mitchell: *The Interstate Compact since 1925* (Chicago: Council of State Governments, 1951).

REVIEW QUESTIONS

1. Explain the nature and scope of Federal grants-in-aid. How has this device altered American federalism?

2. What is the "tax-offset device"? Does its use imply the loss of state rights? How much use of it do you expect in the future?

3. How has Congress used its authority over commerce in order to cooperate with the states?

4. Define interstate compacts. Indicate the extent to which they have been used in the past and are likely to be used in the future.

5. What obligations are imposed by the Constitution upon states in their relations with one another?

6. What are state trade barriers? What can be done about them?

7. Discuss the trend toward centralization in this country. What is the outlook for state governments? What do you propose could be done to strengthen the states?

8. Discuss the following: payments in lieu of taxation, paramount interest in tidelands, equalization through variable grants.

9. Describe current proposals for Federal aid to general education. What are some of the principal issues involved in extending subsidies to the states for elementary and secondary education?

10. If you were a member of a Federal constitutional convention, called for the purpose of general modernization of the Constitution, what changes in our Federal system would you support? Why?

Chapter Seven

Basic Rights
of Free Men

*While it was James Madison who prepared the first
draft of our Bill of Rights, the author was human
experience with tyrannical government in Great Britain,
France, and the United States. It was written with
the blood of men spilled by despots and by revolutions
fought in the name of humanity. Everywhere one heard
the phrase "the still, sad music of humanity," and it
became the progenitor of constitutional guaranties
among nations, old and new, on every continent of
the earth.*

MILTON R. KONVITZ[1]

*But when men have realized that time has upset
many fighting faiths, they have come to believe
even more than they believe the very foundations
of their own conduct that the ultimate good desired
is better reached by free trade in ideas—that the
best test of truth is the power of the thought to get itself
accepted in the competition of the market, and that
truth is the only ground upon which their wishes
safely can be carried out. That, at any rate, is the
theory of our Constitution.*

JUSTICE OLIVER WENDELL HOLMES[2]

The words "liberty," "freedom," and "equality," permeate American history. Familiar to every American are the colonists' quest for religious freedom, William Penn's championship of the rights of conscience and toleration, Peter Zenger's heroic stand for freedom of the press, the stirring words of the Declaration of Independence, the great contest for the Bill of Rights, the fight against slavery, the crusade for the emancipation of women, and the continuing struggle for the equality of workingmen and minorities.

Equally familiar are such phrases as "law and order," "respect for duly constituted authority," and "national interest and security."

[1] *Fundamental Liberties of a Free People: Religion, Speech, Press, Assembly* (Ithaca, N.Y.: Cornell University Press, 1957), pp. 360–361.

[2] Dissenting in *Abrams v. United States,* 250 U.S. 616 (1919).

Except for the few anarchists, Americans have thought both personal liberty and security necessary. They have, however, differed markedly in their emphasis upon these qualities.

So it is today, as this chapter undertakes to show.

THE NATURE OF CIVIL RIGHTS

Rights and Privileges Distinguished. The term "civil rights" has several meanings. As used here, it refers to all the safeguards extended to persons and property by the Constitution which are enforceable by the courts, except so-called "privileges or immunities."

Some rights are mentioned in the body of the Constitution, but most of them are contained in the first ten amendments, which is popularly known as the Bill of Rights. Additional guaranties are to be found in other amendments, especially the thirteenth, fourteenth, fifteenth, and nineteenth.

In addition to rights, the Constitution refers to "privileges or immunities." The actual words are (Amendment Fourteen, Section 1): "No State shall make or enforce any law which shall abridge the privileges or immunities of citizens of the United States. . . ."

Without going into legal complexities, rights are guaranteed to *all persons*, whereas privileges and immunities extend only to *citizens*. Illustrations are plentiful: citizens are entitled to governmental protection on the high seas and in foreign countries; to expatriate; to have access to ports of the United States, to navigable waters, and to agencies of the Federal government; to run for Federal office and vote for Federal officers; to enjoy all rights and advantages secured by treaties; and to petition for writ of habeas corpus. Privileges or immunities

such as these are inherent in national citizenship and cannot be legally denied by state governments.

Absolute or Relative? The Declaration of Independence refers to "natural" and "unalienable" rights. Moreover, certain words used in the Bill of Rights suggest absoluteness. The First Amendment, for example, says Congress shall pass "no law" abridging the rights specified.

One school of thought insists that because of the wording and circumstances surrounding the adoption of the Bill of Rights certain freedoms are near absolute or at least "preferred." A contrary view is that all rights are relative. The former is more partial to personal freedom and limits governmental restraints to situations where the impairment of others' rights is in obvious or immediate danger. The relativists are more partial to governmental action and insist that legislatures, executives, and especially the courts must balance, or weigh, the respective interests involved as problems and cases arise. Jurists split sharply over which view is correct, as will be seen in this chapter.

Governments Are Restrained. The constitutional guaranties of rights protect people from governments, not from one another. The limitations are stated in terms of "Congress shall make no law. . . ." or "no state shall . . . ." Offenses committed by private individuals and groups are covered mainly by state law, both civil and criminal.

When a public official suppresses free speech, a constitutional right is violated; but when a gang of hoodlums breaks up a meeting, the action is probably a violation of state law but not of the Federal Constitution. A Federal law that attempted to impose censorship of the press would violate the guaranty of freedom of press, but a private association may be able to impose a form of censorship without violating the Constitution. State schools cannot discriminate on the basis of race, creed, color, or national origin; but private schools can and keep within the letter of the Federal Constitution.

Both Federal Government and States Limited. The Bill of Rights limits the Federal government only. Similar restrictions on states are found elsewhere in the Constitution; they are listed on page 130.

Until recently, Federal courts were inclined to interpret some of the restrictions on states narrowly. This was particularly true of that part of the Fourteenth Amendment which says that states may not violate the privileges or immunities of citizens of the United States, or take life, liberty, and property without due process of law, or deny to any person under their jurisdiction equal protection of the law.

The courts still refuse to say that all rights guaranteed by the first ten amendments are among the privileges and immunities of national citizenship. But the word "liberty" mentioned in the Fourteenth Amendment has been broadened to include at least freedom of the press, religion, speech, assembly, and petition. In other words, these rights have been "federalized"; neither the states nor local governments can breach them without running afoul of the Federal courts. This protection is of great value, in view of opportunities and temptations that our fifty states and thousands of cities and other local governments have to abridge liberties. Indeed, by far the most civil-rights cases reaching Federal courts challenge state and local action, not Federal.

Both the Courts and Public Opinion Are Guardians. The judiciary plays a crucial role in protecting civil liberties. But the task of protecting rights cannot be left entirely to judges. They are limited in many ways by statutes, precedents, rules, and political considerations. In the long run they tend to reflect prevailing opinions and attitudes.

Furthermore, many meritorious cases never reach the courts. It takes money, friends, and time to face what often is hostile community opinion and persevere through the long and tedious process required to win a favorable verdict. Therefore, public opinion is a powerful, and perhaps decisive, force in determining the quality of freedom.

Scope of Federal Authority. When Federal and state governments trespass upon civil rights guaranteed by the Constitution, the usual procedure is for the injured party to appeal to Federal courts. On such occasions the courts play a negative role. Damage has already been done, and the victim may be unable to make protest, or he may have to wait years for adequate redress. The time has come, critics say, for the Federal government to play an affirmative role in protecting civil rights.

At first glance the Constitution appears to provide ample authority for greater Federal intervention. The Thirteenth, Fourteenth, and Fifteenth Amendments state in their concluding sections that Congress shall have power to enforce their provisions by appropriate legislation. Federal authority to impose penalties for slavery has not been questioned seriously. But Federal attempts to enforce the Fourteenth and Fifteenth Amendments have been contested bitterly.

The scope of Federal authority was challenged shortly after the Civil War when Congress passed several civil-rights acts, making them applicable to both state officials and private parties. In a series of cases [see especially the Civil Rights cases, 109 U.S. 3 (1883)], the Supreme Court drastically narrowed Federal authority. Congress then repealed most of the statutes, and

PROTECTIONS OF AND DANGERS TO CIVIL LIBERTIES

Excessive wartime restrictions
Religious intolerance
Fear of subversion
Trade associations
Race antagonism
Popular hysteria
Political parties
Police brutality
Trade unions

CIVIL LIBERTIES

FEDERAL
AND
STATE
BILLS
OF
RIGHTS

COURTS

POPULAR
SUPPORT
Press
Churches
Schools
Homes
Clubs

Federal and state constitutional guarantees, enforced by the courts and reinforced by popular and group support, stand guard over civil liberties.

Justice Department enforcement of the few that remained has not been impressive. The belief became widespread that Congress was limited to penalizing state and local officials for violating civil rights. Recent decisions of the Supreme Court have broadened Federal authority, although serious constitutional questions remain unanswered.

FIRST-AMENDMENT FREEDOMS

Basic rights that are guaranteed in the First Amendment are freedom of religion, speech, press, assembly, and petition. Although phrased in negative terms, these freedoms are fundamental to the effective functioning of democratic government. For practical purposes, the same restrictions apply to both Federal and state governments.

Religious Freedom. The First Amendment begins: "Congress shall make no law respecting an establishment of religion, or prohibiting the free exercise thereof. . . ." This suggests that the guaranty has two separate aspects.

Church and State. Considerable controversy has arisen from the clause that prohibits laws respecting an *establishment* of religion. Does the amendment erect a wall of separation between church and state, or does it merely prevent the showing of governmental preference toward particular faiths, churches, or sects? In an important decision [*Everson v. Board of Educ.*, 330 U.S. 15–16 (1946)] the Supreme Court had this to say:

The "establishment of religion" clause of the First Amendment means at least this: Neither a state nor the Federal Government can set up a church. Neither can pass laws which aid one religion, aid all religions, or prefer one religion over another. Neither can force nor influence a person to go to or to remain away from church against his will or force him to profess a belief or disbelief in any religion. No person can be punished for entertaining or professing religious beliefs or disbeliefs, for church attendance or non-attendance. No tax in any amount, large or small, can be levied to support any religious activities or institutions, whatever they may be called, or whatever form they may adopt to teach or practice religion. Neither a state nor the Federal Government can, openly or secretly, participate in the affairs of any religious organizations or groups and vice versa. In the words of Jefferson, the clause against establishment of religion by law was intended to erect a "wall of separation between church and state."

Nevertheless, by a 5-to-4 majority, the Court upheld a New Jersey law whereby patrons of Catholic schools were reimbursed with tax funds for bus fares paid going to school and returning. School transportation, the Court majority argued, was in the same category as police and fire protection and other public services. To withhold these, or any one of them, from Catholics would discriminate against them and thereby interfere with their free exercise of religion.

A short time later the Supreme Court ruled [*McCollum v. Board of Educ.*, 333 U.S. 203 (1948)] on an arrangement whereby the public schools of Champaign,

Illinois, released time to local religious groups for instruction on school grounds. Only pupils whose parents gave written consent were required to attend religious classes. Protest was made by one of the parents, who claimed that the Fourteenth Amendment was violated. The Supreme Court agreed, saying the use of a tax-supported school system, with its machinery for compulsory school attendance, for religious instruction was unconstitutional support of an establishment of religion. This decision is difficult for the layman to reconcile with the Everson case mentioned above. It had widespread repercussions, affecting as it did similar arrangements in some 2,200 communities in forty-six states.

Following the McCollum decision, church-school cooperation in religious instruction took the form of released time for instruction off the school premises. New York City's program came before the Supreme Court in 1952 and was upheld by a vote of 6 to 3 (*Zorach v. Clauson*, 343 U.S. 306). The Court held that this form of released time did not violate the Constitution. Later the Supreme Court declared invalid a New York law that required the recitation daily of a prescribed short prayer in public-school classrooms [*Engel v. Vitale*, 370 U.S. 421 (1962)]. Said the Court:

When the power, prestige and financial support of government is placed behind a particular religious belief, the indirect coercive pressure upon religious minorities to conform to the prevailing officially approved religion is plain.

Many other issues have arisen concerning the church-state relationship. A particularly thorny one at present is whether Federal and state financial aid should be granted to church schools for auxiliary services such as transportation, school buildings, and books and supplies. Controversy over this question has raised a major barrier to the passage of Federal aid-to-education bills.

Free Exercise of Religion. The second aspect of the constitutional guaranty of religious freedom concerns its *free exercise.* Religious sects sometimes attempt to justify on religious grounds practices and conduct that society regards as antisocial. According to court decisions, the guaranty is not violated if Congress outlaws bigamous and polygamous marriages in territories, even though they are sanctioned by a particular religious faith, as they once were by some Mormons. Nor is the guaranty violated if religious objectors are required to take military training as a condition for attendance at a state university. Religious objectors may be drafted for military service, and a state may deny them licenses to practice law.

On the other hand, the free exercise of religion is abridged if children of Jehovah's Witnesses are compelled to disobey their religion's precepts by saluting, and pledging allegiance to, the flag; if attendance at private religious schools is forbidden through the device of making attendance at public schools compulsory; if a municipal ordinance makes it illegal to distribute religious tracts without an official permit; if a state law requires persons soliciting funds for religious purposes first to obtain approval of a local public official; or if a municipal ordinance imposes a flat tax rate on persons who make a livelihood by distributing religious tracts.

Freedom of Speech and Press. The First Amendment also provides that "Congress shall make no law . . . abridging the freedom of speech, or of the press." In general, the intent of this provision is to secure the unrestricted discussion of public affairs. Inasmuch as majorities need no special protection, the guaranties have meaning chiefly as they afford safeguards to individuals and

minorities that propagate unpopular, even loathsome, ideas.

Because rights are not absolute, constitutional guaranties do not forbid laws holding people responsible for such things as libel, slander, indecency, or obscenity. [See especially *Roth v. United States,* 354 U.S. 476 (1956)]. The controversy begins when governmental officials attempt to censor or punish people for dissenting utterances about public affairs.

Interpretations. Looking over past experience, some people get the impression that constitutional guaranties of freedom of speech and press are ineffectual, especially during wartime. In 1789 Congress passed the Alien and Sedition Acts, providing severe punishment for anyone found publishing false, scandalous, and malicious criticism of the President and members of Congress. These measures never reached the Supreme Court, but they were generally approved by lower courts. The acts expired in 1801, President Jefferson pardoned all who had been imprisoned, and many years later Congress refunded all fines collected.

During the Civil War, opposition was suppressed by placing large zones under martial law, whether or not actual military operations were in progress within the area. Under the Espionage Act of 1917 (popularly known as the Sedition Act) and its amendments the following year, dozens of pacifist, pro-German, Socialist, and radical publications were excluded from the mails. Hundreds of people were imprisoned for alleged subversive criticism and agitation against the war policies of the government. America's entry into war in 1941 brought with it new strictures on civil liberties, especially for enemy aliens and American citizens of Japanese origin.

The record discloses countless other instances when basic rights have been violated. In several cases the courts held that the Postmaster General had improperly excluded allegedly obscene publications, including the magazine *Esquire,* from the mails. State and local governments likewise have often gone too far in declaring utterances obscene, sacrilegious, vulgar, and slanderous. Labor's right to organize and picket peacefully—forms of speech, press, and assembly—often have been proscribed. Censorship occurs frequently when public officials withhold news at its source. Congressional and state legislative committees often have harassed and intimidated unpopular critics. Anti-Communist measures have impinged severely upon rights of expression. Negroes, Mexicans, Indians, and similar minorities have enjoyed less than a full measure of freedom in parts of the United States. Despite these shortcomings, constitutional guaranties of free expression are far from meaningless, as is demonstrated in the discussion that follows.

"Bad Tendency" versus "Clear and Present Danger" Tests. Because it is difficult to draw the line between permissible restraint and freedom, attempts have been made to find a satisfactory formula upon which to base decisions. In general, *prior censorship* is now forbidden. That is, people cannot be required, under the threat of penalty, to obtain a censor's approval prior to utterance or publication. Rather, the law holds people responsible only for what is actually said or written.

Beyond this there is deep cleavage of opinion. One school contends that speech and the press can be limited if they have a "bad tendency." A more tolerant school insists that the rule should be "clear and present danger." Under the former, persons who merely utter or print revolutionary doctrines may be prosecuted, whether or not their remarks are taken seriously by anyone. Under the latter, one is judged guilty only if revolutionary doctrines are advocated under circumstances that are likely to lead clearly and immediately to force or violence. The bad-tendency rule has prevailed throughout most of our national life, but the more tolerant view has met with greater judicial favor since 1937.

The practical difference between the doctrines is illustrated by two cases. One [*Gitlow v. New York,* 268 U.S. 652 (1924)] involved Benjamin Gitlow, who was indicted by New York State for publishing a Socialist manifesto pleading for organization of industrial workers, mass strikes, destruction of the bourgeois state, and substitution of a new regime dominated by the proletariat. The publication emphasized, however:

It is not a problem of immediate revolution. It is a problem of immediate revolutionary struggle. The revolutionary epoch of the final struggle may last for years and tens of years. . . . The old order is in decay. Civilization is in collapse. The proletarian revolution and the communist reconstruction of society—the struggle for these—is now indispensable.

Although no unlawful action had resulted from the appeal, and none was particularly imminent, a majority of the Supreme Court considered the publication a sufficient threat to justify restricting freedom of speech and press. Here the threat, rather than clear and present danger of illegal action, was the deciding factor.

A second case (*Terminiello v. Chicago,* 337 U.S. 1) was decided in 1949. Terminiello, a Catholic priest, addressed a Chicago meeting. The hall was so heavily picketed that police escort was required to enter the building. Outside, the crowd yelled epithets, threw bricks and ice picks, broke windows, and generally attempted to force entry and break up the meeting. Inside, Terminiello fanatically lashed his critics, praised General Franco, and condemned Jews, Communists, Mrs. Roosevelt, Henry Wallace, and others with whom he disagreed. At the close of the speech, Terminiello was arrested for violating a Chicago ordinance making it illegal to make, aid, countenance, or assist in making any improper noise, riot, disturbance, breach of peace, or diversion tending to breach the peace. He was convicted, and the verdict was upheld by the higher courts of Illinois. But the United States Supreme Court, by a 5-to-4 vote, supported Terminiello, saying:

A function of free speech under our system of government is to invite dispute. It may indeed best serve its high purpose when it induces a condition of unrest, creates dissatisfaction with conditions as they are, or even stirs people to anger. Speech is often provocative and challenging. It may strike at prejudices and preconceptions and have profound unsettling effects as it presses for acceptance of an idea.

Terminiello had not pleaded for violence, and there was no clear and present danger to the community great enough to justify restricting freedom of speech.

Recent Trend. The Terminiello case represented a high point in judicial liberality. After 1949, while professing adherence to the concept of clear and present danger, the Supreme Court was less generous to dissidents. In 1957 it reverted to a more tolerant standard. Several cases will illustrate the trend.

One case [*American Communications Ass'n, CIO v. Douds*, 339 U.S. 382 (1949)], upheld a provision that has since been repealed which required officers of labor unions to file anti-Communist affidavits. Failure to swear would deny unions recourse to the National Labor Relations Board. Among other things, the law required labor leaders to swear that they did not believe in the overthrow of the United States government by force or by any illegal or unconstitutional methods and that they were neither members nor supporters of organizations that believed in or taught the overthrow of the United States government by force.

Leaders of the American Communications Association had not taken the oath when they filed a complaint with the National Labor Relations Board charging their employer with having committed an unfair labor practice. The Board dismissed the complaint, saying the union leaders should first have taken the anti-Communist oath. Here, men and their unions were penalized, not for anything they had done or were about to do, but for refusal to file the required affidavit. Nevertheless, the Supreme Court, in a divided opinion, upheld the legislation, saying Congress might impose penalties for beliefs and memberships as one way of protecting interstate and foreign commerce from possible political strikes.

Another case [*Dennis v. United States*, 341 U.S. 494 (1950)] illustrating current trends involved eleven leaders of the Communist party. Proceeding under the Smith Act, passed in 1940, the government charged the leaders with (1) willfully and knowingly conspiring to organize the Communist party in order to teach and advocate the overthrow and destruction of the American government by force and violence and (2) knowingly and willfully advocating and teaching the duty and necessity of overthrowing and destroying the American government by force and violence. The men were not accused of committing acts of violence, nor was it claimed that their activity provoked an immediate threat of revolution.

Rather, they were accused of conspiring to organize a political party for the purpose of teaching and advocating revolutionary change at some future time.

After a protracted and sensational trial, a jury found the men guilty, and the Supreme Court upheld the conviction. The majority held that it was constitutional to restrict freedom of speech, press, and assembly in advance of any advocacy or overt acts where the intent and purpose of those engaged in the "conspiracy" was to "initiate a violent revolution whenever the propitious occasion appeared." Dissenting sharply, Justice Black said: "This is a virulent form of prior censorship of speech and press, which . . . the First Amendment forbids." Justice Douglas observed: "This record . . . contains no evidence whatsoever showing that the acts charged . . . have created any clear and present danger. . . ."

In a third case [*Yates v. United States*, 354 U.S. 298 (1957)], Yates and thirteen associates had been convicted in California of violating the Smith Act for advocating and teaching the duty and necessity of overthrowing the American government by force and violence and organizing the Communist party to accomplish this result. The Supreme Court reversed the convictions, saying there was a difference between advocacy of abstract doctrine and advocacy of action. Urging others merely to *believe in* something is permissible; urging other to *do* something by force or violence, now or in the future, can be restrained.

Two decisions in 1961 reflect a restrictive mood. One, *Communist Party v. Subversive Activities Control Board* (367 U.S. 1), upheld legislation requiring registration and disclosure of data showing the Communist party's organization and activities. The second, *Scales v. United States* (367 U.S. 203), upheld a conviction for active membership in the Communist party with knowledge that the party advocated the overthrow of government by force and violence. In both instances the Court split 5 to 4 on basic issues.

Motion Pictures and Freedom of Speech and Press. Motion pictures did not exist, of course, when guaranties of freedom of speech and press were written into the Constitution. When they did appear, the problem arose of whether they were to enjoy the same freedoms as other mediums of communication. The issue reached the Supreme Court in 1915 (*Mutual Film Corp. v. Industrial Comm'n*, 236 U.S. 230). Ohio had established a commission authorized to approve for public showing only those films adjudged to be of "a moral, educational or amusing and harmless character."

Had this sort of prior censorship been applied to the press, it would doubtless have been unconstitutional. But the Supreme Court upheld the Ohio law, saying that the exhibition of motion pictures was a "business pure and simple, originated and conducted for profit like other spectacles, not to be regarded, nor intended to be regarded by the Ohio Constitution . . . as part of the press of the country or as organs of public opinion." Motion pictures being thus classed as spectacles, their censorship became common practice in most states.

This decision was controlling until 1952, when it was reversed in *Burstyn v. Wilson* (343 U.S. 495). In this case the Court had before it a decision of the New York Board of Regents revoking a license to show *The Miracle* because of complaints, made chiefly by Catholics, that the film was sacrilegious. The Court met the issue squarely by declaring that the "liberty of expression by means of motion pictures is guaranteed by the First and Fourteenth Amendments."

The new standard is difficult to apply. In 1961 the Court upheld Chicago's prior review of the film *Don Juan* (*Times Film*

Corp. v. Chicago, 365 U.S. 43). Earlier, however, it forbade New York to ban *Lady Chatterley's Lover* merely because it advocated the unpopular idea that adultery might sometimes be justifiable [*Kingsley Pictures Corp. v. Regents*, 360 U.S. 684 (1950)]. Rather than bar all prior censorship the Court insists upon deciding each case on its merits.

Assembly and Petition. Democracy requires that people be permitted to gather in groups to discuss mutual problems and, if they desire, make their opinions known to governmental authorities. These rights of assembly and petition are guaranteed by the First Amendment. Assembly must be peaceful, however, and petitioners are entitled to ask only for objects that are lawful and conducive to public safety.

The right of petition has seldom been violated, but the right of assembly, because it is closely connected with speech and press, has been the subject of considerable litigation. One case occurred when the late Mayor Hague, long-time boss of Jersey City, New Jersey, refused permission to use public parks, halls, and streets as meeting places to persons whom he considered radicals. His action was held to be a denial of the rights of assembly, speech, and press [*Hague v. CIO*, 307 U.S. (1939)].

FOR FURTHER READING

See also references at the end of Chapter 8.

Abernathy, Glenn: *The Right of Assembly and Association* (Columbia, S.C.: University of South Carolina Press, 1961).

Barth, Alan: *The Price of Liberty* (New York: Viking, 1961).

———: *The Loyalty of Free Men* (New York: Viking, 1951).

Berns, Walter: *Freedom, Virtue, and the First Amendment* (Baton Rouge, La.: Louisiana State University Press, 1957).

Carr, Robert K.: *The House Committee on Un-American Activities* (Ithaca, N.Y.: Cornell University Press, 1952).

———: *Federal Protection of Civil Rights: Quest for A Sword* (Ithaca, N.Y.: Cornell University Press, 1947).

Caughey, John W.: *In Clear and Present Danger* (Chicago: University of Chicago Press, 1958).

Chafee, Zechariah, Jr.: *The Blessings of Liberty* (Philadelphia: Lippincott, 1956).

———: *Three Human Rights in the Constitution of 1787* (Lawrence, Kans.: University of Kansas Press, 1956).

———: *Government and Mass Communications* (Chicago: University of Chicago Press, 2 vols., 1947), a report from the Commission on Freedom of the Press.

———: *Free Speech in the United States* (Cambridge, Mass.: Harvard University Press, 1941).

Chenery, William L.: *Freedom of the Press* (New York: Harcourt, Brace, 1955).

Cushman, Robert E.: *Civil Liberties in the United States: A Guide to Current Problems and Experience* (Ithaca, N.Y.: Cornell University Press, 1956).

Dumbault, Edward: *The Bill of Rights and What It Means Today* (Norman, Okla.: University of Oklahoma Press, 1957).

Emerson, Thomas I., and David Haber: *Political and Civil Rights in the United States* (Buffalo, N.Y.: Dennis & Co., 1958 ed., 2 vols.).

Gellhorn, Walter: *Individual Freedom and Governmental Restraints* (Baton Rouge, La.: Louisiana State University Press, 1956).

Gerald, J. Edward: *The Press and the Constitution, 1931–47* (Minneapolis, Minn.: University of Minnesota Press, 1948).

Grant, J. A. C.: *Our Common Law Constitution* (Boston: Boston University Press, 1960).

Hand, Learned: *The Bill of Rights* (Cambridge, Mass.: Harvard University Press, 1958).

Hocking, William E.: *Freedom of the Press: A Framework of Principle* (Chicago: University of Chicago Press, 1947).

Horn, Robert A.: *Groups and the Constitution* (Stanford, Calif.: Stanford University Press, 1956).

Hyman, Harold M.: *To Try Men's Souls* (Berkeley and Los Angeles: University of California Press, 1959).

Jacobs, Clyde E.: *Justice Frankfurter and Civil Liberties* (Berkeley and Los Angeles: University of California Press, 1961).

Johnson, Alvin W., and Frank H. Yost: *Separation of Church and State in the United States* (Minneapolis: University of Minnesota Press, 1948).

Kauper, Paul G.: *Frontiers of Constitutional Liberty* (Ann Arbor, Mich.: University of Michigan Law School, 1957).

Konvitz, Milton R.: *Fundamental Liberties of a Free People: Religion, Speech, Press, Assembly* (Ithaca, N.Y.: Cornell University Press, 1957).

———: *The Constitution and Civil Rights* (New York: Columbia University Press, 1947).

Levy, Leonard W.: *Legacy of Suppression: Freedom of Speech and Press in Early American History* (Cambridge, Mass.: The Belknap Press of Harvard University Press, 1960).

Longaker, Richard P.: *The Presidency and Individual Liberties* (Ithaca, N.Y.: Cornell University Press, 1961).

Meltzer, Milton: *Milestones to American Liberty: The Foundations of the Republic* (New York: Crowell, 1962).

Murray, Robert K.: *Red Scare: A Study in National Hysteria, 1919–1920* (Minneapolis: University of Minnesota Press, 1955).

Oppenheim, Felix E.: *Dimensions of Freedom: An Analysis* (New York: St. Martin's Press, 1961).

Paul, James C. N., and Murray L. Schwartz: *Federal Censorship: Obscenity in the Mail* (New York: Free Press, 1961).

Pfeffer, Leo: *The Liberties of an American: The Supreme Court Speaks* (Boston: Beacon Press, 1956).

———: *Church, State, and Freedom* (Boston: Beacon Press, 1953).

Pound, Roscoe: *The Development of Constitutional Guarantees of Liberty* (New Haven, Conn.: Yale University Press, 1957).

Prichett, C. Herman: *Civil Liberties and the Vinson Court* (Chicago: University of Chicago Press, 1954).

Rourke, Francis E.: *Secrecy and Publicity: Dilemmas of Democracy* (Baltimore: Johns Hopkins University Press, 1961).

Rutland, Robert Allen: *The Birth of the Bill of Rights, 1776–1791* (Chapel Hill, N.C.: The University of North Carolina Press, 1955).

Smith, James Morton: *Freedom's Fetters: The Alien and Sedition Laws and Civil Liberties* (Ithaca, N.Y.: Cornell University Press and Institute of Early American History and Culture, 1956).

Stouffer, Samuel A.: *Communism, Conformity, and Civil Liberties* (New York: Doubleday, 1955).

Torpey, William G.: *Judicial Doctrines of Religious Rights in America* (Chapel Hill, N.C.: The University of North Carolina Press, 1948).

Weinberger, Andrew: *Freedom and Protection: The Bill of Rights* (San Francisco: Chandler, 1962).

REVIEW QUESTIONS

1. What are the differences between privileges and immunities and rights?

2. What is meant when it is said that rights are relative, not absolute? Give illustrations.

3. What rights must the Federal government respect? The states? Both the Federal government and the states?

4. Illustrate with Supreme Court decisions differing interpretations of the constitutional guaranty of freedom of religion.

5. Distinguish between the clear and present danger doctrine and the bad-tendency test. Illustrate both with appropriate Supreme Court decisions.

6. Do you agree with the late Justice Holmes that the "best test of truth is the power of the thought to get itself accepted in the competition of the market"?

Chapter Eight

To Secure These Rights

It is impossible to believe that equality will not eventually find its way into the political world, as it does everywhere else. To conceive of men remaining forever unequal upon a single point, yet equal on all others, is impossible; they must come in the end to be equal upon all.

Now, I know of only two methods of establishing equality in the political world; rights must be given to every citizen, or none at all to anyone. . . .

ALEXIS DE TOCQUEVILLE[1]

I often wonder whether we do not rest our hopes too much upon constitutions, upon laws and upon courts. These are false hopes, believe me, these are false hopes. Liberty lies in the hearts of men and women; when it dies there, no constitution, no law, no court can even do much to help it. While it lies there it needs no constitution, no law, no court to save it.

JUDGE LEARNED HAND[2]

The Constitution extends many more guaranties to persons and property than are discussed in the preceding chapter. Some of them, like the ban on slavery, appear unimportant to modern Americans, but less than a century ago the nation was rent with internal strife over that particular issue. Other

[1] *Democracy in America* (New York: Vantage, 2 vols., 1945), vol. 1, p. 55.

[2] In Irving Dilliard (ed.), *The Spirit of Liberty: Papers and Addresses of Learned Hand* (New York: Knopf, 2d ed., 1953), pp. 189–190.

guaranties, like equal protection, raise burning issues. No human right can be taken for granted; nor can its abuse be ignored. This chapter examines the continuing search for formulas that will preserve both freedom and security.

PROTECTION OF PERSONS AND PROPERTY

Slavery Prohibited. The Thirteenth Amendment provides that "neither slavery nor involuntary servitude, except as a punishment for crime whereof the party shall have been duly convicted, shall exist within the United States, or any place subject to their jurisdiction."

The terms "slavery" and "involuntary servitude" are nearly synonymous, although the latter has a somewhat broader meaning. The obvious purpose of words used was to forbid all shades and conditions of slavery. Though intended to free the Negro, the guaranty extends to other races as well.

Several interesting questions have arisen from the amendment. One of the first inquired whether it applied to an uncivilized tribe of Alaskan Indians whose custom it had been to practice slavery. The Supreme Court ruled the amendment applicable. The question arose later whether slavery could be practiced by Indian tribes within one of the states, inasmuch as such tribes retained the right to govern their internal affairs. Again the Supreme Court said no. Slavery cannot now exist legally anywhere within either the forty-nine states or the American territories.

The amendment has also been held to forbid shipping companies from forcing seamen to work when they have not previously voluntarily contracted to do so; farming out vagrants for hire; making people work under threat of conviction for vagrancy; and compelling laborers, renters, and sharecroppers, by state "peonage laws," to fulfill contracts for labor.

The amendment does not forbid certain types of compulsory service: compelling able-bodied men to work on roads and bridges for six days each year or provide a substitute; drafting manpower for military service; requiring physicians to report contagious diseases without compensation; forcing criminals to work out their fines on the streets or public works; punishing landlords for willful failure to furnish utility and other services promised in leases.

Due Process of Law. The Fifth Amendment forbids Congress to deprive any person of "life, liberty, or property, without due process of law," and the Fourteenth Amendment imposes the same limitation upon the states. This is one of the most important, as well as controversial, of all guaranties. It keeps governments in bounds by prescribing procedures and standards. It extends to both natural persons (human beings) and artificial persons (corporations).

Procedural Due Process. In dealing with people, American governments must follow "settled usages and modes of procedure." The standards are fairly definite. The Constitution specifically mentions certain requirements; others date back to the Magna Charta.

In general, proper procedure requires the following: (1) The government, or subordinate agency, must have jurisdiction over the person or object with which it seeks to interfere. (2) The legislation or order must be properly enacted or prepared and published. (3) Crimes must be clearly defined. (4) Accused persons must be properly apprehended and notified of the nature of the accusation and the time and place of hearing. (5) Opportunity must be given for the accused to prepare and present his defense. (6) The tribunal before which the hearing or trial is to be conducted must be so constituted that it ensures an honest and impartial decision.

Specific procedural requirements stated in the Constitution, such as those related to jury trial, habeas corpus, and double jeopardy, are discussed later in this chapter.

Substantive Due Process. The Fifth Amendment was undoubtedly intended to guarantee the procedures known to common law. But about the middle of the last

RIGHTS GUARANTEED BY THE FEDERAL CONSTITUTION

To Citizens and Aliens Against Encroachment
by National Government

1. Writ of habeas corpus may not be suspended except during rebellion or invasion.
2. No bills of attainder.
3. No ex post facto criminal laws.
4. No class distinction to be created by grants of titles of nobility.
5. Treason is defined in Constitution; Congress may not enlarge number of treasonable offenses.
6. Heirs of persons convicted of treason may not be forbidden to inherit property.
7. No laws respecting religious institutions, and none that interferes with the free exercise of religion.
8. No laws abridging freedom of speech or press.
9. No interference with right to assemble peaceably and petition Congress.
10. No infringement of right of people to bear arms.
11. No soldiers to be quartered in private dwellings in time of peace without owner's consent.
12. No unreasonable searches and seizures and no warrants to be issued but upon probable cause.
13. No criminal prosecution except upon indictment or presentment by grand jury.
14. Cannot be tried twice for the same offense.
15. One accused of crime cannot be compelled to be a witness against himself.
16. Speedy, public, impartial trial by jury of 12 persons whose verdict of guilt must be unanimous.
17. Trial by jury in civil suits involving a sum of more than $20.
18. Those accused of crimes must be informed of charges and right to counsel, be present in courtroom when witnesses are called to testify against them, be given legal power to compel witnesses to testify in their favor.
19. No excessive bail or fines; no cruel or unusual punishment.
20. Slavery or involuntary servitude prohibited.
21. Life, liberty, and property may not be taken without due process of law.
22. Property may not be taken without just compensation.
23. Privilege of voting may not be abridged because of race, color, previous condition of servitude, or sex.

To Citizens and Aliens Against Encroachment
by State

1. Bills of attainder forbidden.
2. Ex post facto criminal laws may not be enacted.
3. No laws impairing obligation of contract.
4. Class distinction not to be created by grants of title of nobility.
5. Slavery or involuntary servitude prohibited.
6. Full faith and credit must be granted to acts, records, and judicial proceedings of other states or of the United States.
7. States must grant citizens of other states same privileges and immunities as are enjoyed by their own citizens.
8. Life, liberty, and property may not be taken without due process of law.*
9. Equal protection of the laws may not be denied.
10. Privileges of voting may not be denied because of race, color, previous condition of servitude, or sex.

* This has been interpreted to include guaranties of freedom of speech, press, religion, and assembly.

century [the first court case appears to have been *Wynehamer v. New York*, 13 N.Y. 378 (1856)] state courts began saying that not only must proper procedures be followed but the law itself should be reasonable. Cautiously at first, then boldly, the Federal courts accepted the doctrine. Henceforth complainants could seek judicial review of the *substance* or *content* of Federal and state laws. To state it differently, the courts came to concern themselves not only with *how* governments proceed, but also with *what* they attempt to do. Gradually the courts became a sort of superlegislature, or "third house," with authority to void any law they considered unreasonable, arbitrary, or capricious. A storm of protest arose as the judges substituted their judgments for those of the political branches of government.

Among the Federal and state laws overthrown by the courts were those regulating wages and hours, requiring workmen's compensation, fixing prices, classifying businesses as public utilities for the purpose of stringent control, and making property valuations. Opinion was often sharply divided within the Supreme Court itself on broad questions of policies like these.

The chief criticism of the substantive doctrine was that conservative courts were restraining popular legislation by the application of standards which at best were incapable of precise definition. Since 1937, Federal courts have shown greater restraint, thus allowing the political branches a freer hand in dealing with current economic and social problems. The substantive concept has not, however, been formally renounced by the Supreme Court.

Just Compensation for Property Taken. Both the Federal and state governments have the power of eminent domain. That is, they may compel private owners to transfer property to them if deemed necessary for the public welfare. Governments can not only take private property themselves but also permit quasi-public agencies, such as public-utility companies, to do so.

Great authority like this is easily abused. The Fifth Amendment states that Congress shall not take private property for public use without just compensation. A similar limitation is placed upon states by the Fourteenth Amendment and by their own constitutions.

Note that the government is obliged to pay only for private property taken for "public use." This would allow the government to collect a fine or penalty for failure to comply with the law. But it would not allow a person's farm to be taken for use as a military camp without his being paid for it. Nor could private property be taken to build a road without owner compensation. What compensation is "just" must be settled by negotiation between interested parties or, in case of disagreement, by an appropriate court.

Equal Protection. States are forbidden to "deny to any person within their jurisdiction the equal protection of the laws," but a similar restraint against the Federal government is not mentioned in the Constitution. Gross denial of equal protection by the Federal government could, however, be held to violate the due-process clause of the Fifth Amendment. Although the provision was inserted in the Fourteenth Amendment to protect Negroes, it stands also as a guaranty to others, including corporations.

The guaranty of equal protection does not require that persons be treated *exactly* alike: minimum-wage laws may be enacted for women without also including men or children; maximum hours may be established for men in hazardous employments without also including less risky occupations; aliens may be forbidden to practice medicine, law, or other professions; taxes may be imposed upon retailers of certain products, such as liquors, and not others; chain stores may be taxed more heavily than independents; the rich may be taxed at higher rates than the poor; etc.

In cases like these, persons are classified. The test is whether the classification is reasonable and appropriate. If it is, everyone within each group must be treated alike.

Equal protection would be denied, however, if a law discriminated against any class or group, e.g., Chinese launderers; if Negroes, women, or wage earners were systematically excluded from juries; if the state courts enforced restrictive covenants barring the sale or transfer of real estate to Negroes and others because of race. In a precedent shattering 1962 decision the Supreme Court held that the equal protection clause sanctioned suits in Federal courts by urban voters who claim they are unfairly represented in state legislatures (*Baker v. Carr*, 369 U.S. 186).

Race Segregation. Although freed by the Civil War, Negroes were not everywhere given social equality. Many prewar restrictions were retained, and others compelling race segregation were promptly adopted. Ultimately these reached the Supreme Court for reconciliation with the equal-protection clause of the Fourteenth Amendment.

In *Plessy v. Ferguson* [163 U.S. 537 (1896)] the now famous "separate-but-equal" doctrine was announced. At issue was a Louisiana law requiring railroads to provide separate coaches for white and colored passengers. The Court upheld the law, saying it was within the scope of the police power to "provide equal but separate accommodations for the white and colored races" as one means of maintaining peace and order.

While this doctrine prevailed, it was fiercely contested. As criticism mounted, Federal courts began to yield. For many

years they took a casual attitude in cases alleging that facilities were not in fact equal under segregation. But in the 1930s they began taking a more realistic view, and in a series of cases [see especially *Missouri ex. rel. Gaines v. Canada*, 305 U.S. 337 (1938)] where evidence clearly indicated that accommodations and facilities were unequal, they ruled segregation unconstitutional. Finally, in 1954, in a momentous and historic decision (*Brown v. Board of Educ.*, 347 U.S. 483), the Supreme Court met the issue head on.

The Desegregation Cases. The principal case gets its name from a Negro family named Brown. Their children were required by school authorities in Topeka, Kansas, to attend segregated elementary schools. Similar cases had arisen in South Carolina, Virginia, and Delaware, and the four were joined by the Supreme Court for review and decision.

In the Brown case the United States district court had ruled that segregation had a detrimental effect upon Negro children, but it denied relief on the ground that Negro and white schools were substantially equal with respect to buildings, transportation, curricula, and educational qualifications for teachers.

In the other three cases the lower courts had found schools for Negroes and whites unequal and ordered either equalization or desegregation. None of the lower Federal courts had ruled against the validity of segregation itself.

The Supreme Court had great difficulty with the issues involved. The cases were argued early in December, 1952; re-argument was permitted a year later; and the decision was announced on May 17, 1954. Even though the decision was unanimous, orders for its implementation were postponed until further hearings were held.

Drawing upon the contributions of psychology and related disciplines, the Supreme Court struck at segregation, saying:

To separate them [children] from others of similar age and qualifications solely because of their race generates a feeling of inferiority as to their status in the community that may affect their hearts and minds in a way unlikely ever to be undone. . . . We conclude that in the field of public education the doctrine of "separate but equal" has no place. Separate educational facilities are inherently unequal. Therefore, we hold that the plaintiffs and others similarly situated for whom the actions have been brought are, by reason of the segregation complained of, deprived of the equal protection of the laws guaranteed by the Fourteenth Amendment.

Late in May, 1955, after extended hearings, the Supreme Court announced its order setting forth how compliance should proceed. In essence, the order (1) reaffirmed and extended desegregation in education, saying: "All provisions of Federal, state or local law requiring or permitting such discrimination must yield to this principle"; (2) charged local school authorities with responsibility for integration under scrutiny of Federal district courts; and (3) instructed the courts to require of school authorities that they make "a prompt and reasonable start" and proceed "with all deliberate speed," but allow reasonable delays if needed to solve administrative problems.

Some Southern states promptly took steps to comply with the Court's decision; several states have resisted. Violence flared in 1957 at Little Rock, Arkansas, when Governor Orval E. Faubus refused to enforce a court order to desegregate the public schools. President Eisenhower ordered Federal troops to perform the task. Further time will be required to obtain full compliance over the nation, but the edict is clear. Meanwhile, the Court's reinterpretation of the equal-protection clause has brought into question legal segregation and discrimination of all types.

RIGHTS OF THE ACCUSED

Treason Defined. Treason is considered one of the highest crimes that can be committed. History is filled with instances in which those in power have sought to destroy their critics and enemies by arbitrarily declaring their conduct treasonable. Because of this experience, the Constitution limits the definition of treason; no acts other than those mentioned can be made to constitute the offense. Congress is limited to prescribing the punishment.

According to the Constitution, only two acts are treasonable: (1) levying of war against the United States and (2) adhering to enemies of the United States or giving them aid or comfort while the United States is at war. In defining the term, the Constitution adopted the very words of the statute of treason enacted during the reign of Edward III. Thus, by implication, the Constitution recognizes the well-settled interpretation of phrases that has prevailed for ages.

Besides defining treason, the Constitution declares "no person shall be convicted of treason unless on the testimony of two witnesses to the same overt act, or on confession in open court." Thus, in addition to its clear statement of *what* treason is, the Constitution also carefully spells out *how* a treason conviction must be gotten. The open-confession provision is an attempt to guarantee that those in authority will not extract confessions behind closed doors, where the temptation to promise favor or use third-degree methods is always present.

Further, the Constitution declares that, although Congress may declare what punishment is to be meted out to those convicted of treason, "no attainder of treason shall work corruption of blood, or forfeiture except during the life of the person attainted." This means that the children or heirs of traitors may not be forbidden, as part of the punishment, to inherit property. Thus children may not be punished for an offense of a dead ancestor.

One can also commit treason against a state. Federal law has become pervasive on this subject, however. The case of *Pennsylvania v. Nelson* [350 U.S. 497 (1956)] is illustrative. Nelson, a member of the Communist party, was convicted by Pennsylvania of violating its sedition act. Upon appeal the conviction was set aside on the ground that the Federal Smith Act had superseded the state law.

The Supreme Court limited the Nelson decision in *Uphaus v. Wyman* (360 U.S. 72, 1959). There an attorney general for New Hampshire sought to compel Dr. Willard Uphaus, a Christian pacifist, to disclose names of persons who had attended an adult summer camp which he directed. Dr. Uphaus refused so as to protect his friends from harrassment. His counsel argued that the state lacked authority to compel disclosure because the Federal government had preempted the field of subversion. By 5-to-4 vote the Supreme Court upheld New Hampshire saying that despite the Smith Act and the Nelson decision the state retained the power to investigate subversion against itself.

Habeas Corpus. A writ of habeas corpus is a command on the part of a judicial officer to have a person held in custody brought before a court for the purpose of determining the legality of detention. The Constitution forbids the Federal government, but not the states, to suspend the writ "unless when in cases of rebellion or invasion the public safety may require it."

Without this guaranty, military and police officers could take people into custody and keep them there indefinitely without hearing or trial. When the Bastille was stormed during the French Revolution, some men who were loosed had been imprisoned for years without trial. Under dictatorial regimes people are frequently spirited away by police to be put to death or confined in concentration camps without being heard of again. The writ of habeas corpus provides protection against such actions. When the writ is issued and the prisoner is produced, adequate cause must be shown for detention. If the judge is unconvinced, the prisoner must be set free.

The writ can be suspended only in the event of rebellion or invasion, and then only when "the public safety may require it." The only occasion since the Civil War when the writ has been suspended occurred in Hawaii during the Second World War. After its suspension, civilian laws were displaced by military orders, and offenders were tried by military tribunals without benefit of jury trial or other normal procedures. Although this system continued throughout most of the war, it was later declared illegal by the Supreme Court [*Duncan v. Kohanamoku*, 327 U.S. 304 (1945)]. Congress had not intended the Hawaiian Organic Act to authorize such drastic subordination of civilian life to the military, the Court said.

Bill of Attainder. A bill of attainder is a legislative act that inflicts punishment without judicial trial. In times of rebellion or political excitement it was not uncommon for Parliament to punish minorities by enacting special bills declaring them guilty of treason or felony. Punishment was often inflicted without allowing the accused party an opportunity to answer the charges, or even without the formality of proof. Indeed, in England it was not uncommon for Parliament to attaint a man after he was dead. To guarantee that such things would not happen, the Constitution forbids both the Federal and state governments to enact bills of attainder. Accordingly, legislatures enact laws defining crimes, but the courts must judge innocence or guilt.

A few attempts to violate the guaranty have occurred. One case involved three Federal employees accused by a House committee of having associated with groups engaged in un-American activities. When the President refused to dismiss the men, who had been duly appointed and had served meritoriously, Congress inserted a provision in a deficiency appropriation bill forbidding payment of salaries. Congress also barred the men from future employment with the Federal government.

This action had the appearance of being legislative punishment without judicial trial. The men continued in office for a brief time, then brought suit for salary, claiming their constitutional rights had been violated. The Court of Claims, before which the case originated, refused to pass on the larger question of constitutionality but ruled that the men were entitled to unpaid salary. Three judges went further and expressed their belief that Congress had violated the constitutional provision forbidding bills of attainder, and the Supreme Court later agreed with this view by unanimous decision [*United States v. Lovett*, 328 U.S. 303 (1946)].

Ex Post Facto Laws. Literally, "ex post facto" means "subsequent to the act." Both the Federal and state governments are forbidden to enact laws that have a retroactive effect. Such laws have been held to include those that (1) make criminal acts which were innocent when done, (2) aggravate a crime or make it greater than it was when committed, (3) alter the rules of evidence, permitting less or different evidence to convict a person of an offense already committed, (4) operate in any way to the dis-

advantage of one accused of a crime committed prior to the enactment of the law.

Although the term "ex post facto" would appear to include any law having a retroactive effect, the courts have given the words their common-law meaning, holding that the prohibition applies only to criminal, and not civil, cases.

Searches and Seizures. In medieval England the King's officers frequently searched people and their property without warrants and seized evidence to prove guilt. A measure of protection was found in the common-law maxim that a man's house is his castle, and this guaranty was written, in effect, into our Constitution.

The Fourth Amendment states, "The right of the people to be secure in their persons, houses, papers, and effects, against unreasonable searches and seizures, shall not be violated, and no warrants shall issue, but upon probable cause, supported by oath or affirmation, and particularly describing the place to be searched, and the persons or things to be seized."

Several things should be noted about the words just quoted. First, people are to be secure in their "persons, houses, papers, and effects." This includes an outbuilding, such as a barn, garage, office, shop, factory, or warehouse. It also restricts the tapping of telephone wires. It includes books and accounts and explains why postal authorities cannot open letters and packages without warrants unless the sender gives permission by writing some such words as "may be opened for postal inspection if necessary." The words quoted from the Fourth Amendment do not include an open field where, for example, an illicit still may be kept.

Second, only "unreasonable" searches and seizures are forbidden. Reasonable ones, not requiring warrants, include those made at the time and scene of a crime and in exceptional circumstances that will not allow or justify delay. In civil proceedings inspections may be made without warrants for reasons of public health or welfare [*Frank v. Maryland,* 359 U.S. 360 (1959)].

Third, when a judge is asked to issue a warrant he must be convinced that the request is justified. The place to be searched and the person to be seized must be described.

The case of *United States v. Jeffers* [342 U.S. 48 (1950)] illustrates how the constitutional guaranty operates. Acting upon a tip and proffering a bribe, Washington, D.C., officers entered a hotel room in search of narcotics. Without a warrant, and during the absence of the two women to whom the room had been let, the officers made a thorough search. They found contraband narcotics and seized them. Later the women were arrested, prosecuted, and found guilty of violating Federal narcotic laws. On appeal, the Supreme Court released the women, saying the evidence used to convict them had been obtained by methods which were proscribed by the Fourth Amendment.

Equally difficult is the question of how far a search may extend while making a valid arrest. In *Harris v. United States* [331 U.S. 145 (1946)], two men were suspected of using the mails for fraudulent purposes. Warrants of arrest, but not of search, were obtained and with these the police arrested Harris and then searched his apartment for nearly five hours looking for two stolen checks. The checks were not found, but draft cards were. Harris was prosecuted and convicted for illegal possession of draft cards.

On appeal, the Supreme Court, in a 5-to-4 decision, upheld the conviction. The majority argued that, because the arrest was made with a valid warrant, the extensive search was incidental and justified. Moreover, evidence of another crime acquired in making a lawful search could be used to convict. The minority opinions protested vigorously. Said Justice Frankfurter:

To find authority for ransacking a home merely from authority for the arrest of a person is to give a novel and ominous rendering to a momentous chapter in the history of Anglo-American freedom. An Englishman's home, though a hovel, is his castle, precisely because the law secures freedom from fear of intrusion by the police except under carefully safeguarded authorizations by a magistrate. . . . the Constitution protects both unauthorized arrest and unauthorized search.

In another case [*United States v. Rabinowitz,* 339 U.S. 56 (1949)] the Supreme Court upheld a conviction based on evidence of postage-stamp forgery found while rummaging through a man's office with an arrest warrant but not a search warrant. A valid arrest, said the court, justified the incidental search of Rabinowitz's office.

The Fourth Amendment does not say whether evidence obtained by illegal search and seizure can be used to convict, but the courts have disallowed the practice in Federal cases [see, for example, *Weeks v. United States,* 232 U.S. 383 (1914)]. The states, however, were permitted to do so if they wished. In 1961 the Supreme Court reversed precedents and brought state practice in line with Federal (*Mapp v. Ohio,* 367, U.S. 643).

More recently the Supreme Court upset the "silver platter" doctrine. Under this precept, evidence illegally obtained by state officers and inadmissible in state courts could be furnished gratuitously—as on a silver platter—to Federal officers and used to convict a person at Federal law. In two 5-to-4 decisions the Court said the practice violated the Fourth Amendment guaranty against unreasonable searches and seizures [*Elkins v. United States,* 364 U.S. 206 (1960); *Rios v. United States,* 364 U.S. 253 (1960)].

Indictment by Grand Jury. The Fifth Amendment provides, among other things, that the Federal government may not hold anyone, except persons employed in the Armed Forces, "for a capital, or otherwise infamous crime, unless on a presentment or indictment of a grand jury." The states are not required by the Constitution to use grand juries, although most of them do.

A "capital" crime is one punishable by death. An "infamous" one has never been clearly defined but is known to include offenses that are punishable by imprisonment, hard labor, or the loss of civil or political privileges.

If a Federal crime is committed, a grand jury composed of from sixteen to twenty-three persons must (unless waived by the defendant) be assembled for the purpose of deciding whether evidence is sufficient to justify trial. The accused cannot insist that he be permitted to appear before the grand jury, but permission to do so is sometimes given. If twelve or more grand jurors believe the evidence justifies trial, a "true bill" is reported to the judge. If not, the accused must be promptly released until convincing evidence is produced. The form of the indictment is of great importance, inasmuch as the accused can be tried only for offenses mentioned in it.

The grand jury is criticized as being clumsy and ill-suited to modern conditions. England has almost completely discarded it. The Federal government permits its waiver in noncapital cases and this is done increasingly by defendants. Its use is also declining in the states. Its place is being taken by a simple affidavit, or "information."

Trial by Jury. The Federal government is

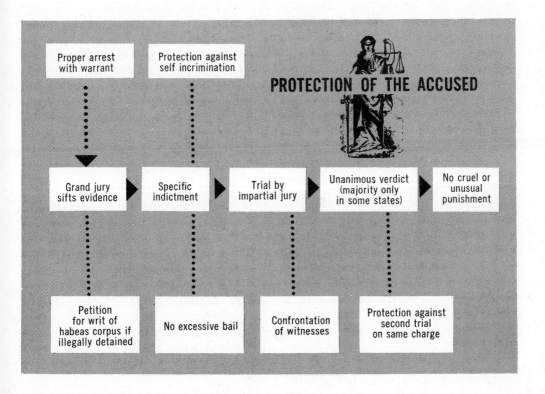

PROTECTION OF THE ACCUSED

Proper arrest with warrant

Protection against self incrimination

Grand jury sifts evidence

Specific indictment

Trial by impartial jury

Unanimous verdict (majority only in some states)

No cruel or unusual punishment

Petition for writ of habeas corpus if illegally detained

No excessive bail

Confrontation of witnesses

Protection against second trial on same charge

required to grant trial by jury in criminal cases by provisions found in the body of the Constitution (Article III, Section 2) and the Sixth Amendment. States may dispense with jury trials as long as their alternative methods accord with due process of law.

So far as the Federal government is concerned, the following observations are pertinent: (1) Every person accused of a criminal offense is entitled to jury trial, except public officials who are subject to impeachment. (2) Jury trial may be waived by the defendant with court approval. (3) Federal juries must be composed of twelve persons, either men or women. (4) Trials must be "speedy," i.e., reasonably prompt. (5) Trials must be "public," so that friends of the accused may see that justice is done. (6) The jury must be "impartial," and to this end attorneys for both parties are permitted to question and challenge prospective jurors and cross-examine witnesses. (7) Members of juries must be drawn from the district in which the crime was committed, and the district must have been defined prior to the trial. (8) The verdict must be unanimous. (9) The trial must be in the presence of a judge having power to instruct the jury as to both law and facts. (10) The verdict of a jury is final unless, upon appeal by the defendant, a new trial is awarded because a mistake was made in law or procedure.

The Seventh Amendment guarantees the right of trial by jury in certain types of civil cases. The provision reads: "In suits at common law, where the value in controversy shall exceed twenty dollars, the right of trial by jury shall be preserved, and no fact tried by a jury shall be otherwise re-examined in any court of the United States than according to the rules of common law."

The words quoted are difficult for the layman to understand. When Congress permits common-law rules to prevail, jury trial must be allowed in cases involving twenty dollars or more.

The civil jury must consist of twelve persons, and procedures are similar to those explained above for criminal trials. Jury trial is frequently waived in civil proceedings, especially where small sums are involved.

Self Incrimination. Among provisions of the Fifth Amendment is one which says: "No person . . . shall be compelled in any criminal case to be a witness against himself." Several rules have emerged from these words: (1) Although the language used suggests that the guaranty extends only to those accused of criminal offenses, the courts hold it applies also to investigations and civil proceedings. (2) The right is personal and may not be invoked to protect someone else. (3) The right does not extend to artificial persons, such as corporations. (4) One may not plead immunity in a Federal case for fear of prosecution by a state or foreign country. (5) The determination of when the right may be invoked rests with the courts. (6) Comment usually may not be made to the jury about a defendant's refusal to testify.

Long taken for granted, this right has become the subject of heated controversy, chiefly because it has been invoked often by persons suspected of Communist activities. Feeling ran so high for a time that it became popular to speak derisively of the constitutional guaranty. One United States senator gained considerable popularity by dubbing those who pleaded the right before congressional committees "Fifth Amendment Communists," whether or not Communist sympathies or activities were proved. Fifth Amendment pleaders frequently suffered extralegal penalties: loss of jobs, for instance. As cases reached the courts, however, the constitutional guaranty stood as a bulwark.

Grants of Immunity. The guaranty of immunity unquestionably makes law enforcement more difficult than it would be if confessions could be forced by torture or otherwise. It is not surprising, therefore, that attempts are made to circumvent the right. This has been done by a number of states through passage of laws providing "immunity baths" for those who confess in response to promises that they will not be prosecuted. Such statutes have been upheld by the United States Supreme Court [see, for example, *Twining v. New Jersey*, 211 U.S. 78 (1908)].

Congress attempted something similar by passage of the Compulsory Testimony Act of 1954. The act provides that, on the application of the Attorney General or a congressional committee, a United States district attorney may order a witness to testify after his claim of privilege. It further provides that one compelled to testify cannot be prosecuted for any matter covered by his answers. To many this appeared to violate the spirit of the Fifth Amendment guaranty of immunity, if not its letter, but the Supreme Court by a 7–2 vote upheld the statute [*Ullman v. United States*, 350 U.S. 422 (1956)].

Reasonable Bail and Punishment. The Eighth Amendment states, "Excessive bail shall not be required, nor excessive fines imposed, nor cruel and unusual punishments inflicted." Bail before trial is normally required to preserve the presumption of innocence which is fundamental to Anglo-Saxon law. The guaranty assumes that offenders will be released on bail and requires that the amount of money to be posted shall not be excessive. What is "excessive" has never been fixed by the courts; the amount must necessarily vary with circumstances and the gravity of the offense.

The provision that cruel or unusual punishments shall not be administered was directed mainly at the barbarity of early English law. It now prohibits punishments that are "so palpably excessive and disproportionate as to schock the sense of justice of all reasonable people." A recent case [*Louisiana v. Resweber*, 329 U.S. 459 (1947)] is one of the very few that have arisen under this provision. It involved a young Negro, Willie Francis, sentenced to death in Louisiana. The electric chair accidentally failed to work when current was first applied, and a second attempt was threatened. The defendant appealed to the courts, contending in part that it was cruel and unusual punishment to force him to suffer the ordeal again. Rejecting his appeal by a 5-to-4 decision, the court said:

The cruelty against which the Constitution protects a convicted man is cruelty inherent in the method of punishment, not the necessary suffering involved in any method employed to extinguish life humanely.

More recently [*Trop v. Dulles*, 356 U.S. 86 (1958)], the Supreme Court declared unconstitutional an act of Congress depriving a wartime deserter from the Armed Forces of citizenship, saying this was cruel and unusual punishment.

Double Jeopardy. According to the Fifth Amendment, an accused person may not be "subject for the same offense to be twice put in jeopardy of life or limb." This was included to prevent persons from being tried several times for the same offense. One is put in jeopardy ". . . when he is put on trial, before a court of competent jurisdiction upon an indictment or information which is sufficient in form and substance to sustain a conviction and a jury has been charged with his deliverance."[1]

One is not in jeopardy when the case is

[1] Thomas M. Cooley, *Constitutional Limitations* . . . (Boston: Little, Brown, 6th ed., 1890), p. 399.

merely before a grand jury; hence the same evidence may be presented more than once for the purpose of obtaining an indictment. One may be tried a second time if the indictment is defective; if the jury cannot come to a decision; if the jury is discharged for some good reason, such as illness of a juror; or if the term of court as fixed by law ends before the trial is finished.

A person may by a single act violate both Federal and state law. If this happens, the person may be tried in both Federal and state courts. The justification is that two offenses are committed.

In one recent case [*Abbate v. United States*, 359 U.S. 187 (1959)] several men were convicted by Illinois for conspiring and dynamiting facilities of a telephone company. After serving short sentences, they were convicted by the Federal government for the same act on the charge that interstate communications had been destroyed.

In another case [*Bartkus v. Illinois*, 359 U.S. 121 (1959)] the defendant was acquitted in Federal court for robbery of a federally insured savings and loan association. He was later convicted by Illinois for robbery. In both cases the Supreme Court held, by 5-to-4 votes, that the guaranty of double jeopardy had not been violated.

THE EXTENSION OF CIVIL RIGHTS

Interest in civil liberties has been high since the Second World War. One evidence of this was the appointment in 1946 by President Truman of a committee of distinguished citizens to explore the subject and make recommendations. The Committee's report, published in 1947 under the title of *To Secure These Rights*, was widely read and highly controversial.

The Committee's Report. The Committee called attention to lynching and to the fact that the culprits are seldom dis-

covered or punished. It reported numerous instances of police brutality in various parts of the nation. Indeed, it quoted testimony given by J. Edgar Hoover, Director of the FBI, to the effect that at a particular jail "it was seldom that a Negro man or woman was incarcerated who was not given a severe beating, which started off with a pistol whipping and ended with a rubber hose."

The Committee reported that Negroes, Mexicans, Indians, and other minorities often find it impossible to obtain justice, partly because of their poverty, partly because of the "complete absence of people of their own kind from jury lists," partly because of the fee system in many communities, which "sometimes stimulates arbitrary arrests and encourages unjust convictions," and partly because in certain states "the white population can threaten and do violence to the minority members with little or no fear of legal reprisals."

The Committee also found some involuntary servitude among the poor, arising from state peonage laws imposing penalties for nonfulfillment of contracts to perform labor. It criticized the curtailment of liberty which resulted when Japanese-Americans along the West Coast were forcibly moved to inland detention and relocation centers during the Second World War. The Committee discovered many instances of discrimination against aliens and even against natives of American territories.

The Committee also noted that the poll tax disfranchised many voters, particularly Negroes, in several Southern states. It found numerous violations of freedom of speech, press, religion, and assembly. It pointed out the dangers of "Red hunting" among civil servants by congressional committees and loyalty boards. It found an abundance of evidence indicating discrimination against Negroes in the Armed

Forces, civil service, District of Columbia, American territories, by state and local governments, landlords, private employers, and in professional and service occupations. The Committee was especially severe in its condemnation of racial segregation.

Proposed Remedies. After reviewing the American scene and finding conditions that were heartening as well as disappointing, the President's Committee on Civil Rights made numerous proposals. Most important of all, the Committee said, it is necessary to have an informed and alert public that is both tolerant and aggressive in defending rights for all, especially minorities and advocates of unpopular causes.

More specific suggestions included (1) reorganization and strengthening of the Civil Rights Section of the Department of Justice; (2) creation by the states of special units for the handling of civil-rights cases; (3) special training for Federal and state police in the handling of cases involving civil rights; (4) establishment of Federal and state permanent commissions on civil rights to maintain constant surveillance; (5) clarification and strengthening of Federal statutes to make it unmistakably clear what conduct is and what is not a Federal crime; (6) Federal legislation outlawing police brutality, lynching, and all forms of peonage; (7) Federal legislation outlawing the poll tax and other serious impediments to voting in primaries and elections; (8) self-government for the District of Columbia; (9) citizenship for the people of Guam and Samoa; (10) repeal of state laws discriminating against aliens; (11) Federal and state action ending "Jim Crow" laws and other serious forms of racial segregation and discrimination; (12) withholding Federal grants-in-aid from public and private agencies that practice discrimination and segregation.

Bitter controversy followed publication of the report, which had serious repercussions in subsequent presidential elections. Nevertheless, the report led to much self-examination and some acceptance of its recommendations. The Supreme Court's decision in 1954 which outlawed race segregation in public schools took the spotlight off the report of the President's Commission.

Civil Rights Acts of 1957 and 1960. Armed with the filibuster, Senate opponents succeeded in blocking Federal civil rights legislation until 1957. The act of that year (1) authorizes a six-member Commission on Civil Rights to investigate and report; (2) approves the appointment of a new Assistant Attorney General to head a division of civil rights within the Department of Justice; (3) outlaws interference with voting in primaries or general elections for Federal officers; (4) empowers the Attorney General to obtain court orders, at public expense, to halt threatened violations of voting rights; (5) makes disobedience to court orders punishable as civil or criminal contempt (in the former compliance is the objective; in the latter, punishment); (6) provides that criminal-contempt proceedings may be tried with or without jury, but if trial is without jury and the judge imposes a fine of over $300 or imprisonment of more than forty-five days, the defendant is entitled to a new trial with jury; (7) fixes uniform qualifications for Federal jurors as a means of preventing state regulations from keeping Negroes off juries that try civil rights cases. This law was weaker than its advocates desired and enforcement proved difficult.

A stronger measure passed in 1960. Obstructing Federal court orders, in civil rights cases or not, was made a crime. To flee in interstate commerce to avoid local prosecution for burning or bombing any building, or giving testimony in such cases, was declared a crime. Transporting explosives in interstate commerce for the purpose of damaging any building was made illegal. State and local officials were required to keep records of Federal elections, including primaries, for twenty-two months. The Attorney General was authorized to inspect and copy such records. Anyone who steals, tampers, or destroys such records was declared subject to Federal prosecution. All members of the Civil Rights Commission, as well as the chairman, were empowered to administer oaths. The United States Commissioner of Education was authorized to arrange free education for children of members of the armed forces in areas where public schools have been closed. Where Federal courts find that the right to vote is denied as a "pattern of practice" because of race or color, they may appoint "voting referees" to ascertain the facts and report. The courts may issue voting certificates which must be honored by state and local election officials.

Rights Extended through United Nations. The United Nations Charter includes a pledge to promote and encourage "respect for, and observance of, human rights and fundamental freedoms for all without discrimination as to race, sex, language, or religion." A Human Rights Commission was established to promote and administer the objectives.

As a step toward fulfilling this pledge, the General Assembly, in December, 1948, adopted the Universal Declaration of Human Rights. This pledges member nations to promote and encourage respect and observance for human rights, but it outlaws nothing. A Covenant on Human Rights has been discussed; if adopted, it would make violations of human rights generally illegal. A covenant which would outlaw all forms of slavery has also received much attention. But the only treaty dealing with human rights that has been adopted by sufficient members to put it into effect is one outlawing genocide, or assaults upon masses,

or groups, of people, as for example Nazi persecution of the Jews.

The United Nations continues its efforts. Much educational work is done, and charges of violations are aired before the Human Rights Commission and the General Assembly. This helps create an awareness of the importance of the individual and his rights. The courts of some nations have taken judicial notice of Charter provisions and the Universal Declaration of Human Rights. Several nations have incorporated parts of the Universal Declaration in newly adopted constitutions.

Because of political and constitutional questions, the United States has been unable to give all-out support for United Nations-sponsored treaties dealing with human rights. It has not ratified the Genocide Convention. Nor has it supported fully the proposed Covenant on Human Rights and a similar treaty on slavery. It is, however, bound by the Charter and Declaration of Human Rights to promote and encourage respect for and observance of human rights.

ON THE TRAIL OF SUBVERSIVES

General Control Measures. Widespread fear of subversion has characterized much of the twentieth century in the United States. The list of Federal and state laws that define treason, espionage, sabotage, and similar crimes has grown long. The Federal government has relentlessly combed its employees, members of the Armed Forces, immigrants, and applicants for visas in search of subversives. All Federal, and many state, employees must take special loyalty oaths. Until 1959 labor-union leaders were required to file anti-Communist affidavits; now Communists are barred from holding union offices. The Attorney General has for some years been publishing a list of subversive organizations. Files on organizations and individuals whose loyalty has been or may someday be subject to suspicion are maintained by Federal and state agencies. Congressional and state legislative committees, the FBI, and other intelligence agencies have probed far and deep. Several states have outlawed the Communist party, forbidden Communists to teach in public schools, and imposed other disqualifications. Meanwhile social pressures have helped induce conformity. The principal Federal laws aimed at subversives in general and Communists in particular are reviewed below.

The Smith Act. Officially known as the Alien Registration Act of 1940, the Smith Act became law at a time of alarm over pro-Nazis and fascists of similar types. Among other provisions it outlawed speech and activities intended to create disloyalty among members of the Armed Forces, overthrow any American government by force or violence, assassinate public officials, or organize groups for these purposes. It declared illegal the being or becoming a member or affiliate of an organization if one knows its purposes to be among those proscribed.

Violations are punishable by fines of not more than $10,000, ten years' imprisonment, or both. Few fascists have been prosecuted under it, but since the Second World War the act has provided the basis for most Federal prosecutions of Communists. Although constitutionality was upheld in *Dennis v. United States*, later Supreme Court decisions made prosecutions more difficult by (1) restricting the term "organize" to mean participation in creating a new organization, and declaring that theoretical advocacy of communism, without intent to instigate revolutionary action, was not prohibited by the Smith Act [*Yates v. United States*, 354 U.S. 298 (1957)], (2) requiring the House Committee on Un-American Activities [*Watkins v. United States*, 354 U.S.

"Everyone is a little subversive but thee and me, and sometimes I think that even thee—." (Fitzpatrick in the St. Louis Post-Dispatch.)

178 (1957)] and state investigators [*Sweezy v. New Hampshire*, 354 U.S. 234 (1957)] to conform with the requirements of due process of law, and (3) forcing the FBI to disclose the nature and source of the evidence relied upon in prosecuting alleged Communists [*Jencks v. United States*, 353 U.S. 657 (1957)]. Congress later mitigated the impact of the Jencks decision by prescribing limits to the disclosure of evidence.

More recently, a sharply divided Supreme Court construed the Smith Act to ban active membership in the Communist party [*Scales v. United States*, 367 U.S. 203 (1961)]. Mere membership in the party, the Court said, is not illegal; only active membership with knowledge that the party intended to overthrow government by force and violence is punishable.

The McCarran Act. This measure, known officially as the Internal Security Act of 1950, is somewhat long and involved. The law declares it illegal "for any person knowingly to combine, conspire, or agree with any other person to perform any act which would substantially contribute to the establishment within the United States of a totalitarian dictatorship" directed from abroad. It tightens laws against espionage. It bars Communists from Federal employment and even from working "in any defense facility."

Federal employees are forbidden to contribute money to Communist organizations. Contributions to Communist organizations are denied tax exemption. It is made illegal for Communists to obtain passports or even to apply for them. Visas to visit or emigrate to the United States are denied to anyone who is or ever was a member of a totalitarian organization or who advocates "the economic, international, and governmental doctrines of world communism or the economic and governmental doctrines of any other form of totalitarianism. . . ."

Naturalization laws are modified and deportations of subversives made easier. The law also outlaws picketing and sound trucks near court buildings when the intent is to influence court officials or proceedings. It also authorizes the arrest and detention during national emergencies of those for whom "there is reasonable ground to believe that such person probably will engage in, or probably will conspire with others to engage in, acts of espionage or of sabotage. . . ."

To help with enforcement, the McCarran Act established a five-man Subversive Activities Control Board and empowered it to investigate and register all Communist-action and Communist-front organizations. Periodic reports disclosing details of organization, finance, and lists of members with addresses are required from such organizations. Before the lists are published, members must be notified that their names appear and be given an opportunity to contest the listing. Such registered organizations can transmit their publications by mail or interstate and foreign commerce only if they are marked "Disseminated by ——, a Communist organization." Moreover, registered organizations may broadcast or televise only after announcing, "The following program is sponsored by ——, a Communist organization."

This is drastic legislation, the constitutionality of which remains to be determined. The measure has been denounced by many as unnecessary and dangerous to civil liberties. In his veto message, President Truman said the measure would help Communists more than it would hurt them, impose a staggering burden upon the Department of Justice and the FBI, aid potential enemies by requiring the publication of complete lists of vital defense facilities, antagonize friendly governments, put the United States "in the thought control business," and "give government officials vast powers to harass all of our citizens in the exercise of their right of free speech." But two-thirds of Congress thought otherwise.

Although this legislation was passed in 1950, the Subversive Activities Control Board's first final order to register was not made effective until 1959. Countless legal problems were encountered by the Board and the courts. In 1961 a sharply divided Supreme Court upheld the registration provisions (*Communist Party v. Subversive Activities Control Board*, 367 U.S. 1) but serious legal and enforcement problems remain.

The Communist Control Act of 1954. Throughout the postwar period the most vocal anti-Communists urged outlawry of the Communist party. Some states did take this step, but doubts over constitutionality, fear of driving the party underground, and theoretical implications caused hesitation elsewhere. Finally, on the eve of a congressional election and with the help of several "liberal" senators who were running for re-election and smarting under the charge of being "soft" toward Communists, an ambiguously worded measure passed Congress, intended to outlaw what was left of the party.

The law purports to outlaw the Communist party, "or any successors of such party regardless of the assumed name" by declaring that it is not entitled to any of the rights, privileges, and immunities which other political parties enjoy under the laws of the United States or any political subdivision thereof. It then proceeds to strike at membership in the party or other organizations advocating overthrow of the government by force or violence, but it stops short of making membership a criminal offense.

Instead, it reverts to the McCarran Act provisions respecting membership in Communist-action organizations. These, it will be recalled, do not make membership a crime; they merely require that membership lists be filed and published.

Other provisions of the Communist Control Act require that Communist-infiltrated organizations register with the Subversive Activities Control Board. The act also withdraws benefits granted by the National Labor Relations Act and the Taft-Hartley Act from unions with Communist officers or employees, from employers who engage Communists to represent them in labor matters, and from Communist-infiltrated unions and employer organizations generally.

FOR FURTHER READING

See also references at end of Chapter 7.

Ashmore, Harry S.: *The Negro and the Schools* (Chapel Hill, N.C.: The University of North Carolina Press, 1954).

Beaney, William M.: *The Right of Counsel in American Courts* (Ann Arbor, Mich.: University of Michigan Press, 1955).

Beisel, Albert R.: *Control over Illegal Enforcement of the Criminal Law: Role of the Supreme Court* (Boston: Boston University Press, 1955).

Dash, Samuel, Richard F. Schwartz, and Robert E. Knowlton: *The Eavesdroppers* (New Brunswick, N.J.: Rutgers University Press, 1959).

Fellman, David: *The Defendant's Rights* (New York: Rinehart, 1958).

Gellhorn, Walter: *Security, Loyalty and Science* (Ithaca, N.Y.: Cornell University Press, 1950).

——— (ed.): *The States and Subversion* (Ithaca, N.Y.: Cornell University Press, 1952).

Griswold, Erwin N.: *The Fifth Amendment Today* (Cambridge, Mass.: Harvard University Press, 1955).

Grodzins, Morton: *The Loyal and the Disloyal: Social Boundaries of Patriotism and Treason* (Chicago: University of Chicago Press, 1956).

Harris, Robert J.: *The Quest for Equality* (Baton Rouge, La.: Louisiana State University Press, 1960).

James, Joseph B.: *The Framing of the Fourteenth Amendment* (Urbana, Ill.: University of Illinois Press, 1956).

Kesselman, Louis C.: *The Social Politics of the FEPC: A Study in Reform Pressure Movements* (Chapel Hill, N.C.: The University of North Carolina Press, 1948).

Lasswell, Harold D.: *National Security and Individual Freedom* (New York: McGraw-Hill, 1950).

Mott, Rodney L.: *Due Process of Law* (Indianapolis: Bobbs-Merrill, 1926).

Ruchames, Louis: *Race, Jobs, and Politics: The Story of FEPC* (New York: Columbia University Press, 1953).

Schaar, John H.: *Loyalty in America* (Berkeley and Los Angeles, Calif.: University of California Press, 1957).

Sibley, Mulford Q., and Philip E. Jacob: *Conscription and Conscience* (Ithaca, N.Y.: Cornell University Press, 1952).

U.S. President's Committee on Civil Rights: *To Secure These Rights* (1947). (Published also by Simon and Schuster, 1947).

Vose, Clement E.: *Caucasians Only* (Berkeley and Los Angeles, Calif.: University of California Press, 1959).

Weintraub, Ruth G.: *How Secure These Rights?* (New York: Doubleday, 1949).

REVIEW QUESTIONS

1. Of what significance today is the ban on slavery contained in the Thirteenth Amendment?

2. Compare the "substantive" concept of due process of law with the "procedural" concept, and illustrate both with appropriate Supreme Court decisions.

3. Review the controversy over the "separate but equal" doctrine and illustrate differing points of view with appropriate Supreme Court decisions.

4. Explain to a person suspected of committing a crime the rights guaranteed him by the Constitution.

5. Defend and criticize findings and recommendations of President Truman's Committee on Civil Rights.

6. Summarize provisions of the Civil Rights Acts of 1957 and 1960. How effective are these?

7. What has the United Nations done on behalf of human rights? What are some of the implications for the United States of UN action in this field?

8. Defend and criticize restrictions placed upon Communists in recent years by the Federal Government.

9. What is meant when it is said that the price of liberty is eternal vigilance?

Chapter Nine

The American People:
Citizens and Aliens

Not like the brazen giant of Greek fame,
With conquering limbs astride from land to land.
Here at our sea-washed, sunset gates shall stand
A mighty woman with a torch, whose flame
Is the imprisoned lightning, and her name
Mother of exiles, from her beacon-hand
Glows world wide welcome; her mild eyes command
The air-bridged harbor that twin cities frame.
"Keep ancient lands, your storied pomp!" cries she
With silent lips. "Give me your tired, your poor,
Your huddled masses yearning to breathe free.
The wretched refuse of your teeming shore.
Send these, the homeless, tempest-tost to me,
I lift my lamp beside the golden door!"[1]

The people of the United States come from many lands and races; they are widely scattered on mainland, in territories, and abroad; they grow in numbers by birth and immigration; they move about in search of opportunity and happiness; and the process of adjustment continues as it has since the founding of the Republic. Most are citizens, many are on the way to naturalization, some retain alien status. From these circumstances arise facts and problems which have an important bearing upon American political institutions and policies.

POPULATION

Growth. From the days of colonial settlement to the time of the Civil War the population of the United States grew more

---

[1] A poem by Emma Lazarus, which is graven on a tablet within the main entrance on the pedestal on which the Statue of Liberty stands.

rapidly than that of any other country in the world. This is one of the outstanding phenomena of world history. From 2½ million in 1776 the numbers increased by leaps and bounds until the First World War; since then the rate of increase has been slower. In 1962 the population of continental United States was about 185 million.

The chart given below makes it apparent that growth has been continuous. The decennial rate of increase declined from 1860 until recently because of a declining birth rate and diminishing immigration. Optimistic predictions reach as high as 228 million for 1975 and 300 million for the year 2000. Obviously, however, whether these predictions come true will depend upon birth rates, life expectancy, and im-

migration. These, in turn, will be influenced by social conditions, the state of the economy, and immigration policies. From the evidence available, it appears doubtful that the United States will, in the foreseeable future, exceed the population of the three most populous nations: China, India, and Russia.

Distribution. Despite the nation's phenomenal growth, its population density is comparatively small. The average square mile of the United States has only 50.7 persons, contrasted with 551 per square mile in the United Kingdom and 643 in Japan. The most closely settled states are those along the Atlantic seaboard. The most sparsely populated state is Alaska, whose average is only 0.4 people for each square mile. The population center of the nation

As population has increased rapidly, there has been a decline in the proportion of Americans living on farms. (Data from Department of Commerce, Bureau of the Census.)

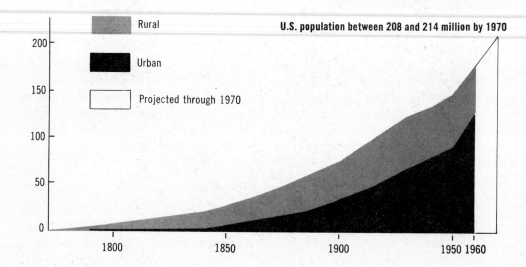

U.S. POPULATION GROWTH AND DISTRIBUTION
1790-1960

Population in millions

Rural

Urban

Projected through 1970

U.S. population between 208 and 214 million by 1970

has moved steadily westward, being near Centralia, Clinton County, Illinois, when the 1960 census was taken.

Rural-Urban Trends. Less than a hundred years ago the chief occupation in the United States was agriculture. Today this nation is one of the most highly industrialized in the world. The change meant an enormous growth of towns and cities. In 1790, some 95 per cent of all Americans lived in rural areas; now about two-thirds dwell in urban places.

The migration to urban areas has profoundly affected American politics and governments. Rural local government has yielded importance to cities and states. Rural voters have lost influence to a new urban middle class.[1]

Although rural voters wield disproportionate influence where geographic areas are represented, as in state legislatures and the national House of Representatives, urban regions have become dominant in choosing officials at large, such as governors, United States senators, and Presidents. It is now theoretically possible for a President to be elected without any support from rural voters. "This dominating position," said Professor Holcombe, "of the urban population in presidential elections marks a revolution in American politics."[2] The scholar quoted predicted that "The new urban class politics will increasingly dominate the national political scene"[3] and subsequent events have confirmed this prophecy.

The shift to urban living has encouraged the growth of pressure groups. Changes in

[1] For further development of this theme, see the writings of Arthur N. Holcombe. Note especially his *The New Party Politics* (New York: Norton, 1933), *The Middle Classes in American Politics* (Cambridge, Mass.: Harvard University Press, 1940), and *Our More Perfect Union* (Cambridge, Mass.: Harvard University Press, 1950).

[2] *The New Party Politics*, pp. 34–35.

[3] *Ibid.*

district boundaries lag behind population shifts, leaving the new urban communities underrepresented. This imbalance partially explains why pressure groups flourish and wield great influence in modern times.

The urban trend also means more governmental intervention in private affairs and added public services. As city dwellers sense their need for better water, light, sewer systems, transportation and schools, improved medical and recreational facilities, modern housing, employment offices and job insurance, attitudes favorable to the "welfare state" emerge. Thus, the movement from country to city must be listed as one of the most important causes of the shift from the individualistic to the positive state mentioned in Chapter 1.

Races. Racially, the people of the United States are diverse. Although white persons account for 88.6 per cent of the total, these represent many different nationalities. Each strain has made important contributions to American life. Besides helping with settlement, expansion, and the development of a high standard of living, each has also made distinctive contributions to the arts and sciences. Indeed, the greatness of America is due in large measure to the use made of the genius inherent in the many racial streams that make up the population.

Through the years there has been little change in the ratio of whites to nonwhites (Negroes, Indians, Orientals, and others). Since 1900, however, there has been a continuing, significant decline in the foreign white stock, i.e., white immigrants and those born here of foreign or mixed parentage.

Historically, concentrations of peoples sharing linguistic, religious, and cultural ties with certain countries of the Old World gave rise to political blocs of considerable significance. Familiar, for example, has been the influence of the Irish who settled in larger cities of New England and Middle

WORLD POPULATION TO DOUBLE

WORLD POPULATION, 1958

(Area of continents in proportion to estimated 1958 population)

WORLD POPULATION, 2000 A.D.

(Area of continents in proportion to estimated population, 2000 A.D.)

WORLD POPULATION, 2000 A.D.

	1958 : 2000 (in millions)	PERCENTAGE INCREASE		1958 : 2000 (in millions)	PERCENTAGE INCREASE
LATIN AMERICA	189 : 592	213	U.S.S.R.	201 : 379	89
ASIA	1500 : 3900	160	NORTH AMERICA	185 : 312	69
AFRICA	220 : 517	135	EUROPE	412 : 568	38
OCEANIA	15 : 29.5	97			

Although the United States grew rapidly in population both by immigration and reproduction during the past century, the phenomenal increases in coming decades are anticipated for Latin America, Asia, and Africa. (Courtesy of the United Nations.)

Atlantic states. In the latter region, especially, settlements of Italian, Austrian, Russian, Polish, and Hungarian peoples attained local and broader political influence, while people of Scandinavian origin became dominant in rural sections of the North Central region.

The Irish-American, Polish-American, and other "hyphenated" voting groups have an importance that is still far from negligible. If present trends continue, however, they

will become less significant. Americanization programs and the number of naturalizations should also diminish as the population becomes increasingly homogeneous.

Age and Sex. The American population has also grown older. The median age has increased every decade since 1800 and stands today at 29.1, compared with 16.7 in 1820. Numerically, only 4 per cent of the people were aged sixty or over in 1850 compared with 11.8 per cent in 1950. Moreover, cur-

By 1970 the population of the United States will probably be somewhere between 208 and 214 million. The largest proportionate increase will be in the youngest and oldest groups. The figures include Alaska and Hawaii. The projections take account of 1960 census results. (Data from Department of Commerce, Bureau of the Census.)

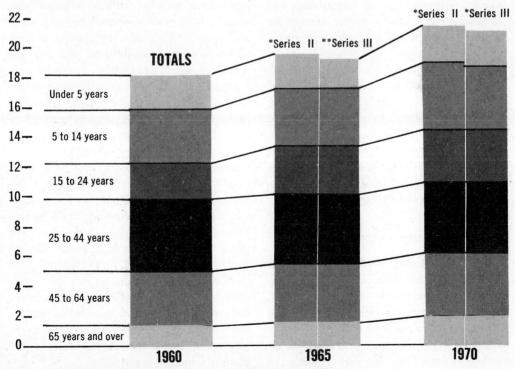

AMERICA'S SHIFTING AGE DISTRIBUTION
1970 estimates based on differing fertility rates

THOUSANDS OF PERSONS

*Series II *Series III

*Series II **Series III

TOTALS

22 —
20 —
18 — Under 5 years
16 —
14 — 5 to 14 years
12 —
       15 to 24 years
10 —
8 —
       25 to 44 years
6 —
4 —
       45 to 64 years
2 —
       65 years and over
0 —

1960   1965   1970

Assumptions of fertility (births per thousand women of childbearing age)
*Series II—1955-1957 level of fertility (approximately same as 1958-60)
          continues to 1965-70
**Series III—1955-57 level declines to 1949-51 level by 1965-70.

rent projections indicate that an increasingly large segment of the American population will be in the older-age brackets. The trend has profoundly affected American politics. The widespread interest in social security is one evidence of this impact.

Men outnumbered women during most of our national history, but 1950 census returns showed this is no longer true. The sex ratio (the number of males per 100 females) dropped from its high of 106.0 in 1910 to 99.2 in 1950. The estimate for 1961 was 97.7. The political consequences of this trend are not clear. Some observers attribute to it greater public interest in education and welfare, more independent voting, and changed campaign techniques.

Legal Distinctions. People now living within the jurisdiction of the United States may be classed as citizens, aliens, and nationals. Citizens are full members of the body politic upon whom rests the primary responsibility of organizing and controlling the nation. Aliens are people who live here but owe permanent allegiance to a foreign country.

The word "national," as commonly used, refers to noncitizens, such as natives of Samoa, who are subject to the jurisdiction of the United States. In a broad sense, the term includes both citizens and noncitizens who owe permanent allegiance to this country. In this latter sense, nationals are entitled to the protection of the American government wherever they may be.

THE NATURAL-BORN CITIZEN

Basic Rules. Modern states use two basic rules to determine citizenship by birth: *jus soli* and *jus sanguinis.* Under the first, citizenship is set by the place of birth. Where *jus sanguinis* is used, the nationality of one's parents and ancestors is the determining factor. The two may conflict, in which case a person is said to possess dual

or multiple nationality. Thus, one born in England of Italian parents is English by *jus soli* and Italian by *jus sanguinis.* Controversies arising from conflicting claims are commonly settled by treaty, otherwise the effective law is that of the country in which the person is located. In practice, states seldom adhere strictly to one principle. They employ both, and such is the case in the United States.

Citizenship Prior to 1868. All colonial charters except William Penn's contained provisions stating that the inhabitants and their children were British subjects. English citizenship was terminated by the Declaration of Independence and passed immediately to the individual colonies. Since the states were admittedly sovereign under the Articles of Confederation, there was no national citizenship; rather, inhabitants were merely citizens of their respective states.

When the Constitution was adopted, persons recognized as citizens in any of the several states became citizens of the United States also. Although recognizing a dual citizenship, the Constitution did not say whether state citizenship depended on United States citizenship or vice versa, but before 1868 the generally accepted view was that United States citizenship, except in cases of naturalization, was subordinate to and derived from state citizenship.

Citizenship Defined. In the Dred Scott case [19 How. 393 (U.S. 1857)], the Supreme Court ruled that neither a state nor the Federal government could confer Federal citizenship upon native-born Negroes, whether slave or free. This, followed by the Civil War, led to the adoption of the Fourteenth Amendment in 1868 which defined citizenship, saying: "All persons born or naturalized in the United States, and subject to the jurisdiction thereof, are citizens of the United States and of the State in which they reside."

Several things should be observed about

this definition: (1) It incorporated the principle of *jus soli*, which had been followed since colonial days. (2) Two methods of acquiring citizenship were acknowledged: birth and naturalization. (3) Only those subject to the jurdisdiction of the United States at the time of birth or naturalization are citizens. (4) Children born anywhere in the United States and subject to its jurisdiction are citizens regardless of laws to the contrary of any particular state. (5) American citizens are also citizens of the state in which they reside.

Citizenship by Birth. Three things must be kept in mind throughout the discussion of rules that follow. One is that the courts have never decided under what circumstances one is a "natural-born" citizen. Another is that some people are citizens at birth because of the Fourteenth Amendment, whereas others are citizens at birth as a result of enactments of Congress.

From the Immigration and Nationality Act of 1952 and innumerable court decisions, the following rules emerge:

One is a citizen by birth if born (1) in the United States and subject to the jurisdiction thereof, or to an Indian, Eskimo, Aleutian, or other aboriginal tribe; (2) in an American outlying possession of parents one of whom is a citizen who has lived in United States territory at least one year; (3) outside the United States of parents (*a*) both of whom are citizens and at least one of whom has resided in the United States or one of its possessions, (*b*) one of whom is a citizen who has resided in the United States at least one year, and the other is a national but not a citizen, or (*c*) one of whom is a citizen, the other alien, if the citizen-parent was in the United States or one of its possessions for ten years, of which five were after attaining the age of fourteen, and provided the child remains in the United States for five years continuously between ages fourteen and

twenty-eight; or (4) in Puerto Rico, the Virgin Islands, Guam, the Canal Zone (if at least one parent is a citizen), and the Republic of Panama (if one parent is a citizen and one is employed by the United States government). One is *not* a citizen by birth (because not subject to United States jurisdiction) if born (1) of foreign sovereigns or diplomatic officials, (2) on foreign public ships in American territorial waters, or (3) of enemies in hostile occupation. Otherwise children born within the United States of alien parents (including those of foreign consular officers) are American citizens, even though the parents are here only temporarily.

Citizenship of Women. Before September 22, 1922, American women who married aliens expatriated themselves. This was true whether the women concerned married or lived in the United States or abroad. On the other hand, alien women, if eligible for naturalization, acquired citizenship by marrying American citizens. Passage of the Cable Act on the date mentioned reversed these provisions. Now American women do not lose citizenship by marriage, nor do alien women acquire citizenship by marriage to Americans. Women who lost citizenship prior to 1922 and alien women who marry Americans may, if eligible for naturalization, be naturalized by a simplified procedure.

THE NATURALIZED CITIZEN

Aliens: Numbers and Status. No cne knows exactly how many aliens are in the United States. The first complete census, made as a consequence of passage of the Alien Registration Act of 1940, disclosed approximately 5 million. Practically all were located in fourteen states, with New York accounting for about one-fourth the total. More recent and comparable figures are unavailable, but the total appears to have

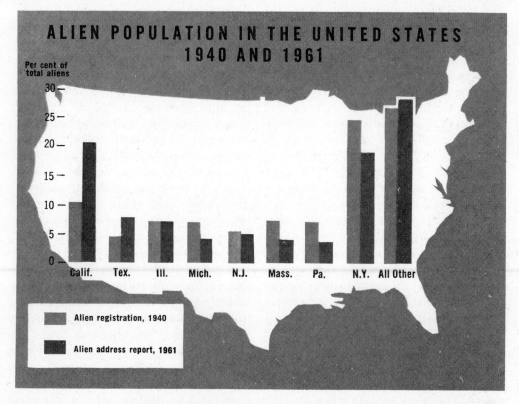

ALIEN POPULATION IN THE UNITED STATES
1940 AND 1961

Per cent of
total aliens

■ Alien registration, 1940

■ Alien address report, 1961

In 1961, about 70 per cent of all aliens reporting resided in the eight states shown.
Note the tendency for aliens to go west to Texas and California. (U.S. Immigration
and Naturalization Service.)

declined. A vigorous alien-address program begun in 1951 by the Immigration and Naturalization Service provides current data. The number of aliens and their distribution among states are shown on the accompanying chart.

Aliens owe temporary allegiance to the country in which they are located and are, therefore, obliged to obey local laws. They must pay taxes that are not discriminatory or confiscatory. They may, with only a few exceptions, own property, engage in business, have access to courts, attend public schools, and use other public facilities. They are generally exempt from jury and military duty. The civil rights guaranteed to citizens by the Constitution extend to aliens

also; the equal-protection clause of the Fourteenth Amendment safeguards them from discriminatory treatment by the states.

Nevertheless, aliens are denied many of the privileges enjoyed by citizens. No state permits them to vote. Most public offices, and many professions, are closed to them. Aliens are frequently denied relief, pensions, workmen's compensation benefits, and employment on public works. Pennsylvania went so far as to forbid aliens to own dogs or firearms, although the ban on dog ownership was repealed in 1957.

Enemy Aliens. When a country goes to war, the nationals of an enemy state who are within its borders present a difficult problem. Before the First World War, nations were more tolerant toward such nationals than now. The general practice was to allow enemy aliens to remain in the country free of special restrictions as long as they did nothing to impede the war effort. Recently, states have shown greater inclination to expel, intern, restrict the activity of, and confiscate the property of enemy aliens.

So far as the United States is concerned, enemy aliens who have established residence are entitled to protection of person and property, but the courts have held that the guaranties of the Fifth and Sixth Amendments, which govern criminal prosecutions, are not applicable to them. During the First World War, enemy aliens were forced to register, were barred from vital zones, and were restricted in what they could say and do. Similar restrictions were imposed during the Second World War; in addition, a large number of enemy aliens were interned. In both wars an Alien Property Custodian seized much enemy-owned property located in the United States. Detailed plans have been laid by the Federal government to deal with enemy aliens in the event of another war.

Control by Federal Law. The term "naturalization" means granting a new nationality to a person. Before the adoption of the Constitution most of the thirteen colonies had naturalization laws which varied widely. Since uniformity is obviously desirable, those who wrote the Constitution inserted a clause giving Congress power "to establish an uniform Rule of Naturalization . . . throughout the United States." The power was first used in 1790; since then naturalization has been controlled exclusively by the Federal government.

Naturalization laws are administered by the Immigration and Naturalization Service in the Department of Justice, although certificates of naturalization are issued by Federal district courts and state courts "having a seal, a clerk, and jurisdiction in actions of law or equity or law and equity, in which the amount in controversy is unlimited." Persons may be naturalized singly upon their own initiative, or collectively by an act of Congress.

The Immigration and Nationality Act of 1952. Because this measure, popularly known as the McCarran-Walter Act, governs most matters related to immigration and nationality, it will be introduced here but explained in detail in pages that follow.

After the Second World War, many refugees and other displaced persons sought entry into the United States. Meanwhile, crises abroad and fears of subversion at home stirred deep feelings in many Americans. Anti-Communist sentiment reached a peak during the Korean "police action," which began in 1950. Developments like these provoked review of immigration and naturalization policies and passage of the McCarran-Walter Act. President Truman vetoed the bill but Congress repassed it. The new law brought into a single statute legislation enacted piecemeal over the years. Leaders of both major political parties have since advocated revisions, but no major changes have been made.

Who May Be Naturalized. The list of qualifications for naturalization has become long. Petitioners must show lawful entry into the country. They must be of good moral character and able to read, write, speak, and understand the English language. They must display knowledge of the history, principles, and form of American government. They must declare their attachment to the principles of American government and say they are disposed to the good order and happiness of the United States. Deserters from the Armed Forces, draft evaders, anarchists, and Communists and other totalitarians are barred. Titles of nobility must be renounced. Enemy aliens cannot be naturalized in wartime. Petitioners must state their attitudes toward bearing arms.

Until recently, religious pacifists were denied the right to naturalize because of their unwillingness to bear arms in defense of the country. In a leading case[*United States v. Schwimmer*, 279 U.S. 644 (1929)], the Supreme Court supported the administrative interpretation that the words "support and defend" in the oath implied the necessity of bearing arms. This stand was reversed, however, in the case of *Girouard v. United States* [328 U.S. 61 (1946)]. Pacifists have since been permitted to naturalize if otherwise qualified. The 1952 Immigration and Nationality Act specifies that an applicant must indicate willingness to bear arms, render noncombatant service in the Armed Forces, or do work of national importance under civilian direction. These options are available only to *religious* objectors, not to those whose pacifism has other bases.

How Individuals Are Naturalized. A declaration of intention, once required, is no longer mandatory. It may be filed, however, by any alien over eighteen who has been lawfully admitted for permanent residence. The first mandatory step is filing a petition. This may be done by any alien of eighteen or more who has resided in the country for five continuous years and in the state where the petition is filed for six months. Then follows investigation, preliminary hearing, and final hearing in open court. The investigation and preliminary hearing are conducted by the Immigration and Naturalization Service; the final hearing is the responsibility of a Federal district court or a state court of record.

The final hearing may be thorough, but usually it is perfunctory, the judge relying upon the recommendations of the officers who conducted the preliminary proceed-

ings. If the judge is satisfied that the petitioner is eligible for naturalization, the oath is administered, a certificate of naturalization is issued, and the alien becomes a full-fledged citizen.

Exceptions to the normal procedure are made for various classes of people. The literacy requirement may be waived for older people. Some of the residence requirement is waived for spouses and children of citizens and aliens with American military service.

Minor children derive American citizenship through the naturalization of their alien parents. Until 1940, children under twenty-one could acquire derivative citizenship; the age was lowered that year to eighteen; in 1952, it was reduced to sixteen.

The President's Commission on Immigration and Naturalization, whose report is referred to at some length below, criticized several features of current procedure. The Commission objected to the reduction of the age of derivative citizenship, the requirement of a neighborhood investigation in every naturalization case, the extended probationary period and tighter residence requirements for spouses of citizens, and the requirement of lawful entry for permanent residence exacted of aliens who are veterans of the American Armed Forces.

Collective Naturalization. At various times large groups of people have been made American citizens by a single legislative enactment. When the Constitution was adopted, all who were citizens of the original states became citizens of the United States. The treaties of acquisition conveyed citizenship to the inhabitants of the territories of Louisiana, Florida, Mexico, and Alaska. In the joint resolution admitting Texas to the Union, American citizenship was substituted for Texan. By special acts Congress collectively naturalized the inhabitants of Hawaii in 1900, of Puerto Rico in 1917, of

Indian tribes in 1924, the Virgin Islands in 1927, and Guam in 1950.

Distinctions between Natural-born and Naturalized Citizens. For the most part, naturalized and natural-born citizens are entitled to the same rights and privileges, but there are several differences. Naturalized citizens may hold any Federal office except that of President or Vice President. Naturalized citizens who seek election to the House of Representatives must have been citizens for seven years, and those who seek election to the Senate must have been citizens for nine years. Natural-born citizens are less in jeopardy of losing citizenship than naturalized, as explained below. Natural-born citizens are entitled to full protection by the American government wherever they may be, but because of claims arising out of dual citizenship, the American government may find it inexpedient to afford full protection to naturalized citizens who return to their native land.

LOSING CITIZENSHIP

American citizenship may be forfeited in three ways: deprivation as punishment for a crime, voluntary expatriation, and denaturalization.

Deprivation of Citizenship. Contrary to a general impression, Federal and state laws do not deprive persons of citizenship for the commission of felonies of all types. State laws frequently deny criminals certain privileges, such as voting, without depriving them of citizenship. Indeed, states could not take away Federal citizenship if they wished to. By Federal law, natural-born citizens are deprived of nationality only for such serious offenses as treason and attempting to overthrow the government by force of arms. For many years desertion from the Armed Forces during wartime was cause for forfeiting citizenship, but in 1958 the Supreme Court ruled this violated the constitutional ban against cruel and unusual punishment (*Trop v. Dulles*, 356 U.S. 86).

Expatriation. Citizenship may be forfeited, however, for a number of reasons unrelated to crimes. One may expatriate, or give up citizenship, by (1) naturalization to a foreign state, taking an oath of allegiance to a foreign state, or by formally renouncing American citizenship before an officer designated by the Attorney General or an American diplomatic or consular officer in a foreign state; (2) voluntary renunciation during wartime if acceptable to the Attorney General; (3) entering or serving in the armed forces of a foreign state; (4) accepting or performing the duties of any office, post, or employment under the government of a foreign state or political subdivision thereof for which only nationals of that state are eligible; (5) voting in a political election in a foreign state or participating in an election or plebiscite to determine the sovereignty over foreign territory; or (6) if a child, by the naturalization of a parent to a foreign state. Several thousand Americans forfeit citizenship annually for one or more of the reasons given. Typically, taking up residence abroad and voting in foreign political elections or plebiscites account for most forfeitures.

Denaturalization. For naturalized citizens the dangers of loss of citizenship are great, especially since passage of the McCarran-Walter Act. For many years the broad formula for revoking citizenship was proof that fraud or illegal means had been used to obtain naturalization. The 1952 act substituted concealment of a material fact or willful misrepresentation.

Under the old formula, citizenship could be revoked for actions that preceded the granting of final papers; the new rule permits revocation for conduct occurring either before or after naturalization. There is no

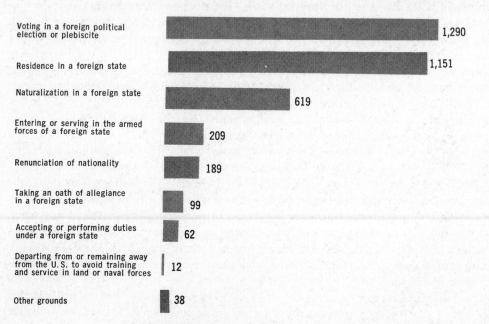

PERSONS EXPATRIATED FROM U.S.
Year Ended June 30, 1961

Voting in a foreign political election or plebiscite	1,290
Residence in a foreign state	1,151
Naturalization in a foreign state	619
Entering or serving in the armed forces of a foreign state	209
Renunciation of nationality	189
Taking an oath of allegiance in a foreign state	99
Accepting or performing duties under a foreign state	62
Departing from or remaining away from the U.S. to avoid training and service in land or naval forces	12
Other grounds	38

Loss of citizenship may result for any one of the reasons stated. Voting in foreign elections and plebiscites and taking up residence in a foreign state account for most expatriations. (U.S. Immigration and Naturalization Service.)

statute of limitations. If it can be proved that a naturalized citizen concealed material facts or made willful misrepresentations in acquiring citizenship, he may be deprived of it years afterwards. If his children acquired citizenship through naturalization of the parent, they, too, will be deprived of citizenship. Cancellation proceedings take place in Federal district courts. Revocation of citizenship may or may not be followed by deportation, depending upon the nature of the offense.

The McCarran-Walter Act made revocation of naturalization compulsory for certain specified conduct. Citizenship is forfeited, for example, if a naturalized person establishes residence in his native land within

three years or establishes it in some other country within five years. It may be revoked if within five years he joins an organization deemed subversive by the Attorney General, or within ten years if he refuses to testify before a congressional committee about alleged subversive activities.

President Truman's Commission on Immigration and Naturalization, reporting in 1953, strongly criticized McCarran-Walter Act changes pertaining to denaturalization. Claiming the new provisions made naturalized persons "second-class citizens," the Commission recommended:

The law should not discriminate against naturalized citizens but should place them in the same status as native-born citizens, except where citizenship was procured by fraud or illegality. The law should minimize or remove restrictions which create statelessness, disrupt family unity, or impose unreasonable conditions or procedures upon the acquisition or retention of citizenship.

The Commission also urged adoption of a statute of limitations that would bar denaturalization unless charges are brought within ten years.

IMMIGRATION

Control Dates Back to Colonial Period. Except for Indians and for most Negroes who came to this country as slaves, or chattels, prior to the Civil War, every person in the United States is either an immigrant or the descendant of one. Restrictive legislation dates from the colonial period, when laws were passed to prevent the entrance of paupers, criminals, and members of certain religious sects, such as Quakers and Catholics.

After the Revolution, the states fell heir to existing restraints but, in general, they added few before 1830. After that date the arrival of increasingly large numbers of immigrants gave rise to new social problems, which led to clamor for more stringent control. Except for a few Federal laws enacted during the period, the states carried the brunt of the burden until 1882. Several states passed laws requiring the bonding of ships' captains as a guaranty that immigrants would not become public charges. They also required payment of a head tax for every immigrant.

State Regulation Unconstitutional. Laws of New York and Massachusetts came before the Supreme Court in the Passenger cases (7 How. 283, 1849) and were declared unconstitutional on the ground that the states were burdening foreign commerce, thus interfering with powers granted exclusively to the Federal government. New

York made two attempts to modify its head-tax legislation but was rebuffed by the Supreme Court on both occasions.

State control of immigration was never entirely satisfactory. Added to questions of constitutionality was the fact that the states were always in competition with one another for desirable immigrants. The confusion that followed New York's failure to

The flow of immigrants to the United States is affected by economic conditions, wars, and—particularly since 1921—restrictive quotas. (U.S. Immigration and Naturalization Service.)

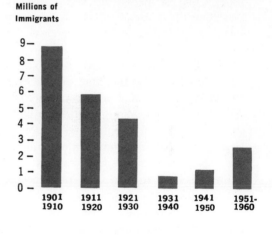

IMMIGRATION
TO THE UNITED STATES
1901- 1961

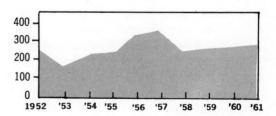

obtain court approval prompted Federal legislation.

Federal Regulation. The first Federal law dealing with immigration was passed in 1819. This measure, the first of a series of so-called "steerage legislation," was designed to prevent the overcrowding of vessels carrying immigrants to American shores. The legislation required captains of all vessels to furnish passenger lists with detailed information about each immigrant. Official immigration statistics date from this enactment.

Later, Federal laws, designed primarily to improve the welfare of immigrants, had the effect of encouraging immigration rather than restricting it as many nativist groups, like the Know Nothing party, demanded. In 1882, Congress passed its first restrictive legislation. This excluded certain "undesirable" classes, including Chinese laborers, for a period of ten years.

One restriction after another was added after 1882 until, by the time of the First World War, there were more than thirty excluded classes. The elimination of "undesirables," coupled with quota control adopted later, greatly curtailed immigration. Indeed, for a brief period the tide was reversed; during the years 1931 to 1936, more people left the country than entered.

The Quota System. At the close of the First World War, a rush of immigrants was expected from European countries. Congress enacted emergency legislation, in 1921, inaugurating a policy of allowing only a certain number of aliens of each nationality to enter annually and granting preference to people who wanted to come from northern and western Europe. Permanent legislation was adopted in 1924, and the quotas that were to prevail until 1953 went into effect in 1929.

Between 1929 and the end of 1952, the law provided that a maximum of 150,000

quota immigrants might enter each year. The total was divided among the various nationalities in proportion to the ratio between their numbers in the census of 1920 and the total population of that year. There were exceptions: no country had a quota of fewer than 100; natives of the Western Hemisphere could enter without quota limits; Orientals were, for the most part, barred.

Supporters of the national-origins quota system maintain that it is an effective method, in that a reasonable quantitative limit is set and that the same kind of people already in the country will enter, thus ensuring assimilation. Opponents charge that the system keeps out desirable immigrants from southern and eastern Europe and Asia, that most of its quotas go unused, and that it is based on untenable theories of racial superiority, economic harmfulness, and personal inferiority.

Figuring the Quota Number. A total of 154,657 quota immigrants per year is authorized by the 1952 act. Each quota area is given an annual quota equal to $\frac{1}{6}$ of 1 per cent of the number of inhabitants from the area who lived in continental United States in 1920; thus the Italian quota, for example, should be $\frac{1}{6}$ of 1 per cent of the number of people of Italian origin in the United States in 1920.

For quota purposes nationality is usually determined by country of birth rather than residence. Thus, if a native of France makes application to immigrate from his present residence in Sweden, he must enter on the French, not the Swedish, quota. This necessitates a point of clearance for each nationality, and for this purpose certain consulates are designated "quota-control offices" by the Department of State. All quota numbers for Frenchmen, for example, are issued by the consulate general in Paris.

QUOTAS VERSUS ADMISSIONS, 1961

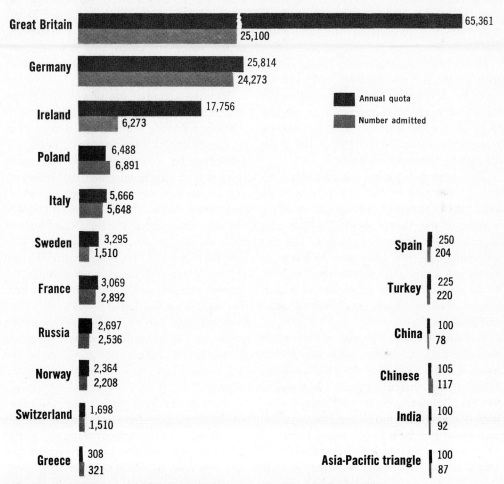

Great Britain — 65,361 / 25,100

Germany — 25,814 / 24,273

Ireland — 17,756 / 6,273

■ Annual quota
■ Number admitted

Poland — 6,488 / 6,891

Italy — 5,666 / 5,648

Sweden — 3,295 / 1,510

Spain — 250 / 204

France — 3,069 / 2,892

Turkey — 225 / 220

Russia — 2,697 / 2,536

China — 100 / 78

Norway — 2,364 / 2,208

Chinese — 105 / 117

Switzerland — 1,698 / 1,510

India — 100 / 92

Greece — 308 / 321

Asia-Pacific triangle — 100 / 87

The annual quotas under the 1952 act assign many more openings for British and Irish immigrants than there are persons applying for admission. Quotas for several other countries, on the other hand, are far below the numbers of desirable applicants. (U.S. Immigration and Naturalization Service.)

Quotas are not cumulative; immigration visas that are not issued during a given year lapse. The ordinary qualified applicant of British or Irish birth can obtain a quota number promptly; applicants of virtually all other nationalities have waiting periods that vary in length. To make matters worse, until recently quotas were "mortgaged" by deductions made for any of several reasons: if a deportation were suspended, if Congress passed a private bill staying a deportation, or if a displaced person were allowed to become a permanent resident. As of December 31, 1955, the Estonian quota was mortgaged until the year 2146, the Greek to 2018, the Latvian to 2275, the Polish to 2000, and the Yugoslavian to 2015. Amendments of 1957 terminated this prohibitive feature.

Under the law, undersubscribed quotas, such as the British or Irish, may not be used by nationals of other countries. In fiscal year 1954, when the desire to migrate from the oversubscribed countries was intense, only about three-fifths of the available quota numbers was used.

The 1952 act further earmarks in each area 50 per cent of the places for persons (and their families) of special training needed in the United States, 30 per cent for parents of American citizens, and the remaining 20 per cent for children or spouses of aliens permanently residing here. If any spots are unused by persons with preference, they are made available to other qualified applicants.

Excluded Classes. The new act continues the exclusion of aliens who are feeble-minded, insane, mentally defective, addicted to drugs or convicted criminals, paupers, and the like. Political grounds for denying visas, both to immigrants and visitors, are expanded and restated to include (1) persons who are believed to be seeking admission to the United States in order to engage in sabotage or to overthrow the government and (2) persons who are or have previously been affiliated with the Communist party or other groups that seek to establish totalitarianism in the United States.

Oriental exclusion is further modified. All nations are assigned at least the minimum quota of 100 per annum, thus removing one of the discriminatory practices that most offended Asian nations. Having conceded this much to international amity, the act then proceeds to nullify much of the good

effect by providing that immigrants of Oriental ancestry, regardless of nationality or place of birth, must be charged to an Oriental quota. Based on national origins in 1920, China has a quota of 105 and Japan of 185. But if a Canadian of Chinese ancestry seeks to enter this country permanently, his quota number is taken from China's meager allotment.

Security screening has proved one of the most difficult parts of the act to administer. The alien seeking a quota visa must answer a questionnaire designed to provide information for a security check. The applicant is then examined under oath concerning his background and is fingerprinted. If the consul has doubt about his admissibility, the case is referred to the Department of State for advice. The quota immigrant who has been issued a visa may be denied entry if the Attorney General finds grounds for barring him. Those denied visas do not have the right to a hearing.

Applicants for visitors' visas and even sailors on foreign ships have been subjected to the safety and security provisions of the act, causing inconvenience and international discord.

Probing the background and the views of the thousands who apply for admission is a difficult and obnoxious task. It invites capriciousness on the part of our officials and reprisals by foreign governments.

Directing Agencies. Responsibility for the administration and enforcement of immigration laws rests primarily with the Secretary of State and the Attorney General.

The Secretary of State discharges most of his responsibilities through the Bureau of Security and Consular Affairs authorized by the 1952 act. This bureau embraces the Passport Office and Visa Office. These, in turn, carry on their work with the aid of American diplomatic and consular officers located at posts abroad.

The Attorney General performs most of his functions in this field through the Immigration and Naturalization Service, which has a staff in all sections of the country and at important ports of entry. A Board of Appeals, established by the Attorney General and responsible to him, reviews appeals from orders and actions of agents of the Immigration and Naturalization Service.

The Public Health Service conducts physical examinations and operates quarantines. The Central Intelligence Agency and the FBI are frequently involved in matters relating to security. The 1952 legislation established a Joint Congressional Committee on Immigration and Nationality Policy, composed of five representatives and five senators. Its task is to review administration of the law and other matters pertaining to immigration and naturalization.

Procedures. Ellis Island and other points of entry used to be scenes of the constant reenactment of that poignant drama: the immigrant who came but was denied admission either because he was not qualified

Over the years there is considerable variation in the principal reasons advanced for excluding aliens, but attempted entry without proper documents tops the list. (U.S. Immigration and Naturalization Service.)

ALIENS EXCLUDED FROM THE UNITED STATES
Year Ended June 30, 1961

Attempted entry without inspection or proper documents ... 634

Subversive or anarchistic ... 21

Stowaways ... 29

Other classes ... 27

Criminals ... 21

Mental or physical defectives ... 7

Immoral classes ... 3

Likely to become public charges ... 1

total 743

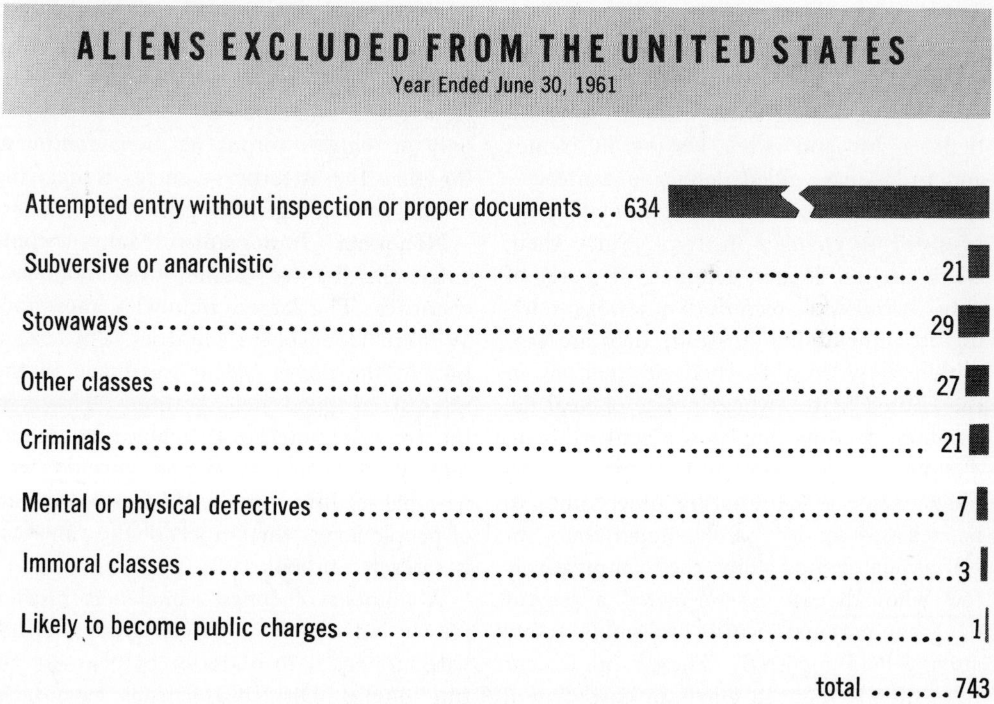

or because his ship arrived too late for him to come within the quota. Much of this was changed by legislation, adopted in 1924, which charged American consuls with primary responsibility for selecting immigrants before they embarked for American shores.

After 1924, the Public Health Service conducted its physical examination while the immigrant was en route or at the port of entry. Travel documents, including passport and visa, were scrutinized by officers of the Immigration and Naturalization Service. Belongings were evaluated by representatives of the Bureau of Customs. If all was in order, the immigrant entered the country. If irregularities were found, he might be detained. Present-day restrictions are so extensive that long investigations often are involved. Until recently, large numbers of immigrants, without constitutional rights and often lacking in friends and funds, have filled detention centers.

Widespread protests of inhuman practices led to changes in 1954. Since then, aliens are no longer detained at ports of entry because of technical questions relating to admissibility. Instead, they are permitted to proceed to their destinations in the United States, where notice of final decision on pending questions is sent to them. The new policy also permits aliens awaiting the outcome of deportation proceedings to be released under parole, supervision, or conditional bond. Only the comparatively few whose release is considered a present danger to national security and public safety are now held in custody. These more lenient rules sharply reduced aliens in custody and permitted the closing of Ellis Island and several other large seaport detention centers.

A detained alien whose right to enter is questioned may plead his case before a special hearing officer. Appeals from exclusion orders may be taken to the Board of Im-

migration Appeals. In exceptional cases the Attorney General may review decisions of the Board.

Controversy over Fairness of Procedures. Much controversy has arisen over whether hearing officers should be bound by the Administrative Procedures Act. This law imposes standards of fairness in hearings and quasi-judicial proceedings of most Federal agencies. To require the same standards of immigration officials, many contend, necessitates large staffs, causes delays, and invites tedious legal controversies by people who are exercising a privilege, and not a right, to emigrate to American shores.

The 1952 act improved procedures somewhat, but exempted the Immigration and Naturalization Service from the Administrative Procedures Act, thus lowering standards of fairness for the alien. Court review for immigrants detained is possible only on habeas corpus petition, complaining that the Attorney General is delaying unduly in holding hearings.

Nonquota Immigrants. Many people enter the United States from nonquota countries. The largest number comes from Western Hemisphere countries. This exception to the quota system was made in the interest of good neighborliness. However, the 1952 act imposes so many rules in the interest of health, economic solvency, and national security that the old free movement of people across the borders of the Americas is severely curbed.

A number of congressional acts provide for the admission of special groups, either without regard to quota or by charging future quotas. Displaced persons have been given special quotas and consideration. Families of citizens of the United States may become nonquota immigrants. Fiancées of veterans were permitted to enter and to remain in this country after their marriages. Special provision was made for admission of skilled sheepherders and for informers from behind the Iron Curtain. Certain aliens who enlist in the American Armed Forces overseas are entitled to enter without quotas. Finally, Congress has been flooded with private bills to waive immigration laws for particularly worthy individuals.

Refugees and Displaced Persons. Since the Second World War, the American government has been swamped by appeals to admit greater numbers of Europe's refugees and displaced people. Additional quotas were needed, as well as financial assistance and liberalized rules. After bitter controversies, Congress made concessions.

Thousands came in under the liberalized rules. The majority were natives of Poland, Germany, and Italy. Many were close relatives of persons admitted under regular quotas. Many were children; some, orphans for whom adoptions were arranged. Some had fled from behind the Iron Curtain. Generous aspects were offset by restrictions requiring passports or other valid travel documents, security investigations and clearances, promises of jobs that would not displace American workmen, and funds enough to prevent applicants from becoming public charges. Restrictive features, coupled with conservative administration, caused many fewer to enter than the law permitted.

Deportation. Aliens are deportable if they are found to have entered the country illegally or to have become members of excluded classes. Deportation is a responsibility of the Immigration and Naturalization Service and the Attorney General.

Legally a deportation order is a civil rather than a criminal procedure; practically it can be an extremely severe penalty. Deporting aliens as punishment for misconduct began as early as 1910 and has been extended steadily, especially by the Immigration and Nationality Act of 1952. The citizen who commits a serious crime may be imprisoned the stipulated length of time; the alien found guilty of the same crime may be imprisoned for the same term and, in addition, may be banished from the United States for life. An offense may be trivial. An offender may have been brought to this country at two months of age and know nothing of the country of his birth. A crime may have been committed and punished many years ago, yet under the retroactive features of the 1952 act, record of it can be the basis for a deportation order now. The law even provides for deportation in case an alien willfully fails to report his current address.

Subversive activities or affiliations are also grounds for deportation. Aliens who are members of the Communist party, and perhaps of other groups, and aliens who entered the country without recording former subversive connections may be deported forthwith. Former Communists may be able to obtain suspension of deportation if membership was involuntary, occurred when the alien was under sixteen years of age, or if membership terminated at least five years ago and the alien has since actively opposed subversive ideologies.

Aliens found deportable have four remedies available to them. First, if not criminal, immoral, or subversive, they may leave voluntarily, without expense to the United States and the stigma of a warrant that would prevent subsequent reentry. Second, they may adjust their status from temporary or irregular to permanent. Before the 1952 act this could be accomplished by preexamination and a brief trip to Canada to pick up a quota number; under the new act, status may be changed by a complicated process available to rather few aliens. Third, deportation may be suspended in cases of "extremely unusual hardship," to quote the words of the 1952 law. Fourth, special acts of Congress may grant relief to particular individuals. The large volume of such private bills is evidence that something is wrong with the general law.

Of those deported under warrant, the principal offenses are irregular entry and disobedience of the rules governing nonimmigrant status. The greatest number are returned to Mexico and Canada, from which illegal entry is comparatively easy. Those arrested and ejected may never reenter the country save on the Attorney General's intervention.

Before an alien can be deported, his native land, or some other nation, must agree to accept him. Some nations are unwilling to accept people who left years ago and have gotten into trouble. Formerly an alien deported within five years of immigration was returned at the expense of the steamship company that brought him; under the 1952 act, the company pays only if it is negligent.

The Wetback Problem. The term "wetback" is commonly used to describe any illegal immigrant from Mexico to the United States; originally it was one who forded the Rio Grande into Texas. The magnitude of the problem is indicated by the fact that during the peak year of 1953 a total of 840,000 wetbacks were apprehended and deported. Wetbacks are attracted by the higher rates of pay and the considerable demand for farm labor in the Southwest. Crossing the border is accomplished easily, frequently with the help of smugglers and "fixers" who supply cheap labor to cooperating employers. Once in the United States, the illegal entrant is difficult to distinguish from the Mexican-American who is domiciled here, or from the Mexican national who is here legally. Serious complaints are made that the illegal entrant brings disease into the country, increases the crime rate, and undermines wage and working standards.

By far the largest number of deportation and voluntary departures are wetbacks who have crossed the border without permit, are apprehended, and returned to Mexico. (U.S. Immigration and Naturalization Service.)

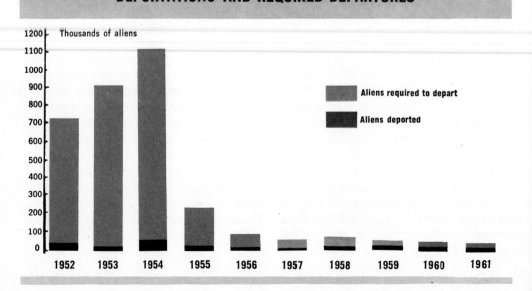

DEPORTATIONS AND REQUIRED DEPARTURES

Thousands of aliens

Aliens required to depart

Aliens deported

1952 1953 1954 1955 1956 1957 1958 1959 1960 1961

The United States has attempted to solve the problem by adding enforcement personnel, improving enforcement techniques, cracking down on smugglers and fixers, establishing more ports of entry, and enlisting the co-operation of the Mexican Government, employers, labor unions, states, and communities most concerned. Current figures indicate that considerable progress has been made.

Whom We Shall Welcome. President Truman's Commission on Immigration and Naturalization, previously mentioned, was critical of American policy in general and the McCarran-Walter Act in particular. In its report *Whom We Shall Welcome*, the Commission concluded that the immigration and nationality law was unwise and injurious to the nation and should be "reconsidered and revised from beginning to end."

More specifically the Commission charged the legislation (1) rested upon an attitude of hostility and distrust against all aliens; (2) discriminated on account of national origin, race, creed, and color; (3) ignored the needs of the nation in domestic affairs and foreign policies; (4) continued unnecessary and unreasonable restrictions and penalties; and (5) was badly drafted, confusing, and in some respects unworkable.

The recommendations made by the Commission were too numerous and detailed to recite fully here. A few of the more important ones relating to immigration were: (1) Abolish the national-origins quota system and substitute a unified quota system which would allocate visas without regard to national origin, race, creed, or color. (2) Calculate the maximum annual quota at $\frac{1}{6}$ of 1 per cent of the latest census rather than the population of 1920. Thus, with 1950 as a base, the annual quota would be raised to 251,162 from the earlier 154,857. (3) Place all immigration and nationality functions in a new independent Commission on Immigration and Naturalization whose members would be appointed by the President and confirmed by the Senate. (4) Permit appeals from consular denial of visas, bring deportation under the Administrative Procedures Act, and generally revise procedures to ensure greater fairness. (5) Bar deportation (as well as denaturalization) unless charges are brought within ten years. (6) Modify provisions that bar or deter scholars, scientists, and other distinguished foreigners from visiting the United States. (7) Relax rules that ban people because of past or involuntary memberships or who have repudiated and now oppose totalitarian ideologies.

It is now possible to appeal visa denials to the Department of State. The bars have been lowered somewhat for distinguished visitors and involuntary members of the Communist Party. Congress has been unwilling, however, to undertake general revision of the McCarran-Walter Act. In a recent message to Congress recommending detailed changes, President Eisenhower said "In the world of today our immigration laws badly need revision."

FOR FURTHER READING

Auerbach, F. L.: *Immigration Laws of the United States* (Indianapolis: Bobbs-Merrill, 1955).

Bernard, William S. (ed.): *American Immigration Policy: A Reappraisal* (New York: Harper, 1950).

Clark, Jane Perry: *The Deportation of Aliens from the United States to Europe* (New York: Columbia University Press, 1931).

Divine, Robert A.: *American Immigration Policy, 1924–1952* (New Haven, Conn.: Yale University Press, 1957).

Fishel, Wesley R.: *The End of Extraterritoriality*

in China (Berkeley, and Los Angeles, Calif.: University of California Press, 1952).

Gettys, Cora Luella: *The Law of Citizenship in the United States* (Chicago: University of Chicago Press, 1934).

Handlin, Oscar: *Race and Nationality in American Life* (Boston: Little, Brown, 1957).

Higham, John: *Strangers in the Land: Patterns of American Nativism, 1860–1925* (New Brunswick, N.J.: Rutgers University Press, 1955).

Hartman, Edward G.: *The Movement to Americanize the Immigrant* (New York: Columbia University Press, 1948).

Holcombe, Arthur N.: *The More Perfect Union* (Cambridge, Mass.: Harvard University Press, 1950).

————: *The Middle Class in American Politics* (Cambridge, Mass.: Harvard University Press, 1940).

"Immigration," *Law and Contemporary Problems* (Durham, N.C.: Duke University, School of Law, Spring, 1956).

Jones, Maldwyn Allen: *American Immigration* (Chicago: University of Chicago Press, 1961).

Kansas, Sidney: *U.S. Immigration, Exclusion and Deportation, and Citizenship* (Albany, N.Y.: Bender, rev. ed., 1940).

Konvitz, Milton R.: *The Alien and the Asiatic in American Law* (Ithaca, N.Y.: Cornell University Press, 1946).

————: *Civil Rights in Immigration* (Ithaca, N.Y.: Cornell University Press, 1953).

Kuznets, S. S., and E. Rubin: *Immigration and the Foreign Born* (New York: National Bureau of Economic Research, 1954).

Lowenstein, Edith (comp.): *The Alien and the Immigration Law* (New York: Oceana Publications, 1957).

Myrdal, Gunnar: *Population, a Problem for Democracy* (Cambridge, Mass.: Harvard University Press, 1940).

Nielson, H. C.: *Population Trends in the United States through 1975* (Stanford, Calif.: Stanford Research Institute, rev. ed., 1957).

Seckler-Hudson, Catheryn: *Statelessness: With Special Reference to the United States* (Washington, D.C.: Digest Press, 1934).

Sellin, Henry (ed.): *Practice and Procedure under the Immigration and Nationality Act (McCarran-Walter Act)* (New York: Oceana Publications and New York University Press, 1954).

Silving, Helen: *Immigration Laws of the United States* (New York: Oceana Publications, 1948).

U.S. President's Commission on Immigration and Naturalization: *Whom We Shall Welcome, Report of the . . .* (1953).

U.S. President's Commission on Migratory Labor: *Migratory Labor in American Agriculture, Report of the . . .* (1951).

Wittke, Carl F.: *We Who Built America* (Cleveland: Western Reserve University Press, 1951).

REVIEW QUESTIONS

1. What are some of the political implications of population trends in the United States?

2. What is the constitutional basis of Federal regulation of immigration? What role may the states play in dealing with this subject?

3. Defend and criticize the restrictions that Congress has placed upon immigration.

4. How are immigration quotas determined for each nationality? How does the process differ since passage of the Immigration and Nationality Act of 1952?

5. What changes have been suggested for making fairer the procedures followed in admitting, debarring, and deporting aliens?

6. Defend and criticize provisions made in recent years for facilitating the emigration of displaced persons to the United States.

7. Compare the rights and privileges of resident aliens and citizens; of naturalized and natural-born citizens.

8. Summarize recommendations made by President Truman's Commission on Immigration and Naturalization as reported in *Whom We Shall Welcome*.

9. Distinguish between the rule of *jus soli* and *jus sanguinis*. What is meant when it is said that a person has dual nationality?

10. Explain the rules that govern the determination of United States citizenship and illustrate each.

11. Explain to an alien the qualifications for naturalization and the steps he would have to take to become a citizen of the United States.

12. How, and for what reasons, may one forfeit citizenship or have it revoked?

Public Opinion and Pressure Groups

All governments, even the most despotic, depend, in a great degree, on opinion. In free republics, it is most peculiarly the case. In these, the will of the people makes the essential principle of the government; and the laws which control the community receive their tone and spirit from the public wishes. It is the fortunate situation of our country, that the minds of the people are exceedingly enlightened and refined.

ALEXANDER HAMILTON[1]

Distress always makes discontent, and men who are in trouble turn with interest and hope to every proposed remedy. It is our duty to treat their views with respect, for, while their theories may be false, their sufferings are real. It is well that we are taught by popular agitation the existence of evils. It is necessary for those who have charge of public affairs to learn what men have in their minds, what views they hold, at what ends they aim. . . . The follies of fanatics frequently teach wisdom better than the words of the wise.

HORATIO SEYMOUR[2]

In its broadest sense, "politics" means the relationship of the governor and the governed in every type of situation and institution involving people, in the state, in industry, a lodge, a club, a church, or a union.[3] The student of government, however limits his concern primarily to the politics of the state. He studies how groups and individuals attempt to control offices and policies of government. Only incidentally is he concerned with how the Reverend Novice was selected moderator of

[1] Speech in the New York State Ratification Convention, June 20, 1788. Quoted in Saul K. Padover, *The Mind of Alexander Hamilton* (New York: Harper, 1958), p. 142.

[2] "The Government of the United States," *North American Review* (November–December, 1878), pp. 360–361.

[3] Harold D. Lasswell, in his *Politics: Who Gets What, When, How* (New York: McGraw-Hill, 1936), p. 1, declared: "The study of politics is the study of influence and the influential."

169

the presbytery or how John L. Lewis managed to rule the United Mine Workers so long. If the church starts a campaign to prohibit pinball games in taverns, or if the union contributes $100,000 to a political fund, the political scientist takes special interest.

Even within the field of political science, the word "politics" has more than one meaning. Sometimes it designates the entire art and science of government and is nearly synonymous with political science. More commonly, the term indicates a subdivision of political science that includes public opinion, pressure groups, political parties, nominations and elections, legislation, and kindred matters. The other great division of political science comparable to politics is *administration*. Politics is policy formation; administration is policy execution. The loose and popular usage of "politics" to imply invidious manipulation and selfish spoils seeking has debased a word of lofty origin. The word "politics" should be reserved to describe the citizen's role in making public policy.

As employed in the next three chapters, politics embraces the entire process of public policy. At about the turn of the century, attention focused on the importance of political parties and their operation. In the 1920s came a fad of emphasizing the pressure group in the role of policy maker. Later, students of politics became intrigued with a new field called "public opinion," which includes some social psychology, propaganda and censorship, opinion measurement, and channels of communication. Each aspect will be discussed in succeeding sections.

PUBLIC OPINION

The Democratic Political Process. The process of public policy making in free countries involves several distinct steps. Individual opinion is the root. Si Perkins's opinion on the tariff is determined by many factors, including emotions, drives, intelligence, and environment. Emotions, motivations, and needs are classified variously by different psychologists. Lists of driving human forces normally include fear, sex, companionship, status, security, and others. Environment influences the formation of the individual opinion; especially important are economic status, social standing, family situation, religious connections, and the like. The individual forms his attitudes within the framework of his impulses, his environment, and his mental abilities. Groups and persons with preconceived notions press the individual to accept their point of view on a subject.

Next, individuals of similar opinions unite to promote and defend their interests. The groups they form—leagues, unions, associations, clubs, institutes, chambers—disseminate propaganda about their cause to influence individuals, other groups, political parties, and public officials. Groups also employ all the techniques of pressure commonly called "lobbying."

Third is the role of the political party. Parties form their policy declarations, or platforms, from the opinions of individuals, often as crystallized by groups. In a two-party system, party platforms are somewhat general, for they represent compromises between diverse points of view. An American party rarely places a plank in its platform until the policy it represents is widely accepted. Parties act in the field of public policy formation as canalizers; taking the lesser streams of group opinion, they merge them into a mighty river. The original character of each contributing stream is thus diluted.

Finally, public policy is formed by those who hold governmental power—executive,

POLICY FORMATION IN A DEMOCRACY

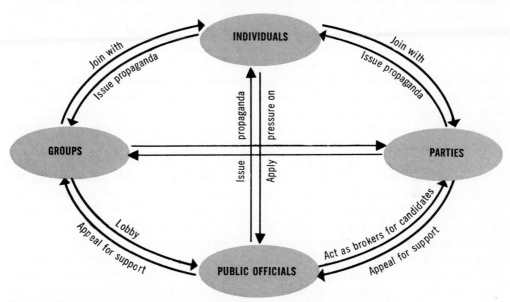

In the political process, the interaction of individuals, groups, parties, and public officials is extremely complicated.

legislative, and judicial. Presidents and governors, legislatures and congresses, perhaps even courts, draw the policies they make public (through orders, laws, decisions) from the three major sources of opinion: individual, group, and party. A President with wide public support may initiate "pet" projects conceived in his own mind or in those of influential advisers. Group pressure may result in congressional action for benefits, regardless of party lines and party platforms. When party discipline is strong, the party may play the major role in the declaration of public policy.

Meaning of Public Opinion. The term "public opinion" is vague. Like many other terms used in politics ("liberal," "reasonable," "sound," "efficient"), it means different things to different people. As

popularly employed, public opinion brings to mind an invisible force, mighty and mysterious, an unseen hand that guides democracies along the paths of righteousness. Used here, it means a belief, judgment, or conclusion on a particular issue shared by a considerable section of the community, usually enough to influence policy. One of the pioneer public relations counselors has called it "an ill-defined, mercurial and changeable group of individual judgments."[1] Public opinion is, then, an aggregate of individual beliefs.

What of the inclusiveness of the word

[1] Edward L. Bernays, *Crystallizing Public Opinion* (New York: Liveright, 1923), p. 61. For recent comment of high quality, see Avery Leiserson, "Notes on the Theory of Political Opinion Formation," *American Political Science Review*, vol. 47 (March, 1953), pp. 171–177.

"public"? Does it mean the whole population? Does it mean only qualified voters? Could the whole population participate in public-policy making? For practical purposes the *public* is that sector of the population which can make a decision on the public question at hand.

Manifestations of Public Opinion. Can one say with finality that public opinion is thus and so on any issue? There are several indexes of value, but each usually may be interpreted in different ways. A careful study of two or more indexes may lead to a valid conclusion regarding an issue.

First, *election returns* show public sentiment, seldom on a single issue, but rather on an aggregate of issues and candidates. A successful candidate will look upon his election as a mandate to follow a certain policy in respect to public problem No. 1, but his personality, his stand on other issues, or his party affiliation might have decided the election results. Rarely does one issue loom so large in a campaign that the verdict is a referendum on that question.

Second, *public referendums* and plebiscites may provide good evidence of the popular attitude on a given subject. Referendums are used in states permitting direct legislation and popular ratification of state constitutional amendments; they are also common in local governmental affairs. But they are not very widely used and lack intelligent participation by the voters. Citizens' inertia or incapacity keep them from tackling complicated propositions.

Third, *lobbying and pressure* sometimes are mistaken for expressions of public opinion. All legislators and many administrators are high-pressured by individuals and groups on every important issue. How can public officials ignore such pressure when

deciding questions of policy? Often the pressure comes from a very small minority. The legislator who determines his stand by counting the telegrams and letters he receives on a question may find himself with the minority so far as real public opinion is concerned. With lobbying and pressure should be classed newspaper editorials and other types of private opinion, publicly expressed. No editor, however gifted or conceited, can claim to express the true voice of the people unerringly.

Fourth, *straw votes,* based on scientific sampling of a cross section of the population, have emerged as reasonably accurate instruments of opinion measurement. Perhaps too much has been claimed for the public-opinion polls, but they do indicate which way the wind of public sentiment is blowing.

Public-opinion Polls. The sampling of public opinion has been attempted for 50 years.[1] The earliest straw votes were conducted by newspapers. Because many polls involved the printing of ballots in the sponsoring journals or handing them out on a very free basis, the results were likely to be highly inaccurate. Later, other publications, notably the *Literary Digest,* undertook nationwide polls of popular sentiment through mail ballots. Although this method proved more accurate than the ballot-in-the-paper scheme, it was not possible to ensure a representative sample or cross section of the people.

During the 1930s, "scientific" quota sampling developed. This method requires a personal interview with great care to ensure the representativeness of the sample. To secure an accurate cross section of the population, the poll taker must obtain the

[1] Claude E. Robinson, *Straw Votes: A Study in Political Prediction* (New York: Columbia University Press, 1932), pp. 47–52.

proper proportion of persons from each state, sex, age group, income class, political party, and occupation. A thoroughly representative sample may be a very small fraction of the whole population. However, error lurks in the natural tendency of the interviewer to approach the most available and articulate among the groups and categories assigned.

Polling methods have changed gradually from straight quota sampling toward probability sampling. The probability, or "pinpoint," method involves choosing barometer precincts or other small districts at random. The interviews are clustered in the adjoining houses, beginning with an assigned starting address. Interviewers call at every nth dwelling unit and maintain age and sex ratios by a rotation plan. Both Gallup and Roper have moved toward probability sampling and have been well satisfied with results obtained. Among the advantages of the newer method for election forecasting are the more systematic selection of neighborhoods for interviewing, the availability of past election returns to judge the political representativeness of the sample, and the possibility of checking an interviewer's results against actual voting figures after the election.[1]

The two best-known polls are the American Institute of Public Opinion, headed by Dr. George Gallup, and the Roper Survey, conducted by Elmo Roper. Both were founded in the mid-1930s. The Gallup poll is conducted from Princeton, New Jersey, and results are sold to subscribing newspapers. Roper's operations stem from a New York headquarters; his clients in 1960 included the Columbia Broadcasting System. Gallup and Roper sample national opinion

[1] George Gallup, "The Future Direction of Election Polling," *Public Opinion Quarterly*, vol. 17 (September, 1953), pp. 202–207.

through 1,500 to 3,000 interviews.

Recently there has been interest in the polling methods of Samuel Lubell, who relies mainly on "depth interviews" conducted by himself. He concentrates on local areas selected for their past voting behavior, and undertakes to record and interpret any swing in sentiment.

Several noncommercial agencies are making substantial contributions to opinion research. The Survey Research Center of the University of Michigan since 1948 has issued a series of books and monographs that provides the best insight available on the American electorate. The Roper Public Opinion Research Center at Williams College, established in 1957, collects and classifies opinion data from polling organizations around the world.

Election Predictions. By far the most dramatic of the tests applied to public-opinion polls is that of predicting election results. The *Literary Digest* poll flourished under the spell of its success in calling the elections of the 1920s and perished after its colossal failure in the 1936 election. Its failure was due mainly to the reliance placed upon securing expressions of opinion by mail from automobile owners and telephone subscribers.

Until 1948, Roper appeared to demonstrate an uncanny ability to predict popular votes in national elections, but in the 1948 presidential election he underestimated the Truman vote by more than 10 per cent. Gallup underrated the Democratic vote at four elections, actually missing by a wider margin in 1936 than in 1948.

Several reasons have been offered to explain the 1948 debacle of the pollsters. Critics declare that the polls consistently have misjudged the opinions of lower-income groups, because such people are tense, insecure, and suspicious of college-trained interviewers. Most of the polls completed their sampling weeks before the election and therefore could not tally last-minute changes in opinions. After the 1948 election, Gallup and Roper looked back over their records and found an unusually high proportion of their interviewees had answered "undecided." In 1952 and after, the polls improved their techniques and interpreted results with great caution.

The significance of the opinion poll is being debated hotly. Enthusiasts claim that polling has opened a new era of democracy in which the masses will become articulate and representatives will hear the authentic voice of the people. Enemies of straw voting claim that polling in advance of an election has a band-wagon effect on voters, who drop their own convictions and vote on what they believe to be the winning side. Critics have expressed fear that the polls might be rigged to show desired results, but they have been answered effectively with the argument that a successful business concern or journal will not risk its reputation lightly. Students of opinion measurement have worked out new techniques for rectifying errors. In general, they conclude that the modern opinion poll is a useful device of democracy but is neither panacea nor taps for our institutions.

Propaganda. In a broad sense, propaganda is the "technique of influencing human action by manipulation of representations."[1] It is effort directed to secure public support for an opinion or a policy; it is special pleading or arguing for one's own convictions. Usage in English has added an invidious connotation, narrowing the scope of meaning. Now the term means special pleading rigged to conceal something or to state the case in overdrawn

terms. Americans describe the arguments of opponents as propaganda and their own pleadings as merely stating the case or presenting the facts. Since few, if any, proponents of an idea present their arguments in a wholly impartial manner, it is well to adhere to a broad definition of the term. Therefore, the terms "propaganda," "special pleading," and "publicity" will be used as meaning much the same thing.

Several years ago, the Institute for Propaganda Analysis issued regular bulletins reviewing various aspects of the propaganda question. A prerequisite of these studies was a classification of propaganda devices that appeared in one of the initial issues.[2] Seven common propaganda devices were isolated: (1) name calling, (2) glittering generalities, (3) transfer, (4) testimonial, (5) plain folks, (6) card stacking, and (7) band wagon.

Name calling is used as a substitute for arguing; bad names like "red" or "fascist" are assigned to opponents, and the core of a controversy need never be reached. To employ glittering generalities or prove a point with a single instance, you devour an adversary with sweeping generalization, such as: "John is a trade unionist and a socialist; therefore all unionists are socialists." "Transfer" means that an existing confidence in something is carried over to the propagandist's cause; thus every political movement calls itself "100 per cent American." The use of testimonials is common in both advertising and politics; the opinion of a person is used to give prestige to a commodity or a candidate. Plain-folks appeal aims to win confidence by plain, homey doings; for example, the office seeker poses with his family or dons overalls and tries to act like a farmer. Card stacking includes

---

[1] Harold D. Lasswell, "Propaganda," *Encyclopedia of the Social Sciences*, vol. 12, p. 521.

[2] *Propaganda Analysis*, vol. 1, no. 2 (November, 1937).

"You Know The Old Saying—No News Is Good News"

WHAT'S GOOD FOR THE ADMINISTRATION IS GOOD FOR THE COUNTRY

PRESS

U.S. GOVT. NOT-TOO-MUCH PUBLIC INFORMATION SECTION

HERBLOCK
©1955 THE WASHINGTON POST Co.

Herblock's view of government agencies that deny access to information of interest to the public. [From *Herblock's Here and Now* (Simon and Schuster).]

any sort of fact juggling or falsification. A band-wagon appeal is an appeal to join the crowd, for "everyone's doing it."

The institute's classification is interesting and useful, but it is not complete, nor is each device mutually exclusive. It leaves out repetition, often called a leading weapon in word warfare. Hitler said:[1]

The masses, however, with their inertia, always need a certain time before they are ready even to notice a thing and they will lend their memories only to the thousand-fold repetition of the most simple ideas.

The need for simplicity is stressed over and over in Hitler's writings; simple ideas must be repeated until the least intelligent

[1] Adolf Hitler, *Mein Kampf* (New York: Reynal & Hitchcock, 1940), p. 239.

can understand or believe. The appeal, therefore, is mainly on the emotional plane. Other rules of propaganda include never admitting virtue on the other side, using the spectacular to attract attention, and avoiding arguments.

Censorship. Propaganda may be made more effective by the simultaneous use of censorship. Censorship is the suppression of facts or opinions that might undermine the existing order or authorities. In peacetime we have a mild form of censorship, in that lewd and immoral publications are denied transit and sale. Also, some states make criminal the utterance of revolutionary sentiments advocating the overthrow of government by force.

Wartime censorship is more extensive; in general, it forbids the publication of any matter that may aid the enemy or handicap the nation's war effort. This is a very broad control. Specific regulation comes from agencies set up for the purpose. During the First World War, both propaganda and censorship were handled by George Creel's Committee on Public Information. During the Second World War, after some preliminary organizing and reorganizing, censorship was assigned to the Office of Censorship, headed by Byron Price. The Office of War Information, directed by Elmer Davis, handled the affirmative publicity task.

Even in wartime, censorship in the United States has been largely of the so-called voluntary type. Newspapers and radio stations were given lists of matters best left unpublicized. A question of whether a certain event should be hushed up might be referred to the appropriate governmental agency for a reply.

Censorship at the source is one of the most potent methods known. If the Armed Forces refuse to give out data on some military action of importance, newsmen must wait until a communique is issued. Many foreign governments close up sources of information and leave correspondents with no news to report. American reporters abroad have developed ingenious methods of evading censorship imposed by foreign governments. Despite censorship at the source, they often manage to eke information out of reluctant officials. If one mode of communication is censored and another is not, the free channel is used; in the 1930s stories were telephoned out of Germany with little restraint, while the same information was forbidden by telegraph and radio. American press and radio-network correspondents frequently are withdrawn from censorship countries and assigned to free ones, from which they write on what really goes on inside the censored country.

An intelligent student of public affairs can keep himself rather well informed regardless of censorship. Libel laws deter the publication or broadcast of some stories originating in this country, but chiefly those of doubtful validity or concerning which there is no conclusive factual proof. Circulation of some books and magazines is halted occasionally by local authorities and by the Post Office Department, but cases of injustice are few. The reader or listener must note the sources of his information and the nature of the channel through which he receives it. His suspicions should be aroused by a sensational story about one country date-lined from another country. The regular press services, especially Associated Press and United Press International, have good reputations, and credence in their dispatches usually is justified; some other services and "special correspondents" frequently slant the news to fit the prejudices of their owners and masters. Radio and television stations are licensed by the Federal Communications Commission and are restrained by the necessity of securing periodic renewal of licenses.

Channels of Communication. Public opinion is influenced actively through the dissemination of information—called propaganda or education, depending on one's prejudices—and by a great number of other forces as well. Various mediums influence opinion. Nearly all social institutions, such as the family, the school, the church, and the club, influence thinking on public questions. All of us acquire opinions from friends and associates, teachers, preachers, lecturers, debaters, novelists, and playwrights. The average person daily adopts points of view or information from newspapers, radio, television, motion pictures, magazines, pamphlets, and other instruments of distributing intelligence.

The Newspaper. The newspaper often is designated as the most potent molder of public opinion in the mass. Newspapers of some sort reach a majority of homes in the United States regularly. In the early 1960's around 12,000 newspapers were published in the United States. Of these, about 2,000 were dailies, with an aggregate circulation of around 50,000,000.[1]

Since newspapers are widely read and, in some cases at least, highly influential, their ownership and policies are matters of vital public interest. Most newspapers are money-making enterprises, conducted mainly for the profit of their owners. To make a profit, a newspaper must build up a circulation, and, intimately connected with that, get advertising. Although the greater income derives from advertising, the newspaper must maintain its circulation at a high level to attract advertisers.

With a few exceptions, the political policy of a newspaper is determined by the opinions of the owner or owners. However, a paper's policy may be influenced by the beliefs and sentiments of both readers and advertisers. Reader censorship often is underestimated; newspaper buyers effectively modify policies by going on strike—refusing to buy or to resubscribe because of disagreement with editorial policy. Pressure by advertisers is frequently overstressed; it is likely to be a subtle restraining or accelerating force, but one unlikely to manifest itself in the crude form of direct threats by advertisers.

Many evils of the newspaper world are blamed on the tendency toward concentrating ownership in fewer hands. News tends to be standardized; the editorial prejudices of one man may be presented to millions daily. A crisis concentrates extra power in those who control chains of newspapers. The outstanding example of multiple newspaper control in America was found in the vast interests of the late William Randolph Hearst. At one time, Hearst controlled twenty-nine daily newspapers in eighteen large cities; in three cities Hearst papers had more than one-half of all daily circulation; in three others they approached one-half.[2] To survive recurring financial crises, Hearst interests have liquidated and consolidated some less profitable holdings. Some eleven papers remain in the chain, but its news and feature services are used by others. Scripps-Howard papers, numbering eighteen, rank close to the Hearst group in national influence. Less policy-oriented, and expanding while the older chains contract, are the Newhouse papers, of which there are nineteen dailies in fourteen cities. Daily newspaper circulation is not growing proportionately to population, a fact which is often attributed to higher costs of production and tougher competition for advertising.

The observing reader will find that a large proportion of the nonlocal dispatches in the average newspaper comes from one of the great wire services. Few newspapers can afford to keep a staff of reporters at the diverse spots in the world from which news may originate. Nearly all dailies and many papers issued less frequently subscribe to one or more of the great news services. The Associated Press (AP) is a cooperative news-gathering agency owned by the newspapers it serves; it maintains bureaus at strategic points throughout the world but relies mainly on member newspapers for local news. The United Press International (UPI) is a private agency that sells its services on contract with newspapers, especially afternoon publications. It maintains its own staff which collects news and wires it to clients.

Both AP and UPI present the news in an

---

[1] *Directory of Newspapers and Periodicals* (Philadelphia: Ayer, annual).

[2] Oliver Carlson and Ernest S. Bates, *Hearst, Lord of San Simeon* (New York: Viking, 1937), pp. 301–303.

objective manner; a paper's local news may be colored and its editorial page may exhibit bias, but the reader desiring impartial treatment of the news may be reasonably certain of the accuracy of AP or UPI news stories. The headlines, however, are composed in the newspaper office and may reflect the bias of the owner or staff; this factor is particularly important because many people scan newspapers superficially, scarcely reading beyond the heads.

Newspapers are not obliged to print all that the wire services send them; obviously they could not, for space is limited and a great bulk of news stories is available. Which dispatches will be used and which thrown away? The editor exercises discretion which may be highly effective in influencing public opinion. Under orders from his owner-publisher, an editor may throw away stories that place a certain political leader in a favorable or neutral light and print only unfavorable ones. More deadly still, newspapers may decline to publish anything about a political enemy; many politicians feel that being ignored by the press is the worst thing that can happen to them.

Radio and Television. The broadcasting industry furnishes two very important modern mediums for influencing public opinion. Advertisers, politicians, and government recognize its importance in conditioning the thinking of people. The number of receiving sets of all sorts was estimated in 1960 at 150 million; it is believed that over 98 per cent of American homes have one or more receivers, a coverage considerably more complete than that of newspapers. Television sets, the census showed in 1960, are in 88 per cent of homes. Then there were the following major broadcasting authorizations: 3,500 AM (amplitude-modulation) standard-band stations, 900 FM (frequency-modulation) short-wave stations, and 650 television stations. In addition there were 180 FM and 65 television educational stations.

Early development of broadcasting was chaotic and haphazard. The Department of Commerce attempted some control under the authority of a weak act of 1912 governing ship-to-shore communications. The Federal Radio Act of 1927 and the Communications Act of 1934 granted extensive powers over broadcasters to a regulatory commission. The system of control that the United States has evolved differs materially from that in most other countries; here private initiative is given greater play, while abroad broadcasting is often a government monopoly in whole or in part, with radio advertising curtailed or forbidden.

The extent of government control bears upon the question of public opinion in several ways. Private owners are cautious about using radio or television stations for the dissemination of their own particular ideas. They are subject to the requirement, imposed by law, that all candidates for public office have equal opportunities to rent time on the air. Moreover, the radio and television audience is fleeting; listeners may tune out easily, so the broadcaster's propaganda must be discreet and entertaining. The broadcaster must also bear in mind that he is engaged in a business vested with public interest. If his record shows an overload of political propaganda on one side, the Federal Communications Commission may refuse the renewal of his license.

Because radio and television time is sold for commercial advertising, political groups wishing broadcasting facilities for a desirable evening hour must either pay large sums for the privilege or ask for "sustaining" (free) time. If a national audience is desired, then it is necessary to negotiate with one of the four great broadcasting systems—the National Broadcasting Company (NBC), the Columbia Broadcasting System (CBS), the Mutual Broadcasting System (MBS) (radio only), or the American Broadcasting Company (ABC)—or with some of the regional networks. The great chains own some stations and make contracts with individually owned ones.

The national networks exercise a fairly rigid supervision—called "editorial discretion" by them and "censorship" by their opponents—to curtail what the broadcasting companies regard as "poor taste" or "propaganda." Until 1945 both NBC and CBS followed the general rule of refusing to sell time for the discussion of public issues, except in the period between the national party conventions and the general election in November every four years. All networks give some free time to opposing sides of important public questions.

News broadcasts constitute a second great means of influencing the public mind. The terse news reports over radio and television give a minimum of information on current events, and rarely any suggestion of editorialization. Many news commentators do express opinions and have considerable influence in determining public reactions to situations.

The number of standard broadcast channels is limited by physical laws and restricted by international agreement. The need for regulation is obvious to most people; the chaos of the 1926 period sufficed to convince even the most doubting that governmental assignment of frequencies was essential. As radio developed, it was inevitable that stations would unite to present common programs of regional and national interest. Around one-third of all AM stations are affiliated with one of the four national radio networks.[1]

After a three-year study of chain broadcasting, the FCC in 1941 ordered stations not to make exclusive contracts with networks, to limit station contracts with networks to one year, and to cease affiliation with any chain owning more than one network. The latter provision forced NBC to dispose of its Blue Network, now the ABC. Both CBS and NBC protested vigorously against the FCC order and challenged its validity in the courts. Mutual favored the report. The court upheld the FCC order, and it is now in effect.

Recently much attention has been given to alleged restrictive practices of the television networks. A staff study for the FCC in 1957 recommended that no licensee be permitted to own more than three stations in the top twenty-five metropolitan areas. It also proposed outright prohibitions on two practices used in relations with affiliates: "option-time" and "must-buy." Option-time gives the network first call on the prime viewing time of its affiliates. Must-buy requires an advertiser, as a condition of using the network, to contract for time on each of a specified group of affiliated stations.[2]

It appears unlikely that American radio and television will follow the broadcasting systems of most other countries in establishing a publicly owned monopoly. For better or for worse, this country may be expected to continue with the existing plan of regulated private enterprise. The principal controversy is more likely to concern

[1] For TV networks, see U.S. House of Representatives, Committee on Interstate and Foreign Commerce, *Network Broadcasting*, H. Rept. 1297, 85th Cong., 2d Sess. (1958).

[2] A discussion of the issues is found in U.S. House of Representatives, *Ibid.*

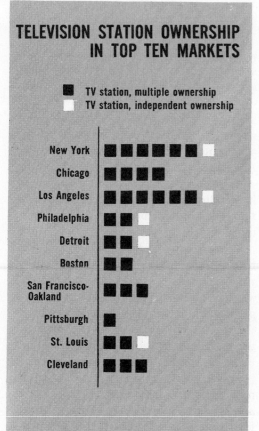

TELEVISION STATION OWNERSHIP IN TOP TEN MARKETS

■ TV station, multiple ownership
☐ TV station, independent ownership

New York
Chicago
Los Angeles
Philadelphia
Detroit
Boston
San Francisco-Oakland
Pittsburgh
St. Louis
Cleveland

Television-station ownership in the great metropolitan areas increasingly falls into the hands of multiple owners (more than one station). Only 5 of the 36 standard channels in the 10 largest centers were licensed to independents (single station owners). And 4 out of the 5 independents were newspaper-owned. (U.S. House of Representatives, Committee on Interstate and Foreign Commerce, *Network Broadcasting,* H. Rept. 1297, 85th Cong., 2d Sess. (1958), p. 731.)

the extent of FCC control. The established interests want their favorable position with a minimum of regulation. The outsiders desire rules and orders permitting them to enter the field. Serious questions of public policy emerge.

In 1946 the FCC issued a "blue book," entitled *Public Service Responsibility of* *Broadcast Licensees,* which laid down the following standards that are taken into account in granting or renewing licenses: (1) a reasonable number of sustaining programs, (2) some local "live" programs, (3) adequate time for discussion of public issues and balanced treatment of controversies, and (4) elimination of advertising excesses. The National Association of Broadcasters protested that these rules would constitute censorship and the loss of freedom of speech.

The ownership pattern has been regulated by FCC rules which limit a single owner to seven stations in each category: AM, FM, and TV. The commission also forbids multiple ownership of AM stations in overlapping primary-coverage areas. The regulatory body has unsuccessfully sought legislation permitting it to control the transfer of station ownership. Stations are being sold for sums far in excess of their physical value. Since the number of available standard-band frequencies is strictly limited, the FCC grants what is in effect a monopolistic privilege. Other public utilities are forced to accept rate regulation, control of earnings, and checking on the quality of their service. Why should broadcast licensees be exempt? In 1949, the FCC further intervened in the program-content field by banning "giveaway" programs; the networks fought the prohibition in court, and the Supreme Court invalidated the FCC regulation. [*FCC v. American Broadcasting Co.,* 347 U.S. 284 (1954)].

Grave issues concerning the freedom of the air remain. The law requires a station permitting one candidate to speak to grant the same privilege to opposing candidates. This has not assured true equality of access to the air to persons of diverse political and economic philosophies. Stations and networks, to avoid being swamped by demands from minor candidates for "equal time,"

CHANNEL 14: A CASE STUDY OF A TELEVISION STATION

	COMPANY	REQUEST	CONSIDERATION	FCC ACTION
1948	A	License to operate	$186,000 est. investment	Granted
1953	A	Permission to sell station to B	$2,400,000 of which $1,200,000 was for license, "goodwill," etc.	Granted
1957	B	Permission to sell station to C	$6,300,000, of which $4,800,000 was for license, "goodwill," etc.	Granted

THE LAW:
1. Gives the Federal Communications Commission authority to grant licenses free to applicants.
2. Provides that the FCC may grant permission for sale of a station, but makes no provision for paying the government for the valuable license.

RESULTS:
1. Fortunes made by early licensees, who later sold out with great capital gains.
2. Tremendous pressure on FCC members, who have power to give away or approve transfer of licenses worth millions.
3. House investigation, in 1958, of charges that five of seven FCC members accepted favors from broadcasters.

virtually ceased giving free time to political candidates. Confronted with proposals in Congress and in the country that stations be required to allocate air time without charge as a condition of broadcast licenses, the networks in 1960 offered to furnish their facilities on a voluntary basis to major-party presidential candidates if the law were amended to make this possible. A bill to confine the guaranty of equal time to major-party candidates was enacted, but it covered the 1960 campaign only. It made possible the series of debates between Kennedy and Nixon, which may set a new pattern in presidential campaigning.

A broader form of equal access to the air may come from fuller utilization of less scarce frequencies—FM in radio and UHF (ultra high frequency) in television—allocated to diverse opinion groups.

The Motion Picture. The motion picture is also a powerful molder of opinions and attitudes. The statistics on the products of filmland are impressive. In 1957 about 46½ million Americans attended motion pictures weekly; the industry had a capital investment of nearly 3 billion dollars; the United States supplied a large share of the world's films.[1] The ownership pattern of production, distribution, and exhibition facilities is similar to that of newspaper and broadcasting chains. Eight major corporations dominate the industry: Metro-Goldwyn-Mayer, Twentieth Century–Fox, Warner Brothers, Paramount, United Artists, Radio-Keith-Orpheum, Universal, and Columbia. Some producers of note are independent, but

[1] *International Motion Picture Almanac* (New York: Quigley Publications, annual).

many have working agreements with one of the major studios.

Regular feature films are more likely to shape attitudes than opinions. There is a strong proclivity to glorify wealth, elaborate homes, and well-dressed people. Producers find it safer and more profitable to stress sex appeal than social problems. Crime is a favorite subject, but the Motion Picture Producers and Distributors of America (Johnston Office) requires among other things that criminals be punished in the film.

Newsreels follow feature films in commercial importance. Generally about ten minutes in length, they are almost invariably shown, even with double-feature programs. The principal producers are Hearst Metrotone, Movietonews, Universal and Televiews. Each does a fairly objective job of reporting.

A related field is that of educational and commercial films. They are made for and financed by organized groups, business concerns, and other bodies. Most of these pictures are shown in schools, churches, clubs, and other groups, although some second-grade movie houses will show them if a fee is paid.

Governments restrain the motion-picture industry comparatively little. A few states have boards of censorship; occasionally a film is banned by some local authority. Most of the regulation of the industry is self-imposed or comes from private associations.

Sporadically, proposals are made in Congress for legislation to break up the centralization of the production-distribution industry. Some are aimed at the device of "block-booking" and "blind-selling." These terms mean that an exhibitor buys a year's supply of films consisting largely of unknowns; if he declines to book blind, the distributor may refuse to supply him with any films, or make the price impossibly high. Although

no bill has yet been enacted by Congress, the companies, when threatened with anti-trust prosecution, agreed to curb the worst abuses. Most of the companies have now reorganized in order to separate their producing and exhibiting functions.

PRESSURE GROUPS

Reason for Pressure Groups. Recognizing that "in unity there is strength," individuals with common interests and points of view join in a mass of associations, clubs, unions, and leagues. These groups, together with business companies, corporations, and partnerships, may have interests that they wish to promote or defend through governmental action or inaction. Increasingly, organized groups and business interests are finding contacts with government essential to their welfare. Therefore, they set up headquarters in Washington and in the state capitals and pressure both legislators and executives. This activity, popularly known as lobbying, is usually quite a legitimate exercise of the right to petition for redress of grievances; normally it operates under the guaranties of freedom of speech and press.

Group representation arises in part from the impossibility of representing perfectly all the diverse elements of society through the regular elective and appointive officials. In this country nearly all legislatures are elected from single-member geographical districts, a situation that notoriously magnifies the strength of a majority or a plurality and minimizes the influence of minorities. Denied direct representation in legislative bodies, or achieving too little, or frustrated in selling their ideas to parties, organizations resort to extralegal means to make their influence felt. Elective officials constantly are concerned that their actions harmonize with that phantom, public opinion. Pressure groups provide a real service in directing and stimulating expressions of opinion by the membership and other interested persons.

Special-interest groups are both numerous and varied. About five hundred significant pressure bodies operate on a national scale. Some groups have large numbers of dues-paying members, such as the great farm groups and labor unions. Others, lacking a definite membership, are effective because they have money and advocate a cause in which many people are vitally interested, like the public-utility companies. Lobbying organizations may also be classified according to their aims: most are interested in the welfare of a special sector of society; some, however, like the moral groups, have programs that are "uplift" in nature, designed to help the other fellow.

Farm Groups in Politics. The leading agrarian organizations on the national scene are the American Farm Bureau Federation and The National Grange. The Farmers Educational and Cooperative Union of America and groups set up on commodity lines, often producers' cooperatives, play a lesser but important role. The Farm Bureau is much younger than the Grange, but it has achieved greater strength in Congress than its rival. It has a large dues-paying membership, a budget of commensurate size, and a staff of well-paid and qualified employees and officers.

The Farm Bureau was launched as a national organization in 1920. Its remarkable growth is due in no small part to the early connection between the bureau and the extension services, cosponsored by the land-grant colleges and universities and the Department of Agriculture. The farm advisers, or county agents, sought to reach farmers in groups; their connections with local Farm Bureau centers followed. There is no uniform pattern over the country, but the county agent is the active promoter

and organizer of the Farm Bureau in many states. Before Congress, the Farm Bureau is vigorous, emphatic, and demanding. The Farm Bureau is strongest among relatively prosperous farmers in the corn belt of the Middle West and the cotton belt of the South.

The Grange has a rich historical background; after a modest beginning in the 1860s, it swept to great strength in the next two decades as the spearhead of agrarian revolt. Retaining the trappings of old—the fraternal-order form, the ritual, the glorification of farm life—the modern Grange has become the conservative among national farm groups. It reflects the attitudes of the Northeastern farmers, who constitute the most influential section of membership. The Grange lobbies in Congress less actively than its rival. It was hostile to many New Deal proposals.

The Farmers Union, influential west of the Mississippi Valley, is devoted to a program of cooperative endeavor. Representing less-prosperous farmers, it takes a somewhat more liberal view on issues than does either the Grange or the Farm Bureau. Some of the organizations in particular commodity fields, such as dairymen, peanut growers, and others, exert great influence upon legislation and administrative policy that concerns them.

Organized Labor. Leading the field of labor organizations in the United States is the American Federation of Labor–Congress of Industrial Organizations (AFL–CIO); unaffiliated but powerful in their own right are the railroad brotherhoods and other independent unions.

The AFL and the CIO merged in 1955 after twenty years of separate existence and recurring warfare. Conventions met in December to liquidate the two rival federations. Delegates from each met to adopt the constitution on which joint committees had worked for months. The former AFL officials took the lion's share of offices in the combined organization, as agreed in the unity committee and justified by numbers.

Political action proved to be one of the most difficult areas in which to combine forces. Because political programs of the former AFL League for Political Education and the former CIO Political Action Committee were so different, the new AFL–CIO approached integration slowly. The Committee on Political Education (COPE) is the political front of the new federation. The political tactics of the combined AFL–CIO represents an amalgam of those developed over the years by the political wings of the separate federations.

The AFL was organized in 1886, after previous experimentation with earlier adaptations of the British Trades Union Congress model. From the beginning the AFL engaged in both economic and political activities. The primary work on the economic front was done by the individual unions that belonged to the federation; the AFL and the state federations of labor emphasized political activities. Samuel Gompers, founder of the AFL, opposed direct participation in politics but sponsored a policy of rewarding friends and defeating enemies. The AFL lobbied vigorously for its objectives in the political field but did not affiliate with any party, preferring to support proved friends and to defeat opponents regardless of party label.

In the early 1930s conflict within the AFL over organizing policies reached an acute stage. Some of the strongest member unions, set up on an industrial as opposed to a craft basis, spurred organization of the unorganized on an industrial basis. They formed a Committee for Industrial Organization, in 1935; in the next year the AFL council ordered these unions to quit the CIO or be suspended from the AFL. Conflicts of personalities over organizing zeal and other factors not directly connected with the industrial-versus-craft controversy widened the split. Most of the unions originally connected with the CIO withdrew from the AFL.

In its new role of rival body, the CIO put organizers into the field in mass-production industries—steel, automobile, rubber, and others—and aroused an enthusiasm for unionism previously unknown. Soon the CIO unions claimed an aggregate membership above that of the AFL. Eventually the CIO was put on a more permanent basis and its name changed to Congress of Industrial Organizations. On the political front, the CIO unions led in the formation of Labor's Nonpartisan League, which entered campaigns with slashing aggressiveness but only modest success.

The independent unions, especially the powerful railroad brotherhoods, maintain separate lobbyists in the national and state capitals, but in common matters they cooperate closely with AFL–CIO representatives.

Although beset with family quarreling and jurisdictional disputes, American organized labor often is substantially united in its general legislative goals and methods. Direct and blunt lobbying is employed widely. Through endorsements of candidates and campaign activities, the unions seek to help friends and defeat enemies. Their success in recent decades in securing favorable legislation, like the National Labor Relations Act and the wages-and-hours law, testifies to the effectiveness of their methods. Many observers predict that American labor someday will follow other labor movements in forming or joining a third party devoted to the interests of labor, perhaps attempting to serve farmers as well.

The unions usually support Democrats. Franklin D. Roosevelt had a wide following in labor; President Truman's 1948 victory may be attributed in part to labor's political activity. Organized labor provided substantial support for Stevenson in 1952 and 1956, and for Kennedy in 1960.

Business Interests. Unlike farm and labor elements, business interests have no membership in the millions. There is less unity in the organization of business than among farmers and workers. Business, however, possesses the power of money to a degree unmatched by the other two great elements in society. As America becomes more and more industrialized, commercial interests gain in relative importance. The Chamber of Commerce of the United States and the National Association of Manufacturers are the mightiest of business groups; behind them rank hundreds of trade associations in every conceivable industry.

Since 1912, the national Chamber of Commerce has been the outstanding group, and it is reasonably representative of the various business interests of the country. With a total affiliated membership of 1 million in good times, it has connections with state and local bodies and branches. The Chamber of Commerce slogan, "less government in business and more business in government," was discredited considerably in the Great Depression but is still adhered to by many. Most proposals for social reform or protective labor legislation have been opposed. One feature of Chamber of Commerce procedure differs from that of the average pressure group. The stand of chamber lobbyists on pending national legislation sometimes is determined by referendum, in which member organizations indicate their opinions by questionnaire answers.

The National Association of Manufacturers (NAM) was established in 1895. This is more vigorously antilabor and hostile toward social legislation than the chamber. Besides lobbying in Congress, the NAM engages extensively in propaganda through motion pictures, radio, television, press, and a variety of its own publications.

During and since the Second World War, forward-looking business interests have joined together to form the Committee for Economic Development, which has issued basic economic studies.

Trade associations have memberships numbering in the thousands and many of them are national in scope. Each exists to defend or promote interests of those who participate in its industry. Although the associations sometimes engage in price fixing and other practices of doubtful legality, it is quite proper for them to seek special representation for their industry or line. These groups, great and small, cover such diverse industries as brewing, tombstone cutting, sugar refining, baking, and liquor distilling. Substantially united on labor and tax issues, they may fight each other over tariff schedules and other matters.

Other Groups. Through professional societies the physician, the attorney, the teacher, the dentist, and the architect, achieve special representation for their professions. Women's groups of influence—the League of Women Voters of the United States, the General Federation of Women's Clubs, the National Federation of Business and Professional Women's Clubs—are interested in a vast range of governmental matters, some affecting women and children, others general in nature. A number of

[1] Unions may be more effective in congressional than presidential politics. For examples of the stands on issues before Congress, see *Labor Looks at the 85th Congress, First Session,* AFL-CIO Legislative Department. Publication No. 59 (October, 1957).

women's groups coordinate their efforts through a Women's Joint Congressional Committee.

Reformers of all shades—antiliquor, anti-vice, anti-spoils-system associations—secure voices in Washington through organized groups. Religious groups often indulge in special pleading for reforms. Various veterans' organizations battle with one another and with the peace groups, which are far from united on the issues. Public employees form organizations or unions to promote their interests; some are AFL–CIO but most are unaffiliated and independent.

Pressure-group Techniques. Men and women who represent organized groups before the legislative and executive branches are known as legislative agents, advocates, counsels, lobbyists, or executive secretaries. Popularly they are known as lobbyists. Many enter this work after serving in Congress or in other public offices; a large proportion of them have practiced law, which combines easily with the work of a legislative agent. Nearly all groups and their representatives are bipartisan in their approach, seeking support from public officers regardless of party affiliation.

Techniques of interest groups and lobbyists vary considerably, but most legislative pressure techniques can be classed under one of four headings: informational, social, propaganda, and campaign. Informational services may begin with the preparation of proposed legislation by attorneys for the interest group. After a legislator who will introduce the bill has been found, he is furnished with considerable information. When the bill is before committee, group proponents present arguments for their side of the question. They then present to legislators supporting literature and data. Actually, special-interest groups oppose more measures than they support.

The social front is attacked by cultivating the acquaintance of many legislators, particularly those strategically placed on the committees with which the lobbyist is most likely to deal. This cultivation may involve any sort of entertainment, such as dinners, all-expense trips, and parties. Propaganda activities demand many kinds of publicity to influence public opinion, through mail appeals, radio talks, newspaper stories, and advertisements. The purpose often is to stimulate interested persons or group members to bring pressure upon a legislator whose support is needed. The individual may be encouraged to telephone, telegraph, write, or visit the legislator in order to win him over to the group's point of view.

Behind the other activities often lie a number of campaign activities. Groups in politics on other than a sporadic basis commonly find it advisable to survey the legislative field before the need of support becomes pressing. The legislator wants help at election time. The campaign period is the logical one in which to sound out the candidates and get them committed to a favorable point of view if possible. This sounding out may be done in writing, as in the answers to a questionnaire, or through a verbal promise, preferably given in a public meeting. If the candidate is favorable, the organization may endorse him openly, or it may prefer to send the word along to membership under cover. Financial support of the candidate may reinforce the memory of the would-be official, and a campaign contribution from the group or from individuals connected with the group is valuable for this purpose. Some interests contribute to more than one candidate for an office, to ensure that they will have influence with the winner, whomever he may be.

Although strict regulation of the lobby was demanded repeatedly, Congress imposed no general controls until the Con-

HOW THE PRESSURE GROUPS WORK

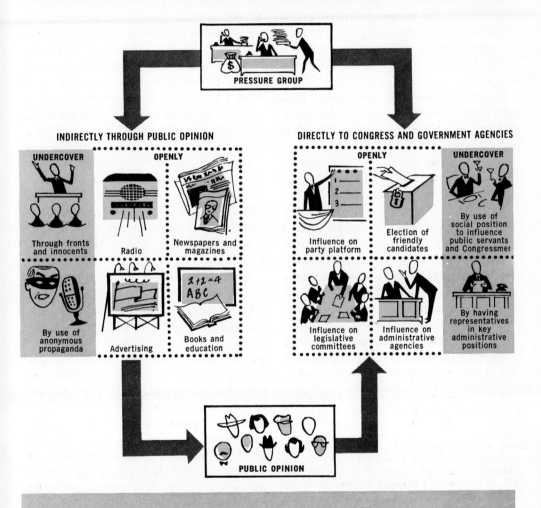

The open and covert activities of organized groups directly and indirectly influence public officials. (Public Affairs Committee, Inc. Used by permission of Maxwell S. Stewart, editor, Public Affairs Pamphlets.)

gressional Reform Act of 1946; the act requires lobbyists to register and file statements of expenditures made to influence legislation.[1]

Registration laws, though, are unlikely to be very effective. If enforced, they do bring pressure groups into the open, a convenience to legislators and press. However, the most effective restriction on campaign expenditures is an occasional legislative investigation.

Pressure Politics and Democracy. Pressure politics constitutes a very important element in American government. The power of pressure groups is demonstrated before Congress and state legislatures, in administrative agencies, and in the several mediums of mass communication effective in the formation of public opinion. On the whole, the activities of special-interest groups probably do more good than harm. Group representation provides a valuable supplement to the usual form of legislative representation, encouraging direct expression of viewpoints by those most affected by a proposed action.

On the other hand, serious abuses have developed. Can these be corrected by carefully drawn and enforced corrupt-practices

[1] For a study of the 1946 act and experience under it during the initial months of operation, see Belle Zeller, "The Federal Regulation of Lobbying Act," *American Political Science Review*, vol. 42 (April, 1948), pp. 239–271. Later developments may be traced in *Congressional Quarterly*. The largest spenders during the first half of 1957 were Campaign for the 48 States (economy in government), U.S. Savings and Loan League, AFL-CIO, Association of American Railroads, and American Farm Bureau Federation.

legislation? Some can, but others pose such complex problems that only general solutions can be proposed. The most serious consequence of pressure-group preponderance is that general or national interests of the great masses of people are subordinated to the special interests of articulate and well-organized minorities. For example, the consumer's voice is completely inadequate in the determination of public policy. Consumers are not organized to compete with farm, labor, and business groups. All Americans are consumers, but their interests as producers often outweigh consumer interests. An individual's own immediate interests may appear to be served by a 50 per cent price increase in the product he is making, yet that price increase may be disadvantageous to users all over the country. Since the consumers have no effective organization, their protests may not be heard.

General or national interests, as opposed to special-group interest, may receive support through (1) coalitions of groups, in opposition to the selfish demands of one group, (2) restoration of party responsibility and discipline in national affairs, and (3) development of a strong consumers' cooperative movement. The first method operates occasionally. Labor and agriculture team up to forestall a tax policy demanded by business, labor and business work together to defeat a farm-subsidy plan, or business and agriculture jointly oppose wage demands by labor. The second and third methods will be discussed in subsequent chapters.

FOR FURTHER READING

Public Opinion, Polls, Propaganda, and Censorship

Albig, William: *Modern Public Opinion* (New York: McGraw-Hill, 1956).

Campbell, Angus, Philip E. Converse, Warren E. Miller, and Donald E. Stokes: *The American Voter* (New York: Wiley, 1960).

Cantril, Hadley: *Gauging Public Opinion* (Princeton, N.J.: Princeton University Press, 1944).

Chase, Stuart, and M. Tyler: *Power of Words* (New York: Harcourt, Brace, 1954).

Christianson, Reo M., and Robert O. McWilliams: *Voice of the People: Readings in Public Opinion and Propaganda* (New York: McGraw-Hill, 1962).

Dobb, Leonard W.: *Public Opinion and Propaganda* (New York: Holt, 1948).

George, Alexander L.: *Propaganda Analysis: A Study of Inferences Made from Nazi Propaganda in World War II* (Evanston, Ill.: Row, Peterson, 1958).

Kelley, Stanley, Jr.: *Professional Public Relations and Political Power* (Baltimore: Johns Hopkins Press, 1956).

Kornhauser, William: *The Politics of Mass Society* (New York: Free Press, 1959).

Lasswell, Harold D.: *Democracy through Public Opinion* (Menasha, Wis.: Banta, 1941).

Lippmann, Walter: *Public Opinion* (New York: Macmillan, 1953).

McPhee, N. William, and William A. Glaser (ed.): *Public Opinion and Congressional Elections* (New York: Free Press, 1962).

Public Opinion Quarterly (since 1937).

Rogers, Lindsay: *The Pollsters* (New York: Knopf, 1949).

Rourke, Francis E.: *Secrecy and Publicity: Dilemmas of Democracy* (Baltimore: Johns Hopkins Press, 1961).

Schettler, Clarence: *Public Opinion in American Society* (New York: Harper, 1960).

Channels of Communication

Ashley, Paul P.: *Say It Safely: Legal Limits in Journalism and Broadcasting* (Seattle: University of Washington Press, 1956).

Chafee, J. Zechariah, Jr.: *Government and Mass Communications* (Chicago: University of Chicago Press, 2 vols., 1947).

Coons, John E. (ed.): *Freedom and Responsibility in Broadcasting* (Evanston, Ill.: Northwestern University Press, 1962).

Drewry, John E.: *Communications Problems and Progress* (Athens, Ga.: University of Georgia Press, 1957).

Ferguson, Leroy C., and Ralph H. Smuckler: *Politics in the Press: An Analysis of Press Content in 1952 Senatorial Campaigns* (East Lansing, Mich.: Michigan State University, Governmental Research Bureau, 1954).

Inglis, Ruth A.: *Freedom of the Movies* (Chicago: University of Chicago Press, 1947).

Klapper, Joseph T.: *The Effect of Mass Communication* (New York: Free Press, 1961).

Merrill, I. R., and C. H. Proctor: *Political Persuasion by Television: Partisan and Public Affairs Broadcasts in the 1956 General Election* (East Lansing, Mich.: Michigan State University, 1959)

Morris, Joe A.: *Deadline Every Minute: The Story of the United Press* (New York: Doubleday, 1957).

Rowse, Arthur E.: *Slanted News: A Case Study of the Nixon and Stevenson Fund Stories* (Boston: Beacon Press, 1957).

Schramm, Wilbur: *Responsibility in Mass Communications* (New York: Harper, 1957).

Siepmann, Charles A.: *Radio Television and Society* (New York: Oxford, 1950).

Smead, Elmer E.: *Freedom of Speech by Radio and Television* (Washington, D.C.: Public Affairs Press, 1959).

U.S. Federal Communications Commission: *An Economic Study of Standard Broadcasting* (1947).

———: *Public Service Responsibility of Broadcast Licensees* ("Blue Book," 1946).

U.S. House of Representatives, Committee on Interstate and Foreign Commerce: *Network Broadcasting*, H. Rept. 1297 85th Cong., 2d Sess. (1958).

U.S. House of Representatives, Committee on the Judiciary: *Report of the Antitrust Subcommittee . . . on the Television Broadcasting Industry*, Committee print (1957).

Pressure Groups

Baker, Roscoe: *The American Legion and American Foreign Policy* (New York: Bookman Associates, 1954).

Blaisdell, Donald C.: *American Democracy under Pressure* (New York: Ronald, 1957).

Fenton, John H.: *The Catholic Vote* (New Orleans, La.: Hauser Press, 1960).

Goldberg, Arthur J.: *AFL-CIO: Labor United* (New York: McGraw-Hill, 1956).

Hamilton, Walton: *The Politics of Industry* (New York: Knopf, 1957).

Herring, E. Pendleton: *Group Representation before Congress* (Baltimore: Johns Hopkins Press, 1929).

Kampelman, Max M.: *The Communist Party vs. the CIO: A Study in Power Politics* (New York: Praeger, 1957).

Kile, Orville M.: *The Farm Bureau through Three Decades* (Baltimore: Waverly Press, 1948).

Kornhauser, Arthur, and others: *When Labor Votes: A Study of Auto Workers* (New York: University Books, 1956).

McCune, Wesley: *Who's Behind Our Farm Policy?* (New York: Praeger, 1956).

Mills, C. Wright: *The Power Elite* (New York: Oxford, 1956).

Odegard, Peter H.: *Pressure Politics: The Story of the Anti-Saloon League* (New York: Columbia University Press, 1928).

————: *Religion and Politics* (New York: Oceana Publications, 1960).

Pinner, Frank A., Paul Jacobs, and Philip Selznick: *Old Age and Political Behavior: A Case Study* (Berkeley and Los Angeles: University of California Press, 1959).

Schattschneider, Elmer E.: *Politics, Pressures and the Tariff* (Englewood Cliffs, N.J.: Prentice-Hall, 1935).

Stokes, Donald E.: *Voting Research and the Businessman in Politics* (Ann Arbor, Mich.: Foundation for Research on Human Behavior, 1961).

Wilson, James Q.: *Negro Politics: The Search for Leadership* (New York: Free Press, 1960).

REVIEW QUESTIONS

1. A foreign scholar (Gunnar Myrdal) says of the American masses: "They do not meet much. They do not organize. They do not speak for themselves: they are listeners in America." How can we have an informed public opinion if this is true?

2. Explain and discuss the concept of propaganda as used by the late Institute for Propaganda Analysis.

3. Explain in detail how the modern cross section or sampling survey of public opinion is made.

4. In what respect might the opinion poll constitute a danger to our usual governmental processes?

5. What are the most important influences molding our opinions? Discuss each and assign an order of importance to your list of determinants.

6. What can a newspaper reader do to follow the news and secure the most accurate possible picture of news events? Discuss the location of, and responsibility for, inaccuracies and bias.

7. An organization (American Civil Liberties Union) reported in 1936: "Of all means of communication, radio today leads the field in affecting public opinion. Scores of programs are carried daily presenting news comment and, less often, political controversy. Each of these programs must face what is in effect a double censorship. . . ." Is radio the *chief* channel of communication now? What is this alleged censorship over radio?

8. "The potency of the motion picture in influencing the thought and opinions of large publics in the fields of politics and economics has not yet been thoroughly tested" (W. Albig). Why has not the full power of the movies been utilized? What factors would condition and control the movies if they were so used?

9. Describe the policies and tactics of farm interests in national politics since the end of the Second World War.

10. How did the AFL and the CIO differ in their approach to politics prior to their amalgamation?

11. What are the principal political goals and methods of organized business in national politics?

12. Why do special-interest groups seek separate, extralegal representation in American government?

13. Can you propose a form of democratic, representative government under which special-group representation would be unnecessary?

Chapter Eleven

Political Parties

There is no natural majority party; we are becoming a genuinely two party nation. The Republican hold on the farmers is broken. The Democratic hold on the big cities is broken, for they are losing the Northern Negroes and many Catholics, the old immigrant groups are assimilated and the "proletariat" is moving to the suburbs, wearing white collars and becoming as concerned about taxes as about wages. All the old groupings have loosened up; we are becoming a standardized middle-class people, moving like interchangeable parts all over the country, losing the old sense of party identification, picking and choosing among individual candidates regardless of party label. Outside the Deep South there hardly remains a state in the union that politicians dare call a "Republican state" or a "Democratic state."

ERIC SEVAREID[1]

Useful as they are in the democratic process, pressure groups cannot do all that is required to make big government operate in a responsible manner. Every large democratic jurisdiction in the modern state system uses political parties to crystallize opinion, to narrow candidate and policy alternatives, and to provide responsibility.

Despite the fact that parties and their activities are subject to much criticism and

[1] "Who Will Win in 1960?" *Esquire* (December, 1957), p. 127.

abuse, the weight of informed opinion supports the contention that they are essential to the operation of large-scale democratic government, and that they require strenghtening rather than weakening.

GENERAL ASPECTS

Nature of the Political Party. A political party is usually defined as an organization of voters adhering to common principles and seeking to control the government. Out-

191

siders often complain that they find it difficult to distinguish between the two major political parties of the United States, which appear to support such similar policies. Some have concluded that Republican and Democratic labels are simply vote-catching arrangements manipulated by professional politicians seeking the spoils of office. The similarities of the two parties in platform and policy arise from a number of factors; prominent among them is party rivalry for the vote of the middle-of-the road independent. Moreover, each party is so broadly based that its platform-making process involves many compromises; the result is very general policy pronouncements.

How does one distinguish between a political party and a pressure group? Organized pressure groups at times take a very active part in political campaigns in support of candidates or parties that they favor. This may take the form of public endorsement and support of certain candidates; more often, it takes the form of urging members to work for and contribute to the campaign funds of favored candidates. Pressure groups often work through the regular party machinery and have a potent voice in the choice of candidates. The primary difference between party and pressure groups is found in the essential aim: parties seek largely to capture offices; pressure groups strive mainly to influence policies.

Neither major American party has a definite membership. Persons may be considered members because they register as such, think themselves to be members, or pay their dues and hold membership cards. The first two are the most common forms of affiliation; the last is limited mainly to small parties of the "left wing."

Factors in Party Allegiance. How is an individual's party affiliation determined, or how does one choose sides in the game of party politics? Exact data on this subject are scarce, but some surveys shed light on certain aspects,

The first, and perhaps the most important, determinant is family tradition. Most voters take the party of their parents. This political ancestor worship in evidenced by such expressions as, "My family is a Republican family" and "We have been Democrats for a hundred years." Because many other factors are influenced by family—economic status, religion, section of residence—this determinant assumes an extraordinary importance.

Economic position ranks second in influence on party bias. No general rule applies to all periods, but recently there has been an increasing tendency for the well-to-do to vote Republican and for the less fortunate to vote Democratic. National origin plays a role too; descendants of Northern Europeans tend to the Republican party, while those of Southern and Eastern Europeans prefer the Democratic party. This choice is probably connected with economic role. Religious connections appear to play little part in pushing adherents into one party rather than the other, but it is an interesting fact that the Republican party is much more strongly Protestant than the Democratic. Sectionalism, or geographic influence, is decisive in many cases and in certain parts of the country. In the South nearly everyone is a Democrat; in Maine and Vermont the Republicans normally are in the majority.

The Two-party System. The two-party system exists in the United States, Great Britain, and some other democracies. Various explanations have been offered. First, some say that the peoples of the English-speaking countries are less doctrinaire and more inclined to compromise than are other peoples. Second, nationality and religion factionalize the people less than in the countries of continental Europe. Third, the early English two-party system, transplanted here in the colonial era, has perpetuated itself. Fourth, the two-party plan is produced by the operation of the American voting systems, especially the electoral college and the single-member district plan of electing legislative representatives.

This fourth point requires elaboration. The importance of the Presidency is such that a third party secures adherents only with great difficulty, for band-wagon sentiment argues against "throwing away your vote" by supporting other than a major party. The electoral-college method of electing the President would be undemocratic should a strong third party emerge. If no majority is won in the electoral college, the election of the Chief Executive is thrown to the House of Representatives, which must select from the highest three, each state casting one vote.

The single-member-district scheme of electing legislative representatives also discourages the development of minor parties. It tends to magnify the strength of the leading party, yielding a proportion of legislative seats far above the proportion of popular votes received. For example, a party polling 52 per cent of the popular vote cast for the representatives in Congress may receive 75 per cent of the seats, not only depriving the major opposition party of representation strictly proportionate to its voting strength, but usually eliminating minor parties almost completely.

The consequences of the two-party system are extremely important. First, it usually produces a situation in which one party actually has the power to govern. Under the parliamentary plan, the two-party scheme usually provides one party with a mandate from the electorate plus a legislative majority strong enough to carry out its program. Under the presidential

plan, the separation of powers occasionally may deadlock the executive and legislative branches. Despite the theoretical advantages of proportional representation (PR) (see page 231), support for it has declined in years of crisis. It is recognized that producing the power to govern through a roughly democratic means is more important than representing all the elements in the body politic exactly in proportion to their strength in the electorate.

Second, major parties under the two-party system become moderate, compromising bodies, highly irritating to those who demand sharp definitions of party policy. Each party faces the task of attracting to the party an aggregation of interests strong enough to win power. Because each major party is at all times either the government or the opposition (alternative government), it can ill afford to make irresponsible policy declarations.

There are some who would exchange the two-party plan for a multiparty scheme, but under our form of government the disadvantages of having many parties would be very great. The multiparty system produces instability, confuses the electorate with a multitude of alternatives, represents local groups and factions on a national scale, and diffuses responsibility for action and inaction. It would make continued functioning of the electoral college virtually impossible.

Third Parties. Third parties have come and gone; during 170 years, only the Republican party has gained sufficient strength to displace an existing major party. Several times, minor-party candidates for the Presidency have polled sufficient votes to hold the balance of power between the two majors, but they have been unable to keep their separate identity or strength for long. Since the Civil War, third parties have made respectable showings on six occasions.

The Populists polled over 1 million votes in 1892; so did the Progressive and the States' Rights Parties, in 1948. Eugene V. Debs, Socialist candidate for the Presidency, secured nearly a million votes in 1912 and again in 1920. With Theodore Roosevelt as a standard-bearer, the Progressives of 1912 polled over 4 million votes, exceeding the vote for President Taft, the Republican candidate. The most recent great revolt came in 1924, when Robert M. La Follette, Progressive presidential candidate, polled 4½ million votes.

Third parties in American national politics have played the role of innovators of policy, not of holders of office. The old parties have taken over many planks from the platforms of the Populists, Greenbackers, Socialists, and Progressives. Much of what the left-wing parties advocated two or three decades ago may be found today in the Democratic and Republican platforms. Those who take part in third-party movements may never enjoy the fruits of office, but the policies for which they work may become, when they gain public approval, law of the land under old-party auspices.

The two old parties are so very similar that many would recast them. They would redesign one into a genuine conservative party and the other into the party of progressive reform. During the 1930s it was thought that the Democratic party might die and a farmer-labor or progressive party would replace it. Since the New Deal era, however, the tendency has been for progressives to concentrate in the Democratic party and for the Republican party to become the conservative organ. This division will be far from sharp, however, until the "Solid South" is broken up and divides along these party lines, and progressive elements of the Republican party are enticed or smoked out. At the moment there appears to be little evidence of either of these developments, despite 1952 and 1956 Republican gains in the South.

Parties in the Past. The Democratic party is a venerable body, more than a century and a half old. It took form during Washington's administration, under the leadership of Jefferson, an exponent of strict construction. Under various names, including Antifederalist, Republican, Democratic Republican, and Democratic, the party has demonstrated enormous ability to survive under difficult circumstances. It took an early stand against high tariffs and enlisted the support of small farmers of the West and of urban workers of the East. The extinction of the Federalist party around 1816 gave the party a period without competition in the political field. Substantial opposition was generated in the Jacksonian era, however. Now labeled Democratic, the party soon faced a formidable Whig opponent. The Civil War made of it a minority party for decades, but it rebounded with vigor in Congress and captured the Presidency twice with Cleveland, twice with Wilson, four times with Franklin D. Roosevelt, and once with Truman.

Today's Republican party is the successor of two earlier major parties. The Federalist party, led by Hamilton, emerged during Washington's administration as the champion of strong national government. It expired after making tactical errors during the War of 1812. When opposition crystallized against Jackson, it called itself National Republican, then Whig. In 1856 a new party, termed Republican, strode upon the scene, nominated John C. Frémont as presidential candidate, and condemned slavery. Its victory in 1860, with Lincoln, precipitated the Civil War, which resulted in Republican predominance in national politics for the greater part of the period since then. Over the years the party

EVOLUTION OF AMERICAN PARTIES

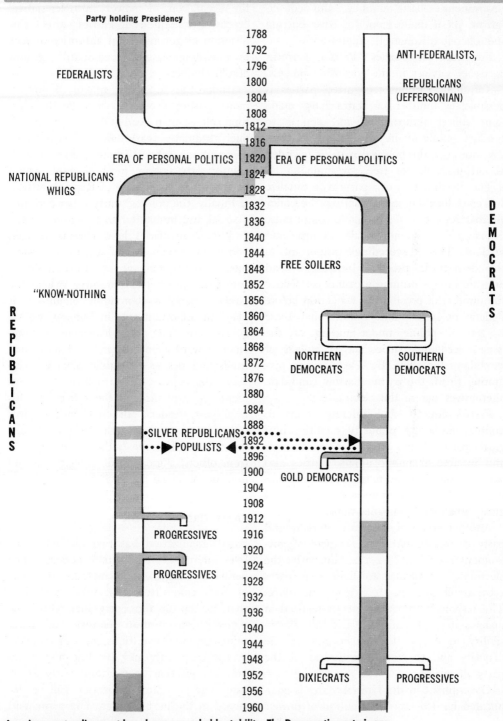

Party holding Presidency

FEDERALISTS	1788
	1792
	1796
	1800
	1804
	1808
	1812
	1816
ERA OF PERSONAL POLITICS	1820
NATIONAL REPUBLICANS	1824
WHIGS	1828

ANTI-FEDERALISTS,

REPUBLICANS
(JEFFERSONIAN)

ERA OF PERSONAL POLITICS

DEMOCRATS

REPUBLICANS

1832
1836
1840
1844
1848   FREE SOILERS
1852
"KNOW-NOTHING   1856
1860
1864
1868
1872   NORTHERN   SOUTHERN
1876   DEMOCRATS   DEMOCRATS
1880
1884
1888
◄•SILVER REPUBLICANS•••••••••
•••►POPULISTS ◄•••••••••••••••►   1892
1896
1900   GOLD DEMOCRATS
1904
1908
1912
PROGRESSIVES   1916
1920
1924
PROGRESSIVES   1928
1932
1936
1940
1944
1948
1952   DIXIECRATS   PROGRESSIVES
1956
1960

American party alignment has shown remarkable stability. The Democratic party is one
of the world's oldest; the Republican has now passed its one-hundredth birthday.
Despite occasional splits, the two-party pattern has prevailed continuously since
the 1820s.

has been for high tariffs, strong national government, "hard" money, and conservatism; yet it made room for trust busting and Theodore Roosevelt progressivism.

Functions of Parties. Parties perform necessary services in the governing process. Government without recognized parties is possible; a number of states have made some offices nonpartisan and appear to conduct public affairs satisfactorily. Generally, however, the political party is regarded as indispensable for free government.

The first function of a party is to canalize and crystallize opinion, to narrow the policy alternatives before the voters, to compromise diverse views of individuals, groups, and sections. This is exceedingly important to the democratic process. Individuals and pressure groups ordinarily cannot so reduce the number of possibilities for action before Federal or state public officers that there is general public understanding of the issues. Secondly, parties act as brokers of candidates for office. By selecting and promoting them, the parties narrow candidate alternatives before the electorate.

Parties educate and interest voters in politics. Elaborate publicity facilities plus great party leaders stimulate enthusiasm and interest in public affairs. Parties also work in the field of naturalization of immigrants, once an important function of great urban party organizations.

Another group of services centers around party responsibility. If the control of government is achieved by a certain party, the electorate is entitled to hold that party accountable for its stewardship in office. This responsibility is imperfectly realized in many states. The minority has the responsibility to expose the weaknesses of the majority and to furnish criticisms of the party in power.

Government in the United States is complicated both by the distribution of powers between the nation and the states and by the separation of power into legislative, executive, and judicial. Parties correct this diffusion of governmental authority in part by providing reasonably compatible groups of officeholders.

Under the American system of government, parties also serve to make the electoral-college plan work. With two parties, one candidate nearly always secures the necessary majority. Without parties, or with a multiparty system, most elections would be thrown to the House of Representatives.

Finally, the political party often performs a social and humanitarian function. Parties and their auxiliaries hold bazaars, dances, and picnics; such events add to the enjoyment of the participants and to the political consciousness of a community. Where the political party is thoroughly organized, it plays an important role in humanizing big government. The party leader in the precinct or ward is an interpreter of individual needs and desires to public officials. Vice versa, the policies and structure of government are explained to the citizen by his local party leaders. Although such services sometimes extend into the field of special favors granted to the faithful and withheld from others, a great deal of legitimate aid may be rendered by a party.

PARTY ORGANIZATION

Party organization has two distinct parts, but interconnections are frequent. The permanent organization includes the tiers of party committees that reach from bottom to top of the party hierarchy. The periodic organization consists of party primaries and conventions, meeting annually or less frequently and deciding highly important questions concerning party structure. The periodic organization will be discussed in the next chapter. The permanent organization, formal and informal, will be described here.

The National Committee. The national committee heads the permanent party organization in the country. In the Democratic party it is composed of one man and one woman from each state and territory. The members most commonly are chosen by state delegations to national party conventions, but some states require selection in state convention or committee, or election in direct primaries. The Republicans in 1952 decided to add, as ex officio members of the national committee, the state chairmen of the states carried by the party in the last election. This change was opposed by women and Southerners, whose representation will be diluted by the move. Nominally, the power of the national committee is great. Increasingly in recent years it has confined its work to ratifying the presidential nominee's choice for chairman, electing other officers, and planning the national convention. There is little significant difference between the Republican and Democratic practices.

By long usage the national chairman is selected by the presidential nominee and formally elected by the committee. He becomes party campaign manager and directs national headquarters. An executive committee, chosen by the chairman, exercises most of the committee's authority for the period between presidential campaigns. Controlled by the national chairman, the central office engages in research, advertising, publicity, money raising, and "stratified electioneering" (appealing to special groups of voters, such as women, veterans, Negroes, farmers, laborers, and foreign-born). Both parties keep some bureaus, especially publicity, open year in and year out.

In each state the national committeeman and committeewoman handle liasion work with the state organization and help to direct patronage matters when their party holds the Presidency. In 1952 the Republicans created a new permanent advisory committee, to be appointed by the national chairman from among Republican senators, representatives, governors, state chairmen, and members of the national committee. Its purpose is to help formulate party policies and campaign strategy.

Campaign Committees. A senatorial campaign committee and a congressional campaign committee are maintained by each party to direct campaign efforts in behalf of party aspirants for national legislative seats. Separate bodies were established to prevent campaigning from falling wholly into executive hands. The Republicans originated this, forming a joint body in 1866 during the struggle between President Johnson and congressional leaders. Subsequently the body split into separate groups for Senate and House. The Republican Senatorial Campaign Committee now is composed of seven members chosen for two-year terms by the Republican caucus of the Senate. The Republican Congressional Campaign Committee is composed of one representative from each state with a Republican in the House; selection is made by the state congressional delegation. The Democratic arrangements are similar.

The committees function chiefly during campaigns, trying to maintain and increase the seats held by their respective parties in the Senate and the House. Each group keeps a small nucleus staff on a permanent basis. Since none has demonstrated much independent money-raising ability, each has relied mainly upon the party national committee. The committees compile the voting records of sitting members, analyze political possibilities in the various states and districts, and in other ways prepare for congressional elections.

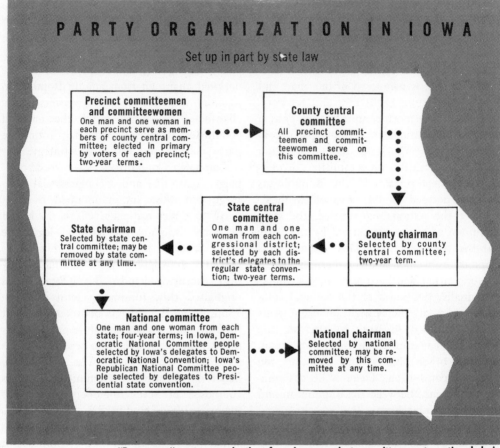

PARTY ORGANIZATION IN IOWA

Set up in part by state law

Precinct committeemen and committeewomen
One man and one woman in each precinct serve as members of county central committee; elected in primary by voters of each precinct; two-year terms.

County central committee
All precinct committeemen and committeewomen serve on this committee.

State chairman
Selected by state central committee; may be removed by state committee at any time.

State central committee
One man and one woman from each congressional district; selected by each district's delegates to the regular state convention; two-year terms.

County chairman
Selected by county central committee; two-year term.

National committee
One man and one woman from each state; four-year terms; in Iowa, Democratic National Committee people selected by Iowa's delegates to Democratic National Convention; Iowa's Republican National Committee people selected by delegates to Presidential state convention.

National chairman
Selected by national committee; may be removed by this committee at any time.

"Permanent" party organization, from Iowa precinct committeemen to national chairman, is well illustrated by this diagram. Conventions and other features of "periodic" organization are not included. [Adapted from George B. Mather, Voting in Iowa (Iowa City, Iowa: Department of Publications, State University of Iowa, 1956), p. 47.]

State Central Committees. A state central committee oversees all party machinery in its area, directs campaigns for state officers and for United States senatorships, and mobilizes state efforts in behalf of the national ticket. State committeemen, chosen by election or by appointment, represent legislative districts, counties, or some other subdivision.

Most state committees are not assigned significant powers, but a few decide whether the party shall use the convention or primary nominating method. They range in number of members from a handful in some states to nearly seven hundred in California. The large committees in practice delegate powers and duties to an executive group which makes the effective decisions. Some state committees have authority to fill vacancies occurring after a convention or primary among the party nominees for office. Occasionally the chairman of the state central committee is a political figure of importance; more commonly he is a front for a stronger man or group in the background.

County Committees. County central committees coordinate the work of all lesser bodies, act on matters affecting county government, and deal in important matters with state central committees. There are over 3,000 counties; virtually all are organized by one or both parties.

District party organizations in considerable number stand between the state and local levels. They are set up in state senatorial, state representative, congressional, and state judicial districts. Their position in the party structure varies considerably from state to state and from urban to rural area.

Local Organization. The precinct, or polling district, is the basic unit in party organization. Its size is determined by population density and the number of voters that election officials can handle conveniently. Between one and five hundred voters are included in the average precinct. About 125,000 precincts exist in the United States; of these perhaps 100,000 have active party organizations. The chairman or executive of the party precinct unit is responsible for the party's direct contacts with voters in their home districts. He provides the personal services in exchange for which people of the precinct may be willing to cast their ballots.

In an urban community a ward committee is usually the next level of organization. (A ward is a district from which local councilmen often are elected.) This party committee coordinates work of precinct units and deals with local political problems, especially with municipal-council politics. A city committee oversees the ward and precinct levels and attends to municipal problems and offices. Township or village committees exist in rural areas to bring together precinct representatives and plan party activities in relation to local governments.

Extralegal Party Groups. The informal organizations of parties often loom large in the political sky. This designation covers a wide range of clubs, associations, and other bodies on levels as diverse as neighborhood caucuses and great national campaign committees.

On the national scene, the most influential and the best financed have been groups seeking the presidential nomination for a particular aspirant, like the National Citizens for Eisenhower and the National Volunteers for Stevenson. Such bodies have demonstrated a capacity to secure support and raise money among people who might shun direct party activity. After securing the nomination they often continue activity through the general election campaign in order to appeal to the independent voters. Although their methods may differ from those of the regular party machines, such groups are likely to supplement national presidential campaigns.

On the state and local fronts, extralegal party organizations are assuming great importance. Official party bodies are closely regulated by state law, which sometimes denies them the discretion to mount a campaign effectively or participate in the primaries. Consequently, informal groups perform functions from which the formal parties are precluded. An aggressive role in the nominating process is a common characteristic. Local clubs and organizations, federated on regional and state levels, search for candidates, narrow the field of aspirants in primaries, raise money and finance campaigns—both primary and general.[1]

[1]For specific examples, see Frank J. Sorauf, "Extralegal Political Parties in Wisconsin," *American Political Science Review*, vol. 48 (September, 1954), pp. 692–704; Hugh A. Bone, "New Party Associations in the West," *ibid.*, vol. 45 (December, 1951), pp. 1115–1125; and Currin V. Shields, "A Note on Party Organization: The Democrats in California," *Western Political Quarterly*, vol. 7 (December, 1954), pp. 673–683.

Machines and Bosses. Although political parties appear essential to the proper functioning of democratic politics on a national scale, parties themselves are often controlled by a single autocrat or group. Political parties in a big democracy are leviathans that must be manned, fed, and directed. In parties and areas with high civic spirit and interest, party affairs may be conducted on a democratic basis. The extent of intraparty democracy varies widely from party to party and from country to country. Commonly, party machinery in democratic countries falls under the control of a small group. A student of Continental European politics has called this the "oligarchical tendency," in which control passes from the masses to professional leadership.[1]

The boss is a political leader who maintains power through corruption, spoils, and patronage. The machine is the organization through which the dominant group or individual rules. Political machines and bosses have flourished in America, utilizing bribery, patronage, special favors, and rigged elections; but since 1940, the number of prominent bosses has declined to almost nil.

Nonpartisanship. Shortly after the turn of the century, criticism of political parties became violent. A progressive reform proposed in many states was the outright abolition of parties. Some argued that, especially in local government, the issues had little relation to national party alignment; there was no Republican or Democratic way to pave a street. Others answered that the vital local problems are connected with state and national issues, and the political party performs functions necessary to a big democracy.

[1] Robert Michels, *Political Parties: A Sociological Study of the Oligarchical Tendencies of Modern Democracy* (New York: Hearst's International Library Co., 1915), pp. 54ff.

In practice, the legislative elimination of parties from state and local affairs has produced disappointing results. In some instances the parties have continued to exist without recognition on the ballot, as in the Minnesota legislature. In most cases, parties cut out of local affairs have withered on what was left of the vine; weakened by the severance of roots from local politics, they have had to live from year to year on the plasma of national-election activity. Denied the leadership of his party, the urban voter in a nonpartisan election is often completely uninformed about the stands of candidates on public issues. Politics degenerates into irresponsibility, with interests, groups, and individuals striving for power and influence.

Seeking to rid themselves of the evils of the party system, reformers abolished the system itself, expecting the evils to expire. Actually, spoils and corruption continued, and the voter no longer had a clear alternative to accepting the officeholders in control. Instead, he was forced to grope through the long ballot, searching, often in vain, for a clue on how to vote. Deploring the trend toward nonpartisanship in local government, the late Edward M. Sait declared:

Very soon there would be no parties anywhere in the United States, if they were left floating in the air without any local base. National organization depends ultimately upon precinct organization. The conduct of national campaigns depends upon continuous experience in fighting local campaigns. Democracy cannot live without parties and parties cannot live in the stratosphere.[2]

[2] Edward M. Sait, *American Parties and Elections* (New York: Appleton-Century-Crofts, 1942), p. 242. Copyrighted by the publishers; quoted by permission. For a study of the effects of nonpartisanship, see Charles R. Adrian, "Some General Characteristics of Nonpartisan Elections," *American Political Science Review*, vol. 46 (September, 1952), pp. 766–776.

Most authorities on local government favor nonpartisanship for municipal and county elections. Since local jurisdictions that have abolished party designations are unlikely to return to partisanship, the party organization must be strengthened by other means. While the detailed steps toward restoring parties will vary from state to state, attention might be given to election of precinct leaders, to preprimary conferences, and to rigid party-affiliation tests for candidates for state and congressional offices.

PARTY FINANCES

Campaigns Cost Money. Money is of key importance in American politics. An enormous amount must be spent to reach the vast electorate. Public inertia is high; to break it down and secure political activity is expensive. The general use of the direct primary doubles the number of elections; elective offices are numerous; and terms of public officers are relatively short. It is necessary to buy the means of reaching voters; radio and television time, newspaper space, and the printing of campaign literature are costly.

No really accurate figures on total campaign costs exist because no adequate system of reporting expenditures has been devised. Each time major changes are made in the law regulating political spending, the parties and candidates accommodate themselves to the changes, but spending continues to increase. There may even be a reduction in the degree of responsibility for expenditures as legal restrictions are extended.

After the Republican and Democratic national committees reported expenditures totaling 14 million dollars in the 1936 campaign, there was a demand for a ceiling. Congress then enacted the 1940 amendments to the Hatch Act, forbidding any party committee to spend more than 3 million dollars in one campaign. The national committees did reduce their income and outgo to fit the legal limit, but the burden of financing party activities was shifted over to various state and auxiliary bodies. The net result is spending by agencies that are less responsible and more obscure.

In 1960 the Republican national committee spent $2,991,221, and the Democratic $3,067,636, including refunded contributions. Combined reported campaign costs for 1960, excluding debts, totaled over $28 million, of which nearly $15 million was spent for Republican candidates and more than $10 million for Democratic. The remainder was spent by groups which could not be identified exclusively with a single party. Private estimates of the aggregate cost of 1960 elections—national, state, and local—ran as high as $175 million.

Sources of Funds. Who puts up the money for election campaigns? Are officeholders placed under obligation to those who have financed their campaigns? The high cost of campaigning is one of the major unsolved problems in politics.

Political funds come from various sources. Perhaps the most meaningful classification places on one side the contributions of well-wishers genuinely interested in the cause; on the other, the donations of those who want something in return. Neither major party has succeeded in getting more than a small proportion of its revenues through small donations ($1 to $25) from individuals, although the Democrats made real progress in this direction in 1940 and 1952. If a Federal income-tax deduction were allowed for campaign contributions, as in some states, political financing might be easier. Revenues other than individual contributions have loomed larger in recent years. Losing out on big donations, the Democrats after 1932 secured much money

REPORTED EXPENDITURES, PRESIDENTIAL AND CONGRESSIONAL CAMPAIGNS, 1960

REPUBLICAN ▬   ## DEMOCRATIC ▬

PARTY NATIONAL COMMITTEES

REPUBLICAN		DEMOCRATIC
$2,991,221	National Committee	$3,067,636
625,724	Senatorial Committee	250,290
2,231,232	Congressional Committee	210,700

OTHER POLITICAL COMMITTEES

	Citizens for Kennedy-Johnson	3,004,900
	Democratic Campaign Committee of Philadelphia	392,920
	National Committee of Business and Professional Men and Women for Kennedy-Johnson	130,633
	Southern California Campaign Committee for Kennedy-Johnson	312,628
1,901,994	Independent Television Committee	
277,623	National Nixon-Lodge Club	
2,125,523	National Volunteers for Nixon-Lodge Finance Committee	
158,620	1960 Republican Campaign Dinner of the Republican State Committee for the District of Columbia	
636,827	Republican Finance Committee of Allegheny County	
318,110	Republican State Committee for the District of Columbia	
115,696	United Republican Finance Committee for the State of New York	
132,310	United Republican Finance Committee of San Mateo County	

LABOR GROUPS (largely favoring Democrats)

Committee on Political Education AFL-CIO	795,140
International Ladies' Garment Workers Union, 1960 Campaign Committee	315,676
Machinists Non-Partisan Political League	193,244
United Steelworkers of America, Voluntary Political Action Fund	239,463

SENATE AND HOUSE CANDIDATES

REPUBLICAN		DEMOCRATIC
$2,523,869	Senate and House	$2,249,719

SUMMARY OF REPORTED EXPENDITURES

12,200,232	Party Committee Totals	7,980,979
	Labor	2,450,944

Expenditures reported under the Federal Corrupt Practices Act represent only a small proportion of the total cost of presidential, congressional, and other campaigns. (Compiled from *Congressional Quarterly*.)

through high-priced dinners, book sales, and trade-union contributions.

Since 1943, trade unions have been forbidden to contribute to political objectives and, under the Taft-Hartley Act, to spend union dues on them. These restrictions do not apply to contributions made from unions' political funds raised through voluntary contributions. Labor political groups reported expenditures aggregating about $2,000,000 each recent presidential election year, largely to help Democrats.

Officeholders are always an important source of financial support for the party in power. The Hatch Act and civil-service rules prevent forced contributions from Federal officers and from state and local employees who engage in federally aided work. Nevertheless, many officeholders continue to make voluntary contributions; the number of substantial contributions from individuals whose offices or homes are in Washington, D.C., is often taken as an index of officeholder interest.

The individual contribution from well-to-do persons remains the mainstay of party finance. Corporations are forbidden by Federal law and by the laws of most states to make campaign contributions. Therefore gifts from corporate sources are made by officers of the concerns, who may be compensated through bonuses or stock options. The Senate subcommittee recorded 1956 contributions in excess of $250 made by officers and directors of 225 corporations. Republicans got the lion's share; Democrats received rather little.

Those who study campaign funds take considerable interest in the volume and direction of political giving by wealthy families. Among the heaviest contributors are the Du Ponts, Rockefellers, Pews, Mellons, and Whitneys. Most of this money goes to the Republican party and candidates.

The Hatch Act provision that no individual may contribute more than $5,000 to

Early in 1958 some Texans gave a $100-a-plate dinner to express appreciation to minority leader Joseph Martin. Herblock pictures the administration's embarrassment. [From *Herblock's Special for Today* (Simon and Schuster).]

'I'VE TOLD YOU FIFTY TIMES—NOT AT THE FRONT DOOR!'

a political committee has not barred those who wish to contribute more; dozens evade this restriction each campaign year by making several contributions, none over $5,000, to several different committees. A wealthy candidate chosen for his ability to carry an important share of the financial burden of the campaign is called a "fat cat."

Legal Regulation. The principal Federal law governing money in elections is the Corrupt Practices Act of 1925, as subsequently amended.[1] It contains three principal elements: financial reports are required; expenditures by candidates are limited; and contributions to campaign

[1] A convenient summary of Federal and state laws governing money in elections is contained in U.S. Senate, Committee on Rules and Administration, *Election Law Guidebook*, 1956, S. Doc. 116, 84th Cong., 2d Sess. (1956).

funds from certain sources are forbidden.

National political committees, defined as those attempting to influence the election of Federal officers in two or more states, are required to report their financial transactions. Each must report quarterly on money received and spent; preliminary to general elections, two reports are required; a cumulative statement is due at the end of each calendar year. Candidates must report twice: before and after the election. Individuals who contribute over $50 to candidates in two or more states, other than through political committees, are required to report. Committee reports must include a detailed and exact account of all contributions and expenditures, including the names and addresses of every person who contributed over $100, and a breakdown of expenditures over $10. A candidate's reports must show amounts and sources of all contributions received "with his knowledge or consent" and expenditures in certain categories; but unitemized totals suffice for other expenditures, and no reports are necessary for some.

The law sets an alternative limit on expenditures of either (1) a flat maximum of $10,000 by a candidate for senator and $2,500 for representative or (2) 3 cents per vote cast, up to $25,000 maximum for senator and $5,000 for representative.

The prohibitions on sources of contributions cover corporations and trade unions. Corporations, as noted above, are able to evade by making indirect contributions through corporate officers. Unions are permitted to collect and spend voluntary political funds.[1] Both corporations and unions pay printing and other bills for candidates, carrying such expenditures on their books as "business expense." This practice is doubly illegal in that it deprives the government of tax revenue and violates the corrupt-practices law.

After a court decision in 1921 indicating that Congress lacked power to regulate primaries, Congress gave up control over political funds in the nominating process. Twenty years later, however, the Supreme Court reversed the earlier decision and held that Congress could regulate primary elections of Federal officers.[2]

The Hatch Act of 1939, as amended, restricts public employee participation in politics and limits expenditures by political committees to 3 million dollars and contributions by individuals to $5,000. The Powers Act of 1944 forbids publication or circulation of political statements relating to candidates for Federal office without containing the names of persons responsible; this legislation applies to primaries as well as general elections. The Taft-Hartley Act of 1947 reiterates restrictions on trade-union spending for political purposes.

Failure of Controls. Many of the provisions of corrupt-practices laws, Federal and state, are disregarded and evaded; on the whole they are archaic and ill suited to present-day conditions. The reporting provisions are badly drawn, and the resultant reports have such lack of uniformity that they defy careful analysis. Primaries ought to be included under the law; the House committee[3] that investigated the 1950 election expenditures found that congressional candidates reported raising and spending

---

[1] During 1957 a Federal jury in Detroit held the United Automobile Workers not guilty of violation of the law in using regular union funds for political television broadcasts. No money was contributed to candidates. The program was one of a year-around "educational" series. Unless overruled, the decision may clear the way for many semipolitical programs by unions and corporations.

[2] The adverse decision was *Newberry v. United States,* 256 U.S. 232 (1921); the favorable one was *United States v. Classic,* 313 U.S. 299 (1941), reaffirmed in *Smith v. Allwright,* 321 U.S. 649 (1944).

[3] U.S. House of Representatives, Special Committee to Investigate Campaign Expenditures, *Report...,* H. Rept. 3252, 81st Cong., 2d Sess. (1951), p. 19. Data were obtained by questionnaire.

CORPORATIONS AND POLITICS

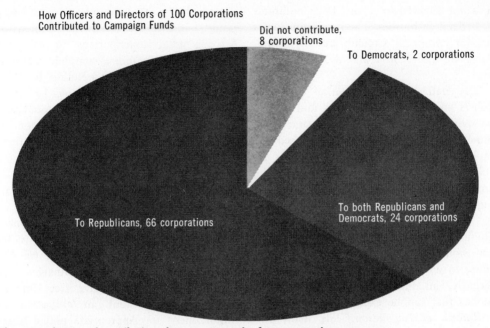

How Officers and Directors of 100 Corporations
Contributed to Campaign Funds

Did not contribute,
8 corporations

To Democrats, 2 corporations

To Republicans, 66 corporations

To both Republicans and
Democrats, 24 corporations

**The preponderance of contributions that come to parties from corporation sources go
to the Republican party. Very little goes to the Democrats. Several contribute to both
Republican and Democratic parties. [From Alexander Heard,** *Money and Politics* **(New
York: Public Affairs Committee, 1956), p. 18.]**

more in the primaries of that year than in the general election.

The House committee probing the 1952 expenditures reported that National Citizens for Eisenhower spent $1,200,000 in pre-convention activities.[1] In many states, nomination is tantamount to election, and nonregulation of the primary means non-regulation of the most crucial part of the electoral process. The "two or more states" test of a political committee excludes from the provisions of the act committees that may spend huge sums on behalf of a

[1] U.S. House of Representatives, Special Committee to Investigate Campaign Expenditures, *Report* . . . , H. Rept. 2517, 82d Cong., 2d Sess. (1953), p. 37.

senatorial candidate in a single state. Logically the law should require all committees seeking to influence the election of one or more Federal officers to report.

The maximum limits on campaign expenditures fixed by Federal law are unrealistic and invite evasion. Consider, for example, the provision limiting the expenditures on behalf of a candidate for the United States Senate to $25,000. In a state with over a million voters this would not pay for a postcard to mail to each voter, much less the cost of printing and addressing. The actual cost in hotly contested campaigns for the Senate in the larger states may exceed a million dollars. The dodge which candidates use is to report only the expenditures which they personally have made or know about, while committees carrying on the campaign spend vast sums of money which go unreported. If a political committee operates only in a single state, it is not required to report its expenditures to Federal authorities. The maximum limits set for campaign expenditures by candidates for the House are also ridiculously low.

The Hatch Act limitation of 3 million dollars on political committees and $5,000 on individual contributions has done much more harm than good. It has induced the proliferation of political committees, a development that actually has reduced the amount of responsibility in political spending.

Ceilings on expenditures or contributions are unworkable with present enforcement provisions. Perhaps the open and honest thing to do is to repeal, as did California recently, all limitations on amounts of money that can be expended.

Reform of Regulation. The main purpose of corrupt-practices laws should be to turn the light of publicity on spending. To do this effectively, a single depository for such reports must be established and given power to prescribe their form and to enforce the law. Greatest emphasis should be placed on getting full reports and fixing responsibility for spending. Political committees ought not to be permitted to receive contributions or make expenditures on behalf of a candidate without his consent.

Improvements in the laws also are needed to eliminate inconsistencies in the categorization of expenditures. The present laws require detailed itemization of some expenditures, only totals for others, and no accounting for a few. Once the responsibility for spending is firmly fixed on the candidate or his authorized agents, the powerful sanction of refusing to seat those who have not complied with the corrupt-practices laws may be invoked.

Although not enacted, a bill proposed in 1956 by Senate majority and minority leaders (with eighty-three cosponsors) may point to better regulation of party campaign funds.[1] Individuals would be limited to $10,000 total contributions in a single year. It would require a complete accounting of contributions and spending. Realistic campaign spending limits would be set; a sum of 20 cents per vote cast was proposed, with an alternate restriction of $75,000 for Senate and $15,000 for House. Others would extend to primaries all the controls that govern general elections.

Among other proposals for reform of campaign finance are the following: (1) Allow an income-tax deduction for contributions within limits. (2) Require radio and television stations to give free time to the parties during political campaigns. (3) Permit broadcasters to give free time to major parties without an obligation to minor ones. (4) Appropriate public funds to finance party activities. (5) Publish a "voter's pamphlet" at public expense. (6) Have political campaign funds audited by public authorities. (7) Create a national foundation to raise money and distribute it to the parties.

PARTY POLITICS IN FLUX

Present Party Alignment. At mid-century the country was beginning to feel the wind that changes the political weather. The impact of Franklin D. Roosevelt and the Depression was fading; the war and postwar periods produced problems that loomed to a younger generation. Whether the present decade marks a long-run and deep-seated change cannot yet be stated with assurance.

[1] It was S. 3308 in the 84th Cong., 2d Sess.

In any case, this is an appropriate time for stock taking. What was the difference, if any, between the Republican party and the Democratic party at the half-century mark?

Adherents. First, consider the composition of the parties, or their patterns of support. After twenty years of intensive public-opinion polling and an even longer period of careful analysis of election returns, we have a fairly clear idea of the habitual voting behavior of various elements in the population.

The Republicans retained, even in the years of the New Deal and Fair Deal (1933–1953), a considerable backlog of support among professional and business-executive people. The GOP remained the overwhelming choice of upper-income groups. The older elements of the population consistently veered toward the Republican side. Regionally, the party was strongest in the Northeast and Middle West. In terms of educational background, the Republicans won the majority of college people. Throughout the years of Democratic ascendancy, the Republicans maintained a bulwark of strength in small towns of most sections of the country.

The Democrats, for two decades after 1932, enjoyed the adherence of the majority of manual workers, skilled and unskilled, union and nonunion. In virtually all sections of the country, the low-income groups voted (if they voted) the Democratic line. The younger elements of the electorate showed pronounced preference for the party of Franklin D. Roosevelt. The South and the Border States supported the Democrats most consistently, but other states of the North and West were fairly faithful. Persons with only grade-school education tended to favor the Democratic party with their votes. The great cities went Democratic in election after election.

Independent Voters. In between the habitual supporters of the Republicans and of the Democrats are several elements that swing political preference. They are often identified as white collar by occupation, middle in income, and small-city and suburban in domicile. These groups have grown rapidly in size and political influence in the postwar period. As long as they divided somewhat evenly between the parties, their influence at the ballot box was not so plainly marked.

In 1952 and 1956, however, independent voters found a champion in General Dwight D. Eisenhower, and a strong majority turned to him. Their support constituted an important element in his victorious coalition. They now retain the balance of power in a number of pivotal Northern industrial states. There is much evidence that they are internationalist on foreign affairs and moderate on domestic issues. An isolationist or ultraconservative Republican is unlikely to win their continued support for the party. The Democrats made some inroads in 1960; whether they can win back a larger share in 1964 remains to be seen. In the meantime, their middle-class attitudes often are shaped by home ownership, acquisition of cars and appliances on credit, and identification with business interests, large or small.

Political Trends. The Democratic victory in House and Senate elections of 1954, 1956, and 1958 reemphasized that President Eisenhower's triumphs were mainly personal: in 1952 he ran over 5½ million votes ahead of Republican congressional candidates; in 1956 his margin was nearly 7½ million.

The Democratic victory in the congressional elections of 1958 was remarkable in several respects. The party complexion of both houses differed from that of the Presidency for the third successive Congress. The Republicans were left with few governors or

THE MAJOR PARTY VOTE SINCE 1904

Major Party Popular Vote
Republican Percentage   Democratic Percentage

1904 — Roosevelt   60.0   40.0

1908 — Taft   54.5   45.5

1912 — Wilson   25.1   74.9

1916 — Wilson   48.3   51.7

1920 — Harding   63.9   36.1

1924 — Coolidge   65.2   34.8

1928 — Hoover   58.8   41.2

1932 — Roosevelt   40.9   59.1

1936 — Roosevelt   37.5   62.5

1940 — Roosevelt   45.0   55.0

1944 — Roosevelt   46.2   53.8

1948 — Truman   47.7   52.3

1952 — Eisenhower   55.4   44.6

1956 — Eisenhower   58.0   42.0

1960 — Kennedy   49.9   50.1

senators of sufficient prominence to compete for the presidential nomination. Democratic majorities in the House and Senate approached those of the 1930s.

The closeness of the 1960 election places added emphasis on the personalities of presidential nominees. Unless war or economic chaos engulf the land, it is probable that the major parties will alternate frequently in control of the presidency. In the 1960 contests for the Senate, the Democrats had several advantages, defending seats that were relatively safe and nonpivotal; the Republicans made gains in the House.

There is likely to be stability in the basic coalitions of support for each party and the elements that constitute them. Elections, then, will be decided by slight shifts of sentiment among independent voters, or disaffection of particular groups or subgroups because of economic conditions or particular issues.

Liberal versus Conservative. The most persistent theme of critics of American parties is that a realignment should take place, making one party clearly left of center and the other right of center. Most assume that the Republican party could take the conservative role by divesting itself of a few Northern and Western mavericks and by adding reactionary Southern Democrats. Some think that the Democratic party could be transformed into a consistently progressive one by shedding certain Southern elements and making a strong appeal to the economically underprivileged of the South and other sections. Others argue that the Democratic party should be replaced by a new party with roots deep in the labor movement, and without the confusing and often contradictory traditions of the past.

Although it is possible to influence party alignment by changes in the electoral system, such as those proposed with respect to the Presidency, parties win their adherents and take on their policy coloration less from deliberate planning than from historical, emotional, and other factors. It appears likely that such changes as are made in the near future will be evolutionary rather than drastic and will take the form of gradual changes in the old parties rather than the launching of new ones.

In point of fact the two major parties differ considerably, not only in the candidates they present for office, but on important domestic and international issues. So long as the system operates on the basis of shifting groups, with each party vying for the support of the larger number, government will be by consensus, and it is apt to be conducted with due regard for the national interest.

Stronger and More Responsible Parties. Reform of the American political party system, discussed since the early years of the republic, came into the spotlight in 1950 and the years following. Interest was focused on the problem by a competent and controversial report, *Toward a More Responsible Two-party System,*[1] made by a committee of the American Political Science Association.

Present Inadequacies. The committee appropriately listed criticisms of the existing party system, including the lack of discipline, the disparity between platforms and performance, and the weakness of leadership. The existing Federal basis of the party organization was criticized as productive of divergent approaches to party strategy and policy. Leadership was considered so diffuse that no individual or body could deal authoritatively with major

[1] Supplement to *American Political Science Review*, vol. 44 (September, 1950); also published separately (New York: Rinehart, 1950). The chairman of the committee was E. E. Schattschneider, and its personnel included many of the leading students of politics.

VOTING PATTERNS OF SELECTED GROUPS

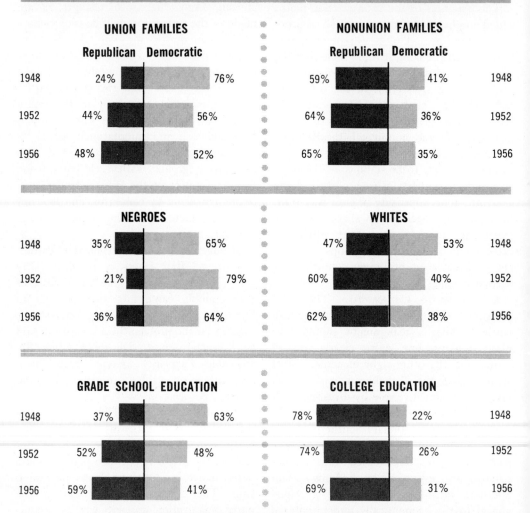

UNION FAMILIES

	Republican	Democratic
1948	24%	76%
1952	44%	56%
1956	48%	52%

NONUNION FAMILIES

Republican	Democratic	
59%	41%	1948
64%	36%	1952
65%	35%	1956

NEGROES

1948	35%	65%
1952	21%	79%
1956	36%	64%

WHITES

47%	53%	1948
60%	40%	1952
62%	38%	1956

GRADE SCHOOL EDUCATION

1948	37%	63%
1952	52%	48%
1956	59%	41%

COLLEGE EDUCATION

78%	22%	1948
74%	26%	1952
69%	31%	1956

In the 1956 presidential election voters of particular groups continued to choose sides much as they had in the past. (Data from the University of Michigan Survey Center.)

party problems. Membership remains a vague concept, scarcely more than a state of mind or a statement of preference.

Many organizational deficiencies were specified. The national convention was judged "an unwieldy, unrepresentative and less than responsible body."[1] Neither the national committees nor the campaign committees of House and Senate were deemed adequate. Party platforms are vague to the

[1] *Ibid.*, p. 3. Conventions are considered in Chap. 12.

point of being meaningless; the atmosphere in which they are written and adopted is far from deliberative; those who make the real decisions in Congress may be virtually unrepresented in the platform-framing process. Popular participation by party members in party affairs is at a low ebb.

Proposed Changes. The report called for stronger, better-integrated, and more responsible parties. National party bodies should be strengthened; the national convention should meet at two-year intervals, and its size should be reduced. Composition of the national committee should be subject to national-convention control, and the strength of the party in all sections of the country should be reflected in the apportionment of the committee. A new body, the "council," was proposed; it would govern the party between conventions and coordinate the various party organizations. Reliance would be placed on the council, a body of fifty members, to prepare advance drafts of the party platform, interpret the adopted platform, and resolve conflicts between national and state platforms.

Another series of recommendations concerned the conduct of party affairs in Congress. Frequent caucuses were suggested, with binding decisions used to carry out party-policy pledges. Congressional leaders of each party should be organized into an effective leadership committee, which would submit policy proposals to party membership, draw up slates for committee assignments, and generally plan party strategy in Congress.

In summarizing its case for action on reform proposals, the committee stressed the dangers of irresponsibility, of overextending the Presidency, of disintegration of the two-party system, and of the emergence of extremism of left and right in the wake of frustration over inaction.

"I've no objection to Adele's condidates, but it's made her drunk with power just from addressing his campaign envelopes!" (George Lichty and Chicago Sun-Times Syndicate.)

Criticisms of the Report. The report stimulated many dissents and critical replies.[1] Some denied the charge that American parties are irresponsible, stressing the different behavior of the two parties in office, especially in Congress. Others rejected tight discipline for political parties representative of a plural society of immense diversity. The American system operates, it was argued, on consensus basis,

[1] Among the many able commentaries on the report are T. William Goodman, "How Much Political Party Centralization Do We Want?" *Journal of Politics*, vol. 13 (November, 1951), pp. 536–561; Julius Turner, "Responsible Parties: A Dissent from the Floor," *American Political Science Review*, vol. 45 (March, 1951), pp. 141–152; Austin Ranney, "Toward a More Responsible Two-party System: A Commentary," *ibid.* (June, 1951), pp. 488–499; Murray S. Stedman, Jr., and H. Sonthoff, "Party Responsibility—A Critical Inquiry," *Western Political Quarterly*, vol. 4 (September, 1951), pp. 454–468.

each party striving to win enough groups and factions to tip the scales in its favor. Individualism, coupled with the tradition that representatives serve sectional rather than national interests, militates against

centralized and well-disciplined parties. Finally, the recommendations are criticized as being mainly mechanical; their application might lead to unexpected and undesired consequences.

FOR FURTHER READING

Acheson, Dean: A Democrat Looks at His Party (New York: Harper, 1955).

Bain, Richard C.: Decisions and Voting Records of the National Party Conventions (Washington, D.C.: Brookings Institution, 1960).

Bone, Hugh A.: American Politics and the Party System (New York: McGraw-Hill, 2d ed., 1955).

————: Party Committees and National Politics (Seattle: University of Washington Press, 1958).

Carney, Francis M., and H. Frank Way: Politics 1960 (San Francisco: Wadsworth, 1960).

Dale, Edwin L., Jr.: Conservatives in Power: A Study of Frustration (New York: Doubleday, 1960).

David, Paul T., Ralph M. Goldman, and Richard C. Bain: The Politics of National Party Conventions (Washington, D.C.: Brookings Institution, 1960).

David, Paul T., and others: Presidential Nominating Politics in 1952 (Baltimore: Johns Hopkins Press, 5 vols., 1954).

Duverger, M.: Political Parties: Their Organization and Activity in the Modern State (New York: Wiley, 1954).

Fenton, John H.: Politics in the Border States (New Orleans: Hauser Press, 1957).

Goodman, William: Two-party System in the United States (Princeton, N.J.: Von Nostrand, rev. ed., 1960).

Harris, Louis: Is There a Republican Majority? (New York: Harper, 1954).

Harris, Seymour E.: The Economics of the Political Parties (New York: Macmillan, 1962).

Heard, Alexander: The Costs of Democracy (Chapel Hill, N.C.: University of North Carolina Press, 1960).

————: A Two Party South? (Chapel Hill,

N.C.: The University of North Carolina Press, 1952).

Hesseltine, William B.: The Rise and Fall of Third Parties . . . (Washington, D. C.: Public Affairs Press, 1948).

Hinderaker, Ivan H.: Party Politics (New York: Holt, 1956).

Holcombe, Arthur N.: The Middle Classes in American Politics (Cambridge, Mass.: Harvard University Press, 1940).

Jonas, Frank H. (ed.): Western Politics (Salt Lake City, Utah: University of Utah Press, 1961).

Key, V. O., Jr.: Politics, Parties, and Pressure Groups (New York: Crowell, 4th ed., 1958).

————: Southern Politics in State and Nation (New York: Knopf, 1949).

————: American State Politics: An Introduction (New York: Knopf, 1956).

Larson, Arthur: A Republican Looks at His Party (New York: Harper, 1956).

Leiserson, Avery: Political Parties: An Introduction to the Study of Political Science (New York: Knopf, 1958).

Lubell, Samuel: The Future of American Politics (New York: Harper, 1952).

————: Revolt of the Moderates (New York: Harper, 1956).

McKean, Dayton D.: Party and Pressure Politics (Boston: Houghton Mifflin, 1949).

Mitchner, James A.: Report of the County Chairman (New York: Random House, 1961).

Moos, Malcolm C.: The Republicans (New York: Random House, 1956).

Nash, Howard P., Jr.: Gadflies of American Politics: A Short History of Third Parties (Washington, D.C.: Public Affairs Press, 1956).

Neumann, Sigmund (ed.): Modern Political Parties (Chicago: University of Chicago Press, 1956).

Odegard, Peter H., and E. Allen Helms: American Politics: A Study in Political Dynamics (New York: Harper, 2d ed., 1947).

Porter, Kirk H., and Donald B. Johnson: Na-

tional Party Platforms, 1840–1960 (Urbana, Ill.: University of Illinois Press, 2d ed., 1962).

Ranney, Austin: *The Doctrine of Responsible Party Government* (Urbana, Ill.: University of Illinois Press, 1954).

——— and W. Kendall: *Democracy and the*

American Party System (New York: Harcourt, Brace, 1956).

Shannon, David A.: *The Socialist Party of America: A History* (New York: Macmillan, 1955).

Turner, Henry A. (ed.): *Politics in the United States* (New York: McGraw-Hill, 1955).

REVIEW QUESTIONS

1. What is a political party?

2. What are the principal determining factors of party allegiance?

3. Various writers (e.g., Ostrogorski, Larned, and MacDonald) have complained that the two-party system falsifies and obscures the democratic political process. How serious are these defects? How would abandonment of the two-party system cure them?

4. The precinct leader has been called the "bone and sinew," "foundation," "real source of strength," and "backbone" of party organization. Why? Explain his methods.

5. Discuss the role of third parties in American politics. What part do they play in presidential elections? Congress? Party platforms?

6. Trace the history of the Democratic party from Jefferson to Stevenson.

7. Trace the history of the Republican party from Frémont to Eisenhower.

8. Describe the composition and functions of the following party committees: national, senatorial campaign, congressional campaign.

9. What are the principal provisions of Federal law governing the expenditure of funds and the raising of money for national elections?

10. A generation ago most large cities of the United States had bosses or machines that were widely known for their power. How many can you name today? To what do you attribute the decline in number or notoriety?

Chapter Twelve

Suffrage, Nominations, and Elections

*[The American masses] . . . are accustomed to being static
and receptive. They are not daring, but long for security.
They do not know how to cooperate and how to pool
risks and sacrifices for a common goal. They do not meet
much. They do not organize. They do not speak for
themselves; they are listeners in America. They seldom
elect representatives from their own midst to Congress,
to state legislatures or to city councils. They rather support
friendly leaders from the upper strata, particularly
lawyers. . . . Political participation of the ordinary citizen
in America is pretty much restricted to the intermittently
recurring elections. Politics is not organized to be a daily
concern and responsibility of the common citizen.*

GUNNAR MYRDAL[1]

Most Americans are confused by the complex ways used to nominate and elect their
officials. Part of the confusion results from
the fact that responsibility is divided between Federal, state, and local governments.
Difficulties are compounded by the diverse
procedures followed in the various states.
Furthermore, the voter is assigned more
work than he can or will perform satisfactorily.

[1] *An American Dilemma* (New York: Harper,
1944), pp. 714, 717.

Although difficult to understand, nomination and election procedures are vital, for
by them the people's will is most directly
expressed. This chapter attempts to clarify
these essential features of the democratic
process and point the way to their reform.

THE RIGHT TO VOTE

Federal Requirements. Matters pertaining
to suffrage are regulated chiefly by the
states. Four Federal requirements are set

forth in the Constitution: (1) Those permitted to vote for the most numerous branch of the state legislature are allowed in each state to participate also in election of Federal officers. (2) The Fourteenth Amendment permits Congress to reduce the congressional representation of any state disfranchising a portion of its adult male population. But this penalty has never been invoked. (3) The Fifteenth Amendment forbids states to deny or abridge the right to vote on account of race, color, or previous condition of servitude. (4) The Nineteenth Amendment prohibits discrimination because of sex. The three amendments have reduced state discretion in suffrage matters, altering the original reliance upon state definition of who might vote.

Under the terms of the Civil Rights Acts of 1957 and 1960, the United States assumes additional responsibility in assuring the right to vote. The Attorney General can inspect and copy voting records and apply for Federal court injunctions to prevent violations. Federal judges may appoint "voting referees" and issue binding "voting certificates." The Civil Rights Commission and the civil rights division of the Department of Justice were created by the legislation. Federal injunctive relief for suffrage was upheld in *United States v. Raines* [362 U.S. 17 (1960)].

State Prerequisites for Voting.[1] One universal requirement for voting is citizenship. All states now insist that a person must be a full-fledged citizen of the United States before exercising the franchise. Formerly, several states permitted aliens to vote if they had declared their intention to become citizens.

A minimum voting age of twenty-one long prevailed in all states, but Georgia in 1944 and Kentucky in 1955 cut it to eighteen. Alaska permits voting at nineteen, Hawaii at twenty. During recent years, the paradox involved in drafting young men of eighteen to fight for their country but denying them the vote inspired a campaign to reduce the voting age. President Eisenhower advocated an amendment to the Constitution to set the voting age at eighteen. It has been argued that the eighteen to twenty-one group is as alert and able to understand political issues as those seventy-five years and over; yet no one has suggested seriously that a maximum age for voting be established. If enfranchised in all states, the eighteen to twenty-one group would add approximately 8 million new voters to the electorate.

Another qualification imposed in all states is period of residence. Most states indicate that a person must have lived in the state for one year. Several states of the North and East demand only six months' residence, and a handful in the Deep South insist upon two years. There are also requirements of residence in counties and precincts; the median is about ninety days in the county and thirty days in the polling district.

Registration is almost uniformly demanded; only one state has no registration plan, but several states require only urban voters to sign up in advance. The purpose of registration is to prevent fraudulent voting.[2] It provides that voters be enrolled in advance of an election; this permits inspection of the rolls by interested persons. A majority of the states have now adopted the permanent type of registration, under which a voter, once enrolled, remains on the rolls until he dies, moves, fails to vote in an important election, or otherwise dis-

[1] Factual data are drawn from *The Book of the States*. See current issue for latest information.

[2] Joseph P. Harris, *Registration of Voters in the United States* (Washington, D.C.: Brookings, 1929), is the standard work on registration.

qualifies himself. A few states still retain the periodic system, which calls for complete reregistration every one, two, four, or six years. Periodic registration is more expensive and more trouble for the public; it is generally considered inferior to permanent registration.

Some form of literacy test is employed in eighteen states. In a few states this check of ability to read and write is carefully administered; it represents a defense against an uninformed electorate and a proper barrier against fraud, for the votes of illiterates might be bought and delivered in the presence of their assisters. On the other hand, it has been administered in some Southern states in such a manner as to disfranchise Negroes, irrespective of their educational qualifications.

Many states disqualify various groups from voting because of insanity, idiocy, feeble-mindedness, or conviction of a felony.

Evidence of tax payment is still required in several states. In the early days of the Republic, the right to vote was reserved carefully for those who held property. As the spirit of democracy spread, property qualifications were lessened and repealed. Today only a few vestigial property qualifications remain, usually as alternatives for other requirements. Five states, however, have retained poll taxes as prerequisites to voting. The poll tax, having become one of the most controversial questions concerning the right to vote, requires fuller examination.

Poll Taxes under Fire. Recent attempts to eliminate poll taxes as prerequisites to voting in Alabama, Arkansas, Mississippi, Texas, and Virginia have aroused bitter arguments. Poll taxes are head taxes of from $1 to $2 on each adult (or each male) within specified age groups. To discourage

payment, usually no bills are sent out and little effort is made to collect; payments are often due far in advance of elections.

The effect of the poll tax has been to disfranchise poor people, both white and Negro. Participation in elections is very low in the states using the device. In 1960 the five states then having poll taxes accounted for 6.4 per cent of the vote for presidential electors, although they had 11.6 per cent of the nation's population in the 1960 census. Critics of the poll tax have stressed the corrupting influence of the requirement for voting. The participating electorate is so small that vested interests or political machines may control elections by buying poll-tax receipts for a few hundred persons. The basic argument against the poll tax is that voting is a right not to be abridged through lack of capacity to pay.

Organizations seeking the elimination of the poll tax have concentrated their attack on three principal fronts. Initially, they sought congressional legislation to abolish the poll tax in Federal elections. First introduced in the House of Representatives in 1940, the bill (under the power of Congress to control the "manner" of electing senators and representatives) would have outlawed poll taxes as fostering pernicious political activities.

In various forms the bill was reintroduced in the next six Congresses and passed by the House of Representatives each time, but it was obstructed in the Senate through filibuster and threat of filibuster. Opponents of the reform charge that the bill is unconstitutional and invades state rights. Proponents cite eminent legal authorities who assert that the Federal government has adequate power to keep the states from denying the franchise to citizens on grounds of nonpayment of the poll tax, which is not a true "qualification."

Second, Southern states are being urged to repeal their poll-tax laws. Six of them have done so since the First World War: North Carolina, 1920; Louisiana, 1934; Florida, 1937; Georgia, 1945; South Carolina, 1950; and Tennessee, 1951.

Third, court proceedings have been instituted to apply the test of constitutionality to poll taxes in both state and Federal courts.

In 1962 Congress submitted to the states a proposed constitutional amendment to ban poll and other tax requirements for voting in Federal elections. It will go into effect if ratified by the legislatures of 38 states within seven years. The measure, when approved by the states, will be the Twenty-fourth Amendment.

The White Primary. The most recent and effective device developed by the Southern states to disfranchise colored people is the white primary. Since the Democratic party usually enjoys supremacy in the Deep South, voting in the Democratic primary is far more important than voting in the general election. The earliest barriers to Negro participation in Democratic party affairs were erected by party rule. In 1923, however, the Texas legislature enacted a law forbidding Negro participation in Democratic primary elections. The United States Supreme Court declared the law a violation of the equal-protection clause of the Fourteenth Amendment [*Nixon v. Herndon*, 273 U.S. 536 (1927)]. Then the Texas legislature repealed the voided statute and substituted a provision that the executive committee of each party might prescribe the qualifications for party membership. The Supreme Court again ruled that equal protection had been denied [*Nixon v.*

Condon, 286 U.S. 73 (1932)]. Subsequently the state convention of the party limited the primary to white voters; since the party was a private association which conducted its own primaries, the Court held that it could exclude colored people without violation of equal protection [*Grovey v. Townsend*, 295 U.S. 45 (1935)]. The Classic case fused primary and general elections into a single instrumentality.[2] The Grovey case was reversed in *Smith v. Allright* [321 U.S. 649 (1944)], which held invalid rules of the Texas Democratic party that forbade Negro voting, on grounds of denial of right to vote under the Fifteenth Amendment. Also invalidated by the Supreme Court was a "pre-primary primary," conducted by a Texas association consisting of all qualified white voters in a county [*Terry v. Adams*, 345 U.S. 461 (1953)].

South Carolina's attempt to retain the white primary by repealing all statutory references to primaries was declared void in the United States circuit court. Despite these rulings, it appears that social and economic pressure will continue to be used to discourage Negro participation in Democratic primaries in some Southern states.

METHODS OF NOMINATING CANDIDATES

Early Presidential Nominations. No nominating methods were necessary in the first three presidential elections. Members of the electoral college considered themselves free agents but managed to agree without difficulty upon Washington twice and Adams once. By 1800 the emergence of political parties emphasized the need for machinery to make the party's choice.

The congressional caucus came to the fore quite naturally to fill the need. Com-

[2] The Classic decision, explained on pp. 204 and 218, did not mention *Grovey v. Townsend*.

©1956, Field Enterprises, Inc.

WELCOME DELEGATES

"Testing . . . in the glorious tradition of the founding fathers . . . We stand on the threshold of destiny . . . as pure as the honor of American womanhood . . . testing . . ."

(George Lichty and Chicago Sun-Times Syndicate.)

posed of the party's senators and representatives in Congress, it was easy to convene and reasonably representative of party sentiment. The chief weakness of the scheme of nominating was that it denied representation to states with no congressmen of a particular party. In 1824, after the Federalist party had expired, the Democratic-Republicans in congressional caucus chose Crawford of Georgia; three other aspirants of the same party, Jackson, John Quincy Adams, and Clay, entered their candidacies. The election was thrown to the House of Representatives, which chose Adams, badly discrediting the congressional caucus.

The national convention, composed of delegates from the various states, replaced the congressional caucus as nominating body for the election of 1832. It has been used

ever since. The Antimasonic party first employed the device in 1831; both the new National Republicans and Jackson's Democrats adopted it promptly.

National Party Conventions. The national conventions have never been governed by Federal law. For twenty years, between 1921 and 1941, the Supreme Court decision *Newberry v. United States* [256 U.S. 232 (1921)] stood as a barrier to congressional attempts to regulate the nominating process. A later decision, *United States v. Classic*, appears to mark a reversal of the Court's attitude.[1] No real attempt, however, has yet been made by Congress to utilize this renewed power. The only legal control is exercised by the states, which by law may establish methods of selecting delegates, as well as rules governing their conduct.

The time of a convention is determined largely by custom. Until recently, Republicans met in the second half of June or in early July, and Democrats about two weeks later. In 1952 and 1960, both conventions were held in July; in 1956 both occurred in August. One reason for the later dates is the great expense, particularly with television, involved in longer campaigns.

The meeting place is decided by the national committee, after considering several factors: (1) Financial inducement is offered by various cities; in recent years about $200,000 has been paid by business people of the city successful in bidding for a major party convention. (2) Strategic location of a city in a pivotal state or section is highly important, for each party hopes to arouse support in the region of the convention city. (3) Facilities and accessibility, including hotel, restaurant, transportation, and communication services on an adequate

[1] 313 U.S. 299 (1941). The Classic case concerned prosecution for frauds perpetrated in a primary election.

scale and a mammoth meeting hall, are necessary.

Convention Representation and Delegates. Until 1916 both parties used the same formula for representation at their conventions: each state was permitted two delegates for each of its two senators plus two for each of its representatives in the House.[1] In the Republican party this basis of representation was attacked on the ground that it gave the same voting strength to delegations from Southern states, where the party had little voting strength, as to Northern and Western states of the same population which regularly elected Republican members of Congress and cast their electoral votes for the Republican candidates. In most Southern states the Republican party was largely a paper organization controlled by a few Federal officeholders when the party was in power; hence a Republican President could always control this sizable block of delegate votes in the national convention. Thus in 1912, President Taft had the solid support of the Republican delegations from the South, which enabled him to defeat Theodore Roosevelt, favored by the majority of delegates from the Republican states outside the South.

This bitter convention fight, leading temporarily to a division of the Republican party, forced the 1916 reforms. They reduced the voting strength of the Southern states in the Republican national conven-

tion. Since then the basis of representation has been revised several times, each time reducing the vote accorded to states where the voting strength of the party is weak. The latest change was made in 1952 after the "regular" delegations from Texas, Louisiana, and Georgia, who supported Senator Robert A. Taft of Ohio for the nomination, were unseated and their seats given to contesting delegations favoring General Eisenhower.

The basis of state representation in the Republican national convention is as follows:

Delegates at large

Four for each state.

Two for each representative elected at large.

Six additional if the state went Republican or elected a Republican governor or United States senator at the last election.

District delegates

One for each congressional district which cast 2,000 Republican votes at the last election.

One additional delegate for each congressional district which cast 10,000 Republican votes at the last election.

In 1956 the Republican Convention had a total voting strength of 1,323, and in 1960, of 1,331.

In 1940 the Democrats yielded to Southern pressure and provided a modest bonus for states showing Democratic voting strength. Each state that went Democratic in a presidential election was given four extra votes at large in the national convention four years later. The method yielded 1,234 votes in 1948 and 1,230 in 1952. For 1956, an additional bonus of four votes was given to each state carried by a Democrat for President, governor, or

---

[1] As used here, "delegate" means vote in convention. In order to honor party bigwigs, the state organizations often send huge delegations to national conventions, each individual casting only a fraction of one vote. In the Democratic convention of 1940, one district in Mississippi sent fifty-four delegates to cast its two votes; each delegate had 1/27 vote. That same convention adopted a rule, effective in 1944, that no delegate may have less than one-half vote. Nevertheless, there were some one-third votes in the 1952 Democratic Convention.

senator in the preceding four years. The 1960 total was 1,521 votes.

In the conventions of both parties, several delegates are also accorded to Canal Zone, Puerto Rico, the Virgin Islands, and the District of Columbia. This is to keep the parties alive in these areas, even though they have no electoral votes.

Delegates are selected in one of two ways: (1) State and district conventions or party committees, in about two-thirds of the states, utilize state and congressional-district machinery to choose delegates and often to direct how they shall vote or (2) presidential primaries, used in approximately one-third of the states, provide a direct choice by the electorate. Three states use a combination of the two. The first method is favored by many party leaders, largely because it is flexible and provides maximum bargaining power for state interests.

Presidential Primaries. Two main forms of the presidential primary are: (1) election of delegates, who may be pledged or unpledged, and (2) popular expression of preference among presidential aspirants. A few states provide for both. The presidential primary is regaining favor, but even in its heyday (1924 with twenty-three states) it was not a decisive force. Leading candidates may remain out of the primaries (as did Stevenson in 1952) or fail utterly in them (as did Hoover in 1928), yet secure the nomination without difficulty. A strong tendency is noted for states using the presidential primary to select delegates pledged to a "favorite son," some man from the home state. Sometimes this tactic is employed in a serious attempt to call the country's attention to his talents. More often it is a subterfuge through which a state delegation is able to be in a better bargaining position and throw its votes to a likely candidate who will reward the state properly.

On the other hand, the three recent preconvention campaigns stimulated a revival of public interest in the presidential primary. In 1952, the sharp contest for delegates between Robert A. Taft and Dwight D. Eisenhower brought out Republican voters in record numbers. The 1956 Democratic primary battle between Adlai Stevenson and Estes Kefauver attracted much attention. John F. Kennedy virtually

California has long elected pledged delegates on an at-large basis. The names of candidates for delegates are not printed on the ballot. In 1964 unpledged delegations will be allowed.

PRIMARY ELECTION

DEMOCRATIC PARTY

FOR DELEGATES TO NATIONAL CONVENTION	Vote for One Group Only
Candidates Preferring EDMUND G. "PAT" BROWN	
Candidates Preferring GEORGE McLAIN	

A presidential-primary short ballot for presidential aspirants: Indiana. Under this plan, delegates are chosen by party bodies, and popular participation is confined to the so-called "popularity contest" among those seeking the presidential nomination.

OFFICIAL PRIMARY BALLOT

REPUBLICAN PARTY

For President of the United States (Vote for one only)		For State Representative Marion County (Vote for eleven only)	
(1-A) LAR DALY	☐	(15-A) WALTER LYNN ABELL	☐
(2-A) DWIGHT D. EISENHOWER	☐	(16-A) WAYNE O. ADAMS, SR.	☐
		(17-A) WALTER H. BARBOUR	☐
For Representative in Congress Eleventh Congressional District (Vote for one only)		(18-A) OLIVER BELL, SR.	☐
(3-A) CHARLES B. BROWNSON	☐		

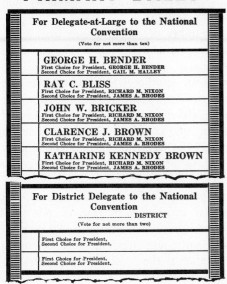

OFFICIAL REPUBLICAN PRIMARY BALLOT

For Delegate-at-Large to the National Convention

(Vote for not more than ten)

GEORGE H. BENDER
First Choice for President, GEORGE H. BENDER
Second Choice for President, GAIL M. HALLEY

RAY C. BLISS
First Choice for President, RICHARD M. NIXON
Second Choice for President, JAMES A. RHODES

JOHN W. BRICKER
First Choice for President, RICHARD M. NIXON
Second Choice for President, JAMES A. RHODES

CLARENCE J. BROWN
First Choice for President, RICHARD M. NIXON
Second Choice for President, JAMES A. RHODES

KATHARINE KENNEDY BROWN
First Choice for President, RICHARD M. NIXON
Second Choice for President, JAMES A. RHODES

For District Delegate to the National Convention

.... DISTRICT

(Vote for not more than two)

First Choice for President,
Second Choice for President,

First Choice for President,
Second Choice for President,

A presidential-primary long ballot for delegates indicating preference: Ohio. Ohio retains the long ballot, listing the names of all candidates for delegate, together with the first and second choices of each for President.

CANDIDATE OF THE

DEMOCRATIC PARTY

FOR

PRESIDENT

OF THE UNITED STATES

I HEREBY DECLARE MY PREFERENCE FOR CANDIDATE FOR THE OFFICE OF PRESIDENT OF THE UNITED STATES TO BE AS FOLLOWS:

PAUL C. FISHER ☐

JOHN F. KENNEDY ☐

For District Delegates:

Vote for not more than Ten:

FRANK T. CONWAY, Manchester ☐
FAVORABLE TO THE NOMINATION OF
JOHN F. KENNEDY FOR PRESIDENT

WILLIAM H. CRAIG, Manchester ☐
PLEDGED TO VOTE FOR THE NOMINATION OF
JOHN F. KENNEDY FOR PRESIDENT

J. FELIX DANIEL, Manchester ☐
FAVORABLE TO THE NOMINATION OF
JOHN F. KENNEDY FOR PRESIDENT

HELEN A. DESJARDINS, Rollinsford ☐
FAVORABLE TO THE NOMINATION OF
STUART SYMINGTON FOR PRESIDENT

HELENE R. DONNELLY, Dover ☐
FAVORABLE TO THE NOMINATION OF
STUART SYMINGTON FOR PRESIDENT

A presidential primary combining election of delegates and preferential votes: New Hampshire. New Hampshire combines the election of delegates and the pledging of the delegation through a preference vote. There is a chance of conflicting results, with one candidate securing the delegates and another the popularity contest.

won the Democratic nomination in 1960 through a series of presidential primary victories. People in states lacking the presidential primary complained about being deprived a voice in choosing their presidential candidate. In 1952, the Gallup poll reported that 53 per cent of those queried said that the people did not have enough to say in choosing presidential candidates; 73 per cent favored a nationwide primary election that would choose presidential candidates, in place of the present national conventions. In 1955, another Gallup poll reported 58 per cent for presidential primaries.

National Convention Procedure. The order of business is much the same in both party gatherings. The national chairman calls the meeting to order. A temporary convention chairman is chosen, and he gives the "keynote" address. Committees of the convention are set up, with one delegate from every state and territory on each committee. The credentials committee determines which are the official delegates for the final roll call; occasionally there is a contest over the authenticity of a delegation's credentials, so control of this committee may affect the choice of candidate for the Presidency. The committee on permanent organization brings in the slate of convention officers; its rejection may forecast a revolt against a leading presidential aspirant. A rules-and-order-of-business committee usually proposes rules of procedure identical with those of previous conventions. Finally, the platform-and-resolutions committee drafts the party declaration of principles and policies. The report on the platform is often hotly debated, but usually the majority report is adopted.

Choosing candidates for President and Vice President comes as the final important action. The roll is called by states, and delegations place in nomination the favored aspirants; this is occasion for elaborate oratory by nominators and seconders and for noisy floor demonstrations. When all contenders for the nomination are before the convention, the first polling begins, by states in alphabetical order. Often, especially in Republican conventions, some candidate secures the requisite majority on the first ballot. Sometimes conventions deadlock and many votes are required; the Democrats took 103 ballots in 1924 before the warring Smith and McAdoo factions could agree on John W. Davis as a compromise candidate.

Voting is done by states, but delegations may be polled individually on demand of a single delegate. The Democrats have a unit rule under which a majority of a state delegation from a nonprimary state may cast the full vote of a state (unless forbidden by that state's law). In 1936 the Democrats abolished the companion two-thirds rule, though Southern Democrats clung to it as vital to the protection of the minority and as an assurance against party splits. Its repeal, and the retention of the unit rule, makes likely in future Democratic conventions quicker victories for aspirants with plurality support.

A number of considerations may decide the vice-presidential contest. The successful presidential aspirant may have traded support with another who received the vice-presidential nomination (Garner, in 1932). Or the ticket may be balanced by nominating one who contrasts with the presidential nominee in section, religion, personality, policy, or other attributes (Sparkman, in 1952).

Reform of the National Convention. The national convention is one of our most criticized political institutions. To pick the major party nominees, we have two aggregations of a thousand or more delegates, chosen by miscellaneous means unlikely to produce majority choice, and meeting in an atmosphere of colossal clowning and high-pressure methods, wholly unregulated by Federal law. Millions of television viewers watched this spectacle in 1952 and 1956 and were disillusioned. Some improvements were made in 1956 to make it a better show, but the basic criticisms remain. On the other hand, the national convention has its strong defenders who maintain that, despite the shenanigans, the party leaders are able to select the most available candidates, and a nationwide primary would place a difficult task on the voters.

Woodrow Wilson, in his first annual message to Congress in 1913, urged the enactment of legislation to provide primary elections so that voters could select nominees for the Presidency without the intervention of nominating conventions. He suggested that platforms be made by a new type of party convention composed of nominees for the Senate and House, national committeemen, and the presidential nominee.

Although Congress took no action, the states moved rapidly to legislate regarding the selection of delegates and the expression of preferences by the electorate. After the Newberry decision, it was assumed for twenty years that Congress lacked power to regulate the nominating process. During this interim, presidential-primary enthusiasm waned, and the old-fashioned national convention with state- and district-convention–selected delegates returned to favor. Professor Overacker classified proposals for a national presidential primary into three: (1) Combine primary with existing conventions; (2) have existing conventions propose nominees but submit to primary for ratification; or (3) eliminate the convention and provide for direct nationwide primary.[1] After examining the difficulties connected with each proposal Overacker concludes that none gives much promise of adoption.

Two proposals to effect reform were before recent Congresses but received little support. The Douglas-Bennett bill provided for Federal inducement for states to conduct presidential primaries. It would authorize the Federal government to enter into agreements with willing states for the conduct of such contests and compensate states up to 20 cents for each vote cast.

The second proposal was a constitutional amendment by Florida Senator George Smathers. This would displace the convention with a uniform nationwide primary for selecting presidential and vice-presidential candidates of the parties. The "nominating votes" (equivalent of electoral vote) of each

[1] Charles E. Merriam and Louise Overacker, *Primary Elections* (Chicago: University of Chicago Press, 1928), p. 191.

state would be divided among presidential candidates in proportion to their popular votes. A majority would be required to nominate; if none were obtained in the first balloting by any candidate, then a second, runoff primary would be held between the two receiving the highest number of votes in the first primary.

A more drastic proposal is one that would restore the presidential caucus (perhaps including the nominees for Senate and House instead of sitting members only). This, it is argued, would help bring the legislative and executive branches closer together and assure greater deliberation and dignity.

Widespread state opposition to both the national primary and the Federal subsidy for state presidential primaries focuses attention on the improvement of state laws. In 1955 the National Municipal League issued a draft of a "model state presidential primary law" as a basis for discussion. The proposed law makes the presidential primary mandatory for larger parties. Voters must register their party affiliations in advance in order to participate. June is proposed as the best month for voting. The state central committee of each party may certify a list of candidates for delegates. Presidential aspirants may file lists of proposed delegates. Voting is by slate, all delegates being elected at large and the various slates winning places on the delegation in proportion to their popular showing. By the proposed law, presidential candidates may not bind their delegates after their support drops below 10 per cent, or after they receive support from only one state.

Nominations for Congressional and State Offices. The development of nominating methods may be indicated chronologically. Self-announcement and selection by informal caucus were used in the early days. This gave way to the legislative caucus, which was composed of partisans in legislative bodies. Criticisms of the unrepresentative character of the legislative caucus led to a modification called the "mixed" (mongrel) caucus, composed of legislators and some outside representatives. Gradually this form was superseded by the delegate convention, set up especially to make nominations. The convention system later was denounced as unrepresentative and controlled by corrupt interests. It was replaced by the direct primary, in which party voters participate directly in the nominating process.

The Convention System. After 1910 the convention was replaced largely by the direct primary. Connecticut, in 1955, was the last state to adopt the primary, but it is in only partial or optional operation in several states. Important use is made of the convention plan of nominating for some state-wide congressional and state offices in Indiana and New York. It is optional with the parties in several Southern states. Subordinate employment is made of conventions for framing party platforms in many other states. The usual pattern of the delegate convention calls for the election of delegates by voters affiliated with the party, or by party groups and committees. The delegates meet in convention under a procedure resembling that of a national convention.

The state- and local-convention method of nominating party candidates, discredited during the reform movement of the first two decades of the century, is restored to favor in the thinking of many students of government. The direct primary has not brought all the improvements predicted by those who believed it a panacea. The direct primary, particularly the open form, makes possible the sudden capture of a party's nomination by a maverick group or colorful individual with no previous party responsibility. Far from removing the control over the nominating process from bosses and machines, adoption of the primary in many states induced a sinister alliance of vested interests with newspapers. This combination succeeds in primaries because of public disinterest, disciplined machine vote, and blind following of newspaper endorsements.

Restoration of the convention system for making nominations of candidates for state-wide offices may produce abler and more responsible leadership. A major party in New York, for example, can offer a nomination to a leading citizen, whereas in some other states a party rarely can avoid a wide-open primary fight of a kind that drives men of reputation from consideration.

The Direct Primary. The direct primary is the most widely adopted of all nominating schemes. It is now mandatory or optional with the parties in the fifty states. Connecticut, in 1955, was the last state to provide it. Party voters indicate on a direct-primary ballot which aspirants they prefer to have as the party's nominees for public office. Usually this is done through a publicly conducted poll with all the safeguards of a general election. Most of the states use the "closed primary," which means that each voter may participate only in the nomination of candidates for the party with which he is registered or affiliated. The other type, the "open primary," is employed in eight states. It allows the voter to decide in the voting booth in which party's primary he wishes to vote without having to register or otherwise publicly disclose his party affiliation.

Advocates of the closed-primary system, usually strong party men, contend that only avowed members of the party, those who have registered as members or who are willing to declare their affiliation publicly,

Democratic-Farmer-Labor Party Ticket

You cannot split your ballot. If you vote for candidates of more than one party, your ballot will be rejected.

▼ Put an (X) opposite the name of each candidate you wish to vote for, in the square indicated by the arrow.

FOR GOVERNOR
VOTE FOR ONE

	THOMAS PAUL DUFFY
	ORVILLE L. FREEMAN
	FRANCIS P. McGRATH
	MAMIE J. NORBY

FOR LIEUTENANT GOVERNOR
VOTE FOR ONE

| | KARL F. ROLVAAG |

FOR SECRETARY OF STATE
VOTE FOR ONE

| | JOSEPH L. DONOVAN |
| | BLOYD GARFIELD KLEVEN |

Republican Party Ticket

You cannot split your ballot. If you vote for candidates of more than one party, your ballot will be rejected.

▼ Put an (X) opposite the name of each candidate you wish to vote for, in the square indicated by the arrow.

FOR GOVERNOR
VOTE FOR ONE

	PAUL INDYKIEWICZ
	ANCHER NELSEN
	W. J. (WALT) WERNER

FOR LIEUTENANT GOVERNOR
VOTE FOR ONE

	MILTON G. BOOCK
	LEONARD R. DICKINSON
	STAN EDDY
	JOHN C. PETERSON

FOR SECRETARY OF STATE
VOTE FOR ONE

| | C. ELMER ANDERSON |

Open primary: Minnesota. Under Minnesota's open-primary scheme, the voter is not limited to a party with which he is affiliated but is free to choose, on primary-election day, the party for which he wishes to help nominate candidates.

should be allowed to vote in a party primary and thus participate in the selection of party candidates.

On the other hand, those who favor the open primary maintain that a man's party affiliation is his own business and that it is an invasion of the secrecy of the ballot to require him to declare publicly with which party he is affiliated. Many voters strongly object to stating their party affiliation publicly. The requirement is particularly distasteful to persons who regard themselves as independents. Proponents of the open system maintain that no good purpose is served by requiring voters to register or state publicly their party affiliation, for they can be relied on to vote in the primary of the party of their choice; the advocates of the closed system argue that the open system permits voters of one party to "raid" the opposite and vote for the weak candi-

dates. Studies indicate that there is actually little raiding carried on in open-primary states; voters almost invariably vote for the candidate they wish to see elected.

Primary Procedures. At the polls in closed-primary states, the voter is given only the ballot of the party with which he has declared affiliation; in open-primary states, he is given the ballots of all parties and selects the one which he will vote in the privacy of the polling booth. Having decided which ballot he will use, the voter is permitted to vote only for the candidates of that party. He may be in favor of certain candidates of another party, but in the primary he must limit his votes to the candidates of the party he selects.

In the State of Washington, however, the voter is given even greater choice. The names of the candidates of all parties are printed on the same "blanket" ballot under

```
┌─────────────────────────────────────────────┐
│                                             │
│  PRIMARY ELECTION BALLOT                    │
│        THURSTON COUNTY                      │
│      SEPTEMBER 13, 1960                     │
│                                             │
├──────────────────────────┬──────────────────┤
│ Representative in Congress │  Two Year Term  │
│ Third Congressional District │  Vote for One │
│ JOHN W. RILEY ............Democrat    ☐     │
│ DALE M. NORDQUIST .......Republican   ☐     │
│ JULIA BUTLER HANSEN .....Democrat     ☐     │
│ HARRY S. ELWAY ..........Republican   ☐     │
│ GENE G. NEVA ............Democrat     ☐     │
│ HENRY "Hank" SCHUMACHER..Republican   ☐     │
│                                       ☐     │
│                                             │
│ Governor                    Vote for One    │
│ LLOYD J. ANDREWS ........Republican   ☐     │
│ ALBERT D. ROSELLINI .....Democrat     ☐     │
│ JOHN PATRIC .............Democrat     ☐     │
│ NEWMAN "Zeke" CLARK .....Republican   ☐     │
│ BRUCE M. SIGMAN .........Democrat     ☐     │
│                                       ☐     │
│                                             │
│ Lieutenant Governor         Vote for One    │
│ JOHN A. CHERBERG ........Democrat     ☐     │
│ WILLIAM J. MILLARD, Sr. ..Republican  ☐     │
│ CLARENCE W. BLEDSOE .....Democrat     ☐     │
│ CHARLES M. STOKES .......Republican   ☐     │
│                                       ☐     │
└─────────────────────────────────────────────┘
```

Blanket or "wide-open primary": Washington. The partisan primary of the state of Washington permits extraordinary freedom to the voter. He receives a comprehensive primary ballot that includes all candidates of all parties. He may choose to vote for a Democrat for one office, a Republican for another.

the office designation, and the voter is free to vote for the candidate of his choice, irrespective of parties. Thus a voter could vote for a candidate for the Republican nomination for governor and a candidate for the Democratic nomination for lieutenant governor.

This system makes no effort to limit the party primaries to the avowed members of the party; rather, it is based on the theory that the primary election is an integral part of the election process and that the voter should be permitted to cast his ballot for the candidate of his choice. This is anathema to advocates of the closed-primary system, who contend that it will break down all semblance of party regularity and division. However, it has not had that effect in Washington. Both the major parties in the state are strong and healthy, and primary and final elections are vigorously contested.[1]

Those seeking party nominations usually are required to file petitions signed by a certain number or percentage of voters. Some states require the payment of a filing fee. In most states the individual obtaining the largest number of votes, even though not a majority, receives the nomination of his party for office. Nine states, all Southern or Border, ensure a majority choice by holding a subsequent runoff primary. If a candidate wins a majority in the first primary, he receives the nomination; otherwise the two highest candidates enter the runoff primary. The Democratic nomination, it may be noted, is tantamount to election in these states.

A few states at various periods have permitted aspirants to enter the primaries of more than one party. In California, where this practice was widely followed from 1914 through 1958, it was called "cross filing." The cross-filer sought to win both party nominations, to avoid a contest in the final election. Until its repeal in 1959, most serious candidates for partisan office in California entered both Republican and Democratic primaries. In New York candidates often get one major and one minor party nomination, but rarely two major ones.

[1] For a good consideration of the direct primary, see National Municipal League, *A Model Direct Primary Election System* (New York: the League, 1951), which was prepared by Joseph P. Harris and a committee of the league.

Variations. Combination schemes using both primary and convention plans have been adopted in several states. Four states —Colorado, Massachusetts, Utah, and Rhode Island—authorize party conventions or committees to propose candidates for nomination at primary elections. Other candidates may run, but without the endorsement of the party organization. Although the laws of these states vary considerably, the purpose of the preprimary endorsement is the same in each case: to indicate to voters which candidates are regarded by the party officers as qualified and dependable supporters of the party's program.

In favor of having official party organizations propose candidates it is argued that better-qualified candidates can be induced to run, more responsibility is placed on party leaders, and a preliminary screening of candidates is needed prior to the primary election. Opponents of the plan say it, in effect, restores the old convention system, grants altogether too much power to party leaders, and places the independent candidate at a disadvantage. The National Municipal League committee on the direct primary favors preprimary endorsements by party bodies and recommends that the candidates so proposed be designated as such on the ballot, but that independent candidates be able to qualify by filing a petition and paying the required fee.[1]

In two states—Iowa and South Dakota— a postprimary convention is used to choose party nominees in case no candidate polls 35 per cent of the vote in the primary election.

The nonpartisan primary, used for certain local and state offices in some states, is in reality a preliminary election rather than a primary in the usual sense. Under this plan, candidates enter their names for the

[1] *Ibid.,* pp. 20–34.

nonpartisan office by filing petitions, paying fees, or both. If any candidate for the office secures a majority in the first election, he is declared elected in some systems. Ordinarily, if there is no majority, the two highest candidates engage in a runoff contest at the general election. No party designations are permitted on the ballot. Mechanically, the nonpartisan primary and election plan is usually superior to the partisan, for it nearly always precludes minority victors.

CAMPAIGNS AND ELECTIONS

Methods of Campaigning. The first step in a political campaign is to man regular party machinery with full force. In a presidential contest the national chairman is in command; in a state-wide campaign, the state chairman or a comparable official is in charge. Headquarters agencies are placed on an active basis.

The strategy depends upon the office sought, the personality of the candidate, and the circumstances. Candidates for the Presidency increasingly take the "swing around the circle," making personal appearances in most sections. An incumbent President sometimes conducts a "front porch" campaign and makes few speeches, except on radio or television. Issues largely are determined by circumstances.

Individual voters are reached in a variety of ways; one of them is canvass by direct personal contact of party workers. It may be a systematic house-to-house canvass or an informal contact at a place where voters gather. Appeals by mail are often easier but less effective than personal canvass. Mail approaches are expensive and require much care in the drafting but make possible stratified electioneering among individuals of different racial, occupational, or other groups.

Voters are reached in the mass by the

following means: (1) Meetings of all kinds are held indoors and outdoors with single speakers and joint debates, sometimes impromptu and occasionally elaborately planned. (2) Radio and television appearances of candidates and other speakers have become important. (3) Printed literature is prepared and distributed; it includes newspaper advertisements and articles, pamphlets, and posters. (4) Motion pictures and recordings are used at meetings and have proved an effective campaign medium. (5) Jewelry and merchandise are used. "Ike" earrings, dress material with designs depicting eras in Eisenhower's life, and pins in the shape of shoes with holes in the soles, advertising Stevenson, were popular in the 1956 campaign.

Authority over Elections. The states are required, by Article I, Section 4, of the Constitution, to provide for the election of members of both houses of Congress: "The times, places, and manner of holding elections for Senators and Representatives shall be prescribed in each State by the legislature thereof; but the Congress may at any time by law make or alter such regulations. . . ."

In 1872 Congress set as election day for Federal officers the Tuesday after the first Monday of November in even-numbered years. Now all states adhere to the congressional date. The manner of holding elections has been regulated by Congress in several respects: (1) In 1842 Congress enacted that representatives be elected by districts composed of contiguous territory. (2) Thirty years later, districts were required to be "as nearly as practicable" of equal population. (3) A 1901 act added the word "compact." (4) Congress has also ruled out oral voting in the election of representatives. Both (2) and (3) were omitted in the 1929 act.

Otherwise, the states have wide authority over elections. As stated above, in providing who shall vote for the most numerous branch of the state legislature, states decide who shall vote for Federal officers. Voting requirements in virtually all states tend to uniformity and include citizenship, an age limit (usually twenty-one years), residence, and registration. Constitutional amendments restrict the authority of the state to discriminate because of race, color, previous condition of servitude, or sex.

Election Administration. In most states, elections are supervised by a state election board or the secretary of state. Counties and cities place in charge of election administration either regular officials with other tasks (e.g., county clerks) or create special officers (registrars or commissioners). Precincts are the essential cell units in elections. The number of officials in each depends upon precinct size, length of the ballot, equipment, and the skill of the officers.

The Australian ballot is in general use in this country. Printed at public expense, it is secret, all-inclusive, and available only on election day, and its use is protected by numerous safeguards. American ballots fall into two general types: (1) the office-block form (Massachusetts) on which candidates are listed by the office they seek, and (2) the party-column type (Indiana) on which all candidates of a particular party are listed together. The voting machine is a mechanical adaptation of the Australian ballot. It has the obvious advantages of speed, accuracy, and simplicity, but it is expensive, fragile, and sometimes discourages split voting.

The method of electing the President is examined in some detail in a later chapter. However, it must be explained here that the voter does not vote directly for his choice for the Presidency; rather, he votes for the electors who go through the for-

STATE

FOR UNITED STATES SENATOR
(For term ending January 3, 1961)   VOTE FOR ONE

103 ☐	MAURINE B. NEUBERGER	Democrat
104 ☐	ELMO SMITH	Republican

FOR UNITED STATES SENATOR
(For term beginning January 3, 1961)   VOTE FOR ONE

105 ☐	MAURINE B. NEUBERGER	Democrat
106 ☐	ELMO SMITH	Republican

**FOR REPRESENTATIVE IN CONGRESS,
THIRD CONGRESSIONAL DISTRICT.**
Multnomah County   VOTE FOR ONE

107 ☐	EDITH GREEN	Democrat
108 ☐	WALLACE L. LEE	Republican

FOR SECRETARY OF STATE   VOTE FOR ONE

109 ☐	HOWELL APPLING, Jr.	Republican
110 ☐	MONROE SWEETLAND	Democrat

FOR STATE TREASURER   VOTE FOR ONE

111 ☐	HOWARD C. BELTON	Republican
112 ☐	WARD H. COOK	Democrat

FOR ATTORNEY GENERAL   VOTE FOR ONE

113 ☐	CARL H. FRANCIS	Republican
114 ☐	ROBERT Y. THORNTON	Democrat

**FOR STATE SENATOR,
TWELFTH SENATORIAL DISTRICT.**
Multnomah County   VOTE FOR FIVE

115 ☐	ROBERT A. BENNETT	Republican
116 ☐	ALFRED H. CORBETT	Democrat
117 ☐	JOHN D. GOSS	Republican
118 ☐	JEAN L. LEWIS	Democrat
119 ☐	THOMAS R. MAHONEY	Democrat
120 ☐	FRED MEEK	Republican
121 ☐	WALTER PEARSON	Democrat
122 ☐	WALTER L. TOOZE	Republican
123 ☐	LEW WALLACE	Democrat
124 ☐	FRANK L. WHITAKER	Republican

COUNTY

FOR COUNTY COMMISSIONER   VOTE FOR ONE

155 ☐	LYLE DEAN	Republican
156 ☐	M. JAMES GLEASON	Democrat

FOR COUNTY CLERK   VOTE FOR ONE

157 ☐	SI COHN	Democrat
158 ☐	HERSCHEL V. THOMPSON	Republican

Office-block ballot: Oregon. The office-block type of ballot makes no provision for straight-ticket voting. The voter must indicate which candidate he wishes for each office. About two-fifths of the states use this type of general-election ballot, which is often called the "Massachusetts type."

mality of casting their ballots for the candidates to whom they have been pledged. Every state now elects presidential electors on a state-wide basis, with each voter able to vote for the whole number of electors to which his state is entitled.

In recent years twenty-five states have adopted the "presidential short ballot," which eliminates the names of the individual electors from the ballot and permits the voter to mark his ballot for the whole slate of electors pledged to the presidential and vice-presidential candidates of his choice. Two other states in effect have the presidential short ballot through their general use of voting machines.

Absentee Voting. Absentee voting, originated for military personnel during the Civil War, has been extended to civilians gradually during the past forty years. All states now permit absentee voting by persons in the Armed Forces. During the Second World War, especially just before the 1944 election, nearly every state extended its provisions for military voting, mainly in the direction of liberalizing registration rules and application forms and in extending the time for returning the ballots.

Absentee voting permits a qualified person who is away from his legal residence or confined for some reason on election day to cast his ballot by mail or in advance of the election. State laws have considerable variety; the following features are common to most:[1] (1) Application is made within

[1] A good source of information on absentee voting is George F. Miller, *Absentee Votes and Suffrage Laws* (Washington, D.C.: Daylion Co., 1949).

DEMOCRATIC	REPUBLICAN
◯	◯
President and Vice President	**President and Vice President**
☐ KENNEDY, JOHN F. PRESIDENT / JOHNSON, LYNDON B. VICE PRESIDENT	☐ NIXON, RICHARD M. PRESIDENT / LODGE, HENRY CABOT VICE PRESIDENT
☐	☐
United States Senator (Vote for One)	**United States Senator** (Vote for One)
☐ BARTLETT, E. L. (Bob)	☐ McKINLEY, LEE L. (Doc)
☐	☐
United States Representative (Vote for One)	**United States Representative** (Vote for One)
☐ RIVERS, RALPH J.	☐ RETTIG, R. L. (Ron)
☐	☐

Party-column ballot: Alaska. Straight-ticket voting is encouraged by permitting one mark at the head of the party column to count for all party candidates.

time limits set by law. (2) The ballot is mailed by election officials. (3) The absent voter fills out the ballot, often before a notary public or a public official. (4) The ballot is returned to the election official by mail. (5) Absentee ballots are either counted in the central election office or sent to the precincts for counting. A few states permit a voter to cast his ballot in person a few days early if he expects to be away on election day. Approximately one-half of the states provide for absentee registration, so that a person who is away at registration time can enter his name on the roll. This is of particular value to people who work in Washington, D.C. but maintain legal residence in their home states and to those from states requiring frequent reregistration.

Servicemen's Voting. During the Second World War, Congress and the country were beset with a great struggle over the right to vote of men and women in the Armed Forces. The necessities of war spread Americans by the millions over every con-

tinent and the seven seas. Servicemen experienced difficulty in voting because of (1) inability to meet one or more of their states' qualifications, such as residence, age, poll tax, literacy, and the like, and (2) the impossibility of either returning to their home states to cast ballots or meeting absentee-balloting deadlines.

In 1942 and in 1944 Federal legislation was enacted to expedite service voting. In each case greatest encouragement was given servicemen to utilize the absentee-voting procedure of their own states. The 1942 law, which permitted voting on a state "war ballot," passed very late and was little used. The 1944 act not only gave the serviceman a form on which to apply for a state ballot but also provided him with an "official Federal war ballot" which he could send to his state if the state absentee ballot did not reach him. Twenty states accepted Federal ballots, totaling less than 85,000.

Existing Federal law provides that, during a *state of war*, absent servicemen have a right to vote for Federal officers without registering. Also, the poll tax is banned as a requirement for voting for Federal officers. The Selective Service Act of 1948 also bans the poll tax as a requirement for voting for President, Vice President, and members of Congress *by inductees*; this applies both in war and peace, but not to volunteers!

Proportional Representation. Proportional representation (PR) is a system of voting that yields to each party or group the approximate strength to which its vote entitles it. PR is applied to the selection of legislative bodies and is designed to correct the absurd disproportion produced by the single-member-district plurality plan. Several methods of PR are in use in different parts of the world, but the Hare plan of single transferable vote is the most common in the United States. Under the Hare system, several representatives are elected from a single district. The voter indicates his choice of candidates by writing numbers—1, 2, 3, 4, etc.—opposite his choice. The ballots are collected and counted centrally.

The first step in counting PR ballots is to establish the "quota." This is done by dividing the number of valid ballots by the number of candidates to be elected plus one. If nine seats in a city council are to be filled, and the number of votes cast is 100,000, then the quota is 10,001. It is figured:

$$\frac{10,000 + 1 = 10,001 \text{ quota}}{9 \text{ councilors} + 1 = 10 \overline{\smash{)}100,000}}$$

The ballots are sorted by first choices. All candidates with more than the quota are declared elected. Their surplus beyond the quota is distributed to second choices on the ballots concerned. Finally, candidates with the lowest number of votes are eliminated and their ballots distributed by second choices until all seats are filled.

Proposed only occasionally for use in selecting members of Congress and of state legislatures, PR has been used successfully

in several cities, including New York and Cincinnati. Proponents maintain that it (1) ensures minority representation, (2) reduces power of small organized machines, (3) makes legislative bodies more truly representative.[1] The case against PR, once the preserve of bosses and others inconvenienced by it, recently has been argued forcefully by competent students of government. The disadvantages are that PR (1) increases the number of groups and parties, (2) reduces the chances of one group securing the power to govern, (3) is too complicated for some voters to understand.[2]

After observing the instability of governments in Continental European countries under the multiparty system, Americans have become increasingly cautious lest PR eliminate the likelihood of a clear majority in legislative bodies. PR is unlikely to be adopted by the Federal government in the United States. It will be proposed seriously to correct some of the ills of state legislatures and might conceivably prove a good remedy. In local affairs, where fewer great policy decisions are made and the work of government is mainly administration, PR provides a fair method of representation. Even in municipal government, however, PR has been losing ground. Its prospects for the future appear dim.[3]

Initiative, Referendum, Recall. Although not employed in Federal politics in the United States, the initiative, referendum,

---

[1] See George H. Hallett, Jr., *Proportional Representation—The Key to Democracy* (Washington, D.C.: The National Home Library Foundation, 1937), pp. 58–74.

[2] Ferdinand A. Hermens, *Democracy or Anarchy? A Study of Proportional Representation* (Notre Dame, Ind.: Review of Politics, University of Notre Dame, 1941).

[3] Its demise in New York is traced in Belle Zeller and Hugh A. Bone, "The Repeal of P.R. in New York City—Ten Years in Retrospect," *American Political Science Review*, vol. 42 (December, 1948), pp. 1127–1148.

and recall play an important part in the government of many states and their subdivisions.

The *initiative* is an electoral device through which an individual or group may propose statutory legislation or constitutional amendment by securing the signatures of the requisite number of voters and place the measure before the electorate for adoption or rejection. The drafting of such measures normally is done by interested groups or their attorneys. The number or proportion of signatures required is set by law or constitution. Some states require initiative propositions to be submitted to the legislature before they are placed before the people; if the legislature takes no action or takes adverse action, the matter is taken up by the electorate. If a majority of the voters favor the measure or change in the constitution, it goes into effect; frequently statutes thus adopted have a privileged status and may not be repealed by the legislature.

The *referendum* is a scheme by which voters may, by petition, force submission to the whole electorate of a bill passed by the legislature. The number or proportion of voters' signatures required usually is less than that for the initiative. Emergency measures commonly are excluded from referendum action. If the voters disapprove of the act as passed by the legislature, it becomes null and void. The referendum is used by more states than the initiative, and it has been proposed seriously for inclusion in the Federal Constitution in connection with a congressional declaration of war. The most common reasons given for adopting the initiative and referendum are that they provide (1) a check on corrupt and inert legislatures and (2) a useful device for the education of voters. Those who oppose direct legislation often argue that these devices (1) place an additional burden on an already overburdened electorate, and (2) modify representative government by destroying legislative responsibility.

The *recall* is an instrument through which voters may, by signing petitions, require a special election to determine whether or not an official shall be superseded before his term expires. The number or proportion of signatures required varies considerably. If the majority of votes are for the recall of an official, the office is declared vacant. A successor may be chosen on the same ballot, elected at a subsequent election, or appointed by some official or body. Various restrictions are placed upon the use of the recall to prevent attempts to remove just after election to office, or repeated attempts. The recall has been adopted in some form in eleven states and a thousand municipalities. Despite the lack of constitutional authority, two states have attempted to inaugurate the recall of Federal officials. Arizona and North Dakota sought to apply their recall to Federal judges, senators, and representatives. Candidates for Congress were requested to state in advance their willingness to abide by a recall vote on their removal; Federal judges serving in the state would be asked to resign in case of an adverse vote in a recall election. The indirect or advisory recall never functioned, and it obviously lacked any real sanction.[1]

The case for the recall is that it (1) provides a continuous control by the electorate over public officials and (2) removes single officials from the shelter of a ticket and forces them to stand on their own merits. Against the recall are the arguments that it (1) gives a powerful weapon to minorities

[1] Frederick L. Bird and Frances M. Ryan, *The Recall of Public Officers* (New York: Macmillan, 1930), pp. 16–17. This is the best general source on the recall.

and factions to use for petty personal and partisan purposes and (2) weakens official courage and independence by rendering the officer vulnerable to momentary fits of public indignation.

The Overburdened Voter. Even a casual examination of American ballots and election returns gives ample evidence that the voter is assigned more work than he can or will perform satisfactorily. In simple and small communities a large amount of direct democracy may be successful. The town meeting of New England and the *landesgemeinde* retained in a few Swiss cantons are examples of government functioning very close to the people. Of course, direct democracy can have only very limited application in modern America where the communities are too large and the problems of government too technical for use of the mass-meeting technique. The other possibility is representative government, in which voters choose representatives who devote such time as is necessary to public affairs.

A hundred years and more ago there arose a mistaken idea that the more offices made elective, the more democratic a government was. The mania for popular election swept through the states and local governments; dozens of minor officials were given their own pedestals and made elective by the people. Although a few states and local governments have experienced reorganizations that reduced the number of elective offices, most of them still elect too many officials. This not only seriously diffuses executive power, but places an impossible burden on the voter. Unable to secure information easily concerning the stewardship in office of a particular obscure incumbent, he relies on the recommendation of a newspaper, the party label, or some other unreliable index.

The Short Ballot. A generation ago critics

of the long ballot were well organized and articulate. They sought:[1]

1. That only those offices should be elective which are important enough to attract (and deserve) public examination.

2. That very few offices should be filled by election at any one time, so as to permit adequate and unconfused public examination of the candidates.

The short-ballot movement made some headway, but its work remained only partially done when the reform tide had ebbed. The Federal government has few elective officers and a rather short ballot—including candidates only for presidential elector, senator, and representative. With the presidential short ballot, eliminating candidates for elector from the ballot, the remaining Federal elective offices certainly qualify as important enough to attract public attention.

Most states, counties, and municipalities continue to burden the voter with the task of selecting officers—ranging from tax commissioner to dogcatcher—who should be appointed by a chief executive. Several states have general-election ballots that include the names of candidates for thirty or more offices plus complicated propositions numbering twenty and over.

The number of elections in the United States is staggering. It has been estimated that about 100,000 separate elections are held in the United States annually. On 151 days of a recent year, elections were going on somewhere in the country. It appears that the second short-ballot principle has been more honored than the first, in that elective offices are filled at scattered times. These minor elections for school and special districts and for local governments often fail to attract any considerable proportion of

[1] Richard S. Childs, *Short Ballot Principles* (Boston: Houghton Mifflin, 1911), p. vii.

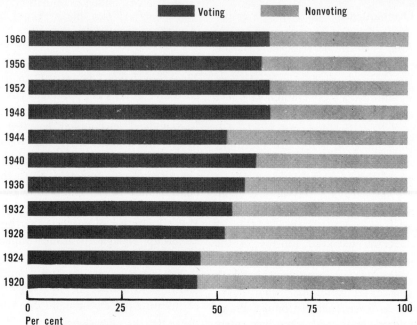

CIVILIAN POPULATION OF VOTING AGE
1920 - 1960

Voting   Nonvoting

1960	
1956	
1952	
1948	
1944	
1940	
1936	
1932	
1928	
1924	
1920	

0   25   50   75   100
Per cent

Although the last three presidential elections brought out more voters than usual, the United States is well below most other democratic nations in electoral participation.

the eligible voters. In the average Northern and Western state, 50 to 80 per cent participation in state and Federal elections is common, while local elections often attract less than 25 per cent of the eligibles.

Getting Out the Vote. It is easy to say that the American voter must be made more alert to his civic responsibilities, but it is difficult to make him so. Certainly all efforts to stimulate interest in and discussion of public affairs are to be encouraged. Compulsory voting has been suggested as a remedy for nonvoting. It has been used with some success in Australia, Belgium, Czechoslovakia, Holland, and other countries. The usual form is to impose a fine upon those who fail to participate in elec-

tions; in some cases the nonvoter is disfranchised as well. Proposed repeatedly in the United States, compulsory voting has not been applied by any state.

Can the task of the voter be made easier? It can be by reducing the number of elective offices and elections. Contrary to uninformed opinion, neither of these steps reduces the measure of democracy; actually, moderate reform along these lines will make more, not less, democracy. If the elective offices are reduced to a reasonable number, the remaining officers can be given the responsibility over a larger sphere of activity and appoint the necessary subordinates to carry out the work. The governor or mayor assigned additional authority, following the abolition of executive offices such as comptroller and commissioner of works, is likely to be more truly responsible to the public. The electorate can judge the general conduct of a mayor or governor but is unable even to name the incumbents of other elective executive offices, much less judge the quality of their work.

Although there are some good arguments against mixing national and local affairs, the multiplicity of elections has been carried too far. The expense of conducting elections is greater than necessary; the participation in local elections is so small that consolidation of elections is urgently needed.

FOR FURTHER READING

Abraham, Henry J.: *Compulsory Voting* (Washington, D.C.: Public Affairs Press, 1956).

Albright, Spencer D.: *The American Ballot* (Washington, D.C.: Public Affairs Press, 1940).

Bain, Henry M., Jr., and Donald S. Hecock: *Ballot Position and Voter's Choice* (Detroit: Wayne State University Press, 1957).

Berelson, Bernard R., and others: *Voting: A Study of Opinion Formation in a Presidential Campaign* (Chicago: University of Chicago Press, 1954).

Blair, George S.: *Cumulative Voting: An Effective Electoral Device in Illinois Politics* (Urbana, Ill.: University of Illinois Press, 1960).

Burdick, Eugene, and Arthur J. Brodbeck (eds.): *American Voting Behavior: How the People Participate in Politics* (Glencoe, Ill.: Free Press, 1956).

Burnham, W. Dean: *Presidential Ballots, 1836–1892* (Baltimore: Johns Hopkins Press, 1955).

Campbell, Angus, Gerald Gurin, and Warren E. Miller: *The Voter Decides* (Evanston, Ill.: Row, Peterson, 1954).

Council of State Governments: *Book of the States* (Chicago: the Council, biennial).

David, Paul T., and others: *Presidential Nominating Politics in 1952* (Baltimore: Johns Hopkins Press, 5 vols., 1954).

Hallett, George H., Jr.: *Proportional Representation: The Key to Democracy* (Washington, D.C.: National Home Library Foundation, 1937).

Harris, Joseph P.: *Election Administration in the United States* (Washington, D.C.: Brookings, 1934).

Heard, Alexander, and D. S. Strong: *Southern Primaries and Elections* (University, Ala.: University of Alabama Press, 1950).

Hermens, Ferdinand A.: *Democracy or Anarchy?*

A Study of Proportional Representation (Notre Dame, Ind.: Review of Politics, University of Notre Dame, 1941).

Janowitz, Morris, and Dwaine Marvick: *Competitive Pressure and Democratic Consent* (Ann Arbor, Mich.: University of Michigan, Institute of Public Administration, 1956).

Johnson, John B., and J. J. Lewis: *Registration for Voting in the United States* (Chicago: Council of State Governments, 1946).

Kelly, Stanley, Jr.: *Political Campaigning: Problems in Creating an Informed Electorate* (Washington, D.C.: Brookings Institution, 1960).

Key, V. O.: *Southern Politics in State and Nation* (New York: Knopf, 1949).

McGovney, D. O.: *The American Sffrage Medley* (Chicago: University of Chicago Press, 1949).

Miller, George F.: *Absentee Voters and Suffrage laws* (Washington, D.C.: Daylion Co., 1949).

National Municipal League: *A Model Direct Primary Election System* (New York: the League, 1951).

———: *Compilation of the 48 Direct Primary Systems* (New York: the League, 1957).

Proceedings of the National Convention (the major parties, quadrennial).

Robinson, Edgar E.: *They Voted for Roosevelt: The Presidential Vote, 1932–1944* (Stanford, Calif.: Stanford University Press, 1947).

———: *The Presidential Vote, 1896–1932* (Stanford, Calif.: Stanford University Press, 1934).

Roseboom, Eugene H.: *A History of Presidential Elections* (New York: Macmillan, 1957).

Scammon, Richard M. (ed.): *America Votes* (New York: Macmillan, vol. 1, 1956; vol. 2, 1958). (Pittsburgh, Pa.: University of Pittsburgh Press, vol. 3, 1960; vol. 4, 1962).

Smith, Constance E.: *Voting and Election Laws* (New York: Oceana Publications, 1960).

Thomson, C. A. H.: *Television and Presidential Politics: The Experience in 1952 and the Problems Ahead* (Washington, D.C.: Brookings Institution, 1956).

———— and Frances M. Shattuck: *The 1956 Presidential Campaign* (Washington, D.C.: Brookings Institution, 1960).

U.S. House of Representatives, Committee on the Judiciary, *Voting Rights, Hearings . . . ,* 86th Cong., 2d Sess., (1960).

U.S. Senate, Committee on the Judiciary, *Poll Tax and Enfranchisement of District of Columbia,* 86th Cong., 1st Sess., (1960).

Williamson, Chilton: *American Suffrage from Property to Democracy* (Princeton, N.J.: Princeton University Press, 1961).

REVIEW QUESTIONS

1. What constitutional authority has the Federal government over the right to vote?

2. Name the most common prerequisites for voting required by the several states.

3. Describe the current status of poll taxes. What Federal and state action has been under active consideration?

4. Trace the historical development of presidential nominating methods.

5. To what legal controls are national party conventions subjected?

6. What factors influence the choice of dates and places for national conventions?

7. Explain the difference between Republican and Democratic methods of computing state representation in national conventions.

8. What is the presidential primary? Describe the various forms used. How extensively is it used today?

9. Describe the procedure and politics of national party conventions, with special reference to those of 1952 and 1956.

10. Trace the evolution of nominating methods for state and congressional offices. What are the several variations of convention and primary in use today?

11. Explain some of the factors that determine the strategy of a candidate campaigning for office.

12. Describe the process of absentee voting. What are the principal issues and problems posed by armed-services-personnel voting?

13. What is proportional representation? How extensively has it been adopted in the United States?

14. Describe the three "instrumentalities of popular control": initiative, referendum, and recall.

15. Do you think the American voter is overburdened? If so, what can be done to relieve him?

Part Two

Federal Institutions

Chapter Thirteen

Congress:

Organization

and Politics

It is the proper duty of a representative body to look diligently into every affair of government and to talk much about what it sees. It is meant to be the eyes and the voice, and to embody the wisdom and will of its constituents. Unless Congress have and use every means of acquainting itself with the acts and disposition of the administrative agents of the government, the country must be helpless to learn how it is being served; and unless Congress both scrutinize these things and sift them by every form of discussion, the country must remain in embarrassing, crippling ignorance of the very affairs which it is most important that it should understand and direct. The informing function of Congress should be preferred even to its legislative function.

WOODROW WILSON[1]

When the founding fathers outlined the legislative branch, in Article I of the Constitution, they had usable models and direct experience from which to draw. Although but recently separated from Britain, the new nation took from the mother country the format of its legislative institutions. The "model parliament" of 1295 had representation from clergy, barons, and commoners;

[1] *Congressional Government* (Boston: Houghton Mifflin, 1885), p. 303.

the two-house tradition flowed from the separate meetings of lords spiritual and temporal in one chamber and of commoners in the other. At the time of the American Revolution, the House of Commons was gaining ascendancy over the House of Lords, and the Parliament's supremacy over the monarch was virtually assured.

The Congress and, indeed, the American Constitution, might have been quite different if framed after Britain experienced

239

broadened franchise (gained under the Reform Acts of 1832 and 1867), or operation of "classical" parliamentary government (as developed in the Gladstone-Disraeli era).

STRUCTURE AND HISTORY

The more immediate models, however, were American legislatures, colonial and revolutionary, which the leaders of this formative era had experienced directly. The colonial legislatures, the revolutionary state assemblies, and the early Congresses, Continental and Confederation, were so influential that they require some examination.

Colonial Legislatures. American colonial legislatures were similar in over-all pattern. Each colony had a legislative assembly, usually a two-house organization. The upper chamber, or "governor's council," often had legislative, executive, and judicial powers. In the royal colonies, as in some British colonies of today, members of the council were appointed by the Crown on recommendation of the governor. In proprietary colonies, the proprietor appointed. The two charter colonies, Connecticut and Rhode Island, elected councilors. Pennsylvania was the only colony with a single-house legislature, having no governor's council.

Intended as a popular body, the lower house was elected by the colonial subjects who could meet the property qualifications required for voting. The members—called "burgesses," "representatives," or "commoners"—represented the people who lived in the districts from which they were selected.

Revolutionary Assemblies. After an initial period of chaotic rule by rump legislatures, eleven of the newly independent states reformed their legislatures in the new constitutions adopted between 1775 and 1780; only Rhode Island and Connecticut kept their old constitutions. In all thirteen states

the legislatures were given broad powers. Eleven states continued with bicameral legislatures; Pennsylvania retained its single-house plan until 1790; Georgia experimented with unicameralism from 1777 to 1789. The two-house states kept the lower house much as before the Revolution. The upper house, soon to be termed "senate" generally, was elected by districts; its members had longer terms than those in the lower house.

Early National Legislatures. The First Continental Congress, assembled in Philadelphia in 1774, was more of a convention than a national legislature, but it must be regarded as stone-age ancestor of the Congress of today. The Second Continental Congress, which provided the national government during the Revolutionary War, may be compared with a modern European constituent assembly, for it both governed the emerging nation and framed the Articles of Confederation. This was a unicameral body to which each state sent its delegates.

Under the Articles of Confederation, Congress principally governed the country. It was a one-house body with a rather fluid membership of delegates from the states. Each state had one vote, which might be cast by the two to seven delegates from that state. States could appoint and recall delegates as they saw fit.

Two-house Plan Established. A strong determinant of congressional structure in the Constitution was the necessity to compromise the differences between large and small states. Under the terms of the Connecticut Compromise, each state was represented equally in the Senate. The seats in the House of Representatives were to be apportioned among the states according to their populations.

Little serious consideration is given today to departure from the two-house plan for Congress. The national utilization of the bicameral plan, however, has led states to imitate. Both Pennsylvania and Georgia promptly abandoned the single-chamber plan after Congress became a two-house body. Vermont, admitted in 1791, used unicameralism until 1836. The bicameral stereotype prevailed in all states for a hundred years, until Nebraska adopted her single-house plan in 1934 and put it into effect in 1937.

THE POWERS OF CONGRESS: GENERAL ASPECTS

Legislative Powers of Congress. Legislative powers may be classified into six groups: (1) delegated, (2) implied, (3) inherent, (4) concurrent, (5) prohibited, and (6) reserved. Since these have been discussed earlier, they will be dealt with only briefly here.

Delegated powers are those specifically enumerated in the Constitution, most of them in Article I, Section 8. These have been given by the sovereign people to the central government at Washington.

Implied powers are those that may reasonably be deduced from delegated powers or, to use the language of the Constitution, those that are "necessary and proper" for carrying delegated powers into execution. Implied powers do not give the Federal government a blank check to do anything it wishes. If that were true, the system would be unitary rather than federal. Implications can be made only from some specifically delegated power.

Inherent powers arise from the fact that the United States is a sovereign state and in its international relations may exercise those powers generally exercised by other national states.

Reserved powers are those that have not been delegated to the Federal government. Some are retained by the states. States have

been prohibited from exercising certain powers that are reserved to the people.

Concurrent powers are those exercised by both national and state governments. The term also refers to powers, like bankruptcy, which may be exercised by the states until Congress decides to assert its authority.

Prohibited powers are denied to both Federal and state governments, to the Nation only, or to the states only.

Restrictions on Congressional Power. Although the powers of Congress, as exercised and construed, are great, there are several limitations, both explicit and implied.

No Emergency Powers. In dealing with domestic affairs, the Federal government has only powers granted to it by the Constitution. In periods of stress it has been claimed, sometimes by Congress but oftener by the President, that the national government is endowed with powers that are neither delegated nor implied but arise from the fact that the government speaks for a sovereign nation. This is true only in the field of international relations.

President Roosevelt urged Congress to enact sweeping legislation beginning in 1933, arguing as partial justification for its constitutionality that emergency conditions demanded it. The Supreme Court acknowledged that extraordinary conditions might justify an *extraordinary use* of existing powers but insisted that critical circumstances could not enlarge the scope of constitutional authority. "Emergency does not create power. Emergency does not increase granted power or diminish the restrictions imposed upon power granted or reserved," said the Court in 1934 (*Home Building and Loan Ass'n v. Blaisdell*, 290 U.S. 398).

A year later a unanimous Court voided the NIRA, saying, among other things, "extraordinary conditions do not create or enlarge constitutional powers [*Schechter v. United States*, 295 U.S. 495 (1935)]. Thus, in emergencies Congress must rely upon some delegated power. If none can be found, the Constitution requires that an amendment be sought or that the matter be left to the states.

No Specific "Police Power." Unitary governments ordinarily have authority to take any steps necessary to protect and preserve the health, safety, morals, and welfare of the people. This is commonly referred to as the "police power." In the United States it is reserved to the states; the national government has police power only within the District of Columbia and other territories.

State and local governments dispose of garbage and sewage, provide hospitals and schools, ensure pure food and water supplies, and do a host of other things simply because the welfare of the population demands them. The Federal government may do such things only if they are reasonably required to regulate interstate and foreign commerce properly, conduct a postal system, raise and support an army and navy, or exercise some other power delegated by the Constitution.

Specific Denials. The delegated powers may not be used to do things expressly forbidden by the Constitution. Congress may not, for example, tax exports, pass ex post facto laws, grant titles of nobility, or impair the liberties guaranteed by the Bill of Rights.

Clearly Granted. It is often difficult to decide what is and what is not a "necessary and proper" use of a delegated power. Although permitting a liberal construction of the phrase, the courts require some clear and direct relationship between a delegated power and the object sought by its exercise. The power to coin money and regulate its value justifies the creation of national banks and the printing of paper notes. The power to regulate interstate commerce justifies the fixing of passenger and freight rates for inter-

state carriers, and also the regulation of intrastate commerce that directly affects interstate commerce. The power to tax to promote the general welfare justifies the establishment of land-grant colleges, a retirement system for aged employees, and the subsidization of farming. In these instances the courts have found a clear and direct relationship between some delegated power and the object or purpose of the enactments.

But when Congress required railroads to establish a retirement system for superannuated employees, the Court construed the act to be "an attempt for social ends" which had nothing to do with interstate commerce [*Railroad Retirement Bd. v. Alton R. R.,* 295 U.S. 330 (1935)]. A revised measure based upon the taxing and spending powers was passed later and has been generally thought to be constitutional. In the NIRA decision, the Supreme Court considered the burden upon interstate commerce caused by depressed local businesses so indirect as to be beyond the scope of the commerce power.

No Delegation of Powers to Executive. One of the fundamental principles of the Constitution is that the legislative, executive, and judicial branches are separate and independent of each other. Many laws that are passed embody general principles and authorize administrative officers to fill in details, but too much cannot be left to the administrators. Congress must clearly declare its will and establish primary standards. If this task is left to the executive, the courts will hold that Congress has illegally delegated powers granted solely to itself.

The first case in which it was held that legislative powers had been so delegated arose from a section of the NIRA [*Panama Refining Co. v. Ryan,* 293 U.S. 388 (1935)]. The Supreme Court ruled that in authorizing the President to make regulations governing interstate shipments of "hot oil"[1] too much discretion had been allowed. Later, major portions of the NIRA were declared unconstitutional, in part because Congress had allowed too much discretion to the President and code authorities.

No Delegation to States. Neither can powers granted to Congress be delegated to the states. This means that Congress cannot authorize states to regulate interstate commerce, coin money, declare war, or exercise any other power conferred exclusively upon it by the Constitution. In 1918, legislation provided that longshoremen injured during the course of employment were entitled to the rights and remedies of the state wherein the injury occurred, but the Supreme Court held that Congress had transferred its authority to the states [*Knickerbocker Ice Co. v. Stewart*, 253 U.S. 149 (1920)]. Thereupon, Congress reenacted the measure, providing a uniform system of federally administered insurance for maritime workers injured on vessels (see page 559).

Sometimes there is overlapping between state and Federal jurisdiction. A state might act under a reserved power on a matter over which Congress has a delegated power. This often happens. When it does, and the matter does not require uniform treatment throughout the country, the state law is allowed to stand until Congress acts; then it must yield.

No Delegation to People. Many states have provisions that permit the use of the initiative and referendum, whereby the voters may participate directly in lawmaking. There is no provision in the Federal Constitution for the use of these devices. All Federal laws must originate in and be approved by Congress; otherwise there would be an illegal delegation of powers.

[1] That is, oil produced in excess of quota established by state law.

No Usurping of State Powers. The states may not invade the domain of Congress, nor may Congress usurp powers reserved to the states. The demarcation line, though, is vague, with the result that political and judicial opinion shifts from time to time. Prior to 1937 the Supreme Court was inclined to halt Federal power in favor of state, declaring unconstitutional Federal laws which taxed the salaries of state judges and state instrumentalities; regulated the employment of children; induced farmers to contract to curtail production; regulated manufacturing, mining, and local businesses; and permitted local governments to reorganize their indebtedness under Federal laws.

More recently, most of these decisions have been reversed. Even so, it is clear that there are still areas in which the Federal government may not trespass. State powers would be usurped if Congress were to regulate commerce that is very local and isolated or to tax with intent to burden or destroy state and local governments and their activities.

No Usurping from Other Branches. Just as all legislative powers belong to Congress, the executive power is given solely to the President and the judicial power entirely to the courts. Congress is precluded, therefore, from usurping executive or judicial powers.

In 1876 Congress provided that postmasters could be removed by the President only with the concurrence of the Senate. Forty years later President Wilson resisted the statute, contending that the power of removal belonged to the executive. The Supreme Court agreed with him, saying that the statute was an unwarranted infringement of the executive power. [*Myers v. United States*, 272 U.S. 52 (1926). See also pp. 311–312.]

Congress cannot invade the province of

the judiciary. In 1792 Congress directed Federal circuit judges to investigate claims and report their findings to the War Department for final action. The courts objected and, in Hayburn's case [2 Dall. 409 (U.S. 1792)], ruled that the legislature had imposed a nonjudicial duty upon them, inasmuch as executive officials were permitted to review and possibly modify or reverse decisions made by the judges.

Nonlegislative Powers. In addition to making laws, Congress performs several other important tasks. A distinction is made, therefore, between legislative powers upon which general laws are based and nonlegislative powers from which Congress gets authority for its other functions. Nonlegislative powers may be classified as (1) constituent, (2) electoral, (3) executive, (4) directory and supervisory, (5) inquisitorial, and (6) judicial.

Constituent powers relate to changing the Constitution, including authority to propose amendments either by the concurrence of two-thirds of both houses or by calling a convention for the purpose when petitioned to do so by two-thirds of the states. Herein is also included authority to decide what method of ratification shall be followed by the states and whether a time limit shall accompany the amendment.

Electoral powers relate to the election of President and Vice President. The electoral votes must be counted in the presence of both houses. In the event of a tie or lack of a majority, election of the President devolves upon the House and that of the Vice President upon the Senate. Congress must provide for settling disputes (if certain electoral votes are contested) and for a method of choosing the President and Vice President upon the death or disqualification of both of these officers before or after their inauguration.

Executive powers are used to perform functions essentially executive in character. The appointment of officers is generally an executive prerogative. When the House and Senate appoint their own officers and committees, they are exercising executive powers. The same is true when the Senate confirms presidential appointees and gives advice and consent to the ratification of treaties.

Directory and *supervisory* powers are closely related. Although the President is the chief administrator, Congress exercises considerable control and supervision over the administrative branch. Congress usually decides whether there is to be a department, commission, board, or major agency. Congress may expand agencies, consolidate them, or abolish them altogether. Congress defines their powers and duties, appropriates funds to operate, authorizes the employment of personnel, and periodically investigates and reviews.

Direction and review go on constantly. Inquiry takes a variety of forms. Almost all agencies are required to make annual reports to Congress. Congressmen often call upon administrators for information and explanations. Congressional committees may undertake review of a particular agency or problem. Senatorial confirmation of an appointment or approval of a treaty may occasion widespread inquiry. Normally, the most thorough review occurs when representatives of the various agencies appear before committees to defend budgetary requests.

Inquisitorial power is a term used to describe congressional authority to conduct investigations (see p. 282). They may be conducted by the House and Senate as a body or, as is commonly the case, by standing or special committees. Congress itself, or its instrumentalities, may issue subpoenas to summon witnesses and compel the production of books and papers. Warrants of arrest may also be issued. Failure to obey congressional writs and orders may be punished by Congress itself. In practice, Congress leaves trial and punishment to the courts.

Judicial powers enable Congress to pass judgment upon certain parties. Each house of Congress is the sole judge of the qualifications of its own members. Each can expel a member, provided two-thirds of the members agree. Impeachment and contempt proceedings are also judicial in nature (see p. 273).

BASIS OF REPRESENTATION

Intended as the popular branch of Congress, the House of Representatives was made larger and more responsive to the public will than the Senate. The latter, as a deliberative upper chamber, was made smaller and more removed from popular pressure.

Constitutional Provisions. As provided in the Constitution, seats in the House of Representatives are apportioned among the states according to population, determined by the census each ten years. Members are elected by the same electorate as that for the most numerous branch of the state legislature. The Fifteenth Amendment forbids states to deny the vote because of race, color, or previous condition of servitude. The Nineteenth Amendment prohibits discrimination on account of sex; the fourteenth provides for penalizing states that deny the vote to adult male citizens by reducing their proportionate representation in the House, although this has never been invoked.

Originally the Senate was composed of two senators from each state, chosen by the state legislature. The rising tide of democracy swept aside the old method of selection and substituted that contained in the Seventeenth Amendment. It provided that the people of each state should elect senators directly. The electorate is the same as that for the House.

Methods of Apportionment. Apportioning House seats has caused periodic controversies. The original sixty-five members of the House were allocated in the Constitution. Thereafter assignments were made by Congress after each census, ranging from the basis of one representative for each 30,000 (1792) to one for 345,000 (1951). Only after the 1920 census did Congress deadlock and fail to carry out the constitutional mandate to reapportion each ten years. The Reapportionment Act of 1929 set the "permanent" number of House members at 435 and provided for automatic reapportionment in case Congress fails to act. The law provides, after each census, for the President to report to Congress the population and the number of representatives to which each state is entitled according to two complex mathematical formulas: (1) equal proportions and (2) major fractions. Should Congress fail to act within sixty days, the reapportionment goes into effect automatically, utilizing the formula which was employed in the last reapportionment.

In 1931 Congress took no action, and the plan based on major fractions was deemed in force. In 1941, however, after the sixty-day period had elapsed, the 1929 act was amended to require the equal proportions method.[1] The admission of Alaska and Hawaii brought House membership to 437, but it dropped back to 435 in 1962.

Apportionment within States. No provision requiring election of representatives by district appears in the Constitution; however, a law imposed it in 1842, and it has prevailed ever since. The original law

[1] In 1951 and 1961 the President submitted the census figures and the proposed reapportionment based on the method of equal proportions. Congress took no action, and the states were notified of their entitlement to House seats.

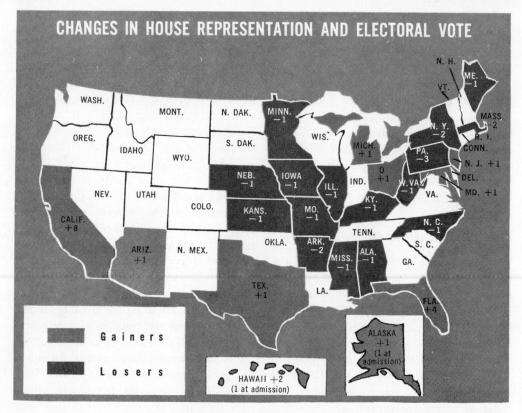

CHANGES IN HOUSE REPRESENTATION AND ELECTORAL VOTE

Gainers

Losers

HAWAII +2
(1 at admission)

ALASKA
+1
(1 at
admission)

How the states fared between 1952 and 1962. The census returns are read with avid interest because they indicate shifts of national power for the decade ahead both in the House of Representatives and in electoral vote. The gains and losses by states recorded on the map above are those computed by the Bureau of the Census and announced in 1960. They were based on existing law, including allocation among the states according to the "equal proportions" method and return to 435 as a total membership of the House. Congress considered amending the law to lessen the impact on states that lost House seats and electoral votes, but the automatic feature of the Reapportionment Act of 1929 put the redistribution indicated above into effect. (Data from U.S. Bureau of the Census.)

required that each district electing a representative be composed of contiguous territory. In 1872 a rule was added to require districts of substantially equal population. In 1901 the feature of compactness was added. Thus the requirement from 1901 until 1929 was for single-member districts of compact and contiguous territory, and as equal in population as practicable.

Requirements of compactness, contiguity, and equality were not included in the law of 1929 and are not now in effect [*Wood*

v. Broom, 287 U.S. 1 (1932)]. Gerrymandering—arranging a district for personal or partisan advantage—was curbed somewhat by these limitations while they existed. The matter now rests primarily with the states. Many have constitutional restrictions against gerrymandering and other districting abuses.[1] In practice many

[1] The most thorough study of apportionment problems is Laurence F. Schmeckebier, *Congressional Apportionment* (Washington, D.C.: Brookings, 1941).

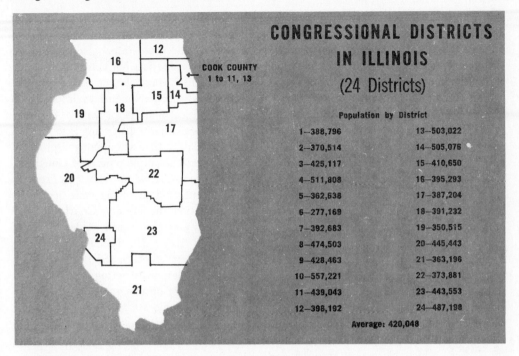

CONGRESSIONAL DISTRICTS IN ILLINOIS
(24 Districts)

COOK COUNTY
1 to 11, 13

Population by District	
1—388,796	13—503,022
2—370,514	14—505,076
3—425,117	15—410,650
4—511,808	16—395,293
5—362,538	17—387,204
6—277,169	18—391,232
7—392,683	19—350,515
8—474,503	20—445,443
9—428,463	21—363,196
10—557,221	22—373,881
11—439,043	23—443,553
12—398,192	24—487,198

Average: 420,048

In November, 1961, the Illinois legislature adopted this congressional redistricting. While population varies, regional and party balance is essentially fair. (Courtesy Illinois Legislative Council.)

states frustrate the goal of representation in the House of all people on the basis of equality. Often this occurs through failure of the States to reapportion congressional districts.

It is well established that a state legislature may not redistrict except by law; two-house resolutions without gubernatorial signature have been ruled inadequate.[1] In 1941 Congress provided by law for the contingency that a state might not redistrict after a national reapportionment. It followed the rules established by the courts. A state gaining seats in the House may elect the new members at large. A state losing seats and not redistricting must elect all members at large.

[1] *Smiley v. Holm*, 285 U.S. 361 (1932), involved Minnesota, and *Koenig v. Flynn*, 285 U.S. 379 (1932), involved New York.

Reapportionment Problems. Some controversy continues over the number of House seats and the mode of allocating them among the states. Several representatives have expressed discontent over the large number of constituents each member must serve when the total membership is held to 437, yet few would enlarge the House except to provide representation for newly admitted states. Some competent students advocate gradual reduction of House size to about 300 for maximum efficiency.

The mathematical formulas by which House seats are allocated are still being disputed by statisticians. The Congress and the public are inclined to judge the rival methods by their results. In general, "major fractions" is slightly more favorable to large states, and "equal proportions" to small states. Two more extreme methods are sometimes discussed: "rejected fractions," used for fifty years, by far the most favorable to the larger states; and the proposed "included fractions," which gives the small states the most generous treatment.[1]

The long-standing (1842–1929) law requiring representatives to be elected by districts was often violated by states that resorted to the device of representative at large. During 1951 the "at large" practice was criticized severely by a committee of the American Political Science Association[2] and by President Truman in a message to Congress.

By 1958 only three states with more than a single representative elected members at large. Beginning in 1962, however, eight states had one or more at large. These included Alabama, Hawaii, and New Mexico—which elect all on a state-wide basis—and Connecticut, Maryland, Michigan, Ohio, and Texas—which elect one at large and the others by districts. Opponents of the at-large method claim that it produces inequities in work load and representation and invites manipulation by the majority party.

Most important is the case for restoring the requirements of equality, compactness, and contiguity. Legislation without some kind of enforcement procedure is unlikely to be effective. Therefore, the leading proposals include sanctions as well as principles. Representative Emanuel Celler had a bill before recent congresses to allow no more than 15 or 20 per cent deviation, for each congressional district in a state, from

the number obtained by dividing the state population by the number of representatives allocated to the state.[3] Representatives elected from districts not conforming to the requirements would be denied seats. The courts have been reluctant to intervene in such "political matters," saying: "The remedy for unfairness in districting is to secure a state legislature that will apportion properly, or to invoke the ample powers of Congress." [Colegrove v. Green, 328 U.S. 549 (1946)]. In a recent case involving state legislative representation, the Supreme Court ruled that such cases might be raised, under the equal protection clause, in the Federal courts. [Baker v. Carr, 369 U.S. 186 (1962)]. Many cases on legislative districting have been filed, but the impact on congressional districts remains uncertain.

Senate Apportionment. Equal representation of the states in the Senate has produced very disproportionate representation by population. The most populous, of course, is New York; it has nearly a hundred times the population of Nevada, yet the same number of senators. The Constitution provides, moreover, that no state may be deprived of equal representation in the Senate without its consent.

As a practical matter, changing the basis of representation in the Senate appears out of the question, short of great upheaval or general alteration of our federal system. The disproportionate influence of small states is especially noticeable in treaty and constitutional-amendment proceedings, in which a two-thirds majority is required. A minority representing a minute fraction of the nation's population can frustrate the will of the majority.

[1] The various plans are discussed in "Legislative Reapportionment," *Law and Contemporary Problems*, vol. 17 (Spring, 1952), pp. 253–469. Equal proportions is favored by Laurence F. Schmeckebier, "The Method of Equal Proportions," pp. 302–313; included fractions is advocated by Walter F. Wilcox, "Last Words on the Apportionment Problems," pp. 290–301.

[2] "The Reapportionment of Congress," *American Political Science Review*, vol. 45 (March, 1951), pp. 153–157.

[3] For a recent review of proposed remedial legislation, see U.S. House of Representatives, Committee on the Judiciary, *Standards for Congressional Districts (Apportionment) Hearings* . . . (1959).

CONGRESSIONAL PERSONNEL

Qualifications. The House of Representatives has a short term (two years) and a low age requirement (twenty-five). Each representative must be a resident of the state from which he is elected and have been a citizen of the United States for at least seven years. Custom decrees that a representative must reside in the district that he represents, but there have been exceptions. The Constitution provides that each house is judge of "the elections, returns, and qualifications" of its members.

Under such authority, the House has barred regularly elected members for their beliefs, faith, and practices. The House has refused admission to a polygamist and to a Socialist who had been convicted of sedition. A simple majority vote may deny the right to take a seat. Expulsion of a sitting member of the House requires a two-thirds vote. Vacancies in the House normally are filled by special election called by the executive authority of the state.

United States senators serve long terms (six years) and have a higher age requirement (thirty years). Like the representative, a senator must be a resident of the state he represents. Nine years of citizenship prior to election are required in the upper house. Power to judge its own membership extends to the Senate, too, and is employed even more vigorously than in the House. The Senate refused to admit two duly elected members (Frank L. Smith, of Illinois, and William S. Vare, of Pennsylvania) because of huge expenditures in primary elections of 1926. Thus, although since the Newberry decision Congress has not attempted to regulate money in primaries, the Senate may bar offenders from the seats they win. Since the adoption of the Seventeenth Amendment, Senate vacancies may be filled by appointment by a governor if state law authorizes it.

It has often been proposed that the term of representatives be increased to four years. This would relieve members of the House from the biennial pressure to repair political fences for reelection; it would reduce considerably the possibility of a deadlock with a President of one party and the House majority of another.

The four-year term for House would introduce problems in connection with the Senate term, for the present scheme requires election of one-third of the senators each two years. Extending the Senate term to eight years with one-half of the senators elected every four years is one possibility, but it might lead to deadlock between President and Senate majority. The Senate term might be reduced to four years. This would virtually eliminate the possibility of deadlock, with all representatives and senators and the President elected at the same time. It is not likely to prove popular with the Senate, two-thirds of which must vote affirmatively to submit the necessary constitutional amendment.

Previous Experience of Congressmen. Nearly 60 per cent of the members of the two houses are attorneys. The second largest occupational group is composed of persons in the various branches of business. Farmers, teachers, and newspapermen follow in order. Getting a start in American politics commonly requires either wealth or an occupation that combines with the erratic periods of service involved. Once successfully established in a safe seat, the representative or senator may abandon his normal occupational pursuits and live on his congressional salary. Certainly membership in Congress constitutes a full-time job, and the salary has been made somewhat commensurate with it. For the lawyer the field of state and local politics has more than the usual glamour; he receives a form of advertising which usually helps his law practice, and he may work himself into line for a judicial post.

A recent review of the personnel of the Congress revealed that the average age of senators was fifty-seven, while that of representatives was fifty-one. Nearly all had previous public experience before election to congressional office. A large majority had attended college or professional schools.[1]

Privileges. Privileges of senators and representatives include certain immunity from arrest and extraordinary freedom of speech. The constitutional provision that national legislators are immune from arrest except for treason, felony, and breach of peace has been interpreted by the courts to prohibit only arrests in civil suits. In criminal cases members are as liable to arrest as other citizens. The same clause declares that "for any speech or debate in either house, they shall not be questioned in any other place." This means that senators and representatives may speak and act freely without fear of criminal prosecutions or civil suits. The House and Senate have full power to determine their own rules, to discipline for excesses, and, in extreme cases, to expel members. For mild offenses and indiscretions a member is called to order. Occasionally a house will censure a member; a leading example was the censure of the late Senator Joseph McCarthy in 1954.

Granting a large measure of privilege to legislators is desirable, but immunity may be abused. From the floor of the House or Senate, or in a committee, persons can be defamed without having practical means of fighting back. In the long run, perhaps, rules of fair conduct by congressional committees

can correct some of the worst abuses. Real progress has been achieved under the House committee "ground rules" adopted in 1955. Acquisition of self-restraint by *all* senators and representatives is highly unlikely.

Since Congress traditionally deals lightly with the misconduct of its members, some other means are needed to protect individuals against false accusations. One proposal is to permit victims of attacks made under congressional immunity to clear their names and secure redress by suing the United States for damages. Additional protection could be provided by making "informing witnesses" subject to civil suits for damages by those against whom they make libelous accusations.

Compensation. Congressional perquisites of office include salary, mileage, stationery, clerk hire, and the postal frank. The salary of senators and representatives is now $22,500 per year, all of which is subject to income taxation, but members may claim business-expense deductions for the extra cost of maintaining a second residence. The Speaker of the House and the President pro tempore of the Senate receive $35,000 each. These salaries are determined and altered by law. Each member is allowed twenty cents per mile traveling expenses to and from Washington once each session. Each member is given an allowance for clerk hire; this he sometimes uses to employ members of his family or political supporters. Official mail may be sent under postal frank free of charge. This privilege is often used for the dissemination of political and partisan speeches and "extensions of remarks" from the *Congressional Record*. There is a contributory retirement plan.

The public reacts unfavorably to proposals for increases in congressional compensation. In 1873 there was a great storm over a "salary grab." In early 1942 there

---

[1] For further information see George B. Galloway, *The Legislative Process in Congress* (New York: Crowell, 1953), pp. 370–375, and recent issues of the *Congressional Quarterly*.

THE COSTS OF RUNNING CONGRESS

A SENATOR GETS THIS	A MEMBER OF THE HOUSE GETS THIS
SALARY . . . $22,500 a year	**SALARY** . . . $22,500 a year
EXPENSES . . . Range from $70,000 to $135,000 a year for staff pay	**EXPENSES** . . . $35,000 or more a year for staff pay
OFFICE HELP . . . Staff of about 16 people	**OFFICE HELP** . . . Staff of about 3 people
OFFICE SPACE . . . A 5-room suite in Washington, plus an office in his home State	**OFFICE SPACE** . . . A two-room suite in Washington, plus an office in his home district

EXTRAS — Free postage • Allowance for long-distance calls • Travel allowance • Allowance for telegrams • $1,200 yearly stationery allowance • Low-cost pension and life insurance

- Cost of Congress, including upkeep of buildings and grounds, over 90 million dollars a year
- Per member of the House and Senate, over $170,000 a year

In the early 1960s these were the estimated average costs of national legislators.

was a controversy over the adoption of congressional pensions, and the legislators were attacked viciously for enacting the new perquisites of office. The law was repealed promptly.

The Legislative Reorganization Act of 1946[1] set the salary at $12,500 and provided a tax-free expense allowance of $2,500. The latter was widely criticized as a special privilege.

Evidence that the $15,000 was not adequate was soon available. A survey by a leading newspaper revealed that the typical senator and representative required an out-

side income to balance his personal budget.[2] The extraordinary demands on the national legislator include maintaining two homes, social entertainment, campaign and political costs, and travel between Washington and home.

In 1955, having received the report of a commission on judicial and congressional salaries, Congress proceeded to pass, and the President to sign, a bill providing both senators and representatives with the sum of $22,500 per year.

Retirement. The retirement plan included in the 1946 act, though quite generous, aroused surprisingly little opposition, in view of the "bundles for Congressmen" campaign that ridiculed an earlier

---

[1] 60 Stat. 831. The chief documents of the committee were U.S. Congress, Joint Committee on the Organization of Congress, *Hearings*, parts 1–4 (1945), and *Organization of the Congress, Report* . . . , S. Rept. 1011, 79th Cong., 2d Sess. (1946). For a fuller coverage of the Committee's work, see Chap. 14.

[2] Cabell Phillips, "The High Cost of Our Low-paid Congress," *The New York Times Magazine*, Feb. 24, 1952, pp. 7, 41–42, 44.

proposal. Although the retirement provisions for members of Congress were incorporated in the civil-service retirement system, they are entirely different from those applicable to civil-service employees. Members are free to elect whether they will come under the system. Those who join are required to pay into the fund 6 per cent of their salaries. This entitles them to receive a retirement allowance, after the age of sixty-two and a minimum of six years of service, of 2½ per cent of their annual salary multiplied by their years of service.

The maximum for congressmen who have served for thirty years was set at $7,500 annually and raised to fit the new salary scale. In contrast to ordinary retirement plans, members are not required to retire when they reach the retirement age, but may continue to serve in Congress as long as reelected. The effect of the plan has not been to induce overage members to retire; rather, it has provided a degree of security for members who have served long in Congress and face the prospect of defeat or retirement without provision for their old age.

Sessions and Congress. A Congress has a life of two years, coinciding with the term of office of representatives. Each Congress since the first (1789–1790) has been numbered consecutively; the Congress elected in 1962 and serving 1963–1964 is the Eighty-eighth.

A regular session occurs once each year. Since the Twentieth Amendment, each regular session begins on January 3, unless another date is provided by law. Under the Legislative Reorganization Act of 1946, the regular session adjourns July 31 unless otherwise provided by Congress. In even-numbered years during normal times, adjournment comes in early summer to leave time for campaigning. In odd years Congress holds forth until middle or late summer. The President has power to call special sessions. Within each two-year Congress, sessions are numbered consecutively, whether regular or special, beginning with "first" for each Congress.

The original constitutional provision called for the assembling of Congress on the first Monday of each December. The first regular session met thirteen months after election. The second regular session convened in December after a new Congress had been elected but with the old personnel. This became known as the "lame-duck" session for many defeated members of Congress continued to function for three months after their rejection by the electorate. The Twentieth Amendment, fathered by Senator Norris and adopted in 1933, abolished the lame-duck session and provided that a new Congress, fresh from the elections of November, begins active legislative work early in January.

PARTY GOVERNMENT

Party lines are rather loosely drawn in the House and Senate. As in the houses of the British Parliament, organization and procedure are linked to partisanship. Congress does not impose the strict discipline of the House of Commons. Groups, sectional and economic, often claim a greater share of a congressman's loyalty than does his party. On the other hand, the parties in Congress play a larger role than do the parties in many state legislatures, especially in the Western states.

The Caucus or Conference. In the House, members elected as Democrats affiliate with the Democratic caucus, while the Republicans join the Republican conference. From these partisan groups the party leaders in the House draw their authority; in their name, the majority and minority perform their important functions. In tangible form, the caucus or conference is a meeting of all representatives elected to the House under the label of a particular party. On the eve of a new Congress, the party group elects its own officers and nominates its candidates for the House offices. Each group has its chairman and secretary.

Only rarely does caucus or conference bind members to vote on the House floor according to the caucus decision. Both parties, upon occasion, attempt to bind their members, but there is often much insurgency. The Democratic rule permits the caucus to set the party "line" if two-thirds of those voting approve. No member is bound, however, on questions of constitutional construction or on matters on which he has made contrary pledges to his constituents. The Republicans get along without formal rules in their conference but take such actions as are deemed necessary by majority vote. A Democratic caucus rule provides that violators of group regulations automatically cease to be members of the caucus. Since 1910, the Republicans have generally been tolerant of independence, but in 1925 thirteen Republicans who supported Senator La Follette for President were not invited to the conference and were read out of the party. Both parties limit caucus attendance to their partisan members of the House.[1] During the last twenty years, caucus action binding members on legislation has practically fallen into disuse.

The Senate party caucuses play less im-

portant roles than do the House groups. As in the House, however, the majority caucus nominates officers for the Senate and determines committee assignments for the majority. The minority caucus provides a list of committee posts for the minority. Binding caucus decisions are exceedingly rare.

Party Leadership. The most sought-after post in the House is the speakership, and it is within the gift of the majority party. Intraparty differences are ironed out in caucus, and the candidate is agreed upon before each new Congress opens. Second most desirable is the majority floor leadership. Often a greater contest for this post develops than over the speakership, for the floor leader in recent years commonly has inherited the speakership. The majority floor leader is chief spokesman and strategist of his party on the floor. The minority caucus goes through the motions of nominating a candidate for the speakership, too. Defeated for election on the floor of the House, he becomes minority floor leader, generalissimo of the opposition forces. Both majority and minority floor leaders keep in touch with members on the floor through whips, who canvass party membership in the House and inform representatives of forthcoming business and of the party's position.

Party organization on the Senate side follows much the same pattern. Assigned the Vice President as a constitutional presiding officer, the Senate selects its next highest officer, the President pro tempore. The nominee of the majorty-party caucus is formally elected on the floor of the Senate. Majority and minority floor leaders are chosen by the respective caucuses.

Strengthening Leadership. The La Follette committee report recommended the establishment of majority and minority policy committees in both the House and

[1] A good description of party government in Congress is in Floyd M. Riddick, *The United States Congress, Organization and Procedures* (Manassas, Va.: National Capitol Publishers, 1949), pp. 42–57. See also his *Congressional Procedure* (Boston: Chapman & Grimes, 1941), pp. 29–40. To the latter he appends the Democratic rules and sample minutes of both Democratic caucus and Republican conference, pp. 352–365.

PARTY COMPLEXION OF CONGRESS

■ Republican ■ Democratic

President	Senate		House of Representatives

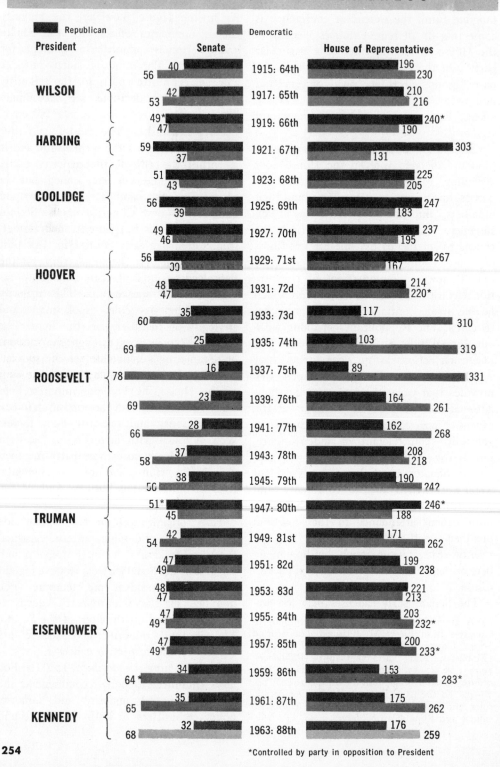

WILSON
- 1915: 64th — Senate: 40 / 56 — House: 196 / 230
- 1917: 65th — Senate: 42 / 53 — House: 210 / 216

HARDING
- 1919: 66th — Senate: 49* / 47 — House: 240* / 190
- 1921: 67th — Senate: 59 / 37 — House: 303 / 131

COOLIDGE
- 1923: 68th — Senate: 51 / 43 — House: 225 / 205
- 1925: 69th — Senate: 56 / 39 — House: 247 / 183
- 1927: 70th — Senate: 49 / 46 — House: 237 / 195

HOOVER
- 1929: 71st — Senate: 56 / 39 — House: 267 / 167
- 1931: 72d — Senate: 48 / 47 — House: 214 / 220*

ROOSEVELT
- 1933: 73d — Senate: 35 / 60 — House: 117 / 310
- 1935: 74th — Senate: 25 / 69 — House: 103 / 319
- 1937: 75th — Senate: 16 / 78 — House: 89 / 331
- 1939: 76th — Senate: 23 / 69 — House: 164 / 261
- 1941: 77th — Senate: 28 / 66 — House: 162 / 268
- 1943: 78th — Senate: 37 / 58 — House: 208 / 218

TRUMAN
- 1945: 79th — Senate: 38 / 56 — House: 190 / 242
- 1947: 80th — Senate: 51* / 45 — House: 246* / 188
- 1949: 81st — Senate: 42 / 54 — House: 171 / 262
- 1951: 82d — Senate: 47 / 49 — House: 199 / 238

EISENHOWER
- 1953: 83d — Senate: 48 / 47 — House: 221 / 213
- 1955: 84th — Senate: 47 / 49* — House: 203 / 232*
- 1957: 85th — Senate: 47 / 49* — House: 200 / 233*
- 1959: 86th — Senate: 34 / 64* — House: 153 / 283*

KENNEDY
- 1961: 87th — Senate: 35 / 65 — House: 175 / 262
- 1963: 88th — Senate: 32 / 68 — House: 176 / 259

254 *Controlled by party in opposition to President

the Senate. These bodies were to formulate legislative policy and expedite consideration and passage of matters on which the party had made commitments to the people. The Legislative Reorganization Act of 1946 failed to include provisions for policy committees, but the Senate secured its policy groups through an appropriation bill in 1947. No such committees have been established in the House, which has continued with its informal steering committees.

Senate majority and minority policy committees meet weekly during sessions. Each has a staff and a substantial budget. Democratic policy committeemen are appointed by the floor leader; Republican ones are elected by the conference for two-year terms.

The record of the Senate policy committees in the initial Congresses after their establishment is generally regarded as disappointing. They have done some useful work, but not the job needed to provide leadership and strengthen party responsibility.

Meanwhile, parties in the House have continued with their steering bodies, which the La Follette committee said "seldom meet and never steer." Party rather than House bodies, they have no budget or staff from the House. Actually they are considerably more active than the above quotation indicates. The Democratic steering committee is an executive committee of the caucus and makes many day-to-day decisions on party strategy. The Republicans now call their steering group "the House Republican policy committee." It is used as an advisory or consultative agency by the Republican leadership in the House.

Neither the formal policy committees of the Senate nor the informal steering committees of the House have fulfilled the need expressed by the La Follette report for "some mechanism which could bring about more party accountability for policies and pledges announced and made in the national platforms of the major political parties."[1]

Party Role in Committees. Until 1911 the Speaker of the House appointed all committees of that body. The principal reform that followed the successful revolt against arbitrary rule by Speaker Joseph Cannon, in March, 1910, was the election of standing committees by the House. Each party receives representation on each standing committee of the House somewhat in proportion to its strength in the whole House. If the Republicans hold two-thirds of the House seats, they take about two-thirds of the places on each committee. Actually, each major party chooses its own representatives for standing-committee assignments. In practice the parties exercise little discretion in individual committee assignments of old members, who receive reassignment, as a matter of course, to committees on which they previously served. For newly elected members, however, the process described below is important. Independent members and those of minor parties secure committee posts through one of the major parties.

The Republican conference uses a committee on committees for selection of committee personnel. This committee is composed of one representative from each state having Republican members of the House. Members are selected by the Republican state delegation and ratified by the conference. The committee on committees draws up a slate of Republican members for the standing committees of the House; it recommends personnel for the party steering committee. In voting within the Republican committee on committees, a member casts votes equal in number to the Republican representatives his state has in Congress.

The Democratic caucus first elects its

[1] *Organization of the Congress*, p. 12.

members of the House Ways and Means Committee; these then determine (sometimes in consultation with the party steering committee) standing-committee assignments for Democratic representatives. After approval by the party caucus, party slates are reported on the floor of the House and accepted quickly and without difficulty.

Senate selection of committee personnel is similar to that of the House. Standing committees are elected, but the nominating within the parties is the crucial matter. The Republicans use the committee on committees device. The Democrats in the Senate employ their steering committee as a committee on committees. In the Republican party, appointment to the committee-selecting body is made by the caucus chairman; in the Democratic, appointment is by the floor leader. Considerations of seniority are influential. The slates of the two parties are accepted almost automatically on the floor of the Senate.

Campaign Committees. Not satisfied that the proper attention would be given by national party organizations to the campaigns of congressional candidates, a joint congressional campaign committee was organized by the Republicans for the campaign of 1866.[1] The Democrats followed suit. In 1916 the senatorial element split off the Republican committee and formed a separate group. The Democrats did likewise in 1918. Today there are four such campaign committees: the Republican and Democratic congressional campaign committees and the Republican and Democratic senatorial campaign committees. In recent years they have been quite active. Each party's House campaign group is composed of one representative from each state represented in the House. The membership of

[1] For an account of origin and functions see: Hugh A. Bone, "Some Notes on the Congressional Campaign Committees," *Western Political Quarterly*, vol. 9 (March, 1956), pp. 116–137.

both Republican and Democratic senatorial campaign committees is appointed by the appropriate caucus chairman.

ORGANIZATION AND LEADERSHIP

Speaker of the House. The House of Representatives chooses its Speaker. The nominee of the majority party invariably is elected by the House. This election takes place at the beginning of each new Congress. The Constitution does not require it, but every Speaker has been at the time of his selection a member of the House. Seniority is important in choosing a Speaker, but personal popularity and political backing are also of importance. The tradition is well established that a Speaker is reelected in subsequent Congresses if his party maintains a majority.

Unlike the impartial and judicious Speaker of the British House of Commons, the American House presiding officer acts as a party leader and uses the powers of his office to promote his party's program. Like the Presidency, the speakership can be an office of great magnitude or one of only modest influence; which it is depends upon the incumbent and the circumstances in his party, in Congress, and in the country. The most powerful Speakers, like Reed, Cannon, and Longworth, built up the authority and prestige of the office to a high level. Some of the others have been content to be merely the presiding officer.

Nominal powers of the Speaker include appointment of select and conference committees, signature of documents in behalf of the House, reference of bills to committees, and general conduct of parliamentary business, which includes recognition of members who wish to have the floor. After the loss in 1911 of the power to appoint standing committees, the Speaker's greatest authority derived from presiding. Speaker

Reed established that members present but refusing to answer to their names could be counted for purposes of securing a quorum. He also refused to put motions that were dilatory or intended to obstruct the business of the House.

The power over recognition, as developed by Speaker Gillette and others, permits the presiding officer to decide who is entitled to the floor. The Speaker may ignore entirely the attempt of a member to claim the floor, unless the member has explained his purpose in a prior interview. More bluntly, the Speaker may turn to one who seeks the floor and ask: "For what purpose does the gentleman rise?" If the purpose is not regarded as proper, the Speaker may reply: "The Chair cannot recognize the gentleman for that purpose." The Speaker rules on all points of order, and his decisions rarely are overruled on appeal to the House. The Speaker may vote or speak to a question if he wishes.

House Floor Leaders. The majority and minority floor leaders, selected by their respective party caucuses, fill posts that have developed into their present form since the turn of the century. The majority leader, when of the same party as the President, often is the administration spokesman. Each floor leader is manager of his party's program on the floor and has effective control, through cooperation with the Speaker, over important aspects of procedure.

House Rules Committee. Over a period of more than a century the House Rules Committee has built up authority over procedure until now it has virtual life-and-death power over legislation in the lower house. Each Congress is deluged with such a mass of proposals (10,000 to 20,000 bills introduced each two years) that full consideration cannot be given to all. Most of the bills fall by the wayside in the committees to which they are referred. But the committees approve and report to the House more bills than it can adequately consider, and some bills opposed by its leadership. Consequently some sifting device must select bills of greater importance to the nation and those likely to win the approval of the House. For many years this function has been performed by the Rules Committee, formerly headed by the Speaker.

The traffic jam of bills awaiting House action is usually so great that only those which receive the blessing of the Rules Committee through a special rule enabling them to be taken up out of order are considered by the House. Bills on certain subjects, like taxation and appropriations, are highly privileged and may be called up without a special rule. On certain days, private bills and noncontroversial minor bills are taken up and passed, normally by unanimous consent. But important legislative measures ordinarily are taken up only as a result of a special rule proposed by the Rules Committee.

This situation gives the Rules Committee great power. It cannot initiate legislation, but it can block that recommended by other committees, virtually exercising a veto power. On occasion it has held hearings on the merits of legislation already considered by other committees. It has refused to bring in a special rule unless a proposed bill was altered to suit its wishes.

If the Rules Committee is controlled by party leaders friendly to the administration, it can block legislation embarrassing to the administration and clear the track for the President's legislative program. If a majority of its members are unsympathetic to the President's legislative program, however, the committee's influence is just the opposite. During President Truman's administration the latter condition generally prevailed. A majority of the members of the Rules Committee of both parties was opposed to the

President's legislative program on labor and other economic issues and prevented these measures from coming before the House. The membership of the committee was largely conservative, consisting of members of both parties who came from safe districts. Many social-reform measures were blocked as a result.

In 1949, after the Democratic victory of the previous year, the House trimmed the powers of the Rules Committee. It provided that, after the Rules Committee held a bill for twenty-one days without acting, the chairman of the committee which recommended the bill could move on a specified day to take it up in the House without a special rule; and if a majority so voted, the bill would be made the order of business. To make the motion, however, recognition by the Speaker was necessary, so the Speaker really decided whether to permit the issue to be raised.

In 1951 the old rule was restored by a conservative combination, including most of the Republican members and many Southern Democrats. Early in the Kennedy administration the Rules Committee was enlarged temporarily from twelve to fifteen members in another effort to overcome conservative obstruction; whether this arrangement will continue in future congresses depends on the will of the House. While a committee with power to screen out unimportant and undesirable bills is needed, critics say its members should be responsible to their parties or the House itself.

Senate Leaders. The Vice President of the United States, as President of the Senate, conducts himself as a rather impartial presiding officer. He votes only in case of a tie. His appointive power is slight. A President pro tempore is elected by the Senate after nomination by the majority-party caucus. He presides over the upper house in the absence of its president, and

succeeds to the Presidency of the United States upon the death or disability of the President, Vice President, and Speaker of the House.

COMMITTEE SYSTEMS

Role of Standing Committees. More than seventy years ago Woodrow Wilson in his doctoral dissertation characterized American government as "government by the Standing Committees of Congress."[1] As the two houses have grown larger in membership and their problems have increased in number and complexity, they have delegated even more important decision making to committees. Standing committees, indeed even their chairmen acting unilaterally, may pigeonhole bills desired by the majority of Congress or the people. They are "little ministries" with enormous power. A member of the British House of Commons serving on a committee to consider a bill must disclaim interest in it by constituents or himself. A member of a House or Senate committee, far from disclaiming such interests, often flaunts his bias and proceeds to champion the case of his district, state, or favorite pressure group.[2]

House Standing Committees. The methods used by the party groups in selecting standing-committee members have been described. Standing committees are the most important class of committees, for they are the screen which sifts the great mass of proposed legislation.

The party slates of committee assign-

[1] *Congressional Government* (Boston: Houghton Mifflin, 1885), p. 56. Dr. George B. Galloway recently declared: "The real locus of the legislative power is not in the House or Senate as such; it is in their standing committees." *The Legislative Process in Congress*, p. 649.

[2] For a valuable study of legislative behavior, see Ralph K. Huitt, "The Congressional Committee: A Case Study," *American Political Science Review*, vol. 48 (June, 1954), pp. 340–365.

ments are formally ratified by the House in a resolution. New members are seldom appointed to one of the more important committees, but must serve on a minor committee until they acquire sufficient seniority or influence to secure assignment to a major one. The chairman of each committee is normally the member of the majority party who is senior in length of service on the committee.

When the Democrats are in the majority, most of the chairmanships are held by members from the South. In 1962, for example, ten of the twenty chairmanships in the House were held by members from seven Southern states: Arkansas, Georgia, North Carolina, South Carolina, Tennessee, Texas, and Virginia, and two other chairmanships were held by members from Border States. When the Republicans are in power, there is a similar concentration of chairmanships in the hands of members from safe Republican districts, mainly in the Northeast and Middle West.

The rule of seniority produces an experienced corps of committee heads, but an aged one. In the Eighty-seventh Congress the group averaged sixty-five years of age. Three-fifths of the chairmen were past the age of compulsory retirement which obtains in most public enterprises and private companies.

The twenty House standing committees range in number of members from nine to fifty, averaging over twenty-nine. With some exceptions, members are now limited to a single standing-committee assignment. Before the enactment of the Legislative Reorganization Act of 1946 there were many more committees. In the Seventy-ninth Congress, the number of regular House committees was forty-seven, and members were permitted to serve on two or more of all but the most important.

The Speaker refers public bills to com-

"It's A Hell Of A Way To Run A Railroad"

Herblock's famous commentary on the seniority system under which chairmen of committees are chosen mainly by longevity. [From *The Herblock Book* (Beacon Press).]

mittees. He sometimes exercises considerable discretion but is ultimately subject to the will of the House. Once a bill is assigned, it is difficult to secure its rereference. Traditionally, standing-committee chairmen wield great power over the meeting, procedure, and action of their committees.

Committees of the House meet and conduct hearings during the morning hours. About one-half have regular meeting days; the remainder meet on call of the chairman. Most committee meetings are open to the public, but some are closed. On important bills committees or subcommittees may hold hearings, with witnesses from various parts of the country testifying. A committee may vote to report the bill out to the House with a favorable recommendation, or it may refuse to report the bill, which has the effect of rejecting or pigeonholing it. The most influential of the House committees, after Rules, are Ways and Means, Appropriation, Commerce, Banking and Currency, Agriculture, Armed Services, and Foreign Affairs.

Other House Committees. House select committees are established for various purposes. Their personnel is appointed by the Speaker. They are created by simple resolution. Usually a select committee studies some problem for a definite period. The best known select committees are investigating committees. Such committees generally are given power to meet, even after Congress has adjourned, to administer oaths, to subpoena persons and records, and the like.

Senate Committees. Senate standing committees are "elected" by the Senate, but this process is actually a ratification of the slates selected by the two major party groups. The majority party receives all chairmanships. The rule of seniority is highly important in the Senate also, but the longer term and the greater tendency to reelect senators make overwhelming sectional domination less likely. In the Eighty-seventh Congress, however, eight of the sixteen standing committees were headed by senators from the Deep South. Some of the most important committees are led by men in their seventies and eighties; the average age of chairmen in 1959 was sixty-five years. Senate committees varied in size from nine members on the smallest to twenty-three on the largest, Appropriations. Each senator is limited to two committees, but when the two parties are rather evenly divided, third-committee assignments are authorized. Before the 1946 reform law, the number of Senate committees in recent Congresses had ranged from thirty-three to seventy-three.

Upon introduction a bill is referred by the presiding officer to the committee which is to consider it. The committee may consider the bill, hold hearings, or report back

to the Senate. Only the Appropriations Committee meets on call of the chairman; all others meet regularly.

The power of the Senate to conduct investigations between sessions was fully assured in *McGrain v. Daugherty* [273 U.S. 135 (1927)], and the Senate has used its power with vigor. Among well-known Senate inquiries were Teapot Dome, munitions, the Truman committee investigating war expenditures, and the Kefauver committee on organized crime. Members of Senate select committees are appointed by the President of the Senate.

Joint Committees. Congress also has numerous joint committees, commissions, and boards. Some of these deal with housekeeping activities of Congress; examples are the joint committees on printing, the Congressional Library, and the Capitol building. Several are of major importance, e.g., the Committees on Atomic Energy, Economic Report, and Defense Production. A number are set up temporarily to plan memorials or commemorations.

Joint investigating committees occasionally are established by two-house resolution or by statute. An example is the Joint Committee on the Organization of Congress. The Temporary National Economic Committee, which reported in 1941, contained members of both houses and representatives of several Federal executive agencies.

The most common joint committees are *conference committees*. They compromise the differences between Senate and House versions of the same bill. The Speaker appoints House conferees, and the Vice President, those of the Senate. The second house amends most important pieces of legislation in some form or other. Then the amended bill goes back to the first house for acceptance. If the first house declines to accept the amendments, it may ask the second to recede from them. If the second house will not, the two houses arrange a conference. Normally, three representatives and three senators constitute the committee, though some are larger. If the conferees agree on a compromise, they report results to each house. Should the House and Senate both agree to accept the conference-committee recommendation, the bill is deemed passed in the form the conference committee proposed. On the other hand, if one or both houses refuse to accept, then the bill dies or another conference must be arranged.

Committee Changes. Reform of the committee system was a prime objective of the Legislative Reorganization Act of 1946 and "the keystone in the arch of congressional reform."[1] The act reduced Senate standing committees from thirty-three to fifteen; House, from forty-seven to nineteen. Jurisdiction was defined with some care. The law limited senators to two standing-committee assignments, with a few exceptions permitted. Although House members were not limited by statute, in practice they are usually not assigned to more than one major standing committee; select and joint committees are in addition.

Special committees were not forbidden by the act, but the report of the La Follette committee urged their abolition. In actual practice few have been authorized. Nearly every proposal for a special investigating committee cuts into the jurisdiction of one or more standing committees. The trend is for standing committees and their subcommittees to conduct most of the investigations.

The number of subcommittees is large. In the House during a recent Congress, eight standing committees had subcom-

mittees, ranging from three for Interstate and Foreign Commerce to seventeen for Agriculture. The Senate, at the same session, had eleven standing committees with subcommittees, ranging from two for Government Operations to fourteen for Judiciary. Some of the leading investigations of the era, including the Army-McCarthy hearings of 1954 and the Kefauver probe of juvenile delinquency, were conducted by subcommittees.

There has also been a significant move toward more joint standing committees. Excluding visiting boards and memorial commissions, twelve existed in 1962.

About half of the House standing committees abide by the law that requires regular meeting days; the Senate committees, with one exception, have established meeting times. Committees have experienced difficulty in meeting the requirement that a majority must be present to report a measure or recommendation. The statutory provision that committees should have witnesses file written statements in advance of proposed testimony is more often ignored than observed.

Largely through standing committees and their subcommittees, Congress since reorganization has conducted a record number of investigations.[2] Relatively few were by special committees. The House conducts more investigations than the Senate, but the upper house often is more generous with funds. Such inquiries make valuable contributions to the understanding of governmental problems by the public and by the Congress.

On the other hand, committees and subcommittees of Congress frequently conduct hearings and other proceedings which

---

[1] George B. Galloway, "The Operation of the Legislative Reorganization Act of 1946," *American Political Science Review*, vol. 45 (March, 1951), p. 41.

[2] *Congressional Quarterly* reported that the committees of the Eighty-seventh Congress, first session, had available more than 9½ million dollars for 198 investigations: 100 House, 76 Senate, and 22 joint.

violate individual rights or fair play. Irresponsible witnesses make sensational accusations, with the result that the victim suffers from loss of reputation and earning power even though he can prove the charges ill founded and false. Persons before congressional inquiries have been deprived of such fundamental safeguards as the rights to have counsel, confront and cross-examine accusers, and be heard. Under the cloak of immunity, both senators and representatives have made charges they could not substantiate. Yet those attacked have no remedy and no way to secure compensation.

The action of the House of Representatives in adopting in 1955 a set of rules on the conduct of committees may prove a turning point. It requires that no fewer than two members of a committee constitute a quorum to take testimony and receive evidence. The subject of investigation must be announced at the outset by the chairman. Committee rules must be made available to witnesses, who may be accompanied by counsel. If testimony tending to defame a person is anticipated, it must be received in executive session; the person concerned must be afforded an opportunity to testify and be given the right to request additional witnesses. Material secured in executive sessions cannot be released without the consent of the committee. Witnesses may submit "brief and pertinent" sworn statements for the record, subject to the discretion of the committee. A witness may obtain a transcript of his testimony on payment of its cost.

Many proposed reforms are not included in the list, but when considered with the Speaker's ban on televised and broadcast committee hearings, renewed in 1962, the rules that were adopted place the House far ahead of the Senate in the safeguards afforded to individuals against maltreatment before congressional committees.

FOR FURTHER READING

See also works listed after next chapter.

Acheson, Dean: A Citizen Looks at Congress (New York: Harper, 1957).

Bailey, Stephen K., and Howard D. Samuel: Congress at Work (New York: Holt, 1952).

Barth, Alan: Government by Investigation (New York: Viking, 1955).

Burnham, James: Congress and the American Tradition (Chicago: Regnery, 1959).

Carroll, Holbert, N.: The House of Representatives and Foreign Affairs (Pittsburgh, Pa.: University of Pittsburgh Press, 1958).

Chiu, Chang-wei: The Speaker of the House of Representatives since 1896 (New York: Columbia University Press, 1928).

Dennison, Eleanor E.: The Senate Foreign Relations Committee (Stanford, Calif.: Stanford University Press, 1942).

Dimock, Marshall E.: Congressional Investigating Committees (Baltimore: Johns Hopkins Press, 1929).

Ewing, Cortez A.: Congressional Elections, 1896–1944 (Norman, Okla.: University of Oklahoma Press, 1947).

Farnsworth, David N.: The Senate Committee on Foreign Relations (Urbana, Ill.: University of Illinois Press, 1961).

Follett, Mary P.: The Speaker of the House of Representatives (New York: Longmans, 1896).

Galloway, George B.: History of the House of Representatives (New York: Crowell, 1962).

——: The Legislative Process in Congress (New York: Crowell, 1953).

Griffith, Ernest S.: Congress: Its Contemporary Role (New York: New York University Press, 3d ed., 1961).

Gross, Bertram M.: The Legislative Struggle: A Study in Social Combat (New York: McGraw-Hill, 1953).

Haynes, George H.: The Senate of the United

States: *Its History and Practice* (Boston: Houghton Mifflin, 2 vols., 1938).

Luce, Robert: *Legislative Principles* (Boston: Houghton Mifflin, 1930).

————: *Congress—An Explanation* (Cambridge, Mass.: Harvard University Press, 1926).

McGeary, M. Nelson: *The Development of Congressional Investigative Power* (New York: Columbia University Press, 1940).

Matthews, Donald R.: *U.S. Senators and Their World* (Chapel Hill, N.C.: University of North Carolina Press, 1960).

Riddick, Floyd M.: *The United States Congress: Organization and Procedure* (Manassas, Va.: National Capitol Publishers, 1949).

————: *Congressional Procedure* (Boston: Chapman & Grimes, 1941).

Rogers, Lindsay: *The American Senate* (New York: Knopf, 1926).

Schmeckebier, Laurence F.: *Congressional Ap-*portionment (Washington, D.C.: Brookings, 1941).

Truman, David B.: *The Congressional Party* (New York: Wiley, 1959).
Illinois Press, 1951).

Taylor, Telford: *Grand Inquest: The Story of Congressional Investigations* (New York: Simon and Schuster, 1955).

Truman, David B.: *The Congressional Party* (New York: Wiley, 1959).

White, William S.: *Citadel: The Story of the U.S. Senate* (New York: Harper, 1957).

Wilson, Woodrow: *Congressional Government* (Boston: Houghton Mifflin, 1885).

Young, Roland: *The American Congress* (New York: Harper, 1957).

————: *Congressional Politics in the Second World War* (New York: Columbia University Press, 1956).

REVIEW QUESTIONS

1. How did the bicameral principle originate? Is there justification for it in Congress today?

2. Compare the House of Representatives and the Senate in respect to qualifications and selection of members?

3. What powers have the Senate and the House to expel or refuse to seat regularly elected members?

4. What are the powers and duties of the Speaker of the House? How does he rank in prestige with other high officials?

5. Describe the committee systems of the United States Senate and House.

6. What is the role of the political party in the legislative process?

7. Name and discuss the American forerunners of the Congress of the United States.

8. What were the principal provisions of the Reapportionment Act of 1929?

9. What is the present status of the traditional principles of apportionment: equality, compactness, and contiguousness?

10. To what privileges and compensation are members of the House and Senate entitled under present law?

11. Explain the following terms: "session," "a Congress," "lame duck," "gerrymander," "equal proportions," "franking privilege."

12. How do the Republicans select House committee members? How do the Democrats?

13. How do the Republicans select Senate committee members? How do the Democrats?

14. Describe the operation of House and Senate standing committees, with special reference to the powers of chairmen.

15. Why are there joint committees of the two houses? Give some examples of joint committees and tell how they operate.

Chapter Fourteen

Congressional
Procedure and Reform

*Because Congress is without leadership and its organization
is disintegrated, the gulf between its promise and its
performance on legislation takes on the proportions,
but not the grandeur, of the Grand Canyon. Without a
center of responsibility there can be no strong leadership and
no coordinated legislative program. National interests are
subordinated to sectional and special interests, and Congress
fails to perform adequately its tremendously important
function of holding the executive accountable.*

*Not only do many needed bills bog down along the
present winding road of the law-making process never to
reach their destination of enactment, but even where
there is agreement to take some of the horseshoe turns
out of the road it is seldom translated into action.
Many hearings are held, and much time is spent, but little
or nothing comes from it. This refers particularly to the
modernization of the law-making machinery.*

*It is actually a vicious progression. Without a center of
responsibility, the machinery isn't fixed; without the
machinery, the legislative job isn't adequately done.
If a center of responsibility were achieved, many of the
shortcomings listed in this letter could and probably
would be overcome.*

NATIONAL COMMITTEE FOR STRENGTHENING THE CONGRESS[1]

To carry on its legislative and nonlegislative
business, Congress needs rules of procedure
and an organization of considerable size
and complexity. Without knowledge of the
rules, both formal and informal, a congressman cannot be effective and certainly will
not be influential. Without knowledge of
the ways of Congress, the citizen may be-

[1] Letter to members of Congress from Robert
Heller, chairman, Jan. 7, 1952, p. 4.

lieve that congressional parliamentary procedures are so much respected merely because they are well established. The citizen
should then recall that the ways of doing
things have been hammered out on the
anvil of controversy over many years. The
compromises reached have set precedents
and these are usually referred to when similar situations arise.

The citizen should remember too that,

although they may change but slowly, congressional practices are constantly being adjusted to reflect the changing pattern of the nation. During the past ten years, much healthy, informed criticism of congressional practices has resulted in substantial improvements. The House of Representatives, in particular, has special problems imposed by its large size and heavy work load. This chapter first sketches some aspects of procedure in the House and Senate and then examines some of the problems which face congressmen, both as individuals and collectively.

PROCEDURE IN THE HOUSE

Introduction of Bills. A bill is introduced in the House of Representatives merely by sending it to the clerk's desk. A member must appear as its sponsor. Before formal introduction, a great deal of planning and drafting is done. Actually, the two main sources of bills are executive agencies and private pressure groups, not the legislators themselves. An idea for legislation may be taken to private attorneys for drafting; in other cases it may be whipped into the bill or resolution form by the staff of the Legislative Counsel.

Simple bills are designated "H.R." or "S." depending upon the house of origin, and are numbered consecutively during a Congress. Joint resolutions, marked "H.J. Res." and "S.J. Res.," differ from ordinary bills only in that they are intended for temporary situations. Neither concurrent resolutions, which deal with matters pertaining to the legislative branch, nor simple resolutions, which concern internal matter in one house only, are submitted to the President for signature.

No limit is imposed on the number of bills a member may introduce. Each Congress in the last twenty years has faced an

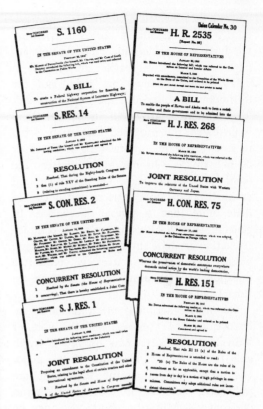

average of about 14,000; slightly less than 1,000 were enacted in an average Congress. All bills not enacted are wiped off the records at the close of a Congress. To secure consideration in the next two-year period, it is necessary to reintroduce the proposed legislation.[1]

Committee Stage. The next step in the legislative process is reference to committee.

[1] Procedure is covered most adequately in Floyd M. Riddick, *Congressional Procedure* (Boston: Chapman & Grimes, 1941), and *The United States Congress: Organization and Procedure* (Manassas, Va.: National Capitol Publishers, 1949). Current developments in congressional procedure were covered in the reviews of each session of Congress, contained in the *American Political Science Review.* For two decades they were written by E. Pendleton Herring, by Orman R. Altman, and by Floyd M. Riddick. Beginning with the Eighty-first Congress, Riddick's reviews were transferred to the *Western Political Quarterly.*

There bills are given a preliminary examination. Most of them are buried as meriting no further consideration. The more important pieces of legislation are studied in detail; public hearings are held, and the testimony of interested persons is heard. The committee arrives at its verdict. If it is favorable, the proposed legislation, often in amended form, is forwarded to the floor of the House. On important matters the committee report may be extensive and exhaustive; on minor matters it may convey little more than a simple affirmative. In general, bills that secure favorable committee action are in a strong position to secure passage in the House; conversely, committee rejection of a measure makes passage extremely unlikely.

Committee action is often taken in executive (closed) session, but the vote of individual committeemen usually is available to the public. Hearings of the major committees on important legislation are published, some in the "documents" series of Congress. Minority reports also may be filed.

Calendars. Each bill reported out of committee to the floor of the House is placed on one of three principal calendars. Bills raising revenue, appropriating money or property, directly or indirectly, are placed on the Union Calendar. All other public bills, not fiscal in nature, go to the House Calendar. All bills of a private character are assigned to the Private Calendar. Noncontroversial bills may be transferred from either Union or House Calendar to the Consent Calendar, if a request is filed. Bills withdrawn from committee by petition are placed before the House on the Discharge Calendar. Members keep track of bills mainly through the daily issue of *Calendars of the United States House of Representatives and History of Legislation*. Listed in this publication are the special orders of the day, unfinished business, bills in conference, the five calendars with all bills on them, a history of active bills, and a summary table on the status of fifteen or twenty major bills.

A rule of the House requires that bills be taken up in their calendar order, but numerous exceptions are made so action may be secured on the more important measures.

Selection for Consideration. Several devices are used to select bills for consideration out of calendar order: (1) A motion may be made to suspend the rules (on first and third Mondays and during last six days of session) and must receive a two-thirds vote. (2) Some committees may bring up privileged matters (especially revenue and appropriation bills). (3) Special orders or rules are highly privileged and may be brought in at any time by the Rules Committee and adopted by a majority vote. (4) Bills may be brought by unanimous consent from the Consent Calendar (on first and third Mondays) for immediate consideration. (5) Committees may call up for passage some of their own bills, otherwise unprivileged, from House or Union Calendars (on Wednesdays except during the last two weeks of a session). (6) Members may secure unanimous consent for immediate consideration of a measure.[1]

The special rules recommended by the Rules Committee and adopted by the House almost invariably call for immediate consideration of a particular bill. In recent Congresses an average of 150 special rules were adopted; of the total, over one-half

[1] A seventh device was created by the Eighty-first Congress (1949–1950) but abolished at the opening of the Eighty-second. It permitted chairmen of committees to move for immediate consideration of bills on two specified days of the month when the Rules Committee refused, after twenty-one days, to report a special rule. See Glendon A. Schubert, "The Twenty-one Day Rule," *Political Science* (New Zealand), vol. 5 (March, 1953), pp. 16–29.

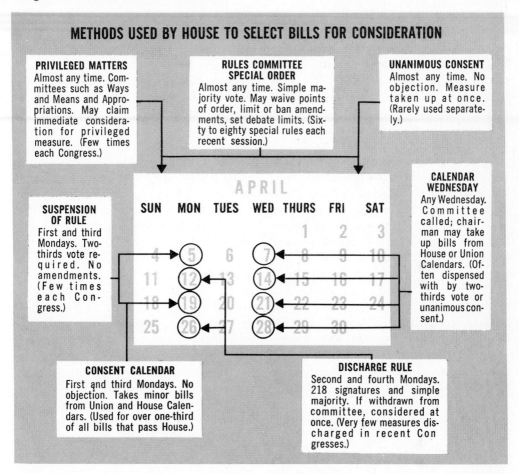

METHODS USED BY HOUSE TO SELECT BILLS FOR CONSIDERATION

PRIVILEGED MATTERS
Almost any time. Committees such as Ways and Means and Appropriations. May claim immediate consideration for privileged measure. (Few times each Congress.)

RULES COMMITTEE SPECIAL ORDER
Almost any time. Simple majority vote. May waive points of order, limit or ban amendments, set debate limits. (Sixty to eighty special rules each recent session.)

UNANIMOUS CONSENT
Almost any time. No objection. Measure taken up at once. (Rarely used separately.)

CALENDAR WEDNESDAY
Any Wednesday. Committee called; chairman may take up bills from House or Union Calendars. (Often dispensed with by two-thirds vote or unanimous consent.)

SUSPENSION OF RULE
First and third Mondays. Two-thirds vote required. No amendments. (Few times each Congress.)

CONSENT CALENDAR
First and third Mondays. No objection. Takes minor bills from Union and House Calendars. (Used for over one-third of all bills that pass House.)

DISCHARGE RULE
Second and fourth Mondays. 218 signatures and simple majority. If withdrawn from committee, considered at once. (Very few measures discharged in recent Congresses.)

were "open" rules that merely set the stage for preferential consideration; less than one-half were "closed" rules that "gagged" the House to a considerable extent. Nearly all closed rules specify that points of order may not be raised against the bill as proposed by a standing committee; many either restrict amendments absolutely or allow only the committee to propose amendments. Both open and closed rules usually set maximum time limits on debate and in other ways provide for expeditious handling of House measures.[1]

[1] The use of special rules may be followed in the annual articles on congressional sessions by Floyd M. Riddick in *The Western Political Quarterly*.

Committee of the Whole. The House, sitting in a more informal capacity, handles all Union Calendar bills as the "Committee of the Whole House on the State of the Union." Private Calendar bills are discussed as in Committee of the Whole. The House resolves itself into such a status by passing a motion directing it. The Speaker appoints a member to act as chairman and retires.

Sometimes the length of debate on a particular bill is set in the motion to resolve; usually time is divided into one-half for those opposing, one-half for those supporting. Procedure in Committee of the Whole is freer than in the House. Attendance of 100 members suffices for a quorum, instead of the usual majority. No record roll-call votes are taken. A bill is read section by section, and amendments may be offered to appropriate sections. When the work at hand is completed, the Committee of the Whole rises and reports its action back to the House. These recommendations may be accepted or rejected by the House.

Consideration on the Floor. When at last the House turns its attention to a certain bill, debate on its merits is in order. Three readings of each bill are required by House rules. The first reading requirement is satisfied by printing the title in the *Record* and *Journal* at the time of introduction. The second reading, the only one in full, occurs as the bill is considered in the House or in Committee of the Whole. General debate precedes second reading. Amendments may be offered as sections are read. Some amendments are general, "considered" amendments, seriously intended as alterations in the bill. Others are *pro forma*, involving the striking out of the last word or two of a section; in the short debate that may ensue, a member may make some point he otherwise could not have made.

In the debate on a particular bill, the chairman or other ranking members of the committee that recommended the measure manages the "pro" side. Ranking minority members of the same committee may be recognized as in charge of the cons.

The House generally predetermines time for debate and divides it equally between sponsors and opponents. The members in control grant time to those who wish to speak. It is very common for one member to ask another who has the floor if he will yield. If the member who holds recognition wishes to step aside for a moment, a question or brief statement may be interposed.

At the conclusion of consideration, the Speaker states, "The question is on the engrossment and third reading of the bill." Then, "The question is upon the final passage of the bill." After the bill is passed, it goes to the Senate.

House Closure. In a body the size of the House of Representatives, the necessity for curbing debate is obvious. Debate is cut off formally by the adoption of a motion calling for the previous question. Such a motion may serve to close debate upon either passage of a bill or upon amendments to a bill. Should the previous question be called for and carried before any debate takes place, each side is given twenty minutes to present its case.

Other methods control the time expended in debate. Special orders brought in by the Rules Committee usually limit debate. Speakers of the House have built up authority to refuse to put dilatory motions. House rules prevent speeches of more than one hour without unanimous consent. Informal agreements on the allocation of time increasingly are made between majority and minority leaders and have proved highly satisfactory in curbing excessive verbosity.

Voting in the House. Four methods of voting are used by the House: (1) Usually the first attempted is viva voce, or voice vote. If this is indecisive, or one-fifth of a quorum requests, another method may be used. (2) Division means standing vote, counted by the Speaker. (3) Voting with tellers involves the members' filing past a given point to be counted for or against a bill. (4) Yeas and nays voting requires a call of the roll by the clerk, each member's vote being recorded. The first three methods are rapid, but provide no record roll call through which a citizen may examine the voting record of his representative. The fourth method takes a great amount of House time, for the names of all members must be called orally, and those who did not respond the first time are called again.

The process often takes a half hour or more.

On one spectacular occasion, in 1935, the Scripps-Howard newspapers recorded the votes of Representatives participating in a teller vote. The vote was upon the so-called "death sentence" on utility holding companies. The press gallery was filled with staff members who knew congressional personnel; they simply put down the names of the members of the House who filed by with the "aye" group and those who appeared with the "no" group. Ordinarily the public is in the dark concerning the votes of individual congressmen, unless a roll call records the yeas and nays.

Several legislative bodies have solved the problem of making record roll-call votes in brief time by installing an electric recording device. The names of the legislators appear on an illuminated board on the front wall of the chamber. Each legislator's desk is fitted with a panel containing "yes" and "no" buttons. When buttons are pushed, the great scoreboard shows how each legislator votes. Great amounts of time have been saved in the states where used, but Congress has not adopted such a scheme.

Laymen often are confused by the pairing of House members for record votes. Pairs are personal contracts between two members; usually they are of opposite points of view and different parties. If one is absent, the other does not vote; the pairing is announced after a roll call.

Discharge Rule. Withdrawal of a bill on which a House committee refuses to report may be obtained under the discharge rule. The rule was first adopted in 1910 and, in several different forms, has persisted since. The present rule, adopted in 1935, provides that, when signatures of 218 members of the House are obtained on a petition to withdraw a bill, a sponsor may move to discharge the committee from further con-

sideration. The matter is placed on a Discharge Calendar for "seven days of grace." The motion may be taken up only on the second and fourth Mondays and requires a simple majority to carry.

The merits of the discharge rule have aroused much controversy. Majority party leaders have been inclined to debunk it as an obstacle to proper handling of business. Independent and minority elements have praised the device as an essential weapon of the forces of democracy in the struggle against domination. Each major party, depending upon its situation in the House, has been friend and then foe of the rule. After the Democrats secured a slight majority in the House, the liberal discharge rule of 1931 was adopted. This permitted a petition to be filed with only 145 signatures. When, however, the Democrats secured a great majority, the 1935 amendment was added, requiring 218 signatures. In practice, many attempts to discharge are made but only a handful receive sufficient signatures. Very few bills actually are withdrawn from committee.[1]

SENATE PROCEDURE

General Aspects. Introduction of a Senate bill is accomplished by the announcement by a senator that he introduces it. Reading the title of the bill constitutes the first reading. Second reading is considered completed if there is no objection, and the bill is sent to the committee requested by the introducer. The Senate committee system has already been described; in important respects it is like that of the House. After a standing committee reports a bill favorably, it is placed on the Senate calendar for at least one day before being taken up. A

[1] In the Seventy-eighth Congress twenty-one discharge motions were filed and three bills actually were discharged; in the first session of the Eighty-seventh, three produced none.

HOW WE GET OUR LAWS

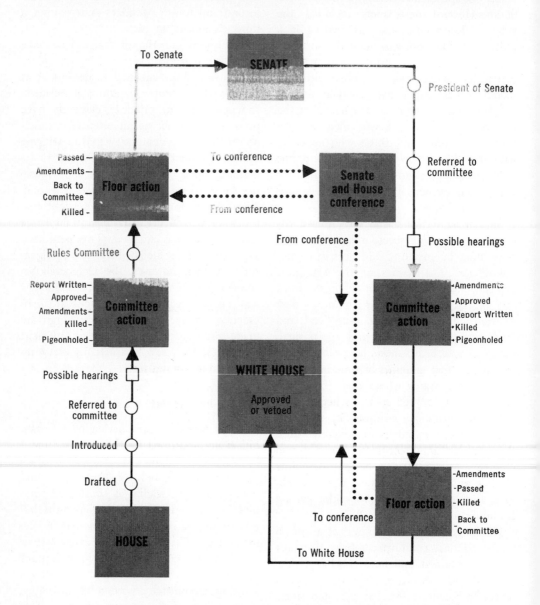

To Senate

SENATE

President of Senate

Passed—
Amendments—
Back to
Committee—
Killed -

Floor action

To conference

From conference

Senate and House conference

Referred to committee

From conference

Possible hearings

Rules Committee

Report Written—
Approved—
Amendments—
Killed -
Pigeonholed-

Committee action

Committee action

•Amendments
•Approved
•Report Written
•Killed
•Pigeonholed

Possible hearings

Referred to committee

Introduced

Drafted

WHITE HOUSE

Approved or vetoed

HOUSE

Floor action

-Amendments
-Passed
-Killed
Back to Committee

To conference

To White House

A simplified diagram of congressional procedure. It shows the several steps through which a House bill might pass. [Adapted from *Under the Dome: How Our Congress Works* (Washington, D.C.: Chamber of Commerce of the United States, 1953).]

rather simple calendar serves Senate needs, and the smaller size of the upper house makes unnecessary the elaborate selective and restrictive devices employed in the House of Representatives.

The Senate normally meets at high noon. During the first hour or more of the day the Senate disposes of prayer, communications, committee reports, introduction of bills and resolutions. After this is completed, the Senate turns to the calendar of bills and takes up those unobjected to in the order listed on the calendar. This is called the "morning hour" and ends at 2 P.M. Thereafter the Senate proceeds to the consideration of other legislation. Voting is by voice vote, standing vote, or roll-call vote. The Senate does not use the teller plan. Roll-call voting takes little time and is used very commonly. Pairing is frequent.[1]

Filibustering and Closure. The reluctance of the Senate to restrict debate is widely known, for the filibuster is the most spectacular of American legislative exploits. Senators have intense pride in the Senate's reputation as a forum of free discussion. Occasionally senators representing a minority point of view obstruct and frustrate the will of the majority through a filibuster. During the filibuster, senators hold the floor for hours, delivering relevant and irrelevant remarks primarily intended to obstruct until some concessions are obtained. The longest filibuster on record is that of Strom Thurmond, who spoke for more than twenty-four hours against the civil-rights legislation of 1957.

The closure rule of the Senate, adopted in 1917, requires a petition to end debate signed by one-sixth of the senators. On the second day after this is filed, the Senate must vote by a two-thirds majority to close debate. After adoption of a closure motion, no senator may speak more than one hour to the question, and other delaying parliamentary tactics are greatly restricted. Closure was invoked in the Senate only five times between 1917 and 1962, but threat of its use headed off or terminated several filibusters. A mild form of closure, capable of stopping spur-of-the-moment filibusters, is found in the unanimous-consent agreements by which debate on particular measures is limited in advance.[2]

In 1949, after a filibuster on civil-rights legislation, the Senate adopted a revised closure rule by which any matter under Senate proceedings (except change of rules) is subject to closure. A mild liberalization took place in 1959, when the rule was changed to permit the imposition of closure by two-thirds of the senators voting, rather than by two-thirds of the total membership of the Senate.

Amendments and Riders. Traditionally, Senate rules governing amendments to bills have not been so strict as those in the House. This is especially true in respect to the requirement that an amendment be "germane," which means pertinent or in close relationship. Except to general appropriation bills, the Senate has felt free to add unrelated amendments. Sometimes a whole bill of subsidiary interest is amended onto another bill. This is called a "rider." The government of Cuba was provided for under the "Platt Amendment," a rider to an Army appropriation bill in 1901; this continued on the statute books, although highly offensive to Cuban pride, until the

[1] The procedure of the Senate is dealt with exhaustively in George H. Haynes, *The Senate of the United States* (Boston: Houghton Mifflin, 2 vols., 1938).

[2] Franklin L. Burdette, *Filibustering in the Senate* (Princeton, N.J.: Princeton University Press, 1940), tells the interesting story of Senate filibuster and closure. Lindsay Rogers, *The American Senate* (New York: Knopf, 1926), presents a convincing case for the freedom of debate of the Senate.

inauguration of the "good-neighbor policy" after 1933. Presidential authority to reduce the gold content of the dollar was granted in a Senate rider to the Agricultural Adjustment Act of 1933. The President has no item veto, so he must sign or veto the whole bill presented to him. The Reorganization Act of 1946 placed new restrictions on amendments to appropriation bills, and curbed the worst abuses.

Appointments and Treaties. The Constitution gives the Senate special powers over appointments and treaties. The President nominates and the Senate confirms officers of the United States by simple majority. The fundamental law speaks of "advice and consent" by the upper house.[1] The development of "senatorial courtesy" and the political contacts of President and senators will be treated subsequently. The procedure of the Senate on appointments is to refer the nominations of the President to appropriate committees. After these committees report, action on the confirmation takes place on the floor.

Treaty ratification requires a two-thirds vote on the floor. A treaty is received from the President and referred to the Committee on Foreign Relations. Upon its report, the Senate usually resolves itself into the Committee of the Whole for deliberation on the treaty. This is the only surviving use of the Committee of the Whole in the upper house. The Committee considers and reports its recommendation back to the Senate.

MATTERS OF JOINT CONCERN

Conference Committees. If both houses pass identical versions of the same bill, it is "enrolled" on parchment paper, signed,

[1] On the confirmation of appointments, see Joseph P. Harris, *The Advice and Consent of the Senate* (Berkeley and Los Angeles, Calif.: University of California Press, 1953).

and sent to the President. If different versions have been passed and neither house will recede, the bill is sent to a conference committee, usually consisting of three or more members from each house, which thrashes out the differences. Each house may choose to instruct its conferees; normally they are left free to negotiate for themselves. After reaching agreement, each set of conferees reports back to its house. The report may be accepted or rejected, with further negotiation ordered. Conference committees, as the late Senator Norris frequently pointed out, have become a sort of third house. They are criticized because proceedings are secret and bills may be rewritten arbitrarily. Their reports seldom are considered carefully.

The Legislative Reorganization Act of 1946 confines the reports of conference committees to legislative controversies submitted and stipulates that where the rule is violated the conference report shall be subject to a point of order. In practice, however, such points of order are not sustained.

Records and Laws. Since 1873, records of debates and proceedings in the Senate and House have been printed in the *Congressional Record*, substantially a stenographic report. It is well known that many speeches that appear in the *Record* were not delivered orally but are "extensions of remarks" included by unanimous consent. In addition to the *Record*, each house keeps a journal of its proceedings and acts. The journal of the previous day is read, usually in part only, at the opening of each session.

Once enacted and signed by the President, measures become laws and may be found in the *Statutes at Large of the United States* for the particular session. From time to time statutes are codified in *The Code of the Laws of the United States of a General and Permanent Character* . . . , commonly called "U.S. Code."

Impeachment. Constitutional authority to impeach is vested solely in the House; power to try impeachment cases rests with the Senate alone. The House usually refers a motion proposing impeachment of an officer to the appropriate standing committee or to a specially created investigating committee. If an impeachment motion is adopted, a committee may be set up to draft articles of impeachment. After their adoption, managers are chosen in whatever manner the House directs. The Senate, upon being informed of House action, sets up a committee to prepare for the trial.

The House managers appear in the Senate at the appointed time and commence their prosecution of the case. If the President is impeached, the Chief Justice of the Supreme Court presides over the Senate trial. The accused officer has a right to appear and testify in his own behalf. A two-thirds vote of the Senate is necessary for conviction. The Senate has sat as a court of impeachment on only twelve occasions. Nine cases involved judges, of whom four were convicted and removed, four were acquitted, and one resigned under fire. The first officer ever impeached was a Senator in 1798, but the Senate dismissed that case for want of jurisdiction. Two reconstruction-era cases were the only ones involving executive officers: President Andrew Johnson was acquitted in 1868; Grant's Secretary of War was acquitted in 1876.

Selection of President and Vice President. The House of Representatives may be called upon to elect a President. The Constitution provides that, if no candidate for President secures a majority of the electoral votes, the House shall choose from among the three highest. In selecting a President, the House votes by states, each state having one vote. The successful candidate must secure the votes of a majority of the states. The House elected Thomas Jefferson President, following the indecisive election of 1800, and John Quincy Adams after that of 1824.

Should no candidate secure a majority of the electoral votes for Vice President, the Twelfth Amendment provides that the Senate shall choose between the two highest candidates. A majority of the total membership of the Senate is necessary to elect. The electoral vote was inconclusive only in 1836; in that case the Senate chose Richard M. Johnson as Vice President during the Van Buren administration.

Staff Services. A significant development of recent years is the providing of professional staff services for Congress. From its earliest days it had clerks, messengers, and page boys, but the "clerk-hire" moneys appropriated rarely were used to employ persons whose expertness in techniques, such as bill drafting, or in subject-matter fields, such as money and banking, qualified them as high-level assistants or advisers. As Congress faced problems of greater and greater complexity, it recognized the need for more than the meager services provided by the clerks previously employed by members and standing committees. To meet the executive branch on a basis of equality, the legislative branch found it advisable to provide a professional staff capable of analyzing executive proposals and formulating and drafting counterproposals.

In 1919 Congress established the Legislative Counsel to provide bill-drafting services. Following the Reorganization Act of 1946, it increased and expanded the staff in size and in immunity from politics.

The Legislative Reference Service of the Library of Congress provides aid to individual legislators and to committees of Congress. In the first five years after reorganization, its staff more than doubled and appropriations for it increased fourfold.

Members' offices still employ a large proportion of congressional staff. The 1946 act provided each senator with funds for a top assistant; clerk-hire allowances have been increased for members of both houses.

Committees received the greatest expansion in terms of both quantity and quality of personnel. The reorganization law authorized each standing committee to appoint up to ten employees, including four professional staff members who should be "permanent," appointed "without regard to political affiliations," and "on the basis of fitness." While most of the professional personnel survived three changes of congressional majorities (1949, 1953, and 1955), the experience is "spotty." Full realization of the ideal of an impartial committee staff, equally able to serve Democrats and Republicans, is still some distance away.[1]

Congress has not appointed a personnel director to supervise staff hiring. Thus some employed in the new positions have not been screened adequately, and other well-qualified staff members have found their abilities utilized to less than the fullest extent.[2]

CONGRESSIONAL PROBLEMS

Among national legislatures and parliaments of the world, Congress stands out as one of the most notable. For over a century and a half it has proved reasonably representative of the nation. The Senate is unquestionably the outstanding second chamber among national parliamentary bodies. The Congress provides one of the few remaining examples of the two-house plan operating on a substantially coordinate basis. Its time and energy have often been frittered away upon unimportant issues chosen because of excessive localism, narrow partisanship, and desire for meddling. But when great national issues have emerged, the Congress has rarely, if ever, failed to serve the country loyally.

Nevertheless, the Congress is ill organized to meet many of the most insistent challenges of today. What progress has been made in retooling Congress? What problems remain unsolved?

The Reorganization of Congress. The reform of Congress, long discussed sporadically in academic and congressional circles, became a major item on the agenda of American democracy in 1945 and 1946. Improvements in organization and procedure had been urged for several years by the Committee on Congress of the American Political Science Association and by many individual critics. The Seventy-ninth Congress accordingly established a joint committee to study its own organization.

After extended hearings, the committee filed its report on March 4, 1946.[3] The committee, headed by Senator Robert M. La Follette, Jr., reached agreement on many of the acute organizational problems facing Congress. The report called for the creation of majority and minority policy committees in each house, a joint legislative-executive council composed of congressional and executive leaders, a fairly drastic reorganization of committee systems of the Senate and House, increases in aids to Congress, reduction of petty duties that take congressional time, and more adequate compensation of members.

[1] For a good discussion of this problem see Max M. Kampelman, "The Legislative Bureaucracy: Its Response to Political Change, 1953," *Journal of Politics*, vol. 16 (August, 1954), pp. 539–550.

[2] Gladys M. Kammerer, "The Record of Congress in Committee Staffing," *American Political Science Review*, vol. 45 (December, 1951), pp. 1126–1136.

[3] U.S. Congress, Joint Committee on the Organization of Congress, *Hearings*, parts 1–4 (1945), and *Organization of the Congress, Report of the . . .* , pursuant to H. Con. Res. 18, S. Rept. 1011, 79th Cong., 2d Sess. (1946).

The committee was unable to reach agreement on reform of the seniority system or of House Rules Committee powers. It considered the proposal of a question hour and of Senate filibusters as beyond its scope. As shown, the Reorganization Act of 1946 fell short of the committee recommendations in several particulars.

Relations with the Executive. The overall leadership of Congress is most likely, under modern conditions, to come from the executive. The President is representative of the whole nation, the generalissimo of the administration, the people's choice. The nation, and its Congress, quite properly looks to him for guidance.

But the Congress should not abdicate its function to the executive. Experience has shown that the American system works best when the President accepts and actively plays the role of chief legislator, with Congress examining critically his every recommendation and checking his performance. Even if the role is granted, however, improvements are required in the mechanism of legislative-executive liaison.

The three leading plans for the reform of Congress called for an improved and formalized congressional body to consult with the President and other representatives of the executive branch. The act failed to make such provision. Four main aspects of the problem will be dealt with under separate headings.

Consultation with President. The proposed forms varied considerably, but all had the idea of a formal council representing Congress that would meet regularly with the President to formulate and carry out national policy. This was dropped from the reorganization bill when the policy committees for each house were stricken out. Until the House officially creates policy committees, it is impossible to carry out the original plan of the two majority policy committees constituting the congressional side of a joint legislative-executive council.

Now informal occasional conferences take place at the White House between the President and his party's congressional leaders to discuss program and strategy and to keep informed. Some of the proposals for an executive-legislative council simply involved the formalization and extension of what already existed. Many legislators prefer the present informal partisan conference to the proposed bipartisan council.

Question Period. At various times in the history of the country, proposals have been made to permit members of the Cabinet to speak on the floor of either house of Congress and answer questions. The act of Congress creating the Treasury Department in 1789 provided that the Secretary of the Treasury should make reports to Congress either in person or in writing, but when Hamilton was ready to make his report on public credit, the House voted that it be submitted in writing. In 1864 and again in 1879 Senator George H. Pendleton introduced bills to permit Cabinet members to speak in Congress and answer questions, but nothing came of them, though select committees of both houses approved them. Presidents Taft and Harding both urged such legislation on Congress, but without result. The proposal was most recently revived by Senator Kefauver, first as a member of the House and later in the Senate, but it found little support in either house.

Obviously this proposal would introduce into the Congress something like the question period used in British legislative bodies. The device has proved effective, in British countries and elsewhere, in producing immediate accountability of an executive officer to parliamentary and public opinion. Applied to the United States, it could narrow the widening gap between

PLANS FOR CONGRESSIONAL REFORM AND THE REORGANIZATION ACT

Features	National Planning Association *	American Political Science Association †	Joint Committee of Congress ‡	Legislative Reorganization Act §
Leadership	Majority and minority policy committees, each house	Legislative council to plan majority program in Congress	Majority and minority policy committees, each house	No provision; Senate policy groups added later
Relations with President	Majority policy committees consult with President	Legislative council to promote liaison and cooperation	Joint council of executive and policy committees	No provision
Question period	Experiment with department heads	No recommendation	No jurisdiction	No provision
Liaison with departments		Committees parallel departments and work with them	Committees review agencies within their jurisdiction	No provision
Control over administration	Broader appropriation bills; control through Accounting Office	House committee on appropriations oversees administrative performance	Service audits by Comptroller General; no more indefinite appropriations	Service audits; definite appropriations
Members' offices	Adequate personal staffs	Substantial clerk-hire increase	An administrative assistant for each	No provision; Senate got assistants later
Library of Congress	Expansion of reference service	More funds and better facilities	Increased funds and services	Increased funds and services
Legislative counsel		More appropriations and services	Expanded funds and personnel	Expanded funds and personnel
Number of committees	15 each house	Eliminate inactive	Senate 16; House 18	Senate 15; House 19
Committee jurisdiction	Equivalent in Senate and House	Parallel committees in the two houses	Clearly defined jurisdiction	Clearly defined jurisdiction
Committee staffs	Adequate staffs	Independent qualified experts	Four added experts per committee	Four added experts per committee
Committee chairmen	Find substitute for seniority	Six-year tenure or party group choose; curb chairman's power	No agreement	No provision
Retirement	Annuity at 55	Contributory plan like civil service	Contributory plan	Contributory plan
Salaries	$25,000	$15,000	$15,000, taxable as businessman's	$12,500 plus $2,500 expenses
Reduction of work load	Reduce or reallocate	Home rule for D.C.; delegate claims; cut private bills	Home rule for D.C.; delegate claims; digest bills	Delegate small claims; allows suits v. U.S.
Lobbyist control	No provision	Groups register; reveal membership and finances	Groups register; list expenditures	Groups register; list expenditures

* Robert Heller,"Strengthening the Congress"(Washington, D.C.: National Planning Association, 1945).
† George B. Galloway and others,"The Reorganization of Congress"(Washington, D.C.: Public Affairs Press, 1945).
‡ Report of the Joint Committee on the Organization of Congress (1946).
§ 60 Stat. 831.

executive and legislative branches by giving each an opportunity to speak to the other officially and frequently. Much misunderstanding arises from the lack of communication.

As Kefauver proposed it, the question period would be limited to two hours per week total. The executive officials could decline to appear. Care would be exercised to see that only pertinent and reasonable questions were asked. It is difficult to understand why the House and Senate have not long since amended their rules to permit, at least on an explanatory basis, the questioning of executives on the floor of the legislative bodies.

However, executive officers are frequently called upon to testify before committees of both houses, which, in a sense, constitutes a question period. The press conference, whether of the President or of a department head, provides some measure of indirect accountability to the public, but it may worsen executive-legislative relations.

Liaison with Departments. One of the most promising levels for legislative-executive collaboration is that of standing committee and administrative department or agency. Two of the reform plans referred to this, but the act of 1946 did little to help, with the exception of simplifying the committee system and clarifying jurisdiction. The way is open, and all that is required is willingness on the part of the committee and agency involved. One such scheme of collaboration was commended to the La Follette committee as a model. During the Second World War, the House Committee on Public Buildings and Grounds consulted monthly with the National Housing Administration and other executive agency heads.

Oversight of Administration. The 1946 act directed standing committees to continually watch over administrative agencies

in their spheres. The report advised against the practice of creating special committees to investigate particular problems. Standing committees can follow the affairs of the agencies through administrative reports to Congress, through their own inquiries into the execution of laws, and through conferences like those described.

Great difficulty is encountered when Congress undertakes oversight of the administration. The line between presidential and congressional authority should be drawn between detailed action and broad policy; nonprecise definition leaves a vast "gray area" that often becomes a battleground. Some committees, acting under instructions given in the 1946 law, use their powers of investigation to dig and delve into administrative minutia in such a way (as in the McCarthy probe of the Army) that demoralization results. On the other hand, most committees perform their "watchdog" functions without undue poaching on presidential prerogative. Senatorial confirmation of appointments offers another formal opportunity to review and criticize the record of the administration. Control of spending, considered under another section, is one of the most potent weapons in the congressional arsenal, yet it has been used often to vent petty and individual spites rather than to criticize broad, general policies.[1]

Fiscal Controls. One of the most needed reforms, and one of the greatest failures of the Reorganization Act, was in the field of fiscal control. The House and Senate Appropriations Committees and the House Ways and Means and Senate Finance Com-

[1] For a detailed analysis of some aspects of oversight, see Cornelius P. Cotter and J. Malcolm Smith, "Administrative Accountability to Congress: The Concurrent Resolution," *Western Political Quarterly*, vol. 9 (December, 1956), pp. 955–966. The same authors wrote "Administrative Accountability: Reporting to Congress," *Ibid.*, vol. 10 (June, 1957), pp. 405–415.

mittees operate with little coordination. Appropriation bills are passed without any over-all limitation upon total appropriations and without precise reference to expected revenues. In short, the Congress adopts no general fiscal policy. The power of the purse, one of the greatest that might be used by Congress to assure accountability of the executive, is dissipated in a maze of numerous appropriation bills, considered at different times, by different committees and subcommittees, amid an atmosphere of pressure and hurry.

The report of the La Follette committee sought to correct some of these evils by (1) the adoption of annual Federal budget totals, (2) strengthening of the appropriations committees, (3) service audits by the Comptroller General, (4) discontinuance of indefinite appropriations, and (5) elimination of legislation from appropriation bills.

The act set up the procedure to determine budget totals or the "legislative budget." The four fiscal committees were directed to meet together to determine over-all receipts and expenditures and to set a ceiling on expenditures. This they have failed to do. In 1950 a consolidated appropriations bill embracing eleven supply bills was used, but in 1951 Congress went back to ten separate ones, each considered by itself.[1] Interest in the legislative budget continues, but real progress will probably have to await formation of a small joint budget committee, employment of more staff, and greater determination to resist pressures for spending.

Staffing changes have been made. The House Appropriations Committee has increased its clerical staff but has relied heavily upon administrative agencies for investigative staff.[2] The Senate did relatively

more in staffing. Neither house has adequate personnel to review the huge expenditures requested.

Other aspects of fiscal controls will be considered in the chapter on public finance.

Work Load. The work load of Congress has not been lightened under the Reorganization Act, but it has been redistributed. The aids and the committee changes mentioned above have had a part in shifting work or in permitting the members to do a better job. Members sit on fewer committees now, but each committee has many more bills.

Title IV of the 1946 act was the "Federal Tort Claims Act," which delegated authority to settle claims of $1,000 or less against the United States to administrative officers. Twelve exceptions were listed, however, and the Congress has been flooded with private claims bills under these exceptions. Private immigration bills also have been introduced in great numbers, for no restriction on them exists.

Home rule for the District of Columbia was recommended by the committee to free Congress from the burden of serving as a municipal council for Washington. The Senate in 1949 passed home-rule legislation, but the House has been unable to agree.

Further reform is needed to divest Congress of additional time-consuming detail. A program for further progress along this line would include reduction of exceptions under the Tort Claims Act, self-government for the District of Columbia, delegation of immigration and deportation cases to an agency or tribunal, and various other means already suggested.

Petty Matters. Even a cursory observer

[1] Paul H. Douglas, *Economy in the National Government* (Chicago: University of Chicago Press, 1952), pp. 56–57.

[2] George B. Galloway, "The Operation of the Legislative Reorganization Act of 1946," *American Political Science Review*, vol. 45 (March, 1951), p. 64. In fiscal 1950 the House had less than one Appropriations staff member for each billion dollars.

of Congress is impressed with the amount of legislative time wasted on relatively minor issues and the hasty fashion (especially in the House) in which matters of great importance are dealt with. A large proportion of the bills on the calendars of the two houses concern petty matters that might more properly be handled by delegating rule-making authority to administrative agencies.

An extreme proposal along this line is one made with reference to the British Parliament. Some years ago, Sir Stafford Cripps urged that the "mother of parliaments" confine its lawmaking solely to one omnibus appropriation and planning bill per session. The American Congress certainly would not be willing to abdicate to this extent, but it might well provide for the settlement of private claims through courts or administrative tribunals and for reduction in the number of minor public bills by the delegation of legislative authority (with appropriate standards) to the executive. Some progress has already been made through the flexible tariff, executive trade agreements, blanket appropriation measures, and the like. In time of war Congress appropriates billions of dollars to the military establishments with a minimum of restrictions on where or how the money shall be spent. In peacetime, the small-town post office, a veterans' hospital, a port-dredging job, all must be authorized according to the political formula worked out in detail by Congress.

The congressman also is expected to serve his constituents as an "errand boy" in fields quite divorced from legislation. One representative estimated that three-fourths of a member's time is taken up by contacting executive agencies, dealing with District of Columbia matters, handling claims against the government, finding jobs for constituents, and various other petty functions. Such work is so time consuming that few members find it possible to study legislation adequately.

Control of Lobbying. Title III of the 1946 act was the Regulation of Lobbying Act. It put into law the requirement that organized groups reveal their expenditures in influencing legislation, their membership, and their contributions. The act does not curb or regulate lobbying activity but merely requires reports on receipts and expenditures.

In the Eighty-first Congress, a House select committee worked at interpreting the meaning of the vaguely drafted act.[1] It declared as covered by the act the following types of activity: pamphleteering; legislative functions of multipurpose organizations; legislative activities of business firms; part- and full-time legislative agents, including attorneys and public relations counselors; and research institutes and foundations that seek to influence legislation. Not included, according to the committee, are publishers of newspapers, magazines, and books that are distributed through the ordinary channels of commerce.

The Lobbying Act has been subjected to much litigation in the Federal courts. The lower courts held some portions constitutional and some unconstitutional. In 1953 and 1954 the Supreme Court spoke. In *United States v. Rumeley* [345 U.S. 41 (1953)] the court held that the term "lobbying activities" meant direct representation before Congress, not indirect attempts to exert influence through the community. In *United States v. Harriss* [347 U.S. 612 (1954)] the constitutionality of the act was upheld. Rejecting contentions of violation of due process, freedom of speech and press, and freedom of petition,

---

[1] U.S. House of Representatives, Select Committee on Lobbying Activities, *General Interim Report*, House Report 1085 (1950), and *Report and Recommendations on Federal Lobbying Act*, House Report 3239 (1951).

Chief Justice Warren, speaking for the court, said:

Present-day legislative complexities are such that individual members of Congress cannot be expected to explore the myriad pressures to which they are regularly subjected. Yet full realization of the American ideal of government by elected representatives depends to no small extent on their ability to properly evaluate such pressures. Otherwise the voice of the people may all too easily be drowned out by the voice of special interest groups seeking favored treatment while masquerading as proponents of the public weal. This is the evil which the Lobbying Act was designed to help prevent.

All Congress wants to know, the Chief Justice declared, is "who is being hired, who is putting up the money, and how much."

A special committee of the Senate reported in 1957 following extensive hearings and study.[1] It possessed extra insight because of the exposure of alleged excesses by lobbyists seeking to amend the Natural Gas Act. The committee proposed a new Legislative Activities Disclosure Act. It defined seven types of activities:

1. Direct contacts with Congress by a person who has been retained or employed for such purpose

2. Direct contacts with Congress to influence legislation by a person employed or retained by a trade association or other membership group to devote a part or all of his time to legislative matters, where such activities form only a part of the association's work

3. Occasional direct contacts with Congress to influence legislation by an officer or employee of a business firm or labor union who devotes the major portion of his time to the regular business of the firm or labor union

[1] U.S. Senate, Special Committee to Investigate Political Activities, Lobbying, and Campaign Contributions, *Final Report* . . . , Rept. 395, 85th Cong., 1st Sess. (1957).

4. Direct contacts with Congress to influence legislation by any other individual not covered by groups 1, 2, and 3

5. Campaigns addressed to the public through newspapers, magazines, television, and radio containing explicit appeals to the public to contact Congress to influence legislation

6. The preparation of books, pamphlets, or data by research groups, which might influence legislation, and the distribution of same without any intent to produce legislative action.

The bill regards persons in the first category and some in the second as "legislative agents"; they must file notices of representation before acting and periodically thereafter; they are subject to criminal penalties for violations. All other persons subject to the act (categories 2, 3, and 4) file periodic reports; they are subject to civil suit to compel filing. Groups in categories 5 and 6 may be forced to file if they spend over $50,000 for the purpose within a twelve-month period. The press, radio, television, and publishers are exempted. The Comptroller General would be given responsibility for enforcement; penalties were to be made more severe. In keeping with its primary purpose of full disclosure, the proposed law emphasizes reporting and record keeping by lobbyists and groups, but excludes small receipts and expenditures.

Congress and the Public. Congress has done a poor job in public relations. The executive branch has great advantages of prestige and concentrated responsibility. The Congress is large and unwieldy, fettered by tradition and handicapped by lack of internal leadership. A number of proposals have been made to improve public understanding of Congress and its problems. First, the House and Senate might reduce the amount of time spent in session, concentrating into one or two days a week the im-

THE COSTS OF AN ELECTION CAMPAIGN

Office: United States Senator

CAMPAIGN COSTS

Total:
$200,000

Newspaper advertising:
$15,000

Billboard advertising:
$30,000

UNITED STATES SENATOR'S
SIX-YEAR SALARY:
$135,000

Headquarters,
mail,
hall rentals,
buttons,
handbills,
filing fees, etc.:
$75,000

Television and radio:
$80,000

SOURCES OF CONTRIBUTIONS:

- Individuals and organizations:
  Allowed up to $5,000 each.
- "Committees" formed for a campaign:
  Allowed up to $3,000,000 in support
  of a candidate or a party.
- Industry associations, fraternal
  societies, farm groups, etc.

PROHIBITED FROM CONTRIBUTING:

- Labor unions (but in practice
  they contribute through officials and
  members, and the provision of services).
- Corporations (but in practice
  they contribute through executives
  and employees, and the provision
  of services).

It costs a great deal of money to conduct a campaign in most states and congressional districts. The candidate incurs obligations to individuals and interests contributing to his campaign. The independence of members of Congress might be increased if alternate means of campaign financing could be found.

portant legislative business that must be conducted on the floor. Second, these sessions could be transmitted directly over radio and television to the whole country and ought to command more attention from the newspapers. Third, public interest should be focused on committee proceedings, where detailed work is done on legislation; this would be made easier by regularizing the meeting times of committees and making provision for public attendance at committee hearings. Fourth, recesses should be taken at appropriate intervals, so that legislators could return to their

districts and report in person to their constituents.

Instead of representing the broad national interest, many members of Congress look first to local and sectional concerns. Senators and representatives commonly regard themselves as "ambassadors of locality," rather than delegates of the whole nation. This is demonstrated many times in every session, but especially in the scramble over the pork barrel of rivers and harbors appropriations, and in the logrolling over economic issues like the tariff and farm relief. The electorate of a district or state then is informed of the glorious service of its legislator, often through an extension of remarks from the *Record* such as: "What Blanton's Twelve Counties, Seventeenth District (Texas), Have Received from Government since 1933." Yet, in another sense, the representative should serve his district; for he is elected by it and is to some extent, at least, expected to represent its views on public questions.

Local interests gain exaggerated importance in this country through the tradition that a representative must live in his district. The custom is so well established that change would be very difficult. The advantages of the British system, under which the member of Parliament need not be, and usually is not, a resident of his district, should not be overlooked.

The interests of the country as a whole occasionally may be served through the alliances and counteralliances of various economic, sectional, and partisan groups. A few congressmen, and especially senators, enjoy such prestige in their home states that on most issues they are free to serve the country with detachment and distinction. In the past, Senators Borah of Idaho, Norris of Nebraska, Cutting of New Mexico, and others enjoyed such popularity in their states that they were able to devote themselves largely to national affairs as they saw them, without the diversion and distortion of localism.

Congressional Investigations. The congressional investigating committee, used and abused so much in recent years in both the legislative-executive struggle and the loyalty-subversion exposé, has become one of the great problems of Congress. Inherited from the House of Commons through the colonial and state legislatures, the power to investigate has been narrowed or broadened according to its exercise by Congress and its interpretation by the courts. The first

Congress, in 1792, appointed a select committee to inquire into a military disaster suffered in an Indian attack in the Northwest Territory.[1] Recent Congresses have conducted about one hundred investigations each, mainly through subcommittees of standing committees.

The early probes were thought justifiable under the legislative power, but the executive from the beginning asserted its power to withhold secret documents. As early as 1798 the power to administer oaths was given by statute to congressional leaders and punishment for perjury prescribed. Unfriendly witnesses were incarcerated directly on orders of House or Senate. In 1857 provision was made by law for one-year imprisonment on conviction of refusal to testify. In *Kilbourne v. Thompson* [103 U.S. 168 (1881)] the Supreme Court sustained a suit for damages against the sergeant at arms of the House, who had jailed for contempt a witness who refused to testify. The resolution directing the inquiry contained no suggestion of remedial legislation; the Court held that it invaded the proper functions of the judiciary. Not until 1897 did the Court specifically hold the act of 1857 constitutional; the conviction of a witness who refused to answer questions of a Senate committee was sustained. The leading case is *McGrain v. Daugherty* [273 U.S. 135 (1927)], in which the Senate's authority to probe the official conduct of a former Attorney General was upheld, but the court did indicate that a witness might refuse to answer if the bounds of power are exceeded by a committee or if the questions are not pertinent to the matter under inquiry.

From earlier decisions, it appears that a congressional investigation is valid if it (1) falls within the Federal legislative power

[1] Telford Taylor, *Grand Inquest: The Story of Congressional Investigations* (New York: Simon and Schuster, 1955), p. 22.

(not invading judicial, executive, or state spheres) and (2) does not violate constitutional guaranties, including self-incrimination. A skillful draftsman can design a resolution in such a way that it minimizes the chances of its being voided for usurpation of the judicial function; a careful chairman or counsel should be able to avoid the state-rights hazard. But the possibilities of conflict with the executive sphere are manifold, and they constitute an abundant source of dispute.

Probes versus Rights. The case of congressional investigations versus individual rights is still more perplexing. Two events of 1953 have an important bearing on the subject. In *United States v. Rumeley* [345 U.S. 41 (1953)] the Supreme Court overruled the conviction of the executive secretary of the Committee on Constitutional Government, who refused to answer a House committee's questions regarding purchasers of alleged propaganda books. The majority opinion relied on an extremely narrow construction of congressional intent in authorizing the particular investigation; the concurring opinion invoked the freedom of the press as the justification for freeing Rumeley.

The other event of 1953 was the enactment of a law granting immunity to witnesses testifying before congressional committees.[1] The grant was confined to probes of threats to national security or defense, and subject in each case to approval by the Federal district court. Obviously, the greater the extension of "immunity baths," the less the possibility of witnesses claiming the privilege against self-incrimination. The possibility that testimony before a congressional committee under a grant of immunity might expose a person to state prosecution was eliminated by a Supreme Court decision

[1] The act was held constitutional in *Ullman v. United States*, 350 U.S. 452 (1956).

"Fair Is Fair." Herblock's devastating criticism of methods used by some Senate committees in conducting investigations. [From *Herblock's Here and Now* (Simon and Schuster).]

[*Adams v. Maryland*, 347 U.S. 179 (1954)].

Congress itself moved to correct some of the most flagrant abuses of individual rights by its committees. The 1955 "ground rules" adopted by the House were a promising beginning; a Speaker's ban on televised House hearings eliminated some sensationalism.

In 1957 the Supreme Court shed additional light upon the difficult line of demarcation between committee powers and individual rights. In *Watkins v. United States* (354 U.S. 178) a witness had refused to tell a House committee the names of persons he believed had left the Communist party. The court held that he was not in contempt. Because he was not accorded a fair opportunity to determine his rights, he was denied due process as guaranteed in the Fifth Amendment. The committee's mandate was so vague that the court could not "ascertain whether any legislative purpose justifies the disclosures sought. . . ."

In 1959 the Court, in a 5-to-4 decision, upheld the contempt conviction of a former college teacher who refused to answer questions of the House Committee on Un-American Activities on his relationship with the Communist party. (*Barenblatt v. United*

States, 360 U.S. 109). The majority opinion maintained that the questions were pertinent to the Committee's investigation of communism in education and that Barenblatt was informed of their pertinency. Having failed to answer questions put to him, he was properly cited for contempt.

FOR FURTHER READING

See also works listed after preceding chapter.

Beck, Carl: *Contempt of Congress* (New Orleans, La.: Hauser Press, 1960).

Berman, Daniel M.: *A Bill Becomes a Law: The Civil Rights Act of 1960* (New York: Macmillan, 1962).

Burdette, Franklin L.: *Filibustering in the Senate* (Princeton, N.J.: Princeton University Press, 1940).

Burns, James M.: *Congress on Trial: The Politics of Modern Lawmaking* (New York: Harper, 1949).

Colegrove, Kenneth: *The American Senate and World Peace* (New York: Vanguard, 1944).

Dangerfield, Royden J.: *In Defense of the Senate: A Study in Treaty-making* (Norman, Okla.: University of Oklahoma Press, 1933).

Finletter, Thomas K.: *Can Representative Government Do the Job?* (New York: Reynal & Hitchcock, 1945).

Freeman, J. Leiper: *The Political Process: Executive Bureau-Legislative Committee Relations* (New York: Doubleday, 1955).

Galloway, George B.: *Congress and Parliament: Their Organization and Operation in the U.S. and the U.K.* (Washington, D.C.: National Planning Association, 1955).

———: *Congressional Reorganization Revisited* (College Park, Md.: University of Maryland, Bureau of Governmental Research, 1956).

——— and others: *The Reorganization of Congress* (Washington, D.C.: Public Affairs Press, 1945). A report of the Committee on Congress of the American Political Science Association.

Graves, W. Brooke: *Administration of the Lobby Registration Provisions of the Legislative Re-*

organization Act of 1946 (Washington, D.C.: Library of Congress, 1950).

Heller, Robert: *Strengthening the Congress* (Washington, D.C.: National Planning Association, 1945).

Horn, Stephen: *The Cabinet and Congress* (New York: Columbia University Press, 1960).

Kammerer, Gladys M.: *The Staffing of the Committees of Congress* (Lexington, Ky.: University of Kentucky, 1949).

Kefauver, Estes, and Jack Levin: *A Twentieth Century Congress* (New York: Duell, Sloan & Pearce, 1947) .

Kraines, Oscar: *Congress and the Challenge of Big Government* (New York: Bookman Associates, 1958).

McCown, Ada C.: *The Congressional Conference Committee* (New York: Columbia University Press, 1927).

Nelson, Harold L.: *Libel in News of Congressional Investigating Committees* (Minneapolis, Minn.: University of Minnesota Press, 1961).

Robinson, James A.: *Congress and Foreign Policymaking* (Homewood, Illinois: Dorsey Press, 1962).

Rogers, Lindsay: *The American Senate* (New York: Knopf, 1926).

U.S. Congress: *Official Congressional Directory.* Issued for each session of each Congress.

———: *Congressional Record.* Issued daily when House or Senate meets. Bound volumes available after close of each session.

U.S. Congress Joint Committee on the Organization of Congress: *Report of the Joint Committee on the Organization of Congress . . .* pursuant to H. Con. Res. 18, S. Rept. 1011 (1946).

————: *Hearings,* parts 1–4, 79th Cong., 1st Sess. (1945).

U.S. Senate, Special Committee to Investigate Political Activities, Lobbying, and Campaign Contributions: *Final Report,* S. Rept. 395, 85th Cong., 1st Sess. (1957). A thorough investigation of "improper influence."

Wahlke, John C., and Heinz Eulau: *Legislative Behavior: A Reader in Theory and Research* (New York: Free Press, 1959).

REVIEW QUESTIONS

1. Trace the progress of a bill from introduction in the House to signature by the President.

2. What is the discharge rule? How has it been used in recent years?

3. What is filibustering? Trace efforts to secure an effective closure rule.

4. Describe Senate appointment-confirmation proceedings. Describe Senate treaty-ratification proceedings.

5. Describe the roles of House and Senate in impeachment proceedings.

6. Explain the role of the House in selecting a President in case no candidate secures a majority of electoral votes.

7. Explain the Senate's role in choosing a Vice President if there is no electoral majority.

8. To what extent are charges of external control of Congress justified?

9. Do you believe that local and sectional influences loom too powerful in Congress?

10. What did the 1946 Legislative Reorganization Act do to improve relations between the executive and legislative branches? What remains to be done?

11. What committee changes were effected by the 1946 act? What additional ones would you propose?

12. How did the 1946 act regulate lobbying? How has the lobbying section of the act worked out in practice?

13. What did the 1946 act provide in the way of additional personnel for committees and congressional services?

14. Propose and defend additional reforms of Congress beyond those provided in the 1946 act.

15. What rules of procedure ensure fair treatment of witnesses and others named before Senate and House committees? What further reforms would you deem desirable?

Chapter Fifteen

The Presidency

*Every four years there springs from the vote created by the
whole people a President over that great nation.
I think the whole world offers no finer spectacle than this;
it offers no higher dignity; and there is no greater object
of ambition on the political stage on which men are
permitted to move. You may point, if you will,
to hereditary rulers, to crowns coming down through
successive generations of the same family, to thrones based
on prescription or on conquest, to sceptres wielded over
veteran legions and subject realms,—but to my mind
there is nothing more worthy of reverence and obedience,
and nothing more sacred, than the authority of the
freely chosen magistrate of a great and free people;
and if there be on earth and amongst men any divine right
to govern, surely it rests with a ruler so chosen and so
appointed.*

JOHN BRIGHT[1]
(in 1861)

When the Constitutional Convention of
1787 discussed the execution of laws, there
was substantial agreement on the necessity
for an executive branch. The Articles of
Confederation provided no separate executive; Congress exercised modest authority
through committees and special agents. This
plan had worked rather badly.

The office of governor, found in all the

[1] Quoted by Clinton Rossiter in *The American
Presidency* (New York: Harcourt, Brace, 1956),
p. 3.

states, was also a possible model. Although
authority, terms, and modes of election
varied, all states were organized separately
with single executives.

The separation of authority between
Crown and Parliament, then undergoing
change in Britain, was cited by those who
desired an independent executive. Those
who wanted no separate executive argued
that the "tyranny" of George III supported
their view. Montesquieu and Locke were
quoted on their advocacy of the separation

of powers by proponents of the separate executive.

In the Convention of 1787, however, little controversy arose over the necessity for a national executive. Madison's notes contain no record of a delegate speaking against an executive branch, although some delegates wanted an executive "absolutely dependent" on the legislative branch.

STRUCTURE AND ROLE

Form of the Executive. If a separate executive were to be established, should it be single or plural? Some proposed vesting executive authority in a group or council, like the two consuls of Rome. This plural type of executive has the obvious disadvantage of dividing authority, which leads to irresponsibility. The Convention decided on a single executive by a vote of seven states to two. Even after the single executive was agreed upon, many wanted executive actions subject to a council of advisers, a device used to curb the powers of many governors. This plan was criticized for division of authority. Eventually the Convention chose to have a single chief magistrate, styled "President," with no advisory council.

The desire to make the President subject to some advisory body did induce the Convention to give the Senate power to advise and consent to appointments and treaties proposed by the executive. On the whole, however, the President was left free to set up his own advisory services. The Cabinet, without a constitutional or statutory status and completely under executive control, is the leading formal agency for consultation. Each chief executive may use such other advisers as he chooses.

Scope of Executive Authority. The question of what powers should be given the separate, single executive was most perplexing and crucial. The heritage of colonial and revolutionary days directed that a weak executive, if any, be established. Years of struggle with royal and proprietary governors taught American colonists to distrust executive power. The aversion of the people to monarchs, and particularly to George III, strengthened the position of those who desired a weak executive.

On the other hand, the breakdown of central government under the Articles of Confederation led some to demand an energetic executive. It was argued that, if the separation of powers were desirable, three coordinate branches were logical. The Convention finally decided to vest in the President most, but not all, of the executive power. Power to confirm appointments and to ratify treaties was reserved for the Senate. The President was given important legislative and some judicial authority. Sections 2 and 3 of Article II of the Constitution were devoted to an enumeration of presidential powers. The President was made Commander in Chief of the Army and Navy, given power to appoint, to make treaties, to receive ambassadors and ministers, to grant reprieves and pardons, to enforce laws, and to perform certain duties in connection with the Congress. The legislative, executive, and judicial functions of the President will be examined in the next chapter.

Much of the President's authority accrues by virtue of factors beyond the formal powers. Prestige as chief representative of the American people, and as leader of his political party, makes him a strong leader if he chooses the role and has the personal qualities to fill it.

THE SELECTION PROCESS

Constitutional Provisions. Direct election of the President was considered a practical impossibility by most of the framers of the

"Don't Expect Me To Get This Real Accurate, Bub"

Oct 48   HERBLOCK

The electoral college is antiquated, but its critics have been unable to unite on proposals for reform. (Herblock and *The Washington Post*.)

Constitution, even though direct election of the governor had been successful in New York and Massachusetts.[1] Selection by Congress was most widely supported in the Convention; this selection method was included in both Virginia and New Jersey Plans and adopted unanimously at one point in the Convention's proceedings.

The electoral-college mode of selection eventually chosen was a compromise. Its craftsmen believed it combined the virtues of independence from the legislative branch with indirect popular participation. Each state chooses, in any way its legislature specifies, electors equal in number to the

[1] James Wilson of Pennsylvania favored direct election. Madison records Wilson as saying that, while apprehensive that he might be regarded as visionary, "in theory he was for an election by the people." C. C. Tansill (ed.), *Documents Illustrative of the Formation of the Union of the American States,*" H. Doc. 398, 69th Cong., 1st Sess. (1927), p. 134.

representatives and senators from that state. All states now use popular election on a state-wide basis. The electors meet in their own states and cast ballots for presidential and vice-presidential candidates. The results, sent to the national capital, are opened in the presence of Congress. Under the original plan each elector voted for two persons; the candidate receiving a majority of electoral votes became President, and the second highest became Vice President.

This scheme caused a tie between Jefferson and Burr, in 1800. Although the electors clearly intended that Jefferson should be President and Burr Vice President, under the terms of the Constitution each had exactly seventy-three votes, and election was thrown to the House of Representatives. In the House some Federalists supported Burr, but eventually Jefferson was elected.

It was clear that the mode of election was defective and must be amended. The Twelfth Amendment corrected this by providing for separate voting for President and Vice President. If no presidential candidate secures a majority of electoral votes, the House of Representatives chooses from the three highest, with each state casting one vote. Two presidential elections have been thrown to the House: the 1800 Jefferson-Burr mix-up and the 1824 contest among Clay, John Quincy Adams, Jackson, and Crawford. If no vice-presidential candidate secures a majority, the Senate chooses from the two highest.

Great confusion can arise over the counting of electoral votes. In 1876, Samuel J. Tilden led Rutherford B. Hayes by 184 to 165 electoral votes, but Congress, with Democratic House and Republican Senate, disagreed over the acceptance of conflicting returns from certain states. Eventually, in 1877, Congress created by statute an Electoral Commission composed of five members of the House, five Senators, and five Supreme Court justices. The verdict of the Commission, rendered on a strictly partisan basis, awarded the twenty disputed votes and the Presidency to Hayes. A law of 1887 declares that each state shall determine the authenticity of its selection of electors.

Procedure in the States. Within this constitutional framework, a standardized state procedure has developed; under it, electors are elected popularly on a general-ticket basis. With few exceptions, this scheme has been followed throughout the country for over a hundred years. Since each state has a number of electoral votes equal to its total of United States senators and representatives, each voter casts his ballot for a considerable group; it ranges from forty-five in New York to three in Nevada, Delaware, Wyoming, Vermont, and Alaska. The list of electors is made up by the official party organization in each state.

The threat, in 1944 and 1948, of some Southern electors chosen under the Democratic label to bolt their party and vote for a third-party presidential candidate spotlighted the law and tradition governing the selection and pledging of electors. Professor Silva found twenty-seven states nominating electors by state party conventions; ten, by other party bodies; seven, in party primaries; three, in optional primary or convention. In Pennsylvania alone the presidential nominee selects his party's candidates for elector.[1]

Most state laws assume that electors will vote automatically for their party's nominees. Only California and Oregon require this directly. States could require pledges of candidates for elector, or direct electors

[1] Ruth C. Silva, "State Law on the Nomination, Election, and Instruction of Presidential Electors," *American Political Science Review*, vol. 42 (June, 1948), pp. 523–524.

concerning their conduct in case their party's presidential or vice-presidential candidate dies before the meetings of the electoral college.

At one time the states followed a uniform practice of printing the names of all would-be electors on the ballots. This was expensive in the large states and virtually impossible when a voting machine was used. Consequently, by 1960, over three-fifths of the states, including most of the larger ones, had adopted the "presidential short ballot," on which, instead of the names of individual electors, is a phrase such as "Twenty-five Electors pledged to vote for John F. Kennedy for President and Lyndon B. Johnson for Vice President."[2]

The electors selected then assemble in the state capital and cast their ballots; a 1934 Federal law requires that the electors meet on the first Monday after the second Wednesday in December.[3] No general official meeting of all electors in the country is held, though in recent years attempts have been made to assemble as many as possible in Washington for unofficial celebrations.

Under the terms of the Twentieth Amendment, the two houses of Congress meet in joint session on January 6 following a presidential election. The electoral votes are counted and the results are an-

[2] The states using the presidential short ballot in 1960 were California, Colorado, Connecticut, Delaware, Hawaii, Florida, Illinois, Indiana, Iowa, Kentucky, Maine, Maryland, Massachusetts, Michigan, Minnesota, Missouri, Nebraska, Nevada, New Hampshire, New Jersey, New Mexico, North Carolina, Ohio, Oregon, Pennsylvania, Rhode Island, Texas, Utah, Washington, West Virginia, and Wisconsin. In addition, New York has, in effect, adopted the short ballot through general use of voting machines.

[3] For a careful statement of how the college meets and does its work, see Robert G. Dixon, "Electoral College Procedure," *Western Political Quarterly*, vol. 3 (June, 1950), pp. 214–224.

METHODS OF CHOOSING PRESIDENTIAL ELECTORS
1788-1836

● Chosen by state legislature
▲ Elected by people by districts
■ Elected by people by general ticket
Each symbol represents one state

Within a half century the states had virtually abandoned other methods of selection in favor of popular election on an at-large basis. The legislature of South Carolina continued to elect presidential electors until 1860.

nounced. Inauguration takes place on January 20.

Electoral-college Shortcomings. It is easy to find fault with the electoral-college system of choosing the President. The original plan anticipated that leading citizens chosen electors as free agents would select the outstanding American who met the formal requirements for President. The emergence of the party system bound electors more and more to vote for the candidates adopted by their party.

The principal methods of selecting presidential electors that emerged in the early years were (1) choice by state legislatures, (2) election by the people through districts, and (3) popular election by statewide general tickets. Selection by legislatures was most widely used in the first eight elections (1788–1816). As sentiment for popular election rose, the district and general-ticket plans grew in importance. Although the district system produced an electoral vote more proportionate to popular vote, states found they could increase their relative influence in presidential elections by shifting to the general-ticket "winner-take-all" plan. After the 1824 election the general-ticket plan rapidly displaced both selection by legislatures and election by districts.[1]

Election by general ticket, at large, seriously distorts the presidential vote in each state. In 1948, for example, Truman won California by a margin of 17,865 over Dewey, and Ohio by 7,107; in these two states Truman won 50 electoral votes with 3,365,925 popular votes, and Dewey received no electoral votes for his 3,340,953. If approximately 12,500 voters had shifted from Truman to Dewey, the latter could have won all 50 electoral votes, and the election would have been thrown to the House of Representatives, despite Truman's popular lead of over 2,000,000 in the nation.

It is a sort of "unit rule," under which the winner of a plurality in each state takes all, and the national total of popular votes counts for nothing officially. This distortion within each state would not be serious if the result were fair and equitable nationally. It is not. Good luck has produced a majority winner in nearly every presidential campaign, but a streak of bad luck may bring repeated minority winners. The charts on page 295 show how the popular and electoral votes were related in past elections. In

three crucial contests, of Truman-Dewey in 1948, of Wilson-Taft-Roosevelt in 1912, of Lincoln-Breckenridge-Bell-Douglas in 1860, an electoral majority was secured without a popular majority, but in each case there was a popular plurality. Hayes in 1876 and Harrison in 1888 were elected with a majority of electoral votes, but with a minority of popular votes.

Reform of Presidential Selection. Four principal proposals have been made for altering the method of choosing the President.

Popular Election. This is simple and direct; it is in keeping with democratic tradition; it assures a majority or plurality choice. Objections to direct election come from the smaller states and the South. The smaller states would lose their advantage of a certain minimum of three electoral votes and its consequent multiplication of their influence in presidential elections. The Southern states would suffer because their participation in voting is low. Influence in presidential elections would drop accordingly. Opposition from these two sources makes proposal of the necessary constitutional amendment by a two-thirds vote in

Presidential-election short ballot: California. About three-fifths of the states used the presidential short ballot in 1960. Names of candidates for elector are eliminated from the ballot, which carries only the names of the presidential and vice-presidential nominees. In California names of would-be electors are not even sent to voters.

PRESIDENTIAL ELECTORS VOTE FOR ONE PARTY		
RICHARD M. NIXON, for President HENRY CABOT LODGE, for Vice President	Republican	
RUTHERFORD L. DECKER, for President E. HAROLD MUNN, for Vice President	Prohibition	
JOHN F. KENNEDY, for President LYNDON B. JOHNSON, for Vice President	Democratic	
for President for Vice President		

[1] Thomas Jefferson wrote James Monroe in 1800: "All agree that an election by districts would be best if it could be general; but while 10 states chuse either by their legislature or by a general ticket, it is folly & worse than folly for the other 6. not to do it." Paul L. Ford (ed.), *The Writings of Thomas Jefferson* (New York: Knickerbocker Press, 1896), vol. 7, p. 401.

each house of Congress a practical impossibility. Ratification by three-fourths of the states also could not be expected.

Abolition of Electors. Although the abolition of electors is an incidental feature of other proposals for reform, it is the sole end sought by one school of electoral-college critics. They would retain the device of electoral votes on the present basis. All states would have, in effect, the presidential short ballot; the electoral vote would be assigned automatically according to the popular-vote returns. In May, 1934, Senator Norris of Nebraska secured much Senate support for a proposed constitutional amendment embodying this plan, but failed by a narrow margin to muster the necessary two-thirds vote. The proposal is mild, indeed, but its adoption would meet the threat of individual electors violating their pledges to vote for the presidential candidate of a specified party. This proposal has generated no great enthusiasm. It is a small matter to take through the many formalities of constitutional amendment, and might divert attention from more fundamental reform.

Election by Districts. A strong case can be made for reverting to this popular method, most favored in the early days of the republic. The plan would divide electors among the parties in rough proportion to that now prevailing in Senate and House. One elector would be elected by each congressional district; additional electors would be chosen at large in each state for each senator (and representative at large, if any). The typical situation would have the voter casting ballots for one district elector and two at-large electors. While each state's

SAMPLE

OFFICIAL BALLOT

STATE OF MISSISSIPPI
REGULAR ELECTION
NOVEMBER 8, 1960

FOR
PRESIDENTIAL ELECTORS

(VOTE FOR EIGHT)

Nominees of the
Democratic Party of the State
of Mississippi
Pledged to Vote for
John F. Kennedy
for President
and
Lyndon B. Johnson
for Vice-President
of the United States of America

Frank K. Hughes	( )
David E. Guyton	( )
Will M. Whittington	( )
Frank E. Shanahan, Jr.	( )
Martin V. B. Miller	( )
Edmund H. Barton	( )
Curtis H. Mullen	( )
Mrs. Lovie Gore	( )

Nominees as
Unpledged Electors of The
Democratic Party of the
State of Mississippi
for President
and
Vice-President
of the United States of America

Henry Harris	( )
George Payne Cossar	( )
Charles L. Sullivan	( )
Clay B. Tucker	( )
Earl Evans, Jr.	( )
Robert R. (Bob) Buntin	( )
Dr. D. M. Nelson	( )
Lawrence Y. Foote	( )

Nominees of the
Mississippi Republican Party
Pledged to Vote for
Richard M. Nixon
for President
and
Henry Cabot Lodge
for Vice-President
of the United States of America

John M. Kaye	( )
Ralph O. White	( )
J. H. Snyder	( )
J. J. Newman	( )
George W. Shaw	( )
C. E. Tolar	( )
Dr. Noel Womack, Jr.	( )
J. B. Snider	( )
	( )

A presidential-election long ballot: Mississippi. About two-fifths of the states print the names of would-be electors on the ballot. The unpledged slate won in Mississippi in 1960; if they had held the balance of electoral votes between Kennedy and Nixon, they could have thrown the election to the House of Representatives.

at-large electors probably would come from a single party, the other party might capture some of the district electors.

The district plan could be reestablished by state action, without Federal constitutional amendment. Its constitutionality appears assured under a decision of the Supreme Court; in 1891 the legislature of Michigan changed to the district system, and its validity was upheld.[1] Adoption of the district plan by a single state or a few states would put it or them at a disadvantage for reasons stated by Jefferson a century and a half ago.

Increasing interest has been shown in imposing the district plan by Federal constitutional amendment. In recent Congresses this has been known as the Mundt-Coudert plan, after its sponsors. Adoption might incite state legislatures to gerrymander congressional districts even more than in the past. The general pattern of rural control of legislatures might give the Republicans some advantage, perhaps enabling them to win without carrying the great metropolitan areas. This would reduce the influence of minorities concentrated in urban centers. It seems likely that presidential elections, under the district system, would be neck-and-neck affairs, occasionally with minority winners, in view of the close margin between the two parties in the House in recent Congresses. The majority party in states where the existing winner-take-all scheme works repeatedly to its advantage would object. Political activists in the pivotal states would regret the loss of the decisive importance of their states.

Proportionate Division of Electoral Vote. This plan, best known as the Lodge-Gossett proposal, would abolish electors and the general-ticket system and substitute a scheme to share the electoral vote of each state between presidential candidates in proportion to their popular vote. The calculations within each state would be carried out to three decimal places; in 1948 the formula would have produced a nationwide electoral-vote distribution of approximately 261.2 for Truman and 222.5 for Dewey, instead of 303 to 189 under the present system. The form adopted by the Senate in 1950 permitted election by a plurality, if 40 per cent or more. Should no candidate receive as much as 40 per cent, the election of President would be thrown to the House and Senate, sitting in joint session. With each legislator voting as an individual, the choice would be between the two highest in electoral vote.

The Lodge-Gossett proposal received surprisingly strong support from the Senate in 1950, when it passed by a substantial majority. Previously a similar plan had secured favorable House committee action on more than one occasion. In 1950, however, the House decisively rejected the Lodge-Gossett proposal, and it has not again reached the congressional high point achieved at that time.

The coalitions supporting and opposing the proposal were indeed strange: Republicans and Democrats were on both sides; some liberals and some conservatives allied to support, others to oppose; large-state and small-state legislators were found in both camps. To some extent this odd alignment arose from the lack of information and understanding, particularly during Senate consideration; in part it stemmed from careful analysis (or misanalysis) of the possible impact of the proposal on national politics.

Among valid arguments of proponents are that Lodge-Gossett would (1) strength-

[1] *McPherson* v. *Blacker*, 146 U.S. 1 (1892). The law, enacted by a temporary Democratic majority that sought a chance to win some presidential electors, was speedily repealed by the Republicans after the 1892 election.

THE HOUSE ELECTS A PRESIDENT

ORIGINAL CONSTITUTION
Electors meet in respective states.
Vote by ballot for **two** persons.
Person with majority shall be President.
Person with second largest number shall be Vice-President.
If no majority for President, then House elects.
House chooses from **five** highest, each state delegation casting one vote, and majority required to elect. [Art. II, Sec. 1.]

1800 controversy
Jefferson and Burr (Democratic Republicans) got 73 electoral votes each, all their partisan supporters having voted the straight ticket. Adams and Pinckney (Federalists) were defeated.
Election thrown to House, where Federalist caucus decided to throw support to Burr.
Deadlock for thirty-five ballots.
Hamilton persuaded Federalists to vote for Jefferson, breaking deadlock.

Twelfth Amendment
Electors vote **separately** for President and Vice-President.
Person with majority shall be President.
If no majority for President, then House elects.
House chooses from **three** highest, each state delegation casting one vote, and majority required to elect. [Amendment XII (1804)]

1824 contest
Electoral votes were divided: Jackson 99, J. Q. Adams 84, Crawford 41, Clay 37; all were nominally of same party.
Clay, eliminated under "rule of three," threw support to Adams.
House voted: Adams 13, Jackson 7, Crawford 4.
Jacksonians charged "bargain and corruption" when Adams appointed Clay Secretary of State.

Both elections thrown into the House of Representatives because of no majority in the electoral college led to bitter controversy. Some plans for reform of the selection process might make House election more common.

en minority parties in one-party states, (2) encourage presidential campaigning in all states instead of the present concentration on large and pivotal states, (3) lessen the strategic leverage of organized minorities— ethnic and ideological—in states with large metropolitan areas, (4) reduce the unfairness inherent in the general-ticket plan that gives all of a state's electoral votes to the winner of a popular plurality, even by the narrowest of margins, and (5) eliminate from the Constitution the manifestly unfair arrangement of having the President chosen by the House, each state voting as a unit, if no electoral majority is secured.

Opponents counter with the contention that the proposal would (1) give the Demo-

SIX PRESIDENTIAL ELECTIONS, 1940-1960

Popular & Electoral Votes

| | DEMOCRAT | | REPUBLICAN | | OTHER |

1940

	Popular	Electoral
Roosevelt (D)	27,243,466	449
Willkie (R)	22,304,755	82
Other	267,091	0

1944

	Popular	Electoral
Roosevelt (D)	25,594,822	432
Dewey (R)	22,017,707	99
Other	356,272	0

1948

	Popular	Electoral
Truman (D)	24,104,836	303
Dewey (R)	21,969,500	189
Other	2,606,080	39

1952

	Popular	Electoral
Stevenson (D)	27,311,316	89
Eisenhower (R)	33,927,549	442
Other	308,996	0

1956

	Popular	Electoral
Stevenson (D)	25,875,408	74
Eisenhower (R)	35,387,015	457
Other	521,125	0

1960

	Popular	Electoral
Kennedy (D)	34,227,096	303
Nixon (R)	34,108,546	219
Other	826,813	15

crats a considerable advantage in presidential elections, (2) increase greatly the influence of Southern elements in the Democratic party, (3) produce more minority winners, through substitution of a 40 per cent plurality for the requirement of a majority of electoral votes, (4) upset the existing balance under which urban influence is preponderant in presidential elections and rural power in congressional politics, (5) endanger the two-party system by fostering the growth of splinter parties that would build up fractional electoral votes.

One answer to the question about the impact of Lodge-Gossett centers around the political future of the "Solid South." If the Republicans succeeded, as former Senator Lodge predicted, in making inroads in the Southern states, a two-party system might emerge in the region. But until or unless that occurred, the South would have its influence augmented both in the Democratic party and in national politics. And in the meantime the Democrats would enjoy, under the Lodge-Gossett proposal, an advantage that the Republicans could overcome only by mustering Northern popular majorities possibly running into the millions of votes.[1]

Variations. Several other proposals for changing the mode of election involve various combinations. The Kennedy plan of 1957 abolishes the electoral college, provides for selection by the whole Congress in case of no electoral majority, and precludes election of a President and Vice President of different parties. The Daniel-Mundt-Thurmond plan of 1956 would give each state the choice of either the district plan (Mundt-Coudert) or the proportionate (Lodge-Gossett). Public-opinion polls show

that a strong majority favors change, but Congress appears unlikely soon to agree which plan should be adopted.

PREREQUISITES AND PERQUISITES

Presidential Term of Office. In the Constitutional Convention sharp controversy arose over the length of a presidential term. Alexander Hamilton once expressed himself as favoring a life term for the executive. The two alternatives considered most carefully, however, were (1) six or seven years without reeligibility, or (2) four years with the possibility of reelection.

The Convention decided in favor of a four-year term, with the President eligible for reelection. Proposals for a single, longer term have since been made, but they have never been seriously considered. A leading advocate was William Howard Taft, who served one term as President and was later appointed Chief Justice of the United States. A seven-year term without reeligibility, Taft once declared, would give the President "courage and independence" and relieve the Federal employee from the "absorbing and diverting" interest in securing his reelection.[2] Against the long term, perhaps the strongest point is that, during six or seven years, popular will may change greatly and become quite out of harmony with the views of the executive.

The Federalist, numbers 71 and 72, probably written by Hamilton, defends the four-year term with reeligibility. This plan was adopted, the author asserted, because it induces a President to do well, gives the public the value of an executive's experience, and secures a stability of policy. A two-year term would be too short to obtain the "desired firmness and independence."

After Washington declined to serve a third term, a tradition grew that the limit

---

[1] For further information see Ruth C. Silva, "The Lodge-Gossett Resolution: A Critical Analysis," *American Political Science Review,* vol. 44 (March, 1950), pp. 86–99; and "Reform of the Electoral System," *The Review of Politics,* vol. 14 (July, 1952), pp. 394–407.

[2] William H. Taft, *The Presidency* (New York: Scribner, 1916), p. 4.

of two terms should apply to all who served as President. The proposal to nominate Grant for a third term aroused a storm of disapproval. Theodore Roosevelt, who reached the office through the vice-presidency and served only one full term, was sharply criticized for seeking election in 1912. Although the Republican forces made the third term a major issue in the 1940 campaign, the tradition was broken with the reelection of Franklin D. Roosevelt.

Those who oppose the third term on principle fear that a man who serves so long in the Presidency may build up a machine that will dominate the government and control the people. This is the consideration that prompted several states and some of the Latin-American republics to forbid even a second term to their governors and presidents.

Proponents of a third term argue that the people should have the right to elect a President to a third term if they wish to do so, and that a fixed limit of two terms will weaken the President's leadership during a second term of office. They maintain that popular controls through elections, legislative controls through Congress, and judicial controls through the courts are adequate to prevent the rise of dictatorship in the country.

The Eightieth Congress submitted to the state legislatures a proposed constitutional amendment which declared: "No person shall be elected . . . more than twice . . ." or more than once if he succeeded to the Presidency and served more than two years of the term of another. This proposal became the Twenty-second Amendment[1] in 1951, when the legislatures of Utah and Nevada voted for ratification. Since its adoption, claims have been made that House action in submitting the amendment to the states was invalid because the required quorum was not present. After 1957, the weakness of the position of a President ineligible for reelection was demonstrated for the first time.[2]

Qualifications and Compensation. The Constitution restricts eligibility for the Presidency to natural-born citizens at least thirty-five years of age and resident in the United States for fourteen years. Few controversies have arisen over these requirements. To provide for those born before the United States existed, citizens at the time of the adoption of the Constitution were made eligible. It is possible that a person born abroad of American parents might be regarded as "natural born." John F. Kennedy, at forty-three, was the youngest to be elected to the Presidency; Theodore Roosevelt reached it at forty-two by succession; only five others reached it in their forties. Some complaints were voiced that Herbert Hoover, who lived abroad for many years, failed to meet the residence requirement, but an interpretation requiring fourteen years continuously and immediately preceding election appears unwarranted.

The compensation of the President is fixed by statutory law;[3] it may not be

---

[1] A similar proposal was the subject of extended hearings in 1940: U.S. Senate, Committee on the Judiciary, *Third Term for President of the United States, Hearings . . .* , 76th Cong., 3d Sess. (1940). See also Charles W. Stein, *The Third Term Tradition* (New York: Columbia University Press, 1942). The full text of the amendment is given in Appendix III.

[2] Various objections to the amendment are considered in Joseph E. Kallenbach, "Constitutional Limitations on Reeligibility of National and State Chief Executives," *American Political Science Review*, vol. 46 (June, 1952), pp. 438–454. Congressional consideration is treated in Paul G. Willis and George L. Willis, "The Politics of the Twenty-second Amendment," *Western Political Quarterly*, vol. 5 (September, 1952), pp. 469–482.

[3] Benjamin Franklin argued in the Constitutional Convention against any salary for the President. Madison recorded concerning this suggestion: "It was treated with great respect, but rather for the author of it, than from any apparent conviction of its expediency or practicability." *Documents*, p. 141.

diminished or increased during a term of office. From 1909 to 1949 it was $75,000 per year; in January, 1949, it was raised to $100,000 and an additional $50,000 tax-free expense allowance was provided. Beginning in 1953 the salary and allowance were both made taxable. Travel, official entertaining, and White House are supported out of separate budget items. Even when all presidential perquisites are considered, however, the chief executive receives less compensation than hundreds in business and entertainment.

Succession. If the President vacates his office, the Vice President succeeds; if both offices fall vacant, Congress determines by law ". . . what officer shall then act as President. . ." (Art. II, sec. 1, cl. 5). In a statute enacted in 1886, Congress provided that the heads of the executive departments should succeed in the following order: State, Treasury, War, Justice, Post Office, Navy, and Interior.[1] The Twentieth Amendment provides that, if no President is chosen by the beginning of the next term, the Vice-President-elect shall serve as President until such time as a President qualifies. If neither President-elect nor Vice-President-elect has qualified, Congress may declare who shall act as President.

Prior to the time Harry S. Truman was sworn in following the death of Franklin D. Roosevelt in April, 1945, six Vice Presidents had succeeded in the Presidency, all because of the deaths of the Presidents. William H. Harrison died in April, 1841, one month after his inauguration, and was succeeded by Tyler. General Zachary Taylor, who died in 1850, was followed by Fillmore. The assassination of Lincoln in 1865 left the Presidency for Andrew Johnson. President James A. Garfield, who died from an assassin's bullet in 1881, was followed by

Chester A. Arthur. McKinley's assassination in 1901 opened the way for the brilliant career of Theodore Roosevelt. Warren G. Harding's death in 1923 left the Presidency to Calvin Coolidge. Only Roosevelt, Coolidge, and Truman managed election for another term in the Presidency. No provision is made in the law or Constitution for succession in case the President becomes disabled. Garfield, Wilson, and Eisenhower had substantial periods of incapacity, but no practical method of removing the executive, except impeachment, exists.

The death of Franklin D. Roosevelt in April, 1945, just at the end of the war in Europe and on the eve of the San Francisco Conference, focused the country's attention on presidential succession. President Truman soon recommended to Congress a new succession law, replacing the heads of the executive departments with the Speaker of the House and the President pro tempore of the Senate. At the time, President Truman's sentiments were believed to be motivated largely by the fact that Secretary of State Edward R. Stettinius, Jr., was almost wholly lacking in political experience. The President repeated his recommendations in his State of the Union message of January, 1946.

In 1947 a new act was passed; it provided that, should both the President and Vice President become unable to discharge the powers and duties of the Presidency, the succession should be the Speaker of the House, President pro tempore of the Senate, and heads of the executive departments in order of the 1886 act except that the posts of Agriculture, Commerce, and Labor were added to the end.[2] The new act has been criticized severely for its

---

[1] 24 Stat. 7. The other cabinet posts did not then exist.

[2] Subsequently, under the National Security Act of 1947, the Secretary of Defense displaced the Secretary of War, and the Secretary of the Navy was eliminated.

failure to define "disability," for the possible unconstitutionality of classifying the Speaker and the President pro tempore as "officers of the United States," as the Constitution requires for succession, and for declaring that he who succeeds becomes President and is entitled to serve the remainder of the full term.[1]

Would the Speaker of the House and the President pro tempore of the Senate be better material for the Presidency than the heads of the executive departments? While the speakership normally is filled by a person öf long experience in legislative matters, proved executive ability is rare in that office. The President pro tempore of the Senate seldom is a man of distinction and sometimes is a party wheel horse of indifferent qualification except that of long seniority. On the other hand, the Secretary of State and the Secretary of the Treasury are often experienced in both administration and politics.

Inability. The Constitution provides that, in case of inability of the President to perform them, the duties of the Presidency shall devolve upon the Vice President, but it is silent on how disability shall be determined. This is a major defect of the Constitution which was brought sharply to public attention after President Eisenhower had suffered severe illnesses. This was not the first time that a President was seriously ill. Garfield lingered for eighty days after being felled by an assassin in 1881. Wilson continued in the Presidency, following his stroke in 1919, to the end of his term in 1921.

Authorities differ considerably on the question of who should decide when a President is disabled. Among those suggested are the Vice President, Congress, Cabinet, Supreme Court, and a special commission created for the purpose. Except for the possibility that the President might declare himself unable to continue, the Vice President appears to be the only one able to act. He would be reluctant, however, to accept the onus of "usurpation" charges that might be made if he attempted succession.

Congress has a considerable measure of authority, either to define in the law procedures to be followed or to initiate the question of the President's inability to discharge his duties. The Cabinet has little standing under the Constitution or law, but it might take the first informal steps toward raising the inability issue. The Supreme Court might ultimately receive on appeal a case involving presidential succession, but its original jurisdiction over such a case is not possible without a constitutional amendment. Several plans for a "Commission on Presidential Inability" have been proposed; typically such a body would be composed of such officials as the Vice President, Secretary of State, Speaker, President pro tempore of the Senate, and the majority and minority leaders of the two houses.

A constitutional amendment may be required to settle the matter beyond doubt. Skillful drafting might produce a statute that could weather the charge of unconstitutionality, but the stakes are so high that it may be better to run no risks. Legislation may be needed to allow the Vice President temporarily to *act as President* under given circumstances, rather than become President.

---

[1] See Ruth C. Silva, *Presidential Succession* (Ann Arbor, Mich.: University of Michigan Press, 1951); also her "The Presidential Succession Act of 1947," *Michigan Law Review*, vol. 47 (February, 1949), pp. 451–476; Everett S. Brown and Ruth C. Silva, "Presidential Succession and Inability," *Journal of Politics*, vol. 11 (February, 1949), pp. 236–256; Joseph E. Kallenbach, "The New Presidential Succession Act," *American Political Science Review*, vol. 41 (October, 1947), pp. 931–941.

Pending determination by law or constitutional amendment, President Eisenhower, in March, 1958, announced an agreement between himself and Vice President Nixon on how they would handle a disability crisis. If the President were unable to function, the Vice President would become "acting President." The declaration of inability would be made by the President, if he were capable, or by the Vice President, if the President were not. When the President decides his disability has ended, he would so declare and resume "the full exercise of the powers and duties of the office." This arrangement was a personal one that could not be binding on future Presidents. It did not remove the constitutional doubt surrounding the recapture of the office by a recovered President from the "acting President."

THE PRESIDENT AND HIS COLLEAGUES

The Cabinet. After the Constitutional Convention eliminated the proposal for a council of advisers, many assumed that the Senate would attempt to fill that role. But the first Senate was reluctant to advise directly with President Washington. Therefore, formal pre-consultation, even on appointments and treaties, was dropped, and never revived.

President Washington began to call department heads into consultation, and these early meetings were soon known as "cabinet" meetings. The Cabinet has remained an informal group without legal sanction, its personnel determined by custom and the President. The Cabinet meets only at the request of the President, it exercises only such authority as he chooses to vest in it, and it may be dissolved if he wishes. In practice, the Cabinet plays an important part in determining executive policy and coordinating administrative work. No votes

are taken, unless the President asks for one; as Lincoln once said, the only vote that counts is the President's own.

Traditionally the Cabinet has been composed of the heads of executive departments. Sometimes the Vice President is included as a member. In Cabinet personnel, as in other Cabinet matters, the President is the master.

During the Eisenhower Administration the Cabinet was composed of the President, the Vice President, and ten heads of departments. Seven others, in the mid-1950s, sat at the Cabinet table and participated in discussion. The Cabinet met rather regularly on Fridays; on at least one occasion a Cabinet meeting was televised.

Mr. Vice President. Vice Presidents often have become the forgotten men in American history. The office is one of importance, and yet it is the butt of endless jokes. Almost the only Vice Presidents remembered from one generation to another are those who succeeded to the Presidency. The Vice President presides over the Senate and becomes President when that office falls vacant. These duties alone should make the office one of the most coveted in the gift of the people. In practice, however, it is looked upon as a political graveyard to be avoided by politicians of promise.

The main reason for the discrepancy between the potentialities of the office and its reputation are found in the method of nominating for the office. Each party, as seen earlier, may use the vice presidency to balance the ticket, or to appease or reward some element. Thus the proper running mate for Alfred E. Smith, Catholic and Eastern, was Joseph T. Robinson, Protestant and Southern; for Wendell Willkie, a novice in politics and identified with Eastern corporate interests, Charles McNary, veteran Senator and champion of farm and progressive interests. In both these cases the vice-presidential candidates were able men, but the method sometimes produces candidates of questionable qualifications.

Second, the constitutional responsibilities of office are not great. The Senate is a body with customs and traditions that the presiding officer must respect and accept. As President of the Senate, he fills a correct and impartial role, voting only in case of a tie. Vice President Dawes tried to modernize the Senate, but found it unwilling to accept his proposals, or even to listen patiently. A vigorous man gets restive under such conditions; his frustration is noticed and the prestige of the office degenerates accordingly.

The considerable possibilities of the office have been demonstrated by recent Vice Presidents, as diverse as Henry A. Wallace and Richard M. Nixon. Both Roosevelt in 1940 and Eisenhower in 1952 and 1956 were strong enough in their respective parties to choose running mates without the usual trading of votes and appeasing of factions. Roosevelt gave Wallace an important role in the war effort. Eisenhower assigned Nixon a variety of congressional, diplomatic and executive tasks, including the honor of presiding over the Cabinet in the absence of the President.[1] In 1955 the salary of the office was set at $35,000 per year.

HEADQUARTERS STAFF

The Chief Administrator. The Constitution vests in the President the "executive power" of the United States. However, the President has less sweeping authority over administration than might be assumed from the language of the fundamental law. Congress frequently determines the structure and authority of administrative agencies; it

[1] The Vice President was made a member of the National Security Council in 1949.

decides what functions require new agencies or remodeled ones, determines powers and duties, and controls in many ways the framework within which administration operates. Many bureaus have been established by executive order rather than act of Congress, and consequently they may be reorganized or abolished and their functions assigned elsewhere by similar executive act. Presidential authority over the administration has been weakened during the last half century by several developments, but the factors operating to strengthen the hand of the President have outweighed them.

Since the turn of the century, especially during the administrations of Theodore Roosevelt, Woodrow Wilson, and Franklin Roosevelt, presidential authority over administration increased markedly. The power to appoint and remove executive officers gives the President a commanding position in the field of personnel. Increasingly complex international situations have dictated more executive discretion in foreign affairs, trade, and defense matters. Economic depression intensified the tendency to delegate more authority in the fields of relief and business regulation.

The emergency nature of many governmental responsibilities is especially important in explaining augmented presidential power over administration. Whereas Congress once was able to stipulate in great detail the precise form, duties, and procedure of administrative agencies, now such variable factors as business conditions, foreign tariff rates, and droughts in farm regions require flexibility and loose construction of statutes. The trend is toward a situation under which Congress lays down broad principles and standards in legislation, leaving to the President and other executive officers the responsibility for details. Such details often include the whole structure and personnel of administrative agencies and the allocation of funds for specific purposes.

The Presidential Secretariat. From the standpoint of the President, the first essential in fulfilling his responsibilities as chief administrator is an able corps of attachés to help him keep abreast of administrative work. For the early Presidents this was no great problem; only a small secretariat was required. To keep informed concerning the administrative leviathan of today requires most careful organization and planning.

President Eisenhower employed a "chief of staff" concept and placed direction of the presidential offices in the hands of his Assistant to the President, Sherman Adams. In 1954 he established a Cabinet secretariat as a part of his executive staff, headed by an officer with the title of Secretary to the Cabinet. This secretariat prepared the agenda for Cabinet meetings, kept the official records of what was decided, and followed through to see that the executive departments carry out the Cabinet decisions. This development indicated the increased role assigned to the Cabinet by President Eisenhower.

President Hoover introduced the pattern of three principal executive secretaries. The number and duties vary from President to President and from time to time. Usually, one is assigned to public relations and the control of information going out of the White House; a second handles visitors of the President, sifting the important from the unimportant and keeping the executive appointment calendar; the third may be given miscellaneous duties. In addition, each President has personal secretaries and clerks.

A later development was the authorization of "administrative assistants" to the President, in addition to the executive secretaries. The President's Committee on Administrative Management urged as a remedy for the lack of staff assistance to the President the appointment of administrative assistants who ". . . should be possessed of high competence, great physical vigor, and a passion for anonymity."[1] The Administrative Reorganization Act of 1939 authorized their appointment. The incumbents of the office have followed the plan outlined by the President's committee: they have carried out the assignments of the President unobtrusively, collecting data, conferring with American and foreign officials, multiplying the eyes and ears of the President in effective fashion.

In addition to the executive secretaries and assistants, the President's staff in the mid-1950s included several special assistants, a special counsel, a Secretary to the Cabinet, and a staff secretary. Their assistants and the Army, Navy, and Air Force aides complete the principal officers of the White House staff.

One student of presidential staffing criticized the White House office organization for permitting too many high-ranking aides direct access to the President.[2] This alleged fault may have been corrected by President Eisenhower's use of a "chief of staff."

Other Executive Office Agencies. The Executive Office also includes the Bureau of the Budget, National Security Council, Council of Economic Advisers, Office of Emergency Planning, Office of Science and Technology, and National Aeronautics and Space Council.

An early concept was that grouping "staff" services in the presidential office gave the executive another form of control over "line," or operating, administrative agencies. Staff types of agencies, housekeeping in nature, might include personnel, budgeting,

[1] U.S. President's Committee on Administrative Management, *Report . . . with Studies . . .* (1937), p. 5.
[2] Bradley D. Nash, *Staffing the Presidency*, National Planning Association Pamphlet 80 (December, 1952), p. 16.

EXECUTIVE OFFICE OF THE PRESIDENT

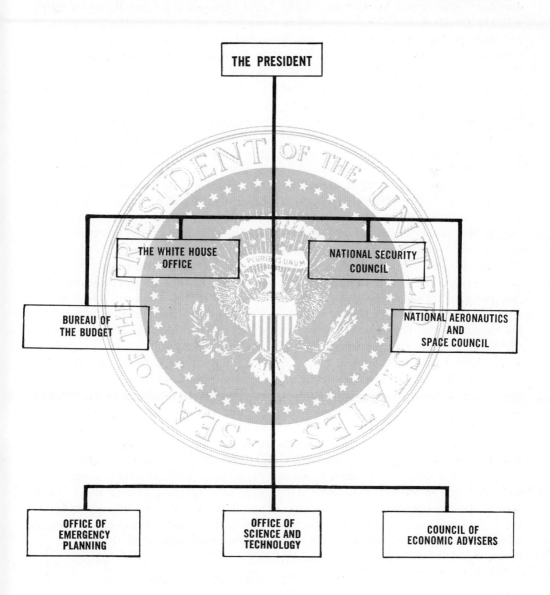

THE PRESIDENT

THE WHITE HOUSE OFFICE

NATIONAL SECURITY COUNCIL

BUREAU OF THE BUDGET

NATIONAL AERONAUTICS AND SPACE COUNCIL

OFFICE OF EMERGENCY PLANNING

OFFICE OF SCIENCE AND TECHNOLOGY

COUNCIL OF ECONOMIC ADVISERS

planning, purchasing, reporting, and other central services provided for operating agencies engaged in such line functions as public health, welfare, conservation, defense, and regulation of business. The objective of well-developed staff agencies, working closely with the President, and thereby giving him a strategic position in the cockpit of control, could not be achieved fully in 1939 when the Executive Office of the President was created. The Reorganization Act of that year forbade transfer of Civil Service Commission and General Accounting Office.

In the war and postwar periods the magnitude of the executive branch has led to some rethinking about staff services. The present tendency appears to be one of allowing the Executive Office to perform a coordinating role with emphasis on program and policy development, leaving routine staff services to the operating departments. The new General Services Administration, created in 1949 to provide central purchasing, property maintenance, transportation, and other services, was made a separate agency outside the Executive Office of the President. Several agencies in the presidential office have been abolished.

Each of the four agencies remaining in the Executive Office is discussed in subsequent chapters; only their general roles will be described here. In its legislative reference work, the Bureau of the Budget provides central clearance to ensure that the legislative proposals of executive agencies conform with the policies of the President.[1] The Bureau also has extensive duties in developing budget policies and estimates, recommending management improvements, coordinating statistical services, and the like. The Employment Act of 1946 created

[1] For an analysis of legislative clearance, see Richard E. Neustadt, "Presidency and Legislation: The Growth of Central Clearance," *American Political Science Review*, vol. 48 (September, 1954), pp. 641–671.

the Council of Economic Advisers. The three economists who constitute the Council help the President prepare his annual economic report to Congress, study economic trends, and recommend to the President appropriate policies. Perhaps anticipating some such public disagreement as developed late in the Truman administration among Council members, the Hoover Commission recommended that the body be displaced by a single-headed Office of Economic Adviser. President Eisenhower transferred administrative authority to the chairman.

The two defense agencies in the Executive Office of the President are the National Security Council and the Office of Civil and Defense Mobilization. The National Security Council was created by the National Security Act of 1947 and assigned the weighty task of advising the President on policies relating to national security. The Central Intelligence Agency and the Operations Coordinating Board operate under the direction of the Council. The Office of Civil and Defense Mobilization exists to plan, direct, and coordinate all mobilization activities.

Calling attention to the useful work of special advisory commissions and of individual consultants appointed by the President, the first Hoover Commission recommended that the chief executive be given adequate funds to operate freely in this sphere. The Hoover group also felt strongly that the President should have power to organize and reorganize his own office without the approval of Congress and to appoint his own staff (except the Civil Service Commission) without confirmation by the Senate.

LINE ORGANIZATION

The Executive Departments. Most important among the line functions are the regular executive departments of the Federal government, now ten in number. According to custom, the heads of the departments are considered members of the President's Cabinet by virtue of their offices. The departments were established by Congress in the following order: State (originally Foreign Affairs), 1789; War, 1789 (lost Cabinet status, 1947); Treasury, 1789; Navy, 1798 (lost Cabinet status, 1947); Interior (originally Home), 1849; Agriculture, 1862 (elevated to full membership status, 1889); Justice (Attorney General, 1789), 1870; Post Office (Postmaster General, 1789), 1872; Commerce (originally Commerce and Labor), 1903; Labor, 1913; Defense (originally National Defense Establishment), 1947; and Health, Education, and Welfare (1953).

The theory underlying the organization of departments is that similar functions should be grouped for convenience and efficiency into a relatively small number of departments, with heads to coordinate the endeavors of the operating services and be responsible to the Chief Executive. While this is the theory, several Federal departments possess functions that are not related to their major functions. Interior, for example, has served as a catchall for miscellaneous agencies that failed to fit elsewhere. At the same time, several activities—like public health, transportation, public works, and conservation—are divided among half a dozen departments.

Each executive department is headed by a secretary, appointed by the President with the advice and consent of the Senate. The department head usually is chosen for political qualifications: political prominence, campaign support, factional affiliation, sectional considerations. It is not surprising, therefore, that his main contribution often proves to be his conduct of departmental external relationships—with President, with Congress, with press, and with public. Usu-

ally he is not prepared to manage the detailed operation of his department; that is better left to the permanent career officials, supervised by the secretary and his political aides. He has important duties in determining departmental policy, appointing and removing officers, and settling disputes and appeals.

The Reorganization Act of 1939 banned new departments but gave the President considerable power to reshuffle bureaus and agencies. President Roosevelt promptly created three new "agencies" which were much like departments in fact but not in name. The "administrator" of each was invited to sit with the President's Cabinet. These agencies were in the fields of welfare, works, and loans.

The first Hoover Commission recommended the creation of a new department in the welfare-education field. Several existing functions of the Federal Security Agency, notably the Public Health Service, Food and Drug Administration, and Bureau of Employment Security, were scheduled for transfer to other departments. The new department would have embraced the remaining social security services, education, vocational rehabilitation, Indian affairs, and certain lesser activities.[1] President Truman, in his 1949 reorganization plan 1, proposed to transform the Federal Security Agency into a Department of Welfare, but his proposal was nullified by adverse congressional action.

In 1953, President Eisenhower's reorganization plan 1 was allowed to go into effect, and the Department of Health, Education, and Welfare took its place among the executive departments. Most Federal activities in the welfare field are now under the new department.

Independent Establishments. After the ten great executive departments come some

[1] Hoover Commission, *Social Security and Education; Indian Affairs* (1949), pp. 3–12.

forty-five agencies. Each is neither a part of any department nor, by itself, sufficient in size or importance to justify the status of a department.

The reasons for their separate establishment are as numerous as the agencies themselves, but a few major arguments are common to many. First, the work of the agency may be so unique that it does not fit into any existing department. Second, the service provided must be fully protected from partisan politics. Third, special interests find it easier to watch and bring pressure on separate agencies than on departmentalized ones. Fourth, possession of quasi-legislative and quasi-judicial powers requires independence from the President.

The more important of existing independent establishments, together with the years in which they were created, are the following: Civil Service Commission, 1883; Interstate Commerce Commission, 1887; Federal Trade Commission, 1914; Tariff Commission, 1916; Federal Power Commission, 1920; General Accounting Office, 1921; Veterans' Administration, 1930; Tennessee Valley Authority, 1933; Securities and Exchange Commission, 1934; Federal Communications Commission, 1935; National Labor Relations Board, 1935; Maritime Commission, 1936 (within Department of Commerce, 1950–61); Civil Aeronautics Board, 1940; Atomic Energy Commission, 1946; and National Aeronautics Space Administration, 1958. Nearly one-half of those listed are regulatory commissions with varying responsibilities for supervising commercial activities.

Congress has assigned much responsibility for the execution of laws to such independent bodies. To some extent this represents a diffusion of the executive power, which the Constitution vests in the President directly and by its charge that he take care that the laws be executed faithfully. In virtually every case, the independent agency is governed by a board or commission appointed by the President for terms sufficiently long that a President is unable to secure control in one term. This insulates the board or commission from the political whim of the executive, but continues in office those whose policies may have been repudiated at the polls. When a change of administration involves a transformation in policy, as in 1953, the disparity between presidential and commission views on public questions may be very critical. It is now settled that Congress may, in the law creating agencies, regulate and limit the power of the President to remove members of regulatory commissions.

"Fourth Branch?" Independent agencies have been condemned as "a headless fourth branch of government," "miniature independent governments," and "irresponsible commissions." Under President Roosevelt's reorganization orders of 1939 some progress was made in incorporating independent agencies into the departmental system, but a large number of the establishments were exempted from any change. The 1939 act withheld from the President the power to alter the status of most of the regulatory commissions. Insistently urged by the President's Committee on Administrative Management was that administrative functions of regulatory commissions be separated from judicial functions. Administrative work would be coordinated with an appropriate regular department; semilegislative and semijudicial work would continue independent of presidential control.

The first Hoover Commission suggested that some commissions be divested of their administrative duties but that the remaining ones should transfer all administrative responsibility to their chairmen.[1] President

---

[1] First Hoover Commission, *The Independent Regulatory Commissions* (1949), pp. 5–6.

Truman took the first steps in his initial plans under the Reorganization Act of 1949. These fixed administrative authority on the chairmen of the Civil Service Commission and the Maritime Board, and in 1950 on the chairmen of the Federal Trade Commission, the Federal Power Commission, the Securities and Exchange Commission, and the Civil Aeronautics Board. Plans proposing the same type of reform for the Interstate Commerce Commission, the Federal Communications Commission, and the National Labor Relations Board were rejected by the Senate.

The problem of effective supervision of agencies outside the regular departments remains unsolved. A former Treasury official has suggested that presidential control might be aided by creating two new cabinet posts "at large." These "ministers without portfolio" would have their assignments fixed by the President, and might achieve a measure of coordination in an area previously known for its uncoordination.[1]

When President Kennedy took office in 1961 he had before him a task force report on regulatory agencies, prepared by James M. Landis; it called for stricter supervision by the chief executive, including presidential appointment of chairmen and the establishment of an office to coordinate regulatory bodies within the Executive Office of the President. No substantial changes were made during the first two years of the new administration.

[1] Daniel W. Bell in Nash, *op. cit.*, p. 12.

FOR FURTHER READING

Adams, Sherman: *Firsthand Report: The Story of the Eisenhower Administration* (New York: Harper, 1961).

Brownlow, Louis: *The American Presidency* (Chicago: University of Chicago Press, 1949).

Corwin, Edward S.: *The President: Office and Powers* (New York: New York University Press, 4th ed., 1958).

——— and Louis W. Koenig: *The Presidency Today* (New York: New York University Press, 1956).

Coyle, David C.: *Ordeal of the Presidency* (Washington, D.C.: Public Affairs Press, 1960).

David, Paul T. (ed.): *The Presidential Election and Transition 1960–1961* (Washington, D.C.: Brookings Institution, 1961).

Fenno, Richard F., Jr.: *The President's Cabinet: An Analysis in the Period from Wilson to Eisenhower* (Cambridge, Mass.: Harvard University Press, 1959).

Fincher, E. B.: *President of the United States* (New York: Abelard-Schuman, 1955).

Finer, Herman: *The Presidency: Crisis and Regeneration, An Essay in Possibilities* (Chicago: University of Chicago Press, 1960).

Hart, James: *The American Presidency in Action* (New York: Macmillan, 1948).

Henry, Laurin L.: *Presidential Transitions* (Washington, D.C.: Brookings Institution, 1960).

Hobbs, Edward H.: *Behind the President: A Study of Executive Office Agencies* (Washington, D.C.: Public Affairs Press, 1954).

Hyman, Sidney: *The American Presidency* (New York: Harper, 1954).

——— (ed.): "The Office of the American Presidency," *Annals of the American Academy*, vol. 307 (September, 1956). Contains articles on many aspects.

Koenig, Louis W.: *The Invisible Presidency* (New York: Holt, Rinehart & Winston, 1960).

Laski, Harold J.: *The American Presidency* (New York: Harper, 1940).

Longaker, Richard P.: *The Presidency and Individual Liberties* (Ithaca, N.Y.: Cornell University Press, 1961).

MacBride, Roger L.: *The American Electoral College* (Caldwell, Idaho: Caxton, 1953).

Moos, Malcolm, and Stephen Hess: *Hats in the Ring, The Making of Presidential Candidates* (New York: Random House, 1960).

Nash, B. D.: *Staffing the Presidency* (Washington, D.C.: National Planning Association, 1952).

Rossiter, Clinton: *The American Presidency* (New York: Harcourt, Brace, 1956).

Silva, Ruth C.: *Presidential Succession* (Ann Arbor, Mich.: University of Michigan Press, 1951).

"The Presidential Office," *Law and Contemporary Problems* (Durham, N.C.: Duke University, School of Law, Autumn, 1956). Covers political and administrative roles and staffing of office.

U.S. Commission on Organization of the Executive Branch of the Government (first Hoover Commission): *Report . . .* (19 vols., 1949). In addition, 18 task-force reports were published.

U.S. Commission on Organization of the Executive Branch of the Government (second Hoover Commission): *Report . . .* (20 vols., 1955). In addition, 19 task-force and subcommittee reports were published.

U.S. House of Representatives: *Amend the Constitution with Respect to Election of President and Vice-President . . . Hearings. . . .* 81st Cong., 1st Sess. (1949). Briefer hearings were held by the same committee in 1947.

————: *Documents Illustrative of the Formation of the Union of the American States.* H. Doc. 398, 69th Cong., 1st Sess. (1927).

U.S. House of Representatives, Committee on the Judiciary: *Presidential Inability,* 84th Cong., 2d Sess. (1956), Committee print.

U.S. National Archives and Records Service: *United States Government Organization Manual* (issued annually).

U.S. President's Committee on Administrative Management: *Report . . . with Studies of Administrative Management in the Federal Government* (1937).

U.S. Senate: *The Electoral College,* S. Doc. 243, 78th Cong., 2d Sess. (1944).

U.S. Senate: *Presidential Succession . . . Hearings . . .* 80th Cong., 1st Sess. (1947).

Waugh, Edward W.: *The Second Consul: The Vice Presidency . . .* (Indianapolis: Bobbs-Merrill, 1956).

Williams, Irving G.: *The Rise of the Vice-Presidency* (Washington, D.C.: Public Affairs Press, 1956).

Wilmerding, Lucius, Jr.: *The Electoral College* (New Brunswick, N.J.: Rutgers University Press, 1958).

REVIEW QUESTIONS

1. What previous experience and knowledge weighed heavily in determining the form and scope of the chief executive office by the Constitutional Convention of 1787?

2. What would the American Presidency be like today if the Convention had persisted in its early inclination for selection by Congress?

3. What defect in the electoral college scheme was corrected by the Twelfth Amendment?

4. Would the following be valid actions under the Federal Constitution? Why? (*a*) State A provides its presidential electors be chosen by the state legislature. (*b*) State B requires that all but two of its electors be elected by voters in congressional districts rather than at large.

5. Describe at least three proposed reforms in the mode of electing a President, and outline the main arguments for and against each one.

6. What are principal arguments pro and con on limiting a President to two four-year terms?

7. Explain the difference in provisions concerning presidential succession before and after the 1947 law on the subject.

8. What are the general responsibilities of the President as "chief administrator"?

9. What are "staff services"? Which have been brought into the Office of the President?

10. Name the regular executive departments of the Federal government, and explain the theory of departmentalizing.

11. How did the Cabinet originate? What are its functions today?

12. What are the "independent establishments"? Should they be grouped into regular departments?

13. Enumerate and discuss the principal recommendations of the two Hoover Commissions regarding organization of the executive branch.

Chapter Sixteen

Powers
of the President

*In spite of vast powers, the office of the Presidency can
become a mere masquerade of power if Congress chooses to
make it so. It is not only that many of the powers of
the President are derived from acts of Congress,
and what Congress gives it may also take away. Even those
Presidential powers derived directly from the Constitution
depend in large measure for their effectiveness upon
congressional cooperation. Without congressional approval
of men and money, the President may be Commander in
Chief, but of a phantom force. Even the President's
foreign policy requires congressional support if it is to
succeed, particularly in the period since World War II
when economic and military assistance to underdeveloped
areas and the associated powers of the free world have
loomed so large. Thus it is literally true that, while the
President proposes, Congress ultimately disposes.
Hence the importance of good relations between the
President and legislature if an administration is to succeed.*

PETER H. ODEGARD[1]

The history of the Presidency, according to
Edward S. Corwin, is a history of aggrandizement. Section II of the Constitution is loosely drawn. What the Presidency
is today depends not only on the letter of
the fundamental law but on the men who

[1] "Presidential Leadership and Party Responsibility," in "The Office of the American Presidency," *Annals of the American Academy*, vol.
307 (September, 1956), p. 66.

have served—especially upon the man who
is serving—and how they have exercised
their authority.

A student who relies exclusively on the
wording of a written constitution may get
a very distorted view of a nation's institution. A stranger, on first reading the British
North America Act, might assume that
Canada is governed by a dictator called the
Governor General. In practice the Gov-

ernor General performs the functions of
a constitutional monarch, and normally
has little discretionary power. The real executive is the Prime Minister and his Cabinet colleagues, who are sustained by majority support in the House of Commons.

The "man from Mars," reviewing the
American Constitution, might see the President as a weak executive, subject to a large
extent to the will of Congress. He might call
our system, as did the young Woodrow
Wilson, "Congressional Government." But
the forceful men who have held the Presidency—Jefferson, Jackson, Lincoln, Cleveland, Theodore Roosevelt, Wilson, and
Franklin Roosevelt—have built the office
into one of the most powerful executive
posts in the modern world.

APPOINTMENT AND REMOVAL

Scope of the Appointing Power. The power
to appoint is one of the most far-reaching of
presidential powers. Through it the President
commands the allegiance of a great number
of Federal officers and secures the support
of many national legislators for his program.

In Article II, Section 2, the President is
given power to ". . . nominate, and by and
with the advice and consent of the Senate,
shall appoint ambassadors, other public
ministers and consuls, judges of the Supreme Court, and all other officers of the
United States . . . which shall be established
by law." The article provides that Congress
may vest appointment of "inferior officers"
in the President alone, in the courts, or in
department heads.

Thus, appointments to the Federal services fall into two general groups: those that
require senatorial confirmation, called "officers," and those that do not, called "inferior
officers." No logical line divides the two.
Included in the officer category are diplomats, judges, department heads, regulatory

commissioners, marshals, and collectors of
customs. Often Congress enlarges this group
to broaden the possibilities of patronage.
Some bureau chiefs and virtually all subordinate employees fall within the inferior-
officer group.

Senatorial Confirmation. The Senate has
interpreted "advice and consent" to justify
withholding confirmation from proposed
officers on grounds that sometimes appear
petty or personal. It rarely interferes with
the President's selection of his own Cabinet;
a notable exception was Charles B. Warren,
nominated by President Coolidge as Attorney General and rejected in 1925 by the
Senate. Appointments to the diplomatic
corps normally secure the Senate's approval
without difficulty, but the Senate's rejection
of Martin Van Buren as Minister to Britain
will be remembered from the Jackson administration. The President may fill Supreme Court justiceships without much interference; yet the Senate refused President
Hoover's appointment of Judge John J.
Parker, in 1930, largely because of Negro
and labor opposition.

Other appointments, especially those of
local nature, are subject to a custom called
"senatorial courtesy." This is an unwritten
rule which requires the President to confer
with and secure the consent of the senator
or senators of his party from a state before
making a nomination to an office in that
state. The rule virtually transfers the nominating power for such offices from the
President to the individual senators of his
party. Almost invariably the Senate rejects
a presidential appointment if personal objection is raised by a senator of the President's party from the state involved.

Senatorial Courtesy in Practice. An example of the operation of senatorial courtesy
arose from President Truman's choice of
two candidates to fill district-court judgeships in Illinois. In August, 1951, Senator

Paul H. Douglas of Illinois, before the Senate Judiciary Committee, opposed the President's nominees on the grounds that he was not consulted and that his own choices were better qualified. The senator produced a poll of the Chicago Bar Association to support his contention. When the nominations reached the floor with an adverse committee recommendation in October, Senator Douglas stated:

I do not want to label the nominees themselves as being personally obnoxious to me. I regard them as estimable men and fine citizens. But I should like to point out that they were nominated without consultation with me, without any indication of the reasons for their selection, and contrary to the recommendations of the much more highly qualified men whose names I had forwarded and who were supported by the heavy preponderance of informed opinion in Illinois.[1]

The Senate rejected both nominees without a roll-call vote.[2]

Sometimes, when senators who are unpopular with their colleagues attempt to obstruct confirmation of an appointment, the Senate will approve in spite of their protest. Only a few rejections occur during each session of Congress; these may be attributed mainly to the fact that the President fails to accept suggestions from senators and appoints those whom they do not recommend.

Reconsideration. After the Senate has confirmed an appointment of the President, can it call the matter back for reconsideration? In a case arising from the desire of the Senate to reconsider confirmation of several appointees of President Hoover to the Federal Power Commission [*United States v. Smith,* 186 U.S. 6 (1932)], the Supreme

Court declared that it could not. Shortly after taking office, the appointees had reversed the policies of the Commission and dismissed several employees. The rules of the Senate allowed reconsideration, but the Court ruled that, once the consent was given and the officers fully installed, the Senate might not withdraw confirmation.

Presidents may fill vacancies that occur during recess of the Senate, but such commissions expire at the end of the next session. Law prohibits the payment of a salary to an officer appointed to fill a vacancy that existed when the Senate was in session. Usually a President will not give a recess appointment to a person previously rejected by the Senate.

Power to Remove. The first Congress declared by law that the President alone might remove all officers appointed by him except judges. In the reconstruction controversies between President Johnson and Congress, the executive was forbidden by law to remove officers without the consent of the Senate. This was repealed about twenty years later.

An act of 1876 provided that first-, second-, and third-class postmasters might be removed only with the consent of the Senate. In spite of the act, President Wilson removed Postmaster Myers of Portland, Oregon. A legal suit arose over Myers's claim for back salary, and he alleged that his removal was illegal under the 1876 law. The statute was declared unconstitutional by the Supreme Court; the power to remove, said the Court, was implied not only from the power to appoint, but also from the general authority of the executive to see that the laws are executed faithfully. [*Myers v. United States,* 272 U.S. 52, 164 (1926)].

The Myers verdict appeared to accord the President an unlimited removal power except with respect to judges. Early in the New Deal, however, another decision modi-

[1] *Congressional Record,* 82d Cong., 1st Sess., Oct. 9, 1951, p. 1310.

[2] For a careful review of this and other instances, see Joseph P. Harris, *The Advice and Consent of the Senate* (Berkeley and Los Angeles, Calif.: University of California Press, 1953).

fied this conception. Humphrey, a Federal Trade Commissioner, was removed by President Roosevelt because the commissioner's philosophy of business regulation differed widely from the President's. Under the law the President was empowered to remove for "inefficiency, neglect of duty, or malfeasance in office," but he gave no such reason. The Court took notice that a regulatory commission's powers are quasi-legislative and quasi-judicial in nature and ruled that the President's removal authority could be limited in respect to officers exercising such powers [*Humphrey's Executor (Rathbun) v. United States*, 295 U.S. 602 (1935)].

Apparently the present rule is that the President may remove executive officers, but that regulatory commissioners with part judicial and part legislative powers may be protected by statutory limitations on the removal power.

WAR AND DIPLOMATIC POWERS

The War Powers. As the Commander in Chief of the Armed Forces, the President has extensive authority over military and foreign policy. The executive shares power over the military establishment with Congress, which may make rules, appropriate money, and declare war; the Senate confirms appointments of military officers. Presidential control of the militia is limited to periods when it is called into the service of the United States. Nevertheless, the President may force Congress to appropriate money, as when Theodore Roosevelt ordered the fleet around the world despite congressional disapproval. A President, by belligerent use of the Armed Forces, may involve the country in a state of war, leaving Congress no alternative but to declare it. Without consulting Congress, Presidents have often ordered marines to land in Central American and Caribbean countries to protect American property and lives.

In war the powers of the President as Commander in Chief are even greater. He directs the Armed Forces on land and sea. He governs conquered territory until Congress provides by law for its civil government. Without much statutory authority, Lincoln suppressed civil rights and seized enemy property. Wilson exercised vast powers, largely conferred upon him by act of Congress.

In the Second World War, President Franklin Roosevelt relied upon a great mass of specific legislation, granting to the executive additional emergency and war powers. His control of radio was assured under the Federal Communications Act of 1934. Congress provided for calling the National Guard into Federal service more than a year before it declared war. Discretion was given the executive in the execution of the selective service law of 1940. A series of laws, beginning not long after war broke out in Europe, step by step gave the President very great authority over industrial facilities, matters of production, priorities, conditions, and contracts. After war was declared, Congress added power over foreign communications, war functions and agencies, alien property, and a host of other matters.[1]

Recent Problems. Hostilities in Korea in June, 1950, focused attention on the length and breadth of presidential power in time of emergency, but without a formal declaration of war. President Truman's prompt action in ordering American Armed Forces to aid the South Koreans was challenged then and subsequently as exceeding his authority as Commander in Chief. He ought, critics

[1] A convenient compilation of war powers previous to the Second World War is contained in the appendix of E. Pendleton Herring, *Presidential Leadership: The Political Relations of Congress and the Chief Executive* (New York: Farrar, Straus, 1940). For powers existing at the outset of the Korean hostilities, see Margaret Fennell, *Provisions of Federal Law Enacted for War and Emergency Periods*, Public Affairs Bulletin 88 (Library of Congress, 1950).

argued, to have consulted Congress and sought congressional approval. The entry of Chinese Communist troops broadened the Korean War far beyond the police action originally anticipated. A substantial body of opinion consistently supported the President's action as a valid exercise of his power to dispose and assign the Armed Forces.

The issue also was raised in 1951 and 1952 over presidential authority to send troops to European duty. In view of the speed with which the nation is likely to become involved in international crises, the President's plenary authority over the Armed Forces no doubt will prevail. Thoughtful citizens, however, fear future misuse of such near-absolute power. The power of the purse is the most effective check, but rigid controls through appropriations are not likely under crisis conditions.

When the President proclaims a national emergency, a number of powers become effective. These were authorized by statutes enacted as early as 1901 and include: calling of personnel of Army, Navy, Air Force, Marines, and Coast Guard; credit control by Federal Reserve Board; suspension of eight-hour day in government employment and contracts; issuance of war-risk insurance; and many others.

In the Formosa Strait crisis, President Eisenhower in 1955 secured from Congress advance "authorization" through a joint resolution to employ the Armed Forces to protect Formosa and the Pescadores. A similar "grant" was made in 1957 to cover possible Communist aggression in the Middle East. The use of the Armed Forces in Lebanon in 1958 was "justified" in part by this authorization.

Foreign Affairs. As in military affairs, the President dominates the field of foreign affairs. The Constitution gives him authority to make treaties (with the consent of two-thirds of the Senate), to appoint diplomats and consuls (subject to ratification by a Senate majority), and to receive foreign diplomatic and consular representatives.

Treaties. Most treaties are negotiated through the usual diplomatic channels, utilizing the regular diplomatic agents of the countries involved. A projected treaty to govern international extradition between the United States and Brazil would be negotiated by the State Department and the Brazilian Ambassador in Washington, or by the Brazilian foreign ministry and the American Ambassador in Rio de Janeiro. A convention or treaty of extraordinary importance or of multilateral nature may be negotiated by the Secretary of State, or some special agent or commission. President Wilson went to Europe to participate in framing the Treaty of Versailles.

Negotiation completed, the Chief Executive sends the treaty to the Senate for its approval. Individual senators are consulted frequently in advance of and during negotiation stages. The Senate Foreign Relations Committee plays the key role in ratification. It holds hearings, at which State Department officials may be called to testify. A two-thirds majority on the floor of the Senate is required to approve a treaty.

The scope of the treaty-making power is not precise. Apparently the power may not be used to accomplish something specifically forbidden to the Federal government by the Constitution. But the treaty power has been used to achieve Federal control in spheres where no other authority existed. In 1916, after adverse lower-court decisions voided attempts under the commerce clause to regulate and protect migratory birds, a treaty was negotiated and ratified with Great Britain, acting for Canada, providing that each country should protect such wild fowl. After the treaty came into force, Congress implemented it by enacting a law providing for the protection of migratory birds. The treaty and act were found constitutional in *Missouri v. Holland* [252 U.S. 416

(1920). See also pp. 434–435]. As a result of this case, the power of Congress to enact laws in support of treaties obviously becomes broader than the ordinary statute-making authority, but the precise limits of such power are as yet unsettled.

Executive Agreements. The President may also make international arrangements without senatorial participation. "Executive agreements" are pledges of certain action by executives of two countries. For example, the President will exchange letters with the Prime Minister of Canada; in them, each executive agrees to permit citizens of the other country to travel without passports. A famous example of this type of arrangement is the "gentlemen's agreement" between President Theodore Roosevelt and the Emperor of Japan under which Roosevelt agreed to try to persuade Congress to kill exclusion legislation and the Japanese agreed to forbid the emigration of coolies.

During the last twenty-five years the "trade agreement" has come into prominence. Neither treaty nor executive agreement, it occupies a special category created by the Trade Agreements Act of 1934 and subsequent renewals. Recognizing its inability to reduce tariff rates due to the pressure of affected groups, Congress vested in the President authority to adjust tariff barriers by negotiation and allowed him to proclaim special trade agreements with individual foreign countries. These reciprocal trade agreements, although not submitted to the Senate for confirmation, are fully enforceable in the courts.

Recognition. Another highly important power of the President in foreign affairs is the authority to recognize countries and governments. This is done by receiving diplomatic representatives of the nation or regime, or by altering the assignments or instructions of our agents abroad. For example, after the Italians completed the conquest of Ethiopia in 1936, the American legation in Addis Ababa was reduced to a consulate. Likewise, the President may indicate dissatisfaction with a nation's representative by dismissing him or asking his recall. A more extreme form of indicating displeasure with a country involves closing its consulates, as was done to those of Germany in 1940.

Recognition may be used as an instrument in foreign policy; it has often been withheld to show disapproval of a government. From the time of the Bolshevik Revolution of 1917 until 1933, this country indicated distaste for the Communist regime by maintaining no official contact with the Soviet government. When President Roosevelt decided to open diplomatic relations, he cabled directly to the President of the Council of Soviets. The Russian government sent M. Litvinov, its foreign commissar, to discuss Soviet-American problems. The talks concluded, the two nations exchanged ambassadors. The extinction of the independence of a nation is recognized by the United States through the closing of a legation or embassy. Recognition by the United States often is a most crucial matter for a new regime in a Latin-American republic. Withholding recognition, as from the Grau San Martín government in Cuba in 1933, may cause the downfall of one regime and the rise of another.

Delegation. Although the question of the delegation of legislative authority by Congress to the President requires more detailed attention in another place, this delegation in the field of foreign affairs has special status.

A case arose over the President's order proclaiming an arms embargo which banned shipments to Bolivia and Paraguay, then at war over the Gran Chaco. Congress had provided that an arms embargo could be put in force by the President whenever he found that a condition of war existed. President Roosevelt's order was attacked by an aircraft concern prevented from exporting planes to the belligerents. The Supreme Court upheld the constitutionality of the legislation and the proclamation on the ground that the President had a very special responsibility in foreign affairs.[1] The neutrality laws of the late 1930s employed the arms embargo as a prominent feature, and their constitutionality was regarded as certain after the Curtiss-Wright case.

Occasionally treaties and laws conflict. Which shall the courts enforce? The two have equal standing; so the courts enforce the latest expression of policy, whether law or treaty.

The Bricker Amendment. Contending that the presidential power over foreign affairs has expanded so much that a curb is required, a bipartisan congressional bloc led by Senator Bricker of Ohio proposed a remedial constitutional amendment. Its sponsors contend that there is a real danger that internal law may be altered by international agreement without legislation, that actions or proposals of the United Nations and its agencies may threaten our constitutional rights.

In its original form the three substantive sections of the proposed amendment were:

Section 1. A provision of a treaty which conflicts with this Constitution shall not be of any force or effect.

Section 2. A treaty shall become effective as internal law in the United States only through legislation which would be valid in the absence of treaty.

Section 3. Congress shall have power to regulate all executive and other agreements with any foreign power or international organization. All such agreements shall be subject to the limitations imposed on treaties by this article.[2]

Proponents argue that the amendment will make it unmistakable that treaties cannot enlarge or violate the Constitution. Treaties affecting internal law must be implemented through legislation which (this is the "which clause") could have been passed without a treaty. Section 3 would bring executive agreements under congressional control and subject them to the "which clause."

The arguments of the opponents of the Bricker amendment are these: It would seriously weaken this country in international relations; there is no valid basis for fear of the abuse of the foreign-affairs power of the President and the Senate under the present provisions of the Constitution; adequate checks are in the hands of Congress and the courts; and the procedure for treaty making and ratifying would be too cumbersome and involved for the necessary flexibility for an age of crisis. In 1954 the Senate joint resolution containing the Bricker amendment secured favorable Senate committee action. By a margin of only one vote it failed to muster the necessary two-thirds majority of the Senate. Resubmitted in revised form in later Congresses, the amendment promises to come up again and again despite vigorous opposition from the executive branch.

JUDICIAL AND ADMINISTRATIVE POWERS

Pardons and Reprieves. The President's power to grant pardons and reprieves is judicial and exclusive. A *pardon* is a release

---

[1] *United States* v. *Curtiss-Wright Export Corp.*, 299 U.S. 304 (1936). For a discussion of the foreign affairs power, see Foster H. Sherwood, "Foreign Relations and the Constitution," *Western Political Quarterly*, vol. 1 (December, 1948), pp. 386–399.

[2] S. J. Res. 1, 83rd Cong., 1st Sess. This is the text given in John W. Bricker, "Making Treaties and Other International Agreements," *Annals of the American Academy*, vol. 289 (September, 1953), pp. 136–137. The wording was later altered.

from liability for punishment. Absolute pardon wipes out all charges and restores the condition that existed before the alleged crime was committed. Conditional pardon may leave certain disabilities or obligations on the offender. A *reprieve*, also issued by the executive, postpones the execution of a penalty; its use may be dictated by humanitarian considerations or by the expectation of new evidence. An *amnesty* is a group pardon, issued by the President to a class of offenders. A good example of amnesty is Jefferson's freeing of all those convicted under the Alien and Sedition Acts of 1798.

In general, Congress cannot restrict the President in the exercise of his pardoning power. A congressional attempt to avoid by statute the full effect of President Johnson's proclamation of amnesty for Confederates convicted of treason was declared unconstitutional on the ground that it interfered with the pardoning power [*Ex parte Garland*, 4 Wall. 333 (U.S. 1867)].

May the President pardon a person found guilty of contempt of a Federal court or one of the houses of Congress? It appears that the President may pardon any offender except one convicted by impeachment. President Roosevelt issued a last-minute pardon to Dr. Francis E. Townsend, old-age-pension advocate, who was held in contempt of a House of Representatives investigating committee; no contest arose, however, for the leading sponsor of the pardon was the chairman of the House committee. Earlier, a presidential pardon for contempt of court was upheld in the Supreme Court [*Ex parte Grossman*, 267 U.S. 87, 122 (1925)].

Execution of the Laws. The constitutional provision that the President "shall take care that the laws be faithfully executed . . ." and the section requiring his oath to preserve, protect, and defend the Constitution give the Chief Executive very broad responsibilities. In practice, Congress confers upon subordinate officials and upon independent agencies law-enforcement duties. The President's role is to oversee execution of the laws. This general responsibility is carried out through the various powers of the President—appointment, war, foreign affairs, legislative—and through an indefinite authority that flows from his oath and the execution-of-the-laws clause.

A striking illustration of this extra authority is found in one of the most dramatic cases in American constitutional law, *in re Neagle*.[1] Because of an adverse court decision, David S. Terry and his adventuress wife threatened bodily harm to Mr. Justice Field of the Supreme Court. Although there was no specific law, a deputy marshal was assigned to protect Field while riding circuit in California. Meeting Field in a railroad-station restaurant, Terry attacked him; the marshal shot and killed Terry. The marshal, Neagle, was charged in the state court with murder. The Federal court issued a writ of habeas corpus directing his release, and it was upheld in the Supreme Court. The highest tribunal declared that the executive possessed authority implied by the nature of government under the Constitution. Therefore, the President may use as much force as necessary or expedient to execute the laws and protect Federal property and agents.

The President has very great discretion in enforcing the law. First he must interpret the law, a process that touches upon both legislative and judicial sides. After interpretation, the President decides which laws to enforce vigorously, slightly, or not

[1] 135 U.S. 1 (1890). The background of the case is described in interesting fashion by Carl B. Swisher, *Stephen J. Field, Craftsman of the Law* (Washington, D.C.: Brookings, 1930), pp. 321–361.

at all. The laws on the statute books are so extensive that the President and his subordinates must pick and choose those for particular attention.

Inherent Power Limited. A highly significant controversy over the powers of the President arose during the Korean conflict over government seizure of the steel industry in 1952. The United Steelworkers of America voted to strike if negotiations failed to produce a satisfactory new contract when the old one expired. On the eve of the strike deadline, President Truman seized and directed the Secretary of Commerce to operate the steel industry. A district-court judge ruled the seizure invalid, and the appeal was hurried into the Supreme Court.

Millowner's counsel argued that the presidential order constituted lawmaking, a function expressly confined to the Congress. The government attorneys based their case on the aggregate of the President's "inherent" powers exercised to avert a national catastrophe. No specific statute was cited as justification for the action. The Court ruled that the President lacked the authority to order the seizure, not possessing the power as Commander in Chief, custodian of executive power, executor of the laws, or Chief Executive acting under the aggregate of his powers.[1] The minority opinion stressed the paramount responsibility of the President faithfully to execute the laws.

LEGISLATIVE POWERS

The Veto Power. The founding fathers also departed from strict separation of powers in authorizing the President to recommend and veto legislation. A bill passed by both houses of Congress must be submitted to the President before becoming law. If he approves, he signs the measure. If he disapproves the measure, he returns it to the house of origin with his objections. The proposed legislation dies unless each house by a two-thirds majority passes it over the veto, in which case it becomes law without presidential approval. If the President does not return the bill within ten days, excluding Sundays, it becomes law without his signature. But if Congress adjourns before the ten days have elapsed, the President may kill the bill by failing to act upon it; this is a "pocket veto" [*Okanogan Indians v. United States*, 279 U.S. 655 (1929)], and it is absolute. The President may approve legislation within the ten-day limit even when Congress has finally adjourned [*Edwards v. United States*, 286 U.S. 482 (1932)].

All bills and joint resolutions except constitutional amendments are sent to the President for approval. Concurrent resolutions, in which both houses join in a declaration of principles or opinion, and simple resolutions, which deal with internal affairs of one house, need not be sent to the President because neither has the effect of law.[2]

Governors in thirty-nine states are empowered to exercise the item veto with appropriation bills, but the President does not possess this power. The item veto empowers

[1] *Youngstown Sheet and Tube Co. v. Sawyer*, 343 U.S. 579 (1952). The majority opinion was written by Mr. Justice Black. The dissenting opinion came from Chief Justice Vinson. The vote was 6 to 3.

[2] In recent years Congress has been encroaching on the President's power by using the concurrent resolution to nullify executive acts and terminate delegated powers. Both the Reorganization Act of 1939 and the Lend-Lease Act of 1941 contained provisions for nullification or termination by concurrent resolution. The problem is discussed in Howard White, "The Concurrent Resolution in Congress," *American Political Science Review*, vol. 35 (October, 1941), pp. 886–889; and Cornelius P. Cotter and J. Malcolm Smith, "Administrative Accountability to Congress: The Concurrent Resolution," *Western Political Quarterly*, vol. 9 (December, 1956), pp. 955–966.

PRESIDENTIAL VETOES, 1909-1962

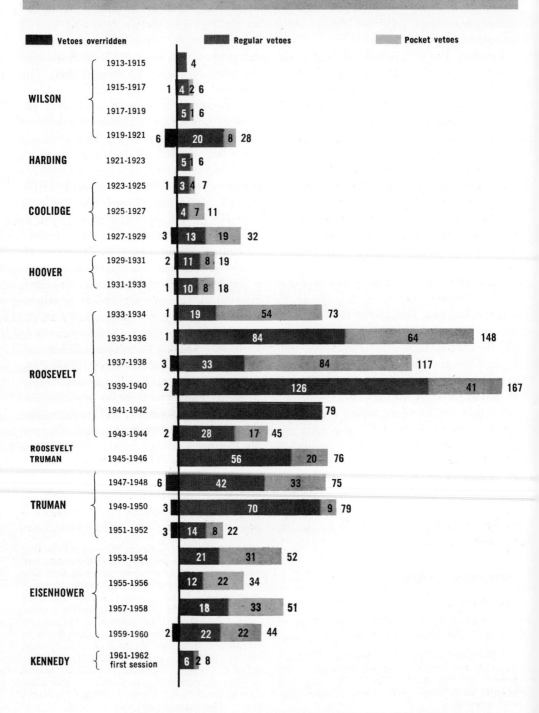

| Vetoes overridden | Regular vetoes | Pocket vetoes |

WILSON
- 1913-1915 — 4
- 1915-1917 — 1 4 2 6
- 1917-1919 — 5 1 6
- 1919-1921 — 6 20 8 28

HARDING
- 1921-1923 — 5 1 6

COOLIDGE
- 1923-1925 — 1 3 4 7
- 1925-1927 — 4 7 11
- 1927-1929 — 3 13 19 32

HOOVER
- 1929-1931 — 2 11 8 19
- 1931-1933 — 1 10 8 18

ROOSEVELT
- 1933-1934 — 1 19 54 73
- 1935-1936 — 1 84 64 148
- 1937-1938 — 3 33 84 117
- 1939-1940 — 2 126 41 167
- 1941-1942 — 79
- 1943-1944 — 2 28 17 45

ROOSEVELT TRUMAN
- 1945-1946 — 56 20 76

TRUMAN
- 1947-1948 — 6 42 33 75
- 1949-1950 — 3 70 9 79
- 1951-1952 — 3 14 8 22

EISENHOWER
- 1953-1954 — 21 31 52
- 1955-1956 — 12 22 34
- 1957-1958 — 18 33 51
- 1959-1960 — 2 22 22 44

KENNEDY
- 1961-1962 first session — 6 2 8

The use of the veto varies widely from President to President and from period to period. Note that the largest number of vetoes overridden (Wilson, 1919–1921, and Truman, 1947–1948) occurred when a President of one party faced a Congress of another.

the executive to strike out specific sections or parts, yet sign the remaining portion of the bill. During the decade of the 1930s, after Congress showed an inability to resist group pressure for higher and higher appropriations, a proposal to give the President an item veto was revived.

A general item-veto power would require a constitutional amendment, and dozens have been proposed in the House and Senate. Considerable support for this has been evident at times, but no action has yet been taken. By inserting a clause into each appropriation bill, giving the President the power to strike out items, Congress might delegate a limited item veto to the executive. Competent attorneys have maintained that this power may be given by Congress without constitutional amendment. Arguments for giving the President an item veto are that it will help reduce extravagance, eliminate pork-barrel legislation, and assure executive responsibility for fiscal affairs. Contrariwise, it is argued that legislative responsibility will be weakened and presidential power increased to an unwarranted extent.

Power to Recommend Legislation. Presidential authority to recommend legislation and call special sessions of Congress is found in Article II, Section 3:

He shall from time to time give to the Congress information of the state of the Union, and recommend to their consideration such measures as he shall judge necessary and expedient; he may, on extraordinary occasions, convene both Houses, or either of them, and in case of disagreement between them, with respect to the time of adjournment, he may adjourn them to such time as he shall think proper; . . .

The President's major annual message, roughly comparable to the Speech from the Throne in British countries, is called the State of the Union message. Both Washing-ton and Adams delivered their important messages in person and orally. Jefferson declined to appear before Congress, preferring to send written messages. Wilson revived the practice of appearing personally, continued since that time. Lesser messages may be sent in considerable number; they are read by a clerk, often inaudibly, and printed in the *Congressional Record*.

The personal appearance of a President before a joint session calls public and congressional attention to his message. This is heard by tens of millions over the radio and heard and seen by additional millions through television and newsreel. The annual and special messages of the Presidents recommend the enactment of certain bills or the adoption of certain policies. Most Presidents also attempt to secure the passage of their proposals through appeals to public opinion and by pressure on Congress.

The President may call Congress into special session, but he lacks the power, possessed by many state governors, to stipulate the exact purpose of the special session. Once assembled, Congress may proceed with any matter within its competence, even the impeachment of the President. Although the President can convene either house separately, this privilege has been used very little. Since the two houses rarely disagree seriously over the date of adjournment, the President's power in this regard is of little practical importance.

Delegation of Legislative Power to President. Congress often delegates power to the President to issue rules and regulations which have the effect of law. Although it is a well-recognized rule of constitutional law that the legislative body may not delegate legislative power to the executive, it may, after determining the policies and standards, delegate power to an executive officer to issue the necessary rules and regulations to carry out those policies.

The Supreme Court has generally upheld such delegations, but on two occasions in recent years the courts ruled that Congress made unconstitutional delegations of legislative authority to the executive. These cases arose out of the National Industrial Recovery Act of 1933. The first concerned a provision in the law giving the President discretion to bar from interstate commerce oil produced in excess of state quotas. Here the Court ruled that Congress failed to establish sufficient standards or policy to guide the executive [*Panama Refining Co. v. Ryan,* 293 U.S. 388 (1935). For a fuller discussion, see p. 242]. The second case arose over the general NRA code-making authority, which the Court found delegated lawmaking to an even greater extent and was therefore more unconstitutional [*Schechter Poultry Corp. v. United States,* 395 U.S. 495 (1935). See also p. 242]. Other instances of delegation have received approval in the courts, or have not been tested. The flexible tariff, under which the President may alter duties on imports as much as 50 per cent, was found constitutional [*Hampton & Co. v. United States,* 276 U.S. 394 (1928)].

The special responsibility of the President for foreign affairs has already been treated; congressional delegation of power to proclaim when a state of war exists between other countries was declared valid in the Curtiss-Wright case. No one has successfully challenged the validity of vesting in the executive the authority to alter the gold content of the dollar.

How may the line between invalid and valid delegation be drawn? The general rule is that Congress must fix primary standards. Power to fill in details may be conferred upon the executive. The Court has not been consistent, and the line of demarcation between proper and improper delegation can only be guessed after careful reading of the cases cited and judging the contemporary temper of the Court.

Emergency Powers. Congress has conferred upon the President many powers that the executive may exercise only during an emergency. The existence of such powers was brought forcibly to the attention of the nation when the newly inaugurated President, Franklin Roosevelt, proclaimed a bank holiday and prohibited gold and silver exports and foreign-exchange transactions. This action was taken under the "Trading with the Enemy Act" of 1917. Some doubted whether the act was still in force, but the Emergency Banking Act three days later validated the President's proclamation and gave him control over gold during a "national emergency."

After this, a decade of controversy over emergency powers followed. Congress repeatedly added to this category of presidential authority, although not without strong opposition. Much of the heat was over delegation of discretionary authority to the President without limitation of emergency periods. The definition of an emergency is left to the President, but it is clear that periods of foreign danger or economic depression are implied in the various statutes.

THE CHIEF MAGISTRATE

The People's Choice. James Bryce, one of the greatest foreign students of American institutions, entitled a short chapter in his *American Commonweath* "Why Great Men Are Not Chosen Presidents."[1] He gave three reasons: (1) A small proportion of first-rate Americans enter politics; (2) American politics offers few opportunities

[1] (New York: Macmillan, 2 vols., 1889), vol. 1, pp. 71–80.

for individual distinction; and (3) prominent men make more enemies than do "safe" men.

Bryce was impressed with the excess of party loyalty and the power of party organization; he blamed party managers for choosing undistinguished candidates rather than risk loss of an election with a prominent one. Looking back over American history, one may see that Bryce was troubled especially by the fact that between Jackson and Lincoln a number of inconspicuous politicans and soldiers served as President, and that Clay, Calhoun, and Webster, the leading men of the time, never reached the executive office.

If Bryce could have reviewed 150 years of the American Presidency, instead of two-thirds of that, he certainly would have been impressed with men who came later. There is evidence in his own subsequent writings that he modified the views previously expressed.[1]

The nominating method affects the quality of presidential timber greatly. The candidate must be reasonably prominent. Public office is almost indispensable—usually as a governor or a Federal department head, seldom as a senator or representative. His policy convictions and beliefs are important in relation to conditions in the country and sentiment in the party. Personal factors, like religion and personality, are considered. The aspirant for the Presidency normally must have some solid political support, especially in his own state. Presidential hopefuls are most likely to get a major-party nomination if they reside in a large and pivotal state; a state ranking below twelfth or fifteenth in population is unlikely to produce a serious candidate.

[1] See especially James Bryce, *Modern Democracies* (New York: Macmillan, 2 vols., 1921), vol. 2, pp. 66–76.

Neither party, under normal conditions, will choose a candidate from a state sure to go for one party. The party naturally takes for granted a state that it wins regularly; the party with a hopeless position in a given state will gain nothing from seeking a candidate there.

The successful candidate for the Presidency may be the active leader of his party if he has the personal qualities and can command the backing. Theodore Roosevelt, Woodrow Wilson, and Franklin D. Roosevelt all made vigorous party leaders. William H. Taft, Warren Harding, and Calvin Coolidge made no real effort to dominate party affairs. Under favorable political conditions and with the requisite personal qualities, the President can be a strong executive. He is elected by the whole people; he can take swift, decisive action.

Increasingly able men are elected President. When two parties are evenly balanced, outstanding candidates tend to be put forward by each. When one party enjoys a considerable majority over the other, the minority party appears to find the stronger candidates, as did the Democrats with Cleveland, Wilson, and Franklin D. Roosevelt.

Future of Executive Power. Although sentiment against additional authority for the President had reached a high pitch by the end of the Second World War, it was obvious that any halt in the expansion of executive powers was likely to be temporary. Under the American system of government, effective national leadership is most likely to come from the President.

Even if the Congress should reorganize itself by concentrating authority in the hands of its own leaders, this action would be unlikely to upset the trend toward placing more and more responsibility on the Chief Executive. Strengthening the

"Let's see, what'll I look into next?" Congressional investigations frequently reach into other branches of government. [From *Herblock's Here and Now* (Simon and Schuster).]

national leadership, and Congress will get most of its proposed bills from the executive agencies that are doing the day-to-day job of administering existing law.

Actually, further expansion of executive power may be expected. Conditions of the modern world, so critical, both in war and in peace, make speedy and positive action necessary. The President alone can provide this kind of leadership. Congress can investigate, criticize, revise, and do certain other things well, but it is unable to act swiftly enough to beat an aggressor to the punch some Sunday morning at 8 A.M. Therefore, contingents of United States Armed Forces might be ordered to meet an invasion of Norway without a declaration of war by Congress. Congress has found itself unable to resist pressure groups sufficiently to reduce tariffs or to reorganize administrative agencies. Finally, the job is delegated to the President.

Congress is essential. The House and Senate should do more of their own thinking, planning, and drafting. The Union will continue to look to the President for broad

Many Americans demand strong executive leadership; others decry the trend, fearing for the future of democracy with so much power in a single executive.

FOR FURTHER READING

See also works listed at end of preceding chapter.

Berdahl, Clarence A.: *The War Powers of the Executive in the United States* (Urbana, Ill.: University of Illinois Press, 1921).

Binkley, Wilfred E.: *The Man in the White House: His Powers and Duties* (Baltimore: Johns Hopkins Press, 1959).

————: *President and Congress* (New York: Knopf, 1947).

————: *The Powers of the President* (New York: Doubleday, 1937).

Chamberlain, Lawrence H.: *The President, Congress, and Legislation* (New York: Columbia University Press, 1946).

Corwin, Edward S.: *The President's Control of Foreign Relations* (Princeton, N.J.: Princeton University Press, 1917).

Finkle, Jason L.: *The President Makes a Decision: A Study of Dixon-Yates* (Ann Arbor, Mich.: University of Michigan, Institute of Public Administration, 1960).

Grundstein, Nathan D.: *Presidential Delegation of Authority in Wartime* (Pittsburgh, Pa.: University of Pittsburgh Press, 1961).

Harris, Joseph P.: *Advice and Consent of the Senate* (Berkeley and Los Angeles, Calif.: University of California Press, 1953).

Herring, E. Pendleton: *Presidential Leadership: The Political Relations of Congress and the Chief Executive* (New York: Farrar, Straus, 1940).

Humbert, William H.: *The Pardoning Power of the President* (Washington, D.C.: American Council on Public Affairs, 1941).

Larkin, John D.: *The President's Control over the Tariff* (Cambridge, Mass.: Harvard University Press, 1936).

May, Ernest R. (ed.): *The Ultimate Decision: The President as Commander in Chief* (New York: George Braziller, 1960).

McClure, Wallace M.: *International Executive Agreements: Democratic Procedure under the Constitution of the United States* (New York: Columbia University Press, 1941).

Milton, George F.: *The Use of Presidential Power, 1789–1943* (Boston: Little, Brown, 1944).

Neustadt, Richard E.: *Presidential Power: The Politics of Leadership* (New York: Wiley, 1960).

Rich, Bennett M.: *The Presidents and Civil Disorder* (Washington, D.C.: Brookings, 1941).

Schubert, Glendon A., Jr.: *The Presidency in the Courts* (Minneapolis, Minn.: University of Minnesota Press, 1957).

Small, Norman J.: *Some Presidential Interpretations of the Presidency* (Baltimore: Johns Hopkins Press, 1932).

Smith, J. Malcolm, and Cornelius P. Cotter: *Powers of the President during Crises* (Washington, D.C.: Public Affairs Press, 1960).

Taft, William H.: *Our Chief Magistrate and His Powers* (New York: Columbia University Press, 1916).

U.S. House of Representatives: *The Powers of the President as Commander in Chief of the Army and Navy of the United States*, H. Doc. 443, 84th Cong., 2d Sess. (1956).

U.S. Senate, Committee on the Judiciary: *Treaties and Executive Agreements: Hearing before a Subcommittee. . . .* 83d Cong., 1st Sess. (1953).

REVIEW QUESTIONS

1. What is the scope of the President's power to appoint and remove?

2. Describe senatorial courtesy and indicate how it operates in practice.

3. What war powers has the President? To what extent could Congress constitutionally restrict his authority to assign the Armed Forces where and when he sees fit?

4. Indicate the length and breadth of the treaty power. To what extent have the rights of citizens under the Constitution and the Bill of Rights been abridged under it?

5. Define "pardon," "reprieve," and "amnesty."

6. Describe the "seizure" of the steel industry in 1952, and explain the Supreme Court's verdict on its constitutionality.

7. To what extent is the title "chief legislator" properly applied to the President of the United States?

8. What options has the President when he receives a bill passed by both houses of Congress? Explain each.

9. Explain the following: "pocket veto," "item veto," "regular veto."

10. What additional authority accrues to the President by virtue of his role as party leader and "the people's choice"?

Chapter Seventeen

Federal Justice

[The American] . . . is probably the most complex
legal system in the world; a system where constitutionally
independent courts of the Nation operate side
by side—and often in identical matters—with the
separate court systems of each of the sovereign forty-eight
states; where federal courts administer state law
and state courts administer federal law; where the very
essence of federalism, the areas where federal and
state law touch and overlap, is made
integral in the national judicial structure to a degree
greater than in any other federated government.

LELAND L. TOLMAN[1]

. . . the power of the Court, for good or evil,
can scarcely be exaggerated. If it cannot actually
shape the destiny of our country, it can exert a
commanding influence in that direction. It can by its
judgments strengthen our institutions in the
confidence and affections of the people, or, more
easily than any other department, it can undermine
the foundations of our governmental system.

MR. JUSTICE HARLAN[2]

Courts are essential in all organized societies. Their organization and role vary with the form of government, political theories, social and economic systems, traditions,

and customs. Thus, in spite of their common origin, British courts differ in organization and function from those of the United States. The courts of France, Switzerland, and the Soviet Union differ even more.

American courts since colonial times have changed little in form but much in the role they perform. To modernize and adapt them to our changing society calls for the wisest statesmanship.

---

[1] *Columbia Law Review*, vol. 54 (April 1954), p. 650.

[2] *American Law Review*, vol. 37 (January–February, 1903), p. 95. Quoted in Charles G. Haines, *The Role of the Supreme Court in American Government and Politics, 1789–1835* (Berkeley and Los Angeles, Calif.: University of California Press, 1944), pp. 48–49.

WHAT COURTS DO

Settle Disputes. To decide who is "right" in a dispute is one of the oldest functions of courts. Disputes reach the courts as "cases" or "controversies." These may be of three types: civil, criminal, and equity.

Civil cases are usually suits between private individuals, although a governmental body or official may be one of the parties. The object of the suit may be property, money, divorce, custody of children, title, or something else of value.

A criminal case is one in which the government accuses someone of violating a law and seeks to inflict punishment upon the accused.

Cases in equity arise when the parties in a dispute cannot secure "substantial justice" by the application of the ordinary rules of law in a civil suit. The party seeking equity must establish to the satisfaction of the court that he has no adequate remedy at law. Historically, judges handed down decisions in equity to accord "substantial justice" without an elaborate body of equity law, but after centuries of experience, equity law has come to have its own elaborate and highly technical code of rules and precedents. To illustrate a case in equity: *A's* property is about to be seriously damaged by *B*. At common law *A* may wait until the property is harmed and sue *B*; but *B* is penniless, and *A* would be unable to recover. Therefore, *A* secures an order from the court in equity to prevent *B* from injuring his property. If *B* violates the order, he is liable to punishment for contempt.

In settling disputes the courts are governed by law, which may be of several types: constitutional, statutory, administrative, international, or common.

Constitutional law in the United States is the fundamental law embedded in written constitutions. *Statutory law* stems from acts of legislative bodies. *Administrative law* arises from orders and decisions of executives, administrators, and so-called "independent establishments." *International law* comes from treaties, agreements, and customs followed by national states in their dealings with one another and with citizens of other states. *Common law,* brought to this country from Britain, is a body of legal precepts founded on reason as applied in past judicial decisions. All American states use the common law except Louisiana, where early French influence left a background of Roman law. Bound as it is by a written constitution and delegated powers, the Federal government does not enforce common law. Federal courts, however, are guided by common-law principles.

Interpret the Law. Courts also interpret the law. The meaning of words and phrases may be obscure when an attempt is made to relate them to concrete situations. The part that is played by the courts in expanding the Constitution is discussed in Chapter 4.

The judicial role is equally significant where other types of law are concerned. When, for example, a statute or executive order uses the word "may," does this mean "shall"? Does the word "acquire" give authority to take by condemnation? Does a nineteenth-century statute governing "vehicles" apply to motorcars and airplanes today? Does the term "innkeeper" refer to one who operates an overnight tourist motel? How undressed must one be to be legally "nude"? When does a tramp become a "vagrant"? How fast is "forthwith"? The law abounds with such words as "due," "reasonable," "fair," "equitable," and "proper." Construing such words is one of the important tasks of courts.

In performing this task, American courts follow the rule of stare decisis; i.e., they follow precedent established in previous cases unless there is some compelling reason why they should break with the past. An example of a compelling reason was the depression of the 1930s, during which the Supreme Court became convinced that the commerce power should be reinterpreted to give Congress authority to regulate businesses that had become national in scope. Another example involves the changed attitudes that caused the Supreme Court in 1954 to rule state laws requiring racial segregation in conflict with the equal-protection clause of the Fourteenth Amendment.

Following precedents may mean projecting into modern times social concepts, cruelties, and injustices from the past. It may also have the effect of causing the judges to make law and thus impinge upon the prerogatives of the political branches of government.

Lawmaking by the judiciary became so pronounced in the United States, especially after the Civil War, that it evoked much controversy. One of the questions raised was this: Is it consistent with democratic theory and practice to permit the judicial branch— the one most insulated from the popular will —to play such an important part in formulating public policies? Why should judges appointed for life terms, critics ask, decide whether there is to be racial segregation by the states, a subject of vast social and political import? Why should judges be permitted to thwart Congress in enacting child-labor legislation for more than twenty years? Why should judges prevent states from establishing minimum-wage laws for women for nearly a quarter of a century? Why should judges make it so difficult for Federal and state governments to regulate large-scale business, as they did before the Second World War? The fact that questions like these are raised makes it clear that courts are less aloof from the political process than formal robes, ancient ritual, and somber courtrooms suggest.

Check and Balance. An important function of the courts is to check the legislative and executive branches. This they do, first, by deciding the meaning of legislative acts when cases come before them; second, by passing on the legality of executive actions; and third, by determining whether statutes and administrative acts are constitutional. The power of judicial review, discussed in Chapter 4, serves as a restraint on the other two branches, although only eighty-one acts of Congress have been held unconstitutional in the entire history of the country.

Disputes will inevitably arise among the three branches of government. Those between the executive and Congress are likely to be short-lived, inasmuch as frequent elections permit the voters to resolve differences. The situation differs, however, in the event of controversy between political branches and the courts. Judges are appointed for life, so their interpretations of the Constitution may paralyze legislation for long periods until amendments can be added. Judicial review is generally accepted, but it is also widely recognized that courts are not to restrain unduly other branches of government.

The 1937 Controversy. Usually when acts of Congress are declared unconstitutional there is a short flurry of criticism which soon subsides, but this is not what happened during the early days of the New Deal.

Between 1933 and 1937 the Supreme Court consisted of nine justices, all of whom had been appointed prior to 1933 and all but two of whom (McReynolds and Brandeis) had been appointed by Republican Presidents. Their average age was seventy-two (in 1937), the highest in Supreme Court history. Also, it so happened that four (McReynolds, Sutherland, Butler, and Van Devanter) of the six who were over seventy were "conservatives," while the fifth (Chief Justices Hughes) was a "middle-of-

AFFILIATION OF SUPREME COURT JUSTICES WITH MAJORITY AND MINORITY GROUPS*

(On basis of 27 important cases decided between 1933 and 1937)

Justice	By whom appointed and when	Age, 1937	Voted for constitutionality (No. of cases)	Voted against constitutionality (No. of cases)	Per cent favorable to New Deal	
BRANDEIS	Wilson '16	81	19	8	0.704	
STONE	Coolidge '25	65	20	7	0.741	"Liberals"
CARDOZO	Hoover '32	67	20	7	0.741	
ROBERTS	Hoover '32	62	15	12	0.555	Held balance
HUGHES	Hoover '30	75	17	10	0.626	of power
VAN DEVANTER	Taft '10	78	6	21	0.222	
SUTHERLAND	Harding '22	75	6	21	0.222	"Conserva-
BUTLER	Harding '22	71	5	22	0.185	tives"
McREYNOLDS	Wilson '14	75	4	23	0.148	

* For a similar chart based upon a smaller sampling of cases, see H. Arthur Steiner,"Significant Supreme Court Decisions, 1934-1937"(New York: Wiley, 2d ed., 1937), p. 6. See also Charles Herman Prichett,"The Roosevelt Court: A Study in Judicial Politics and Values, 1937-1947"(New York: Macmillan, 1948).

the-roader" and only the sixth (Brandeis) a "liberal."

In three years this Court declared New Deal statutes, or provisions thereof, unconstitutional in twelve instances, five of them during the Court term beginning in October, 1935. On most measures the Court was divided into conservative and liberal blocs. Apparently Justices Hughes and Roberts held the balance of power. This meant that in 5-to-4 decisions, of which there were ten during the four-year period, either Hughes or Roberts cast the deciding vote, and in all probability it was the latter oftener than the Chief Justice.

The situation as it existed during President Roosevelt's first term was unprecedented in several ways: (1) The economic crisis was of major proportions, an emergency psychology was present, and the President was one of such character as to act boldly—even rashly, as some insisted. (2) The justices were older than at any other period. (3) No vacancies occurred during the four-year period. (4) Seldom, if ever, had the Supreme Court been so rigidly and evenly divided into blocs. (5) Never had the courts been called upon to pass judgment upon so many measures involving extremely controversial points of constitutional law in such a short period of time, and in no similar period had they declared so many statutes unconstitutional.

Flushed with victory in the election of November, 1936,[1] the President decided upon a showdown with the courts. Less than three weeks after inauguration, on February 4, he sent a message to Congress which

[1] Nothing was said, however, in the platform of the Democratic party or by the President during the campaign which foreshadowed the drastic proposals that the President later submitted.

prompted one of the most exciting debates in American history.

Court Enlargement Plan. The immediate target of the President's proposals was the aged justices on the Supreme and lower courts.[1] Age undoubtedly has its effect upon judicial decisions, and there have been many, including the then Chief Justice,[2] who have advocated retirement at seventy-five or earlier. To compel retirement, however, required a constitutional amendment, and the President was unwilling to brook the delays and difficulties which this would certainly encounter.

Accordingly, he proposed to "rejuvenate" the courts by making it possible to appoint a new judge for every Federal judge who had served ten years and who remained on the bench after reaching the age of seventy, provided the Supreme Court should never exceed fifteen and not more than fifty new judges should be added to the lower courts. This would tend to embarrass older judges into retiring or resigning, but if they chose to remain, it was with knowledge that younger judges might be appointed to "assist" and perhaps might counterbalance their conservatism. Since there were at the time six justices on the Supreme Court over seventy, had they not retired the President might have appointed six additional judges, raising the membership of the Court to the maximum of fifteen. As things then stood, the addition of six liberals to the three already on the Court would have ensured more favorable consideration of New Deal legislation.

Improving Court Management. Three ad-

ditional proposals were less controversial. One was that the Chief Justice be empowered to assign circuit and district judges to serve temporarily in districts other than their own. Another was that the Supreme Court be authorized to appoint a "proctor" who would be a business manager for the judicial system with the expectation that delays and inefficiencies might be eliminated. The third was that, when the constitutionality of a Federal law was challenged in a private suit before a lower court, the Attorney General should be notified and given opportunity to defend the law. Moreover, it was suggested that such cases should be decided only by courts consisting of three judges. Furthermore, if the lower court should declare the law unconstitutional, either the Attorney General or one of the private parties might take an appeal directly to the Supreme Court. This, it was hoped, would eliminate the situation where private parties could rush to district courts and obtain injunctions from a single judge which would render the enforcement of an act of Congress impossible for several months or years while the measure was running the gamut of legal procedures en route to the Supreme Court where final judgment would be rendered.

The proposal that new justices be authorized for those who failed to retire or resign was defeated in its entirety. Out of it, however, came a measure permitting Supreme Court justices with ten years of service to retire at seventy with full pay. Otherwise, all the President's recommendations were adopted at the time or have been since, either in whole or in part. By an act dated August 24, 1937, district judges may be transferred from one district to another within the same judicial circuit by the senior circuit judge, or from within one circuit to another by the Chief Justice. By the same act, the Attorney General must be

[1] Besides the six on the Supreme Court, a total of twenty-four judges who were seventy or over sitting on lower courts were affected by the President's bill. *Adverse Report on Reorganization of the Federal Judiciary*, S. Rept. 711, 75th Cong., 1st Sess. (1937), p. 33.

[2] Charles E. Hughes, *The Supreme Court of the United States* (New York: Columbia University Press, 1928), pp. 73–77.

given notice of proceedings involving the constitutionality of Federal statutes. Moreover, all such proceedings must be conducted before courts consisting of three judges, one of whom must be a circuit judge.[1]

Still further, if the decision is against the constitutionality of a statute, the case may be appealed by either party directly to the Supreme Court, where the matter must be heard "at the earliest possible time and shall take precedence over all other matters not of a like character." The proposal to create a business manager for the courts was defeated at the time but adopted two years later with the establishment of the Administrative Office of the United States Courts.

Court Changes without "Packing." Although failure to enact the principal feature of his program was a serious political defeat, it has been said that the President "lost his battle but won his war." There is truth in the statement. Shortly after the controversy, vacancies occurred by resignation, retirement, or death, permitting the appointment of younger men. By the fall of 1937, the liberals were clearly in the majority, and by September, 1942, only two of the men who constituted the Supreme Court during the President's first term (Stone and Roberts) remained, while the President had appointed 38 of the 55 sitting on the courts of appeals and 138 of the 230 judges sitting on district and other United States courts. It is safe to say that most of these appointees held views acceptable to the President at the time of appointment.

Even before any changes were made in the personnel of the Supreme Court, the Court manifested a change of mind by (1) reversing its previous attitude toward state

minimum-wage laws for women, (2) redefining the commerce clause to include manufacturing, (3) upholding the tax provisions of the Social Security Act, and (4) upholding the Railway Labor Act. Although still not without reverberations, the President's reelection for a third term in 1940 and the outbreak of war in 1941 silenced criticism. Meanwhile, the country adjusted itself to an interpretation of the Constitution that greatly broadened the powers of both the Federal government and the states.

The 1952 Controversy over Inherent Powers. The checking and balancing function was again illustrated in 1952. Then, it will be recalled, President Truman seized the steel mills and kept them operating pending settlement of a dispute between labor and management. The President argued that his constitutional authority to take care that the laws are faithfully executed and to be Commander in Chief of the Army and Navy justified his action even though Congress had passed no legislation stipulating when and how seizure was to be made. First the district court held the President's action unconstitutional, and the steel mills reverted to their owners; then the court of appeals stayed the lower court's order pending review by the Supreme Court, and the mills opened again under government management; finally, in almost recordbreaking time (less than two months after the mills had been seized), the highest court ruled against the President. The mills once more reverted to private owners while the strike recommenced and continued for several weeks afterward. The Supreme Court decision was 6 to 3, and the economic and military consequences were serious, but there was remarkably little indignation registered over the verdict. Once more the American public had witnessed its system of separation of powers and judicial review in full cycle.

---

[1] Temporary restraining orders may still be issued by a single judge when delay would cause irreparable damage.

Restrictions on Courts. The great authority of American courts has encouraged many proposals to restrict court power. Some critics have recommended a constitutional amendment forbidding judicial review. During the period prior to 1937, when Federal courts strongly favored economic *laissez faire*, the suggestion was heard that a special body should be set up with final authority to rule on the constitutionality of social and economic legislation. The recall of judicial decisions by popular vote was advocated in the Bull Moose platform of 1912. The late Senator La Follette proposed a constitutional amendment that would permit Congress by two-thirds vote to override judicial decisions. Some support has been registered for a provision found in a few state constitutions which would require an extraordinary majority vote by the Supreme Court (say 6 to 3 or 7 to 2) before laws could be invalidated.

In the late 1950s the Supreme Court was under heavy fire in Southern states for outlawing the segregation of races. Because a court reversal, or constitutional amendment, is impossible of attainment, critics have attempted to find ways of keeping segregation despite the Court's edict. Some spokesmen for segregation have proposed that Congress forbid United States district courts from accepting cases involving segregation, thus barring them from reaching the Supreme Court. Such a measure is constitutional, it is argued, because of Article III, Section 2, which states that the "Supreme Court shall have appellate jurisdiction, both as to law and fact, with such exceptions, and under such regulations, as the Congress shall make."

Even though such proposals are rejected, Federal courts are not without checks and balances. Judges, being human and sensitive to criticism, are unlikely to resist the persistent pressure of public opinion. Their decisions can be overridden by the slow process of constitutional amendment. Judges die, retire, and resign, providing opportunities for younger men. If sufficiently irked, Congress could refuse to appropriate money for judicial salaries and expenses or impeach judges. In many respects the judiciary is the weakest of the three branches. It possesses neither purse nor sword.

Administer Justice. Courts also perform tasks of an administrative character. They appoint and supervise aides and employees. Each court superintends civil and criminal procedure, involving such tasks as taking bail, appointing juries, admitting attorneys to practice, and assessing and collecting fees. Noncontentious cases (those in which parties are not in dispute) impose duties which are chiefly administrative in nature. Administering estates, appointing receivers in bankruptcy, issuing licenses, performing marriages, and naturalizing aliens, illustrate these. Enforcing court orders, usually through writs,[1] is another administrative task. Disrespect for court orders may be declared contempt and punished by fine or jail. Trial is usually without jury if the contempt is committed in the presence of the court but otherwise with jury if the defendant insists.

---

[1] The most common are "warrants," which are commands for appearance, arrest, search, or seizure; "summonses," which direct plaintiffs in civil suits to appear and make answer to complaints; "subpoenas," which compel the appearance of witnesses or the production of evidence; "writs of execution," which direct defendants to satisfy judgments awarded in civil suits; "writs of ejectment," which eject defendants from real estate held by them which the court has found belongs to plaintiffs; "injunctions," which restrain from threatened damage to property; "mandamuses," which order public officials to perform some act required by law; and "certiorari," which order public officials, especially inferior judicial tribunals, to send up records for review.

Until recently, administration was divided between the Department of Justice and the Federal Courts. Criticism of the inefficient manner in which the judiciary operated led, in 1922, to the establishment of an annual conference of senior circuit judges under the chairmanship of the Chief Justice. This was beneficial, but responsibility for administration remained divided. In 1939, Congress established the Administrative Office of the United States Courts. Subordinate to the annual conference of senior circuit judges and the Supreme Court, it is managed by a director and assistant director appointed by the Supreme Court for indefinite terms.

The Administrative Office. Creation of the Administrative Office made a clearer distinction between judicial administration and law enforcement. The Department of Justice retains full responsibility for the latter, while the task of over-all administration of the judicial system was centralized in the Administrative Office. One interesting result of its work has been periodic conferences in the various circuits, attended by both Federal and state judges and attorneys.

The Office is divided into five main divisions. The Division of Business Administration prepares the budget for all courts but the Supreme Court and provides quarters, supplies, and management services.

The Division of Personnel looks after classification, pay, and related matters.

The Division of Procedural Studies and Statistics furnishes information about the state of judicial business throughout the country and recommends steps that will expedite justice and achieve economies.

The Probation Division supervises the Federal probation system—a task previously performed by the Bureau of Prisons, Department of Justice.

The Bankruptcy Division keeps in touch with bankruptcy proceedings pending in Federal courts and recommends ways to expedite them.

CONSTITUTIONAL COURTS

Constitutional and Legislative Courts Distinguished. Federal courts are of two general types: constitutional and legislative. Constitutional courts are established under Article III to exercise "the judicial power of the United States." These are the Supreme Court, courts of appeals, district courts, Customs Court, Court of Customs and Patent Appeals, and Court of Claims. Legislative courts do not exercise the judicial power; they help administer laws passed by authority of powers delegated to Congress.

Both constitutional and legislative courts are authorized by the Constitution and created by Congress. Their differences lie in the source of their authority and the nature of cases which come to them. Article III mentions the types of cases and controversies to which the judicial power extends, these must all come before constitutional courts.

Legislative courts are created under the implied-power clause as necessary and proper instruments for carrying out authority delegated to Congress. Courts in American territories, for example, are justified by the power given to Congress to acquire and govern such places. The Tax Court is based on the power given to Congress to lay and collect direct and indirect taxes. The Court of Military Appeals rests on authority granted Congress to make rules for the government and regulation of the land and naval forces. The provisions of Article III concerning terms, pay, and removal apply to judges of constitutional courts; Congress has a free hand in providing for judges of legislative courts.

Jurisdiction of Constitutional Courts. Article III of the Constitution extends "the

FEDERAL COURT SYSTEM

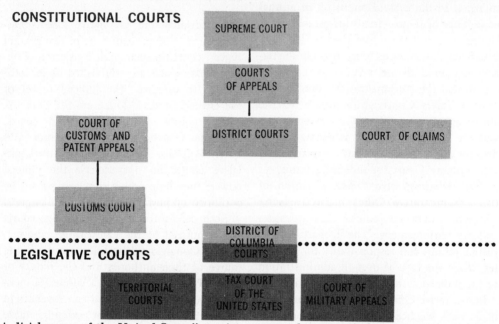

CONSTITUTIONAL COURTS

SUPREME COURT

COURTS OF APPEALS

COURT OF CUSTOMS AND PATENT APPEALS

DISTRICT COURTS

COURT OF CLAIMS

CUSTOMS COURT

DISTRICT OF COLUMBIA COURTS

LEGISLATIVE COURTS

TERRITORIAL COURTS

TAX COURT OF THE UNITED STATES

COURT OF MILITARY APPEALS

judicial power of the United States" to nine classes of "cases" and "controversies." Some of these raise *Federal questions* because they involve the Constitution, acts of Congress, treaties, or vessels on navigable waters. Other cases and controversies reach Federal courts because of the *character or citizenship of the parties* involved.

Item 6 of the accompanying table has been qualified by the Eleventh Amendment, Congress, and the courts in keeping with the precept that a sovereign cannot be sued

FEDERAL QUESTION	1. Cases arising under the Constitution 2. Cases involving Federal laws and treaties 3. Admiralty and maritime cases
CHARACTER OR CITIZENSHIP OF PARTIES	1. Cases affecting ambassadors, other public ministers, and foreign consuls 2. Controversies in which the United States is a party 3. Controversies between two or more states 4. Controversies between citizens of different states (diverse citizenship) 5. Controversies between citizens of the same state claiming lands under grants of different states 6. Controversies between a state or its citizens, and foreign states or their citizens or subjects

without his consent. States may now be sued in Federal courts without their consent only by another state or by the Federal government. If an alien, citizen of another state, or citizen of the same state wishes to sue a state, he can do so only with the consent of the state involved, and then only in state courts. States may, however, initiate suits in Federal courts against aliens, citizens of other states, and foreign governments, although disputes with the latter are often settled by diplomatic negotiation.

Jurisdiction Not Exclusive. The cases and controversies of the table may come before Federal courts, but the Constitution does not so insist. Congress is free to distribute jurisdiction over them as it pleases. Indeed, Congress may completely divest Federal courts of jurisdiction in certain instances. As matters stand, Federal courts have *exclusive* jurisdiction over some of them, *concurrent* jurisdiction over others, and totally *denied* consideration of still others. The division of responsibility is given in the next table.

Supreme Court. Article III states that "The judicial power of the United States shall be vested in one Supreme Court, and in such inferior courts as Congress may from time to time ordain and establish." Only a Supreme Court is specifically mentioned, its creation being mandatory. Others are "inferior courts" which may be created or abolished by Congress.

The Supreme Court was created by the Judiciary Act of 1789. The Court held its first two terms on Wall Street in New York City, but in neither term were there any cases. Its next two terms were held in Philadelphia; thereafter it met in Washington. As first constituted it consisted of a Chief Justice and five associates. Its membership was reduce to five in 1801; increased to seven in 1807; increased to nine in 1837 and ten in 1863; reduced to seven in 1866; and in 1869 it was fixed at nine, where it has remained.

Justices are appointed by the President by and with the advice and consent of the Senate. No qualifications are stated in the Constitution; hence the President is free to

PRESENT JURISDICTION OF FEDERAL COURTS

EXCLUSIVELY FEDERAL	Civil actions in which states are parties (subject to exceptions noted above)
	All suits and proceedings brought against (but not necessarily those initiated by) ambassadors, others possessing diplomatic immunity, and foreign consuls
	All cases involving Federal criminal laws
	All admiralty, maritime, patent-right, copyright, and bankruptcy cases
	All civil cases against the Federal government where consent to sue has been granted
DENIED FEDERAL	Civil suits involving citizens of different states where the amount at issue is less than $10,000
CONCURRENT WITH STATES	Civil suits involving citizens of different states where the amount at issue is $10,000 or more

appoint anyone for whom senatorial confirmation can be obtained. Terms are for good behavior and judges are removable by impeachment only. Only nine judges of constitutional courts have been impeached, and of these four were convicted. Samuel Chase, acquitted in 1805, was the only member of the Supreme Court ever forced to stand trial on impeachment charges.

At the age of seventy, justices may resign and receive full salary for as long as they live, provided they have served on the Federal bench for ten years. Or they may retire at sixty-five with fifteen years of service, and receive full pay for life. If they retire (but not if they resign), they are still Federal judges and eligible for service upon assignment in the lower courts. Salaries are fixed by Congress and, although they can be raised at any time, they cannot be lowered during the incumbency of any particular judge.

Jurisdiction. The Supreme Court has original and appellate jurisdiction. This means that some cases start, or originate, before the Supreme Court, whereas other cases get there by way of lower Federal and state courts.

Only two kinds of cases originate in the Supreme Court: (1) those affecting ambassadors, other public ministers, and consuls and (2) those in which states are parties. All other cases reach the Supreme Court by the appellate route. The Constitution gives the Court appellate jurisdiction, both as to law and fact, "with such exceptions, and under such regulations as Congress shall make." Congress has defined in detail the types of cases that may be taken from lower courts to the highest court.

Cases that do not originate in the Supreme Court come to it by what is technically known as an appeal or by writ of certiorari. Appeals are allowed as a matter of right in cases involving Federal and state powers which obviously require a ruling by the highest court. On petitions for certiorari the Court has the option of granting or denying review. If granted, as comparatively few are, lower Federal or state courts are directed to send up the entire record and proceedings for review or retrial. Typically, about 80 per cent of the Supreme Court's business arises from petitions for certiorari.

Sessions and Conferences. The Supreme Court begins its term annually on the first Monday in October and usually ends early in the following June. Special sessions may be called by the Chief Justice when the Court is adjourned, but the occasion must be of unusual importance and urgency. All sessions are held in the Court's beautiful and spacious white-marble building located across from the capitol building in Washington.

The Chief Justice is the executive officer of the Court; he presides at all sessions and conferences, and announces its orders. Legally, however, his decisions have no greater weight than those of other justices. Associate justices have precedence according to the date of appointment, or, if appointed at the same time, then according to their age. In the absence of the Chief Justice, the associate justice first in precedence performs his duties. The Court divides its time about equally between listening to oral argument and intervening recesses for study and the writing of opinions.

By the time oral argument is finished, the justices have usually made up their minds. After examining records and briefs, the justices compare their views and vote. The Chief Justice states his opinion first but votes last. He also usually decides who will write the Court's opinion. Every judge goes to conference with the knowledge that he may have the responsibility of writing an opinion that will accord with his vote. This encourages each justice to be attentive to

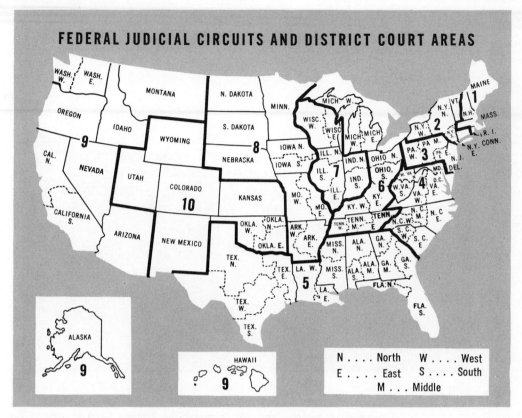

FEDERAL JUDICIAL CIRCUITS AND DISTRICT COURT AREAS

N . . . . North   W . . . . West
E . . . . East   S . . . . South
M . . . Middle

Federal courts below the Supreme Court operate in 10 circuits and 86 districts.

every case and formulate his own views. If a majority cannot reach an agreement, even though the case may be re-argued, the decision of the lower court is allowed to stand.

Decisions and Opinions. Several hundred cases and controversies reach the Supreme Court each year. A large number of appeals and petitions for writs of certiorari are disposed of without serious consideration for want of jurisdiction or merit. Many petitions for certiorari are merely granted or denied upon comparatively short briefs without oral argument. Others involving rather well-settled points of law about which the Court can come to a decision without oral hearings are disposed of as brief per curiam decisions. The remainder are decided after oral argument and in comparatively long written opinions setting forth reasons and justifications.

A decision may be unanimous or divided. If divided, both majority and dissenting opinions are usually written. Often one or more than one justice agrees with the conclusion reached in the majority or the dissenting opinion but for different reasons, in which case concurring opinions may be written. Thus, in a case involving complicated and controversial issues, there may be a majority opinion, a dissenting opinion, and one or more concurring opinions. Six justices constitute a quorum, and at least a majority must concur before a decision is reached. Opinions, as well as information about the disposition of other cases, may be

CASES HANDLED IN FEDERAL COURTS OF APPEALS

Thousands of cases

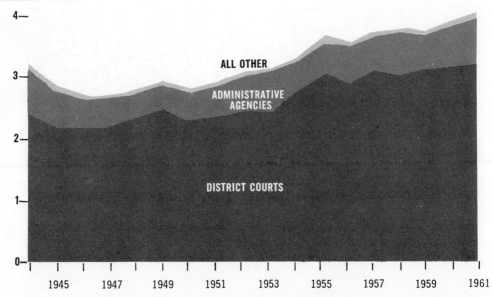

Created about seventy years ago to relieve the Supreme Court of some of the burden of appeals, the court of appeals plays a vital role in the judicial process. (Data from the Administrative Office of the United States Courts.)

found in volumes known, since 1882, as *United States Reports.*[1]

Courts of Appeals. Immediately below the Supreme Court stand the courts of appeals, created in 1891 to facilitate the disposition of cases and ease the burden on the Supreme Court. They operate in the District of Columbia and ten circuits, or regions, into which the nation and its territories have been divided.

Each court has from three to nine judges

[1] Prior to 1882 these volumes were published under the names of the court reporters who prepared them for publication. Their titles, the number of volumes, and dates of issue are as follows: Dallas, 4 vol., 1790–1800; Cranch, 9 vols., 1801–1815; Wheaton, 12 vols., 1816–1827; Peters, 16 vols., 1828–1842; Howard, 24 vols., 1843–1860; Black, 2 vols., 1861–1862; Wallace, 23 vols., 1863–1874; and Otto, 17 vols., 1875–1882.

and usually hears cases in divisions consisting of three judges, but all judges may sit. The justices of the Supreme Court may also sit within circuits to which each has been assigned. Time prevents justices of the Court from "riding circuit," as they did in the early days of the Republic. District judges may also be assigned to serve on the appeals courts, although they may not judge cases which were before them on the lower bench. In some circuits, court is always held in the same city; in others it may be held in two or more designated cities. The courts sit at regular intervals in buildings owned or leased by the Federal government. Appeals judges are appointed by the President with the advice and consent of the Senate for terms of good behavior.

The appeals courts have slight original jurisdiction; they are primarily appellate courts. With few exceptions, cases decided in the district courts, legislative courts, and quasi-judicial boards and commissions go next to the appeals courts. Only the Supreme Court reviews the decisions of the appeals courts.

District Courts. Eighty-six district courts are located in the states. An additional one serves the District of Columbia. Districts have from one to twenty-four judges; in a few instances, one judge serves two or more districts. The judges are appointed by the President with Senate approval for terms of good behavior.

A small state may itself constitute a district; otherwise, districts are arranged with regard for population, distance, and volume of business. Some districts are subdivided into divisions. California, for example, has two districts—northern and southern—but each district is subdivided into a northern and southern division. Nebraska has only one district and eight divisions. In Pennsylvania the three districts—eastern, middle, and western—are not subdivided.

Except for those assigned to the District of Columbia, district judges must reside in the district, or one of the districts, for which they are appointed. A permanent office must be maintained at a principal city, but court is usually held at regular intervals in various cities within each district or division. The court sits in a Federal building if available; otherwise the city or county within which court is held provides facilities.

Most cases and controversies start in district courts. Theirs is chiefly original jurisdiction; no cases come to them on appeal; cases begun in state courts are occasionally transferred to them. In the district courts nearly all accused of committing Federal crimes are tried. Ordinarily, cases are tried with only one judge presiding, but three judges must sit in certain types of cases.

Court of Claims. According to an ancient precept, governments cannot be sued without their consent. Permission to sue has been given by the Federal government for claims of many types. Typically, claims are for unpaid salary, property taken for public use, contractual obligations, and personal injuries for which the Federal government is allegedly responsible. To handle suits like these, the Court of Claims was established in 1855. Claims are barred, however, unless brought within six years. Were it not for the existence of a court of this character, Congress would be swamped with private bills, many involving only petty sums, authorizing payments for injured parties.

The Court of Claims consists of a chief justice and four associate justices who are appointed by the President with Senate approval for terms of good behavior. The court sits in Washington, beginning the first Monday in each December. In 1953 Congress amended the law to provide that this court "is hereby declared to be a court established under Article III of the Constitution of the United States," thus removing it from legislative-court status.

Customs Court. When goods enter the country, customs officers place valuations upon them and collect tariffs. Controversies inevitably arise. To adjudicate these the Customs Court was established in 1890. The court's nine judges are appointed by the President with Senate approval for terms of good behavior. Not more than five may be from the same political party. The court's office is located in New York City, where most of its business is conducted. Congress changed this court from legislative to constitutional status in 1956.

Court of Customs and Patent Appeals. Created in 1910, this court is composed of five members appointed by the President with Senate approval for terms of good behavior. The court usually sits in Washington, but it may convene in any judicial

CASES COMMENCED IN FEDERAL DISTRICT COURTS

Thousands of cases

CIVIL

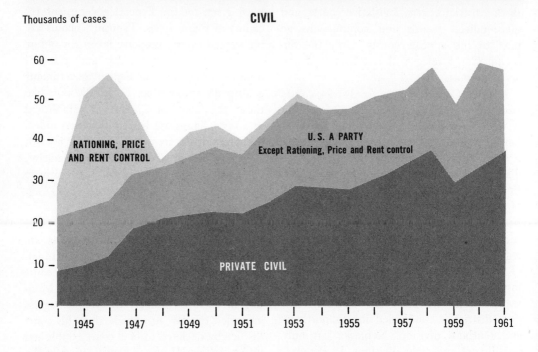

60 –
50 –
40 – RATIONING, PRICE AND RENT CONTROL   U. S. A PARTY
                                            Except Rationing, Price and Rent control
30 –
20 –
10 –   PRIVATE CIVIL
0 –

1945   1947   1949   1951   1953   1955   1957   1959   1961

Thousands of cases

CRIMINAL

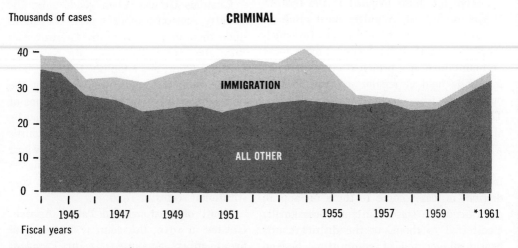

40 –
30 –   IMMIGRATION
20 –
10 –   ALL OTHER
0 –

1945   1947   1949   1951   1955   1957   1959   *1961

Fiscal years

* Figures show defendants in original proceedings commenced.   Figures for other years are for cases commenced.

(Data from the Administrative Office of the United States Courts.)

circuit. The court hears appeals from decisions of the Customs Court and the Patent Office. Its judgments and decrees are final with the exception that they may be reviewed upon certiorari by the Supreme Court. In 1958 Congress shifted this court from legislative to constitutional status.

Court Officers. Attached to each district court are the usual clerks, a reporter, stenographers, bailiffs, and other attendants. These are all appointed by the court and responsible to it. Referees in bankruptcy and probation officers are also appointed by the courts.

In addition, each court appoints one or more commissioners who serve for terms of four years. They are usually part-time quasi-judicial officers who perform about the same functions for the Federal government that justices of the peace handle for the states. Unlike justices of the peace, they do not try petty cases, but they do hold preliminary hearings in criminal cases, issue search and arrest warrants, bind persons over for the grand jury, release them on bail, or discharge them for lack of evidence. They are paid from fees.

LEGISLATIVE COURTS

Legislative courts have diminished in number in recent years. Today they include only the territorial courts, courts of the District of Columbia, Tax Court, and Court of Military Appeals.

Territorial Courts. These are set up by Congress in fulfillment of its power to make all needful rules and regulations respecting American territories. Those with greatest authority are located in Puerto Rico, the Virgin Islands, and the Panama Canal Zone. These differ from district courts in that they have jurisdiction over all matters, local as well as Federal, which Congress may assign directly, or indirectly through the territorial government.

Within each territory there is usually a court resembling a district court with general jurisdiction over the entire area, plus local courts similar to those found in American states. Judges with general jurisdiction serve for a specified number of years. In the Virgin Islands, Canal Zone, and Puerto Rico the term is eight years. In Guam the term is four years.

District of Columbia Courts. Although similar, the Supreme Court draws a distinction between territorial courts and courts of the District of Columbia. Because the District is permanent, and not transitory like territories, the "judicial power" of the United States as defined in Article III operates within it. Accordingly, its courts are constitutional and parallel with other "inferior courts."

The same courts are also legislative, inasmuch as Congress is given full authority to govern the district which constitutes the seat of government. Within the District exist a United States district court, a United States court of appeals, a municipal court, and a municipal court of appeals. The first two deal with Federal cases; the others mentioned handle local controversies.

Other Legislative Courts. The Court of Military Appeals, established in 1950, is a relative newcomer. Although located in the Department of Defense for administrative purposes, it consists of three civilian judges appointed by the President with Senate approval. More details are given later in this chapter.

Certain administrative agencies perform quasi-judicial functions and are sometimes referred to as "legislative courts." Illustrative of these are the Tax Court, the National Labor Relations Board, and the Federal Trade Commission. The Tax Court is a sixteen-member body in the Treasury Department. It hears disputes arising from decisions of the tax-collecting agencies.

CRIMINAL-LAW ENFORCEMENT

The Department of Justice. In the Federal government, as in many of the states, law enforcement is widely dispersed. The Department of Justice, however, is the focal point of much of the responsibility and activity.

The office of Attorney General was among the first established, in 1789, and although a member of the President's Cabinet, the Attorney General did not head a department until 1870. Among its many and expanding duties, this department supervises and directs the work of district attorneys and marshals, operates Federal penal and correctional institutions, conducts all suits in the Supreme Court to which the United States is a party, investigates violations of many types, furnishes legal counsel in Federal cases, and renders legal advice, upon request, to the President and his principal advisers.

Federal Police. No single unified Federal police force exists. The detection and apprehension of lawbreakers is the responsibility of units within several departments. Probably every agency makes investigations of one sort or another, but police work is a major duty of several and an auxiliary function of others. Those having a major responsibility include: Internal Revenue Service (Treasury), Bureau of Narcotics (Treasury), Secret Service (Treasury), Coast Guard (Treasury), Bureau of Customs (Treasury), Federal Bureau of Investigation (Justice), Immigration and Naturalization Service (Justice), Chief Post Office Inspector (Post Office), Food and Drug Administration (Health, Education, and Welfare), Plant Pest Control Branch (Agricul-

ture), Plant Quarantine Branch (Agriculture), Animal Disease Eradication Branch (Agriculture), Animal Inspection and Quarantine Branch (Agriculture), and Meat Inspection Branch (Agriculture).

The general public is not, as a rule, acquainted with the work of these several police agencies, except the FBI, but each agency has a long history, is well established with a highly trained staff, and performs a specialized type of law enforcement. The importance of agency functions is not measured by the number of personnel, which is relatively small. The dispersal of police functions presents problems of definition and coordination of the respective assignments of each agency. Some students of police administration advocate better coordination or consolidation of certain agencies, but a general merger of their activities appears unlikely and perhaps undesirable. Most agencies maintain cooperative relations with other law enforcement officials of Federal, state, and local governments.

The Federal Bureau of Investigation. Of all Federal police agencies, the FBI is best known. Problems of the First World War and prohibition pointed out the need for a permanent body of trained agents to help with law enforcement. The conviction grew that, in order to ensure the closest cooperation with district attorneys, marshals, and the courts, the agents should be under the Department of Justice. As a wave of kidnaping, racketeering, and gangsterism swept over the country, the FBI was organized in 1934. Popularly known as "G men," FBI agents are specially recruited and trained. They have at their disposal almost every device known to modern science for detecting law violators.

The FBI investigates threats to the security of the United States (including the loyalty of its employees and applicants for positions) and all criminal matters not

DEPARTMENT OF JUSTICE

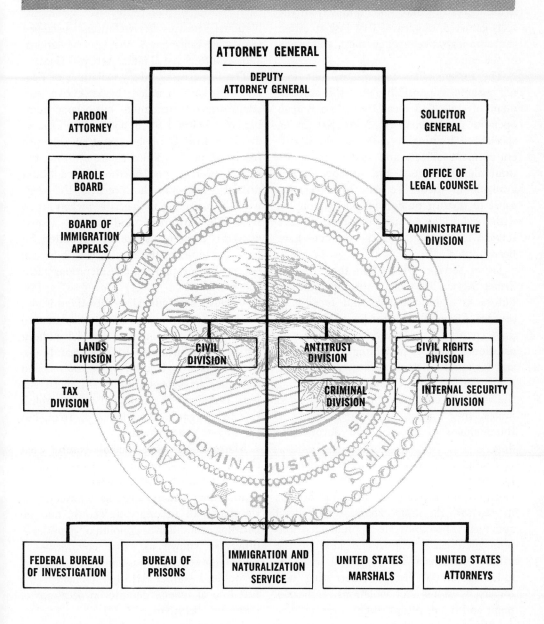

ATTORNEY GENERAL

DEPUTY
ATTORNEY GENERAL

PARDON
ATTORNEY

PAROLE
BOARD

BOARD OF
IMMIGRATION
APPEALS

SOLICITOR
GENERAL

OFFICE OF
LEGAL COUNSEL

ADMINISTRATIVE
DIVISION

LANDS
DIVISION

CIVIL
DIVISION

ANTITRUST
DIVISION

CIVIL RIGHTS
DIVISION

TAX
DIVISION

CRIMINAL
DIVISION

INTERNAL SECURITY
DIVISION

FEDERAL BUREAU
OF INVESTIGATION

BUREAU OF
PRISONS

IMMIGRATION AND
NATURALIZATION
SERVICE

UNITED STATES
MARSHALS

UNITED STATES
ATTORNEYS

specifically assigned to other agencies. The Bureau is primarily a fact-finding agency; it itself does not draw conclusions from the facts gathered, but leaves that task to either the administrative agency most concerned or the courts.

The Bureau offers to assist in, but does not assume responsibility for, the enforcement of state and local laws. The Bureau operates a National Academy for giving specialized training to state and local law-enforcement officers and makes its fingerprint files, laboratory, and advisory services available to them. To date, however, because of distrust of Federal police, coupled with local pride and lack of interest, Bureau services to state and local government have been limited.

Secret Service. Older than the FBI, the Secret Service has more limited jurisdiction but ranks high in quality and breadth of services. Originally created in 1860 to suppress counterfeiting, the Secret Service won additional duties of protecting the President and his family, detecting forgery of government checks, and otherwise safeguarding the fiscal and credit functions of the United States. Its "T men" rival FBI agents in thoroughness of training and devotion to duty.

Common Federal Criminal Offenses. During recent years the number of Federal violations has increased by leaps and bounds in step with the rapid expansion of Federal activities. Thousands are apprehended and prosecuted each year. Some idea of the variety of offenses can be gained from the following partial list: counterfeiting and forgery; Customs Act violations; embezzlement and fraud; escape, flight, mutiny, etc.; extortion and racketeering; Immigration Act violations; Internal Revenue Act violations; Interstate Commerce Act violations; juvenile delinquency; kidnaping; larcency and theft; liquor-law violations; Narcotic Drug

Act violations; National Bank and Federal Reserve Act violations; national-bank robbery; National Bankruptcy Act violations; National Firearms Act violations; postal-law violations; Selective Service Act violations; and White Slave Traffic Act violations.

The Prosecutors. Many violations of Federal laws are handled by executive and administrative procedures, but a large number come before Federal courts. The Department of Justice, upon receipt of evidence from one of the police agencies, turns the matter over to one of the United States district attorneys who prepares the case, with the assistance of specialists when necessary. The attorneys and usually several assistants in each district are appointed for four-year terms by the President with Senate approval. Thus partisan considerations affect the selection.

Within each judicial district there is also a United States marshal and perhaps several deputies. Traditionally these have been partisan appointments for four-year terms. The first Hoover Commission recommended that they be brought under the merit system. President Truman tried to accomplish this by reorganization plan 4 of 1952, but the Senate disapproved.

Marshals are to Federal courts what sheriffs are to states and counties, making arrests, taking charge of prisoners, and executing court orders. They have authority to command all necessary assistance, and on occasion they have appointed deputies—otherwise known as *posse comitatus*—by tens, hundreds, or thousands. Marshals are, to quote a former Attorney General, "the first line of federal defense on occasions of domestic disturbance."

Criminal Procedure. In the background of criminal procedures are the constitutional guaranties of individual rights discussed in Chapter 7. The precise rules that must be followed are prescribed by the Supreme

Court acting under authority granted by Congress. Their purpose is the "just determination" of every criminal proceeding.

Complaint and Examination. A Federal criminal case starts when a sworn complaint is made before a commissioner or other officer charging a person with having committed an offense against the United States. If the complaint indicates that an offense probably has been committed, a warrant for arrest or a summons to appear is issued.

When the accused appears before a commissioner, he is informed of the charges and of his rights to have counsel and preliminary examination. If examination is waived, he is held to answer in the district court. If examined, the defendant may cross-examine witnesses against him and introduce evidence himself. The commissioner then decides whether to discharge or hold for trial.

Indictments and Informations. The next stage is formal accusation of a crime by either indictment or information. Indictment is by grand jury, which consists of from sixteen to twenty-three members, of whom twelve must vote affirmatively to establish a "true bill" of charges. A grand jury remains in existence until discharged by the court, or until its maximum tenure of eighteen months is exhausted. The more populous districts often have several grand juries in existence simultaneously; they do routine criminal indictments or conduct special investigations into particular law-enforcement problems.

Indictment is used in all cases involving the death penalty and other offenses punishable by imprisonment of one year or more. Lesser offenses may be tried on information —a formal statement of charges sworn to by the prosecutor. Cases tried by indictment exceed those where information is used by two-to-one.

The accused is then arraigned. This con-sists of reading (or summarizing) the indictment or information to the defendant in open court and calling upon him to plead. He may plead guilty, not guilty, or —with the consent of the court—*nolo contendere*, a halfway house which is neither an admission of guilt nor a full denial. Surprising as it may seem, the great majority of criminals accused before Federal courts plead guilty. Only about 10 per cent actually run the gamut of full trial.

Trial by Court and Jury. Trial by petit jury is a right that extends, under Article III and the Sixth Amendment, to most Federal criminal proceedings, except when waived by the accused. Only petty offenses are excluded. Juries must consist of twelve members, except when the parties agree to a smaller number. Alternates may be chosen to be on hand in the event that one of the twelve becomes ill or otherwise incapacitated. The rules of evidence, unless otherwise provided by Congress, are governed by common-law principles. The judge is obliged to instruct the parties of their rights and the procedures to be followed. He also instructs the jury on questions of law. The jury verdict must be unanimous to convict.

Before sentencing, the judge gives the defendant an opportunity to make a statement. The judgment of conviction sets forth the plea, verdict or findings, and the sentence. Since 1958 the sentence may be one mandated by law or indeterminate. Legislation in 1958 authorized institutes or joint conferences of Federal judges in the various circuits to make sentencing procedures more uniform. The judgment of conviction may be followed by appeal to an appropriate court.

Probation, Parole, and Detention. Punishment should not only "fit the crime," as Gilbert and Sullivan had their Mikado declare, but the individual concerned. Accordingly, the Juvenile Delinquency Act of 1948 and the Federal Youth Correction

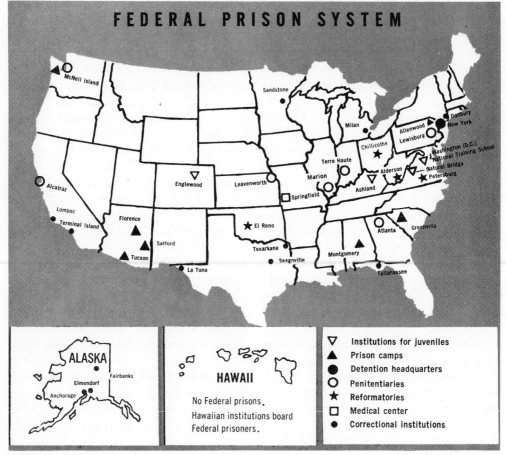

Act of 1950 make possible special handling of youthful offenders. Probation may offer the best promise of reform of an offender, in which case he may be released by a United States district judge for supervision by Federal officers with special training for work of this type. Assignment to Federal prison is based upon diagnosis and classification made during the early days of detention. After a period of imprisonment, parole may be granted by a parole board of five members appointed by the Attorney General. Parolees are supervised by Federal probation officers.

There are no Federal "jails," only "prisons" and other correctional institutions in charge of the Bureau of Prisons, Department of Justice. Many Federal offenders are kept in state and local jails, often found wanting when inspected by the Bureau of Prisons. In 1953, for example, Federal officers inspected 474 jails in thirty-nine states, and of these 11 were rated good, 287 fair, 143 poor, and 33 bad. More recent reports indicate that significant progress is being made in the battle against the notorious jail conditions of insanitation, lack of custodial security, and low nutritional standards, but little against what may be considered jails' most fundamental blights: prisoner idleness and lack of positive rehabilitative programs.

Federal correctional institutions, which now have a capacity of about 20,000, are shown on the map.

MILITARY JUSTICE

Military personnel traditionally has been subject to a different system of justice than have civilians. The British acquired the basis of their system from the Romans. The Second Continental Congress adopted the British court-martial, which has been retained, with some revisions, to the present. The basic pattern is trial by a board made up of military personnel especially appointed for the purpose. This system of administering justice has grown to huge proportions. At the peak of mobilization for the Second World War it handled about one-third of all criminal cases in the nation. The volume of cases remains high because of the abnormally large number of personnel in the Armed Forces.

Military Laws. Under its authority to "make rules for the government and regulation of the land and naval forces," Congress has enacted a large body of military law. Until 1950, each branch of the Armed Forces had its own code of rules, known as Articles of War (Army), Articles for the Government of the Navy, and Disciplinary Laws of the Coast Guard. Enforcement of

(From *Federal Prisons,* **1961.)**

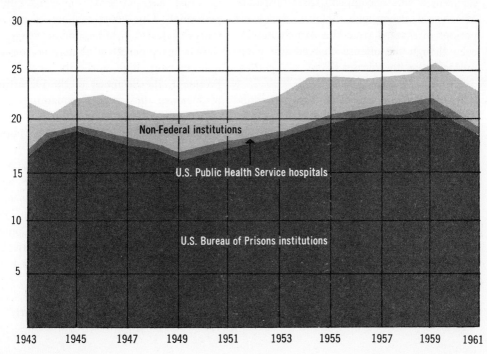

AVERAGE NUMBER OF FEDERAL PRISONERS
1943 to 1961

Thousands

Non-Federal institutions

U.S. Public Health Service hospitals

U.S. Bureau of Prisons institutions

1943   1945   1947   1949   1951   1953   1955   1957   1959   1961

these codes was frequently under attack, especially during the Second World War. Severe penalties were imposed occasionally and publicized widely. The rival interests of command for discipline and of the accused for a fair trial often were resolved in favor of the former. Throughout the services there was a shortage of law officers sufficiently skilled to conduct, prosecute, or defend serious cases. Considerable diversity in procedures and verdicts existed among the several services.

In 1948 a rider on the Selective Training and Service Act made extensive changes in the Army courts-martial, particularly affecting appeals of serious offenses. Two years later Congress passed the Uniform Code of Military Justice, which standardized disciplinary rules for all the services. This new system is explained below.

Civilians are not ordinarily subject to military law. This immunity, the Supreme Court ruled in 1956 (*Reid v. Covert*, 354 U.S. 1), extends in peace time to wives of servicemen who accompany their husbands on overseas assignments. It also extends to persons discharged from the Armed Forces, even though the offense charged was committed prior to release [*Toth v. Quarles*, 350 U.S. 11 (1955)].

Servicemen, on the other hand, are subject to civil authority if permitted by statute or treaty. The Uniform Code allows trial by civil courts for offenses committed off duty within the United States. Treaties and agreements permit trials by civilian courts for off-duty offenses in a number of foreign countries [*Wilson v. Girard*, 354 U.S. 524 (1957)].

Courts-martial. Minor offenses may be punished by commanding officers, but crimes of greater gravity go to courts-martial. Moderate offenses are tried by "summary" courts-martial; other noncapital,

by "special" courts-martial; and the most serious, by "general" courts-martial.

The summary court-martial consists of a single officer, who may try enlisted and noncommissioned-officer personnel and mete out nonsevere punishment. Both trial and defense counsel are appointed by the commanding officer who convened the court, but the accused may request the services of any officer as his defense counsel or may employ civilian counsel at his own expense.

A special court-martial consists of three or more members, who are empowered to punish offenders by penalties of bad-conduct discharges, reduction in rank, two-thirds pay deduction for up to six months, or six months of hard labor. Procedure is rigidly specified to provide maximum protection for the accused. A special court-martial may be convened only by a commanding general or officer of equivalent rank.

A general court-martial consists of five or more members, and if the accused requests it, must have at least one-third enlisted personnel. This court may mete out sentences of death, dishonorable discharge, and similar heavy penalties. It may be convened only by very high authority, such as the President, the Secretary of the Department of Defense, or a top commanding officer designated by the Secretary.

Court of Military Appeals. Decisions of courts-martial are first reviewed by the officers who convened them or by boards established for the purpose. These boards are somewhat comparable to courts of appeals in the civilian court system. Final appeal is to the United States Court of Military Appeals except in those rare cases in which the Supreme Court agrees to rule on questions of law.

The Court of Military Appeals, sometimes called the "GI supreme court," was created in 1950. It consists of three judges appointed by the President from civilian life for fifteen-year terms. The court sits in Washington, D.C. This court is without original jurisdiction but has three types of appellate jurisdiction. It has mandatory jurisdiction over all cases in which the death sentence has been given or in which generals or admirals are involved. It also is required to review cases certified to it by

the judge advocate general of one of the three services. The bulk of cases, however, come from petitions for review from defendants who have received adverse verdicts lower down the military-justice ladder. The court has full discretion in choosing which of the many petitions for review it will grant. It does not, however, review cases that involve sentences of less than one year or the equivalent.

FOR FURTHER READING

Abraham, Henry J.: *The Judicial Process* (New York: Oxford University Press, 1962).

Auerbach, Carl A., et al.: *The Legal Process: An Introduction to Decision-Making by Judicial, Legislative, and Administrative Agencies* (San Francisco: Chandler, 1961).

Aumann, Francis R.: *The Instrumentalities of Justice: Their Forms, Functions and Limitations* (Columbus, Ohio: The Ohio State University Press, 1956).

Aycock, William B., and Seymour W. Wurfel: *Military Law under the Uniform Code of Military Justice* (Chapel Hill, N.C.: The University of North Carolina Press, 1955).

Beisel, A. R.: *Control over Illegal Enforcement of the Criminal Law: Role of the Supreme Court* (Boston: Boston University Press, 1955).

Cahn, Edmund: *Supreme Court and Supreme Law* (Bloomington, Ind.: Indiana University Press, 1954).

Callison, I. P.: *Courts of Injustice* (New York: Twayne Publishers, 1956).

Carr, Robert K.: *Federal Protection of Civil Rights: Quest for a Sword* (Ithaca, N.Y.: Cornell University Press, 1947).

———: *The Supreme Court and Judicial Review* (New York: Rinehart, 1942).

Chute, Charles Lionel, and Marjorie Bell: *Crime, Courts, and Probation* (New York: Macmillan, 1956).

Cummings, Homer, and Carl McFarland: *Federal Justice* (New York: Macmillan, 1937).

Curtis, Charles P.: *Lions under the Throne: A Study of the Supreme Court of the United States* (Boston: Houghton Mifflin, 1947).

Dodge, Arthur J.: *Origin and Development of the Office of Attorney-General*, H. Doc. 510, 70th Cong., 2d Sess. (1929).

Douglas, William O.: *We the Judges* (New York: Doubleday, 1956).

Elliott, Shelden D.: *Improving Our Courts* (New York: Oceana, 1959).

Ewing, Cortez A. M.: *The Judges of the Supreme Court, 1789–1937* (Minneapolis, Minn.: University of Minnesota Press, 1938).

Haines, Charles G., and Foster H. Sherwood: *The Role of the Supreme Court in American Government and Politics, 1835–1864* (Berkeley and Los Angeles, Calif.: University of California Press, 1957).

Harris, Robert J.: *The Judicial Power of the United States* (Baton Rouge, La.: Louisiana State University Press, 1940).

Hart, Henry M., and Herbert Wechsler (eds.): *The Federal Courts and the Federal System* (Chicago: Foundation Press, 1953).

Hughes, Charles E.: *The Supreme Court of the United States* (New York: Columbia University Press, 1928).

Konefsky, Samuel J.: *The Legacy of Holmes and Brandeis: A Study in the Influence of Ideas* (New York: Macmillan, 1956).

Mason, Alpheus T.: *The Supreme Court from Taft to Warren* (Baton Rouge, La.: Louisiana State University Press, 1958).

——— and William M. Beaney: *The Supreme Court in a Free Society* (Englewood Cliffs, N.J.: Prentice-Hall, 1959).

Mayers, Lewis: *The American Legal System* (New York: Harper, 1955).

McCloskey, Robert G.: *The American Supreme Court* (Chicago: University of Chicago Press, 1960).

Mendelson, Wallace: *Justices Black and Frankfurter: Conflict on the Court* (Chicago: University of Chicago Press, 1961).

Murphy, Walter F.: *Congress and the Court: A Case Study in American Politics* (Chicago: University of Chicago Press, 1962).

—— and C. Herman Pritchett: *Courts, Judges, and Politics* (New York: Random House, 1961).

Pound, Roscoe: *Organization of Courts* (Boston: Little, Brown, 1940).

Pritchett, Charles H.: *Civil Liberties and the Vinson Court* (Chicago: University of Chicago Press, 1954).

——: *The Roosevelt Court: A Study in Judicial Politics and Values, 1937–1947* (New York: Macmillan, 1948).

Ramaswamy, M.: *The Creative Role of the Supreme Court of the United States* (Stanford, Calif.: Stanford University Press, 1956).

Rodell, Fred: *Nine Men: A Political History of the Supreme Court from 1790 to 1955* (New York: Random House, 1955).

Schmidhauser, John R.: *The Supreme Court, Its Politics, Personalities, and Procedures* (New York: Holt, Rinehart & Winston, 1960).

Schubert, Glendon A.: *Quantitative Analysis of Judicial Behavior* (New York: Free Press, 1960).

——: *Constitutional Politics: The Political Behavior of Supreme Court Justices. . .* (New York: Holt, Rinehart & Winston, 1960).

Schwartz, Bernard: *The Supreme Court: Constitutional Revolution in Retrospect* (New York: Ronald, 1957).

Smith, Bruce: *Police Systems in the United States* (New York: Harper, rev. ed., 1949).

Spicer, George W.: *The Supreme Court and Fundamental Freedoms* (New York: Appleton-Century-Crofts, 1959).

Umbreit, Kenneth B.: *Our Eleven Chief Justices: A History of the Supreme Court in Terms of Their Personalities* (New York: Harper, 1948).

U.S. Bureau of Prisons: *Federal Prisons* (Leavenworth, Kans.: Federal Prisons Industries, Inc., Press, published annually).

U.S. Director of the Administrative Office of the Courts: *Annual Report.*

U.S. Senate, Committee on the Judiciary: *Adverse Report on Reorganization of the Federal Judiciary,* S. Rept. 711, 75th Cong., 1st Sess. (1937).

——: *Hearings on S. 1392: A Bill to Reorganize the Judicial Branch of the Government,* 75th Cong., 1st Sess. (6 parts, 1937).

Vanderbilt, Arthur T.: *Judges and Jurors: Their Functions, Qualifications and Selection* (Boston: Boston University Press, 1956).

Warren, Charles: *The Supreme Court in United States History* (Boston: Little, Brown, 3 vols., 1922).

Wendell, Mitchell: *The Relations between Federal and State Courts* (New York: Columbia University Press, 1949).

Westin, Alan F. (ed.): *The Supreme Court: Views from Inside* (New York: Norton, 1961).

Whitehead, Don: *The FBI Story* (New York: Random House, 1956).

REVIEW QUESTIONS

1. Why was a dual system of courts decided upon by the Constitutional Convention of 1787? Would it have been better for the Convention to have provided for a single system of Federal courts? A single system of state courts?

2. What do courts do in addition to settling disputes?

3. Distinguish between constitutional and legislative courts and give illustrations of each.

4. Give illustrations of cases over which the Federal courts have exclusive and concurrent jurisdiction. Illustrate also the cases that cannot be taken to the Federal courts.

5. Compare each of the Federal courts as to jurisdiction, organizational detail, and functions.

6. What are the principal police agencies of the Federal government? Would it be better to have a single unified Federal police system?

7. Describe how the Department of Justice is organized and the functions it performs.

8. Describe the Federal penal system. How does this compare with the system in one of the states?

9. What functions are performed by the Administrative Office of the United States Courts? United States commissioners? District attorneys?

10. What steps are customarily taken in a criminal prosecution by the Federal government?

11. Compare the law and procedures that apply under military and civil law.

Chapter Eighteen

Administrative Organization and Procedure

Administration is the capacity of coordinating many, and often conflicting, social energies in a single organism, so adroitly that they shall operate as a unity. This presupposes the power of recognizing a series of relations between numerous special interests, with all of which no single man can be intimately acquainted. Probably no very highly specialized class can be strong in this intellectual quality because of the intellectual isolation incident to specialization; and yet administration and generalization is not only the faculty upon which social stability rests, but is, possibly, the highest faculty of the human mind.

BROOKS ADAMS[1]

Policies and programs adopted by the policy-making bodies—the President and Congress—and passed upon by the courts, do not go into effect until they are carried out by a vast administrative machine. The role of public administration today, however, is much greater than merely that of executing policies decided by others; it has a vital

[1] *The Theory of Social Revolutions* (New York: Macmillan, 1913), pp. 207–208.

part in the preparation of policies for decision by the political officers, and it exercises many delegated policy functions. We live in an administrative age, when the efficiency, effectiveness, and ability of the administrative organization is as important as that of the policy-making bodies whose processes have been described in previous chapters. No sharp line can be drawn between policy and administration. Congress

349

has the duty of checking up to see how its policies are being carried out, and it exercises a continuing control over administration. The highest duty of administrative officers is to prepare policies for consideration by Congress and to exercise policy functions entrusted to them.

The first consideration of public administration is to secure effective machinery to carry out the policies which have been decided upon by the Congress and the responsible executive officers. "A feeble execution," wrote Hamilton in *The Federalist* (70th), "is but another phrase for a bad execution; and a government ill executed, whatever it may be in theory, must be in practice, a bad government." Certain aspects of public administration have been considered in earlier chapters on the executive branch. In this chapter we shall inquire further into the theory and practice of administrative organization and procedure.

ORGANIZATION: THEORY AND PRACTICE

Administrative organization is not an end in itself, but a means to an end. It exists to administer the policies determined by policy formers. A well-organized and well-managed administrative unit will produce the results desired by policy makers, legislative and executive, with efficiency and speed, and with due respect for the rights of the affected parties. Under the most simple circumstances—as in a village with a population of 100—elaborate departmental organization is unnecessary, and responsibilities may be subdivided with ease among part-time officials. A great nation, on the other hand, requires a mighty administrative leviathan with hundreds of thousands of civil servants, plus vast, complex administrative organization.

Staff and Line. The great functions that government provides are usually assigned

to operating departments and are called line functions. They provide the basic services and regulation that government is established to perform. Similar functions are usually grouped together and placed in a common department. In a small city, fire and police services might be included in a department called "public safety," and all health and charitable work grouped in a "public-welfare" department. In a national state, the armed forces could be directed by a department of "national defense," and all services to business could be placed together in a department of "trade and commerce."

To control these operating departments and provide specialized services, staff agencies are created to furnish personnel, planning, finances, or other services needed by the operating or line agencies. Through staff agencies, the administrative head can keep informed of line developments and exert direction and control. The Bureau of the Budget, located in the Executive Office of the President, is an example of a staff agency.

A case often is made for the independence from direct executive or legislative control of a particular staff or line agency. It is argued that a business or entrepreneurial public function ought to be free of the usual governmental restrictions on finance and personnel which were designed to fit ordinary functions. Crusaders for the merit system usually demand independent status for a personnel agency to keep it from the taint of spoils. Making regulatory bodies independent of regular departments is common on the ground that such agencies possess quasi-legislative and quasi-judicial powers and therefore must not be subject to external control under the separation-of-powers principle.

Constitutional and Statutory Provisions. The Federal Constitution is notably silent regarding administrative structure. Article

EXECUTIVE BRANCH OF THE GOVERNMENT

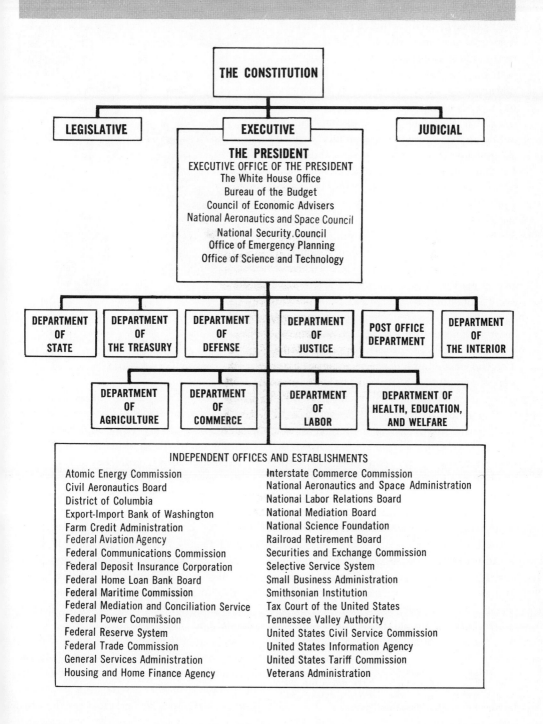

THE CONSTITUTION

LEGISLATIVE — EXECUTIVE — JUDICIAL

THE PRESIDENT
EXECUTIVE OFFICE OF THE PRESIDENT
The White House Office
Bureau of the Budget
Council of Economic Advisers
National Aeronautics and Space Council
National Security Council
Office of Emergency Planning
Office of Science and Technology

DEPARTMENT OF STATE

DEPARTMENT OF THE TREASURY

DEPARTMENT OF DEFENSE

DEPARTMENT OF JUSTICE

POST OFFICE DEPARTMENT

DEPARTMENT OF THE INTERIOR

DEPARTMENT OF AGRICULTURE

DEPARTMENT OF COMMERCE

DEPARTMENT OF LABOR

DEPARTMENT OF HEALTH, EDUCATION, AND WELFARE

INDEPENDENT OFFICES AND ESTABLISHMENTS

Atomic Energy Commission	Interstate Commerce Commission
Civil Aeronautics Board	National Aeronautics and Space Administration
District of Columbia	National Labor Relations Board
Export-Import Bank of Washington	National Mediation Board
Farm Credit Administration	National Science Foundation
Federal Aviation Agency	Railroad Retirement Board
Federal Communications Commission	Securities and Exchange Commission
Federal Deposit Insurance Corporation	Selective Service System
Federal Home Loan Bank Board	Small Business Administration
Federal Maritime Commission	Smithsonian Institution
Federal Mediation and Conciliation Service	Tax Court of the United States
Federal Power Commission	Tennessee Valley Authority
Federal Reserve System	United States Civil Service Commission
Federal Trade Commission	United States Information Agency
General Services Administration	United States Tariff Commission
Housing and Home Finance Agency	Veterans Administration

II, Section 2, states that the President can require an opinion in writing of the principal officer in each of the executive departments on any subject relating to the duties of his office. Congress is given authority to vest by law the appointment of inferior officers in the President alone, in the courts, or in heads of departments. These provisions infer that the framers of the Constitution anticipated executive departments headed by individuals responsible to the President. Certainly the presumption that Congress should establish such departments, functions, and organization as necessary is justified.

Congress acted promptly, and in its first sessions (1789) created the departments of Foreign Affairs,[1] War, and Treasury. Each department was to be headed by a "secretary," appointed by the President. The first Congress also created the offices of Postmaster General and Attorney General, without the status of executive departments. For the next hundred years nearly all Federal functions, as they were created, were grouped into existing or new departments.

The independent agency, responsible to no department, is largely a product of the last seventy years. Its persistence has been due primarily to the conviction that regulatory commissions must be free. The immunity from external control of the Interstate Commerce Commission, for example, is considered of high importance by the common carriers.

Administrative Reorganization. The last quarter century focused attention on improvements for the executive branch of the Federal government. Reorganization efforts have centered around three important surveys: the President's Committee on Ad-

[1] Subsequently changed to State. See Lloyd M. Short, *The Development of National Administrative Organization in the United States* (Baltimore: Johns Hopkins Press, 1923).

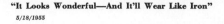
"It Looks Wonderful—And It'll Wear Like Iron"
5/18/1955

Mr. Eisenhower is fitted with the administrative garb recommended by Mr. Hoover. [From *Herblock's Here and Now* (Simon and Schuster).]

ministrative Management, the Commission on Organization of the Executive Branch of the Government (1949), and the second Commission of the same name (1955).

The President's Committee was set up in 1936. Personnel consisted of Louis Brownlow, chairman, Charles E. Merriam, and Luther Gulick. The Committee concentrated on problems of management, considered mainly from the presidential point of view. Its report, issued in January, 1937, was followed by nine special studies. It can be said to have been influential, but Congress failed to adopt many of its recommendations.

Congress established the first Hoover Commission in 1947. The President, the Speaker of the House, and the President pro tempore of the Senate each appointed four of the twelve members. The two parties were represented equally. Task forces were put to work in specialized fields. The Commission and its task forces recommended many changes. About 75 per cent of the first Hoover Commission recommendations have been adopted.

The second Hoover Commission was set up by Congress in 1953. Its composition was similar to that of its predecessor, except that bipartisanship was not required. Seven Republicans and five Democrats were appointed to the Commission. Its powers were greater than the first Hoover group's, in that the new body could recommend the elimination of functions deemed competitive with private industry. Reports of the Commission and of its task forces were published; some of them stirred up much controversy. The record of adoption is lower.

New Departments. Two principal solutions are proposed for the duplication of activities: One is to create new departments; the other is to reshuffle bureaus and agencies within and among existing departments. Most of the reports and studies of reorganization have included both features.

The Department of Health, Education, and Welfare (HEW), finally created under President Eisenhower's reorganization plan 1 of 1953, had been recommended repeatedly by various survey groups for thirty years. Congress held out against the establishment of a new department, despite the urging of Presidents, committees, and the second Hoover Commission. At the time its functions were transferred to the new de-

Vigorous support for the second Hoover Commission's recommendations on taking the government out of business-type enterprises was given by several industrial corporations. (Dowling cartoon, courtesy Basic Incorporated.)

partment, the Federal Security Agency had more employees than three of the executive departments.

Another common recommendation is for a new department to handle the public-works function. The Brookings Institution report in the 1920s and the President's Committee on Administrative Management report in the 1930s favored a Department of Public Works.

A third proposal is for a "Department of Natural Resources," either as a reorganization of Interior or as a new and separate department. A strong minority of the first Hoover Commission supported such a proposal.

Strong sentiment for a department to deal with metropolitan problems preceded President Kennedy's proposal for a "Department of Urban Affairs and Housing" by reorganization order, which was defeated in the House in 1962.

Transfer of Bureaus. The other solution is to reorganize bureaus and services within departments through transfers to bring like functions together and minimize duplication and overlapping of activities. The process is sometimes derisively called "reshuffling" the bureaus. During the last twenty years this type of administrative reorganization has been increased by delegation of authority from Congress to the President. President Hoover asked for power to reorganize at least three times during his administration, but received it only belatedly in 1932 through an amendment to an appropriation bill.

The Committee on Administrative Management advocated "continuing executive responsibility for efficient organization."[1] Changing situations demand organizational flexibility. Again and again it has been

shown that Congress cannot pass reorganization legislation because it is subjected to too great pressure from employees and groups. Consequently, it has been delegating the task to the Chief Executive, subject to congressional veto through a concurrent or a single-house resolution. The accompanying table shows the outlines of the laws permitting reorganization by executive order. These delegations usually are for limited periods; many restrictions are placed on the use of the powers granted; and the Congress normally retains the power to nullify.

The first Hoover Commission recommended strongly that Congress give the President more authority over reorganization than was granted in earlier acts.[2] The Commission declared that many of its most important proposals probably could not be put into effect unless presidential power to reorganize was revived and extended. It called for a forthright delegation, without exceptions, but subject to congressional nullification by passage of a concurrent resolution by both houses within the prescribed time. The Eighty-first Congress enacted the necessary legislation in June, 1949, granting the President sweeping power to reorganize.[3]

The new act authorized presidential reorganization plans affecting nearly every agency of the executive branch. A department cannot be abolished, a term of office increased, or the life of an expiring agency extended. The courts of the District of Columbia are exempt, as are the Comptroller General and the General Accounting Office. Reorganization plans lie before Con-

[1] U.S. President's Committee on Administrative Management, *Report with Special Studies* (1937), pp. 36–38.

[2] First Hoover Commission, *General Management of the Executive Branch* (1949), pp. ix–xii.
[3] A good analysis of the act is Ferrel Heady, "The Reorganization Act of 1949," *Public Administration Review*, vol. 9 (Summer, 1949), pp. 165–174.

EXECUTIVE POWERS OVER ADMINISTRATIVE REORGANIZATION, DELEGATED BY CONGRESS, 1932-1962

Years	Administration	Statute	Exemptions	Nullification	Use
1932-1933	Hoover	Approp. Act, 47 Stat. 413	No abolition of functions	Within 60 days by action of either house	11 Hoover plans killed in House
1933-1935	Roosevelt	Approp. Act, 47 Stat. 1517		No provision; in effect after 60 days	Extensive abolitions and shuffles
1939-1941	Roosevelt	Reorg. Act of 1939	17 exempt agencies; no new depts.	Within 60 days; both houses, concurrent res.	3 great "agencies" created, etc.
1941-1945	Roosevelt	First War Powers Act	Accounting Office; no new depts.	No provision	Several shifts and shuffles
1945-1948	Truman	Reorg. Act of 1945	6 agencies wholly; no new depts.	Within 60 days; both houses	Several orders, 1946-1947
1949-1962	Truman, Eisenhower and Kennedy	Reorg. Act of 1949 (as extended)	Cannot extend life of agency; no abolition of depts.	Within 60 days; either house	Over 50 plans in force 1949-1962

gress for sixty days; if either house disapproves within that period, the plan is dead. The act is stronger than that of 1945 in that there are fewer exemptions. It is weaker in that either house can nullify (both were required under the earlier act).

INTERNAL DEPARTMENTAL ORGANIZATION

Although not always true of other levels of government, Federal executive departments are directed by single heads. This type of overhead management has advantages over the plural, or board-commission, form, in that it concentrates responsibility for action and makes for greater speed and flexibility.

Overhead Management. Within the department, policy is directed by the secretary, who is responsible to the President, but who relies on various aides to keep in touch with a great department employing up to 500,000 persons. He is assisted by undersecretaries and assistant secretaries, usually appointed for political reasons, and by administrative assistants. Most departments develop a group of career men among the top assistants who constitute the management staff. The undersecretaries and assistant secretaries may supervise a group of bureaus, or a certain type of service or function running through several bureaus in the department.[1] Professor Macmahon favors the functional type of assignment for assistants as distinguished from the subject-matter type but recognizes the difficulty of defining responsibilities in precise terms. Department heads convene principal staff aides and bureau chiefs for "departmental cabinet" meetings to iron out policy questions, coordinate efforts, and report progress.

The latest thorough study of departmental management was made by the first Hoover Commission.[2] First, it stressed the necessity for grouping the numerous agencies into departments ". . . by major purposes in order to give a coherent mission to each Department." Within each department, subsidiary bureaus and agencies should be grouped according to major purposes. The Commission further recommended that each department head be empowered to organize his department as he thought best. For the typical department, the department head might have an undersecretary and the necessary number of assistant secretaries to cover the department's functions. Since all these officers would be of policy rank, the Commission proposed that they should be appointed by the President with Senate confirmation.

Another type of administrative unit within a department or an independent agency is the staff office, which performs management services for the operating agencies. These staff services are generally located near the department head. They include offices to provide personnel, legal, financial, research, informational, and other services. As the President watches and controls Federal line functions through his staff agencies, so the department head, within his department, contacts and manages his operating bureaus through personnel, financial, and other staff officers. The first Hoover Commission urged that all major executive agencies be equipped with adequate staff assistants for legal counsel, finances, personnel, supply, management research, information, and congressional liaison.

Bureaus and Other Units. Each department has its own peculiar structure. Line services are divided into "bureaus," but these major units may also be called "services," "offices," or "administrations." Internal organization is determined by both statutes and executive orders. Many of the bureaus in the Federal structure have a statutory basis, a fact that renders reorganization difficult unless the President is delegated authority to transfer units. Bureau heads generally are called "director," "commissioner," or "chief." Civil-service status of the bureau head varies, but a large proportion of heads are found within the classified service, and many others are appointed within the spirit of the merit system.[3]

Below the bureau level, terminology and organizational practice vary even more. The title "division" most commonly indicates a subdivision of a bureau, but "unit," "branch," and "section" are employed also. The lower in the administrative ladder, the less chance that form is bound by statute. This facilitates reorganization by executive action.

The first Hoover Commission proposed a standard nomenclature for agencies within

[1] Arthur W. Macmahon, "Departmental Management," in U.S. President's Committee on Administrative Management, op. cit., pp. 249–270.

[2] First Hoover Commission, op. cit., pp. 29–45.

[3] Arthur W. Macmahon and John D. Millett, Federal Administrators (New York: Columbia University Press, 1939). See also Schuyler C. Wallace, Federal Departmentalization (New York: Columbia University Press, 1941).

a department: service, bureau, division, branch, section, and unit. The bureau would be the prinicpal operating agency, but several bureaus with closely related functions operating in the same department would be grouped into a common "service." Bureaus would be divided further into smaller agencies as required, utilizing the names "division," "branch," "section," and "unit."

ADMINISTRATIVE PROBLEMS

Administrative Areas. In national administration field officers operating from offices spread over the country provide most functions. About 90 per cent of Federal civil employees are in field services, and 10 per cent in Washington, D.C. Obviously, if the Department of Agriculture operated solely in the nation's capital, it would contact directly few agrarian problems and serve few farmers. It must reach out into every section.

This spread over a wide geographic area raises grave problems of organization. Into what administrative areas shall the nation be subdivided? Shall each bureau of each department maintain branch offices in every area, reporting to the bureau in Washington? Or shall all field offices of a department clear through a central field office? Should the field services of the various Federal agencies in a given locality be coordinated, or should each operate independently?

The Federal government employs a bewildering variety of administrative areas. Americans were once reasonably familiar with the old corps areas of the Army Department (now "Army Areas"), but few realized that the country was divided on several different bases by particular services and corps of the Army. For general administrative purposes the Navy uses seventeen naval districts, but it may use other areas for procurement, recruiting, and other purposes. Most Federal administrative areas respect state lines. For each area there is designated a headquarters city, and Federal offices tend to congregate in San Francisco, New York, Chicago, Boston, New Orleans, Denver, and Atlanta.

It is proposed that Federal administrative areas be standardized; this might result in simplification for the public, in some saving in office rent, and in improved coordination of the various field services. Against it may be argued that the regional needs of Federal agencies vary, and that a strait jacket would decrease their effectiveness.[1]

Federal Field Services. The problem of relationship between headquarters and field service is a knotty one. The typical organization has a direct line of authority from bureau in Washington to regional or field offices throughout the country. For example, a field employee of the Department of the Interior works out of the Denver regional office of the Geological Survey, which in turn reports to the Survey office in Washington.

A newer form of organization is in the Social Security Administration, where regional offices supervise the work of several bureaus of the Administration dealing with old-age and unemployment insurance and public assistance. The regional director coordinates operations in his region and sends data to the appropriate bureau of the Administration in Washington. The latter form would be most difficult to apply to a vast executive department.

How obtain regional or area coordination? During the decade of the 1920s "Federal business associations" were or-

[1] See James W. Fesler, *Area and Administration* (University, Ala.: University of Alabama Press, 1949).

ganized to acquaint field workers with the work of other departments and services in their district. Professor Fesler, who studied this problem for the Committee on Administrative Management, recommended the revitalization of these business associations.[1] He advised that a regional coordinator of staff (personnel, purchasing, and like agencies) supervise the associations. Local post offices were urged as clearinghouses for information on Federal functions.

President Roosevelt, however, established field offices of the Office of Government Reports in nearly every state to furnish information to the public, do liaison work with state agencies, and report to Washington public sentiment on the work of Federal agencies.

The two Hoover Commissions studied field-service problems less than did the President's Committee, but the first one did make some pertinent criticisms and a few general suggestions. It found too many separately organized field offices representing departments, bureaus, and even divisions of bureaus. It reported much of the ineffectiveness of field offices due to failure to delegate authority. Lines of direction and supervision between specialized headquarters units and the field often are confused. Inadequate reporting and inspection leave central officials in the dark about field performance. Various Federal field offices lack coordination of effort. Cooperation with state and local governments and with private organizations is far from adequate.[2]

The first Hoover Commission recommended greater standardization of regional boundaries and headquarters, utilization of pooled administrative services (supply,

motor, transport, space, and other), strengthened reporting and inspection practices, and uniformity of relationships with officials of state and local governments.[3]

Boards and Commissions. The plural form of executive, rejected for Federal departments, is common for independent agencies. Boards and commissions have important uses under a number of circumstances. When quasi-legislative and quasi-judicial powers are assigned to an agency, plural headship is considered advantageous, because independence and continuity are important to policy making and adjudication. Teachers, social workers, and others maintain that the board form is desirable for managing educational, welfare, and some other activities, because a "meeting of minds" is valuable and protection from politics is essential. The board-commission used for administrative work often has resulted in confusion of responsibility and "buck passing."

As previously pointed out, the solution of the President's Committee on Administrative Management for the Federal board-commission problems was to place most of them in the executive departments. The regulatory commissions were to give the administrative work to the appropriate department and keep the legislative-judicial aspects in the commission, a relatively autonomous body within the same department. Congress did not accept this solution, preferring to leave the regulatory commissions with their independent status. It is still possible, therefore, for the Federal Trade Commission to follow a policy on

[1] "Executive Management and the Federal Field Service," in U.S. President's Committee on Administrative Management, *op. cit.*, pp. 275–294.
[2] First Hoover Commission, *op. cit.*, pp. 42–45.

[3] Two recent articles on field problems are William J. Gore, "Administrative Decision-making in Federal Field Offices," *Public Administration Review*, vol. 16 (Autumn, 1956), pp. 281–291; and George H. Axinn, "The Milieu Theory of Control," *ibid.*, vol. 17 (Spring, 1957), pp. 97–105.

business regulation out of harmony with that of the Department of Commerce.

The first Hoover Commission found many faults with the independent regulatory commissions, but proposed less drastic changes than its predecessor. It recommended that all administrative responsibility of a commission be vested in its chairman. The Hoover group suggested several transfers of administrative duties from regulatory commissions to the Departments of Commerce and Interior, but rejected the proposal of its task force to establish a consolidated transportation commission. Some critics of the independent commissions regard as a backward step the Hoover recommendation to erect statutory barriers against removal of all regulatory commissioners and to extend the bipartisanship requirement to all commissions.[1]

Some of President Truman's first plans under the Reorganization Act of 1949 made the chairmen of plural bodies the executive officers and administrative chiefs, leaving with the full commissions rule making and adjudicative authority. These were the Civil Service Commission, the Maritime Commission, the Federal Trade Commission, the Federal Power Commission, the Securities and Exchange Commission, and the Civil Aeronautics Board. The Senate nullified plans which similarly would have transferred administrative authority to the chairmen of the Interstate Commerce Commission, the Federal Communications Commission, and the National Labor Relations Board.

In summary, Federal boards and commissions are used for several reasons. First, the plural-headed body is established to ensure the independent exercise of quasi-judicial and quasi-legislative powers. Examples are found in the Interstate Commerce Commission, the Federal Communications Commission, and other regulatory bodies. Second, the board may be used to secure interest-group representation, as on the War Production Board or the War Labor Board. Third, this form may be employed when wide discretionary or policy-forming authority is vested in an agency, as with the Civil Service Commission and the National Labor Relations Board. Finally, it is utilized, coupled with overlapping terms of office, to maintain continuity and prevent abrupt changes when Presidents change. This is important in justifying Tariff Commission independence. The part-time advisory board or commission, much used in state and local affairs to enlist the volunteer services of public-spirited citizens, is employed increasingly in national affairs. Several hundred Federal advisory bodies now exist.[2]

Government Corporations. The corporate form of organization, so common in private business enterprise, has been adapted for use in publicly owned or controlled businesses. Most governmental activities are carried on through the departmental-bureau type of organization. A few have independent status and are not directly responsible to an administrative chief, as are the regulatory boards and commissions, but are subjected to indirect control through appointments and fiscal checks of the Chief Executive.

Even less common is the government corporation, incorporated under state or Federal law, to carry out some Federal function. Several types of government corporations are possible: First, there are wholly government-

---

[1] First Hoover Commission, *The Independent Regulatory Commission* (1949), pp. 5–16.

[2] David S. Brown, "The Public Advisory Board as an Instrument of Government," *Public Administration Review*, vol. 15 (Summer, 1955), pp. 196–204.

owned corporations, such as the farm credit banks and corporations.[1] Second, there are "mixed enterprises" owned in part by the government and in part by others; the banks for cooperatives and the home loan banks fall in this category. Third, the corporation may be owned by private shareholders but wholly controlled by the government; this type of "public-utility trust" is used extensively in Great Britain but not in the United States.

There are several reasons for the adoption of the government-corporation form. It secures independence in management, freedom from dependence on annual appropriations and other fiscal controls, and continuity of policy. Originally some of the federally owned corporations were incorporated under the laws of a particular state, but the advantages of Federal incorporation appear greater. Government corporations have boards of directors, sometimes composed wholly or in part of public officials acting ex officio, to determine the policies of the agencies. The directors employ a general manager who performs functions like those of a manager in private enterprise. Employees generally do not have civil-service status, for this might interfere with businesslike conduct of corporation affairs. Financial independence is considerable, with some corporations empowered to borrow money on their own credit and most having authority to reinvest their own earnings. Government corporations may sue and be sued in the courts, sovereign immunity from suit being dropped under the corporate form.

The Government Corporation Control Act of 1945 established some standard rules and practices. New government corporations must be authorized by law. Those with state incorporation were required to reincorporate by June 30, 1948. Controls over finances were set up, requiring a "business-type" budget, annual audit, and fuller fiscal reports.

The first Hoover Commission made a number of recommendations designed to further increase uniformity and to curb the financial independence of government corporations.[2] Among the changes proposed were that major capital additions should require congressional approval; boards should have advisory powers only; and standardization should prevail in borrowing powers, Federal liability for corporation obligations, and budgetary presentation. The Hoover group also proposed that Federal corporations should surrender to the Treasury government securities held and receive in return non-interest-bearing credit.

The more important Federal government corporations are the Panama Railway, Tennessee Valley Authority, Federal Deposit Insurance Corporation, Export-Import Bank, and more than 5,000 units of the Farm Credit Administration.

The Separation of Powers. One of the cardinal principles of the American constitutional system is the separation-of-powers doctrine. The principal powers of government, according to this formula, are divided into three parts: legislative, executive, and judicial. While governmental problems and functions remained simple, the legislative branch could declare public policy by law, and the executive and judicial branches interpret and enforce such law. This process is found today in many activities of the various levels of government.

For example, Congress adopts and the President signs a bill to forbid counterfeit-

[1] Harold Seidman, "The Theory of the Autonomous Government Corporation: A Critical Appraisal," *Public Administration Review*, vol. 12 (Spring, 1952), pp. 89–96. An extensive literature is available. See reading list at the end of this chapter.

[2] First Hoover Commission, Reorganization of *Federal Business Enterprises* (1949), pp. 5–12.

ing of coins of the realm and provide for ten years' imprisonment of all convicted of the crime. The law comes into force and is published in the *Statutes-at-large*. Secret Service agents of the Treasury apprehend Joe Luger in the act of molding lead 50-cent pieces. He is arrested, jailed, and tried in the courts. The prosecutor is the United States district attorney for the area. On conviction Luger is sentenced to serve ten years in Atlanta penitentiary. In this instance, the conventional methods of policy formation and law enforcement are followed, and the separation-of-powers doctrine proves suitable.

Under modern conditions, however, the problems of government have become so complex and kaleidoscopic that more flexible administration is required in many cases. When, for example, Congress decided that railroad services and rates must be regulated, it created a regulatory commission with extensive powers to make rules and regulations and render decisions in cases of conflict. The alternative to this action would have been to establish rates and standards of service in the law and to make them enforceable through the judicial process. The latter scheme would have proved impossible to operate fairly, for it would have produced uneven returns for operating concerns, ranging from unreasonably large profits to severe losses. Therefore the regulatory commission was established, with powers not only to enforce law (administration), but to make rules (legislation), and to settle disputes over law and fact (adjudication).

For a time the courts declared this development violative of the separation-of-powers doctrine. Eventually it was accepted on the ground that the powers granted to administrative agencies were quasi-legislative and quasi-judicial. While the power of Congress to delegate "rule-making" authority to the President has been restricted, delegation of authority to regulatory bodies to legislate and to adjudicate appears well established.[1]

ADMINISTRATIVE LEGISLATION AND LICENSING

Need for Quasi Legislation. As governmental problems have grown more complex, numerous, and changeable, Congress and the state legislatures increasingly have entrusted to administrative officers and bodies the responsibility to make detailed rules and regulations. Legislative bodies have delegated this authority for good reasons. First, the administrative officials are more expert in technical problems. Second, the legislature saves time for larger problems of public policy. Third, flexibility is secured, so that rules may be adapted to changed conditions and experience.[2]

Most existing authorizations were made in the last half century; they were exercised vigorously during war and crisis, especially in the Wilson and Franklin D. Roosevelt administrations. Administrative rule-making agencies include the President, most of the executive departments, many independent boards and commissions, and other bodies. A rule or regulation validly made is enforceable in the courts as law.

Rules for Rule Makers. While the necessity for administrative legislation has been established, several safeguards are required to avoid abuses of authority. Proper notice of proposed action is required. Opportunity to testify at a public hearing usually is made a prerequisite. A rule or regulation is pub-

[1] See also the discussion of the Panama Refining case and the Schechter case found on pages 319–320.
[2] See Frederick F. Blachly and Miriam E. Oatman, *Administrative Legislation and Adjudication* (Washington, D.C.: Brookings, 1934), pp. 43–53; James Hart, "The Exercise of the Rule-making Power," in U.S. President's Committee on Administrative Management, *op. cit.*, pp. 314–352.

lished in usable form and circulated widely. Some over-all regulation of administrative legislation appears desirable to reduce inconsistencies of content and form.

President Roosevelt by executive order implemented the Federal Register Act of 1935 with details on form for proclamations and orders. The Federal Register Division is located in the National Archives and Records Service, a part of the General Services Administration. The *Federal Register*, issued five times a week, contains presidential proclamations and executive orders and other documents of general applicability and legal effect. While regularization at the departmental level and the prenatal procedural safeguards have not been fully assured, the other proposals—postnatal publicity, coordination, and uniformity—have had some measure of acceptance.

The Attorney General's Committee on Administrative Procedure made a thorough study of these problems. Its report,[1] filed in January, 1941, and the thirteen supporting monographs,[2] constitute the chief data in this field. In 1946 Congress enacted and the President signed the Administrative Procedure Act. Its general provisions require agencies to inform the public regarding organization, procedure, rules, policies, and interpretations. There are some specific requirements about rule making: (1) Notice must be published in the *Federal Register* stating the time, place, nature, and authority for the proposed rules. (2) Interested persons may participate by submitting views, data, and arguments. (3) Rules must be published at least thirty days before the effective date. (4) The right to petition for issuance, change, or repeal of a rule is guaranteed.[3]

Licensing Powers. Another form of delegating authority to administrative officials involves licensing. Licensing laws customarily prohibit the practice of a profession or the operation of a business unless a permit or license has been secured in advance. The discretionary authority possessed by a licensing officer or body sometimes is very great.

Licenses of importance usually are subject to suspension or revocation for cause. A radio station that violates the conditions under which its license was granted may face revocation, suspension, or failure to renew by action of the Federal Communications Commission.

State and local governments utilize licensing more than does the Federal government. The principal Federal uses of licensing are authorized in the following statutes:[4] 1916, Warehouses Act; 1920, Water Power Act; 1921, Packers and Stockyards Act; 1922, Grain Futures Act; 1927, Radio Commission Act (now Communications Act of 1934); and 1934, Securities Exchange Act. To these were added licensing of armament manufacturing in 1935 and of atomic materials in 1946.

A simple example of Federal licensing is found in the live-poultry amendment added to the Packers and Stockyards Act of 1935.[5] To curb fraudulent practices that restrain interstate commerce at large centers of pop-

---

[1] U.S. Attorney General's Committee on Administrative Procedure, *Administrative Procedure in Government Agencies, Report of the . . . ,* S. Doc. 8, 77th Cong., 1st Sess. (1941).

[2] S. Doc. 186, 76th Cong., 3d Sess. (1940). There were also twenty-seven mimeographed monographs.

[3] See Foster H. Sherwood, "The Federal Administrative Procedure Act," *American Political Science Review,* vol. 41 (April, 1947), pp. 271–281.

[4] Charles V. Koons, "Growth of Federal Licensing," *Georgetown Law Review,* vol. 24 (January, 1936), pp. 293–344.

[5] U.S. Attorney General's Committee on Administrative Procedure, *Monograph of the . . . , Part II, Administration of the Packers and Stockyards Act, Department of Agriculture,* S. Doc. 186, 76th Cong., 3d Sess. (1940), pp. 3–4, 10–13.

ulation, the act authorizes the Secretary to designate which markets require regulation. All poultry handlers within a designated market must secure a license from the Secretary to continue in business. Licenses may be denied because of a record of unfair practices or inability to meet financial obligations. In administering the act, the Department proceeds informally and helps applicants fill out forms and prepare the necessary financial statements.

The second Hoover Commission recommended that Congress should be explicit in its delegation of licensing powers to administrative agencies, especially with reference to revocation and suspension.[1] In revocation proceedings, a licensee should be given an opportunity to answer to and rectify alleged violations. In renewal proceedings, administrative action should be taken before expiration date, assuming the application was filed on time and no violation has occurred.

ADMINISTRATIVE ADJUDICATION

Adjudicative Agencies. Administrative adjudication has been defined by Blachly and Oatman as ". . . investigation and settling of a dispute on the basis of fact and law, by an administrative agency which may or may not be organized to act solely as an administrative court."[2] So long as the administrative process remains clear of conflict, adjudication is unnecessary. A dispute, however, requires adjudication. When the decision is rendered by an administrative officer or body, the adjudication is called "administrative." Thereafter litigation continues in the courts and is called "judicial review of administrative action." Court review will be considered in the next subsection.

Why should administrative tribunals exist and administrative bodies be assigned quasi-judicial powers? There are several reasons. These agencies become more expert in their particular field than do judges who must deal with many fields. Personnel of specialized agencies are more apt to understand the social and economic philosophy underlying their problems. An agency can proceed more informally than a court, saving time and money and allowing greater latitude for experimentation with new solutions and procedures. Professor Peter Woll reports that " . . . over ninety per cent of the cases arising within administrative jurisdiction are settled informally."[3] Potential disputes are ironed out by investigation, consultation, mutual consent, and adjustment before resorting to formal procedures.

When formal adjudication is required, the agency acting as a tribunal should have its authority defined and its personnel selected with special care. Several types of agencies act in a judicial capacity: (1) independent specialized courts, such as the Tax Court, Court of Claims, Court of Customs and Patent Appeals, hand down decisions; (2) department heads often are empowered to hear complaints and settle disputes, as does the Secretary of Agriculture in disciplinary proceedings under the Packers and Stockyards Act; (3) administrative adjudication occurs within units of executive departments, such as the Food and Drug Administration (Department of Health, Education, and Welfare) and the Patent Office (Department of Commerce); (4) independent regulatory commissions, discussed in Chapter 15, handle an important share of disputes resolved through the administrative process; typically these commissions exercise administrative, quasi-judicial, and quasi-legislative powers. They include the Interstate Commerce Com-

---

[1] Second Hoover Commission, *Legal Services and Procedure* (1955), pp. 58–59.
[2] Blachly and Oatman, *op. cit.*, p. 91.

[3] Peter Woll, "Administrative Law Reform: Proposals and Prospects," *Nebraska Law Review*, vol. 41 (June, 1962), p. 693.

mission, Federal Trade Commission, Federal Communications Commission, Federal Power Commission, Federal Maritime Commission, Securities and Exchange Commission, and others. Adjudicative powers are also vested in various licensing authorities, discussed on pages 362 to 363, and in the Comptroller General, who renders decisions on the legality of expenditures.

Methods of Adjudication. The first step in formal administrative adjudication is to file a complaint or a request for hearing; the dispute may arise between conflicting private interests or between the public agency and a private interest. Second, a "hearing officer" takes testimony and evidence upon which to base a fair decision; in some cases the officer has power to render an initial decision in the case. Third, the board or commission or head, advised by legal staff, renders the ultimate decision in the case, subject to the court review prescribed by law.

The hearing-examiner problem has claimed much attention in the several studies of the administrative process. In the mid-1950s there were fewer than three hundred such officers, most of whom worked regularly in Washington, D.C. The Administrative Procedure Act assigned the task of selecting and promoting hearing officers to the Civil Service Commission. The Commission set up a board of examiners to give examinations to both incumbents and new applicants. About one-third of the incumbents were disqualified, but the Commission —faced with a barrage of appeals and protests—retained all incumbents.

Reforms Proposed. The second Hoover Commission was concerned over administrative intrusion into judicial functions and made a number of recommendations that tended to separate further the function of prosecuting from the function of deciding.

The most sweeping departure was the proposal for an Administrative Court of the United States with three sections: (1) a Tax Section, with jurisdiction of the existing Tax Court; (2) a Trade Section, which would have the adjudicatory authority now vested in the Federal Trade Commission, the Interstate Commerce Commission, the Federal Communications Commission, the Civil Aeronautics Board, the Federal Reserve Board, the United States Tariff Commission, the Federal Power Commission, and the Interior and Agriculture Departments; (3) a Labor Section, which would take over the unfair-labor-practice cases from the National Labor Relations Board.[1] The Hoover group suggested that Congress study and determine whether the trade and labor sections should have original or appellate jurisdiction.

The second Hoover Commission also suggested an "office of legal services and procedure," in the Department of Justice, to work on simplification, clarification, and uniformity. Like the earlier Attorney General's Committee, the Hoover group proposed the creation of a corps of "hearing commissioners" with fixed terms and independent status. Control and direction would come from the proposed Administrative Court.

For many years the American Bar Association has been actively concerned with the problems and potential dangers of administrative adjudication. Its two basic recommendations are: first, that judicial functions of administrative agencies be more strictly separated from other functions; second, that rules of procedure for administrative adjudication conform more closely to those used by courts. These recommendations and others have been embodied in a proposed "code of Federal administrative procedure" which includes some of the Hoover Commission suggestions. The "code" is intended to replace the Administrative Procedure Act of 1946.

[1] Second Hoover Commission, *Legal Services and Procedure* (1955), pp. 87–88.

Committees of both House and Senate have held numerous hearings in recent years on the conduct of proceedings before regulatory agencies, but the pressures for change have not been strong enough to bring statutory revision. Indeed, the flexibility of the administrative process, as it has evolved, appears more likely to achieve the desired balance between individual rights and public necessities, coupled with expertness in fact-finding. Among the changes likely to come is greater isolation of the trial examiner from the agency with which he works.

CONTROL OVER ADMINISTRATIVE ACTION

Judicial Review of Administrative Action. The right to appeal decisions, rules, and orders by administrative bodies to the courts of law is widely regarded as necessary and proper. Although the great majority of instances of administrative action are accepted without formal dispute, as noted above, the volume of cases before administrative bodies is large. Few such cases are appealed, but they constitute an important share of the total litigation before the Federal courts.

Judicial review has as its objective, according to the Attorney General's Committee on Administrative Procedure, ". . . to serve as a check on the administrative branch of government—a check against excess of power and abusive exercise of power in derogation of private right."[1] The Committee stressed that the courts can review to ensure the fairness of administrative action, but that they cannot assure the correctness of such action. The volume of administrative action is too great for extensive review, and the courts cannot match the administrative bodies in specialization and expertness. The appropriate role of the court in

reviewing administrative action would appear to include examination of the propriety of the interpretation of the law and assurance that the proceedings were reasonable.

These principles have been followed generally by the Federal courts in reviewing administrative action. Faced with a case involving a request for review of administrative action, the court first sees that the Constitution has been followed, especially that there has been no deprivation of liberty or property without due process of law, either procedural or substantive. Next, the court may look to the Federal law under which the administrative body was created or the right of appeal established; considerable variation exists in the right of appeal, the methods of appeal, and the degree of administrative finality. Even in cases where the Constitution is not violated and statutory requirements are met, the remedies of an aggrieved person are not exhausted. He may sue an official for damages or seek an injunction to forbid certain acts by an administrative agency. In general the courts have required due notice and a full and fair hearing on the procedural side.

Congress has provided for appeal of administrative decisions to various court levels. Appeals from several of the regulatory commissions go to the United States courts of appeals. Action of other bodies is reviewable in the district courts. Customs and patent appeals go to the Court of Customs and Patent Appeals.

In considering court reviewability of administrative action, one of the most important aspects concerns control over findings of fact. If the court finds that there are no facts to support the action, it holds due process lacking.[2] Beginning with the Inter-

---

[1] *Administrative Procedure in Government Agencies*, p. 76.

[2] See analysis of Frederick F. Blachly and Miriam E. Oatman, *Federal Regulatory Action and Control* (Washington, D.C.: Brookings, 1940), pp. 119–124.

state Commerce Commission, fact finding by the agency was declared in the statute to be prima facie evidence. Fact finding by several other agencies is conclusive if supported by the weight of evidence. The courts have been inclined to let stand administrative findings of fact unless proved insubstantial; occasionally they have intervened to the extent of reviewing the entire body of facts fully and anew.

Questions of law, however, fall under the full purview of the courts. The court may set aside administrative action because of errors of law. In many cases, questions of fact and law are intermingled, and the court has all necessary discretion to rule as it sees fit. Commenting on the lack of sharp distinction between questions of law and fact, John Dickinson concluded: "The knife of policy alone effects an artificial cleavage at the point where the court chooses to draw the line between public interest and private right."[1]

Reform of Court Review. Complaints over judicial review of administrative action may be divided into two groups. One set is voiced by those who fear administrative finality and who allege that an aggrieved person has insufficient remedies. The other is presented by defenders of the administrative process, who feel the courts have interfered excessively in substituting their own findings of fact and judgment for those of the administrative body. Both sides have agreed that improvements in the judicial review of administrative action are possible; that procedures lack uniformity, clarity, and other attributes of a desirable appellate system.

The Logan-Walter bill became the center of this controversy in 1939. Backed by the American Bar Association, the bill passed

both houses during 1940 but was vetoed by President Roosevelt. This legislation would have given the Court of Appeals for the District of Columbia jurisdiction to hear and determine, within thirty days of issuance, whether an administrative rule conflicted with law or Constitution. Decisions and orders of administrative agencies could be reviewed in the Court of Appeals within thirty days, and set aside on grounds that fact findings were erroneous, due notice or fair hearing was denied, or law or Constitution violated. Appellate-court decisions were to be final except where the Supreme Court called them up for review. The judicial-review features of the bill were attacked vigorously as likely to lead to endless court litigation and to render impossible proper functioning of administrative agencies.

The Administrative Procedure Act of 1946 provided for judicial review to remedy every "legal wrong." Judicial review is authorized except when precluded by law. The law occupies a middle ground between the Logan-Walter school, which wanted every administrative act subjected to judicial review, and some defenders of the agencies, who wished to minimize court appeals.

The proposed "code of federal administrative procedure" would increase considerably the chance that affected parties would try to secure relief through appeals to regular courts. It would eliminate exceptions from judicial review that are provided by the Administrative Procedure Act and open every final agency action to judicial review unless otherwise exempted by law. Moreover, courts would be able to intervene in a case before an agency had rendered a final decision. Advocates of the proposed "code" are not taking as extreme a position as did proponents of Logan-Walter, but their posture points in that direction.

Legislative Control. Administrative action is also subject to external control by legis-

---

[1] John Dickinson, *Administrative Justice and the Supremacy of the Law* (Cambridge, Mass.: Harvard University Press, 1927), p. 55.

lative bodies. (1) Congress determines the statutory framework (structure, powers, duties) within which the Federal administrative agencies operate. Although in recent years this control is less rigid, because of the tendency to draft legislation in general terms, the legislature has retained supremacy in matters of policy. (2) Congressional and state legislative control over appropriations provides a second check on administrative responsibility. The stewardship of a particular agency is reviewed regularly in budget hearings, and the purse strings may be tightened to indicate legislative displeasure with administrative conduct. (3) Congress and nearly all state legislatures possess power to investigate as ancillary to the power to legislate. A large proportion of the investigations are concerned wholly or partially with administrative conduct. The possibility of an investigation is itself an effective deterrent on administrative excesses.

To secure the correct amount and quality of legislative control over administration is an intricate and colossal task. Lack of vigilance by a legislative body may lead to administrative highhandedness. Overintervention in the detail of the administrative process and personnel can bring irresponsible conduct and spoils politics. The legislative branch properly determines general policy and structure and inquires into administrative practices to ensure accomplishment of legislative intent. It should not attempt to administer, directly or indirectly. It should not interfere in a manner to curb initiative, make flexibility impossible, or drive able personnel from public service.[1]

[1] For an able discussion of these problems, see Frank C. Newman and H. J. Keaton, "Congress and the Faithful Execution of Laws: Should Legislators Supervise Administrators?" *California Law Review*, vol. 41 (Winter, 1953–1954), pp. 565–595.

FOR FURTHER READING

See also works at end of Chapter 11.

American Society for Public Administration: *Public Administration Review* (quarterly).

Appleby, Paul H.: *Policy and Administration* (University, Ala.: University of Alabama Press, 1949).

Bernstein, Marver H.: *The Job of the Federal Executive* (Washington, D.C.: Brookings Institution, 1958).

Blachly, Frederick F., and Miriam Oatman: *Federal Regulatory Action and Control* (Washington, D.C.: Brookings, 1940).

Charlesworth, James C.: *Governmental Administration* (New York: Harper, 1951).

Cushman, Robert E.: *The Independent Regulatory Commission* (New York: Oxford, 1941).

Emmerich, Herbert: *Essays on Federal Reorganization* (University, Ala.: University of Alabama Press, 1950).

Fesler, James W.: *Area and Administration* (University, Ala.: University of Alabama Press, 1949).

Gaus, John M.: *Reflections on Public Administration* (University, Ala.: University of Alabama Press, 1947).

—— and L. O. Wolcott: *Public Administration and the United States Department of Agriculture* (Chicago: Public Administration Service, 1940).

Gellhorn, Walter: *Federal Administrative Proceedings* (Baltimore: Johns Hopkins Press, 1941).

Graham, George A.: *America's Capacity to Govern: Some Preliminary Thoughts for Prospective Administrators* (University, Ala.: University of Alabama Press, 1960).

—— and Henry Reining, Jr. (eds.): *Regulatory Administration* (New York: Wiley, 1943).

Graves, W. Brooke: *Public Administration in a Democratic Society* (Boston: Heath, 1950).

——: *Basic Information on the Reorganization of the Executive Branch, 1912–1948*, Public Affairs Bulletin 66 (Washington, D.C.: Library of Congress, 1949).

Latham, Earl, and others: *The Federal Field Service: An Analysis with Suggestions for Research* (Chicago: Public Administration Service, 1947).

Lepawsky, Albert: *Administration: The Art and Science of Organization and Management* (New York: Knopf, 1949).

Malick, Sidney (ed.): *Concepts and Issues in Administration Behavior* (Englewood Cliffs, N.J.: Prentice Hall, 1962).

Millett, John D.: *Government and Public Administration* (New York: McGraw-Hill, 1959).

Millspaugh, Arthur C.: *Toward Efficient Democracy: The Question of Governmental Organization* (Washington, D.C.: Brookings, 1949).

Pfiffner, John M., and R. Vance Presthus: *Public Administration* (New York: Ronald, 3d ed., 1953).

Presthus, Robert: *The Organizational Society* (New York: Knopf, 1962).

Redford, Emmette S.: *Administration of National Economic Control* (New York: Macmillan, 1952).

Rowat, Donald C.: *Basic Issues in Public Administration* (New York: Macmillan, 1961).

Roy, Robert H.: *The Administrative Process* (Baltimore: Johns Hopkins Press, 1958).

Schwartz, Bernard: *The Professor and the Commissions* (New York: Knopf, 1959).

Seckler-Hudson, Catheryn: *Organization and Management: Theory and Practice* (Washington, D.C.: American University Press, 1955).

Simon, Herbert A.: *Administrative Behavior: A Study of Decision-making Processes in Admin-istrative Organization* (New York: Macmillan, 2d ed., 1957).

Thompson, Victor A.: *Modern Organization* (New York: Knopf, 1961).

Truman, David B.: *Administrative Decentralization* (Chicago: University of Chicago Press, 1940).

U.S. Commission on Organization of the Executive Branch of the Government (first Hoover Commission): *Report . . .* (19 vols., 1949). In addition, 18 task-force reports were published.

U.S. Commission on Organization of the Executive Branch of the Government (second Hoover Commission): *Report . . .* (20 vols., 1955). In addition, 19 task-force and subcommittee reports were published.

U.S. President's Committee on Administrative Management: *Report . . . with Studies of Administrative Management in the Federal Government* (1937).

Waldo, Dwight: *Ideas and Issues in Public Administration* (New York: McGraw-Hill, 1953).

————: *Perspectives on Administration* (University, Ala.: University of Alabama Press, 1957).

White, Leonard D.: *The Jeffersonians* (New York: Macmillan, 1951).

————: *The Federalists: A Study in Administrative Management* (New York: Macmillan, 1948).

————: *Introduction to the Study of Public Administration* (New York: Macmillan, 4th ed., 1955).

REVIEW QUESTIONS

1. What is the constitutional relationship between the President and the administrative structure? Between Congress and the administrative structure?

2. How can you explain the reluctance of Congress to establish new departments? Trace the recent history of efforts toward this end.

3. To what extent has Congress been willing to entrust power to reorganize agencies to recent Presidents (Hoover to Eisenhower)? What provisions for nullification were made?

4. Explain some of the problems involved in defining proper administrative areas and in organizing effective field services.

5. Under what circumstances would the board-commission form of organization be appropriate for an administrative-agency headship? Discuss.

6. Describe the recent experience of the Federal government in providing for judicial review of administrative action.

7. What safeguards have been erected to prevent abuses of authority in administrative rule making?

8. Under what circumstances is the government corporation a proper form for organizing a Federal undertaking? Discuss some of the problems connected with public corporations.

9. To what extraordinary stresses and strains is the separation-of-powers doctrine subjected under modern conditions when a single agency of government may not only administer a law but also make rules and regulations and render decisions in case of conflicts?

Chapter Nineteen

The Civil Service

*No amount of care in determining how a government shall
be organized for the performance of its work, the manner
in which the funds necessary for its support shall be
raised and expended, and the particular practices and
procedures that shall be employed in carrying on its
activities, will give even a measurable approach to efficiency
in actual administration of public affairs unless a
technically competent and loyal personnel can be secured
and retained in the service and a system devised whereby
this personnel may be effectively directed and controlled.*

LEWIS MAYERS[1]

*I am all for young (and also old) men of quality going
into public life and government service. . . . Why? . . .
because there is no better or fuller life for a man of
spirit. The old Greek conception of happiness is relevant
here: "The exercise of vital powers along lines of
excellence, in a life affording them scope."*

*This is the Geiger counter which tells us where to dig.
It explains also why to everyone who has ever
experienced it the return from public life to private life
leaves one feeling flat and empty.*

DEAN G. ACHESON[2]

After administrative organization and powers, manpower is the next important prerequisite to effective administration. When the Republic was young, it needed few employees; the task of hiring and firing was like that of a small business concern. Today,

however, the administrative leviathan of the Federal government has reached enormous size, requiring careful management of every phase of personnel work. To cope with this great problem, personnel agencies have been set up by Federal, state, and municipal governments.

No government exists for the purpose of employing people. Public employees are needed to accomplish the goals of fostering

[1] *The Federal Service* (New York: Appleton, 1922), p. vii.

[2] In a letter of the former Secretary of State reprinted in *New York Times*, February 2, 1958.

369

agriculture, regulating commerce, protecting life and property. If the personnel system finds and recruits the person most qualified for the job and maintains his morale at a high level, the public interest is served. If an ill-equipped person is given the job or if the incumbent is dissatisfied, the work suffers. Modern governments, to a large extent, succeed or fail according to the quality of their personnel.

DEVELOPMENT OF AMERICAN MERIT SYSTEMS

Early Personnel Policies. The Constitution charges the President with appointing and the Senate with confirming "officers" of the United States. Authority to appoint "inferior officers" may be vested by law in the President alone, in the heads of executive departments, or in the courts. President Washington established the tradition of appointing for competency. Adams showed preference for those of his own political leanings. Jefferson sought to replace Federalists with his own partisans; this turnover involved about 25 per cent of employees under presidential control.[1] The political complexion of Madison and Monroe was Jeffersonian, minimizing the incentive to change; John Quincy Adams failed to alter the general policy of long continuance in office. This era, from 1789 to 1829, has been termed the "period of relative administrative efficiency."[2]

The Spoils System. When Andrew Jackson took office on March 4, 1829, political opponents occupied many Federal offices.

In his first annual message to Congress, President Jackson recommended limiting appointments to four years:

There are, perhaps, a few men who can for any great length of time enjoy office and power without being more or less under the influence of feelings unfavorable to the faithful discharge of their public duties. Their integrity may be proof against improper considerations immediately addressed to themselves, but they are apt to acquire a habit of looking with indifference upon the public interests and of tolerating conduct from which an unpracticed man would revolt. . . . The duties of all public officers are, or at least admit of being made, so plain and simple that men of intelligence may readily qualify themselves for their performance; and I can not but believe that more is lost by the long continuance of men in office than is generally to be gained by their experience.[3]

The case for rotation in office was strong in Jackson's time. Governmental work was still relatively simple. Jackson's regime, representing a definite break with the past, would not be frustrated by bureaucrats held over from the John Quincy Adams administration.

Between 1829 and the close of the Civil War the spoils system flourished. To job spoils were added other types of spoils—contracts, graft, and the like. In this period of national expansion, opportunities for corruption were plentiful. While the spoils system has not been wholly eliminated even today, important reforms were adopted in the two decades after the Civil War.

Civil-service Reform. Even before the Civil War, steps were taken to bring some order out of the chaos then prevailing in

[1] Carl R. Fish, "Removal of Officials by the Presidents of the United States," *Annual Report of the American Historical Association for the Year 1899* (GPO, 1900), vol. 1, p. 70.

[2] William E. Mosher, J. Donald Kingsley, and O. Glenn Stahl, *Public Personnel Administration* (New York: Harper, 3d ed., 1950), pp. 17–18.

[3] James D. Richardson (ed.), *Messages and Papers of the Presidents* (New York: Bureau of National Literature, 20 vols., 1897–1916), vol. 3, pp. 1011–1012. Fish, *op. cit.*, p. 74, reports that Jackson removed 279 out of a total of about 610 officers.

the personnel field. Acts of 1853 and 1855 established four classes of clerks in Washington departmental offices and set up a scale of salaries. "Pass" examinations were introduced in each department, providing that an appointee must pass some departmental test before taking office. In 1871, during Grant's administration, an appropriation-bill rider authorized the President to set up regulations on appointments and ascertain fitness of candidates for positions. Accordingly, President Grant created an Advisory Board of the Civil Service, and the first competitive examinations were given in 1872. Lacking appropriations for the purpose, Grant abandoned the experiment in 1875. The Hayes administration made progress, especially in relation to Federal employees in New York City.

In July, 1881, a disappointed office seeker fatally wounded President James A. Garfield. Public indignation over the spoils system reached a high pitch and led to the enactment of the Pendleton Act in January, 1883. The law established a Civil Service Commission of three members and provided for open competitive examinations. Discrimination for political reasons was forbidden. Appointment continued to be a function of the President or department head, but his choice was limited to those who ranked in the top four on the eligible list prepared by the Commission. The act left to the President and Congress the extension of the "classified service," those employees coming under the protection of the formal merit system.

State and Local Adoptions. The states followed the Federal government in adopting civil-service systems, and over one-half have enacted laws of general applicability. New York and Massachusetts pioneered with their legislation of 1883 and 1885. Other states followed suit. The list includes all the populous states except Pennsylvania and Texas. All states, to be eligible for social security grants, have established merit systems for employees in aided functions.

A number of counties have adopted civil-service plans. Some have remarkably good records in the personnel field, but perhaps the majority are in the hands of spoilsmen. Most of the large cities and a great many smaller municipalities have some sort of civil-service system. Policemen and firemen often are protected even if other employees are not.

Townships and special districts rarely utilize civil-service systems, but school districts commonly have either formal or informal merit systems. Teacher-tenure plans represent only minor variations from the general pattern of a protected personnel.

PERSONNEL AGENCIES

United States Civil Service Commission. Established under the Pendleton Act, the Commission consists of three members appointed by the President, with Senate confirmation. No more than two may be members of the same political party. Commissioners serve six-year terms. From an original negative conception of eliminating politics in appointments, the Commission has come to play the leading role in a positive and broad personnel-improvement program.

The act charges the Commission with advising the President on civil-service rules. The relationship of Commission and President rarely has been intimate. The body files an annual report, reviewing its work and making recommendations for extension of the classified service. The administrative work of the Commission under a reorganization plan of 1949 is the responsibility of the chairman alone. Acting through an executive director appointed by him, the chairman oversees and supervises the work of the several bureaus, divisions, offices, and boards.

The country is divided into twelve civil-service regions, each with a regional office at a central city. These offices publicize and conduct examinations and serve the personnel needs of the field services of the various Federal agencies.

Other Federal Personnel Agencies. While the Civil Service Commission is the principal Federal personnel agency, other agencies play important parts. The Commission is not, except for its own employees, the appointing agency. The department or agency in which the appointee will serve makes the appointment. The Federal executive departments and other large agencies have directors of personnel. Such officers select from civil-service eligible lists the individuals most likely to prove suitable for particular positions; they also take over many routine personnel duties of heads of departments and other agencies.

The personnel offices in the operating departments and agencies have emerged, since 1938, with key roles in appointing, rating, promoting, and otherwise serving Federal employees. The decentralization program proposed by the first Hoover Commission placed even more stress on the importance of personnel offices in operating units. For some 2,000,000 Federal civil workers, there were about 25,000 employees of personnel offices. The Hoover group criticized overstaffing in the offices of some of the agencies; in some instances it found one personnel worker for as few as thirty-eight employees. Under the reforms proposed, recruiting, examining, and selecting of employees would be conducted largely by the operating agencies, subject to the uniform employment standards and regulations determined and supervised by the Civil Service Commission. Much of this has been achieved.

Reform of Personnel Organization. The Federal government has tried two types of overhead organization for its central personnel agency.

From the beginning of the formal civil service in 1883 until 1949, the full Commission was the dominant force. It possessed administrative, rule-making, and adjudicative powers. This form had the advantage of providing a "council of minds" when policy was being determined or judicial-type decisions were being rendered; it also served to insulate the agency to some extent against partisan political pressures. Over the years, however, a number of disadvantages emerged: responsibility for administration was diffused, expertness often was lacking among lay commissioners, and independent status deprived the chief executive of what could have been a principal managerial "arm."

The net effect of implementing some of the first Hoover Commission recommendations has been to establish a hybrid commission-administrator plan. A reorganization plan of 1949 vested the chairman of the Civil Service Commission with all administrative authority, including the functions of appointing, supervising, and directing personnel and internal organization. In practice, much of the administrative work is delegated by the chairman to the "executive director," appointed by the chairman. The Commission as a body retains power to make rules and regulations, hear appeals, investigate, and recommend improvements.

The office of personnel, which the first Hoover Commission recommended in the Executive Office of the President, has not been created. The experience of the Eisenhower Administration has been described as follows:

Under President Eisenhower a first step was taken: the Chairman of the Civil Service Commission was made personnel adviser to the President with an office in the White House. This really wasn't a satisfactory answer. The Civil Service Chairman personifies the machinery to protect employees from politics, so it only weakened the prestige of the Commission to have its chairman's independence in question. When the first Civil Service Chairman with the dual job resigned, he was replaced by two persons, a new Commission head and a new personnel adviser in the White House.[1]

Many students of public personnel problems believe that the next step is to transfer management of the function to a single administrator. This was the core of the President's Committee on Administrative Management personnel recommendation. The first Hoover report contained a statement of additional views by James K. Pollock, who made a strong case for going the whole distance toward a "modern concept" by vesting management under a single personnel commissioner.

Negative versus Positive Approach. Even more important than the overhead organization of personnel management is the attitude and approach of the managers. American civil service, in its formative years, was developed to the theme of "fighting the spoilsmen." The Commission took the lead in personnel administration from the departments. Between 1938, when personnel offices were authorized in the departments and agencies by executive order, and 1949, when the first Hoover Commission underscored the need for decentralization, much conflict ensued. The Commission held somewhat tenaciously to its negative, policing approach. The departments and agencies sought the best person for the job,

[1] David R. Lindsay, *What's Ahead for Civil Service?* (New York: Public Affairs Pamphlet No. 258, 1957), p. 15.

a task requiring initiative and aggressiveness in a period of relatively full employment.

After 1949 the shift of emphasis and function changed. The Hoover recommendation that primary responsibility for recruiting and examining be placed on departments and agencies was put into force. The Commission reluctantly shifted toward a role of setting standards for the personnel offices of operating agencies, and away from the extreme centralization under which it handled most detailed personnel transactions.

EXTENT OF THE CLASSIFIED SERVICE

Federal civil employment in the early 1960s ranged between 2 and 2½ million. Of these, over 85 per cent were under the classified civil service. The chart shows their distribution among the several departments and agencies and includes the several states and territories.

Expansion of Coverage. The Pendleton Act provided that the "classified service" should be extended by presidential order or by act of Congress. Only 13,900 positions, or 10.5 per cent of executive employees, were included in the classified group in 1883. Each President since then has increased the number of positions included; at times the motivation appears to have been the improvement of the public service; at others, the "blanketing-in" of political appointees. Under the Ramspeck Act of 1940, the President was authorized to include in the classified service, with few exceptions, all non-policy-forming positions. Nevertheless, when President Truman in 1952 issued a reorganization order to bring postmasters, customs officials, and marshals into the classified category, the Senate disapproved and nullified the action.

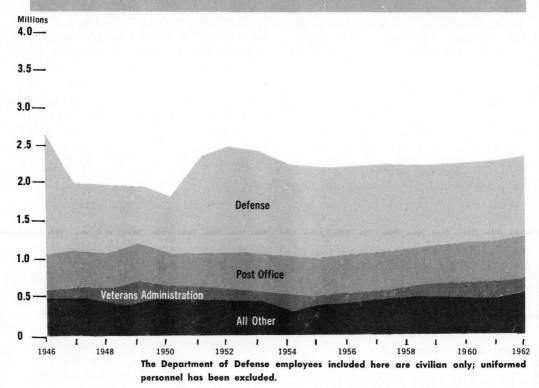

FEDERAL CIVIL EMPLOYEES, EXECUTIVE BRANCH, 1946 - 1962

Millions
4.0—
3.5—
3.0—
2.5—
2.0—
1.5—
1.0—
0.5—
0—

Defense

Post Office

Veterans Administration

All Other

1946   1948   1950   1952   1954   1956   1958   1960   1962

The Department of Defense employees included here are civilian only; uniformed personnel has been excluded.

Who Should Be Exempt? The Federal civil employees outside the formal classified civil service are in two principal groups: those in exempt positions and temporary employees. The task force of the first Hoover Commission identified three exempt category: (1) positions of a policy-forming character, (2) positions of a confidential nature, and (3) positions for which competitive examinations are impractical.[1]

Some agencies have employees exempt from the classified service under specific statutory provision; examples are the TVA and the Foreign Service. Other agencies by tradition have their own merit systems separate and apart from the regular civil

service; examples are the FBI, the Public Health Service, and the Forest Service. In addition there are positions for which it has been deemed impracticable to recruit through the competitive system; some of these require a noncompetitive "pass examination" to assure minimum standards; others have no examinations.

Policy-determining Positions. Not long after a new administration took office in 1953, one of the great personnel issues that emerged was: How high should civil service go?[2] What is the proper line of demarca-

[1] First Hoover Commission, *Task Force Report on Federal Personnel* (1949), p. 19.

[2] For discussion of the issue, see Herman M. Somers, "The President, the Congress, and the Federal Government Service," in *The Federal Government Service: Its Character, Prestige, and Problems* (New York: Columbia University, Graduate School of Business, 1954), pp. 52–80, at p. 69.

tion between the permanent career service and political executives? A few years ago some reformers were inclined to impress even bureau chiefs and assistant secretaries into the classified service; now it seems necessary to reexamine the possibility of a constructive administrative role for the political supporter of the President.

President Roosevelt, from 1933, onwards, brought into Federal employment a large number of able and dynamic administrators. The conditions were favorable: the service was expanding rapidly and private employment conditions were adverse. President Eisenhower, however, beginning in 1953, faced almost opposite conditions: the service was being reduced, and nearly full employment prevailed in the private sector of the economy. Moreover many executives recruited during the Roosevelt-Truman eras were now entrenched as career administrators with classified civil-service protection.

To open up these positions, the President issued an executive order that created "Schedule C" and transferred to it all positions of a "confidential or policy-determining character." By October, 1954, 1,127 positions had been placed in the category;[1] but about one-half of incumbents were retained and a further 20 per cent of new posts filled from the existing service. The able task force of the second Hoover Commission was alarmed over Schedule C mainly because it opened the way to a clean sweep of existing personnel in a future change of administration. Omitting the "confidential" employees, such as private secretaries and chauffeurs, the task force estimated that 755 positions might be considered in the "political executive" category.

Uses of Political Executives. A substantial

part of the 1955 task force report examined ways to strengthen top management through political executives. Correct use of the political executive, according to the task force, is in the top command of departments and agencies, not—as some of the Schedule C posts were—on bureau, divisional, and field-office levels. The positions reserved for political executives are in three groups: (1) heads of agencies and their deputies; (2) assistant agency heads; and (3) aides, assistants, heads of policy offices, etc.

The second Hoover Commission endorsed these recommendations, and urged that non-career executives relieve career administrators of responsibility for advocating or defending policies. Political executives are required at the departmental level. A new Schedule D was proposed for policy-determining positions that should be filled by political executives,[2] Schedule C would be reserved solely for confidential positions.

The Higher Civil Service. The second Hoover Commission and its task force then turned to means of strengthening top management. Like earlier critics of the Federal personnel system, they noted the deficiency in career administrators. They proposed a "senior" civil-service group of top career administrators carefully selected from all parts of the civil service. Senior civil servants would be appointed as individuals—as in the military service with appropriate status, rank, and salary—yet assigned to positions (billets) on a flexible basis. An initial goal of 1,500 senior civil servants was set; ultimately perhaps 3,000 would be required. Each would be politically neutral, and each would be obligated to serve where needed most. A "Senior Civil

[1] Second Hoover Commission, *Task Force Report on Personnel and Civil Service* (1955), pp. 36–37.

[2] Second Hoover Commission, *Personnel and Civil Service* (1955), pp. 31–33. The problems of executive personnel are considered in John A. Perkins, "Staffing Democracy's Top Side," *Public Administration Review*, vol. 17 (Winter, 1957), pp. 1–9.

Service Board" would select, review performance, and set rules and standards.

Jobs Outside the Classified Civil Service. Positions exempted from the classified service include those so provided by (1) statute, (2) Schedule A, for which no examinations are required, (3) Schedule B, for which a noncompetitive examination must be taken to prove minimum qualifications, and (4) Schedule C, which are policy-determining or confidential in character.

Excluding the employees under other merit systems such as those of the TVA, the FBI, the Atomic Energy Commission, the Foreign Service, and the Veterans' Administration (professional), the task force of the second Hoover Commission estimated that 220,000 employees were exempted under Schedules A, B, and C. Well over one-half of these positions are overseas. According to the Hoover report, either these positions should be brought into the competitive civil service or a special merit system should be established to fit their needs. Independent merit systems should be certified by the President. Provision should be made to transfer employees in the smaller

From a tiny fraction in 1884, the competitive sector of the Federal service has grown over 90 per cent by 1960. Uniformed military personnel are not included. [Data from U.S. Civil Service Commission.]

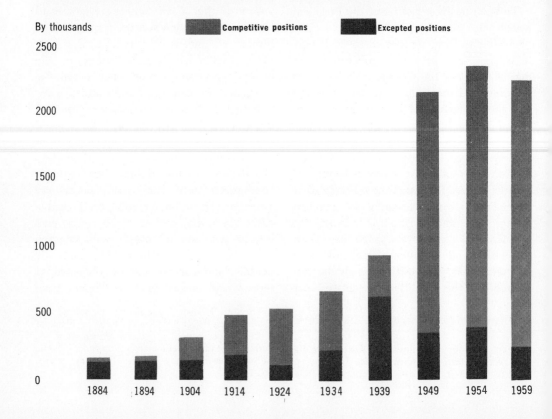

GROWTH OF THE FEDERAL GOVERNMENT SERVICE
showing the division between competitive and excepted positions

By thousands
■ Competitive positions ■ Excepted positions
2500 · 2000 · 1500 · 1000 · 500 · 0

1884 1894 1904 1914 1924 1934 1939 1949 1954 1959

Federal merit systems into the general competitive ranks, and also to make transfers the other way around.

The second Hoover Commission also noted the continued political clearance of appointees to rural-letter-carrier positions and urged that these posts be taken out of politics. It asked for transfer to the competitive category the positions of marshals, customs officials, and mint employees. The Hoover group did not, however, follow its task force in urging inclusion of attorneys in the competitive service, or in freeing the appointment of postmasters from political clearance.

Merit-system Groups. The interest and support of citizens and groups has made possible the expansion and improvement of the merit system. Two national organizations deserve special mention. The Public Personnel Association (formerly the Civil Service Assembly of the United States and Canada) grew out of a conference in Washington in 1906 on the invitation of President Theodore Roosevelt and the United States Civil Service Commission. It is the organization of civil-service commissioners and personnel engaged in public personnel administration. It works mainly in the research and technical fields. Through annual conferences and periodicals—monthly *Personnel News* and quarterly *Public Personnel Review*—the assembly provides mediums for the interchange of views and the discussion of problems by personnel administrators and students.

The National Civil Service League, launched in 1881, is the crusading organization in this field. It has conducted campaigns for the extension of the merit-system idea and for the expansion of the classified service after merit systems have been adopted.[1]

[1] For further information, see Frank M. Stewart, *The National Civil Service Reform League: History, Activities and Problems* (Austin, Tex.: University of Texas Press, 1929).

Many citizens' groups in the states operate wholly or partially in the field of merit-system reform and defense. The League of Women Voters—national, state, and local—has been one of the most vigilant and informed of these groups.

THE SELECTION PROCESS

Recruitment. The first task in a personnel program is to interest potential personnel in applying for positions. On the whole, this work has been done poorly by American public personnel agencies. Those who knock at the gates asking for admission to the Federal service often are largely self-informed about the prospects of public employment. Through passiveness, personnel agencies commonly have failed to cultivate the most promising sources of able recruits. They have been content to publish a formal announcement of forthcoming examinations and have it posted in public places. Recently recruiting practices have improved considerably.

The field from which recruiting is done is limited by the prerequisites stipulated for the position under consideration. Ordinarily American personnel agencies are liberal and permit a great age range for most jobs. Outside pressure is exerted to keep open maximum opportunities for public employment to persons of middle age or after. Authorities in the personnel field favor induction of persons into the public service while they are young, making possible a long and specialized career in the government service.

Closely related to age of recruiting is the question of education. In many instances the idea of giving everyone a chance has been used to justify low or no educational requirements. For professional posts, of course, a license to practice or a professional degree is required, but strenuous opposition develops to allegedly "undemocratic" barriers in the form of educational prerequisites. Examinations may later eliminate untrained persons, but the cost of giving tests to unqualified persons represents waste of public funds. Another important question concerns the desirable type of training. The practical nature of civil-service examinations favors persons with specialized training. British and other great civil-service systems favor the recruiting of those with general education, with specialization to follow induction.

Experience is another qualification commonly required. This varies widely with the position. Personnel agencies often stress experience to the exclusion of education, thus favoring the older applicant over the younger. Citizenship and residence almost invariably are required, although a waiver of the residence requirement is made occasionally for positions for which qualifications are rare. The recruiting announcement usually specifies sex; far more and better paid jobs are available for men than for women.

The common formal printed announcement, inquiries in schools, use of mailing lists, newspaper advertisements and stories, and radio programs inform the public of opportunities in civil service.

Both Hoover Commissions suggested improvement of recruiting through wider distribution of announcements, better information programs, and expansion of college recruiting.

Application. When interested in the available position, the recruit fills out an application form. The blank should call for data necessary to establish the applicant's eligibility for the post to be filled. Spaces are provided for name, address, age, education, experience, references, and a variety of other matters. A photograph of the applicant usually is required. If the application is approved, the candidate for the job may take the examination. The application may be rejected if the applicant lacks some stipulated requirement or has something in his record that disqualifies him.

Private industries place emphasis on the application and carefully evaluate the completed form. Public personnel agencies, as a rule, use the application only to ascertain whether the applicant meets the requirements for taking the examination which has been announced. When no formal test is to be administered, the application form is far more extensive, for it and the references may provide the whole basis for judgment of the applicant.

Examination. Today most of the positions under Federal, state, and local merit systems are filled from eligible lists of persons who have passed a formal written examination. From the beginning, Federal tests were practical in nature, related to the duties of the office sought. Practical examinations are characteristically American and well suited for selecting clerical and manipulative workers. General examinations in Britain have proved superior for the selection of persons capable of filling the higher administrative posts.

These two types of examination have proved valuable, and each has its place in an adequate testing program. It is not enough to test technical abilities without considering capacity for growth, as may be done with "practical" American tests. The general British examination would be misapplied if used as the sole test for mail sorters in the post office. Both achievement and capacity are needed in varying degrees by public employees. In a rare case one is needed to the complete exclusion of the other.

Some governmental departments have conducted careful research studies on the qualities needed for specific positions. Criteria for success are difficult to establish, since supervisors differ in their ideas of effective work. However, if a group of the most successful workers can be compared to the most unsuccessful on their responses to tests, a sort of pattern can be developed. Applicants who come nearest to fitting this pattern will have the best chance of succeeding on the job.

It is more difficult to obtain tests which correlate highly with job performance for complex than for simple jobs. Examinations are designed to test for different qualities.

The amount of intelligence which is most desirable varies from job to job. An intelligence level below that needed for the work would result in feelings of inadequacy and defeat; too much intelligence for a job would tend to make the worker bored and dissatisfied. These attitudes would decrease the morale of the worker and thus production. From research studies of successful workers on each specific job, an intelligence test floor and ceiling can be established.

An attempt is made to evaluate special aptitudes. It is most difficult to separate innate aptitude such as muscular coordination from skill acquired from training. Most aptitude tests include evaluations of both capacity and achievement. Mechanical-aptitude tests, for instance, might test for visualization of objects in space and ask for identification of pictures of tools. Clerical-aptitudes tests evaluate speed of finger movements through demonstrations of speed in placing dots in circles. They test training by vocabulary or the knowledge of how to file certain subject matter.

Personality tests are used in some instances to attempt to measure the applicant's emotional maturity, since much turnover is caused by personality problems. The evaluation is difficult because no applicant wishes to put himself in a bad light by admitting that he blows up often or feels uncomfortable in meeting new people, etc.

The tests do show whether the testee understands socially accepted behavior.

Achievement, or trade, tests measure informational and technical training—such as speed of typing, accuracy of arithmetic, knowledge of laws. They fall distinctly in the category of practical tests specified in so many American civil-service laws.[1]

Forms of Examinations. The usual examination is written and objective. The oral examination has been used very satisfactorily in some places, but it is slow and open to abuses. The interview held by the appointing officer after certification may prove sufficient for ascertaining personality, particularly when he may choose one of the three highest. The short-answer, or objective, type of examination has displaced almost entirely the traditional essay form. The essay examination is slow to read and difficult to grade fairly, especially when a very large number of papers is involved; the essay also places a premium on literary ability and penmanship.

The objective examination has the assets of definite and standardized answers and speedy grading. The machine-scored form can be fed to a counting machine for accurate grading and lightning results. The objective tests take the usual forms: completion, true-false, multiple choice, and matching.

Formerly the United States Civil Service Commission administered virtually all the examinations for the competitive civil service. The first Hoover Commission recommended that primary responsibility be

[1] Experience with the Federal Service Entrance Examination, through which young people with college education or equivalent may begin careers in government, is reviewed in a series of articles in *Public Administration Review*, vol. 16 (Winter, 1956): Philip Young, "The Federal Service Entrance Examination," pp. 1–5; James G. Stochard, "The FSEE and the Staffing of Federal Agencies," pp. 6–10; and Henry Reining, Jr., "The FSEE: The University Point of View," pp. 11–14.

placed on departments and agencies, subject to Commission supervision. The second Hoover Commission favored more use of open, continuous examinations, available at any time; more use of interviews, with improved techniques; and fuller validation of tests and employment standards.

Preparation of Eligible List. Applicants who receive a passing grade in the examination have their names listed on a register in the order of their scores, except that veterans are given preference. The eligible list for a particular position (as stenographer, patrolman, senior attorney) is available to appointing officers. When the eligible list becomes exhausted or obsolete, another examination renews it. Eligible lists are based upon the classification system employed by the jurisdiction. If this classification provides for thousands of minute categories, flexibility is lost; a bookkeeper post in one agency may not be filled by a person on the eligible list for bookkeeper in another agency. Classification will be considered in a subsequent section.

Veterans' Preference. Veterans' preference constitutes one of the most hotly controversial questions in the public personnel field. The first preference law was enacted by Congress at the close of the Civil War; in 1919, preference was extended on a generous scale.

As the Second World War drew to a close, Congress enacted the Veterans' Preference Act of 1944, which virtually closes the greater part of the Federal service to male nonveterans for a long time. The act provides that preference shall be given to (1) ex-servicemen and women with service-connected disabilities, (2) wives of disabled servicemen who are themselves unable to work, (3) unmarried widows of deceased servicemen, and (4) any ex-service person. Those in categories 1, 2, and 3 have ten points added to examination scores;

moreover, certain types of jobs, such as guards, elevator operators, messengers, and custodians, are reserved exclusively for these groups. Veterans in the fourth category receive five extra points. Persons of all categories receive generous credit for military and other experience, some waivers of age, height, weight, and physical and educational requirements, and special privileges when appointments are being made.

Those who favor veterans' preference maintain that it is a proper way for a government to show its appreciation to those who risked their lives in its behalf. Opponents of preference grant the obligation of government to veterans but wish to meet it in ways that will not lower the efficiency of the public service.

The first Hoover Commission sought to put veterans' preference on a defensible basis by grouping all applicants as "outstanding," "well qualified," "qualified," and "unqualified"; within each quality category, veterans would be considered ahead of nonveterans. This proposal should eliminate the appointment of veterans incapable of doing a job, yet give qualified veterans absolute advantage over nonveterans in the same quality group.

Appointment. When the appointing officer wishes to fill a vacancy, he sends to the personnel agency for the eligible list. If he is a Federal official, this process is handled by the director of personnel of his department or establishment. The request for eligibles is called a "requisition" and generally states the title, duties, salary, and qualifications required. Federal law prescribes that the three names ranking highest on the eligible list be certified to the appointing officer. In the various other jurisdictions the number certified ranges from one to seven. The appointing officer is permitted to choose from among those certified. The arguments for allowing some latitude are strong, for personality and other factors not adequately assessed in written examinations may be judged by the appointing officer from oral interview.

Certification of eligibles by a civil-service commission may be made out of regular order. First, veterans' preference in some jurisdictions (including the Federal government under the Preference Act of 1944) requires the disabled veteran to be certified ahead of others on the eligible list. Second, appointments to the Federal positions in Washington are required to be apportioned among the states in proportion to their population. Although the latter has not been rigidly applied, it does place at a disadvantage those from states in which the quotas are filled.

The usual procedure is for the appointing officer to review the information of the personnel agency on the eligible persons. The one he adjudges the most promising candidate is called for interview. If personal qualities and appearance are satisfactory, appointment follows; if unsatisfactory, the second choice may be interviewed and appointed. Sometimes all certified persons are interviewed before a selection is made.

The first Hoover Commission and its personnel task force strongly condemned excessive centralization as a barrier to getting the right person promptly into the correct job. It proved impossible to break the bottleneck so long as a closed central register of eligibles must be maintained for the whole country. An active register containing thousands of names is drawn upon constantly by appointing agencies. The letter of the law appears to require that the top three names must be certified, but in practice dozens of names may be out to different agencies simultaneously.

The appointing officer is in a difficult spot. From the "grab bag" of the active register he receives the names of three people. Their places near the top of the register may have resulted from a high score on a written examination, from veterans' preference, or from the fact that others ahead on the register had been certified, appointed, or declined. From personal interviews, the appointing officer may conclude that none of the eligibles has the personality or ability to do the job. Under existing procedures he must appoint one of the eligibles or allow the position to remain vacant and hope for a better list next time.

To correct the existing defects, both Hoover Commissions recommended decentralization of recruiting and examining and more leeway for appointing officers than the "rule of three" allows.

Abuses appear at the appointing level. A person qualified mainly by political services may be given provisional appointment when no eligible list is available. Later, provisional appointees may be blanketed into the permanent service after noncompetitive examinations. Appointing officers may conspire to appoint political friends by securing "waivers," by threats or promises, from persons higher on the eligible list.

Appointed at last, the new civil servant is not yet fully secure. Normally he must serve out satisfactorily a period of probation, up to six months. Within this period, or at the close of it, the probationer may be dropped from the service if found unsuitable. Few civil-service agencies have adequate systems for efficiency rating; the reluctance of a superior officer to dismiss except for serious deficiency is general. As a result, the probationary test period is much less meaningful than might be expected.

Career-conditional Appointments. One of the most difficult problems of the Federal service is that of emergency expansion of government employment due to the extraordinary demands made by economic depression or war. During the Korean War a rider to an appropriation bill, the Whitten amendment, virtually froze the permanent civil service at September, 1950, levels. For more than four years nearly all appointments to the service were made on an indefinite basis.

In January, 1955, a new system of filling positions went into effect. Employees in the competitive service will serve three years in conditional status before achieving full career standing. Competitive examinations and eligible lists will continue to be used, except that the first year of appointment is probationary and considered part of the examination.

The immediate task was to analyze the records on an estimated 673,000 indefinite employees. Approximately one-third were eligible for full career status; another one-third qualified for career-conditional; the remaining third must remain indefinite unless qualified by future examination.

The keynote of the career-conditional plan is flexibility. In future expansions or contractions of the Federal service, the career employees will enjoy protection, yet the total force can be adjusted to needs without unduly inflating or deflating the permanent ranks. The order also facilitated the transfer of employees from other Federal merit systems, such as the Foreign Service, into the general competitive service.

CLASSIFICATION AND COMPENSATION

Duties Classification. The term "classification" is used in the personnel field in two ways. It is employed in a jurisdictional sense to indicate whether or not positions are within or without the "classified" or merit service. The more common use is in an occupational sense, classifying jobs on the basis of duties performed. A duties or

occupational classification is necessary to simplify the task of personnel management and make possible the elemental justice of equal pay, prestige, and title for equal work.

Occupational classification is accomplished through a process of job analysis. This may be done by the personnel agency or by an outside body. The work and responsibility of a particular job is determined by questionnaires and interviews. Individual positions are arranged into classes, groups, and services. Each class is assigned specifications—including title, duties, and qualifications. The plan is put into force by law or by executive order. The class is the basic unit; it is composed of a number of similar positions, as, for example, typists or clerks. Every position is then placed in a class; within each class the qualifications and scale of compensation for each position are nearly the same.

Under the Classification Act of 1949[1] the policy of equal pay for equal work is supported by varying rates of compensation in proportion to the difficulty, responsibility, and qualifications involved. The act covers about one million positions in the Federal service. A "position" consists of the work, duties, and responsibilities assignable to an officer or employee. A "class" includes those positions sufficiently similar in kind of work, level of difficulty or responsibility, and qualification requirements to warrant similar treatment. A "grade" embraces all classes sufficiently equal in responsibility and qualifications to place them within one range of rates. Each position is placed in the appropriate class and grade. The act established two schedules of grades and salary ranges: a General Schedule (GS) of eighteen grades and a Crafts, Protective,

[1] 63 Stat. 782. The Classification Act of 1923 arranged classes into great services which were, at the time the 1949 act went into effect, (1) professional and scientific, (2) subprofessional, (3) clerical, administrative, and fiscal, (4) custodial, and (5) clerical-mechanical.

and Custodial Schedule (CPC) of ten grades. A law passed in 1954 means the ultimate abolition of CPC by transfer of some positions to GS and others to area wage boards. The Civil Service Commission administers the provisions of the 1949 Act.

The Postal Pay Act of 1945 provides the classification for about 500,000 Federal employees; it contains ninety-two pay schedules. Most of the other Federal employees

The pattern of advancement in the Federal classified service. [Data from basic compensatory schedules of the Classification Act of 1949 as amended.]

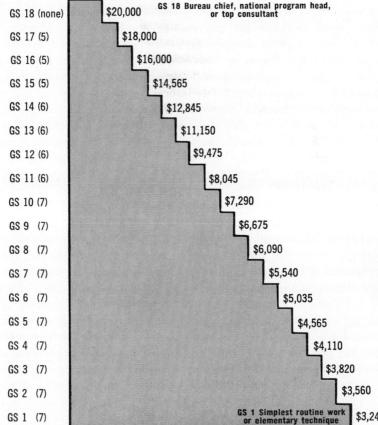

SALARIES AND CLASSIFICATION, FEDERAL CIVIL SERVICE
As of January 1, 1963
(With minimum salary for each grade, and number of steps in parentheses)

GENERAL SCHEDULE GRADE
No. of steps in parentheses

GS = General Schedule

MINIMUM SALARY

Grade	Minimum Salary	Description
GS 18 (none)	$20,000	GS 18 Bureau chief, national program head, or top consultant
GS 17 (5)	$18,000	
GS 16 (5)	$16,000	
GS 15 (5)	$14,565	
GS 14 (6)	$12,845	
GS 13 (6)	$11,150	
GS 12 (6)	$9,475	
GS 11 (6)	$8,045	
GS 10 (7)	$7,290	
GS 9 (7)	$6,675	
GS 8 (7)	$6,090	
GS 7 (7)	$5,540	
GS 6 (7)	$5,035	
GS 5 (7)	$4,565	
GS 4 (7)	$4,110	
GS 3 (7)	$3,820	
GS 2 (7)	$3,560	
GS 1 (7)	$3,245	GS 1 Simplest routine work or elementary technique

are subject to classification-compensation grades established through some sort of wage-board procedure.

The second Hoover Commission and its task force in 1955 complained that the Classification Act had too many grades, was devoid of flexibility to set pay rates, and provided insufficient difference between top and bottom pay rates. To correct these faults, it recommended that grades GS 1–6 be combined into three grades and GS 7–11 be combined into three. The higher grades would be left as is, except that GS 15 and up would be absorbed into the senior civil service. The postal-workers classification plan was criticized, and its eventual transfer to the general scheme was forecast.

Compensation. Once the job of classification is done, the next great task is to fix compensation schedules. Although elemental justice demands like pay for like work, a great range of compensation for comparable work is found in jurisdictions without adequate classification and salary-standardization systems. Proper classification plans establish the basis for salary uniformity for work of a given class and grade.

The public wage scale ought to be kept in some degree of harmony with that of private employment. Wages must be high enough to attract and hold good public employees, but not so high as to make government work overly attractive. Public personnel agencies constantly base salaries upon studies of comparable positions in private employment. If the usual starting wage for a file clerk is $200 per month in private New York offices, a public agency in the same city will have to approximate that amount for a beginner in the same line.

Another problem is to provide justly for differences of education or experience required for the various posts. The occupant of a job requiring a long and expensive professional education, as a physician or attorney, will demand higher compensation than, say, a public relations officer, for whom there may be no educational requirement. It is difficult to allow deference to such considerations, however, and the main reliance must be placed upon competition; if naval architects are hard to find, the compensation must be raised until a sufficient number are attracted.

Several rates of compensation will be provided within each class of positions ranging from a minimum, through some intermediate categories, to a maximum. Thus a typist might enter at $2,690 per year and advance, with some five intermediate salaries, to a maximum of $3,200. Ordinarily a new employee starts at the minimum rate; his aspiration to move on to the next salary rank constitutes an important incentive to do well.

Increments. Some public employees strongly desire to make salary increases within a given position automatic, an annual or biennial increment. Such a plan produces overemphasis on time serving and seniority and fails to evaluate services performed, as decided by superior officers, with or without formal efficiency ratings.

If public salaries are to be based upon rates for comparable private employment, the fluctuations in business conditions must be considered. While public pay may not be so flexible as compensation for private employment, substantial justice may be achieved by the fact that the public salary dips less in depression periods and rises less in prosperity. The civil servant therefore may be envied in bad times and pitied in good times. If a depression is long, the public employee is likely to have a flat-percentage salary cut; if cost of living increases sharply, he may lobby through an increase. A few jurisdictions have attempted to adjust salaries to a cost-of-living index formula.

EFFICIENCY AND MORALE

Service Ratings. How test the efficiency of public employees? Civil-service agencies have experimented with various systems to rate performance. The simplest and surest method of rating is based upon quantity and quality of production at some routine task. Like piecework in industry, this can apply only to a limited number of jobs—a typist or machine operator, for example—capable of unit measurement. It is also possible to rate employees by examinations or tests given at regular intervals, but this method has had little development.

The formal rating schemes have had broader application. They require that the superior officer indicate on a form his evaluation of each employee under his direction. One common method is to rate by traits or level of performance, utilizing a "graphic rating scale" on which the supervisor checks the description appropriate to the employee's qualities and work. Another, called "man-to-man comparison," requires the superior officer to rank his subordinates in terms of best, average, and poorest.

The basic difficulty with efficiency rating schemes lies in securing unprejudiced and frank evaluations by superior officers. In the judgment of authorities on personnel, service ratings are in a rudimentary stage. They are nevertheless improving and represent an advance over the uncoordinated efforts of individual supervisors to judge performance. Certainly at the present stage of development service ratings should not be the only criteria to decide promotion but may properly be used as one factor.

In place of the then-existing Federal rating system, the first Hoover Commission proposed an "ability and service record" rating under which the supervisor would (1) evaluate ability, past performance, pro-gress, and potential usefulness on specific factors and (2) discuss with the employee his strengths and weaknesses. The Hoover group urged that the rating be ignored in determining salary increases, layoffs, or dismissals.

The Eighty-first Congress enacted, however, the Performance Rating Act of 1950. The second Hoover Commission reported in 1955 on the failure of the rating system: approximately 98 per cent of those rated were deemed "satisfactory," while the "outstanding" and "unsatisfactory" categories went practically unused because of onerous restrictions attached to each. Abolition of the system was recommended; an annual report from supervisors on exceptional and unsatisfactory employees was suggested in its place.

Disciplinary Action. It is obvious that civil servants should not be immune from disciplinary action, including removal. They are obliged to perform their duties faithfully, to obey the law, and to avoid conduct unbecoming in a public employee. Sometimes these obligations are set forth in specific detail in an administrative code; most American governments have failed to prescribe employee rights and duties with clarity. The rules for the conduct of Federal employees are found in laws such as the Hatch Act and in the rules of Civil Service Commission and operating agencies. The administrative employee of the United States may not participate in partisan political activities.

An employee of the classified service may be removed only for such cause "as will promote the efficiency of said service" and he must be notified in writing of the charges and given a public hearing. The Civil Service Commission rules give the Commission a restricted power to investigate, but the real authority over removals is in the hands of the appointing officer. Responsibility for discipline and removal in the Federal service rests almost completely with the head of the department or agency.

Many forms of disciplinary action exist. Reprimand or warning is used for minor infractions. Demerits in service ratings, loss of seniority, or transfer to an undesirable location of work may handle intermediate offenses. Suspension, demotion, or dismissal may be used for serious violations. In the Federal service, except in loyalty cases, no appeal is possible from disciplinary action approved by a department head. Proposals have been made to authorize the Civil Service Commission to review disciplinary cases, or to establish a special court to hear appeals from disciplinary action. Some civil service jurisdictions follow the existing Federal scheme of permitting broad discretion on the part of the appointing officer. Others vest important disciplinary authority in the personnel commission or allow appeals to the courts on a liberal basis.

Two principal laws govern the separation of Federal employees from the service. Under the Lloyd–La Follette Act of 1912, non-veterans are subject to what the second Hoover Commission called a "simple and just method consonant with the requirements of an efficient public service."[1] The Veterans' Preference Act of 1944 permits the dismissal of veterans only if elaborate requirements are followed. About one-half of Federal employees are veterans.

Morale and Prestige. Morale is defined as a state of mind, with reference to confidence. Prestige is related to morale but is different: It means the respect for achievement or standing of an individual or group. High morale and high prestige are important to the effective functioning of a public body.

Commonly recognized as prerequisites to

[1] Second Hoover Commission, *Personnel and Civil Service* (1955), pp. 69–70.

high morale in the public service are such factors as security from spoils politics, fairness in wages and working conditions, recognition of good work, and adequacy of retirement system. Group morale, or *esprit de corps*, may be heightened by an agency through attention to its employees' social life, living conditions, credit facilities, unions, and associations.

Many of the same factors that produce high morale also contribute to the prestige of an agency or of public employment generally. A worker wishes to enjoy the admiration of people. The American public service has not enjoyed the prestige value of the British civil service. This low esteem may be traced to several factors, notably to spoils politics, low wages, and insecurity of tenure. Recently advances have been made on these fronts, and prestige has improved. Plenty of room for further improvement remains, however, and the nation should aspire to make employment in its service as attractive as that in any private concern.

Reductions in Force. The fairness or unfairness with which government carries out reductions in force greatly affects morale. In the layoffs of 1953–1954, following the change of administration and the end of the Korean War, existing law and the practices followed undermined the confidence of many civil servants. Here again the Veterans' Preference Act was the controlling factor. For reduction-in-force purposes, employees are initially divided into three groups: (1) career, (2) career-conditional, and (3) indefinite. Permanent employees in the competitive classified service (group 1) may not be laid off before lower-tenure groups (2 and 3) are.

Within each group, however, veterans have preference over nonveterans. Seniority is a minor factor. The very few employees with "outstanding" performance ratings receive some additional credits.

From this complicated set of rules comes the practice of "bumping": A career employee who cannot be retained in his present post because of reductions may accept a lesser position in the same agency, dislodging an employee of a lower group, preference, or seniority. The bumped employee may, in turn, displace someone below him, and the process continues like a chain reaction. Thus one case of bumping high up in an agency may result in demotions in considerable number all along the line. Efficiency, or even seniority, has little to do with this process; typically a veteran with relatively short service may displace a career nonveteran with much longer service and experience.

The second Hoover Commission called for modification of the Veterans' Preference Act to give more credit to years of service, performance, and usefulness.

Turnover. The high turnover rate that plagues the Federal service is evidence of widespread employee dissatisfaction. Between 1951 and 1954, from 445,000 to 988,000 persons had to be recruited yearly to maintain a work force that ranged from 2,330,000 to 2,603, 000; one out of each four positions fell vacant each year.

The task force that surveyed the personnel field for the first Hoover Commission secured the views of nearly 3,500 college seniors toward the public service as a career. Government employment was rated below private industry in salary, opportunities for promotion, incentives to improve efficiency, prestige and recognition, and other categories. Public service was more attractive than private only in security of job, opportunities for service, and leave, retirement, and health benefits.

The second Hoover task force summarized in 1955 the factors affecting morale in the public service as management-employee relations, material rewards, working conditions, and prestige. Prestige, it reported, is most affected by general attitudes of Congress, the public, and the press, behavior of Federal employees and officials, and specific problems such as security and politics in the merit system.

The task force proposed a program to raise morale and prestige by (1) maintaining high standards of personal conduct by Federal employees, (2) defending the public service against sweeping, unsupported charges and acting on accurate, specific charges, (3) protecting public servants against unfair attacks—a task in which the political executive should take the lead.[1]

Loyalty Program. Near the beginning of the "cold war," President Truman, in March, 1947, set up a loyalty program for the Federal service. Later in the same year the Civil Service Commission created a Loyalty Review Board to handle cases arising from it. The Board was abolished by President Eisenhower in April, 1953, and final responsibility for dismissing employees as security risks placed in the hands of department and agency heads. The Bureau of Personnel of the Civil Service Commission directs background security investigative activities. The security appraisal staff of the Commission coordinates agency operations in the employee security field and maintains security-hearing-board rosters for the agencies. About one-third of the Commission's expenditures for fiscal year 1961 were for investigative functions.

The loyalty programs have been criticized both on the ground that they have undermined employee morale and the ground that

[1] This outstanding report was prepared under the chairmanship of President Harold W. Dodds of Princeton University; George A. Graham was director of the task-force staff. Encouraging evidence of increased prestige of public service is contained in Morris Janowitz and Deil Wright, "The Prestige of Public Employment: 1929 and 1954." *Public Administration Review,* vol. 16 (Winter, 1956), pp. 15–21.

"Those Crazy Egghead Scientists—If You Didn't Hold 'Em Down They'd Want To Reach For The Moon"

HERBLOCK
The Washington Post

After the Russians launched their first Sputnik in 1957, Herblock intensified his assault on the restraints imposed upon scientists who work for government. [From *Herblock's Special For Today* **(Simon and Schuster).]**

employees in loyalty proceedings have been denied several basic rights, including presumption of innocence until guilt is proved, nonadmissibility of association evidence, right to be informed of charges, right to confront and cross-examine accusers, and immunity from double jeopardy.[1]

In 1956 the Court ruled that a food and drug inspector (with veteran preference) was improperly dismissed because his post was not shown to affect national security [*Cole v. Young*, 351 U.S. 536]. The immediate result was to limit the employee security program to persons in security-sensitive positions. Later it was held that a short-order cook employed by a private concessionaire within a naval weapons plant could be barred by a security

[1] The operation of the program was reviewed in Robert N. Johnson, "The Eisenhower Personnel Security Program," *Journal of Politics*, vol. 18 (November, 1956), pp. 625–650.

officer without stating grounds or granting a hearing. [*Cafeteria and Restaurant Workers v. McElroy*, 367 U.S. 886 (1961)].

In the meantime, President Eisenhower approved seven revisions in procedure governing security-risk cases: (1) The statement of charges against an employee should be drawn specifically and should be given to the employee at the time of his suspension. (2) The employee should be interviewed prior to suspension, and the final decision to suspend should be made by an Assistant Secretary or above. (3) A legal officer should be present at hearings to advise both the Security Board and the employee, if he is not represented by counsel. (4) Agency heads should review periodically the personnel of Security Boards to ensure high caliber. (5) Before an agency makes an adverse security evaluation of an employee previously cleared by another agency, its head should consult with the head of the other agency to ensure that all relevant information has been considered. (6) Every effort should be made to produce witnesses so that they can be confronted and cross-examined by the employee, so long as such production "would not jeopardize the national security." (7) All violations of law disclosed in security investigations should be reported to the Department of Justice.

Although these new rules improved loyalty proceedings, critics continued to point out alleged deficiencies. Department and agency heads still possessed final authority to fire in security cases. A number of congressional leaders preferred a new independent agency to take appeals from department and agency heads. Other complaints centered around the nonmandatory language of the new procedural "rules"; each one is stated in terms of "should be," rather than "must."

In 1954 a conference of the American Assembly urged that the loyalty-security program be taken out of partisan politics, and, to this end, that the President appoint a commission of outstanding citizens to review it. Acting on this and similar recommendations, Congress created a commission appointed jointly by the President, the Vice President, and the Speaker. The Commission, which was headed by Loyd Wright, reported in June, 1957. It recommended retention, with revisions, of previously existing security programs. It proposed a new "central security office" to:

. . . provide a continuous study of security needs and measures, conduct loyalty and security hearings, and furnish advisory decisions to heads of Government departments and agencies.[1]

The Commission recommended also that disclosure of information known to be classified be made unlawful for persons both in and out of government employment. It urged that evidence of subversion obtained by wiretapping be made acceptable in court. Other suggestions for change have been heard before congressional committees. One would nullify a part of the Cole decision by subjecting employees in nonsensitive positions to security procedures. Another would have given full discretion to an agency head to fire any employee in the interests of national security. No action was taken.

[1] U.S. Commission on Government Security, *Report of . . . .* (1957), p. xvi.

Retirement and Welfare. The national government first adopted a retirement plan for its employees in 1920. Most permanent civil servants receive retirement, disability, and survivor protection under the Civil Service Retirement Act of 1920. An employee contributes 6½ per cent of salary to the retirement fund; the balance comes from appropriations. Employees may retire as early as age fifty-five, after thirty years of service, but the compulsory retirement age is seventy.

The Federal system is based on actuarial reserves, which by adding contribution, appropriation, and compounded interest, produce an appropriate benefit at retirement age. Employee contributions, plus interest, are refundable on separation from the service before qualifying for an annuity.

Some "fringe" benefits are available during working years. Sick leave, rest periods, overtime, vacations with pay, group life, health, unemployment, and accident insurance are among the services provided. A system of cash incentive awards was established in 1954; employees who perform outstanding services or make important inventions can be rewarded by heads of departments or by the President. The most pressing need is to bolster the prestige of the service.

FOR FURTHER READING

American Assembly: *The Federal Government Service: Its Character, Prestige, and Problems* (New York: Columbia University, Graduate School of Business, 1954).

Avery, Robert S.: *Experiment in Management: Personnel Decentralization in the Tennessee Valley Authority* (Knoxville, Tenn.: University of Tennessee Press, 1954).

Blau, Peter M.: *The Dynamics of Bureaucracy* (Chicago: University of Chicago Press, 1956).

Boutecou, E.: *Federal Loyalty Security Program* (Ithaca, N.Y.: Cornell University Press, 1953).

Brown, Ralph S., Jr.: *Loyalty and Security* (New Haven, Conn.: Yale University Press, 1958).

Carpenter, William S.: *The Unfinished Business of Civil Service Reform* (Princeton, N.J.: Princeton University Press, 1952).

Case, Harry L.: *Personnel Policy in a Public Agency: the T.V.A. Experience* (New York: Harper, 1955).

Commission of Inquiry on Public Service Personnel: *Better Government Personnel* (New York: McGraw-Hill, 1935). Twelve monographs were published in 5 volumes.

Corson, John J.: *Executives for the Federal Service* (New York: Columbia University Press, 1952).

David, Paul T., and Ross Pollock: *Executives for*

Government (Washington, D.C.: Brookings Institution, 1957).

Godine, Morton: *The Labor Problem in the Public Service* (Cambridge, Mass.: Harvard University Press, 1951).

Hart, Wilson: *Collective Bargaining in the Federal Civil Service* (New York: Harper, 1961).

Kammerer, Gladys M.: *Impact of War on Federal Personnel Administration, 1939–1945* (Lexington, Ky.: University of Kentucky Press, 1951).

Manning, Bayless: *Conflict of Interest and Federal Service* (Cambridge, Mass.: Harvard University Press, 1961).

Mosher, William E., J. Donald Kingsley, and O. Glenn Stahl: *Public Personnel Administration* (New York: Harper, 3d ed., 1950).

O'Brien, J. L.: *National Security and Individual Freedom* (Cambridge, Mass.: Harvard University Press, 1955).

Powell, Norman J.: *Personnel Administration in Government* (Englewood Cliffs, N.J.: Prentice-Hall, 1956).

Public Personnel Association (formerly Civil Service Assembly of the United States and Canada): *Public Personnel Review* (quarterly, began publication 1940).

———: *Newsletter* (monthly, began publication 1930).

Spero, Sterling D.: *Government as Employer* (New York: Remsen Press, 1949).

Stahl, O. Glenn: *Public Personnel Administration* (New York: Harper, 5th ed., 1962).

Stewart, Frank M.: *The National Civil Service Reform League: History, Activities and Problems* (Austin, Tex.: University of Texas Press, 1929).

Torpey, William G.: *Public Personnel Management* (Princeton, N.J.: Van Nostrand, 1952).

U.S. Civil Service Commission: *Annual Report* (yearly).

U.S. Commission on Government Security: *Report of . . .* (1957).

U.S. Commission on Organization of the Executive Branch of the Government (first Hoover Commission): *Personnel Management* (1949).

———: *Task Force Report on Federal Personnel* (1949).

U.S. Commission on Organization of the Executive Branch of the Government (second Hoover Commission): *Personnel and Civil Service* (1955).

———: *Task Force Report on Personnel and Civil Service* (1955).

U.S. President's Committee on Administrative Management: *Report . . . with Studies. . . .* (1937). Study 1 is "Personnel Administration in the Federal Service," by Floyd W. Reeves and Paul T. David.

Van Riper, Paul P.: *History of the United States Civil Service* (Evanston, Ill.: Row, Peterson, 1958).

Weinstein, Sandra: *Personnel Security Programs of the Federal Government* (New York: Fund for the Republic, 1954).

REVIEW QUESTIONS

1. Sketch the high points in the history of the American civil service and indicate the role of the Pendleton Act of 1883.

2. Indicate the approximate size of the present Federal service, the geographic distribution, and the principal departments affiliated with it.

3. Describe the common forms of personnel agencies, and indicate the advantages and disadvantages of each.

4. What are some of the problems involved in duties classification and salary standardization?

5. What limitations, if any, should be placed upon the right of public employees to organize unions and bargain collectively?

6. Discuss factors which may play a part in building high morale in the public service.

7. To what extent should the higher positions in the public service be exempt from the classified civil service and filled by partisans of the President and congressional majority?

8. What progress have we made toward establishing an attractive career in governmental service?

9. What did the first and second Hoover Commissions recommend regarding the civil service? To what extent have their recommendations been carried out?

10. Describe the loyalty and security programs through which the Federal government has sought to protect the public service from subversive influences.

Part Three

Federal Powers
and Functions

Chapter Twenty

The Tax Power
and Revenues

When one reviews the history of taxation it is difficult to avoid the conclusion that it illustrates
>*"The good old way, the simple plan*
>*That he shall take who has the power,*
>*And he shall keep who can."*

We find that the king took ruthlessly from the common people, while his power to take from those in positions of influence was tempered very materially by his fear of the consequences. Against this there have been numerous uprisings upon the part of those who felt that they were hurt, but knew not exactly how or where.

JACKSON H. RALSTON[1]

It was mainly financial necessities which motivated the Constitutional Convention in 1787, and it was to be expected that any constitution which might be proposed would contain much more adequate taxing powers than the Federal Government had previously possessed. The powers granted were quite extensive compared with previous ones, and they were considerably enlarged by the sixteenth amendment; but they were far from being all-inclusive.

COMMITTEE ON INTERGOVERNMENTAL FISCAL RELATIONS[2]

The power to tax, when exercised, provides the solid fuel necessary to make the mechanism of government operate. It is *sine qua non*, an indispensable ingredient, of government on every level.

The power to raise revenue is, of course, used to gather money for public treasuries; more than that, it may be used in such a way that governments, particularly the Federal government, affect social and economic conditions. Over recent decades, the national government has moved increasingly into regulation hooked to the tax power and into control of economic affairs to level out the peaks and valleys of the business cycle.

[1] *What's Wrong with Taxation?* (San Diego, Calif.: Ingram Institute, 1932), p. 47.

[2] U.S. Senate, *Federal, State, and Local Fiscal Relations*, 78th Cong., 1st Sess. (1943), pp. 54–55.

THE POWER TO TAX

The Tax Clause. The most serious weakness of the Articles of Confederation was that Congress could assess the states but lacked authority to lay and collect taxes directly from the people. It is not surprising that authority to tax stands first on the list of powers delegated to Congress by the Constitution. Article I, Section 8, provides:

The Congress shall have power to lay and collect taxes, duties, imposts and excises, to pay the debts and provide for the common defense and general welfare of the United States; but all duties, imposts and excises shall be uniform throughout the United States.

This brief passage, together with the necessary-and-proper clause, is authority for most Federal taxation.

Four Types of Levies. Congress may lay and collect levies of four types: (1) taxes, (2) duties, (3) imposts, and (4) excises. A tax is an exaction for the support of government. The word "taxes," as used in the tax clause, refers to direct taxes and probably was intended to include only property and capitation (poll) taxes, although in 1895 the Supreme Court ruled that a tax on income from property was also a direct tax.

Direct taxes (other than income) have been levied only five times since 1789, the fifth time to help finance the Civil War. If income taxes are excluded, no Federal revenues are today collected from direct taxes. Duties, imposts, and excises include all indirect taxes. "Duties" and "imposts" are nearly synonymous terms referring to tariffs. An "excise" is an internal tax generally imposed upon manufactures but sometimes upon consumption and retail sales. In recent years, income taxes have accounted for the largest amount of Federal revenue. Excises, taxes, and tariffs (duties and imposts), followed in the order mentioned.

Controversy over Income Taxes. The Constitution requires that all direct taxes be apportioned among the states on the basis of population. Toward the end of the last century this question arose: Is a tax upon incomes a direct or indirect tax? If direct, then income taxes must be apportioned among the states on the basis of population; if indirect, the Constitution would be satisfied if taxes were graduated but uniform within all classifications throughout the country. The controversy arose from a graduated Federal income-tax law enacted in 1894 that did not provide for apportionment among the states.

Pollock, a stockholder in the Farmers' Loan and Trust Company of New York, brought suit to enjoin his company from paying the tax upon its income derived from real estate and from state and local government bonds. The Supreme Court had considerable difficulty in reaching a decision. A similar law, which was enacted in 1861 and had expired in 1872, had been upheld by a unanimous Court [*Springer v. United States*, 102 U.S. 586 (1881)]. But in the cases at hand [*Pollock v. Farmers' Loan and Trust Co.*, 157 U.S. 429 (1895), 158 U.S. 601 (1895)], the Supreme Court ruled that taxes upon incomes were direct, hence unconstitutional, because they were not apportioned among the states.

These decisions precluded the enactment of future income-tax legislation, inasmuch as administration would be difficult if apportionment were undertaken, and it would be impossible to devise a tax schedule that would fall upon people in proportion to their ability to pay. Though from an economic point of view the Court was undoubtedly correct that a tax on income was direct in nature, the decision was a clear reversal of previous decisions. The Court's opinions were the subject of much controversy and have been roundly condemned by many. The decisions stood, nevertheless, until rendered insignificant by adoption of the Sixteenth Amendment.

The Income-tax Amendment. Years of agitation, particularly in the West and South, led to the adoption of the Sixteenth Amendment in 1913. It reads:

> The Congress shall have power to lay and collect taxes on incomes, from whatever source derived, without apportionment among the several States, and without regard to any census or enumeration.

Note that the amendment does not settle the argument of whether a tax upon incomes is direct or indirect. It merely obviates the necessity of apportionment.

Shortly after the adoption of the income-tax amendment, a dispute arose over the meaning of "from whatever source derived." Some argued that the phrase was not intended to enlarge the list of what might be taxed but merely to reverse the Pollock decisions rendering it unnecessary to apportion income taxes. Others interpreted the phrase literally, saying "from whatever source derived" meant just that. If this opinion prevailed, there would be no doubt that Congress could tax incomes cf state employees, or income derived from Federal, state, and local bonds. The argument was temporarily settled in 1916 when the Supreme Court restricted the amendment to its narrowest construction [*Brushaber v. Union P. R. Co.*, 240 U.S. 1 (1916)]. The decision was reaffirmed in 1928 when the Court held that Congress was forbidden to tax interest on state and local government bonds even in an indirect way [*National Life Insurance Co. v. United States*, 277 U.S. 508 (1928)].

In 1938, the Supreme Court endorsed Federal taxation of income paid employees by state governments and created the distinct impression of favoring the broader, more literal interpretation of the Sixteenth

GRIN AND BEAR IT   By Lichty

"I shall continue to promise the voters lower taxes, gentlemen! . . . In my opinion scientific developments haven't changed the facts of political science! . . ."

Lichty comments on the tendency of some congressmen to vote yes on appropriations and no on taxes. (George Lichty and Chicago *Sun-Times* Syndicate.)

Amendment. If this impression is correct, legal obstacles to Federal taxation of income from state and local government securities have been removed.

Purposes for Which Congress Might Tax. The tax clause suggests that there are three purposes for which Congress may lay and collect taxes: (1) to pay the debts, (2) to provide for the common defense, and (3) to provide for the general welfare. These phrases are so general that they arouse endless controversy over their meaning.

For Revenue or Regulation? The primary assumption underlying the tax clause is that taxes are levied to obtain revenue, but Congress often has legislated with mixed motives. Tariff laws, in addition to raising money, have sought to protect American industry, and their constitutionality has never seriously been contested. In 1866 Congress levied a tax of 10 per cent on notes issued by state banks, for the purpose of driving them out of existence, and the measure was upheld [*Veazie Bank v. Fenno,* 8 Wall. 533 (U.S. 1869)]. In 1882 Congress imposed a head tax upon immigrants, the proceeds being earmarked for temporary care of the immigrants and not for the general support of government, and the Supreme Court sustained the legislation [*Head Money cases,* 112 U.S. 580 (1884)].

In 1902 Congress imposed a tax of 10 cents a pound on colored oleomargarine to discourage its consumption in favor of butter; the law was upheld [*McCray v. United States,* 195 U.S. 27 (1904)]. In 1912 a tax of 2 cents a hundred was laid upon matches made with poisonous phosphorus to protect workmen from the horrible occupational disease known as "phossie jaw." Although the law destroyed the white phosphorus industry, it was never challenged. Again, in 1914 and 1919 Congress required dealers in narcotics to pay a tax and submit to regulation, and the legislation was upheld [*United States v. Doremus,* 249 U.S. 86 (1919)].

In all the above cases which reached the Supreme Court, the Court refused to look behind the face of tax legislation into the motives that prompted its enactment.

Court Halts Use. A halt was called, however, in 1922. In two cases coming before it in that year, the Court distinguished between a "true" tax to raise revenue and tax measures intended to penalize or regulate matters reserved for state control. In the first case, the Supreme Court had before it the child labor law of 1919 [*Bailey v. Drexel Furniture Co.,* 259 U.S. 20 (1922). See also p. 555]. That measure levied a tax of 10 per cent upon the net profits of all establishments employing children in violation of standards set up in the act. The Drexel Furniture Company, doing business in North Carolina, permitted a boy under age fourteen to work in its factory during the taxable year 1919. Bailey, the United States collector of internal revenue, notified the company that it was obliged to pay 10 per cent of its net profits for the year. Upon appeal, the Supreme Court declared the law unconstitutional. The tax, it said, was not a true one but a penalty intended to regulate business, a matter reserved to the states.

The second case [*Hill v. Wallace,* 259 U.S. 44 (1922)] involved a Federal law enacted in 1921 intended to abolish dealings in futures upon the grain markets by imposing a tax of 20 cents a bushel upon all contracts for future delivery and subjecting boards of trade to detailed regulations. Hill, representing the Board of Trade of the City of Chicago, brought suit against Wallace, the Secretary of Agriculture, seeking to enjoin collection of the tax and enforcement of the law. The Court declared the law unconstitutional, saying the tax was a penalty enacted to regulate a subject reserved to the states.

The same reasoning was followed later (at least until 1937) and may be illustrated by several decisions. The Revenue Act of 1926 imposed a special excise tax of $1,000 upon retail liquor dealers who carried on business within a state contrary to state and local laws. Tested in 1935, the Supreme Court held the exaction to be not a tax but a penalty for the violation of state laws, the effect of which was to usurp the police powers of the states [*United States v. Constantine,* 296 U.S. 287 (1935)].

A case arose in the following year from the first Guffey Coal Act, which brought the bituminous coal industry under Federal control. The act levied a tax of 15 per cent upon all bituminous coal producers; 90 per cent of the tax was rebated to those who agreed to comply with a code established for the industry. The tax, the Court ruled, was not a true tax but a penalty designed to accomplish results beyond the reach of Federal powers [*Carter v. Carter Coal Co.*, 298 U.S. 238 (1936)].

Suppressing Weapons. A case decided in 1937 raised some doubt about the future attitude of the Court. The National Firearms Act of 1934, in addition to requiring dealers in firearms to obtain an annual license for a fee of $200, required the payment of a tax of $200 on each transfer of sawed-off shotguns, other firearms capable of being concealed (except revolvers and pistols), machine guns, and mufflers or silencers for any firearms. Although expected to produce some revenue, the principal purpose was the suppression of traffic in such weapons. Mr. Justice Stone stated:

Every tax is in some measure regulatory. To some extent it interposes an economic impediment to the activity taxed as compared with others not taxed. But a tax is not any the less a tax because it has a regulatory effect . . . and it has long been established that an Act of Congress which on its face purports to be an exercise of the taxing power is not any the less so because the tax is burdensome or tends to restrict or suppress the thing taxed [*Sonzinsky v. United States*, 300 U.S. 506].

In other words, a tax may be a penalty and the courts decline to inquire into the motives that led to its enactment. This came close to returning to the position adhered to prior to 1922.

The AAA. The controversy took a slightly different turn when the Court considered the Agricultural Adjustment Act of 1933. This set up a far-reaching plan to control farm production. The Department of Agriculture contracted with farmers to pay them for cooperating in a nationwide effort to limit farm production to market needs as one means of raising farm income and contributing to recovery from the Depression. Funds for the program were obtained from a processing tax collected from the first domestic processor of the farm product brought under control. This was an excise tax collected from the miller, the packing company, the cotton ginner, the tobacco manufacturer, and other processors and passed on to consumers in the form of higher prices. The excise met the constitutional requirement of uniformity, since it was collected at the same rate from all producers of particular products regardless of their geographic location. Here, then, was a uniform excise tax levied by Congress to raise revenue to spend among farmers as a means of regulating production and thereby helping recovery.

The constitutionality of the act was challenged, and the case reached the Supreme Court in 1936 [*United States v. Butler*, 297 U.S. 1 (1936)]. The Court majority of six held the measure unconstitutional, chiefly on the ground that the processing taxes were used to coerce farmers as a means of regulating farm production—something reserved to the states by the Tenth Amendment. A strong dissent written by Justice Stone contended that the tax was a uniform excise; that it was used to raise money for the general welfare; that production control was a necessary and proper incident to the primary purpose of helping the nation recover; and hence state powers were not usurped by the Federal government. The decision temporarily halted the farm program, but new devices were discovered to achieve the same end. Subsequent farm legislation has been based primarily on the commerce power, the theory being that production control is incidental to the regulation of the flow of goods to national markets.

The Social Security Act. The issue arose again with the Social Security Act of 1935, but the verdict was different. One feature of this measure imposed a payroll tax on employers and employees to create an old-age and survivors' insurance plan. Immediately challenged, the tax was upheld by the Supreme Court [*Helvering v. Davis*, 310 U.S. 619 (1937)]. The majority of seven insisted that the tax was a uniform excise and income tax, even though exempting a number of employments. They also contended that the revenues were being spent for the general welfare and were not invading powers reserved to the states. The minority countered by contending that the tax was not uniform because many employments were exempted, funds were not being spent for the general welfare but for only a portion of the population, and powers reserved to the states were being usurped.

Another feature of the act levied taxes on employers of workers for the establishment of the unemployment-insurance program now so widely accepted. The law stipulated that employers would be given a 90 per cent credit on the Federal tax if states enacted compensation plans conforming with Federal standards. The Supreme Court upheld this tax offset by a 5-to-4 vote [*Steward Machine Co. v. Davis*, 301 U.S. 548 (1937)]. Again the majority reasoned that the tax was uniform, that it was spent to provide for the general welfare, and that state powers were not violated. The tax-offset device did not unduly coerce the states merely because the law made it attractive for them to cooperate. The minority insisted the tax was not uniform because of its many exemptions, the funds benefited special groups, and the states were improperly coerced and their powers invaded. It is difficult to reconcile this and the other social security tax case discussed above with the Butler case holding the AAA unconstitutional. In consequence of the broader interpretation, Congress may now use the tax power for almost any nationwide welfare program.

Gambling Tax. In 1953 the Supreme Court upheld the validity of an occupational tax on persons in the business of accepting wagers and a percentage tax on all bets except one type licensed by states [*United States v. Kahriger*, 345 U.S. 22 (1953)]. The majority ruled that the tax was not invalid merely because it burdened or discouraged a particular business. Although the tax was accompanied by a registration requirement, the Court held that self-incrimination was not violated. Mr. Justice Black, dissenting, declared that the statute required a man to register and confess he was engaged in gambling; thus "it creates a squeezing device contrived to put a man in federal prison if he refuses to confess himself into a state prison as a violator of state gambling laws."

Limitations on the Taxing Power. Though the taxing power has been broadly interpreted, it is not without limits. Some of these are expressly stated in the Constitution; others are implied.

No Taxes upon Exports. The Constitution expressly forbids only one type of tax. The single prohibition is that Congress may not place any tax or duty on articles "exported from any state." This provision was added upon the insistence of Southern states, who feared discrimination against their exports, particularly of cotton. "Exports" refer to goods shipped from any state to a foreign country and not to articles shipped from one state to another. A tax upon the production of articles, even though applied to that portion which is intended for export, is not considered an export tax. The provision would be violated, however, if a tax were laid on articles in the process of exportation, or if bills of lading and insurance policies for articles being exported were taxed.

Direct Taxes to Be Apportioned. The first restriction is that direct taxes (other than income) must be laid in proportion to the population of each state. In levying direct taxes, Congress must decide how much money it wishes to raise and allot to each state the same proportion that the population of the state bears to the total population.

This provision makes administration cumbersome and it results in taxation that bears no relation to people's ability to pay, hence the infrequent resort to direct taxes throughout our history.

Indirect Taxes to Be Uniform. A second restriction is that indirect taxes must be "uniform throughout the United States." This does not mean that they must be the same for everything and everybody; only geographic uniformity is required. Congress may make classifications for the purpose of taxation, but the tax cannot be more nor less for objects within the same class at any point within the United States.

The tariff on men's shoes, for example, may be higher than the tariff on women's, but the rate on men's cannot be less at the port of New Orleans than at New York. Employers of fewer than eight persons are exempt from paying a payroll tax to the Federal government from which to pay unemployed workmen, but all employers of eight or more must be taxed at the same rate whether they live in Maine or California. Large corporations may be required to pay at higher rates than smaller ones, but all of the same class and size must pay at the same rate whether they operate in Kansas or Ohio.

As a territory Hawaii was an integral part of the "United States," hence the uniformity clause applied there. It does not apply, however, to unincorporated territories. Therefore, people or objects in such a territory as Samoa might be taxed at rates either higher or lower than those charged within the fifty states.

Taxes Not to Discriminate between Ports. The third restriction is that Congress may not levy any tax that gives preference "to the ports of one state over those of another." While Federal levies must be uniform at all ports, Congress is not required to treat all ports alike in *every* respect. Congress has, for example, established ports of entry, erected lighthouses, improved rivers and harbors at some ports and not at others.

Implied Restrictions upon the Taxing Power. In addition to the general limitations, expressed and implied, mentioned above, several others pertaining particularly to the use of the taxing power should be noticed.

State and Federal Governments Not to Burden One Another. In a federal system, especially where the power to tax is shared concurrently by the national government and states, one government is likely to tax the other, either deliberately or otherwise. This happened early in our history when Maryland and several other states imposed taxes upon bank paper issued by the National Bank to impede the operations of the bank. This action led to the famous case of *McCulloch v. Maryland* [4 Wheat. 316 (U.S. 1819)], wherein the Supreme Court held that the Federal government and its agents and instrumentalities could not be taxed by the states, saying that "the power to tax involves the power to destroy." Observing that a Federal tax upon the states would be more justifiable than a state tax upon the Federal government, the Court nevertheless pointed out that Federal taxes that burdened the states would not be permitted.

Following this doctrine of intergovernmental immunity, the Supreme Court held Federal salaries immune from state taxation and state salaries free from Federal taxation. Likewise, Federal securities were declared free from state taxation, and the securities of state and local governments, and the interest on them, immune from Federal taxation. Later the immunity was extended to cover sales of goods to the government. Thus, a state tax on the sale of gasoline to the Federal government was held invalid, while a Federal tax on the sale of motorcycles to a municipal police department was held void. So the Court spun a web of reciprocal immunity.

The doctrine of intergovernmental immunity has always had its critics, but not until 1902 were modifications made. In that year the Court distinguished between functions strictly governmental and those commercial or proprietary in nature. The former were still immune from taxation but the latter were not. This meant that the national government might tax liquor monopolies, the salaries of persons employed in the management of municipally owned railways and other utilities, or the proceeds from the sale of athletic tickets by state universities.

Might states tax Federal instrumentalities engaged in proprietary operations? This has not been judicially determined. In the case of the TVA, the states have not attempted to tax its operations, but the Federal government has expressly authorized the Authority to make in-lieu payments to states in which its projects are located. The amounts are equivalent to the taxes that would be collected from a similar enterprise under private auspices.

Within recent years the courts have gone even further to break down the doctrine of intergovernmental immunities. The first significant break with the past occurred in 1938 when it was held that the salaries of officers of the New York Port Authority were subject to Federal taxation [Helvering v. Gearhardt, 304 U.S. 405 (1938)]. The Supreme Court went still further a year later, holding that the states might tax the salaries of Federal employees and the Federal government might tax the incomes of employees of state and local governments [Graves v. N.Y. ex rel. O'Keefe, 306 U.S. 466 (1939)]. A tax on income, said the Court, is neither economically nor legally a tax upon the source. Hence, there is no basis for the assumption that a tax levied by one government upon the salary of an employee of another government is tantamount to an interference by the first with the second in the performance of its functions. Since these recent decisions, all state and local government employees have become subject to Federal taxation, while at least forty states have imposed taxes upon the incomes of Federal employees living within their jurisdiction.

In 1958 the Supreme Court limited intergovernmental immunities still further by upholding a Michigan law that permitted municipalities to tax subcontractors working on prime contracts to which the United States was a party. The Court admitted that the Federal government "will eventually feel the financial burden of at least some of the taxes" but rationalized by saying:

There was no discrimination against the Federal Government, its property or those with whom it does business. There was no crippling obstruction of any of the Government's functions, no sinister effort to hamstring its power, not even the slightest interference with its property. [City of Detroit v. Murray Corp., 355 U.S. 489 (1958)].

The test in the future of Federal taxes is whether they are discriminatory or impose a burden so direct as to impede the operations of state and local agencies engaged in strictly governmental functions. The test for state taxation appears to be whether taxes discriminate against the Federal government or impose a direct and substantial burden upon it. Before states can tax Federal proprietary enterprises, Congress must grant approval.

Taxation of Judges' Salaries. To ensure judicial independence, the Constitution provides that Federal judges[1] shall be paid compensation which "shall not be diminished during their continuance in office." From this provision, controversy has arisen over whether judges might be required to pay taxes upon their salaries. The issue of immunity from taxation first arose when Congress abolished fees charged by justices of peace in the District of Columbia. This was declared unconstitutional insofar as it applied to incumbent justices [*United States v. More*, 3 Cr. 159 (U.S. 1805)].

During the Civil War, Congress taxed salaries of Federal judges. This legislation, although never judicially tested, was generally thought to be unconstitutional and the money was later refunded. In 1919 Congress enacted a revenue law which did not exempt judges' salaries; but when tested it was declared unconstitutional [*Evans v. Gore*, 253 U.S. 245 (1920)]. A later law imposed a tax upon the salaries of only those judges appointed subsequent to enactment of the legislation, but this, too, proved unacceptable [*Miles v. Graham*, 268 U.S. 501 (1925)]. In this instance the Supreme Court said that the Constitution imposed upon Congress the duty "definitely to declare what sum shall be received by each judge out of the public funds." Less amounted to an unconstitutional threat to judicial independence.

This doctrine prevailed until 1938, when it was overruled [*O'Malley v. Woodrough*, 307 U.S. 277 (1938)]. The case grew out of the revenue acts of 1932 and 1936, which taxed the salaries of judges appointed subsequently. A circuit judge named Woodrough, appointed in 1933, paid under pro-

[1] And, incidentally, the President. What is said here about Federal judges would probably apply to the President as well.

test a tax of more than $600 and then brought suit to recover the amount and prevent future collections. The district court, following precedents mentioned above, held the acts of Congress violative of the Constitution; but the Supreme Court by vote of 7 to 1 upheld the tax measures. The majority concluded that judicial independence was not threatened by subjecting judicial salaries to a general, nondiscriminatory tax. Rather, said the Court:

> To subject them [judges] to a general tax is merely to recognize that judges are also citizens, and that their particular function in government does not generate an immunity from sharing with their fellow citizens the material burden of the government whose Constitution and laws they are charged with administering.

Although the measures here in question applied only to judges appointed after passage of the tax laws, Congress later (in 1939) extended the law to those appointed prior to 1932.

State Powers Not to Be Invaded. Because the power to tax is broad and concurrent, Congress and the states can tax almost anything. Some of the limits to which the courts will allow Congress to go in using the taxing power for regulatory purposes have been indicated. What about possible limits on the so-called "spending power?"

Congress may tax to raise money to spend to provide for the "general welfare." The word "general" refers to that which is designed to benefit a considerable number of people as contrasted with something local or private. But may Congress spend money for any and all general purposes?

One school, led by James Madison, which interpreted the Constitution narrowly, insisted that Congress can spend money only to carry out the delegated powers mentioned in the Constitution. Others, led by

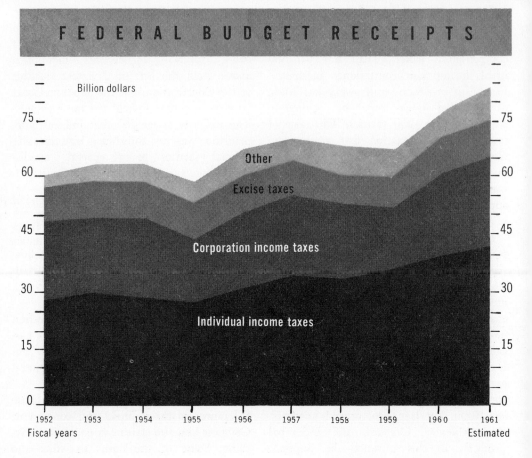

FEDERAL BUDGET RECEIPTS

Billion dollars

Other

Excise taxes

Corporation income taxes

Individual income taxes

1952   1953   1954   1955   1956   1957   1958   1959   1960   1961
Fiscal years   Estimated

(Data from U.S. Bureau of the Budget.)

Alexander Hamilton and Joseph Story, insisted that the taxing-and-spending clause is complete in itself and not limited to the fulfillment of other enumerated powers. The latter interpretation would authorize Congress to tax and spend for *any* purpose to provide for the *general* welfare.

The Supreme Court had never met the issue squarely until reviewing the AAA in the Butler case discussed above. Then, while applying the taxing-and-spending clause narrowly enough to invalidate the AAA, it endorsed the broad interpretation of the power. This interpretation provides the constitutional basis for expenditures for public relief, public works, old-age and sur-

vivors' insurance, unemployment compensation, soil conservation, most Federal education programs, and many other activities. If an expenditure is for a "general" purpose, it would probably not be disallowed for constitutional reasons.

This does not mean that Congress possesses unlimited authority to provide for the general welfare. The tax clause says that "Congress shall have power to lay and collect taxes, duties, imposts and excises, to pay the debts, provide for the common defense and the general welfare of the United States." Some historians contend that a semicolon, rather than a comma, should appear between the word "excises" and the phrase "to pay the debts." A semicolon would divide the sentence into two parallel parts, giving Congress the power to lay and collect taxes and also the power to do whatever it deemed necessary to pay the debts and provide for the common defense and the general welfare. Thus, Congress would possess a general police power. With a comma, the sentence means that taxes may be levied *in order to* pay the debts and provide for the common defense and the general welfare.

The draft of the Constitution reported by the Committee on Style did contain a semicolon, but the semicolon was displaced by a comma in the final draft. Some contend that the copyist took unwarranted liberty with the document. As matters stand, Congress has no separate power to provide for the general welfare but may spend money to obtain such ends. This accounts for the resort to taxation, subsidies to the state and local governments, and Federal spending rather than to more direct methods of providing for the public welfare.

The spending power is subject to two specific restrictions in addition to the general limitations discussed earlier in this chapter. An appropriation may not be made for "armies" for a period longer than two years,[1] and no money may be spent unless appropriated by Congress.

GOVERNMENTAL REVENUES

Income Taxes. Personal and corporate income taxes yield a larger revenue than any other single type of Federal tax.

In recent years the personal income tax brought about one-half and the corporate income tax about one-third of total Federal

[1] Art. I, sec. 8, cl. 12. Appropriations may, however, be made for the Navy and other branches of the government for longer than two years.

tax receipts, exclusive of social security transactions.

The personal income tax is "progressive" in that rates are higher for those with the higher incomes. For a typical year in the late 1950s the tax began at 20 per cent on the first $2,000 of net income, after deductions, and rose to 91 per cent on net income exceeding $200,000. A flat deduction of $600 was allowed to the taxpayer and to each of his dependents.

The corporate income tax has a much-less-marked progressive feature. In the same year the normal tax rate on corporate income was a flat 25 per cent, plus a surtax of 22 per cent for net income over $25,000.

Death and Gift Taxes. Like the income tax, the inheritance tax received its first important application during the Civil War, when every possible source of revenue had to be explored, but it was repealed within a decade. Two appeals from it met adverse court decisions. In 1916 a death tax was enacted and has been retained since. In recent years Federal revenue from death and gift taxes represented less than 2 per cent of Federal tax revenues.

The term "death taxes" includes two different forms: (1) An estate tax is levied on the total estate left by a deceased person; and (2) an inheritance tax applies to that part of a deceased person's estate passing to a particular heir or beneficiary. To guard against evasion by making gifts before death, the Federal government taxes large gifts. Other methods of evasion have been plugged by making subject to death taxes property in joint estates (joint bank accounts), community property (jointly held by husband and wife under the laws of certain states), and certain trusts.

Federal death taxes are progressive, allowing an estate of $60,000 to pass tax free, then rising from 3 per cent on an estate above that figure to a maximum of 77 per

FEDERAL INCOME TAX

If the taxable income* for a single person is	If the taxable income* for a married couple is	The government takes about
$ 2,000	$ 4,000	20 cents out of each $1
$ 4,000	$ 8,000	21 cents out of each $1
$ 6,000	$ 12,000	23 cents out of each $1
$ 8,000	$ 16,000	24 cents out of each $1
$ 10,000	$ 20,000	26 cents out of each $1
$ 14,000	$ 28,000	30 cents out of each $1
$ 20,000	$ 40,000	36 cents out of each $1
$ 50,000	$100,000	54 cents out of each $1
$100,000	$200,000	67 cents out of each $1
$200,000	$400,000	78 cents out of each $1

*Taxable income is the amount left after all deductions and exemptions.

cent. In 1924, as described previously, a Federal tax offset or credit for state taxation was provided. Since 1926, states have been permitted to take as much as 80 per cent of the original or basic Federal tax, but the offset feature does not apply to subsequent levies and surtaxes on estates.

Excise and Sales Taxes. The Constitution mentions excise taxes as part of the Federal taxing power. Such levies soon were made upon liquor and several other commodities and transactions. Reduced, repealed, and restored, excise taxes have had a very shifting history, increasing during war and depression, declining in peace and prosperity. Viewed from the standpoint of revenue, the present excise taxes of greatest importance are on liquor and tobacco, the former yield-

ing about 4 per cent of total revenue in recent years and the latter about 2½.

After these come manufacturers' excise taxes on selective luxury and quasi-luxury items: playing cards, amusement admissions, radios, musical instruments, sporting goods, toilet preparations, and the like. Wartime taxes were added to travel and communication services: rail tickets, telephone calls, telegraph messages, and others. Some taxes, as stated earlier in this chapter, are for purposes of regulation, not revenue; these affect such diverse commodities as narcotics, oleomargarine, and machine guns.

Selective sales or excise taxes employed by the Federal government are not subject to the principal criticism that applies to general sales or manufacturers' taxes used by the states. The burden of the general sales tax falls most heavily upon the individual or family with the least capacity to pay. A family with an annual income of $3,600 must spend a large portion of it for food, clothing, and other items taxable under the general sales tax; the family with $36,000 per year in income spends a much smaller proportion on taxable commodities and therefore pays a smaller proportion of its income in sales tax. Proposals for a general Federal sales tax have often been made, but the opponents in Congress have defeated them.

Customs Duties. Throughout much of American history customs duties constituted the largest source of Federal revenue; the national treasury often was filled to the overflowing point by this means. After the Civil War, customs duties declined in relative importance as a source of revenue; after the First World War, tariff revenue was far outranked in size by income taxes. For recent fiscal years customs receipts were less than 1 per cent of total revenues.

Nontax Revenues. A great variety of nontax revenues accrue to the Federal government. Federal enterprises of a business nature—the Post Office, the Panama Canal and Panama Railroad, the Maritime Administration—return revenues to the Treasury, but little if any net profit is found after deducting operating expenses. Some relatively small amounts are obtained by the sale of public lands and by the rental of lands or of privileges (such as grazing or mineral extraction) on the public domain. Another small source of nontax revenue is Federal profit obtained through minting money. This profit represents the margin between the value of the metals used in minting (plus minting cost) and the face value of coins minted. Other nontax Federal revenues are from fines and penalties exacted for crimes, gifts, interest on loans, and fees.

State and Local Revenues. The largest source of state tax revenues is state sales taxes, including general, motor-vehicle fuel, liquor, and tobacco taxes. Individual and corporate income taxes, license and privilege taxation, property taxes, and death and gift taxes return significant amounts of state income. Federal grants-in-aid and income from state proprietary enterprises, especially liquor stores, constitute the greatest part of nontax state revenue.

The traditional general property tax yields the lion's share of all local tax revenue. Sales taxes now occupy second place; licenses and permits are third. State grants to local governments and income from municipal utility undertakings (especially water and electricity) occupy an important place in local nontax revenues. Municipal enterprises are not leading revenue producers.

FEDERAL-STATE FISCAL RELATIONS

The traditional sources of Federal revenue were customs duties and excise taxes, especially on liquor and tobacco. Adoption of the Sixteenth Amendment and the coming of the First World War transformed and diversified the Federal revenue pattern. State governments, no longer able to subsist on the revenue from the general property tax, turned to other forms of taxation.

Duplicating Taxation. During the last forty years, Federal and state taxes have been increasingly duplicative. This duplication may not be serious in some fields; for example, the Federal tax on gasoline may be justified in view of the large Federal grants-in-aid for state highways. In other fields, however, duplication is costly, awkward, and sometimes unfair; double taxation of incomes has resulted in an erratic pattern and in tax competition between the states. Federal-state duplication is found also in liquor and tobacco.

One solution for the problems arising from duplication is for the Federal govern-

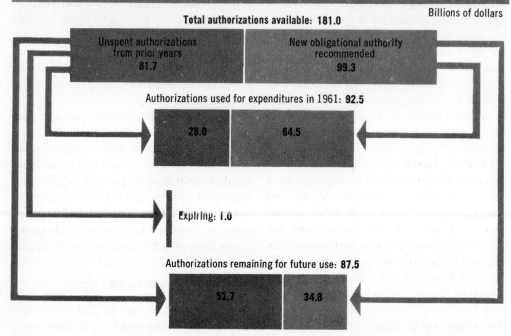

1963 EXPENDITURES RELATED TO AUTHORIZATIONS BY CONGRESS

Billions of dollars

Total authorizations available: **181.0**

| Unspent authorizations from prior years **81.7** | New obligational authority recommended **99.3** |

Authorizations used for expenditures in 1961: **92.5**

| **28.0** | **64.5** |

Expiring: **1.0**

Authorizations remaining for future use: **87.5**

| **52.7** | **34.8** |

In the past Congress often appropriated money far in advance so that agencies could incur obligations. Beginning in 1958 Congress adopted a Hoover Commission recommendation that it go on a pay-as-you-go basis, under which Congress appropriates only such funds as are likely to be spent in the next fiscal year. (1963 Federal Budget in Brief, p. 54.)

ment to allow credits for state taxation. The tax-offset device, as illustrated by Federal death taxes, permits sharing a source of revenue and encourages a measure of uniformity in the states. Only Nevada has no inheritance tax to take advantage of the Federal credit for state taxation.

A similar plan might be suitable for sharing the income tax. Two-thirds of the states had personal income taxes in the late 1950s. The maximum state tax rate is 11 per cent. Many states do not tax individual incomes as such. Consequently, much competition exists between states for the residence of wealthy persons. A tax offset, permitting credit for state taxation up to about 25 per cent of the Federal tax, would regularize personal income taxation in the country and prevent unfair competition.

Another proposal is that the different levels of government should agree on a separation of sources. Usually the plan is that the states should exclusively enjoy the field of general sales taxation, and the Federal government the taxation of personal income. Such plans effectively separate state and local tax sources, for state legislative action alone often suffices to make the separation. To divide sources between Federal and state governments would require either consent of all fifty-one legislative bodies or a Federal constitutional amendment.

More effective would be a tax federally collected, but shared with the states. This alternative would eliminate the expense and trouble of two returns on separate forms. A federally collected state-shared tax would not eliminate the possibility of duplication if any state persisted in taxing separately the commodity or income item concerned.

Tax coordination between Federal and state governments is also found in mutual deductibility, particularly in the income-tax field. The Federal law permits a taxpayer to deduct state individual and corporate income taxes; some states reciprocate by allowing a similar deduction on Federal taxes.

Federal-state cooperation in assessment and collection is achieved through the exchange of information. Since 1950, Federal and state tax authorities have exchanged audit information. The tendency toward uniformity of tax bases and methods of tax computation encourages further cooperation. Utah offers taxpayers the option of paying a fixed percentage of their Federal income-tax payment in lieu of paying on state rates.[1]

Reciprocal Tax Immunity. The constitutional doctrine of reciprocal tax immunity has been traced earlier in this chapter. Blanket immunity of all Federal transactions and instrumentalities from state taxation, and those of the state from Federal taxation, went far beyond the extent necessary to protect one level of government from undue burden by the other. At its height it banned state taxes on salaries of Federal officials, on income from Federal bonds, on sales to Federal agencies; while the states enjoyed similar immunity from Federal taxation. Beginning in 1938, the Supreme

[1] For a full discussion of these problems, see U.S. House of Representatives, Committee on Ways and Means, *Coordination of Federal, State, and Local Taxes*, H. Rept. 2519, 82d Cong., 2d Sess. (1953).

Court reduced considerably the scope of this immunity. The Federal personal income tax is now collected from state and local government employees. Most of the states' income taxes apply to Federal employees as to anyone else.

The greatest controversy arose over a Treasury proposal to eliminate tax exemption on government securities. Standard practice had been that the Federal government make income from its own bond issues exempt from Federal taxation, and most state governments exempted their securities issues from their own taxes. This led to very complete immunity from taxation of most public securities issued in the country. In 1939 the Treasury Department started a campaign to eliminate tax-exempt bonds. The principal opposition came from representatives of state and local governments, who recognized that removal of tax immunity would require them to offer higher interest rates. This point was granted, but would the added interest rates offset the revenue derived from taxing income from public bonds? The greatest beneficiary from the old system of immunity is the person of very large income who invests heavily in tax-exempt state and local securities. Once his income reaches a point where he must pay one-half or more of the additional amount in Federal income tax, the wealthy person can reduce his tax burden by buying tax-exempt bonds.

Abolition of tax exemption is not an easy process. The Federal government took the lead in 1941 by making its own new bond issues subject to Federal income taxation. The states might well be encouraged to take similar action in respect to their own issues. Next, the Federal government might commence taxing income from state and local government securities. This step has been delayed by the vehemence of state and local opposition, but it may be expected eventually. Finally, the states could follow the Federal example and apply their taxation to Federal bonds. These changes probably would apply only to future issues of securities; under the contract clause of the Constitution it might be difficult to make them applicable to existing issues on which tax exemption has been assured. If only future issues are covered, it will take a long time to correct the evils of the existing situation.

An Intergovernmental Fiscal Program. During the 1940s a committee of experts appointed by the Secretary of the Treasury made a thorough study of intergovernmental fiscal relations.[1] Stressing the co-operative approach, the team proposed the establishment of a Federal-state fiscal authority to promote joint administration of selected overlapping taxes, facilitate interstate cooperation, conduct research, and perform other services of mutual interest to

---

[1] U.S. Treasury Department, Committee on Intergovernmental Fiscal Relations, *Federal, State, and Local Government Fiscal Relations . . . a Report . . .*, S. Doc. 69, 78th Cong., 1st Sess. (1943). Members of the committee were Harold M. Groves, Luther Gulick, and Mabel Newcomber.

Federal and state governments. This authority was not established at the time, but the Advisory Commission on Intergovernmental Relations, created in 1959, has provided many of the services suggested by the earlier committee.

The Commission has given a high priority to research and expects to continue to do so. Its studies range over the most important questions arising from intergovernmental relations in a federal system. These include the real property tax, intergovernmental cooperation in tax administration, overlapping taxes, measures of fiscal capacity and tax effort, coordination of Federal and state estate and gift taxes, state and local taxation of property on Federal reservations, centrally collected, locally shared taxes, reassessment of Federal grants-in-aid, state restrictions on local governments, controls accompanying Federal public assistance grants, and intergovernmental responsibilities for mass transit.

The Commission is moving cautiously because of its intergovernmental composition and the complexity of its assignment. The Commission has advisory powers only; upon Federal, state, and local governments rests responsibility for evaluating and adopting the Commission's recommendations.

FOR FURTHER READING

The Tax Power

Bruton, P. W. (ed.): *Cases and Materials on Federal Taxation* (St. Paul, Minn.: West, 1953).

Burdick, Charles K.: *The Law of the Constitution: Its Origin and Development* (New York: Putnam, 1922).

Corwin, Edward S.: *Court over Constitution* (Princeton, N.J.: Princeton University Press, 1934).

Larkin, John D.: *The President's Control over the Tariff* (Cambridge, Mass.: Harvard University Press, 1936).

Powell, Alden L.: *National Taxation of State Instrumentalities* (Urbana, Ill.: University of Illinois Press, 1936).

Seligman, Edwin R. A.: *The Income Tax* (New York: Macmillan, 1911).

Story, Joseph: *Commentaries on the Constitution of the United States* (Boston: Little, Brown, 2 vols., 4th ed., 1873).

Warren, Charles: *The Supreme Court in United States History* (Boston: Little, Brown, 3 vols., 1923).

———: *The Making of the Constitution* (Boston: Little, Brown, 1923).

Taxation and Revenues

Altman, George C.: *Introduction to Federal Taxation* (New York: Commerce Clearing House, rev. ed., 1938).

Anderson, W. H.: *Taxation and the American Economy* (Englewood Cliffs, N.J.: Prentice-Hall, 1951).

Blakey, Roy G., and Gladys C. Blakey: *Sales Taxes and Other Excises* (Chicago: Public Administration Service, 1945).

Blough, Roy: *The Federal Taxing Process* (Engle-wood Cliffs, N.J.: Prentice-Hall, 1952).

Crockett, J. P.: *Federal Tax System of the United States* (New York: Columbia University Press, 1955).

Groves, Harold M.: *Postwar Taxation and Economic Progress* (New York: McGraw-Hill, 1946).

——: *Financing Government* (New York: Holt, 4th ed., 1954).

Lutz, Harley L.: *Public Finance* (New York: Appleton-Century-Crofts, rev. ed., 1947).

Manning, Raymond E.: *Federal Excise Taxes*, Public Affairs Bulletin 59 (Washington, D.C.: Library of Congress, 1947).

Paul, Randolph: *Taxation in the United States* (Boston: Little, Brown, 1954).

Shoup, Carl, and others: *Facing the Tax Problem* (New York: Twentieth Century Fund, 1947).

Smith, Dan T.: *Federal Tax Reform: The Issues and a Program* (New York: McGraw-Hill, 1961).

Shultz, W. J.: *American Public Finance* (Engle-wood Cliffs, N.J.: Prentice-Hall, 6th ed., 1954).

Tax Institute (formerly Tax Policy League, Philadelphia): *Tax Barriers to Trade* (Princeton, N.J.: the Institute, 1941).

——: *Federal-State-Local Tax Coordination* (Princeton, N.J.: the Institute, 1954).

——: *Tax Policy* (Princeton, N.J.: the Institute, monthly).

Taylor, P. E.: *Economics of Public Finance* (New York: Macmillan, rev. ed., 1953).

U.S. Congress, Joint Committee on the Economic Report: *The Federal Revenue System: Facts and Problems* (1956).

U.S. Treasury Department, Committee on Intergovernmental Fiscal Relations: *Federal, State and Local Government Fiscal Relations . . . a Report . . .*, S. Doc. 69, 78th Cong., 1st Sess. (1943).

U.S. Treasury Department, Tax Division, Analysis Staff: *Overlapping Taxes in the United States* (Jan. 1, 1954).

REVIEW QUESTIONS

1. To what extent has the Federal tax power been used to regulate rather than raise revenue?

2. What considerations led to the adoption of the Sixteenth Amendment? How serious are threats of its repeal?

3. As used in the Constitution, what is the meaning of the terms "taxes," "duties," "imposts," and "excises"?

4. What were the main issues raised in the social security tax case? How were they decided?

5. Enumerate and discuss specific limitations on the taxing power.

6. Name and discuss implied restrictions on the taxing power.

7. Explain existing personal and corporate in-come taxes and their importance in the Federal revenue picture.

8. Is it fair to require employers to collect, at their own expense, income taxes and social security taxes from employee payrolls?

9. Compare the main sources of Federal and state-local tax revenues.

10. Discuss the problem of duplicate taxation by Federal and state governments, and suggest possible corrective steps.

11. What is the constitutional basis of reciprocal tax immunity? Discuss some of the problems posed by it.

12. What are the prospects that a comprehensive intergovernmental fiscal program might be placed in operation? Discuss.

Chapter Twenty-One

Fiscal Administration, Money, and Banking

*Increasing emphasis on economic growth necessarily focuses
attention on Federal expenditure policies. The Federal
Government is the largest industry in the United States.
Its direct purchases of goods and services account for
a substantial share of the economy's total output;
its effects on the amount and character of economic
activity are even greater than can be indicated by any such
statistic.*

*In part, these influences stem from the means by which
the Federal Government's activities are financed. . . .
The character and extent of the Federal Government's
spending activities, however, may be of even greater
consequence.*

SUBCOMMITTEE ON FISCAL POLICY[1]

Governments are not created to collect and spend money, but considerations of revenues and expenditures underlie virtually every governmental problem. Governmental services cost a great deal of money, taking about one-fourth of the gross national prod-

[1] U.S. Congress, Joint Economic Committee, Subcommittee on Fiscal Policy, *Federal Expenditure Policies for Economic Growth and Stability*, 85th Cong., 2d Sess., Committee print (1958).

uct in recent years. By managing the purse strings, they who hold governmental power may exert both detailed and general controls over the extent of public activities. For the executive, finance is a control over administration ranking with that of personnel. For the legislative body, finance looms much more important than personnel or any other form of control.

This chapter describes and criticizes

financial administration, with incidental attention to state and local practices.

FINANCIAL ADMINISTRATION

Constitutional Provisions. The Constitution places the primary responsibility for finances upon Congress. Appropriations are made by law, but the President's participation through the veto has not been particularly forceful because he is preoccupied with securing succor for the agencies under his control. Moreover, he possesses no power to veto items or to reduce portions of appropriation bills. The President has used his constitutional power to recommend appropriations to the Congress, but his most effective sanction over congressional action comes from his role as leader of the majority party. With his party in control of both houses and himself accepted as its leader, his influence often is great over fiscal and other matters.

The idea of legislative supremacy in the financial field was established in Britain after centuries of controversy between King and Parliament. Although Parliament is supreme and its approval is necessary for all taxes and appropriations, the administration of finance is largely in the hands of the Cabinet, who, or course, are members of Parliament. Only the government (i.e., the Cabinet) may propose taxes or legislation appropriating money. This places inescapable responsibility on the government in office for the management of fiscal affairs. In the United States, Congress exercises far wider powers over finance and may vote funds not asked for by the executive and revise the budget estimates either up or down.

Early Federal Organization. As American Federal government developed after 1789, the financial responsibilities of Congress multiplied. Various committees of the two

houses, and individual members, pressed for the adoption of fiscal measures raising and expending moneys. It proved difficult to fix specific responsibility for action; the trading of votes for appropriations (logrolling) and the distribution of favors among state and congressional districts (pork barrel) led to immense waste of public funds. The fidelity of financial transactions was inadequately checked and opened opportunities for corruption. Although the Secretary of the Treasury was required to provide Congress with compilations of requests for appropriations, he was given no real authority over those estimates.

The Budget and Accounting Act of 1921. The need for reform in Federal financial practices was first stated prominently by President Taft's Commission on Economy and Efficiency, in 1912. The Commission recommended that the President should submit to each session of Congress a budget, containing a budget message, financial statements, and estimates prepared through the Secretary of the Treasury.

The Budget and Accounting Act of 1921 established the Bureau of the Budget, which now plays a decisive role in fiscal administration. In 1939 the President transferred the Bureau from the Treasury Department to his Executive Office. The Bureau has power "to assemble, correlate, revise, reduce, or increase the estimates of the several departments or establishments." President Roosevelt strengthened the Bureau notably on several occasions after 1933, adding power to apportion appropriations, to require departments to set up reserves, to direct statistical services, and to do research, planning, and investigation.

The Present Bureau of the Budget. The functions of the Bureau of the Budget were enumerated in an executive order in 1939 and now are as follows:

1. To assist the President in budget and fiscal control preparation

2. To supervise and control budget administration

3. To conduct research on administration and to advise departments and agencies on improved organization and practices

4. To aid the President in bringing about more efficient and economical conduct of government service

5. To assist the President by coordinating departmental advice on proposed legislation

6. To assist with proposed executive orders and proclamations

7. To plan the improvement of statistical services

8. To keep the President informed on the work of the government

To accomplish these ends, the Bureau is organized, under a director and his assistants, into appropriate offices and divisions. The offices, each headed by an assistant director, are budget review, legislative reference, management and organization, statistical standards, and accounting. The divisions, each concerned with a broad phase of executive functions, are commerce and finance, international, labor and welfare, military, and resources and civil works.

Reforms instituted in the last few years have brought the personnel and powers of the Bureau near to the level urged by Arthur E. Buck in his able analysis made for the President's Committee on Administrative Management. Each department and larger independent establishment has its own budget officer. He prepares and edits estimates and works with the Bureau of the Budget in the budget conferences and hearings necessary to submit a budget document to Congress.

Much of the legislative reference work is nonfiscal, but it constitutes one of the great tasks of the Bureau. The first Hoover Commission noted that the Bureau, in one Congress, advised the President or executive departments on thousands of bills, including many passed by Congress. After an initial period of getting acquainted, the Eisenhower Administration appeared to rely heavily upon the Bureau's facilities for the central clearance of legislation.[1]

The statistical services of the Bureau include the approval of forms and questionnaires used by Federal agencies, to secure simplification and to avoid overlapping. The administrative management division, for aiding departments to secure efficiency and economy, studies particular agencies or problems and reports to the appropriate authorities. Its contribution, also nonfiscal in nature, is to improve the machinery of administration.

Department of the Treasury. Several tasks of the Treasury Department fall within the field of fiscal management. The Internal Revenue Service is the main tax collector. The Bureau of Customs collects customs duties.

Even more directly related to the matter of over-all financial administration, however, is the function of the Fiscal Service of the Treasury Department. Headed by a Fiscal Assistant Secretary, the Service was created by executive order in 1940 with accounting, debt, and custodial functions. The Fiscal Assistant Secretary keeps in touch with the financial operations of the various departments and agencies and informs the Secretary of the Treasury. Responsible to him is the Commissioner of Accounts, who heads the Bureau of Accounts, supervises the accounting of the Treasury Department, and keeps the central accounts

[1] Richard E. Neustadt, "Presidency and Legislation: The Growth of Central Clearance," *American Political Science Review*, vol. 48 (September, 1954), pp. 641–671.

DEPARTMENT OF THE TREASURY

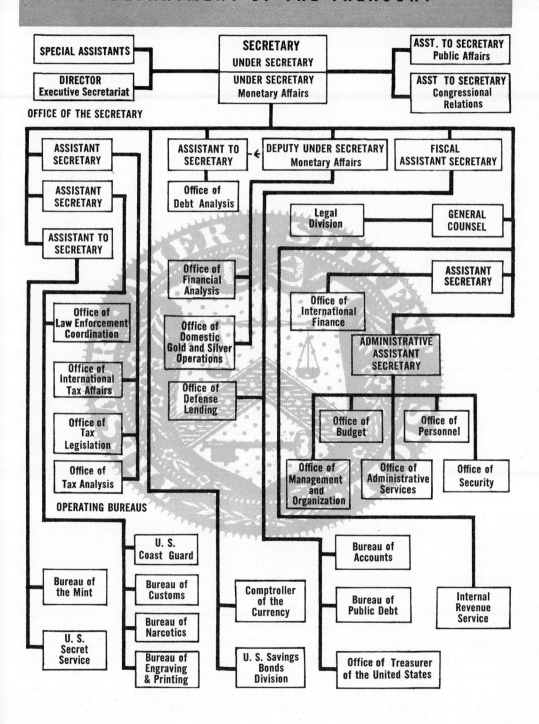

SPECIAL ASSISTANTS

DIRECTOR
Executive Secretariat

OFFICE OF THE SECRETARY

SECRETARY
UNDER SECRETARY
UNDER SECRETARY
Monetary Affairs

ASST. TO SECRETARY
Public Affairs

ASST TO SECRETARY
Congressional
Relations

ASSISTANT
SECRETARY

ASSISTANT
SECRETARY

ASSISTANT TO
SECRETARY

Office of
Law Enforcement
Coordination

Office of
International
Tax Affairs

Office of
Tax
Legislation

Office of
Tax Analysis

OPERATING BUREAUS

ASSISTANT TO
SECRETARY

Office of
Debt Analysis

Office of
Financial
Analysis

Office of
Domestic
Gold and Silver
Operations

Office of
Defense
Lending

DEPUTY UNDER SECRETARY
Monetary Affairs

Legal
Division

Office of
International
Finance

ADMINISTRATIVE
ASSISTANT
SECRETARY

Office of
Budget

Office of
Management
and
Organization

Office of
Administrative
Services

FISCAL
ASSISTANT SECRETARY

GENERAL
COUNSEL

ASSISTANT
SECRETARY

Office of
Personnel

Office of
Security

Bureau of
the Mint

U. S.
Secret
Service

U. S.
Coast Guard

Bureau of
Customs

Bureau of
Narcotics

Bureau of
Engraving
& Printing

Comptroller
of the
Currency

U. S. Savings
Bonds
Division

Bureau of
Accounts

Bureau of
Public Debt

Office of Treasurer
of the United States

Internal
Revenue
Service

413

of the entire government. In addition, the
Bureau of Accounts issues all Treasury warrants, makes disbursements for most of the
Federal agencies, and designates depositories
for government money.

Also in the Fiscal Service is the Bureau
of the Public Debt, headed by the Commissioner of the Public Debt, who handles
Federal borrowing. Special staffs may be
created from time to time to promote bond
selling, but the actual issuance and control
stem from the Bureau of the Public Debt.

Another agency of importance in the
Fiscal Service is the Office of the Treasurer
of the United States. The Treasurer receives
and disburses public funds and is the
custodian of public money. After Congress
has appropriated funds, he credits them to
the proper disbursing officer, following
receipt of a warrant signed by the Secretary
of the Treasury and countersigned by the
Comptroller General.

The Comptroller General. The Budget
and Accounting Act of 1921 created the
General Accounting Office (GAO), headed
by the Comptroller General. It is an agency
of the legislative branch of the government.
The Comptroller General was given wide
powers over accounting, audit, and investigation.

The Comptroller General is appointed by
the President, with Senate confirmation, for
a term of fifteen years. His GAO staff of
about ten thousand employees works in the
several offices and divisions, including
audits, investigations, claims, accounting
systems, transportation, personnel, administrative services, and general counsel.

Under the Budget and Accounting Procedures Act of 1950, the Comptroller
General:

1. Prescribes principles and standards of
accounting for all executive agencies

2. Cooperates with the agencies and the
Treasury in developing accounting systems

3. Approves agency accounting systems
that he deems adequate

4. Reviews accounting systems of the
agencies

5. Audits financial transactions of all
legislative, executive, and judicial agencies

The 1921 act has often been criticized
because it grants to the Comptroller General accounting as well as auditing functions.
It is contrary to accepted principles of
financial administration for the auditor to
also be the chief accounting officer and
through the power of settling accounts to
control the acts of administrative officers.

During the first term of Franklin D.
Roosevelt there were many conflicts between the heads of executive agencies and
the Comptroller General, particularly when
he used his powers of disallowance to block
public policies which he disapproved. Since
the first Comptroller General retired, relations between that officer and executive
departments and agencies have greatly improved. The first Hoover Commission proposed a new "accountant general" under
the Secretary of Treasury, who would set
up methods and procedures, subject to the
approval of the Comptroller General. It also
recommended that the GAO cease bringing
carloads of vouchers to Washington for
audit and do sample audit in the field. The
latter change was made following 1949. The
second Hoover Commission commended the
improvements made in both auditing and
accounting fields by the GAO. It urged
careful study of internal auditing within the
agencies.

THE BUDGETARY PROCESS

Following the confusion and irresponsibility
that characterized early Federal financial
administration, a new era opened with the
enactment of the Budget and Accounting
Act of 1921. State reforms came both before

and after the national, spreading over a period of the last 50 years. Except where otherwise noted, the following analysis of the budgeting process is based primarily upon Federal practice.

Definition of a Budget. A budget is a comprehensive financial plan, the central instrument of financial administration. The budgetary process, according to A. E. Buck, involves three elements: (1) the financial plan, (2) the procedure for formulating, authorizing, executing, and controlling the plan, and (3) some governmental authority responsible for each stage of the procedure.[1]

The budget document is the blueprint in which a government forecasts its expenditures and estimates its revenues. It is for a given fiscal period, usually for one year but sometimes (especially in state governments) for a biennium. The fiscal year of the Federal government is from July 1 to June 30. Some state and local governments use the calendar year or other periods as the fiscal year.

The second of these elements names the four stages in the budgeting process. The first is formulation, involving assembling of estimates from operating agencies and their inclusion in the financial plan. The second is authorization of the budget, through legislative adoption. The third, budget execution, consists of controlling the expenditures authorized. The fourth stage is entered when accounts are checked and transactions audited.

Budget Formulation. The Budget and Accounting Act of 1921 placed the responsibility for budget formulation upon the President, with the assistance of the Bureau of the Budget. The President determines general fiscal policy and then delegates to his budget director power to proceed with budget formulation.

[1] Arthur E. Buck, *The Budget in Governments of Today* (New York: Macmillan, 1934), p. 46.

Assembling Estimates. The Budget Bureau asks the various operating departments and agencies to submit their estimates of expenditures for the forthcoming fiscal period. The Bureau analyzes the preliminary estimates. The Chief Executive is consulted on matters of policy and settles serious disagreements between budget director and operating agency. The revised estimates are then put into final form and printed. Normally the operating departments and agencies request more than they expect to receive but wish to have a safe margin that may be lost in estimate cuts.

The form and contents of budgets vary considerably. A good budget will contain several essential features. First, the executive's budget message reviews the general financial picture: anticipated revenues, business conditions, estimated expenditures, and the like. Second, financial statements compare the fiscal present with the past and with estimated future operations. Then the body of the budget contains the appropriation estimates—the executive's recommendations. The usual practice is to organize the estimates according to departments and agencies. The better budgets often have a parallel column with amounts appropriated for the last one or two fiscal periods.

Review and Revision. Normally the Budget Bureau is saddled with the task of bringing down the expenditure estimates of operating agencies to a level stipulated by the Chief Executive or indicated by estimated revenues. This requires budget hearings, in which departmental officers present their cases to budget officers. The budget officer must decide, and often this decision involves a substitution of his judgment for that of the departmental officer. When a layman decides between the bomber and the carrier in defense estimates, or for or against experimentation with polio vaccine

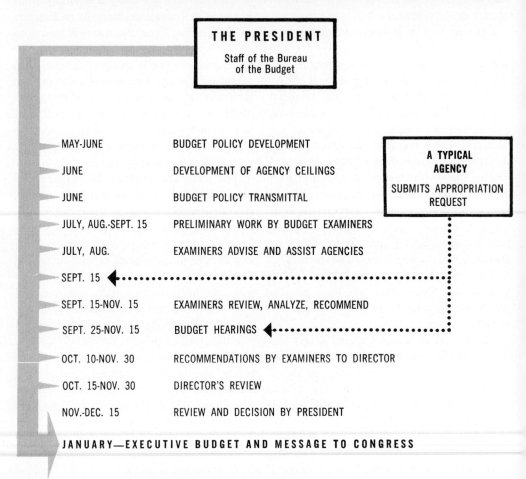

DEVELOPING THE FEDERAL BUDGET

THE PRESIDENT

Staff of the Bureau
of the Budget

MAY-JUNE	BUDGET POLICY DEVELOPMENT
JUNE	DEVELOPMENT OF AGENCY CEILINGS
JUNE	BUDGET POLICY TRANSMITTAL
JULY, AUG.-SEPT. 15	PRELIMINARY WORK BY BUDGET EXAMINERS
JULY, AUG.	EXAMINERS ADVISE AND ASSIST AGENCIES
SEPT. 15	
SEPT. 15-NOV. 15	EXAMINERS REVIEW, ANALYZE, RECOMMEND
SEPT. 25-NOV. 15	BUDGET HEARINGS
OCT. 10-NOV. 30	RECOMMENDATIONS BY EXAMINERS TO DIRECTOR
OCT. 15-NOV. 30	DIRECTOR'S REVIEW
NOV.-DEC. 15	REVIEW AND DECISION BY PRESIDENT

A TYPICAL AGENCY

SUBMITS APPROPRIATION REQUEST

JANUARY—EXECUTIVE BUDGET AND MESSAGE TO CONGRESS

Because Federal budgets are annual and very complicated, formulation is in process
much of each year.

in estimates of the Public Health Service, the necessity for maturity on the part of the budgeteer is painfully obvious. Appeals to budget director or Chief Executive are possible, but not often politic.

Budget Authorization. Budget or appropriation bills are drawn either by the executive budget officer or by a legislative com-

mittee. It is now proper practice for the Chief Executive to submit the budget and be responsible for what it contains. In the Federal and in most state and local governments the legislature can decrease or increase the executive's recommendations. The existence of this power denies the full measure of responsibility possessed by the executive in Great Britain. Only the Ministers can introduce appropriation bills; Parliament cannot increase any item.

Appropriation Bill. Congress and other American legislative bodies have well-established procedures to deal with appropriation measures. The budget bill is introduced in the manner used for other bills. In Congress and in many state legislatures revenue bills must originate in the lower house; although this restriction does not apply to appropriation measures, custom decrees that introduction in the House of Representatives is necessary. The budget goes to the legislature with the executive's budget message, detailing the fiscal picture of past, present, and future.

The printed budget document shows many details not found in the appropriation bill that accompanies it. The bill may be written with considerable detail, or it may include only the principal totals and subtotals. The former is called the "segregated-item" type of appropriation measure; the latter is known as the "lump-sum" variety. The segregated-item bill is unduly restrictive and allows little administrative discretion; the lump-sum plan liberates the executive from detailed limits and permits flexibility for adjustment and economy. Federal appropriation bills are a great mixture; some items provide for millions of dollars and some for only a few dollars.

After introduction, the budget bill is referred to the proper committee. In both the United States Senate and House of Representatives the appropriations committees have subcommittees for each executive department and independent agency. These bodies conduct hearings and call in and question heads of operating agencies. Usually these officers are not permitted to advocate other than the estimate submitted by the Chief Executive. In some badly managed jurisdictions, officers violate the

spirit and sometimes the letter of budget law by lobbying for the restoration of their own unrevised estimates. After hearings are completed, the committee makes its recommendation, and the house debates and acts. The same, or a similar, procedure is followed in the second house.

Executive Action. Having been enacted by both houses, and its differences having been compromised, the appropriation bill is sent to the executive for signature. The President must approve or reject the measure as a whole; naturally he approves almost invariably, for the agencies cannot long operate without money. Many state governors and some local executives have an item-veto power, permitting them to strike out or to reduce any portion of an appropriation measure. Such a power in the hands of the President would strengthen

Congress properly uses the appropriation process to control policy, but occasionally employs it to intervene in detail that should be left to the administration. (From Herblock and *The Washington Post*.)

I'm On My Side of the Fence, Ain't I?

materially his position in the budgetary process.

Widespread abuses still persist in the authorization of budgets by legislative bodies. Appropriations committees rarely have staffs adequate to deal with the intricate problems involved in budget bills. Decisions often, perhaps inevitably, are made with considerations of logrolling and the pork barrel predominating. Most suggestions for improvement involve expansion of the role of the executive in authorization, as well as in other phases of budgeting.

Some features peculiar to Federal budgetary procedure should be noted. The President includes in his budget the appropriations requested by judicial and legislative branches of government, but he has no power to alter these estimates. In some of the best state and local jurisdictions, one single omnibus budget bill is used to cover all the appropriation items proposed by the executive. In Congress, however, a separate bill is introduced for some departments, other departments are grouped together for the purpose, and at least one bill each year is devoted to the independent establishments.

In 1950 Congress combined all appropriations into a single omnibus bill, but it has not repeated the experiment. The chairmen of the appropriations subcommittees of each house have charge of the bills on the floor. Since the budget estimates are made considerably in advance of the fiscal period, it is inevitable that unusual needs will arise and require added appropriations. These demands are handled through "deficiency appropriation" estimates and bills.

Budget Execution. The principal agencies of financial administration of the American national government have been described. Those with roles in budget execution include the Treasury Department, the Bureau of the Budget, and the General Accounting Office and its head, the Comptroller General.

Custody of funds is in the hands of the Treasury. Under current Federal practice, the Treasury notifies the operating departments and agencies of the amount of money they may expend during the fiscal year. The agencies may then incur obligations. Bills are paid through disbursing officers located in various parts of the country. Most disbursing officers are in the Treasury Department, but the Armed Forces and Post Office still have their own. Advances of funds are made available through local depositaries.

Since 1933, the Director of the Bureau of the Budget has been empowered to apportion appropriations for each agency by periods of the fiscal year. This is one of the most important of fiscal powers, for it enables the executive to keep a quarter-by-quarter check of financial transactions of the operating establishments. Under this scheme, spending agencies are given only a certain proportion of their total appropriation to spend in any given period; one common limit in state and local governments is no more than one-tenth in any one month.

The operating departments and establishments keep accounts. The departmental accounting officers report monthly expenditures to the Bureau of the Budget. The Treasury also maintains a set of accounts, showing general transactions. The Fiscal Service of the Treasury, created by executive order in 1940, was directed "to establish and maintain a complete system of central accounts for the entire Government," and to prescribe standards and forms for departmental financial reports. Nevertheless, the Comptroller General still possesses the power to prescribe forms, systems, and procedure for accounting to the departments and establishments. Thus diffusion of responsibility for accounting persists.

After the financial transaction is complete, auditing is in order. It involves the examination of the records to check on the validity of accounts and payments. In governmental circles the theory is current that a postaudit should be conducted by an officer or body independent of the executive or spending agencies. The task of checking to see whether or not expenditures have been made in accordance with law is assigned either to an independent auditor or to one responsible to the legislative branch. The Comptroller General, with fifteen-year term and removal only by Congress, was intended to be such an officer, but only recently has the work been performed effectively.

Budget Reform. The first and second Hoover Commissions gave much attention to budgeting and accounting. The recommendations of the former that were put into effect included statutory provision, in 1949, for performance budgeting in the Department of Defense; improved accounting procedures, under an act of 1950; authorization of the President to prescribe form and contents of the budget; and administrative reorganization of the Bureau of the Budget in 1952.

Despite these changes the second Hoover group found more reform needed. The budgeting process stretches over eighteen months. The budget document exceeds 1,200 pages and weighs more than five pounds. Huge unexpended appropriations are carried forward from year to year; in the mid-1950s the carry-over was from 50 to 75 billion dollars per year. The Commission quoted with approval the conclusions of its task force, adding: ". . . under present procedures there is no effective control over expenditures either by the Congress or the Executive Branch."[1]

Both Hoover groups praised the perform-

[1] Second Hoover Commission, *Budgeting and Accounting*, p. 17.

ance, or program, budget and recommended its adoption or extension. The idea has long been used in state and local governments with progressive budgeting processes. It places emphasis on the work or service to be performed, not merely the salaries, supplies, and equipment required by a particular agency.

Using the Naval Medical Center at Bethesda, Maryland, as an example, the first Hoover Commission reported that the hospital received allotments from twelve different Navy appropriation titles; at no place in the budget was the cost of operating the Bethesda facility totaled or the work of the hospital set forth clearly. The performance budget, on the other hand, describes the significance and scope of the work, gives reasons for increases and decreases, outlines current and future programs, presents per bed and per patient costs for each hospital, and summarizes the complete cost of Navy medical care.

Statutory changes of 1949 and 1950 made performance budgeting mandatory. The budget of fiscal 1951 was the first government-wide program budget.

Cost Basis. Most Federal budgets, the second Hoover Commission pointed out, are based on estimated obligations to be incurred in the budget year. Into the obligations figure go contracts to be awarded, orders to be placed, and other commitments involving future charges against the government. Large sums carried over from previous years are ignored when the obligation basis is used. The Commission recommended that budgets be formulated and administered on a cost basis. To help restore congressional control of the purse, appropriations should be based on anticipated charges for goods and services to be received during the fiscal year.

Agency Comptroller. The head of each Federal agency should have, according to the second Hoover group, an agency comptroller as fiscal adviser, supervisor of accounting, and budget executor. The comptroller of a military department would be responsible only to the civilian Secretary.

Expanded Budget Bureau. Perhaps the outstanding feature of the second Hoover Commission's report in this area was the proposal to expand Bureau managerial functions, including the stationing of its representatives in the agencies, as well as more funds and additional personnel.

PUBLIC EXPENDITURES

Increasing Cost of Government. It is commonplace to observe that the cost of governments is increasing, both absolutely and per capita. The accepted figures show that all levels of American government—national, state, and local—in 1913 expended 2,919 million dollars. The same levels in 1938 spent 16,312 million dollars, and in 1953 they spent 110,600 million dollars. In forty years, the aggregate cost of governments increased thirty-seven times. Federal expenditures rose the most and local the least.

Comparison of governmental costs with national income is perhaps most significant. In 1913 the national income was estimated at 35,400 million dollars; governmental expenditures amounted to 8.2 per cent of that amount. In 1938 national income was figured at 68 billion dollars; the cost of government was 24 per cent of the total. In 1942, when national income was 122 billion dollars, public expenses were more than 38 per cent. In 1953 national income was estimated at 305 billion dollars, and aggregate governmental expenditures were about 36 per cent of the total.

Expenditures by Functions. Federal expenditures, excluding business enterprises, in recent years have been for the following principal functions, listed in order of amount: national defense, interest on debt, agriculture, veterans' services, and labor and welfare.

State expenditures have been for the following, in order of amount: education, highways, public welfare, and health and hospitals.

Similarly, local government expenditures were for the following, in order of the amount of expenditure: education, highways, public welfare, hospitals and health, police, and sanitation.

THE PUBLIC DEBT

The Debt Problem. Failure to keep the revenues of government in balance with the expenditures results more often in deficits than in surpluses. In depression, wars, and expansion, governments borrow. The resulting debt burden is enormous in interest charges and in repayments. Virtually every governmental unit has some power to borrow. Local governments, and some states, are restricted within certain limits. The nation and other states may borrow as much and so long as the public will approve, and lenders will lend. It appears quite reasonable that governments should spend more in times of emergency and repay this in times of peace and prosperity.

During the First World War the country was saddled with a national debt of $25,-500,000,000. This was reduced to $16,185,-000,000 by 1930. Depression spending intervened, and the Federal debt passed the 40 billion dollar mark during 1939. Once in war, budgets were pushed to hitherto undreamed-of heights; for fiscal year 1945, expenditures were over 100 billion dollars; receipts for the same period accounted for over 46½ billion dollars, leaving a deficit of about 54 billion dollars. The debt limit has been raised again and again. At the

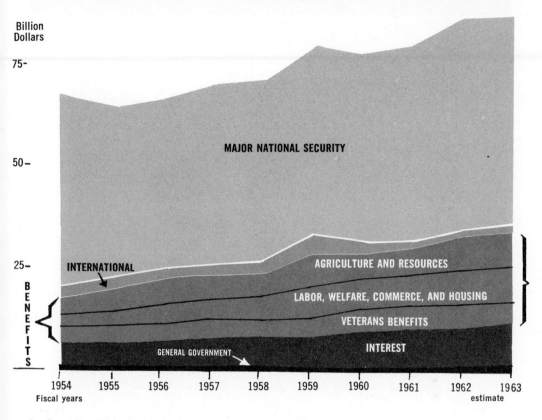

FEDERAL GOVERNMENT EXPENDITURES

Billion
Dollars

75-

MAJOR NATIONAL SECURITY

50-

25-   **INTERNATIONAL**

AGRICULTURE AND RESOURCES

B
E
N
E
F
I
T
S

LABOR, WELFARE, COMMERCE, AND HOUSING

VETERANS BENEFITS

GENERAL GOVERNMENT

INTEREST

1954   1955   1956   1957   1958   1959   1960   1961   1962   1963
Fiscal years   estimate

Federal spending is heavily concentrated in the defense and national security function.
(Data from U.S. Bureau of the Budget.)

moment of writing, the gross debt is about 285 billion dollars.

From their past mistakes, governments have learned some lessons about borrowing. First, do not borrow for a longer period than an improvement will last. Frequently governments will borrow for improvements but leave repayment of the loan until long after the improvement has outlived its utility. Second, do not pay ordinary operating expenses out of borrowed money except in war or extreme crisis. This can be accomplished by issuing term bonds and setting up sinking funds to redeem them when due.

Another satisfactory solution is to issue serial bonds, with redemption periods staggered over the years.

Several states have gone to considerable lengths to limit debts of local governments. Often the limitation is based upon assessed valuation. Restrictions may be avoided by increasing assessed valuation or by forming special districts to perform certain services that require a considerable outlay. Debt-limitation laws have not proved very successful. The states have established central agencies to oversee local budgets and debts with varying degrees of success.

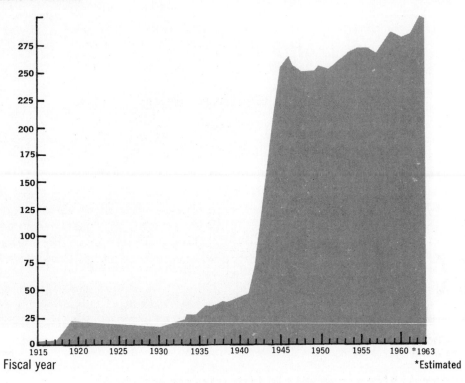

THE PUBLIC DEBT OF THE UNITED STATES, 1915-1963

BILLIONS OF DOLLARS

Fiscal year   *Estimated

The cost of the Second World War and later military burdens have kept the national debt above $250 billion since 1945. (Data from U.S. Bureau of the Budget.)

Debt Policy. During war and depression, people accept the necessity for governmental spending beyond the possible limit of current income. The impossibility of taking all in taxes is obvious. We have accepted a theory that national debt incurred in war and depression should be paid off during peace and prosperity. State and local governments may borrow for improvements, but, like businesses that expand with capital outlay, these obligations are to be paid off as quickly as possible.

Managing the Federal debt is a formidable task. In the early 1960s, the annual interest on it had risen to about 9.0 billion dollars. Although Congress has attempted to put a "ceiling" on the gross amount the government may borrow, the limit has been raised again and again.

One of the knotty problems of debt management is the maturity schedule of the various obligations. The Treasury has been harrassed for several years by the necessity for redeeming short-run issues and savings bonds for which individual and institutional investors demand cash. The government has been handicapped in its efforts to stretch out maturity of its securities by high interest rates. Thus Federal Reserve's "tight" money policies, intended to curb inflation, have contributed to the Treasury's difficulties in managing the debt.

MONETARY POWERS

The Borrowing Power. Article I, Section 8, clause 2 gives Congress authority "To borrow money on the credit of the United States." Congress may authorize the borrowing of money from any source, foreign or domestic, and up to any amount. The only collateral required, at least so far as the Constitution is concerned, is "the credit of the United States."

The power to borrow, together with the power to coin money and regulate its value, implies authority to issue paper money and compel its acceptance as legal tender. The power also justifies the creation of national banks. The Federal government may exempt its securities and the income derived from them from future Federal taxes, although since 1939 it has not done so.

When Congress borrows money, it pledges repayment in currency the value of which Congress itself has power to determine. In this lies the danger that future circumstances might lead to debt repudiation through the expedient of changing the value of the dollar, in which case it would be difficult to find any legal remedy except for injured parties to plead breach of contract or that property had been taken without due process of law.

The Power to Coin Money. To provide money with a fixed and uniform standard of value throughout the country, Congress was authorized "To coin money, regulate the value thereof, and of foreign coin. . . ." Congress authorized the first mint and laid

the foundation of our monetary system in 1792. The monetary power was essential to the new nation.

The words of the Constitution authorize Congress to "coin money." During our early history this was thought to include authority to either make metallic coins or print paper notes. Proceeding upon this assumption, Congress authorized the First and Second National Banks (created in 1791 and 1816) to issue paper notes, and the constitutionality was never questioned. During the Civil War, however, when Congress issued 450 million dollars' worth of treasury notes ("greenbacks") and made them legal tender, the courts were called to pass upon the constitutionality of the issue. The decision was awaited with considerable anxiety, inasmuch as it was bound to have a tremendous effect not only upon the credit of the national government but also upon the banking system and economic life of the country.

The Court announced its decision in the famous case of *Hepburn v. Griswold* [8 Wall. 603 (U.S. 1870)]. "Money" was defined to mean gold, copper, and silver coins; while coinage was defined as "the conversion of metal into money by governmental direction and authority . . . to mold into form a metallic substance of intrinsic value and stamp on it its legal value." Accordingly, said the Court, only metallic coins could be manufactured by the Federal government and made legal tender in payment of debts contracted between private parties before enactment of the law. The law was, therefore, unconstitutional; it exceeded the powers delegated to Congress, violated the spirit of the Constitution, and deprived creditors of property without due process of law.

This decision was reached by a 4-to-3 vote, there being two vacancies on the Court. On the day on which the verdict was announced, President Grant sent to the Senate the names of two men to fill the vacancies existing on the Court. Four days later, by a 5-to-4 vote, with the two new justices joining the three who had dissented in the previous case to make the majority, the Court voted to reconsider the issues involved.[1] Less than fifteen months after the first decision, the Court reversed itself [*Legal Tender cases*, 12 Wall. 457 (U.S. 1871)], this time saying that the power to issue paper notes in wartime and make them legal tender was implied from the power to coin money and fight a war. Authority to make paper money legal tender in time of peace was upheld thirteen years later [*Julliard v. Greenman*, 110 U.S. 421 (1884)].

The Power to Regulate the Value of Money. Congress also has the authority to regulate the value of domestic and foreign money in the United States. This makes possible a uniform monetary standard throughout the country. Since money is the lifeblood of the economic system of the nation, the use of this power has a tremendous effect, for good or for ill, upon domestic and international affairs.

The authorization enables Congress to determine whether the monetary system shall be based on a standard of gold, silver, or something else. It enables Congress to prescribe the relationship that shall exist between precious metals, as, for example, 15 grains of gold to 1 of silver, or as William Jennings Bryan advocated, 16 to 1. The authorization also permits Congress to compel the surrender of money of a particular type, as it did gold and gold certificates in 1933.

Moreover, Congress may abrogate gold clauses in private contracts [*Norman v. Baltimore & O.R.R.*, 294 U.S. 240 (1935)], although it may not abrogate promises to pay in gold or its equivalent contained in contracts between the national government and other parties.[2] Finally, this power, along with the borrowing, taxing, and spending powers, is authority for the establishment and regulation of the banking and credit system.

The Power to Punish Counterfeiting. Article I, Section 8, also empowers Congress "To provide for the punishment of counterfeiting the securities and current coin of the United States." The inclusion of this clause was probably unnecessary, since had it not been expressly granted it would have been implied from the power to coin money. The power is a concurrent one—the states as well as the national government may punish for counterfeiting, although most states leave detection and punishment to the Federal government.

States Denied Authority over Money. Besides granting Congress authority to coin money and regulate its value, the Constitution expressly forbids the states to "coin Money; emit bills of credit; [and] make any thing but gold and silver coin a tender in payment of debts. . . ." Since states are forbidden to coin money, there are no state mints where coins are made. Several states have enacted sales taxes authorizing the issuance and circulation of tokens of various sorts with which to pay taxes when purchases are made. The Supreme Court has upheld the states, inasmuch as the tokens are not to pass currently as coins but are to be used only as evidence that the tax is paid [*Morrow v. Henneford*, 182 Wash. 625 1935)].

---

[1] President Grant was accused of "packing" the Court, but the evidence seems to suggest that no understanding was reached between the President and the two new jurists to the effect that they would act as they subsequently did. The incident was unfortunate, nevertheless, and greatly diminished the prestige of the Court. See Charles E. Hughes, *The Supreme Court of the United States* (New York: Columbia University Press, 1928), pp. 51–53; Charles Warren, *The Supreme Court in United States History* (Boston: Little, Brown, 3 vols., 1923), vol. 3, pp. 220–254.

[2] *Perry v. United States*, 294 U.S. 330 (1935). Although in this case it was said that Congress had exceeded its powers by abrogating gold clauses in its own obligation, the Court added that one must show actual loss or damage before being entitled to recovery.

The states are also forbidden to emit bills of credit. These refer to paper money issued on the credit of a state government with the intention that it will circulate as a common medium of exchange. Although state governments cannot themselves issue paper money, they may authorize state-incorporated banks to do so. In this event the notes are issued on the credit of the banks and not on that of the state; hence, according to definition, they are not legally bills of credit.

Prior to the Civil War, state banks issued bank notes in large amounts. Issued only upon the credit of the banks, their value was ofttimes uncertain; moreover, since the states lacked authority to make them legal tender, many people objected to their use. In consequence, shortly after the Civil War, Congress undertook to force them out of existence by imposing a tax of 10 per cent upon them at the time of issuance. When challenged in the courts, the measure was upheld as a constitutional exercise of the power to tax, coin money, and regulate the value thereof [*Veazie Bank v. Fenno*, 8 Wall. 533, 552 (U.S. 1869); see also p. 395]. The tax accomplished its purpose; state bank notes have been nonexistent for many years.

The states are also forbidden to "make anything but gold and silver coin a tender in payment of debts." When something is made legal tender, it must be accepted by creditors when offered in payment of debt. Since the only thing that the states can make legal tender is gold and silver coin, which must all be supplied by the United States, Congress is solely responsible for the determination of what shall be legal tender.

MONEY, BANKING, AND CREDIT

The Monetary System. Acting under the terms of its constitutional power to coin money and regulate its value, Congress has exercised far-reaching influence over the economic life of the country. The Constitution did not specify what monetary unit should be used. In 1792, Congress, on the recommendation of Secretary of the Treasury Alexander Hamilton, established the decimal system based on the dollar, which is now perhaps the most widely accepted monetary unit in the world. In departing from the traditional British pound, shilling, and pence scheme, this country liberated itself from a cumbersome plan that makes the figuring of interest or tax rates a nightmare of confusion. If an early Congress had been equally farsighted in adopting the metric system of weights and measures, the convenience of posterity would also have been served.

Manufacture of metal coins is carried out in Federal mints located in Philadelphia and Denver. In recent years the mints have produced mainly 1-, 5-, 10-, 25- and 50-cent coins. Gold coin was called in during the crisis of 1933, and production has not resumed. Silver dollars still circulate but are rare in many sections of the country. Since 1950, more than 1½ billion dollars in coin has circulated.

Paper money has circulated in some form or other throughout American history. Although the Constitution forbade states to issue paper money, state-chartered banks continued to issue until their notes were taxed out of existence during the Civil War. After 1863, banks chartered by the national government issued paper money freely. While paper currency of many types circulates today, most of it consists of Federal Reserve notes, backed by commercial paper; silver certificates, backed by Treasury silver bullion; and United States notes, issued and backed by the Treasury.

At many periods of American history there has been sharp controversy over monetary standards. Gold has always been a major factor in the monetary system; over much of the period, silver has also played an important role. William Jennings Bryan's great crusade of 1896 resulted in part from the demonetization of silver in 1873. Support for coinage of silver at that time was motivated largely by debtor aspirations for a cheaper money.

Since the early 1930s, the silver bloc in Congress has been principally interested in assuring a ready market and high price for silver mined in the United States. The United States has been legally off the gold standard since 1933, but it has continued to buy gold and silver at prices above the world market. The store of gold in the vaults of the Federal treasury has reached over 20 billion dollars. Monetary theorists disagree over the utility of this gold, most of it stored at Fort Knox, Kentucky.

The Federal Reserve Plan. The Federal Reserve System was established in 1913, replacing the national banking system created during the Civil War. The power of the Congress to charter banks had been exercised in respect to the first Bank of the United States (1791–1811) and the second Bank (1816–1836) and its constitutionality assured in *McCulloch v. Maryland*. The national banking system of 1863–1864 was designed to stabilize the medium of exchange and to assist the sale of government bonds. After the paper money of state banks was taxed out of existence, the banks chartered by the national government enjoyed a monopoly over the issue of currency.

In successive depressions and panics the national banking scheme was proved inadequate. Senator Carter Glass, author of the 1913 legislation, declared of the old plan: "The Siamese twins of disorder were an inelastic currency and a fictitious reserve system."[1] Inelasticity arose from the re-

[1] Carter Glass, *An Adventure in Constructive Finance* (New York: Doubleday, 1927), p. 60.

quirement that note currency might be issued by national banks only to the extent to which they were holders of government bonds. As national indebtedness was reduced, the volume of currency was reduced. The fictitiousness of the old reserve system, according to Glass, was produced by the tendency of local banks to send their surplus funds to the money centers of the great cities. There funds would be loaned for speculation resulting in panic and depression.

The Federal Reserve System of today is supervised by the Board of Governors, composed of seven members appointed by the President for fourteen-year terms. From its Washington headquarters, the Board determines general monetary and credit policies and oversees the twelve district Federal Reserve banks and member private banks. The Board influences credit conditions mainly through its powers to alter the requirements for reserves against deposits in member banks and to change the rediscount rate (the rate at which Federal reserve banks lend money to private banks). The Federal Reserve Board also sets the margin requirement (proportion of cash that must be paid by investors) on the purchase of securities.

Actually the twelve Federal Reserve banks are privately owned, for their stock is held by the member banks. All national banks are required to subscribe to the capital stock of their districts. State banks may become members; if they do, a similar obligation to purchase stock is incurred. Regional boards of directors govern the Federal Reserve banks. Each board has nine members, six of which are selected by member banks and three by the national Board of Governors.

Reserve banks hold on deposit reserve balances of member banks, extend credit facilities to member banks and other busi-

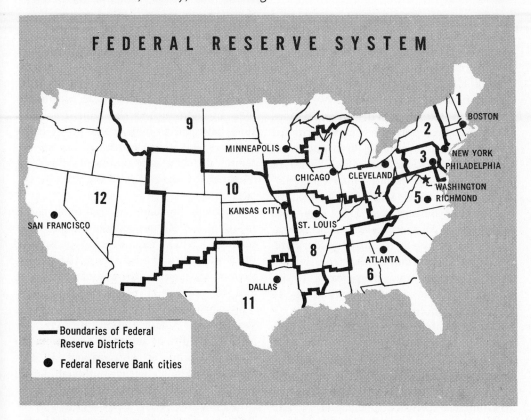

Federal Reserve Districts, although oddly drawn, have considerable influence on economic life of their regions.

ness concerns, and issue Federal Reserve notes which account for most of the money now in circulation. The notes may be backed by commercial paper, thus avoiding the inelasticity of the old national banking system, because the issue of currency can be great when demand for loans is great and less when borrowing is little.

The general utility of the Federal Reserve System has been conceded rather widely. Disagreement remains, however, over the success of the plan to decentralize and regionalize banking operations.

Nationally Chartered Banks and Savings Institutions. The Office of the Comptroller of the Currency oversees the national banking system, including the chartering, opera-

tion, and liquidation of banks. Bank examiners review the books of national banks twice a year. Violators of the law may lose their charters through suits filed by the Comptroller. Although there are more state-chartered banks than national, the national banks do a larger volume of business.

Federal deposit insurance began in 1933, when there was a banking crisis and many "runs" on banks. The Federal Deposit Insurance Corporation (FDIC) was organized to assure the safety of all bank deposits up to $5,000, increased to $10,000 in 1950. Insured banks pay a premium to the FDIC, which builds up a fund to compensate depositors if a member bank fails. Over a hundred million depositors now enjoy insured accounts. Members of the Federal Reserve System are required to belong; most state banks find it to their advantage to join, if they can meet the standards of FDIC. The insurance scheme stands guard against future panics.

Since 1933, savings and loan associations also have been chartered under national authority. The chartering and examining agency is the Home Loan Bank Board of the Housing and Home Finance Agency. A deposit insurance scheme is handled by the Federal Savings and Loan Insurance Corporation. All federally chartered associations are required to participate; state-chartered and certain other credit institutions may apply and, if approved, be insured. Like the FDIC, deposits up to $10,000 are protected.

Business Credit. A complete list of Federal aids to business through provision of credit facilities includes the Federal Reserve System and FDIC, already mentioned in this chapter; the Export-Import Bank of Washington, discussed in Chapter 25; and certain lending and guaranty activities of the General Services Administration and of the Small Business Administration, which are to be covered here.

The General Services Administration has some modest responsibilities for loans to establish productive facilities, stock-pile critical materials, and procure tools and materials for defense.

The Small Business Administration, created in 1953, inherited the small-business-loan portion of the Reconstruction Finance Corporation activity. Proponents justify such activities as necessary to prevent excessive concentration of economic power in the hands of a few giant corporations. Activities take the form of loans and guaranties, contracts with Federal agencies, advice to small concerns on new products, and

disaster loans. Loans are limited to $350,000 and may be made only when financing is not otherwise available at reasonable terms. The second Hoover Commission expressed some doubts about the agency's work. It recommended another two years of life, but with an audit such as government corporations have and an interest rate high enough to cover operating expenses and a fair interest rate on agency borrowings from the Treasury.[1] Congress gave the Administration permanent status in 1958.

Although liquidated by act of Congress in 1953, the Reconstruction Finance Corporation (RFC) requires mention because of its vast size and great role in the Depression of the 1930s, the war of the 1940s, and the period of postwar readjustment. This gigantic institution was set up during the Hoover Administration in 1932. To afford flexibility of action, it was given the corporate form of organization. It was primarily a lending agency, although during the war it operated many productive enterprises. In the early 1950s, criticisms of RFC management and policies reached a climax with disclosures of irregularities and favoritism. In 1954, RFC functions were distributed among other agencies.

Fiscal Policy. Most Americans appear to have accepted the idea that management of public finance, the banking and credit system, and other public concerns should contribute to national economic welfare. Desirable goals include high level of employment, reduced fluctuations of the business cycle, and freedom from excessive inflation or deflation.

Over the years, the Federal government has acquired an arsenal of weapons which it can use to achieve positive goals. Some critics of government intervention prefer to

[1] Second Hoover Commission, *Lending Agencies* (1955), p. 91.

let the economy surge and drift as so-called "natural forces" allow. A leading economist put the opposing case directly:

There is no choice then but to attempt to lead fiscal policy along economically sound rather than destructive channels. Every government always has a fiscal policy whether it realizes it or not. The real issue is whether this shall be a constructive one or an unconscious, bumbling one.[1]

A positive program also involves the use of several devices that are nonfiscal or borderline; they are considered in later chapters. The preceding chapter, and this one, deal with major Federal fiscal "tools" through which economic conditions can be controlled. By raising taxes, government may help curb inflation; by reducing taxes, it may stimulate a lagging economy. The interest rate on the national debt, to take only one aspect, affects other interest rates and hence investment in expansion throughout private sectors of the economy. Federal Reserve alterations of the rediscount rate or reserve requirements influence the availability of credit to producers and consumers, whose consequent behavior may set a distinct economic trend.

Between 1945 and 1951 the Treasury and the Federal Reserve System placed much emphasis on keeping the yields on government securities stable and low. Some economists criticized this policy as stimulating inflationary pressures; demands for goods and services were so great that supply often fell short, resulting in increased prices. In March, 1951, the Treasury and Federal Reserve reached accord; thereafter the powers of the central bank would be used to promote economic stability.

The flexible policy has been tested in two periods of modest recession: 1953–1954

[1] Paul A. Samuelson, *Economics, An Introductory Analysis* (New York: McGraw-Hill, 4th ed., 1958), p. 344.

and 1957–1958. In both cases Federal Reserve played an important role. During 1951–1953, while the Korean War was on, it acted to check inflation by raising the discount rate, increasing reserve requirements, and raising margin requirements on security purchases. Beginning in July, 1953, it took steps to expand credit and money; these included cutting the discount rate, reducing reserve requirements for banks, and purchasing additional government securities. By mid-1954 the short, mild recession was largely over. Federal Reserve, and other government agencies, took similar steps in curbing the recession that began late in 1957.

HOUSING

Governments Intervene. Although housing has always been acknowledged to be a necessity, "adequate" housing has only recently been considered so. Even today millions live in dwellings scarcely fit for human occupancy. All important cities have "slums" or "blighted areas." Many rural sections are covered with dwellings equally bad, if not worse. Social workers and others called attention to this situation for over a generation, but only recently has the public become sufficiently aroused to support vigorous action by the Federal government.

Except for the building done in Washington and other critical areas during the First World War, Federal housing activities began during the Depression. An act creating a system of Federal home-loan banks, in 1932, was the first venture. Then followed legislation to help distressed mortgagees refinance their obligations, make credit more easily available for home renovation and building, clear slums and provide low-cost housing for low-income groups, and, later, provide housing in critical areas for defense and war workers, returning veterans, and others. Since 1947, Federal housing activities have been centered in the Housing and Home Finance Agency, an independent establishment.

Buying and Selling Mortgages. Funds for new homes or for mortgages are usually provided by banks, building and loan associations, insurance companies, and similar institutions. But these companies often sell their mortgages to obtain cash or find better investments. This buying and selling is commonly described as a "secondary mortgage market." The Federal government has helped provide this market since 1935. Today it is the task of the Federal National Mortgage Association. During recent years the Association has bought and sold mortgages totaling billions of dollars. Most of them have been home loans to veterans, farmers, and residents of Alaska.

Home Loan Bank System. Eleven banks located in principal cities comprise the Federal Home Loan Bank System. Each bank has twelve directors, four appointed by the Home Loan Bank Board and eight elected by member institutions. The home-loan banks do not deal directly with individuals who desire to borrow. They are banks for building and loan associations, savings and loan associations, cooperative banks, homestead associations, insurance companies, or savings banks, which in turn lend directly to home builders.

The great bulk of member institutions are of the savings and loan type. Loans are made to member and, in some instances, nonmember institutions, primarily on the basis of first-mortgage collateral. In this way the home-loan banks supply funds with which borrowers can meet the home-financing needs of their communities and the withdrawal demands of savers and investors.

Savings and Loan Associations. Rather than deposit savings in local banks, many people prefer to place them with savings and loan associations either as an investment or with the expectation of later financing a home. Prior to 1933, associations of this type found it necessary to organize under state laws. Since then, Federal law has also permitted them. They may be organized upon application by a responsible group of citizens to the nearest Federal home-loan bank. When approved and established, each association automatically becomes a member of the Federal Home Loan Bank System and must insure its deposits with the Federal Savings and Loan Insurance Corporation. The deposit-insurance plan is similar to the one operated by the FDIC for ordinary commercial banks. The principal function of an association is to help finance home building.

The Federal Housing Administration (FHA). The FHA, which dates back to 1934, is primarily an insurance agency. Its goal is to encourage the improvement of existing housing, the building of new small homes and apartment dwellings, and the manufacture of prefabricated housing.

The FHA does not lend directly to home builders and manufacturers. Local financial institutions lend the money, while FHA guarantees payment of the mortgage, thus diminishing risk of nonpayment to the moneylenders. A premium is charged the financial institution for this service, the income from which is expected to pay the cost of operation. The amount of the loan depends upon the size and cost of the project. Not more than a stipulated rate of interest can be charged on insured loans; the projects must be executed in accordance with approved specifications; and payments must be made periodically until the obligation is fully retired. Thus far, many mortgages have been insured, with few defaults.

Subsidized Low-rent Housing. The housing programs described above are intended to help finance private parties whose credit is good. The role of the Federal Public Housing Authority (FPHA) is quite different. The FPHA is a government corporation whose primary purpose is to clear slums and provide low-rent housing. The authority does not do so directly, however. Rather, it enters into contracts with municipal, county, and state authorities to get the job done.

The procedure is for a local authority to frame plans for slum clearance and new construction, then submit them to FPHA for approval. If approval is given, a contract is entered into whereby the Federal agency agrees to: (1) lend a large part of the cost of the project at prevailing rates of interest plus a small charge for administrative costs, the principal to be repaid over a long period of years, and (2) make annual contributions over a period of years as a subsidy for low rents.

Thereupon, the Federal agency may make grants and loans for clearing and preparing the area for new construction, make long-term loans to local authorities which will be repaid out of rentals, and make annual contributions over a period of years as a subsidy for low rents. Tenants must be citizens and in the low-income category; none may be admitted whose aggregate income exceeds fixed amounts. If, after moving in, the size of the family or income increases beyond prescribed amounts, different quarters must be found. Under the stimulus of this program, the landscapes of many large American cities have been changed by low-rent-dwelling projects.

FOR FURTHER READING

Financial Administration and Budgets

Anderson, William, and others: *Intergovernmental Fiscal Relations* (Minneapolis: University of Minnesota Press, 1956).

Buck, Arthur E.: *The Budget in Governments of Today* (New York: Macmillan, 1934).

Burkhead, Jesse: *Government Budgeting* (New York: Wiley, 1956).

Douglas, Paul H.: *Economy in the National Government* (Chicago: University of Chicago Press, 1952).

Kendrick, M. S., and M. Wehle: *Century and a Half of Federal Expenditures* (New York: National Bureau of Economic Research, 1955).

Kimmel, Lewis H.: *Federal Budget and Fiscal Policy, 1789–1958* (Washington, D.C.: Brookings Institution, 1959).

Mort, Paul R.: *Fiscal Readiness for the Stress of Change* (Pittsburgh, Pa.: University of Pittsburgh Press, 1957).

Mosher, Frederick C.: *Program Budgeting: Theory and Practice with Particular Reference to the U.S. Department of the Army* (Chicago: Public Administration Service, 1954).

Rolph, Earl R., and George F. Break: *Public Finance* (New York: Ronald, 1961).

Smithies, Arthur: *The Budgetary Process in the United States* (New York: McGraw-Hill, 1955).

Studenski, Paul, and H. E. Krooss: *Financial History of the United States* (New York: McGraw-Hill, 1952).

U.S. Commission on Organization of the Executive Branch of the Government (first Hoover Commission): *Budgeting and Accounting* (1949).

———: *Task Force Report on Fiscal, Budgeting, and Accounting Activities* (1949).

U.S. Commission on Organization of the Executive Branch of the Government (second Hoover Commission): *Budget and Accounting* (1955).

———: *Task Force Report on Budget and Accounting* (1955).

Wallace, Robert A.: *Congressional Control of Federal Spending* (Detroit, Mich.: Wayne State University Press, 1960).

Wilmerding, Lucius, Jr.: *The Spending Power: A History of the Efforts of Congress to Control Expenditures* (New Haven, Conn.: Yale University Press, 1943).

Expenditures and Debt

Bator, Francis M.: *The Questions of Government Spending: Public Needs and Private Wants* (New York: Harper, 1960).

Harris, Seymour E.: *The National Debt and the New Economics* (New York: McGraw-Hill, 1947).

Robinson, Marshall A.: *The National Debt Ceiling* (Washington, D.C.: Brookings Institution, 1959).

U.S. Congress, Joint Economic Committee: *Federal Expenditure Policy for Economic Growth and Stability*, 85th Cong., 1st Sess., Joint Committee print (1957).

Money, Banking, Credit, and Housing

Bach, George L.: *Federal Reserve Policy-making* (New York: Knopf, 1950).

Beyer, Glenn H.: *Housing: A Factual Analysis* (New York: Macmillan, 1958).

Fellner, William J.: *Monetary Policies and Full Employment* (Berkeley and Los Angeles, Calif.: University of California Press, 2d ed., 1947).

Goldenweiser, E. A.: *American Monetary Policy* (New York: McGraw-Hill, 1951).

Hansen, Alvin H.: *Monetary Theory and Fiscal Policy* (New York: McGraw-Hill, 1949).

Procknow, Herbert V. (ed.): *The Federal Reserve System* (New York: Harper, 1960).

Wendt, Paul F.: *The Role of the Federal Government in Housing* (Washington, D.C.: American Enterprise Association, 1956).

REVIEW QUESTIONS

1. Describe the process of budget formulation in the Federal government.

2. Explain the various steps in budget authorization.

3. Which United States agencies have roles in budget execution, and what are these roles?

4. What aspects of Federal budget procedure were criticized by the two Hoover Commissions? Why?

5. What justification is there for the argument that automatic budget balancing is unnecessary and may be unwise from the point of view of securing a sound economy?

6. Describe the Federal Reserve System and how it operates today.

7. Trace the growth of the public debt, and discuss the various theories concerning it.

8. Explain the functions of the Comptroller General, Bureau of the Budget, Fiscal Service of the Treasury.

9. Describe Federal regulation of private banking and credit. Under what power of the national government is such supervision justified?

10. How does the Federal government insure deposits in banks and savings and loan associations?

11. What Federal assistance is available to homeowners and home builders?

12. Distinguish between the functions of the Federal Public Housing Authority and the Federal Housing Administration.

Chapter Twenty-Two

Foreign Relations: Powers and Conduct

*The Department [of State] . . . has grown in recent years
from a small group of experts and amateurs to a vast,
sprawling aggregation of specialists, career men, political
appointees, and bureaucrats from other agencies—
so much so that it is no longer feasible to present any
meaningful chart of its structure smaller than a bed sheet.*

FREDERICK L. SCHUMAN[1]

*The millstream that turns the intricately meshed wheels of
the State Department is the flow of reports coming in
from Foreign Service officers all over the world.
These are the raw materials of policy. And they bring
to attention the situations and events that call for executive
action. Thus the reports sent in from missions abroad
eventuate in the instructions, policy guides, messages for
delivery to foreign governments, and other advices which
set the Foreign Service officer himself in motion.*

J. RIVES CHILDS[2]

The resiliency of the American Constitution
is dramatically illustrated in the field of international relations. The constitutional
phrases which grant power in this area are
amazingly brief to provide for large under-

[1] *International Politics, The Destiny of the
Western State System* (New York: McGraw-Hill,
6th ed., 1958), p. 183.
[2] *American Foreign Service* (New York: Holt,
1948), p. 64.

takings and serious commitments in all
parts of the world.

Provisions, like the two-thirds rule for
ratifying treaties, have proved embarrassing
at times. Ambiguous words, such as those
which define the scope of treaties, have
come to be highly controversial. But the
grants of power have proved ample and
flexible enough to permit the nation to

become one of the most powerful nations in the world.

CONSTITUTIONAL POWERS

Specific. By authority of powers delegated to him, the President initiates the formulation of foreign policies; he negotiates treaties and agreements; he decides which governments will be recognized and when to begin and terminate diplomatic and consular relations with other nations; and he chooses, directs, and recalls diplomats and consuls who represent the nation abroad.

The Senate approves treaties and confirms ambassadors and consuls nominated by the President. The two houses of Congress jointly declare war, regulate foreign commerce, lay and collect tariffs, and define violations of international law.

Inherent and Exclusive. The Federal government also has inherent powers in the field of international relations. These derive from the fact that the United States is a sovereign nation and thus may do whatever other national states may rightfully do in their relations with one another.

In *United States v. Curtiss-Wright Export Corp.* [299 U.S. 304 (1936)], the Supreme Court explained inherent powers as follows:

It results that the investment of the Federal government with the powers of external sovereignty did not depend upon the affirmative grants of the Constitution. The powers to declare and wage war, to conclude peace, to make treaties, to maintain diplomatic relations with other sovereignties, if they had never been mentioned in the Constitution, would have vested in the Federal government as necessary concomitants of nationality. . . . As a member of the family of nations, the right and power of the United States in that field are equal to the right and power of the other members of the international family. Otherwise, the United States is not completely sovereign.

Federal powers in the foreign-relations field are exclusive; they are not shared with the states. The states have no standing in international law; they are expressly forbidden by the Constitution to enter into "any treaty, alliance, or confederation," or, without the consent of Congress, to enter into any agreement or compact with a foreign power.

Scope of the Treaty Power. Although the scope of the treaty power is not defined precisely, several general principles are clear: The power extends to all proper subjects of negotiation between the American government and other nations. Treaties must be made under the authority of the United States. Provisions of treaties must be consistent with American institutions and the distribution of powers between the Federal and state governments. The treaty power cannot be used as authority for doing what the Constitution forbids. Treaties are not superior to statutes; if there is conflict between the two, the later supersedes the earlier.

Although these limitations seem clear and reasonable, serious questions have arisen. Many of these originated with the doctrine announced by the Supreme Court in the case of *Missouri v. Holland* [252 U.S. 416 (1920)].

Missouri v. Holland. In 1913, Congress enacted a law that forbade the killing of migratory birds except under strict regulation. The legislation was declared unconstitutional by the lower courts on the ground that migratory birds were property of the state and so not subject to interstate-commerce regulation. In 1916, a treaty was made with Great Britain to assure protection of migratory birds. Two years later

Congress passed a law forbidding the killing, capturing, or selling of birds protected by the treaty except in accordance with regulations set by the Secretary of Agriculture.

Missouri brought suit against Holland, a Federal game warden, to restrain him from enforcing the law, calling it an unwarranted invasion of powers reserved to the states. Missouri lost. The Supreme Court held that the treaty dealt with a proper subject, was made under the authority of the United States, and that the statute in question was a necessary and proper means of making the treaty effective. This decision meant that a treaty could give the Federal government authority to legislate on domestic matters otherwise reserved to the states.

Can the Treaty Power Be Used to Regulate Local Affairs? A dramatic consequence of the decision was that many people argued that the Federal government could make treaties forbidding the exportation or importation of goods produced or distributed by child labor. This, it was argued, was an appropriate subject for negotiation with other nations; the treaty would be enacted under authority of the United States, and it would violate no expressed prohibition of the Constitution.

Although the argument is plausible, the step was never taken. Its serious proposal, however, illustrates the potential scope of the treaty power. The doctrine, if carried to its logical conclusion, could be used to justify Federal regulation of almost any domestic matter. Indeed, if the Federal government could get other nations to cooperate in making a treaty, the distinction between delegated and reserved powers could be almost obliterated.

UN Charter as a Treaty. This question has taken on new importance since the United States joined the United Nations. Article I, Section 3, of the UN Charter, for example, pledges the United States, along with other members, to promote and encourage ". . . respect for human rights, and fundamental freedoms for all without distinction as to race, sex, language, or religion. . . ."

Since Congress has ratified the Charter, does not the logic of the *Missouri v. Holland* decision suggest that Congress can now implement Article I, Section 3, with legislation that otherwise would be considered beyond the scope of Federal powers? If Congress should enact a law implementing the Charter and the courts followed the *Missouri v. Holland* precedent, it would be necessary to examine the following questions: Are human rights and freedoms proper subjects for treaty making? Are the treaty provisions consistent with our institutions and the distribution of powers between the Federal and state governments? Do treaty provisions transgress expressly forbidden provisions of the Constitution? Of course, no one can fortell what the Supreme Court might say, but the decision would probably hinge on whether a majority of the judges thought state-reserved powers were impaired.

Some of these issues have been adjudicated in California courts. A lower court held the state alien-land law unconstitutional on grounds of conflict with the United Nations Charter, which it held to be self-executing. The state Supreme Court, however, held the statute invalid on the ground that it conflicted with the equal-protection clause of the Fourteenth Amendment. All judges agreed that the United Nations Charter was not a self-executing treaty [*Fujii v. California*, 242 P. 2d 617 (1952)].

Apprehension over the probable attitude of the Court helps explain the reluctance of some senators and representatives to approve American adherence to such international commitments as the Genocide

Convention and the Covenant on Human Rights. It also generated support for the proposed Bricker amendment, discussed below.

International Executive Agreements. Arrangements with other nations often are made by executive agreements rather than by treaties. Indeed, since 1900, executive agreements have been used more frequently than treaties. They differ from treaties chiefly in that they do not require senatorial approval. The Constitution does not expressly grant the President authority to make international agreements without the consent of the Senate; his authority must be granted or implied from acts of Congress or treaties, or implied from powers clearly delegated to the President.

Most executive agreements have been made by authority of congressional statutes or treaties. Among these are innumerable postal conventions entered into by authority of legislation dating back to 1792, embargoes upon shipments of munitions to warring South American countries, the much-publicized reciprocal tariff agreements entered into by authority of the Trade Agreements Act of 1934, and international agreements under mutual-security legislation.

Authority for other executive agreements has been implied from constitutional provisions conferring upon the President diplomatic powers, making him Commander in Chief of the Army and Navy, and requiring that the laws be faithfully executed. Theodore Roosevelt's *modus vivendi* of 1907, whereby the American government undertook to collect customs for Santo Domingo to ensure payment of debts owed to foreign bankers, is a conspicuous illustration. The armistice of 1918, the resumption of diplomatic relations with Russia in 1933, the agreement to occupy and defend Iceland in 1941, the Atlantic Charter Agreement of 1941, and the agreements made to terminate the Second World War are other examples.

Executive agreements like those just mentioned are part of the supreme law of the land whether or not they are later implemented by statute or treaty. The President's constitutional authority to make such agreements is incontestable, but he is limited in practice by public opinion and awareness that most agreements of this type cannot be effective without subsequent congressional approval.

One of the principal reasons for the strong backing secured for the Bricker Amendment in the 1950s was the tendency to resort more and more to executive agreements, which are not subject to Senate ratification. (Data from U.S. Department of State.)

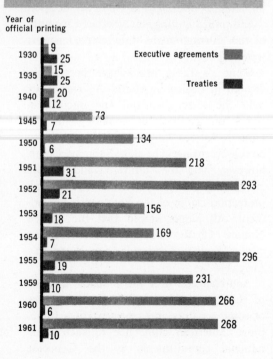

NUMBER OF TREATIES AND EXECUTIVE AGREEMENTS COMPARED

Year of official printing

Year	Executive agreements	Treaties
1930	9	25
1935	15	25
1940	20	12
1945	73	7
1950	134	6
1951	218	31
1952	293	21
1953	156	18
1954	169	7
1955	296	19
1959	231	10
1960	266	6
1961	268	10

The Proposed Bricker Amendment. The frequent use of executive agreements, sometimes under circumstances that suggested deliberate flouting of Congress, has aroused considerable alarm. Critics rallied behind a proposal to amend the Constitution sponsored originally by Senator John Bricker of Ohio. This provided that (1) a treaty would have no force or effect if it conflicted with the Constitution; (2) a treaty would be enforceable within the United States only through legislation which would be valid in the absence of treaty; (3) Congress would have authority to regulate all executive agreements with foreign nations and international organizations, and such agreements would be enforceable within the United States only through legislation which would be valid in the absence of treaty.

Presidential Objections. President Eisenhower and his supporters opposed these changes. They contended the first proposal was unnecessary because the courts had already ruled that treaties must conform with the Constitution. To the second and third proposals, which would have overruled *Missouri v. Holland,* the objection was that the President's hand in foreign affairs would be seriously weakened by doubts over what Congress would approve and disputes over state rights. As a concession, the President indicated willingness to subscribe to the first proposal and to forego requesting Senate approval of the Genocide Convention, which outlaws mass extinction of a people, and the Covenant of Human Rights, a United Nations declaration of civil liberties.

Though defeated by a close vote in the Senate, the Bricker amendment has made the President more cautious in handling foreign relations. The issues are far from dead, and critics of presidential authority can be expected to continue their efforts on behalf of limitations akin to the Bricker proposals.

'*But I Don't Want a SNAFU Car*'

BRICKER PROPOSAL

PRESIDENT

FOREIGN POLICY DUAL CONTROL

(John Stampone in Air Force Daily.)

The Commitment of Troops. The President's authority to commit American troops is ambiguous and highly controversial. Congress has the power to raise and support an army and navy, to levy taxes and make necessary appropriations, and to declare war. The Senate has authority to approve appointments and treaties. But the President executes the laws, acts as Commander in Chief, negotiates treaties, and formulates foreign policy. He may find it desirable, or necessary, to make promises in advance to foreign governments and dispatch troops to various parts of the world, or even order them into action that may lead to war.

When Congress declares war or otherwise authorizes the use of troops abroad, no constitutional problem arises. But in 1950–1951 President Truman wanted to send more troops to central Europe than Congress had authorized. Moreover, in 1950 he ordered American forces to undertake "police action" in Korea without any specific mandate from Congress. Presidents have dispatched troops abroad on many occasions without congressional authorization. President McKinley ordered troops to Peking during the Boxer Rebellion in 1900. President Wilson sent troops into Mexico in 1913 to avenge attacks upon Americans. President Eisenhower directed Marines to take up positions in Lebanon in 1958.

The justification for such steps is that, as Commander in Chief, the President must take risks in committing troops to troubled areas. If the action is routine, or localized and limited, the President is usually not widely criticized. But when the issues are large, costly, and controversial, and when the President lacks overwhelming political support in and out of Congress, this authority is likely to be contested. In short, the limits are political rather than legal.

Problem Posed by UN Charter. The issue came to a head in discussions over American adherence to the UN Charter. The question raised in Congress was how far the President would be allowed to go in committing United States forces in conflicts undertaken by the United Nations.

Only Congress can declare war. But if the President sends American troops into action in cooperation with others, as provided for in the Charter, has the power to declare war been transferred from Congress to the President? Does the Constitution require that congressional approval be obtained in every instance before American forces are ordered into combat?

After much discussion, Congress passed the United Nations Participation Act in 1945. This permitted the President to cooperate with the United Nations but authorized the use of our Armed Forces only in accordance with special agreements between the Security Council and the

United States, to which congressional consent would be required. Such special agreements have not yet been concluded.

The Korean Conflict. Nevertheless, shortly after fighting started in Korea, in June, 1950, the President ordered American troops to provide "cover and support" for South Korean forces. He did not ask for congressional authorization. The order was given before the Security Council voted to apply sanctions. When the Security Council did vote to apply sanctions, it only recommended, rather than ordered, comparable action by other nations. In other words, the President, on his own responsibility, committed the nation to what proved to be serious, bloody, and prolonged military action; later the military effort was continued upon recommendation of the Security Council.

The President was able to do this because Congress acquiesced—indeed, it later supported the action enthusiastically with appropriations and other aids—and the effort met with sufficient popular support or indifference to avoid a serious contest. This suggests that, with or without permissive legislation, a strong-willed President can assert what he deems to be his prerogative, even committing the nation to a course leading to war.

The North Atlantic Treaty. The question came dramatically to the fore again in 1949, during debate on the North Atlantic Pact. After considerable consultation with Senate leaders, the President proposed a treaty, Article V of which read:

The Parties agree that an armed attack against one or more of them in Europe or North America shall be considered an attack against them all; and consequently they agree that, if such an armed attack occurs, each of them, in the exercise of the right of individual or collective self-defense recognized by Article 51 of the Charter of the United Nations, will assist the Party or Parties so attacked *by taking forthwith*, individually and in concert with the other Parties, such action as it deems necessary, *including the use of armed force*, to restore and maintain the security of the North Atlantic Area. (Italics supplied.)

Critics contended that the italicized words could be construed by the President to justify automatic use of force, thus impairing the prerogative of Congress to declare war. Ultimately, Senate approval was given, but only after spokesmen for the President, and Senate supporters, gave repeated assurances that Article V was not to be construed as enlarging executive power or diminishing that of Congress to declare war. In spite of these assurances, a strong President might at some future time invoke Article V as justification for launching an "executive war."

Eisenhower Obtains Advance Approval. President Eisenhower recognized the importance of this balance between the Chief Executive and Congress when he faced a difficult situation early in 1955. Communist China was threatening to invade offshore islands—Formosa and the Pescadores—held by Nationalists Chinese forces with United States support. The President's own political party was sharply split over the proper course to follow in the Far East, and the Democrats controlled both houses of Congress. A misstep by the President would have provoked a political storm and might also have precipitated a third world war. Under these circumstances the President asked Congress in advance for approval of the use of force, if necessary. Congress promptly, and with overwhelming majorities in both houses, approved the request.

In 1957, President Eisenhower made a similar advance request for authority to use force, if necessary, in the troubled Middle East, and Congress responded favorably. As far as constitutional law is concerned, these requests were probably unnecessary. That they were made at all attests the restraining role of Congress, especially where political factors are delicately balanced, and the President's sensitivity to the issues involved.

GENERAL ASPECTS OF DIPLOMATIC AND CONSULAR PRACTICE

Diplomacy is steeped in formality and etiquette, much of which dates back to antiquity. A most important custom concerns the ranking of diplomatic officers.

Classification of Diplomats. Practically all nations follow the classification of diplomats agreed upon by the Congress of Vienna in 1816 and supplemented from time to time. At present there are five classes: the first includes ambassadors, legates (envoys of the Pope chosen from the cardinals for special assignments), and nuncios (envoys of the Pope assigned to permanent posts and chosen from outside the rank of cardinals); the second, envoys extraordinary, ministers plenipotentiary, and apostolic internuncios (envoys of the Pope next in rank to nuncios); the third, ministers resident; the fourth, chargés d'affaires; and the fifth, a group known as diplomatic agents. Envoys rank within each class according to the date of arrival at their post. The one in the highest rank with the most seniority at a given post is known as the *doyen*, or dean of the diplomatic corps.

Envoys of the various classes perform practically the same functions and enjoy the same rights and privileges, the chief difference is a matter of prestige. Diplomats of the first class are supposed to be the personal representatives of the sovereign, while the others are merely representatives of their governments, although in modern times this has little practical significance. Diplomats of the first class occupy embassies; those of the remaining classes, legations. Envoys of the first three classes are accredited to heads of states, those of the fourth and fifth classes to ministers of foreign affairs. There is a tendency to consider chargés d'affaires as temporary officers, while diplomatic agents are as a rule assigned only to states not fully sovereign, such as Morocco.

Classification of Consuls. A diplomat represents his country in its political relations with other governments; a consul is commissioned to help administer American laws in foreign ports, assist American tourists, afford protection to Americans and their interests, and promote trade. The classification of consuls in all states is similar, though there is much less fuss about the matter than with diplomats.

Consular officers of the United States are divided into four classes: consuls general, consuls, vice-consuls, and consular agents. Which is appointed to a particular post depends to a large extent upon the commercial and financial importance of the place so far as American interests are concerned. Some of the consuls general have supervisory jurisdiction over all consular offices of lesser rank within a given area. The one at London has supervisory jurisdiction over all consular offices in the British Isles, except Ireland; the one at Antwerp has supervisory authority over all Belgium and Luxembourg.

Appointment and Reception of Diplomats. Diplomats are invariably appointed by heads of states. In the United States chiefs of important missions are appointed by the President and confirmed by the Senate. Before sending the name of a diplomat to the Senate, the President, acting through the Department of State, usually ascertains whether the person is acceptable to the government to which he is to be accredited. The act of determining whether the envoy is *persona grata* is called *agréation* and the approval *agrément*. When confirmed by the Senate, the diplomat is given a "letter of credence," which is an official commission to be presented to the sovereign upon arrival at his post.

The reverse of this procedure is followed when diplomats come to the United States. The President receives diplomats of higher rank, and the Secretary of State those of lesser rank. The receptions at the White House are formal and stiff, with meticulous regard for ceremony and protocol. They consume considerable time, inasmuch as the largest diplomatic body in the world— over 500 members—is now stationed in Washington.

Appointment and Reception of Consuls. As in the case of diplomats, consuls must be *persona grata*, although *agrément* is not often obtained in advance. They are usually appointed by heads of states or by ministers of foreign affairs. In the United States those above the rank of consular agent are appointed by the President from among career Foreign Service officers; consular agents are appointed by the Secretary of State, usually upon the recommendation of a superior officer located within the country or region to be served.

A consul is given by his own government what is known as a "consular commission," which is presented to the secretary of foreign affairs upon arrival at the point of service. Though as a rule a consul is not received by a sovereign or head of state, he may be, particularly if his government is without diplomatic representation in that country. The receiving government issues an "exequatur" entitling the consul to the rights and duties pertaining to his office. The reverse of this procedure is followed when a foreign consul is sent to the United States. Reception of consuls is a large task.

More than a thousand foreign consular officers are stationed in the fifty states and the American territories.

Privileges and Immunities of Diplomats. International law and treaties grant diplomats privileges not enjoyed by ordinary persons. They are entitled to safe conduct through neutral and friendly states while their own nation is at war; they are exempt from the payment of customs duties and taxes; they may worship as they please in embassies or legations even though their particular mode of worship would otherwise be illegal, as formerly was true in Mohammedan countries; they have certain ceremonial privileges such as displaying their national flag and insignia; they are entitled to certain marks of respect, such as being addressed by appropriate title and seated according to rank at public functions; and they are entitled to perform certain civil functions, such as notarial services.

Diplomats also enjoy certain immunities. Their persons, residences, places of doing business, archives, and mails are inviolable. They cannot be arrested, though their guilt be obvious; nor can they be tried by the courts of the country in which they are stationed for crimes committed while there. They can neither be sued nor compelled to testify in court. These immunities extend also to members of a diplomat's family and his official personnel. If a diplomat misbehaves he may become *persona non grata*, whereupon his recall may be requested or he may be dismissed by the government to which he is accredited. If an offense is serious, he probably will be prosecuted in the courts of his home state.

Privileges and Immunities of Consuls. The privileges and immunities of consuls are less absolute than those of diplomatic agents, since they are based almost entirely upon treaty provisions. The treaties of most countries grant them privileges similar to those enjoyed by diplomats. Though their persons are not absolutely inviolable, they are entitled to protection, and a government failing to provide it is expected to make reparation. Their archives are inviolate, but immunity does not extend to their private papers or personal effects; nor, in the absence of treaty provisions, is the consulate free from visit and search. They are generally liable for civil suit and may be prosecuted on criminal charges unless exempted by treaty.

The Removal of Diplomats and Consuls. As noted above, diplomats and consuls must be *persona grata* at all times to the governments receiving them. Frequently when a foreign representative loses favor, his own government learns of it in time to make a transfer, or asks him to resign, before controversy arises. Where an agent can no longer be tolerated, he may be peremptorily dismissed, although the usual course is to intimate to his government that his recall is desired. Normally, before departing, a diplomat or consul pays a brief formal call to the chief of state or minister of foreign affairs, although where feeling has run high this is sometimes omitted.

ORGANIZATION FOR FOREIGN AFFAIRS

Department of State. This department antedates the Constitution. It can be traced to the Committee on Secret Correspondence appointed by the Continental Congress in 1775. Two years later its name was changed to Committee on Foreign Affairs; in 1781 a Department of Foreign Affairs was established; and in July, 1789, the same name was given to the first executive department created under the Constitution. Later, when assigned a number of duties relating to "home affairs," the name was changed to

Department of State, by which it has since been known.

The Secretary of State is the chief of both the Department of State and the Foreign Service. Next to the President himself, the Secretary is the highest-ranking executive officer (the Vice President, it will be recalled, is a *legislative* officer until he becomes Acting President) in the Federal government. He is the personal choice of the President, and he continues to serve as long as the President desires or until impeached. In ceremonial matters the Secretary ranks first among Cabinet members, always sitting immediately to the President's right at Cabinet meetings. He is the only department head not required to make an annual report to Congress. The Secretary frequently acts as spokesman for the President.

Internal organization has fluctuated considerably in recent years. Both the Department itself and the Hoover Commissions have made intensive studies of the best way to streamline the Department to meet its enlarged responsibilities. In response to these recommendations Congress has authorized the structure and staff shown in the chart on the next page.

Other Agencies Handling Foreign Affairs. Foreign relations involve many more Federal agencies than the Department of State. Indeed, the first Hoover Commission reported in 1949 that it had found "some forty-five other units" of the Federal government participating.

To illustrate: the Departments of Agriculture, Commerce, and Labor are concerned with foreign trade and related matters; the Treasury Department taxes imports and is involved in financial dealings abroad; the Department of Justice handles immigration and naturalization; the Department of Interior administers American overseas territories and international programs to protect fish and wildlife; the Post Office Department handles mail to and from all parts of the world through treaties and agreements with other nations; the Department of Defense has commitments in all parts of the world; practically every major agency is involved with one or more programs of the United Nations. This dispersal of responsibility was a major concern of the first Hoover Commission, but the proliferation of agencies has continued.

The Foreign Service. Because their functions differed, American diplomatic and consular officers were divided into two separate services during most of the nation's history. Appointments were made on a political basis, and positions within the two services were not interchangeable. The spoils system had baneful effects, and morale and efficiency suffered because experienced and competent persons in one service had no way of transferring to the other except by resigning and obtaining reappointment by the President.

Long agitation for change culminated, in 1924, in passage of the Rogers Act, which, among other things, combined the two services, provided for recruitment and promotion of permanent officers on the basis of merit, established what is now called the Foreign Service Institute, classified positions, raised salaries, and provided a retirement system. This legislation, together with amendments added since, particularly by the Moses-Linthicum Act of 1931 and the Foreign Service Act of 1946, is the basic law today.

One of the most significant reforms made by the Rogers Act and subsequent legislation has been the encouragement of the use of career men in high diplomatic positions. Although appointments are still often made on a political basis, the law requires the Board of the Foreign Service to recommend to the President annually a list of the most

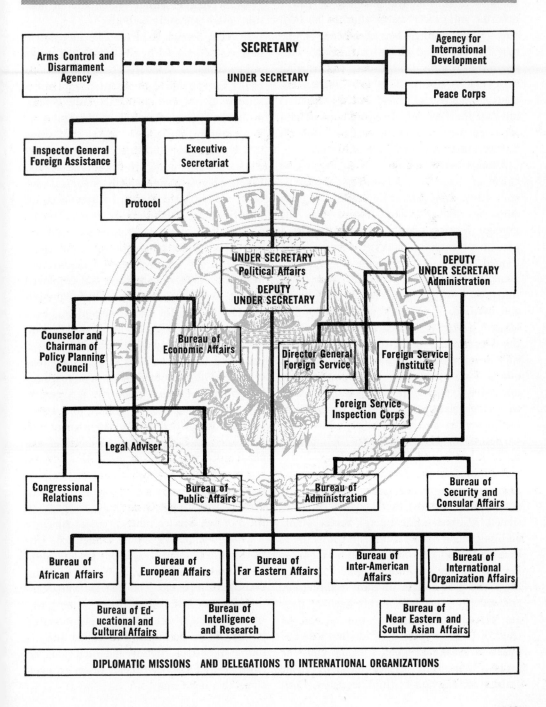

DEPARTMENT OF STATE

Arms Control and Disarmament Agency

SECRETARY

UNDER SECRETARY

Agency for International Development

Peace Corps

Inspector General Foreign Assistance

Executive Secretariat

Protocol

UNDER SECRETARY Political Affairs

DEPUTY UNDER SECRETARY

DEPUTY UNDER SECRETARY Administration

Counselor and Chairman of Policy Planning Council

Bureau of Economic Affairs

Director General Foreign Service

Foreign Service Institute

Foreign Service Inspection Corps

Legal Adviser

Congressional Relations

Bureau of Public Affairs

Bureau of Administration

Bureau of Security and Consular Affairs

Bureau of African Affairs

Bureau of European Affairs

Bureau of Far Eastern Affairs

Bureau of Inter-American Affairs

Bureau of International Organization Affairs

Bureau of Educational and Cultural Affairs

Bureau of Intelligence and Research

Bureau of Near Eastern and South Asian Affairs

DIPLOMATIC MISSIONS AND DELEGATIONS TO INTERNATIONAL ORGANIZATIONS

meritorious senior Foreign Service officers, for consideration when vacancies arise. The law also establishes the positions of career minister and career ambassador, to be held only by top Foreign Service officers. These may be appointed chiefs of mission, with senatorial approval, without jeopardizing their career status. The law further encourages the use of career men by stipulating that the President may, without obtaining senatorial consent, assign Foreign Service officers to head lesser missions.

Foreign Service Officers. Next in rank to chiefs of missions—ambassadors, ministers, and other diplomats who head American embassies and legations abroad—are the Foreign Service officers who constitute a permanent corps of especially recruited and trained people. To be eligible for appointment, one must be between twenty and thirty years of age, a citizen for ten years, and married, if at all, to a citizen of the United States. Experienced employees of the Department of State are eligible, but they must pass the same examinations as others. Promotion from the lowest grade upward is based upon merit ratings. Those who reach class 2 or 3 and fail to be promoted within a reasonable period of time are retired on the principle of "promotion up or selection out."

Examinations are given as often as necessary to obtain needed personnel. The examinations, both written and oral, are designed to test educational achievement, ability, general background, and competence in English and one other modern language. Persons making a combined grade of eighty must also pass a rigid physical examination and security investigation, after which they are placed on a register and chosen as needed. After a period of orientation the officer is usually assigned to some consular post with the rank of vice-consul or to an embassy or legation as third secretary. Dur-

ing his early years he may expect to be shifted from post to post about every three years, serving in either diplomatic or consular establishments or both.

Foreign Service Reserve. The increase in business occasioned by the recent war led to establishing an Auxiliary Foreign Service in 1941. This included presidential appointees to serve during the emergency only. Recognition of their value led to inclusion of provisions in the act of 1946 establishing the Foreign Service Reserve. This has six classes corresponding to those for regular Foreign Service officers. Only citizens of five years' standing are eligible for appointment. The Secretary of State makes appointments on behalf of the President. Reserve officers may come from other governmental agencies, with the approval of the department head concerned, or from those not employed by the Federal government. Their appointments may be for four consecutive years, but when their term has expired they cannot be reappointed until expiration of a period of time equal to the preceding tour of duty. The class to which a reserve officer is appointed depends upon his age, qualification, and experience. While on active duty he is entitled to the same salary and allowances as Foreign Service officers of like class and grade. Creation of this reserve makes possible the employment of qualified specialists for temporary periods without disturbing the independence and integrity of the Foreign Service officers' corps itself.

Foreign-affairs Personnel Integrated. Until recently Foreign Service officers and State Department employees were separate and noninterchangeable. The first Hoover Commission noted that the United States was the only great power that had not integrated foreign-affairs personnel and called this "a source of serious friction and increasing inefficiency." Steps have been taken to overcome this deficiency.

Integration was carried out gradually under a plan drawn up by a committee headed by Henry M. Wriston, a former president of Brown University. In addition to expanding the Foreign Service by lateral entry of Department personnel, vigorous efforts have been made to recruit sufficient young men to staff fully today's far-flung activities.

SELECTED FUNCTIONS
OF THE DEPARTMENT OF STATE
AND FOREIGN SERVICE

The primary function of the Department of State is to provide the President with the facts and advice necessary to determine foreign policy. Next in importance is the Department's duty to execute foreign policy, administer far-flung offices and personnel, and enforce laws relating to external affairs. Basic foreign policies are discussed in the next chapter; only a few routine functions will be mentioned here to illustrate the work done by the Department and the Foreign Service.

Conducting Communications. The work of the Department of State requires endless communication not only with people in the United States, but with Americans and foreigners scattered around the globe. All communications, written, telegraphic, and even telephonic, reaching or leaving the Department are channeled through the Office of Communications and Records.

Of primary importance are communications with American diplomats and consuls in the field and representatives of foreign governments stationed in Washington. Letters to American representatives are called "instructions"; letters from the field are called "dispatches." These are ordinarily forwarded in diplomatic pouches and are entitled to special immunities. There is much communication by cable, by air-grams

(brief messages dispatched by air mail and specially delivered upon arrival), and, in emergencies, by telephone. Telegrams are nearly always sent in code, which must be deciphered by experts.

The Department also broadcasts weekly news reports to officers in the field and sends them a monthly political digest containing materials gleaned from political reports from all parts of the world. Communications to and from the Department and foreign representatives in this country usually take the form of "notes." The originals of all communications, dating back to the days of the Committee on Secret Correspondence, have been preserved in the Department's archives; they constitute an invaluable storehouse of knowledge and one of the priceless assets of the nation. All papers except those of recent years may be consulted for research purposes by qualified scholars.

Making Treaties. The President "makes" treaties by and with the advice and consent of two-thirds of the Senate. The process is a long and complex one. Negotiations are usually begun by the exchange of draft treaties. Throughout the negotiations, representatives keep in touch with their governments and proceed according to instructions. The negotiations may be concluded within a short time or extended over months or even years, depending upon how complex, urgent, or controversial the subject matter is.

When the text finally suits the chief executives of both countries, a time and place are fixed for the signing of the treaty. Meanwhile, the duplicate originals of the treaty are prepared in what is referred to as the *alternat*—that is, with parallel columns containing the two languages side by side, the language of each country being in the left-hand column of the original it is to keep but in the right-hand column of the original to be kept by the foreign government. The authorized plenipotentiaries appear at the appointed hour, sign the document, and place their seals upon it.

The original kept by our government is usually next sent to the Senate, where it is given a first reading and then sent to the Committee on Foreign Relations. The committee considers the matter, sometimes after public or secret hearings, and then reports to the Senate. After debate, the treaty is put to a vote. If two-thirds of those present (assuming the presence of a quorum) approve, the President may proceed; if not, and the signatories still wish to see the treaty adopted, it may be submitted again when the President thinks its chances of obtaining Senate approval more favorable.

The Senate does not formally ratify; it merely gives advice and consent to ratification. When the Senate has spoken, the President notifies the other party, whereupon ratifications are exchanged by plenipotentiaries meeting at an appointed time and place. The treaty is then published and proclaimed, at which time it becomes legally enforceable.

There are strong arguments for and against the requirement of senatorial approval. The intention of the Constitution was to provide the President with advice and counsel and give to the states an effective voice in the making of treaties. The first intention has mostly been frustrated, but the second has often been fulfilled. Although the proportion of treaties rejected by the Senate has been small, it includes many of outstanding importance; an example is the 1920 treaty that would have enrolled the United States as a member of the League of Nations.

The rule requiring senatorial approval of treaties permits minority control and also restrains the President. The point in controversy is whether these results are salutary or otherwise. Feeling runs high on the issue.

Generally speaking, the rule is criticized by those who think the United States should play a larger role in world affairs; defenders include those who believe the contrary and therefore distrust presidential leadership. A constitutional amendment would be necessary to alter or abolish the rule, and at present there is no prospect of one being adopted. Meanwhile, the President often circumvents the Senate by using executive agreements, or tries to assure himself of senatorial support by tactfully inviting members of the Senate to participate in negotiations.

Issuing Passports. Another important function of the State Department is that of issuing passports. This work is headed by the Passport Office in Washington. Passports are permits granted by the American government to its citizens to *leave* the country or another country. Visas are permits to *enter* another country and must be obtained from officials of that country.

The American government will issue passports only to those who owe it allegiance, never to aliens. Within the fifty states, passports are issued only by the Passport Office, although applications may be filed at passport agencies located at a few principal cities, or with the clerk of any Federal or state court having authority to naturalize aliens. In most American territories, passports are issued by the chief executives; abroad they are granted by higher-ranking consuls and, in a few instances, by officers attached to diplomatic posts. Passports are usually valid for two years.

In times past the State Department had nearly unlimited discretion to grant or deny passports. Hearings were not held and explanations were seldom given to those denied passports. Several persons who were denied travel permits because of alleged sympathy for communism challenged the Department's procedures. In *Kent v. Dulles*

[357 U.S. 116 (1958)] the Supreme Court ruled that the right to travel outside the nation was one of the liberties protected by the Fifth Amendment. The Department of State could not, therefore, deny passports arbitrarily as it had done in this instance. The Department has since unsuccessfully urged Congress to authorize specifically the denial of passports to persons who have communistic beliefs and associations.

Issuing Visas. Aliens entering the United States must obtain visas, which are usually merely the word "visa" with seal and signature on a page of the passport. To minimize arbitrariness, recent regulations have narrowed consular authority to reject applications. The Department may demand a justification and then render an advisory opinion to the consul. If the consul acts contrary to advice, he must make further explanation. If disagreement continues, the Department's advice on legal matters prevails while the consul has final word on the facts. Visas are good for six months and are ordinarily renewable for a similar period.

Promotion of Cultural Relations. In recent years the United States has strongly encouraged cultural interchanges. During the 1930s, efforts were directed chiefly toward Latin America, as part of the good-neighbor policy. As the Second World War approached, the program was accelerated by realization of the commercial and strategic importance of Latin America. After the war, less attention was paid to that region and more to parts of the world where communism appeared as a greater threat to American interests. Currently, under the "Alliance for Progress," much emphasis is given to the Latin American sector.

The division of responsibility for the program is something like this: the Assistant Secretary of State for Educational and Cultural Affairs directs the exchange features; the United States Information Agency concentrates on interpreting American objectives abroad; the Agency for International Development focuses upon raising the living standards of friendly nations; the Peace Corps provides specialized educational and technical services in countries that request and facilitate them.

The Exchange Program. Most of the participants fall within one of three categories: trainees in government, visiting professors and leaders, and graduate students.

Some of the government trainees coming to the United States study agricultural economics, soil conservation, rural electrification, and related subjects under the Department of Agriculture; others study matters related to health under the Public Health Service, public administration under the Bureau of the Budget, civil aviation under the Federal Aviation Agency, and so on. Trainees may be sent abroad for similar study. The program is financed by a three-way participation of the Federal government, the foreign government concerned, and the trainee.

Cooperating governments usually assume the expenses of professors and distinguished visitors. The visitors include educators (other than professors), newspapermen, doctors, scientists, directors of radio stations, officials of publishing houses, and persons who have wide popular influence, such as leaders of farm and labor groups. Visitors usually stay for short periods of time.

Students (postgraduate only) desiring to participate in the program apply to the Institute of International Education, where a selection committee makes choices on the basis of ability, without regard to financial standing. Cooperating governments help finance travel and maintenance, and many universities and foundations provide scholarships.

Interpretation and Propaganda. Interpreting American institutions and policies has

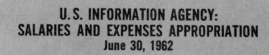

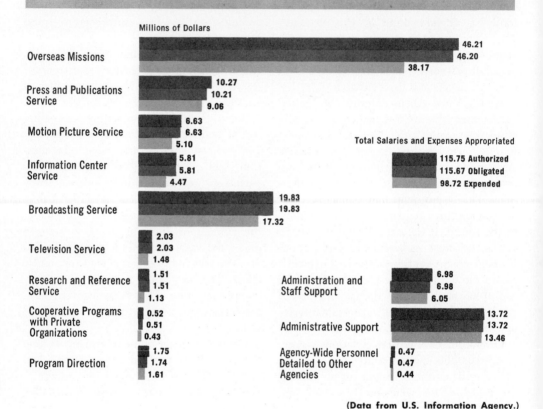

U.S. INFORMATION AGENCY: SALARIES AND EXPENSES APPROPRIATION
June 30, 1962

Millions of Dollars

Overseas Missions — 46.21 / 46.20 / 38.17

Press and Publications Service — 10.27 / 10.21 / 9.06

Motion Picture Service — 6.63 / 6.63 / 5.10

Information Center Service — 5.81 / 5.81 / 4.47

Broadcasting Service — 19.83 / 19.83 / 17.32

Television Service — 2.03 / 2.03 / 1.48

Research and Reference Service — 1.51 / 1.51 / 1.13

Cooperative Programs with Private Organizations — 0.52 / 0.51 / 0.43

Program Direction — 1.75 / 1.74 / 1.61

Total Salaries and Expenses Appropriated
- 115.75 Authorized
- 115.67 Obligated
- 98.72 Expended

Administration and Staff Support — 6.98 / 6.98 / 6.05

Administrative Support — 13.72 / 13.72 / 13.46

Agency-Wide Personnel Detailed to Other Agencies — 0.47 / 0.47 / 0.44

(Data from U.S. Information Agency.)

become another important task. American diplomats and consuls have always done this, of course, but in the modern world of conflicting ideologies their efforts have been expanded and supplemented by special staffs. Libraries and information centers are located in many countries to present American aims and purposes in a favorable light. A steady stream of news and feature releases is fed to the press, radio, and television. Pamphlets, books, and magazines are published especially for this purpose and dis-

tributed by the thousands. Motion pictures and other visual materials are produced and widely disseminated. Fairs, exhibits, and conferences are held in various parts of the world to explain and justify the American point of view. Business, professional, and labor groups are briefed and urged to do their part. The exchange of persons is part of the program. Refugees and others who have special reasons for disliking communism and unfriendly nations are encouraged to assist. Economic and military assistance

U.S. GOVERNMENT EXCHANGE PROGRAMS

	NUMBER OF EXCHANGES, FISCAL YEARS		
	1958	1959	1961
Department of State			8,985
International Educational Exchange Service	6,392	6,503	
International Cooperation Administration	12,930	13,366	
Agency for International Development			8,603
Peace Corps			652
National Aeronautics and Space Administration			1,056
Department of Defense			28,000
Ryukyus Educational Program	78	66	180
Department of Health, Education, and Welfare			492
National Science Foundation			532
TOTAL	19,400	19,935	48,500

Expenditures for information overseas are small when compared with those for military service. (Data from U.S. Information Agency.)

are expected to win friends and influence people.

Not all propaganda is directed toward foreign shores. The department also interprets foreign policy to the American public. This is done by press conferences, press and radio releases, publications, speeches, contacts by liaison officers with Congress and private groups, and conferences for leaders of public opinion.

This "Campaign of Truth," as it is called, has grown tremendously. Its alleged partisanship and the high cost entailed are often the subject of criticism. Spokesmen for the programs are given a "rough time" when they appear before congressional committees to defend expenditures. Congressmen insist on asking: What are the taxpayers getting for their money?

Propaganda directed at foreign listeners is

not intended to be objective and impartial; it is frankly pro-American and pro-free-enterprise. To measure its value is difficult, if not impossible. Those responsible for the program claim great-to-modest success in checking anti-Americanism, winning and keeping allies, checking the spread of totalitarianism, and keeping the hope of freedom alive in the "free world" and even behind the Iron Curtain.

Critics insist that the propaganda is "loaded" in favor of the administration, that it gives a distorted view of American life, that listeners recognize it as propaganda and discount it accordingly, that it reaches only a few behind the Iron Curtain and probably does more to solidify opinion behind totalitarian regimes than it does to gain sympathizers for the American point of view, and that deeds, not words, must win the hearts and minds of men.

The Department of State and other agencies involved justify their informational campaign by pointing to the transcending importance of foreign affairs. They also emphasize that they do not have an organized constituency to rally support, as the

Department of Defense has in veterans' groups, the Department of Labor has in unions, the Department of Commerce has in business organizations, and the Department of Agriculture has in organized farmers.

FOR FURTHER READING

See also references at end of Chapter 23.

Allen, Florence E.: *The Treaty As an Instrument of Legislation* (New York: Macmillan, 1952).

American Assembly: *The Representation of the United States Abroad* (New York: Columbia University, Graduate School of Business, 1956).

American Foreign Service Association: *American Foreign Service Journal* (monthly).

Beloff, Max: *Foreign Policy and the Democratic Process* (Baltimore: Johns Hopkins Press, 1955).

Bemis, Samuel F. (ed.): *American Secretaries of State and Their Diplomacy* (New York: Knopf, 10 vols., 1927–1929).

Brookings Institution: *Administration of Foreign Affairs and Overseas Operations* (Washington, D.C.: Brookings, 1951).

Byrd, Elbert M., Jr.: *Treaties and Executive Agreements in the United States* (The Hague: Martinus Nijhoff, 1960).

Carroll, Holbert N.: *The House of Representatives and Foreign Affairs* (Pittsburgh, Pa.: University of Pittsburgh Press, 1958).

Cheevers, Daniel S., and H. Field Haviland: *Foreign Policy and the Separation of Powers* (Cambridge, Mass.: Harvard University Press, 1952).

Childs, James R.: *American Foreign Service* (New York: Holt, 1948).

Cleveland, Harlan, and Gerald L. Mangone (eds.): *The Art of Overseamanship* (Syracuse, N.Y.: Syracuse University Press, 1957).

Corwin, Edward S.: *The President: Office and Powers* (New York: New York University Press, 4th ed., 1958).

Crabb, Cecil V., Jr.: *American Foreign Policy in the Nuclear Age* (Evanston, Ill.: Row, Peterson, 1960).

Dahl, Robert A.: *Congress and Foreign Policy* (New York: Harcourt, Brace, 1950).

Elder, Robert Ellsworth: *The Policy Machine:*

The Department of State and American Foreign Policy (Syracuse, N.Y.: Syracuse University Press, 1959).

Graebner, Norman A., and others: *An Uncertain Tradition: American Secretaries of State in the Twentieth Century* (New York: McGraw-Hill, 1961).

Graham, Malbone W.: *American Diplomacy in the International Community* (Baltimore: Johns Hopkins Press, 1948).

Hackworth, Green H.: *Digest of International Law* (Washington, D.C.: GPO, 8 vols., 1940–1944).

Ilchman, Warren Frederick: *Professional Diplomacy in the United States: 1779–1939* (Chicago: University of Chicago Press, 1961).

Jenks, C. Wilfred: *International Immunities* (New York: Oceana Publications, 1961).

McCamy, James L.: *The Administration of American Foreign Affairs* (New York: Knopf, 1950).

McClure, Wallace: *International Executive Agreements* (New York: Columbia University Press, 1941).

Macmahon, Arthur W.: *Administration in Foreign Affairs* (University, Ala.: University of Alabama Press, 1953).

Markel, Lester and others: *Public Opinion and Foreign Policy* (New York: Harper, 1949).

Moore, John B.: *A Digest of International Law* (Washington, D.C.: GPO, 8 vols., 1906).

Parks, Wallace Judson: *United States Administration of Its International Economic Affairs* (Baltimore: Johns Hopkins Press, 1951).

Plischke, Elmer: *Conduct of American Diplomacy* (Princeton, N.J.: Van Nostrand, 2d ed., 1961).

Price, Don K. (ed.): *The Secretary of State* (Englewood Cliffs, N.J.: Prentice-Hall, 1960).

Reiff, Henry: *The United States and the Treaty Law of the Sea* (Minneapolis, Minn.: University of Minnesota Press, 1959).

Stuart, Graham: *American Diplomatic and Con-*

sular Practice (New York: Macmillan, 3d ed., 1952).

U.S. Commission on Organization of the Executive Branch of the Government (first Hoover Commission): *Foreign Affairs* (1949).

————: *Task Force Report on Foreign Affairs* (1949).

U.S. Department of State: *Bulletin of the Department of State* (weekly).

Vagts, Alfred: *Defense and Diplomacy: The*

Soldier and the Conduct of Foreign Relations (New York: Columbia University Press, 1956).

Westphal, Albert C. F.: *The House Committee on Foreign Affairs* (New York: Columbia University Press, 1942).

Wilson, Robert R.: *United States Commercial Treaties and International Law* (New Orleans, La.: Hauser Press, 1960).

Wriston, Henry M.: *Diplomacy in a Democracy* (New York: Harper, 1957).

REVIEW QUESTIONS

1. Explain the powers given by the Constitution to the President and Congress for dealing with foreign affairs. What limits are there to each of these powers?

2. How does an executive agreement differ from a treaty? How do you explain the extensive use of the former, especially in recent years?

3. Defend and criticize the proposed Bricker amendment.

4. What are the various classes of diplomats? Of consuls? How are these officials appointed, and what privileges and immunities do they enjoy?

5. Describe the organization and functions of the Department of State. What suggestions for change were made by the first Hoover Commission?

6. Explain to a prospective candidate for the Foreign Service the essential features of the Service. Point out the advantages and disadvantages of entering the Service.

7. What improvements can you suggest in the Foreign Service?

8. What Federal agencies in addition to the Department of State are deeply involved in overseas programs?

9. Explain how a treaty is negotiated and put into effect.

10. Defend and criticize the two-thirds rule for ratifying treaties.

11. Distinguish between a passport and a visa. What rules govern the issuance of each?

12. Defend and criticize the educational and propaganda efforts made by the United States to influence public opinion abroad.

Chapter Twenty-Three

Foreign Policies

and the United Nations

In the years since the Second World War, nothing has happened to disprove the assumption of the founders of the United Nations that the elimination of war is mankind's number-one problem. On the contrary, the phenomenal development of new and extraordinarily destructive weapons has transformed peace from an ideal devoutly to be hoped for into a fundamental necessity of elementary survival. The ranks of the peace-seekers have been expanded to include not only all men of good will but all men of good sense. . . . When war carries with it a threat to the very survival of civilization, the urgency of dealing effectively with all threats to the peace is self-evident.

COMMISSION TO STUDY THE ORGANIZATION OF PEACE[1]

No lesson has been taught more emphatically by two world wars than that of the interdependence of peoples and nations. It now is obvious to all that political units and the people within them must learn to get along together.

For years the American public has been sharply divided over the wisest course in the face of changed circumstances. To many the path of aloofness from Old World entanglements and neutrality appeared to offer the greatest hope of security and peace; but in consequence of the Second World War and the discovery of even more terrible weapons, most Americans believe that the new world interdependence demands collective action to maintain peace.

[1] *Strengthening the United Nations* (New York: Harper, 1957), p. 15.

TRADITIONAL FOREIGN POLICY

Isolation. The American Revolution was won by the revolting Colonies in alliance with France. That alliance was soundly based on the self-interests of the two participants, who agreed to fight until the independence of the United States was recognized. That alliance, the only formal one entered by the United States until the ratification of the North Atlantic Pact in 1949, lasted from 1778 to 1800. For the next century and a half the basic foreign policy was one of aloofness from the political affairs of Europe. Washington set the theme in delivering his Farewell Address, in 1796, when he said that the "detached and distant situation" of the United States made aloofness from Europe's controversies possible. He asked: "Why quit our own and stand on foreign ground?"

As ties increased with the outside world, there were few advocates of absolute isolation but many of limited participation in world affairs. The contemporary "isolationist" would continue United States collaboration in international work along social, cultural, and technical lines, but he opposes membership in a general security organization. He fears it might involve the country in foreign quarrels and jeopardize independence of decision and action.

The Monroe Doctrine. An equally basic foreign policy has been the Monroe Doctrine. Enunciated in 1823 by President Monroe, it warned European powers who, it was feared, were intent upon restoring Spain's authority over recently revolted Latin American republics. The announcement first declared that "in the wars of the European Powers in matters relating to themselves we have never taken any part, nor does it comport with our policy so to do." It then went on to say:

We owe it, therefore, to candor and to the amicable relations existing between the United States and those powers to declare that we should consider any attempt on their part to extend their system to any portion of this hemisphere as dangerous to our peace and safety. With the existing colonies and dependencies of any European power we have not interfered and shall not interfere. But with the Governments who have declared their independence and maintained it, and whose independence we have, on great consideration and on just principles, acknowledged, we could not view any interposition for the purpose of oppressing them, or controlling in any other manner their destiny, by any European power in any other light than as the manifestation of an unfriendly disposition toward the United States.

The audacity of this statement is emphasized by the fact that the population of the United States had just reached 10 million. Success of the policy was due in large measure to British assistance, given because it was also to her interest to ban further European colonization in this hemisphere.

The "America for the Americans" policy has no standing in law, but it has been supported consistently and strongly by Congresses and Presidents for nearly a century and a half. As originally pronounced it said nothing about interrelationships between American states. One authority put it, "The Doctrine states a case of United States *vs.* Europe, not United States *vs.* Latin America." But it came to be interpreted, especially during the administration of Theodore Roosevelt, as a statement of responsibility for the integrity and stability of the American republics. Said President Theodore Roosevelt:

If a nation shows that it knows how to act with reasonable efficiency and decency in social and political matters; if it keeps order and pays its obligations, it need fear no interference from the United States. [But] chronic wrongdoing, or an impotence which results in a general loosening of the ties of civilized society . . . may force the United States, however reluctantly, in flagrant cases of such wrongdoing or impotence, to the exercise of an international police power.[1]

The United States intervened with force in Latin American states on numerous occasions. But this policy has been renounced. No forceful interventions have occurred since the withdrawal of troops from Nicaragua in 1933. Meanwhile, the good-neighbor policy announced in 1933 has produced a friendlier relationship.

Neutrality. During the nineteenth century, the United States was the foremost apostle of neutrality and did much to establish and reinforce a body of rules for protecting those who chose to remain at peace while others fought.

By following this policy the United States remained free of military involvement in all wars between foreign states for a century and a quarter, except for the conflict with Great Britain in 1812 that grew out of the Napoleonic Wars. More recently, the policy delayed America's entering the First World War for two and one-half years; the Sino-Japanese War, which began in 1931, for ten years; the Ethiopian War altogether; and the Second World War for more than two years.

After the First World War a wave of disillusionment swept the country, and isolationism and neutralism were widespread. The Senate refused to vote American membership in the League of Nations and the World Court. Later, in 1935 and 1937, Congress passed "neutrality" legislation designed to prevent a repetition of what happened between 1914 and 1917.

This legislation authorized the President to embargo the sale of arms to warring powers, restrict the travel of citizens and ships in war zones, and require that purchasers pay cash for war materials and carry them in non-American vessels. Most of the provisions were not mandatory, so the President applied them as he saw fit. As war tensions mounted, the neutrality acts were repealed.

Expansion. Until recent years American history was characterized by constant expansion—south to Panama, Puerto Rico, and the Virgin Islands, southwest to Mexico and later to Samoa, northwest to Alaska and the western tip of the Aleutians, and west to the Pacific and then to Hawaii, Guam, and the Philippines.

Expansion led to friction with Great Britain over the Canadian boundary and claims in the Caribbean; with Mexico over Texas and the Southwest; with Spain over Florida, the Southeast, Cuba, and South America; with China and Japan in the Far East; and with Latin American republics.

The desire for additional territory appears to have spent itself. The last important territory acquired by the United States was the Virgin Islands in 1917. In the meantime, the United States has granted independence to the Philippines and has gone through two major wars without annexing former enemy territory.

Foreign Investments and Trade. American citizens have invested billions of dollars in foreign countries. These funds have gone into developing enterprises of various sorts: railroads; mines; ocean shipping; oil lands, wells, and refineries; rubber, sugar, coffee, and banana plantations; churches and mission schools; etc. Needless to say, what happens to these interests is of immediate concern to the investors themselves and also to their government.

Closely related to investments is foreign trade. Although trade with other nations accounts for a comparatively small proportion of the national income, it is important.

[1] Message to Congress, December, 1904, *Foreign Relations of the United States*, 1904 (GPO, 1905), p. 41.

Merely to mention such commonly used articles as tin, natural rubber, cocoa, coffee, tea, silk, bananas, olives, and diamonds—most of which are imported—is to demonstrate the significance of foreign trade. A tremendous amount of effort and treasure has been put into expanding foreign markets.

Americans who invest and trade abroad are normally expected to look after themselves, abide by the laws of the countries in which they do business, and obtain protection from local authorities. The American government, nevertheless, is constantly alert to promote the interests of its citizens and protest against unfair and unjust treatment. Critics of the United States argue that these activities often are only excuses for grabbing and exploiting foreign resources, a process they call "dollar diplomacy."

Protection and promotion are usually provided through diplomats and consuls, but on many occasions the American government has intervened with force, either alone or in concert with other nations. During the Boxer Rebellion, in 1900, the United States, in cooperation with European powers and Japan, sent troops to China to protect lives and property. American intervention in Latin America occurred a number of times between 1898 and 1934 for the same reason. We declared war on the Barbary States because they levied tribute on American commerce entering the Mediterranean. The war with England in 1812 arose over impressing seamen and otherwise interfering with commerce. In 1853 Commodore Perry threatened to bombard Japanese ports not promptly opened to American commerce. After much difficulty with both the Allied and Central Powers during the early part of the First World War, the United States entered the conflict because of Germany's policy of sinking American ships. And involvement in the Second World War occurred, at least in part, because of attacks upon American ships.

The Open Door. The traditional keystone of American policy in the Far East was the open door—free access of all nations to the Chinese economic market. This doctrine remained in force, theoretically, until the end of the Second World War. But in practice it was too difficult to pursue. The Far East was distant and the volume of trade was relatively small. Most Americans felt that keeping the door open was not worth the risks involved. When Japan invaded China in 1931, the American government protested vigorously but did not intervene with armed force.

Events since the Second World War have made the open-door policy obsolete. Even before the Communists came to power in China, the Western nations renounced special rights which had been granted in agreements and treaties. With the Communist regime in control, the whole East Asian picture changed. A new policy is in the making, to fit the new facts. That policy, regardless of what it is, will be based on political and security considerations rather than commercial ones.

NEW AMERICAN POLICY

Collective Security. The traditional policy of isolation has been abandoned for one of collective security, the aim of which is to secure peace for the United States by securing it for all nations. The transition was not sudden or accidental. Although the United States refused to join the League of Nations and World Court, by the 1930s it had affiliated with about forty international administrative unions and had signed more than eighty treaties and agreements dealing with humanitarian, economic, and cultural subjects.

The Second World War convinced

doubting Americans of the need for a world organization to secure peace. A proposed charter was drafted at Dumbarton Oaks (a residence in Washington, D.C.) in the fall of 1944 by representatives of the United States, Great Britain, the Soviet Union, and China. This draft was the forerunner of the United Nations Charter approved at a conference held in San Francisco, April–June, 1945. Ratification by the United States Senate in August of that year completed and formalized the abandonment of isolation and the adoption of collective security.

The Charter provides that member nations unite their resources to remove the causes of war, settle disputes peacefully, and, if necessary, resist aggression by armed might. Primary responsibility for enforcing peace rests in the Security Council, which is given authority to settle disputes by various means, including the use of economic and armed force.

Regional Security. The United Nations Charter assumed that in the postwar era the five big powers would cooperate. The Charter, nevertheless, recognized the need for regional security arrangements subordinate to the United Nations and consistent with its purposes. Soon after the Second World War, the victorious Allies formed rival blocs that resorted to "cold war" against one another. On one side were the United States, Great Britain, France, and most of the countries of the Western World; on the other were the Soviet Union, her allies of Eastern Europe and the Balkans, and Communist China. As time passed, neutralist sentiment increased and other blocs, notably the Arab League, appeared.

This alignment of blocs clearly represents the reemergence of the balance-of-power concept. As in earlier state systems, this situation breeds mutual fear and suspicion, prevents the disarmament anticipated by the Charter, and otherwise leads to the deterioration of international affairs. The outbreak of fighting in Korea in 1950, and in the Middle East in 1956, brought already critical affairs to the verge of a third world war.

Faced with what it considered a threat to peace and security, the United States began a vast program, in 1947, designed to "contain" Communist expansion. The Truman Doctrine, announced in 1947, when the British withdrawal from Greece opened a possible field for Communist penetration, promised American support to all parts of the world threatened by communism. This support has taken many forms: military bases surrounding the Soviet Union, defensive alliances with friendly powers, espionage on a world-wide scale, propaganda and information favorable to the United States and its friends, efforts to foment unrest and revolt in Communist-controlled areas, threats of massive retaliation with nuclear weapons, restricted exports of strategic materials, financial, technical, military, and economic aid to sympathetic countries. The Soviet bloc referred to such efforts as "Anglo-American imperialism."

The North Atlantic Treaty. Ratification of the North Atlantic Pact in 1949 was a momentous event in the history of American foreign affairs. For the first time in a century and a half the United States bound itself by a peacetime alliance that almost certainly would lead to war if one of the allies were attacked. The pact is based upon the assumptions that American security is tied to that of Western Europe and that America's strategic frontier extends from Norwegian Lapland down to the Adriatic Sea.

The key provision of the pact is Article V, which reads: "The parties agree that an armed attack against one or more of them in Europe or North America shall be considered an attack against them all. . . ."

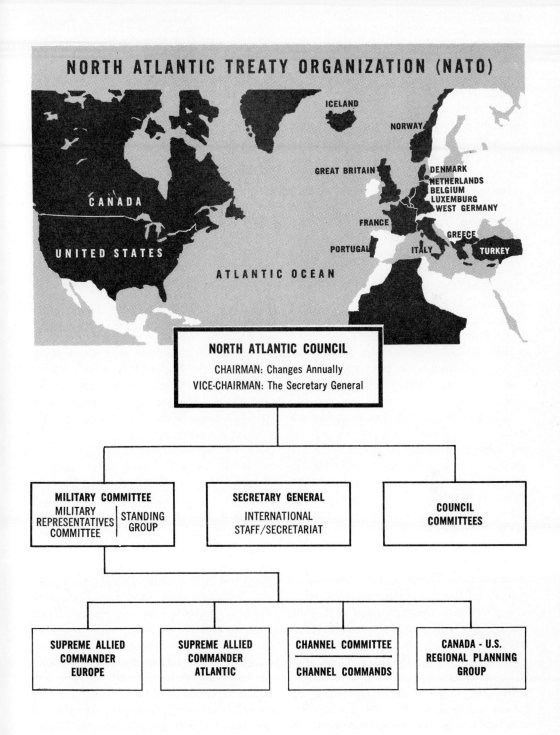

NORTH ATLANTIC TREATY ORGANIZATION (NATO)

ICELAND

NORWAY

GREAT BRITAIN

DENMARK
NETHERLANDS
BELGIUM
LUXEMBURG
WEST GERMANY

CANADA

FRANCE

GREECE

UNITED STATES

PORTUGAL   ITALY   TURKEY

ATLANTIC OCEAN

NORTH ATLANTIC COUNCIL
CHAIRMAN: Changes Annually
VICE-CHAIRMAN: The Secretary General

MILITARY COMMITTEE
MILITARY REPRESENTATIVES COMMITTEE | STANDING GROUP

SECRETARY GENERAL
INTERNATIONAL STAFF/SECRETARIAT

COUNCIL COMMITTEES

SUPREME ALLIED COMMANDER EUROPE

SUPREME ALLIED COMMANDER ATLANTIC

CHANNEL COMMITTEE
CHANNEL COMMANDS

CANADA - U.S. REGIONAL PLANNING GROUP

Signatories are the United States, Great Britain, Canada, France, Belgium, the Netherlands, Luxembourg, Norway, Denmark, Iceland, Portugal, Italy, Greece, Turkey, and Western Germany. The constitutional question, discussed in the previous chapter, of congressional delegation of power to declare war was avoided by not specifying what aid would be furnished to a victim of attack.

Since the pact became effective, a North Atlantic Treaty Organization (NATO) has been created to effect its purposes. A governing North Atlantic Council, composed of the foreign ministers of participating states, has come into existence, plus a permanent Council of Deputies and a number of committees and boards. Headquarters are at Rocquencourt, France. Planning for united and coordinated action in the event of war is their principal function. An international army, popularized by its first Supreme Commander, General Dwight D. Eisenhower, has evolved.

Critics of the pact declare that, like alliances of old, this will not prevent war but will actually encourage it. They say the pact violates both the letter and spirit of the UN Charter, aggravates and even institutionalizes the East-West rift, promises American aid that must of necessity be "too little and too late" to allies whose territories can easily be overrun by invading land forces or obliterated by hydrogen bombs, and that the rearmament of Europe retards economic recovery and thus encourages communism.

Supporters of the pact claim that, since the United Nations security machinery has not been activated, member nations are justified under the Charter in invoking their right of individual and collective self-defense. They argue that any intending aggressor will be deterred by the power of the combination, that economic recovery will be accelerated once security from invasion is assured, that peace is the objective, and that the chances for peace are greater if the United States declares clearly in advance what it will do if aggression comes.

Whatever the merits of the argument, there can be no doubt that the pact signalized the abandonment, at least temporarily, of universal collective security for a system of collective regional defense.

The Pacific Pacts. Similar insecurity in the Western Pacific area has led to American entry into a series of security arrangements with friendly nations. Though several of the pacts mention the possibility of a future general security organization for the Pacific region, the political situation in Asia is not conducive to such a pact. The several pacts vary considerably, but most of them require consultation in case of threat or actual armed attack on the territory or forces of a member power in the Pacific area.

The broadest of these, in terms of membership, is the Manila Pact, which formed the South East Asia Treaty Organization (SEATO) following the 1954 armistice in the Indochina War. The United States—seeking to resist aggression, check subversion, and aid social and economic development—joined with seven other nations: Britain, France, Australia, New Zealand, Pakistan, the Philippines, and Thailand. The pact also provides protection for free Viet Nam, Laos, and Cambodia. In addition, the United States concluded for similar purposes a trilateral treaty with Australia and New Zealand (ANZUS in 1951), and bilateral pacts with the Philippines (1951), Japan (1951), South Korea (1953), and the Republic of China (Nationalist, based on Formosa, in 1954).

Despite these treaties and the outpouring of financial, technical, and military aid, American efforts in the Far East have only partially succeeded. Outright opposition by the Soviet Union and Communist China, aided by strong feelings of nationalism and anticolonialism, has neutralized large sectors of this region.

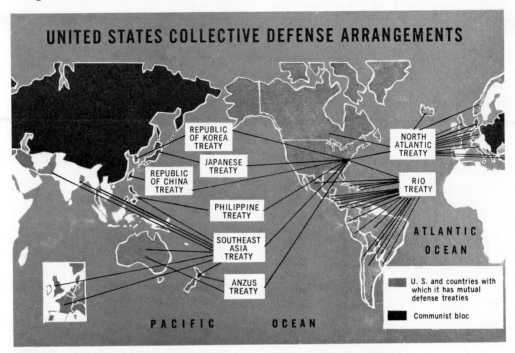

UNITED STATES COLLECTIVE DEFENSE ARRANGEMENTS

REPUBLIC OF KOREA TREATY

JAPANESE TREATY

REPUBLIC OF CHINA TREATY

PHILIPPINE TREATY

SOUTHEAST ASIA TREATY

ANZUS TREATY

NORTH ATLANTIC TREATY

RIO TREATY

ATLANTIC OCEAN

U. S. and countries with which it has mutual defense treaties

Communist bloc

PACIFIC   OCEAN

Existing security pacts bind the United States to nearly one-half of the countries of the world.

The Eisenhower Doctrine. The United States worked for a comprehensive mutual-security pact for the Middle East but with only partial success. Turkey and Greece have joined NATO. The Central Treaty Organization, successor to the Baghdad Pact, allies Britain, Turkey, Iran, and Pakistan; but the United States has limited its membership to economic, military, and counter-subversion committees. Neutralist sentiment produced by Soviet-Western rivalries, Israeli-Arab bitterness, and surging nationalism have balked a strong regional pact.

Israel, with the support of Britain and France, went to war with Egypt over the Suez Canal in 1956. As peace was restored through United Nations auspices, the United States developed what became known as the "Eisenhower doctrine." This pledges American support and assistance when requested by any Middle Eastern power threatened with internal subversion or external aggression. Military aid is implied, as well as financial and economic support. Because aid is promised only *upon request*, the full import of the doctrine awaits future developments. The first serious test of the doctrine occurred in 1958 when revolution in Iraq and disturbances in neighboring countries caused the president of Lebanon to ask for American troops. The American government complied forthwith.

Inter-American Unity. In the Western Hemisphere the big stick, manifest destiny, and dollar diplomacy gave way to Pan-Americanism and the good-neighbor policy.

United States participation in the Pan-American movement dates from 1889. Through numerous conferences held since that year, the American republics have been collaborating in technical, humanitarian, economic, and political and strategic matters. Once known as the International Bureau of American Republics, the common organization became the Pan American Union in 1910. Until 1948 the governing board of the Union was composed of the ambassadors to Washington of the several Latin American nations, with the United States Secretary of State as chairman. The United States usually opposed Union consideration of political questions; Latin Americans, on the other hand, were reluctant to vest much power in the Union, fearing United States domination.

A new spirit entered United States relations with Latin America in the late 1920s. Known during the Franklin D. Roosevelt administration (1933–1945) as the "good-neighbor policy," the new plan involved a cooperative and friendly approach by the United States. Applying something like the golden rule to its relations with the other American republics, this country ceased military intervention, terminated dollar diplomacy, and ended unequal treaties. When the Second World War began, inter-American solidarity had been proclaimed, and the nations took a united stand on various issues. At the Mexico City Conference in 1945 a regional security arrangement was agreed upon, an economic charter adopted, and reform of the composition and powers of the Pan American Union proposed. Eventually every one of the American nations declared war on the Axis countries, and all (Argentina belatedly) took part in the San Francisco Conference and joined the UN.

At Bogotá, Colombia, in early 1948, the American republics agreed to the charter of a broader system known as "The Organization of the American States." The Pan American Union continues as the central organ and secretariat of OAS. The other organs are the Inter-American Conference, which meets every five years or so; meetings of consultation among the foreign ministers; and the Council, which is composed of one representative with rank of ambassador from each member republic. In addition there are specialized conferences and organizations and various subsidiary councils.

The regional security arrangement outlined at Mexico City in 1945 was completed in Brazil in 1947 and is known as the Treaty of Rio de Janeiro. In case of attack on any American state in the Western Hemisphere, all signatories are bound to aid the victim. Twenty-one nations, including the United States, have signed and ratified the treaty.

Distressed over criticisms from south of its borders, the United States has recently paid more attention to the area. In 1959 the Inter-American Development Bank was established through which the United States and member Latin American Republics make loans to governments and private parties for economic development. At the Punta del Este conference of 1961 the United States agreed to step up economic aid under the banner of "Alliance for Progress." Recipient nations are expected to make internal reforms and greater exertions to help themselves.

Economic and Social Cooperation. Turning from isolation, the United States has assumed with other nations a collective responsibility for the social and economic welfare of all. The social and economic agencies and programs of the United Nations are evidence of this commitment. Costly American foreign-assistance programs are additional evidence.

Never before has a country helped others so much in the economic and technical sphere. Beginning with the $3.75 billion loan to Britain in 1946, the United States has poured out vast sums in grants and loans to stimulate the economies and enhance welfare in a third of the countries of the world.

Some of the funds are spent through the United Nations, in which case they are used chiefly to provide economic and technical

THE ORGANIZATION OF AMERICAN STATES

INTER-AMERICAN CONFERENCE

Supreme organ of the organization
decides general action and policy
(meets every 5 years)

MEETING OF CONSULTATION OF MINISTERS OF FOREIGN AFFAIRS

Considers urgent problems
and acts as the organ
of consultation

SPECIALIZED CONFERENCES

Meet periodically
to consider
technical matters

Inter-American
Peace Committee
Washington, D. C.

COUNCIL OF THE ORGANIZATION

Permanent representative body
and provisional organ
of consultation
Washington, D. C.

Advisory Defense Committee

Inter-American Defense Board
Washington, D. C.

Inter-American Cultural Council	Inter-American Council of Jurists	Inter-American Economic and Social Council (IA-ECOSOC)	PAN AMERICAN UNION (PAU)	Specialized Organizations
Committee for Cultural Action, Mexico City	Inter-American Juridical Committee, Rio de Janeiro	Washington, D. C.	Washington, D. C.	Permanent agencies performing technical functions

Technical
Cooperation
Board

Permanent and central organ and
general secretariat of the OAS

Inter-American Institute of
Agricultural Sciences
Turrialba, Costa Rica

Department of Economic and Social
Affairs

Pan American Sanitary Organization
Secretariat: Pan American
Sanitary Bureau
Washington, D. C.

Department of International Law

Inter-American Commission of
Women
Washington, D. C.

Department of Cultural Affairs

Inter-American Children's
Institute
Montevideo

Department of Administrative
Affairs

Pan American Institute of Geography
and History
Mexico City

Office of Public Relations

Inter-American Indian Institute
Mexico City

Office of Statistics

Inter-American Statistical Institute
Washington, D. C.

LEGEND:

—————— Policy direction

·········· Advisory services

●●●●●●● Administrative and secretarial services

✦ ✦ ✦ ✦ Appointment of members

– – – – – The Department is secretariat of the
corresponding Council and its Director is
ex-officio Executive Secretary of the Council

(From The Organization of American States.)

U. S. GRANTS AND CREDITS TO OTHER NATIONS

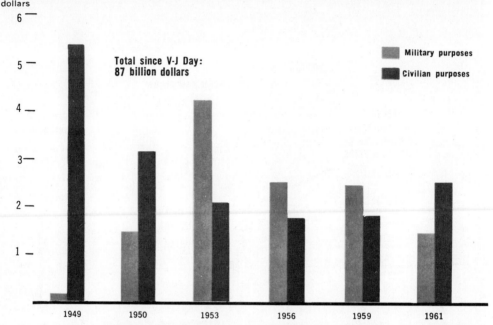

Billions of dollars

Total since V-J Day:
87 billion dollars

■ Military purposes
■ Civilian purposes

Assistance for economic purposes, originally the largest, now is outranked by aid for military purposes. (From U.S. Department of Commerce.)

assistance to underdeveloped areas on the basis of need and willingness to cooperate. Money spent directly by the United States has the same general objectives, but because it is often impossible to disassociate them from the policy of containing communism, a number of needy areas have been skeptical about accepting aid. Although expenditures have been pitifully small in proportion to the need, they have helped improve living standards, reduce disease, decrease mortality, and enhance opportunity. American participation is administered by the Administration for International Development, Department of State.

The Peace Corps, launched in 1961, is a further expression of American desire to help friendly peoples improve their lot. Administered by the Department of State, it enrolls young men and women for specialized services in countries willing to cooperate. The Peace Corps enlists the aid of colleges and universities, religious and welfare agencies, foundations, and other private groups.

The United States also participates in the Colombo Plan, a program of economic and technical assistance launched in 1950 by a group of British Commonwealth nations. Colombo projects are concentrated mainly in the crucial areas of southern and southeast Asia.

THE UNITED NATIONS

The Charter. The Charter opens with an inspiring preamble beginning "We the peoples of the United Nations. . . . " A statement of purposes and principles follows to which members pledged themselves. Then follow 9 chapters and 111 articles. The complete text is Appendix IV of this book.

Membership was open to fifty nations participating in the San Francisco Conference and other "peace-loving" nations subsequently admitted by vote of the General Assembly upon recommendation of the Security Council. The Charter stipulated that it should go into effect when ratified by the United States, the Soviet Union, Great Britain, France, China, and a majority of other signatories. Amendments and general Charter review were authorized.

The United States was the first to ratify, when the Senate approved in early August, 1945, by a vote of 89 to 2. The Charter came into force on October 24, 1945, upon receipt of notice of ratification by the Soviet Union, the twenty-ninth state to approve and the last of the Big Five.

The General Assembly. The General Assembly consists of delegates from all the member nations; each nation has not more than five delegates but only one vote. Decisions on important questions like elections, suspensions, expulsions, budgets, and trusteeship must be made by two-thirds vote, but decisions on matters of less importance are made by ordinary majority.

The functions of the Assembly are to deliberate, administer, elect, approve budgets, and initiate amendments. The late Senator Vandenberg called it a "town meeting of the world." It has general authority to discuss any matter within the scope of the Charter and make recommendations, except in disputes being considered by the Security Council.

The Assembly oversees the work of all organs of the United Nations and is assigned special responsibilities over the Economic and Social Council and the Trusteeship Council. The Assembly's power to elect is considerable, extending to the nonpermanent seats on the Security Council, the judgeships on the International Court of Justice, the Economic and Social Council, and part of the Trusteeship Council. Funds for the UN are secured by the Assembly through the apportionment of expenses among member nations.

Frustrations arising from the cold war have stimulated search for methods of expediting decision making by the United Nations. One of the most important developments was the establishment in 1947 of an Interim Committee, popularly known as the "Little Assembly." Each nation was entitled to one representative, and this committee of the whole was to function between sessions of the parent body. Its primary task was to prepare recommendations for the General Assembly. Temporary at first, the Interim Committee has continued, but its usefulness has been impaired by the refusal of the Soviet bloc to participate.

A second important development came in 1950, when the Assembly approved the "Uniting for Peace" resolution. Inspired by the inability of the Security Council to function on matters pertaining to fighting in Korea, this resolution permits the Assembly to recommend that collective measures be taken by member states against aggressors in the event the Security Council is prevented by the veto from fulfilling its function. That seemed a clear attempt to bypass the Security Council. Whether it conformed with the Charter was debatable, and whether it would prove feasible was doubtful. Nevertheless, under the circumstances, a majority thought it worth trying.

Obviously the General Assembly is not a full-blown "parliament of mankind." Its powers are modest indeed; they include nothing like the lawmaking authority of a national parliament or congress. But when the nations are ready for a more perfect union, the General Assembly may be the key instrument through which that goal may be achieved.

Security Council. Those who drafted the Charter thought peace and security could be maintained only by an international agency

ORGANS OF THE UNITED NATIONS

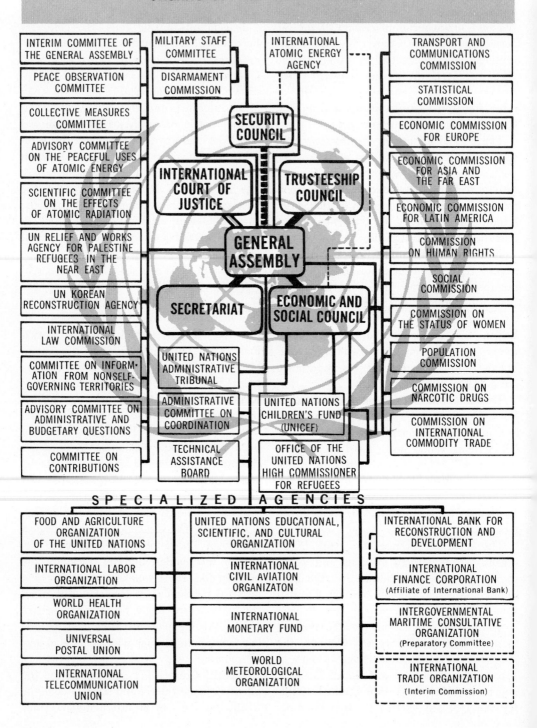

INTERIM COMMITTEE OF THE GENERAL ASSEMBLY

PEACE OBSERVATION COMMITTEE

COLLECTIVE MEASURES COMMITTEE

ADVISORY COMMITTEE ON THE PEACEFUL USES OF ATOMIC ENERGY

SCIENTIFIC COMMITTEE ON THE EFFECTS OF ATOMIC RADIATION

UN RELIEF AND WORKS AGENCY FOR PALESTINE REFUGEES IN THE NEAR EAST

UN KOREAN RECONSTRUCTION AGENCY

INTERNATIONAL LAW COMMISSION

COMMITTEE ON INFORMATION FROM NONSELF-GOVERNING TERRITORIES

ADVISORY COMMITTEE ON ADMINISTRATIVE AND BUDGETARY QUESTIONS

COMMITTEE ON CONTRIBUTIONS

MILITARY STAFF COMMITTEE

DISARMAMENT COMMISSION

INTERNATIONAL ATOMIC ENERGY AGENCY

SECURITY COUNCIL

INTERNATIONAL COURT OF JUSTICE

TRUSTEESHIP COUNCIL

GENERAL ASSEMBLY

SECRETARIAT

ECONOMIC AND SOCIAL COUNCIL

UNITED NATIONS ADMINISTRATIVE TRIBUNAL

ADMINISTRATIVE COMMITTEE ON COORDINATION

TECHNICAL ASSISTANCE BOARD

UNITED NATIONS CHILDREN'S FUND (UNICEF)

OFFICE OF THE UNITED NATIONS HIGH COMMISSIONER FOR REFUGEES

TRANSPORT AND COMMUNICATIONS COMMISSION

STATISTICAL COMMISSION

ECONOMIC COMMISSION FOR EUROPE

ECONOMIC COMMISSION FOR ASIA AND THE FAR EAST

ECONOMIC COMMISSION FOR LATIN AMERICA

COMMISSION ON HUMAN RIGHTS

SOCIAL COMMISSION

COMMISSION ON THE STATUS OF WOMEN

POPULATION COMMISSION

COMMISSION ON NARCOTIC DRUGS

COMMISSION ON INTERNATIONAL COMMODITY TRADE

S P E C I A L I Z E D   A G E N C I E S

FOOD AND AGRICULTURE ORGANIZATION OF THE UNITED NATIONS

INTERNATIONAL LABOR ORGANIZATION

WORLD HEALTH ORGANIZATION

UNIVERSAL POSTAL UNION

INTERNATIONAL TELECOMMUNICATION UNION

UNITED NATIONS EDUCATIONAL, SCIENTIFIC, AND CULTURAL ORGANIZATION

INTERNATIONAL CIVIL AVIATION ORGANIZATON

INTERNATIONAL MONETARY FUND

WORLD METEOROLOGICAL ORGANIZATION

INTERNATIONAL BANK FOR RECONSTRUCTION AND DEVELOPMENT

INTERNATIONAL FINANCE CORPORATION (Affiliate of International Bank)

INTERGOVERNMENTAL MARITIME CONSULTATIVE ORGANIZATION (Preparatory Committee)

INTERNATIONAL TRADE ORGANIZATION (Interim Commission)

with authority and power to apply collective measures against an aggressor nation. The Security Council was born of this conviction. It is composed of eleven member nations, of which five—the United States, the Soviet Union, Great Britain, China, and France—hold permanent seats and six are elected to nonpermanent seats for two-year terms by the General Assembly. The Charter mentions as standards in election to nonpermanent seats equitable geographic representation and the ability to contribute to the maintenance of peace and security.

For settling disputes the Council is given powers ranging from negotiation, conciliation, arbitration, and judicial decision to the interruption of communications, severance of diplomatic relations, economic sanctions, and military action. Plans for the employment of armed forces are to be made by a military staff committee under the Security Council, but the committee has been so deadlocked that little progress has been made. Should agreement be reached, member nations pledge themselves to assign contingents of armed forces for United Nations use. The veto makes certain that military sanctions cannot be used against one of the Big Five.

The Security Council also has power to oversee regional arrangements consistent with the UN Charter. The Council has a major responsibility for the achievement of disarmament. To fulfill this function, a Disarmament Commission has been established; it is now composed of all members of the UN. Disarmament proposals are reviewed in Chapter 24.

Much of the criticism of the UN arises from the predominant position assigned to the major nations in the Security Council. While the spirit of nationalism remains strong, it is difficult, if not impossible, to devise an acceptable alternative to the veto. The United States was as eager for its inclusion in the Charter as was the Soviet Union and has shown no enthusiasm for repealing the feature. The Little Assembly proposed that the veto be abolished when the admission of new members and peaceful settlements are involved, but it went no further. Champions of stronger world government would subordinate national sovereignty to majority will, but how can this be made acceptable in the near future? Other critics question the concept of an international police force with authority to impose sanctions upon national states, especially as long as they remain heavily armed.

Despite the problems it creates, retention of the veto on at least the application of sanctions appears to be a prerequisite to having any international organization with universal membership. Thus the Security Council's usefulness will be limited, as intended, to those items on which the five permanent members agree.

Looking over the first few years of the Security Council, one must exert himself to find achievements to balance the disappointments. The basic cause of the meager record in security matters has been the deep East-West split. The extent of this cleavage was not anticipated by the founding fathers at San Francisco, who counted on continuance of the kind of cooperation that characterized joint efforts in wartime. Obviously the UN, based on a one-world principle, cannot fulfill the expectations of its founders so long as nations are grouped into two hostile armed camps.

Despite the Iron Curtain and the suspicions entertained by those on both sides of it, substantial progress has been made in peaceful settlement of international disputes. Nearly all the major postwar problems among nations have been brought before the UN. Although handicapped by the frequent use of the veto power by Russia, the Security Council has been able to act effectively in some cases. The greatest achievements are the settlements in Palestine, Indonesia, Kashmir, and Egypt, where fighting wars were stopped through UN mediation and intervention. Armed only with the moral power of the world organization, UN representatives have negotiated truces and peaceful settlements. The Security Council provided facilities for airing all sides, investigating, and mediating. Each settlement tends to contribute to the formulation of patterns of good conduct.

Economic and Social Council. The United Nations created the Economic and Social Council and its cooperating agencies to help remove some of the causes of war, through improved standards of living and social and economic progress. The council is composed of eighteen members, elected by the Assembly for three-year terms. Its field of operation is broad, but its actual coercive powers are meager. It can study, report, recommend, prepare agreements, and call conferences.

The council supervises several other United Nations agencies. The oldest of these is the *International Labor Organization* (ILO), the only major agency of the League of Nations to which the United States belonged. The ILO is concerned with labor standards, migration of workers, full employment, public works, workers' health, and welfare of colonial peoples. It functions through its conference, which meets at least once a year and is composed of delegates representing government, labor, and employers of each member country. An executive body, called the governing body, manages its affairs between conferences. The secretariat, headed by the director, is termed the International Labor Office. Headquarters are in Geneva, Switzerland.

The *Food and Agriculture Organization* (FAO) was launched at a conference held at Hot Springs, Virginia, in May and June,

1943. The FAO has been called the "first permanent United Nations agency." It strives to stimulate increased food production and improved nutrition through research, collection of statistics, exchange of expert personnel, and dissemination of information.

The *International Monetary Fund* was one of two agencies established under the Bretton Woods agreement of July, 1944. Its purpose is to encourage world trade and prosperity by stabilizing the value of currencies of participating nations.

The *International Bank for Reconstruction and Development* is the second of the Bretton Woods agencies. This organization tries to guarantee or make direct loans to countries in need of capital for rebuilding after the devastation of war or for developing new productive facilities.

The *United Nations Educational, Scientific, and Cultural Organization* (UNESCO) was born in London in November, 1945. It is the agency through which member nations exchange information and ideas.

The *International Civil Aviation Organization* (ICAO) developed from the Chicago Conference of November-December, 1944. Although its powers are largely technical and advisory, ICAO may later become a highly important regulatory body for world civil aeronautics.

Trusteeship Council. The UN Charter establishes general policy for governing all dependent areas, sets forth rules to govern territories placed under United Nations "trust," and establishes the Trusteeship Council to supervise the system. Charter provisions also admonish nations to ensure the political, economic, social, and educational advancement of dependent areas; to develop self-government of those areas; to report to the UN on progress in their colonies; and to adopt an attitude of good-neighborliness.

The international trusteeship system had no specific territories assigned to it by the Charter. Trust territories were to come later from the following sources: (1) former mandates of the League of Nations, (2) conquered Axis colonies, and (3) other colonies voluntarily placed under the trusteeship plan. All the mandates except Southwest Africa, which the Union of South Africa sought to annex, promptly were transferred to the trusteeship system by action of the mandatory powers. The United States accepted trusteeship over the former Japanese mandates of the Pacific: the Marshalls, the Carolines, and the Marianas. Former Italian colonies in North Africa were placed under temporary UN administration, then launched as the Kingdom of Libya, while Italy was made a trustee of Italian Somaliland. No important colonial power has been willing to place its colonies under trust.

The Trusteeship Council is a principal organ of the UN. It consists of member nations administering trust territories, members of the Big Five, and enough other nations to make an equal number of states administering and not administering trust territories. The council has modest powers of accepting petitions, considering reports, and visiting trust areas. It supervises all ordinary trust territories. Trust areas of strategic importance are supervised by the Security Council, and, as the United States Army and Navy demanded, the trust power has a free hand to maintain bases. Although the system does not contain striking new features, it does obligate all nations with colonies to treat them decently and to report on their stewardship to the UN.

International Court of Justice. The UN Charter established a new International Court of Justice to supersede the World Court of the League of Nations. Charter provisions are brief; details of organization and jurisdiction are contained in a statute annexed to the Charter. The court consists of fifteen judges, no two of whom may be nationals of the same state. The term of office is nine years. The court sits at The Hague. Judges are elected by the General Assembly and the Security Council, each proceeding independently to elect from a a list of nominees proposed by national groups. Membership in the court is automatic for all members of the UN. The statute made the new court successor to existing treaty provisions which named the old court as arbiter in disputes.

Under its statute the court is barred from considering "domestic" questions. A number of nations have bound themselves to accept the court's interpretation of what questions are domestic. The United States, however, added the Connally amendment, which reserved the right to make this decision. Despite strong objection, Congress has been unwilling to repeal this evidence of lack of faith.

ASSESSING THE UNITED NATIONS

Can the UN Keep the Peace? The UN machinery appears to be fairly well suited for achieving the humanitarian objectives of the Charter. It has had modest success in settling legal disputes and codifying international law; it has provided a medium for airing grievances and molding public opinion; it has had considerable success dealing with controversies involving minor powers.

But judging from the experience with the Military Staff Committee, the handling of the Korean conflict, the failure to achieve disarmament, and the constant imminence of new conflicts, the organization seems poorly devised for controlling the conduct of great powers. Its success in preventing war or repelling aggression depends upon the cooperation of the big powers, and upon methods of assuring this that have still to be devised. Although sharp disagreements

"I warned them! If they let one more nation in, I'm getting out." Al Kaufman's comment on admission of new members to the United Nations. [Reprinted from This Week Magazine (February 16, 1958). Copyright 1958 by the United Newspapers Magazine Corporation.]

have marked all sessions, some consolation may be derived from the fact that differences have been openly discussed.

Many proposals have been made to revise the Charter and make the UN a more effective instrument for peace. Article 109 of the Charter provides that two-thirds of the members of the General Assembly and seven members of the Security Council may call a general conference at any time to consider revisions of the Charter, but so far no call has been made. At the tenth-anniversary session of the General Assembly, held at San Francisco in June, 1955, all members pledged their continued support of the UN, but none proposed a Charter-revision conference. The prevailing view is that strengthening the Charter will have to wait until East-West tensions have eased. Earlier attempts, it is feared, might result in weakening rather than strengthening the present organization.

Toward World Government? Strong criticism of the UN is voiced by two groups in the United States: There are still many isolationists who feel that American membership in the UN leads to unnecessary involvement in world affairs. At the opposite pole is another group who advocate world federation. Logical though the advocates of world federation may be, their goal is a beautiful mirage. People are still devoted to their nation-states and are willing to support only limited world government. Americans will remember that it was only a short time ago that their government was unwilling to join the League of Nations.

The solution appears to be to hold the gains embodied in a universal organization like the United Nations until enough people and statesmen are convinced that the nation-state system must be more drastically modified if the interests of civilization are to be served. Perhaps the San Francisco Charter is to the United Nations what the Articles of Confederation were to the United States, a device for preserving unity of diverse states until the necessity for more perfect union became clear to all.

FOR FURTHER READING

American Association for the United Nations: *Changing World* (monthly).

Asher, Robert E., et al.: *The United Nations and Economic and Social Cooperation* (Washington, D.C.: Brookings, 1957).

Atwater, Elton, and others: *World Affairs, Problems and Prospects* (New York: Appleton-Century-Crofts, 1958).

Bailey, Sydney D.: *The General Assembly of the*

United Nations: A Study of Procedure and Practice (New York: Praeger, 1960).

Besterman, Theodore: UNESCO: *Peace in the Minds of Men* (New York: Praeger, 1951).

Bloomfield, Lincoln P.: *The United Nations and United States Foreign Policy* (Boston: Little, Brown, 1960).

Brown, William A., and R. Opie: *American Foreign Assistance* (Washington, D.C.: Brookings, 1953).

Buchan, Alastair: *NATO in the 1960's* (New York: Praeger, 1960).

Carleton, William G.: *The Revolution in American Foreign Policy* (New York: Knopf, 1962).

Chamberlain, Lawrence H., and Richard C. Snyder (eds.): *American Foreign Policy* (New York: Rinehart, 1948).

Chase, Eugene P.: *The United Nations in Action* (New York: McGraw-Hill, 1950).

Claude, Inis L., Jr.: *Swords Into Plowshares: The Problems and Progress of International Organization* (New York: Random House, 1956).

Cleveland, Harlan, Gerard J. Mangone, and John C. Adams: *Overseas Americans* (New York: McGraw-Hill, 1960).

Commission to Study the Organization of Peace: *Strengthening the United Nations* (New York: Harper, 1957).

Council on Foreign Relations: *The United States in World Affairs* (New York: Harper, annual).

Crabb, Cecil V., Jr.: *Bipartisan Foreign Policy: Myth or Reality?* (Evanston, Ill.: Row, Peterson, 1957).

Dizard, Wilson P.: *The Strategy of Truth: The Story of the United States Information Service* (Washington, D.C.: Public Affairs Press, 1961).

Dulles, Foster R.: *America's Rise to World Power, 1898–1954* (New York: Harper, 1955).

Dulles, John F.: *War or Peace* (New York: Macmillan, 1953).

Eichelberger, Clark M.: *The First Ten Years* (New York: Harper, 1955).

Fleming, D. F.: *The Cold War and Its Origins: The Eloquent and Indelible Record of the Great Conflict of Our Time* (New York: Doubleday, 2 vols., 1961).

Fox, William T. R.: *The Super-powers: The United States, Britain and the Soviet Union— Their Responsibilities for Peace* (New York: Harcourt, Brace, 1944).

Gange, John: *American Foreign Relations: Permanent Problems and Changing Policies* (New York: Ronald, 1959).

Goodrich, Leland M.: *The United Nations* (New York: Crowell, 1959).

———: *Korea: A Study of U.S. Policy in the United Nations* (New York: Council on Foreign Relations, 1956).

Graebner, Norman A.: *The New Isolationism: A Study in Politics and Foreign Policy Since 1950* (New York: Ronald, 1956).

Griswold, A. Whitney: *The Far Eastern Policy of the United States* (New Haven, Conn.: Yale University Press, 1962).

Haviland, H. Field: *The Political Role of the General Assembly* (New York: Carnegie Endowment, 1951).

——— and Associates: *The Formulation and Administration of United States Foreign Policy* (Washington, D.C.: Brookings, 1960).

Holborn, Louise W.: *The International Refugee Organization: A Specialized Agency of the United Nations: Its History and Work, 1946–1952* (New York: Oxford, 1956).

Holcombe, Arthur N., and others: *Organizing Peace in the Nuclear Age* (New York: New York University Press, 1959).

Ismay, Lord: *NATO, The First Five Years, 1949–1954* (NATO, 1954).

Kennan, George F.: *Realities in American Foreign Policy* (Princeton, N.J.: Princeton University Press, 1954).

———: *American Diplomacy, 1900–1950* (Chicago: University of Chicago Press, 1951).

Kissinger, Henry A.: *Nuclear Weapons and Foreign Policy* (New York: Harper, 1957).

Leonard, L. Larry: *International Organization* (New York: McGraw-Hill, 1951).

Lerche, Charles O., Jr.: *Foreign Policy of the American People* (Englewood Cliffs, N.J.: Prentice-Hall, 2d ed., 1961).

Lie, Trygve H.: *In the Cause of Peace* (New York: Macmillan, 1954).

Lissitzyn, Oliver J.: *The International Court of Justice* (New York: Carnegie Endowment, 1951).

Logan, John A., Jr.: *No Transfer: An American Security Principle* (New Haven, Conn.: Yale University Press, 1961).

McClure, Wallace: *World Legal Order: Possible Contributions by the People of the United States* (Chapel Hill, N.C.: University of North Carolina Press, 1960).

Murray, James N., Jr.: *The United Nations Trusteeship System* (Urbana, Ill.: University of Illinois Press, 1957).

Newman, Robert P.: *Recognition of Communist China?* (New York: Macmillan, 1961).

Osgood, Robert E.: *NATO. The Entangling Alliance* (Chicago: University of Chicago Press, 1962).

Riggs, Robert E.: *Politics in the United Nations: A Study of United States Influence in the General Assembly* (Urbana, Ill.: University of Illinois Press, 1958).

Russell, Ruth B., and Jeannette E. Muther: *A History of the United Nations Charter: The Role of the United States, 1940–1945* (Washington, D.C.: Brookings, 1958).

Schiffer, Walter: *Legal Community of Mankind* (New York: Columbia University Press, 1954).

Schuman, Frederick L.: *International Politics* (New York: McGraw-Hill, 6th ed., 1958).

———: *The Commonwealth of Man* (New York: Knopf, 1952).

Sharp, Walter R.: *Field Administration in the United Nations System* (New York: Praeger, 1961).

———: *International Technical Assistance Programs and Organization* (Chicago: Public Administration Service, 1952).

Singer, J. David: *Financing International Organization: The United Nations Budget Process* (The Hague: Martinus Nijhoff, 1961).

Snyder, Richard C. (ed.): *Foreign Policy Decision Making: An Approach to the Study of International Politics* (New York: Free Press, 1962).

Stoessinger, John G.: *The Might of Nations: World Politics in Our Time* (New York: Random House, 1961).

Streit, Clarence: *Union Now* (Washington, D.C.: Federal Union, Inc., 1943).

Thompson, Kenneth W.: *Christian Ethics and the Dilemmas of Foreign Policy* (Durham, N.C.: Duke University Press, 1959).

U.S. Department of State: *Papers Relating to the Foreign Relations of the United States* (1861–19—).

Vandenbosch, Amry, and Willard N. Hogan: *The United Nations: Background, Organization, Functions, and Activities* (New York: McGraw-Hill, 1952).

Vinacke, Harold M.: *Far Eastern Politics in the Postwar Period* (New York: Appleton-Century-Crofts, 1956).

———: *The United States and the Far East* (Stanford, Calif.: Stanford University Press, 1952).

Walters, F. P.: *A History of the League of Nations* (New York: Oxford, 2 vols., 1951).

Westerfield, H. Bradford: *Foreign Policy and Party Politics: Pearl Harbor to Korea* (New Haven, Conn.: Yale University Press, 1955).

Whitaker, Arthur P.: *The Western Hemisphere Idea, Its Rise and Decline* (Ithaca, N.Y.: Cornell University Press, 1954).

Wilcox, Francis O., and Carl M. Marcy: *Proposals for Changes in the United Nations* (Washington, D.C.: Brookings, 1955).

Wingenbach, Charles E.: *The Peace Corps: How and Where* (New York: John Day, 1961).

Wood, Bryce: *The Making of the Good Neighbor Policy* (New York: Columbia University Press, 1961).

Wright, Quincy (ed.): *A Study of War* (Chicago: University of Chicago Press, 2 vols., 1942).

REVIEW QUESTIONS

1. Compare "traditional" with "new" foreign policy.

2. How do you explain the shift in American policy in recent times?

3. What provisions are common to the regional security arrangements entered into by the United States in recent years?

4. Defend and criticize regional security arrangements entered into by the United States and the Soviet Union.

5. What basic principles underlie the United Nations?

6. Explain the organization and functions of the principal organs of the United Nations.

7. How is the United Nations supposed to proceed when a dispute arises which threatens the peace?

8. What have been some of the successes and shortcomings of the United Nations?

9. What are some of the proposals made for improving the organization, powers, and procedures of the United Nations?

10. What procedures are required for making changes in the United Nations' Charter?

Chapter Twenty-Four

National Defense

The war power is the most dangerous one to a free government in the whole catalogue of powers.
It usually is invoked in haste and excitement when calm legislative consideration of constitutional limitations is difficult. It is executed in a time of patriotic fervor that makes moderation unpopular, and is interpreted by judges under the influence of the same passions and prejudices.

JUSTICE ROBERT H. JACKSON[1]

What, then, is the source of our strength? That source is our ethical and moral standards and precepts, and our democratic faith in man. This faith is the chief armament of our democracy. It is the most potent weapon ever devised. Compared with it, the atomic bomb is a firecracker.

DAVID E. LILIENTHAL[2]

Terms such as "nuclear weapons," "jet fighters," "intercontinental ballistic missiles," "massive retaliation," and "Sputnik," which headline today's news, were unheard of less than two decades ago. Their appearance signalizes the fast-changing technology of warfare and the preoccupation with na-

[1] In *Woods v. Cloyd W. Miller Co.*, 333 U.S. 138 (1947).
[2] In *The New York Times Magazine*, March 6, 1949, p. 11.

tional defense that has characterized recent times.

The war powers granted by the Constitution were ample. The division of defense responsibilities between the Federal government and the states was both wise and practical. The problem now is not one of winning the next war but of preventing it from starting, for it is difficult to see how the human race can survive a world conflict fought, as it would be, with today's weapons.

How Americans are dealing with this challenge is the subject of this chapter.

WAR POWERS

Federal Government Paramount. More delegated powers contained in Article I, Section 8, of the Constitution relate to defense than to any other subject.

First, Congress is given power to tax and spend "to provide for the common defense." Second, Congress is authorized "to declare war, grant letters of marque and reprisal, and make rules concerning captures on land and water." Third, Congress is empowered "to raise and support armies" and "to provide and maintain a navy." After these are created, Congress may "make rules for the government and regulation of the land and naval forces." Fourth, Congress may "provide for organizing, arming, and disciplining the militia, and for governing such part of them as may be employed in the service of the United States."

Supplementing these grants is the implied-power clause which authorizes Congress to do whatever is necessary and proper for executing them. Moreover, there is strong judicial support for believing that the war powers are inherent ones, like those pertaining to foreign affairs.

While granting the central government broad powers, the Constitution forbade the states to "keep troops, or ships of war in time of peace" without the consent of Congress, or to "engage in war, unless actually invaded, or in such imminent danger as will not admit of delay." Thus, the states were left only with authority to maintain a militia for preserving order and, under remote circumstances, repelling invasion. Even state control over the militia was made tenuous by the constitutional proviso that Congress might provide for its organization, arms, discipline, and use by the Federal Government.

Declaration of War. Only Congress can declare war. A declaration is a formal announcement made, usually, by a joint resolution adopted by at least a majority of both houses and signed by the President. The President may veto the declaration. In turn, Congress could pass it over the veto, but this has never occurred. Congress may declare war at any time and against any political entity—other than a member state in the Union. Congress usually waits for a request from the President.

Although only Congress can declare war, *hostilities* may start by order of the President without prior congressional approval. If the engagement is large and serious, the President usually asks Congress to declare war immediately before or after the start of hostilities; but if it is limited or local, no declaration may be asked for.

An executive war, even of large proportions—as in Korea from 1950 to 1953—can be fought from beginning to end without formal declaration by Congress. Though the President asks Congress to declare war, circumstances have usually reached such a critical stage that Congress has no alternative but to comply with the President's request. Not until Congress acts, however, is a conflict legally war so far as laws of the United States are concerned.

Drafting Manpower. As noted above, Congress has the power to "raise and support armies" and "provide and maintain a navy." The Constitution also contemplates that the states will recruit and train militias according to a discipline prescribed by Congress.

Nowhere does the Constitution state how manpower is to be obtained, but Congress is given authority to do what is necessary and proper to "raise" and "provide" personnel. No constitutional difficulty arises concerning volunteers, but serious questions emerge when men are drafted. The problem divides itself into conscription during or on the eve of war and drafting for peacetime training and service.

Wartime Conscription. Conscription was first used during the Civil War, but it proved to be unpopular and poorly administered. It met with greater success during the First and Second World Wars. The principal objection on legal grounds has been that forcible enrollment is involuntary servitude in violation of the Thirteenth Amendment.

No doubt compulsory service is "involuntary," but is it "servitude"? In a series of cases that arose during the First World War, the Supreme Court distinguished between "servitude" and "duty" or "fundamental obligation" and upheld the draft [*Selective Draft Law cases*, 245 U.S. 366 (1918)]. Although questioned several times since, there has been no serious doubt that conscription is constitutional, at least in time of war or grave danger.

Peacetime Conscription. The first peacetime use of conscription resulted from the passage of the Selective Service and Training Act in September, 1940, more than a year before the United States formally entered the Second World War. The principal legal question involved in peacetime is not whether the citizen's rights are violated, but the states'. Most plans contemplate a Federal draft of young men for a period of training under Federal auspices. But, it is argued, the adult manhood of the nation constitutes the militia whose training is reserved to the states.

A strong case is made to show that those who wrote the Constitution intended Federal forces to be limited in peacetime to a small volunteer army and navy. These, it was assumed, would be buttressed by a citizens' militia under state control and training until called into Federal service.

Assume this to be true and a question remains: Are the courts bound by original intention in the face of modern conditions?

In any event, the power to raise and provide an army and navy, when coupled with the implied power, establishes a strong presumption favoring the constitutionality of peacetime conscription if the system adopted does not dispossess the states of coordinate authority to officer and train militias. Recent peacetime conscription measures have not been seriously contested on constitutional grounds.

Conscripting Labor. Admitting that Congress may draft manpower for service in the Army or government, can a law compel civilian workmen to perform labor for private parties who may profit from the labor expended? Does this amount to involuntary servitude in violation of the Thirteenth Amendment?

A general labor draft failed of enactment during the Second World War, but severe strictures were placed upon the mobility of labor, the penalties being inability to get other jobs or the threat of reclassification and draft into military service. The War Labor Disputes Act did not make it a crime to discontinue working for private employers or plants that had been seized by the government. Had it done so, cases challenging the constitutionality of the act would doubtless have reached the Supreme Court.

There is ample judicial precedent for compelling service on behalf of government, but little in support of compelling workmen to serve private employers. The nearest precedent is found in *Robertson v. Baldwin* [165 U.S. 275 (1896)]. Two seamen who had contracted with a private shipper deserted before completion of the voyage. Apprehended under a Federal law dating back to 1790, they were detained in prison until time for the ship's departure, and compelled to render service until their contract had been fulfilled.

The seamen challenged the Federal statute, charging involuntary servitude in viola-

tion of the Thirteenth Amendment. The
Supreme Court dismissed the idea that the
amendment created a distinction between
involuntary servitude for private persons and
servitude for governmental agencies. It upheld the statute, however, saying that the
amendment was not meant to apply to seamen's contracts because, since time imme-
morial, these had been treated as exceptional
and involved surrendering some personal liberty during the life of the contracts.

According to this decision, whether workmen were forced to labor for the government
or for private parties would make no difference. The test would be whether the amendment was intended to apply to the particular
employments in which labor was forced.
Without showing that, historically, employment contracts in war industries had
been treated as exceptional and permitting
the surrender of a certain amount of personal liberty, a labor draft would be unconstitutional, the precedent reviewed above
would have to be reversed, or the courts
would have to evolve some new basis of
justification.

Drafting Property. If manpower can be
drafted, what of property? Here the question
is whether private property is taken for public use without just compensation or due
process of law. During the last two major
wars Federal laws authorized seizure of war
plants and equipment under certain circumstances, always with the understanding that
owners would be recompensed. The power
to do so has been upheld in the following
words:

The Constitution grants to Congress
power "to raise and support Armies," "to
provide and maintain a Navy," and to make
all laws necessary and proper to carry these
powers into execution. Under this authority
Congress can draft men for battle service.
. . . Its power to draft business organizations

to support the fighting men who risk their
lives can be no less [*United States v. Bethlehem Steel Corp.*, 315 U.S. 289 (1941)].

Curfews. In February, 1942, shortly after
the outbreak of war with Japan, the President created certain military areas and zones
and authorized the military to control conduct in and passage to and from them.
Shortly thereafter the entire West Coast was
declared such a zone and an order was
issued requiring every alien German, Italian,
and Japanese, and all persons of Japanese
ancestry (even though natural-born American citizens) to be in their residences between the hours of 8 P.M. and 6 A.M.

Congress subsequently approved these orders and provided criminal penalties for
their violation. Martial law was not declared;
hence civil courts remained open and available for the trial of offenses. Hirabayashi,
a natural-born American citizen of Japanese
ancestry, was arrested for violating the curfew, and his case ultimately reached the
Supreme Court [*Hirabayashi v. United
States*, 320 U.S. 81 (1942)]. The Court
noted the defendant's citizenship and the
obviously discriminatory character of the
legislation but sustained the conviction on
the ground that the war emergency and the
large number of persons of Japanese ancestry upon the West Coast justified the
curfew.

Internment. More drastic still were orders
issued early in 1942 evacuating all persons of
Japanese ancestry, whether aliens or citizens,
from their homes along the West Coast.
Without any test of loyalty or possible men-
ace to national safety, all Japanese in the
area (approximately 120,000) were compelled to leave, report to control stations,
and thereafter live in internment camps administered by the War Relocation Authority, a civilian agency. Evacuation caused

severe economic hardship, and life in the camps was uncongenial, especially for those accustomed to family life. Once in the camps, persons whose loyalty was unquestioned were permitted to leave provided they did not return to the West Coast and they could find employment or other means of support or educational opportunities elsewhere.

The Hirabayashi case upheld the curfew without expressly passing upon the constitutionality of evacuation and internment. In 1944 a case was brought before the Supreme Court by Korematsu, concededly a loyal American citizen, in which the evacuation program was upheld as justified at the time it was undertaken [*Korematsu v. United States*, 323 U.S. 214 (1944)].

About the same time, another loyal citizen challenged her detention by writ of habeas corpus [*Ex parte Endo*, 323 U.S. 283 (1944)]. She had been detained for two years, first at Tule Lake Relocation Center and then at Central Utah Relocation Center. Without altering approval given to the curfew and evacuation programs in cases previously decided, and without deciding what power the Relocation Authority might have to detain other classes of citizens, the Court ruled that it had no authority to detain loyal citizens for a longer period of time. This decision suggests that evacuation and detention, although justified in wartime, cannot be prolonged beyond a reasonable period required for separating the loyal from the probable saboteurs.

Martial Law. Martial law is the law of necessity. It is sometimes used during grave emergencies when civil authorities fail to maintain law and order. The Constitution nowhere mentions the term. Authority for its use is implied from the power to declare war; to provide for calling forth the militia to execute the laws of the Union, suppress insurrections, and repel invasions; from the President's powers to serve as Commander in Chief and to see that the laws of the Union are faithfully executed; and from the obligation imposed upon the Federal government to guarantee to every state protection against domestic violence.

Nor does the Constitution expressly state whether the President or Congress is to declare martial law. Congress has delegated broad authority to the President, permitting him to use such force as he deems necessary to enforce the laws and preserve order. The President is to decide, therefore, when circumstances justify this drastic remedy.

The most conspicuous instances when martial law has been declared by Federal authorities occurred in 1814, when, during an attack by the British, General Andrew Jackson placed New Orleans and vicinity under military rule, and during the Civil War, when President Lincoln placed the Southern and Border States under martial law. Martial law was not declared anywhere within the Union during the Mexican or Spanish-American Wars or the First World War. During the Second World War, Hawaii was placed under martial law after the attack on Pearl Harbor and remained so during most of the war. This drastic action many thought precipitous and unwarranted and the Supreme Court later declared it illegal [*Duncan v. Kahanamoku*, 327 U.S. 304 (1945)].

Martial Law Distinguished from Use of Troops. Martial law differs from the mere use of troops to patrol or assist police in maintaining order. Under martial law, a military officer is in complete command of a given area, civil courts are closed, and military law and procedure (i.e., trial by courts-martial, etc.) is substituted. But when troops are sent into conflict areas during minor and isolated disturbances, their purpose is usually to aid civil authorities. The troops do nothing on their own responsibility. Lawbreakers are apprehended and prosecuted before civil courts in the usual manner.

Suspension of Habeas Corpus. Martial law is usually accompanied by suspension of the writ of habeas corpus. Authority for doing so is contained in the words, "The privilege of the writ of habeas corpus shall not be suspended, unless when in cases of rebellion or invasion the public safety may require it."

But who is to determine when the public safety requires suspension? The Constitution does not say. At first the Supreme Court took it for granted that the power of suspension lay with Congress, but action taken by President Lincoln during the Civil War clouded the issue. The question is still disputed, but the weight of judicial precedent supports the contention that the President cannot suspend the writ on his own authority but must depend upon congressional authorization.

Whether the writ may be suspended outside zones of actual military operations is also disputed. The weight of opinion appears to dictate that the writ should be suspended only in zones of military operations and then only when civil courts fail to function properly and successfully.

State Militias. The Constitution contemplates cooperative control and use of state militias. The theory is that Congress shall prescribe general rules providing for uniform arms and discipline, but leave to the states the details of organization, appointment of officers, and training. Congress is expressly authorized to provide for calling the militias of the respective states into Federal service. When so called, the states lose all jurisdiction. Although Congress provides for calling militias into Federal service, the principle is

well established that the President alone decides when to call them.

The Constitution states that Congress may call the militia into Federal service for three purposes: (1) to execute the laws of the Union, (2) to suppress insurrections, and (3) to repel invasions. There has been controversy over whether "to repel invasions" authorizes use outside American territory. Although the language appears to forbid use beyond American borders, the issue is academic because under present legislation the militia is also the National Guard, which becomes a part of the Regular Army when called into Federal service. And, of course, the Regular Army can be sent anywhere.

Limits on War Powers. Several limits are implied, but only one is explicitly stated: no appropriation of money "to raise and support armies" shall be for longer than two years. This was copied from the British law at the time, which, however, limited appropriations to one year. The restriction is not repeated in the phrase that authorizes a navy. The restriction prevents the appropriation of permanent funds for the Army and gives every congressman, particularly every member of the House of Representatives, an opportunity to scan the organization and policies of the military. This is one means by which the Army is kept subordinate to the civil branches of government. In recent years this constitutional provision has been interpreted to apply only to salaries and maintenance of the Army and the Air Force, which until 1947 was a part of the Army. It does not prevent long-term appropriations for capital outlays and military equipment, such as airplanes.

Implied Limitations. From a legal point of view, implied limits to war powers are the same as for other powers granted by the Constitution. "No doctrine," said former

Justice Davis, "involving more pernicious consequences, was ever invented by the wit of man than that any of its [the Constitution's] provisions can be suspended during any of the great exigencies of government. Such a doctrine leads directly to anarchy or despotism. . . ." [*Ex parte Milligan*, 4 Wall. 2 (1866)].

Nevertheless, during modern wars there has been a strong tendency for Congress, the courts, and the public to abdicate responsibility in favor of executive action, accepting possible abuse of power as one of war's inevitable concomitants.

DEFENSE AGENCIES

Chief Policy Makers. The President has primary responsibility for setting defense policies. In making decisions the President relies heavily upon two agencies: the National Security Council and the Office of Emergency Planning.

The National Security Council is made up of the President, Vice President, Secretaries of State and Defense, and the Director of the Office of Emergency Planning. Under their direction is the Central Intelligence Agency, which operates in great secrecy and digests information bearing upon security. Also under the Council, until abolished in 1961, was an Operations Coordinating Board, which strove for maximum cooperation of all government agencies in carrying out defense policies.

Since its establishment in 1947, the National Security Council has played a decisive role. More than any other single agency of the Federal government it estimates threats to American security and makes plans to meet them. It determines the emphasis given to nuclear weapons, guided missiles, airpower, civil defense, and similar matters. To the Council is due much of the responsibility for developing programs of foreign aid, NATO, and similar alliances. The Council sanctioned the policy of containing communism, threatening would-be aggressors with "massive retaliation" by air-borne nuclear weapons, and taking the lead in the Korean War. The Council is chiefly responsible for positions taken on such vital issues as disarmament, peaceful uses of atomic energy, and neutral nations.

The Council's great powers have provoked strong criticism. The secrecy that surrounds its deliberations has been attacked. Military considerations have been overemphasized, it has been alleged. The accuracy of information available to the Council has been questioned. In a different vein, critics who favor a more militant course have accused the Council of excessive timidity. The Council, it is contended, "waters down" its decisions to ensure their acceptability to all members, especially the Secretary of Defense, who is vulnerable to interservice rivalries.

The Office of Emergency Planning was established in 1961 to replace the Office of Civil and Defense Mobilization. Its task is to plan, review, coordinate, and advise the President on matters pertaining to civil defense. Other Federal agencies, especially the Department of Defense, are expected to carry out civil defense programs, often in cooperation with state and local governments. The 1961 reorganization was intended to distinguish sharply between staff and line functions with the Office of Emergency Planning confined to the former.

Defense Department. The basic organization of the present Department of Defense was authorized in 1949, although antecedents of the Department date back to the First and Second Continental Congress. The Department is headed by a Secretary appointed from civil life by the President, with the advice and consent of the Senate. Principal staff aides include a Deputy, Director of the Office of Special Operations, Comptroller, and a number of Assistant Secretaries of Defense. The Secretary's principal military advisers are the Joint Chiefs of Staff.

Within the Department of Defense are three subordinate departments (Army, Navy, and Air Force), each headed by a civilian secretary. Advising each secretary is a chief of staff (called Chief of Naval Operations by the Navy), who is the top military officer of his particular department. The three chiefs of staff combine, under the chairmanship of the Chief of Staff to the Secretary of Defense, to form a Joint Chiefs of Staff.

Added to this structure is an Armed Forces Policy Council made up of the several secretaries and their chiefs of staff. The Commandant of the Marine Corps sits with the Joint Chiefs and the Council and has coequal status on matters affecting marines. A host of boards, committees, staff and line officers, and employees, drawn from both military and civilian life, serve this complex hierarchy.

Departmental Military Functions. To help formulate military policies is the foremost function of the Department of Defense. Recommendations of the military agencies carry great weight. Indeed, many critics at home and abroad contend that military leaders have had too much influence in recent times.

Extreme critics have hurled charges of warmongering at the United States; more moderate ones have claimed American policy has become belligerent, domineering, and rigid. Such complaints have caused some reexamination of the role of the military in American life, but none of it has led to organizational changes designed to lessen the influence of the Department of Defense.

Planning strategy and tactics is another important military function of the Department of Defense. Always a difficult task, modern technology has made it more so. Plans adequate for battleships, artillery, tanks, planes, and poison gases of the era before the Second World War have been made obsolete by developments in outer-space missiles, supersonic planes, and hydrogen and bacteriological weapons. Every possible contingency must be anticipated when making plans. Allowances must be made for geography, climate, possible combinations of allies and enemies, quantity and quality of available resources, and enemy potential. Plans are tested in "war games" staged in various defense areas.

Research is also of vital concern to the Department of Defense. Budgets for defense-related research have grown immensely, amounting in fiscal 1961 to an estimate of nearly 4 billion dollars. Most research is of the applied type, which seeks to find new uses for existing knowledge. Besides the Department of Defense, the Atomic Energy Commission is the principal Federal agency engaged in military research. Close liaison is maintained with the National Aeronautics and Space Administration established in 1958. A large amount of research is done indirectly, through grants and contracts with universities and private industries.

Less spectacular military functions of the Department of Defense include recruiting and training manpower; providing shelter, food, medical care, transportation, equipment, supplies, and weapons; acquiring and maintaining bases, ships, and properties; governing occupied areas; providing assistance to friendly nations alone or through the United Nations; servicing reserve and National Guard units; planning for mobilization; and supporting American foreign policies, often with displays of force short of war.

Nonmilitary Functions. Civilian functions

DEPARTMENT OF DEFENSE

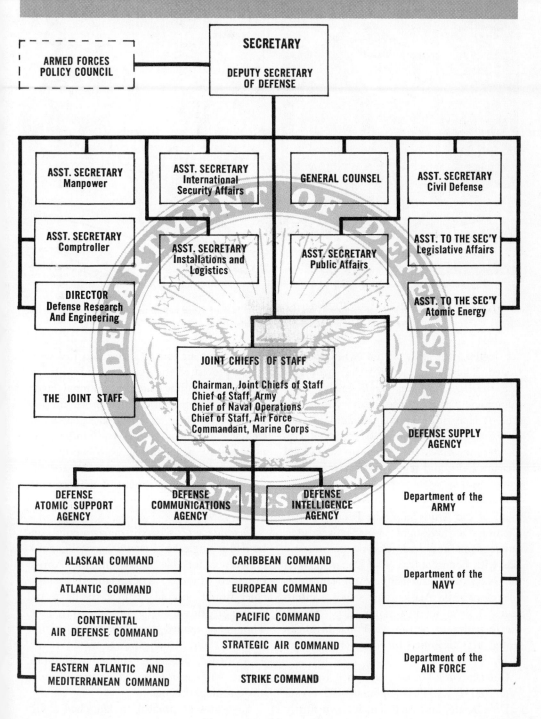

ARMED FORCES
POLICY COUNCIL

SECRETARY

DEPUTY SECRETARY
OF DEFENSE

ASST. SECRETARY
Manpower

ASST. SECRETARY
International
Security Affairs

GENERAL COUNSEL

ASST. SECRETARY
Civil Defense

ASST. SECRETARY
Comptroller

ASST. SECRETARY
Installations and
Logistics

ASST. SECRETARY
Public Affairs

ASST. TO THE SEC'Y
Legislative Affairs

DIRECTOR
Defense Research
And Engineering

ASST. TO THE SEC'Y
Atomic Energy

THE JOINT STAFF

JOINT CHIEFS OF STAFF

Chairman, Joint Chiefs of Staff
Chief of Staff, Army
Chief of Naval Operations
Chief of Staff, Air Force
Commandant, Marine Corps

DEFENSE SUPPLY
AGENCY

DEFENSE
ATOMIC SUPPORT
AGENCY

DEFENSE
COMMUNICATIONS
AGENCY

DEFENSE
INTELLIGENCE
AGENCY

Department of the
ARMY

ALASKAN COMMAND

CARIBBEAN COMMAND

ATLANTIC COMMAND

EUROPEAN COMMAND

Department of the
NAVY

CONTINENTAL
AIR DEFENSE COMMAND

PACIFIC COMMAND

STRATEGIC AIR COMMAND

EASTERN ATLANTIC AND
MEDITERRANEAN COMMAND

STRIKE COMMAND

Department of the
AIR FORCE

ABOUT TIME HE GOT A HEAD   A HECK OF A WAY TO MAKE MISSILES

Don Hesse comments on rivalries and lack of coordination between the Armed Forces. (By permission of McNaught Syndicate, Inc.)

are legion, but only a few will be mentioned. The Department of the Army governs the Panama Canal Zone and manages numerous business enterprises within the area. It constructs national monuments and memorials, assists communities stricken with disaster, preserves the American section of Niagara Falls, and regulates the use of navigable waters within the United States. Through its Corps of Engineers the Department of the Army helps the Federal Power Commission investigate water-power sites, builds dams and hydroelectric plants, and aids with flood control. The Department of the Navy has responsibility for enormous oil reserves in Alaska and other western states. Unlike its two senior departments, the Department of the Air Force has been spared responsibility for distinctly civilian tasks.

Departmental Unification. Until 1947 the War and Navy Departments were organically separate, and each had its own nearly autonomous air force. Critics said this separation prevented integrated planning, led to rivalries for public and congressional favor, encouraged competition in recruitment and procurement, and led to duplication, inefficiency, and confusion. Delays, blunders, and unnecessary costs during both world wars were cited to justify change. The remedy proposed was a department of defense with one head who would direct and unify all armed services.

Defenders of separate departments contended a single head would inevitably show preference for one branch of the Armed Forces or another. They claimed a single chief would become so powerful he would dominate other branches of the government. They also denied that greater efficiency, economy, and striking power would result. As evidence, defenders pointed with pride to the long record of achievements under separate departments.

Advocates of unification launched a vigorous campaign shortly after the Second World War. The Army, backed by President Truman, favored change; the Navy opposed. Washington has seldom, if ever, witnessed a more bitter and intransigent contest. The National Security Act of 1947 was the result. This, as amended in 1949 and since, provides the basis for the present defense organization.

Although a single department exists, the goal sought by champions of unification has not been fully achieved. Particularly serious is a fundamental difference over strategic concepts, especially between leaders of the Air Force and the Army. The former assume a "push-button" war quickly won by "massive retaliation" with air-borne nuclear weapons. This view tends to exalt air power and minimize land and naval forces. Army spokesmen declare such a policy is morally, politically, and practically unjustified. They visualize a long conflict requiring sustained operations by air, land, and sea, similar to those of the Second World War. Acceptance of this view requires "balanced" forces and retention of larger land and sea forces than Air Force leaders think necessary.

The seriousness of this cleavage was made apparent by disclosures that followed Russia's launching of its Sputniks in 1957. Inter-service rivalries had retarded military research and development despite the coordinating devices relied upon to make unification succeed. Many solutions were proposed, some of which became part of the Defense Reorganization Act of 1958. Pertinent provisions: (1) made it unmistakably clear that the secretaries of the three service departments were to function under the direction, authority, and control of the Secretary of Defense; (2) directed all civilian and military·personnel of the service departments to cooperate fully with the personnel of the Office of the Secretary of Defense; (3) gave the President and Secretary of Defense greater authority to shift and consolidate

functions; (4) authorized the Secretary of Defense to establish procedures for the transfer of officers between services; (5) provided a statutory basis for the Naval Air Force, the Marine Corps, and the National Guard Bureau; (6) authorized the Chairman of the Joint Chiefs of Staff to vote on matters decided by that body; (7) required the Secretary of Defense to include in his annual report itemized steps taken to reduce duplication and overlapping.

THE ARMED SERVICES

Land Forces. The Army of the United States consists of the Regular Army, the Women's Army Corps, the Army National Guard, Organized Reserves, and the Reserve Officers' Training Corps.

The Regular Army is a vast organization made up of volunteers and draftees on active duty. The Women's Army Corps (WAC) originated during the Second World War and is presently based on legislation enacted in 1948. It has been integrated into all but the combat phases. It is particularly effective in communications, medical service, personnel administration, and intelligence. Field operations of the Regular Army are carried on through six continental armies, the Army for the Military District of Washington (D.C.), armies in each of the major American territories, and several overseas commands.

The Army National Guard is composed of two parts: one, for the District of Columbia and other American territories, is under the exclusive control of the Regular Army; the other is, during normal times, a group of state organizations. Although largely financed by the Federal government and supervised by the Regular Army, state Guard units are officered and trained by state appointees. Guardsmen are volunteers who take training regularly near home. In wartime or national emergencies the state units may be called into Federal service, during which time they lose their state character and become indistinguishable parts of the Regular Army.

The Organized Reserve is a Federal reserve entirely unrelated to the National Guard. For the most part, it is made up of former members of the Regular Army who served less time than required to fulfill the six- or eight-year military obligation explained on page 484. Reserve officer personnel comes from several sources, of which one of the most important is the Reserve Officers' Training Corps (ROTC) in colleges and universities.

Naval Forces. Components of the naval establishment are more numerous than those of the Army. They include the Regular Navy, Marine Corps, Coast Guard, Naval Reserve, Naval Air Reserve, Naval Reserve Officers' Training Corps (NROTC), and Marine Corps Reserve.

The Regular Navy is by far the largest component and, like the Army, includes both men and women, volunteers and draftees. The Marine Corps, which traces its origin back to 1775, is a semiautonomous force especially trained and equipped for landing operations. The Coast Guard, although a part of the Navy at all times, operates under the Treasury Department in peacetime. It serves as the seaboard police and lifeguard for the nation. It is also an auxiliary to the Navy and the Merchant Marine. The various reserves are much like their Army counterparts.

For administrative purposes the Navy divides the United States and its possessions into seventeen naval districts: the first consists of the New England states, except Connecticut; the seventeenth, of Alaska and the Aleutians. Operating forces include the two major fleets—Atlantic and Pacific—and seagoing, sea-frontier, and district forces.

The Air Force. Air power first demonstrated its military importance during the First World War. Sharp differences of opinion have existed ever since over the proper role of air power. Before 1947, separate departmental air forces were justified on the ground that they could best be developed and directed by the departments whose land or naval operations they were intended to assist. It was assumed that cooperation could be achieved through joint conferences, committees, and the President.

It was obvious that the separate air forces played an important role in the Second World War, but many thought a better job could have been done if responsibility had not been divided. Many also believed that, if left under the Army and Navy, the air force would be neglected by departmental officers whose chief interests lay with other phases of defense. Foreseeing future wars when air power would be even more decisive, champions insisted upon an autonomous air force equipped with sufficient money and manpower to keep abreast of the rapid technological changes that lay ahead. Passage of the National Security Act of 1947 authorized a separate Department of the Air Force with rank equal to that of the Army and Navy. Today, the Army and Navy use their own aircraft chiefly for local supporting operations.

The Air Force is composed of both men and women. The draft has been used very little; most personnel are volunteers. Components consist of the Regular Air Force, the Air Force Reserve, and the Air National Guard, all of which resemble their counterparts in the other branches of the armed services. For operational purposes the Air Force is divided into seventeen major commands bearing such titles as Air Defense Command, Air Research and Development Command, Air University, and Strategic Air Command.

Unified and Specific Commands. Unification carried with it a provision for unified and specific commands. There are now six

DEPARTMENT OF DEFENSE SPENDING,
Fiscal Years, 1952-1963

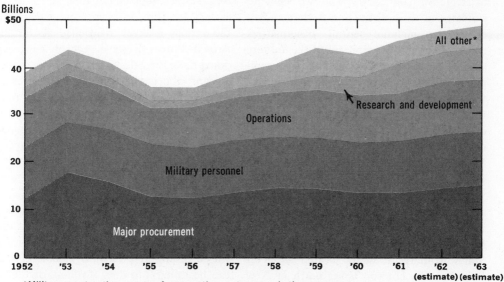

Billions

All other*

Research and development

Operations

Military personnel

Major procurement

1952 '53 '54 '55 '56 '57 '58 '59 '60 '61 '62 '63
(estimate)(estimate)

*Military construction, reserve forces, retirement pay, and other programs

MILITARY SERVICES AND VETERANS AFFAIRS

☐ National Defense   ■ Veterans Benefits and Services   ▨ Other Budget Expenditures

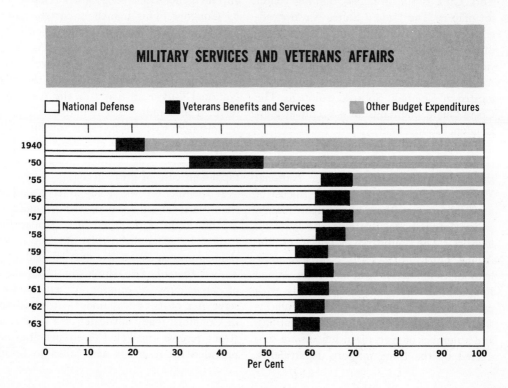

Per Cent

unified commands (Alaska, Atlantic, Caribbean, Continental Air Defense, European, and Pacific) and two specific commands (Eastern Atlantic and Mediterranean, and Strategic Air Command). The two types are similar; the chief distinction is that unified commands include central headquarters composed of officers from each of the military services having forces assigned to the commands. Men assigned remain members of their service components but are subject to the operational direction of the supreme commander of the unified or specific command. The top officer is responsible to the President through the Secretary of Defense and the Joint Chiefs.

Training Schools. Officers are trained for all branches of the service in existing civilian institutions and schools especially provided for the purpose. For the Army, the United States Military Academy located at West Point, on the Hudson River north of New York City, is the principal training center for officers. The United States Naval Academy located at Annapolis, Maryland, a short distance east of Washington, D.C., plays a similar role for the Navy. The United States Air Force Academy, authorized in 1954, is located at Colorado Springs, Colorado. The Coast Guard maintains an academy at New London, Connecticut.

For postgraduate or in-service officers' training, three schools are held jointly by the military departments. The National War College stresses the broad aspects of national policy, with emphasis upon foreign policy, international relations and law, and logistics. The Industrial College of the Armed Forces stresses the economic problems of mobilization and war. The Armed Forces Staff College deals especially with problems of administration. Selected officers study at civilian educational institutions, and a number of specialized schools are conducted by the three military departments.

RESERVES, CONSCRIPTS, AND CIVIL DEFENSE

Reserves. To supplement their active forces, each of the three military services maintains the various reserves mentioned above. The Armed Forces Reserve Act of 1955 lays down the basic rules. This law states that all persons who entered the Armed Forces between June 19, 1951, and August 10, 1955, incurred a military obligation of eight years. Persons who entered after the last date mentioned incur an obligation of only six years. If the obligation is not fulfilled by the time of release from active duty, it must be completed later in one of the reserves.

Reservists form a reservoir of manpower divided into a "ready reserve," "standby reserve," and "retired reserve." The ready, whose ceiling at present is 2,900,000 men, can be called into duty involuntarily during an emergency *declared by the President or by Congress*. This branch is, for the most part, made up of persons who have not fully satisfied their eight- or six-year obligations at the time of release from active duty. The Army National Guard and the Air National Guard are parts of the ready reserve. The standby is a nonorganized pool of personnel that can be called involuntarily only in time of war or emergency *declared by Congress*. The retired group can be tapped in case of great need.

A member of the ready reserve (other than National Guardsmen, who are under a separate code) is required to participate in forty-eight scheduled drills and not more than seventeen days active duty annually, or, in lieu thereof, a maximum of thirty days of active duty for training. When the Reserve Act of 1955 was under consideration in Congress, many advocates of a large and strong reserve urged that severe penalties be provided for reservists who failed to fulfill

COMPOSITION OF THE MILITARY FORCES

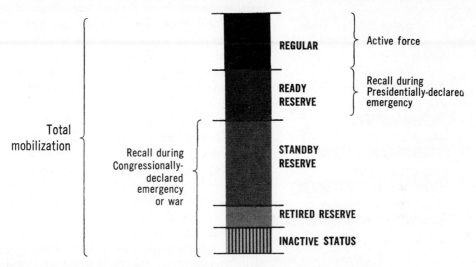

Under the Armed Forces Reserve Act of 1952, the ready reserve may be called to active duty by the President, but congressional action is required to call up the stand-by reserve and the retired reserve. (Data from U.S. Department of Defense.)

training requirements. A mild penalty was finally authorized: A member of the ready reserve who fails or refuses to perform the training prescribed for him may be ordered to train for forty-five days annually instead of thirty. Continued failure or refusal can be dealt with by courts-martial.

Conscripts. Young men have been subject to military draft ever since passage of the Selective Training and Service Act in September, 1940. Administration is the responsibility of the Selective Service System with headquarters in Washington and state capitals. Regional boards exist to handle appeals, and local draft boards of three or more civilians oversee registration, classification, examination, and induction. The law sets the maximum authorized strength for the Army, Navy, Marine Corps, and Air Force, then permits as many to be drafted as necessary to meet these quotas.

Draft Procedures. Registration is the first step in the draft process; it is required of all men between eighteen and twenty-six. Men may not be drafted until eighteen and a half, and then not until those from nineteen to twenty-six have been called. After registration, questionnaires are sent to obtain additional information. Then follows classification, physical examination, and perhaps induction.

Only those in Class I are liable for draft, but those placed in lower classes may be shifted to Class I and become eligible. Men are not chosen by national lottery, as during the First and Second World Wars, but rather by birthday sequence. Twenty-five-year-olds are taken first and then others from older to younger.

Deferments may be granted by local boards to permit high-school students to continue their studies, if their record is satisfactory, until graduation or age twenty-one, whichever is first. College students may be

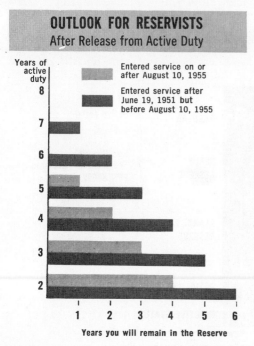

OUTLOOK FOR RESERVISTS
After Release from Active Duty

Years of active duty

Entered service on or after August 10, 1955

Entered service after June 19, 1951 but before August 10, 1955

Years you will remain in the Reserve

deferred until the end of the academic year. Decisions of local boards may be taken to appeal boards and thence to state and national headquarters. The period of service is twenty-four months, plus six years in a reserve after discharge.

Since 1955, men seventeen to eighteen and one half years of age may side-step the draft by enlisting as trainees for six months and serving a prescribed period of time in one of the reserves. Older men now have similar options.

Civil Defense. Defense of the homeland is primarily the function of the Armed Forces, but modern wars require civilian participation. This need was recognized when the Office of Civilian Defense was created in May, 1941. During the Second World War, this agency worked through state and local defense councils composed largely of volunteers. An elaborate air-raid defense system was established; it entailed plane spotting, practice air raids, and black-outs. Emergency first-aid and fire-fighting training were also given in hundreds of communities. Defense councils provided a medium for bringing information to the public on matters pertaining to health, hygiene, dietetics, conservation, and other community needs. These plans were never seriously put to the test here; abroad, even the best home defense could not prevent serious suffering, both physical and economic, and loss of life among civilians. The Office of Civilian Defense was abolished in 1945.

Alarmed over developments in Korea, Congress passed the Civil Defense Act of 1950, which authorized the Federal Civil Defense Administration. This agency was merged in 1958 with the former Office of Defense Mobilization to form the Office of Civil and Defense Mobilization. The latter unit was abolished in 1961 and its functions divided between a new Office of Emergency Planning and the Department of Defense. Civil defense involves cooperation among Federal, state, local, and private agencies. It requires making studies and plans; sponsoring educational programs; providing a nation-wide alert system, storing emergency supplies and equipment; and negotiating interstate and other agreements for mutual assistance.

Much money and effort have been spent on civil defense, but results have been disappointing. It is difficult to arouse and sustain public interest in the absence of an acute emergency; the character of modern weapons leads to a feeling that civil-defense planning is futile and encourages an entirely illusory sense of security. Many believe effective planning requires dispersal of population and industry, but this is costly, disruptive, and unpopular; and opinion varies over the appropriate division of responsibility and cost between the Federal government, the states, and the local governments. These difficulties are likely to continue to plague those responsible for civil defense.

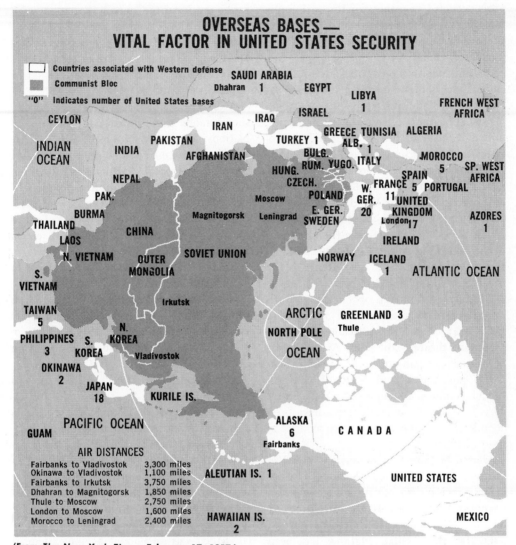

OVERSEAS BASES — VITAL FACTOR IN UNITED STATES SECURITY

☐ Countries associated with Western defense
▨ Communist Bloc
"0" Indicates number of United States bases

SAUDI ARABIA
Dhahran 1
EGYPT
LIBYA 1
ISRAEL
IRAQ
IRAN
PAKISTAN
CEYLON
INDIAN OCEAN
INDIA
AFGHANISTAN
NEPAL
PAK.
BURMA
THAILAND
CHINA
LAOS
N. VIETNAM
OUTER MONGOLIA
SOVIET UNION
S. VIETNAM
Irkutsk
TAIWAN 5
PHILIPPINES 3
S. KOREA
N. KOREA
Vladivostok
OKINAWA 2
JAPAN 18
KURILE IS.
GUAM
PACIFIC OCEAN

GREECE TUNISIA ALGERIA
TURKEY 1
ALB. 1
BULG.
HUNG. RUM. YUGO. ITALY
CZECH.
Moscow POLAND
Magnitogorsk Leningrad
E. GER. 20
SWEDEN
W. FRANCE 5
GER. 11
UNITED KINGDOM
London 17
SPAIN PORTUGAL
MOROCCO 5
SP. WEST AFRICA
FRENCH WEST AFRICA
AZORES 1
IRELAND
NORWAY ICELAND 1
ATLANTIC OCEAN
ARCTIC NORTH POLE OCEAN
GREENLAND 3
Thule
ALASKA 6
Fairbanks
CANADA
UNITED STATES
MEXICO
ALEUTIAN IS. 1
HAWAIIAN IS. 2

AIR DISTANCES
Fairbanks to Vladivostok	3,300 miles
Okinawa to Vladivostok	1,100 miles
Fairbanks to Irkutsk	3,750 miles
Dhahran to Magnitogorsk	1,850 miles
Thule to Moscow	2,750 miles
London to Moscow	1,600 miles
Morocco to Leningrad	2,400 miles

(From *The New York Times*, February 17, 1957.)

MILITARY COMMITMENTS ABROAD

As noted in Chapter 23, the United States has abandoned isolation for collective and regional security. This has meant military commitments in practically all parts of the world; their total reaches startling proportions. Some obligations arose from the necessity for governing areas conquered during the Second World War; some arose from pledges made by joining the United Nations; others have sprung from efforts to contain communism.

Government of Occupied Areas. When enemy territory is occupied, law and order must be maintained, usually by the conquering military forces. Military government at its best is arbitrary and often ruthless, but it is limited by national and international law. Congress has enacted general and special statutes providing the basis for governing areas occupied by American forces. Supplementing these are orders issued from time to time by the President, acting as Commander in Chief.

Within an occupied area the military commander, sometimes called "governor" or "civil affairs administrator," has supreme legislative, executive, and judicial authority, although much of this is delegated to subordinates. Courts-martial enforce military law and orders. Local sovereignty is suspended, and the former governments exist and function solely at the discretion of the commander. Control is as strict and extensive as is necessary to achieve the objectives of the occupying power. Generally speaking, the Bill of Rights does not extend to the inhabitants of occupied territory.

Military government operated in North Africa for many months after invasion in 1942–1943. Later Italy became the most important theater; still later, Austria, parts of Germany, Japan and some of her former island possessions, and South Korea. Although commitments to assist many of these areas continue, occupation forces have been completely withdrawn or severely reduced in most of them.

United Nations Obligations. As noted in Chapter 23, the United Nations Charter makes provision for having armed forces in readiness at all times. It also pledges every member to cooperate to the fullest extent. Thus far the United Nations has been unable to agree sufficiently to provide the police force contemplated. Steps were taken in this direction when the United Nations sent an emergency force to patrol the Israeli-Egyptian border in 1957 and to maintain peace in the Congo in 1960.

If the Charter provisions were fully put into effect, the world police force would consist of "coningents" of soldiers, naval vessels, and air forces kept in readiness by member nations for immediate use when asked

for by the Security Council. How many each would contribute is to be worked out by the Security Council with the advice of a Military Staff Committee, which would also direct whatever military operations might be undertaken.

Thus far none of the great powers has shown much disposition to see the United Nations adequately equipped with military forces. A committee appointed to work on the matter has been stalemated almost from the start. In the meantime, the General Assembly has undertaken the task of planning to meet aggression with collective measures which it has authority to recommend but not to order.

Even though it has not been possible to implement Charter provisions fully, the United States has a continuing obligation to support the United Nations with military strength if ordered or requested to do so. Korea showed how stern this obligation can be.

"Containment." When the Second World War ended, American forces and installations were based at strategic spots around the world. Many bases were retained. The Soviet Union viewed those which remained with alarm, and as East-West tension mounted their number and importance increased. The United States considered them essential for "containing" communism in general and the Soviet Union in particular. Much was said about needing them to deter aggression by threatening "massive retaliation" with nuclear weapons if necessary. Wherever they are, American bases are under military rule. Details surrounding the location, maintenance, and operation of bases on foreign soil are set forth in agreements with governments concerned.

Meanwhile, the United States has entered into regional pacts mentioned in Chapter 23. These do not specifically commit this country to armed intervention in the event of conflict, because to do so would encroach on the congressional prerogative of declaring war. But the obligation to consult and assist is clear and requires preparations for military intervention if this should be decided upon.

The policy of containment has had still another military phase—one of providing aid to friendly powers. Greece, Turkey, Spain, Pakistan, Yugoslavia—indeed practically all "free nations"—have been recipients. Sometimes aid takes the form of technical advice on military matters; sometimes supplies and equipment are furnished; often grants and loans are provided; and steps are taken to improve economic and social life as a means of improving military potential. In all its forms the effort and cost of the containment policy has been great, with far-reaching implications for American defense agencies and personnel.

THE QUEST FOR DISARMAMENT

Wanted: A Disarmed World. Disarmament has been one of the major objectives of national states for well over half a century. But, alas, expenditures for military purposes and armed forces are larger today than ever before in peacetime. The cost in terms of dollars is staggering. For fiscal 1962, expenditures for defense and veterans' benefits cost the United States nearly $50 billion, or about 64 per cent of total Federal expenditures. The cost in terms of social and human values is also great. President Eisenhower, speaking in April, 1953, expressed the problem in this way:

Every gun that is made, every warship launched, every rocket fired signifies—in the final sense—a *theft* from those who hunger and are not fed, those who are cold and are not clothed.

The world in arms is not spending money alone.

It is spending the sweat of its laborers, the genius of its scientists, the hopes of its children.

The cost of 1 modern heavy bomber is this: a modern brick school in more than 30 cities.

It is 2 electric power plants, each serving a town of 60,000 population.

It is 2 fine, fully equipped hospitals.

It is some 50 miles of concrete highways.

We pay for a single destroyer with new homes that could have housed more than 8,000 people.

This—I repeat—is the best way of life to be found on the road the world has been taking.

This is not a way of life at all, in any true sense. Under the cloud of threatening war, it is humanity hanging from a cross of iron.

United Nations Attempts to Achieve Disarmament. The UN has been the scene of most postwar efforts toward disarmament. The Charter authorized the General Assembly to establish principles of disarmament, the Security Council to develop concrete plans. A UN Atomic Energy Commission was established in 1946 and a Commission on Conventional Armaments a year later. In January, 1952, these were merged into a new Disarmament Commission composed of the eleven members of the Security Council plus Canada. In 1957 membership was raised to twenty-five; in 1958, at the insistence of the Soviet Union, the Commission was enlarged to include all UN members. The objective has been a treaty to outlaw weapons of mass destruction and reduce other armaments and armed forces to agreed-upon levels for the purpose of domestic policing and fulfilling international obligations.

American policies have been shaped under the general direction of the Department of State. For a while after 1955 leadership was provided by the Office of Special Assistant to the President on Disarmament. In 1961 Congress authorized the establishment in the Department of State of an Arms Control and Disarmament Agency. The director serves as the principal adviser on disarmament to the Secretary of State and the President.

The Baruch and Other Plans. Shortly after the United Nations Atomic Energy Commission was established, the United States introduced what became known as the Baruch Plan. This was prepared under the direction of Dean G. Acheson, David E. Lilienthal, and Bernard Baruch. Mr. Baruch was then the American representative on the Atomic Energy Commission. Although the plan proved to be acceptable to a majority of the United Nations delegations, Soviet objections stalled attempts to obtain the necessary treaty.

Throughout the long and tedious discussions, agreement has been reached on many features of a disarmament plan. Points of agreement include: (1) The disarmament plan should be established by and administered through the United Nations; (2) all nations having substantial military potential must participate; (3) conventional armaments, weapons of mass destruction (atomic, hydrogen, poison gas, and germs), and military bases must be brought under control; (4) the testing of nuclear weapons should be suspended; (5) the manufacture, possession, and use of weapons of mass destruction must be outlawed; (6) the diversion of nuclear materials for peaceful purposes should begin as soon as possible; (7) conventional weapons and armed forces must be reduced to agreed-upon levels; (8) outer space should be reserved for peaceful uses only; (9) an impartial and dependable system of inspection and enforcement is essential and technically feasible.

The principal points of disagreement relate to whether political settlements must precede disarmament; the composition and powers of the control organ; the time schedule, technically known as "stages," by which the plan would be put into operation; the scope and frequency of inspection; and the nationality of inspection teams.

Much discussion has centered on an "open-sky" proposal made by President Eisenhower in 1955. This called for an exchange of blueprints of American and Soviet military installations followed by unlimited aerial photography to be carried out by both countries. This, the President hoped, would provide almost absolute assurance against surprise attacks and thereby lessen tensions sufficiently to make it possible to find solutions for the technical problems involved.

Spokesmen for the Soviet Union expressed the view that the open-sky plan would neither lessen tensions nor hasten agreement on basic issues unless it were treated as a part of a total control system. As a counterproposal, Soviet spokesmen suggested that control posts be established near large ports, railroad junctions, airfields, and highways, where large military concentrations and preparations for a surprise attack could be observed and reported. Later, Soviet leaders indicated willingness to see the open-sky plan applied to a buffer zone between the Soviet bloc and the NATO countries. Still later, they proposed opening up much of the western United States, eastern Soviet Union, and all of Alaska to aerial and ground inspection if other conditions were met. The Western powers made counterproposals. Meanwhile, negotiations continue chiefly through the United Nations and groups of national experts.

FOR FURTHER READING

Barnet, Richard J.: *Who Wants Disarmament?* (Boston: Beacon Press, 1960).

Bechhoefer, Bernhard: *Postwar Negotiations for Arms Control* (Washington, D.C.: Brookings, 1961).

Bush, Vannevar: *Modern Arms and Free Men* (New York: Simon and Schuster, 1949).

Ekirch, Arthur A., Jr.: *The Civilian and the Military* (New York: Oxford, 1956).

Fitzpatrick, Edward A.: *Universal Military Training* (New York: McGraw-Hill, 1945).

Furniss, Edgar S.: *American Military Policy* (New York: Rinehart, 1957).

Garner, Anthony J.: *Hawaii under Army Rule* (Stanford, Calif.: Stanford University Press, 1955).

Ginzberg, Eli, and others: *The Ineffective Soldier: Lessons for Management and the Nation* (New York: Columbia University Press, 3 vols., 1959).

Hadley, Arthur T.: *The Nation's Safety and Arms Control* (New York: Viking, 1961).

Hammond, Paul Y.: *Organizing for Defense: The American Military Establishment in the Twentieth Century* (Princeton, N.J.: Princeton University Press, 1961).

Hitch, Charles J., and Roland N. McKean: *The Economics of Defense in the Nuclear Age* (Cambridge, Mass.: Harvard University Press, 1960).

Huntington, Samuel P.: *The Soldier and the State: The Theory and Politics of Civil-Military Relations* (Cambridge, Mass.: Harvard University Press, 1957).

————: *The Common Defense: Strategic Programs in National Politics* (New York: Columbia University Press, 1962).

Huzar, Elias: *The Purse and the Sword: Control of the Army by Congress through Military Appropriations, 1933–1950* (Ithaca, N.Y.: Cornell University Press, 1950).

Janowitz, Morris: *The Professional Soldier* (New York: Free Press, 1960).

Kaufmann, W. W. (ed.): *Military Policy and National Security* (Princeton, N.J.: Princeton University Press, 1956).

Kintner, William R.: *Forging a New Sword: A Study of the Department of Defense* (New York: Harper, 1958).

Knorr, Klaus: *The War Potential of Nations* (Princeton, N.J.: Princeton University Press, 1956).

Masland, John W., and Laurence I. Radway: *Soldiers and Scholars: Military Education and National Policy* (Princeton, N.J.: Princeton University Press, 1957).

Millett, John D.: *The Organization and Role of the Army Service Forces* (Washington, D.C.: GPO, 1954).

Millis, Walter, et al.: *Arms and the State: Civil-Military Elements in National Policy* (New York: Twentieth Century Fund, 1958).

————: *Arms and Men: A Study in American Military History* (New York: Putnam, 1956).

Morenus, Richard: *DEW Line: Distant Early Warning, The Miracle of America's First Line of Defense* (Chicago: Rand McNally, 1957).

Morgan, Thomas, and Robert M. Northrop: *Atomic Energy and Congress* (Ann Arbor, Mich.: University of Michigan Press, 1956).

Noel-Baker, Philip: *The Arms Race: A Programme for World Disarmament* (New York: Oceana Publications, 1958).

Peeters, Paul L.: *Massive Retaliation: The Policy and Its Critics* (Chicago: Regnery, 1958).

Rankin, Robert S.: *When Civil Law Fails* (Durham, N.C.: Duke University Press, 1939).

Ransom, Harry H.: *Central Intelligence and National Security* (Cambridge, Mass.: Harvard University Press, 1958).

Rich, Bennett M.: *The President and Civil Disorders* (Washington, D.C.: Brookings, 1941).

Ropp, Theodore: *War in the Modern World* (Durham, N.C.: Duke University Press, 1959).

Rossiter, Clinton L.: *The Supreme Court and Commander-in-Chief* (Ithaca, N.Y.: Cornell University Press, 1951).

————: *Constitutional Dictatorship: Crisis Government in the Modern Democracies* (Princeton, N.J.: Princeton University Press, 1948).

Schelling, Thomas C., and Morton H. Halperin: *Strategy and Arms Control* (New York: Twentieth Century Fund, 1961).

Sibley, Mulford Q., and Philip E. Jacob: *Conscription of Conscience, The American State and the Conscientious Objector, 1940–1947* (Ithaca, N.Y.: Cornell University Press, 1952).

Smith, Dale O.: *U.S. Military Doctrine: A Study and Appraisal* (New York: Duell, Sloan & Pearce, 1955).

Smith, Louis: *American Democracy and Military Power* (Chicago: University of Chicago Press, 1951).

Snyder, Glenn H.: *Deterrence and Defense* (Princeton, N.J.: Princeton University Press, 1961).

Snyder, Richard C.: *The Role of the Military in American Foreign Policy* (New York: Doubleday, 1954).

Stanley, Timothy W.: *American Defense and National Security* (Washington, D.C.: Public Affairs Press, 1956).

Stern, Frederick: *The Citizen Army: Key to Defense in the Atomic Age* (New York: St. Martins, 1957).

Tate, Merze: *The United States and Armaments* (Cambridge, Mass.: Harvard University Press, 1948).

Teeple, David S.: *Atomic Energy: A Constructive Proposal* (New York and Boston: Duell, Sloan & Pearce and Little, Brown, 1957).

Ten Broek, Jacobus, and others: *Prejudice, War, and the Constitution* (Berkeley and Los Angeles, Calif.: University of California Press, 1954).

Tucker, Robert W.: *The Just War* (Baltimore: The Johns Hopkins Press, 1960).

U.S. Commission on Organization of the Executive Branch of Government (first Hoover Commission): *The National Security Organization* (1949).

——: *Task Force Report on National Security Organization* (1949).

U.S. National Security Training Commission: *Universal Military Training, Foundation of Enduring National Strength* (1951).

U.S. Secretary of State's Committee on Atomic Energy: *A Report on the International Control of Atomic Energy* (1946). This is the famous Acheson-Lilienthal report.

Von Glahn, Gerhard: *The Occupation of Enemy Territory* (Minneapolis, Minn.: University of Minnesota Press, 1957).

Wallace, Donald H.: *Economic Controls and Defense* (New York: Twentieth Century Fund, 1953).

REVIEW QUESTIONS

1. What "war powers" does the Constitution give to Congress? To the President?

2. What constitutional problems were involved in (*a*) the wartime treatment of Japanese-Americans along the West Coast, (*b*) martial law in Hawaii, and (*c*) conscription of manpower and property in peace and war?

3. What limits are there to the war powers?

4. What defense powers and responsibilities remain with the states?

5. Compare the national defense establishment before and after unification.

6. Defend and criticize unification of the Armed Forces.

7. What functions are performed by each of the defense agencies?

8. Explain to a prospective draftee how the Selective Service System works.

9. Explain the present program for creating a reserve of trained manpower. What changes should be made in these provisions?

10. Trace disarmament discussions since 1946, and indicate present points of agreement and disagreement.

11. What changes are required to improve the defense organization and policies of the United States?

Chapter Twenty-Five

Government and Business

. . . two-thirds of the economically productive assets of the United States, excluding agriculture, are owned by a group of not more than 500 corporations. This is actual asset ownership. . . . But in terms of power, without regard to asset positions, not only do 500 corporations control two-thirds of the non-farm economy but within each of that 500 a still smaller group has the ultimate decision-making power. This is, I think, the highest concentration of economic power in recorded history. Since the United States carries on not quite half of the manufacturing production of the entire world today, these 500 groupings—each with its own little dominating pyramid within it—represents a concentration of power over economics which makes the medieval feudal system look like a Sunday School party. In sheer economic power this has gone far beyond anything we have seen.

A. A. BERLE, JR.[1]

The economic life of the nation is vitally affected by almost everything the Federal government does. This chapter first reviews the commerce power, which provides the constitutional basis for many Federal activities affecting business. Then follows an account of Federal programs that aid and regulate business generally.

[1] *Economic Power and the Free Society* (New York: The Fund for the Republic, 1957), p. 14.

THE COMMERCE POWER

The Constitutional Provision. One of the most serious defects of the Articles of Confederation was the inability of Congress to regulate interstate and foreign commerce. Accordingly, after compromising conflicting views, the Constitutional Convention approved the following clause without a dissenting vote: "Congress shall have power . . . to regulate commerce with foreign nations, among the several States, and with the Indian tribes."

The words "regulate" and "commerce" were chosen with great care. The authors desired a clause granting the Federal government unquestioned authority over all forms of intercourse affecting two or more states, foreign nations, and the Indian tribes, but leaving to the states authority over affairs that concern only localities.

Interstate Commerce Defined. The term "interstate commerce" is nowhere defined in the Constitution, so its meaning must be sought elsewhere, especially in court decisions. The famous Steamboat case [*Gibbon v. Ogden*, 9 Wheat 1 (1824)] was the first in which the Supreme Court construed the power. Speaking for the Court, in one of his most celebrated opinions, Chief Justice Marshall said: "Commerce, undoubtedly, is traffic, but it is something more; it is intercourse. It describes the commercial intercourse between nations, and parts of nations, in all its branches, and is regulated by prescribing rules for carrying on that intercourse."

Before the Civil War, when society was predominantly rural and businesses small, the line of demarcation between interstate and intrastate commerce could be drawn with comparative ease. Today's situation is different. The transformation from an agrarian society to an industrial nation has commingled all economic activity. As the ripples of a pool radiate to the farthest extremity, so every business transaction may affect the economic life of the nation to some degree. Economically, no clear-cut division can be made between interstate and local commerce.

Nevertheless, the Constitution requires that a distinction be made. While permitting a broad interpretation, the Supreme Court has said that Federal authority may not be pushed to the point of destroying the distinction made by the commerce clause between commerce among the states and the internal concerns of the state. Specific situations determine where the line shall be drawn.

Transportation. Transportation of persons and goods across state lines is the clearest form of interstate and foreign commerce. The method of conveyance is immaterial. People walking, cattle leisurely grazing first in one state and then in another, or travel by ship, train, canoe, airplane, pipeline, motorcar, or bicycle—even logs floated down a navigable stream—are interstate commerce. A carrier may begin and end its journey within a single state; it is, nevertheless, subject to Federal control if it carries passengers or goods destined for points outside the state or if it competes substantially with interstate carriers. If a vehicle begins its journey in one state, leaves the state for a considerable distance en route, and returns to the state of origin, it is engaged in interstate commerce.

Communications. At various times it has been suggested that only the interstate transportation of tangible things, like persons and property, constituted interstate commerce. This idea was rejected long ago. Soon after their invention, Federal regulation of interstate transmission of messages by telephone and telegraph was upheld [*Pensacola Telegraph Co. v. Western Union Telegraph Co.*, 96 U.S. 1 (1878)]. In that case, Mr. Justice Waite said:

The powers thus granted are not confined to the instrumentalities of Commerce or the postal service known or in use when the Constitution was adopted, but they keep pace with the progress of the country, and adapt themselves to the new developments of time and circumstances. They extend from the horse with its rider to the stagecoach, from the sailing vessel to the steamboat, from the coach and the steamboat to the railroad, and from the railroad to the telegraph as these new agencies are successively brought into use to meet the demands of increasing population and wealth.

Later, regulation of radio broadcasting and the transmission of news by wire or wireless were held to come within the scope of the commerce power.

Buying and Selling. Buying and selling goods intended for shipment or use in other states is interstate commerce. Congress has made illegal all sorts of contracts that monopolize interstate commerce; it has outlawed price discrimination between buyers; it has legalized contracts whereby manufacturers may force retailers to maintain resale prices of nationally advertised products; it has regulated the buying and selling of livestock, agricultural products, and stocks and bonds; and it has outlawed unfair trade practices that may injure buyers and sellers.

Moreover, Congress has fixed the rates that sellers may charge and buyers pay for interstate carriers, electric power, natural gas, and bituminous coal. A corollary of this is that states cannot impose burdens upon the buying and selling of interstate products. This explains why salesmen for out-of-state concerns, such as the Fuller Brush Company and the Real Silk Hosiery Mills, who merely take and subsequently deliver orders, cannot be compelled to pay local license fees to do business within a state.

Production and Commerce. Transportation, buying and selling, and transmission of electricity or messages imply movement or conveyance from within one state into another. But what of the actual manufacture of a product or its extraction from the earth? Ultimately bought and sold or transported across state lines, is its production

a part of interstate commerce? The question became important toward the end of the last century when businesses were rapidly becoming national in size.

The pre-1937 doctrine is illustrated by *United States v. Knight* [156 U.S. 1 (1895)]. The American Sugar Refining Company had acquired control of 98 per cent of all the sugar refining in the United States. The Department of Justice charged the company with monopolizing interstate commerce in violation of the Sherman Act. Acknowledging that the company was of enormous size and controlled virtually all sugar refining in the country, the Court nevertheless dismissed the suit saying that the company was not engaged in interstate commerce, hence was beyond the scope of Federal regulation.

The Court distinguished between production and commerce, saying that the former involved merely a change in *form* while commerce involved change of *place*. The refining of sugar was antecedent to commerce but not a part of it. In other words, no matter how large a production unit became, its effect upon economic affairs in other states was so indirect and remote as to be beyond Federal control under the commerce clause. Subsequently, by similar reasoning, Congress was prevented from regulating not only manufacturing but also the production of oil and natural gas, mining, quarrying, and the generation of electric power.

This doctrine prevailed until 1937. Since then the courts have greatly expanded the scope of the commerce power. The entering wedge was a case testing the constitutionality of the National Labor Relations Act [*NLRB v. Jones & Laughlin Steel Corp.*, 301 U.S. 1 (1937)]. Jones and Laughlin Steel Corporation was accused of violating the act by discharging several employees for union activities in production units at its plant at Aliquippa, Pennsylvania. The company admitted the charges but denied that the Federal government could do anything about them because the men were engaged in manufacture which was not interstate commerce.

The company was the fourth largest producer of steel in the country. Though incorporated under the laws of Pennsylvania, it had nineteen subsidiaries which comprised an integrated empire. It owned or leased mines, ships, railroads, stores, mills, plants, factories, pipelines, and refineries in several states and maintained sales offices in twenty cities in this country and one in Canada. Approximately 75 per cent of its products were shipped out of Pennsylvania.

Admitting that the dismissed men were engaged in production, the Supreme Court said that the labor practices of the employer had an immediate and direct effect upon interstate commerce, and so came within the scope of Federal power. Writing for the majority, Chief Justice Hughes observed:

In view of respondent's far-flung activities it is idle to say that the effect would be indirect or remote. It is obvious that it would be immediate and might be catastrophic. . . . When industries organize themselves on a national scale, making their relation to interstate commerce the dominant factor in their activities, how can it be maintained that their industrial labor relations constitute a forbidden field into which Congress may not enter when it is necessary to protect interstate commerce from paralyzing consequences of industrial war?

This meant that manufacturing, or any other form of productive enterprise, was interstate commerce if organized on a national scale and carried on in two or more states. This is a wide departure from the long-standing doctrine enunciated in the Knight case.

Recent Trends. Since the historic shift of 1937, the commerce power has been broadened considerably more. Though agricultural production itself remains local, marketing quotas have been approved [see, for example, *Wickard v. Filburn*, 317 U.S. 111 (1942)]. In 1939, Federal legislation fixing prices for bituminous coal was upheld [*Sunshine Anthracite Coal Co. v. Adkins*, 310 U.S. 381 (1940)]. In the following year the Court upheld Federal regulation of wages, hours, child labor, and working conditions for businesses engaged in the manufacture of lumber products [*United States v. Darby Lumber Co.*, 312 U.S. 100 (1941)]. During the same year, comprehensive Federal regulation of natural-gas companies was approved [*FPC v. National Gas Pipeline Co.*, 315 U.S. 590 (1941); *FPC v. Hope Natural Gas Co.*, 320 U.S. 591 (1943)]. More recently, long-standing decisions have been overruled, bringing insurance [*United States v. South-Eastern Underwriters Ass'n.* 322 U.S. 533 (1944)] and professional amusements within the scope of the commerce power [see, for example, *Radovitch v. National Football League*, 352 U.S. 445 (1957)].

Though the commerce power has been broadened, a huge volume of economic activities remains intrastate. Small locally-owned businesses, such as restaurants, barbershops, retail stores, laundries, and bakeries are still exclusively subject to state control. Agricultural production, very small mines, quarries, factories, and utilities are beyond the pale of the commerce power. The hunting and fishing of game is still local in character. Professionals like doctors, dentists, lawyers, accountants, and architects engage in local commerce, although when they unite in national or regional associations their activities may come under Federal control. Amusements and exhibitions, such as theaters, circuses, games of sport, and movies, are intrastate unless professionalized and involved in business transactions that extend outside the boundaries of a single state.

AIDS TO GENERAL BUSINESS

The Department of Commerce. Having reviewed the basic power used by the Federal government in its dealings with business, we turn to services provided, most of which are centered in the Department of Commerce. Created in 1903, this agency was known as the Department of Commerce and Labor until Labor was made a separate Department in 1913.

Heading the Department is the Secretary, who is a member of the President's Cabinet. The Secretary is nearly always someone who has supported the President's party and usually reflects the attitude of the administration toward business. Principal assistants and internal organization of the Department are shown on the chart on page 498.

The functions of the Department are to foster, promote, and develop the foreign and domestic commerce, the mining, manufacturing, shipping, and fishing industries, and the transportation facilities of the United States. The bulk of its activities are of a service character. Since the Federal Maritime Commission and the Civil Aeronautics Board were given independent status, the Department does little in the way of business regulation.

Economic Planning. Various agencies of the Federal government have long been concerned with planning their particular programs and projects. Not until the Depression, however, was much official recognition given to the need for economic planning.

Federal economic planning was begun in 1934 by an agency ultimately known as the National Resources Planning Board. Its task was to inventory national resources and suggest ways of conserving them, study economic trends and recommend ways of avoiding booms and busts, and plan public works in cooperation with state and local governments. The Board was abolished in 1943, but it established the concept of planning, stimulated the creation of state and local planning bodies, and left behind a number of useful studies.

The demise of the National Resources Planning Board and the threat of unemployment after the Second World War caused much agitation for new legislation, culminating in the Employment Act of 1946. In its original form the legislation would have pledged the government to plan and place into operation a broad economic program whenever required to ensure full employment. As finally passed, after heated argument, the measure was greatly watered down.

The legislation created a three-man Council of Economic Advisers in the Executive Office of the President. The Council, aided by a staff of economists and statisticians, prepares for the President comprehensive economic reports on current conditions and trends. The President later submits these to Congress with his own recommendations. To facilitate their consideration, Congress has created a Joint Committee on the Economic Report, comprised of seven members from each house.

Public Works Planning. Public works consists of those activities that entail construction by, or on behalf of, governmental agencies. Projects that are urgently needed cannot be postponed, but some of them can

DEPARTMENT OF COMMERCE

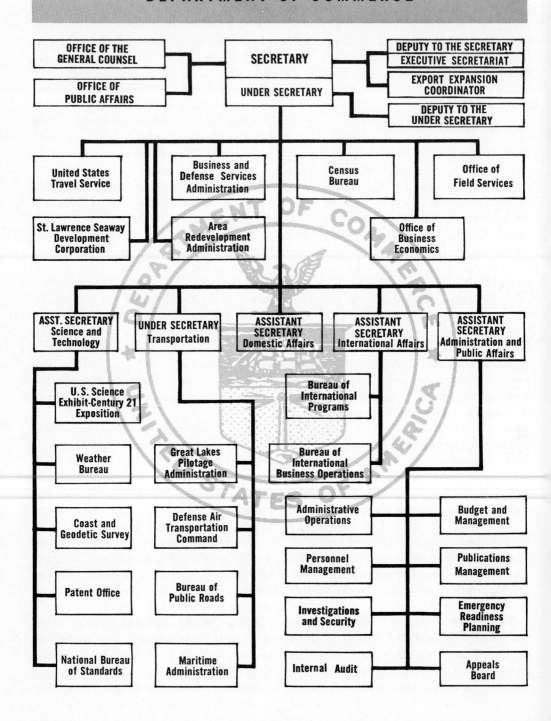

OFFICE OF THE GENERAL COUNSEL

OFFICE OF PUBLIC AFFAIRS

SECRETARY

UNDER SECRETARY

DEPUTY TO THE SECRETARY
EXECUTIVE SECRETARIAT

EXPORT EXPANSION COORDINATOR

DEPUTY TO THE UNDER SECRETARY

United States Travel Service

St. Lawrence Seaway Development Corporation

Business and Defense Services Administration

Area Redevelopment Administration

Census Bureau

Office of Business Economics

Office of Field Services

ASST. SECRETARY Science and Technology

UNDER SECRETARY Transportation

ASSISTANT SECRETARY Domestic Affairs

ASSISTANT SECRETARY International Affairs

ASSISTANT SECRETARY Administration and Public Affairs

U.S. Science Exhibit-Century 21 Exposition

Weather Bureau

Coast and Geodetic Survey

Patent Office

National Bureau of Standards

Great Lakes Pilotage Administration

Defense Air Transportation Command

Bureau of Public Roads

Maritime Administration

Bureau of International Programs

Bureau of International Business Operations

Administrative Operations

Personnel Management

Investigations and Security

Internal Audit

Budget and Management

Publications Management

Emergency Readiness Planning

Appeals Board

be put off until prices are favorable or the economy lags. The omnipresent threat of depression makes it imperative that governments and private concerns maintain portfolios of carefully planned projects the construction of which can be timed to fit in with economic conditions. Recognition of this truth has led to much planning by public and private agencies, especially in recent years.

The General Services Administration plans for meeting Federal space needs. The Armed Forces plan and construct the largest volume of public works. Many other agencies are involved in planning national parks, public roads, river and harbor improvements, water-resource and power developments, irrigation projects, housing, public-health facilities, urban and distressed area redevelopment, and public works in the territories. Much public-works planning is done in close cooperation with state and local governments.

Tariffs. The Constitution gives Congress the power to lay and collect duties and imposts. Such levies on imported goods are now called tariffs. Every American tariff law, including the first, adopted in 1789, has had two purposes: to raise revenue and to protect certain domestic industries.

Protective Tariffs. The intent of a "protective" tariff is to keep foreign products out, thus giving American-made products a competitive advantage. Restriction of foreign selling eases competition and keeps domestic prices higher than they otherwise would be. This process levies a tax upon American consumers; the proceeds serve as a subsidy to the makers of American goods.

Whether this is a sound policy does not concern us here. For good or ill, many American businesses ("infant industries") have come into being and grown to maturity behind tariff walls, without which they might not have been born or might have

fallen by the wayside. Tariffs play a large role in deciding what kinds of goods shall enter the country; they also determine, to a considerable degree, the volume of exports, since countries will not readily buy here unless they can also sell. Indeed, tariffs affect the entire economy, and an unwise tariff policy may have devastating effects not only upon the United States but upon the entire world.

Tariff laws include many schedules, or classifications of commodities, wherein each product is listed with the amount of the tax, if any. Tariffs are either *specific*, i.e., so much per unit, or *ad valorem*, i.e., a stated percentage of the value of the commodity. Before goods leave foreign ports for the United States, invoices must be certified by American consular officers; upon arrival, goods must be appraised by officers of the Customs Bureau of the Treasury Department. Decisions of the customs officers may be reviewed by the United States Customs Court, and further appeal on questions of law may be taken to the Court of Customs and Patent Appeals.

Unless revised frequently, tariff schedules and rules and regulations that must be followed by customs officers tend to become archaic, even ridiculous. Concern over the extent to which the "dead hand of the past" restricts and hampers trade caused Congress to pass the Customs Simplifications Acts of recent years.

The Tariff Commission. Making tariffs is an exceedingly complicated and technical task for which most members of Congress have neither time nor training. Recognizing this, in 1916 Congress created a bipartisan Tariff Commission of twelve members appointed by the President with the advice and consent of the Senate. In 1930 the Commission was reduced to six members, who serve for terms of six years. The Commission is not a quasi-legislative or quasi-

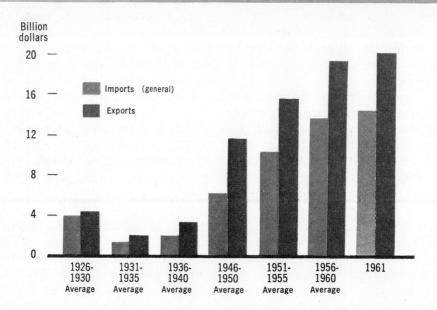

UNITED STATES EXPORTS AND IMPORTS

Billion
dollars

Imports (general)

Exports

20 —

16 —

12 —

8 —

4 —

0

| 1926-1930 Average | 1931-1935 Average | 1936-1940 Average | 1946-1950 Average | 1951-1955 Average | 1956-1960 Average | 1961 |

Some Americans persist in thinking that we can export without importing, but the majority appears to support the principle of reciprocal lowering of trade barriers. (From U.S. Department of Commerce.)

judicial body, nor does it exercise administrative powers. Its primary duty is to conduct research and furnish information to Congress and the President on matters relating to American and foreign tariffs.

"Flexible" Tariffs. Formerly tariff rates fixed by Congress were unalterable until changed by statute. This produced rigidity and invited agitation and lobbying by special interests.

Recognizing the problem, Congress authorized the President to change tariff rates within prescribed limits. The McKinley Tariff of 1890 empowered the President to levy special rates upon certain imports in retaliation for "unjust and unreasonable" charges levied by foreign nations upon American products. Since 1922, rates have

been upon the cost-of-production theory, i.e., the duty fixed is determined by the difference between the cost of production at home and abroad.

When the Tariff Commission finds a difference between foreign and American costs, it reports to the President, who may raise or lower the tariff to the advantage of the American producer. Maximum and minimum rates are stated in the law, and the President is forbidden to raise or lower an existing tariff by more than 50 per cent. Articles covered by reciprocal trade agreements are exempt from these provisions.

Reciprocal Tariffs. Still greater flexibility was provided in the Reciprocal Trade Agreement Act of 1934. To regain vanishing American export markets, the act authorized the President to negotiate trade agreements with willing countries. The agreements resemble treaties but they do not require Senate approval. On the whole, the agreements have generally, but not drastically, lowered tariffs. The legislation had three- or two-year time limits; hence it came up for periodic congressional review. In 1962 it was superseded by the Trade Expansion Act.

While permitting the President to negotiate agreements the former legislation added safeguards. These included the following: (1) Rates could be lowered a total of 20 per cent, but not more than 10 per cent in any one year; (2) rates could be increased to 50 per cent above what they were on July 1, 1934; (3) articles on the dutiable list could not be transferred to the free list, or vice versa; (4) no agreement could be made that would reduce the indebtedness of a foreign government; and (5) "peril-point" and "escape-clause" provisions had to be respected.

Peril-point provisions required the President to notify the Tariff Commission of his intention to negotiate a trade agreement and submit a list of items under consideration. The Tariff Commission then had 120 days to hold hearings and report. The Commission was to indicate a peril point for each item, i.e., a tariff rate that would imperil domestic production. If the President exceeded this point he was required to justify his action in reports to Congress.

Escape-clause provisions required that tariff rates stated in the agreements be adjusted whenever investigation disclosed that they injured, or threatened to injure, domestic producers. Should the President disapprove a Tariff Commission escape-clause recommendation, Congress could override his action by passing a concurrent resolution by two-thirds vote in both House and Senate. Emergency investigation and action was authorized for perishable agricultural products.

The President could make exceptions for imports that threatened national security.

Trade Expansion Act of 1962. This legislation drastically altered American trade policy. Two rival economic blocs had emerged in Europe. One was the Common Market composed of six states (France, West Germany, Italy, Belgium, Luxembourg, and the Netherlands), the other was the European Free Trade Association made up of seven countries (Austria, Denmark, Great Britain, Norway, Portugal, Sweden, and Switzerland). The former, with Britain's entry prospective, promised to absorb the latter bloc. This promised both a threat and an opportunity: a threat to American trade and an opportunity to strengthen the economies of friends and allies.

The new legislation authorizes the President to cut tariffs generally as much as 50 per cent and even 100 per cent in some instances. Injured American producers and workers are entitled to "trade adjustment assistance" financed entirely by the Federal government. For businessmen this means technical assistance and subsidies, for workmen it means retraining and unemployment benefits. Some of the "escape clause" procedures contained in prior legislation were retained but "peril point" provisions were eliminated. The President was given discretionary authority to retaliate against countries imposing import restrictions. Trade agreements will be used as formerly to implement the new legislation.

ITO, GATT, OTC, and OECD. In recent years the nations of the world have given much attention to collective measures designed to reduce trade barriers. A charter to establish an International Trade Organization (ITO) was negotiated at Havana, Cuba, by delegates from fifty-six countries during 1947–1948. It had two purposes: (1) to establish rules of conduct for governing international economic relations and (2) to provide information and technical assistance, interpret and administer the charter, and settle disputes. The charter has not been implemented, chiefly because of the failure of the American government to ratify.

Meanwhile, a General Agreement on Tariffs and Trade (GATT) has been operative. This is an agreement between thirty-four nations to promote trade by reducing such restrictions as tariffs, quotas, and discriminatory taxes. A basic principle is the "most-favored nation" rule, under which each GATT country agrees to give all other members, immediately and unconditionally, any trade advantage, favor, privilege, or immunity it grants to any other country. This rule was welcomed by the United States, since it had been a feature of American commercial policy since 1923, and it greatly facilitated the trade-agreement program.

Unlike the proposed ITO charter, the General Agreement does not establish a formal administrative body. Rather, it provides for periodic sessions of member nations to discuss matters of mutual concern. At these meetings members can also interpret the agreement and decide whether a member nation has lived up to its commitments. They can also release nations from their commitments if circumstances warrant. But aside from asserting moral force, GATT cannot compel a country to do anything.

Several years of experience with GATT convinced members of the need for an administrative body. Accordingly, they proposed creation of an Organization for Trade Cooperation (OTC). This would have a general assembly, an executive committee, and a secretariat. The new organization would administer GATT but have no supranational powers. President Eisenhower laid the proposal before Congress early in 1955, but approval has not been forthcoming.

In 1961 the United States with Canada and eighteen Western European nations established the Organization for Economic Cooperation and Development (OECD). The new body provides a medium through which members confer and cooperate to raise living standards, expand world trade, and eliminate trade restrictions. Authority rests in a council composed of all members, but each may veto decisions or abstain from voting. The growth of the Common Market and passage by the United States of the Trade Expansion Act of 1962 may greatly enhance the role of OECD.

Promotion of Foreign Trade. Foreign trade has always been of great importance to the United States and will continue to be so. Trade promotion is primarily the duty of the Department of Commerce although numerous agencies are involved. Only the Bureau of Foreign Commerce and the Export-Import Bank of Washington will be touched on here.

Bureau of Foreign Commerce. This bureau, of the Department of Commerce, has the difficult task of promoting trade in a badly disorganized and divided world. While it works for a "balanced growth of international trade," it also issues licenses for the control of exports, copes with monetary limitations and restrictions, contends with tariffs and quotas, helps boycott Communist nations, and collaborates with other Federal agencies, the United Nations and its specialized bodies, and private businesses and organizations. This office makes available to those interested a constant stream of economic data from all parts of the world.

The Export-Import Bank of Washington. This corporation dates back to 1934. After being a part of several agencies, it is now a permanent, independent establishment. It is organized under the laws of the District of Columbia, and its capital stock is owned entirely by the Federal government. Originally intended to help finance trade with

Russia, the bank later proved more helpful in Latin America, and it is now aiding trade with American territories and friendly nations.

The bank has two primary functions: (1) to lend money to exporters and importers who cannot obtain desired funds from private sources to take advantage of foreign business opportunities and (2) to make loans to foreign governments to develop their resources, stabilize their economies, market products in an orderly manner, and recover from war.

Subsidies. In addition to tariffs, many direct and indirect subsidies are made to business groups. Only a few can be mentioned here. Generous land grants were made to railroads during the last century. Federal grants for rivers and harbors have been a boon to many localities, businessmen, and shippers. Appropriations for public roads have been an important direct and indirect subsidy to the makers of automobiles and to bus and truck carriers. Generous payments have been made to rail, water, and air carriers of mail; for the benefit of special groups as well as the public, mail has been carried for below-cost rates, or free of charge. Federal contributions to the construction of airlines and airports have been an important stimulus to the aircraft industry. Federal aid in financing mortgages and in making grants and loans for planning, public housing, urban renewal, and industrial development stimulate business.

Several federally owned and operated utilities, such as the former Inland Waterways Corporation and the Alaskan Railroad, have subsidized groups and areas by below-cost operations. Shipbuilders and the Merchant Marine have been generously assisted. During the Depression of the 1930s the Federal government spent huge sums in a deliberate effort to stimulate business

activity. Throughout the Second World War, Federal funds were lavishly spent to encourage the production of war materials and hold prices in line. During recent years large expenditures for national defense have been a boon to many businesses. Stimulation of particular industries or geographic areas is often a consideration in awarding defense contracts.

Postal Service. A postal system that is dependable, universal, and inexpensive is an indispensable aid to business. The authors of the Constitution recognized this when they provided that "Congress shall have power. . . to establish Post Offices and Post Roads."

The Postal Power. This power is granted exclusively to Congress, and the states have never sought to compete. It may be used not only to provide postal service but also for regulatory purposes. Many laws regulate the use of mails and exclude objectionable materials.

Such laws, it is frequently contended, usurp powers reserved by the Tenth Amendment to the states, but the courts have held otherwise. Congress excludes such things as poisons of all kinds, including poisonous animals, insects, and reptiles; explosives; inflammable materials; infernal machines; disease germs and scabs; obscene literature, including that calculated to inform people about contraception and abortion; lotteries; writings calculated to produce sedition or to incite to murder or arson; and fraudulent materials.

During the Depression, Congress went further than ever before in using the postal power, partly because of the narrow construction placed by the courts on the commerce power. The Securities Act of 1933, the Securities Exchange Act of 1934, and the Public Utility Holding Company Act of 1935 were all based in part on the postal power. The first two forbid the use of the mails for selling or dealing in the securities of large corporations unless the securities are first registered with the Securities and Exchange Commission. The third forbids electric and natural-gas holding companies from using the mails except when they have registered and are conducting their affairs according to the act. These are far-reaching measures, imposing a type of restraint many supposed lay within the scope of reserved powers of the states. But their constitutionality has been upheld [see, for example, *Electric Bond & Share Co. v. SEC*, 303 U.S. 419 (1938), *and Jones v. SEC*, 298 U.S. 1 (1936)].

Much controversy has also arisen over the manner in which postal regulations affect personal rights. As with other powers, this one must be reconciled with the Bill of Rights. Especially bothersome, from the standpoint of post office officials, is the guaranty against unreasonable searches and seizures. One's mail is among the "papers" and "effects" that may not be unreasonably searched and seized. Unless the sender consents, no letter, publication, or package sent through the mail can be opened without a search warrant.

Searches and seizures are not made by local postal employees. Postmasters forward suspected mail to the dead-letter office, where an authorized employee goes before a United States Commissioner or district judge, describes the mail to be searched and seized, and presents evidence to justify suspicion. If the warrant is issued, the mail is turned over to the post office inspectors for further investigation and action.

The Post Office Department. The head of the Department is called Postmaster General. Although one of the earliest officers to be appointed in the young republic, he was not accorded Cabinet status until Jackson's time, in 1829, and his office was not given departmental status until 1872.

Till then his office was a unit of the Treasury Department, although the Postmaster General himself was directly responsible to the President. The Postmaster General has nearly always been a politician, often the chairman of the President's political party.

Auxiliary Services. Besides handling the mail, the Post Office Department operates a parcel-post service, a system of registering, certifying, and insuring mail, a money-order system, a postal-savings business for small depositors, a cash-on-delivery collection service, and a special-delivery service. It handles the sale of small-denomination government bonds and stamps and collects several types of taxes.

The Post Office Department owns some of its nearly 35,000 post offices but leases most of them. It operates shops for manufacturing and repairing mailbags, locks, etc., but purchases a huge quantity of its equipment and materials from other agencies, both governmental and private. It uses the railways and other carriers to transport large quantities of mail and parcels, but it also owns and operates a fleet of trucks for that purpose.

Postal Profits and Losses. For the first quarter of a century, the postal service was operated along lines followed by private business and showed a profit practically every year. After 1814, especially during and after the Presidency of Andrew Jackson, three factors influenced the course of management: (1) the spoils system; (2) legislation extending the postal service to all parts of the country, especially the developing West, even though uneconomical; and (3) legislation granting subsidies to special groups in the form of higher prices paid to the railways and other carriers for mail transportation, free postage, or reduced rates.

Uneconomical expansion is a factor of

POST OFFICE DEPARTMENT

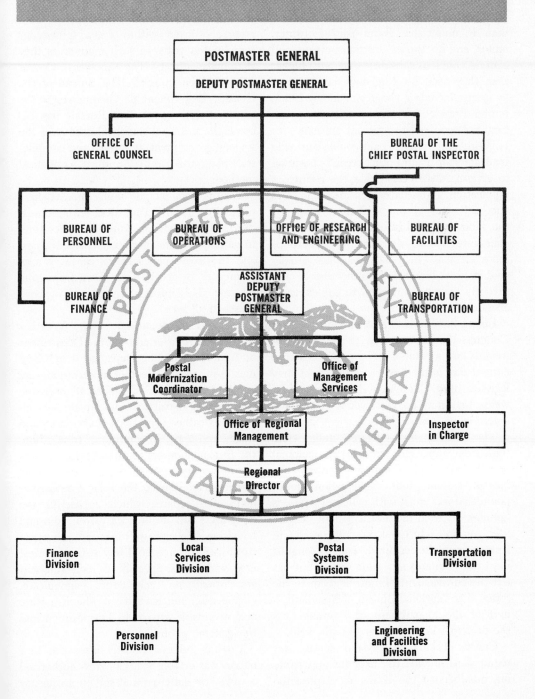

POSTMASTER GENERAL

DEPUTY POSTMASTER GENERAL

OFFICE OF GENERAL COUNSEL

BUREAU OF THE CHIEF POSTAL INSPECTOR

BUREAU OF PERSONNEL

BUREAU OF OPERATIONS

OFFICE OF RESEARCH AND ENGINEERING

BUREAU OF FACILITIES

BUREAU OF FINANCE

ASSISTANT DEPUTY POSTMASTER GENERAL

BUREAU OF TRANSPORTATION

Postal Modernization Coordinator

Office of Management Services

Office of Regional Management

Inspector in Charge

Regional Director

Finance Division

Local Services Division

Postal Systems Division

Transportation Division

Personnel Division

Engineering and Facilities Division

diminishing importance today, since the service now pretty well covers the country. Many postal personnel are political appointees, making management less efficient than it might be. Rates paid to water, motor, and air carriers for transporting mail contain hidden subsidies and are higher than they need be. Mail may be sent free by many, including congressmen, the blind, former Presidents or their widows, agricultural colleges and experiment stations (for bulletins and reports), and publishers who send newspapers and other second-class mail to certain subscribers within the county of publication. Rates have risen in recent years and, following recommendations made by the Hoover Commissions, much effort has gone into making departmental operations more efficient. First-class mail has usually paid its way, but rates for other classes consistently have been too low to pay expenses assignable to them.

Fixing Standards. The Constitution gives Congress the power to "fix the standards of weights and measures." The power is a concurrent one in the sense that the states may legislate until Congress does, and afterwards they may do whatever is not inconsistent with Federal law.

The country first operated under state standards inherited from the colonial period. In 1838 Congress legalized the English system (foot, inch, gallon, quart, pound, ounce, etc.), with which everyone is familiar. In 1866 the metric system (meter, liter, gram, etc.), commonly used in Europe, was also legalized. Today Congress has fixed standards of a wide variety but has left the enforcement of most of them to the states. The National Bureau of Standards, a unit of the Department of Commerce, is the principal Federal agency in this field.

Census Taking. A Federal census was required to provide the data for apportioning members of the House of Representa-

tives and direct taxes. The constitutional mandate reads: "The actual enumeration [of people] shall be made within three years after the first meeting of the Congress . . . and within every subsequent term of ten years, in such manner as they shall by law direct." The Nineteenth Census will be taken in 1970. The Bureau of the Census, Department of Commerce, is the administering agent. The Bureau has become the principal statistical agency of the Federal government. It gathers and compiles statistics and also improves statistical methods.

Census data include much more than a population count. They deal with occupations, unemployment, housing, agriculture, irrigation, manufacturers, mineral industries, and the like. The decennial census is supplemented by special ones taken from time to time. This information is used by businesses of all sorts.

Weather Forecasting. The Weather Bureau was transferred from the Department of Agriculture to the Department of Commerce in 1940. Weather observations are made at thousands of points all over the country. Observations are made of all surface weather conditions, river and flood stages, and upper-air conditions. In addition, the Bureau sponsors research projects aimed at increasing meteorological knowledge. Bureau data provide the basis for weather maps and reports, which appear in the daily press and are broadcast over radio and television. Special warnings are given of storms, hurricanes, cold waves, frosts, forest fires, and floods. Specialized, daily forecasts are issued for aeronautics, agriculture, engineering, and navigation. This is a basic and invaluable service to businessmen and the general public.

Coastal Surveys. Shortly after the new nation was established, Congress authorized a survey of the coast and set up an agency

PATENT APPLICATIONS AND PATENTS GRANTED

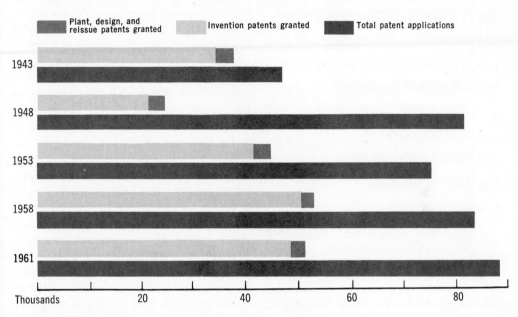

Plant, design, and reissue patents granted | Invention patents granted | Total patent applications

1943
1948
1953
1958
1961

Thousands 20 40 60 80

(From U.S. Patent Office.)

for the purpose, known today as the Coast and Geodetic Survey. Now a unit of the Department of Commerce, this agency has several tasks. It continues to survey and chart the coasts of the United States and its territories, surveys inland waters, determines elevations along the coast and in the interior, studies tides and currents, compiles aeronautical charts, observes the earth's magnetism, makes seismological and astronomical observations, and attempts to improve methods of surveying and mapping.

The agency's surveys, charts, maps and reports are of special value to those interested in navigation, fishing, engineering, aeronautics, building, and radio. The work of the agency is dramatized at times of earthquakes.

Patents. Borrowing from English experience, the Constitution provides that "Con-

gress shall have power . . . to promote the progress of science and useful arts, by securing for limited times to authors and inventors the exclusive right to their respective writings and discoveries." This power is granted exclusively to Congress.

The phrase "to promote the progress of science and useful arts" does not authorize Congress to do whatever it wishes to advance science and the arts. Rather, the phrase merely states the purpose for which patents and copyrights may be issued. Note that exclusive rights can be granted for "limited times" only. This prevents monopolies in perpetuity; but it does not forbid renewals for limited times.

Patents must be issued to "inventors"—not to anyone else, other than bona fide heirs and assigns. Furthermore, patents can be issued only for "discoveries" defined as

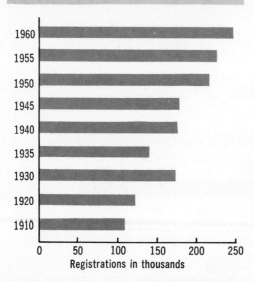

COPYRIGHT REGISTRATIONS

1960
1955
1950
1945
1940
1935
1930
1920
1910

0   50   100   150   200   250
Registrations in thousands

(U.S. Copyright Office.)

new and useful creations or contrivances produced by intellectual labor. This definition precludes a patent for what is merely an ingenious readjustment of existing devices or something found, stolen, or received as a gift.

Patent Legislation. Patent laws, revised and codified in 1952, are administered by the Patent Office, Department of Commerce. When applications are filed, they are carefully studied; if rejected twice, an appeal may be taken to a Board of Appeals. From there appeals may be taken to the United States Court of Customs and Patent Appeals, or civil action may be taken against the Commissioner of Patents in the District Court for the District of Columbia. Although the Patent Office tries to avoid issuing patents that infringe upon those granted to others, it does not guarantee this result. Accordingly, if infringement is detected, an inventor who wishes to protect his interest must bring suit in a Federal district court.

Patents may be issued to the following: (1) anyone who invents or discovers any new and useful process, machine, manufacture, or composition of matter, or any new and useful improvement thereof; (2) anyone who invents or discovers and asexually reproduces any distinct and new variety of plant, other than a tuber-propagated plant; and (3) anyone who invents any new, original, and ornamental design for an article of manufacture.

Patents convey the exclusive right to make, use, refrain from using, and vend the invention throughout the United States and its territories. Patent rights run for 17 years, except for designs, which continue for 3½, 7, or 14 years as elected by the applicant.

Copyrights. Under the constitutional provision quoted above, Congress may grant copyrights to "authors" for "writings." The latter have been defined as original, meritorious works of literature or art created by intellectual labor and published for public use. This would exclude such things as prints, labels, trademarks, ideas expressed in a copyrighted book, titles of books and songs, the news itself, or the mere publication of statutes of a state or ordinances of a city.

Responsibility for handling copyrights rests with the Copyright Office, in the Library of Congress. Copyrights may be obtained only *after* writings are published. To secure them, two copies must be sent to the Copyright Office with an appropriate fee. When issued, the author enjoys the exclusive right to "print, reprint, publish, copy and vend" the work. The privilege extends for a period of twenty-eight years and is renewable for a second, but not a third, period of the same duration.

Notice of copyright must be printed somewhere near the front of the publication; if it is not, others may copy or reproduce the work in any way they please. As

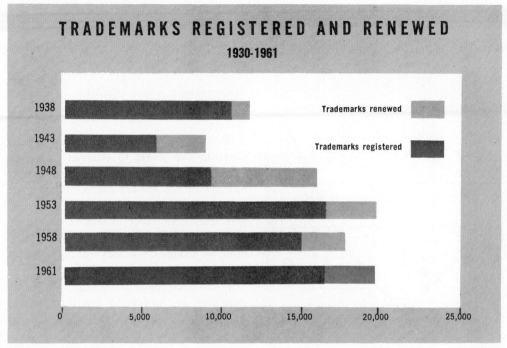

TRADEMARKS REGISTERED AND RENEWED
1930-1961

Trademarks renewed
Trademarks registered

(From U.S. Patent Office.)

compared with the issuance of patents, the procedure is simple and brief. As in the case of patents, the Copyright Office does not guarantee the originality of the writing, nor will it protect the author from infringement. Such protection must be obtained by resort to a United States district court.

At present one may copyright the following: (1) books, including composite and encyclopedic works; directories, gazetteers, and other compilations; (2) periodicals, including newspapers; (3) lectures, sermons, addresses (prepared for oral delivery); (4) dramatic and dramatico-musical compositions; (5) musical compositions; (6) maps; (7) works of art, models or designs for works of art; (8) reproductions of a work of art; (9) drawings or plastic works of a scientific or technical character; (10) photographs; (11) prints and pictorial illustrations; (12) motion-picture photoplays; and (13) motion pictures other than photoplays.

Trademarks. Trademarks are authorized by Congress under its power to regulate interstate and foreign commerce. The Lanham Trade-Mark Act of 1946—a measure long striven for by interested groups—generally codified, revised, and simplified common and Federal statutory law on the subject.

Under this act trademarks, service marks, collective marks, and certification marks may be registered. A trademark is a work, name, symbol, or device, or any combination of these, which identifies and distinguishes a product. Examples are "Kodak" in cameras and "Philco" in radios. A service mark is one that identifies and distinguishes a service, for example, "Greyhound" for bus transportation and "Amos 'n' Andy" in radio entertainment.

A collective mark is one used by a group or association to identify or distinguish goods or services of members, for example, "Indian River" for oranges, "Mohawk Val-

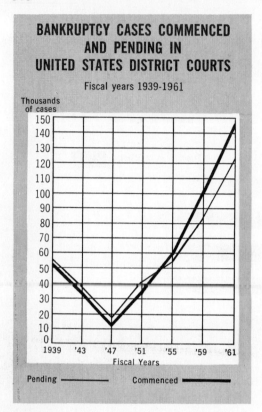

BANKRUPTCY CASES COMMENCED AND PENDING IN UNITED STATES DISTRICT COURTS

Fiscal years 1939-1961

Thousands of cases

Fiscal Years

Pending —————— Commenced ▬▬▬▬

Bankruptcies are inevitable in a free economy, but most of them are suffered by small businesses and often are due to lack of capital or experience. (Administrative Office of the United States Courts.)

ley" for apples, the pine tree for Rochdale cooperatives, and the fleur-de-lis emblem for the Boy Scouts. A certification mark is one used for goods and services of any person other than owners to certify regional origin, quality, accuracy, mode of manufacture, and the like. Examples are various seals, such as the Good Housekeeping Seal of Approval and the labor union symbol used to identify work done by organized labor under collective bargaining.

Marks of all types may be registered with the Patent Office. The procedure is much the same as that explained for obtaining patents. Registrations are good for twenty years provided registrants file affidavits after five years showing their marks are still in use or that nonuse is due to special circumstances. After the first twenty years, registrations may be renewed for subsequent periods of similar length. As with patents and copyrights, registrants must, if the need for protection of their rights arises, resort to the courts.

Bankruptcy. The Constitution grants Congress the power to establish "uniform laws on the subject of bankruptcies throughout the United States." The clause clearly implies that the power is a concurrent one. Like other powers of this type, the states may continue their laws until such time as Congress decides to bring about uniformity.

When Congress does legislate, conflicting state laws are suspended, but those not in conflict remain in effect. If Congress should repeal its provisions, as it did on three occasions during the nineteenth century, old state laws could be enforced without reenactment. Federal law is now so complete and comprehensive that little room is left for state measures, although state insolvency laws are still applicable in some instances.

Except for the three brief periods referred to above, all following major or minor depressions, Congress left the handling of bankruptcies entirely to the states prior to the enactment of the Nelson Act of 1898. Numerous bankruptcy frauds and widespread criticism of the Nelson Act led President Hoover, in 1931, to initiate a nationwide survey of the results of the law. The disclosures, coupled with hardships growing out of the Depression, led to a number of amendments. In 1938 the Chandler Act was passed; while retaining the framework of the Nelson Act, it embodied many changes and codified existing law.

No agency of the executive branch has been set up to administer laws relative to insolvent businesses. The Administrative

Office of the United States Courts acts as a clearing house for matters pertaining to bankruptcies, but litigations originate as civil actions before United States district courts.

With a few exceptions court proceedings may be started either by the debtor or by his creditors. After a debtor has been declared a bankrupt, settlement usually takes place under the supervision of a referee appointed by the court and one or more trustees chosen by the creditors. Appeal may be taken to the United States Courts of Appeals or the Supreme Court.

REGULATION OF GENERAL BUSINESS

Big Business Predominates. Though still the most numerous, small individually owned enterprises are increasingly dwarfed by corporations in assets, income, volume of business, numbers of employees, and economic and political power. The corporation today accounts for half of the national income, with sole proprietorships and partnerships running a poor second and government enterprises third.[1] The corporate form is found in practically all walks of life. In some fields it accounts for almost the entire income. It has even invaded agriculture, and the trend seems likely to continue.

Predominance of the corporate form has had a profound effect upon social, economic, and political life. Among other things, it has changed the once-intimate personal relations among owners, managers, employees, and the public. It has encouraged the movement to cities and the growth of big business. It makes possible the control of business by comparatively few managers, financiers, and investors. It has helped change concepts of property, rights, and

[1] A. D. H. Kaplan, *Big Enterprise in a Competitive Economy* (Washington, D.C.: Brookings, 1954), pp. 118–119.

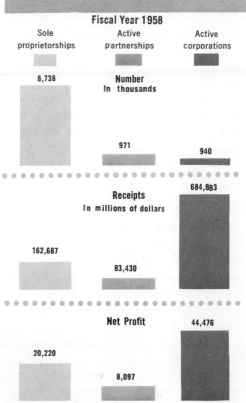

FORMS OF OWNERSHIP RELATED TO RECEIPTS AND NET PROFIT

Fiscal Year 1958

Sole proprietorships	Active partnerships	Active corporations

Number In thousands
8,738 | 971 | 940

Receipts In millions of dollars
162,687 | 83,430 | 684,883

Net Profit
20,220 | 8,097 | 44,476

Small businesses are still numerous in many fields, but there is a tendency for the big to get bigger. (U.S. Department of Commerce.)

democracy and has made the world more interdependent. It has changed the character of competition. It emits a constant and pervasive stream of influence seeking to mold attitudes and public policies favorable to its existence and welfare. Big business invites big government, big labor, and big agriculture, and encourages consumers to organize.

All this in turn paves the way, with the help of wars and depressions, for the "welfare state" of which we are a part. While doing all this, the corporation has helped work scientific, productive, and distributive miracles that have made possible the relatively high standard of living to which Americans have grown accustomed.

Not only do corporations predominate over other types of economic enterprise, but a few have acquired a commanding position in many lines of business—a tendency popularly referred to as "oligopoly." Some corporations have attained ascendancy by natural growth and prosperity. Others have grown large and powerful through mergers, trusts, holding companies, and similar arrangements. These changes have created serious problems of public policy; they also account for many of the controls imposed upon business enterprise, some of which are discussed below.

Securities and Exchanges. When corporations organize, their securities—stocks, bonds, debentures, certificates, etc.—are offered to the public, generally through "stock markets" or "security exchanges." Corporate securities are owned by millions of persons, many of whom own only a few shares. Without governmental regulation, investors may be misled, even by reliable brokers, and many may fall prey to unscrupulous promoters. Moreover, the absence of effective regulation invites the type of speculation that can damage the national economy.

The states have long had "blue-sky laws" —so named because they were designed to prevent the sale of worthless stocks, having no more value than the blue sky, to a gullible public. Today, in addition to antifraud statutes, most states require licenses of dealers, registration of securities, and disclosure of accurate information about securities offered to the public. However, the interstate character of corporate financing makes effective state control virtually impossible.

Federal Legislation. The stock-market crash of 1929 and subsequent disclosures led Congress to enact the Securities Act of 1933 and the Securities Exchange Act of 1934.

These laws are administered by the Securities and Exchange Commission, created in 1934 and composed of five members appointed for five-year terms.

The Securities Act is intended to protect the investor by providing him with accurate information about public offerings of new corporate securities. The law does not guarantee a profitable investment; it merely provides investors with accurate information before they take risks.

Corporations issuing securities which do not fall in an exempt category must file a registration statement with the Commission disclosing information needed to judge the merits of the securities. Issuers of securities must also furnish interested persons with a prospectus, or digest, of information given in the registration statement. Failure to meet requirements of the Commission closes the mails and channels of interstate commerce to the securities involved. Willful violations are punishable by criminal and civil penalties.

The Securities Exchange Act regulates organized national security exchanges, the largest of which is the New York Stock Exchange. Unless exempted by the Securities and Exchange Commission, exchanges, members of exchanges, brokers, and dealers must register or forego the use of mails and channels of interstate commerce. Registrants must keep accounts prescribed by the Commission and make periodic reports. Rules are prescribed and unfair competitive practices are forbidden. As a further means of controlling speculation, the Federal Reserve Board is empowered to fix margins, i.e., the amount of credit that may be extended to buyers of securities.

Trusts and Other Monopolies. Capitalist theory assumes that private business should and will compete freely. However, experience demonstrates that there is a difference between theory and practice, as evidenced by the formation of monopolies. Experience also teaches that many businessmen will resort to the use of unfair competitive practices to gain their ends. Control of business competition was left to the states until near the end of the last century, but the emergence of large-scale trusts in oil, sugar, meat, steel, and other basic industries led Congress to intervene in 1890 with the Sherman Antitrust Act.

Basic Federal Legislation. The Sherman Act is still the basic Federal law dealing with monopolies. It forbids . . .

every contract, combination, in the form of trust or otherwise, or conspiracy in the restraint of trade or commerce among the several states, or with foreign nations. . . .

Every person who shall monopolize, or attempt to monopolize, or combine or conspire with any person or persons, to monopolize any part of the trade or commerce among the several states, or with foreign nations, shall be deemed guilty of a misdemeanor. . . .

The Clayton Act of 1914 supplements these provisions by outlawing three specific evils: (1) price discrimination, (2) exclusive agreements, and (3) interlocking directorates and purchases of stock among competitors. As amended by the Robinson-Patman Act of 1936, also illegal are transactions by which chain stores and other large purchasers receive discounts, rebates, and other concessions that do not correctly reflect legitimate costs. Such concessions are banned where the effect is to diminish competition and injure competitors. The Celler Antimerger Act of 1950 went further and forbade the acquisition of *assets* of rival companies where the effect is to lessen competition substantially or tend to create a monopoly.

The third basic Federal law regulating business competition, the Federal Trade Commission Act of 1914, condemns "unfair methods of competition" in interstate and foreign commerce. The Wheeler-Lea amendment of 1938 forbids "unfair or deceptive acts or practices" and strengthens enforcement powers of the Federal Trade Commission. The amendment also outlaws false advertising of foods, drugs, cosmetics, and curative or corrective devices. Amendments of 1960 strengthened enforcement of the Clayton Act by making procedures identical with those of the Federal Trade Commission Act.

Exemptions. After a bitter contest, labor unions became immune by Supreme Court decision in 1941 (*United States v. Hutcheson*, 312 U.S. 219), except when they combine with nonlabor forces in activities that restrain trade. The Webb-Pomerene Export Trade Act of 1918 permits cooperative arrangements among persons engaged in export trade if agreements are registered with the Federal Trade Commission. The Agricultural Exemption Act of 1922 and later amendments permit farmers, planters, dairymen, and others engaged in agriculture to form marketing associations without risking prosecution.

The National Industrial Recovery Act of 1933, now invalid, and later the Guffey Coal Acts, now expired, exempted industries for which codes had been formed, on the theory that the public was sufficiently protected by code and public authorities. The Miller-Tydings amendment to the Sherman Act, passed in 1937, legalized resale-price-maintenance agreements between manufacturers and distributors in states where such agreements are not illegal so far as local commerce is concerned. The Reed-Bulwinkle Act of 1948 permitted common carriers of particular classes to agree among themselves on rates and charges, provided approval of the Interstate Commerce Commission is first obtained. The McGuire Act of 1952 made resale-price agreements enforceable on both nonsigners and signers of contracts.

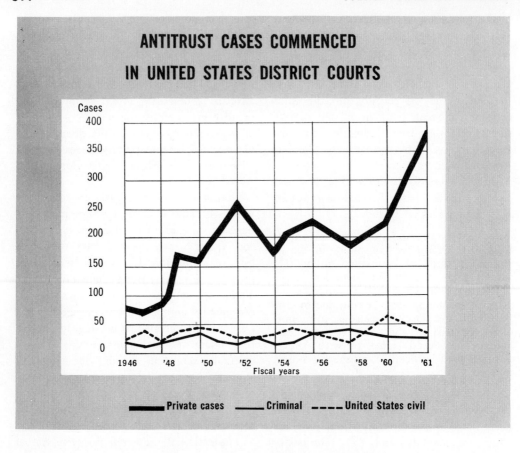

ANTITRUST CASES COMMENCED
IN UNITED STATES DISTRICT COURTS

(Administrative Office of the United States Courts.)

Lastly, most common carriers engaged in interstate and foreign commerce may combine with approval of the Federal regulatory commissions having jurisdiction over them. This extensive list of exceptions makes apparent the fact that the nation follows an inconsistent policy as far as the maintenance of competition is concerned.

The Rule of Reason. Provisions from the Sherman Act quoted above appear to ban "every" contract, combination, etc., and to apply to "every" person. The courts at first interpreted these provisions quite literally but later shifted their position. The turning point came in the famous oil and tobacco decisions of 1911 (*United States v. Standard Oil Co. of N.J.*, 221 U.S. 1; *United States*

v. American Tobacco Co., 221 U.S. 106). Although the Federal government was upheld in both of the cases, Chief Justice White announced that the Court had followed the common-law rule of reason in reaching its decisions. Not every contract leading to monopoly was forbidden, said he, but only those which were "unreasonably restrictive of competitive conditions." This approach, said the Chief Justice, made it necessary to look into the character of the agreement under suspicion, consider surrounding circumstances, and investigate the intent of those forming the agreement.

A storm of protest followed this announcement, but the new rule stuck. Henceforth, the standards were vague and variable,

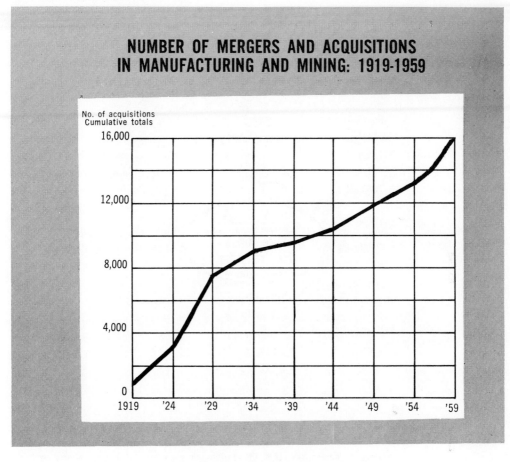

NUMBER OF MERGERS AND ACQUISITIONS IN MANUFACTURING AND MINING: 1919-1959

No. of acquisitions
Cumulative totals

(From U.S. Federal Trade Commission.)

so no one could be certain what conduct was outlawed. Enforcement became a cat-and-mouse game between prosecutors on the one hand and huge business concerns on the other, with both gambling on the probable attitude of the courts.

From 1911 until the late 1930s the courts were rather harsh with pools, trade-association activities, labor unions, and other loose arrangements, but, paradoxically, they were lenient with close combinations such as trusts, holding companies, and mergers.

The Problem of Mergers. Business mergers have been generally looked upon as reasonable combinations even though competitors were "gobbled up." The Clayton

Act outlawed interlocking directorates and intercompany acquisitions of stock but did not forbid the acquisition of assets other than share capital. In consequence, mergers went on apace. One outcome was oligopoly, the domination by a few giant corporations of many lines of industry. The Federal Trade Commission and other investigators repeatedly urged remedial legislation. In 1950 Congress responded favorably by passing the Celler Antimerger Act, amending the Clayton Act. The new provision banned intercompany mergers that substantially lessen competition and tend to create a monopoly.

The Federal Trade Commission and De-

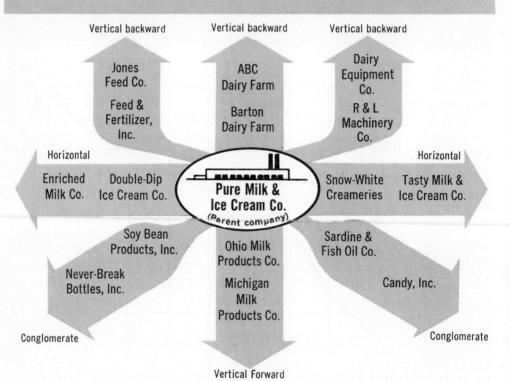

TYPES OF BUSINESS ACQUISITIONS

Vertical backward   Vertical backward   Vertical backward

Jones
Feed Co.

ABC
Dairy Farm

Dairy
Equipment
Co.

Feed &
Fertilizer,
Inc.

Barton
Dairy Farm

R & L
Machinery
Co.

Horizontal   Horizontal

Enriched   Double-Dip   **Pure Milk &**   Snow-White   Tasty Milk &
Milk Co.   Ice Cream Co.   **Ice Cream Co.**   Creameries   Ice Cream Co.
                                        (Parent company)

Soy Bean
Products, Inc.

Ohio Milk
Products Co.

Sardine &
Fish Oil Co.

Never-Break
Bottles, Inc.

Michigan
Milk
Products Co.

Candy, Inc.

Conglomerate   Conglomerate

Vertical Forward

This hypothetical milk and ice cream company has grown big by acquiring a
variety of enterprises. [For illustrations of variations of these patterns, see U.S.
Federal Trade Commission, *Report . . . on the Merger Movement* (1948).]

partment of Justice have great difficulty deciding when mergers "substantially lessen" competition or "tend to create a monopoly." Pillsbury Mills, for example, was prevented from acquiring two other milling companies and thereby raising its share of the market for flour-base mixes from 16 to 45 per cent. Objection was also made to a proposed merger of Bethlehem Steel and Youngstown Sheet and Tube, which would have made the combine's share of the industry's capacity one-fifth of the total.

On the other hand, enforcement agencies did not object to the merger of certain automobile manufacturers: Kaiser and Willys, Nash and Hudson, Packard and Studebaker. In these instances enforcement agencies apparently acted on the assumption that combination of minor companies would strengthen, rather than weaken, competition with the three major producers: General Motors, Chrysler, and Ford. The vagueness and uncertainty of the Celler amendment continues to provoke demand for more stringent control by critics of the merger movement.

Controversy over Basing Points. Another arrangement considered reasonable by the courts for a long time was the system of basing points. If a single basing point was established, all competitors agreed to sell anywhere for a base price plus transportation from a designated point. Thus, in the case of steel, Pittsburgh was made a basing point, and all steel companies, regardless of location, agreed to charge all purchasers of steel a base price plus rail transportation from Pittsburgh.

For example, if a steel mill at Gary, Indiana, sold steel to a firm located in Wheeling, West Virginia, it might charge a base price of $40 a ton plus $10 for transportation, or a total of $50. The $10 for transportation might not actually be the cost of shipping from Gary but, rather, it would be the cost of shipping from the basing point at Pittsburgh. In this case, the Gary firm would absorb the difference ("phantom freight") between what was actually paid for freight and the cheaper cost of shipping from Pittsburgh. By doing so, and taking a smaller net return, both the Gary firm and Pittsburgh firms would sell at identical prices in West Virginia. In some industries, multiple basing points were used. These differed chiefly in that instead of one city, two or more were used by competitors setting identical prices.

This system is strongly defended by many people. Although conceding that the system diminishes price competition, defenders insist both the industry and the nation benefit from price stabilization, and nonprice competition is actually increased. Buyers of steel near Pittsburgh, for example, would normally buy in that area, but if they can buy Gary steel for the same delivered price they might choose to do so. This, it is argued, increases competition for markets even though price is not a factor.

Critics contend this is not the result and that the system leads to economic waste. The Federal Trade Commission ordered the steel industry to discontinue its "Pittsburgh plus" system in 1924, whereupon the in-

dustry substituted the multiple-basing-point system. Finally, in 1945, the Supreme Court agreed with the Trade Commission that single-basing-point systems were illegal (*Corn Products Co. v. FTC*, 324 U.S. 726; *FTC v. Staley Co.*, 324 U.S. 746), and in the famous Cement Institute case decided in 1948 (*FTC v. Cement Inst.*, 333 U.S. 683) the Supreme Court declared multiple basing points illegal also. In the meantime, powerful pressures have developed to get Congress and the President to legalize these price-fixing schemes.

Resale Price Maintenance. If left to their own devices, many producers of nationally advertised brand-name products prefer to dictate prices at which retail dealers must sell their products. One method of dictation is to require dealers to sign contracts in which they promise to maintain prescribed prices and make themselves liable for damage suits if they fail to live up to their agreements. But for producers to require written contracts of all dealers is bothersome and costly and often provokes ill will.

To make the matter simpler, business groups have prevailed upon nearly all states to pass fair trade acts. These legalize resale price maintenance, and most of them say that, when one or a few contracts have gone into effect within a particular state, they become binding upon all dealers handling the products, including both signers and nonsigners. The Supreme Court upheld their application to nonsigners in 1937 (*Old Dearborn Distrib. Co. v. Seagrams-Distillers Corp.*, 229 U.S. 183).

But state laws could validate resale-price-maintenance contracts only for intrastate commerce, and the Supreme Court had outlawed them in interstate commerce as early as 1911 (*Dr. Miles Medical Co. v. Parks & Songs*, 220 U.S. 373). Encouraged by their success with state legislatures, and by the fact that resale price maintenance had been legalized in interstate commerce for the short period when the NRA codes were in effect, business groups turned pressure on Congress to amend the Sherman Act. Their efforts succeeded in 1937 with passage of the Miller-Tydings amendment as a rider to the District of Columbia Appropriations Act. President Roosevelt signed the bill but castigated those who had resorted to the rider tactic to legalize price fixing. The amendment provides that resale-price-maintenance agreements are legal as far as interstate commerce is concerned where states give similar approval for intrastate commerce.

The Miller-Tydings amendment said nothing about nonsigners. The Supreme Court had upheld the constitutionality of nonsigner provisions in state laws, but doubt remained over whether they were enforceable as applied to interstate commerce. The issue was decided by the Supreme Court in 1950 (*Schwegmann Bros. v. Calvert Corp.*, 341 U.S. 384). In this case, Louisiana had a fair trade act applying to both signers and nonsigners of contracts. Calvert Corporation sold liquor in Louisiana and had succeeded in getting over a hundred dealers to sign price-maintenance agreements. Schwegmann Brothers, retailers in New Orleans, refused to sign and sold Calvert's products at cut-rate prices. Since interstate commerce was involved, Calvert invoked the Miller-Tydings amendment and brought suit to compel cooperation. The Supreme Court, however, ruled against Calvert, saying Congress had not intended the Federal amendment to coerce nonsigners.

Pandemonium immediately broke loose all over the country, with Macy's of New York taking the lead in price cutting. Pressure groups again trained their guns on Congress to get legislation legalizing coercion of nonsigners. The desired measure (the McGuire Act) passed Congress in June, 1952. Now if a state permits the co-ercion of signers and nonsigners, Federal law is the same for interstate commerce within that state. Despite statutory support, price setters are often deterred by dealer hostility and consumer resistance. Also, they find it difficult to enforce compliance without involving dealers in a conspiracy as defined by the antitrust laws [see, for example, *United States v. Parke, Davis, & Co.*, 362 U.S. 29 (1960)]. Faced with these obstacles, some large manufacturers have stopped trying to maintain resale prices.

Enforcement of Antitrust Laws. Violations are dealt with in three ways: criminal prosecutions, civil actions initiated by the government or injured competitors, and administrative adjudication by the Federal Trade Commission.

Civil proceedings that have been brought by the government have produced injunctions, consent decrees wherein offenders admit their guilt and agree to mend their ways, and business dissolutions. Injured competitors have won a few damage suits, while the Trade Commission has stopped certain practices by stipulations and by cease-and-desist orders. Government cases are handled in the courts by the Department of Justice, which has a special Antitrust Division for the purpose. The Trade Commission helps make investigations.

Enforcement has been one of the most difficult assignments imaginable. In the Cement Institute case, referred to above, ten years elapsed between the date of the complaint and the Supreme Court decision. Seventy-four corporations were involved in the complaint; it took a trial examiner three years to hear the evidence, consisting of 49,000 pages of oral testimony, and 50,000 pages of exhibits; findings and conclusions of the Trade Commission covered 176 pages; and legal briefs with appendixes contained more than 4,000 pages. Such an investigation requires a large staff with ample funds, a clear legal mandate, and a reservoir of determination that is too often dissipated by time and political processes. A combination of all these has seldom, if ever, existed. In spite of the difficulties, recent years (excepting the war period) have been characterized by growing concern over mounting bigness and declining competition, accompanied by more vigorous enforcement of the antitrust laws. Two developments in 1961 attest the trend: jail sentences for several top officials of large electrical manufacturing companies and a Supreme Court decision upholding an order to E. I. du Pont de Nemours & Co. to divest itself of stock holdings in General Motors valued at billions of dollars [*United States v. du Pont Co.*, 366 U.S. 316 (1961)].

Proposed Remedies. Countless public and private studies of the antitrust laws have been made. A few of the reforms frequently suggested are: (1) Provide enforcement agencies with funds and personnel adequate for the task; (2) clarify what is legal and what is not; (3) stiffen criminal penalties for violations; (4) outlaw basing points by statute; (5) repeal laws permitting resale price maintenance; (6) restrict the scope of patent monopolies; (7) proscribe more activities of trade unions; (8) require trade associations to register; and (9) permit greater use of trade-practice conferences by the Federal Trade Commission to establish rules of business conduct.

Proposed Alternatives. Numerous alternatives have also been proposed. Some suggest that the Federal government license corporations and require them to conform to a stated code of conduct to obtain and keep the license. It has also been suggested that basic industries like steel, automobile manufacturing, and aluminum be declared public utilities and brought under continuous regulation by a Federal commission. Also proposed is a pattern whereby the government and basic industries would undertake joint ownership and control. Some advocate outright government ownership and operation either of all industries or of certain basic industries like steel, oil, coal, etc., somewhat along lines followed in Great Britain and Scandinavian countries.

Some suggest a return to codes, like those used in NRA days. Others suggest expanded use of cooperatives. One occasionally hears that Congress should establish a national economic council composed of representatives of business, labor, and consumers to devise whatever controls may be needed. In other countries these have usually been advisory to parliaments, although ways might be devised whereby they could participate directly in making public law. Many, of course, profess a yearning for *laissez faire* with little or no attempts to restrain business by antitrust laws or other government action.

Unfair Trade Practices. Among other duties, the Federal Trade Commission is charged with responsibility for preventing "unfair methods of competition" and "unfair or deceptive acts or practices" in interstate and foreign commerce. Unfair methods are all attempts to achieve business gains through wrongdoing or undue restraints that injure competitors or the public. The list of methods declared to be illegal, unfair, and deceptive is long. The methods fall into two classes: those that are opposed to good morals and those that tend unduly to hinder competition and foster trade restraints and monopoly. Examples are listed on page 520.

Federal Trade Commission Procedure. The procedure evolved for handling trade-practice violations has received wide acclaim and provided a model for several regulatory agencies more recently established. The function of the Commission is primarily remedial, not punitive. It has

● ● ● ● ● ● ● ● ● ●OPPOSED TO GOOD MORALS ● ● ● ● ● ● ● ● ● ●

1. False and misleading advertising (e.g., selling coffee under the trade name of "Rico Cafe" when it was not a Puerto Rican coffee or blend thereof; claiming "the grape cure" would relieve or cure cancer; stating a metal device "makes hard water feel, taste, and act softer").

2. Misbranding commodities.

3. Falsely representing foreign products as having been made in the United States.

4. Selling rebuilt, secondhand, renovated, or old products as new.

5. Falsely claiming that the customer is being offered an opportunity to make purchases under unusually favorable conditions.

6. Using deceptive containers.

7. Simulating competitors' trade names, labels, counter displays, or catalogues (e.g., using the name "Westinghouse Union Corporation" in simulation of "Westinghouse Electric Corporation"; or using the title "Who's Who and Why" to benefit from the well-known "Who's Who in America").

8. Giving products misleading names (e.g., calling a coat made of rabbit fur "Baltic fox" or "beaver") or falsely suggesting that a product has been approved by some well-known medical, dental, or other professional organization.

9. Using merchandising schemes based on lot or chance, or on a pretended contest of skill.

● ● ● ● ● ● ● ● ● ● FOSTER MONOPOLY ● ● ● ● ● ● ● ● ● ●

1. Conspiring to maintain uniform selling prices through the use of a patent-licensing system.

2. Trade boycotts or combinations of traders to prevent certain wholesale and retail dealers from procuring goods at the same terms accorded to the boycotters or conspirators.

3. Buying up supplies for the purpose of hampering competitors.

4. Using concealed subsidiaries, ostensibly independent, to obtain competitive businesses.

5. Combinations or agreements of competitors to fix, enhance, or depress prices, maintain prices, bring about substantial uniformity in prices, or divide territory or business, to cut off or interfere with competitors' source of supply, or to close markets to competitors.

6. Intimidation or coercion of a producer or distributor to cause him to organize, join, or contribute to, or to prevent him from organizing, joining, or contributing to, a producers' cooperative association or other association, advertising agency, or publisher.

7. Harassing competitors (e.g., by bribing or hiring their employees, by threatening needless and vexatious lawsuits, and by making false and misleading statements about competitors and their products).

8. Selling below cost or giving products without charge to hinder or suppress competition.

9. Coercing and forcing uneconomic and monopolistic reciprocal dealing.

power to impose penalties, but its principal object is to protect the public.

Violations are suspected either as a result of complaints that reach the Commission or through investigations conducted by the Commission's own staff. When a questionable practice is followed by several in the same trade, a trade-practice conference is called; at it, codes of fair competition, wherein members of the trade agree to discontinue the obnoxious practice, may be agreed upon. Where particular individuals are involved, a thorough investigation is made; following that, the case may be dismissed for lack of merit or the suspected

party may enter into what is known as a "stipulation," whereby the charges are admitted and the respondent stipulates that he will mend his ways.

Unless the charges are withdrawn or a stipulation is issued, the Commission makes a formal complaint. Thereupon, a hearing is held before a trial examiner, testimony is taken, and a report is made to the Commission by the examiner. If the Commission finds the respondent guilty, it issues a "cease and desist" order. Appeals may be taken to the United States courts of appeals, but the Commission's findings of facts, if supported by sufficient evidence, are final. Commission orders become effective in sixty days unless appealed. If appealed and sustained, an injunction is issued. If this is violated, a fine may be imposed and collected by the Commission in a civil suit. As noted on page 513, 1960 amendments applied identical enforcement procedures to violations of the Clayton Act.

Food and Drug Regulation. The struggle for adequate food and drug regulation has been a long and difficult one. Federal intervention began in 1906. Credit for this achievement is due in part to Upton Sinclair's sensational novel *The Jungle,* which dramatized the unspeakable conditions under which meats were handled in Chicago packing plants. Today, three Federal agencies are concerned: the Food and Drug Administration (Health, Education, and Welfare), the Federal Trade Commission, and the Meat Inspection Branch of the Agricultural Research Service (Agriculture).

The Food and Drug Administration prevents the misbranding or adulteration of foods, drugs, devices, and cosmetics entering interstate and foreign commerce; the Federal Trade Commission prevents false and misleading advertising of the same products; the Meat Inspection Branch enforces laws on inspection and purity of meats.

Foods are considered adulterated if they contain poisonous, deleterious, putrid, or decomposed substances; if they are produced under unsanitary conditions, or from diseased animals; if their containers are composed of substances injurious to health; or if any substance has been mixed or packed with them to reduce their quality or strength. Similar standards exist for drugs, cosmetics, and devices. Misbranding is carefully defined, and labeling, packaging, etc., must be informative and honest. Food additives were brought under control in 1958. Color is controlled, whether it is added to food, drugs, or cosmetics.

Stricter controls were imposed on drugs in 1962 following disclosures that thalidomide produced deformities in unborn babies. Drug manufacturers must register and permit plant inspections. New drugs must be filed with the Food and Drug Administration, tested, and proven effective before being offered for commercial sale. Clinically tested drugs not yet approved for sale must be safe for patients.

Fixing standards is a lengthy process which requires consultations and hearings with scientific and business interests, for the results may cause drastic changes in methods and costs of production and distribution. Orders often have far-reaching economic consequences.

FOR FURTHER READING

Adams, Walter, and Horace M. Gray: *Monopoly in America: The Government as Promoter* (New York: Macmillan, 1955).

Bailey, Stephen K.: *Congress Makes a Law: The Story behind the Employment Act of 1946* (New York: Columbia University Press, 1949).

Bain, Joe S.: *Barriers to New Competition: Their Character and Consequences in Manufacturing Industries* (Cambridge, Mass.: Harvard University Press, 1956).

Berle, Adolph A., and Gardner C. Means: *The Modern Corporation and Private Property* (New York: Macmillan, 1933).

Bidwell, P. W.: *What the Tariff Means to American Industries* (New York: Harper, 1956).

Corwin, Edward S.: *The Commerce Power v. States Rights* (Princeton, N.J.: Princeton University Press, 1936).

Currie, Brainerd (ed.): "The Patent System," *Law and Contemporary Problems,* vol. 12, no. 4 (Durham, N.C.: Duke University School of Law, 1947).

Edwards, Corwin D.: *The Price Discrimination Law: A Review of Experience* (Washington, D.C.: Brookings, 1959).

——: *Big Business and the Policy of Competition* (Cleveland, Ohio: Western Reserve University Press, 1956).

Fisher, Waldo E., and Charles M. James: *Minimum Price Fixing in the Bituminous Coal Industry* (Princeton, N.J.: Princeton University Press, 1955).

Hickman, Bert G.: *Growth and Stability of the Postwar Economy* (Washington, D.C.: Brookings, 1960).

Humphrey, Don D.: *American Imports* (New York: Twentieth Century Fund, 1955).

Kallenbach, Joseph E.: *Federal Cooperation with the States under the Commerce Clause* (Ann Arbor, Mich.: University of Michigan Press, 1955).

Kaplan, A. D. A.: *Big Enterprise in a Competitive System* (Washington, D.C.: Brookings, 1954).

Kariel, Henry S.: *The Decline of American Pluralism* (Palo Alto, Calif.: Stanford University Press, 1961).

Kaysen, Carl, and Donald F. Turner: *Antitrust Policy: An Economic and Legal Analysis* (Cambridge, Mass.: Harvard University Press, 1959).

Kreps, Clifton H., Jr., and J. M. Kreps (eds.): *Aid, Trade and Tariffs* (New York: H. W. Wilson, 1953).

Latham, Earl: *The Group Basis of Politics: A Study of Basing-point Legislation* (Ithaca, N.Y.: Cornell University Press, 1952).

Lynch, David: *The Concentration of Economic Power* (New York: Columbia University Press, 1946).

Mason, Edward S. (ed.): *The Corporation in Modern Society* (Cambridge, Mass.: Harvard University Press, 1960).

——: *Economic Concentration and the Monopoly Problem* (Cambridge, Mass.: Harvard University Press, 1957).

Redford, Emmette S.: *Administration of National Economic Control* (New York: Macmillan, 1952).

Schattschneider, Elmer E.: *Politics, Pressures and the Tariff* (New York: Farrar, Straus, 1942).

Stocking, George W.: *Basing Point Pricing and Regional Development: A Case Study of the Iron and Steel Industry* (Chapel Hill, N.C.: University of North Carolina Press, 1954).

—— and Myron W. Watkins: *Monopoly and Free Enterprise* (New York: Twentieth Century Fund, 1951).

Thorelli, Hans B.: *The Federal Antitrust Policy* (Baltimore: Johns Hopkins Press, 1955).

U.S. Attorney General: *Report of the . . . National Committee to Study the Antitrust Laws* (Washington, D.C.: Government Printing Office, 1955).

U.S. Congress, Temporary National Economic Committee: *Investigation of Concentration of Economic Power, Final Report and Recommendations*, S. Doc. 35, 77th Cong., 1st Sess., pursuant to Pub. Res. 113 (1941). The hearings were published in 31 parts; there were 43 monographs.

U.S. Council of Economic Advisers: *The Economic Report of the President* (annual).

U.S. House of Representatives, Select Committee on Small Business, *Congress and the Monopoly Problem; 56 Years of Anti-trust Development*, 1900–1956, 84th Cong., 2d Sess. (1956).

U.S. Senate, Committee on the Judiciary: *Proposals for Improving the Patent System*, S. Doc. 21, 85th Cong., 1st Sess. (1957).

——: *The Patent System and the Modern Economy*, S. Doc. 22, 85th Cong., 1st Sess. (1957).

Vaughan, Floyd L.: *The United States Patent System: Legal and Economic Conflicts in American Patent History* (Norman, Okla.: University of Oklahoma Press, 1956).

Warren, Charles: *Bankruptcy in United States History* (Cambridge, Mass.: Harvard University Press, 1935).

Whitnah, Donald R.: *A History of the United States Weather Bureau* (Urbana, Ill.: University of Illinois Press, 1960).

Wilkinson, Joe R.: *Politics and Trade Policy* (Washington, D.C.: Public Affairs Press, 1960).

Wilson, Stephen: *Food and Drug Regulation* (Washington, D.C.: Public Affairs Press, 1942).

REVIEW QUESTIONS

1. Compare recent interpretations of the commerce power with earlier decisions relating to fish and game, insurance, manufacturing, mining, and amusements.

2. Under what circumstances may a state regulate interstate and foreign commerce?

3. List as many important aids or services as you can think of which the Federal government provides primarily for the benefit of general business.

4. Give illustrations of Federal planning activities.

5. Defend and criticize reciprocal-tariff legislation and agreements.

6. Defend and criticize greater American participation in such organizations as GATT for the purpose of eliminating barriers to international trade.

7. Summarize provisions of our patent, copyright, trademark, and bankruptcy legislation. What changes would you recommend?

8. Review the manner and extent to which the Federal and state governments regulate securities and exchanges.

9. Identify (*a*) basing point, (*b*) resale price maintenance, (*c*) interlocking directorate, (*d*) merger, (*e*) oligopoly, and (*f*) unfair trade practice.

10. Summarize provisions of the major antitrust laws enacted by the Federal government.

11. What functions are performed by the Federal Trade Commission? Review the procedure by which the Commission handles an alleged unfair trade practice.

12. Summarize proposals to strengthen Federal regulation of monopoly.

13. Summarize provisions of Federal laws regulating the purity of foods, drugs, and cosmetics.

Chapter Twenty-Six

Public-utility Regulation

Regulation of business is one of the most distinctive activities of American government. No other nation has attempted to control economic activities and business operations through independent commissions on a comparable scale. No other country has placed as much confidence in governmental regulation as opposed to public ownership and management. . . . Despite prolonged political agitation over regulation and the controversial nature of such activity, regulation by commission has not been able to match the ingenuity, imagination, and inventiveness of American business. It has been conventional in method, passive in attitude, and orthodox in the evolution of policy.

MARVER H. BERNSTEIN[1]

Societies—whether primitive or highly complex—have always subjected some businesses to more control than others. Today, many people prefer that such vital businesses as public utilities be privately owned but stringently regulated by government. Others prefer outright governmental ownership and management. This chapter reviews American experience with both systems.

[1] *Regulating Business by Independent Commission* (Princeton, N.J.: Princeton University Press, 1955), p. 296.

THE PATTERN OF CONTROL

Public Utility Defined. A public utility is a business that renders an indispensable service to the community under certain circumstances requiring continuous public regulation. Monopoly is usually present and desirable in such enterprises. Examples are railways, waterways, ferries and bridges, busses, wharves, grain elevators, and suppliers of gas, water and telephone service, and electricity. Each is sufficiently clothed with public interest to warrant regulation that would be unconstitutional if applied to the usual, competitive enterprise.

The classification of an enterprise as a public utility depends upon a number of factors, including whether monopoly is present, geographic location, character of service, immediacy of patron's needs, the amount of capital invested, the scale of operations, and whether it has been considered a public enterprise in times past. Congress and state legislatures make the classification, subject to court approval.

The list of businesses considered to be utilities tends to become longer. The Supreme Court has ruled, however, that ice plants, theater-ticket brokerages, gasoline stations, and meat-packing industries may not be regulated as utilities. Milk and coal productive and distributive agencies lack some of the essentials usually possessed by utilities, but they have a sufficient public interest to permit fixing their prices.

Types of Carriers. Materials that have to do with public utilities often make reference to three types of carriers: common, contract, and self-servers. Common carriers hold out their facilities and service for "common" or general use to all comers. Contract carriers perform services only under terms of specific contracts with customers. A bus, for example, that operates regularly over a given route, stopping for all who wish to ride, would be a common carrier; but one that had to be chartered every time an individual or group wished to use it would be a contract carrier. Self-servers provide service for themselves. Large industries, for example, may own their own railroads, power plants, water systems, or busses. Legislation recognizes differences between these three types of carriers.

Federal and State Spheres. Most utilities are local enterprises and so remain under control of state and local governments. Public-utility commissions exist in the District of Columbia and all the states. It is not easy to decide where their jurisdiction begins and ends. Federal and state activities touch and overlap at many points. In general, business activities that are primarily of local concern, such as the location of grade crossings, the laying of water pipes under city streets, taxi service, and retail sales to ultimate consumers, are regulated by the states, but even such matters as these occasionally become of national concern.

The Regulatory Agencies. All of the regulatory agencies shown in the chart below are independent of the ten executive departments. The Federal Maritime Board (now Commission) was under the Department of Commerce for certain administrative purposes but its successor is independent. The Commission is a regulatory body while the Maritime Administration, which remains in the Department of Commerce, is the administrative arm in this field.

Responsibility is divided similarly in the field of civil aeronautics. Until 1958, a Civil Aeronautics Board and a Civil Aeronautics Administration, which together were known as the Civil Aeronautics Authority, functioned through the Department of Commerce. New legislation made the Board independent, abolished the Administration and Authority, and authorized a new independent administrative Federal Aviation Agency. The present division of duties is explained on page 530.

Members of the regulatory commissions are appointed by the President with Senate approval. Following a Hoover Commission recommendation, the chairman of some of the agencies serves as chief administrator. Terms of office are staggered; most of the agencies are bipartisan. Unlike the state utility commissions, each of which usually regulates a wide variety of utilities,

FEDERAL UTILITY REGULATORY COMMISSIONS

AGENCY	DATE ESTABLISHED	NUMBER OF MEMBERS	TERMS, YEARS	UTILITY JURISDICTION
Interstate Commerce Commission	1887	11	7	Railroads; motor carriers; shipping by coastal, intercoastal, and inland waters; pipelines (except natural gas and water); express companies; carriers using rail-and-water routes; sleeping-car companies
Federal Power Commission	1920	5	5	Water-power sites, electric power, natural-gas pipelines
Securities and Exchange Commission	1934	5	5	Electric and natural-gas holding companies
Federal Communications Commission	1934	7	7	Radio, television, telephone, telegraph
Civil Aeronautics Board	1938	5	6	Civil air commerce
Federal Maritime Commission	1961	5	5	Shipping in foreign commerce

each Federal commission devotes its attention to some particular functional group.

Despite their wide use, regulatory commissions are strongly attacked. Critics say that their independent position makes them "headless," responsibility is dispersed in multi-membered bodies, leadership is unimaginative, procedures are slow and cumbersome, excessive rules and regulations stifle business enterprise, members and staffs are often selected for political reasons, and decisions are often biased in favor of regulated parties in general or particular individuals and companies.

Public confidence in regulation by commission rises and falls with times and events. Some commissions were placed under executive departments, and most chairmen were given greater authority over management to improve administration. Recent disclosures showed that some commissioners yielded to improper influences and this caused codes of conduct to be reexamined. More drastic reforms appear unlikely in the near future.

The Scope of Regulation. As businesses affected with a public interest, utilities are subject to continuous public regulation. Before a new service can be started, approval of the utility commission is required. A company wishing to establish a new bus line, for example, must file an application. The regulatory body may authorize an unlimited number of competitors to enter the field, but more often it allows limited monopoly. Thus, in the case of a railroad application, the Interstate Commerce Commission would probably forbid a competitor to enter the business unless it could be clearly demonstrated that another railroad was necessary to serve the public interest. Authorizations usually take the form of "certificates of public convenience and necessity," licenses, or permits.

Regulation also usually involves control over security issues and intercorporate relationships. Once operations have started, utilities are generally required to submit budgets, reports, and proposed rate schedules. In doing so they must follow a uniform system of accounts, to ensure that each entry has the same meaning to all. The regulatory body may approve the schedule of rates proposed or, after investigation and hearing, insist upon changes. Rate control requires property valuations that usually involve extensive engineering surveys.

Regulatory bodies must also hear and adjust complaints, see that proper safety practices are followed, and otherwise make sure that laws and regulations are obeyed. Approval must be obtained if utilities wish to extend their facilities or services, go out of business, or sell or abandon facilities.

The Problem of Rate Making. Rate fixing is the most difficult and controversial aspect of utility regulation. As a rule the law requires that rates be fixed high enough to earn a "fair return" on the property rendering a public service. What is a fair return is usually easy to determine; the law is generally satisfied if a utility is permitted to earn in the vicinity of 5 to 8 per cent. Far more difficult is the task of ascertaining the value of the property, or of finding the "rate base." If the figure is set too low, investors will lose money, in which case the matter will probably be taken to court, where it could be held that property had been taken without due process of law. On the other hand, if it is set too high, the consumer suffers.

Theories of Valuation. Effective control of utility rates depends upon the theories and methods followed in determining the rate base. Several methods may be followed: one might take the original cost (sometimes referred to as "historical cost") and subtract depreciation; or one might settle for reproduction cost, less depreciation; or one might take the value of outstanding securities; or, finally, one might follow the prudent-investment theory, whereby an attempt is made to ascertain what a prudent investor would have invested in the enterprise. The latter method places great weight upon prudent original cost. There are difficulties with each of these methods. Economic implications are appalling, and these have been aggravated by court decisions.

Smyth v. Ames. The basic case on the subject was for many years *Smyth v. Ames*, decided in 1898 (169 U.S. 466). The dispute arose from rates fixed for a number of railroads by the Board of Transportation for Nebraska. The state board had based its rates chiefly upon the reproduction-cost-less-depreciation theory, but the railroads involved had been constructed in a period of high prices, hence contended for a valuation based upon original cost less depreciation. The Supreme Court, however, refused to accept either theory to the exclusion of the other. It said that in determining fair value a number of factors must be considered, including

. . . the original cost of construction, the amount expended in permanent improvements, the amount and market value of its bonds and stocks, the present as compared with the original cost of construction, the probable earning capacity of the property under particular rates prescribed by statutes, and the sum required to meet operating expenses. . . .

Such a procedure entails extensive investigation, with resultant costly delays. An even greater difficulty is that the Court said nothing about how much weight to give to each of the factors mentioned. It sometimes happens that an original-cost estimate differs from an estimate of the same company by the reproduction-cost-less-depreciation method by millions of dollars. In such an event, what figure represents fair value? Faced with this situation, members of regulatory bodies follow their own predilections, try to guess what the courts might say, and end with a compromise.

Prudent-investment Theory Approved. The Supreme Court has modified its historic position in a series of cases dealing with the fixing of gas rates under the Natural Gas Act [see especially, *FPC v. Hope Natural Gas Co.*, 320 U.S. 591 (1943)]. Now the Federal regulatory commissions are not bound to a single formula or combination of formulas. Prudent investment is the guide, with emphasis on original cost.

Beyond this the approach is a pragmatic one. If rates established by a commission enable a company to operate successfully, attract capital, and compensate investors for the risks assumed, the courts may sustain them regardless of the theory or formula followed by the regulatory body. This new rule gives those responsible for regulation a freer hand in determining value and fixing rates than in the past. A number of states have modified their utility laws to permit commissions similar latitude, but several still prescribe the fair-value formula.

TRANSPORTATION

National Policy. The most recent declaration of national transportation policy was made by Congress in the Transportation Act of 1940. This stated the goal to be one of developing, coordinating, and preserving a national transportation system by water, highway, rail, and other means adequate to meet the needs of commerce, the postal service, and national defense.

As means to this end, Federal regulating bodies are directed to do the following: (1) regulate all modes of transportation so as to preserve the inherent advantages of each; (2) promote safe, adequate, economical, and efficient service; (3) foster sound economic conditions in transportation and among carriers of all types; (4) encourage reasonable charges without unjust discriminations, undue preferences or advantages, or unfair or destructive competitive practices; (5) cooperate with the several states; and (6) encourage fair wages and equitable working conditions.

Transport Problems. Transport policy has been a subject of endless debate, investigation, and study. Crucial questions raised by such inquiries are these: (1) Should Federal responsibility for regulation remain scattered among several agencies or be concentrated in one, perhaps a Department of Transportation? (2) Because of the interstate character of transportation, should state public-utility commissions be permitted to regulate as extensively as they do now? (3) Are private transportation companies overregulated? Would better service at lower rates result from allowing greater private initiative and discretion? (4) How much competition between carriers of a particular type (railroads, for example) is in the public interest? Between carriers of different types (like railroads and motor carriers)? (5) Should transportation services receive governmental subsidy or preference? (6) How can transportation services of all types be best integrated and coordinated? (7) Should transportation services be owned and managed by Federal, state, and local governments in peacetime? In times of war or national emergency?

Recommendations. A Cabinet Committee appointed by President Eisenhower reported in 1955 that "within the short span of one generation this country has witnessed a transportation revolution." No longer, it said, do rail and water carriers have a monopoly; to these traditional forms have been added transportation by passenger car, truck, airplane, and pipeline.

"The net result," continued the Committee, "is a competitive system of transportation that for all practical purposes has eliminated the monopoly element which characterized this segment of our economy some thirty years ago." The Committee then made two general recommendations: (1) adjustment of regulatory programs and policies to allow "greater freedom for competitive experimentation" and (2) restoration and maintenance of a progressive and financially strong system of common carriers in all types of transportation.

A Department of Commerce Study Staff, reporting in 1960, agreed that transport policies should be based on "free enterprise" principles, but it was less sure that competition could be relied upon as a primary regulator. It concluded "that competition remains sufficiently imperfect in a number of situations still to require considerable safeguards." Deregulation was desirable, the Study Staff thought, but it "should proceed gradually over an extended period of years." The Staff also urged better planning under Federal leadership with special attention to the needs and problems of urban areas.

President Kennedy, in 1962, recommended that Congress "consider the nation's transportation network as an articulated and closely linked system rather than an uncoordinated set of independent entities." He particularly urged that the Federal role be reduced for intercity transportation but increased for urban transit. More specifically, he recommended: greater freedom for carriers to reduce rates; tax relief; a clearer policy on mergers; encouragement of through routes and joint rates; experimental rates and services; rate adjustments to encourage carriage by "piggyback" and related techniques; depriving domestic trunk air carriers of operating subsidies; greater flexibility for the transportation of mail by motor common carriers; uniform state registration laws for interstate motor carriers; repealing the law which prevents a railroad from handling cargo it owns; and heavy sub-

sidies for urban mass transit.

Such recommendations always provoke criticism, especially from those who fear that relaxing controls will invite the abuses long associated with transport management.

Railroads. Railroads are subject to statutes, rules, and regulations, many of which date back to the 1800s. For purposes of regulation, railroads are divided into three classes on the basis of total operating revenues. Class I roads, whose annual operating revenues exceed 1 billion dollars, do the bulk of the business. The ICC also divides railroads geographically into districts and regions. The Commission constantly applies the utility controls described above with respect to rates, accounts, security issues, etc. It also considers questions of basic policy and makes recommendations to the President and Congress.

Moreover, the ICC applies and enforces many special laws and regulations. These forbid railroads to transport products made by enterprises they own or control; own or control any competing water carrier unless the ICC finds such ownership is in the public interest and will not reduce competition; use price discrimination and other unauthorized practices; and charge more for short hauls than long hauls over the same route. They require the installation and use of safety devices and uniform bills of lading and prescribe methods for transporting explosives and other dangerous articles.

The ICC also investigates railway accidents, inspects locomotives, checks and limits the hours of service for employees, fixes time zones, and determines fair and reasonable rates for mail transportation by rail and by urban and interurban electric carriers. The enforcement of legislation that regulates labor-management relations and dispute settlement is the responsibility, not of the ICC, but of other agencies.

Motor Carriers. State regulation of motor carriers began in Pennsylvania in 1914.

Other states soon followed and had the field to themselves until 1935, when, after a long and bitter fight, Congress passed the Motor Carrier Act.

In addition to the carriers themselves, transportation brokers and forwarders are of considerable importance to the industry. Brokers are intermediaries who bring users and carriers together. Forwarders are persons, other than carriers, who assemble or consolidate property for reshipment by rail, water, or other carriers. The ICC has authority to regulate these in about the same manner as railroads.

Water Carriers. Water navigation is an ancient industry that has been of vital concern to the American people since they first sailed to these shores. Billions of dollars have been spent on river and harbor development, dredging canals, and subsidizing shipping lines and ship construction. Meanwhile, Federal, state, and local governments have imposed regulations covering practically every phase of water commerce. Water carriers may be divided into four groups: inland, coastal, intercoastal, and foreign.

The Customs Bureau (Treasury) licenses vessels. The Coast Guard (Treasury) enforces safety regulations. The ICC regulates the economic aspects of inland, coastal, and intercoastal carriers. The Federal Maritime Commission is responsible for foreign shipping; the Maritime Administration builds and manages government-owned merchant vessels and administers a subsidy system.

Shipping Abroad. Foreign shippers are freer of governmental controls than is shipping of other types. Since the Maritime Commission does not have control over entry into service, except for ships owned or subsidized by the United States, jungle law prevails among competitors. The Commission lacks power to regulate security issues

and intercorporate relationships. Its authority over rates is limited to seeing that tariffs are filed and are nondiscriminatory, although in the case of charges for wharfage and dockage the Commission may prescribe minimums. The Commission has authority to designate and approve routes; hear and adjust complaints; handle matters pertaining to wages, hours, and working conditions of seamen; and prescribe accounts and reports.

An interesting feature of the regulation of foreign shipping is the degree of cooperation permitted among shipping companies. Those who wish to may join a "conference," which resembles a domestic trade association. The conference pools information and makes agreements regarding such matters as rates, allotment of traffic, pooling of earnings, and methods of meeting competition from nonconference members. If filed with the Maritime Commission and approved, agreements are immune from antitrust laws.

Air Commerce. Most aircraft are engaged in, or affect, interstate and foreign commerce. Thus Federal law is comprehensive; the states have been chiefly concerned with safety, liability, and airports.

Basic Federal legislation was adopted in 1938. Responsibility is divided between the Civil Aeronautics Board and the Federal Aviation Agency. The Board authorizes entry into service, assigns routes, fixes rates and charges, settles complaints over service and competitive practices, and establishes the probable cause of accidents. The Agency makes safety rules, licenses pilots, aircraft, and airports, subsidizes airport construction, builds and operates navigation facilities owned by the Federal government, regulates the use of air space to avoid collisions, and promotes air commerce.

Pipelines. Pipelines are used in the United States chiefly for carrying crude petroleum, gasoline, and natural gas. In rich petroleum centers the earth may be honeycombed with pipes. In the Pittsburgh area pipes crisscross and parallel one another in a most confusing manner.

The Second World War saw rapid expansion and renovation of petroleum pipelines. The most important and dramatic project was the construction of the "Big Inch"—a twenty-four-inch line from east Texas to Philadelphia and New York, the longest and largest pipeline ever installed for transporting petroleum. Oil began moving in it in February, 1943. The line, built by the Federal government, was sold to private enterprise after the war.

Federal control of interstate pipelines began in 1906, when lines were few in number and controlled by one company, Standard Oil. At the time, the ICC was given jurisdiction over all except those for transporting water and gas. The latter were brought under control in 1938, along with other aspects of the industry, but responsibility for administration was placed in the Federal Power Commission. The Holding Company Act of 1935, discussed below, applied to natural-gas companies, many of which own or control interstate pipelines.

The ICC regulates pipelines transporting crude oil, gasoline, and miscellaneous products; the Federal Power Commission deals with those conveying natural gas; and the Securities and Exchange Commission regulates holding-company structures for companies engaged in the production, transportation, and wholesale distribution of natural gas. Pipeline companies are regulated to about the same extent as other common carriers.

ELECTRIC POWER, GAS, AND COMMUNICATIONS

Electric Power. Advent of the power age brought recognition that both Federal and state regulation were necessary. A desire to conserve resources occasioned the first Federal legislation, in 1920. The Water Power Act of that year created the Federal Power Commission to survey the water resources of the nation and pass on applications to establish hydroelectric projects along navigable waters and on public lands. Since then, the commission's powers over interstate operations of electric utilities have been extended; in 1938, to jurisdiction over the interstate transportation of natural gas.

Electric service divides into three parts: generation, transmission, and distribution. Generation involves the manufacture of electric energy; transmission, its transportation from the generating station to the locality in which it is consumed; and distribution, the retail sale and delivery of energy to customers.

Generation and distribution are usually highly localized. They are, therefore, controlled largely by state and local governments. The Federal government is primarily concerned with transmission because this is frequently interstate in character.

Licenses to operate hydroelectric power projects on navigable waters and public lands run for as long as fifty years, but the law reserves the right of the Federal or state government to reacquire the site at any time. The Commission lacks authority to require a showing of public necessity and convenience before electric companies extend their lines across state boundaries, because this would be a matter reserved to the states. The Commission can, however, encourage voluntary interconnections, and even compel them under special circumstances. It also regulates transmission of electric energy to points outside the United States.

The Commission has complete jurisdiction over long-term security issues made by electric utilities under its jurisdiction. It may scrutinize short-term issues of companies organized and operating in states that do not regulate security issues. Service must be adequate, but in this sphere the Commission must cooperate with state agencies. Rates (if wholesale, always interstate; otherwise, state utility commissions have jurisdiction) must be just, reasonable, nondiscriminatory, and nonpreferential. Uniform accounts must be kept and reports filed. Mergers and interlocking relationships must also be approved.

Natural Gas. Very little *manufactured* gas is transported across state lines, so its regulation is left to the states. With *natural* gas the story is different; most of it originates in a few states and is transported, principally by pipelines, to others. Several states attempted regulation, but in a series of decisions the Supreme Court ruled that neither the state in which the gas was produced nor the one in which it was distributed to the ultimate consumer could regulate the interstate rate. These decisions, together with disclosures made in the Federal Trade Commission's sweeping survey of holding-company structures and practices, led Congress to pass the Natural Gas Act of 1938.

Controversy over Independents. Controls exercised by the Federal Power Commission over natural gas are much the same as for interstate electric utilities. Much controversy has arisen in recent years over whether the Commission had authority to regulate independent producers, or "gatherers," of natural gas. The Commission began regulating independent producers in 1942; its action was upheld by the Supreme Court in 1947 (*Interstate Natural Gas Co. v. FPC,* 331 U.S. 682) and again in 1954 (*Phillips Petroleum Co. v. Wisconsin,* 346 U.S. 896, 934). Congress has twice passed bills freeing the industry from Federal regulation; the first was vetoed by President Truman in 1950, and the second by President Eisen-

hower in 1955, chiefly because of unethical tactics used by lobbyists for the legislation.

Federal Control Limited. Controversy has also raged over Federal Power Commission regulation of the *distribution* and *sale* of gas shipped in foreign and interstate commerce. Congress amended the Natural Gas Act in 1954 (the so-called Hinshaw amendment) to provide that a company distributing gas shall not be subject to Federal regulation when the company receives gas at or within a state boundary for use solely within a state. Federal regulation continues up to the state boundary. The new provision applies only in states having commissions that regulate the sales and services of natural-gas companies.

Electric and Gas Holding Companies. A holding company is one organized to "hold" securities of operating companies, supposedly for the purpose of profiting from their reinvestment. Illegal at common law, they were permitted by state statutes, beginning with New Jersey in 1888. By this device, securities of competing companies were brought together under single management, often with monopolistic results.

This was especially true in the electric-power field. By 1932, thirteen holding companies controlled 75 per cent of the entire privately owned electric-utility industry, with more than 40 per cent concentrated in the hands of the three largest: United Corporation, Electric Bond and Share Company, and Insull. Even these three systems were not totally independent. A report in January, 1935, by the Federal Trade Commission disclosed a maze of unsound financial structures, widespread lobbying and propaganda activities intended to disparage government regulation and ownership, and extensive intercompany dealings which saddled operating companies, and ultimately consumers, with exorbitant expenditures.

The Holding Company Act. After a sensational legislative contest, the Holding Company Act was approved on August 26, 1935. This law applied only to electric and gas holding companies involved in interstate and foreign commerce. Some of its provisions are these: (1) Electric and gas holding companies must register with the Securities and Exchange Commission. (2) Commission approval is necessary before new securities are issued or an interest is acquired in any other utility. (3) All holding companies above the second must be abolished, unless excepted by the Commission, and their operations confined to integrated regional systems. (4) Intercompany loans and interlocking directorates with banking institutions were made illegal. (5) Holding companies might not, without Commission approval, sell goods, perform services, or undertake construction work for any associated utility. (6) Holding companies might not contribute to political parties or candidates for public office, nor lobby without disclosing the object sought and expenditures. (7) Holding companies must use uniform accounts, make reports to the Commission, and otherwise follow rules and regulations established by the Commission.

Results of the "Death Sentence." During the legislative battle over the Holding Company Act, much was heard about the so-called "death sentence" provision contained in Section 11 and referred to under item 3 in the list above. This section makes it the duty of the Securities and Exchange Commission to simplify holding-company structures by confining them to integrated regional systems and eliminating all beyond the second degree. There could be an operating company, a holding company controlling the operating company, and a holding company controlling the first holding company, but no more. Moreover, properties had to be regrouped and confined to regional systems.

Thus, holding companies that were pyramided several stories high and spread all over the United States had to be completely revamped. A large number of separate electric, gas, and nonutility operating properties were removed from control by registered holding companies. Many complicated holding-company structures were dissolved or liquidated. Contrary to the dire predictions of those who opposed the law, the industry appears to be in a healthier condition than ever before.

Communications. Prior to 1934, radio and wire communications were partially regulated by several agencies chiefly the ICC, the Postmaster General, and the Federal Radio Commission. The laws were consolidated and broadened in the Communications Act of 1934, and their administration was placed in the hands of one agency, the Federal Communications Commission (FCC). Its jurisdiction extends to all interstate and foreign radio, television, telephone, telegraph, and cable services. Congress charged the Commission with ensuring "a rapid, efficient, nation-wide and world-wide wire and radio communication service with adequate facilities at reasonable charges."

Wire Services. Ownership and management of wire services rest largely in the hands of three companies: the Bell Telephone Company, Western Union, and International Telephone and Telegraph Corporation. Controls are about the same as for other common carriers.

Radio and Television. Broadcasting is regulated exclusively by the Federal government. The first legislation on the subject was in 1910, when Congress enacted a statute requiring steam vessels to have radio equipment for emergency use. A second act, passed in 1912, authorized the

Secretary of Commerce to require and issue licenses for radio transmission, but it failed to make clear his authority to determine frequency, power, hours of transmission, etc.

In 1926 a Chicago station "jumped" its frequency bands and broadcast at hours not permitted by its license. When the station was prosecuted, a United States district court [*United States v. Zenith Radio Co.,* 12 F 2d 614 (1926)] held that the Secretary was without power to enforce his order. Anarchy reigned on the ether, compelling Congress to provide more effective control. The Federal Radio Act of 1927 was the result. This created the Federal Radio Commission and laid down basic rules for radio (and television). The Radio Commission was abolished in 1934, and its functions were transferred to the FCC.

Control by Licensing. Broadcasting systems, or chains of stations, are exempt from regulation, but individual stations must obtain licenses to operate legally. Licenses may run for three years or for shorter periods if the Commission desires a more frequent review of station performance.

Criteria established to guide the Commission in issuing licenses are very general: licenses may not be issued to aliens, foreign governments, or foreign interests; the Commission must be convinced that the public interest and convenience will be served; and licenses must be distributed among the states so as to "provide a fair, efficient, and equitable distribution" of service.

The Communications Act states that broadcasting stations are not common carriers. Regulation is less extensive, therefore, than for other types of utilities. Nor does the Commission have authority to censor programs.

Deceptive contests were outlawed in 1960 to end rigged quiz shows. The same law struck a blow at "payola" by requiring that an advance announcement be made of any agreement with an employee to accept a valuable consideration as a condition for making a broadcast. The Commission's enforcement powers were also strengthened. It may revoke or suspend licenses or issue cease-and-desist orders for willful and continued disobedience. Such orders are enforceable by the courts.

The rules of the Commission require all standard stations to keep daily logs of programs and incidents. No profanity or obscenity is permitted. All legally qualified candidates for particular political offices must be given equal opportunity to present their views. A record must be kept of all requests for political broadcasts. Typical of other regulations are those requiring the filing of tariffs and charges with the Commission, approval of extensions, testing and inspection of stations, and clear identification of stations and sponsors of broadcasts.

FEDERAL POWER PROJECTS

Federal electric-power operations have reached large proportions. As of 1958, they produced over 110 billion kilowatthours— about one-seventh of total national output.

Authority Plan versus Coordinated Development. Two general plans of development and administration have been followed. The valley-authority plan, illustrated by the TVA, empowers a single, independent, Federal corporation to operate within a region. Under this arrangement, a valley authority, headed by a small board, is responsible for planning, building, and operating public works for the conservation and utilization of the water resources of the valley, subject to the statutes defining its authority and to a continuing control by the President and Congress. Its budget must be approved annually. Other Federal agencies continue to operate within the valley, but their programs are affected by the studies and plans of the valley authority The construction and operation of dams,

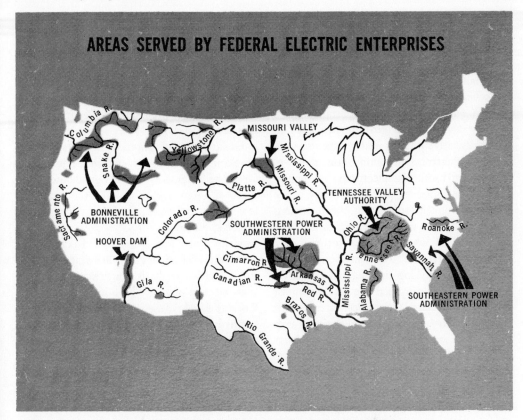

AREAS SERVED BY FEDERAL ELECTRIC ENTERPRISES

The Federal government has assumed heavy responsibilities for power development along our river systems. Note the concentration of projects in the Far West, Mountain states, Southwest, and South, and the paucity of projects in the Middle West, North Atlantic, and New England states.

hydro power plants, and reservoirs become the responsibility of the valley authority. The other plan, illustrated by Missouri Valley activities, calls for coordinated action by several Federal agencies, including the Corps of Engineers, the Bureau of Reclamation, and the Soil Conservation Service.

The valley-authority plan clearly focuses responsibility, permits unified planning and operation, and eliminates duplication, overlapping, and rivalry among the agencies; it should also lessen the possibility of extravagance and waste. For these reasons many have urged a Missouri Valley Authority, Columbia Valley Authority, Southwestern Authority, and perhaps others.

Critics are numerous. The rival agencies insist that they are more competent and efficient than one newly established. Electric-power utilities fear that a valley authority, following the example of the TVA, may drive down power rates and promote public ownership. Many state officials, and even some congressmen, fear a single authority of such enormous powers. A single authority is likely to do much of its own construction and otherwise lessen opportunities for contractors, realtors, and other private interests. These, and other reasons, evoke sympathy from state-rights advocates, champions of free enterprise, and opponents of such Federal projects generally.

Current opposition strategy is to (1) block further expansion, (2) restrict existing Federal operations to generation of electric power at dam sites, leaving transmission and marketing to private enterprise, and (3) when new river-valley projects are inevitable, obtain partnership arrangements whereby the Federal government handles the comparatively unprofitable aspects, such as flood control, irrigation, and defense, while more profitable electric-power operations are assigned to private utilities.

Thus far, opposition has been strong enough to limit valley authorities to one, the TVA, but what does the future hold? The first Hoover Commission, while strongly condemning interagency jealously and overlapping, opposed the establishment of additional valley authorities. It expressed preference for agency consolidation, with direct lines of responsibility running from central headquarters in Washington to the various river-valley projects.

The second Hoover Commission also found lack of central planning, coordination, and cooperation among conservation agencies. The solution proposed, however, was limited to recommending a Water Resources Board located in the Executive Office of the President. The Board would recommend broad policies and "devise methods of coordination of plans and actions of the agencies both at the Washington level and in the field."

One Agency versus Many. Should the river-valley projects be developed and administered separately or be brought together under a single agency? A single agency, it is contended, would be better able to plan, coordinate, and utilize technical services, manpower, and equipment. It could standardize accounting, personnel, and other administrative services. It would give the President and Congress one agency for reports and recommendations instead of the many

that exist now. The first Hoover Commission gave considerable thought to this problem and recommended that, except for the TVA, valley developments should proceed under a single agency, to be called the Water Development and Use Service, and located in a greatly changed Department of Interior.

Department of Interior Projects. Power developments dot the nation. The Army Corps of Engineers has designed and built most of them and continues to operate a few of the hydroelectric plants. Most of the projects, outside the TVA region, are the responsibility of the Bureau of Reclamation (Interior). Most of them are scattered and small, with emphasis on irrigation rather than electric power. Those in the Colorado, Columbia, Arkansas, and Missouri river basins have assumed huge proportions. They are integrated, multiple-purpose, regional projects combining irrigation, electric power, conservation, flood control, and sometimes navigation features.

On the Colorado, the power plants at Hoover and Grand Valley dams are leased for operation to the City of Los Angeles and the Southern California Edison Company. In the Columbia basin, power generated at Bonneville, Grand Coulee, and other dams is marketed by the Bonneville Administration, a subsidiary of the Bureau of Reclamation. In the Arkansas basin, power generated at Dennison, Norfolk, and other dams is marketed by the Southwestern Power Administration, while the Southeastern Power Administration performs a similar function for the Southeastern states outside TVA territory.

In the Missouri Valley, where developments have proceeded slowly because of interagency rivalry, time-consuming consultations with representatives of the various states, and shortages of materials and appropriations, power is marketed by Bureau of

Reclamation representatives. The Bureau sells most of its power wholesale, giving preference to Federal, state, and municipal bodies and farm cooperatives. On the whole, electric rates have been promotional, i.e., low enough to encourage high consumption.

The Tennessee Valley Authority (TVA). The TVA stems from operations begun during the First World War. At that time the government started building Wilson Dam at Muscle Shoals, Alabama, to provide power to transform the rich deposits of nitrate found there. The war ended before plans were completed, leaving the government with a large investment on its hands.

Strong sentiment developed in favor of selling to private bidders, chief of whom was Henry Ford. These attempts were blocked by a small group of "insurgent" senators led by the late Senator George W. Norris, of Nebraska, who later became popularly known as the "father of TVA" and for whom one of the largest dams and the nearby community of Norris, Tennessee, is named. Senator Norris and others envisaged a large-scale regional program designed to bring about coordinated development and utilization of natural resources in the entire Tennessee River Valley.

The Authority is directed by a three-man board; members are appointed by the President with Senate concurrence for nine-year terms. A general manager supervises administration. The chief TVA office is at Knoxville, Tennessee, but activities are carried on in parts of seven states. Constitutionality rests upon the war and commerce powers and the authority granted Congress "to dispose of and make all needful rules and regulations respecting the territory or property belonging to the United States" [*Ashwander v. TVA*, 297 U.S. 288 (1936)].

Status. The TVA is organized as a government corporation outside the executive departments. It is not, however, in the same category as such regulatory agencies as the Interstate Commerce Commission and Federal Trade Commission, chiefly because it does not have quasi-legislative and judicial functions. Speaking of its administrative status in a case arising from the dismissal by President Roosevelt of the former chairman of the Authority, Dr. Arthur E. Morgan, on grounds of contumacy, the district court said [*Morgan v. TVA*, 115 F. 2d, 990 (1940)]:

It requires little to demonstrate that the Tennessee Valley Authority exercises predominantly an executive and administrative function. To it has been entrusted the carrying out of the dictates of the statute to construct dams, generate electricity, manage and develop government property. Many of these activities, prior to the setting up of the T.V.A., have rested with the several divisions of the executive branch of the government. . . . The Board does not sit in judgment upon private controversies, or controversies between private citizens and the government, and there is no judicial review of its decisions, except as it may sue or be sued. . . . It is not to be aligned with the Federal Trade Commission, the Interstate Commerce Commission, or other administrative bodies mainly exercising clearly quasi-legislative or quasi-judicial functions—it is predominantly an administrative arm of the executive department. . . .

Purposes and Functions. The purpose of TVA is to foster the "orderly and proper physical, economic, and social development" of the area. Its first concern must be navigation and flood control. Beyond that it is directed to produce nitrate and phosphate products for use as fertilizers in peacetime and munitions in wartime, operate electric plants for its own use and sale of the surplus, foster afforestation, soil conservation, and diversification of industry. A valuable by-product of its activities is improved recreational opportunities, which include some of the best fishing, camping, swimming, and boating to be found.

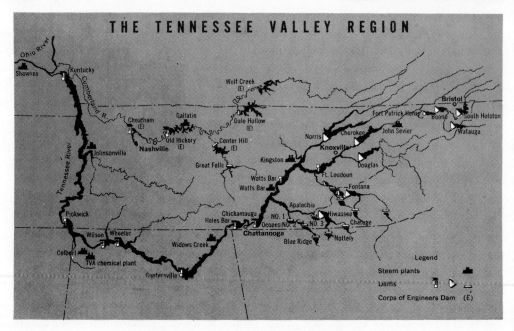

No Federal developmental project in this century has aroused more interest abroad and more controversy at home than the TVA. Its main installations and multipurpose nature are shown here. (From Tennessee Valley Authority.)

Ranging up and down the Tennessee River and its tributaries are numerous dams. Behind these are impounded enormous lakes of water forming a total water line longer than the salt-water boundary of the entire continental United States. Each of the main river dams has a spillway section, a navigation lock, and a powerhouse. The series of dams on the main river provides a navigation channel of 9-foot minimum depth for the 650-mile length of the Tennessee River. Tributary dams are essentially storage dams; none has a navigation lock, but most have, or will have when completed, hydroelectric generating plants.

The Authority directs the operation of Aluminum Company of America dams on tributaries of the Tennessee. TVA also operates a number of steam generating stations and chemical plants for manufacturing nitrate and phosphate products. Until 1959 TVA lacked authority to finance expansion with revenue bonds backed by future earnings. After long and bitter controversy the Authority was permitted to have as much as 750 million dollars in revenue bonds outstanding at any one time. Expansion was restricted, however, to 2,000 square miles or 2½ per cent of the territory served on July 1, 1957, whichever is the smaller.

Electric-power Operations. Most controversy has centered around the sale by the Authority of surplus electric power. The act of 1933 permits the sale either at the generating stations or elsewhere. It also requires that in selecting customers preference be given to cooperative associations and municipalities. The Authority has contracts for sale of power with municipalities, cooperatives, a number of privately owned utility companies, government plants, and large industrial concerns, the largest being the Aluminum Company of America.

All contracts with municipalities and cooperatives stipulate not only the rates to be paid TVA but also the rates at which the energy will be resold. In the beginning the latter were from 40 to 60 per cent lower than rates previously charged by competing private utilities, although now most private utilities in the area have lowered rates to nearer the TVA level.[1] The statistics in the figure on page 540 show comparisons.

Opposition and Criticism. Opposition to TVA came chiefly from private utilities, coal and railway interests, local groups who feared their land would be taken or other interests adversely affected, banking and financial groups, advocates of state rights, manufacturers of fertilizers, and others opposed to the principle of government ownership or increased Federal control. The entire controversy cannot be reviewed here; however, the question of the fairness of the rate policies of TVA and a few general conclusions will be discussed.

Two criticisms have been made of the rate policies of the Authority: (1) that its wholesale rates do not accurately reflect all the cost of generating power and (2) that the retail rates charged by cooperatives and municipalities, but dictated by TVA, do not reflect all proper costs. If either allegation is correct, clearly the users of TVA electricity enjoy a subsidy from the taxpayers of the entire country. At the same time, if either is true, TVA rates are an improper measurement ("yardstick") of what it should cost private utilities to render the same service.

Findings of Investigating Bodies. The nearest to an early impartial study is the report of an investigation made by a joint

[1] Basic TVA-prescribed residential rates are as follows: first 50 kilowatthours per month, 3 cents per kilowatthour; next 150 kilowatthours per month, 2 cents per kilowatthour; next 200 kilowatthours per month, 1 cent per kilowatthour; next 1,000 kilowatthours per month, 0.75 cent per kilowatthour; excess over 1,400 kilowatthours per month, 0.4 cent per kilowatthour. Although these are basic rates, a few municipalities charge less.

committee of Congress in 1939, but even this is not entirely convincing because members of the committee were divided sharply along partisan lines. In general, a majority of the committee approved the Authority's allocation of costs and rate policies.

The first Hoover Commission paid considerable attention to the TVA but made no judgment about merits of the rate controversy. Its task force did, however, make the following observations: (1) It noted, without confirmation or disapproval, that the General Accounting Office in 1949 had concluded that the TVA had allocated to power an insufficient share of the cost of multiple-use facilities. (2) On the basis of this allocation, "power revenues are well in excess of those required to repay over fifty-year periods the cost of facilities allocated to power, even when construction interest is charged at 3 per cent on the unpaid debt balance." (3) TVA made payments to states and counties in lieu of taxes at rates gradually decreasing from 10 per cent to 5 per cent (beginning July 1, 1948) of gross revenue from power sales. By comparison, Class A and B electric utilities paid in taxes for 1946 an average of 19 per cent of gross revenues.[2] (4) TVA annual reports were found to be comprehensive and to present clearly the financial condition of the Authority and the results of operation. The task force noted, again without comment, that the General Accounting Office had said in 1945 of TVA accounts that they "generally were well conceived, supervised, and maintained, and the Authority is to be commended as one of the

[2] This comparison may be unfair to the TVA, as one member of the first Hoover Commission pointed out. Private utilities paid in taxes 19 per cent of gross revenues derived from all phases of their electric activities, including generation, transmission, and distribution. TVA activities, however, are confined largely to generation, transmission, and disposal at wholesale. If taxes paid by distributors of TVA power and the value of free services are added to payments made by TVA in lieu of taxes, the comparison is decidedly favorable to the TVA.

AVERAGE ELECTRIC BILL FOR 100 KWHR RESIDENTIAL SERVICE IN LARGE CITIES*

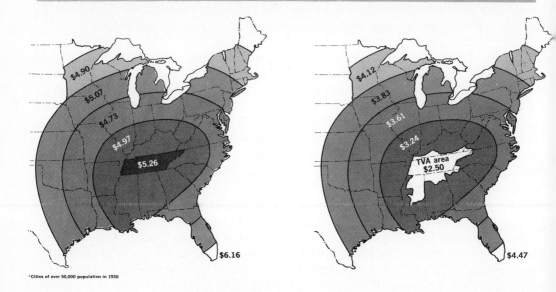

*Cities of over 50,000 population in 1930

Low TVA charges appear to have a substantial impact on electric rates in surrounding areas. The left-hand figure shows average rates in 1932, before TVA; the right-hand figure shows average rates in 1952. (Data from the Tennessee Valley Authority.)

foremost Government corporations in the use of accounting management, comparing quite favorably in this respect with well-managed private corporations."

The second Hoover Commission, and especially its task force, was sharply critical of TVA and Federal power enterprises generally, although there was vigorous dissent. The majority's chief complaints were that Federal power policies were unfair to private utilities, subsidized particular sections of the country at the expense of taxpayers of the entire nation, and sapped state and local governments of their authority.

More particularly, the majority claimed TVA paid less than a fair share of taxes, paid too little interest on capital investment, duplicated private transmission lines, and injured private utilities by giving preference when making sales to cooperatives and public bodies. The majority also objected to further TVA expansion, especially the building of steam plants.

General Observations. Regardless of the merits of the rate issue, several things about the Authority and its operations are clear. All informed neutral observers agree that the corporation has been well run from an administrative point of view; it has been ruthlessly correct in abstention from political favoritism; from an engineering point of view, dams and other structures were soundly and beautifully built; public ownership has been encouraged in the area; electric rates have been lowered throughout the area; low rates have greatly increased the use of electric energy, encouraged population growth, diversified industry, and attracted new capital; great strides have been made in controlling flood waters, conserving soil, and improving navigation; manufacture of nirates and phosphates has helped to lower fertilizer prices and otherwise encourage fertilizer use; and the Authority has been unusually considerate in its handling of personnel and the many social and cultural problems.

The St. Lawrence Waterway and Power Project. Both the United States and Canada have long been interested in developing the St. Lawrence River. Numerous studies were made and projects proposed. In consequence, a series of canals has been constructed, enabling ships, to sail from interior Great Lakes ports to Ogdensburg, New York, and Prescott, Ontario. Unfortunately, from the points mentioned to Montreal, on the Atlantic, a distance of 119 miles, the natural St. Lawrence channel was obstructed; otherwise there would have been an uninterrupted course for ocean-going vessels to travel from Duluth, Minnesota, to the Atlantic, and on to coastal and world ports. The St. Lawrence project contemplated removal of the impediments; construction of dams and locks; dredging canals; and the building of hydroelectric facilities.

All Presidents since Woodrow Wilson advocated completion of the project, and both political parties approved. Canada indicated willingness and completed the Welland Canal, an essential feature in the project. A treaty embodying the proposal was submitted to the Senate but rejected in 1934. In 1941 the proposal was embodied in an executive agreement between Canada and the United States which, although not requiring ratification by two-thirds of the Senate, did require the assent of both houses of Congress and the Canadian parliament. Handling the matter by executive agreement

rather than by treaty evoked considerable criticism. Stiff opposition was encountered chiefly from rail, power, and coal interests and Atlantic seaboard cities, which feared diminished use of their ports. Matters were brought to a head in 1952 after Canada announced her decision to proceed alone if necessary. Congress finally approved in 1954.

The law created a five-member St. Lawrence Seaway Development Corporation, with authority to issue bonds and develop the American share. The Secretary of Defense, through the Army Corp of Engineers, handles the construction phase. The Secretary of Commerce is responsible for general oversight and certain navigation features. The New York Power Authority, under license from the Federal Power Commission, produces electricity at two gigantic stations —St. Lawrence and Niagara—and markets it throughout the area. Power is sold to private utilities, but Federal law prescribes preference for states, municipalities, and nonprofit cooperatives. The Seaway was opened in 1958. Completion of the project will profoundly affect the economy of the region.

THE MERCHANT MARINE

An Essential but Dependent Enterprise. Shipping interests the world over have enjoyed either natural economic advantages or governmental subsidies, making it difficult for the American Merchant Marine to compete successfully. This has led to incessant agitation by powerful lobbies for preferred treatment, which Congress has given abundantly. Although Federal and state law has long dealt preferentially with American shipping interests—improving rivers and harbors, dredging canals, operating lighthouses and other auxiliary services, paying generously for carrying the mail, excluding foreign ships from coastal and intercoastal commerce, etc. —the floodgates were opened during the

First World War. Since then the Federal government has followed two principal courses: it has operated shipping lines of its own and it has built, bought, and sold ships and heavily subsidized both private shipping lines and ship-building industries.

Shipbuilding, Operation, and Sale. During the First World War the Shipping Board built many ships. Most of them were later scrapped or sold under generous terms to private shipping lines, but a few remained under Shipping Board operation. In 1936 the Maritime Commission displaced the Shipping Board and launched an expanded program. It built many ships, but by 1940 most of them had been sold.

When the Second World War began, the Federal government took over all private lines and stepped up its construction program. After the war, lines were restored to former owners, the building program was curtailed, and many government-owned ships were sold. Today, the Maritime Administration builds, reconditions, and remodels ships for sale or charter to private lines; charters war-built ships to private operators; maintains a reserve of ships essential to national defense; and maintains several standby, but inactive, shipyards for emergency use.

Subsidies for Shipbuilders. Since 1936, the Federal government has offered two principal types of subsidies: one to shipbuilders, called a "construction differential," and the other to ship operators, called an "operating differential."

The first works this way: at the request of a private citizen wishing to engage in foreign shipping, the Maritime Administration may contract to have a vessel built in an American shipyard, pay the construction cost, and then sell the vessel to the applicant for an amount equal to the estimated cost of constructing the vessel in a foreign shipyard. In no case may the differential be more than 55 per cent of the cost of the vessel. The applicant is required to post a bond to ensure good faith pending completion of the vessel and to pay part of the purchase price in cash and the remainder plus interest over a period of years.

Subsidies for Shippers. The operating differential works similarly. When a citizen operating a vessel used in an essential service, route, or line in foreign commerce (but not inland, coastal, or intercoastal) finds in his operating expenses items that place him at a competitive disadvantage with foreign operators, the Maritime Administration will pay him a differential high enough to equalize the cost of operation.

The Administration may also aid citizens in the construction of new vessels to be operated in the foreign, coastal, or intercoastal trade when no construction differential is granted. Here the Administration will pay the cost of approved national-defense features and lend a large part of the cost of the vessel, which is repayable, with interest, over a period of years. If the operator makes more than a 10 per cent profit over a ten-year period, the government may recapture half of the excess, up to the full amount of the subsidy paid.

From an economic point of view, Federal operation of shipping lines as described has never been profitable. The same must be said of most of the aids and subsidies. What the nation has paid for is not economical transportation but national defense, international prestige, gratification of patriotic impulses, and assistance to important industries. Whether results justify the expenditures remains a matter of opinion. Few will doubt, however, that ships and shipyards are essential in the event of war.

FOR FURTHER READING

Bernstein, Marver H.: *Regulating Business by Independent Commission* (Princeton, N.J.: Princeton University Press, 1955).

Clapp, Gordon R.: *The TVA* (Chicago: University of Chicago Press, 1955).

Cookenboo, Leslie, Jr.: *Crude Oil Pipe Lines and Competition in the Oil Industry* (Cambridge, Mass.: Harvard University Press, 1955).

Cushman, Robert E.: *The Independent Regulatory Commission* (New York: Oxford, 1941).

Dahir, James: *Region Building: Community Development Lessons from the Tennessee Valley* (New York: Harper, 1955).

Dearing, Charles L., and Wilfred Owen: *National Transportation Policy* (Washington, D.C.: Brookings, 1949).

Dimock, Marshall E.: *Government-operated Enterprises in the Panama Canal Zone* (Chicago: University of Chicago Press, 1934).

Eckstein, Otto: *Water-Resource Development: The Economics of Project Evaluation* (Cambridge, Mass.: Harvard University Press, 1958).

Eldridge, Seba, and Associates: *Development of Collective Enterprise* (Lawrence, Kans.: University of Kansas Press, 1943).

Goodrich, Carter: *Government Promotion of American Canals and Railroads, 1800–1890* (New York: Columbia University Press, 1960).

Hart, Henry C.: *The Dark Missouri* (Madison, Wis.: University of Wisconsin Press, 1957).

Hubbard, Preston J.: *Origins of the T.V.A.: The Muscle Shoals Controversy* (Nashville, Tenn.: Vanderbilt University Press, 1961).

Johnson, Arthur Menzies: *The Development of American Petroleum Pipelines: A Study in Private Enterprise and Public Policy, 1862–1906* (Ithaca, N.Y.: Cornell University Press, 1956).

Klapper, Joseph T.: *The Effects of Mass Communication* (New York: Free Press, 1960).

Krutilla, John V., and Otto Eckstein: *Multiple Purpose River Development in Applied Economic Analysis* (Baltimore: Johns Hopkins Press, 1958).

Lacy, Dan M.: *Freedom and Communications* (Urbana, Ill.: University of Illinois Press, 1961).

Latham, Earl: *The Politics of Railroad Coordination, 1933–1936* (Cambridge, Mass.: Harvard University Press, 1959).

Maass, Arthur, and others: *Design of Water-resource Systems* (Cambridge, Mass.: Harvard University Press, 1962).

McKinley, Charles: *Uncle Sam in the Pacific Northwest; Federal Management of Natural Resources in the Columbia River Valley* (Berkeley and Los Angeles, Calif.: University of California Press, 1952).

Martin, Roscoe C. (ed.): *TVA: The First Twenty Years* (University, Ala., and Knoxville, Tenn.: University of Alabama Press and University of Tennessee Press, 1956).

Nelson, James C.: *Railroad Transportation and Public Policy* (Washington, D.C.: Brookings, 1959).

Pritchett, C. Herman: *The Tennessee Valley Authority: A Study in Public Administration* (Chapel Hill, N.C.: The University of North Carolina Press, 1943).

Redford, Emmette S. (ed.): *Public Administration and Policy Formation: Studies in Oil, Gas, Banking, River Development, and Corporate Investigation* (Austin, Tex.: University of Texas Press, 1956).

Roberts, Elliot: *One River—Seven States: TVA-State Relations in the Development of the Tennessee River* (Knoxville, Tenn.: University of Tennessee, Bureau of Public Administration, 1955).

Selznick, Philip: *TVA and the Grass Roots* (Berkeley and Los Angeles, Calif.: University of California Press, 1949).

Sharfman, Isaiah L.: *The Interstate Commerce Commission* (New York: Commonwealth Fund, 5 vols., 1931–1937).

Strong, Benton J., and Leland Olds: *A Look into Hells Canyon* (Washington, D.C.: Public Affairs Press, 1956).

U.S. Bureau of the Budget: *An Inventory of Certain Commercial-Industrial Activities of the Government* (1956).

U.S. Commission on Organization of the Executive Branch of the Government (first Hoover Commission): see especially *Federal Business Enterprises; Task Force Report on Revolving Funds and Business Enterprises of the Government; Task Force Report on Natural Resources; Regulatory Commissions; Department of Interior* (all 1949).

U.S. Commission on Organization of the Executive Branch of the Government (second Hoover

Commission): *Business Enterprises* (1955).
————: *Task Force Report on Business Enter-prises* (1955).
————: *Transportation* (1955), and a subcommittee report by the same title (1955).
U.S. Congress, Joint Committee on the Investigation of TVA: *Investigation of the Tennessee Valley Authority Report* . . . S. Doc. 56, 76th Cong., 1st Sess., pursuant to Pub. Res. 83 (1939).
U.S. Federal Trade Commission: *Economic, Corporate, and Financial Phases of the Natural-gas-producing, Pipeline and Utility Industries,* S. Doc. 92, part 73A, 70th Cong., 1st Sess. (1936).

————: *Economic, Financial and Corporate Phases of Holding and Operating Companies of Electric and Gas Utilities,* S. Doc. 92, part 72B, 70th Cong., 1st Sess. (1936).
U.S. President's Water Resources Policy Commission: *The Report of* . . . 1950. Vol. 1, *A Water Policy for the American People;* vol. 2, *Ten Rivers in America's Future;* vol. 3, *Water Resources Law* (1950).
Willoughby, William R.: *The St. Lawrence Waterway: A Study in Politics and Diplomacy* (Madison, Wis.: University of Wisconsin Press, 1961).

REVIEW QUESTIONS

1. What is a public utility? How do public utilities differ from businesses of other types?

2. How is responsibility for utility regulation divided between the Federal and state governments?

3. How has substantive due process of law affected utility regulation in the United States?

4. As a practical matter, what difference does it make whether prudent investment or fair value is the formula upon which utility valuations are based?

5. Summarize the manner and extent to which the Federal government regulates (*a*) transportation; (*b*) electric power; (*c*) natural gas; (*d*) communications.

6. Defend and criticize Federal ownership and operation of proprietary enterprises of the types mentioned in this chapter.

7. What justification is there for continuing Federal ownership and operation of each of the enterprises discussed in this chapter?

8. Compare TVA and its operations with developments in other major river valleys.

9. Comparing the various river-valley developments, state the advantages and disadvantages of the TVA approach.

10. What justification is there for continuing Federal subsidies to private shipbuilders and shippers?

11. How successful has Federal operations of shipping lines been?

Chapter Twenty-Seven

Labor and
Welfare Services

*Everyone has the right to work, to free choice of
employment, to just and favorable conditions of work and
to protection against unemployment. . . .
Everyone has the right to form and join unions for
the protection of his interests. . . .
Everyone, as a member of society, has the right to social
security. . . .
The enjoyment of the highest attainable standard of
health is one of the fundamental rights of every human
being without distinction of race, religion, political belief,
economic or social condition. . . .
Everyone has the right to education. . . .* [1]

When American society was largely agrarian,
there was slight need for laws relating to
such things as wages, hours, industrial accidents, housing, and old-age pensions. The
destitute, mentally ill, and indigent aged
were left either to shift for themselves or

to be provided for by relatives or by religious
and philanthropic agencies. Local governments lent assistance through poor boards,
poorhouses, asylums; relations between capital and labor were governed by public
opinion and the common law.

The industrial revolution divorced millions from the land, made them dependent
upon machines, urbanized more than half
the population, and set in motion forces

[1] The first, second, third, and fifth quotations
above are from the Universal Declaration of Human Rights; the fourth is from the Constitution
of the World Health Organization.

DEPARTMENT OF LABOR

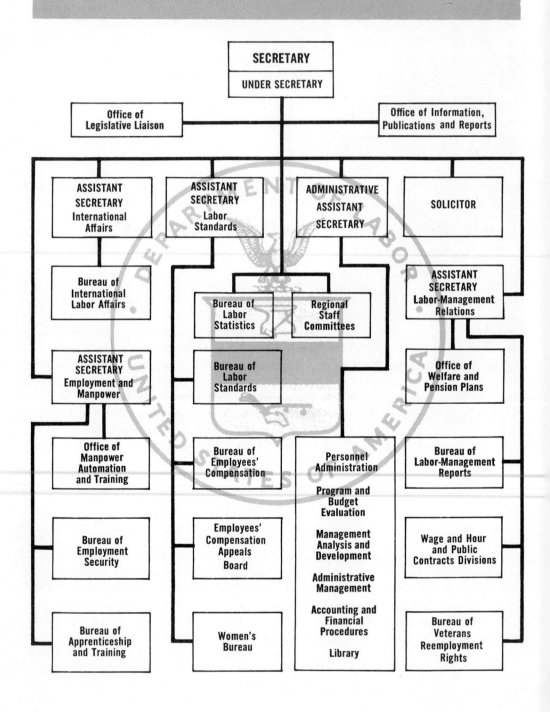

SECRETARY

UNDER SECRETARY

Office of Legislative Liaison

Office of Information, Publications and Reports

ASSISTANT SECRETARY International Affairs

ASSISTANT SECRETARY Labor Standards

ADMINISTRATIVE ASSISTANT SECRETARY

SOLICITOR

Bureau of International Labor Affairs

Bureau of Labor Statistics

Regional Staff Committees

ASSISTANT SECRETARY Labor-Management Relations

ASSISTANT SECRETARY Employment and Manpower

Bureau of Labor Standards

Office of Welfare and Pension Plans

Office of Manpower Automation and Training

Bureau of Employees' Compensation

Personnel Administration

Program and Budget Evaluation

Bureau of Labor-Management Reports

Bureau of Employment Security

Employees' Compensation Appeals Board

Management Analysis and Development

Administrative Management

Wage and Hour and Public Contracts Divisions

Bureau of Apprenticeship and Training

Women's Bureau

Accounting and Financial Procedures

Library

Bureau of Veterans Reemployment Rights

that necessitated governmental intervention. Little labor and welfare legislation was enacted prior to the Civil War; the bulk of it has come since 1910. Local and state governments first entered the field; Federal intervention came full tide with the depression years of the 1930s.

The story for education is similar. Private responsibility has yielded steadily to governmental since the 1830s. Local school boards were the first to share responsibility; later county, state, and Federal governments became partners, although hostility to Federal intervention has limited its role.

POWERS AND AGENCIES

Constitutional Basis for Federal Action. Congress has limited authority to provide for health, education, and the public welfare. The term "general welfare" appears twice in the Constitution: in the Preamble and in the tax clause. Neither of these grants power to Congress to do whatever it thinks necessary on behalf of the public welfare. The Preamble is merely a declaration of purpose, without enforceable provisions; the tax-clause reference merely provides that welfare is one of the objectives for which Congress may tax and spend.

Nevertheless, Congress has authorized countless welfare programs, basing most of them on the tax and commerce powers. The states, however, retain primary authority and responsibility for meeting public-welfare needs.

The Department of Labor. A Bureau of Labor was first established in 1884, under the Interior Department. Soon thereafter the Bureau was made independent as a Department of Labor, but without Cabinet rank. In 1903 it became a bureau in the Department of Commerce and Labor. Ten years later it was organized as a separate department with rank equal to that of the nine other departments.

Heading the Department is a Secretary who, like others of similar rank, is a member of the President's Cabinet and directly responsible to him. This office has the distinction of being the first of Cabinet rank ever held by a woman (Frances Perkins, of New York State, who held the office from March 4, 1933, until early in 1945). Usually the Secretary is a member of the President's party who is closely identified with the ranks of organized labor. Associated with him are the usual staff and line officers and employees.

Reflecting antagonism between management and workers, the Department has often been a storm center. Critics in Congress often charge that the Department is too prolabor and seek to transfer its functions. The Eightieth Congress (1947–1949) was especially harsh, transferring the Children's Bureau (except for its labor functions), the Conciliation Service, and the United States Employment Service.

The first Hoover Commission, reporting in 1949, deplored this dispersion of activities, saying the Department "is now overmanned at the top levels for the functions that remain. The Department has lost much of its significance. It should be given more essential work to do if it is to maintain a significance comparable to the other great executive departments."

Since this recommendation, the Department has been strengthened, chiefly by transferring to it the Bureau of Employment Security, the Bureau of Employees' Compensation, and the Employees' Compensation Appeals Board. The first-mentioned bureau handles employment services and unemployment insurance; the other two handle workmen's compensation for employees of the Federal government and others covered by Federal law.

DEPARTMENT OF HEALTH, EDUCATION, AND WELFARE

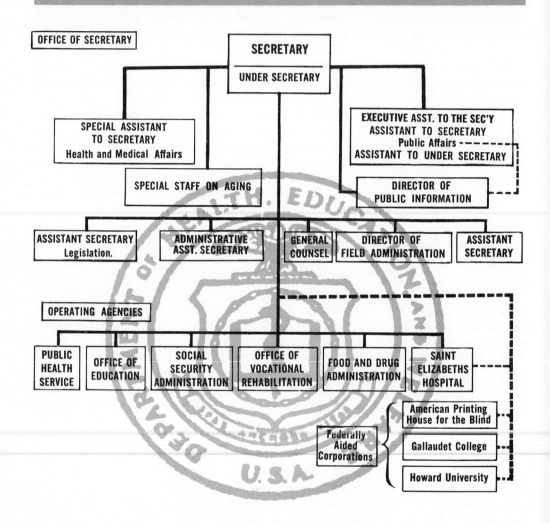

OFFICE OF SECRETARY

SECRETARY

UNDER SECRETARY

SPECIAL ASSISTANT
TO SECRETARY
Health and Medical Affairs

EXECUTIVE ASST. TO THE SEC'Y
ASSISTANT TO SECRETARY
Public Affairs
ASSISTANT TO UNDER SECRETARY

SPECIAL STAFF ON AGING

DIRECTOR OF
PUBLIC INFORMATION

ASSISTANT SECRETARY
Legislation,

ADMINISTRATIVE
ASST. SECRETARY

GENERAL
COUNSEL

DIRECTOR OF
FIELD ADMINISTRATION

ASSISTANT
SECRETARY

OPERATING AGENCIES

PUBLIC
HEALTH
SERVICE

OFFICE OF
EDUCATION

SOCIAL
SECURITY
ADMINISTRATION

OFFICE OF
VOCATIONAL
REHABILITATION

FOOD AND DRUG
ADMINISTRATION

SAINT
ELIZABETHS
HOSPITAL

American Printing
House for the Blind

Federally
Aided
Corporations

Gallaudet College

Howard University

The Department of Health, Education, and Welfare. Federal health, education, and welfare programs traditionally have been scattered among several agencies. Consolidation under a new department was recommended by the first Hoover Commission and by previous studies extending over three decades. President Franklin D. Roosevelt moved toward consolidation when, by executive order, he established the Federal Security Agency in 1939, but departmental status was not achieved until recommended by President Eisenhower in 1953. From the first day of its existence the new Department was one of the largest in terms of employees and appropriations. Its varied programs vitally affect practically every person in the nation. Departmental organization is shown on the accompanying chart.

FEDERAL SERVICES TO LABOR

Organizing and Bargaining Collectively. At common law all combinations, whether of entrepreneurs or workmen, were long considered illegal conspiracies in restraint of trade. Early in the nineteenth century, businessmen were granted the legal right to combine, but not until later did the courts look with favor on combinations of workingmen. The turning point came when the Supreme Court of.Massachusetts recognized the legality of labor unions in the famous case of *Commonwealth v. Hunt* [45 Mass. 111 (1842)]. Labor's right to organize is now legally recognized by all the states and the national government, but the conspiracy doctrine continues to influence the courts when they rule on strikes, boycotts, and certain other union activities.

Antitrust Laws Impeded Unions. Labor's efforts to gain recognition were slowed considerably by Federal antitrust laws, the first of which was the Sherman Antitrust Act of 1890. Whether this act was intended to apply to labor as well as business combines has been hotly disputed. The courts, however, declared the law applicable. Under this ruling, labor leaders and unions were frequently prosecuted and convicted.

The Clayton Act of 1914 brought some relief, but less than appeared on first sight. It declared that the labor of human beings was not a commodity or article of commerce. It also stated that nothing contained in the antitrust laws should be construed to forbid the existence and operation of labor, agricultural, or horticultural organizations instituted for the purpose of mutual help. The courts soon ruled that the words used did not completely remove labor unions and their activities from provisions of the Sherman Act, but did so only in so far as they were "lawfully carrying out their legitimate objects." As a result, labor unions were involved in more litigation after the act than before.

Some relief was provided by the Norris-La Guardia Act of 1932. This limited the circumstances under which Federal courts might restrain union activity by injunctions and forbade enforcement of pledges by workingmen not to affiliate with unions as a condition of employment ("yellow-dog contracts"). But not until 1941, in *United States v. Hutcheson* (312 U.S. 219), did the Supreme Court endorse the apparent intent of Congress to exempt unions from antitrust laws. In the case cited the Court modified previous decisions, saying unions were exempt unless they conspired or combined with nonunion parties to restrain trade. This rule prevails today. Although a boon to labor, this ruling has been of less importance than positive guaranties provided by Federal statutes, like those discussed below.

Railway Labor Leads with Positive Guaranties. Federal legislation designed expressly to protect the right of labor to organize and bargain collectively began with the Erdman

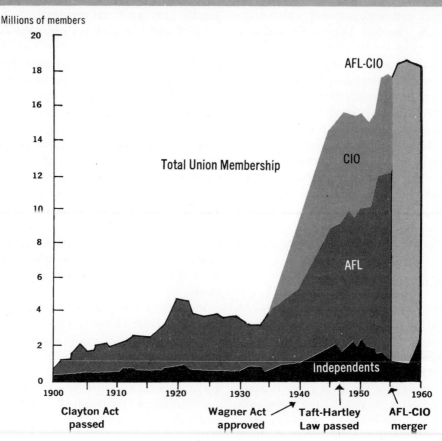

GROWTH OF LABOR UNIONS IN UNITED STATES

Millions of members

AFL-CIO

Total Union Membership

CIO

AFL

Independents

| 1900 | 1910 | 1920 | 1930 | 1940 | 1950 | 1960 |

Clayton Act
passed

Wagner Act
approved

Taft-Hartley
Law passed

AFL-CIO
merger

The National Labor Relations (Wagner) Act, a boon to organized labor, marked the beginning of a great increase in membership. The most important recent developments are the merger of the AFL and CIO, and the increase in the independent group because of the expulsion of the Teamsters and other unions.

Act of 1898. In addition to providing for voluntary mediation and arbitration of railway labor disputes, this measure outlawed yellow-dog contracts for railway employees. However, the latter provision was declared an unconstitutional abridgment of the right of contract in *Adair v. United States* [208 U.S. 161 (1908)].

Railway labor gained much greater recognition of its right to organize and bargain collectively by the Railway Labor Act of 1926. Besides providing the conciliation and arbitration machinery described below, the 1926 act, for interstate carriers, guaranteed the right of employees to organize and bargain collectively through unions of their own choice, authorized the National Mediation Board to hold elections to determine appropriate bargaining units when unions disagreed over which one represented a majority, required both management and labor to bargain in good faith, and outlawed certain unfair labor practices, including yellow-dog contracts, when committed by employers. The courts were given authority to prevent unfair labor practices. Doubts of constitutionality raised by the Adair case were removed when the Supreme Court broadened its rulings [see especially *Texas & New Orleans R.R. v. Brotherhood of Ry. Clerks*, 218 U.S. 548 (1930)]. Since passage in 1926, the Railway Labor Act has been extended to airway labor engaged in interstate commerce.

Labor Triumphs under National Labor Relations Act of 1935. Most of the rights guaranteed to railway and airway employees were extended to other workers engaged in interstate and foreign commerce during the 1930s. The National Industrial Recovery Act, passed in 1933, contained among its many provisions the famous Section 7A. This section guaranteed the right of labor engaged in interstate and foreign commerce to organize and bargain collectively, free from employer interference. Extensive administrative machinery was established to enforce the newly extended right, but this lost its effectiveness when the Supreme Court ruled the act unconstitutional [*Schechter Poultry Corp. v. United States*, 295 U.S. 495 (1935)].

Shortly thereafter Congress reenacted similar provisions in the National Labor Relations Act, sometimes called the Wagner Act. This law established the National Labor Relations Board (NLRB) composed of three members appointed by the President with Senate concurrence for five-year terms. The Board was given jurisdiction over all nongovernmental employees and employers engaged in interstate and foreign commerce except those in the railway and airway industries, who were already covered by the National Mediation Board.

The Board was given two principal functions: one, to supervise elections for determining which union represents a majority within a plant or industry; the other, to prevent employers from committing certain unfair labor practices. The law made it an unfair labor practice for employers to (1) interfere with, restrain, or coerce employees in the exercise of their rights to organize, participate in union activity, and bargain collectively through representatives of their own choosing; (2) dominate or interfere with the formation or administration of any labor organization or contribute financial or other support to it; (3) discriminate with regard to hire or tenure of employment or any term or condition of employment as a method of encouraging or discouraging membership in labor unions; (4) discharge or otherwise discriminate against an employee because he files charges or gives testimony under the act; and (5) refuse to bargain collectively with representatives of his employees.

This legislation was one-sided in that it restrained employers from interfering with unions but placed no similar limitations on unions and employees. The reasoning given for this show of partiality was that employers, being stronger, were able to look after themselves; the evil to be cured was employer interference with the rights of the economically and socially weaker workers.

The National Labor Relations Act was a boon to organized labor. To them it became the most essential of Federal statutes. Employers vehemently objected and fought its enforcement. Objection was made to its assumptions, purposes, controls, and methods of administration. Encouraged by postwar inflation and a series of nationwide strikes, Congress adopted, over the President's veto, the Labor Management Act of 1947, better known as the Taft-Hartley Act. This incurred the uncompromising opposition of organized labor; so the feud continues.

Taft-Hartley Setbacks. The Taft-Hartley law amends the National Labor Relations Act. Because the former National Labor Relations Board was felt to be too partial to organized labor, its membership was increased to five. Reflecting accusations that it had been rule maker, prosecutor, judge, and jury, the Board was given responsibility for general administration and adjudication, but the office of General Counsel was created to investigate charges, issue complaints, and prosecute. The General Counsel was also empowered to supervise most board attorneys and other officers and employees in regional offices.

Other provisions were numerous: Union officers, but not employers, were required to file non-Communist affidavits or be denied benefits of the law. The closed shop was outlawed, but the union shop was permitted if preferred by a majority of employees. (A closed shop employs only union members, whereas a union shop may employ persons who are not union members provided they join within a specified time.)

Supervisors, including foremen, were denied benefits of the law. Employers were granted greater freedom of speech about plant and contract matters. The "checkoff" (employer collection of union dues out of pay) was permitted, but only for employees who gave advance consent in writing. Employer contributions to union health and welfare funds were permitted under certain conditions, one of which was that employers and employees be equally represented in the administration of the funds. Hiring through union halls was forbidden. Union and company contributions to political campaigns were forbidden.

Intention to modify or terminate contracts required thirty-day notice. Suits by employers and unions were authorized for al-

leged violations of collective-bargaining contracts. The Board was authorized to obtain injunctions to prevent certain union conduct. Unions were forbidden to commit unfair labor practices, including refusal to bargain collectively, restraint or coercion of employees in the exercise of their rights, discrimination against employees, engaging in secondary boycotts and jurisdictional strikes, charging excessive or discriminatory initiation fees, and forcing employers to pay or deliver things of value for services not performed. The provisions governing national-emergency work stoppages, explained below, were included.

Landrum-Griffin Controls. A decade elapsed after the Taft-Hartley law passed before Congress made significant changes in labor-management legislation. Meanwhile, foes of organized labor succeeded in getting a number of states to enact "right-to-work" laws prohibiting closed- and union-shop agreements.

Advocates of labor reforms realized some of their hopes in 1959 with passage of the Landrum-Griffin Bill. Among numerous provisions was a "bill of rights" which guarantees union members equal opportunity to nominate candidates, vote for officers, and participate in union meetings. A majority of union members must approve by secret ballot before dues, fees, and assessments are raised. Members are permitted to appear before governmental bodies without union interference. Discipline cannot be administered to members without a full and fair hearing on written charges. Members must be supplied copies of constitutions, bylaws, and collective-bargaining contracts. If rights are infringed, members are entitled to sue in Federal courts, and interference with a member's rights is a Federal crime.

The new law repeals the Taft-Hartley non-Communist affidavit requirement, but stipulates that members of the Communist Party may not hold union offices. Persons who commit certain crimes, and those who withdraw from the Communist Party, must wait five years before holding union offices. Unions must file constitutions, bylaws, and reports with the Secretary of Labor. Local unions must elect officers at least once every three years—national and international unions every five and four years respectively—by secret ballot and majority vote. The misuse of union funds is declared a Federal crime. Taft-Hartley loopholes regarding secondary boycotts and picketing are closed. Taft-Hartley provisions are made applicable to railroad, airline, farm, and local government workers. State labor-relations agencies and courts are allowed to assume jurisdiction over disputes that the National Labor Relations Board declines to handle, but the Board is barred from enlarging the categories of cases it declines to handle.

Labor-Management Disputes. In a free society disputes between capital and management on one hand and labor on the other are inevitable. Other countries have tried various schemes to resolve such disputes, even to the extent of abolishing either the capitalists, as in Russia, or labor unions, as in prewar Germany and Italy. In this country governmental efforts are usually directed toward obtaining voluntary settlements.

Conciliation and Arbitration Distinguished. Most labor-management disputes are settled by conciliation or mediation. These two terms are synonomous and refer to efforts of neutral parties to negotiate and compromise differences. Arbitration also is frequently used; when it is voluntary, both sides agree upon a third party to whom they are willing to submit the dispute for decision. Under compulsory arbitration the law designates a public officer, board, or court to make the award and enforce compliance.

Many persons have advocated compulsory arbitration in the United States, but up to now both the constitutionality and wisdom of such proposals have been doubtful. Compulsory arbitration would probably meet the test of constitutionality today if applied to public-utility enterprises or to other essential industries during periods of national emergency [the leading Supreme Court decision is *Wolff Packing Co. v. Court of Industrial Relations*, 262 U.S. 522 (1923)]. But it is highly doubtful that the courts would approve extended use of this extreme remedy. The prinicpal legal question is whether life, liberty, and property are taken without due process of law. In addition to questioning legality, critics insist compulsory arbitration would lead to undesirable intrusion of government into private enterprise, set back free collective bargaining, inject political considerations into the settlement of disputes, depart from American traditions, and be unenforceable if defied on a large scale.

Federal Mediation and Conciliation Service. The principal Federal agencies engaged in reconciling labor-management disputes are the Federal Mediation and Conciliation Service and the National Mediation Board. Both are independent establishments, although the former was a part of the Department of Labor until separated by the Taft-Hartley Act in 1947. The professed reason given for separation was that the Service had been too prolabor, and independent status would guarantee greater objectivity.

The Service endeavors to prevent disputes from arising by trying to improve human relations in industrial life. It also seeks to create an atmosphere congenial to collective bargaining and the use of the Service's personnel. It works closely with state conciliation agencies. The Taft-Hartley Act requires employers and unions to file notice of every dispute affecting interstate and foreign commerce not settled within thirty days after one or the other party to a collective agreement gives notice of intention to terminate or modify an existing contract. With this information at hand the Service proffers assistance.

Where both parties are willing, commissioners of conciliation intervene, seeking to provide data pertinent to an argument and avoid a strike or lockout. Although many agreements are brought about in this way, agents of the Service are powerless if either party is unwilling to cooperate or accept suggested bases for settlement. Occasionally both parties display enough confidence in a particular agent or panel of agents to request arbitration of a dispute. Agents may render this service, but Federal law makes no provision for enforcing their awards.

National Mediation Board. This three-member board was established by the Railway Labor Act of 1926, mentioned above. The board's authority is restricted to labor-management relations of rail and air carriers engaged in interstate commerce.

When disputes that do not involve the interpretation of contracts between rail and air carriers and their employees arise, the Board first tries mediation. If that fails, it recommends arbitration. If that is rejected, the President may appoint a special fact-finding board to investigate and make recommendations. If such recommendations are unacceptable, a strike or lockout may follow. To prevent this from happening in periods of emergency, Congress has authorized the President to "seize" carriers for temporary periods and operate them under governmental auspices. Seizures occurred several times during and immediately following the Second World War.

When controversies arise over the interpretation of labor-management contracts, the procedure is different. These disputes are handled by the National Railroad Ad-

justment Board, made up of representatives of carriers and unions in equal numbers. The Board operates through four divisions; if a tie vote occurs in one of them, the National Mediation Board appoints a referee to assist in breaking the deadlock. Labor (but not management) may appeal to the courts for enforcement of awards made by the Board. This procedure provides a mild form of compulsory arbitration.

Emergency Disputes under Taft-Hartley Act. Experience with rail and air carriers led to proposals for extending the use of fact-finding boards and "cooling-off" periods to other industries engaged in interstate commerce. A modified version was included in the Taft-Hartley Act of 1947. It provides that, when a work stoppage threatens to cause a national emergency, the President may appoint a board of inquiry with power to compel attendance of witnesses and production of evidence. The board's report, the law states, is to set forth the facts and contentions "but shall not contain any recommendations."

When the report is received, the President is required to file a copy with the Mediation and Conciliation Service and make its contents public. Thereupon, the President may direct the Attorney General to go to court for an eighty-day injunction restraining the threatened stoppage. During the eighty-day cooling-off period, the Service is required to do its best, and the board of inquiry is to be reconvened for study and to make a report that includes the employer's "best offer." This report is to be made public, and the National Labor Relations Board is directed to hold an election to determine whether a majority of workers wishes to accept or reject the best offer.

If at the expiration of eighty days the dispute remains unsettled, the injunction terminates, the President reports to Congress, and the work stoppage may take place, unless Congress by that time approves more drastic action. Although this procedure has been used a few times, authorities are divided over its success and wisdom. That it has not prevented all serious strikes is obvious. Because of the antilabor flavor of the Taft-Hartley law, and the fact that labor usually has more to lose than management has by "freezing" the *status quo* by injunctions, labor leaders are intensely hostile to these procedures.

Other critics point out that the law's time limits force emergency boards to hurry their studies, that the banning of Board recommendations prevents public opinion from rallying around impartial proposals, and that during the eighty-day cooling-off period the penalties and incentives for reaching agreement by collective bargaining merely postpone the date of a showdown. Instead of having government "take sides" or weaken collective bargaining, critics suggest remedies that will ensure impartiality and strengthen the process of collective bargaining.

BRINGING CHILD LABOR UNDER CONTROL

The Quest for Federal Power. Children are special wards of the state, so there has never been any question about the constitutionality of state laws regulating, or even prohibiting, child labor. But the states were reluctant to act for fear of placing their employers at a competitive disadvantage with those in other states. Ultimately it became obvious that only a uniform national law could solve the problem.

Accordingly, in 1916, Congress passed the Keating-Owen Act forbidding the transportation in interstate commerce of products made by factories employing children under fourteen years of age. The act also forbade the employment of children between fourteen and sixteen for more than eight hours a day, or six days a week, or at night. Similar prohibitions applied to products of mines in which children under sixteen were employed. Two years later this legislation was declared unconstitutional [*Hammer v. Dagenhart*, 247 U.S. 251 (1918)]. The chief reason given by the Supreme Court was that Congress was regulating productive facilities that could not properly be considered interstate and foreign commerce. The powers of the states were, therefore, invaded.

Undismayed, Congress turned to the power to tax to provide for the general welfare. Included within the general Revenue Act of February 24, 1919, was a tax of 10 per cent upon the annual net profits of concerns violating certain standards, chief of which was the employment of children under fourteen. This also was declared an unconstitutional invasion of state powers [*Bailey v. Drexel Furniture Co.*, 259 U.S. 20 (1922)].

Following these two unsuccessful attempts, Congress mustered enough votes to propose a constitutional amendment which would give the Federal government the desired authority (text of the proposal is given on p. 746). To date it has been ratified by only twenty-eight states and the prospect of additional ratifications is not bright.

While the amendment was before the states, Congress again tried to abolish child labor by statute, this time by the National Industrial Recovery Act of 1933. All the NRA codes stipulated that the employment of children under sixteen was illegal, and these provisions were generally obeyed until the act was declared unconstitutional in *Schechter Poultry Corp. v. United States* [295 U.S. 495 (1935)].

Federal Restrictions on Child Labor.
Two Federal statutes now govern child
labor: the Public Contracts Act of 1936
and the Fair Labor Standards Act of 1938.[1]
Enforcement is the task of the Wage and
Hour and Public Contracts Divisions, De-
partment of Labor, in cooperation with the
Children's Bureau, Department of Health,
Education, and Welfare.

The Public Contracts Act forbids employers who are performing government
contracts involving more than $10,000 from
employing anyone under nineteen years of
age without a certificate. Even though they
hold certificates, boys under sixteen and
girls under eighteen may not be hired. Exceptions may be granted by the Secretary
of Labor. Certificates are issued in cooperation with the states, usually by public
employment offices or public-school authorities.

The Fair Labor Standards Act is more
flexible. Under it, employments are divided
into three categories: completely exempt,
nonpermissible for fourteen- and fifteen-
year-olds, and too hazardous for youths between sixteen and eighteen years old.

Completely exempt includes retailing,
personal service, street trades (like selling
newspapers), motion pictures, children employed in agriculture outside school hours,
and children working for their parents, except in manufacturing and mining. The list
of nonpermissible employments for four-
teen- and fifteen-year-olds excludes most
children from interstate mining, manufacturing, processing occupations in rooms
where manufacturing is going on, work on
power-driven machinery and hoisting ap-
paratus, operation of motor vehicles or
service as helpers, and public messenger
service.

[1] The former was upheld by the Supreme Court
in *Perkins v. Lukens Steel Co.*, 310 U.S. 113
(1936); the latter in *United States v. Darby Lumber Co.*, 312 (U.S. 100 (1941).

The third category excludes youths between the ages of sixteen and eighteen from
being motor-vehicle drivers and helpers;
operating metalworking and woodworking
machines; working in explosive plants or
coal mines; logging and sawmilling; and
from occupations involving exposure to
radioactive substances.

Violations of Federal and state laws are
more numerous than is commonly believed.
Legal responsibility for obeying child-labor
laws rests with employers rather than with
youths or their parents.

STANDARDS FOR HOURS AND WAGES

The Courts Delay Hour Laws. It is not uncommon to hear people recall working as
many as sixteen or more hours a day.
Agitation for the establishment of legal
limits caused several states to respond toward the end of the last century, but doubts
over constitutionality delayed action. The
basic constitutional question arising from
maximum hour laws is: do they take liberty
and property without due process of law?

The courts finally, albeit reluctantly, admitted that states might reasonably limit
hours for women as a means of promoting
the health, safety, and morals of the community [the two early leading Supreme
Court decisions upholding state hour laws
for women are *Holden v. Hardy*, 169 U.S.
366 (1898), and *Muller v. Oregon*, 208
U.S. 412 (1908)]. Now nearly all states
have such laws. While they vary, they tend
toward an eight-hour day and a forty-four-
hour week. Commonly there are special restrictions upon night work and employment
in certain types of business, such as bar-
rooms and restaurants.

Men were considered by the courts to be
more rugged and less in need of safeguards.
State laws were at first declared unconstitutional; then legislation limiting hours in

hazardous occupations was approved [*Holden v. Hardy*, 169 U.S. 366 (1898)]. Finally, in *Bunting v. Oregon* [243 U.S. 246 (1917)], the Supreme Court upheld state hour laws for men in general occupations. Now most states protect men, but the coverage is less general than for women. The same doubts have enshrouded Federal hour laws, but they disappeared when the Supreme Court upheld the Fair Labor Standards Act.

Wage Laws Given Belated Approval. Massachusetts enacted the first minimum-wage law for women in 1912, and several other states followed suit. In 1923, the United States Supreme Court declared such laws unconstitutional by ruling against a Federal statute establishing minimum wages for women in the District of Columbia (*Adkins v. Children's Hosp.*, 261 U.S. 525). Twenty-four years later the Court reversed itself in a 5-to-4 decision by upholding a statute of the state of Washington [*West Coast Hotel Co. v. Parrish*, 300 U.S. 379 (1937)]. This decision opened the door not only for state, but also for Federal minimum-wage laws for women. The entering wedge having been driven, it was only a short time until the Supreme Court upheld Federal, and incidentally state, wage control for men in the Darby Lumber Co. case cited previously.

Federal Standards Established. The first Federal wage-and-hour legislation providing coverage for general occupations was the National Industrial Recovery Act of 1933, but it was short-lived. Then followed the Public Contracts Act of 1936 regulating hours and minimum wages for employees working on government contracts, and finally the Fair Labor Standards Act in 1938 and subsequent amendments.

The wages-and-hours provisions of the Fair Labor Standards Act apply to all employees in nonexempt businesses engaged in interstate commerce or in the production of goods for interstate commerce. Exemptions are numerous although they have been reduced from time to time. In 1961 coverage was extended to about 3.6 million new workers, mostly in large retail, service, and local transportation enterprises.

The act provided that at the beginning wages might be set by administrative order. Meanwhile, a statutory "floor" would rise gradually from 25 cents an hour to 40 cents by October, 1945. Congress jumped the figure to 75 cents in 1949 and $1 in 1955; 1961 amendments raised it to $1.15 with a further increase to $1.25 in 1963.

The act sets no limit on hours that may be worked but requires time and a half pay for hours worked in excess of a stated number. For most employees overtime pay is required after 40 hours a week; for those covered by 1961 amendments, after 44 hours during the first three years, 42 hours during the fourth year, and 40 hours thereafter. No limit is set on hours worked in one day.

The standards are administered by the Wage and Hour and Public Contracts Divisions of the Department of Labor. Violators may be fined up to $10,000 or, on a second conviction, imprisoned up to six months, or both. Also, workers may collect in court double the back wages due them, plus attorneys' fees and costs.

FINDING JOBS FOR WILLING WORKERS

Private Agencies Prove Inadequate. Employers who need workmen and men who want jobs must get together. A common method is for the employer to hang out a "Help Wanted" sign or advertise in the newspapers, while the employee walks the streets, dropping in where there are signs, or answering advertisements. The procedure is haphazard, inefficient, and destructive of morale. Numerous fee-charging agencies, philanthropic organizations, trade unions, local, state, and Federal governments have tried to meet the need.

Private fee-charging agencies exploited the unemployed so badly that the states tried to regulate them. These efforts were not entirely successful, partly because, until 1941, the Supreme Court forbade the states to prescribe maximum charges [For the pre-1941 attitude of the Court see *Ribnik v. McBride*, 279 U.S. 350 (1928). For its reversal see *Olsen v. Nebraska*, 313 U.S. 236 (1941)]. The Federal government intervened in 1933 with the Wagner-Peyser Act, which established a nationwide, coordinated system of public employment offices.

Federal-State Employment Offices. Originally, the Federal government provided matching grants to states which set up employment offices and operated them according to Federal standards. In 1942, as a war measure, the Federal government took over the employment services. When the war ended, the services were returned to the states. The Federal agency that makes grants and supervises to assure compliance with standards is the Bureau of Employment Security, Department of Labor.

Whether under direct Federal operation or the present Federal-state sponsorship, the employment services provide a ready source of assistance to both employers and employees. Offices exist in the principal towns of every state, and in smaller places representatives call at regular intervals to receive applications for jobs and to put employers in touch with suitable workers. Because they are coordinated, the offices maintain a nationwide clearance system, so that workers who cannot be placed at home can be referred to jobs in other areas. These offices are also integral parts of the social security system; all payments for unemploy-

ment compensation are made through them.

SOCIAL INSURANCE

Present Plans of Recent Origin. Insurance by individuals against hazards to life and property has long been common in the United States, but social insurance is something relatively new. Social-insurance plans are distinctive in that they are established by law and participation is usually compulsory. Borrowing heavily from European ideas and experience, American states haltingly began experiments, about 1900, that have since flourished. The Federal government soon took an interest, but not until the Depression did it launch the large-scale programs now in operation.

The central idea behind all types of social insurance is that the community should help share the risks. Risks and costs are spread, while minimal standards of well-being are maintained for those covered by insurance plans. Thus the community is protected from the failure of its citizens to provide adequately for themselves. The compulsory participation that only governments can require spreads the risks and costs as widely as possible.

Three types of social insurance are found throughout the United States today: workmen's compensation, primarily under state auspices, although the Federal government is involved to a limited extent; unemployment compensation, a cooperative Federal-state program; and old-age and survivors' insurance, administered solely by the Federal government.

Workmen's Compensation. Until recently, employers assumed they had only limited legal responsibility for workmen injured during the course of employment. At common law, an injured employee's only recourse was a civil suit for damages, which usually he could ill afford. Besides being expensive and time consuming, a suit was difficult to win because the workman was required to prove: (1) the employer had been negligent; (2) negligence on his (the worker's) part did not contribute to the accident; (3) the accident was not due to the negligence of a fellow workman; and (4) the accident was not the result of a risk assumed by accepting the job.

Since 1902, all states have passed laws designed to give greater protection to workmen. The Federal government has done likewise for certain types of workmen. The theory behind such legislation is that compensation for on-the-job accidents should be included in the cost of production and borne partly by the employer and the general public rather than solely by the injured and their families.

Insurance for Federal Employees. Most employees of the Federal government are insured for injuries sustained during the course of employment. No insurance fund is established for this purpose; rather, Congress appropriates annually for direct payments to injured workmen. The amounts paid are usually proportionate to the seriousness of the injury and the time and money lost. After a brief waiting period, and within minimums and maximums, payments are made for partial, permanent-partial, and total disability. Payments may also be made for medical, surgical, and hospital service, death, and even burial in the case of death from accident during the course of employment.

Administration involves considerable investigation, hearings, etc., which are handled by the Bureau of Employees' Compensation. Appeals may be taken to a three-man Employees' Compensation Appeals Board and to Federal courts if constitutional issues are involved.

Insurance for District of Columbia, Long-

shoremen, and Harbor Workers. Federal law also compels private employers in the District of Columbia and employers of longshoremen and harbor workers to insure against accidents. Employers may either set up their own insurance funds or insure with a private company approved by the Commissioner of Social Security. A schedule of benefits provides for various types of disability and death; payments are also prescribed for medical, surgical, hospital, and burial service. The cost of insurance is borne by employers; administrative expenses are paid by the Federal government.

These provisions are administered by the Bureau of Employees' Compensation, which functions with the aid of regional offices set up chiefly for the convenience of longshoremen and harbor workers. Appeals are not heard by an administrative board but by Federal district courts.

Special Provisions for Railway Workers and Seamen. No employees other than those mentioned above are covered by workmen's compensation plans prescribed by Federal law. Common-law assumptions have, however, been modified for railway employees and seamen. This occurred for the former by the Employers' Liability Act of 1908, for seamen by the Jones Act of 1920.

As a result of these changes, an injured workman can usually collect damages if an employer violated a safety statute or if the accident occurred because of negligence on the part of an employer. Though both the employer and worker are negligent, the latter can collect, although a jury might reduce damages in proportion to the employee's share of the blame. This legislation is of considerable help to employees, but it still involves them in more litigation, expense, uncertainty, and insecurity than if they were covered by a compulsory-insurance plan.

Disability Insurance under the Social Security Act. Amendments to the Social Secu-

TYPICAL MONTHLY GENERAL ASSISTANCE PAYMENTS

National

High
$113.66

Average
$67.93

Low
$11.96

Exclusive of vendor payments for medical care
and cases receiving only such payments.

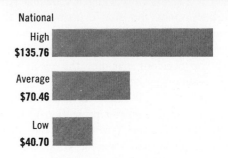

TYPICAL MONTHLY AID TO PERMANENTLY AND TOTALLY DISABLED

National

High
$135.76

Average
$70.46

Low
$40.70

Includes vendor payments for medical care
and cases receiving only such payments.

rity Act made in 1956 launched a new Federal insurance program. This requires that monthly payments be made to insured persons under sixty-five years of age who become totally disabled. Rigid standards for eligibility are set forth in the law. Payments begin after a waiting period of six months; they may be terminated if a disabled employee refuses to accept state rehabilitation services without good cause.

The size of monthly grants is determined by earnings and length of service in insured jobs. The plan is financed by a ½ of 1 per cent payroll tax, paid half by the employer and half by the employee. The tax for self-employed persons is ⅜ of 1 per cent of employment income. An estimated 400,000 persons became eligible when the plan went into effect. The number was expected to jump to 900,000 by 1975. Larger numbers became elegible under 1960 amendments.

Unemployment Insurance. Unemployment is one of the most serious domestic problems facing modern nations. A certain amount of unemployment always exists, even in so-called normal times, and the volume rises sharply when the economy falters. The large and prolonged unemployment of the 1930s hastened a plan that provides a modest income to workers during forced layoffs.

The Social Security Act of 1935 established the present unemployment-insurance plan. The Bureau of Employment Security, Department of Labor, administers the system, in cooperation with the states. As amended, the act required employers of four or more employees to pay a 3.1 per cent tax on their payrolls, exclusive of amounts in excess of $3,000 paid to one employee in a year. It stipulated that a credit of 90 per cent of the amount collected would be allowed employers situated in states that enacted laws which met Federal standards. This placed a heavy penalty upon employers in noncooperating states and forced prompt enactment of state plans. Now all states and most territories have unemployment compensation systems. Amendments added in 1954 extended coverage to most civilian employees of the Federal government.

All the states impose a payroll tax on employers, and a few levy a similar tax on employees. The money is deposited in a federal Unemployment Trust Fund maintained by the United States Treasury. From this each state pays benefits as individuals become unemployed and apply at nearby employment offices. The amount paid varies among the states.

A typical plan provides for a waiting period of two weeks, after which payments are made for about thirteen weeks. The size of the payments depends upon average earnings during a base period. The national average weekly payment amounts to about $34. While unemployed, an employee must be physically able and available for work.

Unemployment Compensation for Railway Workers. Railway employees are covered by separate legislation enacted in 1938. This plan is administered by the Railroad Retirement Board and financed by a payroll tax paid by employers. With the exception that states do not participate in administration, the plan operates much like the general one explained above.

Old-age and Survivors' Insurance (OASI). The Social Security Act also inaugurated a nationwide plan of insurance to guarantee a minimum income, or pension, to most wage earners when they reach sixty-five years of age and retire. This feature of the Social Security Act is administered solely by the Federal Government through the Commissioner of Social Security, Department of Health, Education, and Welfare. Launched in 1935, the program has grown enormously. Today most of the nation's paid workers, and many of its self-employed (farmers, business proprietors, ministers, lawyers, and the like), are covered by some public retirement plan.

At first, participation was compulsory for covered employees, but amendments permitted some groups to join on an optional basis. Among the latter are employees of local and state governments, religious, charitable, educational, and other nonprofit organizations.

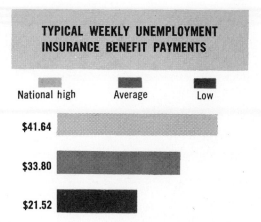

TYPICAL WEEKLY UNEMPLOYMENT INSURANCE BENEFIT PAYMENTS

National high — Average — Low

$41.64

$33.80

$21.52

Employers covered by the act must pay a tax on payrolls, and employees must pay an identical amount on their income. The total tax is collected from the employer. The amount each pays is 3⅛ per cent on the first $4,800 of annual income. The rate is supposed to go up by gradual stages until 1968, when it will amount to 4⅝ per cent for each employer and employee.

The money is deposited in an Old-age and Survivors' Trust Fund in the United States Treasury. It is invested in interest-bearing obligations of the Federal government or securities whose interest and principal are guaranteed by the national government.

Self-employed persons must pay 4.7 per cent on net income up to $4,800 until 1963. Thereafter the figure rises gradually to 6.9 per cent in 1968. Those who enter on an optional basis pay equivalent amounts to those outlined above.

Normal retirement age is sixty-five, but women and certain classes of dependent men may retire at sixty-two. Retirees forfeit benefits if they earn more than $1,200 annually; after seventy-two there are no limits on earnings. Annuities are paid monthly. Upon death, benefits are paid to survivors, although spouses without dependents must wait until retirement age before payments

COVERAGE UNDER THE OLD-AGE, SURVIVORS, AND DISABILITY INSURANCE PROGRAM, December, 1960

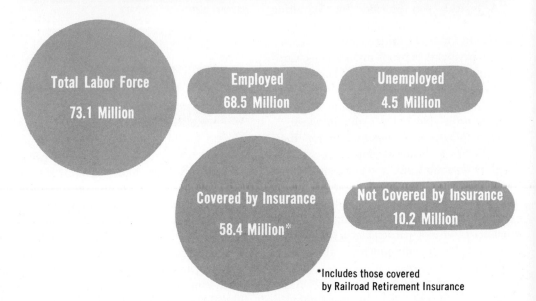

Total Labor Force
73.1 Million

Employed
68.5 Million

Unemployed
4.5 Million

Covered by Insurance
58.4 Million*

Not Covered by Insurance
10.2 Million

*Includes those covered
by Railroad Retirement Insurance

begin. The amounts received are based upon average monthly earnings over a lifetime in covered occupations. The maximum monthly benefit for a family is $254, or 80 per cent of average monthly wage, whichever is less. The minimum for most employees is $40 a month.

WELFARE PROGRAMS

Aids to Veterans. Veterans and their families represent about one-half the population. These large numbers and appeals to patriotism have made veterans' organizations extremely effective in obtaining benefits from the Federal and state governments.

According to the President's Commission on Veterans' Pensions, reporting in 1956, the "United States today has the most liberal and comprehensive veterans' benefit programs in the world." According to the Commission, in 1955 Federal benefits alone

cost $27 for each man, woman, and child in the United States—or about $95 for the average family. Indeed, the cost of caring for veterans is in the long run greater than the military costs of the wars in which they fought! Many veterans receive additional benefits that cannot be measured in dollars, such as preference in civil-service appointments and referrals to job openings by the Public Employment Offices mentioned on page 558.

Types of Benefits. Services and benefits provided for veterans are too numerous to be explained in detail. Many veterans have received bonuses representing the difference between what they earned while in service and what thy might have earned had they remained at home. Many received hospitalization and out-patient medical and dental care. Thousands have gone to school at public expense. Many borrowed for homes, farms, and business with guaranteed loans.

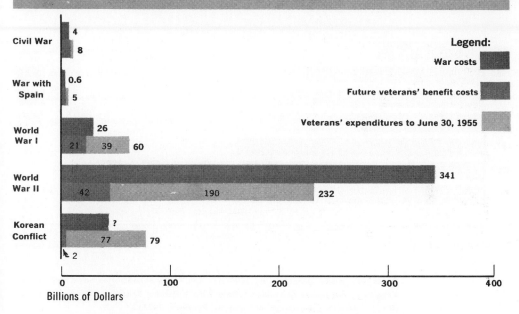

MILITARY COST OF WARS vs. ESTIMATED COST OF VETERANS' BENEFITS, Under Present Laws, Civil War to Korean Conflict

Legend:
War costs
Future veterans' benefit costs
Veterans' expenditures to June 30, 1955

Civil War: 4, 8

War with Spain: 0.6, 5

World War I: 26, 21, 39, 60

World War II: 341, 42, 190, 232

Korean Conflict: ?, 77, 79, 2

Billions of Dollars

Long-range costs will be greater than those reflected because of benefit changes made since the data were assembled. [Data from *Veterans' Benefits in the United States* (U.S. President's Commission on Veterans' Pensions, 1956).]

Large numbers received compensation, popularly known as "pensions" for service-connected disabilities. Many retain life insurance provided at low cost during active service. A great many were given allowances during periods of unemployment after release from service. Special housing and automobiles have been provided for seriously disabled veterans.

Administration. Various governmental agencies administer Federal laws affecting veterans, but the principal one is the Veterans' Administration. This is an independent establishment headed by an Administrator and the usual staff. Two special boards exist: a Board of Veterans' Appeals, which reviews veterans' claims, and the Veterans' Education Appeals Board, which reviews decisions of the Administrator affecting payments to educational institutions for tuition, fees, and similar items. In addition to the Washington office, the Administration maintains a number of regional, insular, and area offices.

The first Hoover Commission stirred up a hornet's nest when it recommended in 1949 that the Veterans' Administration be merged with other important agencies concerned with health and hospitalization. Congress has not approved the plan, chiefly because of resistance from veterans' groups. Critics fear the Administration would be less effective if it lost independent status and became subordinate to a larger organi-

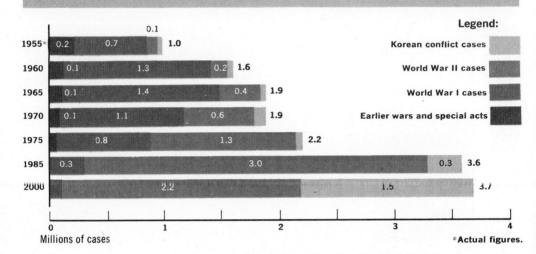

ESTIMATED NUMBER OF VETERAN AND SURVIVOR CASES ON VA PENSION ROLL UNDER PRESENT LAWS
Selected Fiscal Years, 1955-2000

Year				Total
1955*	0.2	0.7	0.1	1.0
1960	0.1	1.3	0.2	1.6
1965	0.1	1.4	0.4	1.9
1970	0.1	1.1	0.6	1.9
1975	0.8	1.3		2.2
1985	0.3	3.0	0.3	3.6
2000	2.2	1.5		3.7

Legend:
Korean conflict cases
World War II cases
World War I cases
Earlier wars and special acts

0   1   2   3   4
Millions of cases   *Actual figures.

Cases will nearly quadruple by 2000 A.D. Still more beneficiaries have been added since these data were assembled. [Data from *Veterans' Benefits in the United States* (U.S. President's Commission on Veterans' Pensions, 1956).]

zation. Neither the second Hoover Commission, which reported in 1955, nor the President's Commission on Veterans' Pensions, referred to above, renewed the recommendation. The latter group recommended, however, that the Administrator be given cabinet status. Both groups recommended extensive changes in benefits and administration.

Old-age Assistance. The Social Security Act provides for assistance to several important groups and functions, including needy old people, the physically handicapped and disabled, dependent children, and public-health services.

Old-age assistance differs from old-age and survivors' insurance. The latter is an insurance plan for employed workers financed by taxes paid by employers and employees. Old-age assistance is given to the needy aged. Old-age and survivors' insurance is administered solely by the Federal government;

old-age assistance is provided by a joint Federal-state arrangement.

Under the latter plan the Federal government pays four-fifths of the first $30 a month per recipient and matches the balance. Since 1958 the states fix the upper limits of grants to individuals. The states are limited inasmuch as the total each may receive monthly from the Federal government is determined by multiplying $65 by the number of persons receiving old-age assistance, aid to the blind, and aid to the permanently and totally disabled. They will rise somewhat due to liberalized benefits authorized for medical care in 1960.

To be eligible for a "pension," as grants are popularly known, one must be at least sixty-five, not an inmate of a public institution, a resident of the state for a prescribed period of time, a citizen (in most states), and in need.

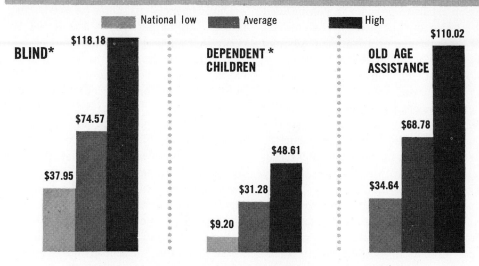

TYPICAL MONTHLY AID TO THE BLIND , DEPENDENT CHILDREN , AND OLD AGE ASSISTANCE

National low   Average   High

BLIND*
$118.18
$74.57
$37.95

DEPENDENT * CHILDREN
$48.61
$31.28
$9.20

OLD AGE ASSISTANCE
$110.02
$68.78
$34.64

*Includes vendor payments for medical care and cases receiving only such payments.

What constitutes need? Most states require applicants to disclose their resources, assets, and income (if any). Grants are then made, if adequate funds are available, which are calculated to meet a minimum budget. Most states allow payments to more then one person in a family if needs warrant.

The states have, on the whole, taken a defensive, miserly attitude in setting up their plans, with the result that complaints are widespread. The most frequent criticisms are that the grants are too low to maintain health and decency, in many instances states require that applicants be destitute before granting assistance, and administration permits too much snooping into personal and family affairs. Critics of higher payments, on the other hand, point to the great costs involved and content that liberality destroys thrift, ambition, and responsibility.

Aid to Dependent Children. The Social Security Act also authorizes the Federal government to make grants to states for the aid of dependent children. A dependent child is a needy person under eighteen years of age who has been deprived of parental support or care by reason of the death, continued absence from home, or physical or mental incapacity of a parent, and who is living and making a home with a father, mother, grandfather, other near relative, or foster-family home. The Federal government will pay monthly for a child $15 and match state grants up to a limit fixed by the state. The total monthly amount contributed by the Federal government for this purpose depends upon each state's per capita income.

Vocational Rehabilitation. In an industrial society many persons need help in retraining and rehabilitating themselves. Unless governmental assistance is given, the burden will fall on relatives, friends, and private agencies. Ultimately many of the handicapped will become beggars or inmates of penal, mental, or other public institutions. Not only is it humane to provide assistance, but it is also sound public policy, even from a financial point of view.

Federal assistance was first provided by the Vocational Rehabilitation Act of 1920. Today an extensive program is administered by the Office of Vocational Rehabilitation under the guidance of a National Advisory Council on Vocational Rehabilitation.

"Vocational rehabilitation" and "vocational rehabilitation services" are defined as any services necessary to render a disabled individual fit to engage in a remunerative occupation. Federal grants are made to states on the basis of need and ability, although certain costs are borne entirely by the Federal government.

In addition to training and guidance, Federal grants may be used for the extension and improvement of state services, research, physical restoration, hospitalization, transportation, occupational licenses, tools, equipment, and prosthetic devices. More physical defects are of the orthopedic type than any other; many result from poliomyelitis, hernia, tuberculosis, defective vision and hearing, and mental illness. As many as 60,000 persons were rehabilitated in a recent year.

Aid for the Blind, Deaf, and Disabled. Federal legislation makes special provision for the blind, deaf, and permanently and totally disabled. Braille reading materials have been entitled to free postage for many years. The Federal government appropriates money to the American Printing House for the Blind, Inc., a privately owned and operated institution in Louisville, Kentucky, whose primary purpose is the production of Braille reading materials for state schools for the blind. Established in 1858, this is the oldest national institution for the blind in the United States and the largest printing house of its kind in the world. Further assistance to the blind was provided by the Randolph-Sheppard Act of 1936, which per-

mits the blind to operate stands in Federal buildings. The act also authorized the Office of Education to conduct surveys and otherwise try to find jobs for the blind.

Direct financial assistance for needy blind persons was authorized by the Social Security Act. The Federal government will match state funds, on the same basis as for old-age assistance. In addition to being needy, blind persons may not be receiving old-age assistance or aid to dependent children. Aid may be given to blind individuals in private and public institutions.

As a special service for the deaf, the Federal government has operated, since 1857, the Columbia Institution for the Deaf, located in the District of Columbia. The advanced department, known as Gallaudet College, is the only one of its kind in the world. A number of scholarships are available for persons interested in attending this department.

Direct financial assistance is also available under the Social Security Act to needy persons who are permanently and totally disabled. Federal matching funds are made to the states on the same basis as for old-age assistance. Typically, the average monthly grant is about $70.

General Assistance a State Program. The Federal government makes no provision for general assistance, or what used to be called "direct relief," to persons in need. Rather, this is a state responsibility.

Programs operating in all states, and most of the territories, are usually administered through state and county welfare departments. The number of cases varies among the states and in response to economic conditions. There is also variation in the size of the grants; typically, the national average is about $69. The Commissioner of Social Security has recommended participation by the Federal government to equalize the burden and payments, but his advice has gone unheeded.

FEDERAL HEALTH SERVICES

Federal Role Expanding. Federal medical services have grown to large proportions. The second Hoover Commission reported in 1955 that these programs entailed annual expenditures of over 2 billion dollars; employed 10 per cent of the nation's doctors, 9 per cent of the dentists, 6 per cent of the graduate nurses; and controlled 13 per cent of the nation's hospital beds.

The Commission also reported that twenty-six Federal departments and agencies had health responsibilities, although three of them—Departments of Defense and Health, Education, and Welfare, and Veterans' Administration—accounted for 90 per cent of the services. Deploring the lack of central direction and coordination, the Commission strongly recommended the establishment of a Federal Advisory Council on Health in the Executive Office of the President. A National Advisory Health Council exists to advise the Surgeon General, but it has not been given the status and authority recommended by the Hoover Commission.

Federal aids to public health have been greatly expanded in recent years. The trend is likely to continue. Aside from what the Federal government does for veterans and persons for whom it has legal responsibilities, its efforts are concentrated on research, business regulation, inspection, and aid to the states.

Public Health Service. More health services for civilians are centered in the Public Health Service than in any other agency. The Service dates back to 1798 and is headed by a Surgeon General appointed by the President with Senate approval. If not one already, the Surgeon General is made a commissioned officer of the military services with the same rank as the Surgeon General of the Army. Principal assistants and administrative officers are also commissioned officers. Many Health Service employees are assigned to other Federal agencies, particularly the Coast Guard, Immigration and Naturalization Service, and Departments of the Army, Navy, and Air Force.

Research. For research purposes Institutes of Health exist to study cancer, heart, mental, dental, and neurological diseases, blindness, and microbiology. The facilities of these institutes are available to research scientists generally. Much research is done in cooperation with other Federal agencies, the states, and private parties.

Hospitals. Federal workmen's compensation laws prescribe medical treatment and care for a large number of people, the most numerous of whom are members of the Coast Guard, longshoremen and harbor workers, and Federal employees. For these the Health Service operates a number of hospitals, outpatient clinics, and offices.

The Department of Health, Education, and Welfare operates other hospitals, but only one of them (Freedmen's) is under the Health Service. Freedmen's is a general hospital located in the District of Columbia. St. Elizabeths, also in the District, serves mental patients. Hospitals for drug addicts are located at Fort Worth, Texas, and Lexington, Kentucky, and one for lepers is at Carville, Louisiana.

Regulation and Inspections. The Department of Health, Education, and Welfare is also involved in business regulation and inspection. Most of this work is centered in the Food and Drug Administration and the Health Service. Activities of the former are discussed elsewhere. The Health Service must license the manufacture and interstate sale of serums, toxins, vaccines, and similar products. In doing so it sets standards and makes investigations and tests. Attention was dramatically focused on this assignment in 1955 by a number of deaths which followed inoculations with the new Salk vaccine for poliomyelitis.

Because insects and germs do not respect geographic boundaries, the Federal government operates an extensive quarantine system in cooperation with the states. The Health Service guards the frontiers by examining immigrants, passengers, crews, vessels, and aircraft entering the country.

Cooperation with the States. Federal-state cooperation on matters pertaining to health is of the utmost importance. The law requires the Surgeon General to call an annual conference of state health authorities. It also stipulates that, upon request of five or more states, the Surgeon General must call special conferences of all states and territories which join in making the request. At such conferences each state has one vote.

Ambitious programs aimed at establishing a coordinated nationwide system of public-health services have been launched. The Federal government leads and assists chiefly through grants, most of which are of the matching type, to the states. All states are cooperating in one or more of the programs, although the number and quality of public-health services is far from uniform over the nation.

Current programs are numerous and varied. Grants for hospital surveys and construction were begun in 1946 and extended in 1954 to chronic-disease hospitals, diagnostic and treatment centers, nursing homes, and rehabilitation facilities. Grants have also been made for general health services, research, prevention and control of particular diseases (such as tuberculosis, venereal, mental, cancer, heart). Other grants are available for maternal and child health, crippled-children's services, medical care for disabled but potentially employable persons, and for the indigent aged.

Although grants for these purposes remain substantial, total sums spent have been reduced somewhat in the past few years for reasons of economy, and because many disapprove of too much Federal intervention in a field historically reserved to the states, local governments, and private agencies. Although the pendulum of public opinion alternates between greater and lesser Federal participation, all signs point to continued, and even greater, exertions by the national government on behalf of public health.

Compulsory Health Insurance Proposed. Concern about the nation's health has led many to advocate compulsory health insurance. The proposal calls for a plan modeled after the social insurance features of the Social Security Act under which insured individuals and families would be entitled to comprehensive hospitalization and medical service as a matter of right. The cost would be borne by a fund derived from taxes on payrolls and income. The right to choose one's own doctor would be preserved.

It is argued that the nation's health demands a bold attack; millions cannot afford adequate medical care; national coverage will reduce the per capita cost; present facilities are inadequate and cannot be sufficiently improved by voluntary efforts; and the proposed plan is not revolutionary, modeled as it is after present social-security programs.

The chief spokesman for the opposition is the American Medical Association, backed by conservative interests generally. Opponents contend that the nation's health is generally good and steadily improving; the present voluntary medical insurance systems provide superior medical practitioners and service; additional low-cost medical care can better be obtained through individual and voluntary cooperative efforts; national insurance will result in a huge government administrative bureaucracy; medical practitioners will inevitably become Federal and state government employees; patients will lose their freedom to choose doctors of preference; and similar plans abroad have failed or are unworthy of emulation.

In Great Britain and most other Western nations, proponents of "socialized" medicine have won. In the United States, bills have been introduced in Congress and state legislatures, hearings have been held, and lobbyists have been at work.

Less extreme plans are also under discussion. Many prefer a plan financed by payroll taxes with hospitalization and medical benefits paid to insured older citizens as a matter of right regardless of financial standing. Opponents prefer that federal assistance be limited to grants-in-aid to states for liberalized medical payments to the needy aged. In 1960 Congress passed a compromise bill embodying the latter features. Doubt remains over whether many states will provide the matching funds required to make the new provisions effective.

Health Reinsurance. Critics of compulsory health insurance have suggested a much more modest plan of "health reinsurance." They point to the rapid growth of group insurance for hospitalization, surgery, medical and dental care, and suggest Federal legislation that will encourage its expansion and "reinsure" against losses.

Federal aid might take the form of long-term loans to groups to help them get started. Or the Federal government might make grants to states willing to subsidize group plans that provide benefits for people in low-income brackets or with abnormal health problems.

Proposals such as these have received serious consideration by Congress, but none has been adopted. Critics point out that private groups have done well without aid. The claim is made that Federal assistance would weaken the initiative and responsibility demonstrated by private groups. Some opponents object to extending Federal grants-in-aid, others disapprove subsidizing services for more people. Extreme critics profess to see in such proposals the entering wedge of socialized medicine.

FEDERAL AIDS TO EDUCATION

Federal Role Limited but Growing. Generally speaking, the American people have viewed with alarm proposals that might diminish local control over education. As a result, primary responsibility rests in more than 125,000 local, popularly elected school boards and numerous private institutions. Centralizing influences have been at work, however, in this field as in most others.

An inventory of Federal educational activities is long. Merely to mention schools for Indians, the GI Bill of Rights, military, naval, coast guard, and air academies, the Foreign Service Institute, UNESCO, land-grant colleges, the Library of Congress, low postal rates for books and periodicals, student and faculty exchanges with foreign nations, agricultural extension services, Bureau of Standards and Atomic Energy Commission scholarships, and school lunches is to suggest the wide scope of Federal interest. On the whole, however, Federal intervention has been for special purposes rather than for general education.

Most Federal activities in aid of education are centered in the Office of Education, which dates back to 1867. At its head is a commissioner who is appointed by the President with Senate approval.

Land-grant Colleges and Universities. Passage of the Morrill Act in 1862 marks the beginning of Federal grants-in-aid of education. That measure, and supplementary legislation, donated 11,367,832 acres of land to the states with the stipulation that it, or the proceeds from the sale thereof, be used for educational purposes. The "leading object," says the act, is "without excluding other scientific and classical studies, and including military tactics, to teach such branches of learning as are related to agriculture and the mechanic arts . . . in order to promote the liberal and practical education of the industrial classes in the several pursuits and professions of life." This legislation provides the basis for land-grant colleges and universities in the fifty states, and in Puerto Rico.

In addition to offering resident instruction, the land-grant institutions maintain experiment stations and extension services which take instruction directly to farms, homes, and communities. Most of them offer courses in military science, but whether these will be compulsory or elective is decided by each institution. Annual reports must be made to the United States Office of Education.

Vocational Education. Both world wars emphasized the need for vocational training. In 1917 Congress passed the Smith-Hughes Act, which provided for grants to states and localities which matched Federal funds for training in agriculture and home economics. The program has since been expanded.

Appropriations are still made under the Smith-Hughes Act, but the scope of instruction and the basis of state and local participation have been altered. This was done by the George-Dean Act of 1936, which made vocational instruction available not only in agriculture and home economics but also in trade and industry. Virtually all the states are participating and sharing the costs on a matching basis with the Federal government. The program is administered by the Office of Education in cooperation with state boards, departments, and school officials.

The National Science Foundation. The role played by science during the Second World War, coupled with an awareness that another conflict would be still more "scientific," led to the suggestion that the Federal government assume greater responsibility for leadership and direction. After much discussion, and a presidential veto of one plan that passed Congress, a National Science Foundation was authorized in 1950 as an independent agency. It has a board of twenty-four members, appointed by the President with senatorial approval, who have distinguished themselves in the basic sciences, medical science, engineering, agriculture, education, and public affairs. The board chooses a nine-member executive committee from its membership; administration is centered in a director appointed by the President with the approval of the Senate.

The law establishing the Foundation requires that it concentrate on the physical sciences. More particularly, this involves initiating and supporting basic research, much of which is defense-related, appraising the impact of research upon industrial development and the general welfare, reviewing scientific research programs and activities of other Federal agencies, awarding graduate scholarships and fellowships, maintaining a roster of scientific personnel, and encouraging the interchange of scientific information among scientists at home and abroad.

Some observers think the greatest research need is not in the physical sciences but in the social sciences and humanities, arguing that people must learn how to live together peacefully and create a richer culture. Attempts to get support for research in these fields have failed.

Increased Federal Aid Proposed. Some states either are too poor or are unwilling to match the higher educational standards of leading states. This has caused many people to advocate that the Federal government make grants to the states as a means of equalizing educational opportunities. Federal aid might take the form of grants or long-term loans, at low rates of interest, for school-building construction. Or Federal aid might be designated for such things as transportation, books and supplies, or scholarships. Or lump-sum grants which state and local school authorities could spend as they choose might be provided. Most advocates of Federal aid suggest using a formula that will help the poorer states most. Most advocates also urge that Federal-aid legislation contain a strict injunction against Federal control of school management or of the substance of what is taught.

Stimulus was given to Federal-aid proposals by the White House Conference on Education, held late in 1955. After the Conference gave strong endorsement, President Eisenhower recommended a plan providing aid to states for school-building construction under terms that would not cause state and local governments to diminish their efforts or forfeit control.

Opponents of Federal aid stress the danger of Federal domination. If Federal funds are taken, they argue, sooner or later Federal control will result. This, they insist, is likely to lead to thought control by the national government and diminution of a sense of responsibility at state and local levels. State and local governments can meet the need, opponents continue, if and when they realize the importance of doing so.

Particularly thorny is the problem of what to do about race segregation. One point of view is that Federal aid should be granted for education but withheld from states and districts that fail to comply with the Supreme Court decision outlawing segregation. A second opinion favors Federal aid but without restrictions relating to race. People holding the latter view contend that to insist on a restrictive clause ensures defeat of all aid for education. They also argue that a restrictive clause is unnecessary because desegregation has been decreed by the courts. A third opinion is hostile to both Federal aid and integration.

Also difficult is the problem presented by private schools, many of which are church-related. Everyone recognizes their great contribution to American education and that they are doing a job which would otherwise need to be done and paid for by taxpayers. To grant Federal aid to public schools and not to private ones adds an additional burden on those who prefer the latter, and perhaps also makes it more difficult for private schools to compete for students and faculty. But to give them aid, it is contended, is contrary to the American doctrine of separation of church and state.

Many spokesmen for private schools do not want Federal aid either for themselves or for public schools; others do not mind Federal aid for public schools but want none of it for themselves; still others, especially spokesmen for the Catholic Church, want Federal aid for all, with assistance for private schools confined to such things as buildings, textbooks, and transportation. Such assistance is now provided by a number of states without running afoul of the Supreme Court.

National Defense Education Act. Spurred by the Soviet Union's Sputniks, Congress passed the National Defense Education Act in 1958. In doing so, Congress reaffirmed the principle "that the States and local communities have and must retain control over and primary responsibility for public education." Federal control was forbidden in the following terms:

Nothing contained in this Act shall be construed to authorize any department, agency, officer, or employee of the United States to exercise any direction, supervision, or control over the curriculum, program of instruction, administration, or personnel of any educational institution or school system.

After expressing these precautions, the act authorizes Federal aid for: (1) loans to students in institutions of higher education; (2) strengthening science, mathematics, and modern foreign-language instruction; (3) national-defense fellowships for the training of college and university teachers; (4) guidance, counseling, and testing; (5) strengthening instruction in modern foreign languages; (6) research and experimentation in more effective use of television, radio, motion pictures, and related mediums for educational purposes; and (7) establishing area

vocational-education programs. Certain of these programs require state matching funds; others do not. Most of the programs require the cooperation of state departments of education although some of them are carried out through direct negotiations between the United States Office of Education and officials of colleges and universities.

Although they consider the act a step in the desired direction, advocates of greater Federal aid to public education remain unsatisfied. The law grants no aid for school construction, payment of teachers, transportation, and other ordinary costs of operation. Some critics object to the fact that the new law is defense centered. They prefer aid to all fields of learning rather than the few singled out for special emphasis.

FOR FURTHER READING

Labor

American Association for Labor Legislation: *American Labor Legislation Review* (quarterly).

Berkowitz, Monroe: *Workmen's Compensation: The New Jersey Experience* (New Brunswick, N.J.: Rutgers University Press, 1960).

Berman, Edward: *Labor and the Sherman Act* (New York: Harper, 1930).

Bernstein, Irving: *The New Deal Collective Bargaining Policy* (Berkeley and Los Angeles, Calif.: University of California Press, 1950).

————, Harold L. Enarson, and R. W. Fleming: *Emergency Disputes and National Policy* (New York: Harper, 1955).

Breen, Vincent I.: *United States Conciliation Service* (Washington, D.C.: The Catholic University of America Press, 1943).

Derber, Milton, and Edwin Young (eds.): *Labor and the New Deal* (Madison, Wis.: University of Wisconsin Press, 1958).

Dunlop, John T., and Arthur D. Hill: *The Wage Adjustment Board* (Cambridge, Mass.: Harvard University Press, 1950).

France, Robert R., and Richard A. Lester: *Compulsory Arbitration of Utility Disputes in New* Jersey and Pennsylvania (Princeton, N.J.: Princeton University, Industrial Relations Section, 1951).

Gregory, Charles O.: *Labor and the Law* (New York: Norton, 1949).

Kelly, Richard D.: *Nine Lives for Labor* (New York: Praeger, 1956).

Kennedy, Thomas: *Effective Labor Arbitration* (Philadelphia: University of Pennsylvania Press, 1948).

Kerr, Clark: *Unions and Union Leaders of Their Own Choosing* (New York: Fund for the Republic, 1958).

Killingsworth, Charles C.: *State Labor Relations Acts: A Study in Public Policy* (Chicago: University of Chicago Press, 1948).

Lecht, Leonard A.: *Experience under Railway Labor Legislation* (New York: Columbia University Press, 1955).

Leek, John H.: *Government and Labor in the United States* (New York: Rinehart, 1952).

Lombardi, John: *Labor's Voice in the Cabinet: A History of the Development of the Department of Labor from Its Origin to 1921* (New York: Columbia University Press, 1942).

McNaughton, Wayne L., and Joseph Lazar: *In-*

dustrial *Relations and the Government* (New York: McGraw-Hill, 1954).

Reede, Arthur H.: *Adequacy of Workmen's Compensation* (Cambridge, Mass.: Harvard University Press, 1947).

Richberg, Donald R.: *Labor Union Monopoly: A Clear and Present Danger* (New York: Regnery, 1957).

Somers, Herman Miles, and Anne Ramsay Somers: *Workmen's Compensation: Prevention, Insurance, and Rehabilitation of Occupational Disability* (New York: Wiley, 1954).

Taft, Philip: *The Structure and Government of Labor Unions* (Cambridge, Mass.: Harvard University Press, 1954).

Ulman, Lloyd: *The Rise of the National Trade Union* (Cambridge, Mass.: Harvard University Press, 1955).

U.S. Commission on Organization of the Executive Branch of the Government (first Hoover Commission): *Department of Labor* (1949).

Welfare

Anderson, Odin W., and Jacob J. Feldman: *Family Medical Costs and Voluntary Health Insurance: A Nationwide Survey* (New York: McGraw-Hill, 1956).

Becker, Joseph M.: *Problems of Abuse in Unemployment Benefits* (New York: Columbia University Press, 1953).

Berelson, Bernard: *Graduate Education in the United States* (New York: McGraw-Hill, 1960).

Bornet, Vaugan Oavis: *Welfare Services Surveyed* (Norman, Okla.: University of Oklahoma Press, 1961).

Burns, Eveline M.: *Social Security and Public Policy* (New York: McGraw-Hill, 1956).

Cohen, Wilbur J.: *Retirement Policies under Social Security* (Berkeley and Los Angeles, Calif.: University of California Press, 1957).

Council of State Governments: *The States and Their Older Citizens: A Report to the Governors' Conference* (Chicago: the Council, 1955).

de Grazia, Alfred, and Ted Gurr: *American Welfare* (New York: New York University Press, 1961).

Douglas, Paul H.: *Social Security in the United States: An Analysis and Appraisal of the Social Security Act* (New York: Random House, 1936).

Eddy, Edward Danforth, Jr.: *Colleges of Our Land and Time: The Land-grant Idea in American Education* (New York: Harper, 1956).

Hales, Dawson: *Federal Control of Public Education; A Critical Appraisal* (New York: Columbia University, Teachers College, 1954).

Harrington, Michael: *The Other America: Poverty in the United States* (New York: Macmillan, 1962).

Hogan, John D., and Francis A. J. Ianni: *American Social Legislation* (New York: Harper, 1956).

Knight, Douglas M., et al.: *Federal Government and Higher Education* (Englewood Cliffs, N.J.: Prentice-Hall, 1960).

Leyendecker, Hilary M.: *Problems and Policy in Public Assistance* (New York: Harper, 1955).

Mustard, Harry S.: *Government in Public Health* (New York: Commonwealth Fund, 1945).

Rivlin, Alice M.: *The Role of the Federal Government in Financing Higher Education* (Washington, D.C.: Brookings, 1962).

Russell, James E. (ed.): *National Policies for Education, Health, and Social Services* (New York: Doubleday, 1955).

Somers, Herman M., and Anne R. Somers: *Doctors, Patients, and Health Insurance* (Washington, D.C.: Brookings, 1961).

Steiner, Peter O., and Robert Dorfman: *The Economic Status of the Aged* (Berkeley and Los Angeles, Calif.: University of California Press, 1957).

U.S. Commission on Intergovernmental Relations: *Federal Aid to Public Health* (1955).

———: *Federal Aid to Welfare* (1955).

———: *Federal Responsibility in the Field of Education* (1955).

———: *Unemployment Compensation and Employment Service* (1955).

U.S. Commission on Organization of the Executive Branch of the Government (first Hoover Commission): *Medical Activities* (1949).

———: *Social Security, Education, Indian Affairs* (1949).

———: *Task Force Report on Public Welfare* (1949).

U.S. Commission on Organization of the Executive Branch of the Government (second Hoover Commission): *Federal Medical Services* (1955).

———: *Task Force Report on Medical Services* (1955).

U.S. President's Commission on Higher Education: *Higher Education for American Democracy* (6 vols., 1947).

U.S. President's Commission on Veterans' Pensions: *Veterans' Benefits in the United States* (1956).

U.S. President's Committee on Education beyond the High School: . . . *Report* . . . (1957).

REVIEW QUESTIONS

1. How do you explain the fact that the bulk of Federal and state labor and welfare legislation is comparatively recent?

2. What constitutional issues were involved in legislation dealing with child labor, wages and hours, the right to organize and bargain collectively, and "yellow-dog" contracts?

3. What is the constitutional basis of Federal intervention in the welfare, health, and education fields?

4. Summarize Federal legislation dealing with (*a*) labor, (*b*) social insurance, (*c*) education, (*d*) aid to veterans, (*e*) vocational rehabilitation, (*f*) aid to dependent children, (*g*) old-age assistance, and (*h*) the physically disabled.

5. Compare the powers, duties, and procedures of the Railway Mediation Board and the National Labor Relations Board.

6. Compare the manner in which national-emergency disputes are handled under the Railway Labor Act of 1926 and the Taft-Hartley Act.

7. To what extent do Federal antitrust laws now apply to the activities of trade unions?

8. Would it be advisable to eliminate the states from participation in (*a*) unemployment compensation and (*b*) the present system of Federal-state employment offices?

9. What common-law presumptions made it difficult for injured workmen to collect damages before the advent of workmen's compensation?

10. Defend and criticize proposals for (*a*) compulsory arbitration of labor-management disputes, (*b*) Federal aid to education, (*c*) compulsory nationwide prepaid medical, surgical, and hospital insurance, and (*d*) reinsurance of voluntary health-insurance plans.

11. What changes would you recommend in present provisions for old-age and survivors' insurance and old-age assistance?

12. Do you think the states are unduly coerced by conditional grants-in-aid for the functions mentioned in this chapter?

Agriculture
and Natural Resources

*The farm problem is complex in the extreme. But the basic
difficulty with present public agricultural policy is simple:
in trying to underwrite farm prices and income it
perpetuates an unreal price structure that encourages
overproduction of farm products and keeps too many people
in farming, resulting in ever-growing surpluses of foods
and fibers in government storehouses, surpluses that
weigh down the very price structure public policy tries to
underpin.*

COMMITTEE FOR ECONOMIC DEVELOPMENT[1]

*Conservation has never been better defined than by
Pinchot's brilliant associate, W. J. McGee, who described
it as "the use of the natural resources for the greatest good
of the greatest number for the longest time."*

DAVID CUSHMAN COYLE[2]

The natural wealth of the United States
makes possible a high standard of living if
its resources are used wisely. But if our
forests, soil, waters, minerals, fish, animals,
and birds are exploited and wasted, future

[1] *Toward a Realistic Farm Program* (New
York: Committee for Economic Development,
1958), pp. 5–6.
[2] *Conservation: An American Story of Conflict
and Accomplishment* (New Brunswick, N.J.: Rutgers University Press, 1957), p. vii.

generations may be condemned to live in
barren poverty.

The fact is that the natural resources of
the United States have been depleted to a
serious extent. Experts estimate that one-
third of the nation's farm land has been
ruined or impoverished by soil erosion.
American farmers have overgrazed the grass-
lands, have farmed land that should have
been untilled, and have cleared land that

575

should have remained forested. With the protective covering of trees, shrubs, and grasses gone, erosion has worn away the fertile topsoil, leaving wastelands. The destruction of vegetation and the uncontrolled activities of hunters and fishers have devastated American wildlife.

The same problem faces us in regard to mineral resources. At the present rate of severance, our deposits of oil, copper, zinc, and lead will soon be gone. The need to import these industrially essential products would necessitate vast changes in our economic life.

AGRICULTURE

Agriculture is America's basic industry: it produces the foods and raw materials upon which our population and manufacturers largely depend. Yet the process of urbanization has steadily reduced the proportion of the population employed in agriculture. Agriculture's share of the national income had been diminishing for a long time when the Second World War temporarily restored farm prices. By the mid-1950s another farm depression loomed on the horizon. The government has tried to meet this emergency by providing extraordinary aid and relief designed to restore agriculture to a position of parity with industry.

The basic agricultural problem is the adjustment of the supply of farm commodities to the demand for them. A manufacturer alert to market conditions is able to predict the production volume of his competitors, and he can cut down or stop production when oversupply threatens the market. But the farmer cannot do this. The large number of competitors and the dependence on uncertain elements, such as weather, plant and animal diseases, and insect plagues, make prediction impossible. It is not surprising that agriculture should have called

upon government for help in stabilizing this chaotic sector of the economy.

Farm Programs of the Past. Since the mid-1920s there have been numerous plans for governmental aid to the farmer. These included proposals for export subsidies, governmental purchase and storage, production control, price supports, acreage allotments and marketing quotas, and a number of other devices.

The McNary-Haugen bill, passed by Congress and vetoed by President Coolidge in both 1927 and 1928, provided export subsidies, financed by fees on domestic sales, but no production control.

During the Hoover Administration, hope was placed in the Agricultural Marketing Act of 1929, which emphasized loans to cooperatives and the purchase and holding of commodities by the Federal Farm Board during critical periods. Prices continued to fall, however, and the government was left with a large accumulation of wheat and cotton.

The Agricultural Adjustment Act (AAA) of 1933, the first of a number of far-reaching farm-aid laws enacted during the Roosevelt Administration, introduced production control as the major method of equalizing supply and demand. Farmers willing to reduce production were paid cash benefits from a tax collected at the processing stage. The tax rate was set at the estimated difference between market price and "parity," which was defined as the price necessary to give farmers purchasing power equal to that existing in the 1909 to 1914 period. Commodity loans were made to encourage withholding from the market; a penalty tax was imposed on excess production of cotton and tobacco.

The AAA of 1933 was declared unconstitutional in January, 1936. The Supreme Court ruled that Congress had exceeded its power in controlling production and that the processing tax with earmarked revenues was discriminatory and invalid.

The Soil Conservation and Domestic Allotment Act of 1936 provided a statutory basis for an interim program in place of the invalidated features of the AAA. Farmers were induced to plant soil-conserving crops in place of soil-depleting ones by the offer of "soil-conservation payments," financed from the general funds of the Treasury up to 500 million dollars annually.

The Agricultural Adjustment Act of 1938 restored much of the voided program of 1933, but employed methods that would not run afoul of the Court. First, farmers who cooperated by reducing acreage of soil-depleting crops were paid for "soil conservation" and for "parity." Second, producers of cotton, corn, wheat, rice, tobacco, and peanuts might, by a two-thirds majority vote in a referendum, establish acreage allotments and marketing quotas. Third, loans were made to farmers on many commodities to keep crops off the market in years of overproduction and low prices. Most of the 1938 program is still in operation.

During the Second World War and in the immediate postwar period, the Steagall amendment set the basic pattern of farm-price support. For the duration of the war plus two years, price supports were made mandatory on the basic commodities at 90 per cent of parity. Other commodities could be included if an increase in production was required; eventually twenty commodities so qualified. Prices of most commodities were well above parity, but the guaranty provided confidence that expanded production. Wartime price-support legislation expired in 1948.

Instead of allowing a full resumption of the 1938 act, Congress enacted the Agricultural Act of 1948, which provided for flexible supports, ranging from 60 to 90 per cent of parity, on nineteen commodities.

Prices would be supported on a sliding scale, depending on the supply of a particular commodity. If the supply were abnormally large, support would be set at 60 per cent; if normal, at 75; if below normal, at 90. The 1948 legislation, enacted by the Republican Eightieth Congress, proved unsatisfactory to key people in the farm population. In the presidential election that followed, Mr. Truman, who advocated rigid 90 per cent support prices and a more favorable parity base, swept the Middle West.

Among the proposals before Congress in 1949 was the Brannan plan, sponsored by the Secretary of Agriculture. It provided for farm prices to find their "natural" levels through the operation of supply and demand. The consumer would enjoy the benefits of any fall in the price level. The farmer would be assisted and protected by direct subsidy payment of an amount representing the deficiency between price received and parity. Congress declined to permit even a trial run of this plan, probably because the largest farm groups were reluctant to have the farm-subsidy issue presented in such open form to the taxpayers.

Congress then enacted the Agricultural Act of 1949, known as the Gore bill, which extended something like the wartime arrangement, including a fixed 90 per cent support program for commodities under production control and marketing quotas. The rigid supports were extended in 1952 to the crops of 1953 and 1954.

The Eisenhower administration changed, at least temporarily, the direction of support activities. Secretary Benson designed the Agricultural Act of 1954 to reestablish flexible supports for five basic commodities, beginning with the 1955 crop. Proponents of flexible supports argue that high and rigid supports stimulate overproduction, saddle the taxpayer with excessive burdens, and

WHO BENEFITS FROM RISING FOOD PRICES?

CHANGE BETWEEN 1950 AND 1958

Selected Foods	in cost to consumer	in farmer's share	in middleman's share
Milk (per qt)	+ 5.2 cents	+ 1.5 cents	+ 3.7 cents
Eggs (per doz)	+ 6.4	+ 7.6	− 1.2
Beef (average per lb, all cuts)	− 2.3	− 8.4	+ 6.1
Pork (average per lb, all cuts)	+ 4.1	− 1.9	+ 6.0
Bread (per lb, loaf)	+ 4.7	+ 0.2	+ 4.5
Apples (per lb)	0.0	+ 0.1	+ 0.8
Potatoes (per 10 lb)	+ 11.7	− 0.8	+ 12.5
Peaches (per can)	+ 5.8	+ 1.5	+ 4.3
TOTAL MARKET BASKET	**+ $122**	**− $12**	**+ $134**

(All foods produced on United States farms purchased in one year by average urban family. Excludes imported foods and meals eaten away from home.)

(Includes processing, transportation, labor costs, taxes, and profits.)

One important reason for the increase in the middleman's share of the consumer's food dollar is that Americans have demanded, and have been willing to pay for, more and more highly refined and packaged foods. (Data from U.S. Department of Agriculture and U.S. Bureau of Labor Statistics, Department of Labor.)

pile up tremendous quantities of commodities.

After the 1954 election, however, advocates of rigid supports had the majority in Congress. They maintained that the device must be used to assure adequate production, to provide the farmer with a fair return, and to stabilize the rural economy. Congress in early 1956 passed a farm bill that embodied both rigid supports and the "soil-bank" plan of the Eisenhower administration.

Soil-bank, an old idea with a new name, involved government payments to farmers for withdrawing land from cultivation. The immediate goal was to remove 12 million acres from wheat production and 3 million

from cotton; land withdrawn could not be used for other crops or grazing. A long range objective was to improve land use and conservation of soil and water resources. Soil-bank had only one year of full operation, but some features were retained.

Recommendations of President Kennedy and his Secretary of Agriculture, Orville Freeman, have centered around a policy of "supply management," under which sales and production quotas on all farm commodities would be controlled strictly to prevent surpluses from reaching the market. The administration early encountered difficulty in securing passage of major farm legislation. In 1961 authority was secured to cut wheat and feed grain acreages and to use marketing orders to cope with surpluses. Price supports on major commodities were raised.

A modified version of the basic plan of the administration—acreage allotments combined with marketing quotas—was defeated early in 1962. Under it farmers who wanted price supports had to accept marketing quotas. Later in 1962 the House and Senate passed quite different versions of farm bills, which were sent to conference, where a compromise omnibus measure was fashioned. The legislation did little more than provide temporarily for the 1963 crop year, and set the stage for later contests. Under the law, supply management of wheat may begin in 1964. Because lower price supports are in prospect, by 1964, for the major commodities, the Eighty-eighth Congress will be under heavy pressure for another farm bill.

The Parity Issue. Parity is a price for farm crops sufficient to give the farmer purchasing power equal to that enjoyed during an earlier "base period." For example, if a farmer in 1912 could take a bushel of wheat to town and buy a shirt, he ought to be able to do the same thing now. The formula takes into account a large number of a farmer's purchases, such as food, clothing, machinery, fuel, and fertilizer.

Actual parity prices for a growing season are worked out by the Department of Agriculture. A rise of the price level on things the farmer buys means an increased parity price; a decline would lead to a reduction.

Parity prices provide a floor, not a ceiling. In times of scarcity, farm prices may soar far ahead of the support level. During the ten years after Pearl Harbor, supports were largely at 90 per cent, but prices averaged 108 per cent.

After the war, the continuation of rigid support levels contributed to the overproduction of several farm commodities. The government had enough wheat and cotton in 1955 for a full year of domestic use.

The limit on Commodity Credit Corporation borrowing authority has been raised repeatedly in order to cover mandatory commitments under the law.

Disposal of surpluses is an extremely troublesome problem. Losses are inevitable unless production decreases sharply or demand rises. From 1933 to 1961 price-support losses were over 9.5 billion dollars. Estimates are that storage costs alone run over 1 million dollars per day. Reduction of inventory by selling on the domestic market normally would drive prices down and further burden the price-support program with purchases of current crops. Dumping in foreign markets might glut them and harm other producers.

The Kennedy administration relied heavily on two programs for utilizing surpluses. The "food stamp plan" was revived; it enables needy families to exchange stamps supplied by the government for surplus and other government-purchased commodities. The "food-for-peace" plan involves food grants to areas abroad for disaster relief and to aid economic development.

The Department of Agriculture. In many ways the Department of Agriculture constitutes a model in departmental organization. Frequently reorganized to improve its services to the American farmer, the Department has placed great stress on management and personnel techniques. Its vast organization has long been admirably administered by first-rate personnel with high morale. The administrative organization prevailing in 1962 grouped the several operating services, administrations, and corporations as shown on the accompanying chart.

Most of the staff offices report to the Administrative Assistant Secretary; these include budget and finance, hearing examiners, information, library, personnel, and plant and operations. The Farm Credit Administration, made independent in 1953, also plays a vital role in serving agriculture.

DEPARTMENT OF AGRICULTURE

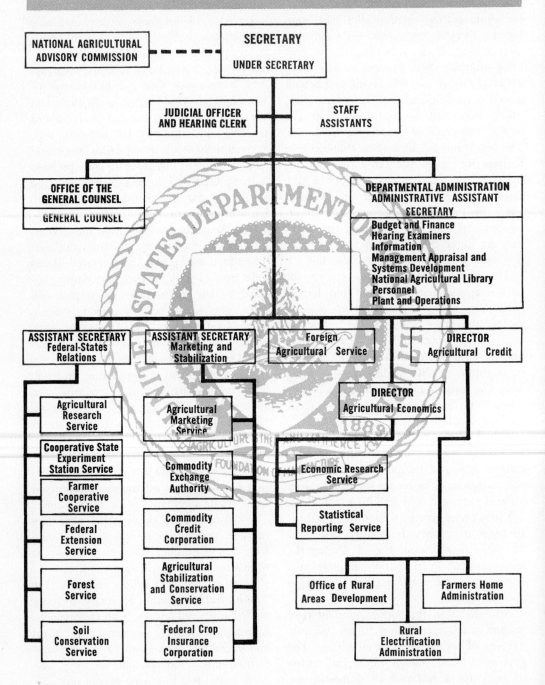

NATIONAL AGRICULTURAL ADVISORY COMMISSION

SECRETARY
UNDER SECRETARY

JUDICIAL OFFICER AND HEARING CLERK

STAFF ASSISTANTS

OFFICE OF THE GENERAL COUNSEL
GENERAL COUNSEL

DEPARTMENTAL ADMINISTRATION
ADMINISTRATIVE ASSISTANT SECRETARY
Budget and Finance
Hearing Examiners
Information
Management Appraisal and Systems Development
National Agricultural Library
Personnel
Plant and Operations

ASSISTANT SECRETARY Federal-States Relations

ASSISTANT SECRETARY Marketing and Stabilization

Foreign Agricultural Service

DIRECTOR Agricultural Credit

Agricultural Research Service

Agricultural Marketing Service

DIRECTOR Agricultural Economics

Cooperative State Experiment Station Service

Commodity Exchange Authority

Economic Research Service

Farmer Cooperative Service

Commodity Credit Corporation

Statistical Reporting Service

Federal Extension Service

Agricultural Stabilization and Conservation Service

Forest Service

Office of Rural Areas Development

Farmers Home Administration

Soil Conservation Service

Federal Crop Insurance Corporation

Rural Electrification Administration

AGRICULTURAL STABILIZATION

Plans to stabilize American agriculture have occupied an important share of congressional time and interest for thirty years. One of the chief functions of the Department of Agriculture is executing these plans.

Machinery of Price Supports. The Commodity Credit Corporation (CCC) is the principal instrumentality through which the Federal government finances its price-support program to achieve parity.

Price support is carried out through agreements to purchase, outright purchase, and conditional purchase of commodities. The latter is most widely used, and takes the form of a loan. If the stored commodity goes down in price the producer may choose to turn it over to the CCC and keep the money advanced to him. If it goes up, he may pay off the loan, plus interest, and redeem his stored crop. Most CCC loans are made through private lending agencies, but the producer may, if he chooses, deal directly with the CCC.

Price support is mandatory on wheat, corn, rice, tobacco, cotton, peanuts, wool, mohair, tung nuts, honey, and butterfat milk. It is permissible on others.

The CCC also has a program to expand capacity either through buying granaries or lending (or guaranteeing private loans) to producers for storage facilities.

Extensive procurement responsibilities are vested in the CCC, which buys farm products for some Federal agencies, foreign governments, and international relief agencies. It is authorized to exchange surplus farm products for strategic materials produced abroad.

Commodity Stabilization. Closely related to the CCC is the Commodity Stabilization Service (CSS), established in 1953 to carry out the nonfiscal aspects of many of the functions assigned to CCC. Personnel and facilities are used interchangeably by the two agencies.

First among the tasks of CSS is the adjustment of supply, when out of line with demand, for a number of farm products. Acreage allotments and marketing quotas are administered through agricultural stabilization and conservation committees on the county level. Under the Agricultural Act of 1949, eligibility for price support requires compliance with acreage allotments and marketing quotas. Penalties may be assessed for marketing in excess of quotas. Allotments and quotas are mandatory when the total supply of a commodity exceeds the normal supply by 20 per cent.

Among the price-support activities of the service is the reduction of the mountains of surplus commodities accumulated under support programs. Under the 1949 act commodities likely to spoil or deteriorate can be exchanged by Federal agencies for goods needed from abroad and not produced here. In the last resort, commodities may be given to the school-lunch program, American Indians and other needy people, and to private welfare groups for use within or outside the United States.

Crop Insurance. Insurance of crops against loss was authorized by the Agricultural Adjustment Act of 1938 and covers all unavoidable hazards, such as hail, flood, drought, wind, disease, and insect damage. The farmer pays a premium computed from the loss history of the farm and other pertinent facts; in case of loss he receives from 50 to 75 per cent of the average yield, in commodities. The program is carried out by the Federal Crop Insurance Corporation, within the Department of Agriculture. Crop insurance appears a practical and essential step toward building security for the farmer comparable to that provided by unemployment insurance for the wage earner. Crop insurance under existing legislation may cover wheat, cotton, flax, corn, tobacco, and other commodities in about one-third of the agricultural counties of the country. The second Hoover Commission concluded that the premiums charged for crop insurance were not sufficient to cover losses and administrative costs and to provide desirable reserves.

MARKETING SERVICES

From its beginning, the United States Department of Agriculture concerned itself with the problems of increasing agricultural productivity. Since the Second World War, however, it has been occupied, in addition, with marketing and handling surpluses.

Agricultural Marketing Service. Since 1954, the marketing and distributive functions of the Department have been concentrated largely in the Agricultural Marketing Service, which handles the Department's economic and statistical work, the national school-lunch program, and the distribution of surplus foods. It carries out its programs, including inducement to greater consumption, new uses, and new markets, through seven commodity divisions: cotton, dairy, fruit and vegetables, grain, livestock, poultry, and tobacco. It has subagencies for food distribution, freight rates, and warehouses.

Its economic and statistical work is mostly for the extremely important purpose of helping the farmer to decide what crops to plant. Estimates are made of acreage, yields, sales, prices, and other facts concerning crops. Regular market-news service is maintained by the Federal Department, giving farmers the benefit of the latest information on prices, demand, and market conditions generally.

The creation of definite standards and grades for farm products benefits both farmer and consumer. Adequate standards,

defined and enforced, assure the farmer a price based upon the actual quality of his products. They ensure the consumer uniform grade of the product. These standards are nationwide, but their application is largely voluntary. The consumer has a great stake in pressing Congress for compulsory grading and labeling of foods. Standardization of containers has been accomplished through use of the Federal power over weights and measures. Mandatory grading of products according to quality probably must rely upon Federal power over interstate and foreign commerce.

Commodity Futures. Traders and speculators buy and sell agricultural commodities long in advance of their availability. Such futures trading serves a useful purpose by establishing a price level on a given commodity at a date sufficiently in advance to create a measure of stability in the market. The first attempt of Congress to regulate futures transactions, in 1921, was declared invalid by the Supreme Court, but a more modest grain-futures act was enacted in 1922. Subsequent legislation has increased the list of commodities under control to include wheat, cotton, corn, oats, rye, barley, flaxseed, grain sorghums, millfeeds, rice, butter, eggs, Irish potatoes, wool tops, fats and oils, cottonseed meal, cotton seed, peanuts, soybeans, and soybean meal.

The Commodity Exchange Authority has power to designate which exchanges may engage in futures trading, to register commission merchants and brokers, to limit the size of transactions, and to forbid manipulative and fraudulent practices.

Disposing of Surpluses. In the depth of the Depression, overproduction of large surpluses of farm products existed side by side with underconsumption by millions of unemployed and hungry people. In 1933 an agency was created to purchase surpluses and divert them to needy families, school lunches, by-product uses, and export. Distribution was handled through regular retail outlets by the use of food stamps, which could be presented as payment for surplus commodities.

The postwar diversion program places heaviest emphasis on the national school-lunch program, which was placed on a regular basis by legislation in 1946. Schools that cooperate receive both Federal funds and surplus commodities. During the 1950s nearly ten million children took part in the lunch program. Large quantities of surplus foods go to charitable institutions and to families on relief or with low incomes.

Marketing Agreements. The "orderly marketing" of farm products is encouraged further by agreements between growers and handlers and by the Secretary of Agriculture's governing of the marketing program of a particular commodity. After being petitioned for an agreement (by producers or handlers), the Department of Agriculture conducts a hearing. An agreement may then be drawn up for the commodity, becoming effective when signed by one-half of the handlers of the commodity; if an order is involved, a two-thirds vote of producers is required on the referendum.

The usual agreement order involving fruits or vegetables covers both quantity and quality control; the volume of the product flowing on the market is regulated, as is the size or grade. Milk-marketing agreements govern minimum prices to producers and modes of payment. Milk-marketing orders were in force in fifty-three areas during the mid-1950s. Programs for commodities other than milk are administered by a committee of growers, handlers, or both.

Agreements and orders cover a variety of fruits, vegetables, potatoes, tree nuts, tobacco, and even hog-cholera serum! The agreement or order must cover the smallest practicable regional production area; for example, south Florida had an avocado program and five New England states (ex-

THE FARM PROBLEM

Although the Federal government has sought many ways to balance the need for an adequate standard of living for farmers with America's capacity to consume farm products:

● **Federal inventory of surplus farm products (storage cost about $1.5 million per day):**

(In billions)

Jan. 1, 1953 ▓▓▓▓ **$2.6**

Jan. 1, 1960 ▓▓▓▓▓▓▓▓▓▓▓ **$8.7**

● **Despite sale, barter, or donation of $18 billion of surplus, 1953-1960.**

● ●

Agricultural production in 1959 equaled all previous records:

Production

1947-1949 average ▓▓▓▓▓▓ **100%**

1959 ▓▓▓▓▓▓▓ **125%**

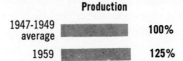

● **Despite lowest acreage (330 million acres) planted since at least 1919; acres not planted under Soil Bank Acreage Reserve program: 23 million; cost of soil-bank program, 1958: over $655 million**

● ●

Farmer's Income

Parity ratio (measure of purchasing power of farm products)

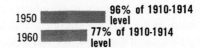

1950 ▓▓▓▓▓▓ **96% of 1910-1914 level**

1960 ▓▓▓▓▓ **77% of 1910-1914 level**

Buying power of farmer's products is at lowest level since 1940

Farmer's share of consumer's food dollar

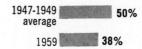

1947-1949 average ▓▓▓▓▓ **50%**

1959 ▓▓▓▓ **38%**

Farmer receives the smallest share of consumer's food dollar since 1939

cluding Maine) joined in a potato program.

Foreign Agriculture. The Foreign Agricultural Service was created in the general departmental reorganization of 1953. It has a variety of responsibilities, in the area of external relationships of American agriculture. It studies foreign markets and represents the Department in foreign relations and technical-assistance matters.

One of its most knotty tasks is to find ways of disposing of surplus farm products in overseas markets without disrupting foreign markets and demoralizing world producers. Although once a leading exporter of farm commodities, the United States, by the Second World War, was no longer so deeply involved in world trade. Domestic costs of production grew higher than foreign costs. Other countries enacted tariffs and import and export controls and otherwise restricted the free movement of trade. We, of course, stimulated such action ourselves by adopting a high tariff law in 1930.

During the Second World War, America again became one of the great granaries of the world, producing not only for itself, but for allies as well. After the war there was an immediate world-wide shortage of food, and the American farmer was able to sell much of his huge production abroad. A great deal of this foreign purchasing was financed by American grants and loans. In the early 1950s it became apparent that foreign markets for farm commodities were shrinking, as foreign aid declined and farm production in other countries was restored. With American farm production costs at a high level, the outlook for export trade was discouraging.

RESEARCH AND EXTENSION

Research to help farmers increase production has always been an important service of the Department of Agriculture. The results of research are made known to the farmer through bulletins, extension services, and demonstrations.

Research. The Department is interested in both basic and applied research carried out either by its own personnel or by that of the states. The areas of research include field crops, management, livestock, nutrition, home economics, and farm-product utilization. Field and horticultural crops are studied to improve yield, raise quality, reduce costs, and solve other problems. Department entomologists study insects, seeking methods to control harmful ones and propagate helpful ones. Plant-quarantine inspectors check plant life entering the United States, cooperate with the states to control insects and diseases attacking plants, and regulate interstate shipments. Extensive investigations are made in the feeding and breeding of farm animals and poultry in the interests of increased productivity. Soil, water, agricultural engineering, and production problems are also studied. Increasingly the Department is placing emphasis on economic research through its own Economic Research Service, which does statistical analysis and market studies.

A large share of national moneys spent for farm research is allocated to state experiment stations. Many of the top-rank research projects in agriculture are cooperative Federal-state ones, jointly conducted by the Department of Agriculture and one or more experiment stations.

Extension. The channels of information through which research results flow to the farmer are many. The Federal Department handles publications and arranges for radio, television, and press releases. The Federal Extension Service supervises the national government's participation in the cooperative extension program operated jointly with the land-grant colleges of the states and with county governments.

Under the program, agricultural, home-demonstration, and 4-H Club agents are located in most of the counties of America. These "county agents" are Federal-state-county missionaries of better agriculture who establish contact with the farmer and provide direct advice, group demonstrations, exhibits, and various organizational contacts. Important agricultural counties often have several county agents with different specialties, such as livestock, field crops, and horticulture. They bring to the attention of the farmer the latest developments from laboratory or experimental farm and put him in touch with the state college or Federal staff member most able to help him with a problem.

AGRICULTURAL CREDIT

To buy land and equip a farm, the average agriculturist must go into debt. If the farmer is to succeed, credit must be available at low interest rates and be repayable over a long period. Private capital is available for farm financing in most sections of the country, but where the risk is great, the interest charges are high. After crop failures the farmers lose their farms to the banks through foreclosures. A small-town bank with heavy investments in farm mortgages may be wiped out by a series of bad crop years. These conditions have forced the government to assume partial responsibility for farm financing.

Farm Credit Administration. The Federal agency that coordinates most of the diverse agricultural loan activities is the Farm Credit Administration (FCA), which since 1953 has been an independent agency. The Federal Farm Credit Board is the policy-determining body of FCA; it also selects the governor, who exercises the administrative functions of FCA. The FCA is not itself a lending agency; it supervises and regulates the agencies created to make farm loans.

The whole system is greatly decentralized in operation. Farmers get their loans from local associations in which they are participants. The local associations are mutual or cooperative in nature and are granted a large measure of self-government.

Long-term Farm Loans. Federal land-bank loans are made through one of the 750 national farm-loan associations. They are long-term borrowings secured by first mortgages upon farms. Interest rates are low, currently from 5½ to 6 per cent. Although these loans are primarily for the purchase of farm lands, the money is available also for improvements of mortgaged farms. If a future farmer, just home from agricultural college, wants to settle down to farming, he locates a piece of suitable land that is for sale. He goes to the offices of the national farm loan association in his county and applies for a loan. If he is judged a good risk and the farm a good buy, the association will advance him up to 65 per cent of the value of the land, taking a first mortgage as security. The applicant must agree to repay his loan in twenty to thirty years by annual or semiannual installments and buy a prescribed amount of stock in the land bank or local association. When the loan is paid off, the stock is redeemed.

Short-term Farm Credit. To produce, harvest, and market crops, farmers need loans for short periods. Credit is obtained for buying seed, feed, machinery, and livestock and many other purposes. The length of time of a short-term loan may be as long as one year. Such a loan is available from one of the 500 local production credit associations, which, like the local farm-loan associations, are cooperative organizations of farmers. The local association obtains the money it lends largely from the Federal intermediate credit bank of the farm-loan district, and from the regional production credit corporations. The overhead financing operations are even more complicated than those connected with long-term farm loans. A farmer needing cash for seed and other production costs of planting his next crop applies to the county production credit association. If the loan is made, he must acquire a share in the association and so becomes a voting member of the cooperative.

Credit for Farm Cooperatives. Special provision is made for financing farmers' cooperatives. Since 1933, cooperative credit needs have been served by the Central Bank for Cooperatives and the twelve district banks for cooperatives in the farm credit districts. Farmers' cooperatives are organized for marketing products, purchasing agricultural supplies, and other purposes.

The Farmer Cooperative Service of the Department of Agriculture performs educational service and research assistance for agricultural cooperatives. Three program divisions—marketing, purchasing, and management—carry out the main work of the service. Among American farmers, 60 per cent are estimated to belong to cooperatives.

Farmers Home Administration. The Farmers Home Administration offers assistance to small farmers unable to obtain credit elsewhere at reasonable rates and terms. The varied programs of the other lending agencies do not cover these farmers, who include some of the most deserving operators of family-sized farms. The Farmers Home Administration also carries out educational and other activities through local offices in about one-half of the counties of the country, duplicating for the marginal farmer many of the services provided by other lending agencies, Federal-state extension organizations, and other groups.

The loans available fall into the following categories:

Operating loans are for purchase of seed, feed, livestock, or fertilizer; they may be used for family living needs; some are made for joint purchase of farm machinery by two or more farmers.

Farm-ownership loans may be used to purchase a farm and to improve it, or to recondition and improve an existing family farm. If the farm is bought by borrowing from a private lending agency, the mortgage may be insured by the Farmers Home Administration.

Water-facility loans are available in Western states both to individuals and to water associations.

Emergency loans may be made, in designated areas, to help farmers who suffer from flood, drought, or other calamity. Special livestock loans have been authorized since 1953.

Veterans' assistance is provided for ex-servicemen with agricultural experience who are eligible for the various types of loans granted by this agency.

The second Hoover Commission criticized the costliness of Farmers Home Administration programs. It urged that applicants for loans be screened more carefully, that charges be increased to cover costs, and that more adequate margins between value of property and amount of mortgage be required. Duplication with the Veterans' Administration and county-agent system were subjects of adverse comment by the Commission. The second Hoover task force showed little appreciation for the special problems of rural poverty when it recommended that the lending and insurance functions of the agency be discontinued.

President Eisenhower, on the other hand, recommended a broad program of expanded services to low-income farmers. In trans-

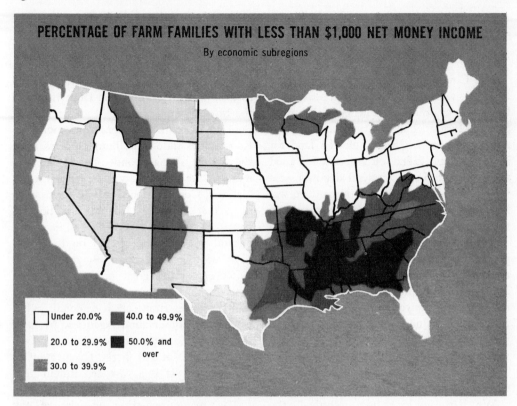

PERCENTAGE OF FARM FAMILIES WITH LESS THAN $1,000 NET MONEY INCOME
By economic subregions

Legend:
- Under 20.0%
- 20.0 to 29.9%
- 30.0 to 39.9%
- 40.0 to 49.9%
- 50.0% and over

Rural poverty is widely distributed among the several regions, but is most heavily concentrated in the South and Border States. [Adapted from the American Assembly, United States Agriculture (1955), p. 92.]

mitting a report to Congress in April, 1955, he declared: "In this wealthiest of nations, where per capita income is the highest in the world, more than one-fourth of the families who live on American farms still have cash incomes of less than $1,000 per year."

Rural Electrification Administration (REA). Created by executive order in 1935, the REA subsequently received statutory authorization, and it has operated in the Department of Agriculture since 1939. Initially its purpose was to provide loans to bring electric service to rural people; since 1949, it has financed rural telephone services as well. The agency lends, not directly to consumers, but to farmers' cooperatives and to public and private enterprises providing utility services. In its first twenty years, REA-financed systems brought electric power to over 4 million farm homes.

The second Hoover Commission pointed out the considerable taxpayer subsidy involved when the REA borrows from the Treasury at 2 per cent money for which the government must pay 3 per cent to bondholders. Administrative costs also add to the burden on the general public, as do tax exemptions on cooperatives and certain other concessions. The Commission recommended that REA be made self-supporting, obtain its financing from private sources, and be subject to the Government Corporation Control Act.

CONSERVATION OF NATURAL RESOURCES

The Coming of Conservation. For three hundred years the North American continent was exploited with little consideration for the future. The frontiersman chopped down trees for his house, cleared land for his fields, and killed off animals for food and for sport. Later, mineral deposits were tapped and exhausted, and the surface was littered with ugly debris. Tractors plowed the prairie grasses that sustained life and held down the soil. Industrial plants and cities poured out their waste, polluting streams and rendering them unable to sustain fish. Forests were ground into pulp to feed the mills for paper, rayon, and a hundred other products. Fabulous wealth was made from petroleum, but the American people have suffered the depletion of their oil resources and the loss of natural gases burned as waste.

We have not yet fully reformed; the spoiler is still around. But increasingly citizens have recognized that the balance of nature must be restored and that the power of the government must be utilized to save what is left and rebuild the resources that have been exploited. Those who have taken part in this work are called "conservationists," and the total program is called the "conservation movement."

The Conservation Movement. Nobody knows who our first conservationist was. Perhaps he was a Pilgrim farmer who alternated his crops or a frontiersman who was careful with his fire and who killed only such game as he could eat; or perhaps it was William Penn, who in 1681 required that one acre out of every five be left in trees. In any case, not all of our forefathers were wasters: many recognized that a devastated farm was no heritage for their sons and did what they could to preserve the land and forests and waters.

The modern conservation movement started during the administration of Theodore Roosevelt (1901–1909). The national forests, previously under the Department of the Interior, were transferred in 1905 to the Forest Service, Department of Agriculture. Roosevelt withdrew millions of acres from the public domain and placed them in national forests. In 1908 he appointed a National Conservation Commission, headed by Chief Forester Gifford Pinchot of Pennsylvania. Its task was to inventory natural resources and report on the possibility of their exhaustion. By the close of Roosevelt's term, great progress had been made toward saving the public lands and their resources from selfish exploitation.

Federal Conservation Agencies. Most of the Federal agencies concerned with conservation are located in the Department of the Interior. It is a vast department that covers many diverse services.

The major operating agencies of the Department concerned directly with natural-resource conservation are the Bureau of Land Management, Bureau of Reclamation, Fish and Wildlife Service, Geological Survey, and National Park Service. Agencies of the Department of Agriculture intimately concerned with resources conservation are the Soil Conservation Service and Forest Service. Also of great importance in this field are the TVA, other agencies engaged in river-valley development, and governments of the various territories.

Soil Conservation. The first approach of the American government to soil conservation was to educate farmers to adopt soil-saving practices. The United States Department of Agriculture and the state experiment stations have for a long time investigated soil building. Their information is passed on to farmers through publica-

DEPARTMENT OF THE INTERIOR

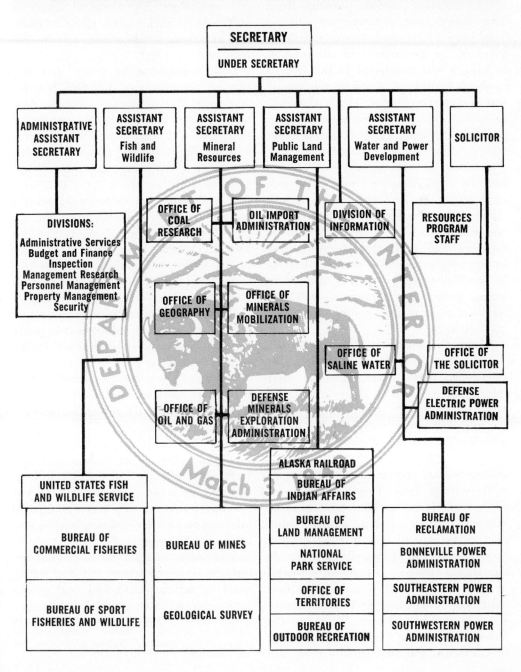

SECRETARY

UNDER SECRETARY

ADMINISTRATIVE ASSISTANT SECRETARY

ASSISTANT SECRETARY
Fish and Wildlife

ASSISTANT SECRETARY
Mineral Resources

ASSISTANT SECRETARY
Public Land Management

ASSISTANT SECRETARY
Water and Power Development

SOLICITOR

DIVISIONS:
Administrative Services
Budget and Finance
Inspection
Management Research
Personnel Management
Property Management
Security

OFFICE OF COAL RESEARCH

OIL IMPORT ADMINISTRATION

DIVISION OF INFORMATION

RESOURCES PROGRAM STAFF

OFFICE OF GEOGRAPHY

OFFICE OF MINERALS MOBILIZATION

OFFICE OF SALINE WATER

OFFICE OF THE SOLICITOR

OFFICE OF OIL AND GAS

DEFENSE MINERALS EXPLORATION ADMINISTRATION

DEFENSE ELECTRIC POWER ADMINISTRATION

ALASKA RAILROAD

UNITED STATES FISH AND WILDLIFE SERVICE

BUREAU OF INDIAN AFFAIRS

BUREAU OF COMMERCIAL FISHERIES

BUREAU OF MINES

BUREAU OF LAND MANAGEMENT

BUREAU OF RECLAMATION

NATIONAL PARK SERVICE

BONNEVILLE POWER ADMINISTRATION

BUREAU OF SPORT FISHERIES AND WILDLIFE

GEOLOGICAL SURVEY

OFFICE OF TERRITORIES

SOUTHEASTERN POWER ADMINISTRATION

BUREAU OF OUTDOOR RECREATION

SOUTHWESTERN POWER ADMINISTRATION

589

tions, demonstrations, and the field work of farm-adviser or county-agent extension services. The chief result of this educational program has been the widespread adoption of crop rotation, contour plowing, check dams, reforestation, and cover cropping.

In 1933 a soil-erosion service was established in the Department of the Interior; in 1935 it was transferred to the Department of Agriculture, where it was named Soil Conservation Service. The Service seeks to spread the use of soil-erosion-control practices through (1) demonstrations in selected areas and (2) assistance of soil-conservation districts organized under state laws. By 1958 there were over 2,000 soil-conservation districts, embracing nearly 1 million farms. The Service aids these farmer-managed districts with technical advice, materials, and equipment. Reorganization in 1953–1954 provoked great controversy by abolishing regional offices and transferring greater responsibility for soil conservation to state headquarters and land-grant colleges.

Water Conservation. Government has played a major role in getting water to the people and to the land. Domestic water supplies are provided by municipally owned projects in most parts of the country. Water for irrigation often is supplied by public irrigation districts. The Bureau of Reclamation of the Department of the Interior has constructed and operates huge dam projects in the western states. These projects generally are multipurpose. They serve to make water available for irrigation, generate hydroelectric power, and aid in flood control. Sometimes they improve navigation, provide recreational facilities, and control salt-water encroachment as well. Some of the most important reclamation projects of recent years have been Hoover Dam on the Colorado River, the Central Valley Project in California, and the Grand Coulee and the Bonneville Dams on the Columbia River. These and similar projects have reclaimed great areas of the West which have rich land but insufficient rainfall to support agriculture. The Corps of Engineers of the Army often plays a complementary, and sometimes a competitive, role in dam building.[1]

Dams constructed for power, flood-control, or domestic and irrigation purposes may serve also to regularize stream flow, which permits fish propagation and recreational uses. Pollution is controlled primarily by state law, prohibiting dumping of industrial waste or raw sewage into rivers. When a stream flows through several states, interstate action may prove necessary for the orderly development of the basin and the correction of pollution. Such is the case with the Delaware River, which is controlled by the Interstate Commission on the Delaware River Basin, an agency of Delaware, New Jersey, New York, and Pennsylvania.

Forest Conservation. In its virgin state, at the beginning of white settlement in North America, the area that is now the United States was about 43 per cent forested. These forests have been seriously depleted: some of the timber has been used for construction, fuel, and industry; the remainder has been wasted and destroyed.

When forests are cleared, soil is exposed to erosion, game is left without protective cover, and streams are filled with silt. Trees also act as windbreaks, reducing wind erosion of the soil, and they have a moderating influence on climate—reducing heat in summer, protecting against cold winds in winter, and providing moisture for crops. The recreational value of forests has been recognized by national, state, and local govern-

[1] Jurisdictional conflicts among Federal agencies are covered in an interesting case study by Robert J. Morgan, "Pressure Politics and Resources Administration," *Journal of Politics*, vol. 18, (February, 1956), pp. 39–60.

CONSERVATION OF LUMBER RESOURCES: A CONTINUING NEED

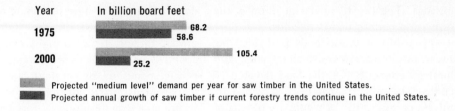

Year   In billion board feet

1975   68.2
        58.6

2000   105.4
      25.2

Projected "medium level" demand per year for saw timber in the United States.
Projected annual growth of saw timber if current forestry trends continue in the United States.

PRODUCTIVITY AND OWNERSHIP OF COMMERCIAL FOREST LAND IN THE U.S.

(total 488.6 million acres, includes coastal Alaska)

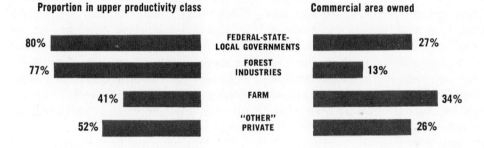

Proportion in upper productivity class		Commercial area owned
80%	FEDERAL-STATE-LOCAL GOVERNMENTS	27%
77%	FOREST INDUSTRIES	13%
41%	FARM	34%
52%	"OTHER" PRIVATE	26%

In order to raise growth to levels needed to meet demand, U. S. Forest Service recommends:

- Immediate planting of 52 million acres (10 per cent of all commercial forest land, 45 per cent of all poorly or nonstocked forest land)
- Better stocking practices, mainly on 4.5 million farms and small ownerships in Great Lakes and southeast parts of the United States
- Improved control of losses from disease, insects, and fire which helps disease get started
- Fuller utilization of dead trees, cull trees, and logging and other residues

A report by the U.S. Forest Service in 1958 forecast a substantial shortage of lumber resources by 1975 and a desperate shortage by 2000. The timber industry disputes these figures and argues that replacement matches logging.

ments, and they have set aside parks, forests, and resorts for public use and enjoyment.

We cannot, of course, stop using our timber resources, but we can wisely regulate their use for ourselves and for future generations. The key to such regulation is the ownership pattern of forest lands.

Ownership of forest lands is divided between private parties and Federal, state, and local governments. Of the land devoted to commercial uses, 75 per cent is owned by private parties, many of whom are owners of small woodlands averaging only sixty-two acres. Of the 25 per cent under public ownership, roughly two-thirds belongs to the Federal government, the remainder to state, county, and municipal governments. Since governments usually hold their forests for purposes other than profit, they are tempted less than private owners to exploit their holdings. In general, logging operations are permitted only on a selective basis, with public foresters marking the trees that may be felled and enforcing rigid specifications for protection of young growth. Farm wood-lot trees are also relatively safe from wholesale devastation, for the farmer commonly regards trees as a crop and recognizes the necessity of replanting.

Private Ownership. The great problem is to regulate the industrial owner of commercial forest lands. He is in the business of cutting and marketing timber products, and his primary motivation often is immediate profit. Mechanized logging operations not only take mature trees but destroy young growth and leave debris that constitutes a serious fire hazard. The more progressive lumbering concerns have cooperated with the Forest Service of the Department of Agriculture in fire prevention and reforestation work, but the great majority have devastated the forests with little thought of the future. Governments can encourage wise use of timber by a tax policy that does not penalize the owner for growing trees to full maturity; some states have done this by exempting forests from ordinary real-property taxes, collecting instead a severance tax at the time the trees are felled. States can do more than they have to require reforestation by laws, based on the state police power, forcing a replanting program upon concerns or individuals who engage in lumbering operations. By constant care and wise management, it is altogether possible to secure an adequate supply of forest products for generations.

Public versus Private Ownership. In recent years there has been much controversy over the continuation and expansion of publicly owned lands. Private grazing, lumbering, and other interests criticize the alleged severity of restrictions imposed upon users of Federal lands. State and local governments are concerned over the large amounts of tax-exempt land within their territorial jurisdiction. Others complain of "creeping socialism." On the other hand, proponents of public ownership point to the long record of ruthless exploitation of natural resources.

The Forest Services lists six categories of forest lands for which it regards public ownership as best: (1) where soil, climate, species, or other factors make for slow growth or poor quality; (2) where large investment and long waiting will be required because of depletion of timber growing stock; (3) where private management is inadequate and a threat to stable supplies and dependent communities; (4) where public management is vital to the control and use of water; (5) where the area has high value for recreation, wildlife propagation, and the like; and (6) where lands are so intermingled with public forests that they hamper proper management of the forests. These principles appear sound, and their application does not call for complete public ownership. The controversy can be eased by fair dealing with affected private interests and generous payments in lieu of taxation to state and local governments.

The Forest Service. The Forest Service is the most influential governmental agency working in the field of forest conservation. Custody of the 160 national forests is entrusted to the Service. It provides fire protection, disease control, recreational facilities, regulation of grazing and timber harvesting, and sale of forest products. In addition, the Forest Service conducts an extensive research program on every aspect of forest management and utilization.

An important phase of the Service's work is its cooperation with state and local governments and private parties. Since 1924, the Federal government has granted financial assistance to state governments for fire control; it also financially aids states that give young trees, or sell them at low cost, to farmers and (since 1949) nonfarmers. An outstanding development in 1950 was the enactment by Congress of the Cooperative Forest Management Act. This aids and encourages state departments of forestry that make trained foresters and other personnel available to advise and consult with owners of small wood lots, small sawmill operators, and other processors of primary forest products. Some 1,000 counties are now served with foresters under this cooperative Federal-state management plan.

The National Parks. Our national park system, containing some of the great natural wonders of the world, is administered by the National Park Service. The primary purpose of the Service is to preserve and develop natural beauty spots and historic monuments for the recreation and enjoyment of the people. The brash commercialization that has spoiled some Eastern works of nature is prevented from entering Yellowstone, Yosemite, Sequoia, Grand Canyon, Smoky Mountain, and the other national parks.

Fish and Wildlife Conservation. Wildlife has been decimated by excessive hunting and trapping, the destruction of natural haunts, lack of food, and other developments. Many types of wildlife have been reduced to extinction or near extinction. The number of buffalo has dropped from some 60 million to a few thousand; wild ducks and geese have been depleted to a fraction of their former numbers; antelope, elk, and moose have become rare. The beautiful passenger pigeon is fully extinct. Certain species of fish have disappeared.

The Fish and Wildlife Service of the Federal government cooperates with state and local agencies to conserve these important resources. It engages in research and administers Federal grants for wildlife restoration. It protects migratory birds covered by treaty, licenses hunters and limits their kill of protected birds, and maintains many wildlife refuges. States also have fish and game agencies to enforce game laws, license hunters, and provide refuges and propagation facilities.

These Federal and state agencies operate hatcheries for the propagation of fishes; the young stock is then planted in suitable waters. State and Federal agencies assist and regulate commercial fishermen; state authority is most extensive, but Federal jurisdiction extends to the highly important Alaskan seal and salmon industry and permits patrol activities on the high seas under treaty arrangements. The enforcement of seasonal limits and quantitative restrictions, mostly imposed by state law, protects the fish supply.

Mineral Resources. The United States is blessed by nature with a great abundance of mineral deposits. But the Second World War dramatically showed that our supplies are not unlimited. The Japanese invasion of Malaya and Netherlands East Indies in 1942 cut off this country's principal source of tin. The needs of modern war for aluminum emphasized our deficiencies in another mineral. And we have little or no chromium, manganese, or nickel.

Our iron supply comes primarily from the deposists around Lake Superior. Although these deposits may be exhausted in the next generation, adequate quantities of lower-grade ore are available for posterity. Vast deposits of high-grade iron ore are being opened in Canada. The United States has about one-third of the copper deposits of the world, but it is using them up at a fairly rapid rate.

Bauxite, the mineral from which aluminum is extracted, is found in Arkansas, but great quantities must be imported. Lead is a major product of Missouri, but the deposits are being mined so rapidly that a serious shortage may result. Zinc is highly important for galvanizing iron to prevent rust; American deposits are mainly in Oklahoma and New Jersey and are sufficiently limited to cause concern over future supply.

H. Ries has pointed out several methods by which mineral resources may be conserved: (1) improved mining methods to reduce waste; (2) better processes of mineral separation to avoid loss; (3) more economical use of finished products; (4) extensive use of scrap materials; and (5) Federal and state measures of conservation to promote saving. The Federal and state governments are working on each of these fronts.

The Bureau of Mines, Department of the Interior, does research concerning the first four points mentioned above. It conducts a safety program directed toward saving life and property from loss in mining accidents, and it produces helium gas for use by the Armed Forces. The Bureau of Mines has extensive responsibilities for carrying out investigations of strategic minerals.

Still broader is the work of the United States Geological Survey, which investigates mineral and water resources, classifies public lands, and prepares topographic maps. The Survey is in a commanding position over governmental lands, in its role of supervisor of oil, gas, and mining operations under leases. It also investigates water supplies. During the war it was given the important task of finding new sources of strategic minerals.

Coal Conservation. Coal is one of the most valuable nonmetallic mineral resources. It is plentiful in the United States, with reserves adequate for the needs of a great population. Anthracite, or hard coal, is found only in the eastern half of Pennsylvania. Bituminous, or soft, coal is found in a belt stretching from Pennsylvania to Alabama, on both sides of the Mississippi River, and in the southern Rocky Mountains. The lower grades of coal, subbituminous coal and lignite, are scattered through the South and West. New England and the Pacific Coast are almost wholly without usable coal deposits.

The Bureau of Mines devotes much attention to coal production and utilization. Because the demand for coal slumped after the First World War, especially in the 1930s, special arrangements were made to care for the sick industry. State governments and universities provide many services to coal miners and coal users.

Federal Land Policy. The greater portion of the country's land has, at one time or another, belonged to the Federal government. Had the government kept title to its lands, the tasks of planning and conservation might be much simpler today. On the other hand, the inducement of land in the West drove men to seek their fortunes on the frontier. Of the total public lands of 1,800 million acres, over 1 billion were

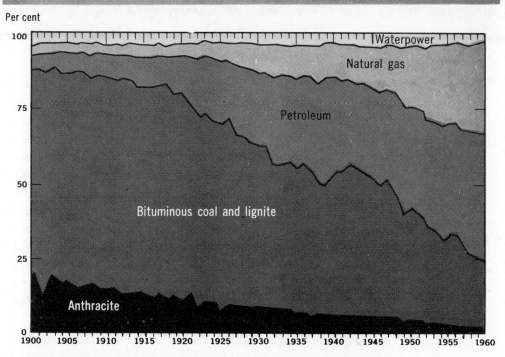

PROPORTIONAL USE OF UNITED STATES ENERGY SOURCES
Continental United States, 1900-1959, Mineral Fuels and Waterpower only

Per cent

Waterpower

Natural gas

Petroleum

Bituminous coal and lignite

Anthracite

The United States is consuming larger and larger amounts of energy, but the share of coal is declining while the roles of natural gas and petroleum are increasing. [Data from *Statistical Abstract*, 1960.]

turned over to state and private owners. These included homesteads, sales, grants to states, and grants to railroads. The acreage remaining under Federal title includes national forests and parks, grazing districts, Indian reservations, and other lands withdrawn from entry by homesteaders.

The Bureau of Land Management is the agency with general custody of public lands. It handles the surveying, management, and disposition of the public domain. Virtually all governmental land suitable for agriculture has long since been granted or sold.

The office issues permits and leases for grazing, mining, and other uses of the land under its jurisdiction. The Bureau also leases land to stock owners under a policy that requires close supervision to prevent overgrazing, with attendant losses through erosion and flood.

Indian Affairs. An aspect of conservation and social welfare frequently neglected concerns the first American, the Indian. Our national history is blotted with episodes of land seizure, massacre, and treaty violation that have reduced the Indian to a pitiful

FEDERAL OWNERSHIP OF LAND

Inventory Report on Real Property Owned by the
United States Throughout the World As of June 30, 1957
General Services Administration — February 18, 1958

Location State	Total Acreage of State	Per cent Owned by Fed. Gov't
ARIZONA	72,688,000	44.6
CALIFORNIA	100,313,600	46.1
COLORADO	66,510,080	36.1
IDAHO	52,972,160	65.1
MONTANA	93,361,920	30.0
NEVADA	70,264,960	87.7
NEW MEXICO	77,767,040	35.4
OREGON	61,641,600	51.3
UTAH	52,701,440	69.2
WASHINGTON	42,743,040	29.6
WYOMING	62,403,840	47.8
Total: (11 Western States)	753.3 million	48.4
Total UNITED STATES	1,903,824,640	21.5
ALASKA	365,481,600	99.2

Government ownership of such a large proportion of land area in the West poses acute problems of financing local governmental services.

condition. Unfortunately, public policy on Indian problems has been inconsistent, neglectful, and sometimes overpaternalistic. It has been estimated that the Indian population in 1492 was close to 850,000; in 1865 it was under 300,000; the 1950 census showed 343,410.

Federal responsibilities have covered two areas: (1) The government is trustee for Indian lands and moneys and (2) it provides welfare, health, educational, and other services not otherwise available.

The lands held for Indian tribes and individuals total more than 54 million acres. Under the Indian Reorganization Act of 1934, Indian societies were recognized and given added power to govern themselves and their property. The Eisenhower administration pushed termination of Federal trusteeship and the disposition of Indian property. Until full termination, however, Indian lands require much help in soil and water conservation, mineral development, and forest management. Few states with large

HOW FEDERAL LANDS ARE USED

(excluding Alaska)

	(Millions of Acres)	
GRAZING	181.0	44.3%
FOREST AND WILDLIFE	171.9	42.1
MILITARY (except Airfields)	18.8	4.6
PARKS AND HISTORIC SITES	15.3	3.7
RECLAMATION AND IRRIGATION	7.9	1.9
FLOOD CONTROL AND NAVIGATION	4.9	1.2
INDUSTRIAL	2.7	0.7
AIRFIELDS	2.4	0.6
POWER DEVELOPMENT AND DISTRIBUTION	2.1	0.5
OTHER	1.5	0.4
TOTAL	**408.5**	**100.0%**

(U.S. General Services Administration.)

Indian populations (Oklahoma, Arizona, and New Mexico have the largest) can or will soon offer Indians the full range of public services available to other citizens.

Critics of quick termination fear that it will intensify the poverty, ill-health, and ignorance so widespread among the Indian population. Legislation in 1953 permitted states, at their discretion, to extend their civil and criminal jurisdiction to Indian communities within their borders. Will this make possible the violation of historic Indian rights and privileges, and perhaps interfere with tribal self-government? Something approaching chaos is feared by some from the pattern of termination set up for the Klamath Indian reservation over a four- to seven-year period. Members of the tribe wishing to withdraw their shares are paid off by selling some tribal property. In view of the valuable timber lands of the Klamath, these individual shares may average more than $20,000; few are expected to make good use of the capital sum; some are likely to sustain complete loss.

The first Hoover Commission recommended that the Bureau of Indian Affairs be transferred to a new department of social security and education. It advised that the best solution of the "Indian problem" was integration of Indians into the rest of the population. Pending integration, it held that social programs for Indians should be transferred to the states. Leading commissioners dissented.

The Continental Shelf. Although the Congress by law in 1953 gave the states jurisdiction over the natural resources of their offshore territorial waters, the same act claimed for the Federal government the "continental shelf" beyond. The extent of state jurisdiction, under the Submerged Lands Act, was to be the seaward limits as they were at the time the state was admitted to the union. In no case, however, were states to reach more than three miles into the Atlantic or Pacific, or three marine leagues (about ten and one-half miles) into the Gulf of Mexico. Not long after the legislation went into effect, the Federal government found itself in conflict with maritime states over proper definition of seaward boundaries.

Petroleum resources of immense value are at stake, particularly in the Gulf area. Texas and Florida entered the union with their historic boundaries of three leagues into the sea set by Spanish usage. Louisiana has claimed submerged lands as far out into the Gulf as twenty-seven miles; Department of the Interior offers to lease for oil drilling the area beyond three miles come into direct conflict with Louisiana claims.

"TIDELANDS" OIL—ITS POTENTIAL VALUE

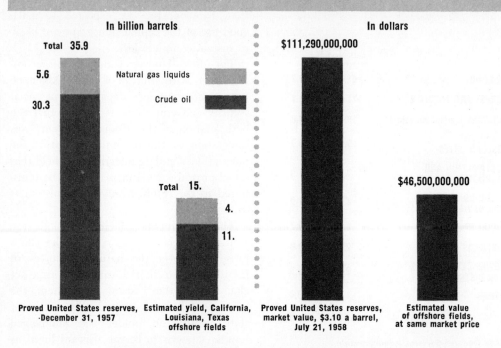

In billion barrels

Total 35.9

5.6   Natural gas liquids

30.3   Crude oil

Total 15.

4.

11.

In dollars

$111,290,000,000

$46,500,000,000

Proved United States reserves, Estimated yield, California,   Proved United States reserves,   Estimated value
·December 31, 1957   Louisiana, Texas   market value, $3.10 a barrel,   of offshore fields,
                            offshore fields   July 21, 1958   at same market price

Some of the maritime states, principally California, Texas, and Louisiana, have collected large sums from those oil companies which they permit to drill under their offshore areas. Potentially greater revenues may accrue to the Federal government under
its claim to the continental shelf beyond territorial waters. (From *Petroleum Week*.)

The three-mile limit is the most widely recognized under international law, and the United States traditionally has supported this definition of territorial waters in the interests of the freedom of the seas. The claim of the continental shelf, however, conflicts sharply with the concept of a three-mile limit. Under contemporary interpretations, the shelf is conceived to be the shallow waters, usually under 600 feet, adjacent to territorial waters. In the Atlantic this definition could mean Federal claim to submerged lands stretching up to 250 miles off shore; in the Gulf the shelf extends as far as 140 miles. The government has been careful to claim not that the boundaries of the

United States extend as far as the continental shelf, but that its jurisdiction over resources does.

The Outer Continental Shelf Lands Act of 1953 authorizes the exploration and development of natural resources on submerged lands. It has been estimated that the "quitclaim" legislation of 1953, giving the states jurisdiction over resources in and under territorial waters, allocated to the states only about 10 per cent of submerged lands. The 90 per cent claimed by the Federal government in the continental shelf included some proved oil producers and a great deal of promising area for exploration. In the Gulf area, despite the hazards of stormy weather, oil drilling has been carried on successfully from platforms resting on piles driven into submerged land through considerable depths. The conflict between the Federal government and the Gulf states was settled by the Supreme Court in 1960. Texas and Florida were awarded resources within three leagues, but Louisiana was confined to one league (about 3.5 miles). The larger problem, which may ultimately be resolved in an international tribunal, concerns the power of an individual nation to make exclusive claims over the resources of an adjacent continental shelf.

FOR FURTHER READING

Agriculture

American Assembly: *United States Agriculture: Perspectives and Prospects* (New York: Columbia University Graduate School of Business, 1955).

Baker, Gladys: *The County Agent* (Chicago: University of Chicago Press, 1939).

Benedict, Murray R.: *Can We Solve the Farm Problem? An Analysis of Federal Aid to Agriculture* (New York: Twentieth Century Fund, 1955).

————: *Farm Policies of the United States, 1790–1950* (New York: Twentieth Century Fund, 1953).

———— and Oscar C. Stine: *The Agricultural Commodity Programs: Two Decades of Experience* (New York: Twentieth Century Fund, 1956).

Benson, Ezra T.: *Freedom to Farm* (Garden City, N.Y.: Doubleday, 1960).

Black, John D.: *Parity, Parity, Parity* (Cambridge, Mass.: Harvard University Press, 1942).

Block, William J.: *The Separation of the Farm Bureau and the Extension Service: Political Issue in a Federal System* (Urbana, Ill.: University of Illinois, 1960).

Christenson, Reo M.: *The Brannan Plan* (Ann Arbor, Mich.: University of Michigan Press, 1959).

Clark, William H.: *Farms and Farmers: The Story of American Agriculture* (Boston: Page, 1945).

Conference on Economic Progress: *Full Prosperity for Agriculture* (Washington, D.C.: the Conference, 1955).

Davis, John H., and Kenneth Hinshaw: *Farmer in a Business Suit* (New York: Simon and Schuster, 1957).

Deering, Ferdie: *USDA, Manager of American Agriculture* (Norman, Okla.: University of Oklahoma Press, 1945).

Gaus, John M., and Leon O. Wolcott: *Public Administration and the United States Department of Agriculture* (Chicago: Public Administration Service, 1940).

Halcrow, Harold G.: *Agricultural Policy of the United States* (Englewood Cliffs, N.J.: Prentice-Hall, 1953).

Hardin, Charles M.: *The Politics of Agriculture* (Glencoe, Ill.: Free Press, 1952).

McConnell, Grant: *The Decline of Agrarian Democracy* (Berkeley and Los Angeles, Calif.: University of California Press, 1953).

McCune, Wesley: *Who's Behind Our Farm Policy?* (New York: Praeger, 1956).

Mighell, Ronald L.: *American Agriculture: Its Structure and Place in the Economy* (New York: Wiley, 1955).

Schickele, Rainer: *Agricultural Policy* (New York: McGraw-Hill, 1954).

Shepherd, Geoffrey S.: *Agricultural Price Income Policy* (Ames, Iowa: Iowa State College Press, 3d ed., 1952).

Soth, Lauren: *Farm Trouble* (Princeton, N.J.: Princeton University Press, 1957).

Truman, David B.: *Administrative Decentralization: A Study of the Chicago Field Office of the United States Department of Agriculture* (Chicago: University of Chicago Press, 1940).

U.S. Commission on Organization of the Executive Branch of the Government (first Hoover Commission): *Department of Agriculture* (1949).

————: *Task Force Report on Agriculture Activities* (1949).

U.S. Commission on Organization of the Executive Branch of the Government (second Hoover

Commission): *Lending Agencies* (1955).

————: *Task Force Report on Lending Agencies* (1955).

Wilcox, Walter W.: *Alternative Policies for American Agriculture*, Public Affairs Bulletin 67 (Library of Congress, 1949).

————: *The Farmer in the Second World War* (Ames, Iowa: Iowa State College Press, 1947).

Natural Resources

Bartley, Ernest R.: *The Tidelands Oil Controversy* (Austin, Tex.: University of Texas Press, 1953).

Callison, Charles H. (ed.): *America's Natural Resources* (New York: Ronald, 1957).

Ciriacy-Wantrup, S. von: *Resource Conservation: Economics and Policies* (Berkeley and Los Angeles, Calif.: University of California Press, 1952).

Clawson, Marion, and Burnell Held: *The Federal Lands, Their Use and Management* (Baltimore: Johns Hopkins Press, 1957).

Coyle, David C.: *Conservation: An American Story of Conflict and Accomplishment* (New Brunswick, N.J.: Rutgers University Press, 1957).

Dewhurst, J. Frederic, and others: *America's Needs and Resources: A New Survey* (New York: Twentieth Century Fund, 1956).

Engler, Robert: *The Politics of Oil: A Study of Private Power and Democratic Directions* (New York: Macmillan, 1961).

Foss, Phillip O.: *Politics and Grass: The Administration of Grazing on the Public Domain* (Seattle, Wash.: University of Washington, 1960).

Frank, Bernard, *Our National Forests* (Norman, Okla.: University of Oklahoma Press, 1955).

Galbraith, John K., et al.: *Perspectives on Conservation: Essays on America's Natural Resources* (Baltimore: Johns Hopkins Press, 1958).

Gulick, Luther H.: *American Forest Policy* (New York: Duell, Sloan & Pearce, 1951).

Gustafson, Axel F., and others: *Conservation in the United States* (Ithaca, N.Y.: Comstock, 2d ed., 1944).

Higbee, Edward: *The American Oasis: The Land and Its Uses* (New York: Knopf, 1957).

Huberty, M. R., and W. L. Flock (eds.): *Natural Resources* (New York: McGraw-Hill, 1959).

Ise, John: *Our National Park Policy: A Critical History* (Baltimore: Johns Hopkins Press, 1961).

Lyons, Barrow: *Tomorrow's Birthright: A Political and Economic Interpretation of Our Natural Resources* (New York: Funk & Wagnalls, 1955).

Neuberger, Richard L.: *Our Natural Resources— And Their Conservation* (New York: Public Affairs Committee, 1956). Pamphlet No. 230.

Nixon, Edgar B. (ed.): *Franklin D. Roosevelt and Conservation, 1911–1945* (Hyde Park, N.Y.: F. D. Roosevelt Library, 1957).

Parks, W. R.: *Soil Conservation Districts in Action* (Ames, Iowa: Iowa State College Press, 1952),

Parson, R. L.: *Conserving American Resources* (Englewood Cliffs, N.J.: Prentice-Hall, 1956).

Peffer, E. Louise: *The Closing of the Public Domain* (Stanford, Calif.: Stanford University Press, 1956).

Pinchot, Gifford: *Breaking New Ground* (New York: Harcourt, Brace, 1947).

Pollak, Franklin S. (ed.): *Resources Development: Frontiers for Research* (Boulder, Colo.: University of Colorado Press, 1960).

Raushenbush, Stephen (ed.): "The Future of Our Natural Resources," *Annals of the American Academy*, vol. 281 (May, 1952).

Sears, Paul B.: *Deserts on the March* (Norman, Okla.: University of Oklahoma Press, 1947).

Simpson, George E., and J. Milton Yinger (eds.): "American Indians and Indian Life," *Annals of the American Academy*, vol. 311 (May, 1957).

U.S. Commission on Organization of the Executive Branch of the Government (first Hoover Commission): *Reorganization of the Department of the Interior* (1949).

————: *Task Force Report on Natural Resources* (1949).

Wengert, Norman: *Natural Resources and the Power Struggle* (New York: Doubleday, 1955).

Zimmerman, Erich W.: *Conservation in the Production of Petroleum* (Princeton, N.J.: Princeton University Press, 1957).

REVIEW QUESTIONS

1. What grounds are there for the argument that general prosperity rests on the productivity and welfare of primary producers?

2. Describe farm programs of the past, with particular emphasis on the question of constitutionality.

3. Explain the controversy over rigid and flexible price supports.

4. What is the soil bank? What is parity?

5. What are the mechanics of price supports? Crop insurance?

6. What does the government do to help the farmer market his products?

7. Discuss the problem of disposing of farm surpluses.

8. What role does the Federal government play in agricultural research? In getting research results to the farmer?

9. What provision is made by the government for farm credit?

10. Trace the coming of conservation and the launching of the modern conservation movement.

11. Describe existing programs for water, soil, and wildlife conservation.

12. What role does ownership play in the preservation of forest resources?

13. What are the prospects for future supplies of the principal mineral resources?

14. Describe recent trends in the administration of Indian affairs.

15. Explain the basis of the Federal government's claim to the resources of the continental shelf. How are they being utilized?

Part Four

State and Local Governments

Chapter Twenty-Nine

State Constitutions

and Powers

State constitutions generally contain too much material that is statutory in nature. As a result, the legislature's efforts to meet public needs effectively are often restricted by unrealistic limitations. The legislature needs broad and flexible powers compatible with basic private rights.

PACIFIC NORTHWEST ASSEMBLY[1]

The basic principles of state and local government in the United States are set forth in the constitutions of the separate states. The state constitution with which most people are familiar is the written constitution, but there are principles and rules of great importance that may not be recorded in the formal document. As with the Federal government, they become part and

[1] *The States in the Pacific Northwest* (Seattle, Wash.: Regional Sponsoring Committee, 1957), p. 3.

parcel of the fundamental law through custom and usage, judicial interpretation, statutory elaboration, and other means. Most of this chapter will be devoted to a consideration of the written constitutions, as construed by the courts.

CONSTITUTIONS PAST AND PRESENT

Study of state constitutions, and indeed of state governments generally, is difficult because of the diversity in form and content.

605

One's natural interest is in the constitution of the state in which he lives. Why, then, should one take the trouble to examine the institutions of other states? The answer is that some comparative study is necessary in order to see a single state government in perspective. Through the experience of other states, one may learn the wisdom or pitfalls involved in a certain course of action or inaction. This is one nation, and it is no longer possible for a person to fulfill his civic responsibilities by being merely a good Vermonter or a good Texan. Migration from state to state is an old American custom, recently revived in intensified form. A general view of American state institutions provides orientation for closer study of a particular state.

FRAMING AND ADOPTING STATE CONSTITUTIONS, 1776-1783*

STATE	FRAMERS	AUTHORITY	RATIFICATION
Delaware	Legislative bodies	Power expressly given	No ratification; proclaimed in effect
Georgia	Legislative bodies	Power expressly given	No ratification; proclaimed in effect
Maryland	Legislative bodies	Power expressly given	Informal ratification through circulation among people, or advance instructions from people
Massachusetts	Constitutional conventions	Chosen for purpose	Popular ratification by vote of people
New Hampshire	Constitutional conventions	Chosen for purpose	Popular ratification by vote of people
New Jersey	Legislative bodies	No express power	No ratification; proclaimed in effect
New York	Legislative bodies	Power expressly given	No ratification; proclaimed in effect
North Carolina	Legislative bodies	Power expressly given	Informal ratification through circulation among people, or advance instructions from people
Pennsylvania	Legislative bodies	Power expressly given	Informal ratification through circulation among people, or advance instructions from people
South Carolina	Legislative bodies	Power expressly given	Informal ratification through circulation among people, or advance instructions from people
Vermont	Legislative bodies	Power expressly given	No ratification; proclaimed in effect
Virginia	Legislative bodies	No express power	No ratification; proclaimed in effect

* For a fuller account see Walter F. Dodd, "The Revision and Amendment of State Constitutions" (Baltimore: Johns Hopkins Press, 1910), pp. 3-29, and James Q. Dealey, "Growth of American State Constitutions" (Boston: Ginn, 1915), pp. 24-31. Rhode Island and Connecticut merely adapted their written charters.

Early State Constitutions. The general situation regarding colonial and early state governments is traced in Chapter 2. Most of the colonial "constitutions" were such in the British sense of basic principles rather than the later American sense of formal documents. The charter and proprietary colonies had fairly definite written limitations; the royal colonies had restrictions placed upon them through instructions to governors and by other means.

Dodd[1] found three principles emerging from colonial experience and thought: (1) written instruments of government, (2) constitutions paramount over statute law, and (3) the theory of social contract. These principles and theories led the states, during the Revolutionary War, either to adopt wholly new constitutions or to revise existing charters, as did Rhode Island and Connecticut. There was no standard pattern by which new constitutions were framed and adopted. The methods used to draft and ratify the new constitutions are shown in the accompanying table.

The legislative bodies that played a key role in framing the new constitutions were variously known as provincial congresses, houses of representatives, general courts, provincial conventions, and assemblies. On three occasions during 1775 and 1776, the Continental Congress urged them to act. Although drafted in haste by revolutionary bodies amid war and turmoil, the constitutions contained principles and provisions that have been in continuous use since. In Massachusetts, much of the original constitution is still in force.

In content these early state constitutions are of considerable interest to present-day students of government. Bills of rights were included in the constitutions of Virginia, Pennsylvania, Massachusetts, and others, but such instruments did not become a uniform feature of state fundamental laws until after the Revolutionary War. The legislature was made the strongest branch of government. A bicameral body except in Pennsylvania (until 1790), Georgia (until 1789), and Vermont (until 1836), the legislature was provided with a second chamber through the transformation of the governor's council into the state senate. Senators usually were elected directly for short terms, as were members of the lower house.

Governors were elected in four of the states and selected by the legislature in the others. In the beginning only Massachusetts permitted the governor to veto legislation. Most of the original constitutions made many actions of the governors subject to approval by an executive council, which was selected by popular or legislative vote.

The judicial systems of colonial days were carried over to the period of statehood with few changes. In most of the states, high-court judges were either elected by the legislatures or appointed by the governors, often with senate or executive-council approval.

The original constitutions were deficient in providing for the amending process. Four states had no provision for amendment; three permitted final action by the legislature; two provided for a council of censors with power to call a constitutional convention; and the others used combinations and variations of the above methods.

Form and Content of State Constitutions. A review of state constitutions of today[2] reveals a general pattern with detailed variations. Just as human beings are long and short, plump and thin, yet possess similar limbs and organs, so the documents of state fundamental law vary in size and arrange-

[1] Walter F. Dodd, *The Revision and Amendment of State Constitutions* (Baltimore: Johns Hopkins Press, 1910), pp. 2–3.

[2] A good compilation is New York State Constitutional Convention Committee, *Constitutions of the States and United States* (Albany: the Committee, 1938).

ment, yet have the same basic features: (1) a bill of rights, guaranteeing civil liberties and rights; (2) an outline of the framework of government, providing for legislative, executive, and judicial branches; (3) enumeration of state powers and responsibilities; (4) provision for local government; (5) an amending clause, indicating the methods of formal constitutional change.

Preamble. The opening clauses of state constitutions uniformly are statements of aspiration and purpose. They are similar to the Preamble of the Federal Constitution, except that the state clauses lean heavily upon divine guidance. The assertion of popular sovereignty is almost invariably found in the enacting clause; most states use "We, the people . . . do ordain and establish. . . ."

Bills of Rights. All state constitutions include bills of rights, although a majority call the article "declaration of rights." Many existing state constitutions were adopted before the Fourteenth Amendment (which protects individual rights against the en-

[Himme cartoon in *Voice of Organized Agriculture* (February, 1957).]

croachment of state governments) was added to the Federal Constitution. Therefore, good reasons existed for a rather full statement of civil liberties, and some of those reasons are valid today. For example, state guaranties in respect to suffrage, judicial trials, and certain other fields are clearly in the area of state competence and are worth retaining.

On the other hand, state bills of rights contain some obsolete and redundant guaranties. Little good purpose is served by the expressions of the social-contract theory, drawn from eighteenth-century philosophers, or the elaborate statements of popular sovereignty so dear to the hearts of phrasemakers. Some of the assertions of property rights are positively harmful; for they add to the already adequate guaranties of the Fourteenth Amendment and thus plague state legislatures that seek solutions to acute social and economic problems. The model state constitution of the National Municipal League confines the bill of rights to twelve brief sections, yet appears to overlook no guaranty of importance. Now that much of the Federal Bill of Rights has been applied to states, many of the provisions of bills of rights could be eliminated without loss.

Structure of Government. The principal branches of state government generally are provided for in this order: legislative, executive, and judicial. About one-half the state constitutions specifically provide for the separation of powers through a "distribution of powers" clause; in the other states separation is presumed, as in the Federal Constitution, from the clauses creating the three branches of government.

Many constitutions include requirements that become impossible to fulfill. An example is the common provision that bills must be read aloud three times; if this were honored in states where the volume of legislation is great, the work of the legislature would never be done. The better constitutions provide only a basic framework for the three branches of government and leave details to be filled in by legislation.

Functions of Government. Most state constitutions specify in some detail what the state's activities may be. They often restrict powers over taxation and finance, make education a state function, and establish the responsibility of the state for regulating various business enterprises.

Local Government. A majority of the state constitutions contain provisions regarding the structure and powers of local authorities. In the home-rule states, the cities —in some states, cities and counties—may, under certain circumstances, frame their own charters and conduct their local affairs without state interference.

Amending Clause. Three modes of proposing amendments are found in state constitutions: (1) by constitutional conventions, (2) by legislatures, and (3) by the people through initiative. Ratification is by popular referendum in nearly all states. A fuller discussion of the amending process appears in the next section.

METHODS OF CALLING A STATE CONSTITUTIONAL CONVENTION*

LEGISLATURE, MAJORITY

Alabama, Alaska, Arizona, Hawaii, New York, Oklahoma, Oregon, Rhode Island, Tennessee, Virginia, West Virginia, Wisconsin

(Kentucky requires a majority in two successive sessions)

LEGISLATURE, TWO-THIRDS

California, Colorado, Delaware, Florida, Georgia, Idaho, Illinois, Kansas, Maine, Minnesota, Montana, Nevada, New Mexico, North Carolina, Ohio, South Carolina, South Dakota, Utah, Washington, Wyoming

LEGISLATURE, THREE-FIFTHS

Nebraska

QUESTION OF CALLING MANDATORY IN A GIVEN PERIOD (YEARS INDICATED OPPOSITE STATE)

Alaska (10), Hawaii (10), Iowa (10), Maryland (20), Michigan (16), Missouri (20), New Hampshire (7), New York (20), Ohio (20), Oklahoma (20)

* Data adapted from **The Book of the States.**

CONSTITUTIONAL AMENDMENT

Although state constitutions, like the Federal Constitution, are constantly subject to change through alterations in usage, legislative action, judicial decisions, and other means, this section considers only formal amendments.

Proposal by Constitutional Convention. The constitutional convention is the recognized device for effecting a general revision of a state constitution. Provision for calling a convention is found in the fundamental laws of thirty-nine states. The methods by which a convention is called may be classified as shown in the accompanying table.

In almost all of the states having definite

provision for constitutional conventions, the question of calling a convention is placed before the people in the form of a referendum proposition. In all cases a majority vote is required to call the convention; in some cases this is a majority of those voting on the proposition, and in others a majority of those participating in the election. Even in some states which have no provision for calling a convention, the courts have held that the legislature possesses such power.

In structure, the constitutional convention is unicameral. As to representation, most delegates are elected by state legislative or congressional districts, but some occasionally are chosen on an at-large basis.

New York's convention of 1938 had 168 delegates, of whom 153 were elected from state senate and assembly districts and 15 at large. Missouri's convention of 1943–1944, which framed the first wholly new constitution adopted in an American state in thirty-five years, had 83 delegates, of whom 68 were elected by state senatorial districts and 15 at large.

In procedure, conventions usually have a free hand. They elect their own officers and make their own rules. Sometimes a legislature limits a convention's powers, but normally the body is left free to propose whatever constitutional changes—complete or partial—it desires. Of necessity, conventions operate through committees so that they can give detailed consideration to particular problems. Approximately one-half the states which authorize constitutional conventions require that the proposals of the convention be placed before the people in a referendum; the legislatures in the remaining states often require a popular referendum on proposed changes when the law creating the convention is passed.

Unless forbidden in constitution or law, a convention could proclaim a new constitution in effect without ratification, as was done in Virginia in 1902 and in Louisiana in 1921. Constitutional changes proposed by the constitutional convention may be in the form of (1) a whole new constitution, (2) a series of amendments, or (3) some alternative propositions. Except in Georgia, Louisiana, Missouri, and New Jersey, no complete revision has been adopted since 1909. Therefore, conventions have been inclined to propose piecemeal constitutional reform, often relegating controversial matters into a series of alternative propositions.

Proposal by Legislatures. The state legislature is by far the most prolific source of proposals to amend constitutions. All states except one authorize the proposal of consti-

tutional changes by the legislature; New Hampshire alone makes no provision. It is common to require more than an ordinary majority vote in the legislature to pass a constitutional amendment for submission to a referendum vote of the people: Twenty states require a two-thirds vote;[1] eight require three-fifths;[2] three require passage by more than a simple majority at two successive sessions. Nine states require a majority vote in the legislature for two successive sessions. In nine states a simple majority in a single session suffices.

The legislature is in a good position to initiate constitutional amendments: It is in session regularly, and its work is of such a nature as to reveal needs for constitutional change. On the other hand, sole responsibility for initiating amendments ought not to be vested in the legislature, for, with the aid of a rotten-borough system of representation, it might hold out against public opinion.

Proposal by Constitutional Initiative. Fourteen states permit the people to originate constitutional amendments directly. The constitutional initiative involves drafting a proposal and circulating it in the form of a petition. If a sufficient number of voters sign, the proposition is placed on the ballot at the next election. The constitutional initiative was adopted mainly between 1902 and 1918. The states now providing for the device are Arizona, Arkansas, California, Colorado, Idaho, Massachusetts, Michigan, Missouri, Nebraska, Nevada, North Dakota, Ohio, Oklahoma, and Oregon.

The number of signatures required to qualify an initiative constitutional amend-

[1] Hawaii is included here; it has an alternative provision for passage by simple majority at two successive sessions.

[2] New Jersey is counted in this category; it also has an alternative arrangement of a majority in each house in two successive sessions.

ment for a place on the ballot usually is stated in terms of percentage of the vote for a certain office, such as governor or justice of the supreme court, at the last general election. The range, among the states actually using the device, is from 8 to 15 per cent; both median and average are 10 per cent.

Although used in less than one-fourth of the states, constitutional initiative is an important device of direct democracy. It makes possible the proposal of amendments despite the opposition of the legislature. It is a "safety valve" through which the electorate can act if sufficiently aroused. As with the initiative and the referendum on ordinary legislation, however, some disillusionment has occurred because signatures can be procured for nearly any proposition for which a sponsor is willing to pay "professional" petition circulators.

Ratification of Constitutional Amendments. All states except Delaware make provision for ratifying amendments by popular vote. Most of the states require only a simple majority of those voting on the amendment; seven require a majority of those participating in the election or voting for candidates for a certain office. The remaining states have special variations. Connecticut ratifies through a majority of voters in town meeting. New Hampshire, which can propose only through constitutional convention, ratifies by a two-thirds vote in town meetings. Illinois ratifies either by a majority of those voting in the election or by a two-thirds vote on the amendment. Rhode Island requires a three-fifths vote on the amendment.

The method of ratifying constitutional changes is a decisive factor in the number of amendments adopted. Except where the mode of proposing amendments is unduly restrictive, each of the thirty-five states requiring only a simple majority of those

voting on the proposition can adapt its constitution to changing times rather readily. The states with more difficult ratification procedures adopt relatively few amendments.

The requirement of popular ratification of amendments places a large burden on the electorate. In a typical biennial election, two-thirds to three-fourths of the states vote on constitutional amendments. Louisiana, which now has the longest constitution, has *adopted* an average of close to nineteen amendments each biennium since its fundamental law went into effect in 1921. California has amended its constitution of 1879 an average of about ten times each two years.

APPRAISAL AND PROPOSALS

No governmental institution is perfect, but state constitutions are among the most imperfect. Depending upon the amending process, some constitutions are too rigid and difficult to change and some are so easily amended that large quantities of statutory matter have gotten into them. General constitutional reform is very difficult to achieve because of the tendency of Americans to glorify their constitutions and to revere what is ancient in government—and, at the same time, embrace every new product of technology. Some of the more acute problems concerning constitutions require further consideration and analysis.

Excessive Length. Early state constitutions were relatively brief statements of basic principles. At that time the distinction between fundamental and statutory law had not been fully made, yet the drafters of those revolutionary state documents understood perhaps better than later constitutional craftsmen that details ought to be left to legislative bodies. The extent to which minute details have been written into state constitutions may be indicated in comparative terms. In 1800 the longest constitution, that of Massachusetts, contained about 12,-000 words; the shortest, New Jersey's, about 2,500 words.[1] Now Louisiana and California compete for long-windedness with documents exceeding 70,000 words; Vermont and Rhode Island, with less than 7,000 each, have the shortest constitutions.[2]

A constitution full of details has many disadvantages. To keep up to date and meet the needs produced by changed situations, a state must amend the law from time to time. If statutory matter is written into the constitution, the extraordinary procedures required for constitutional amendments must be followed in order to secure the desired changes. This burdens the electorate with the necessity of passing judgment on numerous propositions on the ballot, and it greatly diminishes the possibility of securing the reforms thought necessary.

The reasons for the expansion of state constitutions are several: (1) People distrust the legislature and seek to write into the fundamental law provisions that cannot easily be altered. (2) Judicial decisions are overridden effectively by constitutional amendment. (3) Pressure groups attempt to consolidate their gains in permanent fashion by writing them into the constitution. (4) State and local functions have expanded, with a consequent necessity for new authorizations and agencies. (5) The adoption by one-fourth of the states of the constitutional initiative has given the electorate a chance to propose constitutional change; and they have done so.

Excessive Age. Thomas Jefferson maintained that the social contract should be preserved through revolution and through periodic renewals of agreement. Given po-

litical democracy and freedom from barriers that might obstruct the achievement of majority rule, rebellion is not likely to occur in the United States.

The idea of periodic renewals of agreement, however, has influenced state constitutional development considerably. Jefferson argued that each generation should establish its own organic law; for in a dynamic society men and conditions change, and therefore governments should change. The modern manifestation of this sentiment is found in constitutional requirements in nine states making mandatory the periodic submission to the people of the question: Should a constitutional convention be called?

Despite the reasonableness of the idea of periodic renewal, the plain fact is that the forces standing against change are nearly always able to prevent general reform. Most of them, motivated by vested interests in the constitution as it stands, prefer to have things remain as they are rather than risk any change. The utility corporations and others commonly identified with vested interests are involved. Local governments, school districts, civil servants, and many others may be numbered among the opponents of constitutional change. When a convention is proposed, they appeal to the natural conservatism of the people to oppose any general revision.

As a result, most state constitutions have continued through many years without general revision. The oldest are those of Massachusetts, 1780; New Hampshire, 1784; and Vermont, 1793. By way of contrast, the only fully revised constitutions adopted since 1910 are those of New Jersey, 1947; Missouri, 1945; Georgia, 1945; and Louisiana, 1921. In 1958 the average state constitution had been in force for over seventy-nine years.

It is true, of course, that most of the old constitutions have been amended many

[1] James Q. Dealey, *Growth of American State Constitutions* (Boston: Ginn, 1915), p. 39.

[2] For the latest information, see the current issue of *The Book of the States*.

times, but the amendments, as often as not, have added to the disorganization of the documents, making them increasingly worse in form and often contradictory. Until the adoption of the 1945 constitution, Missouri's organic law contained provisions governing the St. Louis Exposition of 1904.

Model State Constitution. In an effort to induce states to modernize their constitutions, the National Municipal League, in 1921, first issued its model state constitution, drafted by a committee of distinguished authorities on government.[1] The model constitution's great assets are its conciseness, its clarity, and its modernity. It is not short, but its present 11,000 words exceed the constitutions of only a few states. It is written in clear and simple language. It provides the features of state and local government regarded by authorities as most essential: the single-house legislature, the concentration of executive power in the governor, a legislative council to plan and carry on research, the initiative and referendum, and county and city home rule.

No state has adopted the model constitution *in toto,* or even considerable parts of it. The Alaskan constitution shows its impact at several points. Some of the improvements of the Missouri constitution may have been inspired by the model. The rapid spread of the legislative-council idea can be traced in part to the same source. Perhaps the model has provided some incentive in the state-executive reorganizations since 1930. The important thing is to have people feel that governmental institutions and instruments can be improved.

[1] The original committee was composed of Charles A. Beard, Arthur E. Buck, Richard S. Childs, Walter F. Dodd, Harold W. Dodds, John A. Fairlie, A. R. Hatton, Arthur N. Holcombe, Raymond V. Ingersoll, Isidor Loeb, Lindsay Rogers, and Clinton Rogers Woodruff. There have been three revisions: in 1928, 1933, and 1941. The current edition is that of 1948.

In its latest form, the model constitution contains 116 sections which are grouped into thirteen articles concerned with: bill of rights, suffrage and elections, legislature, initiative and referendum, executive, judiciary, finance, local government, civil service, public welfare, intergovernmental relations, constitutional revision, and schedule.

Missouri's New Constitution. Because Missouri has fully revised its constitution in the present generation, examination of its charter may give an insight into the kind of constitutional change that may be expected in other states. The first impression that one gets is the reduction of bulk; the number of articles was reduced from fifteen to twelve. Major changes were also made in content. The bill of rights was extended to include guaranties of the right of labor to organize and bargain collectively, of freedom of speech for the press, radio, and other channels of communication, and of the eligibility of women for jury duty.

The bicameral legislature was not changed, but a number of procedural improvements were instituted, including the requirements of record votes in legislative committees and of a permanent committee on legislative research. The changes in the executive branch were most sweeping; the governor was given authority to group scattered agencies into departments; revenue and taxation matters were concentrated into a department of finance; and the merit system was extended, but not to all state functions. The lower judicial system was reorganized, replacing justices of the peace with salaried magistrates.

Local home rule, in which Missouri originally pioneered, was extended to cities of 10,000 and to counties of 85,000 or over. City and county cooperation and functional consolidation, as well as cooperation or consolidation of two or more counties, were authorized. Improvements were made in the field of taxation; especially notable was the provision that the intangible-personal-property taxes be levied and collected by the state but the proceeds be returned to local governments.

The Charter of Alaska. The most modern of constitutions among the American states is that of Alaska. The forty-ninth state framed its fundamental law after the most thorough advance planning by a territory aspiring to statehood. A management firm was retained for professional advice and preparation of background monographs; several consultants were brought in to work with the convention and its committees.

In its final form, the constitution of Alaska is notable in several particulars. The ultimate in the use of the short ballot is achieved in the executive branch, where only the governor is independently elected by the people. The secretary of state, who succeeds to the governorship in case of vacancy, is elected on a joint ticket with the chief executive. The governor exercises great power over administrative reorganization, subject to review and veto by the legislature. He is also dominant in legislative reapportionment.

Although the convention rejected unicameralism, uncommonly great use was made of joint sessions of the two houses on such occasions as the consideration of gubernatorial vetoes. Assuming that Alaska would receive, with statehood, extensive tracts of Federal lands and recognizing the importance of her vast natural resources to the future of the state, the delegates wrote strong provisions on conservation.

Some of the most original provisions are in the local government area: counties were banned; home rule is available to cities and boroughs; flexibility in boundaries and jurisdiction is assured; special districts are discouraged.

To keep the constitution up-to-date, the convention provided that each ten years the voters should be asked whether they wish another convention assembled.

POWERS OF THE STATES

As this book has stressed many times, the Federal government has only delegated powers; all remaining powers of government are left to the states. A closer examination, however, indicates that the Federal government holds a number of powers concurrently with the states. Among these are the power to tax, to borrow, and to maintain defense forces. In addition, the failure of the Federal government to utilize its powers fully has left to the states certain aspects of the regulation of interstate commerce, bankruptcy, weights and measures, and other matters. On the other hand, it is well known that state authority has been reduced considerably in the last few decades by the expansion of the laws and interpretations of Federal powers—such as taxing, commerce, treaty, and monetary.

State Police Power. The police power of a state is its authority to provide for the health, morals, safety, and welfare of the people. It is not to be confused with the police function carried out by police departments. Under its general police power, which is not based on any specific provision of the state constitution but is a residual power, a state may, for example, set automobile speed limits, compel smallpox vaccinations, ban Sunday movies, defer mortgage foreclosures, or regulate the milk industry. To be sure, such legislation must come within the framework set by constitutions, both Federal and state. State regulations must not interfere unreasonably with the rights of liberty and property guaranteed under the Fourteenth Amendment. State laws may not violate any of the express prohibitions on state action listed in the Federal Constitution (see page 86). If they avoid the pitfalls of conflict with the Federal Constitution and laws properly enacted under it and abide by the provisions of the state constitution, legislatures may proceed to legislate in the interests of the general welfare.

Applications of the state police power will be examined in two fields: (1) legislation to promote social welfare and (2) legislation to promote economic interests.

Social-welfare Laws. State efforts to protect the public health through restricting minors to an eight-hour day and women laundry workers to a ten-hour day have been upheld in the Supreme Court as reasonable exercise of the police power. On the other hand, a New York law limiting bakery workers to ten hours a day was found an unreasonable violation of freedom of contract. After repeatedly reversing itself, the Court finally decided that the states might regulate the wages and hours of women workers. A state statute forbidding the advertising of tobacco on billboards, alleged to be an interference with interstate commerce, was upheld as valid. A Massachusetts compulsory-vaccination law was declared not to be an unreasonable invasion of liberty guaranteed by the due-process clause.

Economic Legislation. Beginning in 1877, the United States Supreme Court conceded that states could regulate the rates and services of "businesses affected with public interest." Regulation of meat packing, theater-ticket sales, private employment services, gasoline vending, and ice distribution were all held unconstitutional because they were not sufficiently affected with public interest.

In *Nebbia v. New York, 291 U.S. 502* (1934), the court accepted as constitutional a state milk-control law that involved price fixing and rejected claims that freedom of contract was unreasonably interfered with or due process denied. In the same year the Court held valid the Minnesota moratorium law, which postponed foreclosure sales and extended the redemption period, as a valid exercise of the state police power which did not impair the obligation of contract. In 1941 the Court clearly reversed an earlier decision when it found valid a Nebraska law setting the maximum fees a private employment agency might charge.

Power over Political Subdivisions. States inherently possess authority to create and control units of local government, subject, of course, to any limitations imposed by state constitutions and to the requirement that they qualify under the republican-form-of-government clause. Counties, cities, and other subdivisions of the state are creatures of the state. The Supreme Court is so vigilant to protect this aspect of a state's sovereignty that it declared void a mild bankruptcy law enacted by Congress which would have permitted local public bodies to adjust their debt burden with state approval.

Power over Suffrage and Elections. The Federal government possesses no election machinery of its own but must rely upon the states to provide electoral services. Originally, definition of who might vote was left entirely to the states, but the adoption of the Fifteenth and Nineteenth Amendments prohibits discrimination on account of race and sex. Except for these limitations, each state may prescribe qualifications for voting, subject to the original limitation that the electorate for Federal elections must be the same as that for the most numerous branch of the state legislature. However, recent court decisions indicate added Federal authority over nominations and elections of Federal officers.

Other Powers. Beyond those specifically mentioned, state powers are exceedingly difficult to classify. So long as a state does not violate a limitation placed upon it by the Federal Constitution, it may tax, create and regulate private corporations, enact criminal and civil laws, and provide a wide range of services.

FOR FURTHER READING

State Government, General

American Assembly: *The Forty-eight States* (New York: Columbia University Graduate School of Business, 1955).

Anderson, William, Clara Penniman, and E. W. Weidner: *Government in the Fifty States* (New York: Holt, Rinehart & Winston, 1960).

Babcock, Robert S.: *State and Local Government and Politics* (New York: Random House, 1962).

Bates, Frank G., Oliver P. Field, Pressley S. Sikes, and John E. Stover: *State Government* (New York: Harper, 3d ed., 1949).

Council of State Governments: *The Book of the States* (Chicago: the Council, biennial).

Holloway, William V.: *State and Local Government in the United States* (New York: McGraw-Hill, 1951).

Howard, Vaughan L., and John H. Fenton: *State Government in the South: Functions and Problems* (The Southern Assembly in cooperation with the American Assembly, 1956).

Graves, W. Brooke: *American State Government* (Boston: Heath, 4th ed., 1953).

Macdonald, Austin F.: *American State Government and Administration* (New York: Crowell, 6th ed., 1960).

Maddox, Russell W., and Robert F. Fuquay: *State and Local Government* (New York: Van Nostrand, 1962).

Pacific Northwest Assembly: *The States in the Pacific Northwest: How Can Their Capacity for Responsible Self-government Be Strengthened?* (Pacific Northwest Assembly in cooperation with the American Assembly, 1957).

Peel, Roy V.: *State Government Today* (Albuquerque, N.M.: The University of New Mexico Press, 1948).

Phillips, Jewell C.: *State and Local Government in America* (New York: American Book, 1954).

Snider, Clyde F.: *American State and Local Government* (New York: Appleton-Century-Crofts, 1950).

State Constitutions and Powers

Dealey, James Q.: *Growth of American State Constitutions* (Boston: Ginn, 1915).

Dodd, Walter F.: *The Revision and Amendment of State Constitutions* (Baltimore: Johns Hopkins Press, 1910).

Edwards, Richard A., James L. Blawie, and Marilyn B. Blawie (eds.): *The Index Digest of State Constitutions* (New York: Oceana Publications, 1959). Legislative Drafting Fund, Columbia University.

Graves, W. Brooke (ed.): *Major Problems in State Constitutional Revision* (Chicago: Public Administration Service, 1960).

Hoar, Roger S.: *Constitutional Conventions, Their Nature, Powers, and Limitations* (Boston: Little, Brown, 1917).

Larsen, Christian L., and Conrad Cowan: *South Carolina State Constitution Amendment Procedures* (Columbia, S.C.: University of South Carolina, Bureau of Public Administration, 1948). Contains provisions for amending in forty-eight states.

McCarthy, Mary B.: *The Widening Scope of American Constitutions* (Washington, D.C.: Catholic University of America Press, 1928).

McClure, Wallace: *State Constitution-making* (Nashville: Marshall and Bruce, 1916).

National Municipal League: *Model State Constitution* (New York: the League, 5th ed., 1948).

New York State Constitutional Convention Committee: *Constitutions of the States and the United States* (Albany: 1938).

Official Publications Relating to American State Constitutional Conventions (New York: H. W. Wilson, 1936).

O'Rourke, Vernon, and Douglas W. Campbell: *Constitution-making in a Democracy, Theory and Practice in New York State* (Baltimore: Johns Hopkins Press, 1943).

Steinbicker, Paul G., and Martin L. Faust: *Manual on Amending Procedure and the Ini-*

tiative and Referendum ... (Columbia: 1943).
Missouri Constitutional Convention of 1943,
no. 8.

Sturm, Albert L.: *Methods of State Constitutional
Reform* (Ann Arbor, Mich.: University of
Michigan Press, 1954).

Uhl, Raymond, and others: *Constitutional Conventions* (Columbia, S.C.: University of South
Carolina, Bureau of Public Administration,
1951).

University of Hawaii, Legislative Reference
Bureau: *Manual on State Constitutional Provisions* (Honolulu: 1950).

Wheeler, John P., Jr. (ed.): *Salient Issues of Constitutional Revision* (New York: National
Municipal League, 1961).

REVIEW QUESTIONS

1. Is there a contradiction involved when we embrace the newest in technological developments yet revere the old in constitutions and political institutions?

2. Discuss the transition of state constitutions from the end of the colonial period to 1800.

3. What is the reasoning behind the provision made in a number of state constitutions for a mandatory submission to the voters at given intervals of the question of calling a constitutional convention?

4. Describe the several methods currently in use for proposing and ratifying amendments to state constitutions.

5. Describe the institution of the state constitutional convention, the methods of calling one, and the way in which ones does its work.

6. Why not have a long constitution?

7. Why have so few states been able to renovate their constitutions during the last half century?

8. Compare the powers of state governments with those of the Federal government.

Chapter Thirty

Legislatures
and Legislation

Since policy making is the most important function of state government, confidence in state legislatures must be strengthened. The Southern Assembly believes that state constitutions generally reflect a strong distrust of legislatures. Legislatures need to be freed from outmoded constitutional restrictions in order that they may perform their proper functions.

THE SOUTHERN ASSEMBLY[1]

In most state constitutions, the legislative branch of government is mentioned first. This arrangement has good historical justification. The early state constitutions vested the largest share of governmental power in the hands of the legislatures. Since that time, however, the legislature has lost power, prestige, and importance. As in the

[1] *State Governments in the South: Functions and Problems* (New Orleans: Tulane University, 1956), p. 61.

Federal government, the chief executive has emerged as the champion and leader of the people, even in legislative matters. Excessive localism, obsolete machinery, diffusion of responsibility—all have undermined public confidence in legislatures. Adoption of the initiative and referendum by more than one-third of the states has further reduced the autonomy once enjoyed by legislatures.

On the other hand, the hopes of man for truly responsible government rely more

upon reform of the legislature than upon any other proposal for improvement. In 1946 Congress took a significant step toward bringing its archaic machinery up to date, but by and large state legislatures have changed little in the last hundred years. Action on that front must be placed high on the agenda of democracy.

LEGISLATIVE STRUCTURE

The state legislature's most striking structural feature is bicameralism. Like so many American institutions, the two-house idea originated in England and was transplanted during our colonial period. The evolution of American legislative bodies is traced in Chapter 13.

The Two-house System. With four exceptions, states have adhered to the bicameral plan. Early in the nation's history, single-house legislatures existed in Pennsylvania (1776–1790), Georgia (1777–1789), and Vermont (1777–1836). Nebraska put its unicameral plan into operation in 1937.[1]

The reasons for originally adopting the two-house plan are numerous. It followed the pattern widely used in the colonial era and was therefore familiar. It provided a small second chamber which, in some states, could give "advice and consent" to governors. It erected another barrier and check to the exercise of governmental power, in keeping with the idea of limited government. De Tocqueville viewed the two-house idea with admiration, declaring:

Time and experience, however, have convinced the Americans that, even if these are its only advantages, the division of legis-

lative power is still a principle of the greatest necessity. . . . This theory, nearly unknown to the republics of antiquity, first introduced into the world almost by accident, like so many other great truths, and misunderstood by several great modern nations, has at length become an axiom in the political science of the present age.[2]

This enthusiasm for the checks of the double chamber is shared by few contemporary political scientists. Most experts regard other checks as more adequate and effective and now emphasize clearing obstructions to legislative progress.

Subsequently two additional arguments for bicameralism appeared. After the Federal Constitution was adopted, the desire to conform to the "Federal plan" became strong; this consideration was a major factor in the abandonment of unicameralism by Pennsylvania and Georgia. Also, as states increased in population and diversity of economic endeavors, the two houses in many instances were placed on different bases of representation; many states today apportion one house by population and the other by units of local government.

In evaluating the bicameral principle, proponents urge the importance of the second chamber as a check on the actions of the first, and as a vehicle for providing two bases of representation. Critics argue for other and more effective checks. The standing committee of the first house to consider a particular bill is the most apt to cull it out; eliminations at this stage exceed 50 per cent of the total bills introduced.

Through the veto power, the governor checks the legislature's work. In many states, an additional check is possessed by the people, who act directly through the referendum. Finally, the laws enacted must run the gamut of the courts, which may test

---

[1] Nebraska's first two decades of unicameralism are reviewed in Jack W. Rodgers, "One House for 20 Years," *National Municipal Review* vol. 46 (July, 1957), pp. 338–342, 347; and Richard C. Spencer, "Highest Score Sheet," *ibid.* (November, 1957), pp. 502–505, 510.

[2] Alexis de Tocqueville, *Democracy in America* (New York: Knopf, rev. ed., 2 vols., 1945), vol. 1, p. 84.

the constitutionality of legislation when cases are brought before them.

There is much to be said for having two bases of representation, especially in the more heterogeneous states with their urban-versus-rural and other sectional divisions. The idea has merit, but its fulfillment need not be confined to the bicameral system. A single-house scheme can also provide that some of the legislators be elected by population districts and some by area.

Unicameral Proposals. In the widespread debates and discussions of the single-house legislature during the 1930s, two principal arguments were advanced. First, the one-house plan would definitely fix responsibility for action. The bicameral plan makes "passing the buck" easy and placing the blame difficult. The late Senator Norris once declared that special interests desiring to kill proposed legislation find it twice as easy when they need control only one of two houses. The conference committee, an inevitable institution under bicameralism, actually constitutes a sort of third house that sometimes operates most irresponsibly. Elimination of one house would simplify the legislative process by about 50 per cent and might reduce the army of lobbyists who thrive on the procedural complications that baffle the common man.

Second, reduction to one house should increase the prestige and compensation of legislators. Most one-house plans call for a relatively small-sized legislature. Because the single house would have added responsibilities, legislators ought to be paid more; they might be expected to give more nearly full-time service in the larger states.

Features of unicameral plans vary considerably. Nebraska has forty-three members elected each two years on a nonpartisan basis from districts apportioned according to population. The model state constitution of the National Municipal League is silent on the number of members but would have them elected by proportional representation every two years. Other states seriously considering this reform have proposed members in number up to eighty, often with four-year terms and salaries at $5,000 or more.

The Two-house Plan in Operation. While it is interesting to weigh the relative merits of the two plans, the plain fact is that nearly all states have bicameralism and are likely to retain it for a long time to come. Therefore this section is devoted to the existing structure of state legislatures.

The legislative branch is officially known as "legislature" in half the states; nineteen use "general assembly"; Massachusetts and New Hampshire retain "general court." Upper houses invariably are known as "senates." Lower houses most commonly are called "house of representatives"; four states use "assembly"; three retain "house of delegates"; New Jersey alone prefers "general assembly."

In all bicameral states the senate is the smaller body; it averages one-third the house membership. The range in size of senates is from seventeen in Nevada to sixty-seven in Minnesota, with the average number of senators per state at thirty-seven.

The other house ranges from 35 in Delaware to a maximum of 400 under New Hampshire's recently revised apportionment. The average number of members of the lower house of the American states is just short of 120.

In powers, the two houses are everywhere substantially coordinate in matters of legislation. The lower house traditionally enjoys the privilege of originating financial bills, but the senate usually may amend such bills freely. State senates customarily pass upon certain classes of appointments by the governors. The function of impeachment, judicial in nature, usually involves both houses, the lower house instituting proceedings and the senate sitting as a court and rendering judgment.

LEGISLATORS

Basis of Representation. American states use two principal bases of representation in their legislative bodies: population and units of government. The usual procedure for apportioning legislative seats involves action by the legislature following a decennial census. To avoid the deadlock occasionally encountered in reapportionment controversies, several states have created special boards or commissions for the purpose.

In many instances, population is the sole criterion for apportionment; in a few, the unit of government is the only factor considered; a larger number uses some combination of the two methods. For example, many states provide that the basis of apportionment shall be population but that each county shall have at least one member. On the whole, the legislative districts that emerge from the diverse methods of apportioning in the several states are not unreasonable. Most states that have metropolitan areas underrepresent urban communities and overrepresent rural areas. This has reached a ridiculous extreme in California, which allows one state senator for some 6 million people in Los Angeles County and one for about 14,000 in three rural counties.

In *Baker v. Carr* [369 U.S. 186 (1962)] the Supreme Court invoked the equal protection clause of the Constitution in ruling that urban voters could sue in the federal courts to seek relief from a Tennessee apportionment of state legislative seats that discriminated against metropolitan areas. Suits have been filed seeking the invalidation of legislative apportionment in over one-half of the states, the outcome of which will affect representation in state legislative bodies, and may alter basic rules of the federal system.

As with congressional districts, legislative districts may be drawn for personal or partisan advantage. Occasional requirements in state constitutions that districts must be composed of compact and contiguous territory have not prevented gerrymandering.

Legislative constituencies are normally single-member districts. This plan often magnifies the strength of the strongest group. For over half a century, however, Illinois has used a system which provides minority representation. The state is divided into senatorial districts only. Each district elects one senator and three representatives. In voting for representatives, the voter may cast all three votes for one candidate, or he may divide them. The highest three are declared elected.[1]

Proportional representation does not yet apply to the election of any state legislative body. Although PR, with the Hare plan of a single transferable vote, is technically a good device to secure a majority choice, the difficulty in understanding it, the slowness in counting ballots, and the charge that it aggravates factionalization are all formidable barriers to its adoption.

Sessions. Most of the legislatures convene in regular sessions every two years; eighteen have annual sessions, including Alaska, Arizona, California, Colorado, Delaware, Georgia, Hawaii, Kansas, Louisiana, Maryland, Massachusetts, Michigan, New Jersey, New York, Pennsylvania, Rhode Island, South Carolina, and West Virginia. Governors of most states may call legislators into special session.

[1] George S. Blair, "Cumulative Voting: An Effective Electoral Device in Illinois Politics," *Southwestern Social Science Quarterly*, vol. 34 (March, 1954), pp. 3–18.

The legislatures of the biennial-session states most commonly meet in January of the odd-numbered years; a few meet in even years or in other months. Over one-half the legislatures have their regular sessions limited to a given number of days, ranging from 40 to 195. Other states in effect limit the length of sessions by arranging legislators' pay so that it expires after a stated period. These limitations are motivated, in part, by a desire to save money, especially in states that pay legislators by the day, and, in part, by suspicions that having a legislature in session too long is unsettling and "bad for business."

A few states have experimented with a split-session arrangement, the so-called bifurcated session. It involves convening the legislature for a limited period, usually not more than a month, to organize the houses, introduce bills, and pass urgent measures. Then the legislature recesses for a month or so to confer with constituents and study pending legislation. After the recess, the legislature devotes its time to the passage of bills introduced in the earlier period. The privilege of introducing new measures is rigidly restricted in the second portion. The bifurcated session was intended to remedy the rush that attends the end of a session and to ensure time for full public consideration of proposed measures. While it has not ended the closing rush, it does perform a service by keeping important measures before the public for a longer period.

Terms and Compensation. Senators generally enjoy longer terms of office than do members of the lower house. The most common pattern is four years for the senate and two for the house, but sixteen state senates have only two-year terms and four lower houses have four-year terms.

Compensation of state legislators varies widely. Less than one-third of the states still compensate on a per diem basis, which ranges from $5 in North Dakota to $50 in Louisiana. In the others, pay is stated in terms of so much a period. New York leads with $10,000 per year; New Hampshire, with its host of legislators, manages to pay each one $200 for the two-year term. Most states underpay legislators. In the larger states many of them put in a great part of their time on state work; rarely can they live on the salary. Voters tend to look upon proposals for pay increases as "salary grabs," but substantial increments have been made. Most states have raised salaries since the end of the Second World War, and many have also provided per diem expense allowance during the sessions. The legislator cannot even live in the capital on the low per diem allowed by many states, much less support a family at home and put aside something to finance an election campaign.

Legislative Personnel. What sort of person serves in state legislatures? A number of factors condition the answer to that question. Legislators, as has been shown, are paid rather small amounts. They must serve actively for erratic periods: full time for a few months and at odd times for the remainder of their terms. Occupationally, lawyers and farmers predominate, comprising more than two-fifths of all state legislators; businessmen follow third; the occupations of the remainder scatter over a wide field. A high rate of turnover prevails among legislators, who appear to tire quickly of the low pay, indefinite working period, and frequent election campaigns. The latest tabulation available showed only about 50 per cent of state legislators had served one, or more than one, previous term in legislative office.[1]

Frequently it is alleged that the level of

[1] American Political Science Association, Committee on American Legislatures, *American State Legislatures* (New York: Crowell, 1954), pp. 65–70.

competence among state legislators is low. While this is often overstressed, improvement might be accomplished by reducing the number, adding to prestige and responsibility, increasing compensation, and making available considerably more research, technical, and clerical assistance.

LEADERSHIP AND POLITICS

Legislative Officers. Concerning presiding officers, the standard pattern is for the popularly elected lieutenant governor to preside over the senate and for the house to elect a speaker from among its own members. Ten states make no provision for lieutenant governors, so their senates are chaired by presidents elected by the bodies themselves. Powers of the presiding officers are much the same the country over. All speakers are empowered to appoint committees. Most of the senates allow their presiding officers to do likewise. Some permit a committee to choose. Others vest power of appointment in the president pro tempore, who is elected by the senate.

The presiding officers also have the prerogatives commonly assigned to chairmen of legislative bodies. In presiding they have a considerable amount of discretion in controlling the business of the house. In most states they decide to which committee a bill shall be referred, play a major role in the selection of bills for consideration on the floor, enforce the rules of the house and decide points of order, and control who speaks in debates through the power of recognition. Beyond these formal powers, the speaker of the house is often a political leader and able to influence the course of legislation by throwing his weight to one side or the other. Therefore he has a high place in party and factional councils and may be cultivated carefully by the governor, who seeks the maximum support for his legislative program. The lieutenant governor, an officer of the people's choosing rather than the senate's, normally is much less powerful than the speaker.

In addition to the presiding officers, state legislative bodies have a number of attachés and employees—clerks, secretaries, chaplains, sergeants-at-arms, page boys, stenographers, and others. Usually each house selects them on the basis of personal or partisan sponsorship and patronage.

Legislative Politics. Most, but not all, state legislatures are organized on partisan lines.[1] The usual division is Republicans versus Democrats, and legislative procedure is dovetailed into party rivalry. The caucus is a feature of nearly every state legislative body. Party members meet to discuss matters affecting their party on the legislative front. This formal party caucus dominates the legislative process in some Eastern and North Central states. In these states, party discipline tends to be relatively great, and the party unifies directions taken by the legislative and executive branches. Only Minnesota and Nebraska have formally abolished party designations in their legislatures; in the former, party lines have re-emerged despite their removal from the ballot.

Many states of the West and South have no Democratic-Republican conflict of importance. The battle may be between different factions of the dominant party or among outstanding leaders and their followers. In every state there are great eco-

[1] Useful studies of legislative politics include R. S. Fjelstad, "How About Party Labels?" (Minnesota nonpartisanship) *National Municipal Review*, vol. 44 (July, 1955), pp. 359–364; Malcolm E. Jewell, "Party Voting in American State Legislatures," *American Political Science Review*, vol. 49 (September, 1955), pp. 773–791; and William J. Keefe, "Comparative Study of the Role of Political Parties in State Legislatures," *Western Political Quarterly*, vol. 9 (September, 1956), pp. 726–742.

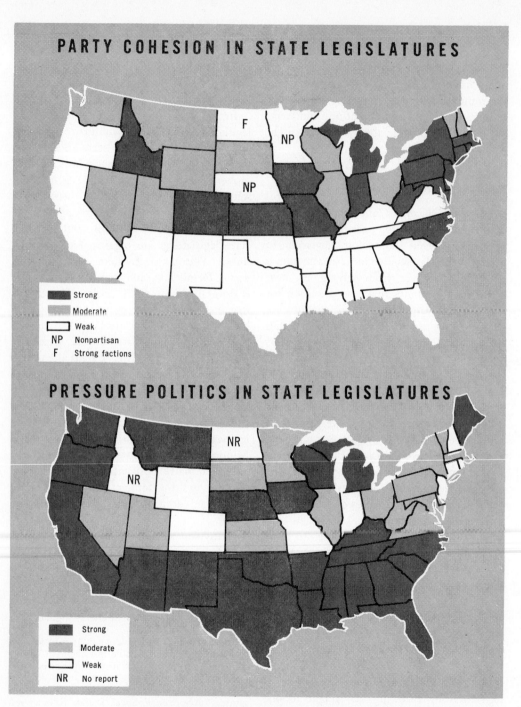

PARTY COHESION IN STATE LEGISLATURES

Strong
Moderate
Weak
NP Nonpartisan
F   Strong factions

PRESSURE POLITICS IN STATE LEGISLATURES

Strong
Moderate
Weak
NR No report

The role of party and pressure group varies widely from state to state. Note how often states with weak parties have strong pressure groups. This information came from competent observers, but there is ample room for differences of opinion. [Data from Belle Zeller (ed.), *American State Legislatures* (New York: Crowell, 1954), pp. 190–191.]

nomic interests that strive for political ascendancy and legislative influence. Where party cleavage is strong, these interests are less obvious; where party lines are weak, pressure groups often play a major part in the alignment of the legislative body. The great importance of the relationship of state legislator to business corporation, labor union, farm group, and other interest often is overlooked. This is not merely a question of lobbying; it involves the whole matter of representation. The representation system cannot represent all interests perfectly. Most lobbyists perform valuable services to the legislature. To suppress group representation would serve no useful purpose; to require lobbyists to register and file statements about their employers and the money they spend to influence legislation is valid. In fact, the requirement is now made of those who represent groups before Congress.

The Legislative Council. As state legislative work has become increasingly heavy and complex, means have been sought to provide the legislature with sorely needed leadership and planning facilities. The legislative-council idea is the major method actually being tried for keeping the legislature abreast of its work. The council is a sort of master interim committee of the legislature, available to study state problems and plan a legislative program.

The legislative council has proven an admirable agency to take charge of a research program. Some of the most notable achievements of existing councils have been in the field of fact finding. By 1962, thirty-nine states had adopted and retained the plan.[1]

Legislative councils range in size from five members in South Carolina to the whole membership of the legislature in Nebraska, Oklahoma, Pennsylvania, and South Dakota. It is usual to select the council membership from the two houses, most commonly on an equal basis. New Hampshire and Utah provide for representatives of the administration. In some states, members of the council are selected by the presiding officers of the two houses; party affiliation is a factor in the choice in most of the states.

The arguments usually advanced against the council idea are that legislative power might become concentrated and that legislators might be tempted to meddle unduly in administrative affairs. Such fears have not been justified in the experience of the states that have used the council plan for a period of time. The spread of the council idea is one of the most encouraging signs in the state legislative field.[2]

LEGISLATIVE PROCEDURE

Legislative Committees. As in Congress, state legislatures do the bulk of their work through standing committees. Therefore, rivalry for good committee assignments is very great. Whether the committees are appointed by the speaker of the house or the president of the senate or chosen by a senate committee, considerations of seniority and political influence are apt to be major factors in determining assignments. In most states seniority is not as potent a factor as it is in Congress. The speaker of the house may use committee appointments to repay political debts incurred in his campaign for the speakership. Pressure groups frequently

[1] Various aspects of legislative councils are covered in David W. Smith, "The Constitutionality of Legislative Councils," *Western Political Quarterly*, vol. 8 (March, 1955), pp. 68–81; and Council of State Governments, *Legislative Councils* (Chicago: the Council, 1957).

[2] See Harold W. Davey, "The Legislative Council Movement in the United States, 1933–1953," *American Political Science Review*, vol. 42 (September, 1953), pp. 785–797.

see that the committees with which they are particularly concerned are loaded with men favorable to their cause.

The number of standing committees varies from state to state and from house to house; the over-all average is thirty-two in the lower houses and twenty-five in the senates. Like congressional committees, state legislative committees have great power over the bills referred to them. The more important bills are deemed to justify public hearings. After the committee completes discussion, it votes on the bill. If the committee is favorable, the bill is reported out to the floor of the legislative body with the recommendation that it be passed. If the committee is unfavorable, the bill may be tabled or pigeonholed. The burying of bills in committee is not as decisive as it is in Congress, however, because nearly one-half the states require that all bills must be reported out. In both these and other states, bills may be withdrawn from committee through a discharge procedure, usually by a majority vote of the whole house.

One simple, highly desirable reform in committee procedure is the joint-committee plan. Of course, every bicameral legislature must have some joint committees to deal with common problems of administering the legislative establishment. This proposal, however, involves the merger of similar standing committees of the two houses into joint committees. This would halve the necessary hearings on a particular bill, thus ending needless duplication of time, testimony, and travel. The plan has been used successfully by Maine, Connecticut, and Massachusetts. It is a mild reform that could be instituted in most states by a mere alteration of legislative rules.

Special or select committees usually are selected by the presiding officers. Such bodies are established for a specific purpose, such as investigation of a problem that is outside or cuts across normal committee jurisdiction. Sometimes these are joint committees, including members of both houses. In some states they may be ad interim committees, empowered to work between sessions of the legislature. However, such bodies have been declared void in several states.

Procedure on the Floor. The legislative process follows rather closely the pattern set by Congress. Any member may introduce a bill; he merely sends the proposed measure to the "hopper" or basket on the clerk's desk. Bills are read the first time, often inaudibly and by title only, and referred to committee. The committee considers the bills, rejects most of them, and recommends passage of some. The house in which the measure was introduced, on second and third reading, debates and amends, then adopts or rejects.

The methods by which roll call is taken and the conditions under which it is necessary vary greatly. A few states make a record roll call mandatory for the passage of all bills. Others require that a record vote be taken if demanded by a relatively small number of legislators, ranging from one to one-fifth of the members present. Illinois and Utah make a roll-call vote mandatory only when demanded by a majority of members. If securing a record vote is made too difficult, there is danger that legislators will hide behind the screen of anonymity when controversial matters arise. Constituents have a right to know how their representatives vote on final passage of every measure.

Oral roll calls take time, but this is no longer a good excuse for not taking a record vote. One-half the states have installed, in one or both houses, electric roll-call devices. The usual electric system provides each legislator with two push buttons at his desk; one is marked "yes," the other, "no." At the front of the chamber is a scoreboard on which the names of all members appear. When the presiding officer calls for a vote, each member pushes the button appropriate to his sentiments, the board lights up, and each legislator's vote is shown opposite his name by a green light for yes and a red light for no. An electrical device punches the roll call on printed sheets, which may then be distributed to the press representatives and go into permanent records of the house.

Final passage having been achieved in the first house, a bill is sent to the second. There the process is repeated, beginning with reference to committee and ending with a vote on final passage. If the two houses pass different versions of the same bill and neither house is willing to recede, a conference committee of an equal number from each house compromises the differences. After the conference committee completes its work, each house votes upon the compromise version of the bill. If accepted, it goes to the governor for signature.

State legislatures are bound by more constitutional and legal restrictions than is the Federal Congress. For example, nearly all states require that bills be read three times, and nearly one-fourth of them require the three readings in full. This is a physical impossibility, so larger states have developed various dodges such as interpreting the printing of the bill as a reading or accepting the mumbling of the title as oral reading. Generally the states have been stricter than has Congress about requiring that bills relate to a single subject and that amendments be germane or appropriate to the original bill; most state procedures would not tolerate riders of the sort commonly added to bills in the Congress.

Nearly all states have by constitution, statute, or rule set a time limit on the introduction of bills, requiring that bills be introduced early enough in a session to permit adequate time for consideration. The limits vary from a deadline set on the fifteenth day of a session to the last three days of a session. A deadline well in advance of halfway through the session is advisable to allow interested persons to examine proposed legislation and to testify on it in committee. Without an adequate deadline, a bill may be introduced and passed in the closing rush without the knowledge of the public.

Governors and Legislation. Governors, in nearly all states, have the power to recommend legislation, call special sessions, and veto bills passed by the legislature. Only the veto power requires much discussion. Every state except North Carolina gives its governor the veto power. This normally extends to ordinary bills but not to constitutional amendments or initiative measures. The great volume of legislation that reaches the governor's desk in the closing weeks of a session makes the time allowed inadequate for consideration. In all states with a gubernatorial veto, a bill becomes law after a stated number of days even if the governor does not sign, provided the legislature has not finally adjourned. The governor is given only three days in several states; the maximum allowed anywhere is thirty days; the median is five days.

If, however, the legislature has adjourned sine die, an entirely different situation prevails. About two-thirds of the states provide that a bill goes into effect if the governor does not sign within the specified time, which ranges from five to forty-five days. Most of the other one-third deem the bill dead ("pocket vetoed") if the governor does not approve in the stated period, which varies from three to thirty days. Of course the latter states give the greatest power over legislation to the chief executive. In case the legislature is still in session when the governor vetoes, it has an opportunity to pass the measure over his veto. Most of the states require a two-thirds vote of those present or elected to override a veto; five require a three-fifths vote; seven permit passage of bills over a veto by a simple majority.

The item veto over appropriation bills might constitute a desirable reform for the Federal government. Thirty-nine states have vested in their governors power to eliminate particular items of appropriation bills. This is appropriate recognition of the governor's primary responsibility for budgetary matters. It has succeeded in controlling state expenditures and constitutes a proper companion authority to the more recent power, granted in many states, of framing and submitting an executive budget.

Legislative Aids. All but three of the legislatures have provided themselves with bill-drafting services. These services are uneven in quality, however, varying from a single handy man who takes part time from other duties to the modern legislative counsel bureau with its full-time staff of expert attorneys. A good bill-drafting agency earns its keep by avoiding loopholes in the law and future trouble in the courts; it also frees the legislature to some extent from undue dependence upon executive-prepared legislation. A sensible use of the legal talent of a drafting agency during the periods between legislative sessions is the preparation of codifications or revisions of state laws.

Most of the legislatures have some assistance from informational services, often a division of the state library or a bureau of the state university. Although good reports do emerge from these sources, the most purposeful research work is done by the legislature's own agencies. Sometimes it comes from fact-finding personnel attached to legislative committees, standing and special, and at other times from research divisions of legislative councils. The important difference between research produced for the legislature by an external agency and that done by the legislature through its own agency is that the latter is more apt to be closely related to legislative needs and more likely to gain legislative confidence.

DIRECT LEGISLATION

The Initiative. The initiative is an electoral device through which an individual or group may propose legislation by securing the signature of the requisite number of qualified voters. The proposition is then placed before the electorate for adoption or rejection. The initiative is called "direct" when filing the petition is followed by the submission of the proposition to the voters. It is "indirect" when submission is first to the legislature. Then, if that body does not approve, it goes before the voters.

Twenty states have adopted the statutory initiative: Alaska, Arizona, Arkansas, California, Colorado, Idaho, Maine, Massachusetts, Michigan, Missouri, Montana, Nebraska, Nevada, North Dakota, Ohio, Oklahoma, Oregon, South Dakota, Utah, and Washington. If this list is compared with that of the states using the constitutional initiative, it will be found that six states— Alaska, Maine, Montana, South Dakota, Utah, and Washington—have adopted the statutory initiative without the constitutional initiative.

The drafting of measures normally is done by interested groups or their attorneys. The official title and the brief summary that appear on the ballot are the work of the attorney general or some other designated officer. The number of signatures required to qualify a proposition for a place on the ballot is set in the state constitution or laws, in terms of a percentage of voters or a flat number. The percentage of voters required to initiate a statute ranges from 3 to 15.[1] Some states require a minimum geographic distribution among those who sign. If a majority of voters vote in favor of an initiated measure, it becomes law; frequently statutes so adopted have a privileged status and may not be repealed by the legislature.

The Referendum. The referendum is a scheme through which voters may, by petition, force submission to the whole electorate of a bill passed by the legislature. The number or proportion of signatures required is usually less than for the initiative. Emergency measures commonly are excluded from referendum action. If the voters disapprove of the act as passed by the legislature, it becomes null and void. A law is postponed from going into effect by the filing of a valid and adequate referendum petition. Twenty-two states have adopted the referendum; they include all those using the initiative plus Maryland and New Mex-

[1] Either of registered voters in the state or of those voting for a particular office in a recent election.

ico. The number of signatures required ranges from 1½ to 25 per cent of the voters, but most states require from 5 to 10 per cent. Some states base the signature requirement on the vote for the governor in the most recent election.

These two instruments of direct legislation have several variations. Most controversy on the matter centers on the general principles outlined above. The people of the states that adopted one or both of these devices were probably influenced by the arguments that they would provide a check on the corrupt and inert legislatures and be a useful instrument for the education of the citizenry. The opponents of direct legislation usually assert that it places an additional load on the already overburdened electorate and modifies representative government by destroying legislative responsibility.

In addition to state use of the initiative and referendum, extensive use of direct legislation is made by hundreds of cities and counties.

FOR FURTHER READING

American Political Science Association, Committee on State Legislatures: *American State Legislatures* (New York: Crowell, 1954).

Baker, Gordon E.: *Rural versus Urban Political Power* (New York: Doubleday, 1955).

Buck, Arthur E.: *Modernizing Our State Legislatures* (New York: American Academy of Political and Social Science, 1936).

Carlyle, Adam: *One House or Two: Nebraska's Unicameral Legislature* (Washington, D.C.: Public Affairs Press, 1957).

Carroll, Daniel B.: *The Unicameral Legislature of Vermont* (Burlington, Vt.: University of Vermont, 1933).

Chamberlain, Joseph P.: *Legislative Processes, National and State* (New York: Appleton-Century-Crofts, 1938).

Council of State Governments: *American Legis-*

latures: Structure and Procedures (Chicago: the Council, 1955).

Epstein, Leon D.: *Politics in Wisconsin* (Madison: University of Wisconsin Press, 1958).

Farmer, Hallie: *The Legislative Process in Alabama* (University, Ala.: University of Alabama, Bureau of Public Administration, 1949).

Faust, Martin L.: *Manual on the Legislative Article* . . . (Columbia: 1943). Missouri Constitutional Convention of 1943, no. 6.

Graves, W. Brooke (ed.): "Our State Legislators," *Annals of the American Academy of Political and Social Science*, vol. 195 (January, 1938).

Guild, Frederic H.: *Legislative Procedure in Kansas* (Lawrence, Kans.: University of Kansas, Governmental Research Center, 1956).

Hounshell, Charles D.: *The Legislative Process in*

Virginia (Charlottesville, Va.: University of Virginia, Extension Division, 1951).

Key, V. O., Jr.: *American State Politics: An Introduction* (New York: Knopf, 1956).

New York State Constitutional Convention Committee: *Problems Relating to Legislative Organization* (Albany: the Committee, 1938).

Staniford, Edward F.: *Legislative Assistance* (Berkeley, Calif.: University of California, Bureau of Public Administration, 1957).

Steiner, Gilbert Y., and Samuel K. Gove: *Legislative Politics in Illinois* (Urbana, Ill.: University of Illinois Press, 1960).

Willoughby, William F.: *Principles of Legislative Organization and Administration* (Washington, D.C.: Brookings, 1934).

Young, Clement C. (ed.): *The Legislature of California, Its Membership, Procedure, and Work* (San Francisco: Commonwealth Club, 1943).

REVIEW QUESTIONS

1. Why must legislatures be freed from constitutional restraints in order to "perform their proper functions"?

2. Do you regard bicameralism, as did de Tocqueville, as "an axiom of the political science of the present age"? Discuss.

3. What are the principal arguments for unicameralism? Why have states, except Nebraska, been unwilling to adopt it?

4. Discuss the major problems involved in finding a proper basis of representation in state legislatures.

5. Prepare a list of arguments for or against banning political parties from state legislative politics.

6. What is the legislative-council idea? Where and in what form has it been put into effect?

7. Describe the legislative-committee system found in American states. How could it be improved?

8. Trace normal state legislative procedure from introduction of a bill through gubernatorial action on it.

9. Explain the initiative and referendum as used in the states.

Chapter Thirty-One

The Governor

and Administration

The Model State Constitution, in its fifth edition, continues to stand firmly for the time-honored American principle of concentration of administrative power and responsibility in a single popularly-elected chief executive. This principle, until the present century, was consistently recognized in our federal government, and in spite of frequent Congressional encroachments, it is still the theory of our federal constitution. Unfortunately, it has been greatly weakened in many of the state constitutions.

GEORGE C. S. BENSON[1]

The American governorship is central to the improvement of both executive and legislative processes. The chief executive is the only logical leader for the administration, and most students of state government look to the governor to provide direction to the legislature as well. The experience of the American colonists with arbitrary royal and proprietary

[1] National Municipal League, *Model State Constitution with Explanatory Articles* (New York: the League, 5th ed., 1948), p. 31.

governors evoked deep-seated distrust of executive power. Thus the early state constitutions minimized executive authority in providing for the office of governor. Many states elected governors by legislatures and checked them with executive councils.

EVOLUTION OF THE STATE EXECUTIVE

Colonial Governors. The office of governor existed in each of the thirteen colonies. In

631

the royal colonies the governor was a sort of viceroy sent out from London to represent the British government. Proprietary governors were appointees of the proprietors and carried out their wishes. Only in Massachusetts (before 1684), Connecticut, and Rhode Island did charters permit the colonists to choose their own executives. After the Massachusetts Company moved to the continent, the body of freemen chose John Winthrop governor. This body found it difficult to assemble, with the result that legislative authority and gubernatorial selection were vested in the general court. The voters of Connecticut and Rhode Island chose the governors but did not endow them with any of the coercive powers possessed by royal and proprietary governors or by state governors today.

In both royal and proprietary colonies the governor was a powerful officer. On the executive side, he possessed the power to appoint and was commander in chief of the military. On the judicial front, he was head of the colonial high court and dispenser of pardons and reprieves. He appointed the members of the upper house of the legislative branch, recommended legislation, exercised the veto power, and dissolved the legislature at his own discretion. The governor's powers were limited, on the other hand, by the legislative control of the purse strings. The popularly elected chamber of the legislature insisted upon and received generally the financial prerogatives that had been won by the British House of Commons.

First State Governors. Constitutions framed and adopted by the states in the revolutionary and confederation eras invariably included the office of governor but subordinated it to the legislature. Most of the states vested power to select the governor in the legislature; only Massachusetts, New Hampshire, and New York provided for popular election. The gubernatorial veto, today used in all but one state, was granted originally only in Massachusetts; New York had a modified veto power vested in governor and council. The majority of the original states further held the executive accountable to the legislature or the voters by limiting his term to one year.

Development of the Governorship, 1800–1900. During the first half of the nineteenth century, governors were gradually made elective by the people and executive councils were abandoned in many states. But the process of making the governor strong was not yet complete. A mania for popular election spread to other state executive offices. Attorneys general, auditors, controllers, treasurers, secretaries of state, and other officers were given their own constitutional pedestals and made elective by the people. Although substantial gubernatorial independence of the legislature was at last achieved, the executive power was diffused by popular election of other executive officers and boards. This might be called "the era of the plural executive," and it continues in several states today.

Toward the latter half of the last century, the powers of the governors were strengthened somewhat. The veto power was gradually granted in nearly all states. The power to veto items of appropriation bills had been granted in about one-third of the states by the turn of the century. Most executive councils were abolished. Often referred to as "chief executive," the governor continued to wield only a part of the executive authority. Woodrow Wilson, near the end of the period under review, contrasted the offices of Federal and state executives:

Of state officials associated with the governor it may, on the other hand, be said that both in law and in fact they are colleagues of the governor, in no sense his agents, or even his subordinates, except in formal rank in precedence. They, like himself, are elected by the people; he is in no way concerned in their choice. Nor do they serve him after election. They are not given him as advisers; they are, on the contrary, coordinated with him.[1]

Through the years, governors received added independence through a lengthened term of office—two or four years in nearly all states. Higher salaries also indicated the growing prestige of the office.

Trends in the Twentieth Century. Since 1900, earlier tendencies to make the governor a weak executive have been reversed in a majority of the states. Beginning in the first decade of this century, several states reexamined their administrative establishments and proposed reforms. During the second and third decades, state after state put reorganization plans into effect. With few exceptions, the changes centered around the expansion of gubernatorial powers over administration.

The normal pattern was to abolish dozens of boards and commissions and to transfer their functions to regular departments, the heads of which were appointed by and responsible to the governor. In only a few states, however, was the number of elective executive officers reduced. Elsewhere the reorganizations related mainly to agencies the legislature controlled. Departmentalization of most state activities expanded the authority of the governor substantially.

Hand in hand with administrative consolidation went the creation of the executive-budget system. The usual pattern in the reorganized states was to make the governor responsible for the preparation and submission of a financial plan, including both revenues and expenditures. The chief executive's authority over the administration also was increased greatly by vesting fiscal controls in his hands or in those of a director

[1] Woodrow Wilson, *The State: Elements of Historical and Practical Politics* (Boston: Heath, 1898), p. 499.

of finance or other officer responsible to him. Among these controls are expenditure control, central purchasing, and others that will be discussed later.

Although many states strengthened their chief executives' role, several have not. In the latter the governorship remains weak, the executive authority being shared with a large number of other elective administrative officers, boards, and commissions.

SELECTION PROCESS

Qualifications, Terms, and Pay. The governor and lieutenant governor, if there is one, usually have identical formal qualifications for office. These almost always are thirty or more years of age, United States citizenship, and residence in the state for a minimum period of time. It is perhaps unnecessary to specify such rules, because it is unlikely that the electorate would break any of them even if they were left out of the constitution.

The governor's term of office is four years in thirty-five states and two years in fifteen states. There has been a tendency to make the term longer; the average of more than three years prevailing today may be contrasted with the average of slightly over one year at the time of the adoption of the Federal Constitution. Two-fifths of the states, including Pennsylvania, New Jersey, and Indiana, forbid governors to serve more than one, two, or three successive terms, but this device has not led, as it has in some Latin-American countries, to *coup d'état* to keep the incumbent in by violence. The rest of the states have kept their executives available for reelection in case the electorate so desires.

Salaries of state executives are on the upgrade. The largest are those of New York ($50,000) and California ($40,000); the median, which has risen recently, is nearly

$20,000. In most states, governors also have the use of a residence and receive an allowance for entertaining. Even in the agricultural states of the West and South, the type of man chosen for governor usually could make more money by staying out of political office. It is certainly poor policy to pay public servants very much less than is received by the businessmen and other people with whom they deal.

Election. Governors are everywhere elected under party designations. They are nominated for office, in most states, by the direct primary. Even in primary states, however, there has been a recent tendency, led by New York and Indiana, to exempt the governorship from the primary and to nominate through party conventions. The return to the convention system of nominating candidates for the post of chief executive has added much interest to party organizational matters, has reduced campaign expenditures of aspirants, and may have improved the quality of the candidates chosen. The great majority of the states continue to use the primary, but in order to assure a majority choice, a few conduct runoff primary elections.

Most gubernatorial elections occur in even-numbered years, combined with congressional elections. A few states, especially some in the South, have chosen odd-numbered years for state elections. Virtually all states elect governors on the highest vote cast, whether plurality or majority, but a few insist upon a majority and throw the election to the legislature if none is obtained. The popular-vote, at-large system of voting for governor is often assumed to be in universal use, but in Mississippi an electoral-vote scheme is still in effect. In Georgia the "county-block" plan, which has been used in party primaries, has been proposed for general elections as well.

The governorship regularly attracts a considerable number of aspirants and candidates. Those who are successful generally have had some experience as a legislator or a county prosecutor. The office commands respect, and the powers make it a post to be desired. Governors frequently vault to United States senatorships and occasionally to the Presidency. With such stakes, it is not surprising that competition for the office is keen.

Removal. The governor can be removed from office by impeachment. Indictment is by the lower house, trial by the upper. In many states the chief justice of the supreme court presides. Impeachment has not been used to any great extent. New York, Texas, and Oklahoma each removed governors by impeachment in the period 1913–1923. The mere existence of the power may be a deterrent upon some governors. The fact that the legislature is in session for only limited periods in most of the states restricts the possibility of impeachment proceedings. Since the governor usually has the sole power to call special sessions and may even specify what the legislature can do in such sessions, there is little chance of impeaching him except at regular sessions.

Twelve states have provision for removal by recall. This device, explained in Chapter 12, permits voters, by signing petitions, to require a special election to determine whether or not an official should be superseded before his term expires. It removed a governor on only one occasion, in the state of North Dakota. With adequate safeguards to ensure that it is not abused, the recall offers a weapon to dismiss an officer whenever a sufficiently large proportion of the electorate judges such action to be desirable.

Whether the office of governor is vacated through impeachment, recall, death, or resignation, the constitution provides for a successor. In most cases this is the lieutenant governor. When there is no such officer, usually the president of the senate or the speaker of the lower house succeeds to the governorship.

POWERS OF THE GOVERNOR

Appointment and Removal. One of the most decisive powers of the executive is that of appointment and removal. Through his power to appoint, the governor may surround himself with fellow administrators who share his views and will carry out his policies. The governor also may secure, through his use of this power, the support of legislators. Although greatly reduced in volume since the adoption of merit systems in many states, gubernatorial appointments still loom important because of the increasing integration of authority in the major department heads and bureau chiefs.

The scope of the appointing power is limited by the persistence of many constitutional offices that are filled by popular election. Normally subject to confirmation, mostly senatorial, governors appoint secretaries of state in seven states, attorneys general in seven, controllers in ten, auditors in three, treasurers in four, and superintendents of public instruction in five. These offices, in most other states in which they exist, are elective, usually by the people but occasionally by the legislature.

The mode of selection of other department heads likewise varies. Taken as a whole, the most common pattern is to vest appointment in the governor, with or without senatorial confirmation, but a surprisingly large number of major state administrators are chosen by some means other than gubernatorial appointment. Almost inevitably this leads to some measure of irresponsibility; neither the electorate nor the legislature is able to coordinate the functions or even judge the stewardship of a large number of semi-independent officials.

Legislative Powers. The role of the governor in legislative procedure was referred to in Chapter 30. The governor's major legislative powers are (1) to call special sessions, (2) to recommend policies and legislation, and (3) to veto bills.

Authority to convene extraordinary sessions of the legislature is universally vested in the governor. In most cases, the governor's power is an exclusive one, not shared with the legislature. New Hampshire alone permits the legislature to call itself into special session, but this power has not been exercised. In a few states, the governor is required to convene the legislature if requested to do so by a fixed proportion of the legislators.[1] It appears that about one-half the states further empower the governor to specify what matters may be taken up by the legislature in a special session.

Depending greatly on the prevailing political situation and on the personal qualities of a governor, the power to recommend legislation can be one of the most influential possessed by the chief executive. Assembling not long after its election (usually in January after a November election), the legislature almost inevitably looks to the governor to propose a positive legislative program. If the governor produces a well-conceived plan and has the ability to sell it to the legislators, his program is likely to become the principal focus of attention during the session. On the other hand, if the legislature is hostile to the governor, or if he is weak, it may proceed to devise a program of its own. Happily, the former situation com-

[1] New York State Constitutional Convention Committee, *Problems Relating to Legislative Organization and Powers* (Albany: the Committee, 1938), pp. 402–405.

monly prevails, and the governor is able to exert positive leadership. He often delivers his principal messages in person to the legislature and via radio and television throughout the state.

The veto power, already described in some detail, is not as negative as it might at first appear. It arms the governor with a weapon to defend his positive program, to protect the financial position of the state, to curb excessive localism, and to ferret out poorly drafted and unconstitutional measures. Often the threat of veto keeps the legislature off a course of action opposed by the governor. In recent years, governors of many states have held public hearings on major bills to permit proponents and opponents an opportunity to air their views. Because of the great volume of legislation passed in the closing rush, the governor's veto is often absolute; after the legislature has adjourned finally, it is impossible for him to return a disapproved bill to the house of origin. The power to pocket veto and to veto items of appropriation bills adds greatly to the total of gubernatorial authority in the states permitting those practices.[1]

Military Powers. Early state constitutions stressed the governor's role as commander in chief of the armed forces of the state. After the adoption of the Federal Constitution and the assumption by the Federal government of paramount authority in military matters, this aspect of the governor's power diminished in importance. The enactment of National Guard legislation at the close of the First World War emphasized even more the supremacy of Federal control over the former state militias. In time of national emergency and war, the various state units

of the National Guard are called into active duty and operate as integral parts of the United States Armed Forces.

The governor has retained, however, a great deal of control over state armed forces. Except when in Federal service, National Guard units are under his command. Subject to the provisions of state constitution and law, the governor commissions officers and calls out the militia to suppress insurrections or deal with emergencies. During the last two decades, for example, governors have used state troops to restore order during strikes; quell outbreaks in state penitentiaries; do rescue and police work in flood, earthquake, and other disasters; and block school desegregation.

In practice, governors place little importance upon their functions as commanders in chief. They delegate military matters to an adjutant general and his staff. Some governors pervert their power to commission officers to political purposes and honor untrained citizens with high rank. When this rank is purely honorary, no great harm is done. Loading National Guard units with officers selected on a political basis, however, may undermine the effectiveness of that force in emergencies.

Financial Powers. As the reorganization of the administrative branches of state governments has proceeded, governors have been given more and more authority over finances. Originally, the governor had control only over the expenditures of that portion of the administrative establishment under his direct jurisdiction. The spread of the veto power to state after state gave the chief executive at least a negative authority over proposed expenditures. The item veto has expanded his control greatly.

The twentieth-century reorganizations gave governors the most potent of their fiscal controls. Centering in the budget, they

[1] For a thorough study of the gubernatorial veto see Frank W. Prescott, "The Executive Veto in American States," *Western Political Quarterly*, vol. 3 (March, 1950), pp. 89–112.

were (1) the power to formulate the financial plan and (2) the power to execute it. The executive budget is a comprehensive financial plan, usually containing estimates of revenues, recommendations of new revenues (if any), and proposals of amounts to be expended for each purpose and agency. In most reorganized states, the responsibility for formulating the budget is placed squarely on the shoulders of the governor. After the budget is authorized, the governor usually possesses powers which may be used to control the pattern of expenditures by executive agencies. The most effective of these controls affect purchases, construction, allocation of expenditures to particular financial periods (months or quarters), and the imposition of compulsory savings.

The Pardoning Power. The governor's power to grant pardons and reprieves is judicial in nature, deriving from the role of the royal colonial governor as chancellor. It exists to provide a remedy for mistakes that are made in the trial and conviction of alleged criminals and a way to release offenders who are deemed to have reformed.

In the early days while populations were small and other duties of office not too heavy, governors could give applications for executive clemency personal attention. The busy state executive of today rarely can find time to examine more than the most spectacular cases. Twenty states do not entrust the governor with the sole authority for pardoning. Of the states that have modified gubernatorial responsibility for pardons, sixteen have pardon boards, which may or may not include the governor, and four require ratification of executive action by either council or senate. Even in the states that have retained the pardoning power solely in the hands of the governor, nineteen states have established advisory pardon boards to investigate and make recommendations.

Few governors relish this aspect of their job. Applications for pardons and commutation of sentence consume great amounts of time and nervous energy and are among the most distasteful tasks of a state executive. The present trend is to place primary emphasis on the decision or recommendation of a full-time board or staff, preferably one trained in the field of penology.

Chief Administrator. State constitutions, commonly referring to the governor as "chief executive," assign him the task of seeing that laws are faithfully executed. Some even follow the Federal Constitution in giving him power to require department heads to render reports to him in writing. Although not always stated in so many words, the governor is usually expected to head the executive branch of state government and to use such powers as are delegated to him to get some order out of the chaos created by constitutional provisions written to fit another age and inspired by an outmoded political philosophy. In addition, in nearly every state public opinion expects him to serve as chief legislator, despite constitutional provisions, express or implied, that the doctrine of separation of powers must prevail. Thus the modern governor, facing the often difficult task of asserting himself as a real leader, must utilize such powers as he has been given or can assume.

That it has been possible for the governor to emerge from figurehead to leader, as Leslie Lipson aptly puts it,[1] has been due less to formal powers vested by legal sanction than to the position of the chief executive as party leader and representative of all the people. At the head of the state ticket of his party, the gubernatorial candi-

[1] *The American Governor from Figurehead to Leader* (Chicago: University of Chicago Press, 1939).

date commands a special position in party councils and is frequently the outstanding leader of his party. Like the President in the national field, the governor is selected by a process involving the whole electorate. With some justice, therefore, he can claim to be its spokesman and leader.[1]

STATE ADMINISTRATION

Constitutional Officers. In addition to the governor, a number of state officials usually are popularly elected.

The *lieutenant governor* succeeds to the governorship in case of vacancy and is usually the presiding officer of the state senate. Sometimes he also has minor administrative assignments, such as serving on boards and commissions.

The *secretary of state* is the official custodian of records, keeper of the seal, issuer of corporate charters, and supervisor of election administration. His duties, largely routine, seldom affect policy.

The *attorney general*, the chief legal officer, performs many types of legal services for the state, including prosecution, the overseeing of local law-enforcement officials, defense of the state, and the furnishing of legal advice to state agencies.

The *treasurer* is custodian of the state purse; sometimes he collects taxes; and he disburses money when payments are authorized by appropriate authority.

The *auditor, controller,* or *comptroller* usually possesses power to authorize those payments provided by law; in most states such an officer also audits state accounts.

The *superintendent of public instruction* directs the state school system through his supervisory and financial powers over elementary, secondary, and teacher-training schools.

Most of these officers, with the exceptions noted earlier, are elected by the people and therefore are independent of direct gubernatorial control. When such officers are the heads of executive departments, the latter have a similar independence.

Departments. A department is an organization into which related functions are assigned for direction, control, and efficient operation. Before the administrative reorganizations carried out in many states since 1925 it was common to have up to a hundred or more uncoordinated agencies—bureaus, commissions, boards, offices, and the like—either directly responsible to the governor or independent of his control. Since reorganization, most states have set up departments presided over by single heads, called "directors" or "secretaries," but several states have retained boards or commissions to control departments. In some fields, notably education and public welfare, boards—with or without an executive officer—are common.

Because states vary considerably in the nomenclature they use and the duties they assign to departments, it is possible to present no more than a list of the departments most commonly found in the American states: administration,[2] budget, or finance; justice; revenue or taxation; public instruction; military; agriculture; conservation; health; highways; mental hygiene; insurance; labor; public works; and welfare.

The typical department is further sub-

---

[1] For a good case study, see *Gladys M. Kammerer*, "The Governor as Chief Administrator in Kentucky," *Journal of Politics*, vol. 16 (May, 1954), pp. 236–256.

[2] There has been a significant recent trend to concentrate management functions in a "department of administration." For a case study of one, see Ferrel Heady and Robert H. Pealy, "The Michigan Department of Administration: A Case Study in the Politics of Administration," *Public Administration Review*, vol. 16 (Spring, 1956), pp. 82–89.

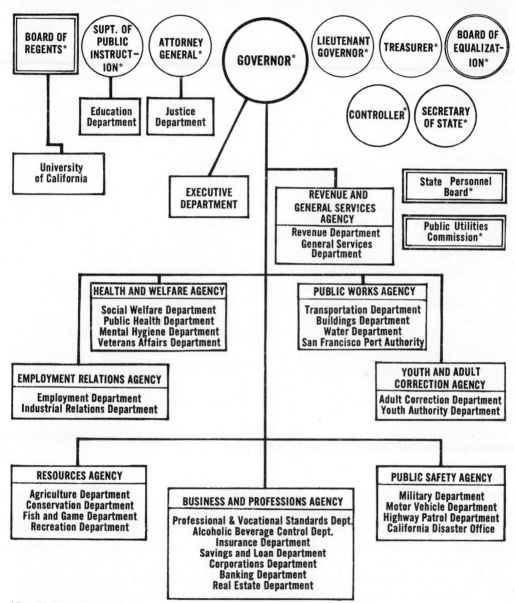

RECOMMENDED ORGANIZATION
STATE OF CALIFORNIA

BOARD OF REGENTS*

SUPT. OF PUBLIC INSTRUCT-ION*

ATTORNEY GENERAL*

GOVERNOR*

LIEUTENANT GOVERNOR*

TREASURER*

BOARD OF EQUALIZAT-ION*

CONTROLLER*

SECRETARY OF STATE*

Education Department

Justice Department

University of California

EXECUTIVE DEPARTMENT

REVENUE AND GENERAL SERVICES AGENCY
Revenue Department
General Services Department

State Personnel Board*

Public Utilities Commission*

HEALTH AND WELFARE AGENCY
Social Welfare Department
Public Health Department
Mental Hygiene Department
Veterans Affairs Department

PUBLIC WORKS AGENCY
Transportation Department
Buildings Department
Water Department
San Francisco Port Authority

EMPLOYMENT RELATIONS AGENCY
Employment Department
Industrial Relations Department

YOUTH AND ADULT CORRECTION AGENCY
Adult Correction Department
Youth Authority Department

RESOURCES AGENCY
Agriculture Department
Conservation Department
Fish and Game Department
Recreation Department

BUSINESS AND PROFESSIONS AGENCY
Professional & Vocational Standards Dept.
Alcoholic Beverage Control Dept.
Insurance Department
Savings and Loan Department
Corporations Department
Banking Department
Real Estate Department

PUBLIC SAFETY AGENCY
Military Department
Motor Vehicle Department
Highway Patrol Department
California Disaster Office

*Constitutional Office or Board

California is in the process of reorganizing its state administration along the lines of the "Recommended Organization" shown above. Departmentalization began in 1921, and was extended in 1927 and 1929. As time passed, however, the number of departments became excessive, and many independent units were established. After careful study, it was decided to group nearly all of the administrative entities under gubernatorial control into eight great "agencies," the administrators of which would coordinate activities as deputies of the governor.

divided into bureaus, divisions, offices, or
agencies, each with a chief responsible to
the department head. In some states the
governor appoints bureau chiefs; in others,
civil service selects them.

Independent Agencies. In states that
have not yet reorganized, and in many that
have, a confused array of scattered agencies,
boards, commissions, and officials remains.
These independent agencies are administered in a variety of ways. Some have single
heads chosen by the governor, functioning
much like bureaus but reporting directly to
the governor rather than through a department. Others have full or part-time boards,
which may either divide administrative responsibilities among themselves or choose
a full-time administrator to do the job. The
use of a board or commission has often
been justified for a new function, or when
the work to be done involves a combination
of administrative, legislative, and judicial
functions.

State Merit Systems. As recorded in
Chapter 19, over one-half of the states have
adopted general civil-service systems on the
merit basis. The remainder of the states
have merit systems covering employees only
in certain functions or departments. The
latter are mainly the result of a requirement imposed by Social Security Act
amendments, in 1939, which made it
mandatory for states receiving Federal
social security aid to use the merit system in
the agencies concerned with its administration. The usual state agencies covered are
social welfare, public health, unemployment
compensation, and employment services.

Most of the state-wide civil-service systems are directed by an agency called either
civil-service commission or personnel board,
although a few have experimented with
single-headed bodies. The agency classifies
positions by the kind of work involved and
by the relative degree of skill or responsi-

bility required. The appropriate compensation is fixed for each job, and a complete
salary-standardization plan is drawn up.

The trend toward comprehensive state
merit systems has been strong since the
Second World War. If it continues at the
same rate in the future, nearly all states
will have state-wide plans within another
twenty years. State civil-service reform is
opposed by many practicing politicians on
the ground that those who work in campaigns must be rewarded. There is a good
argument for making all policy-forming
offices appointive by the governor, since he
is entitled to surround himself with major
officers who share his views and enjoy his
full confidence. For the great bulk of state
jobs, however, there is little rational defense
for the old-fashioned spoils methods belonging to a bygone age.

**The Administrative Reorganization Move-
ment.** As the American states acquired new
population and new problems, the functions
of state government multiplied. Lacking an
over-all plan, or even a philosophy of
administrative organization, legislatures
created new agencies with little thought of
their relationship to existing agencies. The
result was like that achieved by a farmer
who began with a small shed, which was
quite adequate to shelter himself and his
team of horses. Later the farmer chose a
wife, and in due time they acquired several
children. In the meantime, farming operations having multiplied several times over,
the farmer required barns for hay, cover
for animals and farm machinery, eventually
even a garage. Each expansion brought new
demands for buildings, and the Topsy-like
growth of farm structures—here a room,
there a lean-to, over yonder an outhouse,
a new porch on the front, and new store-
room on the rear—was very similar to that
of state governments.

The time came, about 1910, when public

officials and students of government recognized that the scattered agencies often were inefficient and sometimes worked at cross-purposes. Several states made studies of the need for reorganization. Illinois, in 1917, adopted the first definite reforms. It abolished more than one hundred agencies, boards, and commissions and regrouped their functions into nine departments which were headed by directors appointed by the governor. It created an executive-budget system which concentrated a great deal of authority in a new department of finance.

Most of the thirty-odd states that have instituted some degree of administrative reorganization have followed the Illinois model. A few, notably Virginia and New York, went further and reduced the number of elective constitutional officers. On the other hand, Wisconsin and Michigan reorganized their agencies but avoided increasing the governor's power by placing responsibility for coordination in the hands of agencies beyond his direct control.

The pattern of modern state administrative organization, then, is to concentrate most agencies and functions into a limited number of executive departments. These departments, headed by appointees of the governor, consist of appropriate bureaus and other subdivisions. Great emphasis is placed upon the establishment of the executive budget and the concentration of fiscal-control powers in a department of finance or similar agency. Many of the reorganized states have created central purchasing agencies and installed uniform accounting systems. Another feature of many reformed administrations is the organization of department heads into a cabinet presided over by the governor.

Following the creation of the first Commission on Organization of the Executive Branch of Government by Congress in 1947, two-thirds of the states set up bodies to survey their administrative problems. These "little Hoover groups," as they were popularly called, studied a variety of problems in the several states, but the central focus was administrative organization. A common theme in most of the reports was that the governor should be placed in command of most or all of the administrative agencies, and that he should discharge his responsibility through departments headed by individuals rather than boards and commissions. Many of the reports stressed the desirability of strengthening financial controls in the hands of governors and legislatures.

In an evaluation written after the initial impact of little Hoover reports, Karl A. Bosworth[1] found only two states—New Hampshire and New Jersey—in which legislatures moved positively and wholeheartedly to put recommendations into effect. Some of the states did nothing, or practically nothing. Perhaps one-half or more of the states acted favorably on at least some of their little Hoover recommendations.[2]

[1] "The Politics of Management Improvement in the States," *American Political Science Review*, vol. 47 (March, 1953), pp. 84–99. For a later review, see W. Brooke Graves, "Some New Approaches to State Administrative Reorganization," *Western Political Quarterly*, vol. 9 (September, 1956), pp. 743–754.

[2] For case studies of particular states, see F. M. Landers and H. D. Hamilton, "State Administrative Reorganization in Michigan: The Legislative Approach," *Public Administration Review*, vol. 14 (Spring, 1954), pp. 99–111; S. K. Gove, "Reorganization in Illinois," *National Municipal Review*, vol. 42 (November, 1953), pp. 502–506; R. H. Weir, "Reorganization—1954 Style," *State Government*, vol. 27 (April, 1954), pp. 72–74; Bennett M. Rich, "Administrative Reorganization in New Jersey," *Public Administration Review*, vol. 12 (Autumn, 1952), pp. 251–257.

FOR FURTHER READING

Brooks, Glenn: *When Governors Convene: The Governors' Conference and National Politics* (Baltimore: The Johns Hopkins Press, 1961).

Buck, Arthur E.: *Administrative Consolidation in State Governments* (New York: National Municipal League, rev. ed., 1930).

——: *The Reorganization of State Government in the United States* (New York: Columbia University Press, 1938).

Carleton, Roderick L., and Staff: *The Reorganization and Consolidation of State Administration in Louisiana* (Baton Rouge, La.: Louisiana State University Press, 1937).

Governors' Conference: *Proceedings of the . . .* (Chicago: Council of State Governments, annual).

Jensen, Christen: *The Pardoning Power in the American States* (Chicago: University of Chicago Press, 1922).

Lipson, Leslie: *The American Governor from Figurehead to Leader* (Chicago: University of Chicago Press, 1939).

New York State Constitutional Convention Committee: *Problems Relating to Executive Administration and Powers* (Albany: 1938).

Ransone, Coleman B.: *The Office of Governor in the United States* (University, Ala.: University of Alabama Press, 1956).

Rohr, Charles J.: *The Governor of Maryland: A Constitutional Study* (Baltimore: Johns Hopkins Press, 1932).

Scace, Homer E.: *The Organization of the Executive Office of Governor* (New York: Institute of Public Administration, 1950).

Webster, Donald H., and others: *Washington State Government: Administrative Organization and Functions* (Seattle: University of Washington, Bureau of Governmental Research and Services, 1956).

REVIEW QUESTIONS

1. Trace the evolution of the office of the governor and indicate the problems involved in developing a strong state executive.

2. To what extent is executive authority in the American states divided between elective constitutional officers and departments under gubernatorial control?

3. What are the principal powers of the American governor?

4. Explain the administrative-reorganization movement in the states, and indicate how far it has proceeded.

5. Describe the appointive power of the governor. How extensively have the states adopted the merit system?

6. What are the ways by which a governor can influence lawmaking?

7. Would you strengthen or weaken the office of governor? What specific changes would you advocate?

8. Compare the office of governor with that of the President of the United States.

9. Outline a plan for making the administrative branch of the government of your state the best possible.

Chapter Thirty-Two

The State Judiciary

Our system of government is no stronger than our courts, and our courts are no stronger than the strength of the public's confidence in them.

CHARLES S. RHYNE[1]

In America, where the stability of Courts and of all departments of government rests upon the approval of the people, it is peculiarly essential that the system for establishing and dispensing Justice be developed to a high point of efficiency and so maintained that the public shall have absolute confidence in the integrity and impartiality of its administration.[2]

AMERICAN BAR ASSOCIATION

Each of the states has responsibility for enforcing its laws. The institutions and procedures used by the various states have many similarities but they also differ. They are separate and independent of one another and the Federal system explained in

[1] "Defending our Courts: The Duty of the Legal Profession," *American Bar Association Journal*, vol. 44 (February, 1958), p. 121.

[2] Preamble to the Cannons of Professional Ethics as promulgated by the American Bar Association.

Chapter 17. Upon them falls the primary responsibility of maintaining domestic order and protecting life and property. Of all the tasks reserved by the Constitution to the states, these are the most essential and important.

AREA OF STATE RESPONSIBILITY

State Law. The states have legal competence to deal with any matter, as long as they stay

643

within the limits imposed by the Federal Constitution. Their law consists of the state constitution, legislative enactments, orders of the executive and judicial branches, charters and ordinances of local governments, and common law (except in Louisiana, where the Napoleonic civil code prevails).

The legal authority of a state stops at its boundaries. If a state wishes to reach beyond its territorial limits, it can do so only through the Federal government or with the cooperation of other states. Within state boundaries, responsibility must be shared with the Federal government.

State-court Jurisdiction. State courts have jurisdiction over all cases and controversies arising under state law. The Eleventh Amendment makes them also responsible for settling disputes between the state and its citizens or citizens of other states. Acts of Congress give states additional authority: exclusive jurisdiction over civil suits arising from Federal laws between parties with diverse citizenship if less than $10,000 is involved; concurrent jurisdiction in similar cases when larger sums are at issue; and permission to share in the administration of a few matters such as naturalization, passport applications, and bankruptcies. When concurrent jurisdiction exists, the parties in dispute usually choose between launching the suit in a state or Federal court.

Types of Cases. In the discussion of the Federal courts (Chapter 17), disputes are classified as criminal, civil, equity, and those arising under international law. Virtually all disputes at international law come before Federal courts; state judiciaries seldom encounter them. Most cases before state courts are, therefore, of the other types mentioned.

In criminal cases the state is a party and prosecutes persons charged with violating state laws. Civil cases are contests between private parties who are seeking settlements, usually in the form of monetary payments. Cases in equity seek judicial determination of matters for which there are no readily available remedies "at law." Illustrations are given in Chapter 17.

JUDICIAL ORGANIZATION

State Systems Decentralized. Central direction of the Federal judicial system is provided by the Department of Justice, the Annual Judicial Conference of Senior Circuit Judges, and the Administrative Office of the United States Courts. The state judicial systems, organized on a district or county basis with elective judges, are characterized by extreme decentralization. Usually each court acts as a nearly autonomous unit.

Some uniformity is provided by constitutional provisions, acts of the legislature, and rules of procedure established by higher courts. In judicial administration, however, state courts often lack even the power to appoint and direct minor court personnel. "Even the pettiest agency," says Roscoe Pound, "has much more control than the average state court."[1]

Greater unification of state courts has been proposed for years. The American Judicature Society has pleaded for this reform since its foundation in 1913,[2] the National Municipal League embodied the suggestion in its model state constitution,[3] and many others have endorsed the change.

Judicial reforms have been adopted in a few states. The Missouri constitution adopted in 1946 gave the Supreme Court broad rule-making authority and limited

[1] *Organization of State Courts* (Boston: Little, Brown, 1940), p. 286.

[2] See its *Journal,* published bimonthly.

[3] The League's views also have been set forth in its monthly publication *National Municipal Review.*

power to transfer judges. North Carolina made similar changes in 1950, and several other states have followed suit. The most sweeping reform was made by New Jersey, which in 1947 adopted a unified and flexible system. Alaska's new court system is a similar one.

Judicial Administration. Decentralized as their judicial systems are, states had until recently no central source of leadership or information on matters pertaining to the administration of justice. The need is now being met in many states through judicial conferences, judicial councils, and administrative offices.

Conferences are formal meetings of representative jurists of a particular state to discuss matters of mutual concern, adopt rules, and make recommendations concerning the administration of justice. Judicial councils exist in over thirty states. These are composed of jurists, members of the bar, leading citizens, and sometimes members of the state legislature. They often employ full- or part-time executive secretaries and a small staff. Their functions are usually limited to conducting studies, compiling statistics, and making recommendations. In no instance have they been given authority to direct and supervise the courts.

A recent trend is for the states to establish an agency resembling the Administrative Office of the United States Courts, discussed in Chapter 17. Illustrative of these is an administrative office of the courts established in Maryland. Its director, appointed by the chief judge of the court of appeals, is empowered to examine dockets, determine the need of any court for assistance, make recommendations concerning the assignment of judges, collect and compile statistical data, prepare budget estimates for the judicial system, and recommend improvements.

Supreme Courts. The pinnacle of the judicial structure of every state is a supreme tribunal usually called a supreme court. The great majority of states have five or seven judges on their highest court; a few have only three. Judges are usually elected. Except for the issuance of writs, their work is confined almost exclusively to hearing appeals from the lower courts.

These courts never "try" cases; nor do they permit the introduction of new evidence. Rather, they merely review the law and the record and sustain, reverse, or modify decisions made by lower courts. If more testimony seems necessary or retrial appears appropriate, the case is remanded to trial courts. Decisions are written and are published in volumes generally known as "state supreme court reports."

Supreme courts are the ultimate interpreters of state constitutions and laws except where appeals may be taken to the Federal courts because of alleged conflicts between state and Federal constitutions and laws. A few states have authorized them to render advisory opinions upon important questions of law when so requested by the governor or legislature.

Intermediate Courts. The more populous states have established one or more intermediate courts immediately below the highest court for the purpose of reviewing cases that need not demand the time of overburdened supreme tribunals. These are also appellate courts.

Their names vary: Tennessee has one intermediate court called the court of appeals; Pennsylvania and New Jersey each has one called the superior court; California has several known as district courts of appeals; in Oklahoma there is a court which has jurisdiction in criminal cases only and is known as criminal court of appeals. Courts like these consist of from three to nine judges, who are usually elected. Their

TYPICAL STATE COURT SYSTEM

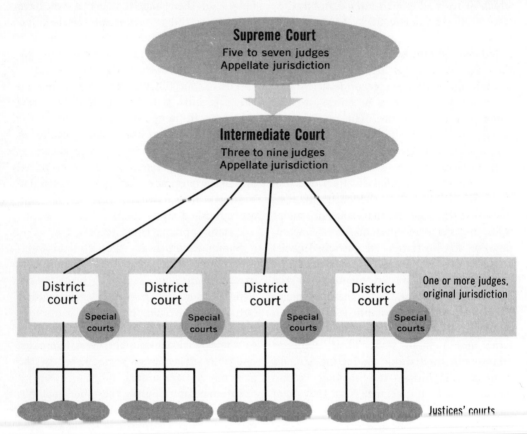

Supreme Court
Five to seven judges
Appellate jurisdiction

Intermediate Court
Three to nine judges
Appellate jurisdiction

District court   District court   District court   District court   One or more judges, original jurisdiction

Special courts   Special courts   Special courts   Special courts

Justices' courts

organization and procedures are much like those of supreme tribunals.

District or County Courts. Beneath the courts of appeals stand the trial courts that handle the great majority of cases litigated throughout the country. These try the home-town cases of murder, burglary, assault and battery, rape, and suit for damages. They function within districts outlined by state legislatures to include at least one county, and frequently more in sparsely settled regions. California, for example, has fifty-eight districts—one for each county; New York has nine; Illinois has

seventeen; and Pennsylvania has fifty-eight —nine fewer than the number of counties. The number of judges in each district varies from one to several, and in most states judges are chosen by popular election.

The names of these courts vary. In Pennsylvania they are known as district courts; in California, superior courts; elsewhere, county or circuit courts or something else. Some cases reach them on appeal from summary courts, like those of justices of the peace; in these instances it is customary to ignore the trial heard before summary court and rehear the entire case from beginning to end. Most cases, however, originate here. Most end here, also, because there are comparatively few appeals. Sometimes the same judges sitting in the same courts handle cases of all types but at separate and distinct periods of time. Again, some states have different courts with different judges for cases of various types. Still other states have different courts but the same judges for various types of cases. Thus, in Pennsylvania the same judge or judges at different times preside over courts of quarter sessions, oyer and terminer, orphans, and common pleas.

Where separate courts exist, those handling civil cases are often called courts of common pleas; those handling criminal cases may be called courts of sessions, courts of oyer and terminer and general jail delivery, or, for less serious offenses, courts of quarter sessions; those handling equity cases are commonly known as courts of equity or courts of chancery; those dealing with probate matters are called probate, orphans', or surrogate courts.

Minor Courts. At the base of state judicial systems are numerous courts for handling minor disputes with little formality. In rural areas and small municipalities these are justices' courts presided over by justices of the peace. In larger places similar courts may be manned by magistrates, or occasionally aldermen.

Uusually two officers are chosen within each town, township, ward, or district for terms varying from two to six years. They usually need not be lawyers, nor for that matter possess any special qualifications other than the ability to get nominated and elected. Vacancies are numerous for lack of interested candidates and many who accept office have little official business. Justices come from all walks of life. A recent Kansas poll showed farming as the chief occupation. Others mentioned were teacher,

barber, druggist, garageman, insurance agent, secretary, hail adjuster, professor and minister, grain-elevator operator, purchasing agent, and motel owner. An earlier Pennsylvania study disclosed fifty housewives filling the office. Justices usually hold other jobs; their compensation for official services ordinarily comes from fees, although a few states have put justices on a salary basis.

The duties of justices are extremely varied. Besides performing marriage ceremonies and notarial duties, they handle both civil and criminal cases. Civil suits, like those involving breaches of contract, trespass, action on notes, and bill collection, ordinarily involve sums of less than $300. Where sums of less than $100 are involved, the justices' decisions are usually final; otherwise an appeal may be taken to a higher court.

Often a justice's court exercises a concurrent jurisdiction with a district court, parties having the option of starting their suit in either place. In criminal matters where serious offenses are involved, the justice may hold only a preliminary hearing, but where the offense is minor he may try the case and pronounce judgment. Records of proceedings need not be kept, hence the term "court not of record." In most cases the trial is without jury. Invariably decisions may be appealed to district or county courts.

Criticisms and Proposed Reforms. The minor judiciary has been widely criticized in recent years, with the result that it has been subjected to extensive study. Critics insist that there are far too many justices for modern times; that justices lack desirable training; that many justices are uninterested in their work, so much so that it is many times impossible to find anyone to run for the office; that the nature of the office leads to inefficiency, excessive costs, and dispersion of responsibility; that the fee system often leads to undesirable

NEW JERSEY'S COURT SYSTEM

SUPREME COURT

Chief Justice and Six Associates

with broad powers of administration over all courts in the state. Jurisdiction: final appeals in all important cases. First term: seven years. Tenure on reappointment; retirement at seventy.

SUPERIOR COURT

Minimum of twenty-four judges; term, tenure, and retirement same as Supreme Court

LAW DIVISION	APPELLATE DIVISION	CHANCERY DIVISION
General jurisdiction in all causes, civil and criminal. Review in lieu of prerogative writ except state agencies.	Jurisdiction in questions of general equity, and matrimonial and probate matters.	Decides appeals from Law Division, Chancery Division, county courts, county district courts, juvenile and domestic relations courts, and state agencies.

21 COUNTY COURTS

Minimum of one county judge in each county

LAW DIVISION	PROBATE DIVISION
Jurisdiction: civil and criminal within each county.	Concurrent with superior court within county, and has such equity jurisdiction as required to resolve matters in controversy. Decides appeals from municipal courts and in workmen's compensation cases.

INFERIOR COURTS

May be established, altered or abolished by appeals therefrom as provided by law

MUNICIPAL COURTS	COUNTY DISTRICT COURTS	JUVENILE AND DOMESTIC RELATIONS COURTS	SURROGATE COURTS

All judges appointed by governor with approval of senate, except municipal judges and surrogates.

(Administrative Office of the Courts, State of New Jersey, July, 1958.)

solicitation of business and to petty extortion; that justices in large places have become integral parts of corrupt machines; and that justices do not render impartial justice but too often decide in favor of the plaintiff because it is easier, more popular, or more profitable to do so—hence the accusation that the initials "J.P." mean "justice for the plaintiff."

The case in favor of reform is convincing. In England, home of the justices' courts, their use has steadily declined in favor of appointive, full-time, legally trained "stipendiary magistrates." The Federal courts have functioned for years with United States Commisioners who are not elective lay justices like those of the states.

The remedy most commonly advocated is abolition of the justices' courts and transfer of their functions to district or county courts in rural areas and metropolitan courts in urban areas. A possible adaptation is to retain the justice of the peace but only as an assistant to the judge of the county court. The least that might be done would be to consolidate jurisdictional areas, establish higher qualifications, provide for a larger measure of supervision by district courts, and abolish the fee system.

An increasing number of states have taken steps to substitute magistrates who are appointive, trained, and salaried for the old-fashioned justices of the peace. States that have moved in this direction include Alaska, Arizona, Colorado, Connecticut, Hawaii, Illinois, Iowa, Maine, Missouri, New Jersey, New Mexico, New York, North Carolina, North Dakota, Tennessee, Washington, and Wisconsin.

Special Courts. The courts described above provide the warp and woof of state judiciaries. To them must be added a wide variety of special courts found particularly in metropolitan centers. Most common are municipal courts set up for handling problems peculiar to congested areas. They are usually headed by several elective judges, each of whom presides over one or more divisions specializing in criminal, civil, traffic, domestic-relations, or juvenile cases.

In addition to handling disputes arising from municipal law, these courts nearly always have concurrent jurisdiction with the usual district or county courts. This means that, for violating a city ordinance, one would be prosecuted in the municipal court, but for a state offense committed within the city's limits one might be tried in the municipal court, a justice's court, or a county (or district) court. This is often quite confusing, especially where cities have spread out to include an entire county or more.

COURT OFFICIALS

Judges. The principal court officers are the judges. As indicated above, there may be one or several for each court. Where there are several they may sit en banc (as a body), or one or more may preside over each of the divisions of the court. Except for justices of the peace and their counterparts, most states require that judges be "learned in the law." A few states specify that a judge must be of "good character," while North Carolina required that he "believe in God."[1] Methods of selection and appointment of judges are discussed below.

Terms vary from two years in Vermont to life in Masschusetts. The usual method of removal is by impeachment; several states permit removal by the governor upon the address of two-thirds of both houses of the legislature; several states provide for popular recall; a few permit removal by the state supreme court; others follow variations of one or more of these methods.

[1] Qualifications and other data may be found in *The Book of the States* for various years.

POPULAR ELECTION OF JUDGES: NEW YORK

4	5	6	7	8	9	10	11	12	13	14	15	16	17	18	19	20	21	22	23
Chief Judge of the Court of Appeals	Associate Judges of the Court of Appeals			Justices of the Supreme Court, 1st Judicial District								Justices of the City Court				Judges of the Court of General Sessions		Justices of the Municipal Court, 9th District	
Vote for one	Vote for three			Vote for eight								Vote for four				Vote for two		Vote for two	

The great burden imposed on the electorate by popular election of judges in large jurisdictions is indicated by a portion of the Manhattan-voting-machine face in 1954. Rather than struggle with individual candidates, the voter is encouraged to pull the party lever and vote for all executive, legislative, and judicial candidates of his party.

Appointment versus Election of Judges. During the colonial period judges were appointive. After the Revolution, appointment by state legislatures became the rule. Mississippi broke with tradition in 1832 by providing for popular election. Other states were quick to follow, with the result that, by the time of the Civil War, election had become most common.

Today, although as many as seven different methods are used, three predominate: (1) popular election, (2) appointment by governors, and (3) selection by legislatures. The first is by far the most common, appointment by governors or legislatures being confined to about a dozen states, nearly all located along the Atlantic seaboard.

The adoption of popular election reflected a suspicion of aristocracy and control by financial and corporate interests. It also indicated a feeling that the best place to obtain judicial responsibility was at the ballot box. These views are still dominant throughout most of the country. Additional reasons advanced in defense of the practice

are these: The elective method has produced judges as competent as those chosen by other methods; evils attributable to state jurisprudence are due to other causes than the manner of selecting judges; with all their faults, elected judges render decisions more in keeping with popular desires and interests; and election prevents governors, or the dominant party in the legislature, from building powerful machines by rewarding partisans with judgeships.

Against popular election, these arguments are advanced: Political bosses and machines dictate and control nominations and elections; elective judges must of necessity be politically conscious and are usually strongly partisan; voters are unlikely to give sufficient consideration to candidates' judicial temperament and legal expertness; ably qualified men, to whom "playing politics" and campaigning may be distasteful, are deterred from seeking office; elective judges decide cases with an eye to reelection rather than on merits; and election produces a highly decentralized judiciary without uniform standards and practices and one that defies effective administration.

Despite the popular favor in which election is held, most professional students of government prefer selection by other methods. They conclude that, of the methods used, executive appointment has worked best and legislative appointment worst, with other methods in between. However, in view of the entrenched position of the elective procedure, many critics question the advisability of concentrating reform efforts on complete abandonment of the method. Instead, compromises are suggested; one of them is contained in the model state constitution proposed by the National Municipal League. This suggests election every eight years of a chief justice who would be authorized to appoint all other state judges from a list of eligibles presented by the judicial council. Terms would run for twelve years, except that after four years every judge would be required to stand for approval or rejection at the polls.

Growing interest has been shown in the plan just outlined. California adopted a modified version in 1934. Missouri's new constitution of 1946 provided that judges should be nominated by an impartial commission of lawyers, laymen, and jurists. The governor appoints from this list with the proviso that after a short term incumbent judges will present themselves to the people for approval or rejection. Under New Jersey's constitution of 1947 the governor appoints judges, with senate confirmation, who serve for seven-year terms and then submit themselves to the voters for approval or rejec-

tion. If approved, judges continue to serve for terms of good behavior or until the age of seventy. Alaska and Iowa have adopted similar plans. Kansas and Maryland approved the arrangement for some of their judges and interest has been manifested elsewhere.

Most other states continue using older methods, often attempting to mitigate evils by providing for election on nonpartisan or independent ballots, coupling election with rather long terms (as in Pennsylvania where elected district judges serve for ten years and the Supreme Court judges for twenty-one), recall of judges or even judicial decisions, and other devices.

The Clerk of Court. Next to the judge, the principal court officer is the clerk, who is sometimes called the "prothonotary." This officer handles the large volume of administrative work arising from the judicial process. Among his duties are the issuing of writs and court processes; keeping the court's financial records; arranging dockets; collecting court costs, fees, and fines; and recording, indexing, and filing the court's decisions and awards.

Despite his close relationship to the court and the fact that his work is entirely administrative, the clerk is seldom directly responsible to the court. Rather, he is usually popularly elected. Careful students are agreed that the substitution of appointment for election would result in greater responsibility, efficiency, and economy in both time and money. They also urge that the clerk be paid a salary rather than fees.

FOR FURTHER READING

American Judicature Society: *Journal of the . . .* (Chicago: bimonthly).

Aumann, Francis R.: *The Instrumentalities of Justice: Their Forms, Functions and Limitations* (Columbus, Ohio: The Ohio State University Press, 1956).

Callender, Clarence N.: *American Courts* (New York: McGraw-Hill, 1927).

Callison, I. P.: *Courts of Injustice* (New York: Twayne Publishers, 1955).

Carpenter, William S.: *Judicial Tenure in the United States* (New Haven, Conn.: Yale University Press, 1918).

Chute, Charles Lionel, and Marjorie Bell: *Crime, Courts, and Probation* (New York: Macmillan, 1956).

Council of State Governments; *Courts of Last Resort in the Forty-eight States* (Chicago: the Council, 1950).

———: *Trial Courts of General Jurisdiction in the Forty-eight States* (Chicago: the Council, 1951).

Elliott, Sheldon D.: *Improving Our Courts: Collected Essays on Judicial Administration* (New York: Oceana, 1960).

Fairlie, John A., and Charles M. Kneier: *County Government and Administration* (New York: Appleton-Century-Crofts, 1930).

Fosdick, Raymond, et al.: *Criminal Justice in Cleveland* (Cleveland: The Cleveland Foundation, 1922).

Gavit, Bernard C.: *Procedure in State Courts* (New York: Practicing Law Institute, 1946).

Lancaster, Lane W.: *Government in Rural America* (Princeton, N.J.: Van Nostrand, rev. ed., 1952).

Orfield, Lester B.: *Criminal Procedure from Arrest to Appeal* (National Conference of Judicial Councils, 1947).

Pound, Roscoe: *Organization of Courts* (Boston: Little, Brown, 1940).

Robinson, William M.: *Justice in Grey* (Cambridge, Mass.: Harvard University Press, 1941).

Vanderbilt, Arthur T.: *Judges and Jurors: Their Functions, Qualifications and Selection* (Boston: Boston University Press, 1956).

———: *Minimum Standards of Judicial Administration* (New York: Law Center of New York University for the National Conference of Judicial Councils, 1949).

Warren, George: *Traffic Courts* (Boston: Little, Brown, 1942).

Willoughby, William F.: *Principles of Judicial Administration* (Washington, D.C.: Brookings, 1929).

REVIEW QUESTIONS

1. Distinguish between the types of cases which come before state courts and those that are tried by Federal courts.

2. How does the court system of a typical state differ from what it was during the colonial period? The revolutionary period?

3. Compare the judicial system of a typical state with the Federal court system.

4. What is meant when it is said that state judicial systems are decentralized?

5. Which is preferable, the appointment or election of judges? Which method is most widely used among American states? What method is recommended in the model state constitution?

6. Suggest changes that should be made in state courts and their procedures.

7. What is a judicial council? What factors have encouraged its adoption in a number of states?

8. What is the role of each of the principal state judicial officers mentioned in this chapter? How is each usually chosen?

Chapter Thirty-Three

Cities and Their Government

Each year more American communities grow to metropolitan size. As their populations increase and their activities expand beyond one political jurisdiction into one or more others, they assume many of the attributes of a crazy quilt. Like the quilt itself, they are both haphazard and planned. Every metropolis is characteristically a practical patchwork of income, race, and age; of private and public ownership; of the new and the old; of identical and of mixed land uses; of households, firms and institutions whose interests converge, diverge, conflict with, and complement each other. . . . Compromises, conflicts, congruities, incongruities, agreements, and disagreements in behavior and interest come together in that colorful make-do, the metropolis.[1]

Throughout the United States are thousands of urban communities, usually organized under state law into "municipalities" for purposes of local self-government. Such communities are designated variously as cities, boroughs, villages, and towns. The Census Bureau reported 17,997 of these existing in 1962.[2] Larger municipalities commonly known as "cities" will be discussed here and smaller units in the next chapter.

Chapter 9 noted that, since 1789, the United States has been transformed from a sparsely populated rural nation to one in which nearly two-thirds of the people live

[1] Martin Meyerson and Barbara Terrett, "Metropolis Lost, Metropolis Regained," *The Annals,* vol. 314 (November, 1957), p. 1.

[2] Bureau of the Census, *Governmental Units in 1962* (Preliminary Report No. 6, 1962).

in urban centers, many of them gigantic metropolitan areas. Some of the implications of this change for the political scientist were also considered.

STATE-MUNICIPAL RELATIONS

Municipalities Created by States. Municipalities are creatures of the state. They owe their corporate existence to the legislature. Formerly, whenever a group wished to incorporate for self-government, it petitioned the legislature for a special act. Special legislation of this kind produced extreme diversity; it led to excessive meddling by the legislature in municipal affairs; and it was often accompanied by unconscionable lobbying and graft on the part of those desiring laws favorable to their personal interests.

To correct this, most states inserted provisions in their constitutions prohibiting special legislation. This led to classification of municipalities and the enactment of codes for each class. Legislatures continue to devise methods to circumvent the ban on special legislation, but the worst abuses have been eliminated. Municipalities now are usually classified, codes exist for each class, and charters are granted in accordance with the general provisions. Charters are usually issued by some state agency upon receipt of petitions signed by the duly constituted authorities, a certain number of residents, or both.

Nature of Municipal Corporations. The municipal charter is a very formal and precise document stating the purposes, powers, functions, rights, privileges, and form of government. The powers granted usually vary with the class into which a municipality falls. Generally they include authority to sue, tax, and borrow money; promote and protect health, safety, and morals; exercise the power of eminent domain for certain purposes; operate certain utilities; and enforce the law.

Although municipalities may have considerable home rule, they are agents of the states. Accordingly, they possess the immunity from suit usually enjoyed by states. This means that when municipalities engage in strictly "governmental," as distinguished from "proprietary" or "nongovernmental," affairs they cannot be sued except by permission of state law. Thus, if city police use unnecessary violence, the city cannot be sued, although the policemen as individuals can be. If a traffic accident results from negligently maintained and operated traffic signals, the city is not liable. Or if a city fire engine en route to a fire crashes into private property, the city cannot be forced to pay damages.

It is only when municipalities engage in "proprietary" or "nongovernmental" activities such as operating markets, street railways, waterworks, liquor stores, and toll bridges that they can be held responsible. The paradoxical situation is that, if one were run over by a police car, the city would not be liable, but if one were hit by a truck operated by a municipal electric department, damages could be collected.

Being state agents, municipalities enjoy the same immunity from Federal interference as do states. The Federal government does not tax their bonds, nor their revenues, nor purchases of supplies for "governmental" functions, nor payrolls for social security unless the municipality elects to participate. Nor can the Federal government otherwise burden municipalities. Again immunity generally does not apply to "nongovernmental" functions.

Classification of Cities. The classification systems followed by the states are extremely varied and confusing. Most states require that a community have a minimum number

COMPARISON OF CLASSIFICATION SYSTEM IN TWO STATES

CITIES	INDIANA POPULATION	PENNSYLVANIA POPULATION
1st class	250,000 or over	1,000,000 or over
2d class	35,000 - 50,000	500,000 - 999,999
2nd class, A		135,000 - 499,999
3d class	20,000 - 35,000	Under 135,000
4th class	10,000 - 20,000	
5th class	2,000 - 10,000	
Boroughs		No limit stated
Towns	Under 2,000	Only 1 incorporated by special act

of people before it can incorporate. A few states prescribe a minimum area. Illinois, for example, requires cities to have at least 1,000 people and a four-square-mile area. The requirement for towns is 100 people and a two-square-mile area. Indiana and Pennsylvania typify other aspects of classification (see table). Where such classifications exist, the law varies for each class. Some have more home rule than others. The forms of government may differ.

Overlapping Jurisdictions within Cities. Five levels of government are usually at work simultaneously within municipal limits: school district, city, county, state, and Federal governments. Often there are still others in the form of special districts or authorities. The nature and extent of these operations and interrelationships defy simple description.

All levels of government employ and direct personnel. Nearly all tax and borrow money. All spend money, maintain buildings, and execute governmental functions. Most of them participate in the detection and prosecution of law violators. Counties and states usually handle elections, although cities often participate; the Federal government has a measure of interest and responsibility. All but school and special districts have some responsibility for roads and highways. Cities and states exercise control over local businesses, but the Federal government steps in where taxes and interstate commerce are involved. Cities, states, and the Federal government frequently cooperate to plan, promote public health, and provide better housing, public works, relief and welfare services, and national defense.

State-controlled Functions. In addition to state controls imposed by charters, some municipal functions are especially supervised by the state. Municipal tax-assessment methods are usually prescribed. Sources of municipal revenue are usually limited by state law. Borrowing limits are commonly fixed either by the state constitution or by statutes, and frequently cities are required to report their indebtedness to state administrative agencies. The exercise of eminent domain is usually circumscribed.

Often financial budgets, accounts, and reports are prescribed and required to be filed with a state agency, where they are subject to scrutiny. The acquisition, construction, and operation of municipal utilities are usually subject to regulation by public-utility commissions. State law governs the establishment of municipal courts and their methods of operation. Municipal penal, correctional, and welfare institutions are commonly subject to some state supervision. The layout and construction of streets, highways, bridges, tunnels, traffic lights, airports, etc., are often state-supervised; the source and purity of the public water supply and other matters likely to affect public health are also of state concern.

This overlapping and long list of state-controlled functions, which is by no means all-inclusive, makes it difficult for the citizen to know where responsibility lies. Municipal officials themselves are often confused and irritated by the uncertainty of their powers and their limits.

Home Rule. As a result of this muddled situation, heated and persistent controversy surrounds state-local relations. Obviously, all the people of a state have a legitimate interest in what happens within the municipalities, but this interest is never as direct, intimate, and compelling as that of local residents. The state legislature, often composed of a majority of representatives from rural parts of the state, may deny legislation sought by the cities. Time and again cities have pleaded with state legislatures for charter amendments desired by overwhelming majorities, only to be rebuffed by members from rural areas. State administrators, too, often appear unnecessarily meddlesome to local officials.

The persistence of the problem has led to many attempted solutions. The home-rule movement started in 1875 when a Missouri constitutional amendment gave the city of St. Louis extensive powers of self-government. Today, about half of the states grant cities varying amounts of home rule.

Despite its apparent success, the home-rule movement is waning. Several factors have been responsible for this decline. One has been the unwillingness of state legislatures to implement home-rule provisions contained in their constitutions. In Pennsylvania, for example, a home-rule amendment was adopted in 1922. But not until 1949 was the state legislature willing to implement the amendment for Philadelphia, and not until 1957 was each third-class city allowed to substitute a form of its choice for the commission plan, which had been mandated by state law. Again, Utah and Nevada adopted home-rule amendments in 1925, but neither state has a self-governing city.

Meanwhile, legal ambiguities and narrow construction by the courts have deprived municipalities of gains they thought had been won. The general trend to centralization in business, industry, labor, social life, and government has retarded home rule. Slow, inefficient, and corrupt municipalities have handicapped the movement. Depressions and wars brought problems that caused municipalities to look to the states and, especially, to the Federal government for financial assistance and leadership.

FORMS OF GOVERNMENT

Strong Mayor-Council Form. This form, usual in large cities, is patterned after the state and Federal governments. It is based on the separation of executive and legislative powers and their operation within a framework of mutual checks and balances.

THE MAYOR-COUNCIL FORM: TYPICAL OF LARGE CITIES

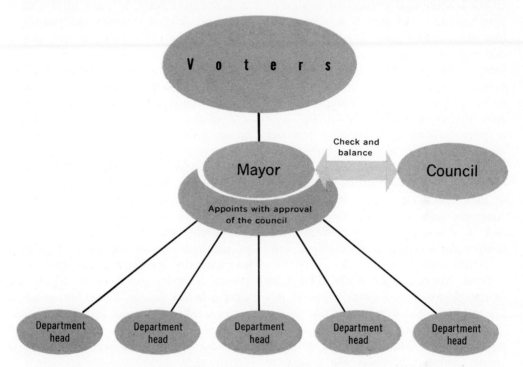

Soon after the Revolution, most American cities adopted bicameral legislatures, which remained predominant until after the Civil War. The tide then turned—today they remain only in Atlanta, Georgia, New York City, and a few New England communities.[1]

Present-day councils, which are mostly unicameral, vary considerably in size. A few have only two members; Chicago, with fifty, has the largest. Philadelphia has twenty-four;

[1] *The Municipal Yearbook* gives current figures about the forms of city governments. New York City has a peculiar arrangement where, in addition to a council, there exists a Board of Estimate consisting of the mayor, the elected comptroller, the president of the council, and the five borough presidents, each of whom has weighted voting power. The board shares responsibility with the council for certain financial legislation.

Los Angeles, fifteen; St. Louis, thirty; Cleveland, thirty-three; New York City has twenty-six on the council and eight on the Board of Estimate; and until recently Newport, Rhode Island, had as many as one hundred and ninety-five. Two-thirds of the larger cities have fixed the membership at five or nine.

Nearly everywhere councilmen are elected rather than appointed. Election remains on the ward basis in a considerable number of places, but there is a strong trend toward election at large. The partisan ballot is most common in mayor-council cities, but nonpartisan elections are increasingly popular. Councilmen's terms vary from one to six years, with two or four the most common. Salaries vary from nothing to $13,000, in

Washington, D.C. In smaller places the median salary is $500 or less.

In the strong mayor-council form, the mayor is usually not a member of the council but is nominated and elected to serve as chief executive. His term is usually two or four years, and he generally is paid a salary. Although ordinarily not a member of the council, he may recommend legislation, maneuver to obtain councilmanic approval of his proposals, vote to break a tie, and veto. The mayor is said to be "strong" if he is given control over budgets; possesses power to appoint, remove, and direct department heads; has responsibility for administration; and is authorized to veto items or total bills. This form is found in most American cities with over 500,000 people and in a number of medium-sized cities. Smaller places usually prefer the weak mayor-council form.

Weak Mayor-Council Form. This form of city government is much like that just described except that it has a mayor (called "burgess" in boroughs) with fewer and less potent powers. The mayor has little effective control over either the council or administrative affairs. He may suggest legislation, but unless he is unusually popular and influential the council does not look to him for leadership. He may veto, but his action is likely to be overridden. The council usually appoints and removes officers and supervises administration, often through committees.

Deprived of important functions, the mayor is often little more than a figurehead. He usually convenes newly elected councils; he sometimes may vote to break a tie; he is often the chief police officer and justice of the peace; and he attends to certain ceremonial matters. These are not impressive powers and duties, but this form of city government remains the one most widely used in the United States.

The Commission Form. A third form of city government found in the United States is the commission type. Although previously used, it was first popularized by adoption in Galveston, Texas, in 1901, after a tidal wave had deluged the city, precipitating a crisis that the old regime was too incompetent and corrupt to handle. The "Galveston Plan" was long afterward the reformer's goal, but its popularity has waned. Although losing ground, it is found in about 8.6 per cent of all cities over 5,000 population. Some of the larger cities using the commission form are Washington, D.C.; Tulsa, Oklahoma; Memphis, Tennessee; Birmingham, Alabama; Portland, Oregon; and St. Paul, Minnesota.

The commission plan is very simple. It completely abandons the idea of separation of powers and concentrates all legislative and executive authority in a single, small, governing body, members of which are elected by the people. Three, five, or seven persons, called "commissioners," are elected to serve collectively as a city council and individually as administrators of the several departments.

One commissioner is usually the mayor, who, in addition to heading a department, acts as chairman, performs certain ceremonial duties, and sometimes has the power of veto. Terms are usually two or four years; election is usually from the city at large. The nonpartisan ballot is found in about two-thirds of the places using the commission form. Since the commissioner is legislator and department chief, he usually serves full time and is better paid than councilmen under other forms.

Many variations of the original commission form have been made; the most notable is the "Des Moines Plan." In its early days the principal objections to the commission form were its lack of checks and balances and its failure to deal with the spoils sys-

THE COMMISSION FORM

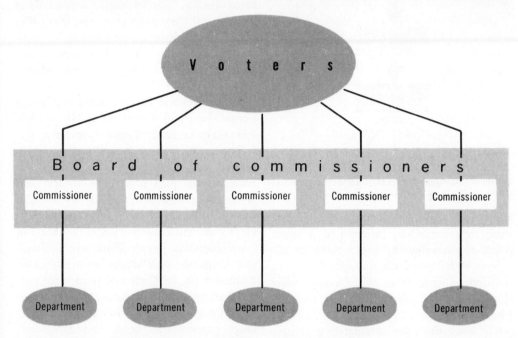

Voters

Board of commissioners

Commissioner | Commissioner | Commissioner | Commissioner | Commissioner

Department | Department | Department | Department | Department

tem. The Des Moines Plan, inaugurated in 1907, was intended to correct these shortcomings. The plan superimposed several features on the Galveston charter; among them were the merit system, nonpartisan primary and election, and the initiative, referendum, and recall. The addition of these features strengthened the voters' confidence and hastened the spread of the commission form. In 1949 Des Moines turned its back on the commission plan in favor of the council-manager form.

The Council-Manager Form. Although first used in Staunton, Virginia, in 1908, the council-manager plan was popularized when introduced four years later in Dayton, Ohio, following a devastating flood. Today the plan is used in about 38 per cent of all cities with a population of over five thousand. Among the largest are Cincinnati,

Ohio, and Dallas, San Antonio, and Fort Worth, Texas.

This plan provides for a strong council and a weak mayor, with responsibility for administration in the hands of a trained, professional manager elected by the council for an indefinite term and responsible to the council at all times. This arrangement leaves policy formation where it belongs, with politically minded councilmen and mayors, but places administration in the hands of a professional, nonpartisan expert. A variation of this plan, found in several large cities, is the mayor-manager form noted below.

Other reforms sometimes urged as indispensable to the success of the manager plan include the short ballot, nonpartisan ballot, election at large, proportional representation, and the initiative, referendum,

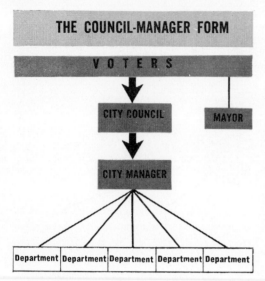

THE COUNCIL-MANAGER FORM

Under the new arrangement, the mayor retains his strong powers but is aided by an officer called chief administrator, managing director, city administrator, or something similar. The manager, supposedly a professional administrator, relieves the mayor of much of his administrative work and so frees him for dealing with policy matters, public relations, ceremonial affairs, and politics.

Advantages and Disadvantages of Various Forms. Fear and distrust of public officials and their exercise of power underlie the separation of powers found in the mayor-council form. Besides providing checks and balances, the plan sometimes attracts and produces colorful leaders such as Fiorello

and recall. Although commendable, and sweeping reforms may be required in some places to guarantee any improvement at all, success or failure of the manager plan does not depend upon them. The manager plan can be adopted, where state law permits, whenever the council, the mayor, and the public sense the value of separating politics from administration sufficiently to employ a competent manager and make him administrative head.

La Guardia, of New York; Daniel W. Hoan, of Milwaukee; Harold Burton, of Cleveland; and Joseph Clark and Richardson Dilworth, of Philadelphia—men who dramatize public issues and press vigorously for their adoption. Its defenders claim that it brings government closer to the people, keeps expenditures, taxes, and debts low, and still gets essential tasks done.

The Mayor-Manager Form. Despite its success, the council-manager form has not appealed to many large cities. Cincinnati is the only city with more than half a million people that uses it today. The strong mayor-council plan is preferred chiefly because of reluctance to give up checks and balances and the belief that a strong mayor is needed to lead and speak for the populace as a whole.

Critics insist that, at the municipal level, powers can be effectively checked by other means. They also contend that, although the form may occasionally attract able and colorful leaders, it has produced more bosses, such as William M. Tweed, of New York

[*The Municipal Year Book (1962)*, p. 100.]

To retain these values, and at the same time incorporate some of the desirable features of the council-manager plan, a number of large cities, among them New York City, Philadelphia, New Orleans, and San Francisco, have recently installed the mayor-manager form.

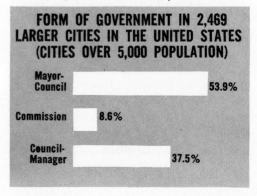

FORM OF GOVERNMENT IN 2,469 LARGER CITIES IN THE UNITED STATES (CITIES OVER 5,000 POPULATION)

Mayor-Council	53.9%
Commission	8.6%
Council-Manager	37.5%

City; Frank Hague, of Jersey City; and Edward Crump, of Memphis.

Separating powers, critics continue, so dissipates responsibility that the public is at a loss to know whom to praise or censure. This situation, it is argued, invites behind-the-scenes domination by bosses, political machines, and vested interests. Politics and administration become so inextricably mingled that competence and efficiency are rarely possible, with resultant inconvenience, expense, and contempt on the part of the public. Large American municipalities have been, on the whole, badly managed. The conclusion is drawn that the mayor-council form has fundamental defects.

The case for the commission form is that it corrects one of the fundamental weaknesses of the mayor-council form by focusing responsibility upon a few commissioners; it shortens the ballot; it changes election by wards to choice at large; it diminishes corruption and behind-the-scenes domination; and it sometimes leads to improved services at lower cost.

Professional students of government concede that many of the claims made for the commission form are valid, but they agree that it contains inherent defects too. Chief of these is that, because commissioners are at once politicians, lawmakers, and department heads, politics and policy formation cannot be separated from administration. Accordingly, partisanship tempers administration, with loss in efficiency, economy, and public confidence.

Because the exact number of commissioners is fixed and each commissioner must head a department, an inflexible administrative situation prevails. Department heads who are elected are rarely qualified administrators. The possibility exists that they will be of different persuasions, or even hostile to one another, making unified direction of administration impossible. Fundamental differences of opinion are desirable in a legislative body, but effective administration is obtained from a unified command.

The council-manager plan has the unqualified endorsement of professional students of government, especially for medium-sized and smaller municipalities. It focuses responsibility for policy formation in the hands of a comparatively few elected councilmen. Thus, voters can watch what happens and place praise or blame where it belongs. By relegating the mayor to a minor role, rivalries between the legislative and executive branches are diminished. It separates politics from administration, unifies the direction of city management, and, by placing a professional manager at the helm, introduces expert leadership and devotion to the best principles of the manager's profession. Only a few cities, of which Cleveland is the largest, having once introduced the manager form, have abandoned it.

The mayor-manager form is too new to assess with finality. That it is a decided improvement over the old-fashioned mayor-council plan is obvious. Its recent popularity among large cities is encouraging. But whether it will prove superior in the long run to the council-manager form remains to be seen.

INTERNAL ADMINISTRATIVE STRUCTURE

Municipal Officials. Municipal officials other than the mayor or manager are the treasurer, clerk, assessor, auditor, and attorney. Election is the rule in more than half of the cities. This makes for a long ballot and seriously fragments responsibility. Election of the officers mentioned is often the rule regardless of the form used, although adoption of the commission form, and especially the council-manager

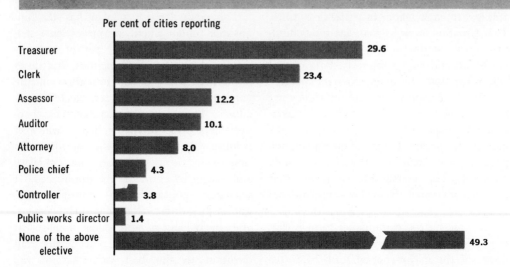

PER CENT OF SUBORDINATE MUNICIPAL OFFICES CHOSEN BY ELECTION IN LARGER CITIES IN UNITED STATES

Per cent of cities reporting

Office	Per cent
Treasurer	29.6
Clerk	23.4
Assessor	12.2
Auditor	10.1
Attorney	8.0
Police chief	4.3
Controller	3.8
Public works director	1.4
None of the above elective	49.3

Most cities with over 5,000 population fill their lesser executive offices by appointment rather than election. The extent of the elective feature is shown for each office. [Data from *The Municipal Year Book* (1962), p. 105.]

form, has discouraged election in favor of appointment.

Municipal Boards and Departments. It was once customary to center administrative responsibility in bipartisan boards, with the result that almost every city had boards for health, police, water, poor relief, schools, and other purposes. Such boards are still widely used, but their popularity has declined and there is a tendency to make them advisory rather than administrative. Accompanying this trend has been a shift to single-headed administrative departments, especially in cities using the commission or manager form.

In a large city one finds a bewildering array of boards, commissions, and departments. Where so many exist it is obviously difficult, if not impossible, for the mayor or manager to direct and supervise

properly. This fact has led to numerous reorganizations, during which the agencies have been consolidated into as few as five or six principal departments. Those serving the people directly, such as departments of health, safety, education, and welfare, are commonly known as "line" agencies; those that service and coordinate the primary agencies but serve the public only indirectly are called "staff" or "auxiliary" agencies. Included in the latter are those handling finance, accounting, law, personnel, central purchasing, and planning.

METROPOLITAN AREAS

Definition and Growth. The most dramatic and probably the most important development of recent decades has been the mushrooming growth of huge metropolitan areas. According to the Census Bureau, a "standard metropolitan statistical area" is a county or group of contiguous counties (except in New England) which contains at least a city of 50,000 inhabitants or "twin cities" with a combined population of at least 50,000. A total of 212 was reported for 1960. Almost 63 per cent of the American people lived in them; ten years earlier the figure was 56.8 per cent; in 1900 it was only 31.7 per cent. It is in these regions that most of the population increase has taken place during the present century. Many areas overlap two or more states.

First in population was the New York region with about 12 million (in 1960). Then followed Chicago, Los Angeles–Long Beach, Philadelphia–New Jersey, and Detroit. Like huge magnets, these centers draw people from the small town, farm, and foreign shore. Even if the international situation becomes stable, the rapid growth of population coupled with economic and social changes is almost certain to bring about further concentration in metropolitan areas.

Jurisdictional Confusion. Metropolitan areas have grown rapidly, and governments have not kept pace. The people of the areas come under the varying and frequently conflicting jurisdiction of scattered cities, towns, and other units of government.

The metropolitan area itself is not a governmental unit but a conglomeration of them. In 1957 a total of 1,074 local governments were reported for the New York area and 954 for the Chicago region. Annexations and consolidations have occurred, but the process has been slow. In consequence, a number of baffling problems exist.

Problems of Metropolitan Areas. Overlapping is one of the most serious problems. A city police department, for example, is concerned over what happens in the city's environs. At the same time, sheriffs, constables, and town police serving outlying areas cannot ignore the city. Since there is no common administration, there is a great deal of duplication, friction, and jealousy. Frequently there is a wide disparity between the protection offered in the respective units of government. One of the worst features is that criminals and shady operators often make the city's periphery their base of operations. A unification or integration of services might result in better protection at a lower per capita cost. This is true of fire, street, health, transportation, and other municipal services.

Disparity between assessments and taxes is also a problem. With several hundred units, each having its own assessor and tax schedule, intercommunity differences and often multiple taxation are inevitable. In addition to confusion and unfairness, property owners within the central city may be lured by lower taxes to suburban communities, thereby adding to the financial worries of the city. Business regulations may differ among the units, making it difficult for any one of them to maintain effective standards. Planning and zoning are made exceedingly difficult. Streets, sidewalks, street lighting, and the like may be uncoordinated and lack uniformity. There may be unnecessary duplication of schools, parks and playgrounds, water supply, electric power, and sewage-disposal systems, all of which mean cost and inconvenience to the taxpayer.

Solutions Involving Nonstructural Changes. Necessity has spurred a number of arrangements and proposals which do not entail drastic structural changes in existing governmental patterns. The simplest is a sort of informal cooperation where municipal officers confer with one another, borrow equipment, exchange information, and the like.

A second arrangement is one in which one municipality, usually the central city, agrees to furnish services to other communities in the area. Interjurisdictional agreements such as these are numerous. It is quite common for suburban children to attend city schools with their tuition paid by their own governments. Cities often agree to provide fire protection, water, or electricity to nearby communities, which pay for the service.

Two or more cities may jointly operate a service such as a bridge or sewer system. Sometimes the states or governmental units concerned superimpose a special corporation, called an authority or district, upon an area, with authority to perform specified functions. The Chicago Sanitary District is an example. It has jurisdiction over the surrounding area and operates to keep Lake Michigan free from pollution. Another is the Boston Metropolitan District, with authority over a number of cities and towns for providing sewage disposal, water supply, recreational facilities, and planning. Another example is the Port of New York Authority, jointly organized by New York and New Jersey, which now operates interstate bridges, parking facilities, airports, tunnels and transportation terminals.

A fourth possibility is for the state to give the central city extraterritorial powers. Cities may be authorized to build and maintain a water supply outside their borders, lay sewers, establish parks, extend highways, or build bridges. Some cities may control contagious diseases within a radius of several miles; others may prohibit slaughterhouses, hog farms, and houses of prostitution in adjacent territory; others may inspect milk in the entire milkshed. The principal difficulty is that occupants of outlying areas are governed without representation, and are likely to be resentful and uncooperative.

A fifth possibility is for the county, with its board consisting of representatives of cities or towns within a county, to serve as the integrating unit. The difficulties include (1) hitting upon a satisfactory apportionment of representatives; (2) the lack of effective and efficient county administration; and (3) the fact that metropolitan areas usually extend over more than one county.

Solutions Involving Structural Changes. The arrangements just mentioned provide only a partial solution. They continue the existence of the multiplicity of governmental units that obstructs district integration. Structural changes are extremely difficult to obtain, nevertheless, some have occurred and others have been seriously advocated.

The structural changes that have occurred oftenest are annexations and consolidations. Annexation takes place when one governmental unit merely acquires or absorbs additional unincorporated territory, but a consolidation occurs when two or more governmental units are merged. Virtually every city has grown by annexation or consolidation, but the process has been slow and it presents almost insuperable problems where the metropolitan area straddles two or more states. Sometimes annexations and consolidations are voluntary, with the people in all units giving consent. Sometimes they may be compulsory, in which case the state legislature usually makes the change with or without the consent of one or all the parties concerned.

Another proposal involving structural changes is that cities and counties separate entirely. Each would remain but neither one would have jurisdiction within the boundaries of the other. Or a federated-district plan might be worked out, as at Toronto, Canada, and Dade County, Florida. This would entail creation of a central government with delegated powers, leaving the participating units with authority over matters that are distinctly local. A more extreme proposal is that the largest cities be transformed into city-states and have direct relations with the Federal government.

Annexations and consolidations will doubtless continue, but the increasing difficulties may slow the rate. County-city merger, or even separation, might well take place, but since most metropolitan areas encompass more than one county, often parts of two or more states, intracounty changes offer only a partial solution.

The federated-district plan is being considered in several places, but problems of apportionment and allocation of powers are formidable. Unless the federation cut across state boundaries, its effectiveness would be limited. The city-state idea theoretically has much to commend it, but is probably unobtainable for political reasons and because the Federal Constitution forbids changing state boundaries without the consent of every state concerned. Unless annexations and consolidations can be expedited in some manner not now apparent, nonstructural solutions, though inadequate, are likely to be the most practical. The continued use of voluntary cooperative arrangements, and especially the authority or special district, offers the greatest promise.

FOR FURTHER READING

Adrian, Charles R.: *State and Local Governments* (New York: McGraw-Hill, 2d ed., 1960).

——: *Governing Urban America: Structure, Politics and Administration* (New York: McGraw-Hill, 2d ed., 1961).

Alderfer, Harold F.: *American Local Government and Administration* (New York: Macmillan, 1956).

Anderson, William: *The Units of Government in the United States: An Enumeration and Analysis* (Chicago: Public Administration Service, 1949).

Banfield, Edward C.: *Political Influence* (New York: Free Press, 1961).

—— (ed.): *Urban Government, A Reader in Administration and Politics* (New York: Free Press, 1961).

Bogue, Don J.: *The Structure of the Metropolitan Community* (Ann Arbor, Mich.: University of Michigan Press, 1949).

Bollens, John C.: *Special District Governments in the United States* (Berkeley and Los Angeles, Calif.: University of California Press, 1957).

——: *Appointed Executive Local Government* (Los Angeles: Haynes Foundation, 1952).

—— and others: *Exploring the Metropolitan Community* (Berkeley and Los Angeles, Calif.: University of California Press, 1961).

Colean, Miles L.: *Renewing Our Cities* (New York: Twentieth Century Fund, 1953).

Coleman, Woodbury: *The Future of Cities and Urban Redevelopment* (Chicago: University of Chicago Press, 1953).

——: *Urban Redevelopment: Problems and Practices* (Chicago: University of Chicago Press, 1953).

Connery, Robert H., and Richard H. Leach: *The Federal Government and Metropolitan Areas* (Cambridge, Mass.: Harvard University Press, 1960).

Council of State Governments: *The Book of the States* (Chicago: the Council, biennial).

——: *The States and the Metropolitan Problem* (Chicago: the Council, 1956).

Dahl, Robert A.: *Who Governs? Democracy and Power in an American City* (New Haven, Conn.: Yale University Press, 1961).

Gulick, Luther H.: *The Metropolitan Problem and American Ideas* (New York: Knopf, 1962).

Jones, Victor: *Metropolitan Government* (Chicago: University of Chicago Press, 1942).

Kneier, Charles: *City Government in the United States* (New York: Harper, rev. ed., 1947).

MacDonald, Austin F.: *American City Government and Administration* (New York: Crowell, 6th ed., 1956).

Martin, Roscoe C., Frank J. Munger, and others:

Decisions in Syracuse (Bloomington, Ind.: Indiana University Press, 1961).

McKenzie, Roderick D.: *The Metropolitan Community* (New York: McGraw-Hill, 1933).

Meyerson, Martin, and Edward C. Banfield: *Politics, Planning and the Public Interest* (Glencoe, Ill.: Free Press, 1955).

Morlan, Robert L. (ed.): *Capitol, Courthouse and City Hall* (Boston: Houghton Mifflin, 2d ed., 1960).

National Municipal League: *Model City Charter* (New York: the League, 1941).

Pate, James E.: *Local Government and Administration: Principles and Problems* (New York: American Book, 1954).

Phillips, Jewell Cass: *Municipal Government and Administration in America* (New York: Macmillan, 1960).

Reed, Thomas H.: *Municipal Management* (New York: McGraw-Hill, 1941).

Ridley, Clarence E., and Orin F. Nolting (eds.): *The Municipal Year Book* (Chicago: International City Managers' Association, annual).

Robson, William A. (ed.): *Great Cities of the World: Their Government, Politics and Planning* (New York: Macmillan, 2d ed., 1957).

Ross, Peter H., and Robert H. Dentler: *The Politics of Urban Renewal, The Chicago Findings* (New York: Free Press, 1962).

Sayre, Wallace S., and Herbert Kaufman: *Governing New York City* (New York: Russell Sage Foundation, 1960).

Schattschneider, Elmer E.: *Local Political Surveys* (New York: Holt, Rinehart & Winston, 1962).

Schultz, Ernst B.: *American City Government* (Harrisburg, Pa.: Stackpole, 1949).

Studenski, Paul, et al.: *The Government of Metropolitan Areas in the United States* (New York: National Municipal League, 1930).

Sweeney, Stephen B., and George S. Blair (eds.): *Metropolitan Analysis* (Philadelphia, Pa.: University of Pennsylvania Press, 1958).

Tableman, Betty: *Governmental Organization in the Metropolitan Areas* (Ann Arbor, Mich.: University of Michigan Press, 1951).

U.S. Department of Commerce, Bureau of the Census: *Governments in the United States in 1957* (1957).

Vernon, Raymond: *Metropolis, 1985* (Cambridge, Mass.: Harvard University Press, 1960).

Vigman, Fred K.: *Crisis of the Cities* (Washington, D.C.: Public Affairs Press, 1955).

Wood, Robert C., with Vladimir V. Almendinger: *1400 Governments: The Political Economy of the New York Metropolitan Region* (Cambridge, Mass.: Harvard University Press, 1961).

REVIEW QUESTIONS

1. How are municipalities classified in a typical state? Why are separate codes required for each class?

2. Summarize the contents of a city charter.

3. How do functions of cities compare with those performed by counties and local governments of other types?

4. What are the advantages and disadvantages of each of the forms of municipal government mentioned in this chapter?

5. Define and criticize greater home rule for American cities.

6. What is a metropolitan area? What problems does it present?

7. Distinguish between a nonstructural and a structural solution for problems confronting metropolitan areas. Which of these offers greater promise of success?

8. How do you explain the fact that American cities, especially the large ones, have been so poorly governed?

9. Suggest changes required to improve municipal government in a typical state.

Chapter Thirty-Four

Governments
of Counties
and Smaller Units

*What is required more than any other thing for the
administrative rehabilitation of rural government is
a system that will command the confidence and respect
of the citizen. A government which has no important
services to perform, or which does not have resources
adequate to its needs, or which is so inconsequential that
it must content itself with part-time and amateur service,
or which is satisfied to drift along an administrative
channel marked out a century ago and not changed since,
or which approaches the public's problems timidly and
half-heartedly, or which shares responsibilities with
a dozen or so of a hundred other units and agencies—such a
government will not enjoy, because it will not have
earned, the confidence of the people.*

ROSCOE C. MARTIN[1]

The transition from a predominantly rural
to an urban nation has caused the Federal,
state, and municipal governments to over-
shadow smaller units of local government.
In consequence, the citizen is often ill-
informed about them and they have been
the last to modernize. Those governments
are still of great importance, nevertheless.
They serve millions of people; employ

[1] *Grass Roots* (University, Ala.: University of
Alabama Press, 1957), p. 55.

numerous personnel; tax, borrow and spend
large sums of money; and help shape
attitudes toward government and politics.

LOCAL GOVERNMENTS ESTABLISHED
BY STATES

Units of Local Government. Over 91,000
units of local government exist in the
United States. Illinois has the largest number of any state, and the West North

Central region is the most crowded general area. When they were founded, their size and number may have been suitable for prevailing conditions, but there are now too many local units. To reduce them is an essential but difficult task.

Local Governments Are State Agents. Small local governments, like cities, owe their powers, forms, and functions to state legislatures. They are agents, or mere portions of the states, and hence possess privileges and immunities similar to those of the states. This means that they cannot be sued for torts, except where state law permits, and that they cannot be unreasonably burdened by the Federal government. Where breach of contract is involved, however, the immunity enjoyed by states has generally not been extended to counties, townships, school districts, or other local units, and they usually can be sued for performance. An architect, for example, can usually sue a local government for unpaid fees due him for designing a public building.

State Legislatures Are Limited. The authority of state legislatures over local government is broad but not unlimited. Constitutional provisions restricting state authority vary widely but they can be reduced to four categories: (1) Many state constitutions proscribe special legislation; thus all local governments of a particular type must be either treated alike or grouped into classes, with general laws enacted for each class. (2) Some constitutions prohibit specific acts. To avoid legislative tampering with the number of counties, Oklahoma sets up its counties in the constitution itself. Some constitutions stipulate that boundaries can be changed only by following certain procedures, such as obtaining a two-thirds vote. Some forbid boundary alterations moving the line closer than a specified number of miles from the county

seat. Others prohibit the creation of new counties unless the proposed area has a certain assessed valuation. It is sometimes stipulated that boundaries may not be changed until the proposal is ratified by the voters concerned. (3) Most state constitutions forbid legislatures to move county seats. (4) A number of constitutions deny legislatures the power to abolish local offices or to alter election by popular vote.

Such restrictions call for constitutional amendments before changes may be made.

State Control Expanding. In spite of constitutional restraints, the same centralizing trend noted elsewhere is conspicuous in the area of local government. Everywhere, power and responsibility have shifted from small to larger units, bringing with them the familiar conflict and the demand for home rule.

Although a number of state constitutions and statutes accord home rule to counties and smaller places, the amount of state administrative control and supervision has increased. This is true of assessments, taxation and debts, budgets and accounts, schools, highways, roads, health, sanitation, police, courts, welfare, and nearly every function. The trend toward centralization, which is largely the result of technical change and population growth, is not likely to slow down in the foreseeable future. The multitude of units must be regrouped and reorganized to conform more nearly with the requirements of our industrial age.

COUNTIES

Origin and Development. When the American colonies were first settled, England was divided into shires, which, in turn, were subdivided into parishes, hundreds, manors, and boroughs. When transplanted to the colonies, the term "shire" soon gave way to its synonym "county." The county, which was first instituted in Virginia, later became the primary unit of local government and administration in the South. The middle states established both counties and townships. New England used counties and towns, but the former were relegated to a subordinate position.

This general pattern remains along the Atlantic seaboard. West of the original Southern states and west of the Rockies, the county pattern was followed, but elsewhere the mixed county-township system was copied. Counties exist in forty-seven states, including Louisiana where such units are "parishes." Alaska and Rhode Island have none. Connecticut abolished hers in 1960.

Number and Size of Counties. Counties number from 3 in Delaware to 254 in Texas, with a state average of over 60. Each state has used its own criteria to determine the number of counties and draw boundaries. The largest county is San Bernardino, California, with 20,131 square miles; the average is 961 square miles. The most populous in the 1950 census was Cook County, Illinois, with over 4½ million; one of the smallest was Loving County, Texas, with a population of 227. The average county had approximately 44,000 people.

Counties are seldom abolished or merged, despite the fact that students of government agree that most states have too many of them. Between 1952 and 1962, nine counties were eliminated.

Classification of Counties. There is urgent need in many states for the classification of counties. For state legislatures to deal separately with each county is time-consuming and leads to needless meddling, chaotic variation, and connivance for undesirable ends. The constitutional prohibitions against special legislation enacted about the turn of the century stimulated classification, but the movement has not gone nearly so far as with cities.

Even though counties are classified, legislatures often employ ingenious devices for dealing with particular ones. Classifications are frequently devised so as to leave only one or two counties in a class. Indeed, on one occasion California provided fifty-eight classes—one for each county!

County Boards. The internal organization of most counties has changed little since colonial times. The classifications mentioned above are chiefly for legislative purposes, rather than for structural organization.

Some states require that all counties have exactly the same form of government. Others make the general pattern uniform but allow variations.

Oddly enough, the separation-of-powers doctrine so entrenched elsewhere has had little acceptance at the county level. British precedent did not decree separation; nor have the powers and functions of counties been great enough to inspire the fear of abuse that prompts and sustains this form of government.

Usually, no county office compares in power with mayor, governor, or President. Many executive functions not delegated to administrative officers are given to a body that performs legislative and often judicial functions as well. That body is given various names: board of supervisors, board of county commissioners, county court, board of revenue, fiscal court, board of chosen freeholders, and police jury.

County boards are generally of two types. The "commission form" usually consists of three members elected at large by county voters. The other is larger and known as the "supervisor form." It is comprised of representatives chosen from townships, cities, or districts within the county. Boards of the second type in rural areas have memberships varying between fifteen and twenty-five, whereas boards in counties with large

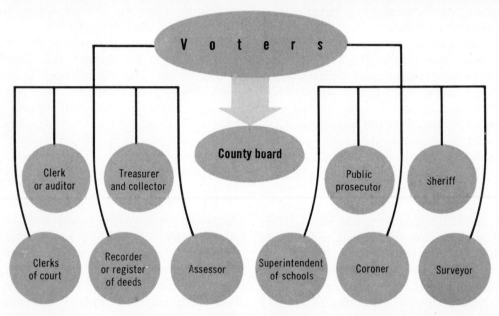

A TYPICAL COUNTY GOVERNMENT

Voters

County board

Clerk or auditor

Treasurer and collector

Public prosecutor

Sheriff

Clerks of court

Recorder or register of deeds

Assessor

Superintendent of schools

Coroner

Surveyor

cities may have as many as fifty or even a hundred.

Some states have boards of both types. Where townships do not exist, as in the South, the county is frequently subdivided into districts and each of these is represented on the county board. In this region, justices of the peace, chosen from the districts, often constitute the county board. Large boards customarily meet quarterly or oftener, while small ones meet more frequently. Meetings are held in the county courthouse and ordinarily are open to the public. Terms are usually two or four years. Compensation in a majority of states is on a per diem basis with allowance for mileage, although many small-board counties pay modest salaries.

Opinions differ as to which of the two types of board is the better. Certainly the large one provides representation for more

areas, and this may increase both local interest and a sense of responsibility. For legislative purposes it might well be superior. But a small body is without doubt better for purposes of administration. This suggests the desirability of a compromise: a numerous body to formulate policy but a smaller one—or better still, a manager—for administration.

Elective Officers. A typical county has a plethora of elected officers. Among others the list includes judges, sheriff, prosecuting attorney, county clerk or prothonotary, coroner, treasurer, auditor and comptroller, recorder of deeds, surveyor, jury commissioners, and superintendent of schools. A large number of elective officers make unified administration impossible and the ballot excessively long. The offices are often established by the state constitution; if so, they cannot be altered or abolished except by constitutional revision. This fact, more than almost any other, slows the modernization of county governments.

New Forms for Counties. Two alternative plans have some prospect of acceptance. One is modeled after the strong mayor-council form widely used in cities. The county board is retained in this plan, but administrative officers, now elective, become appointive and responsible to the county mayor or president.

This plan has several advantages: it separates legislative from executive functions, focuses administrative responsibility

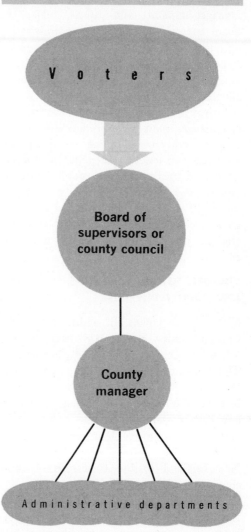

APPOINTIVE COUNTY MANAGER FORM

Voters

Board of supervisors or county council

County manager

Administrative departments

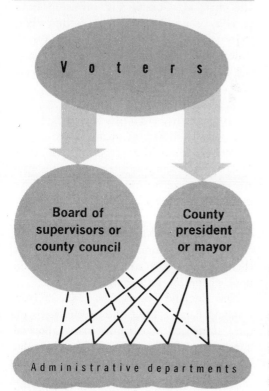

ELECTIVE COUNTY EXECUTIVE FORM

Voters

Board of supervisors or county council

County president or mayor

Administrative departments

― ― ― ― **Approves appointments**

in the mayor or president, and shortens the ballot. A few counties, most of them urban, have adopted it. The reform, if thorough, would be an improvement, but it has all the weaknesses of the mayor-council form discussed in Chapter 33.

The second proposal is the manager plan

so successful in cities. The county board devotes itself to policy formation and legislation, leaving administration to a professional expert hired by and responsible to the board. Under ideal circumstances the manager appoints and directs, subject to board approval, all the other administrative officers of the county. Although this plan is endorsed by most professional students of government, only a few counties have adopted it.

Stirred by population pressures and social changes, many counties are showing increased vitality by grappling with planning, zoning, urban renewal, air pollution, conservation, libraries, recreation, commutation facilities, and similar problems peculiar to our age. Pressed to meet critical needs, progressive counties are taking steps to revise charters and modernize forms and procedures.

VILLAGES, TOWNS, TOWNSHIPS, AND COUNTY DISTRICTS

Villages and Towns. In addition to counties and cities, most areas have smaller urban or semiurban units of government. The nomenclature varies. The South and West use "town"; the Northeastern and Middle Western states, "village"; and a few Eastern states, "borough." These units are more like cities than counties; they should not be confused with the towns of New England or the townships of rural areas, both discussed below.

William Anderson has listed the principal characteristics of villages and towns as follows: (1) Their areas are usually small but vary from less than one to several hundred square miles; (2) population within them is usually denser than in the surrounding countryside; (3) the units remain a part of the county in which they are situated, yet are set off by law as separate corporations for providing services required in

urban places; (4) their corporate status is generally the same as that of larger municipal corporations; (5) many have special charters or are incorporated under general laws often referred to as the local charter; and (6) their functions are quite numerous and highly varied.[1]

The governments of villages and towns resemble those of cities. The weak mayor-council form is almost universal. The chief executive, known as a president, mayor, or burgess, is nearly always popularly elected. The legislative body, called council or board of trustees, usually has from three to nine members chosen at large by popular vote. Members are generally unsalaried.

Other municipal officers, also commonly elected, are a clerk or secretary, treasurer, street commissioner, attorney or solicitor, and marshal. County and township functions may also be carried on within these units either by the municipality or by county and township officers. In either case, the most common officers are an assessor, tax collector, justice of the peace, constables, and auditors.

Although they are much like cities, towns and villages differ in many ways. Their powers are fewer; their governmental structure is much simpler; their council is usually smaller and unpaid; the chief executive is usually much weaker, and administrative functions are dispersed widely among elected officers. Nevertheless, millions of citizens know simple governments like these better than any other and depend upon them for indispensable services.

New England Towns. The towns of New England date to the earliest settlements on the "stern and rockbound coast." Several hundreds exist, usually within irregular boundaries encompassing between twenty-

[1] William Anderson, *The Units of Government in the United States* (Chicago: Public Administration Service, 1942), p. 16.

five and thirty-five square miles. The entire area may be rural, in which case the town is virtually indistinguishable from townships that exist elsewhere. They may be partly rural but have within them one or more populous centers that have not incorporated for purposes of municipal government. Unlike the general practice elsewhere, they remain under the general town government. The New England town is really a combined township and municipality.

Political power in New England towns flows from town meetings. These assemblies of qualified voters gather annually or oftener to deliberate on matters of policy and choose officers for the ensuing year. During the interim between town meetings, responsibility rests in a board of selectmen (usually three) and a number of elective officers, including a clerk, constable, school board, tax collector, treasurer, and often others. The town-manager plan, similar to the city-manager plan, is used often.

The towns also serve as the units of representation in the state legislature. Because the towns are small and numerous, the lower houses of the legislatures have large memberships—240 in Massachusetts, 294 in Connecticut, and 400 in New Hampshire.

In form, modern town governments are little changed from colonial times. The town meeting, however, has lost most of its social value and much of its authority. Only a small proportion of a densely populated town attends town meetings. Even though more people attended, their diversity of background and interests, coupled with the unwieldiness of large assemblies and the complexity of current issues and problems, would render the meetings ineffective. Although town meetings are still important gatherings, the boards of selectmen have assumed more responsibility, while Federal, state, and municipal governments have absorbed functions and injected an increasing amount of direction and control.

Townships. The township exists in sixteen states outside New England, mostly in the area between New Jersey on the east and the Dakotas and Kansas on the west. Washington is the only Far Western state in which a few counties are organized into townships; there are no townships in the South. In New York, Pennsylvania, and New Jersey, townships sprang up erratically, with highly irregular boundaries. From Ohio westward, townships were artificially plotted on the square, with regular boundaries usually enclosing thirty-six square miles.

People clustering in these areas are likely to incorporate into villages, towns, cities, or boroughs to provide local self-government. This is not always the case, however. Many populous communities, usually in the environs of cities, prefer township status.

Half the states with townships provide for township meetings modeled after those held in New England towns. Whether such assemblies are permissible or not, governmental machinery remains much alike. The principal governing body is an elective board known as a board of trustees or board of supervisors. These are of two types: one is composed of members (usually three) specifically chosen for the position; the other is an ex officio board composed of such township officers as supervisor, clerk, treasurer, and justices of the peace. The former type is found in the Dakotas, Indiana, Iowa, Minnesota, Missouri, Ohio, Pennsylvania, and Wisconsin; the latter in other township states.

Many students believe that townships have outlived their usefulness. The fact that more than half the states get along without them is proof that they are not indispensable. Many of them have already atrophied, and others have lost functions to larger units of government. Although many townships, especially those in suburban areas, are still virile, modern trends are against them. If the number of governmental units is to be materially reduced, the township is a good place to start.

County Districts. In the South and the Far West, where neither town nor township exists, counties are usually divided into districts. These have no corporate status and exist merely for administrative and political convenience. Unlike towns and townships, which have a general governmental responsibility, county districts usually perform only a few special functions.

Districts are known by several names. In Virginia and West Virginia they are called magisterial districts; in Tennessee, civil districts; in Georgia, militia districts; in Maryland, Florida, and Alabama, election districts or precincts; in Mississippi, supervisors' districts; in Delaware, the English term "hundred" is still used. In Western states, similar districts are commonly called precincts, townships, or judicial townships. Whatever their name, they serve similar purposes. Most commonly they serve as electoral units for choosing members on the county board and other county officers. They also are convenient areas for handling elections, administering justice, law enforcement, tax assessment and collection, and for road, health, and school administration.

SPECIAL DISTRICTS

Number and Types. In addition to the hierarchy of governmental units described above, all states have special, or *ad hoc*, districts. The most numerous of these are the school districts. They still flourish, but their number has declined noticeably during the last two decades, chiefly because of the consolidation movement at work among school districts. Of the 53,001 districts reported in

1962, a total of 34,678 were school districts; the rest served other purposes.

School Districts. In most places school administration is handled by special school districts. A comparative few districts are county-wide; cities and other urban places usually have only one school district; and rural areas are generally divided into small districts for school purposes. Many of the latter are very small and sparsely populated; consequently they are short of money for salaries, equipment, and supplies. Consolidations have improved the situation, but rural instruction generally remains inferior.

School districts are properly regarded as governmental units; they have the power to tax, borrow, and spend public funds for community purposes, and they are usually not liable for torts. This nonliability makes it impossible to sue them for injuries suffered by pupils, teachers, or laborers. They can, however, usually be sued for breach of contract.

With a few exceptions, school matters are the primary responsibility of nonsalaried boards elected by the voters. Urban school systems are supervised by superintendents appointed by the school boards; rural schools, by popularly elected county superintendents. At a higher level, most states have elective or appointive superintendents of public instruction to enforce and administer state laws pertaining to public schools.

Other Districts. Districts for purposes other than school administration exist in all the states. A variety of reasons account for their separate existence. Sometimes they were created to remove them from politics. Often they were formed to circumvent debt limitations on regular governments. Sometimes new agencies that could operate more flexibly and freely across traditional boundaries were needed. Sometimes it was thought unwise to saddle poorly paid and busy municipal officials with additional responsibilities.

Districts were often created to permit the appointment of specially qualified persons as directors of operations.

All such districts are specially incorporated for operating independently of, or in close cooperation with, regular governments. Some have been given the power to tax, others have not. Most of them may borrow money, and their legal status is generally like that of other small governmental units.

Because the more than 18,000 districts follow no common pattern of organization or function, they are difficult to classify and describe. Roughly, they can be placed in three groups: general government, public-service enterprise, and combined general government and public-service enterprise. The first, or general-government type, is dependent upon taxation or special assessments. It includes most nonschool special districts. Among them are fire, highway, navigation, health and hospital, sewer, library, drainage, soil conservation, cemetery, and combinations of one or more of these. The second, or public-service-enterprise type, provides services for rates or charges just as do private corporations. Among them are water supply, power, light, gas, housing, and a number of multipurpose districts. The third, or combined general-government and

public-service-enterprise type, is a very small percentage of the total. It collects taxes and assessments and sets rates and charges. Chief examples of the type are conservation, power, and a few miscellaneous districts.

Districts or authorities such as those just mentioned differ widely in governmental organization. The most common form is an elective or appointive board that either divides administrative responsibility among its members or, more frequently, selects a director, supervisor, or manager to superintend operations. As noted in Chapter 33, bodies of this type often conduct functions that transcend municipal boundaries, especially in metropolitan areas.

The creation of special districts may be the best practicable solution for particular situations, but students of government look upon them with some skepticism. They add to the number of governmental units, thus further confusing the public, lengthening the ballot, and scattering responsibility. Moreover, their creation gives the appearance of solving problems and thus distracts attention from the basic need to consolidate and reorganize governmental units to make them adequate for modern governmental needs.

FOR FURTHER READING

Alderfer, Harold F.: *American Local Government and Administration* (New York: Macmillan, 1956).

Anderson, William: *The Units of Government in the United States: An Enumeration and Analysis* (Chicago: Public Administration Service, 1949).

Bollens, John C.: *Special District Governments in the United States* (Berkeley and Los Angeles, Calif.: University of California Press, 1957).

Council of State Governments: *The Book of the States* (Chicago: the Council, biennial).

Fairlie, John A., and Charles M. Kneier: *County*

Government and Administration (New York: Appleton-Century-Crofts, 1930).

Gilbertson, Henry S.: *The County: The "Dark Continent" of American Politics* (New York: The National Short Ballot Organization, 1917).

Humes, Samuel, and Eileen M. Martin: *The Structure of Local Government Throughout the World* (The Hague: Martin Nijhoff, 1961).

Jones, Victor: *Metropolitan Government* (Chicago: University of Chicago Press, 1942).

Lancaster, Lane W.: *Government in Rural America* (Princeton, N.J.: Van Nostrand, rev. ed., 1952).

Maass, Arthur (ed.): *Area and Power: A Theory of Local Government* (New York: Free Press, 1959).

Martin, Roscoe C.: *Grass Roots* (University, Ala.: University of Alabama Press, 1957).

Porter, Kirk H.: *County and Township Government in the United States* (New York: Macmillan, 1922).

Ridley, Clarence E., and Orin F. Nolting (eds.): *The Municipal Year Book* (Chicago: International City Managers' Association, annual).

Stein, Clarence: *Toward New Towns for America* (Chicago: Public Administration Service, 1951).

Studenski, Paul, et al.: *The Government of Metropolitan Areas in the United States* (New York: National Municipal League, 1930).

U.S. Department of Commerce, Bureau of the Census: *Governmental Units in 1962* (Preliminary Report No. 6, 1962).

Wager, Paul W. (ed.): *County Government across the Nation* (Chapel Hill, N.C.: The University of North Carolina Press, 1950).

Weidner, Edward W.: *The American County— Patchwork of Boards* (New York: National Municipal League, 1946).

Wells, Roger H.: *American Local Government* (New York: McGraw-Hill, 1939).

REVIEW QUESTIONS

1. What is a county? How many counties are there in a typical state? What functions do they perform?

2. Describe the forms of county government in the United States. Which form do you think is best?

3. What local governments in addition to municipalities and counties exist in the United States?

4. How are towns and townships governed? What functions do they perform?

5. With so many local governments already in existence, how do you account for the growth of special districts or authorities in recent times?

6. Do you agree or disagree with those who say that the county is the dark continent of American politics?

7. Would you advocate more or less home rule for counties and smaller units of local government?

8. Why do students of government look with skepticism upon the creation of special districts and authorities?

9. Suggest changes that should be made in counties and smaller units of local government.

10. If the number of local governments is to be reduced, which ones would you eliminate? How could this be done?

Chapter Thirty-Five

Finance:
State and Local

Stated positively, the States and localities have to overcome greater disabilities than does the National Government in raising revenues. Among the problems faced by the States are the possibility of interstate tax competition, jurisdictional conflicts associated with the allocation of tax bases, and the need for avoiding interstate trade barriers. The growing complexity of our industrial economy places the larger units in a relatively stronger position in the imposition and collection of taxes.

U.S. COMMISSION ON INTERGOVERNMENTAL RELATIONS[1]

Public finance is a field of extraordinary importance to the whole economy. In these days, the average citizen is apt to think of it mainly in terms of taxation—who pays, how much, and on what. Subconsciously, of course, people may recognize that they get services of importance to them from governments, but their primary concern is usually concentrated on the point at which dollars and cents are separated from the individual by the tax collector. Governments have a big job to convince the public that tax money is prudently spent to provide the greatest good for the greatest number. Beyond that, it is increasingly apparent that governmental revenue and expenditure patterns drastically affect the national economy. If the country is to enjoy full employment and rising living standards, governments

[1] *Report . . . (1955), p. 94.*

677

GENERAL REVENUE OF STATE AND LOCAL GOVERNMENTS
by Major Source

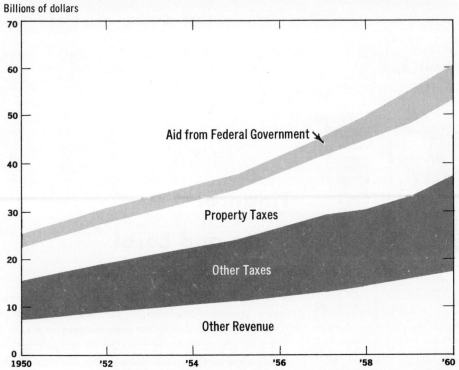

Billions of dollars

Aid from Federal Government

Property Taxes

Other Taxes

Other Revenue

As state and local revenues have increased the property tax has declined in relative importance. Other taxes, especially sales taxes, and Federal aid have shown great increases. (Data from U.S. Department of Commerce, Bureau of the Census.)

must exert their influence to those ends mainly through their power to tax and power to spend.

REVENUES

A general picture of national revenues has been presented in Chapter 20. The purpose of this section is to examine in more detail the nature of revenue sources for state and local governments, to explore possible new sources, and to appraise from the state and local point of view some of the proposals for an intergovernmental tax program.

Tax Program. General revenues of the state governments ranged from 13.4 billion dollars in 1952 to 27.4 billion in 1960. Taxes provided about two-thirds of these sums, rising from 9.9 billion dollars in 1952 to 18.0 billion in 1960.[1] The leading taxes and their actual yields for 1961 were:

[1] These data are drawn from various publications of the Bureau of the Census.

	Millions of dollars
General sales	4,510
Motor-fuel sales	3,431
Individual income	2,355
Motor-vehicle licenses	1,517
Corporate income	1,266
Tobacco sales	1,001

Significant proceeds also came from levies on property, severance of natural resources, insurance and utilities, corporation licenses, and death and gifts.

Three sources accounted for nearly all tax revenue collected by local governments: property, general sales, and licenses and permits.

Sales and Gross-receipts Taxes. Having emerged during the Depression, sales taxes have become the most important single source of state revenue. State and local governments employ several types. The most productive is the "general sales tax," levied on the retail sale of most commodities. More than one-half the states now use the general retail sales tax of 1 to 3 per cent. Of course, the tax is hardly ever "general," for it is common to exempt food and some other commodities to reduce the regressiveness of the tax. As explained earlier, the burden of a general sales tax falls more heavily upon the low-income group than upon the high, for those with low earnings must spend a higher proportion of their income for commodities than do wealthy persons. That is why the general retail sales tax has been fought so vigorously when it has been proposed in Congress. During the Depression, however, this tax, with its steady flow, low collection cost, and enormous returns, rescued many a state from near insolvency.

A second type is the "selective sales tax," levied on the sale of particular items, especially luxuries. Similar to the excise taxes of the Federal government are the state levies on motor fuels, alcoholic beverages, tobacco,

and other commodities. Actually, gasoline is not regarded as a luxury item, but state taxation of it is justified in terms of providing revenue for highways. It is now taxed by all states. Likewise, all states tax liquor—and some of them secure a much larger revenue by operating state liquor stores. Many other commodities are subject to selective sales taxes in the several states.

A third type is the "gross-receipts tax," or "gross tax," which involves the collection of a small percentage of all receipts or income. Sometimes grouped with it and sometimes in a separate category is the "turnover tax," under which transactions are taxed. Gross income often bears little relation to net income. Thus a retail merchant might have $100,000 in gross receipts in a given year, yet suffer a net loss of $5,000 for the period. A professional man might gross $20,000 and net $10,000. Therefore, several different rates may be necessary to provide even a rough measure of justice. If the tax applies to all gross receipts or income, there is bound to be pyramiding, which is likely to increase the price of a commodity considerably because each person or concern through which the commodity has passed has been liable to a tax on its value. Perhaps the most successful of gross-receipts taxes have been those applied to companies with a generally stable relationship between gross receipts and net returns, such as insurance and public-utility corporations.

After sales taxes became a major source of state revenue, some cities and counties sought to share in this new and lucrative levy. Their boundaries are rarely so arranged that a sales tax is administratively feasible. New York City and a few other large municipalities have enjoyed modest success with a general retail sales tax but are plagued with exemptions for out-of-city sales. If sales-tax revenues are to be shared by local governments, the state will probably

STATE AND LOCAL TAX COLLECTIONS, PER CAPITA, FISCAL 1953

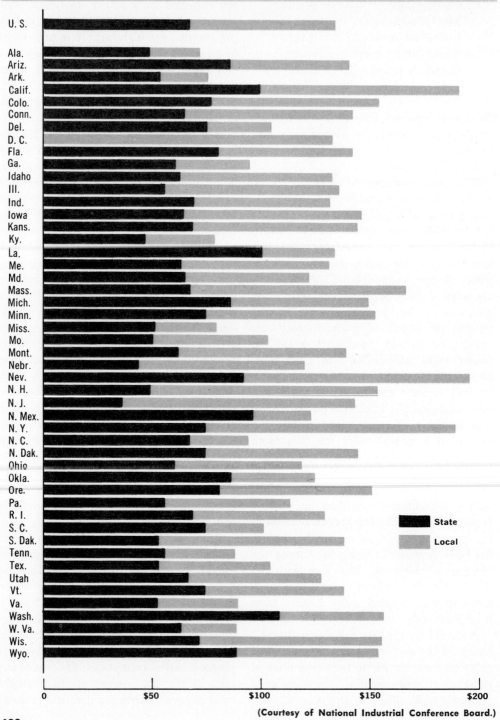

U. S.
Ala.
Ariz.
Ark.
Calif.
Colo.
Conn.
Del.
D. C.
Fla.
Ga.
Idaho
Ill.
Ind.
Iowa
Kans.
Ky.
La.
Me.
Md.
Mass.
Mich.
Minn.
Miss.
Mo.
Mont.
Nebr.
Nev.
N. H.
N. J.
N. Mex.
N. Y.
N. C.
N. Dak.
Ohio
Okla.
Ore.
Pa.
R. I.
S. C.
S. Dak.
Tenn.
Tex.
Utah
Vt.
Va.
Wash.
W. Va.
Wis.
Wyo.

State

Local

0        $50 $100 $150 $200

(Courtesy of National Industrial Conference Board.)

680

collect the tax for cities and counties and share the proceeds with them.

Regressive as it is, the sales tax is likely to remain indefinitely as a major state-revenue producer. The incidence of the general retail sales tax, however, falls most heavily upon those least able to pay and least heavily upon those most able to pay. Although retained, the sales tax may well in the next generation be supplemented to a greater extent by other taxes, such as personal and corporate income taxes, which adhere to the ability-to-pay principle.

Property Taxes. Property taxes constitute the major source of revenue for American local governments, accounting for about 85 per cent of their tax revenue in the 1950s. Until the events of crisis and war vastly increased the collection of Federal income tax and state sales tax, the property tax was *the* major source of American governmental revenue. Despite the development of new forms of taxation during the Depression, most states still make some use of property taxation. But in 1956 only 2.5 per cent of state general revenue was derived from this source.

Property taxes generally are thought to apply to real property only, but this is not always the case. Property can be either tangible or intangible. A man who owns a farm has tangible property in the form of land, house, machinery, livestock, and the like. Another man may own very little real or personal property but own a million dollars' worth of bank deposits, stocks, and bonds, which are called "intangible property." The intangibles may or may not be taxed, depending upon the provisions of state law or local ordinance.

The first job in collecting the property tax is assessment. Taxing bodies set the rate of taxation at so much in dollars and cents for each one hundred dollars of assessed valuation. The local tax assessor estimates the value of all kinds of property, and reduces it to an "assessed valuation," which is some given fraction of estimated true value. The job of an assessor is an almost impossible one. It is difficult enough to work out a proper formula for assessing real property, but it is next to impossible to make a fair assessment of intangibles.

Another problem that plagues property-tax administrators is that of exemptions. Every state and community releases some property owners from liability for payment. It is common practice to exempt real property up to a certain maximum valuation if owned by a veteran. Similar exemptions often are extended to widows of veterans and to the physically handicapped. Churches, schools, and charitable instutions usually are excepted. Several states have extended exemptions of farms and homes up to a set maximum if used as a "homestead" by the owner. Each exemption narrows the base on which the property tax is built and reduces the number of taxpayers but is defended by many on grounds of social justice.

Income Taxes. Nearly three-fourths of the states have some form of income tax, personal or corporate. Unlike the inheritance or estate tax, the Federal government allows no offset or credit for state taxation. A sort of credit is given, however, in that a taxpayer may deduct from the income on which he pays a Federal tax any amounts paid out in state income taxes. Therefore the existence of a state income tax means a reduction in the amount of Federal revenue from this source. Personal income taxes in the 1950s ranked first among Federal revenues and third among state revenues; they were negligible sources for local governments because of the difficulty of collecting them at that level.

The question of levying a personal income tax has been controversial; thirty-one states have now adopted it in some form. The corporate income tax is used by thirty-three states.

State personal income-tax rates vary from 1 to 11 per cent, but most states have a maximum of 5, 6, or 7 per cent. The high Federal rates on large incomes have been a deterrent to higher state rates. State tax rates have also been held down by the fear of competition with other states which have little or no income tax.

On the other hand, the progressive features of the personal income tax offset the regressive features of sales and property taxes. The tax effectively reaches some persons who own no tangible property yet reap income from intangibles. Its incidence is in little doubt; it falls directly upon the taxpayer and cannot be shifted to others.

Inheritance-estate Taxation. All states except Nevada have an inheritance or estate tax. Both are death duties; the estate tax is levied on a deceased person's estate; the inheritance tax is exacted from a beneficiary's share of the estate. As previously explained, Federal law permits an offset or credit for state death duties up to 80 per cent of the 1926 estate-tax rate. The offset does not apply to later Federal estate levies. Existence of the credit device was a powerful incentive for states to enact inheritance-tax laws, thus putting an end to the competition among states seeking to provide tax-free havens for elderly rich people.

State inheritance taxes not only have progressive rates that increase with the size of a beneficiary's share, but they are also graduated according to the relationship of the beneficiary to the deceased. The largest exemption and lowest rates are usually allowed for a widow, followed by those for a widower and children. More distant relatives have a much smaller exemption and higher rates. Those who are not related have little or no exemption and the highest rates.

The inheritance and estate taxes have had problems, but many of the enforcement difficulties have been solved. In the beginning, gifts were used to avoid death taxes; both Federal and state governments plugged this loophole by enacting gift-tax laws, setting the rates nearly as high as the death duties. Next, states locked horns over jurisdictional matters, seeking to tax every estate over which they could establish any shred of jurisdiction. This situation was eased by reciprocity arrangements and later by Federal court decisions defining state jurisdiction. Death duties have great social significance, for they offer an opportunity to redistribute at least a portion of accumulated wealth. This function of the tax is more in the hands of the Federal than the state governments, for only the nation is in a position to apply the high rates necessary to accomplish the social purpose.

Business Taxation. Business taxes include corporation income taxes, license and privilege taxes, capital-stock taxes, and various levies on particular types of businesses. Taken together, they account for a good share of national, state, and local tax revenues.

The state corporate income tax, used by thirty-three states, poses many puzzling problems for the tax administrator. Here again the problem is one of jurisdiction. Business corporations that hold charters from one state often operate in many others. Which, then, can tax corporate net income? The question is not finally answered, but agreement is being reached. Using a standard worked out by the National Tax Association, several states are now allocating corporate income among themselves for taxation purposes on the basis of business done in each state. The three criteria employed in making the allocation are location of tangible property, distribution of sales, and distribution of payrolls.

Corporations are also taxed through capital-stock taxes, which are levied against the assessed valuations of business-concern stocks. Formerly used in all states, more than one-third of the states have dropped the plan in favor of a corporate income tax. Some states use both.

Some states also derive a considerable amount of revenue from the taxation of insurance companies, often a percentage of gross premiums in the state. This is usually justified on the basis that companies should pay something for the privilege of doing business in the state. State taxation of banks is complicated by the fact that most of the larger banks have national charters, and therefore the state power to tax these Federal instrumentalities is restricted. Federal law does not permit state taxation of the personal property of national banks, or levies on bank shares in excess of most other intangibles. To permit states to tax national banks on the same basis that they do state banks appears reasonable but has not yet been accepted.

Motor-vehicle Taxes. All states levy taxes on motor vehicles, presumably for the privilege of operating them. They net the states an important share of revenue too, reaching over $1,500,000,000 in recent years. Most Americans are familiar with this tax. It is usually graduated according to weight, type, age of the vehicle, ranging from steep fees for trucks to insignificant ones for motorcycles. Collection is handled through the sale of license plates or tags, which makes compliance rather easy to secure. Like the gasoline tax, the proceeds of the motor-vehicle tax often are earmarked for use on the highways only. Nearly every state has controversy between those who wish to use vehicle and fuel money for general purposes and those who want it used only on highways.

Other Revenues. State and local governments also receive large amounts of revenue from nontax sources, especially from public enterprises they operate. This category of revenue is relatively more important to municipal than to other levels of government.

State Nontax Revenues. Liquor is the principal state proprietary enterprise. Sixteen states[1] have adopted the monopoly plan of liquor control, involving the operation of state stores. Established primarily as a means of maintaining effective control over the sale of alcoholic beverages, the plan has produced large amounts of revenue for the states. In 1960, for example, sixteen state liquor authorities had revenue that exceeded expenditures by $221,000,000. In addition, these states received revenue from liquor taxes and fees. The licensing-plan states also secure revenue from liquor, but it comes via taxation only and is relatively smaller in amount.

Other state enterprises net little profit. They are in diverse fields: California operates a short railway in San Francisco harbor; New York runs vestiges of its once-great canal system; North Dakota is in the grain-elevator business. Most of these enterprises have a heavy burden of debt and can only service that debt and pay operating expenses.

Local Nontax Revenues. Local governmental enterprises, mainly municipal, are sources of a good deal of nontax revenue but usually have even greater expenditures. Cities commonly operate their own water-supply systems. Fewer municipalities run light and power systems. Other enterprises of American cities are transportation, gas, port, airport, and market. Some cities deliberately subsidize their transportation facilities as a service to the people.

[1] Alabama, Idaho, Iowa, Maine, Michigan, Montana, New Hampshire, North Carolina, Ohio, Oregon, Pennsylvania, Utah, Vermont, Virginia, Washington, and West Virginia. Wyoming's plan involves the operation of wholesale facilities only.

County enterprises are few and far between. Several counties in North Carolina, Maryland, and Georgia themselves operate liquor stores. They profit from their liquor enterprises by a comfortable margin. Other county enterprises are negligible.

Special districts often are created solely to provide utility services, such as water supply, light and power, and housing.

Although they handle rather large amounts of money, local enterprises as a whole show a net loss.

EXPENDITURES

Pattern of State Expenditures. The three functions for which nearly two-thirds of state expenditures are made are (1) education, (2) highways, and (3) public welfare. The remainder of state services—general government, public safety, conservation of natural resources, corrections, hospitals, recreation, debt service, and all the rest—are financed out of the remaining one-third.

Actually, a state legislature rarely if ever is in a position to evaluate state functions anew and make appropriations according to its appraisal of their worth to the state. To a great extent the appropriations for education, highways, public welfare, unemployment compensation, and debt service are beyond the control of the legislature. Most expenditures for education are in the form of grants-in-aid to local school districts, and it is common to have the basis for this allocation fixed in the state constitution. Highway appropriations catch the legislature in a double squeeze: motor-vehicle and fuel taxes are usually earmarked for highway purposes, and Federal highway grants must be matched.

A large portion of public-welfare expenditures is for assistance and other programs under the Social Security Act; state matching of Federal funds is required, and a good deal of the money is spent through local governments with which the state may have a constitutional or contractual arrangement. Unemployment compensation is financed through payroll taxes, the proceeds of which are transferred to a trust fund; the function is so closely supervised by the Social Security Administration that there is little chance for state legislative discretion. Interest and principal repayment on state debts constitute a top claim on the resources of a state and can be deferred or adjusted only with difficulty.

Local Governmental Expenditures. Counties make their largest expenditures for highways, public welfare, general control, and hospitals. *Welfare* is a traditional county function in most sections of the country, and states have been inclined to keep counties involved in financing the expanded assistance program under the Social Security Act. *General control* includes charges for maintenance of the legislative, executive, and judicial branches, the conduct of elections, the operation of county buildings, and many other expenses; county expenditures in this category are higher than in any other level of government, probably because of the heavy burden imposed by election administration. Counties still control many *highways*, but states are assuming more and more responsibility for maintenance and construction of secondary highways formerly under county control. The extent of *health* and *hospital services* provided by counties varies greatly from state to state; few jurisdictions provide services for the average citizen, since the emphasis is placed mainly on serving the underprivileged who cannot afford private facilities.

The largest expenditures of cities are for public safety, schools, streets and highways, sanitation, and health and hospitals. In *public safety*, police protection costs more than fire protection, and the two together con-

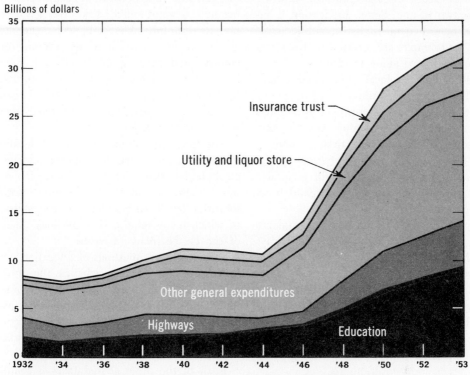

HOW STATE AND LOCAL GOVERNMENTS SPEND THEIR FUNDS

Billions of dollars

Insurance trust —

Utility and liquor store —

Other general expenditures

Highways

Education

1932 '34 '36 '38 '40 '42 '44 '46 '48 '50 '52 '53

(Historical Statistics on State and Local Government Finances, 1902–1953, p. 13.)

stitute the largest single expenditure of American municipalities. The large amount of city money spent for *schools* is rather surprising; this expenditure is greatest in the vast urban centers where, in some cases, school districts have been abolished and combined with city governments. The amount of *welfare service* varies greatly from city to city and state to state, depending upon the program of city officeholders plus the extent and adequacy of county welfare services.

Townships may include wholly urban, wholly rural, or mixed areas. They spend the largest amount on schools, roads and highways, sanitation, public safety, and public welfare. The diversity of the township group is great, ranging from the New England mill town through the prairie-state rural township to the suburban township that provides high-class residential facilities for commuters from a great city.

School districts quite naturally spend most of their resources for schools, but they do have minor expenditures for overhead administration, health, and other services.

INTERGOVERNMENTAL FISCAL RELATIONS

State Grants to Local Governments. Just as Federal grants to the states have become a fixed part of the fiscal system, so state grants-in-aid to counties, cities, school districts, and other units of local government have come to play a major role. Indeed, in amounts of money involved, state grants to localities exceed Federal grants to states by nearly two to one. Some duplication is involved here; Federal funds for public assistance, for example, are received by the states and often passed along to counties.

State grants to local governments have developed for two principal reasons: (1) Taxation, based on the property tax, has proven inadequate to produce the new revenues required to provide desired services. (2) The states, aided and abetted by the Federal government, have sought to induce local governments to enter or expand functions deemed of social value.

The purposes for which local governments are given state grants are nearly always specified. In order of size of grant, the local functions aided by states in recent years have been schools, public assistance, and highways. Lesser amounts are granted for health and hospital services, libraries, and other functions. Schools account for approximately one-half of all moneys granted by states to local governments.

Sources of state-aid moneys are specified only in a minority of cases. It is considered better practice to take moneys from the general fund, but many states allocate a portion of the proceeds of the gasoline tax to counties and cities, and several earmark other sources in whole or in part for aid to localities. The basis of allocation employed in state aid is sometimes the amount of collections of a certain tax, such as the gasoline tax, in each political subdivision; more often allocation is on a number-aided basis. In one sense this is fair, but to provide the same per-pupil state aid for a wealthy district as for an impoverished one overlooks the important element of need in determining allocations.

State-administered Locally Shared Taxes. A recent tendency is for states to levy taxes and share a portion of all the proceeds with local governments. It is sometimes difficult to draw the line between a locally shared tax and a grant-in-aid. Take the gasoline tax, for example. The state levies the tax and earmarks a portion of its revenue for counties and cities, specifying that it must be used for streets, roads, and highways. Is this a grant-in-aid or a shared tax? It can be classed as either, but is considered here in the shared category.

The principal state-administered locally shared taxes are on gasoline, motor vehicles, alcoholic beverages, income, sales, and business. Gasoline taxes are shared with localities by about one-half of the states, of which many require that the local share of the tax be spent on roads.

Several distinct methods of allocation are in use, including collections in the unit, equality among units, area, population, highway mileage, motor-car registration, assessed valuation, and statutory percentages. Motor-vehicle taxes are subject to similar controls.

Each of the other shared taxes is found in only a few states, and the purposes for which it may be spent are less likely to be specified. In some cases—for example, alcoholic beverages—a distinct local problem is created by the commodity taxed, and it appears fair that tax money collected by the state should be handed over to aid in its solution. Naturally, local governmental officials and property taxpayers welcome the state's contribution and seek its expansion along other lines.

State Financial Controls over Local Units. During the last thirty years, state controls over local finances have increased considerably. These restrictions have taken the form of debt and tax limitations and state administrative supervision. Debt limitations on local government may be stated in terms of relationship between debt and assessed valuation, or they may involve state review of proposals for bond issue. Although deemed necessary to protect the credit of local taxing units, debt limitations are often honored more in the breach than in the observance. They have often been evaded through the creation of special districts, to which may be assigned expensive new functions of government, and by various other expedients.

Tax limitations are usually imposed in terms of either assessed valuation or restrictions on the amount of increase permitted in any given fiscal period. The first occasionally is avoided through an increase in the assessed valuation of property or the utilization of new sources of revenue. The latter is more restrictive. Indeed, its operation may greatly handicap a city or county in which there is a rapid increase in population and a resulting necessity for expanded services

The state administrative controls over local finance developed in Indiana in the 1920s attracted a great deal of attention. The state tax board was given power to review local budgets and to disallow or reduce excessive ones. New York and some other states provide for state auditing of local accounts and installation of uniform accounting systems. Many variations in types of administrative controls are found.

FINANCIAL ADMINISTRATION

Chapter 21 dealt with both the budgetary process and financial administration in a general way. The present section will examine in more detail how state and local governments have developed their fiscal processes.

State Agencies. Officers, boards, commissions, departments, and other bodies collect taxes in the various states. The diversity of nomenclature is so great that it is difficult to ascertain any pattern at first glance. However, states may be classified into three groups by types of tax-collecting agencies: (1) Some states have departments of revenue or finance; (2) others have tax commissions or boards; (3) still others have two, three, four, or five officers or agencies involved in tax collection. A tendency, favorably regarded by students of public finance, is to concentrate tax collection in the hands of a single officer, commission, or department.

The comprehensive financial plan, called the budget, is formulated from the estimates of needs and revenues submitted by the various agencies of government. Most states, reorganized on a modern basis, place the governor or some officer or agency directly responsible to him in charge of preparing the budget for submission to the legislature. Most of the states require that all estimates be submitted in advance of a date fixed in one of the final months of the year. The budget document is then prepared and placed before the legislature on or before the appointed day, which is most commonly in January, February, or March.

In authorizing the budget, many state legislatures have unlimited power to increase, decrease, or eliminate items. The power to increase is denied to the Maryland and West Virginia legislatures and restricted in the cases of Nebraska and Rhode Island. This represents an important departure from the traditional legislative supremacy over money matters. Actually, however, the same effect might be secured in many other states through the exercise of the item veto, but such action might be overridden by the legislature.

After the legislature passes the budget, the more advanced states place responsibility for administering it in the hands of a finance officer or agency almost always directly responsible to the governor. At this stage various controls may be imposed. It is common practice to set, either by statute or administrative rule, a maximum proportion of the annual or biennial budget that may be spent in a single month. If an agency wishes to deviate, it must secure permission from the finance authority. Controls also may be established over purchase of supplies and employment of personnel. Discretionary power is often given a finance officer to reduce the amount of an agency's appropriation in order to effect savings.

When expenditures are proposed by an operating agency, the purchase order is checked against the appropriation or balance of account. This function, called "preaudit," is usually vested in the finance officer but sometimes is retained by an elective comptroller. The payment is actually made by a treasurer, who is chief custodian of state funds. Finally, the transaction is in many states postaudited by the auditor or comparable official, who usually is popularly elected or chosen by the legislature. Legislative choice is increasingly favored.

Local Agencies. The financial procedures and officers of counties, cities, towns and townships, school districts, and special districts are so diverse that only a very general description can be given. The budget ought to be formulated directly under the supervision of the chief executive authority, if one exists. It should be comprehensive, including all proposed expenditures and full statements concerning revenues and debt.

In some local governments there is a great need for a unified finance department. Financial functions are often widely distributed among many officers and agencies, making central control and direction virtually impossible. Cities are apt to be better organized in this regard than are counties, for in the former, whether the mayor-council plan exists or has been replaced by the council-manager form, a single executive has fiscal authority. Except where the county-manager plan has been installed, the typical plural executive of that level of government, like the cities under the commission plan, so diffuse executive power that it is difficult to unify financial functions.

FOR FURTHER READING

American Municipal Association: *State-collected Municipally Shared Taxes* (Chicago: the Association, 1946).

Buck, Arthur E.: *The Budget in Governments of Today* (New York: Macmillan, 1934).

———: *Budgeting for Small Cities* (New York: National Municipal League, 1931).

Council of State Governments: *Postwar State Taxation and Finance: Report and Recommendations* (Chicago: the Council, 1947).

Due, John F.: *Sales Taxation* (Urbana, Ill.: University of Illinois Press, 1957).

Durfee, Waite D., Jr.: *Intergovernmental Fiscal Relations* (Minneapolis: University of Minnesota Press, 1950).

Griffin, William M.: *State Supervision of Local Assessments* (Tallahassee: Florida State University, Bureau of Governmental Research and Service, 1957).

Kilpatrick, Wylie: *State Supervision of Local Finance* (Chicago: Public Administration Service, 1941).

MacMillan, T. E.: *State Supervision of Municipal Finance* (Austin, Tex.: University of Texas, Institute of Public Affairs, 1953).

Sigafoos, Robert A.: *The Municipal Income Tax: Its History and Problems* (Chicago: Public Administration Service, 1955).

U.S. Department of Commerce, Bureau of the Census: *Compendium of State Government Finances in 1956* (1957).

REVIEW QUESTIONS

1. What are the principal sources of state tax revenue? Discuss.

2. What are the principal sources of local tax revenue? Discuss.

3. Discuss state grants to local governments.

4. What justifications are there for state-administered locally shared taxes? Mention the principal uses of this device.

5. Describe state financial controls over local governments.

6. What state agencies are charged with responsibility for financial administration?

Chapter Thirty-Six

State and Local
Law Enforcement

*But the unfortunate fact remains that all laws, however
perfect, must in the end be administered by imperfect men.
There is, alas! no such thing as a government of laws
and not of men. You may have a government more of laws
and less of men, or vice versa, but you cannot have an
auto-administration of the Golden Rule. Sooner or later
you come to a man—in the White House, or on a wool sack,
or at a desk in an office, or in a blue coat and brass buttons
—and then, to a considerable extent, the question of
how far ours is a government of laws or men depends
upon him.*

ARTHUR TRAIN[1]

All levels of American government join in the task of protecting life and property, but primary responsibility falls upon state and local governments. How this crucial assignment is performed is the subject of this chapter.

STATE AND LOCAL POLICE

Detection and Arrest. Detecting crimes and offenders is preliminary to all else. It is done by private individuals, administrative officers, Federal agents who detect violations of state law during the course of their own activities, and especially by state and local police.

When there is sufficient evidence of suspected crime, criminal proceedings are started by making arrests. Although arrests can sometimes be made without them, war-

[1] *Courts and Criminals* (New York: Scribners, 1926), p. 11.

rants are usually necessary. Warrants are obtained from judicial officers who must first be convinced that a law has probably been broken. After arrest follows preliminary hearing before a minor judicial officer, unconditional or conditional release on bail or on the offender's own recognizance, detention perhaps, investigation, grand-jury review, and trial. Following detection and apprehension, the police officer's task is usually confined to acting as state's witness.

State Police. Governors have long been charged with seeing that state laws are faithfully executed. Until comparatively recent times they have had no forces constantly at their command with which to fulfill this duty. They were dependent upon sheriffs, municipal police, constables, or, in emergencies, the militia. This situation often proved embarrassing. On one occasion the governor of Indiana, finding himself without power to compel locally elected sheriffs and constables to do his bidding, was forced to call out the militia to enforce a law prohibiting race-track gambling.[1] Former Governor Pennypacker of Pennsylvania emphasized the situation by saying:

In the year 1903, when I assumed the office of Chief Executive of the State I found myself thereby invested with supreme executive authority. I found that no power existed to interfere with me in my duty to enforce the laws of the State, and that, by the same token, no conditions could release me from my duty so to do. I then looked about to see what instruments I possessed wherewithal to accomplish this bounden obligation—what instruments on whose loyalty and obedience I could truly rely. I perceived three such instruments—my private secretary, a very small man, my woman stenographer, and the janitor, a Negro. So I made the State Police.[2]

[1] Bruce Smith, *Police Systems in the United States* (New York: Harper, 1949), pp. 166–167.
[2] Katherine Mayo, *Justice to All* (New York: Putnam, 1918), pp. 5–6. See also Smith, *loc. cit.*

Circumstances like these, coupled with the growth of cities, the advent of trains and automobiles, and the continued breakdown of the sheriff-constable system, led to the establishment of state police systems. The Texas Rangers, organized for border patrol while Texas was a republic, were the first. Massachusetts, in 1865, established a system of state constables; Arizona, in 1901, and New Mexico, in 1903, created border patrols modeled after the famed Texas Rangers; Connecticut established a small state force in 1903 and Pennsylvania its motor police in 1905. Other states have followed, until today about two-thirds of them have police with general authority to enforce state laws; the remaining states have police with authority over traffic violations only.

In addition to the basic agencies, a number of states have set up supplemental forces. Some are responsible for criminal investigations, others for special aspects of motor-vehicle law enforcement, and others for liquor law enforcement.

State police are usually directed by an agency in the state government called a department of public safety, highway patrol, or simply state police department. In addition to a central headquarters, such officers are commonly based upon substations scattered throughout the state.

State Police Jurisdiction. Defining state police jurisdiction has been exceedingly difficult, partly owing to public distrust of officers beyond local control and partly to pride and jealousy on the part of the local officials. The present situation may be summarized as follows: (1) Most of the states have police forces with general criminal jurisdiction, which means that they are competent to act anywhere within state limits where state laws are violated. (2) Upon the governor's request, state police are usually required to assist state administrative and regulatory agencies, like those concerned with public health, pure food and drugs, school attendance, etc. (3) State police are universally prohibited from enforcing laws and ordinances of local governments except when invited to do so. (4) State forces usually refrain from operating within incorporated places, even for the enforcement of state laws, except when invited to do so, when it is necessary to continue pursuit started outside such places, or when they witness crimes committed. (5) Legislation usually prohibits or carefully restricts the use of state police in industrial (labor) disputes. (6) State police are usually forbidden to serve civil processes such as warrants, subpoenas, writs, and the like.

Special Policing Agents. A visit to any state capital or city hall discloses a welter of administrative agencies engaged in policing activities. Most of them begin by registering or licensing buildings, restaurants, hotels, saloons, pool halls, drugstores, fishermen and hunters, automobiles and their drivers, public utilities, airports, hospitals, factories, mines, and many others. Then follow periodic or special inspection and perhaps the filing of reports.

Offenders may have licenses and permits revoked, or pay fines, or be hauled before courts. To catalogue the agencies involved is impractical. The ones employing the largest staffs are likely to be those responsible for enforcing laws relating to the use of motor vehicles, hunting and fishing, banking, school attendance, building location and design, health, sanitation, safety, food, drugs, narcotics, and liquor.

Sheriffs. The office of sheriff is one of the oldest in England and America. The sheriff is, at least in theory, the principal peace officer of the county. In colonial days, sheriffs were generally appointed by the governor; the march of democracy during the early nineteenth century made them elective. Today, except in Rhode Island, where the legislature appoints the sheriffs, and in Alaska, which has no counties, election by county voters is the rule. The terms of sheriffs are generally two years. Often they are forbidden to succeed themselves. Their remuneration is usually derived from fees, mileage allowance, boarding prisoners in the county jail, and selling supplies to prisoners. Sheriffs are among the best-paid county officers, netting from $1,200 in small rural counties to $100,000 annually in some metropolitan centers. They detect and apprehend criminals, summon *posse comitatus* (groups of deputies) on rare occasions when emergencies make it necessary, care for prisoners, administer county jails, execute court orders and processes, make up jury rolls and summon jurors, and in some places, assist with tax collection and election administration. Many times sheriffs are assisted by deputies, constables, bailiffs, jailers, and others.

The office of sheriff, like so many others inherited from the rural past, is often under fire. Under modern conditions, elective police are seldom qualified to detect and combat crime. The emergence of trained and well-equipped municipal, state, and Federal police forces has caused sheriffs to slough their police role and confine themselves to the other duties mentioned above. Referring to this situation, a leading authority has said, "In a vast majority of American counties the sheriff system has already collapsed."[1] Some counties, however, have competently manned, well-organized, and modernly equipped sheriff's offices.

No state has abolished the office, although a few have taken steps to end the fee system and prevent sheriffs from enriching themselves by collecting fixed prices for prisoners' meals while serving cheap and

[1] Smith, *op. cit.*, p. 89.

inadequate food. Those who would abolish the office would turn what police functions remain over to state, municipal, or appointive county police. They would transfer the handling of prisoners and jails to state officers responsible for correctional institutions, and they would turn court duties over to some administrative officer responsible to the court. The entrenched position of the office, written into state constitutions and supported by local pride and resistance to change, makes abolition unlikely; meanwhile, milder reforms are long overdue.

Municipal Police. As cities grew, more protection was needed than could be provided by sheriffs and constables. At first a force of night watchmen to patrol the streets was thought sufficient; then followed day as well as night shifts; finally, in 1853, New York established the first uniformed force such as is common today. Early police forces were locally controlled, but because of mismanagement and collusion with corrupt political machines and the underworld, state control became the rule between 1860 and 1890.

The cure proved worse than the disease. Too often it merely meant transferring responsibility from one corrupt setting to another. Today, local control has been restored in all the largest cities except Boston; Baltimore; St. Louis and Kansas City, Missouri, where the head of the police department is appointed and removed by the governor. In smaller cities local direction is also the rule. Although locally controlled, municipal police are invariably responsible for the enforcement of state as well as municipal law within city limits.

The administration of municipal police, especially in large cities, presents a major problem. Cities like New York, Chicago, and Los Angeles employ police personnel of several thousands and spend huge sums for police protection. It is important that the taxpayers get their money's worth—something which is unlikely unless administration is divorced from politics and sound principles of public management are followed. This entails a high degree of civic consciousness on the part of citizens, a clear line of authority untrammeled by partisan considerations, a modern civil-service system which will ensure recruitment on the basis of merit, adequate pay scales, systematic promotion, security of tenure, provision for retirement, and a highly trained personnel outfitted with the most modern equipment. Considerable improvement has taken place since the orgies of the past century but much remains to be done. Fortunately, many national and state agencies, associations of police officers, and civic groups have organized to help with the problem.

Constables. Like so many local offices, that of constable was brought over from England and so dates to earliest colonial days. The bailiwick of the constable has been the town, township, districts, into which Southern counties are divided, and small incorporated places where the constable is often known as "town marshal." Constables are generally chosen by popular election for terms of two or four years, and their compensation comes from fees. Theoretically the local police officers are chiefly responsible for maintaining the peace, but they are almost invariably ill qualified for crime control. Either their areas of operation are poorly policed or municipal, county, and state police have taken over. Their time is spent almost entirely in serving warrants, summonses, subpoenas, and other processes of justices of the peace. Occasionally they help collect taxes and serve as pound-keepers.

The prestige of constables has steadily diminished until today it is often difficult to find candidates for the office. In England the office was swept away in 1856, while in this country it either has been abandoned or has virtually ceased to function in most places employing full-time uniformed police. Advocates of abolition suggest that full-time police take over the small amount of criminal work remaining and that the assistance now given justices of the peace be performed either by police officers or, better still, by an administrative officer attached to a unified county court.

State Militias. All the states maintain militias to help with law enforcement and the maintenance of public peace. The Federal government, it will be recalled, may intervene within states when invasion, rebellion, or insurrection is involved, when it is necessary to enforce Federal law and protect Federal property, or when state governments ask for Federal help. Federal intervention with military force is comparatively rare. The use of state forces is much more frequent, but county and local police are usually adequate.

State militias consist of two parts: the unorganized, which includes all able-bodied adult males, and the organized, better known as the National Guard. The unorganized militia is seldom called up either for training or duty but conceivably might be in the event of a serious emergency like a flood, fire, invasion, or widespread civil disorder. National Guard units, although financed largely by Federal funds and trained according to standards set by the United States Army, are nevertheless normally state bodies. When not mobilized for Federal service, National Guard personnel is appointed by state governors and is responsible to them.

Administrative supervision is commonly provided through a department of military affairs with a director often called "adjutant general." Detailed work consists in coordinating state and Federal military ac-

tivity; organizing, training, maintaining, disciplining, servicing, and equipping the National Guard; protecting Federal military stores and properties; maintaining state arsenals, armories, camps, and reservations; administering state veterans' hospitals and state laws pertaining to ex-servicemen; and helping with law enforcement upon command of the governor.

Membership in the National Guard usually requires occasional training at some nearby armory followed by attendance at summer encampments. National Guard units were called into Federal service during both world wars but demobilized shortly after fighting ended. To fill the gap occasioned by their absence during the Second World War and the Korean War, most states organized special state or home guards.

PROSECUTION OF OFFENDERS

After their detection and arrest, those suspected of crime are "arraigned" before appropriate judicial officers who may dismiss them, release them on their own recognizance or on bail, or put them in prison to await trial. Those accused are presumed to be innocent until proved guilty; responsibility for proof rests upon the state.

State Departments of Justice. Each of the states has an attorney general usually presiding over a department of justice. The attorney general is occasionally appointed but oftener elected, in which case he may be not only independent of the governor but actually hostile to him and his party. Terms for attorneys general vary from two to eight years. A majority of states restrict their taking part in private practice during tenure. Regardless of how chosen, the attorney general seldom heads and directs a unified organization of public prosecutors throughout the state as does the United States Attorney General for the nation.

In Rhode Island and Delaware, both small states, the attorneys general conduct all criminal prosecutions. A direct line of responsibility and control also exists in New Jersey and Florida, where district attorneys are appointed by governors. In a number of states where district attorneys are elective, attorneys general may intervene, supersede, or even remove them either when so ordered by the governor or so invited by local authorities. Actually this seldom occurs, with the result that in most counties elected prosecuting attorneys function with little or no direction or supervision from central agencies. Because of this highly decentralized system, attorneys general confine their activities largely to advising the governor and administrative officers and representing the state in civil cases in which it is a party. Many persons favor more centralized direction and supervision of law enforcement throughout the state.

Prosecuting Attorneys. As suggested above, virtually all criminal prosecutions are handled by local officials. In rural areas the task is performed by "district" or "county" attorneys who are usually elected for terms of two or four years. Thus, unlike their counterparts in England and the Federal government, the office is highly political. Indeed, it is the local office from which political careers are most likely to be launched. In urban areas prosecutions may be conducted either by the district attorneys or by special solicitors or prosecutors appointed by municipal authorities.

Holders of this office do more than merely prosecute those accused of crime. In cooperation with police they often carry on campaigns to uncover organized crime. Also, within their territorial jurisdiction, they defend the state and county, or their offi-cials, in actions brought against them. They attend and participate in habeas corpus proceedings brought before county judges. They advise and represent the attorney general on many occasions. They advise county officers and justices of the peace on questions of law.

Despite its frequent shabbiness, the office of prosecuting attorney is one of importance and power. Vigilance and tact of the prosecuting attorney can greatly aid and stimulate local police and judicial officers. Upon him rests the decision of whether those who have been apprehended will stand trial; indeed, his power to decide whether to prosecute is almost absolute. He has great influence over grand and petit juries. He can cause a case to drag or kill it by entering a plea of nolle prosequi.[1] His recommendation has great weight with the judge when fixing punishment. From start to finish, he exercises a dominating influence over prosecution. Whether crime will flourish within the community depends to a large extent upon him.

The Coroner. Another local enforcement office hoary with age is that of coroner. The holder of the office is nearly always elected; his area of operation is the county; his compensation usually comes from fees; and his term varies from two to six years. His principal function is to investigate and hold inquests in cases of death under violent or suspicious circumstances. The coroner is supposed to fix the cause of death and name the party responsible. He may make his inquiries alone or impanel a jury, commonly of six persons. The report becomes the offi-

---

[1] This is either a record entry that the prosecutor does not care to proceed further with a case or an entry showing that an agreement has been reached not to proceed further with a particular suit. This is often done, frequently under circumstances suggesting collusion with powerful criminals and their allies.

cial basis for action in all subsequent matters relating to the deceased.

This office has outlived its usefulness. Although doctors and undertakers often fill the post, the fact that it is political and poorly paid makes it unattractive to competent professional men. In the Federal government the same function is performed by physicians employed at the instance of district attorneys. A more practical solution for the states would be the plan followed in Massachusetts and New York. There the office of coroner has been abolished. His medical duties have been turned over to appointive medical examiners who are always physicians, and his judicial and legal duties given to judges, grand juries, and district attorneys.

The Grand Jury. Grand juries are used by the Federal government and by all the states. They are employed for two purposes: (1) to investigate the conduct of public affairs and officials and (2) to decide whether available evidence is persuasive enough to justify bringing to trial someone accused of committing a crime. If general investigation suggests guilt, the grand jury returns a "presentment"; if hearings suggest that someone held for crime is guilty, the grand jury returns a "true bill" of "indictment." In both cases the charges listed become the basis for subsequent court proceedings. Federal grand juries must be comprised of the number required at common law—not fewer than sixteen nor more than twenty-three—but among the states grand jurors number between six and twenty-three, with twelve common. Women may now serve unless prohibited by statute. A vote of a majority is usually sufficient to indict.

Grand juries are usually appointed by district courts as often as thought desirable. In some states the law compels the calling of one jury to serve for an entire year or for each term of court; in large cities they are often in continuous session. The accused may not appear as a matter of right—that is to say, proceedings are ex parte—but they may occasionally be permitted to testify.

The prosecuting attorney usually dominates proceedings, although the jury always makes its decision in secret. If the evidence of guilt is unimpressive, "no bill" is recorded and the accused must be discharged; if persuasive, the accused is charged with specific crimes mentioned and described in the bill of indictment, then held for trial. One's life and limb are not in jeopardy in grand-jury proceedings; hence the evidence may be reconsidered an indefinite number of times.

Today, the grand jury is frequently used to expose affairs of public concern such as ballot frauds, brutal treatment of mental-hospital patients, and conspiracies to tamper with justice, but it steadily falls into desuetude. Federal authorities avoid using it whenever possible; a majority of states permit the use of alternative methods; and a few states, notably Michigan, almost never use the grand jury.

The trend is toward a simpler, more expeditious, more expert, and less expensive device. The alternate oftenest used is the "information." Where this is permissible, the district attorney appears before a judge with such evidence and witnesses as he deems necessary. The hearing is often perfunctory, as it commonly is with grand juries, but at best it is thorough and the accused is allowed to testify. If the judge is impressed, he issues a document called an "information," similar to a bill of indictment. After extensive use of this method, competent observers are agreed that it amply protects personal liberties while at the same time expediting the administration of justice. This trend is likely to continue, but it would be a mistake to dispense with the

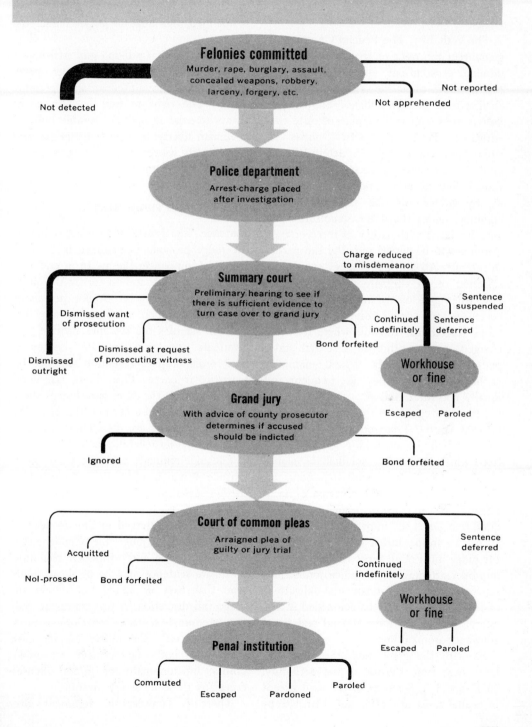

THE FLOW OF FELONIES THROUGH THE CRIMINAL PROCEDURE

Felonies committed
Murder, rape, burglary, assault, concealed weapons, robbery, larceny, forgery, etc.

Not detected

Not reported

Not apprehended

Police department
Arrest-charge placed after investigation

Summary court
Preliminary hearing to see if there is sufficient evidence to turn case over to grand jury

Charge reduced to misdemeanor

Sentence suspended

Sentence deferred

Continued indefinitely

Bond forfeited

Dismissed want of prosecution

Dismissed at request of prosecuting witness

Dismissed outright

Workhouse or fine

Grand jury
With advice of county prosecutor determines if accused should be indicted

Escaped

Paroled

Ignored

Bond forfeited

Court of common pleas
Arraigned plea of guilty or jury trial

Sentence deferred

Continued indefinitely

Acquitted

Nol-prossed

Bond forfeited

Workhouse or fine

Escaped

Paroled

Penal institution

Commuted

Escaped

Pardoned

Paroled

697

grand jury altogether, lest the community lose a potent device for probing public affairs.

The Petit Jury. The Federal Constitution guarantees the right of trial by jury "in all criminal prosecutions" and in all "suits at common law, where the value in controversy shall exceed twenty dollars." Similar provisions are found in a number of state constitutions. Petit, or "petty," juries sit throughout court trials to determine the guilt or innocence of accused parties. Although Federal petit juries must consist of exactly twelve and the same number is common among the states, some states provide for juries with as few as three or even a number to be agreed upon by the parties in interest. All but a few states permit the selection of an alternate juror who serves only when one of the regular number becomes incapacitated or disqualified. Unanimous verdicts are the rule where felony is charged, but in other suits several states permit divided verdicts. Where unanimity is the rule, "hung juries" are frequent and usually necessitate retrial.

Juries are called into existence by order of trial courts. Prospective jurors are selected, usually by lot, from a list of citizens from which have been excluded the names of those whose occupations or personal affairs would suffer because of absence. As in Federal law, state constitutions usually require that juries be "impartial." Counsel for all parties are permitted to challenge, while the judge must at all times be alert to avoid improper attempts to prejudice jurors. Jury service is one of the fundamental obligations of citizenship and may be compelled if necessary. A small per diem stipend and travel allowance are paid jurors.

As with the grand jury, the trend has been away from the use of the petit jury. In England it is almost never used except in capital cases, and often not then. Use by Federal courts has declined, and the same trend is seen in the states. If the petit jury is not used, the judge or judges render the verdict.

Many insist that waiving jury trial makes the administration of justice cheaper, speedier, and fairer without jeopardizing personal liberty. The right to trial by jury ought always to exist as an indispensable bulwark of human liberty, but the states might well facilitate its waiver whenever agreeable to the parties concerned.

SENTENCE AND PUNISHMENT

Sentence. Shortly after the verdict is known, the judge pronounces sentence in criminal cases and announces the award in civil proceedings. He is bound to follow the jury's determination of facts but not necessarily its recommendations, if it makes any. For criminal offenses the law may provide "determinate" or "indeterminate" sentences. The former implies a definite sentence for a particular crime. This allows the judge little discretion; the exact punishment specified by statute must become the sentence. When the term is up, the offender must be released whether rehabilitated or not.

The indeterminate sentence allows more latitude. It may be of the limited type where the law sets a minimum and maximum, like five to ten years for larceny, leaving the exact time to be served or fine to be paid to the committing judge, the offender's conduct, and parole authorities. Or the indeterminate sentence may be of the absolute type that fixes no limits but allows the judge full discretion. A few states use only the determinate sentence for felonious cases; a few use only the indeterminate; most states use both—determinate for major crimes, indeterminate for minor offenses, especially those involving juveniles.

There is considerable argument over

which of the two is better. Modern criminologists tend to favor the indeterminate form because it provides greater incentives for offenders and makes parole easier. The Federal government uses only the determinate sentence, but strong sentiment favors a change.

Civil Awards. As with criminal offenses, the jury in civil cases is limited to finding the facts. When its verdict is known, the judge makes an award. Inasmuch as civil cases are suits between private parties or between private individuals and governmental bodies, the settlement usually involves money, property, custody of children, and the like. The "judgment," as it is often called, becomes binding and enforceable in any state of the Union. While nonpayment of an obligation is not of itself punishable by fine or imprisonment, willful disobedience may become punishable as contempt of court.

The Problem of Capital Punishment. Putting persons to death for crimes is an old custom. It was most unrestrained during the medieval period and was transferred by the colonists to America. The practice has greatly diminished with the passing of time, but it is still followed by the Federal government and all but a few states. Offenses punishable by death have been reduced until today they usually include only treason and willful homicide, although a few states continue the extreme penalty for rape. Most state governments carry out executions in their own prisons and reformatories, but several leave the unpleasant task to local sheriffs. Electrocution is the method oftenest used; hanging is next; lethal gas is third. Utah permits a choice between hanging and shooting.

Defenders of capital punishment, when not attempting to justify revenge, usually begin with a concept of "justice" that assumes individuals are free moral agents who must personally accept full responsibility for right and wrong choices. Such being the case, an individual must be prepared to pay with his life whenever his conduct becomes a threat to the community or its members. It is also contended that the death sentence deters would-be criminals and that society ought not to be financially burdened to keep heinous criminals in prison for life or long terms.

Opponents often admit the fundamental moral and legal right of the community to execute human beings but insist that a policy of love and mercy represents a higher state of civilization and is more consistent with religious ideals and ethics. Others believe that every human being is endowed with a spark of divinity which no one, not even society, ought to destroy. The testimony of sociologists is marshaled to show that men are not necessarily free moral agents but are conditioned by their heritage, the social climate in which they were born and raised, and their opportunities for guidance and growth. Modern psychologists deny that fear of consequences is an effective deterrent, and they are supported by the fact that most capital crimes are unpremeditated and that statistics show either no correlation, or an adverse one, between the number of crimes and the severity of punishment.

Other arguments are these: With capital punishment there is always the risk of executing the innocent; the act of killing tends to cheapen human life and demoralize those who must carry out the ordeal; it causes unnecessary shame, grief, and often illness to relatives and friends; it makes the community think it is solving the problem of crime and by so doing causes indifference to social conditions that contribute to delinquency; in well-run prisons offenders more than pay their keep by work done in workshops, factories, and on farms; and, when the choice lies between freedom or death, juries often acquit those who should receive some punishment.

The arguments against capital punishment are persuasive. Fear of the consequences which might follow if the practice were dropped is doubtless the primary reason why states are slow to change. Still, writes a competent scholar:

Again and again in European and American states capital punishment has been abolished without any resulting increase in the homicide rate, and in many cases its revival has not resulted in the slightest diminution. Statistical evidence is uniformly negative. . . . Fear of capital punishment is probably much less of a deterrent than fear of a less extreme but more certain punishment would be.[1]

Types of Prisons. The Federal prison system has been noted elsewhere. Coexistent with it is a wide variety of state and local penal and correctional institutions: penitentiaries, prisons, reformatories, houses of correction, workhouses, jails, industrial and training schools, prison farms, and chain gangs. Some are for men, others for women, and still others are for juveniles. States now directly operate some penal and correctional institutions, but most are operated and maintained by counties, cities, and towns.

Prisons for long-term convicts are nearly all built on the old cell-block plan, the cell of which has been aptly described as "a diminutive box with an opening of some 15 inches square for inlet of light and air from the outside corridor." Even in this day of "enlightenment," many prisons, including some of the largest, are still without any internal plumbing.

Prison Administration. The administrative pattern varies so widely among states as

[1] George W. Kirchwey, *Encyclopedia of the Social Sciences*, vol. 3, p. 195.

to defy simple classification. Most states operate some prisons and correctional institutions directly from the state capital. The chief exceptions are Georgia and South Carolina, where most offenders are turned over to county officials for control and supervision. In addition to direct operation, most states have reposed in some central agency a measure of responsibility for maintaining and enforcing standards in the county and municipal penal and correctional institutions. The same agencies are frequently charged with responsibility for state institutions such as mental hospitals.

Despite the trend toward giving state bodies more control, the administration of county and municipal institutions remains highly decentralized. As a rule, county penal and correctional institutions are controlled directly by the governing bodies themselves or by special boards of trustees, a board being appointed for each institution. Councils, departments, general boards, or boards of trustees control municipal institutions.

In general, prison and correctional administration within the fifty states is deplorable. As noted elsewhere, inspections made by the Federal Bureau of Prisons find comparatively few fit for the care of Federal prisoners. Partisan considerations have dictated the selection and handling of personnel. Prison architecture and equipment are often archaic. Prison industries, which might make many institutions self-supporting, are often so inefficient that they net huge financial losses. The emphasis generally is upon punishment rather than correction and rehabilitation. Willingness to profit by the discoveries of modern psychiatrists, criminologists, and others has been conspicuously lacking. Overcrowding is general. Poor diets, brutality, and riots are common.

The conclusion reached in 1931 by the

National Commission on Law Observance and Enforcement that our prisons had failed as business, educational, and disciplinary institutions remains true today. There are scattered instances of progressive features, but rarely does one find a model institution. The progressive features of particular institutions should be extended until a new general pattern is established.

PROBATION AND PAROLE

Probation. Instead of imprisoning all offenders, many states allow their judges to continue cases or suspend sentences while placing guilty parties under strict supervision by probation officers. Massachusetts, in 1836, was the first to authorize the practice. At first only volunteer supervisors were used; but salaried probation officers were later engaged. Creation of juvenile courts, first in Chicago in 1899 and then in a number of states, greatly encouraged the practice.

Today in some states as many as one-third of all persons tried and convicted are placed on probation, with the result that it is not unusual to find more at large under supervision than are incarcerated in prisons. Indeed, some see in the further development and use of probation and parole the eventual abolition of prisons except possibly for a few of the more hopeless offenders. While on probation, the offender carries with him constant awareness of his special status; he is supposed to make periodic reports to a probation officer; and he knows that a misstep is likely to result in imprisonment with little ceremony.

Parole. Parole refers to the practice of releasing prisoners before the expiration of terms as a reward for good behavior and with the expectation that they will "go straight." It is to be distinguished from probation (which also provides for freedom under supervision) by the fact that probation is granted before imprisonment, parole afterward. Parole is not the same as a pardon. The latter, if unconditional, restores all civil rights and freedom under no supervision, without the possibility of reimprisonment. Parole is most effectively used with the indeterminate sentence. Nearly all prisoners are ultimately released, the bulk of them by parole. Most are released within two years.

Until after the Civil War, parole as we now know it was not used in the United States. Instead, release was obtained, if at all, by conditional pardon or by commutation laws adopted by legislatures. Ohio, in 1884, became the first state to parole inmates of state prisons; today all states use it for offenders of certain types. Although permitted in most states, its practice is not uniform, and in some states parole is infrequent and difficult to obtain. Generally, parole is less frequent in the South than elsewhere in the country.

Probation and Parole Administration. Invariably, committing judges decide whether offenders will be placed on probation. In making the decision, judges are often guided by recommendations of probation officers, social workers, or friends of the parties concerned.

Parole is handled much differently. The decision to release is almost invariably made by a board known as parole board, board of pardons, court of pardons, or something similar. Usually such boards have state-wide jurisdiction. It is only through them and/or the governor, who retains his pardoning power, that long-term offenders can be released from any penal institution in the state. Statutes determine how soon after incarceration a prisoner is eligible for parole; experience demonstrates that sentences are reduced from 10 to 20 per cent for sentences up to three years and from 30 to 40 per cent or more for longer sentences.

Probation and parole administration are woefully inadequate. The decision to place on probation or parole is often made on an insufficient and unscientific basis. After release, the offender is frequently forgotten, so he again falls into evil company and soon lands back in jail. A handful of states, and some counties and cities, have established central offices with sufficient trained personnel to make constant checks and provide friendly counsel, but all authorities agree that they are exceptional. A number of states and local subdivisions attempt to

keep in touch with released persons merely by correspondence. Some states have no salaried probation and parole officers; neither do they make use of sponsors, employers, or "first friends" to guarantee good conduct.

The obvious answer to the problem is to create central offices equipped with enough trained officers to provide constant supervision and counsel. This is the humane thing to do, and it can pay cash dividends by greatly reducing crime. Merely to create offices for spoilsmen to plunder, as some jurisdictions have done, provides no solution.

FOR FURTHER READING

Beattie, Ronald H., and Leland L. Tolman: "State Sentencing Practices and Penal Systems," in *Report to the Judicial Conference of the Committee on Punishment for Crime* (Washington, D.C.: GPO, 1942).

Council of State Governments: *The Book of the States* (Chicago: the Council, biennial).

Fosdick, Raymond: *Criminal Justice in Cleveland* (Cleveland: The Cleveland Foundation, 1922).

Frank, Jerome: *Courts on Trial* (Princeton, N.J.: Princeton University Press, 1949).

Haynes, Fred E.: *The American Prison System* (New York: McGraw-Hill, 1939).

Mayo, Katherine: *Justice to All* (New York: Putnam, 1918).

Millspaugh, Arthur C.: *Local Democracy and Crime Control* (New York: Brookings, 1936).

National Commission on Law Observation and Enforcement: *Report on the Cost of Crime* (12 reports, 1931), no. 12.

———: *Report on Penal Institutions, Probation and Parole* (1931), no. 9.

Pigeon, Helen D.: *Probation and Parole in Theory and Practice* (New York: National Probation Association, 1942).

Shalloo, Jeremiah P.: *Private Police: With Reference to Pennsylvania* (Philadelphia: The American Academy of Political and Social Science, 1933).

Smith, Bruce: *Police Systems in the United States* (New York: Harper, 1949).

———: *Rural Crime Control* (New York: Institute of Public Administration, Columbia University, 1933).

———: *The State Police* (New York: Macmillan, 1925).

Willoughby, William F.: *Principles of Judicial Administration* (Washington, D.C.: Brookings, 1929).

Wilson, O. W.: *Police Administration* (New York: McGraw-Hill, 1950).

REVIEW QUESTIONS

1. Compare the police system of a state with that found in a city, county, and smaller unit of local government.

2. Which, if any, of the law-enforcement agencies and officers mentioned in this chapter should be discontinued?

3. How do you explain the fact that state police are of comparatively recent origin and usually have very limited jurisdiction?

4. How satisfactory is the office of district attorney? Attorney general? How can the work of these officers be improved?

5. Would you favor more or less use of grand and petit juries?

6. What is required to ensure competent municipal police systems?

7. Outline a plan for making the prison system of a typical state the best one possible.

8. Defend and criticize capital punishment.

9. What are the essentials of good probation and parole administration?

10. Trace the handling of a criminal case from detection to imprisonment.

Chapter Thirty-Seven

Services:

State and Local

The major task of state government—for the long pull—
is to maintain, strengthen and vitalize our federal system
while providing to the people the material services
they need and demand.

FRANK BANE[1]

Streets, schools, water supply, garbage disposal, protection—these and many more services provided by state and local governments are essential to safe and orderly living. Many Americans take such services for granted; their essentiality and cost merit widespread citizen interest and demand for performance of high quality.

Services Classified. State and local services may be divided into three broad classes.

[1] "Progress and Opportunities of the States," *State Government*, vol. 27 (January, 1954), pp. 11–16.

General services provide for the public at large or for special groups. Included are maintaining the public peace; protecting life and property; promoting health, safety, morals, and economic well-being; providing public roads, schools, and recreational facilities; caring for veterans, the aged, handicapped, and mentally ill; conducting elections; keeping vital statistics; and recording documents.

The second class includes those with emphasis on regulation of private economic enterprise. Such services regulate public utilities; supervise banking; control the issuance of stocks and bonds; fix and maintain prices, wages, and hours; prevent monopolistic practices; and the like.

The third class includes governmental activities of proprietary character. Illustrations are governmentally owned and operated water, light, power, and transportation companies, liquor monopolies, banks, and insurance plans.

SELECTED GENERAL SERVICES

Health. State and local health departments or offices are found in every state. State health departments are usually headed by a director of health appointed by the governor. Most states also have boards of health, usually with advisory powers only.

Health Services. State and local agencies constantly engage in many activities for the protection and betterment of health. They set standards for medical colleges and examine and license doctors, dentists, veterinarians, nurses, druggists, barbers, and others. They test drinking water and milk; inspect restaurant kitchens and dishes; test animals for diseases; check stream pollution; inspect hospitals, mines, factories, and workshops. They also control child labor and enforce laws related to hours of work, pure food and drugs, vaccination, sterilization, and quarantines.

Special Health Programs. The states also sponsor special health programs, at times in cooperation with the United States Public Health Service or private institutions. Clinics for free or inexpensive medical care are maintained in some areas, especially cities. Some states require frequent physical and dental examinations in public schools and provide public-health nurses. Free or inexpensive X rays are sometimes provided to aid in detecting tuberculosis. Most states, and many large municipalities, maintain

mental and general hospitals, sanatoria for persons afflicted with tuberculosis and addictive diseases, and rehabilitation centers. Health services are also provided for veterans and recipients of public assistance.

Federal aid for state and local health services is a phenomenon of recent years. Grants have been made for research and control of tuberculosis, cancer, heart and venereal disease; general and mental health services; hospital surveys, planning, and construction; and water-pollution studies. Grants are made on the basis of health needs, population, and the financial ability of the state and local governments. All the states now accept Federal grants, but public-health facilities and standards are not uniform throughout the nation. Many counties still lack full-time health organizations.

Education. Public-school education, which began scarcely more than a century ago, is now the largest and most costly of state and local services. All states make attendance at public or private schools compulsory to age sixteen or above, although in some states exceptions are numerous and the laws are indifferently enforced.

All states provide elementary and secondary schools. State-owned or -aided junior and teacher's colleges are common. Vocational education, spurred by Federal funds, has been stressed for years. Special facilities and services are provided for the blind, deaf, retarded, and other handicapped. States often license private schools and require them to conform with minimum standards. Every state has a land-grant college or university, and often other institutions of higher learning. Financial aid is given in a few states to private colleges and universities. Some states, and the number is increasing, grant scholarships to college students on the basis of either demonstrated merit or politics.

State-wide administration is almost always

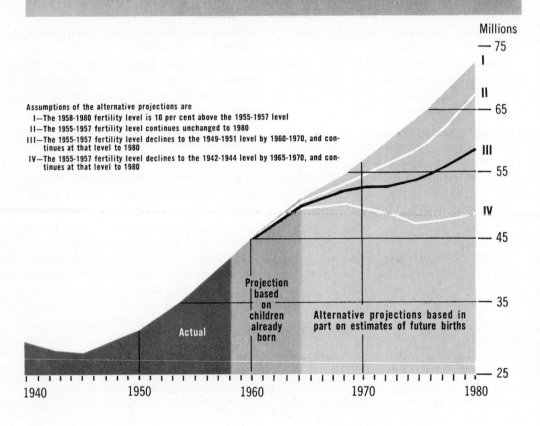

ACTUAL AND PROJECTED SIZE OF THE
SCHOOL AGE POPULATION (Ages 5 to 17), 1940-1980

Assumptions of the alternative projections are
 I—The 1958-1980 fertility level is 10 per cent above the 1955-1957 level
 II—The 1955-1957 fertility level continues unchanged to 1980
 III—The 1955-1957 fertility level declines to the 1949-1951 level by 1960-1970, and continues at that level to 1980
 IV—The 1955-1957 fertility level declines to the 1942-1944 level by 1965-1970, and continues at that level to 1980

Millions
— 75

Projection based on children already born

Actual

Alternative projections based in part on estimates of future births

[Committee for Economic Development, *Paying for Better Schools* (New York: The Committee, 1959), p. 21.]

centered in a department of education headed by a superintendent or commissioner. The chief state school officer is elected in some states but appointed by the governor in others, often upon the recommendation of a state board or council of education. Such boards or councils exist in all the states, but their authority varies. Typically they have great power, especially over the issuing of licenses. At other levels of government, control is usually the responsibility of school boards or special boards of trustees.

Despite all that has been done on behalf of education, there are large areas of need. Teachers' salaries and other emoluments are pitifully low for the nation as a whole. Special instruction for the gifted and handicapped is available in only a few schools, mostly in large cities. School health and recreational programs leave much to be desired. The quality of instruction is low in many places, and curricula need revision. Funds for visual aids, books, scholarships, laboratories, school lunches, busses, and the like are too few to maintain the highest standards. Farm and Negro children have the least educational opportunity. Despite their decrease, school districts are still too numerous.

The sums spent for public-school education appear large, but the total is small compared with the number of people benefited or expenditures for other purposes (liquor and tobacco for example). Expenditures by states are shown on the accompanying chart. Most poorer states at the bottom of the list spend a greater proportion of their income for education than do the wealthier states at the top. Because this is true, many people advocate Federal aid to the states based on their financial needs and tax efforts.

Welfare Services. Society usually proceeds on the assumption that all people are capable of managing their affairs providently enough to take care of their needs throughout life. But experience demonstrates that large numbers will find themselves in dire straits for brief or prolonged periods of time.

Having learned this, governments, especially those of industrialized countries, provide gratuitous services and social insurance against times of need. The former tendency was for society to blame the needy individual and offer aid with pity and scorn. This approach is being replaced; society now admits at least partial responsibility and offers assistance as a matter of respect or right.

Welfare services are now provided by governments at all levels. At state capitals, there is usually a department of welfare headed by an officer called secretary, director, or something similar. Several states prefer administrative boards. Seldom are all welfare activities centered in one department; they are scattered throughout several agencies, mostly the departments of educa-

The outlook is for increased demand for education. The rate of increase may slow down somewhat at the elementary level but it is likely to accelerate at high school and college levels. [Committee for Economic Development, *Paying for Better Schools* (New York: The Committee, 1959), p. 20.]

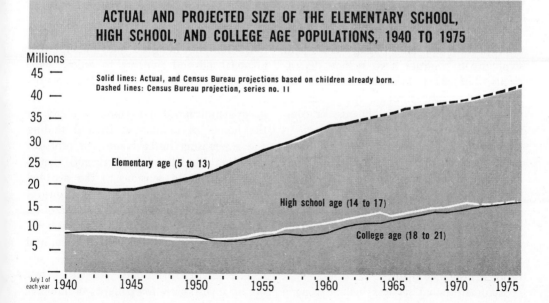

ACTUAL AND PROJECTED SIZE OF THE ELEMENTARY SCHOOL, HIGH SCHOOL, AND COLLEGE AGE POPULATIONS, 1940 TO 1975

Millions

Solid lines: Actual, and Census Bureau projections based on children already born.
Dashed lines: Census Bureau projection, series no. II

Elementary age (5 to 13)

High school age (14 to 17)

College age (18 to 21)

July 1 of each year 1940 1945 1950 1955 1960 1965 1970 1975

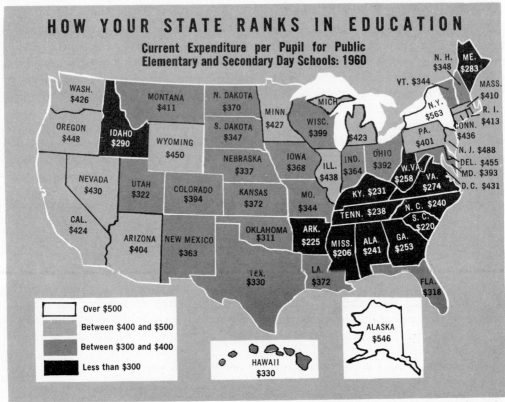

HOW YOUR STATE RANKS IN EDUCATION

Current Expenditure per Pupil for Public Elementary and Secondary Day Schools: 1960

WASH. $426
OREGON $448
IDAHO $290
MONTANA $411
N. DAKOTA $370
MINN. $427
S. DAKOTA $347
WISC. $399
MICH
N.Y. $563
VT. $344
N. H. $348
ME. $283
MASS. $410
R. I. $413
WYOMING $450
NEBRASKA $337
IOWA $368
ILL. $438
IND. $364
OHIO $392
PA. $401
CONN. $436
N. J. $488
NEVADA $430
UTAH $322
COLORADO $394
KANSAS $372
MO. $344
KY. $231
W.VA $258
VA. $274
DEL. $455
MD. $393
D.C. $431
CAL. $424
ARIZONA $404
NEW MEXICO $363
OKLAHOMA $311
ARK. $225
TENN. $238
N. C. $240
S. C. $220
TEX. $330
LA. $372
MISS. $206
ALA. $241
GA. $253
FLA. $318

Legend:
- Over $500
- Between $400 and $500
- Between $300 and $400
- Less than $300

ALASKA $546

HAWAII $330

This rating shows current expenditures per pupil in average daily attendance for public elementary and secondary day schools in 1960. The average expenditure per pupil was $376. (Data from U.S. Department of Commerce, Bureau of the Census.)

tion, health, and labor. Large cities and some urban counties have welfare departments, but other local governments are likely to operate through the governing bodies themselves, special boards, or committees.

Welfare services vary from boarding overnight guests in the town jail to administering billion-dollar insurance plans. A distinction is made between noninstitutional cases and those requiring institutional confinement and care. A distinction is also made between services that are provided free to needy persons and those made available through insurance plans.

Noninstitutional services include general relief for the indigent and unemployed; financial aid and guidance to widows with minor children; supervision for law violators on probation and parole; assistance for needy handicapped and crippled children in the homes of families or friends; finding and supervising foster homes for orphans; providing outpatient medical and dental care; and paying pensions to the disabled or to aged people in need. The institutions most commonly operated are reformatories, orphans' homes, mental hospitals, schools for handicapped and deficient children, and homes for elderly people.

The services mentioned are either free or on a cost basis for patients or families able to pay. Insurance plans require contributions by recipients, employers, or both. The most widely found state insurance plans are those which pay benefits to workmen injured on the job and to the unemployed.[1]

Public Safety. Police systems, courts, and militias have been discussed in an earlier chapter. In addition to their activities, state and local governments promote safety by other means. Administration of such services is probably more dispersed than that

[1] For a fuller discussion see Chap. 27. The old-age and survivors' insurance plan, it will be recalled, is operated entirely by the Federal government.

of the other services discussed in this chapter.

Next to police, fire protection is the most important safety service. State governments usually confine their activities to enacting general laws and protecting forests and public lands, although state police or inspectors sometimes check theaters, dry-cleaning establishments, and other especially hazardous places. Otherwise, fire protection is usually left to municipalities. Larger cities invariably employ full-time fire-fighting forces; smaller places depend upon a full-time skeleton crew supplemented with volunteers when necessary, or they may rely entirely upon volunteers. Volunteer depart-

Per capita expenditures for public education grew from $8.15 in 1890 to an estimated $90.33 in 1958. Per capita expenditures in 1958 for all education (both public and private) reached an estimated $111.67. [Roger A. Freeman, *School Needs in the Decade Ahead* (Washington, D.C.: The Institute for Social Science Research, 1958), p. 4.]

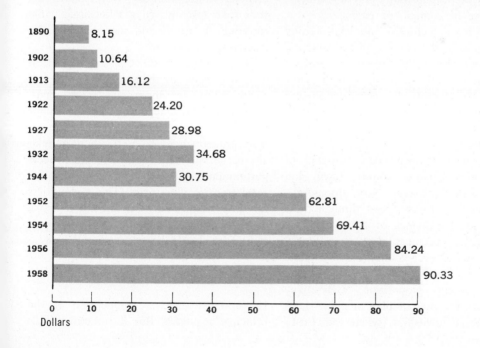

PER CAPITA EXPENDITURES FOR PUBLIC EDUCATION IN 1955-1956 DOLLARS, 1890 to 1958

Year	Dollars
1890	8.15
1902	10.64
1913	16.12
1922	24.20
1927	28.98
1932	34.68
1944	30.75
1952	62.81
1954	69.41
1956	84.24
1958	90.33

ments are often partly subsidized by local governments.

Other safety services are extremely varied. Usually standards are established by general laws; then follows education and inspection to ensure compliance. Usually subject to inspection are buildings, bridges, automobiles and other vehicles, elevators, mines, factories, and other hazardous places. Safety education is a state function of growing importance.

Highways, Roads, and Streets. All levels of government have some responsibility for highways, roads, and streets. Planning, designing, construction, and maintenance are important tasks.

At the state level, administration is the responsibility of a highway department, commission, board, or department of public works, headed by a director, engineer, commissioner, secretary, or an officer bearing a similar title. Elective road commissioners or supervisors are common among counties and townships. In municipalities the work is usually the responsibility of a department, committee of council, or engineer.

Aside from technical problems arising from planning, designing, and construction, two important questions constantly arise to complicate road administration: How should responsibility for construction and maintenance be shared among the various levels of government? How should the costs be divided?

In horse and buggy days, division of responsibility between county, town, and township was fairly easy. Now, automobile, truck, and bus drivers speed through these places almost oblivious of their existence. The problem becomes more complicated as cities spread over county and even state lines.

As a general proposition, with many exceptions, the present plan in many states is this: Rural townships (where they exist)

retain responsibility for construction and maintenance of only minor rural roads; cities have jurisdiction over their streets, except where they are also interconnecting county roads or through state highways; counties build and maintain principal rural roads, except where they are also state highways; and the state accepts responsibility for primary intercity and intercounty routes. Even though legislation attempts a precise division of responsibility, controversies inevitably arise. An almost universal tendency is for smaller units to yield jurisdiction to larger and higher levels of government.

Assessing costs is equally difficult. The principal source of local tax revenues is the property tax. But why should city, county, or township property owners bear the full cost of providing arteries for cars, busses, or trucks that speed over their roads, often without stopping? Why shouldn't the car owner pay something for the privilege? Meanwhile, states (but seldom local governments) collect gasoline taxes from all users of motor vehicles. Why should the state take revenues on gasoline used while traveling on streets and roads paid for by local property holders?

One solution is for the larger political divisions, especially the state, to assume full responsibility for more and more roads. This has been happening, but it might unfairly shift too much of the tax burden from property holders. A still more popular alternative is for the state to return to local governments a portion of the revenues derived from gasoline taxes. This is doubtless fair in principle, but it is difficult to make an equitable determination of the proportions that should be returned and kept.

SELECTED REGULATORY SERVICES

In capitalist societies competition is the principal regulator. But it sometimes fails or is deliberately eliminated, in which event governmental regulation or ownership is usually instituted. Economic regulation, i.e., the control of prices, wages, hours, and the like, is almost always done by the state government itself (except where the Federal government has jurisdiction), but on matters pertaining to health, safety, and morals, cities and other local governments may be permitted to undertake the job alone or in cooperation with one another or the state. There may even be concurrent regulation by local, state, and Federal governments.

Utilities. Public utilities, most of which are complete or partial monopolies, are among the most stringently regulated private economic enterprises. In all the states the task is assigned to a public-utility commission, which is usually, but not always, an independent establishment. Commissions vary in size from one member in

Rhode Island to seven in South Carolina, with three members nearly universal. In a majority of states, commissioners are appointive; elsewhere, mostly in the South, they are popularly elected. Terms vary from ten years, in Pennsylvania and New York, to two years, with six years the most common.

There is much variation, but most states give their commissions authority to regulate private companies of the following types: electric light and power, manufactured and natural gas, street railways, interurban railways, motor busses, taxicabs, water, telephone, telegraph, and oil and gas pipelines. A number of commissions also regulate municipally owned and operated utilities, either in their entirety or when they serve customers living beyond the municipal limits. Several states also authorize their commissions to regulate motor trucks, even though these are not, strictly

[Data from *The Municipal Year Book* (1962), p. 106. Percentages shown are for cities which reported]

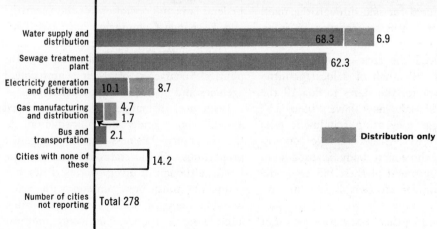

speaking, public utilities. Regulation usually involves control over entrance into service, extensions, reorganizations, abandonments, capital structures, rates, services, and accounts.

Commission control is now universal, but it is viewed by many as inadequate. This is due to many factors. Most important is the failure to give commissions adequate funds and place their staffs under merit systems. Insistence by the courts upon excessive legal formulas, including a complicated valuation basis, has favored the utilities and hampered commissions at nearly every turn. Meanwhile, utilities and their holding-company superstructures have become so closely related to interstate commerce that jurisdictional uncertainties and conflicts have arisen to obstruct effective regulation. More lenient judicial interpretation, increasing intervention by the Federal government, the increase of public ownership, and more effective criticism from labor and consumer groups have brought some improvement. Even so, commission regulation is still widely viewed with skepticism.

Security Issues. Since the Securities Act of 1933 and the Securities Exchange Act of 1934, the Federal government has regulated the larger exchanges and most of the securities offered for sale through the mails and those of businesses engaged in interstate and foreign commerce. This has greatly reduced the area of state activity, but there is still much of a local or intrastate character for the states to do. All the states but Nevada now have "blue sky" laws aimed at preventing fraudulent sales (see also p. 512). Either a single commissioner or a three-man body is usually in charge. Appointment of these officers is the rule, but popular election is not uncommon.

State laws, like the Federal ones, are not intended to guarantee buyers a profitable investment. Rather, they aim to prevent fraud and enforce full disclosure of information. In general, the laws are of three types: (1) fraud laws; (2) licensing laws, which seek to concentrate marketing in the hands of honest dealers; and (3) registration laws, which require that securities be registered with information to enable investors to decide if they are sound investments. Those of the first type are corrective in that they permit prosecution only after fraud has been perpetrated; the other types attempt to prevent fraud and other illegal practices before people are victimized. The latter types are now found in a majority of states.

Enforcement involves issuing, revoking, and suspending licenses, examining the practices and financial status of dealers and issues, promulgating rules and regulations, and aiding with criminal prosecution where that becomes necessary. Before Federal regulation, state laws were generally ineffective. This was due to the interstate character of many of the operations, the many exemptions allowed by the laws, and inefficient administration. Suspected weaknesses became tragically apparent after the stock-market crash of 1929.

Today, state laws are more uniform, while Federal laws and operations of the Securities and Exchange Commission have raised administrative standards. Nevertheless, state operations are still handicapped by the political character of their enforcement agencies and inadequate appropriations.

Insurance. Insurance was long considered a field wholly under state jurisdiction. As the insurance business grew to gigantic proportions, all the states introduced regulation, although of diverse forms. Insurance companies must now contend with a formidable body of widely varying statutes, administrative rulings, and court interpretations. The universal pattern of administration is a single state commissioner or superintendent, who may be placed in a department with banking and business regulation or operate separately.

Although considered a business "affected with public interest," and subjected to close regulation, insurance is a field which permits much competition. Regulation begins with incorporation, which requires that many standards be met. Licenses are issued to *domestic* companies (operating in the state of incorporation), *foreign* companies (incorporated in other states), and *alien* companies (incorporated in other countries). The insurance commissioner has power to issue or refuse and suspend or revoke the licenses of a company, broker, or agent. He may examine a company's books, approve or disapprove its investments, and enforce laws governing standard policy forms.

In 1944 the Supreme Court held [*United States v. South-Eastern Underwriters Assoc.*, 322 U.S. 533 (1944). See also Chap. 25.] that insurance companies were within the scope of the Federal commerce power and upheld a conviction for violating the antitrust law. Under the decision, Congress might at once have enacted Federal legislation that would have superseded state regulation. It did not do so. The states continue to play their ancient role, with the Federal government insisting that insurance companies comply with Federal antimonopoly laws. The insurance companies have made it clear that they prefer state regulation.

Food and Drugs. At least forty-three states have undertaken food and drug regulation, some even before the Federal government intervened in 1906. Since 1938, about half the states have enacted new statutes patterned after the Federal Food, Drug, and Cosmetic Act of that year. The remainder have usually followed closely earlier Federal laws. There now exists a nearly uniform body of law applicable to both interstate and intrastate commerce.

Administration is usually the primary responsibility of state departments of health and agriculture. State laws may be enforced directly from state headquarters or field offices, or considerable reliance may be placed upon the officers of county and city governments. In California, for instance, the state board of health may appoint special agents; sheriffs are also enforcement agents; and responsibility for prosecution rests with district attorneys.

States emulating recent Federal laws have statutory provisions generally considered adequate. But enforcement often leaves much to be desired. Appointments for political reasons, inadequate inspectional and laboratory staffs, and insufficient funds are the principal handicaps at state and local levels.

Weights and Measures. Dependable weights and measures are essential if competition is to be fair and consumers are to be protected. The Federal government is limited to "fixing" uniform standards, maintaining standards for the products it buys, collaborating with private parties and state governments, and policing a few standards set for products moving in interstate commerce. States may legalize Federal standards, as most have, or enact supplementary ones of their own. Practically all enforcement of commercial standards is left to state and local governments.

Three plans of administration are in use by the states. The simplest is centering responsibility in a state office of weights and measures. Under this plan, state inspectors operate at large; no county or city officials perform similar functions. A second plan is a dual one in which both state and local governments engage in the task. This arrangement calls for a state office with inspectors operating at large and sealers of weights and measures in counties and cities. A third plan is for all inspectional and testing work to be left to local governments.

The first of the three plans provides the greatest uniformity. The second is most common. One of its advantages is that the presence of both state and local officers engaged in similar duties tends to check, balance, and stimulate activities. Another is that it permits regulation by local officers close to the scene. On the other hand, it makes for widely varying standards within a state, gives rise to jurisdictional disputes between local and state officers, and often permits considerable overlapping. Very little can be said in favor of the third plan.

Activities are of two types. The first, ordinarily referred to as "mechanical activities," involves inspection and testing of equipment varying in size from the smallest prescription weights to huge scales. This requires considerable expertness and exact standards. Licenses may be required as an evidence of approval. It is common practice to charge fees for inspections, although there is a growing opinion that the fee system should be discontinued.

The second division, consisting of "supervisory activities," is concerned with the way equipment is used. This involves such duties as check-weighing and check-measuring loads of coal, ice, wood, and packaged merchandise; investigating complaints; educating buyers and sellers about their rights under the weights and measures laws; assisting with prosecution; and the like.

Complaints are common over the fact that some state standards differ from those fixed by the Federal government, thus causing inconvenience and confusion. There is greater lament over the lackadaisical, if not downright incompetent, manner in which present laws are often administered and enforced. Some states have been so indifferent as to ignore the dangers inherent in providing little or no protection for the public. These problems are being attacked through associations of weights and measures officials existing in several states and through annual conferences called by the United States Bureau of Standards. More citizen interest and participation are required to hasten progress.

PROPRIETARY SERVICES

State and local governments, like the Federal, often own and operate enterprises similar to those commonly under private ownership for profit. For present purposes, proprietary enterprises may be divided into those created by and responsible to the state itself, and those created by and responsible to local governments. The former are fewer in number than the latter.

Liquor Monopolies. The most lucrative state enterprises are the liquor monopolies. One state (Wyoming) monopolizes wholesale distribution, while sixteen states own and operate retail establishments. Administration is generally the responsibility of a board or commission that functions with a central staff, field officers, and store personnel. In a few of the monopoly states, licensing and other administrative functions are shared with counties, municipalities, or both. The state board is given broad powers to regulate other handlers of alcoholic beverages, although a majority of states make prosecutions the responsibility of the attorney general or district attorneys.

Too little literature is available to make sound conclusions about the administrative competence of proprietary operations of this sort. That they are money-makers is obvious, but is the net return as great as it might be? Only a few have placed personnel under merit systems. On grounds of public policy there is considerable justification for believing that monopoly states, like others, subordinate considerations of temperance and sobriety to those of maximum revenues.

Other State Enterprises. A complete list of other state projects would be long. All states own land and derive proceeds either from sales of the land itself or from rentals and sales of mineral and forest products. Extensive proprietary operations are carried on at state prisons, hospitals, and other institutions. Many of the states are engaged in the insurance business, chiefly because of the passage of workmen's compensation, unemployment compensation, and civil-service retirement laws. Educational institutions, hospitals, research laboratories, and the like were once almost entirely provided by private enterprise, but all the states are now involved. Most of the states operate toll bridges, and some of them, ferries. A few maintain garages with mechanics for automobile inspections.

California owns a short railroad in San Francisco's harbor area. New York operates a barge system on its historic canal, a power authority for the development of the St. Lawrence project (including distribution of electric power), a health resort at Saratoga Springs at which mineral water is also bottled and sold, bridges and tunnels (in cooperation with New Jersey) through the Port of New York Authority. North Dakota is involved in an ambitious program operating mills, grain elevators, a state bank, insurance (fire, tornado, bonding, hail), and the financing of land sales. Alabama operates an elaborate system of docks, wharves, warehouses, and other terminal facilities at Mobile.

Generalizations about operations so divergent in character and scattered in location are dangerous. Some of them need to modernize administrative policies and procedures. Some are heavily in debt, but continued state operation may be justified on grounds of public policy. More studies

of the enterprises are needed for the benefit of those intimately affected and students interested in broad aspects of public administration and policy.

Local Enterprises. The list of proprietary projects under the management of local governments would duplicate many mentioned above. If public schools are eliminated, most of them fall under the heading of utilities and housing.

Public Utilities. Recent years have witnessed a considerable increase in the number of utilities owned and operated by local governments. In cities public ownership of water-supply and distribution systems is the rule rather than the exception. Sewage-treatment plants are next most numerous, followed by airports, incinerators, electric generating and/or distribution systems, and auditoriums.

Utilities are usually the responsibility of a committee of city council, city manager, special board, authority, or district created for the purpose. The governing body usually appoints a utility superintendent or engineer to oversee operations. There has been endless controversy over private versus public ownership of utilities. Experience suggests that, while there are dangers involved, governmental ownership can prove highly advantageous where the public is willing and able to insist upon efficient management.

Housing. California began subsidizing homes for veterans following the First World War, and New York enacted legislation, in 1926, providing encouragement to limited-dividend housing corporations. It was not until Depression years, however, that local governments stepped boldly into the business of building and operating housing projects. The impetus came chiefly from the United States Housing Act of 1937. This encouraged the states to enact legislation permitting local governments to establish housing authorities to clear slums and build low-cost dwellings. A number of states cooperated, with the result that several hundred local units created authorities. These are locally operated subject to state and Federal laws, with the Federal government granting subsidies to help keep rents low.

As a further aid a number of states have enacted urban-redevelopment legislation. This authorizes and assists private and municipal corporations to assemble and clear sites for housing. When done by local governments, the acquisition of property and work may be carried out by the governmental bodies themselves, or by authorities created especially for the purpose.

It is too early to evaluate the work of local governments in the housing field. Experience in Europe, England, and the United States suggests that private capital cannot or will not fully meet the need; hence governments are likely to become increasingly involved.

FOR FURTHER READING

Anderson, Odin W., and Jacob J. Feldman: *Family Medical Costs and Voluntary Health Insurance: A Nationwide Survey* (New York: McGraw-Hill, 1956).

Cleaveland, Frederic N.: *Science and State Government* (Chapel Hill, N.C.: University of North Carolina Press, 1959).

Colean, Miles L.: *American Housing: Problems and Prospects* (New York: Twentieth Century Fund, 1944).

Council of State Governments: *The Book of the States* (Chicago: the Council, biennial).

Daland, Robert T.: *Government and Health: The Alabama Experience* (University, Ala.: University of Alabama, Bureau of Public Administration, 1955).

Eddy, Edward Danforth, Jr.: *Colleges of Our Land and Time: The Land-grant Idea in American Education* (New York: Harper, 1956).

Ferguson, John H., and Charles F. LeeDecker: *Municipally Owned Electric Plants in Pennsylvania* (University Park, Pa.: The Pennsylvania State University, Institute of Local Government, 1951).

——— and ———: *Municipally Owned Waterworks in Pennsylvania* (University Park, Pa.: The Pennsylvania State University, Institute of Local Government, 1948).

Ferrell, John A., and Pauline A. Mead: *History of County Health Organization in the United States, 1908–1933* (Washington, D.C.: GPO, 1936).

Harper, Donald V.: *Economic Regulation of the Motor Trucking Industry by the States* (Urbana, Ill.: University of Illinois Press, 1959).

Hogan, John D., and Francis A. J. Ianni: *American Social Legislation* (New York: Harper, 1956).

Leyendecker, Hilary M.: *Problems and Policy in Public Assistance* (New York: Harper, 1955).

Marketing Laws Survey: *State Liquor Legislation* (Washington, D.C.: GPO, 1941).

McGeary, M. Nelson: *The Pittsburgh Housing Authority* (University Park, Pa.: The Pennsylvania State University, 1943).

Moos, Malcolm C., and Francis E. Rourke: *The Campus and the State* (Baltimore: Johns Hopkins Press, 1959).

Mountin, Joseph W., and others: *Distribution of Health Services in the Structure of State Government, 1950* (Washington, D.C.: GPO, 1952).

Municipal Fire Administration (Chicago: International City Managers' Association, 5th ed., 1950).

Municipal Police Administration (Chicago: International City Managers' Association, 4th ed., 1954).

Mustard, Harry S.: *Government in Public Health* (New York: Commonwealth Fund, 1945).

Patterson, Edwin W.: *Essentials of Insurance Law* (New York: McGraw-Hill, 2d ed., 1957).

———: *The Insurance Commissioner in the United States* (Cambridge, Mass.: Harvard University Press, 1927).

Pierce, T. M., and others: *White and Negro Schools in the South* (Englewood Cliffs, N.J.: Prentice-Hall, 1955).

Ridley, Clarence E., and Orin F. Nolting (eds.): *The Municipal Year Book* (Chicago: International City Managers' Association, annual).

Smillie, Wilson G.: *Public Health Administration in the United States* (New York: Macmillan, rev. ed., 1947).

Steiner, Peter O., and Robert Dorfman: *The Economic Status of the Aged* (Berkeley and Los Angeles, Calif.: University of California Press, 1957).

Toulmin, Harry A., Jr.: *A Treatise on the Law of Food, Drug, and Cosmetic Regulation* (Cincinnati: W. H. Anderson Co., 1942).

Tyler, P. (ed.): *Social Welfare in the United States* (New York: H. W. Wilson, 1955).

U.S. Advisory Committee on Education: *Report of the Committee* (1938).

U.S. Commission on Intergovernmental Relations: *Federal Aid to Public Health* (1955).

————: *Federal Aid to Welfare* (1955).

————: *Federal Responsibility in the Field of Education* (1955).

————: *Unemployment Compensation and Employment Service* (1955).

U.S. Congress, Subcommittees of the Committees on the Judiciary: *Hearings on Insurance*, 78th Cong., 1st Sess. (6 parts, 1943).

U.S. Department of Commerce, Bureau of the Census: *Governmental Finances in the United States* (annual).

U.S. Department of Commerce, National Bureau of Standards: *Units and Systems of Weights and Measures* (NBS Circular 570, 1956).

U.S. President's Commission on Higher Education: *Higher Education for American Democracy* (6 vols., 1947).

U.S. President's Committee on Education beyond the High School: *... Report ...* (1957).

White, R. Clyde: *Administration of Public Welfare* (New York: American Book, 2d ed., 1950).

Wyatt, Laurence: *Intergovernmental Relations in Public Health* (Minneapolis, Minn.: University of Minnesota Press, 1951).

REVIEW QUESTIONS

1. Do you think present public-health services are adequate? How can they be improved?

2. Is the administrative structure of your state government properly organized for effective administration of the various services performed?

3. To what extent are the health, education, and welfare services of your state and local governments financed and controlled by the Federal government?

4. How do you explain the differences between expenditures for education in the various states? How can educational opportunity be equalized among the several states?

5. How effective is the regulation of public utilities in your state as compared with other states?

6. How do the laws of your state concerning the regulation of securities, insurance, food and drugs, and weights and measures compare with Federal laws dealing with these subjects?

7. In what ways do Federal and state governments cooperate in regulating the matters mentioned in question 6?

8. What circumstances have led state and local governments to own and operate proprietary enterprises?

9. When proprietary businesses are owned and operated by governments, how can efficient management be ensured?

10. How can responsibility for highways, roads, and streets be most effectively apportioned among the various levels of government?

Chapter Thirty-Eight

Frontiers of Civic Responsibility

*But good government entails more than courage and
high-mindedness on the part of official leadership.
In the last analysis, civic decency stems from the people
themselves. Where there is misgovernment, where
criminals exert tremendous influence in local affairs,
where standards of official conduct are low, the people
usually have received exactly what they demanded.
In every locality the people who want good government
far outnumber those who represent the lawless and
corrupt elements. But the criminal minority is organized;
it is thoroughly familiar with its objectives and it is
willing to expend sustained effort as well as money to
achieve them. True democracy cannot be had for the
asking. The good citizens must have organization [and]
direction; and the effort must be a continuing one.
. . . The responsibility cannot be shifted. The
counterparts of rights and privileges are duties and
obligations. No privilege is possible nor can it remain
secure without the acceptance of the corresponding
responsibility. There is no escaping the truism of
Thomas Paine, "Those who expect to reap the blessings
of freedom must, like men, undergo the fatigues of
supporting it."*

VIRGIL W. PETERSON[1]

Men who think of themselves as Virginians
or Rhode Islanders first and Americans
second are about as rare as a surrey with
a fringe on top in a present-day city street.
After a century and three-quarters of nationhood, the old economic and cultural self-
sufficiency that formerly characterized

states, local communities, and even families,
has given way to a complex interdependency.
Economic progress has been rooted in division of labor and given great opportunity in
a vast free-trade area tied together with
efficient transport by land, water, and air.
Interstate movement of people and ideas
has contributed to a national culture. Foreign wars have stimulated national patriotism, caused men of different states to rub
shoulders in training and combat, and taken

---

[1] Reprinted by special permission of the *Journal
of Criminal Law and Criminology* (Northwestern
University School of Law), Vol. 39, No. 3, 1948.

those in the Armed Forces far beyond the confines of their home states.

STATE PROBLEMS AND PROSPECTS

Federalism Reappraised. Such unifying factors have made problems formerly regarded as state or local matters the concern of the national government. Federal centralization has proceeded a considerable distance, but the states retain much power. Their relative status has diminished since 1800, but their absolute importance has increased. While losing some functions to the national government, they have taken on new ones that compensate for the loss. Today, the states have far larger budgets, perform a greater variety of services, and affect more intimately the lives of their people than ever before.

Meanwhile, states are learning to work together to an extent undreamed of a few decades ago. The Council of State Governments, the various associations of officials, compacts and agreements, and public and private bureaus of research seek common solutions for common problems exceeding state lines. Progress, often discouragingly slow, appears to be sure. Purged of many of the responsibilities for which they were ill equipped, the states are now in a better position to win public confidence by doing well the functions that properly fall within their jurisdiction.

Constitutional Reform. For almost a whole generation the states seemed to have lost their capacity for full constitutional revision. From 1909 to 1945 no state secured popular ratification for a fully revised constitution. Interest groups fought violently against any change that might deprive them of some special protection from a clause long since incorporated in the constitution. In many states frequent amendments added to the already great bulk of the organic law.

This deadlock was broken in 1945. Missouri, through the method of constitutional convention and popular ratification, secured a concise, modern, and vastly improved constitution. In Georgia a special commission drafted a full revision, accepted by the voters in 1945. Although defeated in 1944, revision succeeded in New Jersey in 1947, giving that state one of the most up-to-date organic laws in the union. Tennessee in 1953 adopted eight amendments, proposed by a limited constitutional convention, to its previously unamended 1870 constitution. These victories for reform have encouraged other state movements for constitutional conventions. Proposals for conventions to revise fundamental law are almost constantly before sessions of the several state legislatures. Alaska's and Hawaii's modern constitutions may induce other states to act.

Many proponents of constitutional revision believe that the ordinary amending process offers the best way to accomplish it. But piecemeal amendment will not, in most states, suffice to accomplish the general revision that is long overdue. Experience has shown that the convention method is best for a general overhaul job.

Legislative Problems. The legislature remains the weakest link in the chain of state government. There have been some improvements since Bryce recorded that the "real blemishes" were in the legislative branch, but, on the whole the composition and conduct of the legislature are still unsatisfactory.

Apportionment. The apportionment of representatives in most state legislatures overrepresents rural areas in one or both houses and underrepresents cities. Most of the distortions of the democratic principle in state legislative representation arise from the use of units of government as a basis of representation. To justify the representing of counties or towns on a basis of equality or near equality, regardless of population, proponents of such schemes often cite the equal representation of states in the national Senate. But in no state do units of local government play a role comparable to that of the states in the Federal Union. Political subdivisions of a state are creatures of the state; neither historically nor constitutionally are they units from which the central whole was constructed. Early transportation limits, historical accident, and other factors no longer operative usually determined town and county boundaries.

The "rotten borough" has a great impact on lawmaking in many states. Disagreement between the governor, elected by the people of the whole state and reasonably representative of them, and the nonpopular house of the legislature often threatens deadlock. Conflict between popular and nonpopular houses is also a common source of legislative paralysis. Obviously, a legislature of two houses with different bases of representation provides a "check" against hasty action. It may block *any* action on critical problems by handing the representatives of a minority of the population a virtual veto power over the wishes of a majority. Is such a check necessary? Already in existence are gubernatorial veto, judicial review of constitutionality, and, in one-third of the states, the referendum. Reform of nonpopular houses of the state legislatures would hasten solutions of the great social and economic problems that plague urban and industrial society.

Legislative Councils. The most conspicuous alteration in American state legislatures in the last generation has come through the establishment of legislative councils. Although they vary widely in composition and powers, the essential idea common to most of the councils is to provide a continuing body to study problems and plan a legislative program. State legislatures are large and

noncontinuous assemblies, composed of quasi, often inexperienced, laymen who meet for relatively short periods during their brief terms of office. Hemmed in by constitutional limits on the length of sessions and by the restricted compensation allowed, legislators function in a hectic atmosphere that is almost directly opposite to that of orderly deliberation. Since strong leadership is scarce in the legislatures, governors, with or without the whip of party, have emerged as chief legislators.

By vesting the power to study and plan in a council of its own choosing, many legislatures have restored to the legislative branch the ingredients prerequisite to exercise of the deliberative function. A few states, by including representatives of the governor on the council, have expanded the functions of that body to include legislative-executive collaboration. Instead of creating a committee that would become the legislature's master, as many critics of the idea feared, the legislative council has proved to be a useful instrument; it has improved the quality of legislation through better fact finding and advance planning. The legislative-council idea extended to the remaining one-half of the states that have not adopted it will strengthen democracy; it will assure that the proper foundations are laid before legislative action is taken.

Some states secure the benefits of fact finding and informed recommendations in specific fields through the device of interim committees of the legislature. The constitutionality of such committees and the rules under which they must operate, if they may be used at all, vary greatly from state to state. States that make generous financial provision for compensating legislators while on interim-committee duty are apt to have a large number of such committees.

As a general rule, when the standing committees (or their subcommittees) that would normally have jurisdiction over the subject matter in question conduct inquiries between legislative sessions, they obtain better results. Interim committees that are not coordinated with the regular committee arrangement may produce solutions out of harmony with the thinking of the legislators who have the primary responsibility for scrutinizing proposals in that sector. Another danger is that the interim committee may be used for getting publicity for the chairman or making sensational disclosures on the basis of hearsay or quite inadequate evidence. Neither on the national nor on the state level has enough thought been given to devising standards of conduct for legislative investigative committees.

Legislative Reform. Bicameralism remains the chief structural feature of American state legislatures. Only Nebraska has yielded to the many arguments for unicameralism. After more than a decade of experience with a one-house legislature, Nebraska has shown that neither the proponents who heralded the millennium nor the opponents who predicted doom were right. Unicameralism has simplified Nebraska's legislative procedure and thereby reduced public bewilderment over legislative matters. It has reduced "passing the buck" to a minimum; no longer can members of one house blame those of another for some legislative failure. The record has been one of modest achievement.

One of the great barriers to further expansion of the one-house idea is concern lest unicameralism mean the end of two different bases of representation in the legislature. A state wishing to adopt a single-house plan, yet retain two apportionment bases, could do so simply by providing that members of the former two houses meet together in a single chamber. It would be possible to elect legislators on two or more bases, yet secure the advantages of a single tier of committees, fixed responsibility for the fate of legislation, public convenience from one hear-

ing rather than two, reduced printing and attaché personnel costs, and a single debate heard by all members of the legislature. Despite all these considerations, however, attachment to the old ways has kept all but one of the states on the bicameral stereotype.

Lesser reforms have proved more palatable. There is a commendable tendency to increase legislative salaries. Nevertheless, even in the states with the highest compensation, legislative service often involves financial sacrifice. Some of the largest budgets now exceed the billion-dollars-per-year level; entrusting such a responsibility to underpaid, part-time legislators just does not make sense. Other badly needed improvements in the larger states are annual sessions of the legislature and annual budgets to provide for closer control over financial operations.

The State Executive "New Look." The state administrative reorganization movement, begun nearly a half century ago, had pretty well run its course by the Second World War. Renewed interest and some action has marked the period since 1945. Missouri, Georgia, New Jersey, Alaska, and Hawaii, in their new constitutions, made substantial administrative improvements.

"Little Hoover Commissions." The example of the Hoover Commission and its broad study of Federal administration led many states to launch inquiries of their own. Although the bodies that conducted these investigations varied widely in composition and in terms of reference, they were promptly referred to as "little Hoover Commissions." By the mid-1950s committees or commissions in two-thirds of the states were studying state organization, which in some cases included constitutional revision and legislative reorganization as well as administrative reforms. Some of the probing bodies were executive-appointed; others were legislative committees; a few were created in

the image of the Hoover Commission, with some members designated by the chief executive and some by the legislative branch. Not for a generation has so much intelligent attention been given to the problems of state management.

One big problem faced by all study groups is the extent to which the governor should be strengthened and given effective command over the executive branch. Should he, for example, be made the only elected executive officer or should some of his colleagues also be elected as is customary? Should other states go the whole way, as did New Jersey and Alaska, and provide for the popular choice of only the governor?

Closely related is the question of whether the governor's "span of control" should be reduced by consolidating some of the many departments and agencies. Should the independent boards and commissions be made subordinate to the governor? Should they be headed by a single administrator or by a plural body? Should they be stripped of administrative authority and left to play only advisory roles?

Also related is the problem of staffing the executive branch. Should the governor be given more professional staff? How can sufficient qualified manpower be recruited, retained, and kept productive? Some states still make extensive use of the spoils system. How can this be reconciled with the principles of good management? What type of organization and what statutory provisions are essential for effective personnel administration? These are some of the many difficult problems with which administrative reformers come to grips.

The Governorship: Opinion divides sharply over whether the governorship should be strengthened. There is, nonetheless, a growing awareness of the governor's need for help. More than half the states have created departments of administration or something similar with different names.

Ideally these are headed by skilled administrators in which case the arrangement resembles the mayor-manager form discussed in Chapter 33. Typically the new agencies serve as the governor's "eyes and ears" and assist him with such duties as planning, budgeting, personnel administration, accounting, organization and procedures, program evaluation, and purchasing.

But more than professional staffs is needed. Most political scientists recommend: a term for the governor of at least four years with the right to serve for two or more consecutive terms; the governor should be the only elective state-wide executive officer; agencies should be consolidated into twenty or fewer departments whose heads are responsible to the governor; civil service for all non-policy-forming positions.

Thus far no state, not even recently admitted Alaska and Hawaii, has seriously considered installing the parliamentary form. The suggestion is sometimes made that the legislature should appoint a manager and give him control over administration as under the council-manager plan of city government. Such a plan, it is argued, would create legislative supremacy and provide a responsible executive. Critics insist that such an arrangement would be both unattractive and undesirable because the people need and want the unifying political influence of a state governor as they do a President.

In any event, the American addiction to separation of powers precludes any radical departure from the traditional arrangement. One thing is certain, however: the office of governor remains high in prestige and is steadily, albeit slowly, achieving what it takes to be the chief executive in fact.

State Judicial and Legal Reforms. Less conspicuous, but equally important, are rumblings of discontent over judicial systems and legal procedures. Judicial councils —now used in nearly two-thirds of the states—are on the increase, with an expanding area of activity and public confidence. Equally significant is the growth of administrative offices of the courts. These exist in about half the states for the purpose of expediting lagging justice. Another step forward was the establishment in 1949 of a Conference of Chief Justices of the States to do for state jurisprudence what the annual conference of Federal jurists has done for the national.

Most spectacular has been the movement toward unified court systems, notably in New Jersey and Alaska. The "Missouri Plan" for choosing judges has proved itself and is taking hold elsewhere. A few states require that minor justices be lawyers or undergo special training. The fee system of paying justices has been eliminated in several states and brought under stricter control elsewhere. Small-claims courts have gained popularity and greater use is made of arbitration in civil cases.

Great strides have been made in modernizing, simplifying, unifying, and codifying the law. Some states are seriously studying revision of rules of evidence. There are numerous indications that judges, bar associations, and law schools are becoming increasingly concerned over legal ethics, the training of future lawyers, restrictions upon admission to legal practice, and the high cost of justice.

Police-force training and professionalization have gone forward, especially at state and municipal levels. Prison facilities and care are generally bad, but there is improvement in spots. Work programs suffer increasingly because of lobbying by "free enterprise" and drastic Federal and state restrictions on the sale of prison-made products. The chain gang is gone except in a few Southern counties.

Probation, parole practices, and supervision show some improvement, but inadequate appropriations and the spoils system continue to plague these efforts. Traffic violations remain a serious problem, with vari-

ous experiments under way. Several states have evolved traffic tickets that are supposed to be "fix-proof." Meanwhile, the National Committee on Traffic Law Enforcement has proposed standards toward which many state officials aspire.

Considerable progress has been made in handling juvenile offenders. California, for example, led the way by establishing a Youth Authority. New York and New Jersey have adopted similar programs. Minnesota has established a Youth Conservation Commission; Wisconsin, a Youth Service Division; and Massachusetts, a Youth Service Board. These agencies emphasize the importance of clinical analysis followed by varied practicable programs to correct and eliminate the causes of delinquency. Outdoor work is an integral part of most of the programs. The Federal government has recently entered the field with grants to state and local governments which desire to improve their juvenile correctional services.

TOWARD LOCAL DEMOCRACY

Local government is bound to have a place in any conceivable political system. Although counties, cities, and other local units may change individually and internally, their basic pattern is apt to survive. Those who know the mood of the community can better perform certain types of services. Local self-government allows a rather broad form of local option; acting through their elected representatives, the people decide what they want and what they will spend for it. One of the strongest arguments for retaining a large measure of discretion in the hands of local authorities is that it permits experimentation, the results of which may be of great value to other localities and to higher units of government. It also provides greater vitality in local government, which becomes the training ground for future members of state legislatures and Congress.

State-Local Relations. The changing pattern of intergovernmental relationships must be assessed in terms of the trend toward Federal centralization, and attention must be given to the shift of power and responsibility from local to state government. The problems involved in the latter sphere were examined in a report of the Council of State Governments in 1946. The report stressed four major problem areas: finances, functions, legal relationships, and multiplicity of local units.[1]

Finances. On the financial front, local governments have relied most heavily on the property tax, which is often badly assessed and unevenly collected. Local governments frequently find themselves without revenues to perform the services legally required by the state or strongly demanded by the people. During the Depression, hundreds of local governments went broke. Schools were closed, services abandoned, and grass grew in the streets. Property taxpayers became delinquent in wholesale numbers. After some improvement in economic conditions, property-tax collections improved too, but local government remained vulnerable. Dependent almost completely on a single source of revenue, local governments run the risk of a man with all his eggs in one basket. They are unable to finance ever-growing functions upon a rigid tax base. According to the Council report, they should be given broader taxing powers rather than be aided by expanding state grants-in-aid or shared revenues. The higher costs of city government since the end of the Second World War and increased demands have forced many cities to adopt new forms of taxes to broaden the tax base.

[1] Council of State Governments, *State-Local Relations, Report of the Committee on . . .* (Chicago: the Council, 1946).

Functions. Each level of government should be assigned the functions it is capable of performing with both efficiency and maximum participation by those affected. The Council report stressed that local discretion is important to democracy and democratic procedures. Local government is an important fountainhead from which democracy flows. In counties, cities, and other local units, large numbers of men and women officeholders are getting experience in government and interpreting its problems to people in their constituencies. Local home rule quickens the sense of civic responsibility by assuring that decisions on local matters shall be made locally.

Legal Relationship. Local government remains everywhere the creature of the state. Most states impose detailed restrictions on local activities through constitutional and statutory provisions and through administrative supervision. One-third of the states have granted constitutional home rule to some cities, involving the privilege of drawing up their own charters and governing so far as "municipal affairs" are concerned. Home rule has been circumscribed, in some of the states that have adopted it, by restrictive judicial interpretations and constitutional and statutory amendments. Nevertheless, this frees local governments to find their own solutions to local problems and relieves state legislatures of some of the mass of detailed legislation on local matters. States like Michigan and California have demonstrated that home rule, while not a panacea for all local ills, can enlarge the scope of self-government and sharpen civic alertness.

Even more important than the formal limitations on local powers, however, are the forces of modern life that make communities interdependent and formerly local problems state- and nationwide.

The story of relief illustrates this. Poor

relief was a traditional function of English local government transplanted to America. Local units bore the burden of caring for the poor for over a century and a quarter after nationhood was achieved. Then the Great Depression, following the crash of 1929, struck with unprecedented violence. At first counties, cities, and townships struggled valiantly to take care of their unemployed. When their resources were exhausted, the states began to help. Finally, in 1933, the Federal government assumed a large share of the obligation by providing work for the able-bodied unemployed. Under the social security program inaugurated in 1935, the Federal government financed a share of state and local public-assistance programs, launched a Federal system of old-age insurance, and induced the states to begin unemployment-compensation schemes.

Multiplicity of Units. Few, if any, governmental situations are more impervious to suggestions for change than is the multiplicity of local units. Like the weather, everyone talks about it but no one does very much about it. Governmentally speaking, the United States is divided into about 91,000 units, of which over one-third are school districts. Nearly every state has too many counties and other general local units of government. The typical urban resident pays taxes to two or more taxing authorities and is confused over which services from what level of government he receives in return. Most metropolitan areas have chronic problems arising from the common pattern of development. A central city is incorporated, with boundaries that embrace the greater part of the urban population in the vicinity. As the city grows, population spills beyond the city limits. Annexation by the central city may operate for a time, but usually the satellite city emerges to play the role of dormitory for people who work in the city. Eventually as much as half or more of the population of a metropolitan area is outside the jurisdiction of the central city; it does not share directly in the solution of many of the problems that rightfully belong to the metropolitan area as a whole— health, transportation, delinquency, dependency, and poverty.

There is some possibility of consolidating counties, since they are creatures of the state and usually subject to its will. But fervid county pride is aroused by such proposals, and a howl goes up that can be heard around the state. The number of counties has remained so static in most states that one might think they were defined in the Federal Constitution. Establishment of a county is likely to mean its eternal existence unless some new plan of inducing consolidations can be worked out. The states that allow their legislatures to determine county boundaries and jurisdictions are in a good position to merge smaller counties and otherwise recast outmoded arrangements on the county-government level.

One of the most needed consolidations is that of cities and counties. Metropolitan areas require an instrument of government that will permit central administration of metropolitan-district problems and local solutions for community ones. The separate existence of city and county governments in great urban centers usually involves duplication, waste, and confusion.

The greatest quantitative consolidation, however, is possible in school districts. The small rural district, operating only a single one-room school, rarely has the facilities and resources necessary to provide the best educational services. District consolidation can be accomplished without consolidating schools. Retention of the one-room school or merger into a consolidated school is a question quite apart from the larger unit. The enlarged district can effect savings through purchase of supplies, maintenance of buildings, provision of nursing facilities, and in many other ways.

Most urgent of all is the incorporation of special districts into other local units. Many states have left the door for the formation of special districts so wide open that hundreds of these jurisdictions have been established. Some of them have important functions that are best performed by special units, but most of them ought to be assigned to a general local unit.

Local Organization. Generally speaking, local governments are ill organized to provide the services thrust upon them by the Federal system and modern technology. With few exceptions they have continued institutions established generations ago to deal with problems vastly simpler than those of today and to serve relatively small populations. Of course, there have been changes. Bicameral city councils have been reduced to unicameral ones. Many city councils and a few county boards of supervisors have appointed managers.

Basically, however, the old forms still prevail. Except in counties and school and other districts, the line between the legislative and executive branches is too strictly drawn. Except where the manager plan is in use, the line between politics and administration rarely is drawn strongly enough. Separation of powers may prevent autocratic government, as its proponents allege, but it also often produces deadlock unless the breach is healed over under the binding sinews of party or the pressure of a strong executive. County government, once called "the dark continent of American politics," remains dusky except in a few advanced counties that have created executives. Council-manager cities constitute the only considerable number of local units that have developed an organizational form that meets modern demands for a responsible executive whose tenure depends upon the majority will of the legislative body.

Too many state and local officers are elected by the people; ballots are so long that even moderately alert citizens can know little of the stewardship in office of their representatives. The urge to separate national, state, and local elections has produced so many election days that participation has been seriously diminished.

Need for Stronger Executives. Within local governments, the most pressing single need is for stronger and more responsible executives. Many local governments, especially counties and cities with the commission plan, have no real executive. Other cities have weak mayors whose executive powers are slight. The manager plan of cities and counties and the wise use of the school superintendent as the executive officer of boards of education are encouraging beginnings. If local units are to be well governed, a responsible executive is a first essential. The local executive of the future may well be modeled on the office of the city manager, as developed in the municipalities effectively using that form.

The manager plan is on the march. More than one-fourth of the incorporated municipalities have city managers. It appears entirely possible that, during the 1960s, the manager plan will be used by a majority of American cities. Municipal progress in the next generation may well turn largely upon the soundness of the charters, statutes, and ordinances creating these managerships, and upon the training and professional integrity of those appointed as managers. In many ways the need for the manager plan is even more acute in counties than in cities, but its spread in the county sphere has been slow.

The Metropolitan Area. Not discounting the many forces and vested interests that support the *status quo*, one may say with some assurance that the development of metropolitan-area governments will have high priority on the agenda of American democracy in the next generation. The great cities of today, in almost all cases, had their basic physical layouts determined before the development of the automobile. With few exceptions, the great metropolitan areas sprawl over many units of government—cities, counties, townships, school districts, special districts, and even states. Even where a bold consolidation is carried through, as in London in 1888 and in New York in 1898, the old problems of outgrown boundaries recur in another decade or two as the metropolis expands and improved transportation permits suburbanites to commute from greater and greater distances.

The outlines of metropolitan reform are far from clear. In most drastic form, local government might be replaced by a centralized single government. This solution has few champions and runs counter to deeply embedded home-rule sentiments buttressed by entrenched local governments. More promising are the new federal-district arrangements at Toronto, Canada, and Dade County, Florida, whereby powers are divided between an area government and local units; this plan is particularly attractive for metropolitan regions confined to one state.

More likely, however, order will be brought out of the existing metropolitan chaos in piecemeal fashion. Far from simple, this might result from a maze of contractual obligations among local units to provide each other with certain services, for payment. It is even possible that a considerable degree of functional consolidation might be achieved through the organization of metropolis-wide special districts, later brought together into a single government.

Arousing Citizen Interest. In the America that de Tocqueville visited in the 1830s, as indeed in some rural communities of today, the level of citizen interest was high. Government belonged to the people. Participation in town affairs was expected of all New England freemen who went to town meetings and accepted and discharged civic responsibilities. By way of contrast, de Tocqueville mentioned the civic sterility that existed in the communes of his native France. Because of centralization, he thought, people had no sense of belonging to the communes in which they lived, and they participated little in local affairs.

Today an overseas observer might get an entirely different impression of American local institutions. The typical American is more urban than rural. In the great metropolitan areas, he may not even know in which municipality he lives. He has little conception of governmental functions and is often unable to distinguish between state, county, municipal, and district services. The chances are that he votes occasionally in state elections but seldom in local elections. If he does vote, he is likely to support blindly the political party with which his parents were affiliated, or if no party labels are available, to vote as his daily newspaper or some friend recommends.

Far from the active, participating freeman of the early days of the republic, today's average citizen is a drone, quite impotent in local affairs. Once in a while, of course, he becomes aroused over something. It may be that a new ordinance steps on his own toes, or a crime wave reaches his neighborhood, or local services break down. Sometimes he becomes enthusiastic over the prospects of unseating a local boss or turning out a political machine.

American state and local governments, traditionally the fountainheads of democracy, are not abreast of the needs and requirements of our urban-industrial civilization. Thrice in the last forty years we have sent American soldiers forth to foreign battlefields, and each time the justifications for the enormous sacrifices were "free government," "freedom," and "democracy." We have been disappointed afterward, because democracy and freedom did not follow automatically in the countries defeated or liberated. If, in the period of postwar disillusionment, Americans would rededicate themselves wholeheartedly to the study and improvement of their institutions, perhaps some positive good would come from the investment of men and money in war.

Mind Your Own Business was the title of a book written by R. B. Suthers in 1905.[1] In it the author presented "the case for municipal housekeeping" in England, arguing convincingly for Britons to participate in local affairs. We in the United States need someone to inspire us to mind our own business. We need citizens in every county and city and town to agree to spend enough time on civic affairs to keep abreast of public business. President Eliot's famous bookshelf offered the equivalent of a college education through fifteen minutes of reading a day. A quarter hour of intelligent

[1] The latest revision (London: Fabian Society and G. Allen Unwin) was published in 1938.

attention applied daily to civic problems might transform a drone into a civic worker and lack of interest into informed opinion. A little more time and energy invested through participation in the political party of their choice and through nonpartisan civic groups like the League of Women Voters will make leaders out of formerly indifferent citizens.

Startling international and national news focuses our attention upon the government at Washington. In a decade that has required the sacrifices of total war, it is both proper and inevitable that an alert citizen should devote time and attention to foreign affairs. In an era haunted by the nightmare of the Depression, we look to the national capital to formulate economic policies that will secure full employment and promote free enterprise. Preoccupation with national affairs must not be carried so far that we neglect our state and locality, for there are the roots from which much of our political democracy stems.

FOR FURTHER READING

Arkansas:

Alexander, Henry M.: *Organization and Function of State and Local Government in Arkansas* (Fayetteville, Ark.: University of Arkansas, Bureau of Research, 1947).

California:

Crouch, Winston W., and Dean E. McHenry: *California Government: Politics and Administration* (Berkeley and Los Angeles, Calif.: University of California Press, 2d ed., 1949).
———— and others: *California Government and Politics* (Englewood Cliffs, N.J.: Prentice-Hall, 2d ed., 1960).
Harris, Joseph P., and Leonard Rowe: *California Politics* (Stanford, Calif.: Stanford University Press, 2d ed., 1959).
Hyink, Bernard L., et al.: *Politics and Government in California* (New York: Crowell, 1959).
Schlessinger, Phillip J., and Richard Wright: *State and Local Government in California*

(New York: Holt, Rinehart & Winston, 1962).
Turner, Henry A., and John A. Vieg: *The Government and Politics of California* (New York: McGraw-Hill, 1960).

Colorado:

Martin, Curtis W.: *Colorado Politics* (Denver, Colo.: Big Mountain Press, 1960).

Delaware:

Dolan, Paul: *The Government and Administration of Delaware* (New York: Crowell, 1956).

Florida:

Doyle, Wilson K., and others: *The Government and Administration of Florida* (New York: Crowell, 1954).

Georgia:

Gosnell, Cullen B., and C. D. Anderson: *The Government and Administration of Georgia* (New York: Crowell, 1956).

Illinois:

Garvey, Neil F.: *The Government and Administration of Illinois* (New York: Crowell, 1959).

Gore, S. K., and others (eds.): *State and Local Government in Illinois* (Urbana, Ill.: University of Illinois, Institute of Government and Public Affairs, 1953).

Ranney, Austin: *Illinois Politics* (New York: New York University Press, 1960).

Indiana:

Sikes, Pressley S.: *Indiana State and Local Government* (Bloomington, Ind.: Principia Press, rev. ed., 1951).

Iowa:

Ross, Russell M.: *The Government and Administration of Iowa* (New York: Crowell, 1957).

Kansas:

Drury, James W.: *The Government of Kansas* (Lawrence, Kan.: University of Kansas Press, 1961).

Louisiana:

Havard, William C.: *The Government of Louisiana* (Baton Rouge, La.: Bureau of Public Administration, Louisiana State University, 1958).

Massachusetts:

Latham, Earl, and George Goodwin, Jr.: *Massachusetts Politics* (Medford, Mass.: Tufts Civic Education Center, 1960).

Michigan:

LaPalombara, Joseph: *Guide to Michigan Politics* (East Lansing, Mich.: Bureau of Social and Political Research, Michigan State University, 1960).

Minnesota:

Mitau, G. Theodore: *Politics in Minnesota* (Minneapolis, Minn.: University of Minnesota Press, 1960).

Mississippi:

Highsaw, Robert B., and C. N. Fortenberry: *The Government and Administration of Mississippi* (New York: Crowell, 1954).

Missouri:

Karsch, Robert F.: *Essentials of Missouri Government* (Columbia, Mo.: Lucas Bros., 5th ed., 1957).

New Jersey:

Rich, Bennett M.: *The Government and Administration of New Jersey* (New York: Crowell, 1957).

New Mexico:

Donnelly, Thomas C.: *The Government of New Mexico* (Albuquerque, N.M.: The New Mexico Press, 1947).

Judah, Charles B., and Frederick C. Irion: *The 47th State: An Appraisal of Its Government* (Albuquerque, N.M.: Division of Government Research, University of New Mexico, 1956).

New York:

Caldwell, Lynton K.: *The Government and Administration of New York* (New York: Crowell, 1954).

Moscow, Warren: *Politics in the Empire State* (New York: Knopf, 1948).

Straetz, Ralph A., and Frank J. Munger: *New York Politics* (New York: New York University Press, 1960).

North Carolina:

Rankin, Robert S.: *The Government and Administration of North Carolina* (New York: Crowell, 1955).

Wager, Paul W.: *North Carolina: The State and Its Government* (New York: Oxford, 1947).

Ohio:

Aumann, Francis R., and Harvey Walker: *The Government and Administration of Ohio* (New York: Crowell, 1956).

Rose, Albert H.: *Ohio State and Local Government* (Dayton, Ohio: University Book Store, 1948).

Oklahoma:

Thornton, H. V., and others: *Problems in Oklahoma State Government* (Norman, Okla.: Bureau of Government Research, University of Oklahoma, 1957).

Pennsylvania:

Cooke, Edward F., and Edward G. Janosik: *Guide to Pennsylvania Politics* (New York: Holt, Rinehart and Winston, 1957).

Tanger, Jacob, and others: *Pennsylvania Government* (State College, Pa.: Penns Valley Press, 3d ed., 1950).

South Carolina:

Organization of the State Government of South Carolina (Columbia, S.C.: University of South Carolina, Bureau of Public Administration, 1952).

Tennessee:

Combs, William H., and W. E. Cole: *Tennessee: A Political Study* (Knoxville, Tenn.: University of Tennessee Press, 1940).

Texas:

Benton, Wilbourn E.: *Texas: Its Government and Politics* (Englewood Cliffs, N.J.: Prentice-Hall, 1961).

MacCorkle, Stuart A., and Dick Smith: *Texas Government* (New York: McGraw-Hill, 4th ed., 1960).

Patterson, Caleb P., and others: *State and Local Government in Texas* (New York: Macmillan, 2d ed., 1948).

Stewart, Frank M., and Joseph L. Clark: *The Constitution and Government of Texas* (New York: Heath, 4th ed., 1949).

Washington:

Ogden, Daniel M., and Hugh A. Bone: *Washington Politics* (New York: New York University Press, 1960).

Webster, Donald H., and others: *Washington State Government* (Seattle: University of Washington Press, 1956).

Wyoming:

Trachsel, Herman H., and Ralph M. Wade: *The Government and Administration of Wyoming* (New York: Crowell, 1953).

REVIEW QUESTIONS

1. To what extent do you believe our economic prosperity rests upon the vastness of our free-trade areas?

2. Is federalism "finished"? Discuss changes that have taken place. What do you expect in the future?

3. Has the deadlock on American state constitutional reform been broken by Missouri and New Jersey, or were those instances exceptions which prove the rule that general renovation is nearly impossible under present conditions?

4. What are the persistent problems that plague state legislatures with respect to apportionment, legislative councils, and general renovation and reform?

5. What are the prospects for state administrative reorganization?

6. Discuss some of the problems of state-local relations.

7. What structural and organizational improvements look promising in the field of local government?

8. What can be done to penetrate the indifference of the American people toward public affairs?

The Declaration

of Independence

IN CONGRESS, JULY 4, 1776: THE UNANIMOUS DECLARATION OF THE THIRTEEN UNITED STATES OF AMERICA

When in the Course of human events, it becomes necessary for one people to dissolve the political bands which have connected them with another, and to assume among the Powers of the earth, the separate and equal station to which the Laws of Nature and Nature's God entitle them, a decent respect to the opinions of mankind requires that they should declare the causes which impel them to the separation.

We hold these truths to be self-evident, that all men are created equal, that they are endowed by their Creator with certain unalienable Rights, that among these are Life, Liberty and the pursuit of Happiness. That to secure these rights, Governments are instituted among Men, deriving their just powers from the consent of the governed, That whenever any Form of Government becomes destructive of these ends, it is the Right of the People to alter or to abolish it, and to institute new Government, laying its foundation on such principles and organizing its powers in such form, as to them shall seem most likely to effect their Safety and Happiness. Prudence, indeed, will dictate that Governments long established should not be changed for light and transient causes; and accordingly all experience hath shown, that mankind are more disposed to suffer, while evils are sufferable, than to right themselves by abolishing the forms to which they are accustomed. But when a long train of abuses and usurpations, pursuing invariably the same Object evinces a design to reduce them under absolute Despotism, it is their right, it is their duty, to throw off such Government, and to provide new Guards for their future security.— Such has been the patient sufferance of these Colonies; and such is now the necessity which constrains them to alter their former Systems of Government. The history of the present King of Great Britain is a history of repeated injuries and usurpations, all having in direct object the establishment of an absolute Tyranny over these States. To prove this, let Facts be submitted to a candid world.

He has refused his Assent to Laws, the most wholesome and necessary for the public good.

He has forbidden his Governors to pass Laws of immediate and pressing importance, unless suspended in their operation till his Assent should be obtained; and when so suspended, he has utterly neglected to attend to them.

He has refused to pass other Laws for the accommodation of large districts of people, unless those people would relinquish the right of representation in the Legislature, a right inestimable to them and formidable to tyrants only.

He has called together legislative bodies at places

731

unusual, uncomfortable, and distant from the depository of their Public Records, for the sole purpose of fatiguing them into compliance with his measures.

He has dissolved Representative Houses repeatedly, for opposing with manly firmness his invasions on the rights of the people.

He has refused for a long time, after such dissolutions, to cause others to be elected; whereby the Legislative Powers, incapable of Annihilation, have returned to the People at large for their exercise; the State remaining in the mean time exposed to all the dangers of invasion from without, and convulsions within.

He has endeavoured to prevent the population of these States; for that purpose obstructing the Laws of Naturalization of Foreigners; refusing to pass others to encourage their migration hither, and raising the conditions of new Appropriations of Lands.

He has obstructed the Administration of Justice, by refusing his Assent to Laws for establishing Judiciary Powers.

He has made Judges dependent on his Will alone, for the tenure of their offices, and the amount and payment of their salaries.

He has erected a multitude of New Offices, and sent hither swarms of Officers to harass our People, and eat out their substance.

He has kept among us, in times of peace, Standing Armies without the Consent of our legislature.

He has affected to render the Military independent of and superior to the Civil Power.

He has combined with others to subject us to a jurisdiction foreign to our constitution, and unacknowledged by our laws giving his Assent to their acts of pretended legislation:

For quartering large bodies of armed troops among us:

For protecting them, by a mock Trial, from Punishment for any Murders which they should commit on the Inhabitants of these States:

For cutting off our Trade with all parts of the world:

For imposing taxes on us without our Consent:

For depriving us in many cases, of the benefits of Trial by jury:

For transporting us beyond Seas to be tried for pretended offences:

For abolishing the free System of English Laws in a neighboring Province, establishing therein an Arbitrary government, and enlarging its Boundaries so as to render it at once an example and fit

instrument for introducing the same absolute rule into these Colonies:

For taking away our Charters, abolishing our most valuable Laws, and altering fundamentally the Forms of our Governments:

For suspending our own legislature, and declaring themselves invested with Power to legislate for us in all cases whatsoever.

He has abdicated Government here, by declaring us out of his Protection and waging War against us.

He has plundered our seas, ravaged our Coasts, burnt our towns, and destroyed the lives of our people.

He is at this time transporting large armies of foreign mercenaries to compleat the works of death, desolation and tyranny, already begun with circumstances of Cruelty & perfidy scarcely paralleled in the most barbarous ages, and totally unworthy the Head of a civilized nation.

He has constrained our fellow Citizens taken Captive on the high Seas to bear Arms against their Country, to become the executioners of their friends and Brethren, or to fall themselves by their Hands.

He has excited domestic insurrections amongst us, and has endeavoured to bring on the inhabitants of our frontiers, the merciless Indian Savages, whose known rule of warfare, is an undistinguished destruction of all ages, sexes and conditions.

In every stage of these Oppressions We have Petitioned for Redress in the most humble terms: Our repeated Petitions have been answered only by repeated injury. A Prince, whose character is thus marked by every act which may define a Tyrant, is unfit to be the ruler of a free People.

Nor have We been wanting in attention to our British brethren. We have warned them from time to time of attempts by their legislature to extend an unwarrantable jurisdiction over us. We have reminded them of the circumstances of our emigration and settlement here. We have appealed to their native justice and magnanimity, and we have conjured them by the ties of our common kindred to disavow these usurpations, which would inevitably interrupt our connections and correspondence. They too have been deaf to the voice of justice and of consanguinity. We must, therefore, acquiesce in the necessity, which denounces our Separation, and hold them, as we hold the rest of mankind, Enemies in War, in Peace Friends.

We, therefore, the Representatives of the united

States of America, in General Congress, Assembled, appealing to the Supreme Judge of the world for the rectitude of our intentions, do, in the Name, and by Authority of the good People of these Colonies, solemnly publish and declare, That these United Colonies are, and of Right ought to be Free and Independent States; that they are Absolved from all Allegiance to the British Crown, and that all political connection between them and the State of Great Britain, is and ought to be totally dissolved; and that as Free and Independent States, they have full Power to levy War, conclude Peace, contract Alliances, establish Commerce, and to do all other Acts and Things which Independent States may of right do. And for the support of this Declaration, with a firm reliance on the Protection of Divine Providence, we mutually pledge to each other our Lives, our Fortunes and our sacred Honor.

John Hancock[1]

[1] The remaining signatures are omitted.

Articles

of Confederation

ARTICLES OF CONFEDERATION AND PERPETUAL UNION BE-
TWEEN THE STATES OF NEWHAMSHIRE, MASSACHUSETTS-BAY,
RHODEISLAND AND PROVIDENCE PLANTATIONS, CONNECTI-
CUT, NEW-YORK, NEW-JERSEY, PENNSYLVANIA, DELAWARE,
MARYLAND, VIRGINIA, NORTH-CAROLINA, SOUTH-CAROLINA
AND GEORGIA

Article I. The stile of this confederacy shall be "The United States of America."

Article II. Each State retains its sovereignty, freedom and independence, and every power, jurisdiction and right, which is not by this confederation expressly delegated to the United States, in Congress assembled.

Article III. The said States hereby severally enter into a firm league of friendship with each other, for their common defence, the security of their liberties, and their mutual and general welfare, binding themselves to assist each other, against all force offered to, or attacks made upon them, or any of them, on account of religion, sovereignty, trade, or any other pretence whatever.

Article IV. The better to secure and perpetuate mutual friendship and intercourse among the people of the different States in this Union, the free inhabitants of each of these States, paupers, vagabonds and fugitives from justice excepted, shall be entitled to all privileges and immunities of free citizens in the several States; and the people of each State shall have free ingress and regress to and from any other State, and shall enjoy therein all the privileges of trade and commerce, subject to the same duties, impositions and restrictions as the inhabitants thereof respectively, provided that such restrictions shall not extend so far as to prevent the removal of property imported into any State, to any other state of which the owner is an inhabitant; provided also that no imposition, duties, or restriction shall be laid by any State, on the property of the United States, or either of them.

If any Person guilty of, or charged with treason, felony, or other high misdemeanor in any State, shall flee from justice, and be found in any of the United States, he shall upon demand of the Governor or Executive power, of the State from which he fled, be delivered up and removed to the State having jurisdiction of his offence.

Full faith and credit shall be given in each of these States to the records, acts and judicial proceedings of the courts and magistrates of every other State.

Article V. For the more convenient management of the general interest of the United States, delegates shall be annually appointed in such manner as the legislature of each State shall direct, to meet in Congress on the first Monday in November, in every year, with a power reserved to each State, to recall its delegates, or any of them, at any time within the year, and to send others in their stead, for the remainder of the year.

No State shall be represented in Congress by less than two, nor by more than seven members; and no person shall be capable of being a delegate for more than three years in any term of six years; nor shall any person, being a delegate, be capable of holding any office under the United States, for which he, or another for his benefit receives any salary, fees or emolument of any kind.

Each State shall maintain its own delegates in a meeting of the States, and while they act as members of the committee of the States.

In determining questions in the United States, in Congress assembled, each State shall have one vote.

Freedom of speech and debate in Congress shall not be impeached or questioned in any court, or place out of Congress, and the members of Congress shall be protected in their persons from arrests and imprisonments, during the time of their going to and from, and attendance on Congress, except for treason, felony, or breach of the peace.

Article VI. No State without the consent of the United States in Congress assembled, shall send any embassy to, or receive any embassy from, or enter into any conference, agreement, alliance or treaty with any king, prince or state; nor shall any person holding any office of profit or trust under the United States, or any of them, accept of any present, emolument, office or title of any kind whatever from any king, prince, or foreign state; nor shall the United States in Congress assembled, or any of them, grant any title of nobility.

No two or more States shall enter into any treaty, confederation or alliance whatever between them, without the consent of the United States in Congress assembled, specifying accurately the purposes for which the same is to be entered into, and how long it shall continue.

No State shall lay any imposts or duties, which may interfere with any stipulations in treaties, entered into by the United States in Congress assembled, with any king, prince or state, in pursuance of any treaties already proposed by Congress, to the courts of France and Spain.

No vessels of war shall be kept up in time of peace by any State, except such number only, as shall be deemed necessary by the United States in Congress assembled, for the defence of such State,

or its trade; nor shall any body of forces be kept up by any State, in time of peace, except such number only, as in the judgment of the United States, in Congress assembled, shall be deemed requisite to garrison the forts necessary for the defence of such State; but every State shall always keep up a well regulated and disciplined militia, sufficiently armed and accoutered, and shall provide and constantly have ready for use, in public stores, a due number of field pieces and tents, and a proper quantity of arms, ammunition and camp equipage.

No State shall engage in any war without the consent of the United States in Congress assembled, unless such State be actually invaded by enemies, or shall have received certain advice of a resolution being formed by some nation of Indians to invade such State, and the danger is so imminent as not to admit of a delay, till the United States in Congress assembled can be consulted; nor shall any State grant commissions to any ships or vessels of war, nor letters of marque or reprisal, except it be after a declaration of war by the United States in Congress assembled, and then only against the kingdom or state and the subjects thereof, against which war has been so declared, and under such regulations as shall be established by the United States in Congress assembled, unless such State be infested by pirates, in which case vessels of war may be fitted out for that occasion, and kept so long as the danger shall continue, or until the United States in Congress assembled shall determine otherwise.

Article VII. When land-forces are raised by any State for the common defence, all officers of or under the rank of colonel, shall be appointed by the Legislature of each State respectively by whom such forces shall be raised, or in such manner as such State shall direct, and all vacancies shall be filled up by the State which first made the appointment.

Article VIII. All charges of war, and all other expenses that shall be incurred for the common defence or general welfare, and allowed by the United States in Congress assembled, shall be defrayed out of a common treasury, which shall be supplied by the several States, in proportion to the value of all land within each State, granted to or surveyed for any person, as such land and the buildings and improvements thereon shall be estimated according to such mode as the United States in Congress assembled, shall from time to time direct and appoint.

The taxes for paying that proportion shall be

laid and levied by the authority and direction of the Legislatures of the several States within the time agreed upon by the United States in Congress assembled.

Article IX. The United States in Congress assembled, shall have the sole and exclusive right and power of determining on peace and war, except in the cases mentioned in the sixth article—of sending and receiving ambassadors—entering into treaties and alliances, provided that no treaty of commerce shall be made whereby the legislative power of the respective States shall be restrained from imposing such imposts and duties on foreigners, as their own people are subjected to, or from prohibiting the exportation or importation of any species of goods or commodities whatsoever—of establishing rules for deciding in all cases, what captures on land or water shall be legal, and in what manner prizes taken by land or naval forces in the service of the United States shall be divided or appropriated—of granting letters of marque and reprisal in times of peace—appointing courts for the trial of piracies and felonies committed on the high seas and establishing courts for receiving and determining finally appeals in all cases of captures, provided that no member of Congress shall be appointed a judge of any of the said courts.

The United States in Congress assembled shall also be the last resort on appeal in all disputes and differences now subsisting or that hereafter may arise between two or more States concerning boundary, jurisdiction or any other cause whatever; which authority shall always be exercised in the manner following. Whenever the legislative or executive authority or lawful agent of any State in controversy with another shall present a petition to Congress, stating the matter in question and praying for a hearing, notice thereof shall be given by order of Congress to the legislative or executive authority of the other State in controversy, and a day assigned for the appearance of the parties by their lawful agents, who shall then be directed to appoint by joint consent, commissioners, or judges to constitute a court for hearing and determining the matter in question: but if they cannot agree, Congress shall name three persons out of each of the United States, and from the list of such persons each party shall alternately strike out one, the petitioners beginning, until the number shall be reduced to thirteen; and from that number not less than seven, nor more than nine names as Congress shall direct, shall in the presence of Congress be drawn out by lot, and the persons whose names shall be so drawn or any five of them, shall be

commissioners or judges, to hear and finally determine the controversy, so always as a major part of the judges who shall hear the cause shall agree in the determination; and if either party shall neglect to attend at the day appointed, without showing reasons, which Congress shall judge sufficient, or being present shall refuse to strike, the Congress shall proceed to nominate three persons out of each State, and the Secretary of Congress shall strike in behalf of such party absent or refusing: and the judgment and sentence of the court to be appointed, in the manner before prescribed, shall be final and conclusive; and if any of the parties shall refuse to submit to the authority of such court, or to appear or defend their claim or cause, the court shall nevertheless proceed to pronounce sentence, or judgment, which shall in like manner be final and decisive, the judgment or sentence and other proceedings being in either case transmitted to Congress, and lodged among the acts of Congress for the security of the parties concerned: provided that every commissioner, before he sits in judgment, shall take an oath to be administered by one of the judges of the supreme or superior court of the State, where the cause shall be tried, "well and truly to hear and determine the matter in question, according to the best of his judgment, without favour, affection or hope of reward:" provided also that no State shall be deprived of territory for the benefit of the United States.

All controversies concerning the private right of soil claimed under different grants of two or more States, whose jurisdiction as they may respect such lands, and the States which passed such grants are adjusted; the said grants or either of them being at the same time claimed to have originated antecedent to such settlement of jurisdiction, shall on the petition of either party to the Congress of the United States, be finally determined as near as may be in the same manner as is before prescribed for deciding disputes respecting territorial jurisdiction between different states.

The United States in Congress assembled shall also have the sole and exclusive right and power of regulating the alloy and value of coin struck by their own authority, or by that of the respective States—fixing the standard of weights and measures throughout the United States—regulating the trade and managing all affairs with the Indians, not members of any of the States, provided that the legislative right of any State within its own limits be not infringed or violated—establishing and regulating post-offices from one State to another, throughout all the United States, and exacting such postage on the papers passing thro' the same as may be requisite to defray the expenses of the said office—appointing all officers of the land forces, in the service of the United States, excepting regimental officers—appointing all the officers of the naval forces, and commissioning all officers whatever in the service of the United States—making rules for the government and regulation of the said land and naval forces, and directing their operations.

The United States in Congress assembled shall have authority to appoint a committee, to sit in the recess of Congress, to be denominated "a Committee of the States," and to consist of one delegate from each State; and to appoint such other committees and civil officers as may be necessary for manageing the general affairs of the United States under their direction—to appoint one of their number to preside, provided that no person be allowed to serve in the office of president more than one year in any term of three years; to ascertain the necessary sums of money to be raised for the service of the United States, and to appropriate and apply the same for defraying the public expenses—to borrow money, or emit bills on the credit of the United States, transmitting every half year to the respective States an account of the sums of money so borrowed or emitted,—to build and equip a navy—to agree upon the number of land forces, and to make requisitions from each State for its quota, in proportion to the number of white inhabitants in such State; which requisition shall be binding, and thereupon the Legislature of each State shall appoint the regimental officers, raise the men and cloath, arm and equip them in a soldier like manner, at the expense of the United States; and the officers and men so cloathed, armed and equipped shall march to the place appointed, and within the time agreed on by the United States in Congress assembled; but if the United States in Congress assembled shall, on consideration of circumstances judge proper that any State should not raise men, or should raise a smaller number than its quota, and that any other State should raise a greater number of men than the quota thereof, such extra number shall be raised, officered, cloathed, armed and equipped in the same manner as the quota of such State, unless the legislature of such State shall judge that such extra number cannot be safely spared out of the same, in which case they shall raise, officer, cloath, arm and equip as many of such extra number as they judge can be safely spared. And the officers and men so cloathed, armed and equipped, shall march to the place appointed, and within the time agreed on by the United States in Congress assembled.

The United States in Congress assembled shall never engage in a war, nor grant letters of marque and reprisal in time of peace, nor enter into any treaties or alliances, nor coin money, nor regulate the value thereof, nor ascertain the sums and expenses necessary for the defence and welfare of the United States, or any of them, nor emit bills, nor borrow money on the credit of the United States, nor appropriate money, nor agree upon the number of vessels of war, to be built or purchased, or the number of land or sea forces to be raised, nor appoint a commander in chief of the army or navy, unless nine States assent to the same: nor shall a question on any other point, except for adjourning from day to day be determined, unless by the votes of a majority of the United States in Congress assembled.

The Congress of the United States shall have power to adjourn to any time within the year, and to any place within the United States, so that no period of adjournment be for a longer duration than the space of six months, and shall publish the journal of their proceedings monthly except such parts thereof relating to treaties, alliances or military operations, as in their judgment require secrecy; and the yeas and nays of the delegates of each State on any question shall be entered on the journal, when it is desired by any delegate; and the delegates of a State, or any of them, at his or their request shall be furnished with a transcript of the said journal, except such parts as are above excepted, to lay before the Legislatures of the several States.

Article X. The committee of the States, or any nine of them, shall be authorized to execute, in the recess of Congress, such of the powers of Congress as the United States in Congress assembled, by the consent of nine States, shall from time to time think expedient to vest with them; provided that no power be delegated to the said committee, for the exercise of which, by the articles of confederation, the voice of nine States in the Congress of the United States assembled is requisite.

Article XI. Canada acceding to this confederation, and joining in the measures of the United States, shall be admitted into, and entitled to all the advantages of this Union; but no other colony shall be admitted into the same, unless such admission be agreed to by nine States.

Article XII. All bills of credit emitted, monies borrowed and debts contracted by, or under the authority of Congress, before the assembling of the United States, in pursuance of the present confederation, shall be deemed and considered as a charge against the United States, for payment and satisfaction whereof the said United States, and the public faith are hereby solemnly pledged.

Article XIII. Every State shall abide by the determinations of the United States in Congress assembled, on all questions which by this confederation are submitted to them. And the articles of this confederation shall be inviolably observed by every State, and the Union shall be perpetual; nor shall any alteration at any time hereafter be made in any of them; unless such alteration be agreed to in a Congress of the United States, and be afterwards confirmed by the Legislatures of every State.

Constitution

of the United States

# of America

We, the people of the United States, in order to form a more perfect union, establish justice, insure domestic tranquility, provide for the common defence, promote the general welfare, and secure the blessings of liberty to ourselves and our posterity, do ordain and establish this Constitution for the United States of America.

Article I

Section 1. All legislative powers herein granted shall be vested in a Congress of the United States, which shall consist of a Senate and House of Representatives.

Section 2. (1) The House of Representatives shall be composed of members chosen every second year by the people of the several States, and the electors in each State shall have the qualifications requisite for electors of the most numerous branch of the State legislature.

(2) No person shall be a Representative who shall not have attained to the age of twenty-five years, and been seven years a citizen of the United States, and who shall not, when elected, be an inhabitant of that State in which he shall be chosen.

(3) Representatives and direct taxes shall be apportioned among the several States which may be included within this Union, according to their respective numbers, [which shall be determined by adding to the whole number of free persons,][1]

including those bound to service for a term of years, and excluding Indians not taxed, [three fifth for all other persons].[2] The actual enumeration shall be made within three years after the first meeting of the Congress of the United States, and within every subsequent term of ten years, in such manner as they shall by law direct. The number of Representatives shall not exceed one for every thirty thousand, but each State shall have at least one Representative; [and until such enumeration shall be made, the State of New Hampshire shall be entitled to choose three, Massachusetts eight, Rhode Island and Providence Plantations one, Connecticut five, New York six, New Jersey four, Pennsylvania eight, Delaware one, Maryland six, Virginia ten, North Carolina five, South Carolina five, and Georgia three.][3]

(4) When vacancies happen in the representation from any State, the executive authority thereof shall issue writs of election to fill such vacancies.

(5) The House of Representatives shall choose

[1] Modified by Fourteenth Amendment.

[2] Superseded by Fourteenth Amendment.

[3] Temporary provision.

their Speaker and other officers; and shall have the sole power of impeachment.

Section 3. [(1) The Senate of the United States shall be composed of two Senators from each State, chosen by the legislature thereof, for six years; and each Senator shall have one vote.]¹

(2) Immediately after they shall be assembled in consequence of the first election, they shall be divided as equally as may be into three classes. The seats of the Senators of the first class shall be vacated at the expiration of the second year, of the second class at the expiration of the fourth year, and of the third class at the expiration of the sixth year, so that one third may be chosen every second year; [and if vacancies happen by resignation, or otherwise, during the recess of the legislature of any State, the executive thereof may make temporary appointments until the next meeting of the legislature, which shall then fill such vacancies.]²

(3) No person shall be a Senator who shall not have attained to the age of thirty years, and been nine years a citizen of the United States, and who shall not, when elected, be an inhabitant of that State for which he shall be chosen.

(4) The Vice President of the United States shall be president of the Senate, but shall have no vote, unless they be equally divided.

(5) The Senate shall choose their other officers, and also a president pro tempore, in the absence of the Vice President, or when he shall exercise the office of President of the United States.

(6) The Senate shall have the sole power to try all impeachments. When sitting for that purpose, they shall be on oath or affirmation. When the President of the United States is tried, the Chief Justice shall preside: and no person shall be convicted without the concurrence of two thirds of the members present.

(7) Judgment in cases of impeachment shall not extend further than to removal from office, and disqualification to hold and enjoy any office of honor, trust, or profit under the United States: but the party convicted shall nevertheless be liable and subject to indictment, trial, judgment, and punishment, according to law.

Section 4. (1) The times, places, and manner of holding elections for Senators and Representatives shall be prescribed in each State by the legislature thereof; but the Congress may at any time by law make or alter such regulations, except as to the places of choosing Senators.

[(2) The Congress shall assemble at least once in every year, and such meeting shall be on the first Monday in December, unless they shall by law appoint a different day.]³

Section 5. (1) Each House shall be the judge of the elections, returns, and qualifications of its own members, and a majority of each shall constitute a quorum to do business; but a smaller number may adjourn from day to day, and may be authorized to compel the attendance of absent members, in such manner, and under such penalties, as each House may provide.

(2) Each House may determine the rules of its proceedings, punish its members for disorderly behavior, and, with the concurrence of two thirds, expel a member.

(3) Each House shall keep a journal of its proceedings, and from time to time publish the same, excepting such parts as may in their judgment require secrecy; and the yeas and nays of the members of either House on any question shall, at the desire of one fifth of those present, be entered on the journal.

(4) Neither House, during the session of Congress, shall, without the consent of the other, adjourn for more than three days, nor to any other place than that in which the two Houses shall be sitting.

Section 6. (1) The Senators and Representatives shall receive a compensation for their services, to be ascertained by law, and paid out of the Treasury of the United States. They shall in all cases, except treason, felony, and breach of the peace, be privileged from arrest during their attendance at the session of their respective Houses, and in going to and returning from the same; and for any speech or debate in either House, they shall not be questioned in any other place.

(2) No Senator or Representative shall, during the time for which he was elected, be appointed to any civil office under the authority of the United States, which shall have been created, or the emoluments whereof shall have been increased, during such time; and no person holding any office under the United States shall be a member of either House during his continuance in office.

Section 7. (1) All bills for raising revenue shall originate in the House of Representatives; but the Senate may propose or concur with amendments as on other bills.

(2) Every bill which shall have passed the House of Representatives and the Senate, shall,

---

¹ Superseded by Seventeenth Amendment.
² Modified by Seventeenth Amendment.

³ Superseded by Twentieth Amendment.

before it become a law, be presented to the President of the United States; if he approve he shall sign it, but if not he shall return it, with his objections, to that House in which it shall have originated, who shall enter the objections at large on their journal, and proceed to reconsider it. If after such reconsideration two thirds of that House shall agree to pass the bill, it shall be sent, together with the objections, to the other House, by which it shall likewise be reconsidered, and if approved by two thirds of that House, it shall become a law. But in all such cases the votes of both Houses shall be determined by yeas and nays, and the names of the persons voting for and against the bill shall be entered on the journal of each House respectively. If any bill shall not be returned by the President within ten days (Sundays excepted) after it shall have been presented to him, the same shall be a law, in like manner as if he had signed it, unless the Congress by their adjournment prevent its return, in which case it shall not be a law.

(3) Every order, resolution, or vote to which the concurrence of the Senate and House of Representatives may be necessary (except on a question of adjournment) shall be presented to the President of the United States; and before the same shall take effect, shall be approved by him, or being disapproved by him, shall be repassed by two thirds of the Senate and House of Representatives, according to the rules and limitations prescribed in the case of a bill.

Section 8. (1) The Congress shall have power to lay and collect taxes, duties, imposts, and excises, to pay the debts and provide for the common defense and general welfare of the United States; but all duties, imposts, and excises shall be uniform throughout the United States;

(2) To borrow money on the credit of the United States;

(3) To regulate commerce with foreign nations, and among the several States, and with the Indian tribes;

(4) To establish a uniform rule of naturalization, and uniform laws on the subject of bankruptcies throughout the United States;

(5) To coin money, regulate the value thereof, and of foreign coin, and fix the standard of weights and measures;

(6) To provide for the punishment of counterfeiting the securities and current coin of the United States;

(7) To establish post offices and post roads;

(8) To promote the progress of science and useful arts, by securing for limited times to authors and inventors the exclusive right to their respective writings and discoveries;

(9) To constitute tribunals inferior to the Supreme Court;

(10) To define and punish piracies and felonies committed on the high seas, and offenses against the law of nations;

(11) To declare war, grant letters of marque and reprisal, and make rules concerning captures on land and water;

(12) To raise and support armies, but no appropriation of money to that use shall be for a longer term than two years;

(13) To provide and maintain a navy;

(14) To make rules for the government and regulation of the land and naval forces;

(15) To provide for calling forth the militia to execute the laws of the Union, suppress insurrections, and repel invasions;

(16) To provide for organizing, arming, and disciplining the militia, and for governing such part of them as may be employed in the service of the United States, reserving to the States respectively the appointment of the officers, and the authority of training the militia according to the discipline prescribed by Congress;

(17) To exercise exclusive legislation in all cases whatsoever, over such district (not exceeding ten miles square) as may, by cession of particular States, and the acceptance of Congress, become the seat of the government of the United States, and to exercise like authority over all places purchased by the consent of the legislature of the State in which the same shall be, for the erection of forts, magazines, arsenals, dock-yards, and other needful buildings; and

(18) To make all laws which shall be necessary and proper for carrying into execution the foregoing powers, and all other powers vested by this Constitution in the government of the United States, or in any department or officer thereof.

Section 9. [(1) The migration or importation of such persons as any of the States now existing shall think proper to admit, shall not be prohibited by the Congress prior to the year one thousand eight hundred and eight, but a tax or duty may be imposed on such importation, not exceeding ten dollars for each person.][1]

(2) The privilege of the writ of habeas corpus shall not be suspended, unless when in cases of rebellion or invasion the public safety may require it.

---

[1] Temporary provision.

(3) No bill of attainder or ex post facto law shall be passed.

[(4) No capitation, or other direct, tax shall be laid, unless in proportion to the census or enumeration hereinbefore directed to be taken.][1]

(5) No tax or duty shall be laid on articles exported from any State.

(6) No preference shall be given by any regulation of commerce or revenue to the ports of one State over those of another: nor shall vessels bound to, or from, one State, be obligated to enter, clear, or pay duties in another.

(7) No money shall be drawn from the Treasury, but in consequence of appropriations made by law; and a regular statement and account of the receipts and expenditures of all public money shall be published from time to time.

(8) No title of nobility shall be granted by the United States: and no person holding any office of profit or trust under them, shall, without the consent of the Congress, accept of any present, emolument, office, or title, of any kind whatever, from any king, prince, or foreign State.

Section 10. (1) No State shall enter into any treaty, alliance, or confederation; grant letters of marque and reprisal; coin money; emit bills of credit; make anything but gold and silver coin a tender in payment of debts; pass any bill of attainder, ex post facto law, or law impairing the obligation of contracts, or grant any title of nobility.

(2) No State shall, without the consent of the Congress, lay any imposts or duties on imports or exports, except what may be absolutely necessary for executing its inspection laws: and the net produce of all duties and imposts, laid by any State on imports or exports, shall be for the use of the treasury of the United States; and all such laws shall be subject to the revision and control of the Congress.

(3) No State shall, without the consent of Congress, lay any duty of tonnage, keep troops, or ships of war in time of peace, enter into any agreement or compact with another State, or with a foreign power, or engage in war, unless actually invaded, or in such imminent danger as will not admit of delay.

Article II

Section 1. (1) The executive power shall be vested in a President of the United States of America. He shall hold his office during the term of four years, and, together with the Vice President, chosen for the same term, be elected, as follows:

(2) Each State shall appoint, in such manner as the legislature thereof may direct, a number of electors, equal to the whole number of Senators and Representatives to which the State may be entitled in the Congress: but no Senator or Representative, or person holding an office of trust or profit under the United States, shall be appointed an elector.

[The electors shall meet in their respective States, and vote by ballot for two persons, of whom one at least shall not be an inhabitant of the same State with themselves. And they shall make a list of all the persons voted for, and of the number of votes for each; which list they shall sign and certify, and transmit sealed to the seat of the government of the United States, directed to the president of the Senate. The president of the Senate shall, in the presence of the Senate and House of Representatives, open all the certificates, and the votes shall then be counted. The person having the greatest number of votes shall be the President, if such number be a majority of the whole number of electors appointed; and if there be more than one who have such majority, and have an equal number of votes, then the House of Representatives shall immediately choose by ballot one of them for President; and if no person have a majority, then from the five highest on the list the said House shall in like manner choose the President. But in choosing the President, the votes shall be taken by States, the representation from each State having one vote; a quorum for this purpose shall consist of a member or members from two thirds of the States, and a majority of all the States shall be necessary to a choice. In every case, after the choice of the President, the person having the greatest number of votes of the electors shall be the Vice President. But if there should remain two or more who have equal votes, the Senate shall choose from them by ballot the Vice President.][2]

(3) The Congress may determine the time of choosing the electors, and the day on which they shall give their votes; which day shall be the same throughout the United States.

(4) No person except a natural-born citizen, or a citizen of the United States, at the time of the adoption of this Constitution, shall be eligible to the office of President; neither shall any person be eligible to that office who shall not have attained

---

[1] Modified by Sixteen Amendment.

[2] This paragraph superseded by Twelfth Amendment, which, in turn, is modified by the Twentieth Amendment.

to the age of thirty-five years, and been fourteen years a resident within the United States.

(5) In case of the removal of the President from office, or of his death, resignation, or inability to discharge the powers and duties of the said office, the same shall devolve on the Vice President, and the Congress may by law provide for the case of removal, death, resignation, or inability, both of the President and Vice President, declaring what officer shall then act as President, and such officer shall act accordingly, until the disability be removed, or a President shall be elected.

(6) The President shall, at stated times, receive for his services a compensation, which shall neither be increased nor diminished during the period for which he shall have been elected, and he shall not receive within that period any other emolument from the United States, or any of them.

(7) Before he enter on the execution of his office, he shall take the following oath or affirmation: "I do solemnly swear (or affirm) that I will faithfully execute the office of President of the United States, and will, to the best of my ability, preserve, protect, and defend the Constitution of the United States."

Section 2. (1) The President shall be commander in chief of the army and navy of the United States, and of the militia of the several States, when called into the actual service of the United States; he may require the opinion, in writing, of the principal officer in each of the executive departments, upon any subject relating to the duties of their respective offices, and he shall have power to grant reprieves and pardons for offenses against the United States, except in cases of impeachment.

(2) He shall have power, by and with the advice and consent of the Senate, to make treaties, provided two thirds of the Senators present concur; and he shall nominate, and by and with the advice and consent of the Senate, shall appoint ambassadors, other public ministers and consuls, judges of the Supreme Court, and all other officers of the United States, whose appointments are not herein otherwise provided for, and which shall be established by law: but the Congress may by law vest the appointment of such inferior officers, as they think proper, in the President alone, in the courts of law, or in the heads of departments.

(3) The President shall have power to fill up all vacancies that may happen during the recess of the Senate, by granting commissions which shall expire at the end of their next session.

Section 3. He shall from time to time give to the Congress information of the state of the Union, and recommend to their consideration such measures as he shall judge necessary and expedient; he may, on extraordinary occasions, convene both Houses, or either of them, and in case of disagreement between them, with respect to the time of adjournment, he may adjourn them to such time as he shall think proper; he shall receive ambassadors and other public ministers; he shall take care that the laws be faithfully executed, and shall commission all the officers of the United States.

Section 4. The President, Vice President, and all civil officers of the United States, shall be removed from office on impeachment for, and conviction of, treason, bribery, or other high crimes and misdemeanors.

Article III

Section 1. The judicial power of the United States shall be vested in one Supreme Court, and in such inferior courts as the Congress may from time to time ordain and establish. The judges, both of the Supreme and inferior courts, shall hold their offices during good behavior, and shall, at stated times, receive for their services a compensation, which shall not be diminished during their continuance in office.

Section 2. (1) The judicial power shall extend to all cases, in law and equity, arising under this Constitution, the laws of the United States, and treaties made, or which shall be made, under their authority;—to all cases affecting ambassadors, other public ministers, and consuls;—to all cases of admiralty and maritime jurisdiction;—to controversies to which the United States shall be a party;—to controversies between two or more States; [—between a State and citizens of another State;]¹—between citizens of different States;— between citizens of the same State claiming lands under grants of different States, and between a State, or the citizens thereof, and foreign States, citizens, or subjects.

(2) In all cases affecting ambassadors, other public ministers, and consuls, and those in which a State shall be party, the Supreme Court shall have original jurisdiction. In all the other cases before mentioned, the Supreme Court shall have appellate jurisdiction, both as to law and fact, with such exceptions, and under such regulations, as the Congress shall make.

(3) The trial of all crimes, except in cases of impeachment, shall be by jury; and such trial shall

¹ Limited by Eleventh Amendment.

be held in the State where the said crimes shall have been committed; but when not committed within any State, the trial shall be at such place or places as the Congress may by law have directed.

Section 3. (1) Treason against the United States shall consist only in levying war against them, or in adhering to their enemies, giving them aid and comfort. No person shall be convicted of treason unless on the testimony of two witnesses to the same overt act, or on confession in open court.

(2) The Congress shall have power to declare the punishment of treason, but no attainder of treason shall work corruption of blood, or forfeiture except during the life of the person attained.

Article IV

Section 1. Full faith and credit shall be given in each State to the public acts, records, and judicial proceedings of every other State. And the Congress may by general laws prescribe the manner in which such acts, records, and proceedings shall be proved, and the effect thereof.

Section 2. (1) The citizens of each State shall be entitled to all privileges and immunities of citizens in the several States.

(2) A person charged in any State with treason, felony, or other crime, who shall flee from justice, and be found in another State, shall, on demand of the executive authority of the State from which he fled, be delivered up, to be removed to the State having jurisdiction of the crime.

[(3) No person held to service or labor in one State, under the laws thereof, escaping into another, shall, in consequence of any law or regulation therein, be discharged from such service or labor, but shall be delivered up on claim of the party to whom such service or labor may be due.]¹

Section 3. (1) New States may be admitted by the Congress into this Union; but no new State shall be formed or erected within the jurisdiction of any other State; nor any State be formed by the junction of two or more States, or parts of States, without the consent of the legislatures of the States concerned as well as of the Congress.

(2) The Congress shall have power to dispose of and make all needful rules and regulations respecting the territory or other property belonging to the United States; and nothing in this Constitution shall be so construed as to prejudice any claims of the United States, or of any particular State.

¹ Superseded by Thirteenth Amendment so far as it relates to slaves.

Section 4. The United States shall guarantee to every State in this Union a republican form of government, and shall protect each of them against invasion; and, on application of the legislature, or of the executive (when the legislature cannot be convened), against domestic violence.

Article V

The Congress, whenever two thirds of both Houses shall deem it necessary, shall propose amendments to this Constitution, or, on the application of the legislatures of two thirds of the several States, shall call a convention for proposing amendments which, in either case, shall be valid to all intents and purposes, as part of this Constitution, when ratified by the legislatures of three fourths of the several States, or by conventions in three fourths thereof, as the one or the other mode of ratification may be proposed by the Congress; provided [that no amendment which may be made prior to the year one thousand eight hundred and eight shall in any manner affect the first and fourth clauses in the ninth section of the first article; and]² that no State, without its consent, shall be deprived of its equal suffrage in the Senate.

Article VI

(1) All debts contracted and engagements entered into, before the adoption of this Constitution, shall be as valid against the United States under this Constitution, as under the Confederation.

(2) This Constitution, and the laws of the United States which shall be made in pursuance thereof; and all treaties made, or which shall be made, under the authority of the United States, shall be the supreme law of the land; and the judges in every State shall be bound thereby, anything in the constitution or laws of any State to the contrary notwithstanding.

(3) The Senators and Representatives before mentioned, and the members of the several State legislatures, and all executive and judicial officers, both of the United States and of the several States, shall be bound by oath or affirmation to support this Constitution; but no religious test shall ever be required as a qualification to any office or public trust under the United States.

Article VII

The ratification of the conventions of nine States shall be sufficient for the establishment of

² Temporary provision.

this Constitution between the States so ratifying the same.

Done in convention by the unanimous consent of the States present the seventeenth day of September in the year of our Lord one thousand seven hundred and eighty-seven, and of the independence of the United States of America the twelfth. In witness whereof, we have hereunto subscribed our names.

AMENDMENTS

Article I

Congress shall make no law respecting an establishment of religion, or prohibiting the free exercise thereof; or abridging the freedom of speech, or of the press; or the right of the people peaceably to assemble, and to petition the government for a redress of grievances.

Article II

A well regulated militia, being necessary to the security of a free State, the right of the people to keep and bear arms shall not be infringed.

Article III

No soldier shall, in time of peace, be quartered in any house, without the consent of the owner, nor in time of war, but in a manner to be prescribed by law.

Article IV

The right of the people to be secure in their persons, houses, papers, and effects, against unreasonable searches and seizures, shall not be violated, and no warrants shall issue, but upon probable cause, supported by oath or affirmation, and particularly describing the place to be searched, and the persons or things to be seized.

Article V

No person shall be held to answer for a capital or otherwise infamous crime, unless on a presentment or indictment of a grand jury, except in cases arising in the land or naval forces, or in the militia, when in actual service in time of war or public danger; nor shall any person be subject for the same offence to be twice put in jeopardy of life or limb; nor shall be compelled in any criminal case to be a witness against himself, nor be deprived of life, liberty, or property, without due process of law; nor shall private property be taken for public use, without just compensation.

Article VI

In all criminal prosecutions the accused shall enjoy the right to a speedy and public trial, by an impartial jury of the State and district wherein the crime shall have been committed, which district shall have been previously ascertained by law, and to be informed of the nature and cause of the accusation; to be confronted with the witnesses against him; to have compulsory process for obtaining witnesses in his favor, and to have the assistance of counsel for his defense.

Article VII

In suits at common law, where the value in controversy shall exceed twenty dollars, the right of trial by jury shall be preserved, and no fact tried by a jury shall be otherwise re-examined in any court of the United States than according to the rules of the common law.

Article VIII

Excessive bail shall not be required, nor excessive fines imposed, nor cruel and unusual punishments inflicted.

Article IX

The enumeration in the Constitution of certain rights shall not be construed to deny or disparage others retained by the people.

Article X

The powers not delegated to the United States by the Constitution, nor prohibited by it to the States, are reserved to the States respectively, or to the people.[1]

Article XI[2]

The judicial power of the United States shall not be construed to extend to any suit in law or equity, commenced or prosecuted against one of the United States by citizens of another State, or by citizens or subjects of any foreign State.

Article XII[3]

The electors shall meet in their respective States, and vote by ballot for President and Vice President, one of whom, at least, shall not be an inhabitant of the same State with themselves; they shall name in their ballots the persons voted for as Presi-

[1] The first ten amendments appear to have been in force from Nov. 3, 1791.
[2] Proclaimed Jan. 8, 1798.
[3] Proclaimed Sept. 25, 1804.

dent, and in distinct ballots the persons voted for as Vice President, and they shall make distinct lists of all persons voted for as President, and of all persons voted for as Vice President, and of the number of votes for each, which lists they shall sign and certify, and transmit sealed to the seat of the government of the United States, directed to the president of the Senate;—the president of the Senate shall, in the presence of the Senate and House of Representatives, open all the certificates, and the votes shall then be counted;—the person having the greatest number of votes for President, shall be the President, if such number be a majority of the whole number of electors appointed; and if no person have such majority, then from the persons having the highest numbers not exceeding three on the list of those voted for as President, the House of Representatives shall choose immediately, by ballot, the President. But in choosing the President, the votes shall be taken by States, the representation from each State having one vote; a quorum for this purpose shall consist of a member or members from two thirds of the States, and a majority of all the States shall be necessary to a choice. And if the House of Representatives shall not choose a President whenever the right of choice shall devolve upon them, before the fourth day of March next following, then the Vice President shall act as President, as in the case of the death or other constitutional disability of the President.—The person having the greatest number of votes as Vice President, shall be the Vice President, if such number be a majority of the whole number of electors appointed, and if no person have a majority, then from the two highest numbers on the list, the Senate shall choose the Vice President; a quorum for the purpose shall consist of two thirds of the whole number of Senators, and a majority of the whole number shall be necessary to a choice. But no person constitutionally ineligible to the office of President shall be eligible to that of Vice President of the United States.[1]

Article XIII[2]

Section 1. Neither slavery nor involuntary servitude, except as a punishment for crime whereof the party shall have been duly convicted, shall exist within the United States, or any place subject to their jurisdiction.

[1] This amendment modified by the twentieth.
[2] Proclaimed Dec. 18, 1865.

Section 2. Congress shall have power to enforce this article by appropriate legislation.

Article XIV[3]

Section 1. All persons born or naturalized in the United States, and subject to the jurisdiction thereof, are citizens of the United States and of the State wherein they reside. No State shall make or enforce any law which shall abridge the privileges or immunities of citizens of the United States; nor shall any State deprive any person of life, liberty, or property, without due process of law; nor deny to any person within its jurisdiction the equal protection of the laws.

Section 2. Representatives shall be apportioned among the several States according to their respective numbers, counting the whole number of persons in each State, excluding Indians not taxed. But when the right to vote at any election for the choice of electors for President and Vice President of the United States, Representatives in Congress, the executive and judicial officers of a State, or the members of the legislature thereof, is denied to any of the male inhabitants of such State, being twenty-one years of age, and citizens of the United States, or in any way abridged, except for participation in rebellion, or other crime, the basis of representation therein shall be reduced in the proportion which the number of such male citizens shall bear to the whole number of male citizens twenty-one years of age in such State.

Section 3. No person shall be a Senator or Representative in Congress, or elector of President and Vice President, or hold any office, civil or military, under the United States, or under any State, who, having previously taken an oath, as a member of Congress, or as an officer of the United States, or as a member of any State legislature, or as an executive or judicial officer of any State, to support the Constitution of the United States, shall have engaged in insurrection or rebellion against the same, or given aid or comfort to the enemies thereof. But Congress may by a vote of two thirds of each House, remove such disability.

Section 4. The validity of the public debt of the United States, authorized by law, including debts incurred for payment of pensions and bounties for services in suppressing insurrection or rebellion, shall not be questioned. But neither the United States nor any State shall assume or pay any debt or obligation incurred in aid of insurrection or rebellion against the United States, or any claim for

[3] Proclaimed July 28, 1868.

the loss or emancipation of any slave; but all such debts, obligations, and claims shall be held illegal and void.

Section 5. The Congress shall have power to enforce, by appropriate legislation, the provisions of this article.

Article XV[1]

Section 1. The right of citizens of the United States to vote shall not be denied or abridged by the United States or by any State on account of race, color, or previous condition of servitude.

Section 2. The Congress shall have power to enforce this article by appropriate legislation.

Article XVI[2]

The Congress shall have power to lay and collect taxes on incomes, from whatever source derived, without apportionment among the several States, and without regard to any census or enumeration.

Article XVII[3]

The Senate of the United States shall be composed of two Senators from each State, elected by the people thereof, for six years; and each Senator shall have one vote. The electors in each State shall have the qualifications requisite for electors of the most numerous branch of the State legislature.

When vacancies happen in the representation of any State in the Senate, the executive authority of such State shall issue writs of election to fill such vacancies:

Provided, That the legislature of any State may empower the executive thereof to make temporary appointments until the people fill the vacancies by election as the legislature may direct.

This amendment shall not be so construed as to affect the election or term of any Senator chosen before it becomes valid as part of the Constitution.

Article XVIII[4]

Repealed by the Twenty-first Amendment.

Section 1. After one year from the ratification of this article the manufacture, sale, or transportation of intoxicating liquors within, the importation

[1] Proclaimed Mar. 30, 1870.

[2] Passed July, 1909; proclaimed Feb. 25, 1913.

[3] Passed May, 1912, in lieu of Article I, Section 3, paragraph 1, of the Constitution and so much of paragraph 2 of the same section as relates to the filling of vacancies; proclaimed May 31, 1913.

[4] Passed Dec. 3, 1917; proclaimed Jan. 29, 1919.

thereof into, or the exportation thereof from the United States and all territory subject to the jurisdiction thereof for beverage purposes is hereby prohibited.

Section 2. The Congress and the several States shall have concurrent power to enforce this article by appropriate legislation.

Section 3. This article shall be inoperative unless it shall have been ratified as an amendment to the Constitution by the legislatures of the several States, as provided in the Constitution, within seven years from the date of the submission hereof to the States by the Congress.

Article XIX[5]

(1) The right of citizens of the United States to vote shall not be denied or abridged by the United States or by any State on account of sex.

(2) Congress shall have power, by appropriate legislation, to enforce the provisions of this article.

Article XX[6]

Section 1. The terms of the President and Vice President shall end at noon on the 20th day of January, and the terms of Senators and Representatives at noon on the 3rd day of January, of the years in which such terms would have ended if this article had not been ratified; and the terms of their successors shall then begin.

Section 2. The Congress shall assemble at least once in every year, and such meeting shall begin at noon on the 3rd day of January, unless they shall by law appoint a different day.

Section 3. If, at the time fixed for the beginning of the term of the President, the President elect shall have died, the Vice President elect shall become President. If a President shall not have been chosen before the time fixed for the beginning of his term, or if the President elect shall have failed to qualify, then the Vice President elect shall act as President until a President shall have qualified; and the Congress may by law provide for the case wherein neither a President elect nor a Vice President elect shall have qualified, declaring who shall then act as President, or the manner in which one who is to act shall be selected, and such person shall act accordingly until a President or Vice President shall have qualified.

Section 4. The Congress may by law provide for the case of the death of any of the persons from whom the House of Representatives may choose a

[5] Proclaimed Aug. 26, 1920.

[6] Proclaimed Feb. 6, 1933.

President whenever the right of choice shall have devolved upon them, and for the case of the death of any of the persons from whom the Senate may choose a Vice President whenever the right of choice shall have devolved upon them.

Section 5. Sections 1 and 2 shall take effect on the 15th day of October following the ratification of this article.

Section 6. This article shall be inoperative unless it shall have been ratified as an amendment to the Constitution by the legislatures of three fourths of the several States within seven years from the date of its submission.

Article XXI[1]

Section 1. The eighteenth article of amendment to the Constitution of the United States is hereby repealed.

Section 2. The transportation or importation into any State, Territory, or possession of the United States for delivery or use therein of intoxicating liquors, in violation of the laws thereof, is hereby prohibited.

Section 3. This article shall be inoperative unless it shall have been ratified as an amendment to the Constitution by conventions in the several States, as provided in the Constitution, within seven years from the date of submission hereof to the States by the Congress.

Article XXII[2]

Section 1. No person shall be elected to the office of the President more than twice, and no person who has held the office of President, or acted as President, for more than two years of a term to which some other person was elected President shall be elected to the office of the President more than once. But this Article shall not apply to any person holding the office of President when this Article was proposed by the Congress, and shall not prevent any person who may be holding the office of President, or acting as President, during the term within which this Article becomes operative from holding the office of President, or acting as President during the remainder of such term.

Section 2. This Article shall be inoperative unless it shall have been ratified as an amendment to the Constitution by the legislatures of three-fourths of the several States within seven years

[1] Proclaimed Dec. 5, 1933. This amendment was ratified by state conventions.

[2] Adopted Feb. 27, 1951.

from the date of its submission to the States by the Congress.[3]

[3] Six amendments have been proposed but not ratified. The first and second were proposed on Sept. 25, 1789, along with ten others which became the Bill of Rights. The first of these dealt with the apportionment of members of the House of Representatives. It was ratified by ten states, eleven being the necessary three-fourths. The second provided that "No law, varying the compensation for the services of the Senators and Representatives, shall take effect, until an election of Representatives shall have intervened." It was ratified by six states, eleven being necessary. A third was proposed on May 1, 1810, which would have abrogated the citizenship of any persons accepting foreign titles or honors. It was ratified by twelve states, fourteen being necessary. A fourth was proposed on Mar. 4, 1861, which prohibited the adoption of any amendment "to abolish or interfere, within any state, with the domestic institutions thereof, including that of persons held to labor or service by the laws of that state." This was approved by three states. The fifth, the proposed child-labor amendment, was proposed on June 2, 1924. It provides:

Section 1 —The Congress shall have power to limit, regulate, and prohibit the labor of persons under eighteen years of age.

Section 2 —The power of the several States is unimpaired by this article except that the operation of State laws shall be suspended to the extent necessary to give effect to legislation enacted by Congress.

This has been ratified by twenty-eight states and rejected in eleven. The approval of thirty-eight states is probably necessary. The sixth was proposed on August 27, 1962, and must be ratified within seven years. It provides:

Section 1—The right of citizens of the United States to vote in any primary or other election for President or Vice President, for electors for President or Vice President, or for Senator or Representative in Congress, shall not be denied or abridged by the United States or any state by reason of failure to pay any poll tax or other tax.

Section 2—The Congress shall have power to enforce this article by appropriate legislation.

Charter
of the United Nations

We the peoples of the United Nations determined to save succeeding generations from the scourge of war, which twice in our lifetime has brought untold sorrow to mankind, and to reaffirm faith in fundamental human rights, in the dignity and worth of the human person, in the equal rights of men and women and of nations large and small, and to establish conditions under which justice and respect for the obligations arising from treaties and other sources of international law can be maintained, and to promote social progress and better standards of life in larger freedom, *and for these ends* to practice tolerance and live together in peace with one another as good neighbors, and to unite our strength to maintain international peace and security, and to ensure, by the acceptance of principles and the institution of methods, that armed force shall not be used, save in the common interest, and to employ international machinery for the promotion of the economic and social advancement of all peoples, *have resolved to combine our efforts to accomplish these aims.*

Accordingly, our respective Governments, through representatives assembled in the city of San Francisco, who have exhibited their full powers found to be in good and due form, have agreed to the present Charter of the United Nations and do hereby establish an international organization to be known as the United Nations.

CHAPTER I. Purposes and Principles

Article 1

The Purposes of the United Nations are:

1. To maintain international peace and security, and to that end: to take effective collective measures for the prevention and removal of threats to the peace, and for the suppression of acts of aggression or other breaches of the peace, and to bring about by peaceful means, and in conformity with the principles of justice and international law, adjustment or settlement of international disputes or situations which might lead to breach of the peace;

2. To develop friendly relations among nations based on respect for the principle of equal rights and self-determination of peoples, and to take other appropriate measures to strengthen universal peace;

3. To achieve international cooperation in solving international problems of an economic, social, cultural, or humanitarian character, and in pro-

moting and encouraging respect for human rights and for fundamental freedoms for all without distinction as to race, sex, language, or religion; and

4. To be a center for harmonizing the actions of nations in the attainment of these common ends.

Article 2

The Organization and its Members, in pursuit of the Purposes stated in Article 1, shall act in accordance with the following Principles.

1. The Organization is based on the principle of the sovereign equality of all its Members.

2. All Members, in order to ensure to all of them the rights and benefits resulting from membership, shall fulfil in good faith the obligations assumed by them in accordance with the present Charter.

3. All Members shall settle their international disputes by peaceful means in such a manner that international peace and security, and justice, are not endangered.

4. All Members shall refrain in their international relations from the threat or use of force against the territorial integrity or political independence of any state, or in any other manner inconsistent with the Purposes of the United Nations.

5. All Members shall give the United Nations every assistance in any action it takes in accordance with the present Charter, and shall refrain from giving assistance to any state against which the United Nations is taking preventive or enforcement action.

6. The Organization shall ensure that states which are not Members of the United Nations act in accordance with these Principles so far as may be necessary for the maintenance of international peace and security.

7. Nothing contained in the present Charter shall authorize the United Nations to intervene in matters which are essentially within the domestic jurisdiction of any state or shall require the Members to submit such matters to settlement under the present Charter; but this principle shall not prejudice the application of enforcement measures under Chapter VII.

CHAPTER II. Membership

Article 3

The original Members of the United Nations shall be the states which, having participated in the United Nations Conference on International Organization at San Francisco, or having previously signed the Declaration by United Nations of January 1, 1942, sign the present Charter and ratify it in accordance with Article 110.

Article 4

1. Membership in the United Nations is open to all other peace-loving states which accept the obligations contained in the present Charter and, in the judgment of the Organization, are able and willing to carry out these obligations.

2. The admission of any such state to membership in the United Nations will be effected by a decision of the General Assembly upon the recommendation of the Security Council.

Article 5

A Member of the United Nations against which preventive or enforcement action has been taken by the Security Council may be suspended from the exercise of the rights and privileges of membership by the General Assembly upon the recommendation of the Security Council. The exercise of these rights and privileges may be restored by the Security Council.

Article 6

A Member of the United Nations which has persistently violated the Principles contained in the present Charter may be expelled from the Organization by the General Assembly upon the recommendation of the Security Council.

CHAPTER III. Organs

Article 7

1. There are established as the principal organs of the United Nations: a General Assembly, a Security Council, an Economic and Social Council, a Trusteeship Council, an International Court of Justice, and a Secretariat.

2. Such subsidiary organs as may be found necessary may be established in accordance with the present Charter.

Article 8

The United Nations shall place no restrictions on the eligibility of men and women to participate in any capacity and under conditions of equality in its principal and subsidiary organs.

CHAPTER IV. The General Assembly

Composition

Article 9

1. The General Assembly shall consist of all the Members of the United Nations.

2. Each Member shall have not more than five representatives in the General Assembly.

Functions and Powers

Article 10

The General Assembly may discuss any questions or any matters within the scope of the present Charter or relating to the powers and functions of any organs provided for in the present Charter, and, except as provided in Article 12, may make recommendations to the Members of the United Nations or to the Security Council or to both on any such questions or matters.

Article 11

1. The General Assembly may consider the general principles of cooperation in the maintenance of international peace and security, including the principles governing disarmament and the regulation of armaments, and may make recommendations with regard to such principles to the Members or to the Security Council or to both.

2. The General Assembly may discuss any questions relating to the maintenance of international peace and security brought before it by any Member of the United Nations, or by the Security Council, or by a state which is not a Member of the United Nations in accordance with Article 35, paragraph 2, and, except as provided in Article 12, may make recommendations with regard to any such questions to the state or states concerned or to the Security Council or to both. Any such question on which action is necessary shall be referred to the Security Council by the General Assembly either before or after discussion.

3. The General Assembly may call the attention of the Security Council to situations which are likely to endanger international peace and security.

4. The powers of the General Assembly set forth in this Article shall not limit the general scope of Article 10.

Article 12

1. While the Security Council is exercising in respect of any dispute or situation the functions assigned to it in the present Charter, the General Assembly shall not make any recommendation with regard to that dispute or situation unless the Security Council so requests.

2. The Secretary-General, with the consent of the Security Council, shall notify the General Assembly at each session of any matters relative to the maintenance of international peace and security which are being dealt with by the Security Council and shall similarly notify the General Assembly, or the Members of the United Nations if the General Assembly is not in session, immediately the Security Council ceases to deal with such matters.

Article 13

1. The General Assembly shall initiate studies and make recommendations for the purpose of:

a. promoting international cooperation in the political field and encouraging the progressive development of international law and its codification;

b. promoting international cooperation in the economic, social, cultural, educational, and health fields, and assisting in the realization of human rights and fundamental freedoms for all without distinction as to race, sex, language, or religion.

2. The further responsibilities, functions, and powers of the General Assembly with respect to matters mentioned in paragraph 1 (b) above are set forth in Chapters IX and X.

Article 14

Subject to the provisions of Article 12, the General Assembly may recommend measures for the peaceful adjustment of any situation, regardless of origin, which it deems likely to impair the general welfare or friendly relations among nations, including situations resulting from a violation of the provisions of the present Charter setting forth the Purposes and Principles of the United Nations.

Article 15

1. The General Assembly shall receive and consider annual and special reports from the Security Council; these reports shall include an account of the measures that the Security Council has decided upon or taken to maintain international peace and security.

2. The General Assembly shall receive and consider reports from the other organs of the United Nations.

Article 16

The General Assembly shall perform such functions with respect to the international trusteeship system as are assigned to it under Chapters XII and XIII, including the approval of the trusteeship agreements for areas not designated as strategic.

Article 17

1. The General Assembly shall consider and approve the budget of the Organization.

2. The expenses of the Organization shall be borne by the Members as apportioned by the General Assembly.

3. The General Assembly shall consider and approve any financial and budgetary arrangements with specialized agencies referred to in Article 57 and shall examine the administrative budgets of such specialized agencies with a view to making recommendations to the agencies concerned.

Voting

Article 18

1. Each member of the General Assembly shall have one vote.

2. Decisions of the General Assembly on important questions shall be made by a two-thirds majority of the members present and voting. These questions shall include: recommendations with respect to the maintenance of international peace and security, the election of the non-permanent members of the Security Council, the election of the members of the Economic and Social Council, the election of members of the Trusteeship Council in accordance with paragraph 1 (c) of Article 86, the admission of new Members to the United Nations, the suspension of the rights and privileges of membership, the expulsion of Members, questions relating to the operation of the trusteeship system, and budgetary questions.

3. Decisions on other questions, including the determination of additional categories of questions to be decided by a two-thirds majority, shall be made by a majority of the members present and voting.

Article 19

A Member of the United Nations which is in arrears in the payment of its financial contributions to the Organization shall have no vote in the General Assembly if the amount of its arrears equals or exceeds the amount of the contributions due from it for the preceding two full years. The General Assembly may, nevertheless, permit such a Member to vote if it is satisfied that the failure to pay is due to conditions beyond the control of the Member.

Procedure

Article 20

The General Assembly shall meet in regular annual sessions and in such special sessions as occasion may require. Special sessions shall be convoked by the Secretary-General at the request of the Security Council or of a majority of the Members of the United Nations.

Article 21

The General Assembly shall adopt its own rules of procedure. It shall elect its President for each session.

Article 22

The General Assembly may establish such subsidiary organs as it deems necessary for the performance of its functions.

CHAPTER V. The Security Council

Composition

Article 23

1. The Security Council shall consist of eleven Members of the United Nations. The Republic of China, France, the Union of Soviet Socialist Republics, the United Kingdom of Great Britain and Northern Ireland, and the United States of America shall be permanent members of the Security Council. The General Assembly shall elect six other Members of the United Nations to be non-permanent members of the Security Council, due regard being specially paid, in the first instance to the contribution of Members of the United Nations to the maintenance of international peace and security and to the other purposes of the Organization, and also to equitable geographical distribution.

2. The non-permanent members of the Security Council shall be elected for a term of two years. In the first election of the non-permanent members, however, three shall be chosen for a term of

one year. A retiring member shall not be eligible for immediate re-election.

3. Each member of the Security Council shall have one representative.

Functions and Powers

Article 24

1. In order to ensure prompt and effective action by the United Nations, its Members confer on the Security Council primary responsibility for the maintenance of international peace and security, and agree that in carrying out its duties under this responsibility the Security Council acts on their behalf.

2. In discharging these duties the Security Council shall act in accordance with the Purposes and Principles of the United Nations. The Specific powers granted to the Security Council for the discharge of these duties are laid down in Chapters VI, VII, VIII, and XII.

3. The Security Council shall submit annual and, when necessary, special reports to the General Assembly for its consideration.

Article 25

The Members of the United Nations agree to accept and carry out the decisions of the Security Council in accordance with the present Charter.

Article 26

In order to promote the establishment and maintenance of international peace and security with the least diversion for armaments of the world's human and economic resources, the Security Council shall be responsible for formulating, with the assistance of the Military Staff Committee referred to in Article 47, plans to be submitted to the Members of the United Nations for the establishment of a system for the regulation of armaments.

Voting

Article 27

1. Each member of the Security Council shall have one vote.

2. Decisions of the Security Council on procedural matters shall be made by an affirmative vote of seven members.

3. Decisions of the Security Council on all other matters shall be made by an affirmative vote of seven members including the concurring votes of the permanent members; provided that, in decisions under Chapter VI, and under paragraph 3 of Article 52, a party to a dispute shall abstain from voting.

Procedure

Article 28

1. The Security Council shall be so organized as to be able to function continuously. Each member of the Security Council shall for this purpose be represented at all times at the seat of the Organization.

2. The Security Council shall hold periodic meetings at which each of its members may, if it so desires, be represented by a member of the government or by some other specially designated representative.

3. The Security Council may hold meetings at such places other than the seat of the Organization as in its judgment will best facilitate its work.

Article 29

The Security Council may establish such subsidiary organs as it deems necessary for the performance of its functions.

Article 30

The Security Council shall adopt its own rules of procedure, including the method of selecting its President.

Article 31

Any Member of the United Nations which is not a member of the Security Council may participate, without vote, in the discussion of any question brought before the Security Council whenever the latter considers that the interests of that Member are specially affected.

Article 32

Any Member of the United Nations which is not a member of the Security Council or any state which is not a Member of the United Nations, if it is a party to a dispute under consideration by the Security Council, shall be invited to participate, without vote, in the discussion relating to the dispute. The Security Council shall lay down such conditions as it deems just for the participation of a state which is not a Member of the United Nations.

CHAPTER VI. Pacific Settlement of Disputes

Article 33

1. The parties to any dispute, the continuance of which is likely to endanger the maintenance of international peace and security, shall, first of all, seek a solution by negotiation, enquiry, mediation, conciliation, arbitration, judicial settlement, resort to regional agencies or arrangements, or other peaceful means of their own choice.

2. The Security Council shall, when it deems necessary, call upon the parties to settle their dispute by such means.

Article 34

The Security Council may investigate any dispute, or any situation which might lead to international friction or give rise to a dispute, in order to determine whether the continuance of the dispute or situation is likely to endanger the maintenance of international peace and security.

Article 35

1. Any Member of the United Nations may bring any dispute, or any situation of the nature referred to in Article 34, to the attention of the Security Council or of the General Assembly.

2. A state which is not a member of the United Nations may bring to the attention of the Security Council or of the General Assembly any dispute to which it is a party if it accepts in advance, for the purposes of the dispute, the obligations of pacific settlement provided in the present Charter.

3. The proceedings of the General Assembly in respect of matters brought to its attention under this Article will be subject to the provisions of Articles 11 and 12.

Article 36

1. The Security Council may, at any stage of a dispute of the nature referred to in Article 33 or of a situation of like nature, recommend appropriate procedures or methods of adjustment.

2. The Security Council should take into consideration any procedures for the settlement of the dispute which have already been adopted by the parties.

3. In making recommendations under this Article the Security Council should also take into consideration that legal disputes should as a general rule be referred by the parties to the International Court of Justice in accordance with the provisions of the Statute of the Court.

Article 37

1. Should the parties to a dispute of the nature referred to in Article 33 fail to settle it by the means indicated in that Article, they shall refer it to the Security Council.

2. If the Security Council deems that the continuance of the dispute is in fact likely to endanger the maintenance of international peace and security, it shall decide whether to take action under Article 36 or to recommend such terms of settlement as it may consider appropriate.

Article 38

Without prejudice to the provisions of Articles 33 to 37, the Security Council may, if all the parties to any dispute so request, make recommendations to the parties with a view to a pacific settlement of the dispute.

CHAPTER VII. Action with Respect to Threats to the Peace, Breaches of the Peace and Acts of Aggression

Article 39

The Security Council shall determine the existence of any threat to the peace, breach of the peace, or act of aggression and shall make recommendations, or decide what measures shall be taken in accordance with Articles 41 and 42, to maintain or restore international peace and security.

Article 40

In order to prevent an aggravation of the situation, the Security Council may, before making the recommendations or deciding upon the measures provided for in Article 39, call upon the parties concerned to comply with such provisional measures as it deems necessary or desirable. Such provisional measures shall be without prejudice to the rights, claims, or position of the parties concerned. The Security Council shall duly take account of failure to comply with such provisional measures.

Article 41

The Security Council may decide what measures not involving the use of armed force are to be employed to give effect to its decisions, and it may call upon the Members of the United Nations to apply such measures. These may include complete or partial interruption of economic relations and of rail, sea, air, postal, telegraphic, radio, and other means of communication, and the severance of diplomatic relations.

Article 42

Should the Security Council consider that measures provided for in Article 41 would be inadequate or have proved to be inadequate, it may take such action by air, sea, or land forces as may be necessary to maintain or restore international peace and security. Such action may include demonstrations, blockade, and other operations by air, sea, or land forces of Members of the United Nations.

Article 43

1. All Members of the United Nations, in order to contribute to the maintenance of international peace and security, undertake to make available to the Security Council, on its call and in accordance with a special agreement or agreements, armed forces, assistance, and facilities, including rights of passage, necessary for the purpose of maintaining international peace and security.

2. Such agreement or agreements shall govern the numbers and types of forces, their degree of readiness and general location, and the nature of the facilities and assistance to be provided.

3. The agreement or agreements shall be negotiated as soon as possible on the initiative of the Security Council. They shall be concluded between the Security Council and Members or between the Security Council and groups of Members and shall be subject to ratification by the signatory states in accordance with their respective constitutional processes.

Article 44

When the Security Council has decided to use force it shall, before calling upon a Member not represented on it to provide armed forces in fulfillment of the obligations assumed under Article 43, invite that Member, if the Member so desires, to participate in the decisions of the Security Council concerning the employment of contingents of that Member's armed forces.

Article 45

In order to enable the United Nations to take urgent military measures, Members shall hold immediately available national air-force contingents for combined international enforcement action. The strength and degree of readiness of these contingents and plans for their combined action shall be determined, within the limits laid down

in the special agreement or agreements referred to in Article 43, by the Security Council with the assistance of the Military Staff Committee.

Article 46

Plans for the application of armed force shall be made by the Security Council with the assistance of the Military Staff Committee.

Article 47

1. There shall be established a Military Staff Committee to advise and assist the Security Council on all questions relating to the Security Council's military requirements for the maintenance of international peace and security, the employment and command of forces placed at its disposal, the regulation of armaments, and possible disarmament.

2. The Military Staff Committee shall consist of the Chiefs of Staff of the permanent members of the Security Council or their representatives. Any Member of the United Nations not permanently represented on the Committee shall be invited by the Committee to be associated with it when the efficient discharge of the Committee's responsibilities requires the participation of that Member in its work.

3. The Military Staff Committee shall be responsible under the Security Council for the strategic direction of any armed forces placed at the disposal of the Security Council. Questions relating to the command of such forces shall be worked out subsequently.

4. The Military Staff Committee, with the authorization of the Security Council and after consultation with appropriate regional agencies, may establish regional subcommittees.

Article 48

1. The action required to carry out the decisions of the Security Council for the maintenance of international peace and security shall be taken by all the Members of the United Nations or by some of them, as the Security Council may determine.

2. Such decisions shall be carried out by the Members of the United Nations directly and through their action in the appropriate international agencies of which they are members.

Article 49

The Members of the United Nations shall join in affording mutual assistance in carrying out the measures decided upon by the Security Council.

Article 50

If preventive or enforcement measures against any state are taken by the Security Council, any other state, whether a Member of the United Nations or not, which finds itself confronted with special economic problems arising from the carrying out of those measures shall have the right to consult the Security Council with regard to a solution of those problems.

Article 51

Nothing in the present Charter shall impair the inherent right of individual or collective self-defense if an armed attack occurs against a Member of the United Nations, until the Security Council has taken the measures necessary to maintain international peace and security. Measures taken by Members in the exercise of this right of self-defense shall be immediately reported to the Security Council and shall not in any way affect the authority and responsibility of the Security Council under the present Charter to take at any time such action as it deems necessary in order to maintain or restore international peace and security.

CHAPTER VIII. Regional Arrangements

Article 52

1. Nothing in the present Charter precludes the existence of regional arrangements or agencies for dealing with such matters relating to the maintenance of international peace and security as are appropriate for regional action, provided that such arrangements or agencies and their activities are consistent with the Purposes and Principles of the United Nations.

2. The Members of the United Nations entering into such arrangements or constituting such agencies shall make every effort to achieve pacific settlement of local disputes through such regional arrangements or by such regional agencies before referring them to the Security Council.

3. The Security Council shall encourage development of pacific settlement of local disputes through such regional arrangements or by such regional agencies either on the initiative of the states concerned or by reference from the Security Council.

4. This Article in no way impairs the application of Articles 34 and 35.

Article 53

1. The Security Council shall, where appropriate, utilize such regional arrangements or agencies for enforcement action under its authority. But no enforcement action shall be taken under regional arrangements or by regional agencies without the authorization of the Security Council, with the exception of measures against any enemy state, as defined in paragraph 2 of this Article, provided for pursuant to Article 107 or in regional arrangements directed against renewal of aggressive policy on the part of any such state, until such time as the Organization may, on request of the Governments concerned, be charged with the responsibility for preventing further aggression by such a state.

2. The term enemy state as used in paragraph 1 of this Article applies to any state which during the Second World War has been an enemy of any signatory of the present Charter.

Article 54

The Security Council shall at all times be kept fully informed of activities undertaken or in contemplation under regional arrangements or by regional agencies for the maintenance of international peace and security.

CHAPTER IX. International Economic and Social Cooperation

Article 55

With a view to the creation of conditions of stability and well-being which are necessary for peaceful and friendly relations among nations based on respect for the principle of equal rights and self-determination of peoples, the United Nations shall promote:

a. higher standards of living, full employment, and conditions of economic and social progress and development;

b. solutions of international economic, social, health, and related problems; and international cultural and educational cooperation; and

c. universal respect for, and observance of, human rights and fundamental freedoms for all without distinction as to race, sex, language, or religion.

Article 56

All Members pledge themselves to take joint and separate action in cooperation with the

Organization for the achievement of the purposes set forth in Article 55.

Article 57

1. The various specialized agencies, established by intergovernmental agreement and having wide international responsibilities, as defined in their basic instruments, in economic, social, cultural, educational, health, and related fields, shall be brought into relationship with the United Nations in accordance with the provisions of Article 63.

2. Such agencies thus brought into relationship with the United Nations are hereinafter referred to as specialized agencies.

Article 58

The Organization shall make recommendations for the coordination of the policies and activities of the specialized agencies.

Article 59

The Organization shall, where appropriate, initiate negotiations among the states concerned for the creation of any new specialized agencies required for the accomplishment of the purposes set forth in Article 55.

Article 60

Responsibility for the discharge of the functions of the Organization set forth in this Chapter shall be vested in the General Assembly and, under the authority of the General Assembly, in the Economic and Social Council, which shall have for this purpose the powers set forth in Chapter X.

CHAPTER X. The Economic and Social Council

Composition

Article 61

1. The Economic and Social Council shall consist of eighteen Members of the United Nations elected by the General Assembly.

2. Subject to the provisions of paragraph 3, six members of the Economic and Social Council shall be elected each year for a term of three years. A retiring member shall be eligible for immediate reelection.

3. At the first election, eighteen members of the Economic and Social Council shall be chosen. The term of office of six members so chosen shall expire at the end of one year, and of six other mem-

bers at the end of two years, in accordance with arrangements made by the General Assembly.

4. Each member of the Economic and Social Council shall have one representative.

Functions and Powers

Article 62

1. The Economic and Social Council may make or initiate studies and reports with respect to international economic, social, cultural, educational, health, and related matters and may make recommendations with respect to any such matters to the General Assembly, to the Members of the United Nations, and to the specialized agencies concerned.

2. It may make the recommendations for the purpose of promoting respect for, and observance of, human rights and fundamental freedoms for all.

3. It may prepare draft conventions for submission to the General Assembly, with respect to matters falling within its competence.

4. It may call, in accordance with the rules prescribed by the United Nations, international conferences on matters falling within its competence.

Article 63

1. The Economic and Social Council may enter into agreements with any of the agencies referred to in Article 57, defining the terms on which the agency concerned shall be brought into relationship with the United Nations. Such agreements shall be subject to approval by the General Assembly.

2. It may coordinate the activities of the specialized agencies through consultation with and recommendations to such agencies and through recommendations to the General Assembly and to the Members of the United Nations.

Article 64

1. The Economic and Social Council may take appropriate steps to obtain regular reports from the specialized agencies. It may make arrangements with the Members of the United Nations and with the specialized agencies to obtain reports on the steps taken to give effect to its own recommendations and to recommendations on matters falling within its competence made by the General Assembly.

2. It may communicate its observations on these reports to the General Assembly.

Article 65

The Economic and Social Council may furnish information to the Security Council and shall assist the Security Council upon its request.

Article 66

1. The Economic and Social Council shall perform such functions as fall within its competence in connection with the carrying out of the recommendations of the General Assembly.

2. It may, with the approval of the General Assembly, perform services at the request of Members of the United Nations and at the request of specialized agencies.

3. It shall perform such other functions as are specified elsewhere in the present Charter or as may be assigned to it by the General Assembly.

Voting

Article 67

1. Each member of the Economic and Social Council shall have one vote.

2. Decisions of the Economic and Social Council shall be made by a majority of the members present and voting.

Procedure

Article 68

The Economic and Social Council shall set up commissions in economic and social fields and for the promotion of human rights, and such other commissions as may be required for the performance of its functions.

Article 69

The Economic and Social Council shall invite any Member of the United Nations to participate, without vote, in its deliberations on any matter of particular concern to that Member.

Article 70

The Economic and Social Council may make arrangements for representatives of the specialized agencies to participate, without vote, in its deliberations and in those of the commissions established by it, and for its representatives to participate in the deliberations of the specialized agencies.

Article 71

The Economic and Social Council may make suitable arrangements for consultation with non-governmental organizations which are concerned with matters within its competence. Such arrangements may be made with international organizations and, where appropriate, with national organizations after consultation with the Member of the United Nations concerned.

Article 72

1. The Economic and Social Council shall adopt its own rules of procedure, including the method of selecting its President.

2. The Economic and Social Council shall meet as required in accordance with its rules, which shall include provision for the convening of meetings on the request of a majority of its members.

CHAPTER XI. Declaration Regarding Non-Self-Governing Territories

Article 73

Members of the United Nations which have or assume responsibilities for the administration of territories whose peoples have not yet attained a full measure of self-government recognize the principle that the interests of the inhabitants of these territories are paramount, and accept as a sacred trust the obligation to promote to the utmost, within the system of international peace and security established by the present Charter, the well-being of the inhabitants of these territories, and, to this end:

a. to ensure, with due respect for the culture of the peoples concerned, their political, economic, social, and educational advancement, their just treatment, and their protection against abuses;

b. to develop self-government, to take due account of the political aspirations of the peoples, and to assist them in the progressive development of their free political institutions, according to the particular circumstances of each territory and its peoples and their varying stages of advancement;

c. to further international peace and security;

d. to promote constructive measures of development, to encourage research, and to cooperate with one another and, when and where appropriate, with specialized international bodies with a view to the practical achievement of the social, economic, and scientific purposes set forth in this Article; and

e. to transmit regularly to the Secretary-General for information purposes, subject to such limitation as security and constitutional considerations may require, statistical and other information of a technical nature relating to economic, social, and educational conditions in the territories for which they are respectively responsible other than those territories to which Chapters XII and XIII apply.

Article 74

Members of the United Nations also agree that their policy in respect of the territories to which this Chapter applies, no less than in respect of their metropolitan areas, must be based on the general principle of good-neighborliness, due account being taken of the interests, and well-being of the rest of the world, in social, economic, and commercial matters.

CHAPTER XII. International Trusteeship System

Article 75

The United Nations shall establish under its authority an international trusteeship system for the administration and supervision of such territories as may be placed thereunder by subsequent individual agreements. These territories are hereinafter referred to as trust territories.

Article 76

The basic objectives of the trusteeship system, in accordance with the Purposes of the United Nations laid down in Article 1 of the present Charter, shall be:

a. to further international peace and security;

b. to promote the political, economic, social, and educational advancement of the inhabitants of the trust territories, and their progressive development towards self-government or independence as may be appropriate to the particular circumstances of each territory and its peoples and the freely expressed wishes of the peoples concerned, and as may be provided by the terms of each trusteeship agreement;

c. to encourage respect for human rights and for

fundamental freedoms for all without distinction as to race, sex, language, or religion, and to encourage recognition of the interdependence of the peoples of the world; and

d. to ensure equal treatment in social, economic, and commercial matters for all Members of the United Nations and their nationals, and also equal treatment for the latter in the administration of justice, without prejudice to the attainment of the foregoing objectives and subject to the provisions of Article 80.

Article 77

1. The trusteeship system shall apply to such territories in the following categories as may be placed thereunder by means of trusteeship agreements:

a. territories now held under mandate;

b. territories which may be detached from enemy states as a result of the Second World War; and

c. territories voluntarily placed under the system by states responsible for their administration.

2. It will be a matter for subsequent agreement as to which territories in the foregoing categories will be brought under the trusteeship system and upon what terms.

Article 78

The trusteeship system shall not apply to territories which have become Members of the United Nations, relationship among which shall be based on respect for the principle of sovereign equality.

Article 79

The terms of trusteeship for each territory to be placed under the trusteeship system, including any alteration or amendment, shall be agreed upon by the states directly concerned, including the mandatory power in the case of territories held under mandate by a Member of the United Nations, and shall be approved as provided for in Articles 83 and 85.

Article 80

1. Except as may be agreed upon in individual trusteeship agreements, made under Articles 77, 79, and 81, placing each territory under the trusteeship system, and until such agreements have been concluded, nothing in this Chapter shall be construed in or of itself to alter in any manner the rights whatsoever of any states or any peoples

or the terms of existing international instruments to which Members of the United Nations may respectively be parties.

2. Paragraph 1 of this Article shall not be interpreted as giving grounds for delay or postponement of the negotiation and conclusion of agreements for placing mandated and other territories under the trusteeship system as provided for in Article 77.

Article 81

The trusteeship agreement shall in each case include the terms under which the trust territory will be administered and designate the authority which will exercise the administration of the trust territory. Such authority, hereinafter called the administering authority, may be one or more states or the Organization itself.

Article 82

There may be designated, in any trusteeship agreement, a strategic area or areas which may include part or all of the trust territory to which the agreement applies, without prejudice to any special agreement or agreements made under Article 43.

Article 83

1. All functions of the United Nations relating to strategic areas, including the approval of the terms of the trusteeship agreements and of their alteration or amendment, shall be exercised by the Security Council.

2. The basic objectives set forth in Article 76 shall be applicable to the people of each strategic area.

3. The Security Council shall, subject to the provisions of the trusteeship agreements and without prejudice to security considerations, avail itself of the assistance of the Trusteeship Council to perform those functions of the United Nations under the trusteeship system relating to political, economic, social, and educational matters in the strategic areas.

Article 84

It shall be the duty of the administering authority to ensure that the trust territory shall play its part in the maintenance of international peace and security. To this end the administering authority may make use of volunteer forces, facilities, and assistance from the trust territory in carrying out the obligations towards the Security Council undertaken in this regard by the administering authority, as well as for local defense and the maintenance of law and order within the trust territory.

Article 85

1. The functions of the United Nations with regard to trusteeship agreements for all areas not designated as strategic, including the approval of the terms of the trusteeship agreements and of their alteration or amendment, shall be exercised by the General Assembly.

2. The Trusteeship Council, operating under the authority of the General Assembly, shall assist the General Assembly in carrying out these functions.

CHAPTER XIII. The Trusteeship Council

Composition

Article 86

1. The Trusteeship Council shall consist of the following Members of the United Nations:

a. those Members administering trust territories;

b. such of those Members mentioned by name in Article 23 as are not administering trust territories; and

c. as many other Members elected for three-year terms by the General Assembly as may be necessary to ensure that the total number of members of the Trusteeship Council is equally divided between those Members of the United Nations which administer trust territories and those which do not.

2. Each member of the Trusteeship Council shall designate one specially qualified person to represent it therein.

Functions and Powers

Article 87

The General Assembly and, under its authority, the Trusteeship Council, in carrying out their functions, may:

a. consider reports submitted by the administering authority;

b. accept petitions and examine them in consultation with the administering authority;

c. provide for periodic visits to the respective trust territories at times agreed upon with the administering authority; and

d. take these and other actions in conformity with the terms of the trusteeship agreements.

Article 88

The Trusteeship Council shall formulate a questionnaire on the political, economic, social, and educational advancement of the inhabitants of each trust territory, and the administering authority for each trust territory within the competence of the General Assembly shall make an annual report to the General Assembly upon the basis of such questionnaire.

Voting

Article 89

1. Each member of the Trusteeship Council shall have one vote.

2. Decisions of the Trusteeship Council shall be made by a majority of the members present and voting.

Procedure

Article 90

1. The Trusteeship Council shall adopt its own rules of procedure, including the method of selecting its President.

2. The Trusteeship Council shall meet as required in accordance with its rules, which shall include provision for the convening of meetings on the request of a majority of its members.

Article 91

The Trusteeship Council shall, when appropriate, avail itself of the assistance of the Economic and Social Council and of the specialized agencies in regard to matters with which they are respectively concerned.

CHAPTER XIV. The International Court of Justice

Article 92

The International Court of Justice shall be the prinicpal judicial organ of the United Nations. It shall function in accordance with the annexed Statute, which is based upon the Statute of the Permanent Court of International Justice and forms an integral part of the present Charter.

Article 93

1. All Members of the United Nations are *ipso facto* parties to the Statute of the International Court of Justice.

2. A state which is not a Member of the United Nations may become a party to the Statute of the International Court of Justice on conditions to be determined in each case by the General Assembly upon the recommendation of the Security Council.

Article 94

1. Each Member of the United Nations undertakes to comply with the decision of the International Court of Justice in any case to which it is a party.

2. If any party to a case fails to perform the obligations incumbent upon it under a judgment rendered by the Court, the other party may have recourse to the Security Council, which may, if it deems necessary, make recommendations or decide upon measures to be taken to give effect to the judgment.

Article 95

Nothing in the present Charter shall prevent Members of the United Nations from entrusting the solution of their differences to other tribunals by virtue of agreements already in existence or which may be concluded in the future.

Article 96

1. The General Assembly or the Security Council may request the International Court of Justice to give an advisory opinion on any legal question.

2. Other organs of the United Nations and specialized agencies, which may at any time be so authorized by the General Assembly, may also request advisory opinions of the Court on legal questions arising within the scope of their activities.

CHAPTER XV. The Secretariat

Article 97

The Secretariat shall comprise a Secretary-General and such staff as the Organization may require. The Secretary-General shall be appointed by the General Assembly upon the recommendation of the Security Council. He shall be the chief administrative officer of the Organization.

Article 98

The Secretary-General shall act in that capacity in all meetings of the General Assembly, of the

Security Council, of the Economic and Social Council, and of the Trusteeship Council, and shall perform such other functions as are entrusted to him by these organs. The Secretary-General shall make an annual report to the General Assembly on the work of the Organization.

Article 99

The Secretary-General may bring to the attention of the Security Council any matter which in his opinion may threaten the maintenance of international peace and security.

Article 100

1. In the performance of their duties the Secretary-General and the staff shall not seek or receive instructions from any government or from any other authority external to the Organization. They shall refrain from any action which might reflect on their position as international officials responsible only to the Organization.

2. Each Member of the United Nations undertakes to respect the exclusively international character of the responsibilities of the Secretary-General and the staff and not to seek to influence them in the discharge of their responsibilities.

Article 101

1. The staff shall be appointed by the Secretary-General under regulations established by the General Assembly.

2. Appropriate staffs shall be permanently assigned to the Economic and Social Council, the Trusteeship Council, and, as required, to other organs of the United Nations. These staffs shall form a part of the Secretariat.

3. The paramount consideration in the employment of the staff and in the determination of the conditions of service shall be the necessity of securing the highest standards of efficiency, competence, and integrity. Due regard shall be paid to the importance of recruiting the staff on as wide a geographical basis as possible.

CHAPTER XVI. Miscellaneous Provisions

Article 102

1. Every treaty and every international agreement entered into by any Member of the United Nations after the present Charter comes into force shall as soon as possible be registered with the Secretariat and published by it.

2. No party to any such treaty or international agreement which has not been registered in accordance with the provisions of paragraph 1 of this Article may invoke that treaty or agreement before any organ of the United Nations.

Article 103

In the event of a conflict between the obligations of the Members of the United Nations under the present Charter and their obligations under any other international agreement, their obligations under the present Charter shall prevail.

Article 104

The Organization shall enjoy in the territory of each of its Members such legal capacity as may be necessary for the exercise of its functions and the fulfillment of its purposes

Article 105

1. The Organization shall enjoy in the territory of each of its Members such privileges and immunities as are necessary for the fulfillment of its purposes.

2. Representatives of the Members of the United Nations and officials of the Organization shall similarly enjoy such privileges and immunities as are necessary for the independent exercise of their functions in connection with the Organization.

3. The General Assembly may make recommendations with a view to determining the details of the application of paragraphs 1 and 2 of this Article or may propose conventions to the Members of the United Nations for this purpose.

CHAPTER XVII. Transitional Security Arrangements

Article 106

Pending the coming into force of such special agreements referred to in Article 43 as in the opinion of the Security Council enable it to begin the exercise of its responsibilities under Article 42, the parties to the Four-Nation Declaration, signed at Moscow, October 30, 1943, and France, shall, in accordance with the provisions of paragraph 5 of that Declaration, consult with one another and as occasion requires with other Members of the United Nations with a view to such joint action on behalf of the Organization as may be necessary for the purpose of maintaining international peace and security.

Article 107

Nothing in the present Charter shall invalidate or preclude action, in relation to any state which during the Second World War has been an enemy of any signatory to the present Charter, taken or authorized as a result of that war by the Governments having responsibility for such action.

CHAPTER XVIII. Amendments

Article 108

Amendments to the present Charter shall come into force for all Members of the United Nations when they have been adopted by a vote of two thirds of the members of the General Assembly and ratified in accordance with their respective constitutional processes by two thirds of the Members of the United Nations, including all the permanent members of the Security Council.

Article 109

1. A General Conference of the Members of the United Nations for the purpose of reviewing the present Charter may be held at a date and place to be fixed by a two-thirds vote of the members of the General Assembly and by a vote of any seven members of the Security Council. Each Member of the United Nations shall have one vote in the conference.

2. Any alteration of the present Charter recommended by a two-thirds vote of the conference shall take effect when ratified in accordance with their respective constitutional processes by two thirds of the Members of the United Nations including all the permanent members of the Security Council.

3. If such a conference has not been held before the tenth annual session of the General Assembly following the coming into force of the present Charter, the proposal to call such a conference shall be placed on the agenda of that session of the General Assembly, and the conference shall be held if so decided by a majority vote of the members of the General Assembly and by a vote of any seven members of the Security Council.

CHAPTER XIX. Ratification and Signature

Article 110

1. The present Charter shall be ratified by the signatory states in accordance with their respective constitutional processes.

2. The ratifications shall be deposited with the Government of the United States of America, which shall notify all the signatory states of each deposit as well as the Secretary-General of the Organization when he has been appointed.

3. The present Charter shall come into force upon the deposit of ratifications by the Republic of China, France, the Union of Soviet Socialist Republics, the United Kingdom of Great Britain and Northern Ireland, and the United States of America, and by a majority of the other signatory states. A protocol of the ratifications deposited shall thereupon be drawn up by the Government of the United States of America which shall communicate copies thereof to all the signatory states.

4. The states signatory to the present Charter which ratify it after it has come into force will become original Members of the United Nations on the date of the deposit of their respective ratifications.

Article 111

The present Charter, of which the Chinese, French, Russian, English, and Spanish texts are equally authentic, shall remain deposited in the archives of the Government of the United States of America. Duly certified copies thereof shall be transmitted by that Government to the Governments of the other signatory states.

In faith whereof the representatives of the Governments of the United Nations have signed the present Charter.

Done at the city of San Francisco the twenty-sixth day of June, one thousand nine hundred and forty-five.

Index